UNDERSTANDING Psychology

Features and Benefits

A STRONG READING STRAND

...ENCOURAGES ACTIVE READING AND LEARNING FOR STUDENTS OF ALL READING LEVELS

- Places special emphasis on vocabulary and reading comprehension, transforming students into active readers.
- In-text definitions, dozens of graphic organizers, and reading checks at point-of-use keep students on track as they read the narrative.

DIFFERENTIATED INSTRUCTION

...MAKES *UNDERSTANDING PSYCHOLOGY* ACCESSIBLE TO STUDENTS OF ALL LEARNING LEVELS

- A complete program with a full complement of ancillaries and technology gives this program the flexibility to meet the needs of all students.
- The *Reading Essentials and Study Guide* is a shorter version of the text that reduces reading demands while keeping key content and vocabulary.

A VARIETY OF ASSESSMENT OPTIONS

...MAKE IT EASY TO SUPPORT INSTRUCTION AND ACCOMMODATE THE NEEDS OF ALL STUDENTS

- All assessment options were approved by the program's authors, academic consultants, and experienced educators.
- Includes the Exam*View*® Assessment Suite with hundreds of test items that can be easily modified.

A VARIETY OF ACTIVITIES AND FEATURES

...ARE ESSENTIAL FOR STUDENT SUCCESS AND TO GET STUDENTS EXCITED ABOUT PSYCHOLOGY

- The TIME Reports feature from TIME Magazine brings up-to-the-minute, real-life issues concerning the field of psychology to the classroom.
- Interdisciplinary features such as Readings in Psychology help students make the connection between psychology and other disciplines.

TEACHER RESOURCES

...PROVIDE TIME-SAVING SOFTWARE PRODUCTS THAT CREATIVELY ENGAGE STUDENTS AND REDUCE PREP TIME.

- TeacherWorks™ Plus, the most powerful and user-friendly lesson planner available, makes it easy and fast to plan for the day, week, month, or even year.
- The Online Learning Center, a text-specific Web site found at glencoe.com, provides study tools such as chapter overviews, student self-check quizzes, and Web-based activities.

Teacher Wraparound Edition

GLENCOE

UNDERSTANDING Psychology

Teacher Wraparound Edition

GLENCOE

UNDERSTANDING Psychology

Richard A. Kasschau, Ph.D.

With Features From TIME

McGraw Hill Glencoe

New York, New York Columbus, Ohio Chicago, Illinois Woodland Hills, California

Author

Richard A. Kasschau, Ph.D., is Professor of Psychology at the University of Houston. Dr. Kasschau is a fellow of the American Psychological Association, a former president of the Society for Teaching Psychology, a charter fellow of the Association for Psychological Science, and former chair of the Educational Testing Service task force that recommended the establishment of the Advanced Placement Exam in Psychology. He has written extensively for magazines, newspapers, and professional journals, and has over a dozen books to his credit, including the nation's first all-electronic college-level introductory psychology text. An award-winning and distinguished teacher who has taught psychology for 42 years, Dr. Kasschau has twice won the University of Houston's Teaching Excellence Award.

McGraw Hill Glencoe

The McGraw·Hill Companies

Send all inquiries to
Glencoe/McGraw-Hill, 8787 Orion Place, Columbus, Ohio 43240-4027

ISBN 978-0-07-874518-8 (*Teacher Wraparound Edition*)
MHID: 0-07-874518-7 (*Teacher Wraparound Edition*)
ISBN 978-0-07-874517-1 (*Student Edition*)
MHID: 0-07-874517-9 (*Student Edition*)

Printed in the United States of America

2 3 4 5 6 7 8 9 10 027/043 10 09 08 07

Senior Consultant-Writers

Ronald Foore, Ed.D.
Booker T. Washington Magnet High School
Tulsa, Oklahoma

Jim Matiya
Carl Sandburg High School
Orland Park, Illinois

Academic Consultants

Martha Alcock, Ph.D.
Capital University
Columbus, Ohio

Shirley DeLucia, Ed.D.
Capital University
Columbus, Ohio

Maureen Hester, Ph.D.
Holy Names College
Oakland, California

Judith R. Levine, Ph.D.
State University of New York at Farmingdale
Farmingdale, New York

Joel Stellwagen, Ph.D.
Hinsdale South High School
Darien, Illinois

Educational Reviewers

Jerry Agner
Marion Harding High School
Marion, Ohio

Lynn Erven
Lake Forest High School
Lake Forest, Illinois

Dale Kinney
Ralston High School
Omaha, Nebraska

Patrick Mattimore
South San Francisco High School
San Francisco, California

Nathan McAlister
Highland Park High School
Topeka, Kansas

Gale Ow
Lowell High School
San Francisco, California

Introducing the *Understanding Psychology*
Integrated Internet Support for Your

PSYCHOLOGY *Online*

Psychology Online boxes at point of use in the unit and chapter direct students to use Web curriculum as part of an integrated study of psychology.

You Need: Help with Assessment

✓ **We Provide:** Self-Check Quizzes and Interactive Puzzles

You Need: Integration of Web Resources into Your Lessons

✓ **We Provide:** Complete Student Activities, Teacher Strategies, and Additional Links

Use our Web site for additional resources. All essential content is covered in the Student Edition.

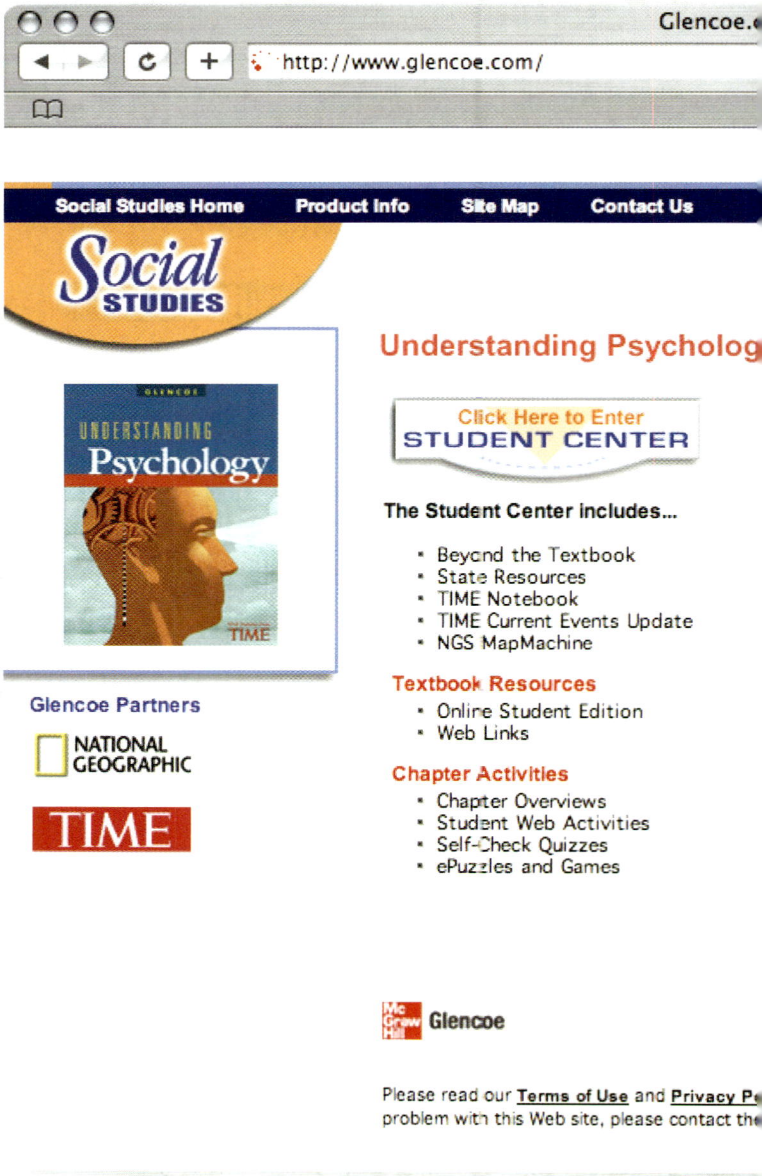

Web Site: glencoe.com

Student Edition

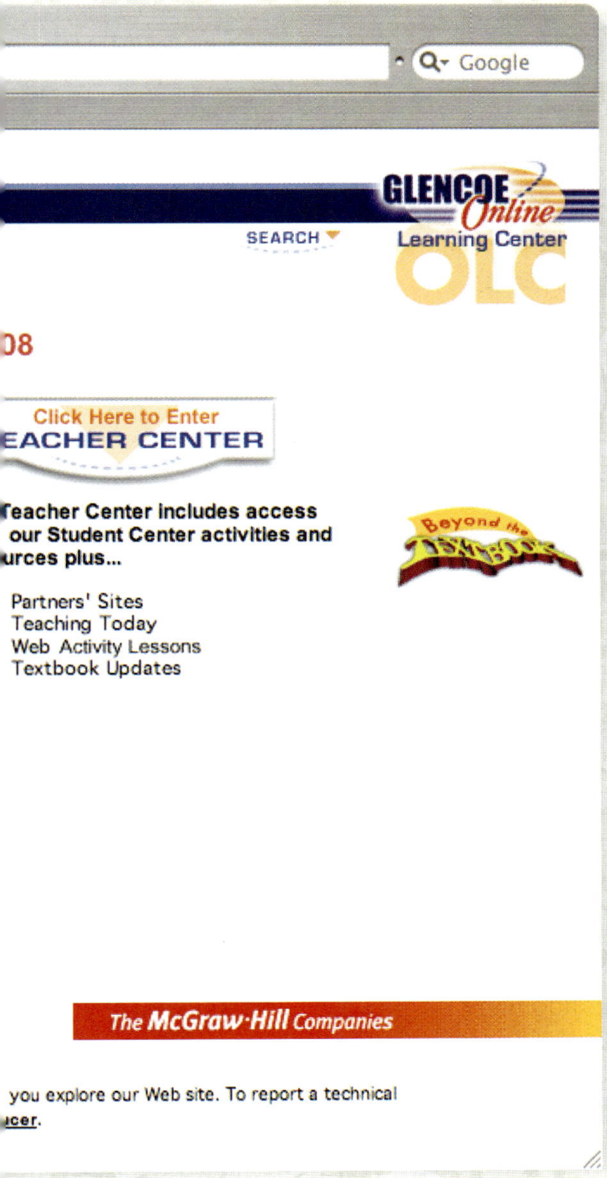

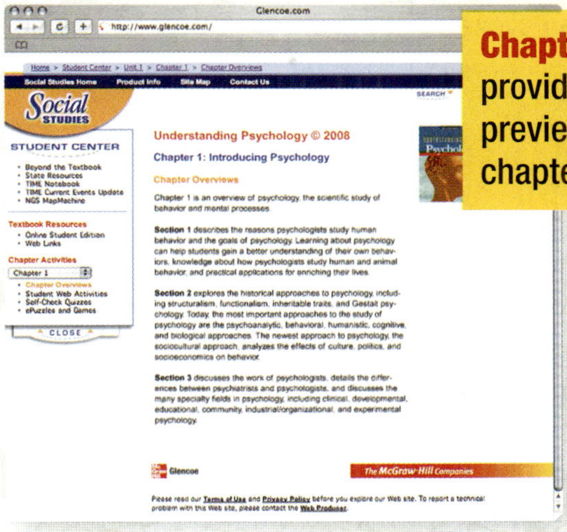

Chapter Overviews provide a quick preview or review of chapter content.

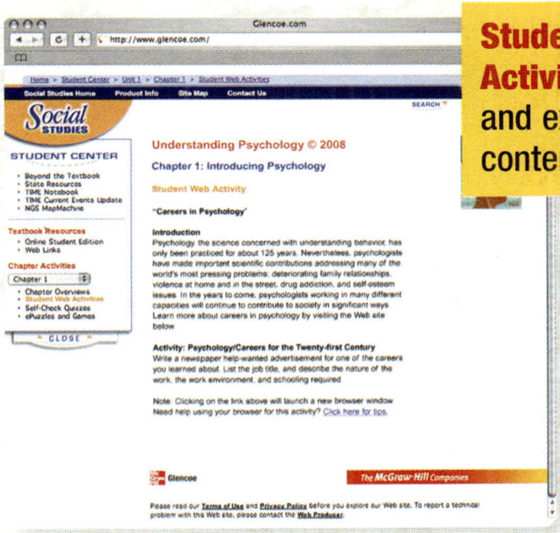

Student Web Activities enrich and extend chapter content.

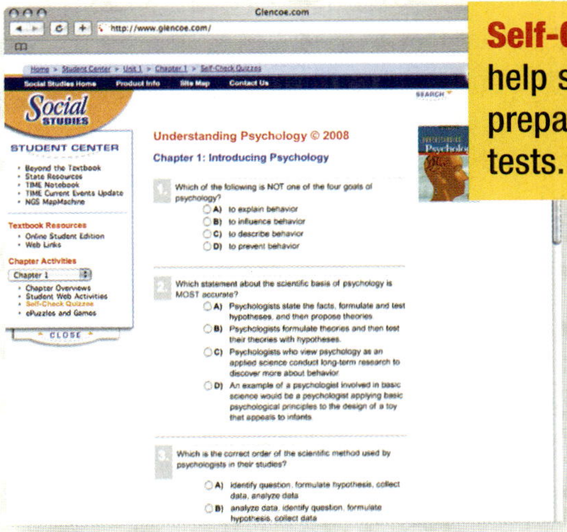

Self-Check Quizzes help students prepare for chapter tests.

Table of Contents

Table of Contents

Parapsychology unit at end

Table of Contents

Visit the *Understanding Psychology* Web site!

All essential content is covered in the Student Edition, but use our Web site for additional resources including:

- **Chapter Overviews** for quick view of the chapter.
- **Student Web Activities** take you into the real world of psychology.
- **Self-Check Quizzes** to help prepare you for the Chapter Test.

Profiles In Psychology

Case Studies

Quick Lab

Psychology and You

More About...

TIME REPORTS

Readings in Psychology

Table of Contents

Charts, Tables, and Graphs

Table of Contents

Charts, Tables, and Graphs

National High School Psychology Standards

Glencoe's *Understanding Psychology* provides extensive coverage of the content standards developed by a coalition of psychologists and educators that includes the Task Force for the Development of National High School Psychology Standards and the American Psychological Association (APA).

This chart correlates chapter and section content to the APA's five domains and 15 content areas according to the main themes of each chapter and section. In addition, each set of unit planning pages in the Teacher's Wraparound Edition includes a diagram that correlates the material covered in each unit to the national standards.

For a complete discussion of the standards, see www.apa.org or contact *National Standards for the Teaching of High School Psychology*, American Psychological Association, 750 First Street, NE, Washington, DC 20002 for information.

Domain and Content Area:	*Understanding Psychology* Chapter and Section Coverage:
Methods: *Introduction and Research Methods* defines the science of psychology, describes its history, identifies the methods for examining behavior and mental processes, and reviews scientific careers available in the discipline.	**Chapter 1 Introducing Psychology** **Section 1** Why Study Psychology? **Section 2** A Brief History of Psychology **Section 3** Psychology as a Profession **Chapter 2 Psychological Research Methods and Statistics** **Section 1** What Is Research? **Section 2** Problems and Solutions in Research **Section 3** Statistical Evaluation **Chapter 21 Psychology: Present and Future** **Section 1** Careers in Psychology **Section 2** Psychology's Contributions
Biopsychological: *Biological Bases of Behavior* addresses how the brain processes information and how the body adapts to the demands of its environment.	**Chapter 6 Body and Behavior** **Section 1** The Nervous System: The Basic Structure **Section 2** Studying the Brain **Section 3** The Endocrine System **Section 4** Heredity and Environment
Biopsychological: *Sensation and Perception* examines how the brain makes meaning out of the physical sensations generated by the environment.	**Chapter 8 Sensation and Perception** **Section 1** Sensation **Section 2** The Senses **Section 3** Perception

Textbook Correlation to APA Standards

Domain and Content Area:	*Understanding Psychology* Chapter and Section Coverage:
Biopsychological: *Motivation and Emotion* examines the drives and needs that direct behavior, including sex, thirst, hunger, and social needs, as well as the range of human emotion.	**Chapter 12 Motivation and Emotion** **Section 1** Theories of Motivation **Section 2** Biological and Social Motives **Section 3** Emotions
Biopsychological: *Stress, Coping, and Health* identifies how stress reactions hinder our effectiveness and proposed alternatives that lead to a healthier existence.	**Chapter 15 Stress and Health** **Section 1** Sources of Stress **Section 2** Reactions to Stress **Section 3** Coping With Stress **Section 4** Stress in Your Life
Cognitive: *Learning* demonstrates how we make changes in our behavior through experience with the environment, usually focusing on classical conditioning, instrumental conditioning, and cognitive learning.	**Chapter 9 Learning: Principles and Applications** **Section 1** Classical Conditioning **Section 2** Operant Conditioning **Section 3** Social Learning
Cognitive: *Memory* addresses how we remember as well as how we can improve our memory.	**Chapter 10 Memory and Thought** **Section 1** Taking in and Storing Information **Section 2** Retrieving Information
Cognitive: *Thinking and Language* examines the role of language, problem-solving skills, creativity, multilingualism, and intelligence testing as primary interests of researchers in this area.	**Chapter 11 Thinking and Language** **Section 1** Thinking and Problem Solving **Section 2** Language
Cognitive: *States of Consciousness* explores varying stages of awareness, including sleep, reactions to drugs, daydreaming, and controlled conscious processes.	**Chapter 7 Altered States of Consciousness** **Section 1** Sleep and Dreams **Section 2** Hypnosis, Biofeedback, and Meditation **Section 3** Drugs and Consciousness

Textbook Correlation to APA Standards

Domain and Content Area:	*Understanding Psychology* Chapter and Section Coverage:
Developmental: *Lifespan Development* examines how nature and nurture influence our development from conception until death.	**Chapter 3 Infancy and Childhood** **Section 1** Physical, Perceptual, and Language Development **Section 2** Cognitive and Emotional Development **Section 3** Parenting Styles and Social Development **Chapter 4 Adolescence** **Section 1** Physical and Sexual Development **Section 2** Personal Development **Section 3** Social Development **Section 4** Gender Roles and Differences **Chapter 5 Adulthood and Old Age** **Section 1** Adulthood **Section 2** Old Age **Section 3** Dying and Death
Sociocultural: *Individual Differences* focuses on how psychologists measure and compare individuals' abilities and characteristics. This unit emphasizes test construction, test selection appropriate to the context, and objective and fair-minded interpretation.	**Chapter 13 Psychological Testing** **Section 1** Characteristics of Psychological Tests **Section 2** Intelligence Testing **Section 3** Measuring Achievement, Abilities, and Interests **Section 4** Personality Testing
Sociocultural: *Personality and Assessment* demonstrates scientific explanations of personality development along with methods psychologists use to measure personality concepts.	**Chapter 13 Psychological Testing** **Section 1** Characteristics of Psychological Tests **Section 2** Intelligence Testing **Section 3** Measuring Achievement, Abilities, and Interests **Section 4** Personality Testing **Chapter 14 Theories of Personality** **Section 1** Purposes of Personality Theories **Section 2** Psychoanalytic Theories **Section 3** Learning Theories **Section 4** Humanistic and Cognitive Theories **Section 5** Trait Theories

Textbook Correlation to APA Standards

Domain and Content Area:	*Understanding Psychology* Chapter and Section Coverage:
Sociocultural: *Psychological Disorders* investigates patterns of behavior that are considered deviant or distressful in our culture and includes how psychologists diagnose these patterns.	**Chapter 16 Psychological Disorders** **Section 1** What Are Psychological Disorders? **Section 2** Anxiety Disorders **Section 3** Somatoform and Dissociative Disorders **Section 4** Schizophrenia and Mood Disorders **Section 5** Personality Disorders and Drug Addiction
Sociocultural: *Treatment of Psychological Disorders* discusses the various intervention methods, including psychotherapy and medical interventions, that mental health practitioners use in treating abnormal conditions.	**Chapter 17 Therapy and Change** **Section 1** What Is Psychotherapy? **Section 2** Psychoanalysis and Humanistic Therapy **Section 3** Cognitive and Behavior Therapies **Section 4** Biological Approaches to Treatment
Sociocultural: *Social and Cultural Dimensions of Behavior* explores how we perceive the social world and how we behave in relation to other people. This unit explores how social and cultural contexts influence behavior.	**Chapter 18 Individual Interaction** **Section 1** Interpersonal Attraction **Section 2** Social Perception **Section 3** Personal Relationships **Chapter 19 Group Interaction** **Section 1** Group Behavior **Section 2** Conformity and Obedience **Section 3** Conflict and Cooperation **Chapter 20 Attitudes and Social Influence** **Section 1** Attitude Formation **Section 2** Attitude Change and Prejudice **Section 3** Persuasion

Reading for Information

Think about your textbook as a tool that helps you learn more about the world around you. It is an example of nonfiction writing—it describes real-life events, people, ideas, and places. Here is a menu of reading strategies that will help you become a better textbook reader. As you come to passages in your textbook that you don't understand, refer to these reading strategies for help.

✓ BEFORE YOU READ

Set a Purpose

- Why are you reading the textbook?
- How does the subject relate to your life?
- How might you be able to use what you learn in your own life?

Preview

- Read the chapter title to find what the topic will be.
- Read the subtitles to see what you will learn about the topic.
- Skim the photos, charts, graphs, or maps. How do they support the topic?
- Look for vocabulary words that are boldfaced. How are they defined?

Draw From Your Own Background

- What have you read or heard about concerning new information on the topic?
- How is the new information different from what you already know?
- How will the information that you already know help you understand the new information?

AS YOU READ

Question

- What is the main idea?
- How do the photos, charts, graphs, and maps support the main idea?

Connect

- Think about people, places, and events in your own life. Are there any similarities with those in your textbook?
- Can you relate the textbook information to other areas of your life?

Predict

- Predict events or outcomes by using clues and information that you already know.
- Change your predictions as you read and gather new information.

Visualize

- Pay careful attention to details and descriptions.
- Create graphic organizers to show relationships that you find in the information.

LOOK FOR CLUES AS YOU READ

- **Comparison-and-Contrast Sentences:**

  Look for clue words and phrases that signal comparison, such as *similarly, just as, both, in common, also,* and *too.*

  Look for clue words and phrases that signal contrast, such as *on the other hand, in contrast to, however, different, instead of, rather than, but,* and *unlike.*

- **Cause-and-Effect Sentences:**

  Look for clue words and phrases such as *because, as a result, therefore, that is why, since, so, for this reason,* and *consequently.*

- **Chronological Sentences:**

  Look for clue words and phrases such as *after, before, first, next, last, during, finally, earlier, later, since,* and *then.*

AFTER YOU READ

Summarize

- Describe the main idea and how the details support it.
- Use your own words to explain what you have read.

Assess

- What was the main idea?
- Did the text clearly support the main idea?
- Did you learn anything new from the material?
- Can you use this new information in other school subjects or at home?
- What other sources could you use to find more information about the topic?

How to Think Like a Psychologist

Why Study Psychology?

Many people begin their study of psychology without a clear definition or understanding of the subject. They may have images of a laboratory where scientists run rats through mazes, or they may assume that it deals only with abnormal emotional disturbances. These, however, are only small parts of the study of psychology. Psychology provides tools to help us gain insight into our own behavior, as well as our relationships with others.

What to Expect

As you begin your study of psychology, you will find that it is different from any of your other classes. This is because psychology is connected to both the social sciences, such as history or economics, and the natural sciences, such as biology and chemistry. As a social science, psychology explores the influences of society on individual behavior and group relationships. As a natural science, psychology looks for biological explanations for human behavior. You will learn more about the social and biological aspects of human behavior as you draw from the course material to gain insight into your life and the lives of those around you.

Your study of psychology can help you gain insights into explaining your and others' behavior.

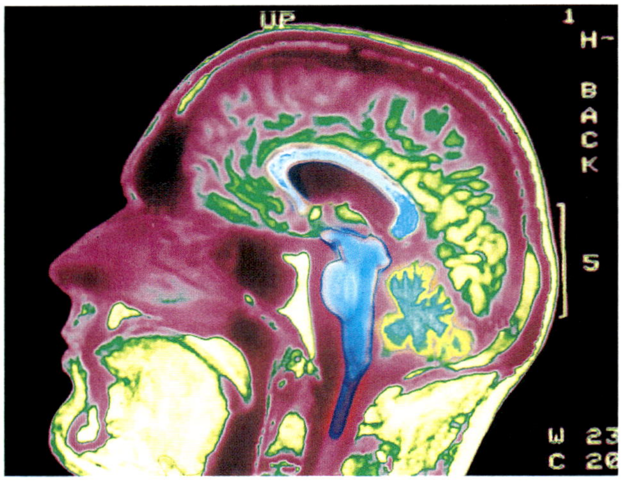

PET scan of a human brain

How Do Psychologists Think?

In your study of psychology, you will learn to think like a scientist. Scientists constantly question their own assumptions and look for alternative evidence and conclusions.

Scientists, including psychologists, use the **scientific method** as a problem-solving tool. It teaches them to think critically by encouraging open-mindedness, intellectual curiosity, and evaluation of reasons. Using the scientific method will help you think critically and be objective when applying principles to everyday issues, people, and problems.

How to Think Like a Psychologist

The Scientific Method

The scientific method consists of five steps that help the scientist integrate theory and research, as well as compare empirical—or factual—data with common sense ideas. Using the scientific method will help you think like a psychologist.

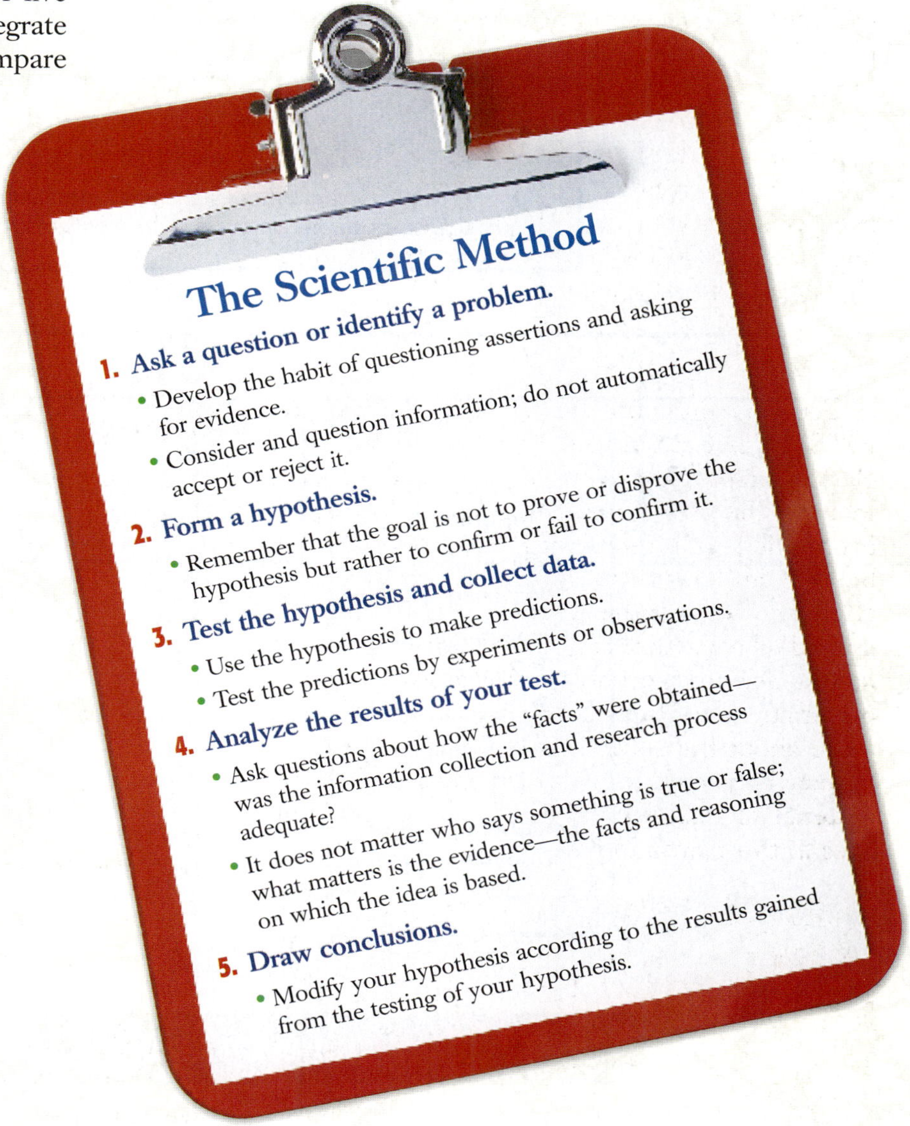

Research, Projects, and Problem Solving

In your psychology course, you will also need to solve problems through individual research or group projects—whether they are the Psychology Projects in this textbook or other activities your teacher may assign. Solving problems involves a series of processes including analyzing the problem, breaking it into component parts, and establishing goals. Here are the steps involved in problem solving:

- Identify the problem.
- Brainstorm possible solutions.
- Evaluate the proposed solutions.
- Choose and implement the best solution.
- At a later time, review the success of the solution.

To begin any project, you need to establish your goals—what you want to accomplish, how you will accomplish it, and by when. Intermediate goals address parts of the problem that must be solved in order to arrive at the terminal goal—the final solution to the problem. Use intermediate goals to establish a time line for completing the assignment, which will help you keep track of your progress. As you work, monitor and evaluate your work for schedule, accuracy, and whether it is focused on the final goal. Ask yourself: Are things working as expected? Do you need to adjust anything?

Unit 1 Planning Guide

National High School Psychology Standards

The national high school psychology standards identify what students in an introductory high school psychology course should learn. **The material covered in Unit 1 reflects content from one of the five content domains: *Methods*.** To see a chapter-by-chapter correlation to the national standards, refer to the Teacher pages.

Content Domains for National High School Psychology Standards

Use this diagram to review the standards areas that are covered in Unit 1. Standards areas covered in this unit are highlighted in red in the diagram.

Methods
- **Introduction and Research Methods**

Sociocultural
- Individual Differences
- Personality and Assessment
- Psychological Disorders
- Treatment of Psychological Disorders
- Social and Cultural Dimensions of Behavior

Developmental
- Lifespan Development

Cognitive
- Learning
- Memory
- Thinking and Language
- States of Consciousness

Biopsychological
- Biological Bases of Behavior
- Sensation and Perception
- Motivation and Emotion
- Stress, Coping, and Health

BIBLIOGRAPHY

Readings for the Student

Colman, A.M. (2006). *A Dictionary of Psychology.* New York: Oxford University Press.

Hergenhahn, B.R. (2005). *An Introduction to the History of Psychology.* Boston, MA: Wadsworth/Thomson.

Kuther, T.L., & Morgan, R.D. (2006). *Careers in Psychology: Opportunities in a Changing World.* Boston, MA: Wadsworth/Thomson.

Readings for the Teacher

Benjamin, L.T., Jr. (2006). *A History of Psychology in Letters.* Malden, MA: Blackwell Publishing.

Millon, T. (2004). *Masters of the Mind.* Hoboken, NJ: Wiley.

Sani, F., & Todman, J. (2006). *Experimental Design and Statistics for Psychology.* Malden, MA: Blackwell Publishing.

Multimedia Resources

Videocassette. *Psychology: Scientific Problem Solvers—Careers for the 21st Century.* American Psychological Association.

Videocassette. *Psychology: Understanding Ourselves, Understanding Each Other.* (29 minutes). American Psychological Association.

Audiotape. *The Evolution of a Clinical Psychologist.* Jeffrey Norton.

Unit 1 Resource Manager

Note: The following materials may be used when teaching Unit 1. Chapter level support materials may be found on the chapter resource pages.

GLENCOE'S ASSESSMENT ADVANTAGE

Use the following tools to easily assess student learning in a variety of ways:

- Authentic Assessment with Rubrics
- Section Quizzes, Chapter Tests, and Unit Tests
- glencoe.com
- SAT/SAT II Test Practice
- *ExamView® Assessment Suite* CD-ROM

APPLICATIONS AND HANDS-ON

Psychology Lab Activities 1–1 and 1–2

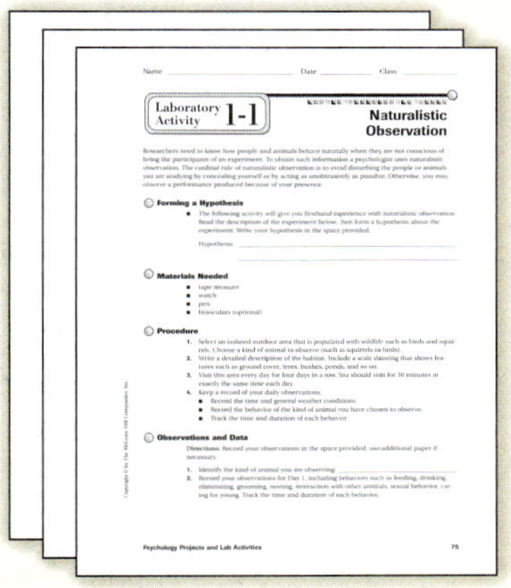
Laboratory Activity 1-1 Naturalistic Observation

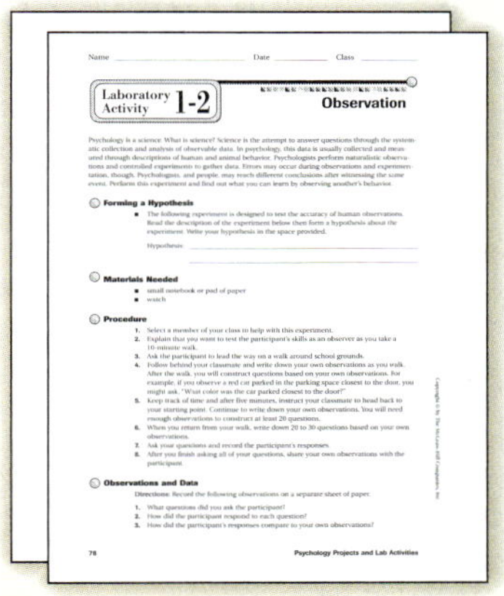
Laboratory Activity 1-2 Observation

ASSESSMENT

GLENCOE'S ASSESSMENT ADVANTAGE

Unit 1 Test, Form A

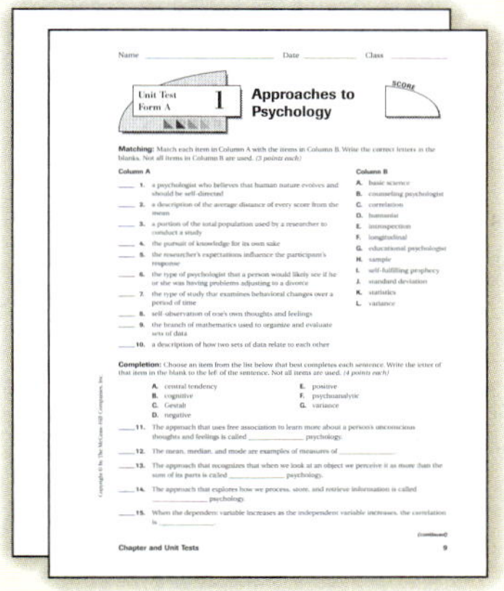
Unit Test Form A 1 Approaches to Psychology

Unit 1 Test, Form B

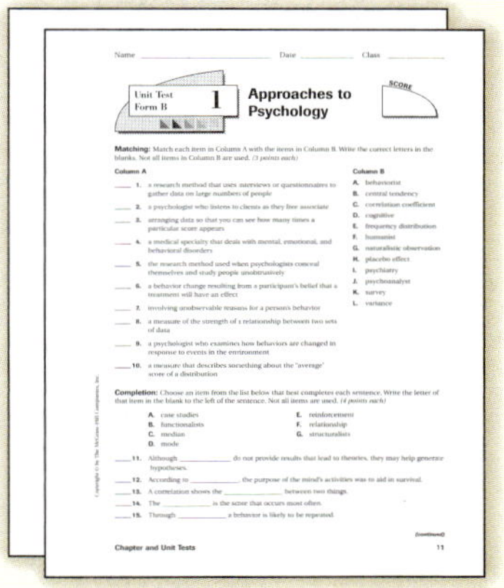
Unit Test Form B 1 Approaches to Psychology

PRESENTATION Plus!

Use Glencoe's ***Presentation Plus!*** multimedia teacher tool to easily present dynamic lessons that visually excite your students. Using Microsoft PowerPoint® you can customize the presentations to create your own personalized lessons.

Unit Overview

This unit introduces psychology and its most common research methods. **Chapter 1** explains why it is useful to study psychology. It also explores the relatively brief history of psychology and previews the large number of professions available to those interested in psychology. **Chapter 2** discusses the importance of scientific research to psychology. It introduces the basic techniques used to conduct sound research. Common statistical techniques used to analyze research results are introduced.

Unit Objectives

After studying this unit, students will be able to:

1. Identify various approaches to the study of psychology.
2. Examine experimental procedures psychologists use to avoid bias.

UNIT 1

Approaches to Psychology

Contents

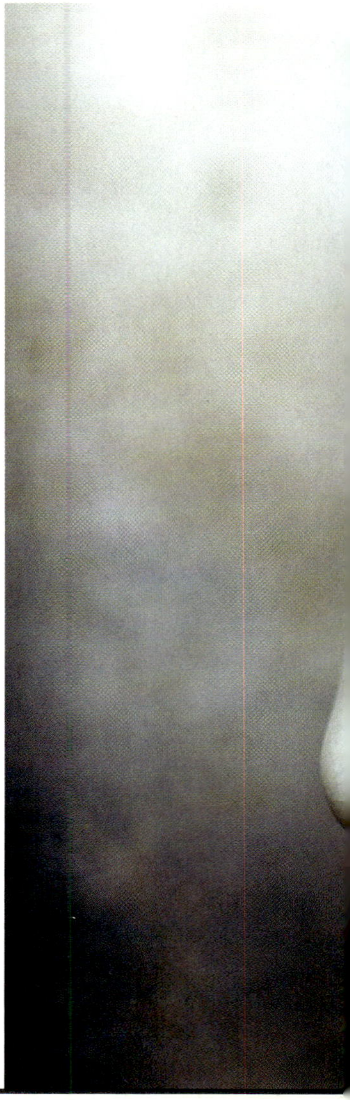

Psychology is the study of the human mind and human behavior.

EXTRA CREDIT PROJECT

Conducting Research Ask students to investigate the variables that influence how well students perform in school. Tell them to consider the following questions: **What exactly are we studying?** (definition of problem) **Who is included in the study?** (sample) **How will this group be studied?** (selection of sample) **How will data be collected?** (methods of research) **How will the data be interpreted?** (evaluation) Have the students present their plans to the entire class for review. Then challenge them to put the finalized plan into action. **BLOCK SCHEDULING**

Why It's Important

What do you expect to learn in this introductory psychology course? You may learn more about yourself and more about others. This unit will explain why psychologists study human and animal behavior. Psychologists attempt to explain and predict why people behave, feel, and think as they do. They attempt to learn ways in which people can improve the quality of life.

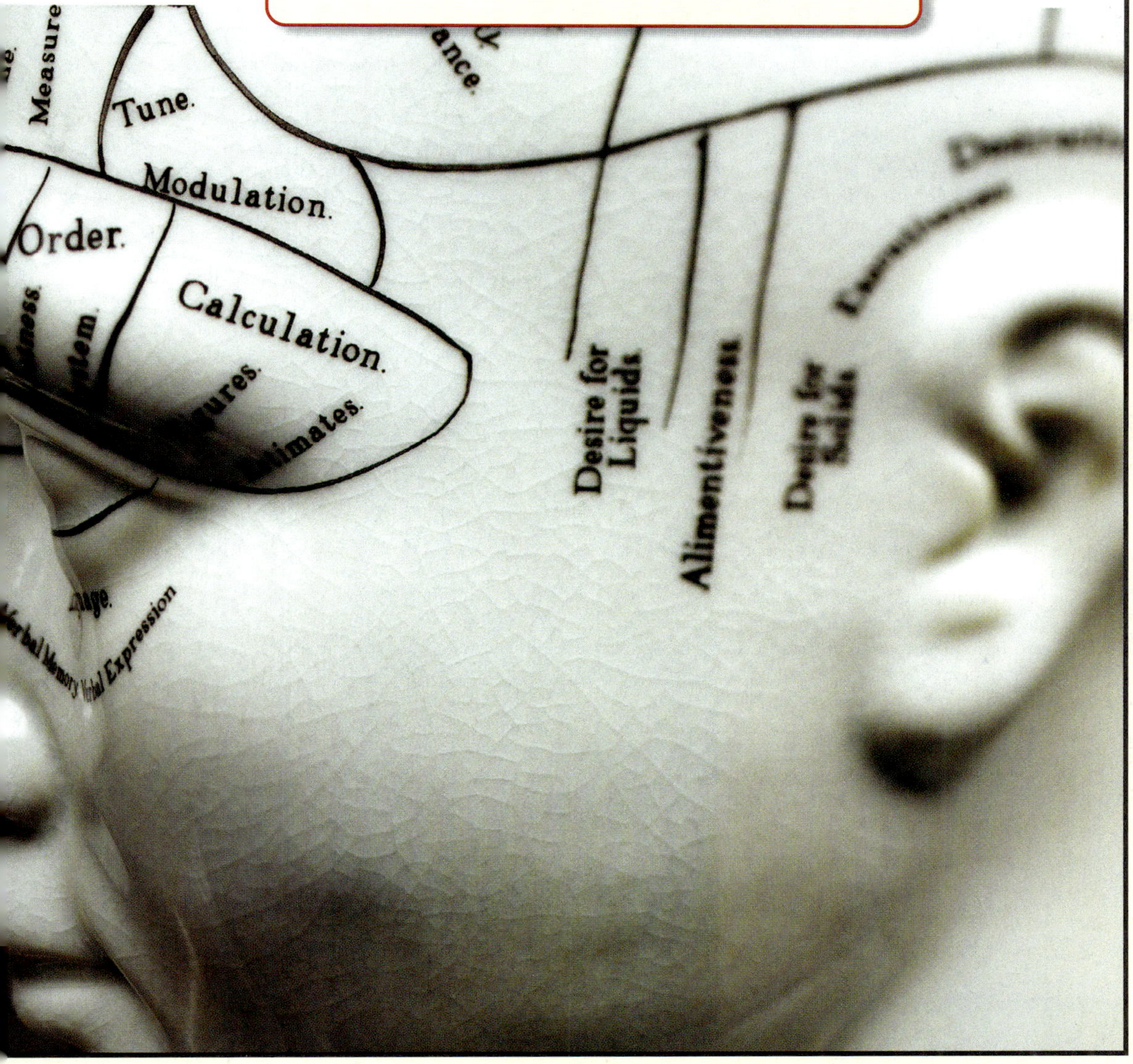

Psychology Fair Suggestion Box

Encourage students to get involved with a psychology fair. Here are some project suggestions for **Unit 1—Approaches to Psychology:**

- Research the historical schools of psychology.
- Explore emerging professions or fields of study in psychology.
- Design a research study that will yield scientific results.
- Describe the application of statistics in analyzing the results of opinion polls.

Refer to ***Psychology Projects and Lab Activities*** in the TCR for help with organizing a psychology fair.

PSYCHOLOGY *Online*

Visit glencoe.com, the *Understanding Psychology* Web site, for Chapter Overviews, Student Web Activities, Interactive Puzzles, and Self-Check Quizzes for every chapter of the text.

PORTFOLIO PROJECT

Conducting an Interview Explain to students that psychologists specialize in one or more areas of psychology. Ask students to select a specialty in psychology and develop a list of interview questions designed to learn as much as possible about the jobs and careers available in the specialty. Have students locate and then contact a person in the specialty they have chosen. If possible, have students conduct the interviews either by phone or in person. Students should present their interview questions and completed interview in report format to the teacher.

BLOCK SCHEDULING

Readings in Psychology

Block Schedule

This activity works well for a block-scheduling framework.

Reinforcing Vocabulary

Review the **Reader's Dictionary** terms with students to be sure they understand any unfamiliar items.

Background Information

Through the centuries, humans have been fascinated with predicting, explaining, and attempting to change behavior. For most of human history, our fascinations have been limited by nonscientific approaches. Psamtik did use relatively sound scientific processes, but his assumptions were not valid. Jean-Marc-Gaspard Itard attempted a noble act without any knowledge of developmental issues. Their attempts, however, contributed to a body of knowledge that has come to be known as *psychology*.

Consider the ethical implications of the actions of Psamtik and Phillipe Pinel. **Ask:** **Would we sacrifice the social and cognitive development of young children to conduct an experiment?** The American Psychological Association (APA) would certainly not approve of this type of experiment. The set of binding ethical principles established by the APA to help govern researchers' work would guarantee that this type of experiment not be conducted.

READINGS IN PSYCHOLOGY

These excerpts describe two experiments. The first experiment, related in *The Story of Psychology*, took place in an ancient time, when humans were just beginning to question the origin of their own thoughts. The second excerpt appeared in *History of Psychology* and details the attempts of one scientist to change the behavior of a wild boy.

Reader's Dictionary

Assyrians: people of an empire in the Middle East, c. 650 B.C.

spontaneously: arising naturally, without external influence

Phrygians: people of an ancient country located in Anatolia, or present-day Turkey

innate: existing in an individual from birth

inarticulate: incapable of understandable speech

erratic: strange; not normal

An Experiment in the Seventh Century B.C.

BY MORTON HUNT

A most unusual man, Psamtik I, King of Egypt. During his long reign, in the latter half of the seventh century B.C., he not only drove out the Assyrians, revived Egyptian art and architecture, and brought about general prosperity, but found time to conceive of and conduct history's first recorded experiment in psychology.

The Egyptians had long believed that they were the most ancient race on earth, and Psamtik, driven by intellectual curiosity, wanted to prove that flattering belief. Like a good psychologist, he began with a hypothesis: If children had no opportunity to learn a language from older people around them, they would spontaneously speak the primal, inborn language of humankind—the natural language of its most ancient people—which, he expected to show, was Egyptian.

To test his hypothesis, Psamtik commandeered two infants of a lower-class mother and turned them over to a herdsman to bring up in a remote area. They were to be kept in a sequestered cottage, properly fed and cared for, but were never to hear anyone speak so much as a word. The Greek historian Herodotus, who tracked the story down and learned what he calls "the real facts" from priests of Hephaestus in Memphis, says that Psamtik's goal "was to know, after the indistinct babblings of infancy were over, what word they would first articulate."

The experiment, he tells us, worked. One day, when the children were two years old, they ran up to the herdsman as he opened the door of their cottage and cried out *"Becos!"* Since this meant nothing to him, he paid no attention, but when it happened repeatedly, he sent word to Psamtik, who at once ordered the children brought to him. When he too heard them say it, Psamtik made inquiries and learned that *becos* was the Phrygian word for bread. He concluded that, disappointingly, the Phrygians were an older race than the Egyptians.

We today may smile condescendingly; we know from modern studies of children brought up under conditions of isolation that there is no innate language

ADDITIONAL READINGS ABOUT THE TOPIC

Mordicai, G. (1998). *Victor: A Novel Based on the Life of Victor, the Savage of Aveyron.* New York: Farrar Straus & Giroux.

Healy, M. (2000). *The Ancient Assyrians.* Harrisburg, PA: Stackpole Books.

Golding, W. (1959). *Lord of the Flies.* New York: Putnam.

Shattuck, R. (1994). *The Forbidden Experiment: The Story of the Wild Boy of Aveyron.* Tokyo: Kodansha International.

and that children who hear no speech never speak. Psamtik's hypothesis rested on an invalid assumption, and he apparently mistook a babbled sound for an actual word. Yet we must admire him for trying to prove his hypothesis and for having the highly original notion that thoughts arise in the mind through internal processes that can be investigated.

THE WILD BOY OF AVEYRON

BY DAVID HOTHERSALL

In 1799 [Phillipe] Pinel was asked to examine a wild boy, believed to be about twelve years old, who had been found by three hunters in the woods of Saint-Serin near Aveyron in southern France. From reports of hunters who had caught glimpses of him, it was believed that he had lived in the woods for some years. He was virtually naked, covered with scars, dirty, and inarticulate. Apparently he had survived on a diet of acorns and roots. He walked on all-fours much of the time and grunted like an animal. News of the capture of this wild boy caused a sensation in Paris. The newly formed Society of Observers of Man arranged for him to be brought to the capital for study. . . . Taken to Paris in 1800 and exhibited in a cage, the wild boy sat rocking back and forth and was completely apathetic. He was a great disappointment to the hordes of curious spectators. . . .

After examining the boy, Pinel concluded that far from being a noble savage, the boy was an incurable idiot. Despite this conclusion, one of Pinel's assistants, Jean-Marc-Gaspard Itard (1744–1835), undertook to care for the wild boy and to try to educate him. First he gave him a name, Victor, and then made a working assumption that Victor's behavior was due to his social isolation rather than the result of brain damage or some other organic condition. Itard had five aims:

1st Aim—To interest him in social life by rendering it more pleasant to him than the one he was then leading, and above all more like the life which he had just left.

2nd Aim—To awaken his nervous sensibility by the most energetic stimulation, and occasionally by intense emotion.

3rd Aim—To extend the range of his ideas by giving him new needs and by increasing his social contacts.

4th Aim—To lead him to the use of speech by inducing the exercise of imitation through the imperious law of necessity.

5th Aim—To make him exercise the simplest mental operations upon the objects of his physical needs over a period of time, afterwards inducing the application of these mental processes to the objects of instruction. (Itard, 1894)

So Itard undertook Victor's rehabilitation. With the assistance of a Madame Guerin, Itard succeeded, after truly heroic efforts, in teaching Victor to pay attention, to keep clean and to dress himself, to eat with his hands, to play simple games, to obey some commands, and even to read and understand simple words. However, despite all their efforts, Victor never learned to talk. At times he showed signs of affection, but often, and especially under stress, his behavior was erratic, unpredictable, and violent. Victor learned simple discriminations, but when they were made more difficult, he became destructive, biting and chewing his clothes, sheets, and even the chair mantlepiece. After working with Victor for five years, Itard gave up hope of ever attaining his goals. Victor's background and the "passions of his adolescence" could not be overcome. Victor lived with Madame Guerin until 1828, when he died at the age of forty.

Analyzing the Reading

1. What was Psamtik's hypothesis? Why was it invalid?
2. Why was Psamtik's experiment important even though his hypothesis was flawed?
3. **Critical Thinking** Do you think Itard's experiment was worthwhile? Why or why not?

ACTIVE READING STRATEGY

Encourage students to react to what they read. **Ask: How did the selection make you feel? Did you enjoy the selection? Did you learn anything? What surprised you about the selection?**

PSYCHOLOGY JOURNAL

Ask students to imagine that they were one of the people who came to view the wild boy in the cage. Have students write a letter to Phillipe Pinel expressing their feelings and thoughts on seeing a human being treated this way. Tell students to remember the time period in which they are writing. ■

FYI

Ancient Greek philosophers asked many of the same questions as modern psychologists. Their quest for knowledge of how and why the human mind operates as it does laid the foundation for the critical thinking techniques used by modern thinkers.

Answers to Analyzing the Reading

1. Psamtik's hypothesis stated that if children had no opportunity to learn a language from imitating those around them, they would spontaneously speak an innate language. The hypothesis was invalid because the capacity for language is innate, but the specific language is learned.
2. He demonstrated that thoughts arise from the mind and used a systematic experiment in an attempt to prove his hypothesis. Psamtik demonstrated that internal (mental) processes can be investigated.
3. Answers will vary. Challenge students to consider what was learned and not learned from the experiment. Ask students how researchers would likely treat such a person if found today. Would researchers seek to learn from such a boy today?

Chapter 1 Resource Guide

SECTION RESOURCES

Daily Objectives	Reproducible Resources	Multimedia Resources
Section 1 **Why Study Psychology?** Describe how, through the study of human and animal behavior, people can discover psychological principles that have the potential to enrich the lives of humans.	Guided Reading Activity 1–1 Vocabulary Activity 1–1 Section Quiz 1–1	Daily Focus Transparency 1–1 *ExamView® Assessment Suite* CD-ROM Presentation Plus! Software
Section 2 **A Brief History of Psychology** Discuss the set of questions, theories, methods, and possible answers in psychology that have been passed on, studied, and changed over time.	Guided Reading Activity 1–2 Vocabulary Activity 1–2 Section Quiz 1–2	Daily Focus Transparency 1–2 Vocabulary PuzzleMaker CD-ROM *ExamView® Assessment Suite* CD-ROM Presentation Plus! Software
Section 3 **Psychology as a Profession** Summarize how psychologists are trained to observe, analyze, and evaluate behavior patterns, and to apply what they have learned.	Guided Reading Activity 1–3 Vocabulary Activity 1–3 Section Quiz 1–3	Daily Focus Transparency 1–3 Vocabulary PuzzleMaker CD-ROM *ExamView® Assessment Suite* CD-ROM Presentation Plus! Software

Blackline Master   CD-ROM   Transparency

Block Schedule

Activities that are particularly suited for use within the block-scheduling framework are identified throughout this chapter by the following designation: **BLOCK SCHEDULING**

KEY TO ABILITY LEVELS

Teaching strategies have been coded for varying learning styles and abilities.

- **L1 BASIC** activities for all students
- **L2 AVERAGE** activities for average to above-average students
- **L3 CHALLENGING** activities for above-average students
- **ELL ENGLISH LANGUAGE LEARNER** activities

Chapter 1 Resource Guide

Timesaving Tools

TeacherWorks™ All-In-One Planner and Resource Center

- **Interactive Teacher Edition** Access your Teacher Wraparound Edition and your classroom resources with a few easy clicks.
- **Interactive Lesson Planner** Planning has never been easier! Organize your week, month, semester, or year with all the lesson helps you need to make teaching creative, timely, and relevant.

Use Glencoe's **Presentation Plus!** multimedia teacher tool to easily present dynamic lessons that visually excite your students. Using Microsoft PowerPoint® you can customize the presentations to create your own personalized lessons.

Activity

From the Classroom of...

Nathan McAlister
Highland Park High School
Topeka, Kansas

Pavlovian Dog Experiment

Purpose
This experiment is an introduction to classical conditioning.

Materials Needed
1 large bag of instant lemon crystals (lemonade will do)
1 set of cupcake forms (one for each student)
1 bell (a cowbell works best)

Procedure
It is important that you not tell the students the purpose of the experiment. Fill a cupcake paper form approximately one-quarter full of instant lemon crystals. Give a cupcake form to each student and give the following instructions.

Remain silent throughout the experiment. Lick one finger and at the sound of the bell, place the wet finger in the lemon crystals and immediately put that finger on the tongue, then remove the finger from the mouth.

Take the bell out and following the instructions above, strike the bell, producing one tone and one tone only. Repeat this procedure 20 times. After the twentieth time, tell students to stop. Sound the bell once more and ask students if they salivated at the sound of the bell. The students should have salivated like a Pavlovian dog at the sound of the bell. **Note:** This experiment may not work on all students.

Psychology Online

Use our Web site for additional resources. All essential content is covered in the Student Edition.

You and your students can visit glencoe.com, the Web site companion to *Understanding Psychology*. This innovative integration of electronic and print media offers your students a wealth of opportunities. The student text directs students to the Web site for the following options:

- Chapter Overviews
- Student Web Activities
- Self-Check Quizzes

Answers are provided for you in the **Web Activity Lesson Plan.** Additional Web resources and Interactive Puzzles are also available.

Chapter 1 Resource Guide

Note: The following materials may be used when teaching Chapter 1. Section level support materials are shown at point of use in the margins of the Teacher Wraparound Edition.

TEACHING TRANSPARENCIES

Chapter 1 Concept Transparencies

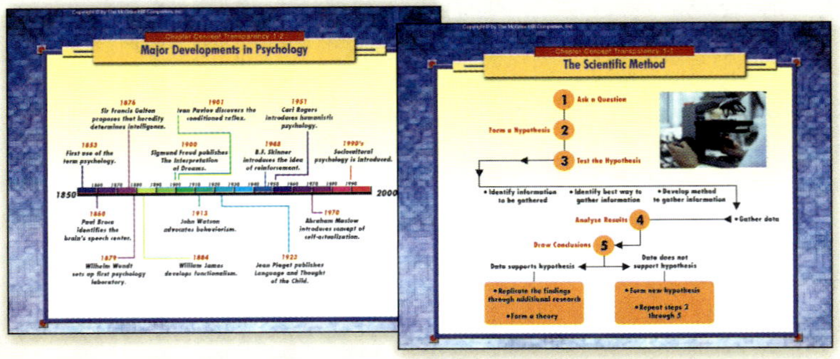

MULTIMEDIA

- **Vocabulary PuzzleMaker CD-ROM**
- ***ExamView® Assessment Suite* CD-ROM**
- **TeacherWorks™ CD-ROM**
- **Glencoe Skillbuilder Interactive Workbook, Level 2**
- **Presentation Plus! Software**

REVIEW AND REINFORCEMENT

Reteaching Activity 1

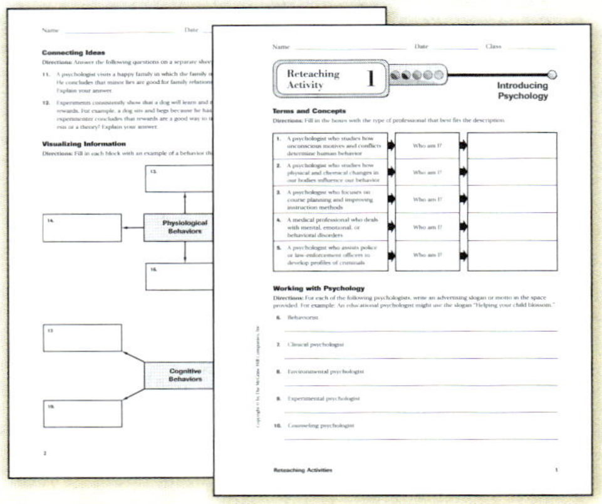

Graphic Organizer Activity 1

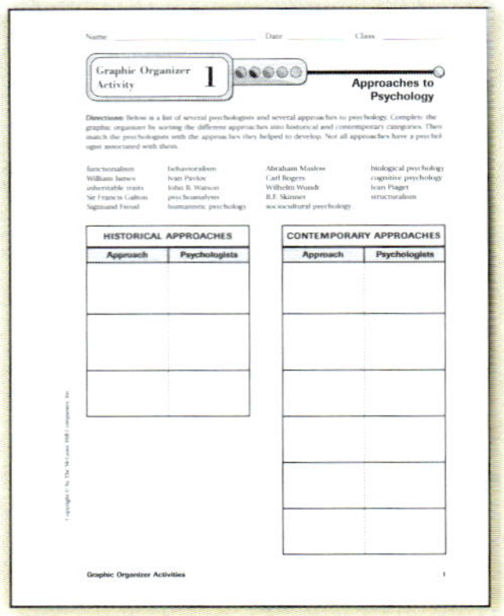

APPLICATION AND HANDS-ON

Psychology Project 1

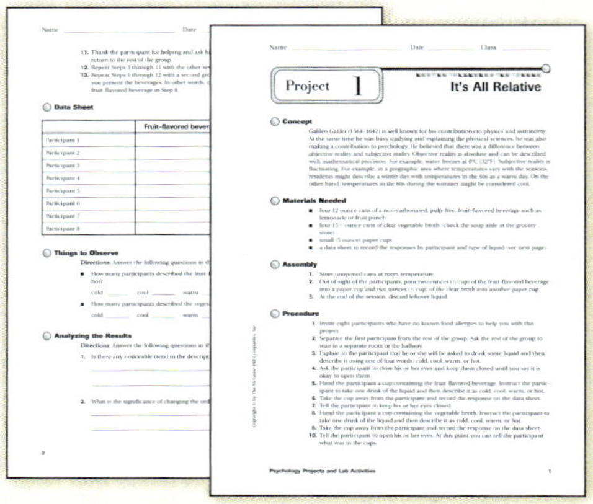

Application Activity 1

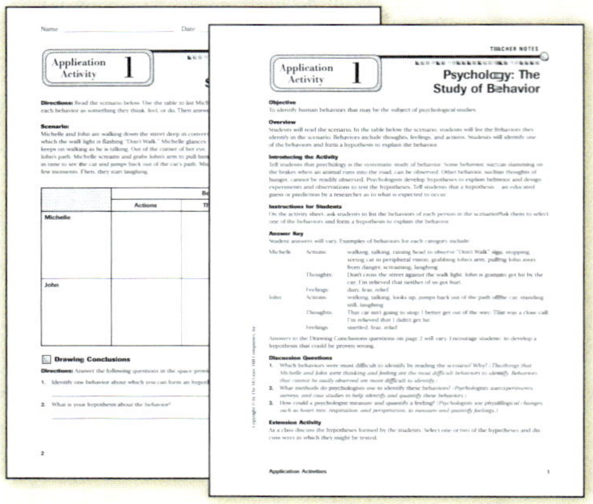

Chapter 1 Resource Guide

ASSESSMENT

Chapter 1 Test, Form A

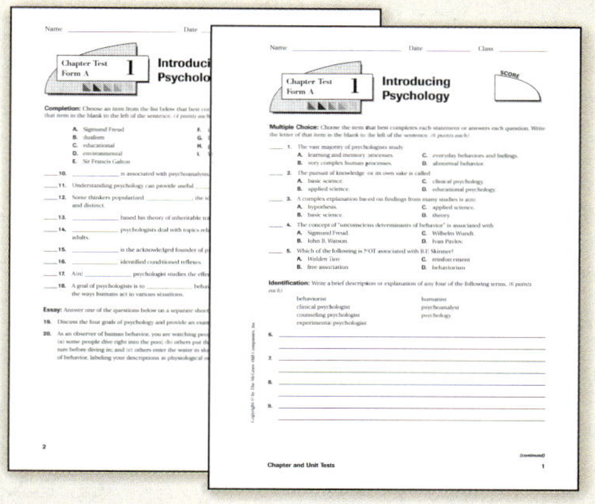

Chapter 1 Test, Form B

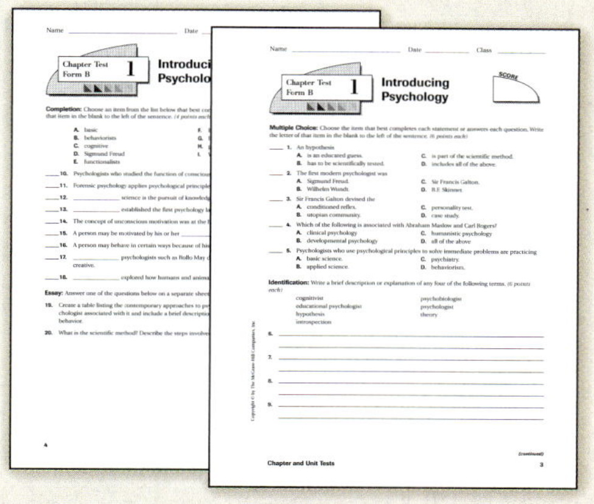

Authentic Assessment Activity 1

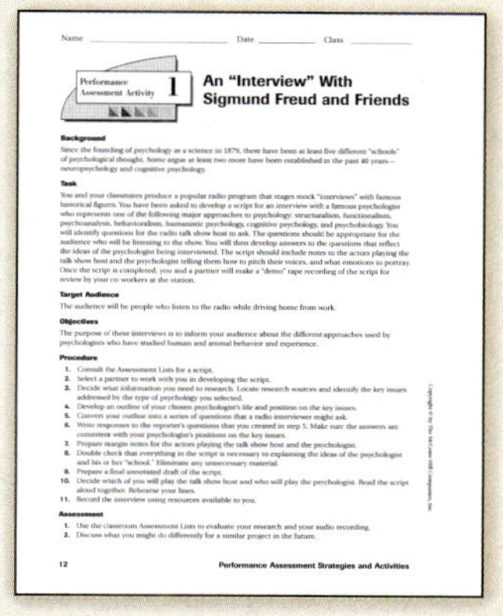

EXTENSION AND ENRICHMENT

Enrichment Activity 1

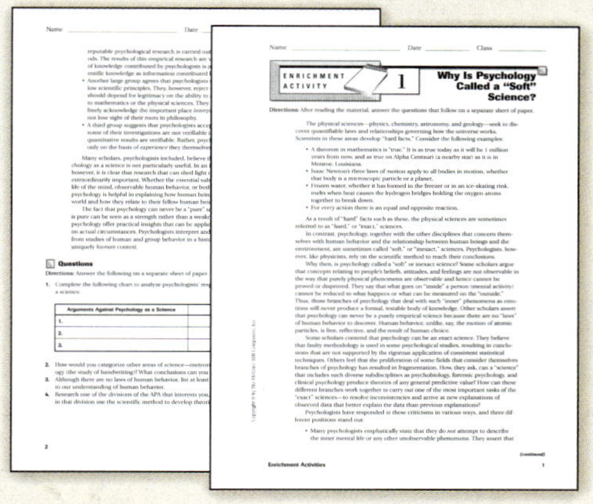

Critical Thinking Skills Activity 1

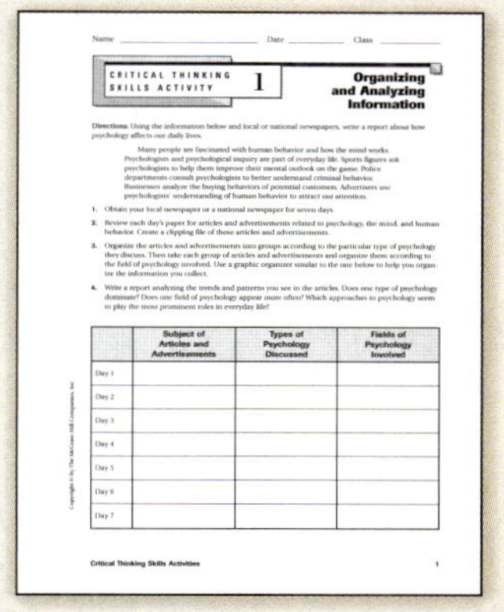

Psychology Reading 1

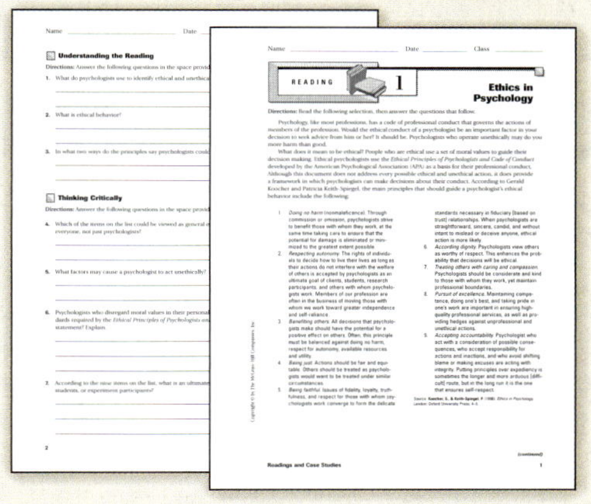

Psychology Case Study 1

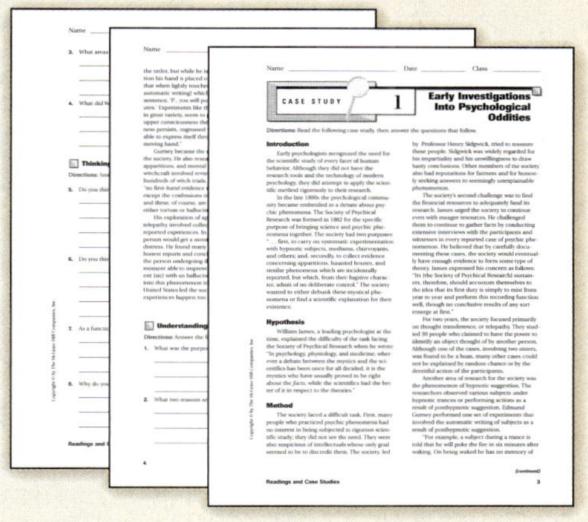

PSYCHOLOGY Online

Visit glencoe.com for a Chapter Overview for **Chapter 1—Introducing Psychology.**

GLENCOE TECHNOLOGY

Presentation Plus!

For a preview of Chapter 1 content, see MindJogger Checkpoint on **Presentation Plus!**

PSYCHOLOGY JOURNAL

Have students generate a list of reasons the study of psychology can be useful in their lives. Suggest that they set specific goals for the course.

This journal activity provides the basis for the Psychology Journal activity exercise in the Chapter Assessment. ■

CHAPTER 1 Introducing Psychology

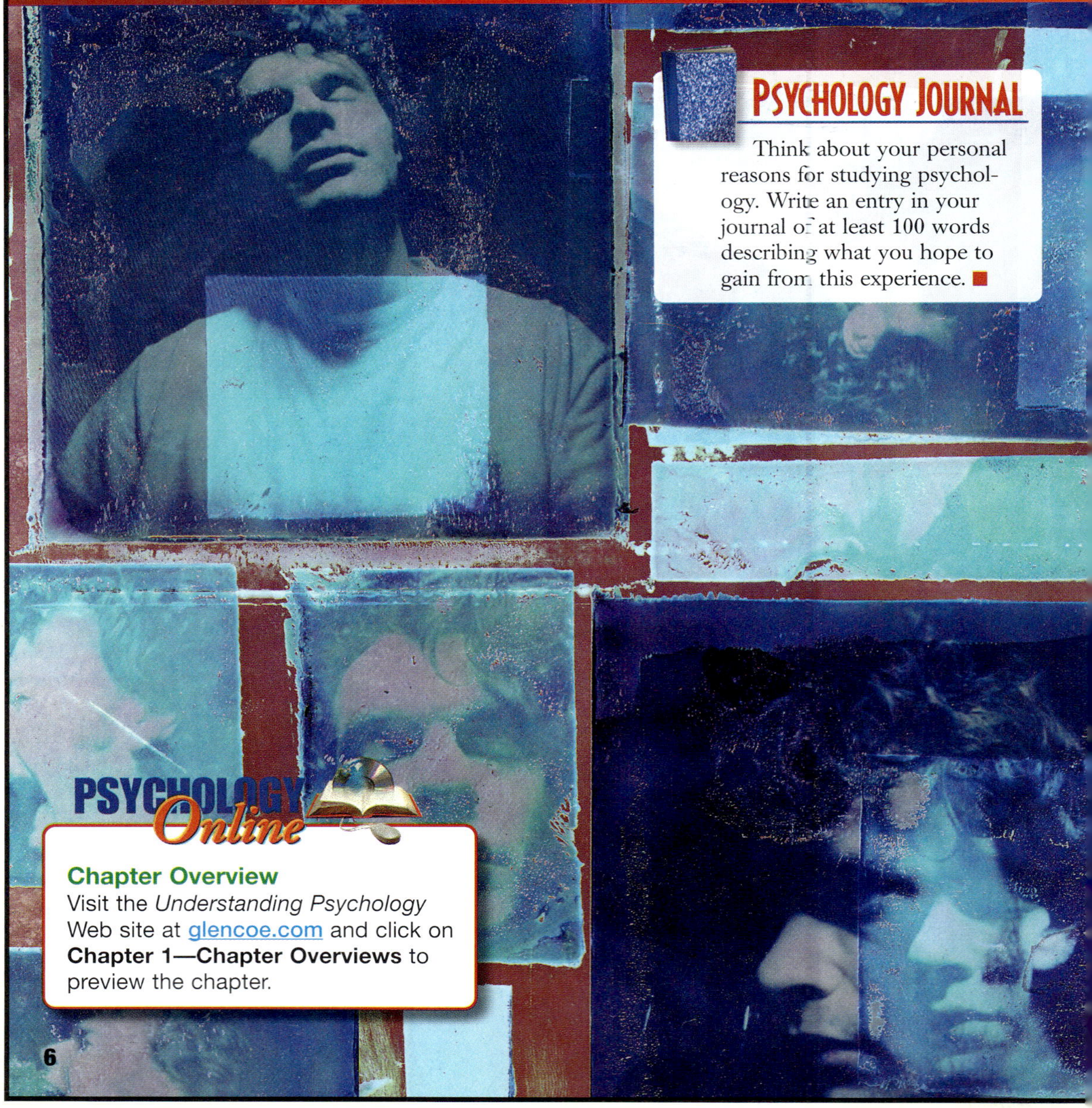

PSYCHOLOGY JOURNAL

Think about your personal reasons for studying psychology. Write an entry in your journal of at least 100 words describing what you hope to gain from this experience. ■

PSYCHOLOGY Online

Chapter Overview
Visit the *Understanding Psychology* Web site at glencoe.com and click on **Chapter 1—Chapter Overviews** to preview the chapter.

TWO-MINUTE LESSON LAUNCHER

Students often begin their study of psychology with only a fuzzy image of a psychologist. Many assume that all psychologists deal with abnormal emotional disturbances. Investigate student assumptions by brainstorming a list of all the traits and functions associated with the term *psychologist*. Record all student responses on the board. Based on these responses, ask students to complete the following sentence: **A psychologist is a person who ________.** Discuss any stereotypes that are found in these responses. At various points throughout the course, revisit these statements and see what changes the students would make.

SECTION 1 Why Study Psychology?

Reader's Guide

Main Idea

Through the study of human and animal behavior, people can discover psychological principles that have the potential to enrich the lives of humans.

Vocabulary

- physiological
- cognitive
- psychology
- hypothesis
- theory
- basic science
- applied science
- scientific method

Objectives

- Describe the range of topics that are covered in an introductory psychology course.
- Cite the goals and scientific basis of psychology.

EXPLORING PSYCHOLOGY

Addicted to the Internet

It's 4 A.M. and "Steve" is engulfed in the green glare of his computer screen, one minute pretending he's a ruthless mafia lord masterminding a gambling empire, the next minute imagining he's an evil sorcerer or an alien life form.

Steve, a college student, is playing a . . . fictional Internet game that is played by sending online messages to other players. But as he continually logs on for hours, Steve finds himself sleeping through classes, forgetting his homework, and slipping into "Internet addiction" . . .

—from the *APA Monitor*

From a psychologist's point of view, Steve is demonstrating complex behavior. Steve stays on his computer from midnight until morning, often ignoring **physiological,** or physical, needs such as sleep and hunger. He engages in this behavior because of **cognitive,** or private, unobservable mental, reasons. For example, Steve may go online because he likes the intellectual challenge of outwitting the other players. Or Steve's behavior may be motivated by emotions—he goes online to avoid the pressures of college life. There may also be subconscious, emotional, and behavioral reasons. For instance, does the Internet reinforce his behavior? Does this Internet use reflect a weak self-concept? Learning about psychology can help you gain a better understanding of your own behavior, knowledge about how psychologists study human and animal behavior, and practical applications for enriching your life.

physiological: having to do with an organism's physical processes

cognitive: having to do with an organism's thinking and understanding

SECTION RESOURCES

Reproducible Masters

- Guided Reading Activity 1–1
- Vocabulary Activity 1–1
- Section Quiz 1–1

Transparencies

- Daily Focus Transparency 1–1

Multimedia

- *ExamView® Assessment Suite* CD-ROM
- Presentation Plus! Software

1 FOCUS

Section Objectives

1. Describe the range of topics that are covered in an introductory psychology course.
2. Cite the goals and scientific basis of psychology.

BELLRINGER
Motivational Activity

Project Daily Focus Transparency 1–1 and have students answer the questions.

Available as blackline master

Daily Focus Transparency 1–1

Reader's Guide

Use the Reader's Guide to introduce concepts and vocabulary.

Exploring Psychology

Ask students to read the **Exploring Psychology** feature and then discuss the following: **Why do you think Steve is spending so much time on the Internet when he knows that his schoolwork is suffering?**

Vocabulary Precheck

Have students read the Glossary definition of each vocabulary term. Then ask them to restate each definition in their own words.

2 TEACH

L1 Previewing the Book Have students locate the table of contents at the front of the text. Ask for volunteers to select a heading that interests them and turn it into a question. For example, if a heading reads *Storing Information,* the question might be, *How do we store information?* or *Where is information stored in our brains?* Discuss the ways in which the study of psychology helps us gain practical information and answer many intriguing questions.

BLOCK SCHEDULING

Reading Check Answer The study of psychology offers insights into human behavior. Many of these insights have practical applications to daily life.

Guided Reading Activity 1-1

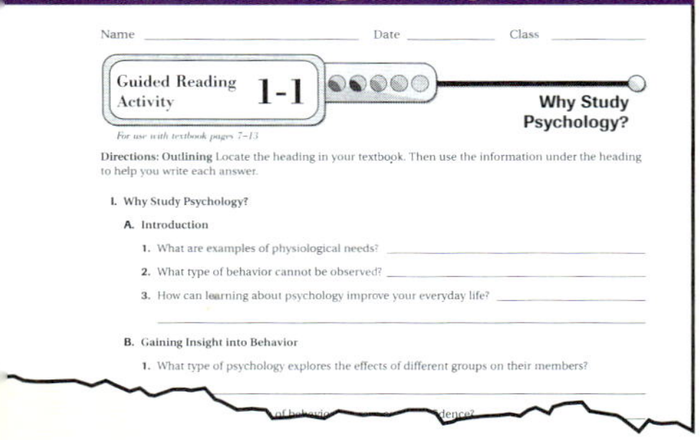
Name ______ Date ______ Class ______

Guided Reading Activity 1-1

Why Study Psychology?

For use with textbook pages 7–13

Directions: Outlining Locate the heading in your textbook. Then use the information under the heading to help you write each answer.

I. Why Study Psychology?
   A. Introduction
      1. What are examples of physiological needs? ______
      2. What type of behavior cannot be observed? ______
      3. How can learning about psychology improve your everyday life? ______
   B. Gaining Insight into Behavior
      1. What type of psychology explores the effects of different groups on their members? ______

Figure 1.1

Caption Answer Psychology is the scientific study of behavior and mental processes.

Reading Check What insights might you gain from studying psychology?

GAINING INSIGHT INTO BEHAVIOR

Psychology can provide useful insight into behavior. For example, suppose a student is convinced that he is hopelessly shy and doomed forever to feel uncomfortable in groups. Then he learns through social psychology that different kinds of groups tend to have different effects on their members. He thinks about this. He notes that although he is miserable at parties, he feels fine at meetings of the school newspaper staff and in the group he works with in the biology laboratory. In technical terms, he is much more uncomfortable in unstructured social groups than in structured, task-oriented groups. Realizing that he is uncomfortable only in some groups brings him relief. He is not paralyzingly shy; he just does not like unstructured groups. He is not alone in his feelings—and thinking about his feelings helps him gain confidence in himself.

ACQUIRING PRACTICAL INFORMATION

Most of the chapters in this book include material that has a practical application in everyday life. You will learn concrete and detailed ways to carry out a number of useful procedures psychologists have developed.

For example, Chapter 9 describes a systematic way of dispensing rewards and punishments that psychologists call shaping. You will definitely find this useful if you ever have to train a puppy. (You give the puppy a treat after it obeys a command.) You may find yourself wondering how you are shaping the behavior of people around you. Perhaps you have two friends who are always happy to join you for a soda or a movie but who never bring any money along. You have loaned them money many times, and just as many times, they have failed to pay you back. You know they can afford to pay their share, and you have repeatedly told them so. They are good friends, however, so you end up paying their way again and again. In doing so, you are rewarding or reinforcing an undesirable behavior pattern. Is that what you really want to do?

Figure 1.1 Psychology and You

Studying psychology may help you gain a better understanding of human behavior. ***What is psychology?***

Chapter 10 includes a description of several mnemonic devices, or memory aids, that help you retain information. The poem beginning "Thirty days has September," which helps many people remember the number of days in

COOPERATIVE LEARNING ACTIVITY

Creating a Display Organize the class into small groups to create displays about the influence of psychology in the popular media. Ask each group to collect newspaper or magazine articles that cite behavioral studies. For example, many polls and surveys seek to describe, explain, or predict behavior. For each sample gathered, have the group identify the goal of psychology that is being met. Each group should prepare a display showing the samples and identifying the goals of psychology that have been met. After the groups have presented their displays to the class, set up an area in the classroom for the displays.

each month, is an example. With mnemonic devices, you usually associate each item on a list with something easier to remember, such as a picture, rhyme, or phrase. Although this may require time and effort, memory experts have shown that it is worth the trouble.

In reading about child development in Chapter 3, you may recall similar experiences you had in your own childhood. Chapter 16, on disturbance and breakdown, may help you understand difficult periods in your own life and in the lives of those around you.

Psychology and You

Why You Overreact

Your friend makes a simple comment about your hair or clothes, and you blow up, getting violently angry and feeling deeply hurt. Why? Emotions occur as the result of a physical stimulation paired with some social or personal event. If an emotional event occurs, but you do not have a physical reaction—such as a pounding heart or a tense stomach—you will not feel that emotion in the usual sense. Yet consider the following situation: You just drank two cans of caffeinated soda. Your heart is beating hard, and your stomach is tense. Then your friend makes a critical comment. When you hear the comment, you get angry—but you get angrier than usual because your body is already stimulated. If you are very tired, you may react mildly or not at all to an emotional event.

OVERVIEW OF PSYCHOLOGY

Psychology is the scientific study of behavior and mental processes. Such study can involve both animal and human behaviors. When applied to humans, psychology covers everything that people think, feel, and do. Psychologists differ in how much importance they place on specific types of behavior. For example, some psychologists believe that you should study only behavior that you can see, observe, or measure directly. Steve's behavior of logging on and remaining on the Internet for hours at a time is an observable behavior. Some psychologists believe that our thoughts, feelings, and fantasies are also important, even though these processes are not directly observable. Steve may log on because he feels intimidated by others or by schoolwork, but psychologists cannot directly observe that these are the reasons that Steve is engaging in this behavior.

psychology: the scientific study of behavior that is tested through scientific research

While psychologists may differ on which types of behavior are important, they do agree that the study of behavior must be systematic. The use of a systematic method of asking and answering questions about why people think, act, and feel as they do reduces the chances of coming to false conclusions. Consider the story of the blind men and the elephant. A long time ago, three very wise, but blind, men were out on a journey when they came across a sleeping elephant. Because they could not see the elephant, they did not know what was blocking their way, so they set about to discover what they could about the obstacle.

As it happened, each man put his hands on a different section of the elephant, examining it in great detail and with much thought. The first man, having felt the elephant's trunk, described a creature that was long, wormlike, and quite flexible. "No, no! You must be mistaken," said the second man, who was seated astride the elephant. "This creature is wide, very round, and does not move very much." The man who was holding one of the elephant's tusks added his description of a small, hard, pointed creature.

L1 Creating a Chart Organize students into small groups and ask each group to appoint a recorder. Tell students that when people use the word *behavior* they generally mean the way a person acts. Explain that behavior can be observable (actions) or unobservable (thoughts, feelings, and fantasies). Provide an example of each type of behavior. Give the groups a few minutes to create a chart listing as many observable and unobservable behaviors as possible. Then ask each group to identify connections between the observable and unobservable behaviors. For example, if eating is listed as an observable behavior, it could connect with hunger as an unobservable behavior. Ask the recorder to read these connections as you compile a list on the board.

Psychology and You

Use the following question to direct a class discussion after students have read the **Psychology and You** feature.

Ask: What other types of physical stimulation can cause a strong emotional response?

MEETING SPECIAL NEEDS

Learning Style: Kinesthetic Demonstrate how easy it is to reach false conclusions by knowing only part of the whole. In a small opaque trash bag, place a variety of objects of different textures, sizes, and shapes. Hold the bag open and ask students to close their eyes and reach inside the bag for five seconds. Ask them to make a list describing the items in the bag in as much detail as possible. Discuss students' lists and show them the actual items. Have students compare this activity to understanding human behavior. L2

Refer to ***Inclusion for the High School Social Studies Classroom Strategies and Activities*** in the TCR for strategies for students with different learning styles.

Looking @ the Issues

Behavior The December 1998 edition of *PsychNews International* contained the responses received to a hypothetical situation in which someone confesses to murder in an online newsgroup. The majority of respondents (56.4 percent) said that they would notify the police immediately. This unscientific survey varies sharply from an actual incident in which Larry Froistad made such a confession and was later convicted of the murder. Only 3 of the 200 newsgroup members actually phoned the police. **Ask: What explains the difference between people's self-reported reactions and people's actual behavior?**

Figure 1.2

Visual Instruction Remind students that stereotypes reflect cultural beliefs; and almost everyone has stereotypes of one sort or another. Encourage students to review the questions and evaluate which answers may have been affected by stereotypes.

Caption Answer Answers to the survey are found on page 12 of the student text. All the statements are false.

PSYCHOLOGY Online

Links and instructional guidelines can be found in the **Web Activity Lesson Plan** at glencoe.com.

Figure 1.2 Test Your Intuitions

Test your intuitions about behavior by answering true or false to the statements below.
Turn to page 12 to check your answers.

1. The behavior of most lower animals—insects, reptiles and amphibians, most rodents, and birds—is instinctive and unaffected by learning.
2. For the first week of life, a baby sees nothing but shades of gray-blue regardless of where he or she looks.
3. A child learns to talk more quickly if the adults around the child habitually repeat the word he or she is trying to say, using proper pronunciation.
4. The best way to get a chronically noisy child to settle down and pay attention is to punish him or her.
5. Slow learners remember more of what they learn than fast learners.
6. Highly intelligent people, geniuses, tend to be physically frail and socially isolated.
7. On the average, you cannot predict from a person's grades at school and college whether he or she will do well in a career.
8. Most stereotypes are completely true.
9. In small amounts, alcohol is a stimulant.
10. The largest drug problem in the United States, in terms of the number of people affected, is marijuana.
11. Psychiatry is a subdivision of psychology.
12. Most developmentally disabled people also have psychological disorders.
13. A third or more of the people suffering from severe psychological disorders are potentially dangerous.
14. Electroshock therapy is an outmoded technique rarely used in today's mental hospitals.
15. The more severe the disorder, the more intensive the therapy required to cure it; for example, schizophrenics usually respond best to psychoanalysis.
16. Nearly all the psychological characteristics of men and women appear to be inborn; in all cultures, for example, women are more emotional and sexually less aggressive than men.
17. No reputable psychologist takes seriously such irrational phenomena as ESP, hypnosis, or the bizarre mental and physical achievements of Eastern yogis.

Each of these men was correct in his description of what he felt, but in order to understand the elephant fully, they needed to combine their accumulated knowledge. The study of human behavior is similar. We cannot rely on simplistic explanations. In order to understand our observations, we have to combine the results of many psychological studies.

We each like to think we understand people. We spend time observing others (and ourselves) and form conclusions about people from our daily interactions. Sometimes the conclusions we draw, however, are not accurate because we are not systematic in our efforts.

PSYCHOLOGY Online

Student Web Activity
Visit the *Understanding Psychology* Web site at glencoe.com and click on **Chapter 1—Student Web Activities** for an activity about the study of psychology.

The Goals of Psychology

As psychologists go about their systematic and scientific study of humans and animals, they have several goals. Overall, psychologists seek to do four things—describe, explain, predict, and influence behavior.

Description The first goal for any scientist or psychologist is to describe or gather information about the behavior being studied and to present what is known. For example, we described Steve's behavior at college.

Explanation Psychologists are not content simply to state the facts. Rather, they also seek to explain why people (or animals) behave as they

CRITICAL THINKING ACTIVITY

Demonstrating Reasoned Judgment Dr. Alfred Pontificate developed a controversial theory that one's birth order determines one's course in life. He characterized personality and behavior solely on the basis of one's position among siblings. Ask students to consider the following questions: **Can behavior be explained based on one factor such as birth order? What factors other than birth order should be considered when explaining human personalities and behaviors? What methods could you use to verify or refute Dr. Pontificate's theory? What is the difference between a theory and a principle? L2**

do. Such explanations can be called psychological *principles*–generally valid ideas about behavior. Psychologists propose these explanations as hypotheses. A **hypothesis** is an educated guess about some phenomenon. It is a researcher's prediction about what the results of a study are expected to be. As research studies designed to test each hypothesis are completed, more complex explanations called theories are constructed. A **theory** is usually a complex explanation based on findings from a large number of experimental studies. Theories change as new data improves our understanding, and a good theory becomes the source of additional ideas for experiments. A number of theories taken together may validate or cause us to alter the principles that help explain and predict observed behavior.

Prediction The third goal of psychologists is to predict, as a result of accumulated knowledge, what organisms will do and, in the case of humans, what they will think or feel in various situations. By studying descriptive and theoretical accounts of past behaviors, psychologists can predict future behaviors.

Influence Finally, some psychologists seek to influence behavior in helpful ways. These psychologists are conducting studies with a long-term goal of finding out more about human or animal behavior. They are doing **basic science,** or research. Other psychologists are more interested in discovering ways to use what we already know about people to benefit others. They view psychology as an **applied science** and are using psychological principles to solve more immediate problems.

Psychologists who study the ability of infants to perceive visual patterns are doing basic research. They may not be concerned with the implication their findings might have on the design of a crib. Psychologists studying rapid eye movement in sleep research are also involved in basic science. If they discover that one individual has a sleep disturbance, they will try to understand and explain the situation, but they may not try to correct it. That is a job for applied scientists, such as clinical psychologists, industrial/organizational psychologists, counseling psychologists, or engineering psychologists.

An example of a psychologist involved in applying psychological principles rather than discovering them is a consultant to a

hypothesis: an assumption or prediction about behavior that is tested through scientific research

theory: a set of assumptions used to explain phenomena and offered for scientific study

basic science: the pursuit of knowledge about natural phenomena for its own sake

applied science: discovering ways to use scientific findings to accomplish practical goals

Figure 1.3 Gaining Perspective

Psychology involves gaining new perspectives on your own and others' behavior. Upon examination, René Magritte's painting *The Human Condition* becomes more and more complex. ***How does your perspective of this painting change upon closer examination of it?***

Figure 1.3

Caption Answer Students may realize that the scene outside the window is partly a painting.

Vocabulary Activity 1-1

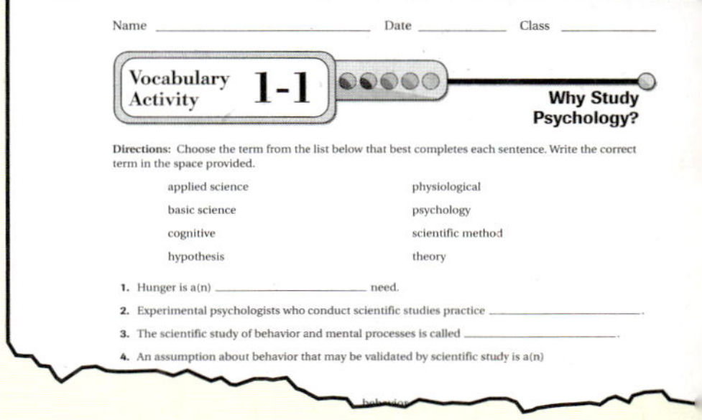

Name ______ Date ______ Class ______

Vocabulary Activity 1-1

Why Study Psychology?

Directions: Choose the term from the list below that best completes each sentence. Write the correct term in the space provided.

applied science	physiological
basic science	psychology
cognitive	scientific method
hypothesis	theory

1. Hunger is a(n) ______ need.
2. Experimental psychologists who conduct scientific studies practice ______.
3. The scientific study of behavior and mental processes is called ______.
4. An assumption about behavior that may be validated by scientific study is a(n)

TEACHER Tip

Introduce the term *naturalistic observation,* which is analyzing the behavior of humans and animals in their environment. Ask students to assess the advantages and disadvantages of naturalistic observation. Why might some psychologists prefer *controlled observation,* which is observation done under laboratory conditions?

PSYCHOLOGY JOURNAL

Have students record examples of observable and unobservable behaviors. Encourage students to analyze how their unobservable behaviors influence their observable behaviors. ■

PSYCHOLOGY LAB EXPERIMENT

Observable Behavior To understand the concept of observable behavior, ask students to watch you (or a student volunteer) for three or four minutes. Have students record everything they observe. Instruct them to be as objective as possible, avoiding any value judgments or inferences about your physical appearance or behavior. Sample student responses, and point out any subjective comments or observations. Explore the importance of and difficulties with objectivity as an aspect of information gathering. **Ask:** **Do you think psychologists can learn everything they need to know about people by observing only their behaviors? Why or why not?** **L1** **BLOCK SCHEDULING**

CHAPTER 1
Section 1, pages 7–13

Figure 1.4

Visual Instruction Explain that psychologists use a variety of research methods to study behavior and mental processes. However, regardless of what method they are using, they tend to follow the same general procedure known as the scientific method.

Caption Answer The conclusion may lead to a theory, new hypotheses, or new avenues of investigation.

3 ASSESS

Assign Section 1 Assessment as homework or as an in-class activity.

Section Quiz 1-1

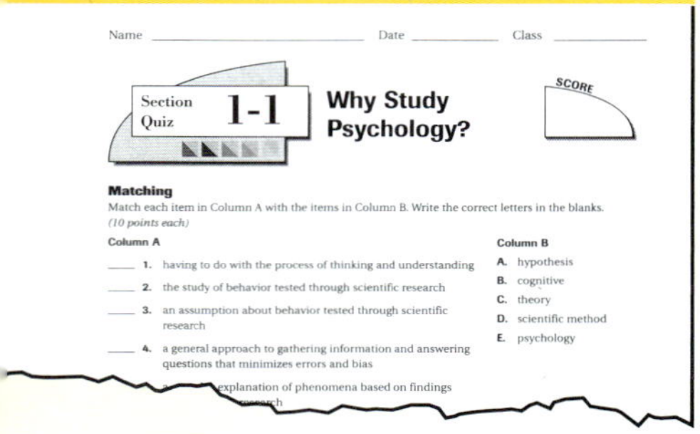
Name ______ Date ______ Class ______

Section Quiz 1-1 **Why Study Psychology?** SCORE

Matching
Match each item in Column A with the items in Column B. Write the correct letters in the blanks. *(10 points each)*

Column A	Column B
____ 1. having to do with the process of thinking and understanding	A. hypothesis
____ 2. the study of behavior tested through scientific research	B. cognitive
____ 3. an assumption about behavior tested through scientific research	C. theory
____ 4. a general approach to gathering information and answering questions that minimizes errors and bias	D. scientific method
explanation of phenomena based on findings ... research	E. psychology

Reading Check Answer

A principle is a generally valid idea about behavior. A theory is a complex explanation based on findings from a large number of studies. Principles are the general ideas or questions that psychologists have to begin an inquiry, while theories are constructed on the basis of research.

Reteach

Ask students to select a common, observable behavior. Have them list as many unobservable behaviors as possible that are commonly associated with the observable behavior.

Figure 1.4 The Scientific Method

Scientists investigate a question they have by using the scientific method. ***What may occur after a psychologist reaches a conclusion?***

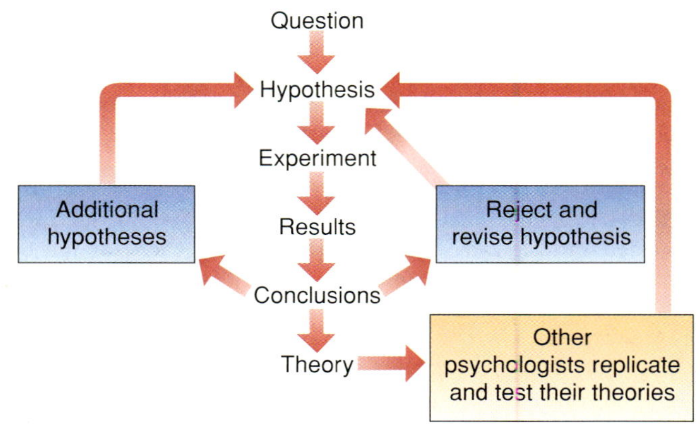

Answers to Figure 1.2
All of the statements in Figure 1.2 are false. As you read the different chapters in *Understanding Psychology,* you will learn more about the correct answers to these statements and the research that psychologists have conducted to demonstrate why these statements are false.

toy manufacturer. A toy manufacturer tries to develop toys that appeal to children. The manufacturer may apply, or use, psychological principles when designing those toys. Since the transfer of findings from basic to applied science can be tricky, the distinction between basic and applied science is important. The following example illustrates this.

Psychologists doing basic research have found that babies raised in institutions such as orphanages become seriously delayed in their physical, intellectual, and emotional development. Wayne Dennis (1960), among others, traces this to the fact that these babies have nothing to look at but a blank, white ceiling and white crib cushions, and are handled only when they need to be fed or changed. However, we have to be very careful not to apply this finding too broadly. Even though children who lack stimulation tend to develop poorly, it does not follow that providing infants with maximum stimulation will cause them to grow up emotionally sound and intellectually superior. Quite the contrary, most babies do best with a medium level of stimulation (White, 1969). Even more significantly, social interaction seems much more important than visual stimulation. Normal development is more likely to result from long-term interactions with a responsive caregiver (Rice, Cunningham, & Young, 1997). Basic science provides specific findings—what happens in one study conducted at one time and in one place.

Reading Check Define the concepts of principle and theory, and differentiate between the two.

THE SCIENTIFIC BASIS OF PSYCHOLOGY

scientific method: a general approach to gathering information and answering questions so that errors and biases are minimized

To ensure that data are collected accurately, psychologists rely on the **scientific method** (see Figure 1.4). In psychology, facts are based on data. The data are obtained from methods such as experiments, surveys,

INTERDISCIPLINARY CONNECTIONS ACTIVITY

Literature The stories we heard as children sought to influence our behavior in helpful ways. Explain to students that many fairy tales and fables end with a moral, or lesson about acceptable and unacceptable behavior. Ask students to reread a tale told to them as a child. Have them prepare a chart with the following columns: *Behaviors Identified in the Story, The Moral,* and *How the Story Could Influence Children's Behavior.* Ask for volunteers to read or retell the story and to share their charts with the class. **L2** **ELL**

and case studies. This means that psychologists reach their conclusions by identifying a specific problem or question, formulating a hypothesis, collecting data through observation and experimentation, and analyzing the data.

The scientific basis of psychology goes back many years. Today people are very sophisticated about scientific procedures, but that has not always been true. Wilhelm Wundt is credited with setting up the first psychology laboratory in Leipzig, Germany, in 1879. He proposed that psychological experience is composed of compounds, much like the compounds found in chemistry. Psychology, he claimed, has two kinds of elements—sensations and feelings. Wundt tried to test his statements by collecting scientific data.

Wilhelm Wundt

Although Wundt's methods proved cumbersome and unreliable, the importance of Wundt's work is the procedure he followed, not the results he obtained. He called the procedure "introspection," and in psychology it led to what we now call the scientific method. Whereas in Wundt's introspection an individual observes, analyzes, and reports his or her own mental experiences, the scientific method developed as an objective method of observation and analysis. Researchers thus are better able to share and retest findings.

Although psychologists use the scientific method to test and support many theories, many questions about behavior remain unanswered. Psychological theories are continually reviewed and revised. New theories and technological developments are constantly generating new questions and new psychological studies.

Reading Check What is the scientific method?

SECTION 1 Assessment

1. **Review the Vocabulary** What is the difference between a hypothesis and a theory?
2. **Visualize the Main Idea** In a graphic organizer similar to the one below, list and describe the goals of psychology.

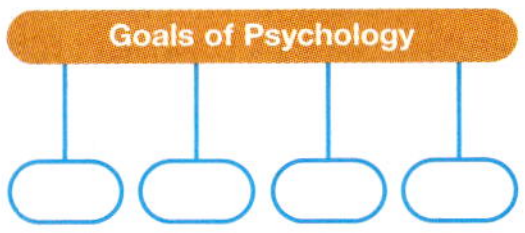

3. **Recall Information** Why do psychologists use the scientific method?
4. **Think Critically** How might a psychologist doing basic science and a psychologist practicing applied science differ in their approach to the issue of Internet addiction?
5. **Application Activity** Use the four goals of psychology to outline how a psychologist might approach the following question: Why are you sitting here in psychology class when there are other things you could be doing?

Reading Check Answer
The scientific method is a general approach to gathering information and answering questions so that errors and biases are minimized.

Enrich

Divide the class into small groups. Ask each group to select one of the false statements from Figure 1.2. They should research the topic and prepare a short essay entitled "Setting the Record Straight." Have groups share their essays with the entire class. Discuss how actual evidence can contradict popular attitudes and ideas.

4 CLOSE

Ask students to make a prediction of a future behavior based on past behaviors. Students may select their own behaviors or behaviors they observe in others.

SECTION 1 Assessment Answers

1. A hypothesis is an assumption or prediction that can be scientifically tested. A theory is an explanation based on numerous scientific studies.
2. Graphic organizers should include description, explanation, prediction, and influence of behavior.
3. For psychology to be considered a science, psychologists must base their conclusions on studies that are free of errors and biases.
4. Psychologists using basic science would seek to explain the behavior; applied scientists would seek ways to alter the destructiveness of the addiction.
5. Students' answers will vary. For example, you are attending a high school psychology class (description). You are interested in the study of human behavior (explanation). Your interest in the subject will affect your grade (prediction). Interesting activities will help you retain what you learn (influence).

1 FOCUS

Section Objectives

1. Explain important trends in the history of psychology.
2. Identify various approaches to the study of psychology.

BELLRINGER
Motivational Activity

Project Daily Focus Transparency 1–2 and have students answer the questions.

Available as blackline master

Daily Focus Transparency 1–2

Reader's Guide

Use the Reader's Guide to introduce concepts and vocabulary.

■ **Exploring Psychology**
Ask students to read the **Exploring Psychology** feature and then discuss the following question: **Why is phrenology called a pseudoscience?**

■ **Vocabulary Precheck**
Have students create a set of flash cards with the terms on one side and the definitions on the other.

Use the **Vocabulary PuzzleMaker CD-ROM** to create crossword and word search puzzles.

SECTION 2 A Brief History of Psychology

Reader's Guide

■ **Main Idea**
Psychology involves sets of questions, theories, methods, and possible answers that have been passed on and changed from generation to generation.

■ **Vocabulary**
- structuralist
- introspection
- functionalist
- psychoanalyst
- behaviorist
- humanist
- cognitivist
- psychobiologist

■ **Objectives**
- Explain important trends in the history of psychology.
- Identify various approaches to the study of psychology.

EXPLORING PSYCHOLOGY

The Science of Skull Bumps

S.S. . . . was sent to the State Prison for five years for assault and battery, with intent to kill, . . . Before his mind became deranged, he exhibited great energy of passion and purpose, but they were all of a low character, their sole bearing being to prove his own superiority as an animal. . . . The drawing shows a broad, low head, corresponding with such a character. The moral organs are exceedingly deficient, . . . If the higher capacities and endowments of humanity were ever found coupled with such a head as this, it would be a phenomenon as inexplicable as that of seeing without the eye, or hearing without the ear.

—from "Mathew B. Brady and the Rationale of Crime: A Study in Daguerreotypes," *Library of Congress Quarterly Journal*, Madeleine B. Stern

In the 1800s Marmaduke B. Sampson wrote the account above to explain why crime occurs. According to Sampson, the behavior of S.S. was the direct result of the shape of his head. Phrenology—the practice of examining bumps on a person's skull to determine that person's intellect and character traits—became an important practice in the United States in the mid-1800s. Although this pseudoscience may appear ridiculous to us, modern scientists credit phrenology for encouraging study into the role of the brain in human behavior. Phrenology may have inspired scientists to consider the brain, instead of the heart, as responsible for human behavior.

SECTION RESOURCES

Reproducible Masters
- Guided Reading Activity 1–2
- Vocabulary Activity 1–2
- Section Quiz 1–2

Transparencies
- Daily Focus Transparency 1–2

Multimedia
- Vocabulary PuzzleMaker CD-ROM
- *ExamView® Assessment Suite* CD-ROM
- Presentation Plus! Software

THE ORIGINS OF PSYCHOLOGY

Psychology has come a long way since the days of studying bumps on skulls. In the fifth and sixth centuries B.C., the Greeks began to study human behavior and decided that people's lives were dominated not so much by the gods as by their own minds: people were rational.

These early philosophers attempted to interpret the world they observed around them in terms of human perceptions—objects were hot or cold, wet or dry, hard or soft—and these qualities influenced people's experience of them. Although the Greek philosophers did not rely on systematic study, they did set the stage for the development of the sciences, including psychology, through their reliance on observation as a means of knowing their world.

In the mid-1500s, Nicolaus Copernicus (1473–1543) published the idea that Earth was not the center of the universe, as was previously thought, but revolved around the sun. Later, Galileo Galilei (1564–1642) used a telescope to confirm predictions about star position and movement based on Copernicus's work. The individuals of the Renaissance were beginning to refine the modern concept of experimentation through observation.

Seventeenth-century philosophers popularized the idea of *dualism,* the concept that the mind and body are separate and distinct. The French philosopher René Descartes (1596–1650) disagreed, however, proposing that a link existed between mind and body. He reasoned that the mind controlled the body's movements, sensations, and perceptions. His approach to understanding human behavior was based on the assumption that the mind and body influence each other to create a person's experiences. Exactly how this interaction takes place is still being studied today.

As one psychologist has expressed it, "Modern science began to emerge by combining philosophers' reflections, logic, and mathematics with the observations and inventiveness of practical people" (Hilgard, 1987). By the nineteenth century, biologists had announced the discovery of cells as the building blocks of life. Later, chemists developed the periodic table of elements, and physicists made great progress in furthering our understanding of atomic forces. Many natural scientists were studying complex phenomena by reducing them to simpler parts. It was in this environment that the science of psychology was formed.

HISTORICAL APPROACHES

The history of psychology is a history of alternative perspectives. As the field of psychology evolved, various schools of thought arose to compete and offer new approaches to the science of behavior.

Structuralism

In 1879 in Leipzig, Germany, Wilhelm Wundt (1832–1920) started his Laboratory of Psychology. Because of his efforts to pursue the study of human behavior in a systematic and scientific manner, Wundt is generally acknowledged as establishing modern psychology as a separate,

Figure 1.5 Phrenology

This 1893 advertisement endorsed the "science" of phrenology. ***How did phrenology contribute to psychology?***

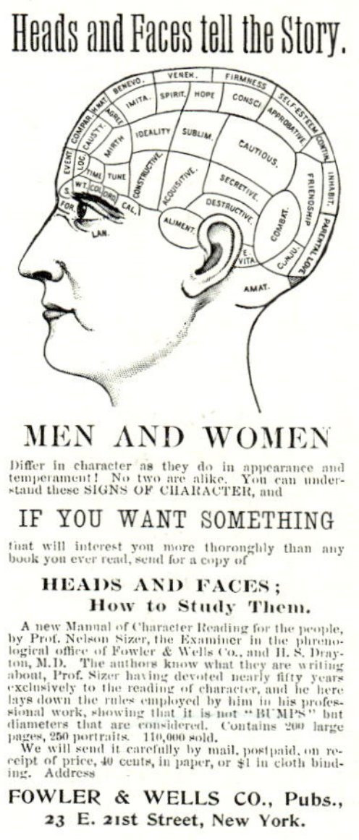
Heads and Faces tell the Story.

MEN AND WOMEN

Differ in character as they do in appearance and temperament! No two are alike. You can understand these SIGNS OF CHARACTER, and

IF YOU WANT SOMETHING

that will interest you more thoroughly than any book you ever read, send for a copy of

HEADS AND FACES;
How to Study Them.

A new Manual of Character Reading for the people, by Prof. Nelson Sizer, the Examiner in the phrenological office of Fowler & Wells Co., and H. S. Drayton, M.D. The authors know what they are writing about, Prof. Sizer having devoted nearly fifty years exclusively to the reading of character, and he here lays down the rules employed by him in his professional work, showing that it is not "BUMPS" but diameters that are considered. Contains 200 large pages, 250 portraits. 110,000 sold.

We will send it carefully by mail, postpaid, on receipt of price, 40 cents, in paper, or $1 in cloth binding. Address

FOWLER & WELLS CO., Pubs.,
23 E. 21st Street, New York.

2 TEACH

L1 Designing a Time Line

Organize students into small groups. Supply newsprint, poster board, or continuous feed computer paper to each group. Have students design a time line showing the major events in the history of psychology. Based on the time lines, have each group discuss major changes or trends in psychology. Ask each group to share its answers with the class.

You may want to compile a master time line for the wall. As the course continues, have students add pivotal events. **BLOCK SCHEDULING**

Guided Reading Activity 1–2

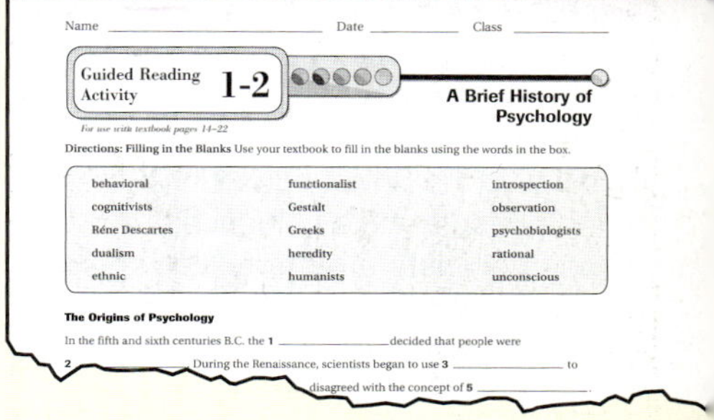
Name ______ Date ______ Class ______

Guided Reading Activity 1-2

A Brief History of Psychology

For use with textbook pages 14–22

Directions: Filling in the Blanks Use your textbook to fill in the blanks using the words in the box.

behavioral	functionalist	introspection
cognitivists	Gestalt	observation
Réne Descartes	Greeks	psychobiologists
dualism	heredity	rational
ethnic	humanists	unconscious

The Origins of Psychology

In the fifth and sixth centuries B.C. the **1** ______ decided that people were **2** ______. During the Renaissance, scientists began to use **3** ______ to

disagreed with the concept of **5** ______.

Figure 1.5

Caption Answer Phrenology encouraged psychologists to study the role of the brain, rather than the heart, in human behavior.

COOPERATIVE LEARNING ACTIVITY

Preparing a Classroom Presentation Organize the class into small groups to prepare a classroom presentation about the historical era of one of the philosophers, scientists, or psychologists presented in the text. For example, what was happening in Freud's Austria during the late 1800s and early 1900s? Each group should seek to answer the question: **How did the events of the era influence the person?** Each group should prepare a classroom presentation. Have the groups make their presentations in chronological order from past to present. Remind the students that during group work they will sometimes be leaders and other times followers; but at all times they should work to create a supportive group climate.

L3 Analyzing a Statement
Read aloud the following remark made by Freud near the end of his life.

Looking back, then, over the patchwork of my life's labors, I can say that I have made many beginnings and thrown out many suggestions. . . . I can [only] . . . hope that I have opened up a pathway for an important advance in our knowledge.

Discuss as a class how Freud opened the door to new topics of inquiry.

CULTURAL CONNECTIONS
Cuban psychologists live in a Soviet-styled environment. Although they are familiar with the work of Freud, Skinner, and Adler, they base much of their work on Lev Vygotsky, the father of Russian psychology. His theories of sociocultural influence were used to develop the Soviet educational system. As a result of his influence, Cuban psychologists are more likely to counsel a would-be defector to suppress individual needs and yield to government demands for loyalty.

structuralist: a psychologist who studied the basic elements that make up conscious mental experiences

introspection: a method of self-observation in which participants report their thoughts and feelings

formal field of study. Although he was trained in physiology—the study of how the body works—Wundt's real interest was in the study of the human mind. Wundt was a **structuralist,** which means that he was interested in the basic elements of human experience. In his laboratory, Wundt modeled his research on the mind after research in other natural sciences he had studied. He developed a method of self-observation called **introspection** to collect information about the mind. In carefully controlled situations, trained participants reported their thoughts, and Wundt tried to map out the basic structure of thought processes. Wundt's experiments were very important historically because he used a systematic procedure to study human behavior. This approach attracted many students who carried on the tradition of systematic research.

Functionalism

William James (1842–1910) taught the first class in psychology at Harvard University in 1875. James is often called the "father of psychology" in the United States. It took him 12 years to write the first textbook of psychology, *The Principles of Psychology* (1890). James speculated that thinking, feeling, learning, and remembering—all activities of the mind—serve one major function: to help us survive as a species. Rather than focusing on the structure of the mind as Wundt did, James focused on the functions or actions of the conscious mind and the goals or purposes of behaviors. **Functionalists** study how animals and people adapt to their environments. Although James was not particularly interested in experimentation, his writings and theories are still influential. In Chapter 12 you will learn more about James's ideas on motivation and emotion.

Did You Know?
Studying Scientists Some researchers study how scientists do science. Their findings point out misconceptions:
- Scientists are not always objective. They sometimes ignore data that does not support their theories rather than impartially examining all available evidence.
- Some scientists are not all that open-minded. Critics accused Isaac Newton, Charles Darwin, and Albert Einstein of intolerance.
- The best scientists are not always the brightest. Studies demonstrate that no strong relationship exists between scientists' IQs and their contributions.

functionalist: a psychologist who studied the function (rather than the structure) of consciousness

Inheritable Traits

Sir Francis Galton (1822–1911), a nineteenth-century English mathematician and scientist, wanted to understand how heredity influences a person's abilities, character, and behavior. (*Heredity* includes all the traits and properties that are passed along biologically from parents to child.) Galton traced the ancestry of various eminent people and found that greatness runs in families. He therefore concluded that genius or eminence is a hereditary trait. This conclusion was like the blind men's ideas about the elephant. Galton did not consider the possibility that the tendency of genius to run in distinguished families might be a result of the exceptional environments and socioeconomic advantages that also tend to surround such families. He also raised the question: Wouldn't the world be a better place if we could get rid of the less desirable people? Galton encouraged "good" marriages to supply the world with talented offspring. Later, scientists all over the world recognized the flaws in Galton's theory. A person's heredity and environment interact to influence intelligence.

MEETING SPECIAL NEEDS

Learning Style: Verbal/Linguistic Explain that some psychologists view psychology as an art, not strictly a science. They claim that creativity and intuition play as much of a role in psychology as hard-and-fast scientific laws. Other psychologists believe that the field should be treated as a science only. Have students take one of the following positions: psychology is an art only, psychology is a science only, or psychology is both an art and a science. Ask students to prepare and present a persuasive speech supporting their positions. **L2**

Refer to ***Inclusion for the High School Social Studies Classroom Strategies and Activities*** in the TCR for strategies for students with different learning styles.

Figure 1.6 **Sir Francis Galton**

Galton declared that the "most fit" humans were those with high intelligence. He assumed that the wealthiest people were also the most intelligent. ***What factors did Galton fail to take into account in his studies?***

The data Galton used were based on his study of biographies. Not content to limit his inquiry to indirect accounts, however, he went on to invent procedures for directly testing the abilities and characteristics of a wide range of people. These tests were the primitive ancestors of the modern personality tests and intelligence tests.

Although Galton began his work shortly before psychology emerged as an independent discipline, his theories and techniques quickly became central aspects of the new science. In 1883 he published a book, *Inquiries into Human Faculty and Its Development,* that is regarded as the first study of individual differences. Galton's writings raised the issue of whether behavior is determined by heredity or environment—a subject that remains a focus of controversy today.

Gestalt Psychology

A group of German psychologists, including Max Wertheimer (1880–1943), Wolfgang Köhler (1887–1967), and Kurt Koffka (1886–1941), disagreed with the principles of structuralism and behaviorism. They argued that perception is more than the sum of its parts—it involves a "whole pattern" or, in German, a *Gestalt.* For example, when people look at a chair, they recognize the chair as a whole rather than noticing its legs, its seat, and its other components. Another example includes the perception of apparent motion. When you see fixed lights flashing in sequence as on traffic lights and neon signs, you perceive motion rather than individual lights flashing on and off (see Figure 1.8). Gestalt psychologists studied how sensations are assembled into perceptual experiences. This approach became the forerunner for cognitive approaches to the study of psychology.

"HAVE A COUPLE OF DREAMS, AND CALL ME IN THE MORNING."

Figure 1.7 **Dream Analysis**

Freud believed that dreams can represent past, present, or future concerns or fears. Most contemporary psychologists, though, disagree with the symbols Freud found in dreams. ***How do you think the psychologist in the cartoon plans to help his patient?***

CONTEMPORARY APPROACHES

Many ideas taken from the historical approaches to psychology are reflected in contemporary approaches to the study

CHAPTER 1
Section 2, pages 14–22

Figure 1.6

Caption Answer Galton failed to consider the stimulation in one's environment and social and economic factors as influences on intelligence.

TEACHER Tip

Help students understand how the history of psychology fits into the larger historical picture by examining the major events of the nineteenth and early twentieth century.

PSYCHOLOGY JOURNAL

Ask students to write one paragraph expressing how understanding the history of psychology will be helpful in learning about modern psychological methods. ■

Figure 1.7

Caption Answer He plans to use his patient's dreams to interpret their unconscious thoughts and motivations.

CRITICAL THINKING ACTIVITY

Making Comparisons Tell students that Hippocrates, the Greek physician known as the father of medicine, once said: "Men ought to know that from the brain, and the brain only, arise our pleasures, joys, laughter, and jests, as well as our sorrows, pains, grief, and tears." Explain to students that they will compare this view of behavior to those of the psychological pioneers mentioned in this chapter. Ask students to answer the following questions: **Which psychological pioneers would be *most* likely to agree with Hippocrates? Which psychological pioneers would be *least* likely to agree?** **L2**

Figure 1.8

Caption Answer Both images are examples of how we see the whole rather than just its individual parts.

Vocabulary Activity 1–2

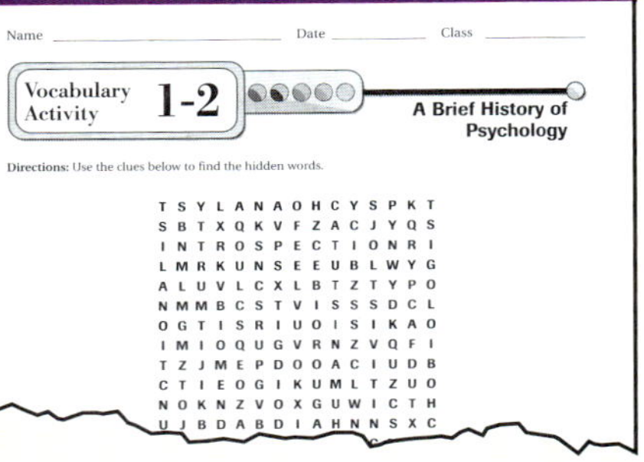
Name ______ Date ______ Class ______

Vocabulary Activity 1-2

A Brief History of Psychology

Directions: Use the clues below to find the hidden words.

T	S	Y	L	A	N	A	O	H	C	Y	S	P	K	T
S	B	T	X	Q	K	V	F	Z	A	C	J	Y	Q	S
I	N	T	R	O	S	P	E	C	T	I	O	N	R	I
L	M	R	K	U	N	S	E	E	U	B	L	W	Y	G
A	L	U	V	L	C	X	L	B	T	Z	T	Y	P	O
N	M	M	B	C	S	T	V	I	S	S	S	D	C	L
O	G	T	I	S	R	I	U	O	I	S	I	K	A	O
I	M	I	O	Q	U	G	V	R	N	Z	V	Q	F	I
T	Z	J	M	E	P	D	O	O	A	C	I	U	D	B
C	T	I	E	O	G	I	K	U	M	L	T	Z	U	O
N	O	K	N	Z	V	O	X	G	U	W	I	C	T	H
U	J	B	D	A	B	D	I	A	H	N	N	S	X	C

PSYCHOLOGY Update

Therapy Model In the era of managed care, even the amount of psychotherapy that may be required to treat various types of disorders has been studied. Kenneth Howard, Ph.D., and Mark Kopta, Ph.D., have developed a dosage model that estimates the number of psychotherapy sessions that a person needs to achieve normal psychological functioning. The model takes into account such things as the psychologist's listening and empathizing skills. In general, they estimated that one year of psychotherapy sessions would be needed to have a 75 percent chance of regaining normal psychological functioning.

Figure 1.8 Gestalt Psychology

Artist Giuseppe Arcimboldo (1527–1593) played with perceptual images in his painting *Autumn.*

An electric sign in which the bulbs go on and off in turn, with the appropriate timing, gives the impression of motion. ***How do these two images represent the ideas of Gestalt psychology?***

of psychology. The most important approaches to the study of psychology today are the psychoanalytic, behavioral, humanistic, cognitive, biological, and sociocultural approaches.

Psychoanalytic Psychology

While the first psychologists were interested in understanding the conscious mind, Sigmund Freud (1856–1939), a physician who practiced in Vienna until 1938, was more interested in the unconscious mind. He believed that our conscious experiences are only the tip of the iceberg, that beneath the surface are primitive biological urges that are in conflict with the requirements of society and morality. According to Freud, these unconscious motivations and conflicts are responsible for most human behavior. He thought that they were responsible for many medically unexplainable physical symptoms that troubled his patients.

Freud used a new method for indirectly studying unconscious processes. In this technique, known as *free association,* a patient said everything that came to mind—no matter how absurd or irrelevant it seemed—without attempting to produce logical or meaningful statements. The person was instructed not to edit or censor the thoughts.

PSYCHOLOGY LAB EXPERIMENT

Free Association Tell students that this experiment explores the concept of free association. Have students write down the first thought that comes into their minds as you read aloud the following list of words: *time, death, red, mother, fear, home, school, friend, love, hate.* Direct students not to write their names on their papers. Also, they should remain silent so that their responses do not influence anyone else. Collect the papers and redistribute them. Working in pairs, students should review the responses. **Ask: What, if anything, can you determine about the person whose list you are reviewing?** Discuss how psychologists use this free-association technique. Also, discuss the difficulties in analyzing personalities on the basis of a few responses. **L2** **BLOCK SCHEDULING**

Freud's role, that of **psychoanalyst,** was to be objective; he merely sat and listened and then interpreted the associations. Free association, Freud believed, revealed the operation of unconscious processes. Freud also believed that dreams are expressions of the most primitive unconscious urges. To learn more about these urges, he used *dream analysis*—basically an extension of free association—in which he applied the same technique to a patient's dreams (Freud, 1940) (see Figure 1.7).

While working out his ideas, Freud took careful, extensive notes on all his patients and treatment sessions. He used these records, or case studies, to develop and illustrate a comprehensive theory of personality (Ewen, 2003). Freud's theory of personality will be discussed in Chapter 14.

In many areas of psychology today, Freud's view of unconscious motivation remains a powerful and controversial influence. Modern psychologists may support, alter, or attempt to disprove it, but most have a strong opinion about it. The technique of free association is still used by psychoanalysts, and the method of intensive case study is still a major tool for investigating behavior. A *case study* is an analysis of the thoughts, feelings, beliefs, experiences, behaviors, or problems of an individual.

psychoanalyst: a psychologist who studies how unconscious motives and conflicts determine human behavior, feelings, and thoughts

Behavioral Psychology

The pioneering work of Russian physiologist Ivan Pavlov (1849–1936) charted another new course for psychological investigation. In a now-famous experiment, Pavlov rang a tuning fork each time he gave a dog some meat powder. The dog would normally salivate when the powder reached its mouth. After Pavlov repeated the procedure several times, the dog would salivate when it heard the ring of the tuning fork, even if no food appeared. It had been conditioned to associate the sound with the food.

Profiles In Psychology

Mary Whiton Calkins

1863–1930

"What we most need to know about any man is surely this: whether he is good or bad."

Mary Whiton Calkins, a female pioneer in psychology, contributed greatly to the field of psychology despite numerous obstacles. In the 1800s, North American universities barred women from Ph.D. programs. Despite this, Harvard's William James admitted Calkins into his graduate seminar. When Calkins joined the seminar, all the other students dropped it in protest, so James tutored her alone.

Calkins taught and studied, petitioning Harvard to admit her as a Ph.D. candidate. Harvard refused and, instead, held an informal examination for Calkins. Calkins completed the requirements for the doctoral degree and outperformed all her male counterparts on the examination. When Radcliffe University offered her the doctoral degree, she refused to accept the compromise.

Calkins served as a full professor of psychology at Wellesley College and became the first female president of both the American Psychological Association (APA) and the American Philosophical Association.

Profiles In Psychology

Ask students to read the **Profiles In Psychology** feature and then discuss the following questions:

1. What educational barriers did Calkins face? *(She could not be admitted as a doctoral student at Harvard. When she convinced William James to let her attend the graduate seminar, all the other students dropped the course.)*
2. How did Calkins respond to these barriers? *(She stayed in the seminar, receiving James's full attention. She completed all requirements to receive her Ph.D. When Harvard refused to grant the degree, Radcliffe University offered to confer the degree. Calkins refused to accept this compromise.)*

CURRICULUM CONNECTION

The Arts In the 1930s, psychiatrist William Menninger used works of fiction as a therapy tool for some psychiatric patients. Today, some therapists are using movies as a therapy tool. In a survey of therapists attending a marriage and family therapy conference, the majority used discussions about movies as a regular tool in psychotherapy sessions.

INTERDISCIPLINARY CONNECTIONS ACTIVITY

Daily Life Assign students to observe the characters in a television program, movie, or video of their own choosing. As they watch, have students make a list of observed behaviors in the characters. **Ask:** **What factors shaped these behaviors?** Have students share their observations with the class. In a follow-up discussion, **ask:** **How might the behaviors of the entertainers affect the behavior of the viewers? How did this activity influence the way you view the media?** **L3**

CHAPTER 1

Section 2, pages 14–22

Quick Lab

Purpose Students will examine why they behave as they do.

Process Skills Relating cause and effect

Teaching Strategies

- Review the concepts of observable and unobservable behavior.
- Discuss the relationships between a behavior and its cause.

Analysis

1. Students will list many different types of behavior. They should be able to readily connect both observable and unobservable behaviors with the events that caused the behavior. Students may notice that one behavior is the cause for another behavior.
2. Students' answers will vary. Each behavior should be linked to specific positive and negative reinforcements.

Readings and Case Studies in Psychology
Have students read the Chapter 1 Reading selection in *Readings and Case Studies in Psychology* and answer the questions that follow the reading.

Quick Lab

Why do you do what you do?
Throughout the course of a day, you perform many activities. Why?

Procedure

1. Observe and keep careful notes of your behavior on a particular day.
2. You may want to make a chart listing each action, such as "woke to the alarm clock's ring," "ate breakfast," and "yelled at little brother."

Analysis

1. Beside each behavior you have noted, list what caused your behavior. For example, "I woke up at 7:00 A.M. because school starts at 8:00 A.M., and I hate being late. I ate breakfast because I was hungry."
2. Using the behaviorist approach, describe how rewards and punishments affected each of the behaviors on your list.

See the Skills Handbook, page 622, for an explanation of designing an experiment.

behaviorist: a psychologist who analyzes how organisms learn or modify their behavior based on their response to events in the environment

humanist: a psychologist who believes that each person has freedom in directing his or her future and achieving personal growth

cognitivist: a psychologist who studies how we process, store, retrieve, and use information and how thought processes influence our behavior

The conditioned reflex was a response (salivation) provoked by a stimulus (the tuning fork) other than the one that first produced it (food) (see Chapter 9 for a complete explanation). The concept was used by psychologists as a new tool, as a means of exploring the development of behavior. Using this tool, they could begin to account for behavior as the product of prior experience. This enabled them to explain how certain acts and certain differences among individuals were the result of learning.

Those psychologists who stressed investigating observable behavior became known as **behaviorists.** Their position, as formulated by psychologist John B. Watson (1878–1958), was that psychology should concern itself only with the *observable* facts of behavior. Watson further maintained that all behavior, even apparently instinctive behavior, is the result of conditioning and occurs because the appropriate stimulus is present in the environment.

Although it was Watson who defined and solidified the behaviorist position, it was B.F. Skinner (1904–1990) who introduced the concept of reinforcement. (*Reinforcement* is a response to a behavior that increases the likelihood the behavior will be repeated.) Skinner attempted to show how his laboratory techniques might be applied to society as a whole. In his classic novel *Walden Two* (1948), he portrayed his idea of Utopia—a small town in which conditioning, through rewarding those who display behavior that is considered desirable, rules every conceivable facet of life.

Humanistic Psychology

Humanistic psychology developed as a reaction to behavioral psychology. In the 1960s, **humanists** such as Abraham Maslow, Carl Rogers, and Rollo May described human nature as evolving and self-directed. It differs from behaviorism and psychoanalysis in that it does not view humans as being controlled by events in the environment or by unconscious forces. Instead, the environment and other outside forces simply serve as a background to our own internal growth. The humanistic approach emphasizes how each person is unique and has a self-concept and potential to develop fully. This potential for personal growth and development can lead to a more satisfying life.

Cognitive Psychology

Since 1950, cognitive psychology has benefited from the contributions of people such as Jean Piaget, Noam Chomsky, and Leon Festinger. **Cognitivists** focus on how we process, store, retrieve, and use information

EXTENDING THE CONTENT

Wilhelm Wundt Wilhelm Wundt showed little interest in scholarship as a child and teen. In fact, he was barely able to finish school because of his daydreaming. Nobody could guess that in 1855, the daydreamer would rank first on the state medical examinations. As Wundt's fame grew, leading psychologists made their way to Wundt's laboratory. To Wundt, all sound psychological theory rested upon experimental science. **Ask:** **What do you think Wundt thought of William James?** *(Wundt commented once on William James's writing: "It is literature, it is beautiful, but it is not psychology.")*

and how this information influences our thinking, language, problem solving, and creativity. They believe that behavior is more than a simple response to a stimulus. Behavior is influenced by a variety of mental processes, including perceptions, memories, and expectations.

Reading Check How do cognitive psychologists differ from behaviorists?

Biological Psychology

This viewpoint, today often referred to as *behavioral neuroscience*, emphasizes the impact of biology on behavior. **Psychobiologists** study how the brain, the nervous system, hormones, and genetics influence our behavior. PET, CT, fMRI, and MEG/MSI scans (explained in Chapter 6) are the newest tools used by psychobiologists. Psychobiologists have found that genetic factors influence a wide range of human behaviors. Recently, psychobiologists have discovered a link between chemicals in the brain (neurotransmitters) and human behavior. For example, researchers found that autistic children share a genetic defect in regulating the neurotransmitter serotonin. Serotonin plays an important role in brain functioning. In many ways, our behavior is the result of our physiological makeup.

psychobiologist: a psychologist who studies how physical and chemical changes in our bodies influence our behavior

Sociocultural Psychology

The newest approach to psychology involves studying the influence of cultural and ethnic similarities and differences on behavior and social functioning.

Figure 1.9 Contemporary Approaches to Psychology

Modern psychologists use many different approaches to study the same behavior. Each viewpoint offers additional information to understanding behavior and reflects a different view of human nature. ***What other questions might a cognitivist study?***

Approach	What influences our behavior?	Sample research question
Psychoanalytic Psychology	Unconscious motivations influence our behavior.	How have negative childhood experiences affected the way I handle stressful situations?
Behavioral Psychology	Events in the environment (rewards and punishments) influence our behavior.	Can good study habits be learned?
Humanistic Psychology	Individual or self-directed choices influence our behavior.	Do I believe I can prepare for and pass the test?
Cognitive Psychology	How we process, store, and retrieve information influences our behavior.	How does caffeine affect memory?
Biological Psychology	Biological factors influence our behavior.	Do genes affect your intelligence and personality?
Sociocultural Psychology	Ethnicity, gender, culture, and socioeconomic status influence our behavior.	How do people of different genders and ethnicities interact with one another?

Reading Check Answer Cognitive psychologists believe that behavior is influenced by a variety of mental processes, whereas behaviorists believe that all behavior is the result of conditioning.

Applying Psychology

Tell students that more than 100 years ago, Hermann Ebbinghaus found that studying a list of new information once a day for several days led to better recall than studying that same list several times in one day. Have students select one subject for which they will have a test in one to two weeks. Tell students to try Ebbinghaus's advice by studying that subject each day. After the test, have students report whether this form of study improved their recall.

Figure 1.9

Visual Instruction Explain that most psychologists tend to lean toward one approach, but they often borrow ideas from other theories.

Caption Answer An example of a question a cognitivist might ask is "How does darkness affect our perception of colors?"

3 ASSESS

Assign Section 2 Assessment as homework or as an in-class activity.

EXTENDING THE CONTENT

Behaviorism B.F. Skinner's confidence in behaviorism diminished in later years, as the following excerpt reflects: "I used to believe that a science of behavior could show us how to solve the problems confronting us—pollution, overpopulation, poverty, the threat of nuclear war. But I am forced to conclude that what the science of behavior shows us is that we can't solve these problems. . . . [T]he people who are in a position to deal effectively with these problems . . . are working under the wrong sort of reinforcement contingencies. People in business are reinforced for doing what produces the most number of dollars. . . . People in government are reinforced for doing what pleases voters—and business."

Section Quiz 1–2

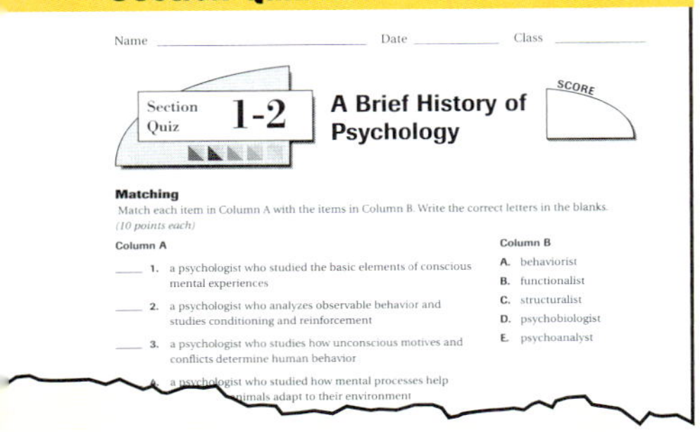
Name ______ Date ______ Class ______

Section Quiz 1-2 **A Brief History of Psychology**

SCORE

Matching

Match each item in Column A with the items in Column B. Write the correct letters in the blanks. *(10 points each)*

Column A

____ 1. a psychologist who studied the basic elements of conscious mental experiences

____ 2. a psychologist who analyzes observable behavior and studies conditioning and reinforcement

____ 3. a psychologist who studies how unconscious motives and conflicts determine human behavior

4. a psychologist who studied how mental processes help animals adapt to their environment

Column B

A. behaviorist
B. functionalist
C. structuralist
D. psychobiologist
E. psychoanalyst

Reteach

Ask students to compare and contrast how the contemporary approaches to psychology view humans and their environment.

Enrich

Ask students to search newspapers and magazines for cartoons that seek to explain behavior. Have students classify their examples by psychological approach.

4 CLOSE

An old cliché states that "a little learning is a dangerous thing." Ask students whether they agree or disagree with the statement as it relates to understanding human behavior. Students should be able to defend their answers.

For example, a sociocultural psychologist considers how our knowledge and ways of thinking, feeling, and behaving are dependent on the culture to which we belong. Think about all the perspectives and behaviors you share with other people of your culture. Psychologist Leonard Doob (1990) illustrated the cultural implications of a simple, reflexive behavior—a sneeze. Doob asks, "Will [the person who senses the urge to sneeze] try to inhibit this reflex action? What will he say, what will bystanders say, when he does sneeze? What will they think of him if he fails to turn away and sneezes in their faces? Do they and he consider sneezing an omen and, if so, is it a good or bad omen?" To answer such questions, we would have to understand the cultural context in which the sneeze occurred, as well as the cultural beliefs associated with the sneeze.

Sociocultural psychologists also study the impact and integration of the millions of immigrants who come to the United States each year. The character of the U.S. population is rapidly changing. By the year 2020, Americans of Hispanic origin will make up almost 18 percent of the population, while those of African American and Asian descent will make up nearly 19 percent (U.S. Census Bureau, 2004). Psychologists study the attitudes, values, beliefs, and social norms and roles of these various racial and ethnic groups. They also study methods to reduce intolerance and discrimination.

The sociocultural approach is also concerned with issues such as gender and socioeconomic status and is based on the idea that these factors impact human behavior and mental processes. For instance, how might you be different if you had been born female instead of male, or male instead of female? Would you be different if you had been born in poverty, or into an extremely wealthy family?

SECTION 2 Assessment

1. **Review the Vocabulary** Using your own words, describe the structuralist, functionalist, behaviorist, and humanist approaches to the study of psychology.
2. **Visualize the Main Idea** Use a graphic organizer similar to the one below to list the different historical approaches to the study of psychology.

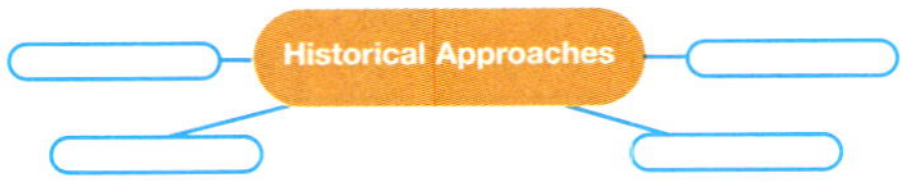

3. **Recall Information** Identify some issues that sociocultural psychologists might research.
4. **Think Critically** With which approach to psychology do you most agree? Why?
5. **Application Activity** Consider the following question: Why do you sometimes daydream in your classes? Compare how the various approaches to the study of psychology would address this question differently. Describe the differences and similarities.

SECTION 2 Assessment Answers

1. Students' answers will vary. Their descriptions should accurately express the positions of the various approaches.
2. The graphic organizers should include structuralism, functionalism, inheritable traits, and Gestalt.
3. Students' answers will vary. Examples include the long-term effects of war and the effects of poverty on the ability to learn.
4. Students' answers will vary. Students should be able to defend their answers.
5. Students' answers will vary. Behaviorists would dismiss the daydreams since they are not based on observable facts, while psychoanalysts would say that the daydreams represent unconscious conflicts.

Case Studies

The Four Humors

Period of Study: Around A.D. 150

Introduction: Hippocrates (460–375 B.C.), often referred to as the "father of medicine," became one of the first people to claim that illness had natural, not supernatural, causes. Hippocrates associated the four elements—earth, air, fire, and water—with four humors in the body. He associated earth with phlegm (mucus), air with blood, fire with yellow bile, and water with black bile. Humans with balanced humors were healthy; an imbalance among the humors resulted in sickness. Galen (A.D. 130–200) extended Hippocrates' theory to include characteristics of human personalities.

Hypothesis: Galen identified four personality characteristics called *melancholic, sanguine, choleric,* and *phlegmatic.* Galen associated these four characteristics with the four humors of the body. Each humor was thought to give off vapors that rose to the brain. An individual's personality could be explained by the state of that person's humors.

Method: If a person had excess phlegm, that person was probably dull, pale, and cowardly. Cheerful and generous personalities resulted from the dominance of blood. Laziness and gloominess were associated with cold and dryness (black bile). If a person had too much choler (yellow bile) in his system, he was probably a violent or vengeful person. The perfect personality resulted when none of the four humors dominated.

At that time, treatment of a psychological disorder involved restoring a balance among the humors. Doctors often gave patients poisonous herbs to eat. This caused vomiting, a sign that the imbalanced humor was leaving the patient's body. Balancing the diet could also balance the humors.

Results: The theories of Hippocrates and Galen proved unfounded, and their prescribed treatments for various disorders did not prove reliable. The relationship between your physical makeup and your personality is not yet firmly established. Your mental state can make the symptoms of some diseases more distressing, or factors such as stress can make you more liable to getting sick. However, the dominance of, say, black bile in your system does not lead to depression. Galen's notion, though, that a healthy personality is a balanced one may indeed be sound.

A Personality Wheel

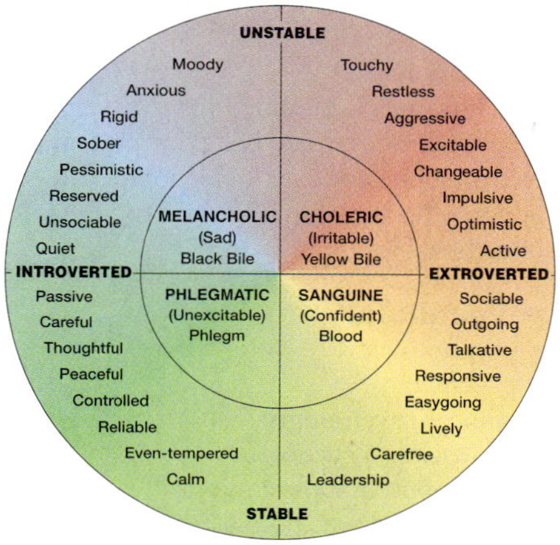

Humor	Principal Source	Temperament	Characteristic
Phlegm	Brain	Phlegmatic	Sluggish, unemotional
Blood	Heart	Sanguine	Cheerful
Yellow bile	Liver	Choleric	Quick-tempered, fiery
Black bile	Spleen	Melancholic	Sad

Analyzing the Case Study

1. According to Galen's hypothesis, how are a person's physical and mental states related?
2. How did Galen treat psychological disorders?
3. **Critical Thinking** How can Galen's original theory be used today as a prescription for a healthy personality?

Going Further

Galen's Influence

Galen was both a physician and a philosopher. As a young man he studied the healing arts at Asclepius's sanctuary. Asclepius was the Roman god of healing. After studying there, Galen traveled widely and continued his learning. He was eventually appointed to the prestigious position of physician to the gladiators. For four years, he honed his skills in treating traumas and training injuries.

Galen was a prolific medical and philosophical writer. Throughout his writings, he freely combined medicine and philosophy. At the time, philosophy enjoyed a place of prominence. Galen argued that medicine should be given the same status as philosophy. His influence on Western medical thought and practice continued through the Middle Ages.

Like all physicians of his day, Galen used a variety of herbs to treat medical conditions. Many in the medical community today are reexamining the usefulness of herbal remedies to treat a variety of ailments.

Discussing the Case Study

Ask: **How are mental and physical health related?** Discuss the question in class and have students collect samples from newspapers and magazines that cite the importance of maintaining a balanced life both physically and mentally.

Answers for Analyzing the Case Study

1. Galen hypothesized that the four humors gave off vapors that rose to the brain. A mentally healthy individual exhibited a balance in the humors. An unhealthy personality had an imbalance in the humors.
2. Galen gave people poisonous herbs to induce vomiting. This was thought to bring the humors back into balance. Galen also recognized the value of a balanced diet in maintaining mental health.
3. Galen stressed maintaining balance in the four humors. Although his theory of humors was wrong, his concept of maintaining balance can be applied to personality and lifestyle. Extremes in personality, such as extreme anger or depression, can result in a variety of physical and psychological ailments.

1 FOCUS

Section Objectives

1. Explain the work of a psychologist.
2. Summarize the careers and specialized fields in psychology.

BELLRINGER
Motivational Activity

Project Daily Focus Transparency 1–3 and have students answer the questions.

Available as blackline master

Daily Focus Transparency 1–3

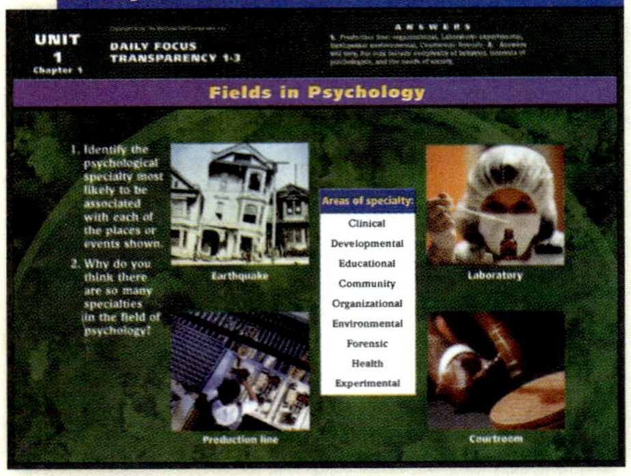

Reader's Guide

Use the Reader's Guide to introduce concepts and vocabulary.

Exploring Psychology

Ask students to read the **Exploring Psychology** feature and then discuss: **How did the patient express his depression?**

Vocabulary Precheck

Have students work with a partner to create a crossword puzzle using the vocabulary terms. Then have pairs of students exchange and complete each other's puzzles.

Use the **Vocabulary PuzzleMaker CD-ROM** to create crossword and word search puzzles.

SECTION 3 Psychology as a Profession

Reader's Guide

Main Idea

Psychologists are trained to observe, analyze, and evaluate behavior patterns, to develop theories of behavior, and to apply what they have learned to influence behavior.

Vocabulary

- psychologist
- psychiatry
- clinical psychologist
- counseling psychologist
- developmental psychologist
- educational psychologist
- community psychologist
- industrial/organizational psychologist
- experimental psychologist

Objectives

- Explain the work of a psychologist.
- Summarize the careers and specialized fields in psychology.

EXPLORING PSYCHOLOGY

The Thoughts of a Patient

Everything seems to be contradictory. I don't seem to know what else to tell you, but that I am tearful and sad—and no kick out of Christmas. And I used to get such a boot out of it. . . . It's an awful feeling. . . . I don't get a bit of a kick out of anything. Everything seems to get so sort of full of despair. . . . I feel so sort of what I call "empty"—nothing in back of you like when you're feeling yourself. . . . You go to bed and you dread each day when you feel low like that. . . . And I try to keep saying to myself, like you say, that I haven't been that bad that I should have to punish myself. Yet my thinking doesn't get cheerful. When it doesn't get cheerful it makes you wonder will it all end in suicide sometime. . . .

—from *The Encyclopedia of Behavior* by Robert M. Goldenson, 1970

The thoughts above are the reflections of a patient. The patient is suffering from depression—an emotional state of dejection and sadness, ranging from mild discouragement to feelings of utter hopelessness and despair. Some psychologists conduct research to collect information and form theories about disorders such as depression. Other psychologists apply that information in the form of therapy to help people cope with depression. What else do people in the field of psychology do? Let's start by defining a psychologist.

SECTION RESOURCES

Reproducible Masters

- Guided Reading Activity 1–3
- Vocabulary Activity 1–3
- Section Quiz 1–3

Transparencies

- Daily Focus Transparency 1–3

Multimedia

- Vocabulary PuzzleMaker CD-ROM
- *ExamView® Assessment Suite* CD-ROM
- Presentation Plus! Software

WHAT IS A PSYCHOLOGIST?

Psychologists are people who have been trained to observe, analyze and evaluate behavior. They usually have a doctorate degree in psychology. There are many different fields of psychology. The principal ones are described in this section.

People often confuse the terms *psychologist* and *psychiatrist*. These are different professions. **Psychiatry** is a specialty of medicine. After a student completes medical school, he or she continues training in psychiatric medicine and learns to treat people with disturbed behavior. A psychiatrist is a medical doctor who can prescribe medication or operate on patients. Sometimes a psychiatrist works with a psychologist in testing, evaluating, and treating patients.

As the field of psychology expanded, it divided into a number of subfields. Clinical and counseling psychology are the most popular. **Clinical psychologists** help people deal with their personal problems. They work mainly in private offices, mental hospitals, prisons, and clinics. Some specialize in giving and interpreting personality tests designed to determine whether a person needs treatment and, if so, what kind. (About one-half of all psychologists specialize in clinical psychology.) **Counseling psychologists** usually work in their own office, in schools, or industrial firms, advising and assisting people with the problems of everyday life. They help people adjust to challenges. In most states a doctorate is required to be a clinical or counseling psychologist.

School psychologists, educated in principles of human development, clinical psychology, and education, help young people with emotional or learning problems. Other specialists study personality, social psychology, or developmental psychology. These psychologists are usually involved in basic rather than applied science. Psychologists who study personality investigate its development, study personality traits, or may create personality tests. Social psychologists study groups and how they influence individual behavior. Some are particularly interested in public opinion and devote much of their time to conducting polls and surveys.

psychologist: a scientist who studies the mind and behavior of humans and animals

psychiatry: a branch of medicine that deals with mental, emotional, or behavioral disorders

clinical psychologist: a psychologist who diagnoses and treats people with emotional disturbances

counseling psychologist: a psychologist who usually helps people deal with problems of everyday life

Figure 1.10 Psychologists at Work

All psychologists, no matter what their area of expertise, are interested in theories about behavior and mental processes. ***Can you name the type of psychologist at work in each photo?***

COOPERATIVE LEARNING ACTIVITY

Identifying Functions of Psychologists Organize the class into small groups of four or five students. Ask each group to make a list of behavioral disorders, areas of research, and job functions of psychologists. Next to each item on the list, have the group write which type of psychologist would most likely be associated with the item. The groups should then use index cards or small slips of paper to record each item from the list of disorders, areas of research, and job functions. Next, have the groups exchange cards. Challenge each group to guess which type of psychologist might best handle each item. Have the group that prepared the cards check the answers. **BLOCK SCHEDULING**

2 TEACH

L1 Researching Careers

Ask students to collect newspapers for at least two weeks from the nearest major city. Have students work in pairs to clip help-wanted advertisements for different occupations within the field of psychology. Each pair will categorize the clippings by field of psychology and mount the clippings onto poster board. Next to each ad, the students should name the career or occupation described in the ad. **ELL**

Guided Reading Activity 1–3

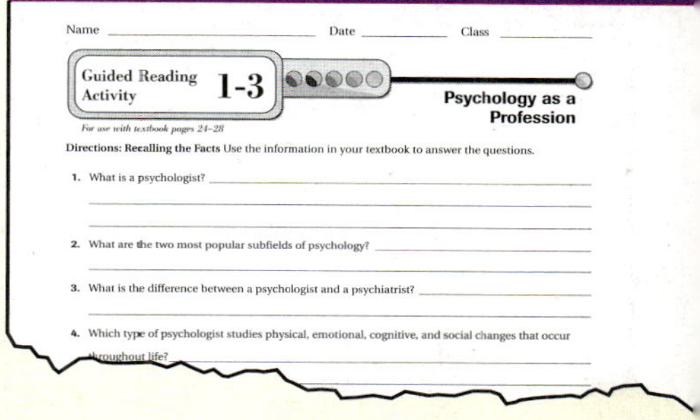

Name ______ Date ______ Class ______

Guided Reading Activity 1-3

Psychology as a Profession

For use with textbook pages 24–28

Directions: Recalling the Facts Use the information in your textbook to answer the questions.

1. What is a psychologist? ______
2. What are the two most popular subfields of psychology? ______
3. What is the difference between a psychologist and a psychiatrist? ______
4. Which type of psychologist studies physical, emotional, cognitive, and social changes that occur throughout life? ______

Figure 1.10

Caption Answer Students' answers may vary, but they may mention clinical or counseling psychologists and developmental psychologists.

Readings and Case Studies in Psychology

Have students read the Chapter 1 Case Study selection in *Readings and Case Studies in Psychology* and answer the questions that follow the case study.

Figure 1.11

Visual Instruction Ask students how they think the large number of psychologists employed by academic institutions helps expand our knowledge of psychology and assists psychologists in practice.

Caption Answer Business and government agencies hire psychologists to aid in hiring employees, to improve work conditions, to conduct research, and to counsel workers.

TEACHER Tip

In discussing the many specialties within psychology, compare it to other fields such as medicine and engineering. Help students understand that most professions are subdivided into specialties.

PSYCHOLOGY JOURNAL

Have students write about what they think a psychologist might do on a day-to-day basis if he or she were employed by a large business. ■

Vocabulary Activity 1–3

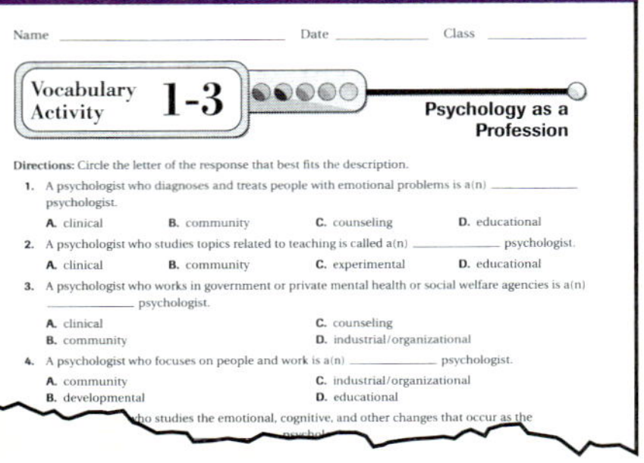
Name ______ Date ______ Class ______

Vocabulary Activity 1-3

Psychology as a Profession

Directions: Circle the letter of the response that best fits the description.

1. A psychologist who diagnoses and treats people with emotional problems is a(n) ______ psychologist.
   A. clinical **B.** community **C.** counseling **D.** educational
2. A psychologist who studies topics related to teaching is called a(n) ______ psychologist.
   A. clinical **B.** community **C.** experimental **D.** educational
3. A psychologist who works in government or private mental health or social welfare agencies is a(n) ______ psychologist.
   A. clinical **B.** community **C.** counseling **D.** industrial/organizational
4. A psychologist who focuses on people and work is a(n) ______ psychologist.
   A. community **B.** developmental **C.** industrial/organizational **D.** educational

...ho studies the emotional, cognitive, and other changes that occur as the

Figure 1.11 Where Psychologists Work

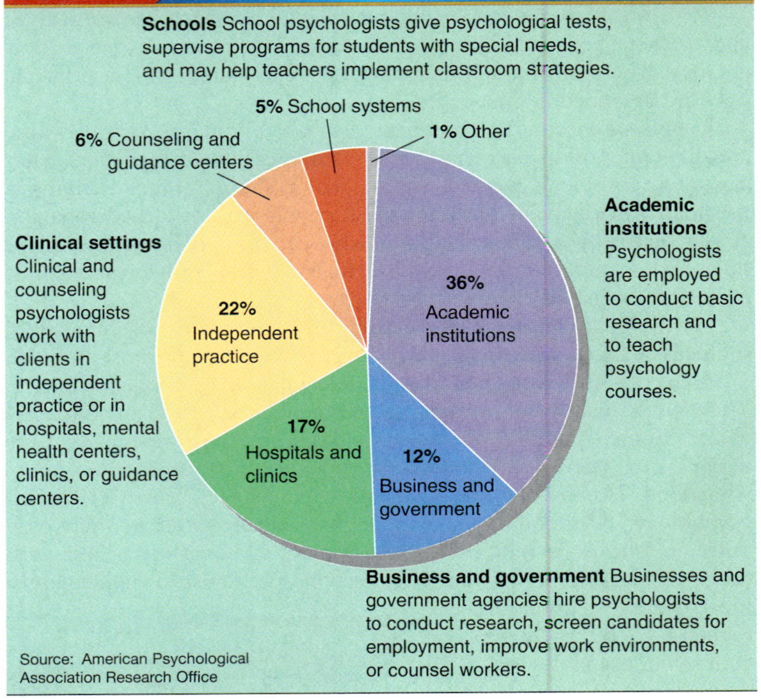

Most psychologists in the United States are engaged in clinical psychology. ***Why do businesses and government agencies hire psychologists?***

developmental psychologist: a psychologist who studies the emotional, cognitive, biological, personal, and social changes that occur as an individual matures

educational psychologist: a psychologist who is concerned with helping students learn

community psychologist: a psychologist who may work in a mental health or social welfare agency

industrial/organizational psychologist: a psychologist who uses psychological concepts to make the workplace a more satisfying environment for employees and managers

Developmental psychologists study physical, emotional, cognitive, and social changes that occur throughout life. Specialists in this field study children, the elderly, and even the process of dying.

Educational psychologists deal with topics related to teaching children and young adults, such as intelligence, memory, problem solving, and motivation. Specialists in this field evaluate teaching methods, devise tests, and develop new instructional devices. A **community psychologist** may work in a mental health or social welfare agency operated by the state or local government or by a private organization. A community psychologist may help design, run, or evaluate a mental health clinic. **Industrial/organizational psychologists** are employed by business firms and government agencies. Industrial psychologists study and develop methods to boost production, improve working conditions, place applicants in jobs for which they are best suited, train people, and reduce accidents. Organizational psychologists study the behavior of people in organizations such as business firms.

MEETING SPECIAL NEEDS

Learning Style: Naturalist Some fields of psychology are concerned with research (basic science), while others apply research to improve people's lives (applied science). Have students use the list in Figure 1.12 and various research tools, including electronic, to identify divisions that are dedicated to basic science and divisions that focus on applied science. Based on their research, students should create a chart that categorizes at least 20 divisions. **L2** **BLOCK SCHEDULING**

Refer to ***Inclusion for the High School Social Studies Classroom Strategies and Activities*** in the TCR for strategies for students with different learning styles.

Environmental psychologists work in business settings or within the government to study the effects of the environment on people. They may look at the effects of natural disasters, overcrowding, and pollution on the population in general as well as individuals and families. *Psychobiologists* study the effect of drugs or try to explain behavior in terms of biological factors, such as electrical and chemical activities in the nervous system. *Forensic psychologists* work in legal, court, and correctional systems. They assist police by developing personality profiles of criminal offenders or help law-enforcement officers understand problems like abuse. *Health psychologists* study the interaction between physical and psychological health factors. They may investigate how stress or depression leads to physical ailments such as ulcers, cancer, or the common cold.

Figure 1.12 Divisions of the APA

The divisions of the American Psychological Association (APA) represent the many areas in which a psychologist may specialize. ***Under which divisions might the work of a clinical psychologist fall?***

1. Society for General Psychology
2. Society for the Teaching of Psychology
3. Experimental Psychology
4. There is no Division 4
5. Evaluation, Measurement, and Statistics
6. Behavioral Neuroscience and Comparative Psychology
7. Developmental Psychology
8. Society for Personality and Social Psychology
9. Society for the Psychological Study of Social Issues - SPSSI
10. Psychology and the Arts
11. There is no Division 11
12. Society of Clinical Psychology
13. Consulting Psychology
14. Society for Industrial and Organizational Psychology
15. Educational Psychology
16. School Psychology
17. Counseling Psychology
18. Psychologists in Public Service
19. Military Psychology
20. Adult Development and Aging
21. Applied Experimental and Engineering Psychology
22. Rehabilitation Psychology
23. Society for Consumer Psychology
24. Theoretical and Philosophical Psychology
25. Experimental Analysis of Behavior
26. History of Psychology
27. Society for Community Research and Action: Division of Community Psychology
28. Psychopharmacology and Substance Abuse
29. Psychotherapy
30. Psychological Hypnosis
31. State Psychological Association Affairs
32. Humanistic Psychology
33. Mental Retardation and Developmental Disabilities
34. Population and Environmental Psychology
35. Psychology of Women
36. Psychology of Religion
37. Child, Youth, and Family Services
38. Health Psychology
39. Psychoanalysis
40. Clinical Neuropsychology
41. American Psychology-Law Society
42. Psychologists in Independent Practice
43. Family Psychology
44. Society for the Psychological Study of Lesbian, Gay, and Bisexual Issues
45. Society for the Psychological Study of Ethnic Minority Issues
46. Media Psychology
47. Exercise and Sport Psychology
48. Peace, Conflict and Violence: Peace Psychology Division
49. Group Psychology and Group Psychotherapy
50. Addictions
51. Society for the Psychological Study of Men and Masculinity
52. International Psychology
53. Clinical Child Psychology (Division 12, Section I)
54. Society of Pediatric Psychology (Division 12, Section V)
55. American Society for the Advancement of Pharmacotherapy
56. Trauma Psychology

Source: American Psychological Association, 2006.

CHAPTER 1
Section 3, pages 24–28

Figure 1.12

Visual Instruction Explain that the work of psychologists in different divisions may overlap.

Caption Answer Clinical psychologists may be found in many divisions. The most obvious are Divisions 8, 12, 29, 30, 39, 42, 49, and 53.

3 ASSESS

Assign Section 3 Assessment as homework or as an in-class activity.

Section Quiz 1–3

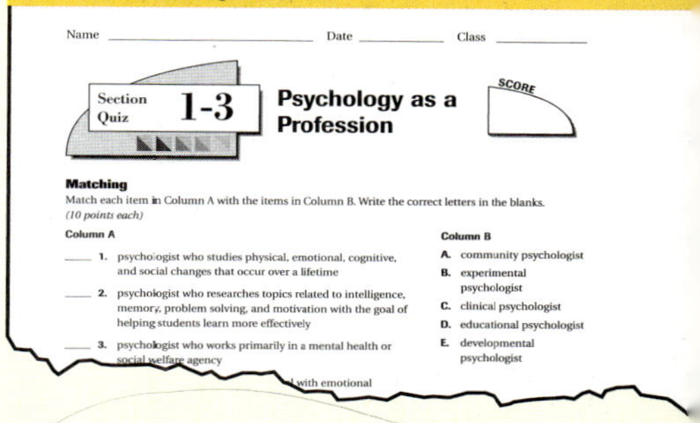
Name ______ Date ______ Class ______

Section Quiz 1-3 **Psychology as a Profession**

SCORE

Matching
Match each item in Column A with the items in Column B. Write the correct letters in the blanks. *(10 points each)*

Column A	Column B
____ 1. psychologist who studies physical, emotional, cognitive, and social changes that occur over a lifetime	A. community psychologist
____ 2. psychologist who researches topics related to intelligence, memory, problem solving, and motivation with the goal of helping students learn more effectively	B. experimental psychologist
____ 3. psychologist who works primarily in a mental health or social welfare agency	C. clinical psychologist
	D. educational psychologist
	E. developmental psychologist

Reteach

On the board, copy key statements from Section 3 but change them in some way to make the statements false. Ask students to write the statements correctly.

CRITICAL THINKING ACTIVITY

Classifying Information Challenge students to research the salary ranges of various fields of psychology. One useful source is the *Occupational Outlook Handbook,* prepared annually by the U.S. Department of Labor. Ask students to organize the information by specialty, by region of the country, or by gender and ethnicity. Students should present their findings in table or chart format. Ask students to write answers to the following questions: **What surprised you about your findings? How do you think the salary ranges compare with those of other professions? L2**

Reading Check Answer

developmental psychologists: emotional, cognitive, biological, personal, and social development; educational psychologists: cognitive learning processes, intelligence, and memory of children and young adults

Enrich

Have students write an essay on why they would or would not like to become a psychologist.

4 CLOSE

Challenge students to brainstorm ways in which psychologists have improved our lives. Record students' ideas on the board.

experimental psychologist: a psychologist who studies sensation, perception, learning, motivation, and/or emotion in carefully controlled laboratory conditions

Reading Check

How does developmental psychology differ from educational psychology?

Finally, some psychologists are **experimental psychologists.** These psychologists perform research to understand how humans (and animals) operate physically and psychologically. Experimental psychologists do everything from testing how electrical stimulation of a certain area of a rat's brain affects its behavior, through studying how disturbed people think, to observing how different socioeconomic groups vote in elections. Experimental psychologists supply information and research used in psychology.

The American Psychological Association (APA), founded in 1892, is a scientific and professional society of psychologists and educators. It is the major psychological association in the United States and is the world's largest association of psychologists. The APA is made up of 54 divisions, each representing a specific area, type of work or research setting, or activity. Some divisions are research-oriented, while others are advocacy groups. Together they are a cross section of the diverse nature of psychology (see Figure 1.12). The APA works to advance the science and profession of psychology and to promote human welfare.

What psychologists think about, what experiments they have done, and what this knowledge means form the subject of *Understanding Psychology.* Psychology is dedicated to answering some of the most interesting questions of everyday life: What happens during sleep? How can bad habits be broken? Is there a way to measure intelligence? Why do crowds sometimes turn into mobs? Do dreams mean anything? How does punishment affect a child? Can memory be improved? What causes psychological breakdowns? In trying to answer such questions, psychologists tie together what they have discovered about human behavior, thoughts, and feelings in order to look at the total human being. The picture is far from complete, but some of what is known will be found in the chapters that follow.

SECTION 3 Assessment

1. **Review the Vocabulary** Describe the work of a clinical psychologist, a counseling psychologist, a developmental psychologist, and a community psychologist.
2. **Visualize the Main Idea** Use a graphic organizer similar to the one below to name several specialty fields of psychology.

3. **Recall Information** How might the work of environmental psychologists differ from that of industrial/organizational psychologists?
4. **Think Critically** If you decided to continue in the field of psychology, what type of psychologist would you want to be? Why?
5. **Application Activity** Create a pamphlet that answers some basic questions concerned with psychology as a profession, for example: What is psychology? What is the difference between psychiatry and clinical psychology? What kinds of jobs can I get with a psychology degree?

SECTION 3 Assessment Answers

1. Clinical psychologists diagnose and treat emotional disturbances. Counseling psychologists help people deal with problems of everyday life. Developmental psychologists study human developmental changes. Community psychologists design, run, or evaluate mental health clinics.
2. Graphic organizers may include any of the specialty fields covered in this section.
3. Environmental psychologists explore how the environment affects people; industrial/organizational psychologists try to improve business by boosting productivity and improving working conditions.
4. Students' answers will vary. Their descriptions should display an understanding of the basic goals of their chosen specialty.
5. Students' answers will vary. Evaluate the pamphlets on both content and design.

CHAPTER 1

Summary and Vocabulary

Psychologists study human behavior to attempt to explain and predict why people behave and feel as they do.

Section 1 Why Study Psychology?

Main Idea: Through the study of psychology, people can discover psychological principles that have the potential to enrich the lives of humans.

- Psychology is the scientific study of behavior and mental processes.
- The goals of psychology are description, explanation, prediction, and influence.
- Psychologists rely on the scientific method when researching an issue.
- Psychology can provide insight into behavior and has practical applications in everyday life.

Section 2 A Brief History of Psychology

Main Idea: Psychology involves sets of questions, theories, methods, and possible answers that have been passed on, studied, and changed from generation to generation.

- Historical approaches to psychology include structuralism, functionalism, inheritable traits, and Gestalt psychology.
- Psychoanalytic psychology involves interpretation of unconscious thoughts.
- Behaviorists investigate observable behavior.
- Humanists believe that human behavior is self-directed.
- Cognitive psychologists focus on mental processes and rationally motivated behavior.
- Psychobiologists are interested in the physiological basis of behavior in humans and animals.
- Sociocultural psychology is a modern influential movement that views human behavior from a political and cross-cultural point of view.

Section 3 Psychology as a Profession

Main Idea: Psychologists are trained to observe, analyze, and evaluate behavior patterns, to develop theories of behavior, and to apply what they have learned to influence behavior.

- Psychiatrists and clinical psychologists both treat people with psychological disorders. Psychiatrists are medical doctors, whereas clinical psychologists are trained in psychology.
- There are many specialty fields in psychology, including clinical, developmental, industrial/organizational, experimental, and community psychology.

Chapter Vocabulary

physiological (p. 7)
cognitive (p. 7)
psychology (p. 9)
hypothesis (p. 11)
theory (p. 11)
basic science (p. 11)
applied science (p. 11)
scientific method (p. 12)
structuralist (p. 16)
introspection (p. 16)
functionalist (p. 16)
psychoanalyst (p. 19)
behaviorist (p. 20)
humanist (p. 20)
cognitivist (p. 20)
psychobiologist (p. 21)
psychologist (p. 25)
psychiatry (p. 25)
clinical psychologist (p. 25)
counseling psychologist (p. 25)
developmental psychologist (p. 26)
educational psychologist (p. 26)
community psychologist (p. 26)
industrial/organizational psychologist (p. 26)
experimental psychologist (p. 28)

1 Summary and Vocabulary

Using the Chapter 1 Summary and Vocabulary

Use the Chapter 1 Summary and Vocabulary to preview, review, condense, or reteach the chapter.

Preview/Review

Use the Chapter Vocabulary list to help students review and study.

Activity Have students create a crossword puzzle using selected terms from the chapter. Then encourage students to exchange their puzzle with someone else in the class to complete.

Vocabulary PuzzleMaker CD-ROM reinforces the vocabulary terms used in Chapter 1.

Condense

Have students read the Chapter 1 Summary.

Chapter 1 Guided Reading Activities

Reteach

Reteaching Activity 1

AUTHENTIC ASSESSMENT ACTIVITY

Selecting a Psychologist Ask students to select one of these topics: psychological testing, child development issues, or treatment for depression. Students should develop a one-page FAQ (frequently asked questions) sheet, with answers, that indicates what type of psychologist would be qualified to help, how appointments are made, the typical time required for testing and treatment, and so on. **BLOCK SCHEDULING**

Refer to the ***Authentic Assessment*** booklet for additional activities and information about evaluating student performance.

1 Assessment

PSYCHOLOGY Online

Have students visit the Web Site at glencoe.com to review Chapter 1 and take the **Self-Check Quiz.**

GLENCOE TECHNOLOGY

Presentation Plus!

For a review of Chapter 1 content, see MindJogger Checkpoint on **Presentation Plus!**

Reviewing Vocabulary

1. i	**6.** a
2. d	**7.** b
3. e	**8.** c
4. g	**9.** f
5. j	**10.** h

Recalling Facts

1. Psychology is the scientific study of behavior that is tested through scientific research.
2. The steps of the scientific method are (1) identifying a specific problem/question, (2) formulating a hypothesis, (3) collecting data, and (4) analyzing data.
3. The four goals of psychology are description, explanation, prediction, and influence.
4. Wundt developed a self-observation technique known as introspection. This technique is based on Wundt's experiments in which trained participants reported their thoughts to Wundt. Wundt then tried to map out the basic structure of the human thought process.
5. functionalists only: concerned with the functioning of the conscious mind and how it helps organisms adapt to their environment; behaviorists only: concerned with learning and behavior modification that result from environmental events; both explore the connection between behavior and environment

Critical Thinking

1. Students' answers will vary. Their definitions should indicate the scientific nature of psychology, including an understanding of the scientific method.
2. Students' answers will vary. Evaluate their responses based on the proper connection between their positions and the theories presented in the chapter.
3. Psychologists involved in basic science would research such things as how the fear of the dark developed. Psychologists involved in applied science would explore ways to help people overcome their fear of the dark. Basic science seeks to explain the fear, while applied science seeks to eliminate the individual's fear.
4. Yes, humanistic psychologists present an optimistic world view because they recognize individual potential and encourage people to reach that potential.
5. The history of psychology lays the groundwork for study of the subject. The history demonstrates the ways in which psychology has contributed to the quality of modern human life. It also helps us understand that psychology is a complex field that will continue to grow and develop.

Psychology Projects

1. Answers will vary. Students should demonstrate an understanding of the four goals of psychology.
2. Answers will vary. Students should demonstrate an understanding of the differences between Freud and Skinner. Charts should show that Freud is most commonly identified as a psychoanalyst, while Skinner is known as a behavioral psychologist.
3. Answers will vary. Students' ads should reflect a basic understanding of the different types of psychologists and the work in which they are involved. The advertisements should clearly describe the various services available at the clinic.

CHAPTER 1 Assessment

PSYCHOLOGY Online

Self-Check Quiz
Visit the *Understanding Psychology* Web site at glencoe.com and click on **Chapter 1—Self-Check Quizzes** to prepare for the Chapter Test.

Reviewing Vocabulary

Choose the letter of the correct term or concept below to complete the sentence.

- **a.** psychobiologist
- **b.** hypothesis
- **c.** structuralist
- **d.** functionalist
- **e.** behaviorist
- **f.** theory
- **g.** clinical psychologist
- **h.** developmental psychologist
- **i.** experimental psychology
- **j.** industrial/organizational psychology

1. Psychologists who do research in memory, perception, and learning are involved in ________.
2. A(n)________ wants to learn how various mental processes help people adapt to their environment.
3. A psychologist who focuses on studying objectively verifiable phenomena is known as a(n)________.
4. The type of psychologist who usually works in a mental health clinic, mental hospital, or prison is called a(n) ________.
5. ____________ is concerned with using psychological concepts to make the workplace a more satisfying environment for employees.
6. A(n) ___________ would study the influence of biological factors on behavior and mental processes.
7. An educated guess, or ________, predicts what the results of testing will be.
8. A(n) ___________ would attempt to describe the basic elements of human experience.
9. A belief or set of beliefs that is used to explain observed facts and to predict new facts is called a(n) ________.
10. A(n) ___________ charts changes in behavior as people grow older, trying to understand the factors that influence those changes.

Recalling Facts

1. What is psychology?
2. What are the steps of the scientific method?
3. What are four goals of psychology?
4. What method of study did Wundt develop to collect information about the mind?
5. Using a graphic organizer similar to the one below, compare and contrast functionalism and behaviorism.

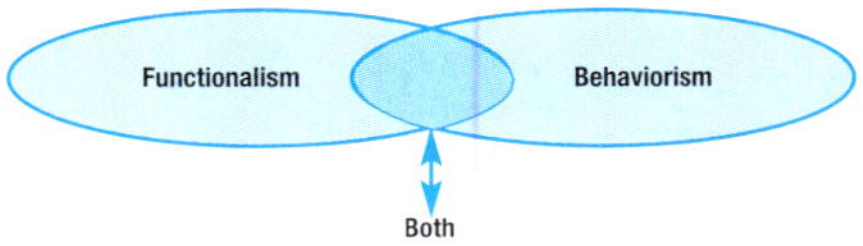

Critical Thinking

1. **Synthesizing Information** Write your own definition of psychology. Is your definition different from one you would have written before reading the chapter? Put the definition in your Psychology Journal and read it at the end of the course to see if you still agree with it.
2. **Demonstrating Reasoned Judgment** Do you think human behavior is free or determined? Defend your answer using theories from the different approaches to psychology.
3. **Making Comparisons** Consider the issue of fear of the dark. How would the work of a psychologist involved in basic science and a psychologist involved in applied science differ in regard to the study of this issue?
4. **Making Inferences** Do you think that humanistic psychology presents an optimistic view of the world? Explain.
5. **Drawing Conclusions** Why do you think it is important to study the history of psychology?

CHAPTER 1 Assessment

Psychology Projects

1. **Why Study Psychology?** Imagine that you are a psychologist and a patient has arrived at your office to discuss a problem. (Create a problem—such as stress or shyness—for the assignment.) Using the four goals of psychology, outline a possible plan to help the patient. Your plan should meet all the goals.
2. **A Brief History of Psychology** Create a chart that explains the differences in the study of psychology between Sigmund Freud and B.F. Skinner. Your chart should include motivations of behavior, reward structures, and procedures for diagnosis and treatment. You may illustrate your text with cartoons or drawings to clarify certain points.
3. **Psychology as a Profession** Create an advertisement for a psychology clinic. In the ad, describe the services of the types of psychologists that work at your clinic. You should include at least six types of psychologists, such as clinical, environmental, and so on. When creating your ad, keep in mind the types of problems that people might want to bring to the clinic. You may want to create a magazine, newspaper, or Internet ad. Be sure to monitor and evaluate your project for time lines, accuracy, and goal attainment (see page 1).

Technology Activity

Use the Internet or the computerized card catalog in your local or school library to find information on careers in psychology. Choose one field of psychology and detail the education, experience, and qualities needed for a job in that field. Present your research in an informational pamphlet.

Psychology Journal

Review the journal entry that you wrote at the beginning of the chapter on your reasons for studying psychology. Based on what you have learned from studying the chapter and classroom discussions, assess the ideas you presented in the original entry. Ask yourself:

- Are any of the ideas based on misconceptions, false premises, or faulty reasoning?
- What ideas would you revise or delete?
- What other ideas for studying psychology would you now include?

Write a new entry in your journal. Describe the three biggest benefits you feel you can derive from studying psychology. Provide reasons to justify your choices.

Building Skills

Identifying Cause-and-Effect Relationships

Review the cartoon and answer the questions that follow.

1. How might this girl have "learned" to avoid the intended bad consequences of pulling the string?
2. Which approach to psychology might this cartoon illustrate?

See the Skills Handbook, page 624, for an explanation of identifying cause-and-effect relationships.

Practice and **assess** key social studies skills with **Glencoe Skillbuilder Interactive Workbook CD-ROM, Level 2.**

Assessment

Building Skills

1. She may have encountered this situation before. Now she has learned (from experience) to avoid the bad consequences.
2. behaviorism (Her behavior is the result of conditioning.)

GLENCOE TECHNOLOGY

CD-ROM

Glencoe Skillbuilder Interactive Workbook, Level 2

This interactive CD-ROM is designed to reinforce student mastery of essential social studies skills.

Chapter Bonus Test Question

This question may be used for extra credit on the Chapter Assessment.

Answer the following question:

I am a new approach to psychology that studies how cultural and ethnic similarities and differences influence behavior. What approach am I?

Answer: sociocultural psychology

Technology Activity

Students' pamphlets should identify the education, experience, and qualities needed for the specific field chosen. Ask students to share the addresses of the Web sites they found.

Psychology Journal

Students' answers should express ways in which the student can benefit from studying psychology. Students should be able to justify their choices.

TIME REPORTS

Reader's Dictionary

Review the following terms with students to help them read and understand the article.

prolific: productive
cognitive theory: explores the difference between inborn knowledge and what is learned from the environment
genetic epistemology: the study of the limits of inborn abilities and traits
anthropology: the study of human and animal cultures and societies
pedagogical theory: explores the art of teaching
psyche: the mind
neurotic: having emotional instabilities
Oedipus complex: a child's attraction to the parent of the opposite gender
neurasthenics: mental disorders characterized by fatigue, listlessness, feelings of inadequacy, and other symptoms of emotional instability
introspection: an examination of one's own thoughts and feelings

TIME REPORTS

CHILD PSYCHOLOGIST

Jean Piaget

He found the secrets of human learning hidden behind the seemingly illogical notions of children

By SEYMOUR PAPERT

JEAN PIAGET, THE PIONEERING SWISS philosopher and psychologist, spent much of his professional life listening to children, watching children and poring over reports of researchers around the world who were doing the same. He found, to put it most succinctly, that children don't think like grownups. After thousands of interactions with young people often barely old enough to talk, Piaget began to suspect that behind their cute and seemingly illogical utterances were thought processes that had their own kind of order and their own special logic. Einstein called it a discovery "so simple that only a genius could have thought of it."

Piaget's insight opened a new window into the inner workings of the mind. By the end of a wide-ranging and remarkably prolific research career that spanned nearly 75 years—from his first scientific publication at age 10 to work still in progress when he died at 84—Piaget had developed several new fields of science: developmental psychology, cognitive theory and what came to be called genetic epistemology. Although not an educational reformer, he championed a way of thinking about children that provided the foundation for today's education-reform movements. It was a shift comparable to the displacement of stories of "noble savages" and "cannibals" by modern anthropology. One might say that Piaget was the first to take children's thinking seriously.

CORBIS/ FARRELL GREHAN

JEAN PIAGET: A towering figure of 20th-century psychology

Others who shared this respect for children—John Dewey in the U.S., Maria Montessori in Italy and Paulo Freire in Brazil—fought harder for immediate change in the schools, but Piaget's influence on education is deeper and more pervasive. He has been revered by generations of teachers inspired by the belief that children are not empty vessels to be filled with knowledge (as traditional pedagogical theory had it) but active builders of knowledge—little scientists who are constantly creating and testing their own theories of the world. And though he may not be as famous as Sigmund Freud or even B.F. Skinner, his contribution to psychology may be longer lasting. As computers and the Internet give children more autonomy to explore ever larger digital worlds, the ideas he pioneered become ever more relevant.

Piaget grew up near Lake Neuchâtel in a quiet region of French Switzerland. His father was a professor of medieval studies and his mother a strict Calvinist. He was a child prodigy who soon became interested in the scientific study of nature. When, at age 10, his observations led to questions that could be answered only by access to the university library, Piaget wrote and published a short note on the sighting of an albino sparrow in the hope that this would influence the librarian to stop treating him like a child. It worked. Piaget was launched on a path that would lead to his doctorate in zoology and a lifelong conviction that the way to understand anything is to understand how it evolves.

After World War I, Piaget became interested in psychoanalysis. He moved to Zurich and then to Paris to study logic and abnormal psychology. Working with Theodore Simon in Alfred Binet's child-psychology lab, he noticed that Parisian children of the same age made similar errors on true-false intelligence tests. Fascinated by their reasoning processes, he began to suspect that the key to human knowledge might be discovered by observing how the child's mind develops.

The core of Piaget is his belief that looking carefully at how knowledge develops in children will clarify the nature of knowledge in general. Whether this has in fact led to deeper understanding remains, like everything about Piaget, controversial. But for those who still see Piaget as the giant in the field of cognitive theory, the difference between what the baby brings and what the adult has is so immense that the new discoveries do not significantly reduce the gap but only increase the mystery. ■

32 TIME, March 29, 1999

C L I C K H E R E

TIME REPORTS

Visit **www.time.com/teach** for the complete text of this article as well as related articles on the subject.

Block Schedule

This activity works well for a block-scheduling framework.

COOPERATIVE LEARNING ACTIVITY

Analyzing Piaget's Interviews Organize the class into small groups. Ask students to find examples of some of Piaget's interviews with children. Have each group copy one of these dialogues. Then have them underline "errors in thinking" made by the child. Ask each group to explain how these errors in thinking actually show insight into the topic being discussed. Students should present their findings in a written report. Have each group present its examples and analyses to the class. **BLOCK SCHEDULING**

PSYCHOANALYST

Sigmund Freud

He opened a window on the unconscious and changed the way we view ourselves

By PETER GAY

MORE THAN ANY OTHER EXPLORER of the psyche, Sigmund Freud has shaped the mind of the 20th century. The very fierceness and persistence of his detractors are a wry tribute to the staying power of Freud's ideas.

His fundamental idea—that all humans are endowed with an unconscious in which potent sexual and aggressive drives, and defenses against them, struggle for supremacy, as it were, behind a person's back—has struck many as a romantic, scientifically unprovable notion. His contention that the catalog of neurotic ailments to which humans are susceptible is nearly always the work of sexual maladjustments, and that erotic desire starts not in puberty but in infancy, seemed to the respectable nothing less than obscene. His dramatic evocation of a universal Oedipus complex, in which (to put a complicated issue too simply) the little boy loves his mother and hates his father, seems more like a literary conceit than a thesis worthy of a scientifically minded psychologist.

Freud first used the term *psychoanalysis* in 1896, when he was already 40. He had been driven by ambition from his earliest days and encouraged by his doting parents to think highly of himself. After an impressive career in school, he enrolled in 1873 in the University of Vienna and drifted from one philosophical subject to another until he hit on medicine. As he pursued his medical researches, he came to the conclusion that the most intriguing mysteries lay concealed in the complex operations of the mind. By the early 1890s, he was specializing in "neurasthenics" (mainly severe hysterics); they taught him much, including the art of patient listening. At the same time he was beginning to write down his dreams, increasingly convinced that they might offer clues to the workings of the unconscious, a notion he borrowed from the Romantics. He saw himself as a scientist taking material both from his patients and from himself, through introspection. By the mid-1890s, he was launched on a full-blown self-analysis, an enterprise for which he had no guidelines and no predecessors.

The book that made his reputation in the profession—although it sold poorly—was *The Interpretation of Dreams* (1900), an indefinable masterpiece—part dream analysis, part autobiography, part theory of the mind, part history of contemporary Vienna. The principle that underlay this work was that mental experiences and entities, like physical ones, are part of nature. This meant that Freud could admit no mere accidents in mental procedures. The most nonsensical notion, the most casual slip of the tongue, the most fantastic dream, must have a meaning and can be used to unriddle the often incomprehensible maneuvers we call thinking. ■

—For the complete text of this article and related articles from TIME, please visit www.time.com/teach

POST-FREUDIAN ANALYSIS

Other psychologists continued the work that Freud began, though not always in ways that he would have approved.

CARL JUNG A former disciple of Freud's, Jung shared his mentor's enthusiasm for dreams but not his obsession with the sex drive. Jung said humans are endowed with a "collective unconscious" from which myths, fairy tales and other archetypes spring.

ALFRED KINSEY A biologist who knew little about sex and less about statistics, Kinsey nonetheless led the first large-scale empirical study of sexual behavior. The Kinsey reports shocked readers by documenting high rates of what some considered atypical sexual behavior.

B.F. SKINNER A strict behaviorist who avoided all reference to internal mental states, Skinner believed that behavior can best be shaped through positive reinforcement. Contrary to popular misconception, he did not raise his daughter in the "Skinner box" used to train pigeons.

FROM TOP TO BOTTOM: STEPHAN BRETSCHER, ARCHIVE PHOTOS, JAMES F. COYNE

ANALYZING THE ARTICLES

1. What was Piaget's contribution to psychology?
2. **CRITICAL THINKING** How might the ways we think about children and ourselves be different today if Piaget and Freud had not proposed their theories?

TIME REPORTS

ACTIVE READING STRATEGY

Explain to students that connecting means relating what they already know about a subject with what they are now reading about the subject.

Questions for Discussion

Use the following questions for a class discussion after students have read the article.

1. How does Einstein's comment "so simple that only a genius could have thought of it" apply to children's thinking? *(Children think in simple terms but often have profound insights.)*
2. What technique did both Piaget and Freud employ? *(They listened and talked to people.)*
3. What part of Freud's theories is most difficult for you to accept? Why? *(Answers will vary. Many will question his theories of sexual drives in young children. Others will question his view that every mental experience has meaning.)*

ANSWERS TO ANALYZING THE ARTICLES

1. He promoted the idea that children build their knowledge; they are not empty vessels. His exploration of how children gain knowledge helped distinguish inborn knowledge from knowledge gained through learning.
2. If Piaget had not proposed his theories, we would see children's thought processes as illogical. His ideas provided the foundation for today's education-reform movements. If Freud had not proposed his theories, we would be less aware of unconscious desires and struggles that exist from infancy. Also, Freud's theories motivated many others to research psychological concepts. Many of these psychologists have proposed theories of their own that contribute to our understanding of human behavior.

Chapter 2 Resource Guide

SECTION RESOURCES

Daily Objectives	Reproducible Resources	Multimedia Resources
Section 1 **What Is Research?** Describe the process in which psychologists approach a research issue and conduct the research to test a hypothesis, solve a problem, or confirm previous research.	Guided Reading Activity 2–1 Vocabulary Activity 2–1 Section Quiz 2–1	Daily Focus Transparency 2–1 *ExamView® Assessment Suite* CD-ROM Presentation Plus! Software
Section 2 **Problems and Solutions in Research** Discuss how psychologists must recognize and resolve errors as they conduct research.	Guided Reading Activity 2–2 Vocabulary Activity 2–2 Section Quiz 2–2	Daily Focus Transparency 2–2 Vocabulary PuzzleMaker CD-ROM *ExamView® Assessment Suite* CD-ROM Presentation Plus! Software
Section 3 **Statistical Evaluation** Recognize that psychologists must collect and evaluate evidence to support their hypotheses.	Guided Reading Activity 2–3 Vocabulary Activity 2–3 Section Quiz 2–3	Daily Focus Transparency 2–3 *ExamView® Assessment Suite* CD-ROM Presentation Plus! Software

Blackline Master   CD-ROM   Transparency

Block Schedule

Activities that are particularly suited for use within the block-scheduling framework are identified throughout this chapter by the following designation: **BLOCK SCHEDULING**

KEY TO ABILITY LEVELS

Teaching strategies have been coded for varying learning styles and abilities.

- **L1** **BASIC** activities for all students
- **L2** **AVERAGE** activities for average to above-average students
- **L3** **CHALLENGING** activities for above-average students
- **ELL** **ENGLISH LANGUAGE LEARNER** activities

Chapter 2 Resource Guide

Timesaving Tools

TeacherWorks™ All-In-One Planner and Resource Center

- **Interactive Teacher Edition** Access your Teacher Wraparound Edition and your classroom resources with a few easy clicks.
- **Interactive Lesson Planner** Planning has never been easier! Organize your week, month, semester, or year with all the lesson helps you need to make teaching creative, timely, and relevant.

Use Glencoe's **Presentation Plus!** multimedia teacher tool to easily present dynamic lessons that visually excite your students. Using Microsoft PowerPoint® you can customize the presentations to create your own personalized lessons.

Activity

From the Classroom of...

James Matiya
Carl Sandburg High School
Orland Park, IL

Survey

In this activity, students are asked to conduct a survey. Each student should ask four people of different age groups to read the following paragraph and declare whether the substance should be banned or not. After conducting the survey, all students should combine their answers. Students should tally their answers and then calculate mean, mode, and median. Then ask students to separate and tally the answers between males and females, different age groups, and different class levels. Discuss the results as a class.

Ban Dihydrogen Monoxide!

This substance has been found in many different forms. It may be found in solid, gaseous, and liquid states. In the solid state, people have been known to lose their lives to falling parts of it. In solid and liquid states, it is responsible for the death and injury of millions of people. It has destroyed millions of miles of roads as well. In the gaseous state, people have been burned, have difficulty breathing, and it has made people extremely warm even to the point of becoming physically sick. Government agencies monitor the levels of this substance. The substance has been used as an industrial coolant, especially in nuclear power plants. It has been found along the highways in different states, despite the fact that it may cause erosion to the soil and will weaken the effectiveness of cars' brakes. Would you support a ban of this substance?

Psychology Online

Use our Web site for additional resources. All essential content is covered in the Student Edition.

You and your students can visit glencoe.com, the Web site companion to *Understanding Psychology*. This innovative integration of electronic and print media offers your students a wealth of opportunities. The student text directs students to the Web site for the following options:

- Chapter Overviews
- Student Web Activities
- Self-Check Quizzes

Answers are provided for you in the **Web Activity Lesson Plan.** Additional Web resources and Interactive Puzzles are also available.

Chapter 2 Resource Guide

Note: The following materials may be used when teaching Chapter 2. Section level support materials are shown at point of use in the margins of the Teacher Wraparound Edition.

TEACHING TRANSPARENCIES

Chapter 2 Concept Transparencies

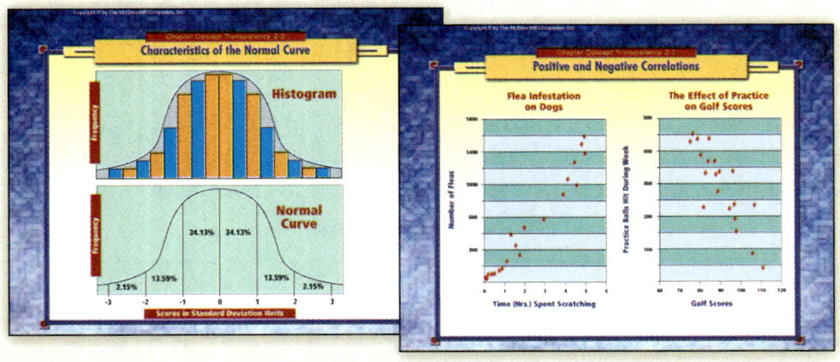

MULTIMEDIA

- Vocabulary PuzzleMaker CD-ROM
- *ExamView® Assessment Suite* CD-ROM
- TeacherWorks™ CD-ROM
- Glencoe Skillbuilder Interactive Workbook, Level 2
- Presentation Plus! Software

REVIEW AND REINFORCEMENT

Reteaching Activity 2

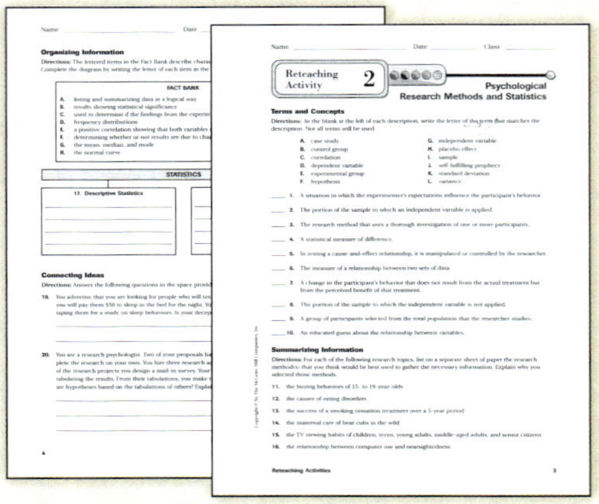
Reteaching Activity 2
Psychological Research Methods and Statistics

Graphic Organizer Activity 2

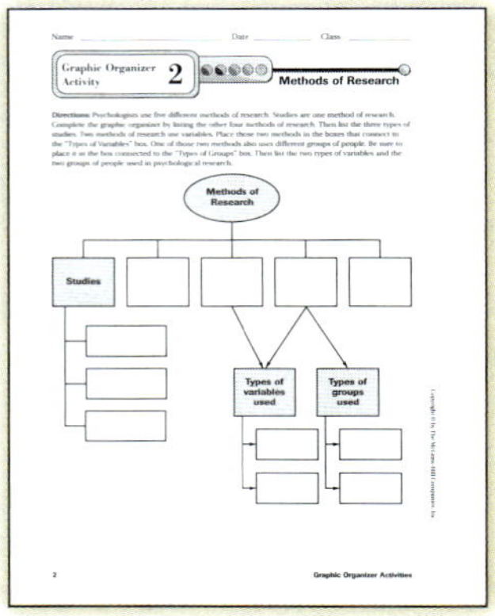
Graphic Organizer Activity 2
Methods of Research

APPLICATION AND HANDS-ON

Psychology Projects 2–1, 2–2, and 2–3

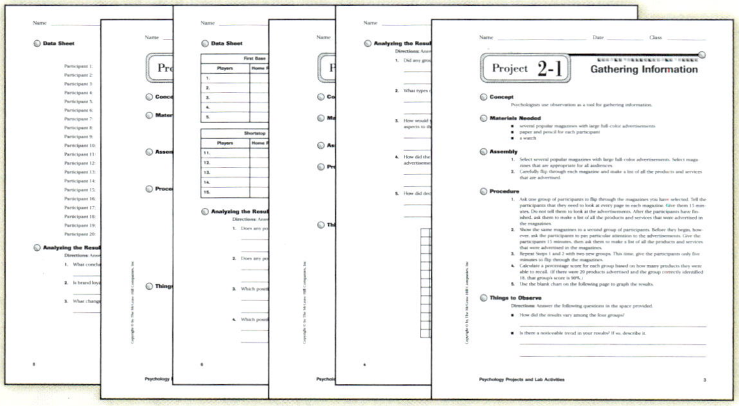
Project 2-1
Gathering Information

Application Activity 2

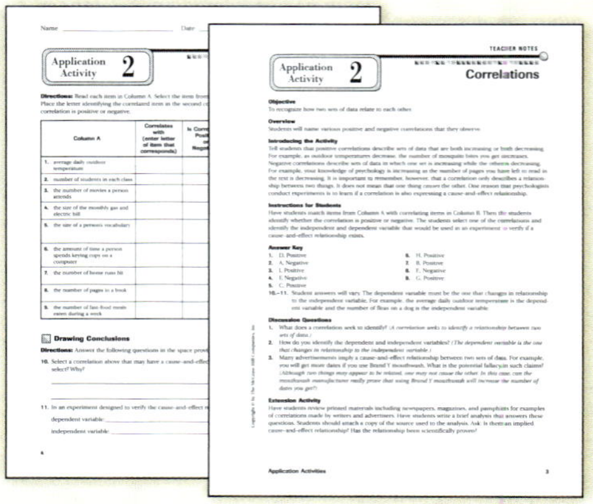
Application Activity 2
Correlations

Chapter 2 Resource Guide

ASSESSMENT

Chapter 2 Test, Form A

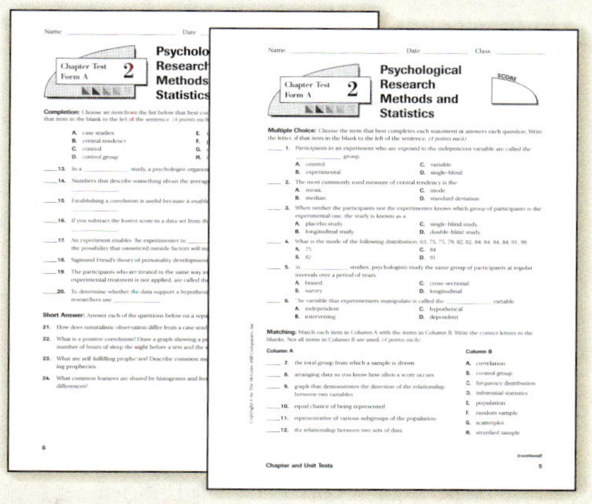

Chapter 2 Test, Form B

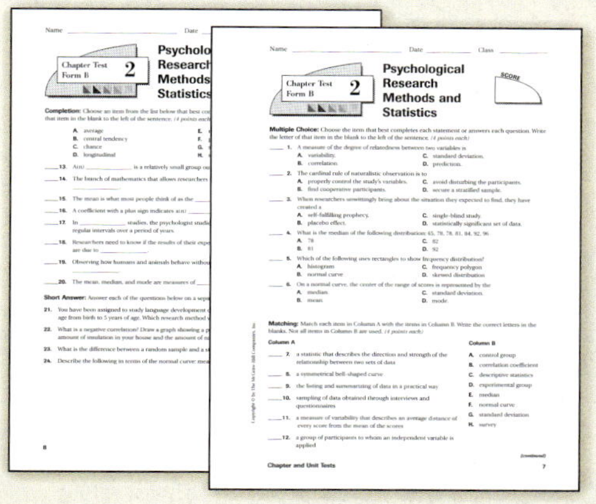

Authentic Assessment Activity 2

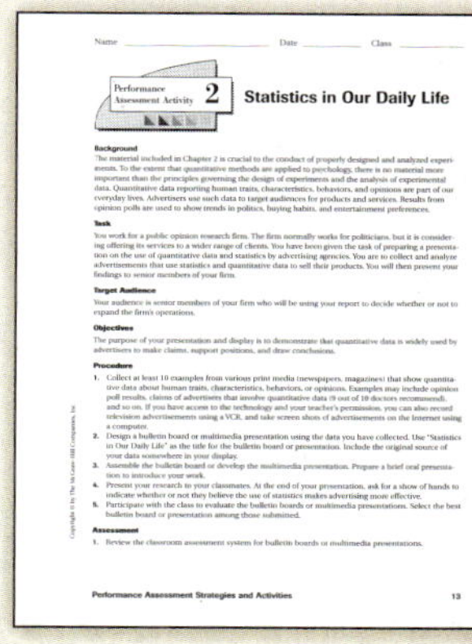

EXTENSION AND ENRICHMENT

Enrichment Activity 2

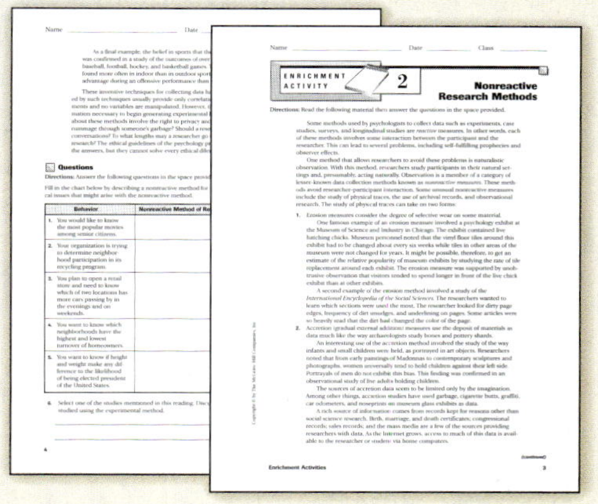

Critical Thinking Skills Activity 2

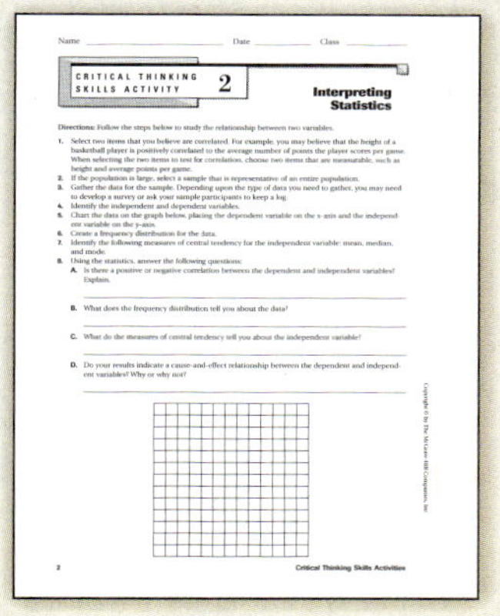

Psychology Reading 2

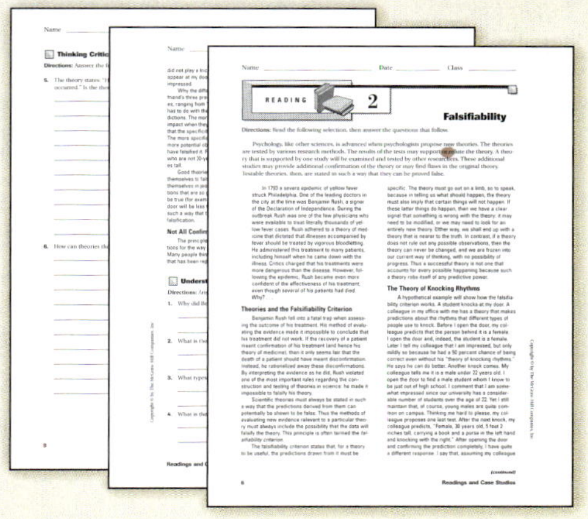

Psychology Case Study 2

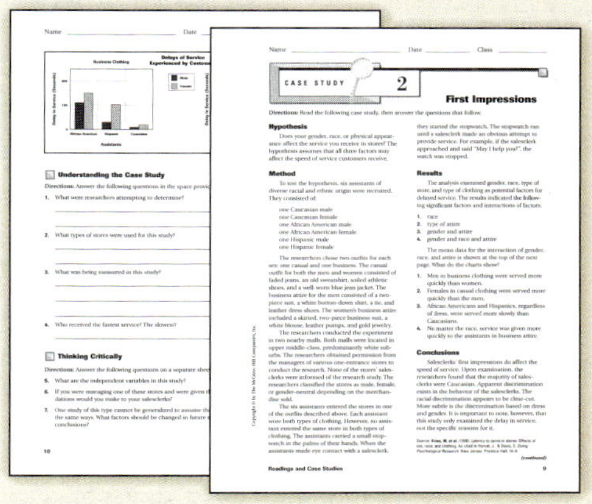

PSYCHOLOGY Online

Visit glencoe.com for a Chapter Overview for **Chapter 2—Psychological Research Methods and Statistics.**

GLENCOE TECHNOLOGY

PRESENTATION Plus!

For a preview of Chapter 2 content, see MindJogger Checkpoint on **Presentation Plus!**

PSYCHOLOGY JOURNAL

Have students bring in examples of print advertisements that use statistics. Discuss how the information was likely gathered and what claim the advertisers are promoting.

This journal activity provides the basis for the Psychology Journal activity exercise in the Chapter Assessment. ■

CHAPTER 2

Psychological Research Methods and Statistics

PSYCHOLOGY JOURNAL

For the next seven days, observe how statistics are used in the media. In your journal, describe the examples you find. ■

PSYCHOLOGY Online

Chapter Overview
Visit the *Understanding Psychology* Web site at glencoe.com and click on **Chapter 2—Chapter Overviews** to preview the chapter.

34

TWO-MINUTE LESSON LAUNCHER

On the board, list subjects that students are currently taking in school (other than psychology). For each subject, have students brainstorm a problem or issue that might arise. **Ask: What method of research would you use to solve the problem or address the issue?** (Tip: Pose the following examples to get students started. In math, people often use *formulas* to solve a problem; in science, they may use a *lab experiment;* in auto mechanics, they might refer to *engine specifications* or *computer diagnostics.*) Explain that Chapter 2 will introduce the common research methods and tools used by psychologists. As students study the chapter, ask them to note methods that overlap with those used in other disciplines.

SECTION 1

What Is Research?

Reader's Guide

Main Idea

Psychologists must first decide how to approach the research issue. Then psychologists conduct the research in one of a variety of ways to test a hypothesis, solve a problem, or confirm previous findings.

Vocabulary

- sample
- naturalistic observation
- case study
- survey
- longitudinal study
- cross-sectional study
- correlation
- hypothesis
- variable
- experimental group
- control group

Objectives

- Describe the process of psychological research and the scientific method.
- Name the different types of psychological research.

EXPLORING PSYCHOLOGY

Do You Act This Way?

There are some chimps who, far more than others, constantly seem to try to ingratiate themselves with [win over] their superiors. Melissa, for one, particularly when she was young, used to hurry toward and lay her hand on the back or head of an adult male almost every time one passed anywhere near her. If he turned toward her, she often drew her lips back into a submissive grin as well. Presumably Melissa, like the other chimps who constantly attempt to ingratiate themselves in this way, is simply ill at ease in the presence of a social superior, so that she constantly seeks reassurance through physical contact. . . . There is much controversy as to how the human smile has evolved. It seems fairly certain, though, that we have two rather different kinds of smiles, . . . We smile when we are amused and we smile when we are slightly nervous, on edge, apprehensive. . . .

—from *In the Shadow of Man* by Jane Goodall, 1988

Jane Goodall observed the behavior of chimpanzees in Tanzania, Africa, to obtain data. She observed the behavior of chimps over a period of 30 years and provided much information about the animals' lives. Whereas Goodall used the research method of naturalistic observation, other scientists conduct experiments and surveys. All of these researchers, however, follow scientific methods.

SECTION RESOURCES

Reproducible Masters

- Guided Reading Activity 2–1
- Vocabulary Activity 2–1
- Section Quiz 2–1

Transparencies

- Daily Focus Transparency 2–1

Multimedia

- *ExamView® Assessment Suite* CD-ROM
- Presentation Plus! Software

1 FOCUS

Section Objectives

1. Describe the process of psychological research and the scientific method.
2. Name the different types of psychological research.

BELLRINGER
Motivational Activity

Project Daily Focus Transparency 2–1 and have students answer the questions.

Available as blackline master

Daily Focus Transparency 2–1

Reader's Guide

Use the Reader's Guide to introduce concepts and vocabulary.

Exploring Psychology

Ask students to read the **Exploring Psychology** feature and then discuss: **What problem may exist in using observation as a tool to gather research information?**

Vocabulary Precheck

Have students review the vocabulary terms and list the words they do not recognize.

2 TEACH

L1 Generating Research Lists Place seven sheets of newsprint (or poster board) around the room. Label each sheet with one of the seven methods of research discussed in the text. Ask students to help you create a list of questions they have about human behavior. Begin by providing the following example: *I have always wondered why the same students seem to be consistently late to class.*

Ask for volunteers to identify which of the seven research methods would be a good way to research an item from the list. Have the volunteers write the item on the appropriate sheet. An item may be placed on two or more sheets. During the study of Chapter 2, revisit these lists and ask students to make any changes based on what they have learned. Remind students that during group work they will sometimes be leaders and other times followers; but at all times they should work to create a supportive group climate. **BLOCK SCHEDULING**

Profiles In Psychology

Ask students to read the **Profiles In Psychology** feature and then discuss the following questions:

1. What did Jane Goodall especially like about naturalistic observations? *(She loved the variety each day brought.)*
2. What behaviors previously thought to be only human did Goodall observe? *(She saw chimps hunting, using tools, and one group killing another group even though the first group wasn't threatened.)*

Psychologists collect information somewhat like most people do in everyday life—only more carefully and more systematically. When you turn on the television and the picture is out of focus, you experiment with different knobs and dials until you find the one that works. When you ask a number of friends about a movie you are thinking of seeing, you are conducting an informal survey. Of course, there is more to doing scientific research than turning dials or asking friends what they think. Over the years psychologists, like other scientists, have transformed these everyday techniques for gathering and analyzing information into more precise tools.

sample: the small group of participants, out of the total number available, that a researcher studies

PRE-RESEARCH DECISIONS

Researchers must begin by asking a specific question about a limited topic or hypothesis. The next step is to look for evidence. The method a researcher uses to collect information partly depends on the research topic. For example, a social psychologist who is studying the effects of group pressure is likely to conduct an experiment. A psychologist who is interested in personality might begin with intensive case studies. Whatever approach to gathering data a psychologist selects, however, he or she must make certain basic decisions in advance.

Profiles In Psychology

Jane Goodall

1934–

"Every individual matters. Every individual has a role to play. Every individual makes a difference."

Jane Goodall, a British zoologist, became known for her work with chimpanzees in the wild. In 1960 she began her research at what is now Gombe Stream National Park in Tanzania. By living among the chimpanzees, she won their trust, observing their daily activities and writing detailed reports. She wrote, "The most wonderful thing about fieldwork, whether with chimps, baboons or any other wildlife, is waking up and asking yourself, 'What am I going to see today?'"

Goodall discovered while doing 30 years of research that chimps hunt and eat larger animals and make and use tools more than any other species except humans. Goodall also witnessed the first known instance in which one group of chimps systematically killed another group, even though the first group's survival was not threatened. This discovery surprised naturalists and suggested that behaviors like hunting, using tools, and warfare are not uniquely human.

Samples

Suppose a psychologist wants to know how the desire to get into college affects the attitudes of high school juniors and seniors. It would be impossible to study every junior and senior in the country. Instead, the researcher would select a **sample,** a relatively small group out of the total *population* under study—in this case, all high school juniors and seniors.

COOPERATIVE LEARNING ACTIVITY

Conducting a Survey Organize the class into groups of four to six students. Tell them that a local restaurant wants to gather statistics to help support its claim that it has a better hamburger than its competitors. Have each group define the topic to be surveyed, select a sample, write the survey using multiple choice questions, conduct the survey among the identified sample, score the data, and analyze the results. Explain and have students apply evaluation rules to their quantitative information. If time permits, have the groups develop an advertising campaign that uses the statistics gathered in the survey.

A sample must be *representative* of the population a researcher is studying. For example, if you wanted to know how tall American men were, you would want to make certain that your sample did not include a disproportionately large number of professional basketball players. Such a sample would be *nonrepresentative;* it would probably not represent American men in general.

There are two ways to avoid a nonrepresentative sample. One is to take a purely *random sample* so that each individual has an *equal chance* of being represented. For example, a psychologist might choose every twentieth name on school enrollment lists for a study of schoolchildren in a particular town. Random sampling is like drawing names or numbers out of a hat while blindfolded.

The second way to avoid a nonrepresentative sample is to deliberately pick individuals who represent the various subgroups in the population being studied. For example, the psychologist doing research on schoolchildren might select students of both sexes, of varying ages, of all social classes, and from all neighborhoods. This is called a stratified sample. In a *stratified sample,* subgroups in the population are represented proportionately in the sample. For example, if about 30 percent of schoolchildren in the United States are ages 5–8, then in a stratified sample of schoolchildren in the United States, 30 percent of those studied will be ages 5–8.

Reading Check How does a random sample differ from a stratified sample?

METHODS OF RESEARCH

The goals of research are to describe behavior, to explain its causes, to predict the circumstances under which certain behaviors may occur again, and to control certain behaviors. Psychologists use various methods of research to accomplish each of these goals.

Naturalistic Observation

Researchers need to know how people and animals behave naturally, when they are not conscious of being observed during an experiment. To obtain such information, a psychologist uses **naturalistic observation.** The cardinal rule of naturalistic observation is to avoid disturbing the people or animals you are studying by concealing yourself or by acting as unobtrusively as possible. Otherwise you may observe a performance produced because of the researcher's presence.

naturalistic observation: research method in which the psychologist observes the subject in a natural setting without interfering

Case Studies

A **case study** is an intensive study of a person or group. Most case studies combine long-term observations with diaries, tests, and interviews. Case studies can be a powerful research tool. Sigmund Freud's theory of personality development, discussed in Chapter 14, was based on case studies of his patients. Jean Piaget's theory of intellectual development, described in Chapter 3, was based in part on case studies of

case study: research method that involves an intensive investigation of one or more participants

CHAPTER 2
Section 1, pages 35–41

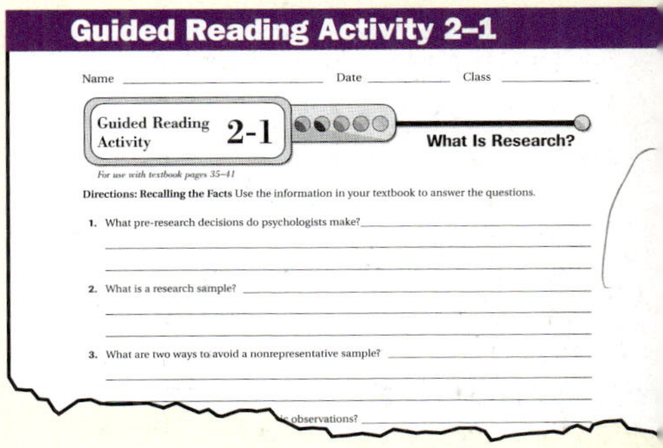
Guided Reading Activity 2–1

Name ______ Date ______ Class ______

Guided Reading Activity 2-1 — What Is Research?

For use with textbook pages 35–41

Directions: Recalling the Facts Use the information in your textbook to answer the questions.

1. What pre-research decisions do psychologists make?
2. What is a research sample?
3. What are two ways to avoid a nonrepresentative sample?

observations?

Reading Check Answer In a random sample, each potential participant has an equal chance of being selected. In a stratified sample, the entire population of potential participants is divided into subgroups. A random sample is then taken from each subgroup.

Applying Psychology

Tell students that the Internet gives us greater access to information than ever before. Some researchers and students are using the Internet to conduct surveys. Recent surveys posted to the Internet include surveys about absolute pitch, taste preferences, dating preferences, creativity, and visual perceptions. Describe to students the types of research being conducted or have them go online to find sample surveys. Ask students what potential sampling problems exist with these online surveys.

MEETING SPECIAL NEEDS

Learning Style: Logical/Mathematical For one 24-hour period, direct students to keep a list of all the correlations they experience. Explain that a correlation is a relationship between two things. Remind them that a correlation does not necessarily indicate cause and effect. To prepare students for this activity, you may want to provide a few examples. An example in daily life includes the amount of traffic and the time it takes to get home. Have students review their lists and place a check mark beside any correlations that appear to have a cause-and-effect relationship. Ask students to explain why these correlations may be cause and effect. **L2**

CHAPTER 2

Section 1, pages 35–41

L2 Making Observations

During the discussion of naturalistic observation, point out that a researcher using this method records or writes down only what can be seen. Emphasize that the researcher must not make inferences about what the behaviors mean or what the subject might be feeling.

Ask students to use naturalistic observation to observe an individual or a group for at least 30 minutes. Students should write a list of the behaviors as they observe them. Have students rewrite the list removing all inferences and judgments. Have each student work with a partner to review another student's list and circle any remaining inferences and judgments.

CURRICULUM CONNECTION

Civics Have students select state or national elected officials. Ask students to review newspaper articles for the two months before the last election. **Ask: How did the polling data change during the two-month period? Did the polling results taken immediately before the election select the correct candidate? How did the actual percentage of votes received compare to the polling numbers?**

Vocabulary Activity 2-1

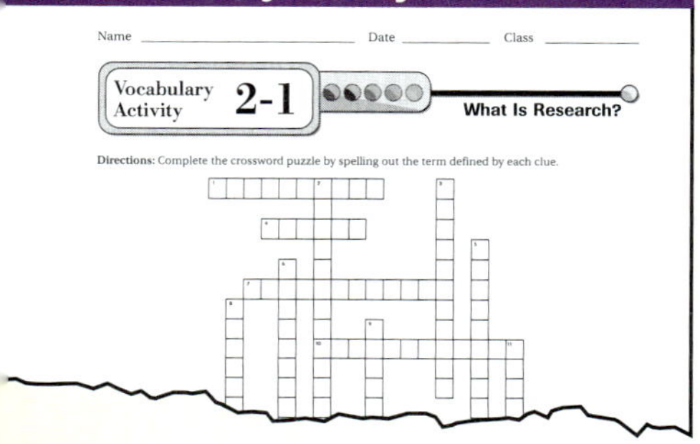
Name ______ Date ______ Class ______

Vocabulary Activity 2-1 — What Is Research?

Directions: Complete the crossword puzzle by spelling out the term defined by each clue.

Did You Know?

A Polling Fiasco To predict the presidential election of 1936, the *Literary Digest* mailed 10 million ballots as a poll (a survey of citizens' votes). With 23% responding, the *Literary Digest* predicted Alfred M. Landon would win comfortably. But Franklin D. Roosevelt won with 61% of the popular vote! The *Digest* sampled mainly owners of telephones and cars and members of clubs. This represented a significant over-sampling of the wealthy, who preferred Landon in the election. These, and other sampling errors, created one of the greatest polling fiascos of all time.

his own children. By itself, however, a case study does not prove or disprove anything. The results cannot be generalized to anyone else. The researcher's conclusions may not be correct. Case studies, though, provide a wealth of descriptive material that may generate new hypotheses that researchers can then test under controlled conditions with comparison groups.

Surveys

One of the most practical ways to gather data on the attitudes, beliefs, and experiences of large numbers of people is through **surveys.** A survey may consist of interviews, questionnaires, or a combination of the two. Interviews allow a researcher to observe the participant and modify questions if the participant seems confused by them. On the other hand, questionnaires take less time to administer and the results are more uniform because everyone answers the same questions. Questionnaires also reduce the possibility that the researcher will influence the participant by unconsciously frowning at an answer he or she does not like. In interviews, there is always a danger that participants will give misleading answers in order to help themselves gain approval.

survey: research method in which information is obtained by asking many individuals a fixed set of questions

Longitudinal Studies

When conducting **longitudinal studies,** a psychologist studies the same group of people at regular intervals over a period of years to determine whether their behavior and/or feelings have changed and if so, how. Longitudinal studies are time-consuming and precarious; participants may disappear in midstudy. Longitudinal studies, however, are an ideal way to examine consistencies and inconsistencies in behavior over time. A good example was the New York Longitudinal Study begun in 1956. Psychologists followed 133 infants as they grew into adulthood, discovering that children are born with different temperaments (Thomas, Chess, & Birch, 1968).

longitudinal study: research method in which data are collected about a group of participants over a number of years to assess how certain characteristics change or remain the same during development

Cross-Sectional Studies

An alternative approach to gathering data is cross-sectional studies. In a **cross-sectional study,** psychologists organize individuals into groups on the basis of age. Then, these groups are randomly sampled, and the members of each group are surveyed, tested, or observed simultaneously. Cross-sectional studies are less expensive than longitudinal studies and reduce the amount of time necessary for the studies.

In 1995 researchers conducted a cross-sectional study in which they showed three-, four-, six-, and seven-year-olds a picture of a serious-looking woman. The psychologists then asked the participants what they thought the woman was thinking about. The psychologists found that the older children seemed to have a clearer picture of mental processes. From

cross-sectional study: research method in which data are collected from groups of participants of different ages and compared so that conclusions can be drawn about differences due to age

CRITICAL THINKING ACTIVITY

Classifying Information Students will design a study to determine the variables that influence how well students perform in school. Students should consider the following questions: **What exactly am I studying?** (definition of problem) **Who am I being asked to study?** (population sample) **How will I study this group?** (selection of sample) **How will the data be collected?** (method of research) **How will the data be interpreted?** (evaluation) Have students present their plans to the class. Have students work in pairs or groups to put their finalized plans into action. **L2**

this discovery, the psychologists proposed that as children mature, their understanding of mental processes improves (Flavell, Green, & Flavell, 1995).

Correlations and Explanations

A researcher may simply want to observe people or animals and record these observations in a descriptive study. More often, however, researchers want to examine the *relationship* between two sets of observations—say, between students' grades and the number of hours they sleep.

Scientists use the word **correlation** to describe how two sets of data relate to each other. For example, there is a *positive correlation* between IQ scores and academic success. High IQ scores tend to go with high grades; low IQ scores tend to go with low grades. On the other hand, there is a *negative correlation* between the number of hours you spend practicing your tennis serve and the number of double faults you serve. As the hours of practice increase, errors decrease. In this case, a high rank on one measure tends to go with a low rank on the other (see Figure 2.1).

It is important to keep in mind that a correlation describes a relationship between two things. It does not mean, though, that one thing causes the other. In some cases, a third factor exists that may account for the positive correlation. Correlations do not identify what causes what. For example, although you might detect a positive correlation between sunny days and your cheerful moods, this does not mean that sunny days cause good moods.

correlation: the measure of a relationship between two variables or sets of data

Experiments

Why would a researcher choose experimentation over other research methods? Experimentation enables the investigator to *control* the situation and to decrease the possibility that unnoticed, outside variables will influence the results.

Figure 2.1 A Correlational Study

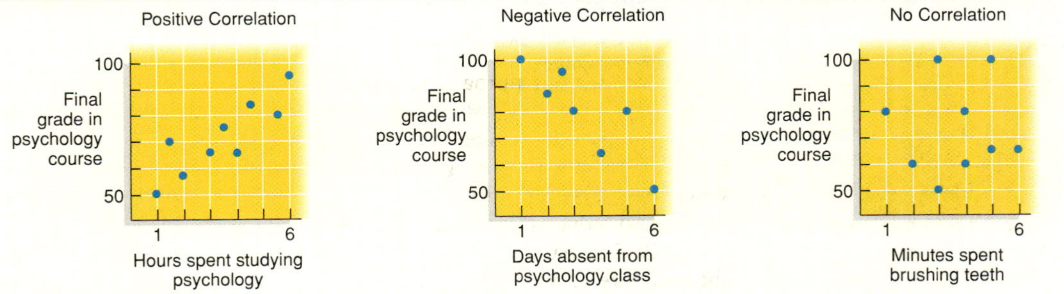

These charts display possible correlations between different variables. ***How does time spent studying psychology correlate to the final grade in a psychology course?***

Readings and Case Studies in Psychology

Have students read the Chapter 2 Case Study selection in *Readings and Case Studies in Psychology* and answer the questions that follow the case study.

Figure 2.1

Visual Instruction Explain that each dot represents an observation of one person. When two factors show a positive correlation, one rises as the other rises. When two factors show a negative correlation, one rises as the other falls.

Caption Answer There is a positive correlation between the time spent studying psychology and the final grade for the course. The more hours spent studying, the higher the grade.

Psychology Journal

Have students record examples of surveys, studies, and experiments in which they have participated. Ask them to explain the researcher's hypothesis for one of the items listed. ■

PSYCHOLOGY LAB EXPERIMENT

Designing a Research Study Explain to students that they will be using the information discussed in this section to help them design a research study. Divide the class into small groups and provide each group with a local or national newspaper. Ask the members of each group to identify a topic or event that they would like to research based on an item in the newspaper. Have the groups select the most appropriate research method for the topic and design an experiment, survey, or study to research it. Ask the groups to share their work with the class. If time permits, have students conduct the research and prepare a written report of their findings. **L1** **BLOCK SCHEDULING**

Figure 2.2

Visual Instruction Remind students that the independent variable is the *if* part of the hypothesis, and the dependent variable is the *then* part of the hypothesis.

Caption Answer dependent: people engage in violent/aggressive behavior; independent: people watch violent TV programs

3 ASSESS

Assign Section 1 Assessment as homework or as an in-class activity.

Section Quiz 2–1

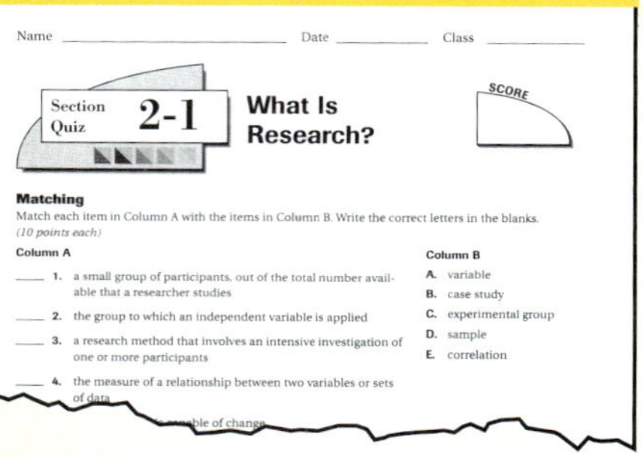
Name ______ Date ______ Class ______

Section Quiz 2-1 **What Is Research?**

SCORE

Matching
Match each item in Column A with the items in Column B. Write the correct letters in the blanks. *(10 points each)*

Column A

____ **1.** a small group of participants, out of the total number available that a researcher studies

____ **2.** the group to which an independent variable is applied

____ **3.** a research method that involves an intensive investigation of one or more participants

____ **4.** the measure of a relationship between two variables or sets of data

...ble of change

Column B

A. variable
B. case study
C. experimental group
D. sample
E. correlation

Reteach

Write examples on the board that describe a pair of variables. Ask students to identify the dependent and independent variable in each situation. *(Example: The number of hours a person sleeps* [independent variable] *affects test performance* [dependent variable]*).*

hypothesis: an educated guess about the relationship between two variables

variable: any factor that is capable of change

experimental group: the group to which an independent variable is applied

control group: the group that is treated in the same way as the experimental group except that the experimental treatment (the independent variable) is not applied

Every experiment has a **hypothesis,** or an educated guess, about the expected outcome; the researcher has some evidence for suspecting a specific answer. In a hypothesis, a psychologist will state what he or she expects to find. The hypothesis also specifies the important variables of the study.

In designing and reporting experiments, psychologists think in terms of **variables,** conditions and behaviors that are subject to change. There are two types of variables: independent and dependent. The *independent variable* is the one experimenters change or alter so they can observe its effects. If an effect is found, the *dependent variable* is the one that changes in relation to the independent variable. For example, the number of hours you study (the independent variable) affects your performance on an exam (the dependent variable).

Participants who are exposed to the independent variable are in the **experimental group.** Participants who are treated the same way as the experimental group, except that they are not exposed to the independent variable, make up the **control group** (see Figure 2.2). A control group is necessary in all experiments. Without it, a researcher cannot be sure the experimental group is reacting to what he or she thinks it is reacting to—a change in the independent variable. By comparing the way control and experimental groups behaved in an experiment (statistically), the researchers can determine whether the independent variable influences behavior and how it does so.

The results of any experiment do not constitute the final word on the subject, however. Psychologists do not fully accept the results of their own or other people's studies until the results have been *replicated*—that is, duplicated by at least one other psychologist with different participants. Why? Because there is always a chance that the studies may have hidden flaws.

Figure 2.2 Experimental Research

Psychology is an experimental science. Psychologists follow the same general procedures when conducting experimental research. ***What are the dependent and independent variables of this experiment?***

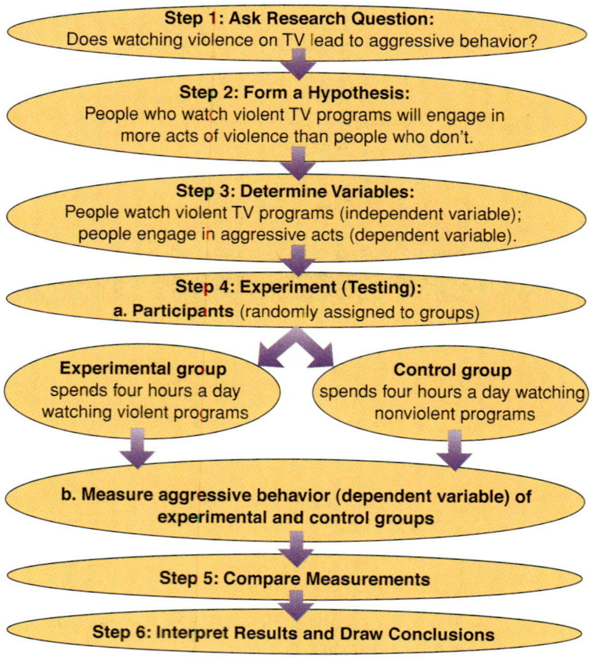

Ethical Issues

Ethics are the methods of conduct, or standards, for proper and responsible behavior. In 1992 the American Psychological Association published a set of ethical principles regarding the collection, storage, and use of psychological data. These principles, revised in 2002, include:

- Using recognized standards of competence and ethics, psychologists plan research so as to minimize the possibility of misleading results. Any ethical

INTERDISCIPLINARY CONNECTIONS ACTIVITY

Science The National Aeronautics and Space Administration (NASA) conducts numerous experiments that involve psychology. For example, humans tend to use facial clues as part of everyday communication. Research has shown that humans process these facial expressions from the top to the bottom of the face. In space, astronauts float freely and may converse with one another "upside down," making facial clues more difficult to read. Have students write a research report on other psychological experiments that NASA has conducted. Suggest that the NASA Ames Research Center is a good place to begin this research. **L3**

problems are resolved before research is started. The welfare and confidentiality of all participants are to be protected.

- Psychologists are responsible for the dignity and welfare of participants. Psychologists are also responsible for all research they perform or is performed by others under their supervision.
- Psychologists obey all state and federal laws and regulations as well as professional standards governing research.
- Except for anonymous surveys, naturalistic observations, and similar research, psychologists reach an agreement regarding the rights and responsibilities of both participants and researcher(s) before research is started.
- When consent is required, psychologists obtain a signed, informed consent before starting any research with a participant.
- Deception is used only if no better alternative is available. Under no condition is there deception about (negative) aspects that might influence a participant's willingness to participate.
- Other issues covered include sharing and utilizing data, offering inducements, minimizing evasiveness, and providing participants with information about the study.

Recently the use of animals in research has caused much concern and debate. Researchers have attempted to balance the rights of animals with the need for advancing the health of humans through research. While some people oppose subjecting animals to pain for research purposes, others point to the enormous gains in knowledge and reduction in human suffering that have resulted from such research.

PSYCHOLOGY Online

Student Web Activity Visit the *Understanding Psychology* Web site at glencoe.com and click on **Chapter 2—Student Web Activities** for an activity about psychological research.

SECTION 1 Assessment

1. **Review the Vocabulary** Explain how a psychologist might select a sample for a survey.
2. **Visualize the Main Idea** In a chart similar to the one below, list and describe the advantages and disadvantages associated with each method of research.

Research Method	Description	Advantages	Disadvantages

3. **Recall Information** What pre-research decisions must a psychologist make?
4. **Think Critically** Why should psychologists question the results of an experiment that they have conducted for the first time?
5. **Application Activity** Suppose you wanted to find out whether there was a correlation between hours spent watching television and test grades in psychology class. Design a plan using one or more of the methods of research to help you study this correlation.

SECTION 1 Assessment Answers

1. A psychologist may select a random sample from the population to be studied or a stratified sample using participants from subgroups of the entire population.
2. Students' answers should demonstrate an understanding of the seven methods of research discussed in this section.
3. research question, selection of research method, identification of sample, ethical considerations
4. to look for errors in conducting the research, to determine if any outside variables influenced the result, and to seek replication for verification
5. Students' answers will vary but should identify surveys, longitudinal studies, or experiments as the research method.

PSYCHOLOGY Online

Links and instructional guidelines can be found in the **Web Activity Lesson Plan** at glencoe.com.

Enrich
Divide the class into small groups. Ask each group to select one of the ethical principles presented in the section. Suggest that students visit the APA Web site at www.apa.org for a complete version of the ethical principles, revised in 2002. Each group will brainstorm ways in which violating the principle could cause harm to a human or animal participant. Ask students to discuss if there is ever an acceptable reason for violating the principle.

4 CLOSE

Ask students to predict the positive and negative ways that the computer, the Internet, or artificial intelligence will affect psychological research.

1 FOCUS

Section Objectives

1. Summarize the methodological hazards of doing research.
2. Examine experimental procedures psychologists use to avoid bias.

BELLRINGER
Motivational Activity

Project Daily Focus Transparency 2–2 and have students answer the questions.

Available as blackline master

Daily Focus Transparency 2–2

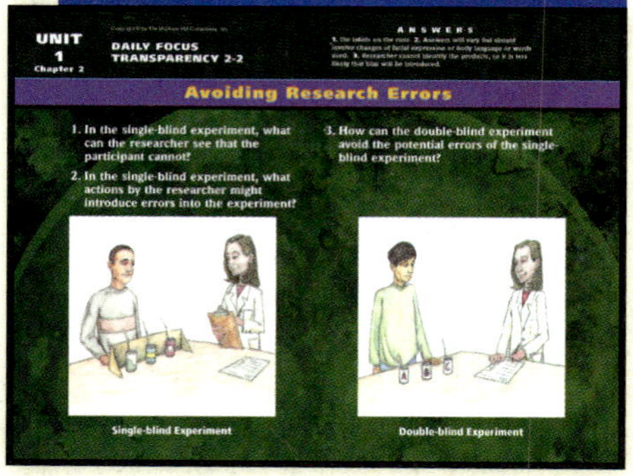

Reader's Guide

Use the Reader's Guide to introduce concepts and vocabulary.

Exploring Psychology

Ask students to read the **Exploring Psychology** feature and then discuss the following question: **How can self-fulfilling prophecies affect behavior?**

Vocabulary Precheck

Have students read the Glossary definition of each vocabulary term. Then ask them to restate each definition in their own words.

Use the **Vocabulary PuzzleMaker CD-ROM** to create crossword and word search puzzles.

SECTION 2

Problems and Solutions in Research

Reader's Guide

Main Idea

The investigation of psychological issues is a painstaking process. Psychologists must recognize and resolve errors while doing research.

Vocabulary

- self-fulfilling prophecy
- single-blind experiment
- double-blind experiment
- placebo effect

Objectives

- Summarize the methodological hazards of doing research.
- Examine experimental procedures psychologists use to avoid bias.

EXPLORING PSYCHOLOGY

Was She Doomed?

One young woman died of fear in a most peculiar way: When she was born, on Friday the 13th, the midwife who delivered her and two other babies that day announced that all three were hexed and would die before their 23rd birthday. The other two did die young. As the third woman approached her 23rd birthday, she checked into a hospital and informed the staff of her fears. The staff noted that she dealt with her anxiety by extreme hyperventilation (deep breathing). Shortly before her birthday, she hyperventilated to death.

—from *Introduction to Psychology* by James W. Kalat, 2005

Once an expectation is set, we tend to act in ways that are consistent with that expectation. How did the woman in the excerpt above die? Technically, when people do not breathe voluntarily, they breathe reflexively—the amount of carbon dioxide in the blood activates breathing. By breathing so deeply for so long (hyperventilating), the woman exhaled so much carbon dioxide that she did not have enough left in her bloodstream to trigger the breathing reflex. When she stopped breathing voluntarily, she stopped breathing altogether and died. In effect, the woman believed in the Friday the 13th hex and unintentionally fulfilled its prediction.

This is what we mean by a self-fulfilling prophecy. A **self-fulfilling prophecy** involves having expectations about a behavior and then acting in some way, usually unknowingly, to carry out that behavior.

self-fulfilling prophecy: a situation in which a researcher's expectations influence that person's own behavior, and thereby influence the participant's behavior

In everyday life, we consciously or unconsciously tip off people as to what our expectations of them are. We give them cues, such as nodding

SECTION RESOURCES

Reproducible Masters

- Guided Reading Activity 2–2
- Vocabulary Activity 2–2
- Section Quiz 2–2

Transparencies

- Daily Focus Transparency 2–2

Multimedia

- Vocabulary PuzzleMaker CD-ROM
- *ExamView® Assessment Suite* CD-ROM
- Presentation Plus! Software

and raising our eyebrows. People pick up on those cues and act as expected. Psychologists must be aware of such cues when conducting experiments. They must not allow their expectations to influence the results. The results must be unbiased. Science is a painstaking, exacting process. Every researcher must be wary of numerous pitfalls that can trap him or her into mistakes. In this section, we will look at some of the most common problems psychological researchers confront and how they cope with them.

AVOIDING A SELF-FULFILLING PROPHECY

Sometimes an experimenter's behavior may unwittingly influence the results. The experimenter may unintentionally raise an eyebrow or nod when posing a question, thus influencing the person being studied. One way to avoid this self-fulfilling prophecy is to use a double-blind technique. Suppose a psychologist wants to study the effects of a particular tranquilizer. She might give the drug to an experimental group and a placebo (a substitute for the drug that has no medical benefits) to a control group. The next step would be to compare their performances on a series of tests. This is a **single-blind experiment.** The participants are "blind" in the sense that they do not know whether they have received the tranquilizer or the placebo. What does it mean, then, if the participants taking the placebo drug report that they feel the effects of the tranquilizer? It means that their expectations have played a role—that they felt the effects because they believed they were taking a tranquilizing drug, not because of the drug itself.

The researcher will not know who takes the drug or the placebo. She may, for example, ask the pharmacist to number rather than label the pills. *After* she scores the tests, she goes back to the pharmacist to learn which participants took the tranquilizer and which took the placebo. This is a **double-blind experiment.** Neither the participants nor the experimenter knows which participants received the tranquilizer. This eliminates the possibility that the researcher will unconsciously find what she expects to find about the effects of the drug. The researcher remains unbiased.

THE MILGRAM EXPERIMENT

In the 1960s Stanley Milgram wanted to determine whether participants would administer painful shocks to others merely because an authority figure had instructed them to do so. Milgram collected nearly 1,000 male

More About...

The Hawthorne Study

In 1939 a group of industrial psychologists set out to determine how to increase workers' productivity at a General Electric plant in Hawthorne, Illinois (Roethlisberger & Dickson, 1939). The participants were eight assembly line workers. In the first experiment, the psychologists gradually increased the lighting in the room (the independent variable) and observed the effect on productivity (the dependent variable). Productivity improved as the lighting was increased. In a second experiment, the participants were permitted to take rest breaks. This also increased the productivity of the workers. Next, the psychologists reduced the lighting levels, and again productivity increased. The psychologists found that no matter what they did, productivity increased. Why? The psychologists soon recognized that the participants realized they were receiving special attention. This motivated the workers to work harder, thus increasing their productivity.

The results of the experiment in Hawthorne generated studies in human relations and management that apply to work situations today.

single-blind experiment: an experiment in which the participants are unaware of which participants received the treatment

double-blind experiment: an experiment in which neither the experimenter nor the participants know which participants received which treatment

2 TEACH

L1 Discussion Explain to students that critical thinking skills are important in psychology because they help people recognize and resolve errors in research. Ask students to provide examples of the principles of critical thinking. Then ask them to discuss how the principles can be applied to psychological research.

Guided Reading Activity 2-2

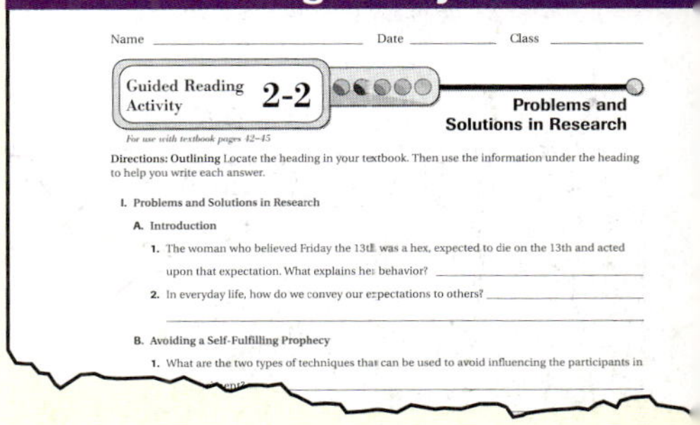
Name ______ Date ______ Class ______

Guided Reading Activity 2-2 — Problems and Solutions in Research

Directions: Outlining Locate the heading in your textbook. Then use the information under the heading to help you write each answer.

I. Problems and Solutions in Research

A. Introduction

1. The woman who believed Friday the 13th was a hex, expected to die on the 13th and acted upon that expectation. What explains her behavior? ______

2. In everyday life, how do we convey our expectations to others? ______

B. Avoiding a Self-Fulfilling Prophecy

1. What are the two types of techniques that can be used to avoid influencing the participants in

Vocabulary Activity 2-2

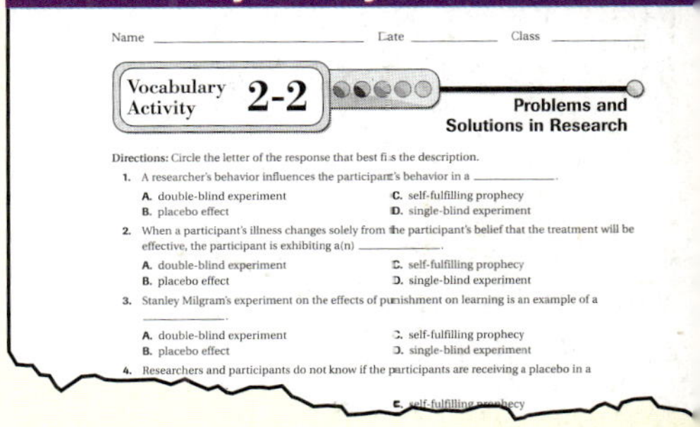
Name ______ Date ______ Class ______

Vocabulary Activity 2-2 — Problems and Solutions in Research

Directions: Circle the letter of the response that best fits the description.

1. A researcher's behavior influences the participant's behavior in a ______.
A. double-blind experiment C. self-fulfilling prophecy
B. placebo effect D. single-blind experiment

2. When a participant's illness changes solely from the participant's belief that the treatment will be effective, the participant is exhibiting a(n) ______.
A. double-blind experiment C. self-fulfilling prophecy
B. placebo effect D. single-blind experiment

3. Stanley Milgram's experiment on the effects of punishment on learning is an example of a
A. double-blind experiment C. self-fulfilling prophecy
B. placebo effect D. single-blind experiment

4. Researchers and participants do not know if the participants are receiving a placebo in a

COOPERATIVE LEARNING ACTIVITY

Conducting an Interview Organize the class into small groups to conduct interviews with research psychologists, marketing research professionals, or human resource specialists who design and conduct studies. Each group member should write at least three questions to be asked. The questions should be designed to identify the type of research the person conducts and how the researcher avoids bias and errors. The group will review each member's questions and develop an interview form to be used. The group will conduct the interview with one person appointed to ask the questions and one appointed to record the answers. Ask the group to summarize its findings in a brief report or table.

Figure 2.3

Visual Instruction Tell students that double-blind studies are required by the Food and Drug Administration (FDA) before new drugs can be made available to the public. Since neither the participants nor the researchers know who is taking the real drug or the placebo, the people who measure the effects can remain unbiased.

Caption Answer to avoid introducing any bias into the experiment

Readings and Case Studies in Psychology

Have students read the Chapter 2 Reading selection in *Readings and Case Studies in Psychology* and answer the questions that follow the reading.

Reading Check Answer

The participants did not know that they were not administering a shock, but the experimenter did know.

3 ASSESS

Assign Section 2 Assessment as homework or as an in-class activity.

Section Quiz 2–2

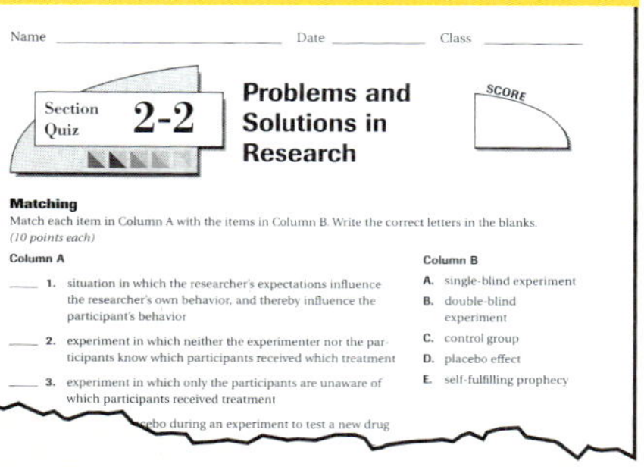
Name ____________ Date ________ Class ________

Section Quiz 2-2 **Problems and Solutions in Research**

SCORE

Matching
Match each item in Column A with the items in Column B. Write the correct letters in the blanks. *(10 points each)*

Column A

____ 1. situation in which the researcher's expectations influence the researcher's own behavior, and thereby influence the participant's behavior

____ 2. experiment in which neither the experimenter nor the participants know which participants received which treatment

____ 3. experiment in which only the participants are unaware of which participants received treatment

...cebo during an experiment to test a new drug

Column B

A. single-blind experiment
B. double-blind experiment
C. control group
D. placebo effect
E. self-fulfilling prophecy

Figure 2.3 Single-Blind and Double-Blind Experiments

Researchers must take measures during experimentation to guard against seeing only what they expect to see. ***Why would a researcher conduct a double-blind experiment?***

	Experimenter	Participants	Organizer of Experiment
Single-Blind Experiment	aware	unaware	aware
Double-Blind Experiment	unaware	unaware	aware

participants, including college students and adults in different occupations. Milgram told the group of paid volunteers that he was studying the effects of punishment on learning. Milgram introduced each volunteer to a "learner"—actually someone posing as a learner. The volunteer watched the learner attempt to recite a list of paired words that he supposedly had memorized earlier. Each time the learner made a mistake, the volunteer, or "teacher," was ordered to push a button to deliver an electric shock to the learner. The volunteers were told that the shocks, mild at first, would increase with each mistake to a painful and dangerous level of 450 volts.

The volunteers at this point did not realize that the shocks were false because the learners displayed distress and pain, screaming and begging for the electric shocks to stop. Although the task did not seem easy for them, most of the volunteers delivered a full range of the fake electric shocks to the learners. (Sixty-five percent of the volunteers pushed the shock button until they reached maximum severity.)

Reading Check
Why can the Milgram experiment be classified as a single-blind experiment?

The results implied that ordinary individuals could easily inflict pain on others if such orders were issued by a respected authority. Later, Milgram informed the volunteers that they had been deceived and that no shocks had actually been administered. This was a good example of a single-blind experiment because the participants were unaware that they were not administering a shock. Critics raised the following questions, though. How would you feel if you had been one of Milgram's participants? Did Milgram violate ethical principles when he placed participants in a position to exhibit harmful behavior? Was the deception Milgram used appropriate? Did the information gained outweigh the deception? Before the start of any experiment today, the experimenter is required to submit a plan to a Human Subjects Committee that can either approve or reject the ethics of the experiment.

Milgram's hypothesis and experiment has been applied in similar studies. In Milgram's original study, more than half of the participants (26 of 40, or 65 percent) administered the highest level of shock. Researchers at Swarthmore College hypothesized that Milgram's findings were due, in part, to the fact that his participants were mostly

MEETING SPECIAL NEEDS

Logical/Mathematical Have students locate magazine, newspaper, or journal articles about a psychological experiment. Ask them to write a summary indicating the hypotheses that the experiment was designed to test, the method used to test the hypotheses, the dependent and independent variables, the nature of the experimental and control groups, and the results of the experiment. Ask students to discuss their findings with the class. **L3**

Refer to ***Inclusion for the High School Social Studies Classroom Strategies and Activities*** in the TCR for strategies for students with different learning styles.

middle-aged, working-class men. Most had probably served in the military during World War II and thus had experience taking orders and obeying authority. Young, liberal, highly educated Swarthmore students would obey less. Yet, surprisingly, 88 percent of the Swarthmore undergraduates administered the highest level of shock!

THE PLACEBO EFFECT

When researchers evaluate the effects of drugs, they must always take into account a possible placebo effect. The **placebo effect** is a change in a patient's illness or physical state that results solely from the patient's knowledge and perceptions of the treatment. The placebo is some sort of treatment, such as a drug or injection, that resembles medical therapy yet has no medical effects.

In one study (Loranger, Prout, & White, 1961), researchers divided hospitalized psychiatric patients into two experimental groups and a control group. They gave the experimental groups either a "new tranquilizer" or a "new energizer" drug. The control group received no drugs at all. After a six-week period, the researchers evaluated the experimental groups. Fifty-three to eighty percent of the experimental groups reported that they had indeed benefited from the drugs. Yet all the drugs administered during the experiment were placebos. The participants had reacted to their own expectations of how the drug given to them would affect them. Neither the researchers nor the patients were aware that the drugs were placebos until after the experiment.

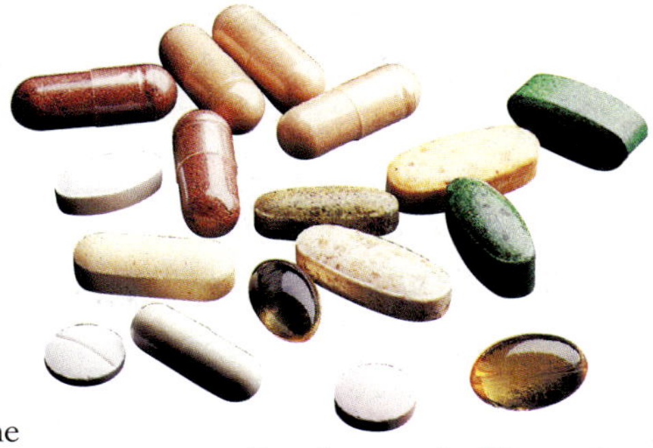

People spend millions of dollars a year on herbal remedies such as these, which have not been proven to cure their ills.

placebo effect: a change in a participant's illness or behavior that results from a belief that the treatment will have an effect rather than from the actual treatment

SECTION 2 Assessment

1. **Review the Vocabulary** Explain how psychologists try to avoid the self-fulfilling prophecy.
2. **Visualize the Main Idea** Use a diagram similar to the one below to outline an experiment discussed in this section.

Hypothesis: ____________
Independent Variables: ________ Dependent Variables: ________
Results: ____________
Conclusions: ____________

3. **Recall Information** What questions about the Milgram experiment did critics raise? How are today's experiments restricted in regards to ethics?
4. **Think Critically** How can the expectations of the participants bias the results of an experiment? How can the expectations of the experimenter bias the results of an experiment?
5. **Application Activity** Describe a single-blind experiment you might set up. Explain your hypothesis and the participants' tasks.

SECTION 2 Assessment Answers

1. by using single-blind and double-blind experiments
2. Students' answers will vary. Answers should reflect an understanding of the steps involved in a scientific experiment.
3. How would you feel if you had been a participant? Were ethical principles violated? Was deception warranted? Did the information gained outweigh the deception? Experiments can be rejected or approved based on the ethical principles followed or disregarded.
4. Participants may behave in ways that match their expectations, creating a self-fulfilling prophecy. Experimenters may do the same in the creation, observation, and interpretation of the experiment.
5. Students' answers will vary. The key factor is to create a study in which the participants do not know what they are receiving.

Reteach

Ask students to list examples of self-fulfilling prophecies from their own experience.

Enrich

Bring a market researcher to the class to present an overview of how research is conducted in a "real world" environment. Inform the researcher beforehand of your study of self-fulfilling prophecies, single-blind and double-blind studies, and the placebo effect.

4 CLOSE

Conduct a brief in-class debate on the ethical implications of using placebos in research studies. The debate can extend to medical research in addition to psychology.

Going Further

Facilitated Communication

The Clever Hans case has a parallel in the late twentieth century. Autism is a disability that in its severest form causes otherwise intelligent children to be unable to communicate with the outside world. A technique from Australia called *facilitated communication* was widely reported in the media as a means of allowing autistic children to communicate with the outside world.

Facilitated communication involves a facilitator supporting the hand and arm of the autistic individual while he or she types on a computer keyboard. The messages display on a computer monitor. Media coverage showed previously nonverbal individuals typing complete sentences and thoughts.

Repeated studies have unanimously concluded that the autistic individual is reacting to tactile cues from the facilitator. For example, when a child and facilitator were shown the same picture and asked to name the item, the child named the object correctly. However, when the child and facilitator are shown different pictures, the child typed the name of the facilitator's object.

Discussing the Case Study

Ask: Why are carefully controlled studies necessary to avoid deceiving the public? Discuss the question in class and have students research other intentional or unintentional deceptions that have been, at least for a time, believed.

Case Studies

The Case of Clever Hans

Period of Study: 1911

Introduction: A horse, Clever Hans, grew famous throughout Europe for his startling ability to answer questions. Taught by his owner, Mr. von Osten, Hans seemed to be able to add, subtract, multiply, divide, spell, and solve problems, even when his owner was not around. Oskar Pfungst decided to investigate the humanlike intelligence of the horse.

Hypothesis: Two different hypotheses are involved in this case. First, Mr. von Osten, believing that horses could be as intelligent as humans, hypothesized that he could teach Hans some problem-solving abilities. Pfungst, on the other hand, believed that horses could not learn such things and, while investigating this theory, developed a hypothesis that Hans, the horse, was reacting to visual cues to answer questions.

Method: Mr. von Osten, a German mathematics teacher, started by showing Hans an object while saying "One" and at the same time lifting Hans's foot once. Von Osten would lift Hans's foot twice for two objects, and so on. Eventually Hans learned to tap his hoof the correct number of times when von Osten called out a number. For four years, von Osten worked with Hans on more and more complex problems, until Hans was able to answer any question given him.

Upon hearing of the amazing horse, Pfungst grew skeptical and investigated. Pfungst soon discovered that Hans responded correctly to questions only when the questioner had calculated the answer first. Then Pfungst realized that Hans's answers proved wrong when the horse could not see the questioner. To test his hypothesis, Pfungst fitted the horse with blinders. The horse failed to answer the questions. Eventually Pfungst realized that the questioner would unknowingly give Hans clues as to the right answer. For example, after asking a question, the questioner would lean forward to watch Hans's foot. This was a cue for Hans to start tapping. Pfungst observed that "as the experimenter straightened up, Hans would stop tapping, he found that even the raising of his eyebrows was sufficient. Even the dilation of the questioner's nostrils was a cue for Hans to stop tapping." (Pfungst, 1911) Questioners involuntarily performed these actions, and Hans responded to the visual signals.

Results: Von Osten believed that he had been teaching the horse how to solve problems and answer questions, when in fact he had been teaching Hans to make simple responses to simple signals. Pfungst had uncovered errors in von Osten's experiments. Von Osten had practiced a self-fulfilling prophecy—he had unintentionally communicated to Hans how he expected the horse to behave. Pfungst had learned the truth by isolating the conditions under which Hans correctly and incorrectly answered questions. He had carefully observed the participant's reactions under controlled conditions.

Analyzing the Case Study

1. How did Mr. von Osten test his hypothesis?
2. What errors did von Osten make while testing his hypothesis?
3. **Critical Thinking** If Pfungst had not come along and found the truth, how could we discover today how Hans answered the questions?

Answers for Analyzing the Case Study

1. He trained Hans initially by raising and lowering his foot the correct number of times for the number he was shown. Hans soon learned to tap his foot the correct number of times in response to various math problems.
2. He did not set up controls to eliminate other explanations for Hans's ability.
3. The best way to discover how Hans performed his feat would be to train another horse, closely following von Osten's method, then use controls similar to Pfungst's to investigate possible explanations for its ability.

SECTION 3

Statistical Evaluation

Reader's Guide

Main Idea

Psychologists must collect and evaluate evidence to support their hypotheses.

Vocabulary

- statistics
- descriptive statistics
- frequency distribution
- normal curve
- central tendency
- variance
- standard deviation
- correlation coefficient
- inferential statistics

Objectives

- Recognize types of descriptive statistics.
- Describe inferential statistics.

EXPLORING PSYCHOLOGY

When Statistics Lie

Long ago, when Johns Hopkins University had just begun to admit women students, someone not particularly enamored of [happy with] coeducation reported a real shocker: Thirty-three and one-third percent of the women at Hopkins had married faculty members! The raw figures gave a clearer picture. There were three women enrolled at the time, and one of them had married a faculty man.

—from *How to Lie With Statistics* by Darrell Huff, 1954

Although people may use statistics to distort the truth (such as in the example above), people may also use statistics honestly to support their hypotheses. In order to allow statistics to validly support a hypothesis, psychologists must collect meaningful data and evaluate it correctly.

How many times have you been told that in order to get good grades, you have to study? A psychology student named Kate has always restricted the amount of TV she watches during the week, particularly before a test. She has a friend, though, who does not watch TV before a test but who still does not get good grades. This fact challenges Kate's belief. Although Kate hypothesizes that among her classmates, those who watch less TV get better grades, she decides to conduct a survey to test the accuracy of her hypothesis. Kate asks 15 students in her class to write down how many hours of TV they watched the night before a psychology quiz and how many hours they watched on the night after the quiz. Kate collects additional data. She has her participants check off familiar products on a

SECTION RESOURCES

Reproducible Masters

- Guided Reading Activity 2–3
- Vocabulary Activity 2–3
- Section Quiz 2–3

Transparencies

- Daily Focus Transparency 2–3

Multimedia

- *ExamView® Assessment Suite* CD-ROM
- Presentation Plus! Software

1 FOCUS

Section Objectives

1. Recognize types of descriptive statistics.
2. Describe inferential statistics.

BELLRINGER
Motivational Activity

Project Daily Focus Transparency 2–3 and have students answer the questions.

Available as blackline master

Daily Focus Transparency 2–3

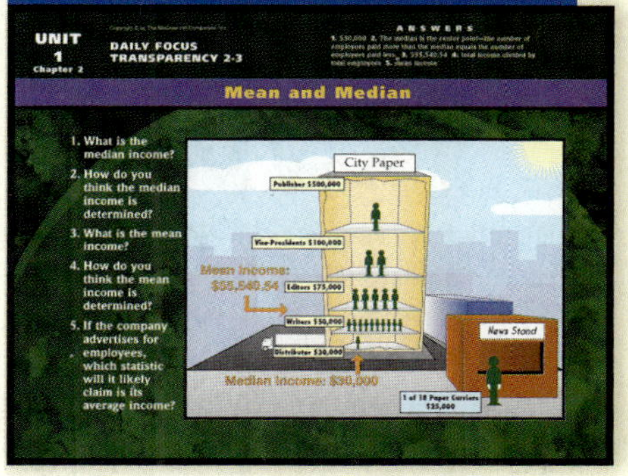

Reader's Guide

Use the Reader's Guide to introduce concepts and vocabulary.

Exploring Psychology

Ask students to read the **Exploring Psychology** feature and then discuss the following question: **How did the reporter seek to mislead using an accurate statistic?**

Vocabulary Precheck

Have students work in pairs to create a set of flash cards with the terms on one side and the definitions on the other. Students should take turns quizzing each other.

CHAPTER 2
Section 3, pages 47–54

2 TEACH

L2 Analyzing Statistics Divide students into small groups, and give each group a different newspaper or different days of the same newspaper. Direct each group to identify three to five examples of statistics. Instruct students to analyze how the various statistics are used. **Ask:** **Are any of the statistics used to present a misleading picture or to slant an argument? Which statistics are the most objective? Which statistics open the door for speculation beyond the written material?** Have each group present its findings to the class. ELL

Psychology and You

Use the following question to direct a class discussion after students have read the **Psychology and You** feature.
Ask: **What statistics are kept for your favorite sport (other than baseball)?**

Figure 2.4

Visual Instruction From the data, what tentative conclusions can students draw? **Ask:** **Have you identified a correlation, a solid cause-and-effect relationship, or both?**

Caption Answer 1/2 hour and 1 hour

Psychology and You: Baseball Statistics

Let's look at how statistics are used in one of our most popular sports, baseball. A batting average is the number of hits per official "at bats" (walks do not count). If a player has a batting average of .250, it means that on average he or she gets a hit every fourth time at the plate.

The earned run average represents the number of runs a pitcher allows per 9 innings of play. Consider the pitcher who pitches 180 innings in a season and allows 60 runs. On the average, this pitcher allows one run every 3 innings (180 innings divided by 60 runs). One run every 3 innings equals 3 runs every 9 innings, so the earned run average is 3. The next time you watch your favorite sport, think about the part that statistics plays in it.

list of 20 brand-name items that were advertised on TV the night before the quiz. Kate also asks her participants to give their height.

When the data are turned in, Kate finds herself overwhelmed with the amount of information she has collected. Her data are presented in Figure 2.4. How can she organize it all so that it makes sense? How can she analyze it to see whether it supports or contradicts her hypothesis? The answers to these questions are found in **statistics,** a branch of mathematics that enables researchers to organize and evaluate the data they collect. We will explore the statistical procedures that help psychologists make sense out of the masses of data they collect.

statistics: the branch of mathematics concerned with summarizing and making meaningful inferences from collections of data

descriptive statistics: the listing and summarizing of data in a practical, efficient way

DESCRIPTIVE STATISTICS

When a study such as Kate's is completed, the first task is to organize the data in as brief and clear a manner as possible. For Kate, this means that she must put her responses together in a logical format. When she does this, she is using **descriptive statistics,** the listing and summarizing of data in a practical, efficient way, such as through graphs and averages.

Figure 2.4 Kate's Data

Before	After	Grade*	Products	Height
0.0	1.5	5	2	71
0.5	2.5	10	4	64
0.5	2.5	9	6	69
1.0	2.0	10	14	60
1.0	2.5	8	10	71
1.0	1.5	7	9	63
1.5	3.0	9	7	70
1.5	2.5	8	12	59
1.5	2.5	8	9	75
1.5	3.0	6	14	60
2.0	3.0	5	13	68
2.5	2.5	3	17	65
2.5	3.5	4	10	72
3.0	3.0	0	18	62
4.0	4.0	4	20	67

Kate's data show the number of hours of television watched before and after the quiz, the grade on the quiz, the number of products recognized, and participants' height in inches. ***How much television did the two students with the best grades watch the night before the quiz?***

* Highest grade possible is 10.

Guided Reading Activity 2-3

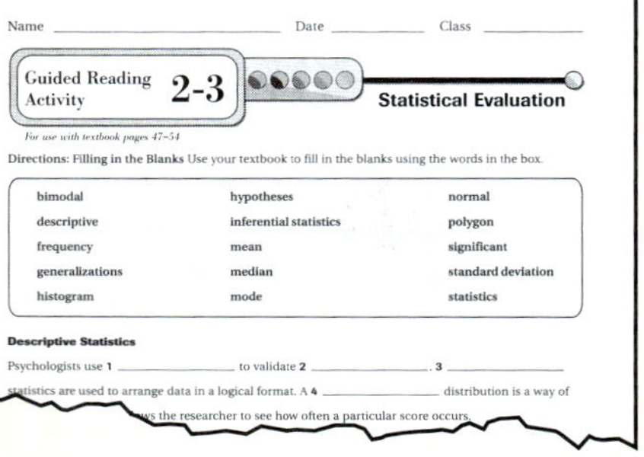
Name ____ Date ____ Class ____
Guided Reading Activity 2-3 Statistical Evaluation
For use with textbook pages 47–54
Directions: Filling in the Blanks Use your textbook to fill in the blanks using the words in the box.

bimodal	hypotheses	normal
descriptive	inferential statistics	polygon
frequency	mean	significant
generalizations	median	standard deviation
histogram	mode	statistics

Descriptive Statistics
Psychologists use 1 ____ to validate 2 ____ 3 ____
statistics are used to arrange data in a logical format. A 4 ____ distribution is a way of
...s the researcher to see how often a particular score occurs.

COOPERATIVE LEARNING ACTIVITY

Frequency Distributions Organize the class into groups of four students. Ask each group to identify a statistic for which 15 observations can be easily gathered—for example, the high temperature in your location for the past 15 days. Each group should gather its data and create a frequency distribution table and at least three different graphs or charts showing the data. The graphs or charts should be clearly labeled so that someone looking at them for the first time can readily understand the information. Finally, have students choose the distribution table and the graph or chart that most clearly expresses the data and use them to create a bulletin board display. **BLOCK SCHEDULING**

Figure 2.5 A Frequency Distribution

A frequency distribution shows how often a particular observation occurs. ***How many students watched three or more hours of television the night before the quiz?***

Hours	Frequency Before*	Frequency After*
0.0	1	0
0.5	2	0
1.0	3	0
1.5	4	2
2.0	1	1
2.5	2	6
3.0	1	4
3.5	0	1
4.0	1	1
Total	15	15

*Number of students

Distributions of Data

One of the first steps that researchers take to organize their data is to create frequency tables and graphs. Tables and graphs provide a rough picture of the data. Are the scores bunched up or spread out? What score occurs most often? Frequency distributions and graphs provide researchers with their initial look at the data.

Kate is interested in how many hours of TV her participants watched the night before and the night after the quiz. She uses the numbers of hours of TV viewing as categories, and then she counts how many participants reported each category of hours before and after the quiz. She has created a table called a frequency distribution (see Figure 2.5). A **frequency distribution** is a way of arranging data so that we know how often a particular score or observation occurs.

frequency distribution: an arrangement of data that indicates how often a particular score or observation occurs

What can Kate do with this information? A commonly used technique is to figure out percentages. This is done simply by dividing the frequency of participants within a category by the total number of participants and multiplying by 100. Before the quiz, about 13 percent of her participants (2 divided by 15) watched TV for 2.5 hours. On the night after the quiz, 40 percent of her participants watched 2.5 hours of TV (6 divided by 15). If you are familiar with the use of percentages, you know that test grades are often expressed as percentages (the number of correct points divided by the total number of questions times 100). Sometimes frequency distributions include a column giving the percentage of each occurrence.

Figure 2.6 A Frequency Polygon

This graph shows the number of hours of TV watched the night before the quiz and the night after the quiz. ***How do the two lines compare?***

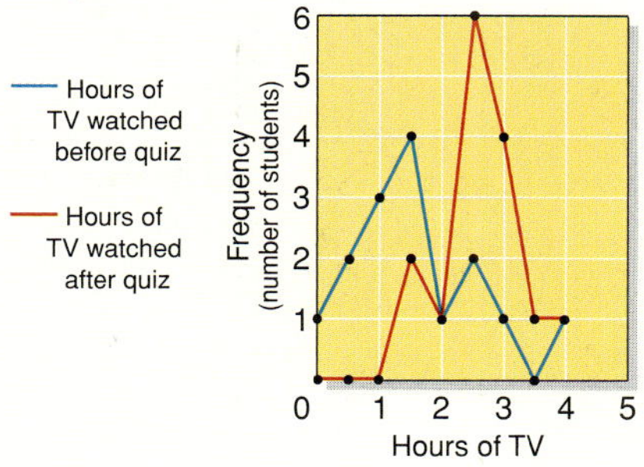

CHAPTER 2
Section 3, pages 47–54

Figure 2.5

Visual Instruction Explain that descriptive statistics help researchers accomplish two important goals: showing at a glance how scores in a sample are distributed and conveying in a shorthand manner how closely two factors are related.

Caption Answer two

TEACHER Tip

In discussing statistics, always begin with statistics that are easy to understand and fun to work with, such as baseball or weather statistics. It is far more important for students to understand what these statistics measure and how to interpret findings than to make direct applications to psychology.

Figure 2.6

Visual Instruction To interpret a frequency polygon, or line graph, students should determine if the line connecting a group of data points has an upward or downward slope. A downslope indicates a lowering of frequency, for example.

Caption Answer Answers may vary. Students may note that the hours of TV watched after the quiz vary more widely and that more students watched more hours of TV after the quiz.

MEETING SPECIAL NEEDS

Learning Style: Verbal/Spatial Explain that graphs and charts can sometimes mislead. Ask students to identify a government statistic that is measured over time—for example, the national debt. Have students create two line graphs plotting time on the x-axis. On the y-axis of one graph, have them use large increments, such as \$100 billion. On the other y-axis, have them use small increments, such as \$10 billion. The size of the two graphs should be the same; just the increments on the y-axis should vary. Have students write a paragraph explaining which graph the government would prefer to distribute and why. **L2** **BLOCK SCHEDULING**

CHAPTER 2
Section 3, pages 47–54

L2 Determining Validity

Review the importance of replication as a means of determining the validity of any experiment. Ask small groups of students to develop and conduct a study similar to Kate's (see Figure 2.4). Instruct students to review information on conducting a survey, especially selection of a sample. Have the groups complete the study and analyze the results by preparing graphs or charts. **Ask: Did the surveys validate Kate's findings? Why or why not?**

Figure 2.7

Visual Instruction Tell students that you cannot tell for sure whether a curve is a normal curve just by looking at it and observing that it is roughly bell shaped. Normal curves are formed by only a very specific distribution of scores.

Caption Answer the highest point of the curve

Figure 2.8

Visual Instruction Remind students that measures of central tendency, the mean, median, and mode, are not identical in all distributions.

Caption Answer If your score matched the median, you scored better than 50 percent of your classmates and worse than 50 percent.

Figure 2.7 A Normal Curve

The maximum frequency lies in the center of a range of scores in a perfect normal curve. The frequency tapers off as you reach the edges of the two sides. ***Where is the mean located in a normal curve?***

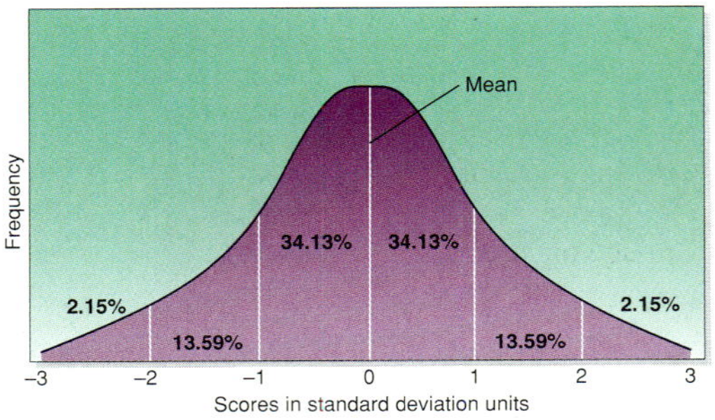

It is often easier to visualize frequency information in the form of a graph. Since Kate is most interested in how much TV her classmates watched, she decides to graph the results. Kate constructs a histogram. *Histograms* are very similar to bar graphs except that histograms show frequency distribution by means of rectangles whose widths represent class intervals and whose areas are proportionate to the corresponding frequencies.

Another kind of graph is the frequency polygon or frequency curve. Figure 2.6 is a frequency polygon. It shows the same information presented in a different way. Instead of boxes, a point is placed on the graph where the midpoint of the top of each histogram bar would be. Then the points are connected with straight lines.

Frequency polygons are useful because they provide a clear picture of the shape of the data distribution. Another important feature is that more than one set of data can be graphed at the same time. For example, Kate might be interested in comparing how much TV was watched the night before the quiz with the amount watched the evening after the quiz. She can graph the "after quiz" data using a different kind of line. The comparison is obvious; in general, her participants watched more TV on the night after the quiz than on the night before the quiz.

Figure 2.8 Measures of Central Tendency

My friends' scores on the last psychology quiz

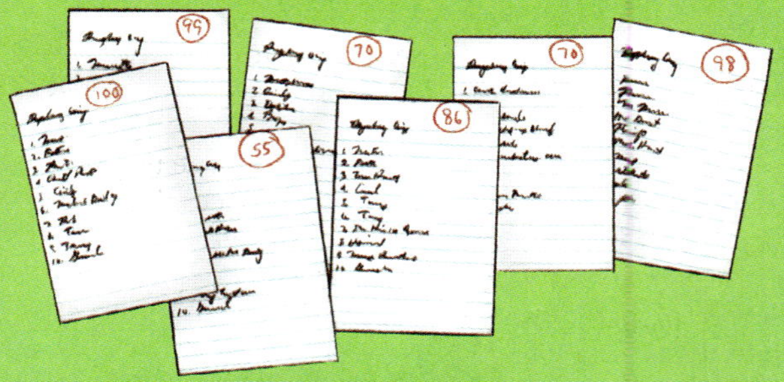

What is the mean? The mean is the "average." [55+70+70+86+98+99+100=578÷7=83]

What is the median? The median is the middle score after the scores are ranked from highest to lowest. [86]

What is the mode? The mode is the most common score. [70]

It is often useful to summarize a set of scores by identifying a number that represents the center, average, or most frequently occurring number of the distribution. ***If your score matched the median on the last psychology quiz, how did you do in comparison to your classmates?***

CRITICAL THINKING ACTIVITY

Analyzing Information Ask students to work in pairs to select an issue in the news that interests them. Challenge students to use statistics to develop both a pro and a con position on the issue. Ask for volunteers to share their pro and con positions with the class, presenting the statistics that support each view. Direct the rest of the class to take notes on how each person makes use of numbers and surveys. **L2**

Imagine that Kate could measure how much TV everyone in Chicago watched one night. If she could graph that much information, her graph would probably look something like Figure 2.7. A few people would watch little or no TV, a few would have the TV on all day, while most would watch a moderate amount of TV. Therefore, the graph would be highest in the middle and taper off toward the tails, or ends, of the distribution, giving it the shape of a bell.

This curve is called the **normal curve** (or bell-shaped curve). Many variables, such as height, weight, and IQ, fall into such a curve if enough people are measured. The normal curve is symmetrical. This means that if a line is drawn down the middle of the curve, one side of the curve is a mirror image of the other side. It is an important distribution because of certain mathematical characteristics. We can divide the curve into sections and predict how much of the curve, or what percentage of cases, falls within each section.

normal curve: a graph of frequency distribution shaped like a symmetrical, bell-shaped curve; a graph of normally distributed data

Measures of Central Tendency

Most of the time, researchers want to do more than organize their data. They want to be able to summarize information about the distribution into statistics. For example, researchers might want to discuss the average height of women or the most common IQ test score. One of the most common ways of summarizing is to use a measure of **central tendency**—a number that describes something about the "average" score. We shall use Kate's quiz grades (refer back to Figure 2.4) in the examples that follow.

central tendency: a number that describes something about the "average" score of a distribution

The *mode* is the most frequent score. In a graphed frequency distribution, the mode is the peak of the graph. The most frequently occurring quiz grade is 8; that is, more students received an 8 than any other score. Distributions can have more than one mode. The data for height presented in Figure 2.4 have two modes: 60 and 71. Distributions with two modes are called *bimodal.*

Reading Check What is the difference between the mean and the mode?

When scores are put in order from least to most, the *median* is the middle score. Since the median is the midpoint of a set of values, it divides the frequency distribution into two halves. Therefore, 50 percent of the scores fall below the median, and 50 percent fall above the median. For an odd number of observations, the median is the exact middle value.

The *mean* is what most people think of as an average and is the most commonly used measure of central tendency. To find the mean (or $\bar{X}$), add up all the scores and then divide by the number of scores added. The mean equals the sum of the scores on variable X divided by the total number of observations. For the quiz grades, the sum of the scores is 96, and the number of scores is 15. The mean equals 96 divided by 15, giving us a mean quiz grade of 6.4.

The mean can be considered the balance point of the distribution, like the middle of a seesaw, since it does reflect all the scores in a set of data. If the highest score in a data set is shifted higher, the mean

Figure 2.9 Standard Deviation

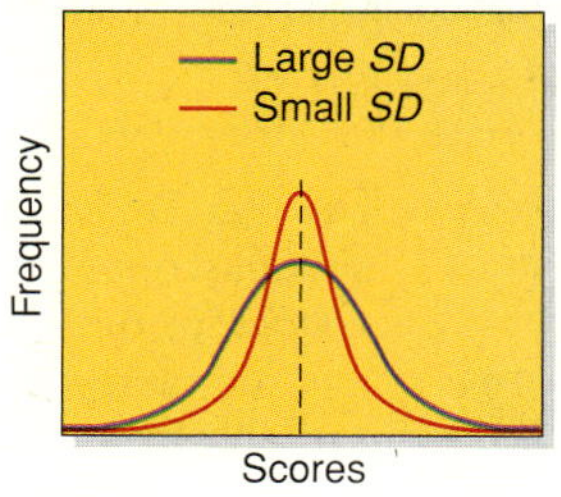

Two distributions with the same mean and different standard deviations are shown. ***What information does the standard deviation supply?***

CHAPTER 2
Section 3, pages 47–54

PSYCHOLOGY JOURNAL

Have students gather the height and shoe size from every member of their family. Ask them to graph the information in their journals. Ask students to consider if any useful insights can be drawn from this data. ■

Reading Check Answer Whereas the mean is the average of scores, the mode is the most frequently occurring score.

Vocabulary Activity 2–3

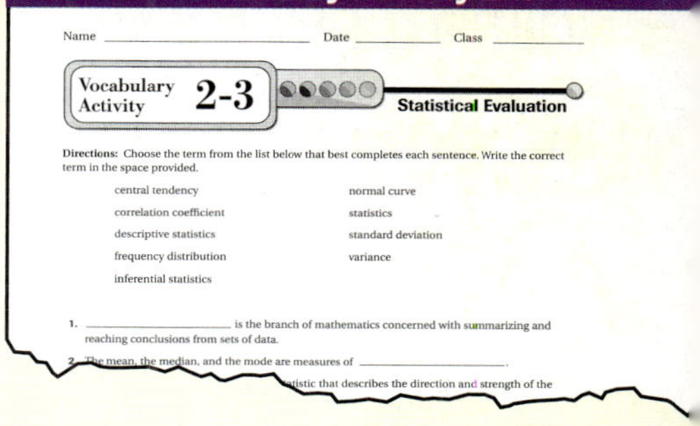
Name ______ Date ______ Class ______

Vocabulary Activity 2-3 Statistical Evaluation

Directions: Choose the term from the list below that best completes each sentence. Write the correct term in the space provided.

central tendency	normal curve
correlation coefficient	statistics
descriptive statistics	standard deviation
frequency distribution	variance
inferential statistics	

1. ______ is the branch of mathematics concerned with summarizing and reaching conclusions from sets of data.
2. The mean, the median, and the mode are measures of ______.

Figure 2.9

Visual Instruction Remind students that the standard deviation tells you immediately whether a set of scores varies widely from the mean or is clustered around it.

Caption Answer the average distance of every score from the mean

PSYCHOLOGY LAB EXPERIMENT

Analyzing Results Students will compute statistics and use them to analyze information. Supply students with actual test scores from past classes. Replace all names identifying the students with a letter system (A–Z). Have students compute the mean, median, and mode. Next have students determine the range and the standard deviation to measure variability. Have students use the statistics to prepare charts and graphs that clearly express their findings. (Tip: A more challenging activity would be to have the students gather data about a subject that interests them.) **L2** **BLOCK SCHEDULING**

CHAPTER 2
Section 3, pages 47–54

L3 Distinguishing Differential and Inferential Statistics Assign students to review Figures 2.6, 2.7, and 2.10. **Ask: If you wanted a full description of the data compiled by Kate, which figure would you use?** *(Figure 2.6)* Suppose you wanted to draw a conclusion about the relationship between height and TV viewing time before the quiz. **Ask: Which figure would provide the quickest and easiest-to-read answer?** *(Figure 2.10)* **What can you conclude from Figure 2.10?** *(There was no relationship between height and viewing time.)*

CULTURAL CONNECTIONS

Milgram's experiment was conducted in Germany and Japan. Both cultures rate high in measures of respect for and compliance with authority. The German and Japanese participants showed an even higher rate of obedience—more than 80 percent for both groups.

More About...

Transforming Scores

Suppose you take the ACT and score a 26. Then you take the SAT and get a 620. The college you want to go to will accept either test score. Which score should you send? (Which score is better?) To make a comparison between two scores that have different distributions, different means, and different variabilities, you must transform the scores.

ACT

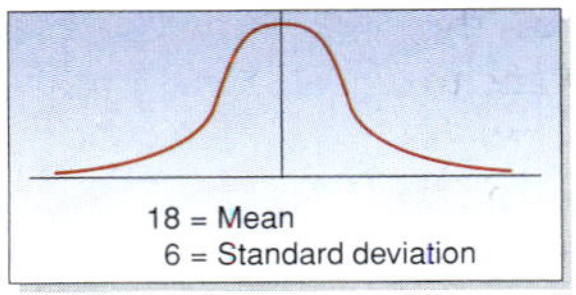

SAT

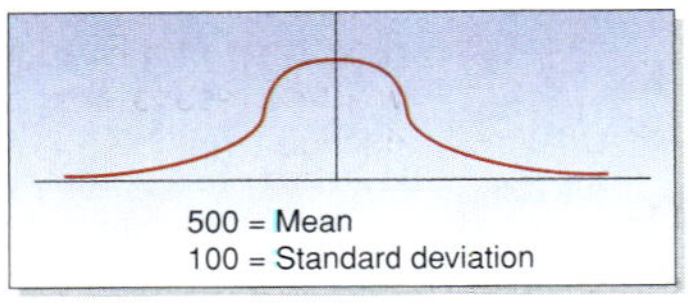

If you look at the distributions of the ACT and SAT, you will find that the ACT has a mean of 18 and a standard deviation of 6. So you take your score on the ACT (26) and subtract the mean from it (26 − 18) to get 8; 8 is 1.33 standard deviations above the mean (8/6). Do the same for your SAT score [620 − 500 = 120; so 620 is 1.2 standard deviations above the mean (120/100)]. So which score would you submit to the college of your choice? (The correct answer is your ACT score because 1.33 is greater than 1.2.)

What we just did was to make a standard score. A standard score is a transformed score that provides information about its location in a distribution.

will shift upward also. If we change the highest quiz grade from 10 to 20, the mean changes from 6.4 to 7.1.

Measures of Variability

Distributions differ not only in their average score but also in terms of how spread out, or how variable, the scores are. Figure 2.9 shows two distributions drawn on the same axis. Each is symmetrical, and each has the same mean. However, the distributions differ in terms of their variability. Measures of **variability** provide an index of how spread out the scores of a distribution are.

Two commonly used measures of variability are the range and the standard deviation. To compute the *range*, subtract the lowest score in a data set from the highest score and add 1. The highest quiz score is 10 and the lowest is 0, so the range is 11, representing 11 possible scores 0–10. The range uses only a small amount of information, and it is used only as a crude measure.

The **standard deviation** is a better measure of variability because, like the mean, it uses all the data points in its calculation. It is the most widely used measure of variability. The standard deviation is a measure of distance. It is like (but not exactly like) an average distance of every score to the mean of the scores. This distance is called a *deviation* and is written: $X - \bar{X}$. Scores above the mean will have a positive deviation; scores below the mean will have a negative deviation. The size of the typical deviation depends on how variable, or spread out, the distribution is. If the distribution is very spread out, deviations tend to be large. If the distribution is bunched up, deviations tend to be small. The larger the standard deviation, the more spread out the scores (see Figure 2.9).

Correlation Coefficients

A **correlation coefficient** describes the direction and strength of the relationship between two sets of observations (recall the discussion of correlations in Section 1). The most commonly used measure is the Pearson correlation coefficient (r). A coefficient with a plus (+) sign indicates a *positive correlation*. This means that as one variable *increases,* the second variable also *increases.* For example, the more you jog, the better your cardiovascular system works. A coefficient with a minus (−) sign indicates a *negative correlation;* as one variable *increases,* the second variable *decreases.* For example, the more hours a person spends watching TV, the fewer hours are available for studying. Correlations can take any value between +1 and −1 including 0. An r near +1 or −1 indicates a strong relationship (either positive or negative), while an r near 0 indicates a weak relationship.

variability: a measure of difference, or spread of data

standard deviation: a measure of variability that describes an average distance of every score from the mean

INTERDISCIPLINARY CONNECTIONS ACTIVITY

Sports Ask the coaches of your various high school teams to supply the statistics for a complete season for at least 10 (anonymous) athletes. Supply different sets of data to pairs of students. Direct them to analyze the data using all of the valid measures introduced in this section. (Note: Do not tell students exactly which statistics to compute; allow them to discover which can and cannot be computed from the information.) Have them use the statistics to create charts or graphs that explain the information. Direct students to write their conclusions in a one-page report. **L2**

Generally, an r from ±0.60 to ±1.0 indicates a strong correlation, from ±0.30 to ±0.60 a moderate correlation, and from 0 to ±0.30 a weak correlation. A correlation of ±1.0 indicates a perfect relationship between two variables and is very rare.

To get an idea of how her data look, Kate draws some scatterplots. A *scatterplot* is a graph of participants' scores on the two variables, and it demonstrates the direction of the relationship between them. Figure 2.10 illustrates one of Kate's correlations. Note that each point represents one person's score on two variables.

correlation coefficient: describes the direction and strength of the relationship between two sets of variables

INFERENTIAL STATISTICS

The purpose of descriptive statistics is to describe the characteristics of a sample. Psychologists, however, are not only interested in the information they collect from their participants, but they also want to make generalizations about the population from which the participants come. To make such generalizations, they need the tools of inferential statistics. Using **inferential statistics,** researchers can determine whether the data they collect support their hypotheses, or whether their results are merely due to chance outcomes.

inferential statistics: numerical methods used to determine whether research data support a hypothesis or whether results were due to chance

Probability and Chance

If you toss a coin in the air, what is the probability that it will land with heads facing up? Since there are only two possible outcomes, the probability of heads is 0.50. If you toss a coin 100 times, you would expect 50 heads and 50 tails. If the results were 55 heads and 45 tails, would you think the coin is fair? What if it were 100 heads and zero tails?

When a researcher completes an experiment, he or she is left with lots of data to analyze. The researcher must determine whether the findings from the experiment support the hypothesis (for example, the coin is fair) or whether the results are due to chance. To do this, the researcher must perform a variety of statistical tests, called measures of statistical significance. When researchers conclude that their findings are statistically significant, they are stating, at a high level of confidence, that their results are not due to chance.

Figure 2.10 A Scatterplot

When there is little or no relationship between two variables, the points in the scatterplot do not seem to fall into any pattern. ***What conclusions can you draw from this scatterplot?***

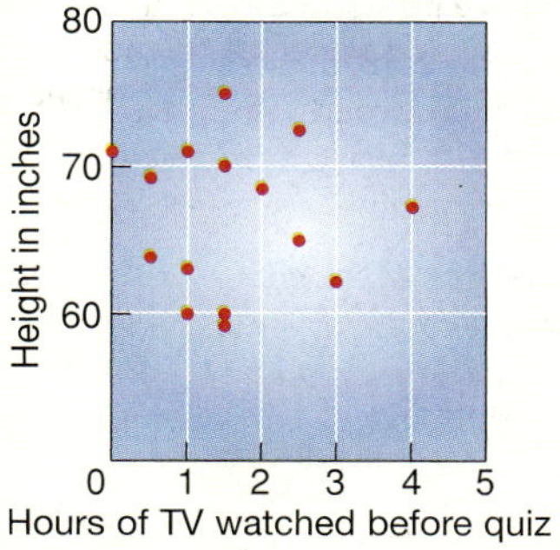

Statistical Significance

For many traits in a large population, the frequency distribution follows a characteristic pattern, called the normal curve (see Figure 2.7). For example, if you measured the heights of 500 students chosen at random from your high school, you would find very few extremely tall people and very few extremely short people. The majority of students

Figure 2.10

Visual Instruction The first step in determining the direction and strength of a correlation between two sets of data is creating a scatterplot.

Caption Answer There is no correlation between height and TV viewing time before the test.

3 ASSESS

Assign Section 3 Assessment as homework or as an in-class activity.

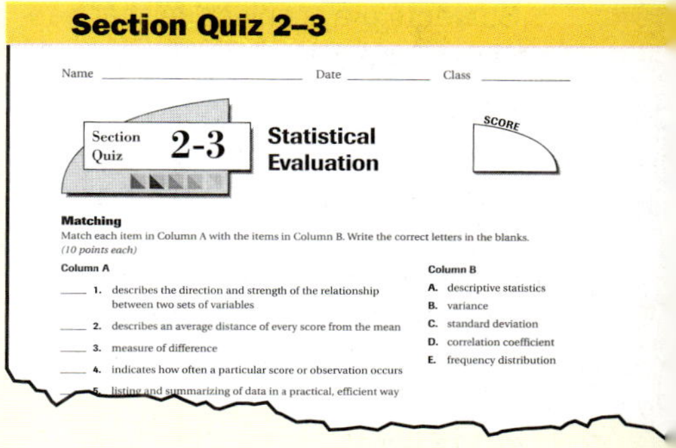
Section Quiz 2–3

Name ______ Date ______ Class ______

Section Quiz 2-3 **Statistical Evaluation**

SCORE

Matching
Match each item in Column A with the items in Column B. Write the correct letters in the blanks.
(10 points each)

Column A
____ 1. describes the direction and strength of the relationship between two sets of variables
____ 2. describes an average distance of every score from the mean
____ 3. measure of difference
____ 4. indicates how often a particular score or observation occurs
____ 5. listing and summarizing of data in a practical, efficient way

Column B
A. descriptive statistics
B. variance
C. standard deviation
D. correlation coefficient
E. frequency distribution

Reteach

As a class, create a list of questions that students should ask themselves each time they read a statistic used to support a point of view.

EXTENDING THE CONTENT

Artificial Intelligence In recent years, research psychologists have attempted to solve problems through the use of artificial intelligence (AI), the science of having computers perform tasks that would ordinarily require human cognitive abilities. Artificial intelligence psychologists work to develop computer programs that mimic human thought processes, including learning from mistakes. Goals include teaching computers to make decisions, recognize visual patterns, and even offer creative insights. AI is already being employed in areas ranging from voice recognition software to medical diagnoses to diagnosing car problems.

CHAPTER 2

Section 3, pages 47–54

Quick Lab

Purpose Students will examine how statistics can be used to make predictions.

Process Skills Organizing information, drawing conclusions, demonstrating reasoned judgment

Teaching Strategies

- State the hypothesis to be researched.
- Discuss the statistical tools that will be useful to the would-be psychic.

Analysis

1. 13, 15, 17, 19, 31, 35, 37, and 39. Answers will vary.
2. Students' answers will vary. Students may conjecture that people will begin at number 13 and not proceed much further.

Enrich

Have students write an essay entitled "Numbers Don't Lie, Do They?"

4 CLOSE

Revisit the lists created during the Two-Minute Lesson Launcher. Ask students how the research methods used in psychology compare with the methods used in other fields. **Ask: In what ways are they similar? In what ways are they different?**

Quick Lab

Do some people really have psychic powers?

A well-known psychic sometimes begins his performance by saying the following: "Think of a number between 1 and 50. Both digits must be odd numbers, but they must not be the same. For example, it could be 15 but it could not be 11. Please choose a number and I will tell you what number you are thinking of."

Procedure

1. Develop a hypothesis that explains how the psychic is performing this feat. (Hint: The psychic uses statistics, not magic.)
2. Try out the psychic's act on several of your classmates and record their responses.

Analysis

1. Based on the psychic's directions, decide which numbers can be used and which numbers will most likely be used.
2. How do your observations support or contradict your hypothesis?

See the Skills Handbook, page 622, for an explanation of designing an experiment.

would fall somewhere in the middle. Suppose Kate wants to know if her classmates watch more TV than the "average American." Since daily TV viewing is probably normally distributed, she can compare her results to the normal distribution if she knows the population's mean number of TV viewing hours.

When psychologists evaluate the results of their studies, they ask: Could the results be due to chance? What researchers really want to know is whether the results are so extreme, or so far from the mean of the distribution, that they are more likely due to their independent variable, not to chance.

The problem is that this question cannot be answered with a yes or no. This is why researchers use some guidelines to evaluate probabilities. Many researchers say that if the probability that their results were due to chance is less than 5 percent (0.05), then they are confident that the results are not due to chance. Some researchers want to be even more certain, and so they use 1 percent (0.01) as their level of confidence. When the probability of a result is 0.05 or 0.01 (or whatever level the researcher sets), we say that the result is *statistically significant.* It is important to remember that probability tells us how likely it is that an event or outcome is due to chance, but not whether the event is *actually* due to chance.

When does a statistically significant result *not* represent an important finding? Many statistical tests are affected by sample size. A small difference between groups may be magnified by a large sample and may result in a statistically significant finding. The difference, however, may be so small that it is not a meaningful difference.

SECTION 3 Assessment

1. **Review the Vocabulary** What is the difference between a frequency distribution and a histogram? Between a normal curve and a scatterplot?
2. **Visualize the Main Idea** Using an organizer similar to the one at right, list and describe the measures of central tendency.

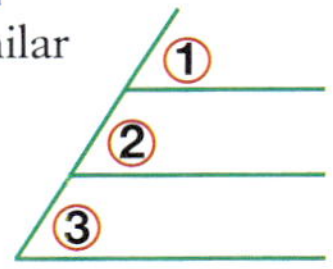

3. **Recall Information** What is the importance of the normal curve?
4. **Think Critically** What does correlation tell you about the relationship between two variables?
5. **Application Activity** Conduct a class or family survey on an issue, then display your findings in a frequency distribution, frequency polygon, or scatterplot. Apply evaluation rules. What conclusions can you reach from your results?

SECTION 3 Assessment Answers

1. A frequency distribution is a table listing the frequency with which a particular score occurs. A histogram is the graphical representation in bar format of the frequency distribution. A normal curve is a bell-shaped frequency distribution. A scatterplot is a graph consisting of coordinates whose values represent two variables under study.
2. mean: an arithmetic average; median: the middle score; mode: the most frequent score
3. The normal curve is a graph that has the ability to predict what percentage of the cases falls within each segment of the curve.
4. A correlation describes the strength and direction of the relationship between two variables.
5. Students' answers will vary. Evaluate the results based on a clear understanding of the statistics.

CHAPTER 2 Summary and Vocabulary

Psychologists learn about what they do not know by carefully and systematically collecting information. They then must describe and analyze their research findings through various statistical measurements and interpret their results.

Section 1 What Is Research?

Main Idea: Psychologists must first decide how to approach the research issue. Then psychologists conduct the research in one of a variety of ways to test a hypothesis, solve a problem, or confirm previous findings.

- Researchers begin their research by asking a specific question about a limited topic; determining the validity of a claim, hypothesis, or theory; and choosing an unbiased sample.
- Psychologists use several methods of research to accomplish their research goals. These methods include naturalistic observation, case studies, surveys, and experiments.
- Psychologists follow a set of ethical principles that govern their research.

Section 2 Problems and Solutions in Research

Main Idea: The investigation of psychological issues is a painstaking process. Psychologists must recognize and resolve errors while doing research.

- In a self-fulfilling prophecy, an experimenter has expectations about a participant's behavior and then acts in some way, usually unknowingly, to influence that behavior.
- In single-blind experiments, the participants do not know which participants have received the treatment.
- Researchers can avoid a self-fulfilling prophecy by using the double-blind technique in their experiments.
- When researchers evaluate the effects of drugs, they must always take into account a possible placebo effect.

Section 3 Statistical Evaluation

Main Idea: Psychologists must collect and evaluate evidence to test their hypotheses.

- Researchers use descriptive statistics to organize data in a practical, efficient way.
- Descriptive statistics include distributions of data, measures of central tendency, measures of variability, and correlation coefficients.
- Researchers use inferential statistics to make generalizations about the population from which the participants come.
- Researchers perform a variety of statistical tests, called measures of statistical significance, to determine whether findings from their experiment support the hypothesis or whether the results are due to chance.

Chapter Vocabulary

sample (p. 36)
naturalistic observation (p. 37)
case study (p. 37)
survey (p. 38)
longitudinal study (p. 38)
cross-sectional study (p. 38)
correlation (p. 39)
hypothesis (p. 40)
variable (p. 40)
experimental group (p. 40)
control group (p. 40)
self-fulfilling prophecy (p. 42)
single-blind experiment (p. 43)
double-blind experiment (p. 43)
placebo effect (p. 45)
statistics (p. 48)
descriptive statistics (p. 48)
frequency distribution (p. 49)
normal curve (p. 51)
central tendency (p. 51)
variability (p. 52)
standard deviation (p. 52)
correlation coefficient (p. 52)
inferential statistics (p. 53)

2 Summary and Vocabulary

Using the Chapter 2 Summary and Vocabulary

Use the Chapter 2 Summary and Vocabulary to preview, review, condense, or reteach the chapter.

Preview/Review

Use the Chapter Vocabulary list to help students review and study.

Activity Have students write the vocabulary terms and their definitions, one to a card, on 3" x 5" index cards. Create three heading cards: *Research Methods, Statistical Measurements,* and *Other.* Ask students to classify each of the terms by placing them in a stack beneath the correct heading.

Vocabulary PuzzleMaker CD-ROM reinforces the vocabulary terms used in Chapter 2.

Condense

Have students read the Chapter 2 Summary.

Chapter 2 Guided Reading Activities

Reteach

Reteaching Activity 2

AUTHENTIC ASSESSMENT ACTIVITY

Composing a Letter As students have learned, statistics can be used to enlighten and to mislead. Have students compose letters to their state or federal representatives asking them to protect consumers from the misleading use of statistics. The letters should cite examples of the deception and include specific recommendations to protect the consumer. Remind students to use standard grammar, sentence structure, and punctuation.

Refer to the ***Authentic Assessment*** booklet for additional activities and information about evaluating student performance.

PSYCHOLOGY Online

Have students visit the Web site at glencoe.com to review Chapter 2 and take the **Self-Check Quiz.**

GLENCOE TECHNOLOGY

PRESENTATION Plus!

For a review of Chapter 2 content, see MindJogger Checkpoint on **Presentation Plus!**

Reviewing Vocabulary

1. h
2. e
3. a
4. i
5. d
6. g
7. j
8. b
9. f
10. c

Recalling Facts

1. A biased sample can be avoided by using a random sample so that each individual has an equal chance of being represented. A researcher can also avoid a biased sample by using a stratified sample. In a stratified sample, subgroups in the population are proportionately represented.
2. Naturalistic observations are useful for observing visible behaviors in a natural setting where the human or animal is unaware of, or not bothered by, the experimenter.
3. Participants or experimenters may have expectations about the research or experiment that can influence or bias the results.
4. Graphic organizers should include the following: distributions of data (frequency distributions); measures of central tendency (mean, median, and mode), measures of variability, and correlation coefficients.
5. Researchers use inferential statistics to show that the data verifies or refutes the hypothesis. Descriptive statistics describe the characteristics of a sample; they list and summarize the data. Inferential statistics are numerical methods that help the researcher make generalizations about the sample.

CHAPTER 2 Assessment

PSYCHOLOGY Online

Self-Check Quiz

Visit the *Understanding Psychology* Web site at glencoe.com and click on **Chapter 2—Self-Check Quizzes** to prepare for the Chapter Test.

Reviewing Vocabulary

Choose the letter of the correct term or concept below to complete the sentence.

a. variability
b. sample
c. longitudinal study
d. control group
e. single-blind experiment
f. double-blind experiment
g. placebo effect
h. statistics
i. normal
j. frequency distribution

1. __________ is a branch of mathematics that helps researchers organize and evaluate data.
2. In a(n) __________, only the participants of the experiment do not know whether they are in the experimental group or the control group.
3. Measures of __________ indicate how spread out the scores of a distribution are.
4. A bell-shaped curve is a(n) __________ curve.
5. In an experiment, the __________ includes the participants who are not exposed to experimental variables.
6. The __________ is a change in a patient's physical state that results from the patient's perceptions of the treatment.
7. Researchers use a(n) __________ to arrange data so that they know how often a particular observation occurs.
8. Researchers generally select a(n) ________, which is a relatively small group of the total population that is being studied.
9. In a(n) __________, neither the participants nor the experimenter knows whether the participants are in the experimental group or the control group.
10. In a(n) __________, a researcher studies a group of people over a period of years.

Recalling Facts

1. What are two ways that a researcher can avoid a biased sample?
2. When do researchers use naturalistic observation?
3. How does a self-fulfilling prophecy present a problem for researchers?
4. Using a graphic organizer similar to the one below, identify and explain the kinds of descriptive statistics.

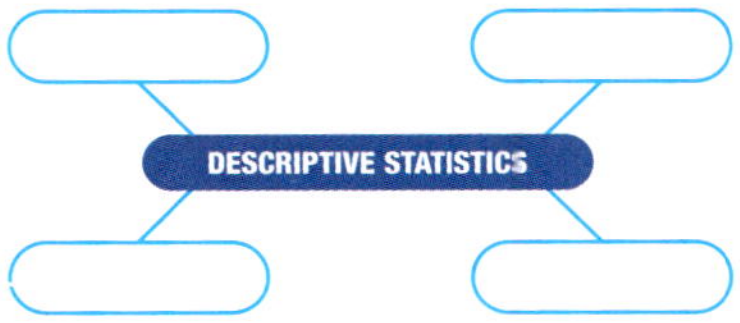

5. Why do researchers use inferential statistics? How do inferential statistics describe data differently than descriptive statistics?

Critical Thinking

1. **Synthesizing Information** How could you attempt to disprove the following hypothesis? You can raise blood pressure by making a participant anxious.
2. **Analyzing Statements** Explain the following statement: "Correlation does not imply causation."
3. **Making Inferences** What correlation would you expect between students' grades and class attendance?
4. **Applying Concepts** How are statistics used within your classroom? Within your school?
5. **Analyzing Information** Various kinds of statistics are used in sports. Provide examples of statistics from various sports.

Critical Thinking

1. Students' answers will vary. The most obvious research techniques would be experiments. You cannot use naturalistic observations because a rise in blood pressure is not an observable behavior.
2. Correlations simply indicate that two sets of data are related; they make no claim about how they are related or whether the relationship has any significance.
3. You would expect a positive correlation; as attendance increases, the grades increase.
4. Students' answers will vary. Obvious examples include grades and sports statistics.
5. Students' answers will vary. Examples include batting average, free throw percentage, and quarterback ratings.

Psychology Projects

1. Answers will vary. Students should demonstrate that they can plan and conduct research. Encourage students to use statistics to help them answer their research questions.
2. Answers will vary. The graphs are likely to be similar in having more occurrences clustered in the middle of the range. They are likely to be dissimilar in the absolute values of the heights.

CHAPTER 2

Assessment

Psychology Projects

1. **What Is Research?** Choose a traffic intersection near your home or school that has a stop sign. Design a study to assess whether or not motorists stop at the posted sign. Consider the research questions you need to answer, such as how to determine whether motorists comply with the sign, the number of vehicles, and the time of day. Conduct your study and record your observations.
2. **Statistical Evaluation** Collect heights from 20 women and 20 men. Create a frequency distribution for each group, and divide them into 5-inch intervals before counting. Graph your data for men and women separately as frequency polygons on the same axis. Compute means, medians, modes, ranges, and standard deviations for women and men separately. How are the two distributions alike and different?

Technology Activity

Does smoking cause lung cancer? Some scientists cite animal studies as proving that it does. Representatives of the tobacco industry state that animal studies cannot be generalized to humans. Search the Internet to find arguments and data from each side of this debate. Use that information to support both viewpoints in an essay.

Psychology Journal

For each of the examples of statistics you listed in your journal (at the beginning of the chapter), indicate whether you feel that enough information was provided to evaluate the validity of any reported claims. What other information should have been provided? How might additional information change the reported conclusions?

Building Skills

Interpreting Graphs Review the graphs, then answer the questions that follow.

1. What does each of the graphs illustrate?
2. Which of the age groups shown is least likely to use the Internet?
3. How has the number of adult Internet users changed since 1996?
4. Do most Internet users today use a dial-up connection or a broadband connection? How do you think this will change in the future?
5. Do you think a higher percentage of teens use the Internet than the age groups shown? Explain.

Practice and **assess** key social studies skills with **Glencoe Skillbuilder Interactive Workbook CD-ROM, Level 2.**

See the Skills Handbook, page 628, for an explanation of interpreting graphs.

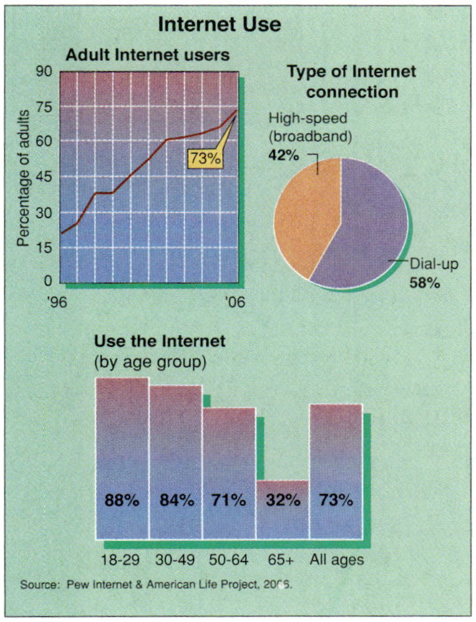

Building Skills

1. the percentage of adult Internet users between 1996 and 2006; the percentage of Internet users who use dial-up versus broadband connections; the percentage of Internet users by age group
2. ages 65 and older
3. The number of adult Internet users has increased steadily over time.
4. dial-up; more broadband users
5. Students probably will say that teenagers are more comfortable with and exposed to new technology than older people.

GLENCOE TECHNOLOGY

CD-ROM

Glencoe Skillbuilder Interactive Workbook, Level 2

This interactive CD-ROM is designed to reinforce student mastery of essential social studies skills.

Chapter Bonus Test Question

This question may be used for extra credit on the Chapter Assessment.

Answer the following question:

I am the numerical method used to determine whether research data support a hypothesis or whether results are due to chance.

Answer: inferential statistics

Technology Activity

Students' essays should use statistics to support both sides of the argument. Encourage students to share the addresses of the Web sites they found. If possible, ask students to use their findings to conduct a class debate on the question of whether smoking causes lung cancer.

Psychology Journal

Students' answers should express their understanding of the use of statistics in everyday circumstances. Remind students that people can sometimes use statistics to mislead.

Unit 2 Planning Guide

National High School Psychology Standards

The national high school psychology standards identify what students in an introductory high school psychology course should learn. **The material covered in Unit 2 reflects content from two of the five content domains: *Cognitive* and *Developmental*.** To see a chapter-by-chapter correlation to the national standards, refer to the Teacher pages.

Content Domains for National High School Psychology Standards

Use this diagram to review the standards areas that are covered in Unit 2. Standards areas covered in this unit are highlighted in red in the diagram.

Methods
- Introduction and Research Methods

Sociocultural
- Individual Differences
- Personality and Assessment
- Psychological Disorders
- Treatment of Psychological Disorders
- Social and Cultural Dimensions of Behavior

Developmental
- **Lifespan Development**

Cognitive
- Learning
- Memory
- **Thinking and Language**
- States of Consciousness

Biopsychological
- Biological Bases of Behavior
- Sensation and Perception
- Motivation and Emotion
- Stress, Coping, and Health

BIBLIOGRAPHY

Readings for the Student

Cushman, K. (2005). *What We Can't Tell You: Teenagers Talk to the Adults in Their Lives.* Providence, RI: Next Generation Press.

Elkind, D. (2001). *The Hurried Child: Growing Up Too Fast Too Soon.* Cambridge, MA: Perseus Press.

Singer, D.G., & Revenson, T.A. (1998). *A Piaget Primer.* Madison, CT: International Universities Press.

Readings for the Teacher

Pence, K.L., & Justice, L.M. (2006). *Language Development: From Theory to Practice.* Saddle Brook, NJ: Prentice-Hall.

Pressley, M., & McCormick, C.B. (2006). *Child and Adolescent Development for Educators.* New York: Guilford Press.

Trawick-Smith, J. (2005). *Early Childhood Development: A Multicultural Perspective.* Saddle Brook, NJ: Prentice-Hall.

Multimedia Resources

Videocassette. *Childhood—The Enchanted Years.* (2 parts of 26 minutes each) Films Incorporated, Education. This video shows the development of children from birth to four years, including reaching, perception, walking, and talking.

Videocassette. *Cognitive Development.* (22 minutes) McGraw-Hill Training. Piaget's theory of cognitive development is explained through animation.

Unit 2 Resource Manager

Note: The following materials may be used when teaching Unit 2. Chapter level support materials can be found on the chapter resource pages.

Use the following tools to easily assess student learning in a variety of ways:

- Authentic Assessment with Rubrics
- Section Quizzes, Chapter Tests, and Unit Tests
- glencoe.com
- SAT/SAT II Test Practice
- *ExamView® Assessment Suite* CD-ROM

APPLICATIONS AND HANDS-ON

Psychology Lab Activity 2

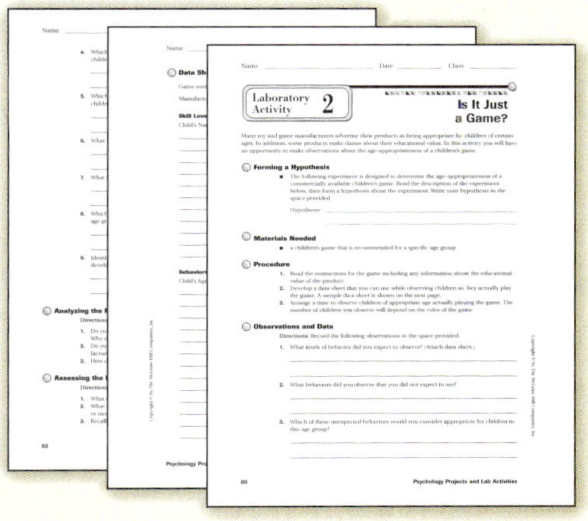

ASSESSMENT

Unit 2 Test, Form A

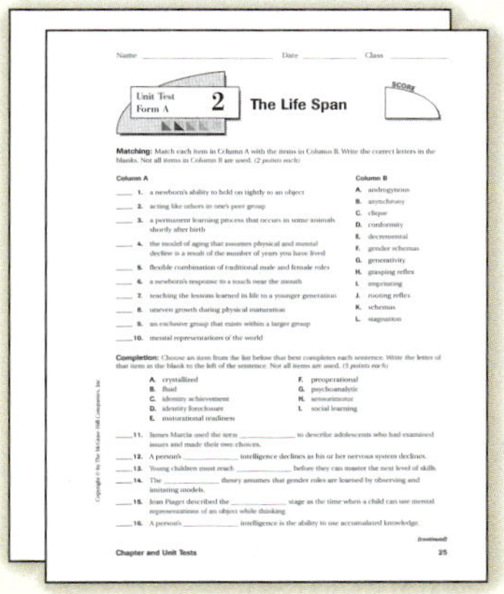

Unit 2 Test, Form B

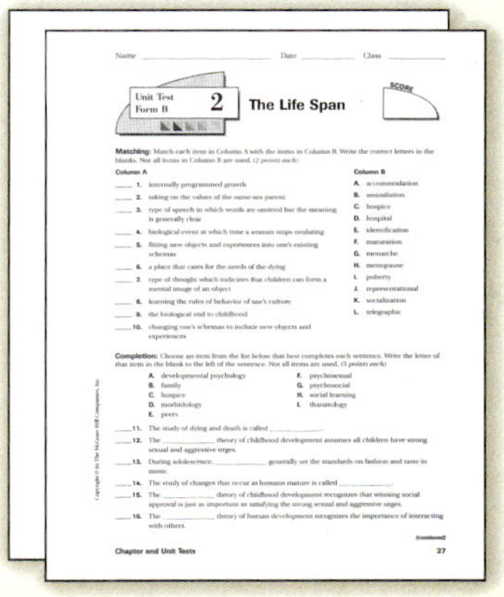

Use Glencoe's ***Presentation Plus!*** multimedia teacher tool to easily present dynamic lessons that visually excite your students. Using Microsoft PowerPoint® you can customize the presentations to create your own personalized lessons.

Introducing
UNIT 2

Unit Overview

This unit explores human development from birth through old age. **Chapter 3** explains the physical, cognitive, social, and emotional development of infants and children. **Chapter 4** describes the physical and sexual developments that occur during adolescence. Personal and social development are also explored. **Chapter 5** examines the psychological issues that arise in adulthood. The issues involved with dying and death are addressed.

Unit Objectives

After studying this unit, students will be able to:

1. Describe the physical and perceptual development of newborns and children.
2. Describe the role of family and peers during adolescence.
3. Identify changes that occur in health and life situations during old age.

UNIT 2

The Life Span

Contents

As we go through the stages of our lives, we develop a sense of ourselves and the world. ▶

EXTRA CREDIT PROJECT

Observing Children at Play Obtain permission from parents or a preschool for students to observe children at play. Tell students to observe two or more children at play from the following age groups: toddlers (15 to 24 months), 2-year-olds, 4-year-olds, and 6-year-olds. For each age group observed, students should answer the following questions: **How well do the children interact? How well do they use language to communicate with other children? What other forms of communication do they use? What is their level of cognitive development? Social development? Moral development?** Students should compare their results for each age group with the other age groups and create a chart to show their findings.

Why It's Important

Each of us is born into a world in which we must adapt. From childhood to adolescence to adulthood to old age, we change physically, emotionally, cognitively, socially, and morally. Developmental psychologists study the changes through which human behaviors pass as we grow older. This unit seeks to answer the question: How did we become who we are?

Psychology Fair Suggestion Box

Encourage students to get involved with a psychology fair. Here are some project suggestions for **Unit 2—The Life Span:**

- Research the development of language in infants and young children.
- Research one of the primary theories of childhood development.
- Explore the role of adolescents in various cultures.
- Examine the gender differences in physical and psychological development.
- Describe the physical and psychological changes that occur during middle age or old age.

Refer to ***Psychology Projects and Lab Activities*** in the TCR for help with organizing a psychology fair.

PSYCHOLOGY Online

Visit glencoe.com, the *Understanding Psychology* Web site, for Chapter Overviews, Student Web Activities, Interactive Puzzles, and Self-Check Quizzes for every chapter of the text.

PORTFOLIO PROJECT

Role Playing Ask students to work in pairs or in small groups to role-play a demonstration of a specific principle or theory of child development. For example, a pair of students might role-play the process involved in a child's developing awareness of object permanence, or a group of students might demonstrate the kind of learning that occurs when small children invent a game. The role playing should clearly present a picture of the specific developmental process involved. The groups should share their role playing with the rest of the class. **BLOCK SCHEDULING**

Chapter 3 Resource Guide

SECTION RESOURCES		
Daily Objectives	**Reproducible Resources**	**Multimedia Resources**
Section 1 **Physical, Perceptual, and Language Development** Understand that as infants grow physically, they also develop cognitive skills, perceptions, and language.	Guided Reading Activity 3–1 Vocabulary Activity 3–1 Section Quiz 3–1	Daily Focus Transparency 3–1 *ExamView® Assessment Suite* CD-ROM Presentation Plus! Software
Section 2 **Cognitive and Emotional Development** Discuss how as the thought processes of children develop, they begin to think, communicate and relate with others, and solve problems.	Guided Reading Activity 3–2 Vocabulary Activity 3–2 Section Quiz 3–2	Daily Focus Transparency 3–2 Vocabulary PuzzleMaker CD-ROM *ExamView® Assessment Suite* CD-ROM Presentation Plus! Software
Section 3 **Parenting Styles and Social Development** Describe the social decisions children face as they grow and progress through the stages of life.	Guided Reading Activity 3–3 Vocabulary Activity 3–3 Section Quiz 3–3	Daily Focus Transparency 3–3 Vocabulary PuzzleMaker CD-ROM *ExamView® Assessment Suite* CD-ROM Presentation Plus! Software

Blackline Master   CD-ROM   Transparency

Block Schedule

Activities that are particularly suited for use within the block-scheduling framework are identified throughout this chapter by the following designation: **BLOCK SCHEDULING**

KEY TO ABILITY LEVELS

Teaching strategies have been coded for varying learning styles and abilities.

- **L1** **BASIC** activities for all students
- **L2** **AVERAGE** activities for average to above-average students
- **L3** **CHALLENGING** activities for above-average students
- **ELL** **ENGLISH LANGUAGE LEARNER** activities

Chapter 3 Resource Guide

Timesaving Tools

TeacherWorks™ All-In-One Planner and Resource Center

- **Interactive Teacher Edition** Access your Teacher Wraparound Edition and your classroom resources with a few easy clicks.
- **Interactive Lesson Planner** Planning has never been easier! Organize your week, month, semester, or year with all the lesson helps you need to make teaching creative, timely, and relevant.

Use Glencoe's **Presentation Plus!** multimedia teacher tool to easily present dynamic lessons that visually excite your students. Using Microsoft PowerPoint® you can customize the presentations to create your own personalized lessons.

Activity

From the Classrooms of...

Patricia H. Rousseau and Dana Winterholler Conway
Pine Crest Preparatory School
Ft. Lauderdale, FL

Receptive Language Development

Objective: To demonstrate the importance of receptive or open-minded language development

Rationale: Comprehension of specific content is imperative for understanding. The activity demonstrates that the whole context is altered when words are excluded or changed. This activity can also be used to show cultural diversity.

Directions: Read the following passage and translate the underlined words or phrases. Then have a class discussion to compare students' translations of the passage.

Once upon a time there was a yani player named James. He was acking down the hall and found a bini. James knew he had to use the bini ketit. First, James asked his bubu, "What should I tikle for? Should I tikle for selchul, sabor, a soung, or you? She hesitated and then said, "Sabor, of course." Next, James asked his buddy Bill, "What should I tikle for?" Bill chose selchul. Finally, James thought to ask a wise arch and sought out his psychology ista to help him decide. James found her and asked her the same question. She replied, "Soung!" James thought and made a decision and wished for selchul! Is James happy with his tikle? Would this have been your tikle?

Psychology Online

Use our Web site for additional resources. All essential content is covered in the Student Edition.

You and your students can visit glencoe.com, the Web site companion to *Understanding Psychology*. This innovative integration of electronic and print media offers your students a wealth of opportunities. The student text directs students to the Web site for the following options:

- Chapter Overviews
- Student Web Activities
- Self-Check Quizzes

Answers are provided for you in the **Web Activity Lesson Plan.** Additional Web resources and Interactive Puzzles are also available.

Chapter 3 Resource Guide

Note: The following materials may be used when teaching Chapter 3. Section level support materials are shown at point of use in the margins of the Teacher Wraparound Edition.

TEACHING TRANSPARENCIES

Chapter 3
Concept Transparencies

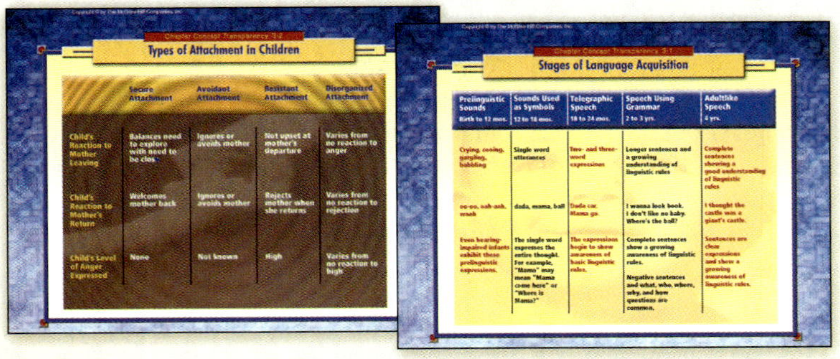

MULTIMEDIA

- Vocabulary PuzzleMaker CD-ROM
- *ExamView® Assessment Suite* CD-ROM
- TeacherWorks™ CD-ROM
- Glencoe Skillbuilder Interactive Workbook, Level 2
- Presentation Plus! Software

REVIEW AND REINFORCEMENT

Reteaching Activity 3

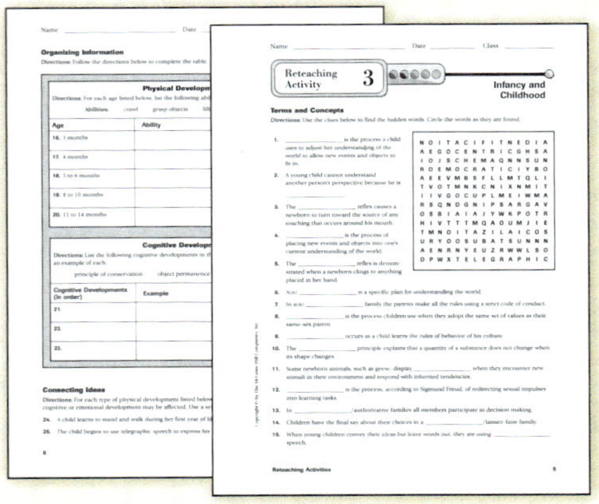

Graphic Organizer Activity 3

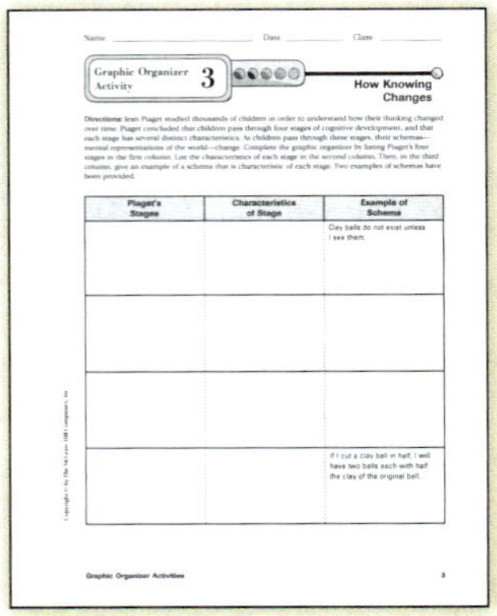

APPLICATION AND HANDS-ON

Psychology Project 3

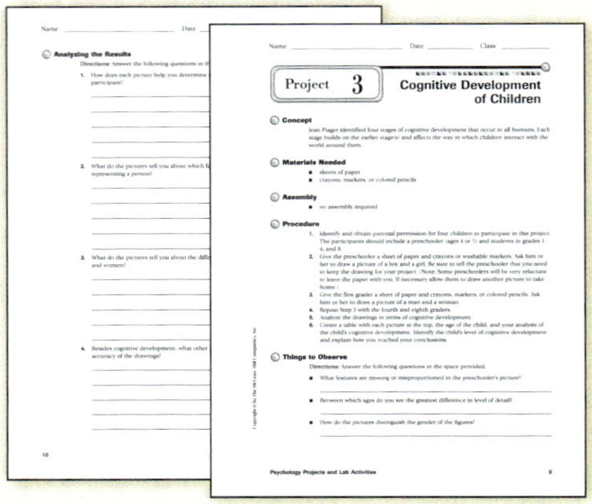

Application Activity 3

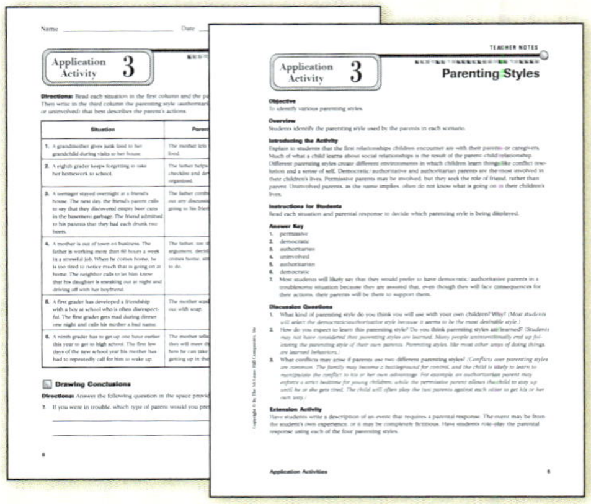

Chapter 3 Resource Guide

Glencoe's Assessment Advantage

ASSESSMENT

Chapter 3 Test, Form A

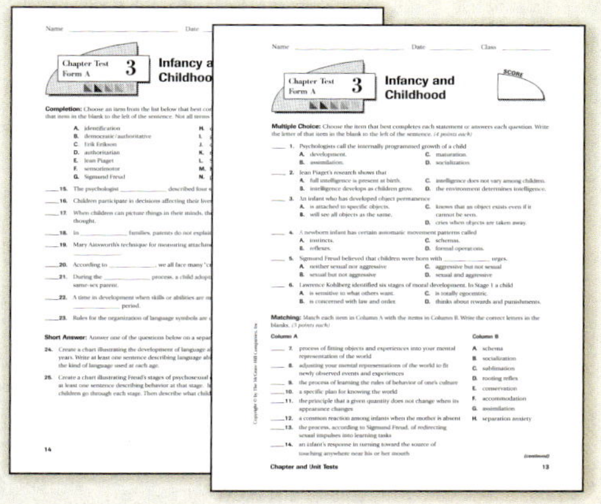

Chapter 3 Test, Form B

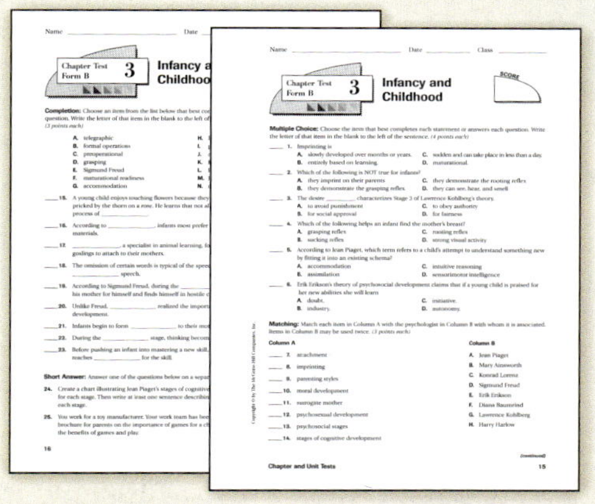

Authentic Assessment Activity 3

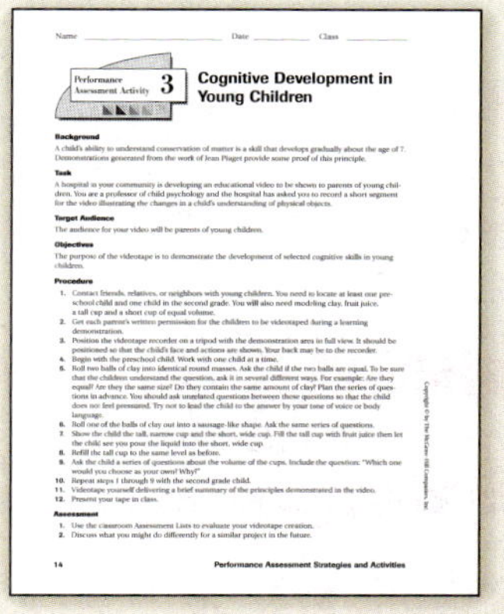

EXTENSION AND ENRICHMENT

Enrichment Activity 3

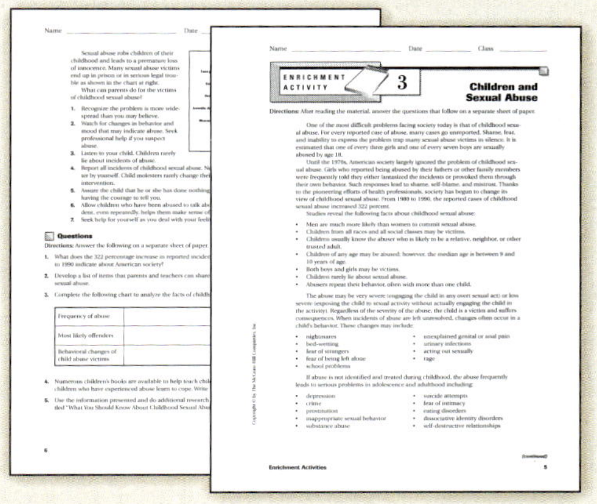

Critical Thinking Skills Activity 3

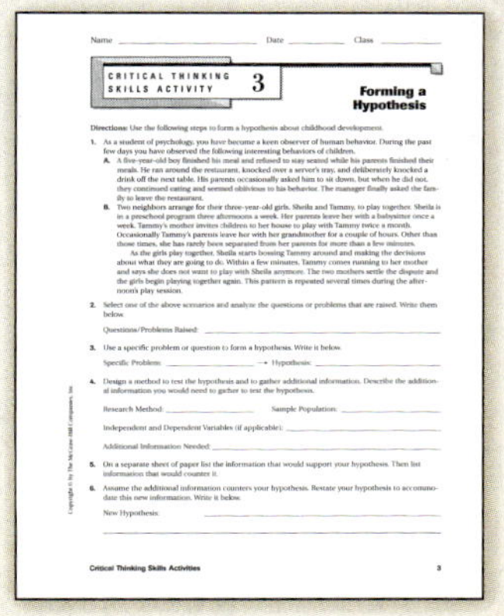

Psychology Reading 3

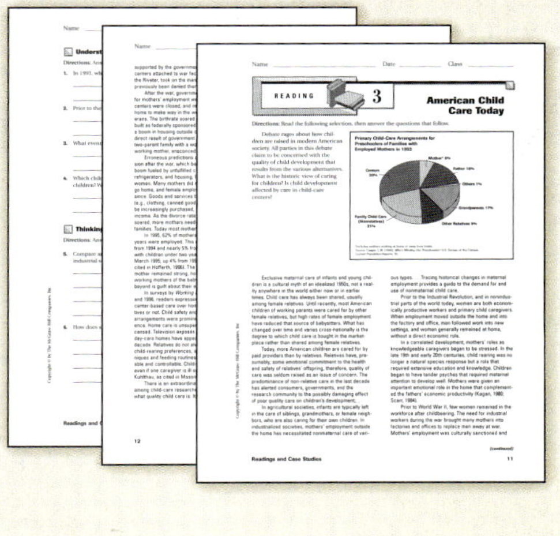

Psychology Case Study 3

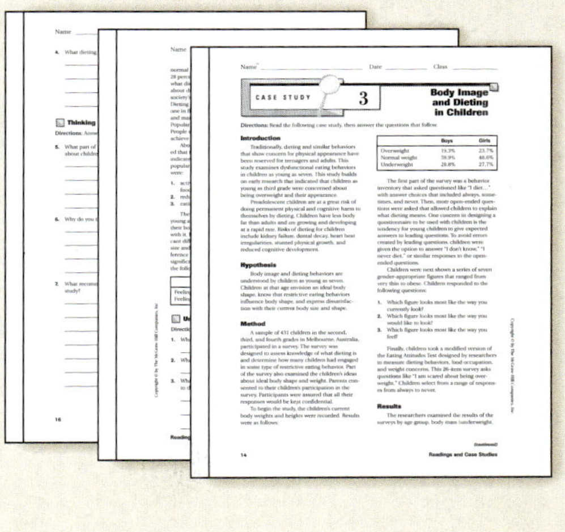

PSYCHOLOGY Online

Visit glencoe.com for a Chapter Overview for **Chapter 3—Infancy and Childhood.**

GLENCOE TECHNOLOGY

PRESENTATION Plus! For a preview of Chapter 3 content, see MindJogger Checkpoint on **Presentation Plus!**

PSYCHOLOGY JOURNAL

Suggest that students observe several 2-year-old children in a variety of settings as they interact with parents, peers, and strangers.

This journal activity provides the basis for the Psychology Journal activity exercise in the Chapter Assessment. ■

CHAPTER 3 Infancy and Childhood

PSYCHOLOGY JOURNAL

Observe a group of 2-year-old children. Record in your journal the two-word sentences you hear. ■

PSYCHOLOGY Online

Chapter Overview
Visit the *Understanding Psychology* Web site at glencoe.com and click on **Chapter 3—Chapter Overviews** to preview the chapter.

60

TWO-MINUTE LESSON LAUNCHER

Humans learn faster and learn more in their early years of life than at any other time. Explore any preconceptions that students may have about infancy and childhood. **Ask: How much of the world do you believe babies might comprehend? What are the earliest memories that you recall? How do children use play to understand social situations? How do parenting styles affect development?** Tell students that children develop physically, socially, emotionally, cognitively, and morally. Throughout the chapter, refer back to these five types of development. During class discussions, include a time to categorize various types of development into one or more of these five categories.

SECTION 1

Physical, Perceptual, and Language Development

Reader's Guide

Main Idea

Infants are born equipped to experience the world. As infants grow physically, they also develop cognitive skills, perceptions, and language.

Vocabulary

- developmental psychology
- grasping reflex
- rooting reflex
- maturation
- telegraphic speech

Objectives

- Describe the physical and perceptual development of newborns and children.
- Discuss the development of language.

EXPLORING PSYCHOLOGY

What Do Babies See?

Propped against my knees in the delivery room, my son, minutes old, peered at me with wide, unblinking eyes. He looked so intent. So serious. So thoughtful. What could earth's freshest arrival possibly be thinking about? Maybe he was wondering who all the giants looming over him might be, especially the pair with the goofy grins who kept counting his fingers and toes over and over. Maybe his head still ached from the incredibly narrow trip out of my womb. Maybe he was asking himself, "Hey, who turned on the lights?" It's hard to know how the world appears to a new baby. But in recent years, researchers have deduced plenty about what infants sense, remember, prefer, and need. And such knowledge is more than academic for new parents.

—from *Parent* magazine, Paula Spencer, 1999

Do you remember anything from when you were a baby? Less than 15 years ago, you were probably only two feet tall and just taking your first step. Just a year or two after that, you spent your days intently playing. Most of those events from your life are long forgotten, but you changed faster and learned more in early childhood than you ever will again.

In this chapter you will learn about **developmental psychology**—the specialized study of how an individual's physical, social, emotional, moral, and intellectual development occur in sequential interrelated stages throughout the life cycle.

developmental psychology: the study of changes that occur as an individual matures

SECTION RESOURCES

Reproducible Masters
- Guided Reading Activity 3–1
- Vocabulary Activity 3–1
- Section Quiz 3–1

Transparencies
- Daily Focus Transparency 3–1

Multimedia
- *ExamView® Assessment Suite* CD-ROM
- Presentation Plus! Software

1 FOCUS

Section Objectives

1. Describe the physical and perceptual development of newborns and children.
2. Discuss the development of language.

BELLRINGER
Motivational Activity

Project Daily Focus Transparency 3–1 and have students answer the questions.

Available as blackline master

Daily Focus Transparency 3–1

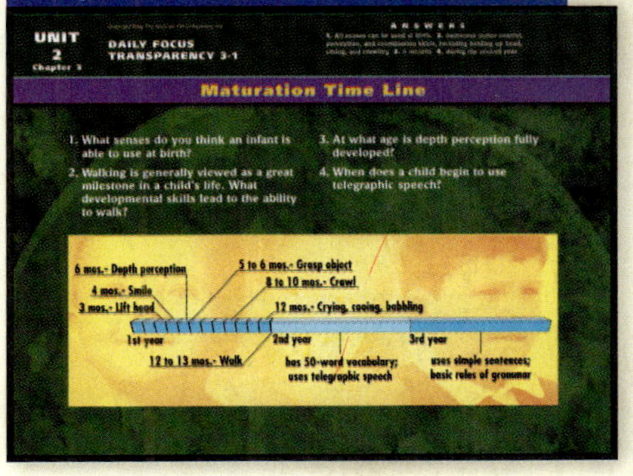

Reader's Guide

Use the Reader's Guide to introduce concepts and vocabulary.

Exploring Psychology
Ask students to read the **Exploring Psychology** feature and then discuss the following question: **What objects do you think tend to fascinate babies?**

Vocabulary Precheck
Have students read the Glossary definition of each term. Ask them to provide an example that explains each term.

CHAPTER 3
Section 1, pages 61–68

2 TEACH

L1 Brainstorming Point out that learning begins from the moment of birth, as newborns direct their gazes toward bright patterns and faces. Have the class brainstorm a list of sensations that a typical newborn might experience within the first few days of life. **BLOCK SCHEDULING**

Guided Reading Activity 3–1

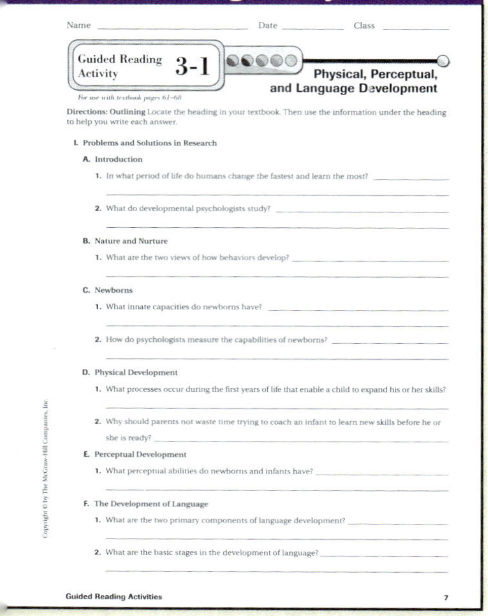
Name ________ Date ________ Class ________

Guided Reading Activity 3-1

Physical, Perceptual, and Language Development

For use with textbook pages 61–68

Directions: Outlining Locate the heading in your textbook. Then use the information under the heading to help you write each answer.

I. Problems and Solutions in Research

A. Introduction

1. In what period of life do humans change the fastest and learn the most? ________
2. What do developmental psychologists study? ________

B. Nature and Nurture

1. What are the two views of how behaviors develop? ________

C. Newborns

1. What innate capacities do newborns have? ________
2. How do psychologists measure the capabilities of newborns? ________

D. Physical Development

1. What processes occur during the first years of life that enable a child to expand his or her skills? ________
2. Why should parents not waste time trying to coach an infant to learn new skills before he or she is ready? ________

E. Perceptual Development

1. What perceptual abilities do newborns and infants have? ________

F. The Development of Language

1. What are the two primary components of language development? ________
2. What are the basic stages in the development of language? ________

Guided Reading Activities 7

Reading Check Answer The argument focuses on how much of human development is dependent on our genetic makeup and how much is dependent on our environment and the developmental opportunities we experience.

NATURE AND NURTURE

Reading Check What is the argument of nature versus nurture?

Developmental psychologists study the following main issues: (1) continuity versus stages of development, (2) stability versus change, and (3) nature versus nurture. On the question of nature versus nurture, psychologists ask: How much of development is the result of inheritance (heredity), and how much is the result of what we have learned? Some psychologists believe that most of our behaviors are the result of genetics or inheritance. Others believe that most of our behaviors are the result of experience and learning. Separating biological and environmental causes of behavior is very complicated. Usually behavior develops as a result of the interaction of both heredity and environment.

grasping reflex: an infant's clinging response to a touch on the palm of his or her hand

rooting reflex: an infant's response in turning toward the source of touching that occurs anywhere around his or her mouth

NEWBORNS

Development begins long before an infant is born. Expectant mothers can feel strong movement and kicking—even hiccuping—inside them during the later stages of pregnancy. It is common for a fetus (an unborn child) to suck its thumb, even though it has never suckled at its mother's breast or had a bottle.

More About...

Reflexes

The *rooting* and *sucking* reflexes, present in all human infants, gradually decline in strength. The *grasping* reflex disappears during the first six months in those infants where it is present at birth. The Moro, or *startle,* reflex is quite unusual. An infant lying on its back when startled by a loud noise out of sight above his or her head will show a very complex response. The arms will spread out at right angles to the body and grasp upwards, and the legs will spread outward.

Now consider this situation. What would happen if someone ran a thumbnail right up the center bottom of your foot? Your toes would curl, and your foot would withdraw. Before her first birthday, an infant will do exactly the opposite—the toes flare outward, and the foot presses against the stimulus. This is called the *Babinski* reflex. Pediatricians use the shift in the Babinski from infantlike to adultlike form around the first birthday as a sign of normal neurological development.

Capacities

Newborns have the ability at birth to see, hear, smell, and respond to the environment. This allows them to adapt to the new world around them. Psychologists have found that birth puts staggering new demands on a baby's capacity to adapt and survive. He goes from an environment in which he is totally protected from the world to one in which he is assaulted by lights, sounds, touches, and extremes of temperature. The newborn is capable of certain inherited, automatic, coordinated movement patterns, called reflexes, that can be triggered by the right stimulus (see Figure 3.1). Many, but not all, infants are born with many such reflexes. The **grasping reflex,** for example, is a response to a touch on the palm of the hand. Infants can grasp an object, such as a finger, so strongly that they can be lifted into the air.

Also vital is the **rooting reflex.** If an alert newborn is touched anywhere around the mouth, he will move his head and mouth toward the source of the touch. In this way the touch of his mother's breast on his cheek guides the infant's mouth toward her nipple. The sucking that follows contact with the nipple is one of the infant's most complex reflexes. The infant is able to suck, breathe air, and swallow milk twice a second without getting confused.

COOPERATIVE LEARNING ACTIVITY

Creating a Time Line Organize the class into small groups to create time lines showing the typical development of children through the first year of life. Ask the groups to research the reflex abilities of newborns, their perceptual development, their physical development, and their language development. The time line should show the progressive abilities of children through their first year. Most abilities occur at different times in different infants. The time line should show the typical range that doctors and psychologists have identified as normal development. Ask each group to self-monitor their completed time line for accuracy and completeness.

Figure 3.1 **Newborn Reflexes**

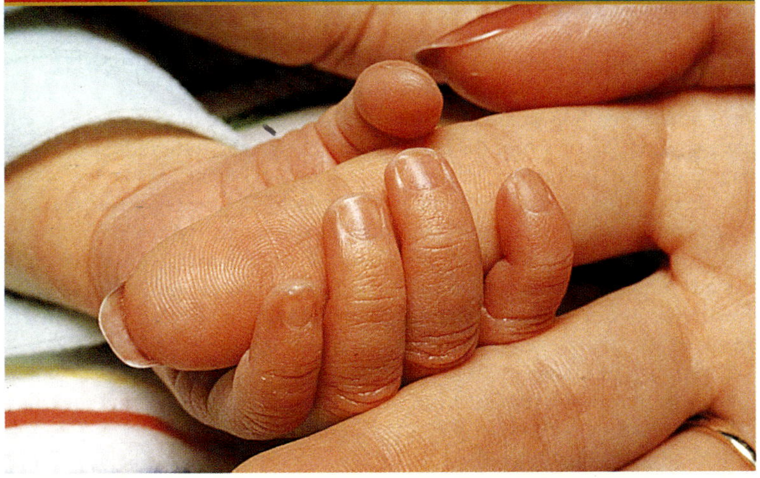

Reflexes are important in determining the health of an infant. In the grasping reflex, newborns close their fingers tightly around objects placed in their hands. ***What seems to be the purpose of these reflexes?***

How do we measure the capabilities of newborn infants who cannot speak or understand the questions of curious psychologists? One reasonable way to answer these questions is to take advantage of the things infants *can* do. What they can do is suck, turn their heads, look at things, cry, smile, and show signs of surprise or fright. The vigor of an infant's sucking, the patterns of eye movements, and expressions of pleasure and displeasure are all closely tied to how the infant is being stimulated. By measuring these behaviors while stimulating the infant in different ways, we can infer how the infant perceives the world.

PHYSICAL DEVELOPMENT

Infants on average weigh 7.3 pounds at birth. Some infants can weigh as much as 20 or 25 pounds by the end of the first year. At birth, 95 percent of infants are between 5.5 and 10 pounds and are 18 to 22 inches in length. In the space of two years, the grasping, rooting, searching infant will develop into a child who can walk, talk, and feed herself or himself. This transformation is the result of both maturation and learning.

Did You Know?

SIDS Infants have been known to quietly and mysteriously die in their sleep. Physicians call this "sudden infant death syndrome," or SIDS. SIDS takes more lives in the first year than any other cause of infant death. We do not know why SIDS happens. One theory suggests that it results from a failure in the infant's central nervous system in learning how to turn a reflex into a voluntary action. That is, the infant fails to learn to keep passages open for breathing. There is no known way to predict or prevent SIDS. Recent studies report a decreased incidence of SIDS when the infant is positioned on the sides or back to sleep instead of on the stomach.

Figure 3.1

Caption Answer The purpose of these reflexes is basic survival. The grasping reflex results from a safety instinct.

FYI

Heredity places limits on development despite all the efforts that a person may make to improve the environment in which a child is nurtured. For example, no diet or program of education will significantly increase the general level of intelligence with which a normal child is born. Similarly, heredity limits the height a child will attain and puts a cap on physical performance. No child alive today, for example, will ever be capable of high-jumping 50 feet. Nurturing allows heredity potentials to emerge fully.

PSYCHOLOGY JOURNAL

Direct students to write about an early childhood experience. Tell them to write it as though it happened just yesterday. ■

MEETING SPECIAL NEEDS

Learning Style: Auditory/Musical Have students select a children's story that is told in rhyme and practice reading it aloud. Then students should arrange with a parent to read the book to a 2- or 3-year-old. Students should read the book aloud, letting the child look at the pictures. After they have finished, have students ask the child questions about the story to see what he or she remembered. **Ask:** **What did the child like about the story? Do you think the rhymes contributed to interest in the story? Do you think the rhymes helped the child remember details of the story?** L2 ELL BLOCK SCHEDULING

L1 Analyzing Data Ask students to speculate about the psychological drawbacks of pushing a small child to master new skills too soon. *(Answers will vary. For example, the child might experience frustration and give up. This may actually delay his or her mastery of the skill.)* You may want to introduce the concept of learned helplessness, which will be discussed in Chapter 9.

Figure 3.2

Visual Instruction Have students examine the chart and describe the various progressions, such as initial body control, sitting erect, standing, crawling, and walking. Ask the students to conjecture how the child's learning in one progression is utilized in attempting the next.

Caption Answer You expect infants to begin standing at 8 to 9 months and to start walking at 11 to 15 months.

Looking @ the Issues

Drug Use and Child Development
A child's mental and emotional development can be seriously affected by the mother's lifestyle, even before the child is born. Children born to women who drink large amounts of alcohol during pregnancy may suffer from *fetal alcohol syndrome.* These children may suffer mental retardation, poor motor development, and unusual facial features. The use of crack cocaine or other psychoactive drugs can also cause a range of developmental problems. A major problem for babies born to drug users is that they may be addicted to the drug at the time they are born. **Ask: What should society do to protect children from such developmental and emotional consequences?**

Maturation

To some extent an infant is like a plant that shoots up and unfolds according to a built-in plan. She will begin to lift her head at about 3 months, smile at 4 months, and grasp objects at 5 to 6 months. Crawling appears at 8 to 10 months. By this time the infant may be able to pull herself into a standing position, although she will fall if she lets go. She will begin to walk 3 or 4 months later, tentatively at first, but gradually acquiring a sense of balance.

maturation: the internally programmed growth of a child

Psychologists call internally programmed growth **maturation.** Maturation is as important as learning or experience, especially in the first years. (*Learning* is a relatively permanent change in behavior that occurs as a result of experience.) Unless a child is persistently underfed, severely restricted in her movements, or deprived of human contact and things to look at, she will develop more or less according to this schedule. Purely as a matter of efficiency, it is worth a parent's time to wait until infants reach *maturational readiness* before pushing them into mastering new skills. No amount of coaching will push a child to walk or speak before she is physiologically ready.

The process of maturation becomes obvious when you think about walking. An infant lacks the physical control walking requires. By the end

Figure 3.2 Physical and Motor Development

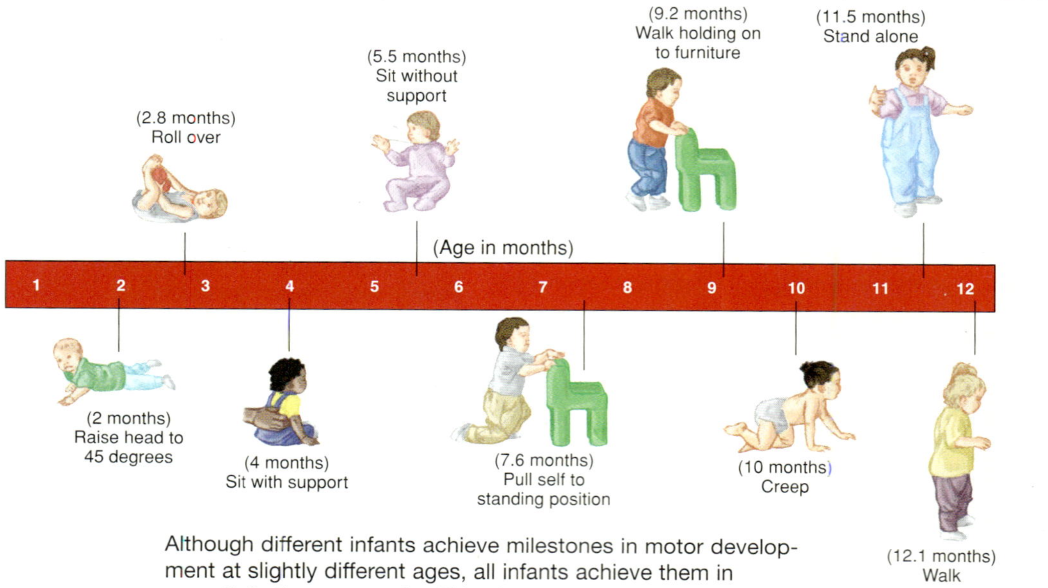

Although different infants achieve milestones in motor development at slightly different ages, all infants achieve them in essentially the same order. This chart shows the average ages when milestones are usually achieved. ***At what age would you expect an infant to start standing? Start walking?***

CRITICAL THINKING ACTIVITY

Demonstrating Reasoned Judgment Ask students to go to the public library and browse the shelves to see how many different books are available on the psychological aspects of child rearing. Tell the students to select one book and read a chapter with a critical eye. **Ask: How much of the book's advice is based on psychological and other scientific research? How much seems to be based on the author's own philosophical biases?** Ask students to write a review of the book. Encourage students to submit their book reviews to the family or parenting column of the local newspaper. **L3** **BLOCK SCHEDULING**

of the first year, however, the nerves connected to the child's muscles have grown. He or she is ready to walk.

By recording the ages at which thousands of infants first began to sit upright, to crawl, and to try a few steps, psychologists have been able to develop an approximate timetable for maturation (see Figure 3.2). This schedule helps doctors and other professionals spot problems and abnormalities. If a child has not begun to talk by the age of 2½, a doctor will recommend tests to determine if something is wrong.

One of the facts to emerge from this effort, however, is that the maturational plan inside each child is unique. On the average, infants start walking at 12 to 13 months. Some, though, are ready at 9 months, and others delay walking until 18 months. Each infant also has his or her own temperament. Some infants are extremely active from birth, and some are quiet. Some are cuddly and some stiff. Some cry a great deal while others hardly ever whimper. Although no two infants are exactly alike and no two mature according to the same timetable, most infants progress through the same sequential steps. Identifying similarities and differences in growth patterns is the challenge for developmental psychologists.

Figure 3.3 **The Visual Preferences of Infants**

Three- or four-month-old infants show a strong preference for faces and patterns, suggesting that infants are born with and develop visual preferences. ***How do researchers measure the capabilities of infants?***

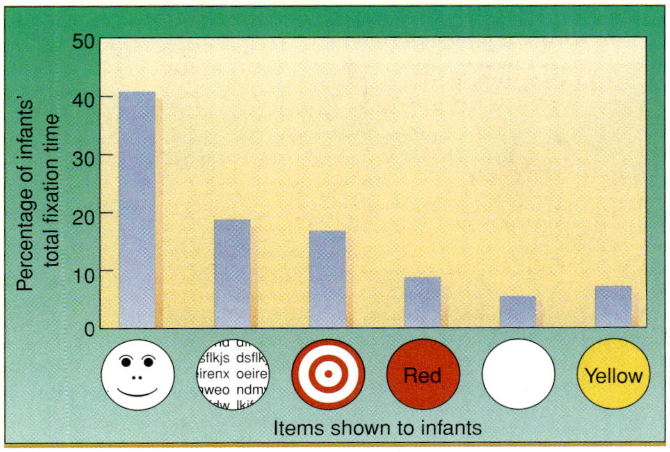

PERCEPTUAL DEVELOPMENT

Besides grasping and sucking, newborns look at their bodies and at their surroundings. Newborns have mature perception skills. Robert Fantz (1961) showed infants different faces and discovered that they prefer looking at human faces and patterned materials the most (see Figure 3.3). They also benefit greatly from being touched by their parents (Eliot, 2000).

Two experimenters (Gibson & Walk, 1960) devised the visual cliff to determine whether infants had depth perception. The visual cliff is a platform, part of which has a checkerboard pattern. The other part consists of a sheet of glass with the checkerboard pattern a few feet below it. It creates the illusion of a clifflike dropoff (see Figure 3.4). Whereas very young infants seemed unafraid, older infants (6 months and older) who were experienced at crawling refused to cross over the cliff. The older infants had explored the world, apparently finding that dropoffs are dangerous. Also, researchers found that there were changes in the heart rates of very young infants even if they would crawl farther, implying that newborns are born with some perceptual capabilities.

Figure 3.3

Visual Instruction Discuss research or theories about what newborns and infants really see. Ask students to research and determine if newborns and infants see colors, shapes, and faces.

Caption Answer They conduct experiments, such as the visual cliff experiment, with infants to identify abilities. The experiments involve infants making choices such as what to watch, what object to grasp, or what sound to turn one's head toward.

Vocabulary Activity 3-1

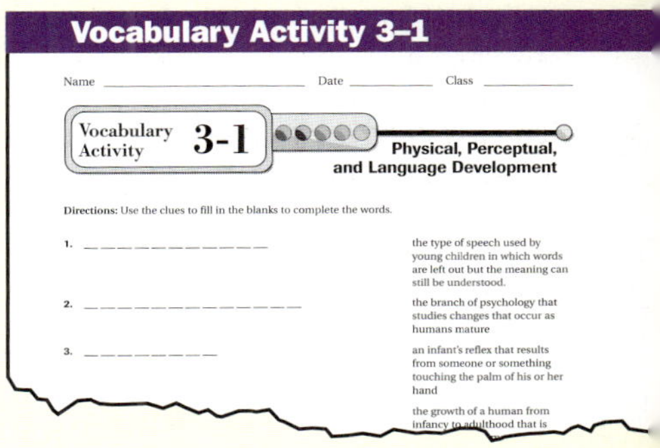
Name ______ Date ______ Class ______

Vocabulary Activity 3-1

Physical, Perceptual, and Language Development

Directions: Use the clues to fill in the blanks to complete the words.

1. ___________ the type of speech used by young children in which words are left out but the meaning can still be understood.

2. ___________ the branch of psychology that studies changes that occur as humans mature

3. ___________ an infant's reflex that results from someone or something touching the palm of his or her hand

the growth of a human from infancy to adulthood that is

TEACHER Tip

Remind students that development occurs at different rates for different children. While parents should be observant of the development process, they should not interpret these developmental charts too rigidly. Caution students not to raise alarms with friends or family members if a child does not progress according to schedule.

PSYCHOLOGY LAB EXPERIMENT

Observing Language Development Encourage students to obtain parental permission to tape-record and observe a 3-year-old child for 30 minutes. Students may use preplanned questions to prompt the child's conversation. Have them listen to the different words the child uses and write down as many as possible. Students should repeat this process with a 4-year-old. After completing the experiment, ask students to write a one-page report that answers the following questions: **How many different words did the 3-year-old use? How many different words did the 4-year-old use? What other differences did you notice about the words and language skills of the two children? L2**

CHAPTER 3
Section 1, pages 61–68

Figure 3.4

Caption Answer Changes in heart rate would indicate if the child experienced fear or worry, even if the child's physical response did not indicate any anxiety.

Cultural Connections

In a 1992 study comparing the ethnic differences in mothers' responsiveness to their children, researchers found that cultural differences exist. The study compared mothers with second- or third-born children in middle-class America and in rural Kenya. Though both groups responded equally when their babies were distressed, their form of response varied. Kenyan mothers made physical contact with their crying infants 58 percent of the time and talked to them about 8 percent of the time. The American mothers touched or held their infants about 35 percent of the time when they cried and talked to them about 25 percent of the time. *Source:* Richman, A.L., Miller, P.M., & LeVine, R.A. (1992). Cultural and educational variations in maternal responsiveness. *Developmental Psychology,* 28, 614–21.

Figure 3.4 The Visual Cliff

Infants display the ability to perceive three-dimensional space. Infants' heart rates increased as they approached the perceived dropoff of the visual cliff. ***Why do you think researchers measured the infants' heart rates during this experiment?***

THE DEVELOPMENT OF LANGUAGE

Language and thought are closely intertwined. Both abilities involve using symbols. We are able to think and talk about objects that are not present and about ideas that are not necessarily true. A child begins to think, to represent things to himself, before he is able to speak. The acquisition of language, however, propels the child into further intellectual development (Piaget, 1926). We have been able to learn a good deal about the acquisition of language from animals.

Can Animals Use Language?

Psychologists believe that chimpanzees must develop at least as far as 2-year-old humans because, like 2-year-olds, they will look for a toy or a bit of food that has disappeared. They can represent the existence of that toy or bit of food in their minds. Can they be taught to "talk" about it? Allen and Beatrice Gardner raised a baby chimp named Washoe in their home and, since chimps are very good with their hands, taught her to use the American Sign Language for the deaf. At 3½ years of age, Washoe knew at least 87 signs for words like *food, dog,* and *toothbrush.* By age 5, Washoe used more than 160 signs.

Several chimpanzees have been taught to converse in other ways. Chimpanzees have been trained on special typewriters connected to computers. One chimpanzee, Panzee, used a special computer keyboard with symbols to communicate with humans (see Figure 3.5).

The chimps use only aspects of the human language. Chimps use words as symbols but do not apply grammatical rules. The ability to arrange symbols in new combinations to produce new meanings is especially well developed in the human brain. The rules for such organization of symbols are called *grammar.* Grammatical rules are what make the sentence "the rhinoceros roared at the boy" mean the same thing as "the boy was roared at by the rhinoceros." It may be in our ability to use such grammatical rules that we surpass the simpler language of the chimpanzee.

How Children Acquire Language

Some psychologists argue that language is reinforced behavior, while others claim it is inborn. Some people claim there is a critical period, or a window of opportunity, for learning a language. For example, songbirds

INTERDISCIPLINARY CONNECTIONS ACTIVITY

Science When zoologists work with endangered species in recovery programs, they often must guard against letting the newborn animals become imprinted with the images of their human caregivers. Instruct students to investigate a current effort to raise endangered species in captivity and then release them into the wild. **Ask: What do zoologists do to ensure that the wild birds or animals do not become accustomed to living among humans? Why do they need to take these precautions?** Have students present an oral report on their findings. **L2**

learn their song more easily during an early sensitive period of life. Humans may also have a sensitive period early in life in which acquisition of language is easier.

The example of Washoe shows that there are several steps in learning language. First, one must learn to make the signs—whether by hand or by mouth. Also, one must learn the meaning of the signs. Finally, one must learn grammar. Each child takes these steps at his or her own rate (see Figure 3.6). During the first year of life, the average child makes many sounds. Crying lessens, and the child starts making mostly cooing sounds, which develop into a babble that includes every sound humans can make—Chinese vowels, African clicks, German rolled *r*'s, and English *o*'s.

Late in the first year, the strings of babbles begin to sound more like the language that the child hears—French babies babble French sounds, Korean babies babble Korean sounds. Children imitate the speech of their parents and their older brothers and sisters, and are greeted with approval whenever they say something that sounds like a word. In this way children learn to speak what becomes their native language even though they could just as easily learn any other.

The leap to using sounds as symbols occurs sometime early in the second year. The first attempts at saying words are primitive, and sounds are incomplete. "Ball" usually sounds like "ba," and "cookie" may even sound like "doo-da." The first real words usually refer to things the infant can see or touch. Often they are labels or commands ("dog!" "cookie!").

By the time children are 2 years old, they have a vocabulary of 500 to 1,500 words. Near the end of the second year, they begin to express themselves more clearly by joining words into two-word phrases. From about 18 months to 5 years of age, children are adding approximately 5 to 10 words a day to their vocabulary (Carey, 1978).

At age 2, though, a child's grammar is still unlike that of an adult. Children use **telegraphic speech**—for example, "Where my apple?" "Daddy fall down." They leave out words or use the wrong verb tense but still get the message across. As psychologists have discovered, 2-year-olds already understand certain rules (Brown, 1973). They keep their words in the same order adults do. Indeed, at one point they overdo this, applying grammatical rules too consistently. For example, the usual rule for forming the past tense of English verbs is to add *-ed.* Many verbs, however, are irregular, such as *go/went.* At first children imitate the correct form of the verb: "Daddy went yesterday." Once children discover the rule for forming past tenses, they replace the correct form with sentences like

telegraphic speech: the kind of verbal utterances in which words are left out, but the meaning is usually clear

Reading Check
At what age do children start to use sounds as symbols?

Figure 3.5 How Animals Talk

Panzee, the chimpanzee, used the computer keyboard to type requests and answer questions. ***Which aspects of human language do chimps use?***

CHAPTER 3
Section 1, pages 61–68

Reading Check Answer
Children start to use sounds as symbols during their second year of life (between 12 and 24 months).

Figure 3.5
Caption Answer Chimps use words as symbols but do not acquire grammatical understanding as humans do.

3 ASSESS

Assign Section 1 Assessment as homework or as an in-class activity.

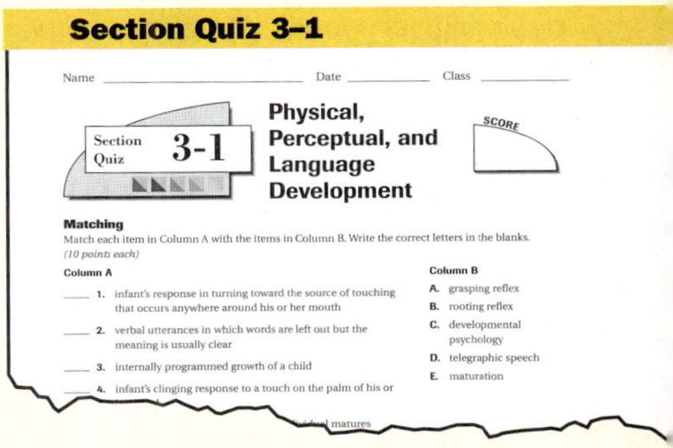
Section Quiz 3-1

Name ______ Date ______ Class ______

Section Quiz 3-1 **Physical, Perceptual, and Language Development**

SCORE

Matching
Match each item in Column A with the items in Column B. Write the correct letters in the blanks.
(10 points each)

Column A
____ **1.** infant's response in turning toward the source of touching that occurs anywhere around his or her mouth
____ **2.** verbal utterances in which words are left out but the meaning is usually clear
____ **3.** internally programmed growth of a child
____ **4.** infant's clinging response to a touch on the palm of his or

Column B
A. grasping reflex
B. rooting reflex
C. developmental psychology
D. telegraphic speech
E. maturation

EXTENDING THE CONTENT

Development of the Senses At birth, a newborn's vision is approximately 20/600. The preferred distance for objects at birth is about 8 inches from the eyes. Acuity, or sharpness, improves throughout the child's first year of life. Bold, contrasting colors hold more interest for newborns because their ability to detect changes in light, shading, and color is immature. The newborn has shape constancy but lacks a mature sense of size constancy. An infant's auditory development is also immature at birth. It develops quickly, however, so that the infant will turn his or her head toward sounds when he or she is a few days old. Infants do not distinguish low tones well but are sensitive to high-pitched tones and human voices.

Figure 3.6

Visual Instruction Tell students that when infants reach the stage of uttering single words, parents often respond by speaking in parentese. This is a way of speaking to young children in a slower and higher-than-normal voice.

Caption Answer New parents should expect to hear their child's first words near the end of the first year of life.

Reteach

Have students make a list of the things that a child accomplishes physically, cognitively, perceptually, and with language development during the first two years of life.

Enrich

Ask students to review nature films depicting very young primates or other mammals clinging to their mothers. **Ask: What other inherited, automatic, coordinated patterns of newborn behavior can you identify?** For example, newborn kangaroos crawl unassisted into their mother's pouch.

4 CLOSE

Ask students to predict whether animals such as chimpanzees can ever be taught to develop rules of grammar, even if the rules are different from human rules.

Figure 3.6 The Flowering of Language

Between the ages of 2 and 5, the typical child learns an average of 10 words a day—nearly 1 word every hour awake! ***When should new parents expect to hear their baby's first word?***

Age	*Language Abilities*	*Example*
1 year	Babbling begins and increases; by year's end, infant masters sounds of own language and usually says his or her first word	baba mama
2 years	Infant will progress to saying dozens of words; begins to speak in paired words; to ask a question, child issues a declaration in a rising tone; to negate something, child uses nouns with a negative word	Allgone ball. More ball. Jenny go? No ball.
3 years	Child acquires more grammatical knowledge; says appropriate sentences; uses simple declaratives; produces correct negative sentences; average size of vocabulary is over 5,000 words	I eating. I'm eating. Don't go.
4 years	Child uses more grammatical rules and future tense; asks questions in adult form; average vocabulary is about 9,000 words	Will Jenny go? I can't go. Why is Jenny crying?
5 years	Child uses more complex clauses; joins two or more ideas in one sentence; has problems with noun/verb agreement	I see what you did.

Source: Adapted from *Developmental Psychology* by Howard Gardner, 1963.

"Daddy *goed* yesterday." *Goed* is a positive error because it indicates the child is applying rules. When the correct form appears, the child has shifted from imitation through *overgeneralization* to rule-governed language. By the age of 4 or 5, children have a vocabulary of several thousand words. Their ability to use words will continue to grow with their ability to think about and understand the world around them.

SECTION 1 Assessment

1. **Review the Vocabulary** Describe two reflexes that infants display.
2. **Visualize the Main Idea** Using a flowchart similar to the one below, list the steps involved in learning language.

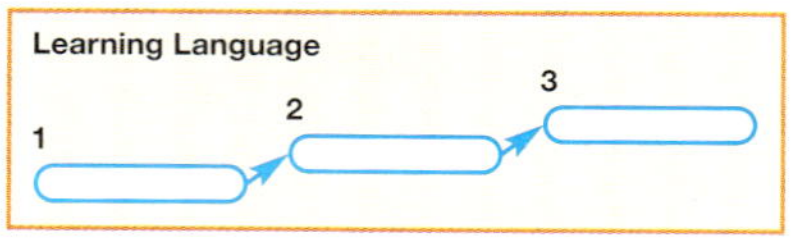

3. **Recall Information** What questions do developmental psychologists raise concerning nature versus nurture?
4. **Think Critically** How does human language acquisition differ from the acquisition of human language by an animal?
5. **Application Activity** Interview a younger sibling, cousin, or friend (5 years old or younger). Use what you have learned about the development of language to describe that child's use of language.

SECTION 1 Assessment Answers

1. grasping reflex: the ability to grab and hold on to objects; rooting reflex: the ability to move toward the source of the touch whenever touched near the mouth
2. babbling, first words, speaks in paired words, says appropriate sentences, asks questions in adult form, joins two or more ideas in a sentence
3. How much of human development results from heredity and how much results from learning?
4. Humans progress beyond animals in that they learn grammatical rules that allow them to express complex thoughts.
5. Students' answers will vary. The student should identify the age of the child and then identify his or her ability to use grammatical rules.

Case Studies

Too Late for Words: The Case of Genie

Period of Study: 1981

Introduction: In 1970 an unusual and unfortunate discovery was made in California. A 13-year-old girl known as "Genie" had spent all 13 years of her life locked in a room isolated from the world. Her parents had kept her harnessed to a potty-chair, which allowed only small movements of her hands and feet. At night Genie was put in a type of straitjacket and forcefully placed in a wire cage. Her parents refused to communicate with her in any way and demanded Genie's siblings avoid any form of communication with her as well.

Genie was discovered by a combined effort of people in social services and the police. When she was discovered, she had no bowel or bladder control, could not chew solid food, had severely damaged posture from years of sitting, and she could not speak or understand language. Nursing Genie back to physical health became the top priority. Then psychologists were to be called upon to evaluate her mental and emotional conditions, as well as to begin teaching her how to communicate.

Hypothesis: The unfortunate case of Genie provided psychologists with some clues in defining whether language can be learned at any point in time or if there is a specific stage of development in which humans need to learn language and communication skills. The function of language has been traced to the left hemisphere of the brain. However, it is undetermined if a window exists in early childhood that allows language to be learned easily.

Method: Placed in a hospital, Genie was described as being "a pitiful, malformed, incontinent, unsocialized, and severely malnourished creature" (Pines, 1981). Genie was given various tests that were designed to measure social maturity and school-level placement. She scored at a level equal to that of a normal 1-year-old child. As time passed, Genie learned to recognize her written name. After 7 months passed, she began to develop spoken use of the phrases "stopit" and "nomore," one-word utterances similar to what toddlers use. One-word use progressed to two-word use; however, Genie's development was slower than that of a toddler with similar language skills.

Results: Genie made limited progress in language development. After 7 years had passed, she had learned as much language skill as a normal child learns in 2 to 3 years. When she was 24 years old, she had the language skills of a 5-year-old. Even though Genie learned much about language, she could not fully understand grammar or the use of pronouns and was unable to control the pitch of her voice. Perhaps Genie's window for learning language had passed; thus her brain could only understand language in a simplified form. However, the physical, emotional, and mental abuse that Genie sustained during her first 13 years of life undoubtedly played key roles in her development as a whole.

Analyzing the Case Study

1. Why, when found, was Genie unable to speak coherently or understand language?
2. Describe Genie's ability to learn to use language properly. How much progress in language development did Genie make? Explain.
3. **Critical Thinking** What conclusions can you draw from this case about a window of opportunity to learn language? Are the results conclusive? Explain.

Answers for Analyzing the Case Study

1. Students' answers may vary. An obvious explanation is that her own utterances were not reinforced; therefore she did not learn to form words or sentences.
2. She could use words as symbols, but she was not able to master the rules of grammar or control the pitch of her voice.
3. The case gives support to the theory that language develops during a "window of opportunity." However, it is not conclusive because the abuse she received may have influenced her ability to learn language.

Going Further

Research With Development of a Second Language

Anecdotal evidence and several studies suggest that children have a much easier time learning a second language than do adults. Some researchers point to this evidence as supporting the critical period theory of language development.

Psychologist Elissa Newport, Ph.D., has compared how children and adults learn a second language. She has found, "that children can only handle small bits of information at a time because they have a more limited perspective than adults."

Children's limited perspective works well for language development, which is composed of many small pieces (phonemes and morphemes). Their perspective allows them to steadily acquire both the sounds of a new language and its grammatical rules. They can truly learn to think in the second language. Adults, however, find this level of comfort with a second language difficult to achieve.

Discussing the Case Study

Ask: **How does Genie's difficulty with acquiring language skills compare and contrast to an adult learning a second language?**

1 FOCUS

Section Objectives

1. Summarize the cognitive-development theory.
2. Discuss how children develop emotionally.

BELLRINGER
Motivational Activity

Project Daily Focus Transparency 3–2 and have students answer the questions.

Available as blackline master

Daily Focus Transparency 3–2

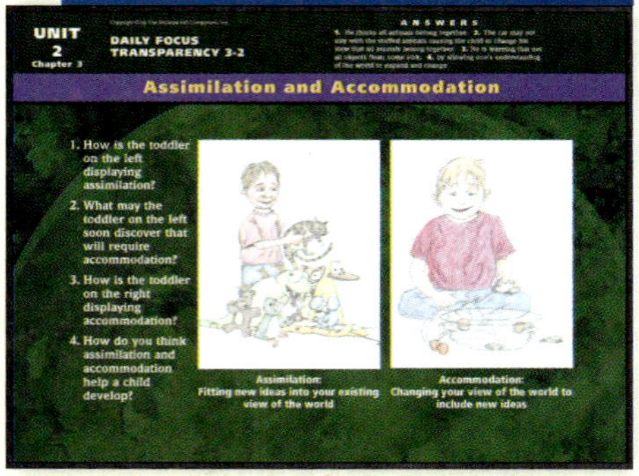

Reader's Guide

Use the Reader's Guide to introduce concepts and vocabulary.

■ Exploring Psychology

Ask students to read the **Exploring Psychology** feature and then discuss the following question: **Have you ever experienced a child's (unusual) logic? How can you explain that logic?**

■ Vocabulary Precheck

Have students read the Glossary definition of each term. Ask them to create a word search puzzle with clues to the terms. Pairs of students should exchange and complete each other's puzzles.

Use the **Vocabulary PuzzleMaker CD-ROM** to create crossword and word search puzzles.

SECTION 2

Cognitive and Emotional Development

Reader's Guide

■ Main Idea

As the thought processes of children develop, they begin to think, communicate and relate with others, and solve problems.

■ Vocabulary

- schema
- assimilation
- accommodation
- object permanence
- representational thought
- conservation
- egocentric
- imprinting
- critical period

■ Objectives

- Summarize the cognitive-development theory.
- Discuss how children develop emotionally.

EXPLORING PSYCHOLOGY

What Is She Thinking?

At [2 years and 4 months old] L. heard water running in the bathroom upstairs. She was with me in the garden and said to me: *"That's daddy up there."* At [2 years and 5 months old] L. went with her uncle to his car and saw him drive off along the road. She then went back into the house, and went straight to the drawing-room, where he had been earlier, and said: *"I want to see if uncle C. has gone."* She went in, looked all round the room and said: *"Yes, he's gone."*

—from *Plays, Dreams and Imitation in Childhood* by Jean Piaget, 1962

Psychologist Jean Piaget (1896–1980) chronicled the development of thought in his own daughter ("L."). From the stories Piaget described above, it is obvious that children think differently from adults in many ways. Children form their own hypotheses about how the world works.

COGNITIVE DEVELOPMENT

If you have a younger brother or sister, you may remember times when your parents insisted that you let the little one play with you and your friends. No matter how often you explained hide-and-seek to your 4-year-old brother, he spoiled the game. Why couldn't he understand that he had to keep quiet or he would be found right away?

SECTION RESOURCES

Reproducible Masters

- Guided Reading Activity 3–2
- Vocabulary Activity 3–2
- Section Quiz 3–2

Transparencies

- Daily Focus Transparency 3–2

Multimedia

- Vocabulary PuzzleMaker CD-ROM
- *ExamView® Assessment Suite* CD-ROM
- Presentation Plus! Software

This is a question Swiss psychologist Jean Piaget set out to answer more than 60 years ago. According to him, intelligence, or the ability to understand, develops gradually as the child grows. The sharpest, most inquisitive 4-year-old simply cannot understand things a 7-year-old grasps easily. What accounts for the dramatic changes between the ages of 4 and 7?

Piaget spent years observing, questioning, and playing games with babies and young children—including his own. He concluded that young children think in a different way than older children and adults; they use a different kind of logic. A 7-year-old is completely capable of answering the question "Who was born first, you or your mother?" but a 4-year-old is not (Chukovsky, 1963). Intellectual development involves quantitative changes (growth in the *amount* of information) as well as qualitative changes (differences in the *manner* of thinking).

More About...

Imaginary Playmates

There's nothing new about imaginary playmates—children have always had them. Our understanding about the role of imaginary playmates in the development of children, though, has grown. Dr. Jerome L. and Dr. Dorothy G. Singer studied a group of 3- and 4-year-olds and found a number of differences between children with imaginary playmates and those without. For example:

- Children with imaginary playmates are less aggressive and more cooperative than other children.
- They are rarely bored and have a rich vocabulary, far advanced for their age.
- They watch fewer hours of television than other children.
- They have a greater ability to concentrate.
- More than half of the children studied had imaginary playmates.

Above all, imaginary playmates seem to fill a gap in children's lives and are especially important to children who are first-born or who have no brothers and sisters. They are an adaptive mechanism that helps children get through the boring times in life.

How Knowing Changes

Understanding the world involves the construction of **schemas,** or mental representations of the world. Each of us constructs intellectual schemas, applying them and changing them as needed. We try to understand a new or different object or concept by using one of our preexisting schemas. In the process of **assimilation,** we try to fit the new object into this schema. In the process of **accommodation,** we change our schema to fit the characteristics of the new object.

For example, suppose an infant encounters a new block. The block fits his schema for other blocks he has encountered before. He may fit it into his stacking schema. The infant has stacked blocks before and can easily assimilate the new block into the existing schema. Suppose the infant then encounters an open box. He may at first try to fit the box into his stacking schema but finds that a block just falls inside the box. Now the stacking schema must be altered to accommodate this new object.

Assimilation and accommodation work together to produce intellectual growth. When events do not fit into existing schemas, new and grander schemas have to be created. The child begins to see and understand things in new ways.

Object Permanence An infant's understanding of things lies totally in the here and now. The sight of a toy, the way it feels in her hands, and the sensation it produces in her mouth are all she knows. She does not imagine it, picture it, think of it, remember it, or even forget it. When an infant's toy is hidden from her, she acts as if it has ceased to exist. She does not look for it. Instead, she grabs whatever else she can find and

schema: a conceptual framework a person uses to make sense of the world

assimilation: the process of fitting objects and experiences into one's schemas

accommodation: the adjustment of one's schemas to include newly observed events and experiences

Reading Check How are assimiliation and accommodation different?

2 TEACH

L1 Creating a Visual Chart

Organize students into small groups, supplying newsprint or poster board to each. Have each group create a visual chart of Piaget's stages of cognitive development, using drawings or pictures to represent the major accomplishments of each stage. Have the class select one or two of the charts to display in the classroom.

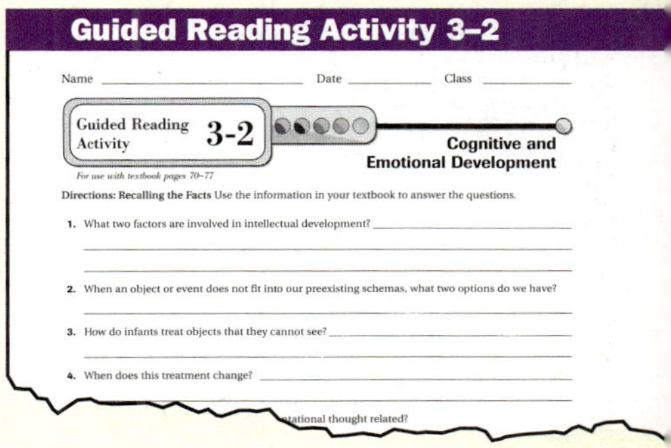

Guided Reading Activity 3–2

Name ______ Date ______ Class ______

Guided Reading Activity 3-2

Cognitive and Emotional Development

For use with textbook pages 70–77

Directions: Recalling the Facts Use the information in your textbook to answer the questions.

1. What two factors are involved in intellectual development? ______
2. When an object or event does not fit into our preexisting schemas, what two options do we have? ______
3. How do infants treat objects that they cannot see? ______
4. When does this treatment change? ______

...ational thought related?

Reading Check Answer When a child uses assimilation, he or she fits new objects and experiences into an existing schema; when using accommodation, he or she alters the schema to fit in new information.

COOPERATIVE LEARNING ACTIVITY

Writing a Children's Story Organize the class into small groups to write a short children's story without illustrations. Tell students that their stories should address a realistic obstacle that a child might encounter, such as fear of the dark. The story should encourage the child to face and overcome the obstacle. Have students read their completed stories to a preschool child. After the story is read, students should ask the child to draw pictures to illustrate the story. Have the groups share their stories and the children's pictures. Discuss how the pictures show representational thought. **BLOCK SCHEDULING**

CHAPTER 3
Section 2, pages 70–77

PSYCHOLOGY Online

Links and instructional guidelines can be found in the **Web Activity Lesson Plan** at glencoe.com.

Figure 3.7

Caption Answer A child should begin to understand object permanence at 7 to 12 months.

Readings and Case Studies in Psychology

Have students read the Chapter 3 Reading selection in *Readings and Case Studies in Psychology* and answer the questions that follow the reading.

TEACHER Tip

Point out that according to Piaget, both the concept of object permanence and the motor skills shown in Figure 3.2 occur during the first, or sensorimotor, stage of cognitive development.

PSYCHOLOGY Online

Student Web Activity Visit the *Understanding Psychology* Web site at glencoe.com and click on **Chapter 3—Student Web Activities** for an activity about infancy and childhood.

plays with that, or she may simply start crying. At 7 to 12 months, however, this pattern begins to change. When you take the infant's toy and hide it under a blanket while she is watching, she will search for it under the blanket. However, if you change tactics and put her toy behind your back, she will continue to look for it under the blanket—even if she was watching you the whole time.

You cannot fool a 12- to 18-month-old quite so easily. A child this age watches closely and searches for the toy in the last place she saw you put it. Suppose you take the toy, put it under the blanket, conceal it in your hands, and then put it behind your back. A 12-month-old will act surprised when she does not find the toy under the blanket—and keep searching there. An 18- to 24-month-old will guess what you have done and walk behind you to look (see Figure 3.7). She knows the toy must be somewhere (Ginsburg & Opper, 1969).

This is a giant step in intellectual development. The child has progressed from a stage where she apparently believed that her own actions created the world, to a stage where she realizes that people and objects are independent of her actions. Piaget called this concept **object permanence.** This concept might be expressed in this way: "Things continue to exist even though they cannot be seen or touched." It signifies a big step in the second year of life.

object permanence: a child's realization that an object exists even when he or she cannot see or touch it

representational thought: the intellectual ability of a child to picture something in his or her mind

Representational Thought The achievement of object permanence suggests that a child has begun to engage in what Piaget calls **representational thought.** The child's intelligence is no longer one of

Figure 3.7 Showing Object Permanence

A child who lacks object permanence will reach for a visible toy but not for one that is hidden behind a barrier—even if the child has seen someone place the toy behind the barrier. The child below, however, displays object permanence. ***At what age should a child begin to understand the concept of object permanence?***

MEETING SPECIAL NEEDS

Learning Style: Verbal/Spatial Ask students to create a game that is designed to help children practice assimilation and accommodation. For example, a matching game designed for preschool children could help children match things that belong together, like a raincoat and an umbrella. Students should have children of various ages play the game and critique it. **L2**

BLOCK SCHEDULING

Refer to ***Inclusion for the High School Social Studies Classroom Strategies and Activities*** in the TCR for strategies for students with different learning styles.

action only. Now, children can picture (or represent) things in their minds. At 14 months of age, Piaget's daughter demonstrated this. When she was out visiting another family, she happened to witness a child throwing a temper tantrum. She had never had a tantrum herself, but the next day she did—screaming, shaking her playpen, and stamping her feet as the other child had. She had formed so clear an image of the tantrum in her mind that she was able to create an excellent imitation a day later (Ginsburg & Opper, 1969). To Piaget, this meant that his daughter was using symbols. Soon she would learn to use a much more complex system of symbols—spoken language.

conservation: the principle that a given quantity does not change when its appearance is changed

egocentric: a young child's inability to understand another person's perspective

The Principle of Conservation

More complex intellectual abilities emerge as the infant grows into childhood. Between the ages of 5 and 7, most children begin to understand what Piaget calls **conservation,** the principle that a given quantity does not change when its appearance is changed. For example, if you have two identical short, wide jars filled with water and you pour the contents of one of these jars into a tall, thin jar, a child under 5 will say that the tall jar contains more water than the short one. If you pour the water back into the short jar to show the amount has not changed, the child will still maintain that there was more water in the tall container. Children under 5 do not seem to be able to think about two dimensions (height and width) at the same time. That is, they do not understand that a change in width is made up for by a change in the height of the tall glass (see Figure 3.8). This happens because children are **egocentric.** Egocentric thinking refers to seeing and thinking of the world from

Profiles In Psychology

Jean Piaget

1896–1980

"[T]he child no longer tends to approach the state of adulthood by receiving reason and the rules of right action ready-made, but by achieving them with his own effort and personal experience; in return society expects more of its new generations than mere imitation: it expects enrichment."

Born in Switzerland, Jean Piaget sought to answer one question in his life work: How does knowledge grow? He studied his three children and thousands of other children to answer this question. Piaget spent his time watching children play and playing with them. He told them stories and listened to their stories, asking them questions about why things are as they are. He invented problems for them to solve and asked them what they dreamt about.

What did Piaget discover? He discovered that knowledge builds as children grow. Children develop logic and think differently at different ages. Psychologists regard Piaget's discovery as revolutionary and insightful. Piaget's theory challenged the behaviorists' view that the environment determines behavior. Piaget stressed a child's active role in gaining knowledge. For these contributions, many consider Piaget the greatest child psychologist of the twentieth century.

L1 Summarizing Information
Assign groups of students to create a one-page handout for new parents who will be attending an informational session entitled "How Your Child Learns to Think." The handout should summarize the order in which children will learn cognitive skills and provide examples to help parents recognize how their children are thinking.

Profiles In Psychology

Ask students to read the **Profiles In Psychology** feature and then discuss the following questions:

1. Why are Piaget's discoveries considered by some to be revolutionary? *(Piaget suggested that children purposefully interact with their environment, learning and thinking in different ways during four developmental stages.)*
2. What do you think Piaget means by his statement that "[S]ociety expects more of its new generations than mere imitation. . . ."? *(Answers will vary. He means that a society's well-being depends on new generations for diversity of thought and action. To be successful, society needs new generations to creatively build on the achievements of the previous generation.)*

CRITICAL THINKING ACTIVITY

Demonstrating Reasoned Judgment Surrogate mothers can be beneficial in a child's development—up to a point. Ask students to consider other kinds of surrogate attachments that children form. To what extent are a child's attachments to pets, dolls, and stuffed animals, for example, a replacement for interactions between the child and other humans? Do students see any danger in a child's preferring the company of a doll over that of a peer? Have students give reasons to support their opinions. **L2**

Vocabulary Activity 3–2

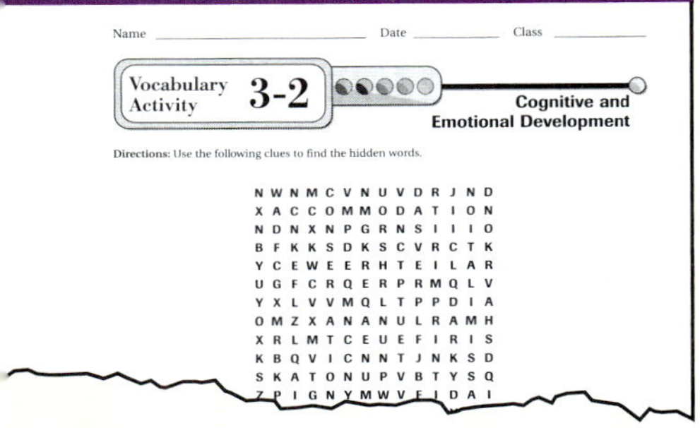
Name ____________ Date ________ Class ________

Vocabulary Activity 3-2

Cognitive and Emotional Development

Directions: Use the following clues to find the hidden words.

N W N M C V N U V D R J N D
X A C C O M M O D A T I O N
N D N X N P G R N S I I I O
B F K K S D K S C V R C T K
Y C E W E E R H T E I L A R
U G F C R Q E R P R M Q L V
Y X L V V M Q L T P P D I A
O M Z X A N A N U L R A M H
X R L M T C E U E F I R I S
K B Q V I C N N T J N K S D
S K A T O N U P V B T Y S Q

PSYCHOLOGY JOURNAL

Ask students to write about an experience they have had with a young child that showed that the child's level of cognitive development is sensorimotor or preoperational. ■

Figure 3.8

Visual Instruction Demonstrate other types of conservation as follows. (1) Place four playing cards on a table so that they form a simple rectangle. Now move the cards apart so that there is space between them. A child who does not understand conservation will perceive a change in total surface area. (2) Place 20 pennies spaced apart in two parallel lines of 10 pennies each. Now move the pennies in one line farther apart. The young child will think there is a change in the number of pennies.

Caption Answer Children who are egocentric see the world from their own viewpoint without considering other options. Conservation requires the child to consider other options.

your own standpoint and having difficulty understanding someone else's viewpoint and other perspectives. By age 7, the same child will tell you that the tall jar contains the same amount of water as the short one.

Piaget's Stages of Cognitive Development Piaget described the changes that occur in children's understanding in four stages of cognitive development (see Figure 3.9). During the *sensorimotor stage,* the infant uses schemas that primarily involve his body and sensations. The *preoperational stage* emerges when the child begins to use mental images or symbols to understand things. By the third stage, *concrete operations,* children are able to use logical schemas, but their understanding is limited to concrete objects or problems. In the *formal operations stage,* the person is able to solve abstract problems. According to Piaget, a person's development through these four stages depends on both the maturation of his or her nervous system and on the kinds of experiences he or she has had. Everyone goes through the stages in the same order, but not necessarily at the same age.

EMOTIONAL DEVELOPMENT

While the child is developing his ability to use his body, to think, and to express himself, he is also developing emotionally. He begins to become attached to specific people and to care about what they think and feel.

Figure 3.8 Tasks to Measure Conservation

The concept of conservation can be used to show that children think less logically than adults do. Children in the preoperational stage do not understand that the property of a substance remains the same although its appearance may change. ***How is conservation related to egocentric thinking?***

Type of conservation	*First display*	*Second display*	*Child is asked*
Length	 The child agrees that the sticks are of equal length.	 The experimenter moves one stick closer to the child.	*Which stick is longer?* Preconserving child will say that one stick is longer. Conserving child will say that they are the same length.
Substance amount	 The child acknowledges that the two balls have equal amounts of clay.	 The experimenter rolls out one of the balls.	*Do the two pieces have the same amount of clay?* Preconserving child will say that the long piece has more clay. Conserving child will say that the two pieces have the same amount of clay.

PSYCHOLOGY LAB EXPERIMENT

Personal Maturation Present the following research question: **How did I progress through the stages of the maturation process?** Direct students to find out specific things about at least one of the following types of development: physical, motor, emotional, and language. Interviewing family members and caregivers, collecting pictures, and reading baby books and scrapbooks are excellent starting points. Some of the facts students should try to uncover include height and weight at birth; age when they first crawled, walked, rode a bicycle, played a sport; age when they spoke their first word and what it was; and age when they developed special skills, such as dancing or singing. Students should present their findings in a time line. **L2** **BLOCK SCHEDULING**

Figure 3.9 **Piaget's Stages of Cognitive Development**

Piaget stressed the active role of the child in gaining knowledge. He also stressed the differences in the way a child thinks during different stages of maturity. ***At which of Piaget's stages do children lack the concept of conservation?***

Stage	Approximate Age	General Characteristics
Sensorimotor	Birth–2 years	Behavior consists of simple motor responses to sensory stimuli; lacks concept of object permanence
Preoperational	2–7 years	Lacks operations (reversible mental processes); exhibits egocentric thinking; lacks concept of conservation; uses symbols (such as words or mental images) to solve simple problems or to talk about things that are not present
Concrete operations	7–11 years	Begins to understand concept of conservation; still has trouble with abstract ideas; classification abilities improve; masters concept of conservation
Formal operations	11 years–onward	Understands abstract ideas and hypothetical situations; capable of logical and deductive reasoning

Experiments With Animals

Experiments with baby birds and monkeys have shown that early in life there is a maturationally determined time of readiness for attachment. If the infant is too young or too old, the attachment usually cannot be formed, but the attachment itself is a kind of learning. If the attachment is not made, or if a different attachment is made, the infant will develop in a different way as a result.

Imprinting Konrad Lorenz (1903–1989) became a pioneer in the field of animal learning. Lorenz discovered that baby geese become attached to their mothers in a rapid, virtually permanent learning process called **imprinting.** A few hours after they struggle out of their shells, goslings are ready to start waddling after the first thing they see that moves. Whatever it is, they usually stay with it and treat it as though it were their mother from that time on. Usually, of course, the first thing they see is the mother goose. Yet Lorenz found that if he substituted himself or some moving object like a green box being dragged along the ground, the goslings would follow that. Lorenz's goslings followed him wherever he went and ran to him when frightened (see Figure 3.10). Goslings are especially sensitive just after birth, and whatever they learn during this critical period, about 13 to 16 hours after birth, makes a deep impression that resists change. A **critical period** is a time in development when an animal (or human) is best able to learn a skill or behavior. If a gosling has imprinted on a human being instead of a goose, it will correct its imprinted response when later exposed to its actual mother. Thus, imprinting is important for survival purposes.

imprinting: inherited tendency of some newborn animals to follow the first moving object they see

critical period: a specific time in development when certain skills or abilities are most easily learned

Figure 3.9

Visual Instruction Remind students that Piaget's stages are not as distinct as they seem. Skills within each stage develop gradually.

Caption Answer Children lack conservation at the sensorimotor and preoperational stages.

PSYCHOLOGY Update

Imprinting Today nearly 300 free-flying condors live in the United States. All of these birds were born in captivity; nearly half have been released into the wild. In the late 1990s the release of condors caused problems for the birds and for humans. Even though zoologists had minimized the contact between the condors and people, imprinting was inevitable. The birds did not fear humans and were comfortable living among them. This created problems in Grapevine, California, where 15 of the birds had taken up residence. They entered people's homes, tore up screens, destroyed patio furniture, and ripped open garbage. In recent years some condors have died from electrocution when they perched on power lines. Today, the California Condor Recovery Program ensures that condors living in unsafe areas are retrapped and released in more remote areas. Condors subject to release also are given human aversion training. *Source*: Zoological Society of San Diego (2006). California condor recovery program. http://cres.sandiegozoo.org/projects/sp_condors_recovery_program.html

INTERDISCIPLINARY CONNECTIONS ACTIVITY

The Arts Have students review what they have learned about children's cognitive development. Then play Stephen Sondheim's song "Children Will Listen" from the Broadway musical *Into the Woods.* In a classroom discussion, ask students what common sense and psychological advice they would have for parents whose attitude is "Don't worry, the baby doesn't understand what is going on." **L2**

CHAPTER 3
Section 2, pages 70–77

Figure 3.10

Caption Answer Imprinting provides a measure of protection to the newborn by creating a safe response to stimuli.

3 ASSESS

Assign Section 2 Assessment as homework or as an in-class activity.

Section Quiz 3–2

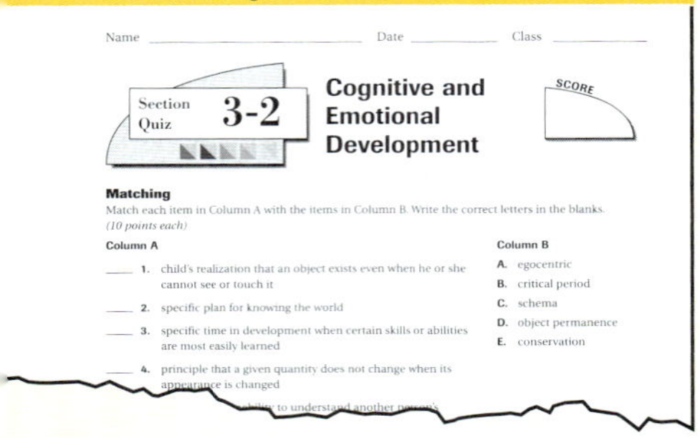
Name ______ Date ______ Class ______

Section Quiz 3-2 **Cognitive and Emotional Development** SCORE

Matching
Match each item in Column A with the items in Column B. Write the correct letters in the blanks. *(10 points each)*

Column A	Column B
____ 1. child's realization that an object exists even when he or she cannot see or touch it	A. egocentric
____ 2. specific plan for knowing the world	B. critical period
____ 3. specific time in development when certain skills or abilities are most easily learned	C. schema
____ 4. principle that a given quantity does not change when its appearance is changed	D. object permanence
	E. conservation

Reteach
Ask students to give an example of a child's behavior at each of Piaget's cognitive development stages.

Figure 3.10 The Process of Imprinting

Konrad Lorenz was the first moving object these goslings saw after they hatched, so they became imprinted on him. ***How is imprinting related to survival?***

Surrogate Mothers An American psychologist, Harry Harlow (1905–1981), studied the relationship between mother and child in a species closer to humans, the rhesus monkey. His first question was: What makes the mother so important? He tried to answer this question by taking baby monkeys away from their natural mothers as soon as they were born. (This is described further in Chapter 12.) Harlow raised the monkeys with two surrogate, or substitute, mothers. Each monkey could choose between a mother constructed of wood and wire and a mother constructed in the same way but covered with soft cloth. In some cages, the cloth mother was equipped with a bottle; in others, the wire mother was.

The results were dramatic. The young monkeys became strongly attached to the cloth mother, whether she gave food or not, and for the most part ignored the wire mother. If a frightening object was placed in the monkey's cage, the baby monkey would run to the cloth mother for security, not to the wire mother. It was the touching—physical contact—that mattered, not the feeding. Harlow called this contact comfort, or tactile touch. He concluded that the monkeys clung to their mothers because of the need for contact comfort.

Human Infants

Is there a critical period when infants need to become attached to a caregiver, as Lorenz's experiments suggest? Some psychologists would answer this question with a firm "yes." Infants begin to form an attachment to their mothers (or to a surrogate mother) at about 6 months, when they are able to distinguish one person from another and are beginning to develop object permanence. This attachment seems to be especially strong between the ages of 6 months and 3 years. (Attachment is a deep, caring, close, and enduring emotional bond between an infant and caregiver.) By 3 years, the child has developed to the stage where he is able to remember and imagine his mother and maintain a relationship with her (in fantasy) even if she is absent.

This monkey went to the cloth surrogate mother for comfort and reassurance.

When an attachment bond to one person has been formed, disruption can be disturbing to the infant. For example, when a 1-year-old child encounters a stranger, that child may display anxiety even when the mother is present. If the mother remains nearby, this *stranger anxiety* will pass. *Separation anxiety* occurs whenever the child is suddenly separated from the mother. If the separation persists, the child may develop psychological disorders.

Mary Ainsworth, with John Bowlby, studied attachment in families (Ainsworth & Bowlby, 1991). Ainsworth devised a technique called the

EXTENDING THE CONTENT

Separation Anxiety A clear picture of the development of cognitive abilities sheds light on some other areas of child behavior. For example, at about 10 to 12 months, many children go through a period of separation anxiety. They become upset when their mothers leave. They did not have any problems with the mothers leaving at 5 months of age. Why? The answer may be that the older child is more confused by the mother's disappearance. One study showed that infants were not particularly upset when their mothers left a room through a familiar door, but when the mothers left in a surprising way—by stepping into a closet, for example—the infant became upset. Thus, separation anxiety arose when the mother's disappearance led to uncertainty.

Strange Situation to measure attachment. In this technique, mothers and children underwent a series of episodes that sometimes involved the mother leaving and coming back into the room when a stranger was present and when a stranger was not present. From her research, she found there were three patterns of attachment in children: *secure attachment, avoidant attachment,* and *resistant attachment.* Psychologists have since identified a fourth attachment, called *disorganized attachment.*

Infants who demonstrate secure attachment balance the need to explore and the need to be close. They welcome the mother back when she returns and are free of anger. In avoidant attachment, the infants avoid or ignore the mother when she leaves and returns. The infants with resistant attachment are not upset when the mother leaves but reject her or act angrily when she returns. The infants with disorganized attachment behave inconsistently. They seem confused and act in contradictory ways. They may not be upset when the mother leaves but then they avoid her when she returns. This attachment seems to be the least secure attachment. (Mothers who are sensitive and responsive tend to have securely attached infants. However, there is a complex interplay between caregivers and infants.)

Quick Lab

How do children exhibit attachment?

How do children show emotional attachment to their parents or caregivers?

Procedure

1. Observe a 1- or 2-year-old child with a parent or caregiver for signs of emotional attachment. A day care center, a pediatrician's waiting room, or a play area in a shopping mall are good places to observe.
2. Watch for the following: How often does the child make contact with his or her parent? Does the child move away and explore? How does the child respond to unfamiliar people or objects?

Analysis

1. Did the child exhibit separation anxiety? What were the signs?
2. In a short paragraph, assess the emotional attachment of the child you observed.

See the Skills Handbook, page 622, for an explanation of designing an experiment.

SECTION 2 Assessment

1. **Review the Vocabulary** Why do infants construct schemas?
2. **Visualize the Main Idea** Using Piaget's stages, create a time line that tracks the cognitive development of a child. See the example below.

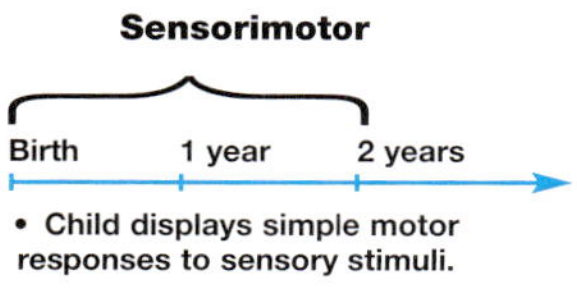

3. **Recall Information** What does it mean when people say children are egocentric?
4. **Think Critically** How might a child who displays avoidant attachment react when placed alone in a strange room?
5. **Application Activity** Design your own test for object permanence. Use several objects and test a younger sibling, cousin, or your pet dog or cat to see if he or she searches for hidden objects. Describe the results of your experiment.

SECTION 2 Assessment Answers

1. Schemas allow children to explain the world around them and to classify information in logical ways.
2. Students should use the information from Figure 3.9 to construct the time line.
3. Children view the world from their own perspective and cannot look at things from someone else's point of view.
4. Children may avoid or ignore the mother when she leaves and returns.
5. Students' answers will vary. The point is not the objects chosen but what the child's inclination reveals about the child's stage of development. It would be interesting to continue this experiment over several months with a very young child to determine when they develop object permanence.

Quick Lab

Purpose Students will explain why children show emotional attachment.

Process Skills Synthesizing information

Teaching Strategies

- Discuss what signals emotional attachment between parent and child.
- Discuss separation anxiety and explain how it is a common part of development for children.

Analysis

1. Students' answers will vary. Signs may include crying and fear if the parent or caregiver suddenly disappears.
2. Students' answers will vary but should include a discussion of physical affection and anxiety at separation.

Enrich

Ask students to collect brochures or articles on child development designed for parents. Have students review the examples to see if Piaget's theories are represented.

4 CLOSE

Have students recall instances of anxiety from their childhoods. **Ask: How did the element of uncertainty contribute to your feelings?** *(Students might recall, for example, being left with an unfamiliar babysitter.)*

1 FOCUS

Section Objectives

1. Describe theories of social development.
2. Outline Kohlberg's stages of moral reasoning.

BELLRINGER
Motivational Activity

Project Daily Focus Transparency 3–3 and have students answer the questions.

Available as blackline master

Daily Focus Transparency 3–3

Reader's Guide

Use the Reader's Guide to introduce concepts and vocabulary.

Exploring Psychology

Ask students to read the **Exploring Psychology** feature and then discuss: **How do children learn behavior that society finds acceptable and unacceptable?**

Vocabulary Precheck

Have students read the Glossary definition of each term. Then ask students to rewrite each definition in their own words.

Use the **Vocabulary PuzzleMaker CD-ROM** to create crossword and word search puzzles.

SECTION 3 Parenting Styles and Social Development

Reader's Guide

Main Idea

Children face various social decisions as they grow and progress through the stages of life.

Vocabulary

- authoritarian family
- democratic/authoritative family
- permissive/laissez-faire family
- socialization
- identification
- sublimation
- role taking

Objectives

- Describe theories of social development.
- Outline Kohlberg's stages of moral reasoning.

EXPLORING PSYCHOLOGY

A Day in the Life of a Preschool Teacher

"Hey you two—just pretend to eat, remember? If you put those spoons in your mouth, you'll pick up germs. Just pretend to use them."

That afternoon, the same two boys engaged in a mock karate battle on the playground. Hitting and kicking is forbidden in my class, regardless of whether it hurts anyone or not. To listen to them protesting the time-out, you'd think they'd never heard the rule.

"We weren't fighting!"

"You were kicking," I said sternly. "We don't kick here."

"But we weren't kicking!" they protested. "We were pretend-kicking, just like pretend-eating."

—from "Little People's Logic" by Sarah Starr

The story above comes from a preschool teacher. She concluded that children do not necessarily draw the conclusions you intend them to. The children involved in the "pretend-eating" and "pretend-kicking" did not follow the teacher's logic. The teacher explained the difference between acceptable "pretend-eating" and "pretend-fighting" by stating, "Sometimes people get hurt even when you pretend to fight." Children learn the rules for behavior in society through experiences such as this one.

SECTION RESOURCES

Reproducible Masters

- Guided Reading Activity 3–3
- Vocabulary Activity 3–3
- Section Quiz 3–3

Transparencies

- Daily Focus Transparency 3–3

Multimedia

- Vocabulary PuzzleMaker CD-ROM
- *ExamView*® *Assessment Suite* CD-ROM
- Presentation Plus! Software

PARENTING STYLES

The way in which children seek independence and the ease with which they resolve conflicts about becoming adults depend in large part on the parent-child relationship. Diana Baumrind (1971, 1973) observed and interviewed nursery school children and their parents. Follow-up observations when the children were 8 or 9 led to several conclusions about the impact of three distinct parenting styles on children.

In **authoritarian families** parents are the bosses. They do not believe that they have to explain their actions or demands. In fact, such parents may believe the child has no right to question parental decisions.

In **democratic** or **authoritative families** children participate in decisions affecting their lives. There is a great deal of discussion and negotiation in such families. Parents listen to their children's reasons for wanting to go somewhere or do something and make an effort to explain their rules and expectations. The children make many decisions for themselves, but the parents retain the right to veto plans of which they disapprove.

Figure 3.11 Parents and Children

Diana Baumrind's research focused on European-American children, but parenting styles may differ across cultures and groups. ***According to research on European-American children, which parenting style seems to lead to more confident children?***

In **permissive** or **laissez-faire families** children have the final say. The parents may attempt to guide the children but give in when the children insist on having their own way. Or the parents may simply give up their child-rearing responsibilities—setting no rules about behavior, making no demands, voicing no expectations, virtually ignoring the young people in their house.

Psychologists (Maccoby & Martin, 1983) later identified a fourth parenting style: *uninvolved parents.* These parents were typically egocentric in their child rearing and seemed uncommitted to their roles and quite distant from their children.

authoritarian family: parents attempt to control, shape, and evaluate the behavior and attitudes of children and adolescents in accordance with a set code of conduct

democratic/authoritative family: children and adolescents participate in decisions affecting their lives

permissive/laissez-faire family: children and adolescents have the final say; parents are less controlling and have a nonpunishing, accepting attitude toward children

Effects of Parenting Styles

Numerous studies suggest that adolescents who have grown up in democratic or authoritative families are more confident of their own values and goals than other young people. This seems to come from two features—the *establishment of limits* on the child and *responding* to the child with warmth and support (Bukatko & Daehler, 2004). The children of democratic families are more likely to want to make their own decisions with or without advice. There are several reasons for this: First, the child is able to *assume responsibility gradually.* He or she is not denied the opportunity to exercise judgment (as in authoritarian families) or given too much responsibility too soon (as in permissive families). Second, the child is more likely to *identify with parents* who love and respect him or her than with parents who treat him or her as incompetent or who seem

2 TEACH

* **L1 Explaining Parenting Styles** Write the four parenting styles on the board. Ask students to brainstorm examples of situations that demonstrate the various parenting styles described in this section.

BLOCK SCHEDULING

Guided Reading Activity 3-3

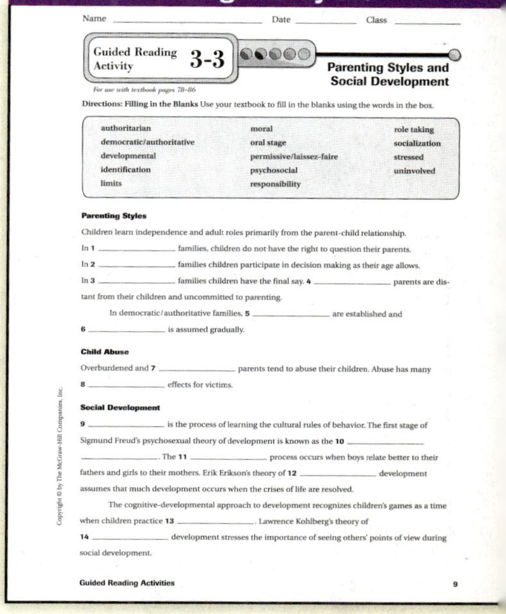

Name ______ Date ______ Class ______

Guided Reading Activity 3-3

Parenting Styles and Social Development

For use with textbook pages 78–86

Directions: Filling in the Blanks Use your textbook to fill in the blanks using the words in the box.

authoritarian	moral	role taking
democratic/authoritative	oral stage	socialization
developmental	permissive/laissez-faire	stressed
identification	psychosocial	uninvolved
limits	responsibility	

Parenting Styles

Children learn independence and adult roles primarily from the parent-child relationship.

In **1** ______ families, children do not have the right to question their parents.

In **2** ______ families children participate in decision making as their age allows.

In **3** ______ families children have the final say. **4** ______ parents are distant from their children and uncommitted to parenting.

In democratic/authoritative families, **5** ______ are established and **6** ______ is assumed gradually.

Child Abuse

Overburdened and **7** ______ parents tend to abuse their children. Abuse has many **8** ______ effects for victims.

Social Development

9 ______ is the process of learning the cultural rules of behavior. The first stage of Sigmund Freud's psychosexual theory of development is known as the **10** ______ ______. The **11** ______ process occurs when boys relate better to their fathers and girls to their mothers. Erik Erikson's theory of **12** ______ development assumes that much development occurs when the crises of life are resolved.

The cognitive-developmental approach to development recognizes children's games as a time when children practice **13** ______. Lawrence Kohlberg's theory of **14** ______ development stresses the importance of seeing others' points of view during social development.

Guided Reading Activities 9

Figure 3.11

Caption Answer The democratic/authoritative parenting style seems to lead to more confident children because children are permitted to make their own decisions with parental approval.

COOPERATIVE LEARNING ACTIVITY

Building Self-Image Explain to students that acquiring an identity and learning to live with oneself are important elements of socialization. Have students work in small groups to list specific phrases, events, body language, and so on, that build a positive self-image in a child. Then ask them to list things that could be a factor in creating a negative self-image. After the lists are complete, have each group discuss these questions: **(1) Should parents say and do only things that promote a positive self-image? (2) What are some disciplinary techniques that would not damage a child's self-image but would change his or her behavior? (3) Can a child affect his or her own self-image? How?**

L1 Discussing Family Relationships In addition to parents, siblings play a role in the social development of a child. Have students consider their own relationships with siblings or the relationships their friends have with siblings. List on the board or on an overhead the types of influences older and younger siblings have on children. (If you have someone in your class who is a twin, ask this person to share how having a twin affects his or her social development.) ELL

Psychology and You

Use the following question to direct a class discussion after students have read the **Psychology and You** feature.

Ask: **Do you agree or disagree with Harris's theory? How could you test the theory?**

TEACHER Tip

Discuss as a class what students should do if they become aware of a child who is being abused.

Psychology and You

Nature vs. Nurture

Do you think that the way parents treat their children influences how those children will turn out? Judith Rich Harris does not think so (Harris, 1999). Harris argues that other than the genes parents contribute to their children, virtually nothing they do or say makes a difference in what kind of adult the child becomes. Harris further proposes that a child's natural, genetic tendencies make her parents behave a certain way.

Harris claims that peer groups, not parents, teach children how to behave in the world. So the only influence parents have over their children, then, is by supplying the environment in which their children meet other peers. For example, parents should live in a good neighborhood so their children associate with the "right" peers.

Many psychologists passionately criticize Harris's theory. Critics claim that there is a very strong relationship between parenting styles and the social development of children. They argue that although two children may share the same parents, they may be treated differently by them and, thus, turn out differently.

indifferent. Finally, through their behavior toward the child, democratic parents *present a model of responsible, cooperative independence* for the growing person to imitate.

Although the style parents adopt in dealing with their children influences adolescent development, it would be wrong to conclude that parents are solely responsible for the way their children turn out. Children themselves may contribute to the style parents embrace, with consequences for their own personal development. Parents may adopt a laissez-faire attitude simply because they find that style the easiest way to cope with a teenager who insists on having his or her own way. Adolescents experiencing rapid physical and emotional changes may force their parents to make major adjustments in their parenting style.

CHILD ABUSE

Child abuse includes the physical or mental injury, sexual abuse, negligent treatment, or mistreatment of children under the age of 18 by adults entrusted with their care. Accurate statistics are difficult to compile, since many incidents of child abuse go unreported. In 2003 nearly 3 million cases of child abuse were reported. After investigation, an estimated 906,000 children were confirmed as victims of actual abuse or neglect situations (Child Maltreatment 2003, 2005).

Child abuse is viewed as a social problem resulting from a variety of causes. Many abusive parents were themselves mistreated as children, suggesting that (in contrast to Harris's view in "Psychology and You" above) these parents may have learned an inappropriate way of caring for children. Such parents tend to use the harsh physical discipline that they saw their own parents using. Many abusive parents have little patience with their children. Often they have unrealistic expectations.

Overburdened and stressed parents are more likely to abuse their children. Low-birthweight infants and those children who are hyperactive or mentally or physically disadvantaged experience a higher than normal incidence of abuse. One reason for this higher incidence may be that such children are less responsive and more difficult to care for, thus making greater demands on and providing fewer rewards for the parents (Belsky, 1984; Pianta, Egelands, & Erikson 1989). Social-cultural stresses such as unemployment and lack of contact with family, friends,

MEETING SPECIAL NEEDS

Learning Style: Verbal/Linguistic Have students select one of the educational television shows designed for very young children; for example, *Sesame Street* or *Barney and Friends.* Tell the students to watch an entire episode of the show, examining its content for specific examples of how such shows encourage social and moral development in children. Have students write a one-page evaluation of how well the show conveys developmental principles to children.

L2 BLOCK SCHEDULING

Refer to ***Inclusion for the High School Social Studies Classroom Strategies and Activities*** in the TCR for strategies for students with different learning styles and groups in the community are other factors associated with child abuse.

Several strategies show promise in reducing child abuse. For example, parent education for abusive parents allows them to learn new ways of dealing with their children. By providing information about resources and a support system for these families, communities may reduce the incidence of child abuse.

Abuse has many developmental effects for its victims. It may rob children of their childhood and create a loss of trust and feelings of guilt. In turn, this may lead to antisocial behavior, depression, identity confusion, loss of self-esteem, and other emotional problems. Every state and most counties have social services agencies that provide protective services to children. They have legal authority to investigate reported incidents of child abuse.

SOCIAL DEVELOPMENT

Learning the rules of behavior of the culture in which you are born and grow up is a process known as **socialization.** To live with other people, a child has to learn what is considered acceptable and unacceptable behavior. This is not as easy as it sounds. Some social rules are clear and inflexible. Other social rules leave room for individual decisions, so that sometimes there seems to be a gray area between right and wrong. Some rules change from situation to situation. Some apply to certain categories of people. For example, some rules for boys in our society are different from the rules for girls. We tend to encourage boys to express aggression but not fear; traditionally, girls have been raised to express emotions but not ambitions. Of course, the rules for feminine behavior have changed over the years.

Learning what the rules are—and when to apply or bend them—is, however, only one dimension of socialization. Every society has ideas about what is meaningful, valuable, worth striving for, and beautiful. Every society classifies people according to their family, sex, age, skills, personality characteristics, and other criteria. Every culture has notions about what makes individuals behave as they do. In absorbing these notions, a child acquires an identity as an individual member of a society, a member of different social categories, and a member of a family. Acquiring these identities is the second dimension of socialization.

Finally, socialization involves learning to live with other people and with yourself. Anyone who has seen the shock of a 2-year-old's face when another child his age takes a toy he wants, or the frustration and humiliation a 4-year-old experiences when she discovers she is unable to hit a baseball on the first try, knows how painful it can be to discover that other people have rights and that we all have limitations.

Figure 3.12 Socialization

Through socialization, children learn the beliefs and behaviors valued by their society. ***What are the three dimensions of socialization?***

Reading Check What is an effective way of stopping child abuse?

socialization: the process of learning the rules of behavior of the culture within which an individual is born and will live

CHAPTER 3
Section 3, pages 78–86

Figure 3.12

Caption Answer The three dimensions of socialization are (1) learning the rules and when to apply them; (2) acquiring an identity as a member of a particular society, as a member of a family, and as an individual; and (3) learning to live with other people and yourself.

Reading Check Answer Future incidents of child abuse can be effectively prevented by providing parent education and family and community support systems.

Vocabulary Activity 3–3

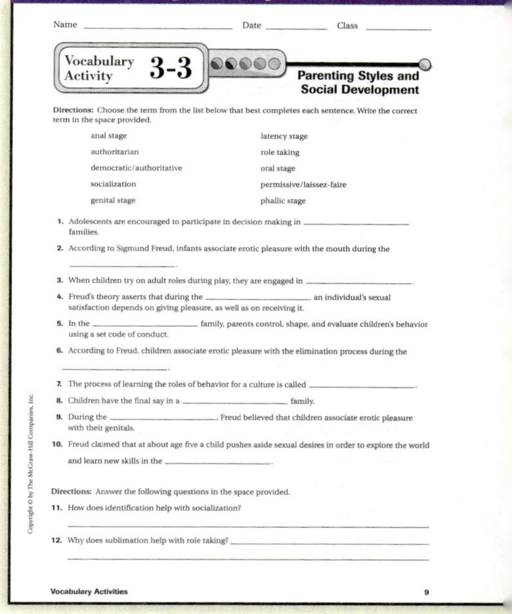

Name ________ Date ________ Class ________

Vocabulary Activity 3-3

Parenting Styles and Social Development

Directions: Choose the term from the list below that best completes each sentence. Write the correct term in the space provided.

anal stage	latency stage
authoritarian	role taking
democratic/authoritative	oral stage
socialization	permissive/laissez-faire
genital stage	phallic stage

1. Adolescents are encouraged to participate in decision making in ________ families.
2. According to Sigmund Freud, infants associate erotic pleasure with the mouth during the ________.
3. When children try on adult roles during play, they are engaged in ________.
4. Freud's theory asserts that during the ________ an individual's sexual satisfaction depends on giving pleasure, as well as on receiving it.
5. In the ________ family, parents control, shape, and evaluate children's behavior using a set code of conduct.
6. According to Freud, children associate erotic pleasure with the elimination process during the ________.
7. The process of learning the roles of behavior for a culture is called ________.
8. Children have the final say in a ________ family.
9. During the ________, Freud believed that children associate erotic pleasure with their genitals.
10. Freud claimed that at about age five a child pushes aside sexual desires in order to explore the world and learn new skills in the ________.

Directions: Answer the following questions in the space provided.

11. How does identification help with socialization? ________
12. Why does sublimation help with role taking? ________

Vocabulary Activities 9

CRITICAL THINKING ACTIVITY

Understanding Cause and Effect Ask students to consider the following situation: A 3-year-old child has an almost exclusive attachment to her mother. When the mother tries to leave the girl alone or with other children, the girl either cries or tries to follow the mother. The mother usually gives in and allows the girl to stay at her side. In fact, the mother has quit her part-time job because whenever the girl was left at day care or at her grandmother's house, she threw tantrums or became withdrawn. **Ask: Which theory of social development addresses the behavior of the mother and the child? What advice would you give to the mother? L2**

PSYCHOLOGY JOURNAL

Ask students to write how imitation plays a part in explaining violent acts committed by young children (children under 13 years of age). ■

Figure 3.13

Visual Instruction Explain that by identifying the stages of psychosexual development, Freud was trying to emphasize that all human beings are born with biological drives.

Caption Answer Children compete with the parent of the same sex during the phallic stage.

Applying Psychology

One of the most devastating effects of sexual abuse is that the child is often tricked into participating in the activity but later believes the act to be his or her fault. If the offender is someone the child knows well, the child not only experiences the trauma and stress of abuse but is also forced to keep the incident a secret for fear of getting the grownup in trouble. Often, parents and other usually responsible adults unintentionally dismiss the child's attempts to tell about the incident because the idea of sexual abuse is too horrifying for them to accept. Discuss with students how to identify signs that may indicate a child has suffered from sexual abuse.

Freud's Theory of Psychosexual Development

Sigmund Freud believed that all children are born with powerful sexual and aggressive urges. In learning to control these impulses, children acquire a sense of right and wrong. The process—and the results—are different for boys and girls.

According to Freud, in the first few years of life, boys and girls have similar experiences. Their erotic pleasures are obtained through the mouth, sucking at their mother's breast. Weaning the child from nursing is a period of frustration and conflict—it is the child's first experience with not getting what he wants. Freud called this the *oral stage* of development (see Figure 3.13). Later the anus becomes the source of erotic pleasure, giving rise to what Freud called the *anal stage*. Through toilet training the child learns to curb freedom and establish social control.

A major conflict comes between the ages of 3 and 5, when children discover the pleasure they can obtain from their genitals. As a consequence, they become extremely aware of the differences between themselves and members of the opposite sex. In this *phallic stage*, according to Freud, the child becomes a rival for the affections of the parent of the opposite sex. The boy wants to win his mother for himself and finds himself in hostile conflict with his father. The girl wants her father for herself and tries to shut out her mother. These struggles take place on an unconscious level. Generally, the child and the parents do not have any clear awareness that it is going on. In this process, which is called **identification** with the aggressor, the boy takes on all his father's values and moral principles. Thus, at the same time that he learns to behave like a man, he internalizes his father's morality. His father's voice becomes a voice inside him, the voice of conscience. The girl also goes through this process and begins to identify with her mother. She feels her mother's triumphs and failures as if they were her own, and she internalizes her mother's moral code.

Freud believed that at about age 5 or 6 children enter a *latency stage*. Sexual desires are pushed into the background, and children explore the world and learn new skills. This process of redirecting sexual impulses into learning tasks is called **sublimation.** Ideally, when one reaches the *genital stage* at adolescence, one derives as much satisfaction from giving pleasure as from receiving it. For Freud, personality development is essentially complete as we enter adolescence. Today relatively few psychologists believe that sexual feelings disappear in childhood.

identification: the process by which a child adopts the values and principles of the same-sex parent

sublimation: the process of redirecting sexual impulses into learning tasks

Figure 3.13 Freud's Stages of Psychosexual Development

According to Freud, there is often conflict between child and parent. The conflict occurs because the child wants immediate gratification of needs while the parent restricts that gratification in some way. ***At what stage do children compete with their parents?***

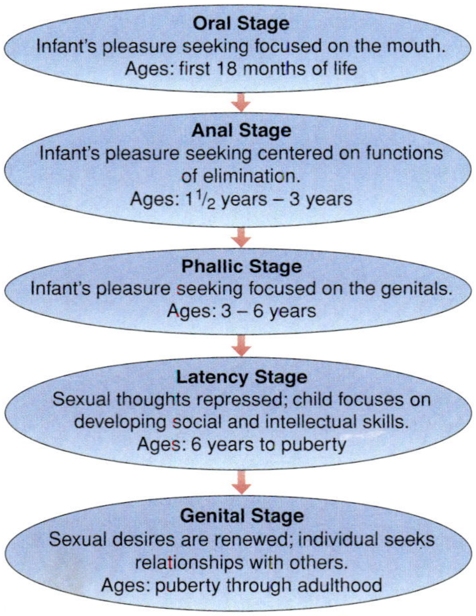

PSYCHOLOGY LAB EXPERIMENT

Moral Development in Children Have students work in small groups to analyze if children's moral reasoning develops with age. The groups should devise a moral dilemma to which children can relate. Suggest the groups use the dilemma as a survey instrument for various ages of children. Each group should interview two children from each of the following age groups: 4–5, 6–7, 8–9, and 10–12. The groups should pose the moral dilemma and record the children's responses. Using Kohlberg's stages of moral development, the groups should analyze each child's response and indicate the moral stage at which each child is operating. Have the groups prepare charts showing the various levels and brief reports explaining their findings. **L2** **BLOCK SCHEDULING**

Erikson's Theory of Psychosocial Development

Erik Erikson (1902–1994) takes a broader view of human development than Freud in terms of both time and scope. Although he recognizes the child's sexual and aggressive urges, he believes that the need for social approval is just as important. Erikson studied what he called *psychosocial* development—life periods in which an individual's goal is to satisfy desires associated with social needs. Although Erikson believes that childhood experiences have a lasting impact on the individual, he sees development as a lifelong interactive process between people (see Figure 3.14).

Erikson argues that we all face many crises as we grow from infancy to old age, as we mature, and as people expect more from us. Each of these crises represents an issue that everyone faces. The child, adolescent, or adult may develop more strongly in one way or another, depending on how other people respond to his or her efforts.

For example, the 2-year-old is delighted with his newfound ability to walk, to get into things, to use words, and to ask questions. The very fact that he has acquired these abilities adds to his self-esteem, and he is eager to use them. If the adults around him applaud his efforts and acknowledge his achievements, he begins to develop a sense of autonomy, or independence. However, if they ignore him except to punish him for going too far or being a nuisance, the child may begin to doubt the value of his achievements. He may also feel shame because the people around him act as if his new desire for independence is bad.

Reading Check How does Erikson's view of development differ from Freud's?

Learning Theories of Development

Both Freud and Erikson stress the emotional dynamics of social development. Their theories suggest that learning social rules is altogether different from learning to ride a bicycle or to speak a foreign language. Many psychologists disagree. They believe children learn the ways of their social world because they are rewarded for conforming and because they copy older children and adults in anticipation of future rewards. In other words, social development is simply a matter of conditioning (learning) and imitation. (See Chapter 9 for a discussion of these concepts.)

The Cognitive-Developmental Approach

Theorists who emphasize the role of cognition or thinking in development view the growing child differently. Learning theory implies that the child is essentially passive—a piece of clay to be shaped by experience. The people who administer rewards and punishments and serve as models do the shaping. Cognitive theorists see the child as the shaper. Taking their cue from Jean Piaget, they argue that social development is the result of the child's acting on the environment and trying to make sense out of his experiences. The games children play illustrate this.

Games and Play Children's games are serious business. When left to their own devices, youngsters spend a great deal of time making up rules. This enables them to learn for themselves the importance of agreeing on

Reading Check Answer
Erikson adds the importance of social approval as a key component of development. He also viewed development as a lifelong process.

CURRICULUM CONNECTION

The Law When lawyers argue for damages in wrongful death and dismemberment cases, the usual practice has been to compensate the person or family for the physical loss suffered. Lawyers have recently begun taking another approach. They are arguing that compensation should be based not just on the physical loss but on the impact the loss has on social relationships. For example, if a parent is killed in an automobile accident, what is the value of the disruption to the family's life for the loss? This system is being called the "Whole Family" systems theory. To support their compensation requests, lawyers are asking developmental psychologists to serve as expert witnesses in defining the effects of the loss on the family.

FYI

Even when an infant forms a strong attachment to both the mother and the father, and they nurture the baby equally, the child will still tend to prefer being soothed by the mother.

INTERDISCIPLINARY CONNECTIONS ACTIVITY

The Arts Your students might enjoy having a close look at *Children's Games* by Pieter Brueghel the Elder. (Hundreds of games are depicted on a single canvas.) Use an opaque projector to show a copy of the painting to the class. Have students try to find examples of children trying on adult roles and learning various aspects of competition in the games that Brueghel depicts. **L2** **ELL**

L2 Debating an Issue Assign students to research some of the studies that have been done to determine the effect on children of having mothers work outside the home. Debate the following issue: *Resolved*—Mothers should remain in the home to ensure the normal development of their children.

Figure 3.14

Visual Instruction Compare Piaget's cognitive development stages with Erikson's stages of psychosocial development. Ask students how cognitive development plays a role in social development.

Caption Answer The issues during the first year of life revolve around trust versus mistrust.

TEACHER Tip

Point out that one of the major criticisms of the Freudian theory is that it is not supported by compelling scientific research. Nevertheless, Freud's ideas have had a profound and lasting impact on how people think about the unconscious forces that affect our lives.

Looking @ the Issues

Sigmund Freud Although Freud remains a household name, his theories have come under increasing attack with the passage of time. Ask students to research some of these challenges and to write a summary of the controversial issues involved. Have students discuss their findings with the class.

a structure for group activities. A child can relax and enjoy himself without fear of rejection as long as he does not break the rules. The world of play thus becomes a miniature society, with its own rules and codes. Games also teach children about aspects of adult life in a nonthreatening way. In young children's games, it is the experience of playing, not winning, that counts.

role taking: children's play that involves assuming adult roles, thus enabling the child to experience different points of view

Much of the children's play involves **role taking**. Youngsters try on such adult roles as mother, father, teacher, storekeeper, explorer, and rock star. Role taking allows them to learn about different points of view firsthand. Suppose a child plays a mother opposite another child who plays a whiny, disobedient baby. When she finds herself totally frustrated by the other child's nagging, she begins to understand why her mother gets mad. You are unable to cook even a pretend meal when the baby keeps knocking over the pots and pans.

Moral Development Lawrence Kohlberg's studies show just how important being able to see other people's points of view is to social development in general and to moral development in particular. Kohlberg (1968) studied the development of moral reasoning—deciding what is right and what is wrong—by presenting children of different ages with a series of moral dilemmas. Kohlberg gave the following example: In Europe, a

Figure 3.14 Erikson's Stages of Psychosocial Development

According to Erikson, a child encounters a psychosocial challenge at each stage. If the child successfully resolves the issue, the child develops a positive social trait and progresses to the next stage. ***What issues concern a child in the first year of life?***

Stage 8: Ego integrity versus despair
Ages: older adult
Have I lived a full life?

Stage 7: Generativity versus stagnation
Ages: middle adult
Will I succeed in life?

Stage 6: Intimacy versus isolation
Ages: young adult
Shall I share my life with someone or live alone?

Stage 5: Identity versus role confusion
Ages: early teens
Who am I?

Stage 4: Industry versus inferiority
Ages: 6 – 12
Am I successful or worthless?

Stage 3: Initiative versus guilt
Ages: 3 – 6 years
Am I good or bad?

Stage 2: Autonomy versus shame and doubt
Ages: 1 – 3 years
Can I do things myself or must I rely on others?

Stage 1: Trust versus mistrust
Ages: early infancy
Is my world predictable and supportive?

EXTENDING THE CONTENT

Emotional Intelligence Kohlberg's description of the highest level of moral development mentions a "principled conscience" in which an individual balances his or her own needs with those of the group. Intelligence theorists use the term "emotional intelligence" to describe the ability to show empathy. This relatively new theory of intelligence, discussed in Chapter 13, may be related to higher levels of moral development. Those with a high level of emotional intelligence base moral decisions on what feels right and wrong and how their actions will affect others. Discuss with the class how such people would address situations such as paying taxes, registering to vote, or obeying the speed limit.

woman was near death from cancer. One drug might save her, a form of radium that a druggist in the same town had recently discovered. The druggist was charging $2,000, ten times what the drug cost him to make. The sick woman's husband, Heinz, went to everyone he knew to borrow the money, but he could get together only about half of what it cost. He told the druggist that his wife was dying and asked him to sell it cheaper or let him pay later. But the druggist said, "No." The husband got desperate and broke into the man's store to steal the drug for his wife. Should the husband have done that? Why? (Kohlberg, 1969b)

What interested Kohlberg was how the children arrived at a conclusion. He wanted to know what sort of reasoning they used. After questioning 84 children, Kohlberg identified six stages of moral development (see Figure 3.15). He then replicated his findings in several different cultures.

Stages of Moral Development In stage one, children are totally egocentric. They do not consider other people's points of view and have no sense of right and wrong. Their main concern is avoiding punishment. A child in this stage will say that the man should steal because people will blame him for his wife's death if he does not, or that he should not steal because he will go to jail when he's caught.

Children in stage two have a better idea of how to receive rewards as well as to avoid punishment. Youngsters at this level interpret the Golden Rule as "help someone if he helps you, and hurt him if he hurts you." They are still egocentric and premoral, evaluating acts in terms of the consequences, not in terms of right and wrong.

In stage three, children become acutely sensitive to what other people want and think. A child in this stage will say that the man in the story should steal because people will think he is cruel if he lets his wife die, or that he should not steal because people will think he is a criminal. In other words, children want social approval in stage three, so they apply the rules other people have decreed literally and rigidly.

In stage four, a child is less concerned with the approval of others. The key issue here is law and order—a law is seen as a moral rule and is obeyed because of a strong belief in established authority. For example, a woman may stay married because she took a vow, or a driver may obey the speed limit when no police are around. Moral thinking here, as at stage three, is quite rigid.

In the remaining two stages, people continue to broaden their perspective. The stage-five person is primarily concerned with whether a law is fair or just. He believes that laws must change as the world changes, and they are never absolute. The important question is whether a given law is good for society as a whole. Stage six involves an acceptance of ethical principles that apply to everyone, like the Golden Rule: "Do unto others as you would have them do unto you." Such moral imperatives cannot be broken; they are more important than any written law.

Critics point out a gender bias in Kohlberg's theory (Gilligan, 1977). Whereas girls might argue that both stealing and letting Heinz's wife die are wrong, boys might logically argue that life has greater value than

CULTURAL CONNECTIONS

Who runs the largest corporate-sponsored day care system in the United States? Surprisingly, the answer is the Department of Defense (DOD), which serves more than 200,000 children worldwide. Military families have unique needs that can challenge any child care system. Personnel work odd schedules and can be deployed on short notice. Some types of service involve long separation from families. In addition, families typically move every three years. When families are stationed in foreign countries, extended family is unavailable to assist with child care. To fill the gap, the DOD runs 800 child development centers and oversees 9,700 licensed family child care homes.

3 ASSESS

Assign Section 3 Assessment as homework or as an in-class activity.

Section Quiz 3–3

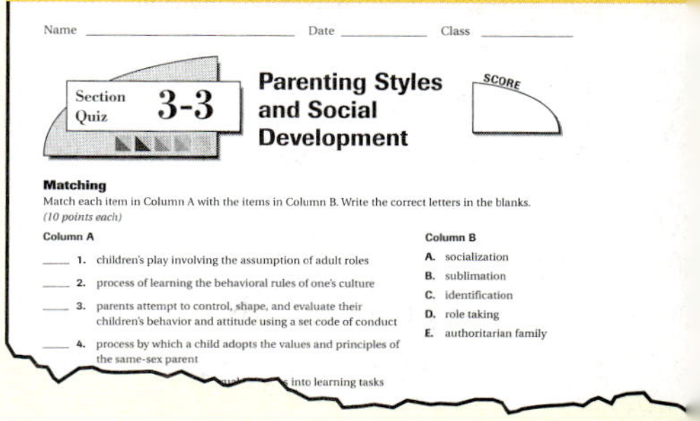
Name ______ Date ______ Class ______

Section Quiz 3-3

Parenting Styles and Social Development

SCORE

Matching

Match each item in Column A with the items in Column B. Write the correct letters in the blanks. *(10 points each)*

Column A

____ 1. children's play involving the assumption of adult roles

____ 2. process of learning the behavioral rules of one's culture

____ 3. parents attempt to control, shape, and evaluate their children's behavior and attitude using a set code of conduct

____ 4. process by which a child adopts the values and principles of the same-sex parent

into learning tasks

Column B

A. socialization

B. sublimation

C. identification

D. role taking

E. authoritarian family

EXTENDING THE CONTENT

Effective Parenting Parenting is perhaps the most important responsibility a person can have, and yet most people receive little or no formal training for this responsibility. Instead, people tend to parent in the way that they were parented. Ask students to suggest what should be done to improve parenting skills in American society. Encourage students to identify community resources that might already be in place to help people become more effective parents. **L2**

Figure 3.15

Visual Instruction Ask students to compare Kohlberg's moral development with Erikson's theory of social development.

Caption Answer The child is primarily motivated to obey in order to avoid punishment.

Reteach

On the board, copy key statements and facts from Section 3, but change them to make them false. Ask students to write the statements correctly.

Enrich

Have students write an essay defending one of the theories of social development.

4 CLOSE

Ask students to brainstorm ways in which conditioning and imitation are commonly used to aid children in their social development.

Figure 3.15 Kohlberg's Stages of Moral Development

Each stage of Kohlberg's theory is cognitively more complex than the last. *Why would a child in the first stage choose to listen to her parents?*

Level	Stage	Orientation	Reference Group	Example
Pre-conventional	1	Obedience and punishment	Self	It's OK for Heinz to steal if he doesn't get caught.
	2	Instrumental relativist	Immediate family	Stealing the drug helps his wife.
Conventional	3	Good boy/Nice girl	Extended family	His in-laws will respect him if he steals the drug.
	4	Law and order	Self-serving view of society	It's illegal to steal.
Post-conventional	5	Social contract	Interactive view of society	It's OK to steal because the druggist is charging too much.
	6	Universal ethics principle	Balanced cost/benefit analysis of self/society	If the situations were reversed, would the druggist steal from Heinz?

property. Using these arguments, Kohlberg would place boys at higher levels of moral development. Girls are taught to be empathetic, whereas boys are taught the goal of justice.

To reach the highest levels of moral development, a child must first be able to see other people's points of view. Yet this understanding is no guarantee that a person will respect the rights of others. Thus, the development of thinking or cognitive abilities influences moral development.

SECTION 3 Assessment

1. **Review the Vocabulary** Describe Freud's theory of socialization.
2. **Visualize the Main Idea** Describe parenting styles using a chart similar to the one below.

Parenting Style	Role of Parents	Role of Children

3. **Recall Information** What are the functions of children's games? How do these games illustrate the cognitive-developmental approach?
4. **Think Critically** What questions might you ask a child to determine what stage of moral development he or she is in?

5. Application Activity Go to a public place where you can observe children, such as a playground, park, or shopping mall. Note the behaviors between parents and child and among the children as they play together. Record and analyze your observations. Describe the different parenting styles you observed.

SECTION 3 Assessment Answers

1. Freud's theory centered on how children deal with their innate sexual and aggressive urges.
2. Students' charts should reflect an understanding of the four parenting styles discussed in this section.
3. Children use games to learn social rules. Games allow children to take on different roles, allowing them to experience situations from different points of view. Games also allow children to explore the importance of agreeing on rules for group activities. Games resemble a miniature society.
4. Why don't you misbehave? Why don't you steal?
5. Students' answers will vary. Students should be able to identify all the parenting styles in a relatively short period. Discuss with students that judgments based on short-term observations may not be completely valid.

CHAPTER 3 Summary and Vocabulary

Developmental psychology is the study of the changes that occur as people grow up and grow older. It covers the entire life cycle, from conception to death.

Section 1 Physical, Perceptual, and Language Development

Main Idea: Infants are born equipped to experience the world. As infants grow physically, they also develop perceptions and language.

- Some psychologists believe that most behaviors are the result of genetics—nature. Others believe that most behaviors are the result of experience and learning—nurture.
- The newborn is capable of certain inherited, automatic, coordinated movement patterns, called reflexes, which are triggered by the right stimulus.
- Infants experience rapid development through maturation and learning.
- Depth perception increases in older infants.
- There are several steps involved in learning language.

Section 2 Cognitive and Emotional Development

Main Idea: As the thought processes of children develop, they begin to think, communicate and relate with others, and solve problems.

- Children's knowledge of the world changes through the processes of assimilation and accommodation.
- Piaget described the changes that occur in children's understanding in four stages of cognitive development.
- Infants begin to develop emotionally by attaching to specific people, usually their mothers.

Section 3 Parenting Styles and Social Development

Main Idea: Children face various social decisions as they grow and progress through the stages of life.

- There are four basic parenting styles—authoritarian, democratic or authoritative, permissive or laissez-faire, and uninvolved.
- Socialization is the process of learning the rules of behavior of one's culture.
- Freud's theory of psychosexual development suggests that all children are born with powerful sexual and aggressive urges, and in learning to control these impulses, children acquire a sense of right and wrong.
- Erikson's theory of psychosocial development suggests that the need for social approval is important.
- The cognitive-developmental theories of development suggest that social development is the result of the child trying to make sense out of his experiences.
- Kohlberg suggested that humans progress through six stages of moral reasoning.

Chapter Vocabulary

developmental psychology (p. 61)
grasping reflex (p. 62)
rooting reflex (p. 62)
maturation (p. 64)
telegraphic speech (p. 67)
schema (p. 71)
assimilation (p. 71)
accommodation (p. 71)
object permanence (p. 72)
representational thought (p. 72)
conservation (p. 73)
egocentric (p. 73)
imprinting (p. 75)
critical period (p. 75)
authoritarian family (p. 79)
democratic/authoritative family (p. 79)
permissive/laissez-faire family (p. 79)
socialization (p. 81)
identification (p. 82)
sublimation (p. 82)
role taking (p. 84)

3 Summary and Vocabulary

Using the Chapter 3 Summary and Vocabulary

Use the Chapter 3 Summary and Vocabulary to preview, review, condense, or reteach the chapter.

Preview/Review

Use the Chapter Vocabulary list to help students review and study.

Activity Ask for student volunteers to give the psychological definition for each term presented in the chapter. Ask another student to use the term in a sentence that gives an example or provides further explanation of the term.

Vocabulary PuzzleMaker CD-ROM reinforces the vocabulary terms used in Chapter 3.

Condense

Have students read the Chapter 3 Summary.

Chapter 3 Guided Reading Activities

Reteach

Reteaching Activity 3

AUTHENTIC ASSESSMENT ACTIVITY

Creating Advertisements Have students work in small groups to select four toys from toy catalogs—one for each stage of Piaget's stages of cognitive development. Students should work together to develop an ad for each toy that tells parents why it is appropriate for their child's particular stage of development. Ads should mention the age range that the toy is designed for as well as what concepts it is designed to teach.

Refer to the ***Authentic Assessment*** booklet for additional activities and information about evaluating student performance.

PSYCHOLOGY Online

Have students visit the Web site at glencoe.com to review Chapter 3 and take the **Self-Check Quiz.**

GLENCOE TECHNOLOGY

PRESENTATION Plus!

For a review of Chapter 3 content, see MindJogger Checkpoint on **Presentation Plus!**

Reviewing Vocabulary

1. f
2. c
3. a
4. g
5. b
6. d
7. i
8. e
9. j
10. h

Recalling Facts

1. They can see, hear, smell, and have reflexes such as grasping, rooting, and sucking reflexes.
2. No amount of coaching can push a child to walk before he or she is physiologically ready to walk.
3. Children babble and make sounds throughout infancy. Their first words occur at about 1 year of age. By 2 years of age, children speak two-word sentences that indicate a basic understanding of grammar. By 3 years of age, children understand more grammatical rules and speak in more complete sentences. Language development continues for the next two years as children's language skills mature.
4. Socialization is the process of learning the rules of behavior of the culture within which the person is born and lives. Social rules are often complex and flexible, but they allow us to live together peacefully.
5. Obedience and punishment: obedience to avoid punishment; instrumental relativist: obedience to earn a reward; good boy/nice girl: obedience to earn another's respect; law and order: moral belief based on recognition of authority; social contract: fairness and justice of law; universal ethics principles: acceptance of ethical principles that apply to everyone in all situations

CHAPTER 3 Assessment

PSYCHOLOGY Online

Self-Check Quiz
Visit the *Understanding Psychology* Web site at glencoe.com and click on **Chapter 3—Self-Check Quizzes** to prepare for the Chapter Test.

Reviewing Vocabulary

Choose the letter of the correct term or concept below to complete the sentence.

a. rooting reflex
b. maturation
c. democratic/authoritative families
d. telegraphic speech
e. schemas
f. object permanence
g. egocentric
h. socialization
i. sublimation
j. developmental psychology

1. __________ is the awareness that objects exist even when they cannot be perceived.
2. In __________, adults develop a parenting style in which children participate in decisions affecting their lives.
3. Because of the __________, a newborn who is touched anywhere around the mouth will move her head and mouth toward the source of the touch.
4. Seeing and thinking of the world only from one's own standpoint is called __________ thinking.
5. __________ is internally programmed growth.
6. Children at around age 2 use __________, in which words are left out but the message gets across.
7. The process of redirecting sexual impulses into learning tasks is __________.
8. To understand the world, children construct __________, or mental representations of the world.
9. The study of changes that occur as an individual matures is __________.
10. Learning the rules of behavior of one's culture is called __________.

Recalling Facts

1. Describe capacities newborns display.
2. How does the maturation process explain why a 4-month-old infant cannot be taught to walk?
3. Describe the process by which children learn to talk.
4. Define socialization and explain why it is so important to development.
5. Using a diagram similar to the one below, list and explain Kohlberg's stages of moral development.

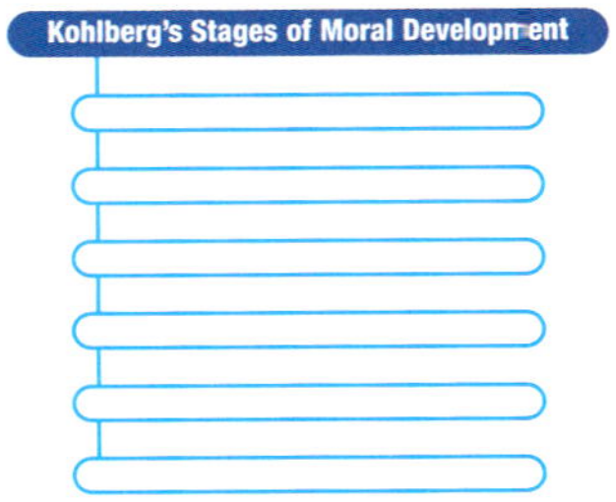

Critical Thinking

1. **Demonstrating Reasoned Judgment** Do you think development is the result of heredity, learning (experience), or both? Why?
2. **Making Inferences** Should young children be treated as "little adults"? Based on what you have learned about development, do you think that is reasonable? Why or why not?
3. **Applying Concepts** Young children are egocentric. Provide some examples of children's egocentric thinking.
4. **Analyzing Concepts** What do you assume might happen when a boy plays with action-figure dolls? How does this behavior fit into the learning theories of development?
5. **Evaluating Information** Determine how well your beliefs agree with those of your parents. How important do you think your early social training was for what you believe?

Critical Thinking

1. Students' answers will vary. Most will likely recognize both as integral to development based on specific examples from their own experience.
2. Students' answers will vary. Piaget's theory suggests that this is inappropriate because children are not cognitively prepared to use adult reasoning to make decisions.
3. Students' answers will vary. Examples may include the principle of conservation, separation anxiety, and understanding rules of games like "hide and seek."
4. Boys use the action figures to imitate the aggressiveness seen on TV, in the movies, or in video games. This fits the cognitive-developmental approach in which children take on various roles.
5. Students' answers will vary. Students may cite differences and similarities in beliefs. Most students will recognize that early social training was effective in forming beliefs; this is especially true in children raised in democratic and authoritative families, as they were allowed to make their own decisions within boundaries established by parents.

CHAPTER 3

Assessment

Psychology Projects

1. **Physical, Perceptual, and Language Development** Investigate recent findings about the role of heredity and environment on a child's development. Present your information in an oral report.
2. **Social Development** How are sex roles communicated to people in American society? Look through magazines and newspapers, watch television commercials, and listen to the radio. Present your findings in an illustrated, captioned poster.
3. **Cognitive Development** Using information from the chapter as well as from other sources, present 10 ideas that people can use with children to increase their language and intellectual development. Explain how these 10 suggestions will increase a child's language and intellectual development.

Technology Activity

Use the Internet and computer software catalogs to find examples of computer software that parents and other adults can use with infants and small children. Explain what aspect of the child's development—physical, language, emotional, intellectual, and social—the software addresses.

Psychology Journal

Reread your journal entry about the sentences spoken by 2-year-olds. What sorts of words are used and in what context? Can you specify the grammatical rules children of this age use in combining words? Write your answers in your journal.

Building Skills

Interpreting a Graph Doctors often record infants' and young children's weight and height on growth charts similar to the one for girls here. The measurements are presented in the form of percentiles. For example, a 30-month-old girl who weighs 28.7 pounds falls into the 50th percentile. This means that half of all 30-month-old girls weigh less than that child and half weigh more. Review the growth chart, then answer the questions that follow.

1. Into what percentiles does an 18-month-old girl fall who weighs about 28 pounds and is 34 inches tall?
2. Into what percentile would a 9-month-old girl fall who weighs 22 pounds?
3. How do growth charts illustrate that a child's physical development is unique?

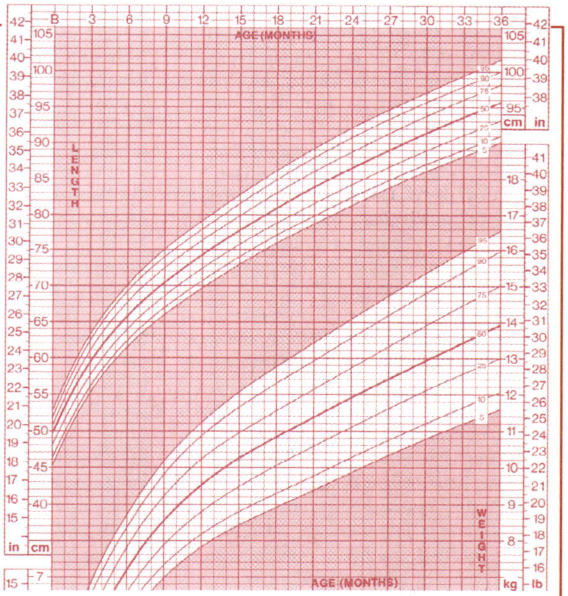

Practice and **assess** key social studies skills with **Glencoe Skillbuilder Interactive Workbook CD-ROM, Level 2.**

See the Skills Handbook, page 628, for an explanation of interpreting graphs.

Assessment

Building Skills

1. 94th percentile; about 95th percentile
2. about 93rd or 94th percentile
3. Growth charts demonstrate that children may fall into various ranges at different ages. No two children are exactly alike, but most progress through the same sequential steps of development.

GLENCOE TECHNOLOGY

CD-ROM

Glencoe Skillbuilder Interactive Workbook, Level 2

This interactive CD-ROM is designed to reinforce student mastery of essential social studies skills.

Chapter Bonus Test Question

This question may be used for extra credit on the Chapter Assessment.

Answer the following question:

My theories on cognitive development help explain why young children cannot reason abstractly. Who am I?

Answer: Jean Piaget

Psychology Projects

1. Answers will vary. Students' reports should be well organized and informative.
2. Posters will vary. Sex roles are communicated by parents, peers, social groups, and various forms of media. The influence of each depends on the child and the way in which he or she has been raised.
3. Answers will vary. Students' ideas should support an understanding of language and intellectual development.

Technology Activity

Students' lists of software should correctly identify the type of development that is targeted by the software. Language, intellectual, and physical development will be most common. Social development can be fostered by games played by two or more children.

Psychology Journal

Students will identify various words that they heard when they were with the 2-year-old. Most words will be nouns or verbs.

TIME REPORTS

Reader's Dictionary

Review the following terms with students to help them read and understand the article.

gruesome: horrible, repulsive
testosterone-driven: being controlled by the male hormone testosterone
psychically: sensitivity to spiritual or mystical experiences
pathologize: to treat as abnormal
emotive: showing emotion
repression: removing unwanted desires or thoughts from consciousness and leaving them in the unconscious
bulimia: an eating disorder characterized by compulsive overeating followed by self-induced vomiting or laxative use
precarious: uncertain, unstable
self-mutilation: self-inflicted physical pain performed as a relief from, or an expression of, mental pain

CLICK HERE

TIME REPORTS

Visit **www.time.com/teach** for the complete text of this article, as well as related articles on the subject.

Block Schedule

This activity works well for a block-scheduling framework.

ACTIVE READING STRATEGY

Explain to students that as they read, they should evaluate whether the details support the author's thesis. After completing the selection, readers should compare their opinions and interpretations with those expressed by the author.

TIME REPORTS

Is It More Than Boys Being Boys?

Two books examine the emotional development of boys

By HARRIET BAROVICK

UNTIL KIP KINKEL OPENED FIRE ON his schoolmates in Springfield, Ore., in May, everyone thought he was just a regular kid. A little angry, maybe, with a gruesome sense of humor. Mostly, just a boy. But even before the frantic second-guessing over the tragedy began came two books to suggest that boys being boys—or what the world tries to make of boys—may have been a big part of the problem. Michael Gurian, a Spokane, Wash., therapist and author of *A Fine Young Man*, and Harvard psychiatry professor William Pollack, author of *Real Boys: Rescuing Our Sons from the Myths of Boyhood*, argue that boys are in crisis from emotional undernourishment. Though our culture views them as testosterone-driven demons, boys are much more fragile than many adults realize. And that's about all they agree on; where they clash is on the origin of the difficulties and how to avert them.

Both grapple with a universal truth: boys have complicated relationships with their mothers. Pollack, who is alarmed by what he calls the "silent crisis" of "normal" boys, says we live in a confused society in which mothers are afraid to cling to their sons. On the one hand, we ask 1990s boys to be sensitive and expressive, and on the other, we saddle them with the culture's outdated notions of masculinity. The result is what Pollack calls the ever present "boy code"—a stoic, uncommunicative, invulnerable stance that does not allow boys to be the warm, empathic human beings they are. The "gender straitjacketing" starts, Pollack says, during the early years, when boys suffer their first and most momentous trauma: premature separation from their well-meaning mothers. Fearful that maintaining a close connection will result in the shaming of their sons (name calling from peers, disapproval from adults), mothers disconnect, usually by the time their boys are five or six. When boys feel ashamed of their dependence on Mom, when they are discouraged from emotional expression, they withdraw, creatively and psychically. They become lost.

COLIN MULVANY

IRON JOHNNIES: Boys, says Gurian, love the rough and tumble but need attention, too.

Not exactly, insists the anthropologically oriented Gurian, who focuses on adolescent boys. Boys—who are just being who they are—are making a natural, and critical, separation. And by the way, moms cling too much. Boys are more independent than girls at ages 5 and 6. To suggest something is wrong with this is to "pathologize" boys. Indignant about society's ignorance of male biology, Gurian says we're basing our expectations on female models.

One of the biggest problems for boys in our culture, says Gurian, is that adults, especially female ones, need to be educated about "what a boy is." Evolved from hunter-gatherer primates whose main purpose was survival, boys' uniquely fragile brains are not equipped to handle emotive data in the same way girls' are. So boys are by their nature emotionally insecure. At the same time, their several daily surges of testosterone "hardwire" them to be dominant and physically aggressive and to solve problems quickly. It is the job of parents—in particular, fathers or male mentors—to help them resolve this contradiction and channel their natural attributes productively.

Gurian concedes that a solid relationship with Mom is important during infancy and early childhood. But by age 10 or so, boy raising should largely be a man's game, where values such as honor, compassion, integrity and respect for women are handed down with discipline and understanding. The ability to talk about feelings is worth striving for, but boys don't come to it naturally. Besides, there are other, equally important ways of achieving intimacy.

So is there any agreement at all on how to help avert crises? Sort of. Both advise boy-specific nurturing techniques, like engaging in action-oriented activity that will lead to conversation instead of asking direct "How do you feel?" questions.

COOPERATIVE LEARNING ACTIVITY

Finding Evidence to Support or Oppose Hypotheses Organize the class into small groups. Have each group select one of the two articles—the one about boys or the one about girls. Have the group identify the author's hypothesis. Then have the groups find evidence in addition to that presented in the article to support or counter the author's hypothesis. Have the groups prepare an oral presentation offering their support or opposition to the hypothesis using the evidence they have gathered. Afterwards, discuss the basic methods of social scientific reasoning.

What Gurian and Pollack both bitterly lament—and convincingly illustrate—is the peculiar pain, and the potential loneliness, of being a boy in America today. Especially acute are the adolescent years, when boys look hulking and powerful but are in fact needy and terrified. The statistics are scary: adolescent boys are five times as likely to commit suicide as adolescent girls; adolescent boys are 1.5 times as likely as girls to be victims of violent crime; boys are more likely to be diagnosed with attention deficit disorder and mental illnesses; and boys commit violent crime at a higher rate than adults.

Sure, Gurian says, boys can't process emotional trauma as well as girls can, and without proper guidance can go haywire. And Pollack says misdirected rage is a response to emotional repression and to society's message that anger is an acceptable male emotion. The latter argument—like Pollack's overall idea—seems more expansive and more convincing. But either way, we clearly ought to be paying more attention. ■

Surviving Your Teens

Reviving Ophelia chronicles the traumas of troubled girls

By ELIZABETH GLEICK

IN THE LAND OF POPULAR PSYCHOLOGY books, nothing works so well as a bunch of case studies, paired with a lot of enthusiastic word of mouth. The No. 1 paperback best seller, Mary Pipher's *Reviving Ophelia: Saving the Selves of Adolescent Girls*, has the combination just right. Dozens of troubled teenage girls troop across its pages: composite sketches of Charlottes, Whitneys and Danielles who have faced traumatic psychological issues ranging from bulimia to enduring their parents' bitter divorce. There's a girl here for everyone: either the girl the reader once was or the sullen one now lolling about the reader's house listening to Hole. "The book put a name and a face on something I was already sensing," says Annette Davis, a San Jose, California, mother of two, who has given copies of the book to her children's teachers. "It wasn't just about my daughter, though. It was about me. It spoke to something in my experience in adolescence and some of the pain I still carry around."

Thanks to readers like Davis, who are buying the book by the dozens to give to friends and showing up to hear Pipher, a Lincoln, Nebraska, clinical psychologist, speak, *Reviving Ophelia* has become a phenomenon. Originally rejected by 13 publishers, the hard-cover book was published in 1994 by Putnam. The book really took off, though, when the paperback came out last March.

GAIL FOLDA

PHENOMENON: Best-selling author Mary Pipher

Certainly the premise of *Reviving Ophelia* (which takes its title from the doomed Hamlet heroine) is a familiar one. Pipher believes adolescence is an especially precarious time for girls, a time when the fearless, outgoing child is replaced by the unhappy and insecure girl-woman. "Something dramatic happens to girls in early adolescence," Pipher writes. "Just as planes and ships disappear mysteriously into the Bermuda Triangle, so do the selves of girls go down in droves." She decided to write the book because her own practice was increasingly occupied by girls—mostly white and middle class, she says—coping with such problems as eating disorders, depression, substance abuse and self-mutilation.

Pipher's view—and what, no doubt, helps make her work so popular—is that, for the most part, the culture, not the parents, are to blame. Pipher points out that girls enter junior high school faced with daunting magazine and movie images of glossy, thin, perfect women. She argues that pop culture is saturated with sex; violence against women is rampant; and drugs and alcohol are far more accessible than they were during her 1950s girlhood in a small Nebraska town.

Pipher does offer commonsensical, unthreatening solutions. She suggests that parents immerse themselves in their daughters' life and take the trouble to learn about the pressures at school. And through therapy she tries to teach the girls to turn their pain outward: to write their angry thoughts in journals, rather than cut, starve or kill themselves; to get involved in charity work when they feel shunned by classmates; and to remind themselves daily of the ways in which they are valuable and unique. ■

—**For the complete text of this article and related articles from TIME, please visit www.time.com/teach**

ANALYZING THE ARTICLES

1. What is the "boy code"? Do you think such a code exists?
2. **CRITICAL THINKING** According to the books reviewed, what are the crises that adolescent males and females encounter? Are those crises really so different?

Questions for Discussion

Use the following questions for a class discussion after students have read the article.

1. What do both books mentioned in the first article identify as a universal truth about boys? How does each book describe this universal truth? *(Boys have complicated relationships with their mothers. Pollack believes that boys suffer from a premature separation from their mothers around the age of five or six. Gurian, however, believes that boys are more independent than girls. They need a solid relationship with their mothers, but by the age of 10 they need the strong influence of a male figure in their lives.)*
2. According to Michael Gurian, what is a boy? *(Boys evolved from hunter-gatherer primates whose main goal was survival. Their brains are not equipped to handle emotions and they are emotionally insecure. They are dominant and physically aggressive and quick problem solvers.)*
3. According to Mary Pipher, what happens as girls move from childhood to adolescence? *(They change from a fearless, outgoing child to an unhappy, insecure girl-woman. They are faced with media images of thin, perfect women.)*
4. Do you agree with Pipher's analysis of girls' selves as they become adolescents? *(Answers will vary. Many will agree with her analysis. Challenge them to consider what factors contribute to this change.)*

ANSWERS TO ANALYZING THE ARTICLES

1. It is a stoic, uncommunicative, invulnerable stance that does not allow boys to express empathy and concern. Answers will vary on whether students think these codes exist. Encourage students to provide examples to support their positions.
2. For boys, we often expect them not to express emotion and give them no effective outlets for their feelings, especially their feelings of anger and rage. For girls, culture provides unrealistic expectations of what the ideal woman should be. Students should be able to identify similarities in the culture's expectations of what boys and girls should be.

Chapter 4 Resource Guide

SECTION RESOURCES

Daily Objectives	Reproducible Resources	Multimedia Resources
Section 1 **Physical and Sexual Development** Describe the physical development and biological changes that all adolescents experience.	Guided Reading Activity 4–1 Vocabulary Activity 4–1 Section Quiz 4–1	Daily Focus Transparency 4–1 *ExamView® Assessment Suite* CD-ROM Presentation Plus! Software
Section 2 **Personal Development** Outline the changes in patterns of reasoning, moral thinking, and the development of one's identity during the transition from childhood to adulthood.	Guided Reading Activity 4–2 Vocabulary Activity 4–2 Section Quiz 4–2	Daily Focus Transparency 4–2 *ExamView® Assessment Suite* CD-ROM Presentation Plus! Software
Section 3 **Social Development** Discuss the changes that adolescents undergo in their social relationships.	Guided Reading Activity 4–3 Vocabulary Activity 4–3 Section Quiz 4–3	Daily Focus Transparency 4–3 *ExamView® Assessment Suite* CD-ROM Presentation Plus! Software
Section 4 **Gender Roles and Differences** Describe the physical and psychological gender differences of males and females, and discuss how beliefs about these differences influence behavior.	Guided Reading Activity 4–4 Vocabulary Activity 4–4 Section Quiz 4–4	Daily Focus Transparency 4–4 Vocabulary PuzzleMaker CD-ROM *ExamView® Assessment Suite* CD-ROM Presentation Plus! Software

Blackline Master   CD-ROM   Transparency

Block Schedule

Activities that are particularly suited for use within the block-scheduling framework are identified throughout this chapter by the following designation: **BLOCK SCHEDULING**

KEY TO ABILITY LEVELS

Teaching strategies have been coded for varying learning styles and abilities.

L1 **BASIC** activities for all students
L2 **AVERAGE** activities for average to above-average students
L3 **CHALLENGING** activities for above-average students
ELL **ENGLISH LANGUAGE LEARNER** activities

Chapter 4 Resource Guide

Timesaving Tools

TeacherWorks™ All-In-One Planner and Resource Center

- **Interactive Teacher Edition** Access your Teacher Wraparound Edition and your classroom resources with a few easy clicks.
- **Interactive Lesson Planner** Planning has never been easier! Organize your week, month, semester, or year with all the lesson helps you need to make teaching creative, timely, and relevant.

Use Glencoe's **Presentation Plus!** multimedia teacher tool to easily present dynamic lessons that visually excite your students. Using Microsoft PowerPoint® you can customize the presentations to create your own personalized lessons.

Activity

From the Classroom of...

Gary Cockman
Davison High School
Davison, MI

Kohlberg's Theory of Moral Development

Goal: To introduce Lawrence Kohlberg's theory on moral development

1. Assign students to work in pairs. Tell them that they will be part of an experiment.
2. One person will be the experimenter and the other will be the participant. Tell them that they will trade roles later in the experiment.
3. Ask the experimenters to use their index finger and thumb to hold the participant's skin on the bottom of their forearm.
4. Tell them to begin pinching harder as you count to 15.
5. Have the students reverse roles and repeat Steps 3 and 4.
6. On a piece of paper, have each student write answers to the following questions. Tell them NOT to put their names on the paper.
   - **a.** Did you participate in the experiment?
   - **b.** If you did, why?
   - **c.** Did you fully participate or did you only pretend to pinch harder? Why did you make this choice?
7. Collect the papers.
8. Show Kohlberg's phases of moral development and explain each of the six stages. Read some of the responses to question **c** aloud. Have students identify the stage of moral development that best fits the statement.

Psychology Online

Use our Web site for additional resources. All essential content is covered in the Student Edition.

You and your students can visit glencoe.com, the Web site companion to *Understanding Psychology*. This innovative integration of electronic and print media offers your students a wealth of opportunities. The student text directs students to the Web site for the following options:

- Chapter Overviews
- Student Web Activities
- Self-Check Quizzes

Answers are provided for you in the **Web Activity Lesson Plan**. Additional Web resources and Interactive Puzzles are also available.

Chapter 4 Resource Guide

Note: The following materials may be used when teaching Chapter 4. Section level support materials are shown at point of use in the margins of the Teacher Wraparound Edition.

TEACHING TRANSPARENCIES

Chapter 4 Concept Transparencies

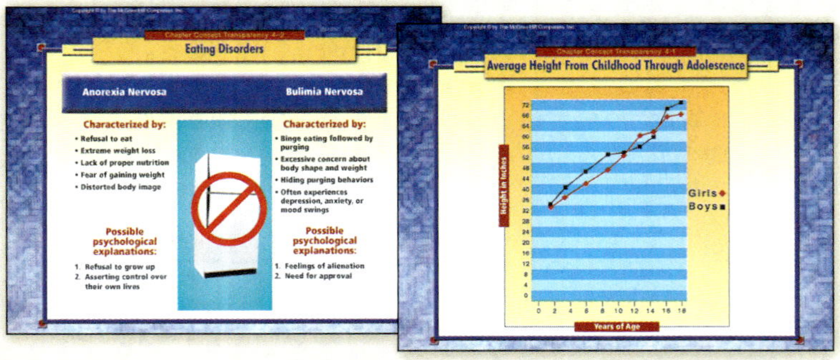

MULTIMEDIA

- **Vocabulary PuzzleMaker CD-ROM**
- ***ExamView® Assessment Suite* CD-ROM**
- **TeacherWorks™ CD-ROM**
- **Glencoe Skillbuilder Interactive Workbook, Level 2**
- **Presentation Plus! Software**

REVIEW AND REINFORCEMENT

Reteaching Activity 4

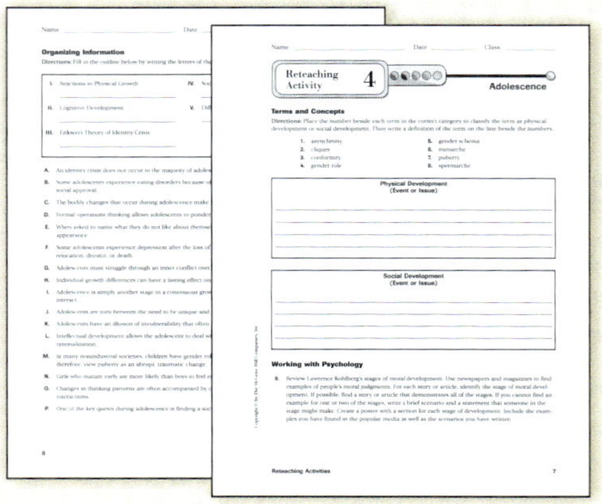

Graphic Organizer Activity 4

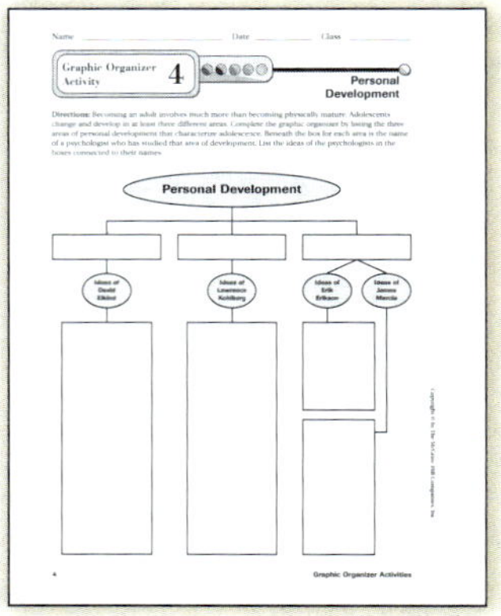

APPLICATION AND HANDS-ON

Psychology Projects 4–1 and 4–2

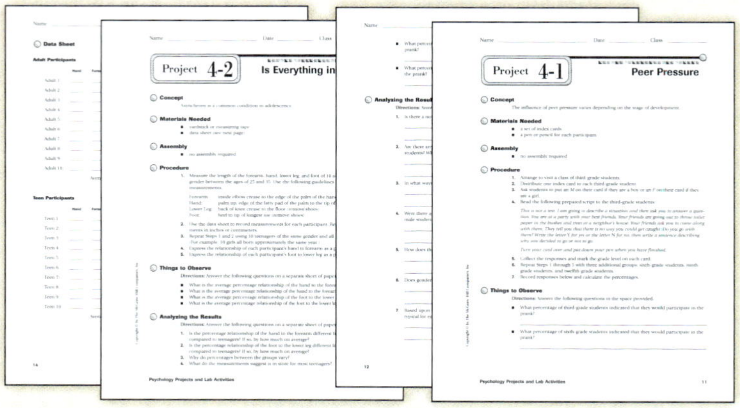

Application Activity 4

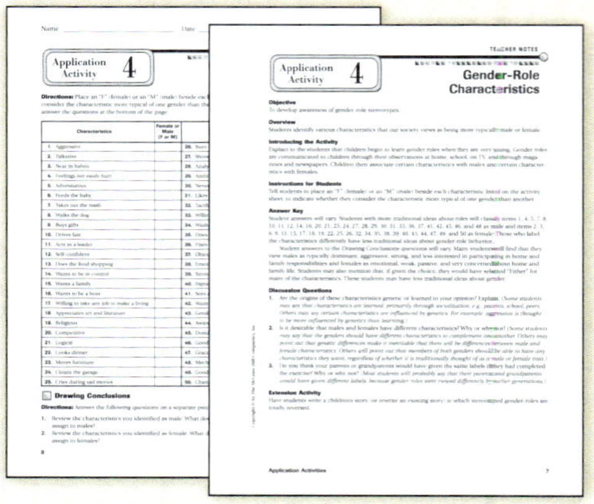

Chapter 4 Resource Guide

Glencoe's Assessment Advantage

ASSESSMENT

Chapter 4 Test, Form A

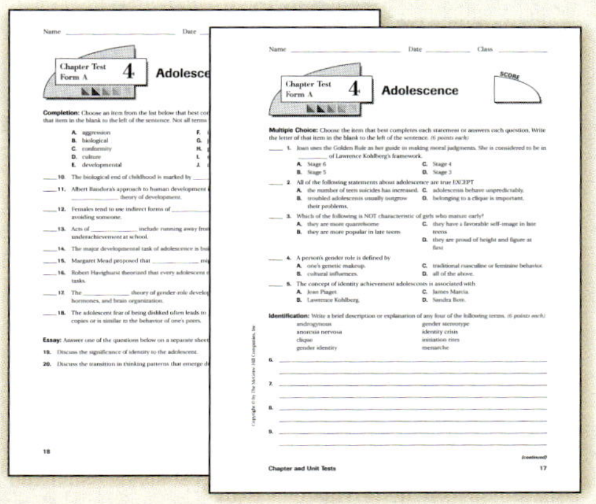
Chapter Test Form A 4 Adolescence

Chapter 4 Test, Form B

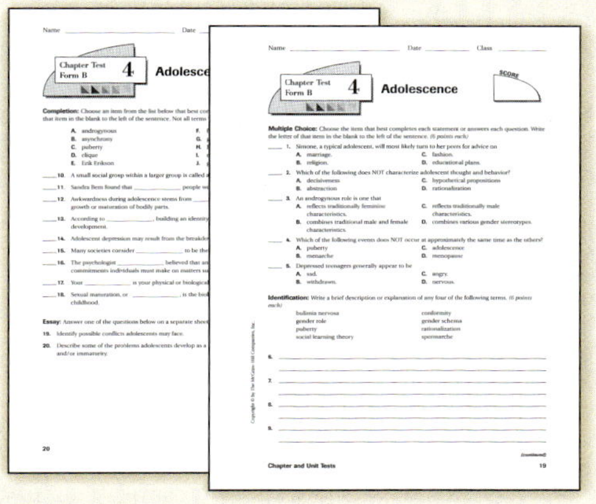
Chapter Test Form B 4 Adolescence

Authentic Assessment Activity 4

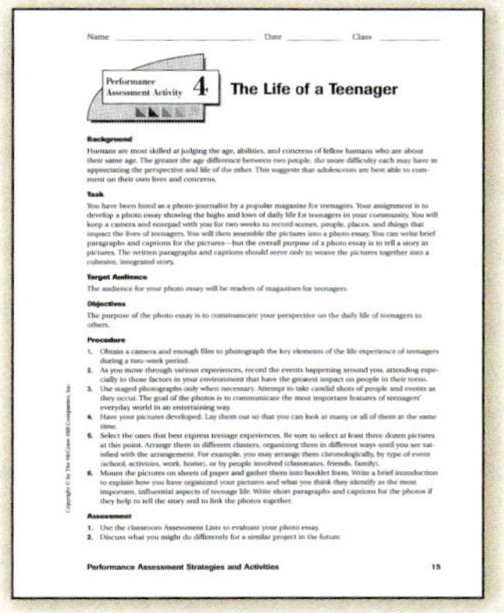
Performance Assessment Activity 4 The Life of a Teenager

EXTENSION AND ENRICHMENT

Enrichment Activity 4

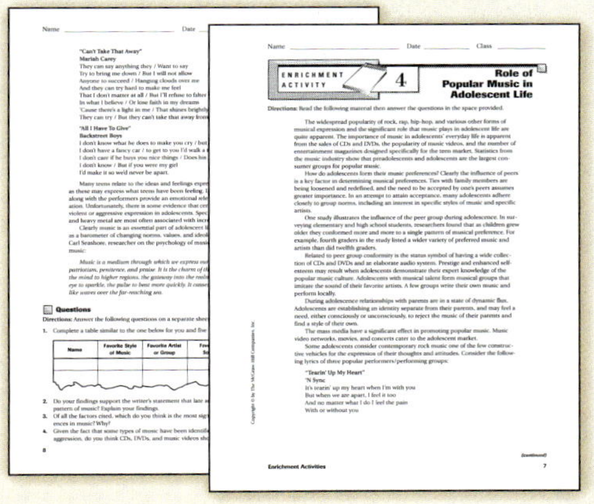
Enrichment Activity 4 Role of Popular Music in Adolescent Life

Critical Thinking Skills Activity 4

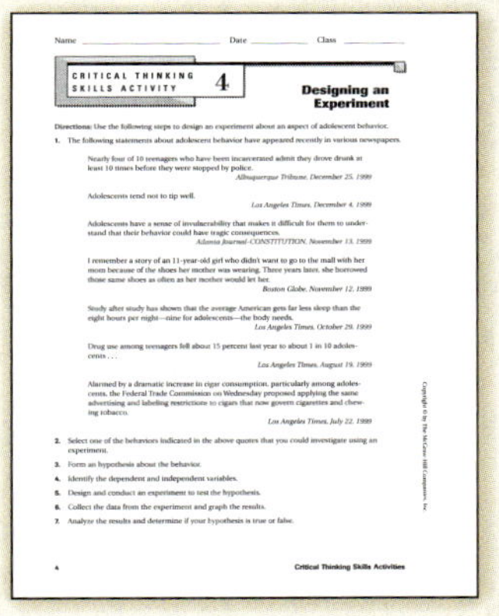
Critical Thinking Skills Activity 4 Designing an Experiment

Psychology Reading 4

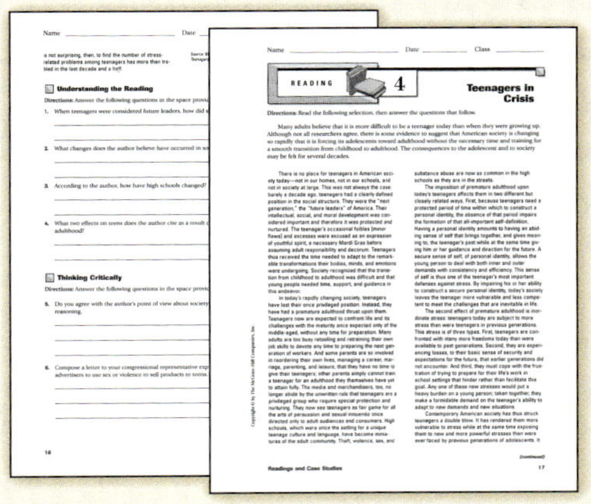
Reading 4 Teenagers in Crisis

Psychology Case Study 4

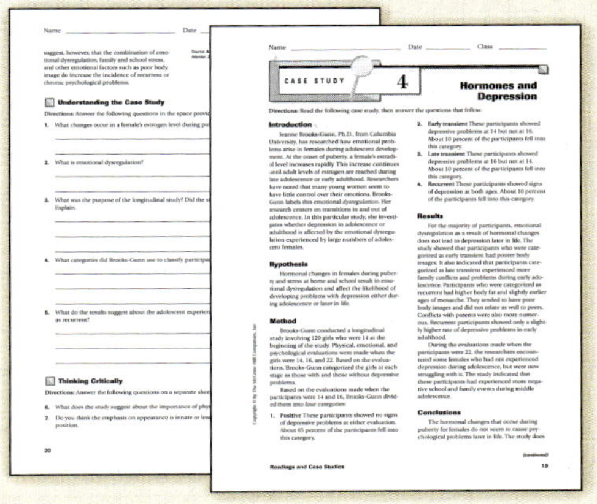
Case Study 4 Hormones and Depression

PSYCHOLOGY Online

Visit glencoe.com for a Chapter Overview for **Chapter 4—Adolescence.**

GLENCOE TECHNOLOGY

Presentation Plus! For a preview of Chapter 4 content, see MindJogger Checkpoint on **Presentation Plus!**

PSYCHOLOGY JOURNAL

Have a class discussion about the types of issues or decisions that teenagers face and how such factors affect personality development.

This journal activity provides the basis for the Psychology Journal activity exercise in the Chapter Assessment. ■

CHAPTER 4 Adolescence

PSYCHOLOGY JOURNAL

According to psychologist Erik Erikson, building an identity is unique to adolescence. Write in your journal two paragraphs that support Erikson's point of view, citing one of his stages and using an example. ■

PSYCHOLOGY Online

Chapter Overview
Visit the *Understanding Psychology* Web site at glencoe.com and click on **Chapter 4—Chapter Overviews** to preview the chapter.

92

TWO-MINUTE LESSON LAUNCHER

Tell students that society recognizes adolescence as a transition between childhood and adulthood. Explain, however, that society's views on adolescence have changed over time. For example, until the 1800s, it was common for boys as young as 9 years old to leave home to work or to become an apprentice. By the mid 1800s, the concept of adolescence as we know it today had become established. Educators began telling parents that adolescence was the time when children most needed guidance to protect them from the temptations of the adult world. As a class, brainstorm transitions that occur during adolescence. Provide students with categories of transitions such as physical, emotional, and social.

SECTION 1 Physical and Sexual Development

Reader's Guide

■ Main Idea

All adolescents experience dramatic changes in their physical size, shape, and capacities, as well as biological development related to reproduction.

■ Vocabulary

- initiation rites
- puberty
- menarche
- spermarche
- asynchrony

■ Objectives

- Describe the physical changes that characterize adolescence.
- Describe research related to the sexual attitudes and roles of adolescents.

EXPLORING PSYCHOLOGY

The Nature of Adolescence

Of all the periods in human life in which the instinctual processes are beyond question of paramount importance, that of puberty has always attracted most attention. Adolescents are excessively egotistic, regarding themselves as the center of the universe and the sole object of interest, and yet at no time in later life are they capable of so much self-sacrifice and devotion. . . . On the one hand they throw themselves enthusiastically into the life of the community and, on the other, they have an overpowering longing for solitude. They oscillate between blind submission to some self-chosen leader and defiant rebellion against any and every authority.

—from *The Ego and the Mechanisms of Defense* by Anna Freud, 1946

As Anna Freud described above, adolescent development is complicated. Adolescence is the transition period between childhood and adulthood, and while we all have an idea about what adolescence is, defining it precisely is difficult. Some define it in psychological terms: a time period of mixed abilities and responsibilities in which childlike behavior changes to adultlike behavior. In some societies, adolescence is not recognized as a separate stage of life; individuals move directly from childhood to adulthood.

In our own society, however, adolescence is looked upon as a time of preparation for adult responsibilities (Hall, 1904). There are many

1 FOCUS

Section Objectives

1. Describe the physical changes that characterize adolescence.
2. Describe research related to the sexual attitudes and roles of adolescents.

BELLRINGER
Motivational Activity

Project Daily Focus Transparency 4–1 and have students answer the questions.

Available as blackline master

Daily Focus Transparency 4–1

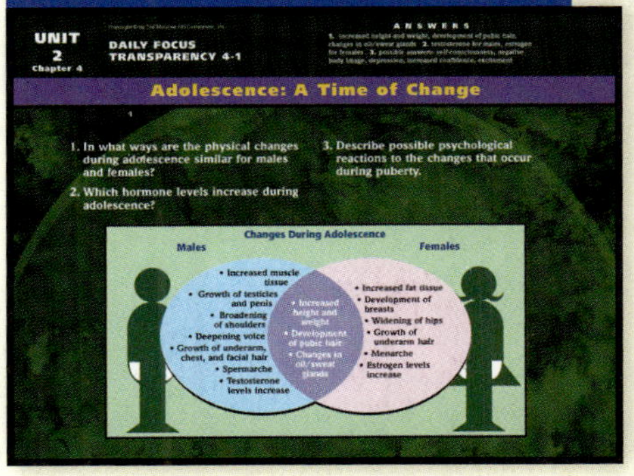

Reader's Guide

Use the Reader's Guide to introduce concepts and vocabulary.

■ Exploring Psychology

Ask students to read the **Exploring Psychology** feature and then discuss: **Do Anna Freud's statements, written over 50 years ago, describe today's adolescents?**

■ Vocabulary Precheck

Have students read the Glossary definition of each vocabulary term. Ask them to restate each in their own words.

SECTION RESOURCES

Reproducible Masters

- Guided Reading Activity 4–1
- Vocabulary Activity 4–1
- Section Quiz 4–1

Transparencies

- Daily Focus Transparency 4–1

Multimedia

- *ExamView® Assessment Suite* CD-ROM
- Presentation Plus! Software

2 TEACH

L1 Exploring Firsts Most students know that adolescence is synonymous with the teen years. They also know that the term defines their stage of life. Few, however, have given much thought to more concrete parameters. Challenge students to think of initiation rites, or events unique to this period of human development (at least in the United States). **Ask: What first-time physical, intellectual, and emotional experiences and changes do young people encounter during their teenage years?** Make a list of students' ideas on the board.

Figure 4.1

Caption Answer The period is often characterized as a period of confusion and frustration that leads to stress.

FYI

Some experts view G. Stanley Hall's *Adolescence*, published in 1904, as the beginning of developmental psychology. His *Senescence* (1922) marked one of the first efforts made to study the elderly.

initiation rites: ceremonies or rituals in which an individual is admitted to new status or accepted into a new position

initiation rites, or rites of passage, that mark admission into adulthood. These rites include informal celebrations such as birthdays—at 16 or 18 or 21—as well as more formal events such as bar mitzvahs and bat mitzvahs, graduation from high school or college, and even weddings. Many of the new burdens of adulthood are assumed just when young people are undergoing complex physical and emotional changes that affect them both personally and socially. The end of adolescence and the beginning of adulthood is often blurry because it varies for each person.

Because so much is happening in these years, psychologists have focused a great deal of attention on the period of adolescence. We will concentrate on some of the major changes adolescents encounter.

THEORIES OF ADOLESCENCE

The contradictory views of society at large are reflected not just in the behavior of adolescents but in the theories of psychologists. Controversy concerning the nature of adolescent experience has raged since 1904, when G. Stanley Hall presented his pioneering theory of adolescence. Hall saw the adolescent as representing a transitional stage. Being an adolescent for Hall, figuratively speaking, was something like being a fully grown animal in a cage, an animal that sees freedom but does not know quite when freedom will occur or how to handle it. Thus, the adolescent was portrayed as existing in a state of great "storm and stress," as a marginal being, confused, troubled, and highly frustrated.

Through the years many psychologists and social scientists have supported Hall's theories, but there have been others who disagreed, mildly (Arnett, 1999) or more strongly. The latter theorists regard adolescence as a period of growth that is in no way discontinuous with the period of childhood that precedes and the period of young adulthood that follows.

One major proponent of this latter theory was Margaret Mead (1901–1978). In a series of classic anthropological studies in the late 1920s and early 1930s, Mead (1935) found that in some cultures, adolescence is a highly enjoyable time of life and not at all marked by storm and stress. She proposed that adolescent storm and stress was a by-product of an industrialized society. Mead proposed that culture might play a role in development.

Other studies conducted since then have tended to support Mead. They point to a relative lack of conflict in the lives of adolescents and a continuous development out of childhood that is based on individual reactions to their culture. In 1988 a report indicated that

Figure 4.1 Adolescence

Adolescents are stuck somewhere between childhood and adulthood. Most adolescents remain closely tied to their parents but spend more and more time with their peers. ***Why has adolescence been characterized as a time of "storm and stress"?***

COOPERATIVE LEARNING ACTIVITY

Making an Introduction Separate the class into pairs, and assign each student to answer the following questions: **(1) Who are you? (2) How would your parent(s)/guardians describe you? (3) How would your teachers and/or employer describe you? (4) How would a good friend describe you?** Direct students to exchange this information with their partners. Have students prepare short statements introducing their partners to the rest of the class. Allow each student to fix any incorrect information. **BLOCK SCHEDULING**

adolescence may be a difficult time period, but only 11 percent of adolescents encounter serious difficulties. About 32 percent have sporadic problems, while 57 percent enjoy basically positive, healthy development during the teenage years (Peterson, 1988).

Although adolescence may not be as crisis-ridden as some psychologists think, few would deny that there is at least some stress during that period. Great physical, mental, and emotional changes occur during adolescence. As psychologist Robert Havighurst (1972) pointed out, every adolescent faces challenges in the form of developmental tasks that must be mastered. Among the tasks that Havighurst lists are the following:

1. Accepting one's physical makeup and acquiring a masculine or feminine gender role
2. Developing appropriate relations with age-mates of both sexes
3. Becoming emotionally independent of parents and other adults
4. Achieving the assurance that one will become economically independent
5. Deciding on, preparing for, and entering a vocation
6. Developing the cognitive skills and concepts necessary for social competence
7. Understanding and achieving socially responsible behavior
8. Preparing for marriage and family
9. Acquiring values that are harmonious and appropriate

Although the tasks present challenges, adolescents generally handle them well. Most face some stress but find ways to cope with it. There are, of course, exceptions. A small percentage of young people experience storm and stress throughout their adolescent years. Another small group confronts the changes all adolescents experience with no stress at all. Perhaps the only safe generalization is that development through adolescence is a highly individualized and varied matter.

The pattern of development a particular adolescent displays depends upon a great many factors. The most important of these include the individual's adjustment in childhood, the level of adjustment of his or her parents and peers, and the changes that occur during adolescence. This time period is marked by major physical, social, emotional, and intellectual changes. It is to these changes that we now turn.

Reading Check How do Hall's and Mead's theories of adolescence differ?

PHYSICAL DEVELOPMENT

Sexual maturation, or **puberty,** is the biological event that marks the end of childhood. Hormones trigger a series of internal and external changes. These hormones produce different growth patterns in boys and girls. Some girls start to mature physically as early as 8, while boys may start to mature at age 9 or 10. On average, girls begin puberty between ages 8 and 10. The age for boys entering puberty is typically between 9 and 16. Just before puberty, boys and girls experience a growth spurt.

puberty: sexual maturation; the end of childhood and the point when reproduction is first possible

CHAPTER 4
Section 1, pages 93–99

Reading Check Answer Hall saw adolescence as a period when the human is making a major transition that involves much storm and stress. Mead saw it as a stage in a continuous process that moves from childhood to adolescence to adulthood.

Guided Reading Activity 4–1

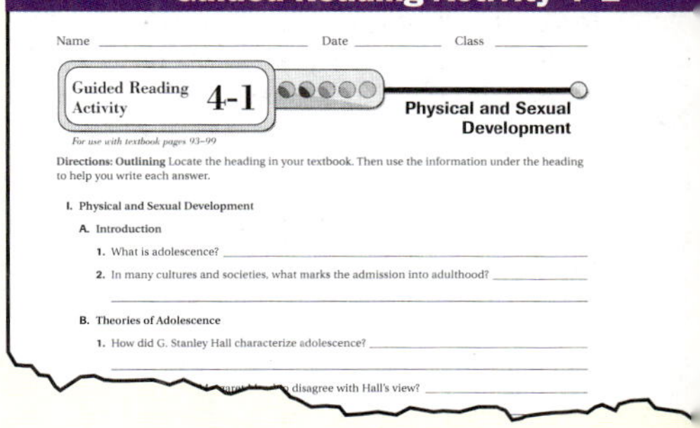
Name ______ Date ______ Class ______

Guided Reading Activity 4-1 — Physical and Sexual Development

For use with textbook pages 93–99

Directions: Outlining Locate the heading in your textbook. Then use the information under the heading to help you write each answer.

I. Physical and Sexual Development
A. Introduction
1. What is adolescence? ______
2. In many cultures and societies, what marks the admission into adulthood? ______
B. Theories of Adolescence
1. How did G. Stanley Hall characterize adolescence? ______
... disagree with Hall's view? ______

CURRICULUM CONNECTION

The Media Assign students to watch at least three different television shows or movies that include adolescent characters. Instruct students to take notes on the decisions or activities that involve these characters. Direct them to pay particular attention to the emotional responses. Based on these programs, ask students whether the media portrayal of adolescence most closely mirrors the picture painted by G. Stanley Hall, Margaret Mead, Robert Havighurst, or a combination of these researchers.

MEETING SPECIAL NEEDS

Learning Style: Intrapersonal Robert Havighurst's research indicated that all adolescents face developmental challenges. Direct students to illustrate one of the tasks Havighurst identified. The illustration may take one of the following forms: a drawing, a series of photographs with captions, a cartoon, a speech, or an essay. **L2**

Refer to ***Inclusion for the High School Social Studies Classroom Strategies and Activities*** in the TCR for strategies for students with different learning styles.

PSYCHOLOGY JOURNAL

Ask students to research their own growth through puberty. Have them write when their growth spurt occurred and how much they grew during that time. Also, ask them to write how they felt during this time of physical growth. ■

Readings and Case Studies in Psychology

Have students read the Chapter 4 Reading selection in *Readings and Case Studies in Psychology* and answer the questions that follow the reading.

TEACHER Tip

Have a class discussion about the pressures teens face in their lives. Categorize the pressures as occurring within the family, among peers, and at school.

Figure 4.2

Visual Instruction Point out to students the dramatic increase in height that takes place during adolescence, which occurs approximately two years earlier in girls.

Caption Answer between the ages of 10 and 14; between the ages of 11 and 16

The growth spurt is a rapid increase in weight and height (see Figure 4.2). It reaches its peak at age 12 for girls and just after age 14 for most boys. The growth spurt generally lasts two years. Soon after the growth spurt, individuals reach sexual maturity. At about the age of 10, girls rather suddenly begin to grow. Before this growth spurt, fat tissue develops, making the girl appear chubby. The development of fat tissue is also characteristic of boys before their growth spurt. Whereas boys quickly lose it, progressing into a lean and lanky phase, girls retain most of this fat tissue and even add to it as they begin to spurt.

Once their growth spurt begins, females can grow as much as 2 to 3.5 inches a year. During this period, a girl's breasts and hips begin to fill out, and she develops pubic hair. Between 10 and 17 she has her first menstrual period, or **menarche.** Another 12 to 18 months will pass before her periods become regular and she is capable of conceiving a child, although pregnancies do sometimes occur almost immediately following menarche. Most societies consider menarche the beginning of womanhood.

menarche: the first menstrual period

At about 12, boys begin to develop pubic hair and larger genitals. Normally, between 12 and 13 they achieve their first ejaculation, or **spermarche.** Though their growth spurt begins 24 to 27 months later than that of girls, it lasts about 3 years longer. Once their growth spurt begins, boys grow rapidly and fill out, developing the broad shoulders and thicker trunk of an adult man. They also acquire more muscle tissue than girls and develop a larger heart and lungs. Their voices gradually deepen, and hair begins to grow on their faces and later on their chests.

spermarche: period during which males achieve first ejaculation

asynchrony: the condition during adolescence in which the growth or maturation of bodily parts is uneven

Figure 4.2 Average Annual Gains in Height

Hormones controlled by the endocrine system can cause dramatic growth spurts; a boy may experience a yearly increase of 4–6 inches (10–15 cm), while a girl may increase 3–5 inches (8–13 cm) in height. ***When does the growth spurt occur in girls? In boys?***

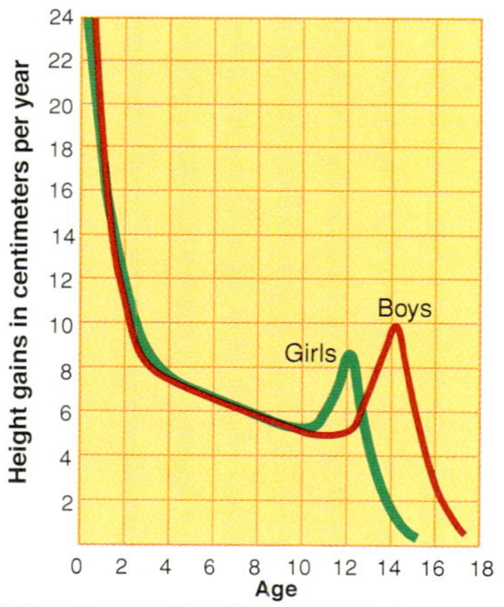

The rate and pattern of sexual maturation varies so widely that it is difficult to apply norms or standards to puberty. In general, however, girls begin to develop earlier than boys and for a year or two may tower over male age-mates.

This period of adolescent growth can be an awkward one for both boys and girls because of **asynchrony**—the condition of uneven growth or maturation of bodily parts. For example, the hands or feet may be too large or small for the rest of the body. As the adolescent grows older, however, the bodily parts assume their correct proportions.

Reactions to Growth

In general, young people today are better informed than they were two or three generations ago. Most do not find the signs of their sexual maturation upsetting. Nevertheless, the rather sudden bodily changes that occur during puberty make all adolescents somewhat self-conscious. This is particularly true if they are early or late to develop.

CRITICAL THINKING ACTIVITY

Making Generalizations Challenge students to draw a two-frame cartoon that captures their opinions on how adults see adolescents and how adolescents see themselves. Remind students of the tools used by political cartoonists—symbols, caricatures, exaggerated features, labels, and so on. Have students share their cartoons with the class. Explore whether there is any consensus among student opinions. For example, how do most students feel that adults tend to view them? Why? **L2**

Figure 4.3 **Rates of Physical Development**

Rapid physical changes occur during adolescence. Normally the changes that occur in adulthood are gradual. ***Why do you think there are psychological reactions to physical growth?***

Adolescents usually want to be accepted by their peers. They conform to ideals of how a male or female their age should act, dress, and look. For both young men and women, there is a strong correlation between having a negative body image and feelings of depression (Rierden, Koff, & Stubbs, 1988). Adolescents are very aware of these rapid physical changes. They are very concerned that they measure up to idealized standards. As you can imagine, very few ever meet these expectations. Most adolescents mention physical appearance when they discuss what they do not like about themselves. Most tend to evaluate themselves in terms of their culture's body ideal. Youths of both sexes are particularly sensitive about any traits they possess that they perceive to be sex-inappropriate. For example, boys tend to be very shy about underdeveloped genitalia, lack of pubic hair, or fatty breasts. Girls are likely to be disturbed by underdeveloped breasts or dark facial hair.

Individual differences in growth greatly affect the personality of young adolescents. For example, research indicates that boys who mature early have an advantage. They become heroes in sports and leaders in social activities. Other boys look up to them; girls have crushes on them; adults tend to treat them as more mature. As a result, they are generally more self-confident and independent than other boys. Some late-maturing boys may withdraw or exhibit deviant behavior. The effects of late maturation for boys may last into young adulthood (Graber et al., 2004).

Variations in the rate of development continue to have an effect on males even into their thirties. Those who matured earlier have been found to have a higher occupational and social status than those who matured later. The correlation weakens, however, as males enter their forties (Jones, 1965).

With girls the pattern is somewhat different. Girls who mature early may feel embarrassed rather than proud of their height and figure at first. Some begin dating older boys and become bossy with people their own

Reading Check How do female and male growth spurts differ?

PSYCHOLOGY LAB EXPERIMENT

Evaluating Stereotypes Students will examine the following research question: **What stereotypes about body image does the media hold?** Ask students to collect pictures from advertisements or newspaper and magazine articles showing the "ideal body type" as portrayed by the media. Have students mount the examples on poster board. Students should survey five teenage friends, asking them the following questions: **What stereotypes does the media hold in terms of body image? Do these stereotypes place any pressure on adolescents? If so, why? If not, why not?** Students should prepare a written summary of the survey results to add to the poster. **L2**

Figure 4.3

Caption Answer Most adolescents feel somewhat self-conscious. This self-consciousness and uneasiness about their bodies may lead to a negative body image and feelings of depression.

Vocabulary Activity 4–1

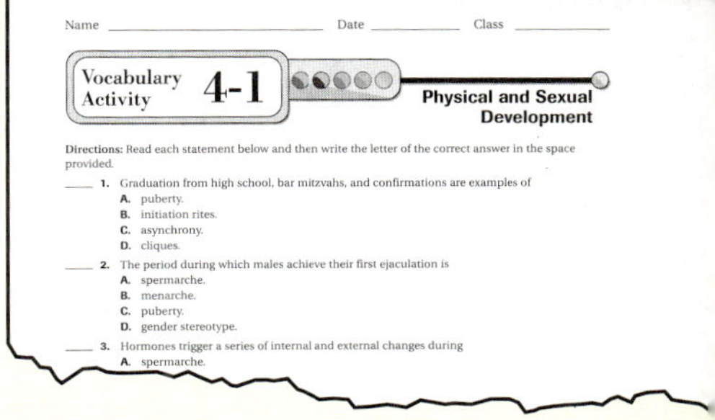
Name ______ Date ______ Class ______

Vocabulary Activity 4-1

Physical and Sexual Development

Directions: Read each statement below and then write the letter of the correct answer in the space provided.

____ **1.** Graduation from high school, bar mitzvahs, and confirmations are examples of
A. puberty.
B. initiation rites.
C. asynchrony.
D. cliques.

____ **2.** The period during which males achieve their first ejaculation is
A. spermarche.
B. menarche.
C. puberty.
D. gender stereotype.

____ **3.** Hormones trigger a series of internal and external changes during
A. spermarche.

Reading Check Answer Female growth spurts generally occur at a younger age, and females retain more of the fat tissue that they had before the growth spurt.

FYI

Upon reaching puberty, many adolescents can grow more than five inches in one year.

Figure 4.4

Caption Answer Increases in sexual awareness and sexual activity have raised questions over the role of family, religion, and government in providing information and guidance about sex to young people. The fear of sexually transmitted diseases and the AIDS epidemic have boosted education efforts to teach young people about practicing safe sex.

3 ASSESS

Assign Section 1 Assessment as homework or as an in-class activity.

Section Quiz 4–1

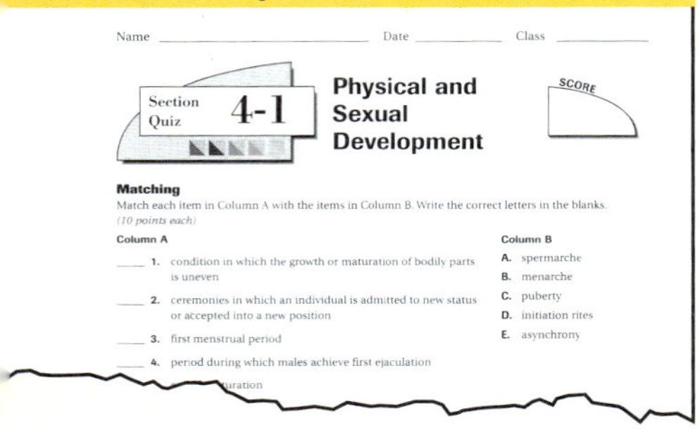
Name ______ Date ______ Class ______

Section Quiz 4-1 **Physical and Sexual Development**

SCORE

Matching
Match each item in Column A with the items in Column B. Write the correct letters in the blanks. *(10 points each)*

Column A
____ **1.** condition in which the growth or maturation of bodily parts is uneven
____ **2.** ceremonies in which an individual is admitted to new status or accepted into a new position
____ **3.** first menstrual period
____ **4.** period during which males achieve first ejaculation

Column B
A. spermarche
B. menarche
C. puberty
D. initiation rites
E. asynchrony

Reteach
Create a chart on the board or overhead projector with a column labeled *Female* and a column labeled *Male*. Have students list the major physical and sexual changes that occur for each. Many of the changes will be listed in both columns.

Figure 4.4 Sexual Growth

During puberty, boys and girls begin to produce higher levels of hormones. Those hormones spark sexual development. ***How have sexual attitudes changed in the past 30 years?***

age. Late-maturing girls tend to be less quarrelsome and may get along with their peers more easily. In their late teens, girls who matured early may be more popular and have a more favorable image of themselves than girls who matured slowly.

Why does physical growth have such powerful psychological effects? According to one widely held theory, the psychological reactions to physical growth may be the result of a self-fulfilling prophecy. For example, the boy who believes he does not meet his culture's physical ideal may think less of himself and not pursue success as doggedly as the next person. His belief actually helps bring about the failure he feared.

SEXUAL DEVELOPMENT

As we noted earlier, adolescence is accompanied by puberty, which is when individuals mature sexually. The physical changes that occur are accompanied by changes in behavior. Adolescence is also the time when an individual develops attitudes about sex and expectations about the gender role he or she will fill. Early sexual maturity and cultural patterns of sexual behaviors have changed from one generation to the next generation. For example, the average age of marriage is about 26 years, some three or four years later than it was in the 1950s and about 12 years after sexual maturation (*World Almanac and Book of Facts*, 2006).

Sexual Attitudes

Attitudes affect the way we feel about sex and the way we respond sexually. Around the world there are wide variations in what children are told about appropriate sexual behavior and how they respond. In some societies children are kept in the dark about sex until just before they are married, whereas in others preadolescent children are encouraged

INTERDISCIPLINARY CONNECTIONS ACTIVITY

Science Assign students to prepare an in-depth biographical portrait of Margaret Mead. Students should mention Mead's contributions to the field of anthropology and explore how this work paved the way for Mead's speculations on developmental psychology. Have students present their portraits to the whole class. **Ask:** **What variable in Mead's research created conditions unlike those addressed by Hall? Given these variables, do you think Mead's studies can still be used as a standard to judge Hall's theories on adolescence? Why or why not? L3**

to engage in sexual play in the belief that such play will foster mature development.

Although middle- and upper-class females who attend college seem to be more sexually active than college females were 30 or 40 years ago, in general in the United States sexual behavior in other social categories is about the same today as it was in the 1970s. In terms of attitudes, however, there has been a change.

The increase of sexual awareness and activity of today's teens has raised many questions over the role of family, religion, and government in providing information and guidance about sex. The Youth Risk Behavior Surveillance Report (2004) claims that approximately 870,000 pregnancies occur each year among adolescents, along with 3 million cases of sexually transmitted diseases. The teen birthrate has fallen steadily since 1991, but teen-related pregnancies and births continue to be societal issues. Studies show that children of teenage mothers are more likely to become teenage parents themselves, to do poorly in school, and to serve time in prison.

Fear of sexually transmitted diseases and the AIDS epidemic have also affected sexual attitudes. The number of U.S. AIDS cases has been holding fairly steady in recent years. At first associated only with homosexual sex and intravenous drug use, AIDS was ignored by many Americans. Efforts at increasing condom use have been successful, though. The use of condoms by young people rose from about 46 percent in 1991 to 63 percent in 2003. (Centers for Disease Control and Prevention, 2004).

Many teens are examining the risks of sexual behavior and deciding that the only safe choice is abstinence from sexual intercourse. *Abstinence* is a choice to avoid harmful behaviors including premarital sex and the use of drugs and alcohol. By choosing abstinence some teens hope to avoid unwanted pregnancies, sexually transmitted diseases, and loss of self-respect.

SECTION 1 Assessment

1. **Review the Vocabulary** What do menarche and spermarche have to do with physical development?
2. **Visualize the Main Idea** Create two flowcharts similar to the one below to characterize physical changes in a male and female adolescent and possible reactions to those changes.

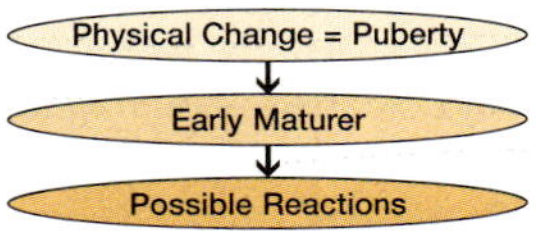

3. **Recall Information** According to Margaret Mead, how does one's culture influence adolescent development?
4. **Think Critically** What are the problems with defining the start and end of adolescence? Why do these problems exist?
5. **Application Activity** Think back over the stages of your life from childhood to the present. Which were the best and worst years of your life and why? Compare your responses to your classmates, and as a class debate whether adolescence is a time of "storm and stress."

SECTION 1 Assessment Answers

1. Spermarche and menarche are the beginning of reproductive capability and are accompanied by physical maturation.
2. Flowcharts should demonstrate an understanding of the physical development that occurs during adolescence.
3. One's culture affects the way in which adolescence is viewed. In some cultures it is a highly enjoyable and celebrated time of life not marked with storm and stress. Only in industrialized societies does the stress seem so pronounced.
4. The start and end of adolescence are difficult to define because they vary for each person. For example, puberty generally begins earlier in girls. The transition known as adolescence also varies from culture to culture.
5. Students' answers will vary. The best and worst years may be signaled by puberty or by other life changes (death of a family member, move, change of schools, and so on). In the debate, challenge students to argue the side that they do not support.

Enrich

Tell students that less than two centuries ago the onset of puberty opened the door to adulthood—marriage, children, and so on. Ask them to consider the following question: **What economic and technological conditions have allowed society in the U.S. to support the adolescent age group?** Have students write a one-page essay discussing their answers to this question.

4 CLOSE

In many cultures, formal rites of passage from childhood to adulthood occur during adolescence. Ask students to list ways in their lives that the transition from childhood to adulthood has been or will be recognized and celebrated.

Going Further

Effect of Early Maturation on Social Interaction

For the past century, especially in industrialized countries, the onset of puberty has been occurring at earlier ages in both females and males. Improved health care and better nutrition are generally cited as the reasons for this change.

One problem for adolescents who experience early-onset puberty is that they have not really finished being children when their bodies are thrust into puberty. Self-esteem suffers, especially in females. Their peers often reject them.

Like most adolescents, those with precocious puberty want to fit in with their peers. Some studies indicate that early maturation propels females to socialize with older, more physically mature adolescents. These relationships make the early-maturing females more susceptible to sexual pressure and deviant behaviors.

Discussing the Case Study

Ask: **Does early maturation tend to be more difficult for females or for males?** Discuss the question with the class. Also discuss the different points of view expressed by males and females in the class. Point out that the endocrine system controls the release of hormones and monitors their levels.

Case Studies

Early Maturation

Period of Study: 1992

Introduction: In 1986 a 9-year-old Brazilian girl, Maria Eliana Jesus Mascarenhas, amazingly gave birth to a healthy 7-pound daughter.

How can a 9-year-old girl bear children? Maria suffered from a hormone imbalance that produced premature puberty, also known as *precocious puberty.* (Sexual development normally begins around age 11 in girls.) For reasons unknown, this disorder tends to affect females more than males. Children who start puberty prematurely are tall for their age because of the growth spurt triggered by hormones. However, since their skeleton matures and growth stops at an earlier age than normal, they never achieve their full height potential as adults.

There are also countless psychological difficulties for the child and parents who encounter this disorder. At the time of her child's birth, doctors estimated that Maria's body matched those of normal 13- or 14-year-old girls. This case inspired psychologists to study the influence of psychological factors on the maturation of females in general.

Hypothesis: Psychological factors, including stressors revolving around family, social relationships, and school, will cause an earlier menarche in some females (Rice, 1992a).

Method: Researchers conducted a longitudinal study on a group of 16-year-old girls. Psychologists assessed the living conditions in which the participants grew up, including the absence of a father, mother, or both; family conflict; and parental marital difficulty.

Results: The study found that females who grow up in conditions of family stress experience behavioral and psychological problems that stimulate earlier pubertal onset, leading to reproductive readiness, as in Maria's case. These stressful conditions caused a slower metabolism, resulting in weight gain and triggering early menarche.

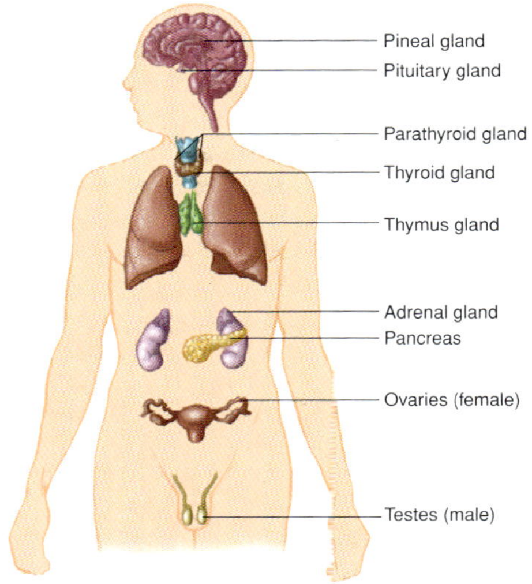

Further studies have indicated that girls who experience precocious puberty may go through periods of moodiness or irritability, while boys may become aggressive. These children may also become self-conscious about their bodies. Treatment for precocious puberty is usually aimed at changing the hormonal imbalance in the body through drug therapy. Psychologically, the behavior of children usually improves, becoming more age-appropriate, as their bodies return to normal development.

Analyzing the Case Study

1. How was a 9-year-old child able to give birth?
2. What are the psychological causes of precocious puberty?
3. **Critical Thinking** What considerations might a psychologist take into account when treating a child suffering from precocious puberty?

Answers for Analyzing the Case Study

1. She suffered from a hormone imbalance that resulted in precocious puberty.
2. The psychological causes include stressors revolving around family, social relationships, and relationships with peers.
3. Students' answers will vary. Psychologists would focus primarily on self-esteem issues. They would also treat symptoms of moodiness, depression, or aggressiveness.

SECTION 2 Personal Development

Reader's Guide

Main Idea

The transition from childhood to adulthood involves changes in patterns of reasoning and moral thinking, as well as the development of one's identity.

Vocabulary

- rationalization
- identity crisis
- social learning theory

Objectives

- Describe the cognitive and ideological changes that characterize adolescence.
- Outline the process by which adolescents find a personal identity.

EXPLORING PSYCHOLOGY

The Tattoo

"I had this tiny butterfly in a circle of roses tattooed on my left shoulder. No one else knew it was there, but I did, and whenever I thought about it I felt happy, like a different person. My mother was furious when she found out I'd had it done, but I think it's really pretty." (Barbara, age 19)

—from *Adolescence: The Survival Guide for Parents and Teenagers* by Elizabeth Fenwick and Dr. Tony Smith, 1994

During adolescence, a sense of identity and self-esteem are very important and depend very much on friends. Barbara's butterfly tattoo served as a statement of identity and made her happy and confident. Also during adolescence, many changes are occurring in ways of thinking and feeling. Becoming an adult involves much more than becoming physically mature, although that is an important part of the process. The transition from childhood to adulthood also involves changes in patterns of reasoning and moral thinking, and adjustments in personality and sexual behavior.

COGNITIVE DEVELOPMENT

During adolescence, the thinking patterns characteristic of adults emerge. Jean Piaget described this as *formal operations* thinking (Piaget & Inhelder, 1969). From about age 11 or 12, most people's thinking becomes more abstract. For example, the adolescent can consider the

Reading Check How does an adolescent's thinking differ from that of a child?

1 FOCUS

Section Objectives

1. Describe the cognitive and ideological changes that characterize adolescence.
2. Outline the process by which adolescents find a personal identity.

BELLRINGER
Motivational Activity

Project Daily Focus Transparency 4–2 and have students answer the questions.

Available as blackline master

Daily Focus Transparency 4–2

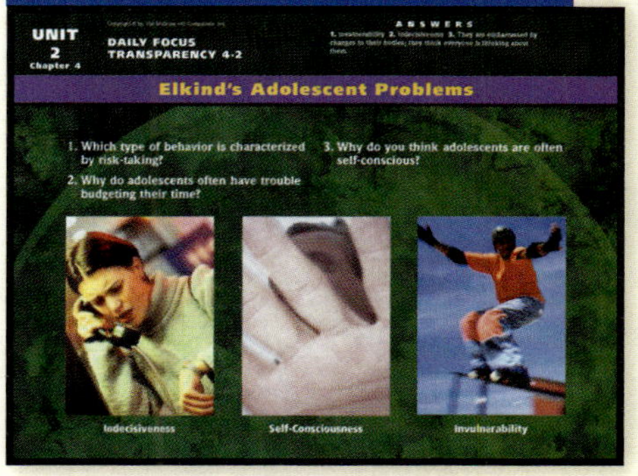

Reader's Guide

Use the Reader's Guide to introduce concepts and vocabulary.

Exploring Psychology

Ask students to read the **Exploring Psychology** feature and then discuss: **What identity statements are common among teens that you know?**

Vocabulary Precheck

Have students divide each term into smaller, recognizable parts. Ask them to define each of the smaller parts in their own words.

Reading Check Answer

Adolescents begin to use more abstract thinking and reasoning.

SECTION RESOURCES

Reproducible Masters

- Guided Reading Activity 4–2
- Vocabulary Activity 4–2
- Section Quiz 4–2

Transparencies

- Daily Focus Transparency 4–2

Multimedia

- *ExamView® Assessment Suite* CD-ROM
- Presentation Plus! Software

2 TEACH

L1 Analyzing a Quote Jean Piaget made the following remark about adolescents:

The great novelty of this stage is that … the subject becomes capable of reasoning correctly about propositions he or she does not believe;… that is … propositions [that are] pure hypotheses. He or she also becomes capable of drawing conclusions from truths that are merely possibilities.

Ask: **How did Piaget explain this new reasoning ability? What examples can you think of in which you could logically reason both sides of an argument? How does this ability expand a teen's view of the world? How does this ability create stress in teens' lives?**

Guided Reading Activity 4–2

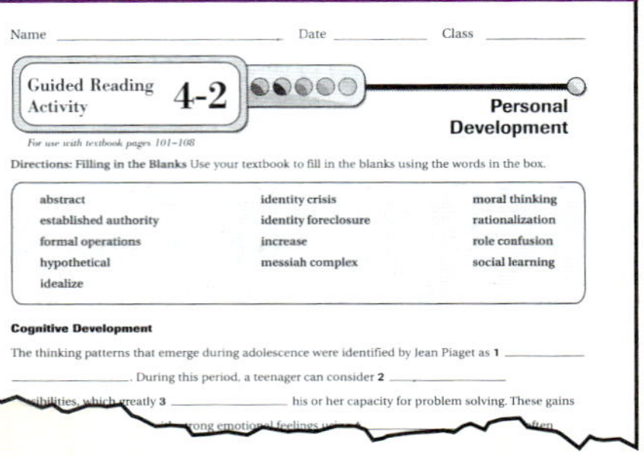
Name ________ Date ________ Class ________

Guided Reading Activity 4-2 — Personal Development

For use with textbook pages 101–108

Directions: Filling in the Blanks Use your textbook to fill in the blanks using the words in the box.

abstract	identity crisis	moral thinking
established authority	identity foreclosure	rationalization
formal operations	increase	role confusion
hypothetical	messiah complex	social learning
idealize		

Cognitive Development

The thinking patterns that emerge during adolescence were identified by Jean Piaget as 1 ________ ________. During this period, a teenager can consider 2 ________ ________ possibilities, which greatly 3 ________ his or her capacity for problem solving. These gains

Figure 4.5

Caption Answer Formal operations thinking expands problem-solving capabilities and allows adolescents to consider their own motives and thoughts.

Make charts w/ examples

answer to a hypothetical question like "What would the world be like if people lived to be 200?" He or she can entertain such hypothetical possibilities in a way that a young child cannot. This ability expands the adolescent's problem-solving capacity. A teenager who discovers that her car's engine has a knock can consider a number of possible causes and systematically test various adjustments and auto parts until she finds the root of the problem. This is the same ability that a scientist must have to conduct experiments.

With comprehension of the hypothetical comes the ability to understand abstract principles and deal with analogies and metaphors. Not only is this capacity important for studying higher-level science and mathematics, but it also leads the adolescent to deal with abstractions in his or her own life such as ethics, conformity, and phoniness. It allows for introspection—examining one's own motives and thoughts. One adolescent noticed, "I found myself thinking about my future, and then I began to think about why I was thinking about my future, and then I began to think about why I was thinking about why I was thinking about my future."

These new intellectual capacities also enable the adolescent to deal with overpowering emotional feelings through **rationalization.** After failing a test, for example, an individual may rationalize that it happened "because I was worried about the date I might be going on next week." An 8-year-old is too tied to concrete reality to consider systematically all the reasons why he or she might have failed.

rationalization: a process whereby an individual seeks to explain an often unpleasant emotion or behavior in a way that will preserve his or her self-esteem

Do all adolescents fully reach the stage of formal operations thinking at the same age? As you might suspect, just as there are variations in physical maturity, so there are variations in cognitive maturity. In general, the rate of mental growth varies greatly both among individual adolescents and among social and economic classes in this country. One study showed that less than half of the 17-year-olds tested had reached the stage of formal operations thinking (Higgins-Trenk & Gaite, 1971).

Differences have also been noted among nations. Formal operations thinking is less prevalent in some societies than in others, probably because of differences in the amount of formal education available. People who cannot read and write lack the tools to separate thought from concrete reality, and hence they cannot reach, or do not need to reach, more advanced levels of thinking (Dasen & Heron, 1981).

The change in thinking patterns is usually accompanied by changes in personality and social interactions as well. For example, adolescents tend to become very idealistic. This is because, for the first time, they can imagine the hypothetical—how things might be. When they compare this to the way things are, the world seems a sorry place. As a result, they can grow rebellious.

Figure 4.5 Introspection

Adolescents display an egocentrism—the tendency to be overly concerned with the sudden changes in their lives. Usually this period of intense introspection decreases as adolescents become young adults. ***Why does formal operations thinking bring about introspection in adolescents?***

COOPERATIVE LEARNING ACTIVITY

Creating a Chart Organize the class into small groups to create charts that give examples of problems adolescents face as their reasoning capacity is maturing. Use the six problems identified by Dr. David Elkind on page 103. The chart should list the problem and then provide examples of typical teen statements and mature statements for each. **BLOCK SCHEDULING**

Some adolescents even develop a "messiah complex" and believe they can save the world from evil. In addition, the adolescents of each generation typically become impatient with what they see as the adult generation's failures. They do not understand why, for example, a person who feels a job compromises his or her principles does not just quit. In other words, adolescents tend to be somewhat unrealistic about the complexities of life. Evidence suggests that adolescent risk-taking behavior may be based in underdeveloped self-regulation (Eccles et al., 2003).

Dr. David Elkind (1984) described some problems adolescents develop as a result of immaturity and abstract thought processes:

- **Finding fault with authority figures:** Adolescents discover that people they admired for years fall short of their ideals and let everyone know it.
- **Argumentativeness:** Adolescents practice building their own viewpoints by arguing any problem that presents itself.
- **Indecisiveness:** Aware of many choices, adolescents often have trouble making even simple decisions.
- **Apparent hypocrisy:** Adolescents have difficulty understanding an ideal and living up to it.
- **Self-consciousness:** Adolescents assume that everyone is thinking about the same thing they are—themselves!
- **Invulnerability:** Adolescents begin to feel special, that their experiences are unique, and that they are not subject to the same rules that govern everyone else. This special feeling of invulnerability underlies adolescent risk-taking behavior and self-destructive behavior.

MORAL DEVELOPMENT

Besides experiencing physical and cognitive changes, some adolescents, though by no means all, also go through important changes in their moral thinking. You will recall that according to Lawrence Kohlberg (whose theory was reviewed in Chapter 3), moral reasoning develops in stages. Young children in the early stages of their moral development are very egocentric. They consider an act right or wrong depending on whether or not it elicits punishment (Stage 1) or on whether it has positive or negative consequences for themselves (Stage 2). At later stages they judge an action by whether or not it is socially approved (Stage 3) or is sanctioned by an established authority (Stage 4).

Many people never get beyond Stage 4, and their moral thinking remains quite rigid. For those who do, however, adolescence and young adulthood are usually the periods of the most profound development. Individuals who progress to Stage 5 become concerned with whether a

More About...

Teenagers and Work

By high school graduation, 70 to 80 percent of students have had some kind of job. Most take low-skilled jobs that provide an opportunity to make some extra money. While most people tend to believe that any kind of job experience is good, especially for economic reasons, research indicates that such work can, in fact, be harmful.

One reason for this is that students who work evenings or weekends have less time to study. If you work, you need to set time aside for schoolwork. Another reason is that students gain a false impression of the workplace from their work experience. The jobs they take tend to be low paying, boring, and unchallenging.

Finally, working while still in school can create false ideas about money. Most students work to pay for luxury items, such as brand-name clothes or concert tickets. There is a danger that they will experience a false sense of affluence because what they earn is spending money, not money to pay for necessities such as food and rent. Realizing that spending money may, in fact, be less available when you take a full-time job will help you avoid this trap.

PSYCHOLOGY JOURNAL

Ask students to select an issue about which they have mixed feelings. They should write about the issue, expressing their feelings and examining their motives. **Ask: How does this process help you reach a conclusion about the issue?** ■

Applying Psychology

David Elkind identified three types of stressful situations: Type A are foreseeable and avoidable (riding a roller coaster, driving recklessly). Type B are not foreseeable or avoidable (death of a loved one, accidents). Type C are foreseeable but not avoidable (exams, the consequences of coming home past curfew). Elkind found that Type B was the most stressful. Have students research which type of stress is most difficult to manage and how a teen's self-esteem affects how he or she manages the different types of stress.

Vocabulary Activity 4–2

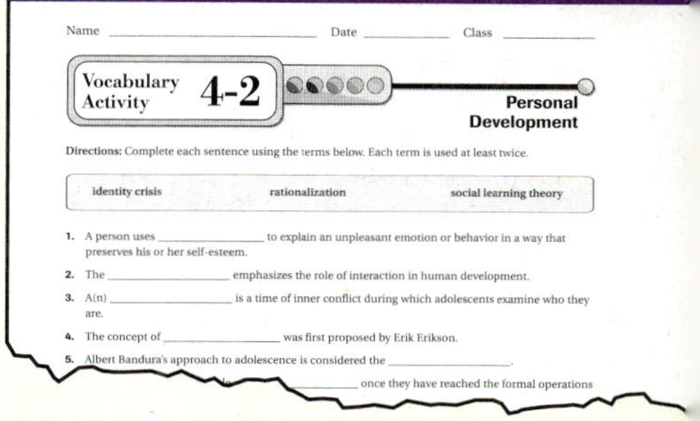
Name ______ Date ______ Class ______

Vocabulary Activity 4-2

Personal Development

Directions: Complete each sentence using the terms below. Each term is used at least twice.

identity crisis	rationalization	social learning theory

1. A person uses ______ to explain an unpleasant emotion or behavior in a way that preserves his or her self-esteem.
2. The ______ emphasizes the role of interaction in human development.
3. A(n) ______ is a time of inner conflict during which adolescents examine who they are.
4. The concept of ______ was first proposed by Erik Erikson.
5. Albert Bandura's approach to adolescence is considered the ______.

______ once they have reached the formal operations

MEETING SPECIAL NEEDS

Learning Style: Interpersonal Organize students into small groups. Have the groups write five different scenarios that involve an identity crisis that a teen might face. The scenarios should be open-ended. Each group should select one scenario to role-play for the entire class. After each role play, the class should discuss possible resolutions for the crisis. **L2**

BLOCK SCHEDULING

Refer to ***Inclusion for the High School Social Studies Classroom Strategies and Activities*** in the TCR for strategies for students with different learning styles.

Quick Lab

Purpose Students will examine how the media portrays adolescents.

Process Skills Analyzing information, identifying central issues, drawing conclusions, demonstrating reasoned judgment

Teaching Strategies
- State the topic to be analyzed.
- Discuss the developmental tasks faced by adolescents.

Analysis
1. Answers will vary. In analyzing other ways to solve the problem, students should use specific concepts discussed in this section.
2. Answers will vary. In analyzing the developmental tasks, students should use specific concepts discussed in this section.
3. Answers will vary. Remind students that the ways in which television characters master tasks or handle conflicts sometimes does not mirror real life.

FYI

Kohlberg theorized that humans progress from one stage of moral development to the next in the same sequence, not skipping any stage or returning to any previously completed stage. Kohlberg's theory seems to apply across cultures. Cross-cultural studies have been done in Britain, Canada, Honduras, India, Israel, Turkey, Taiwan, the United States, and the Yucatan region of Mexico.

Quick Lab

How does the media portray adolescents?
Many television shows feature teenagers as the main characters. How are these teenagers featured? What are their concerns and how do they handle problems?

Procedure
1. Watch a television show that features teenagers as the main characters.
2. List the problems presented in the show and how the teenager attempted to resolve them.
3. Have students role-play the show's protagonists and debate alternative solutions.

Analysis
1. In a report, describe other ways the teenager might have solved the problems or issues that he or she faced.
2. Which of the developmental tasks of adolescence was the teenager in the television show mastering?
3. How well did the television teenager's solutions compare with those of your classmates?

See the Skills Handbook, page 622, for an explanation of designing an experiment.

law is fair or just. They believe that the laws must change as the world changes and are never absolute. For example, an individual who has progressed to Stage 5 might ignore a law to save a human life. Individuals who reach Stage 6 are also concerned with making fair and just decisions. However, they differ from Stage 5 individuals in that they formulate absolute ethical principles, such as the Golden Rule, that they have worked through for themselves. They believe such moral laws apply to everyone, cannot be broken, and are more important than any written law.

Reaching higher levels of moral thinking involves the ability to abstract—to see a situation from another's viewpoint. That is why such moral development tends to occur in adolescence, when individuals gain the capacity for formal operations thinking. Not all adolescents who display such thinking simultaneously show higher levels of moral reasoning, though. In fact, only about 1 in 10 do (Kohlberg & Tunel, 1971). Thus, formal thought, while necessary for higher moral development, does not guarantee it. Interestingly, by the mid-1980s, Kohlberg began to question whether differentiating between Stages 5 and 6 was necessary. He concluded that only one stage—combining the key features of both stages—adequately identified the most advanced form of moral development and thinking.

Overall, psychologists agree that a person's moral development depends on many factors, especially the kind of relationship the individual has with his or her parents or significant others. Evidence shows that during high school, adolescent moral development does not progress much. During college, however, when the individual is away from home more and experiencing different cultures and ideas, more pronounced changes in moral development occur.

IDENTITY DEVELOPMENT

The changes adolescents undergo affect many facets of their existence, so it is hardly surprising that cumulatively they have a shaping influence on personality. Psychologists who have studied personality changes in adolescence have focused on the concept of identity. One psychologist in particular, Erik Erikson, has shown that the establishment of identity is key to adolescent development. His theory of how individuals arrive at an integrated sense of self has inspired a great deal of argument.

CRITICAL THINKING ACTIVITY

Demonstrating Reasoned Judgment Tell students that some people have criticized Kohlberg's Stage 6 because they feel it encourages asocial behavior by recognizing the right to break laws that conflict with moral principles. Ask students to research civil disobedience as practiced by Mohandas Gandhi or Dr. Martin Luther King, Jr. Have students present short speeches in which Gandhi or King offers his interpretations of Stage 6. **L3**

Close

Erikson's Theory of the Identity Crisis

According to Erikson, building an identity is a task that is unique to adolescence. Children are aware of what other people (adults and peers) think of them. They know the labels others apply to them (good, naughty, silly, talented, brave, pretty, etc.). They are also aware of their biological drives and of their growing physical and cognitive abilities. Children may dream of being this or that person and act out these roles in their play. Yet they do not brood about who they are or where they are going in life. Children tend to live in the present; adolescents begin to think about the future.

To achieve some sense of themselves, most adolescents must go through what Erikson termed an **identity crisis**—a time of inner conflict during which they worry intensely about their identities. Several factors contribute to the onset of this crisis, including the physiological changes and cognitive developments described earlier in this chapter, as well as awakening sexual drives and the possibility of a new kind of intimacy with the opposite sex. Adolescents begin to see the future as a reality, not just a game. They know they have to confront the almost infinite and often conflicting possibilities and choices that lie ahead. In the process of reviewing their past and anticipating their future, they begin to think about themselves. The process is a painful one that is full of inner conflict, because they are torn by the desire to feel unique and distinctive on the one hand and to fit in on the other. Only by resolving this conflict do adolescents achieve an integrated sense of self.

identity crisis: a period of inner conflict during which adolescents worry intensely about who they are

According to Erikson, adolescents face a crisis of identity formation versus identity confusion. The task of an adolescent is to become a unique individual with a valued sense of self in society. This issue is never completely resolved. The issue surfaces many times during a lifetime.

Adolescents need to organize their needs, abilities, talents, interests, background, culture, peer demands, and so on, to find a way to express themselves through an identity in a socially acceptable way. Identity forms when the adolescent can resolve issues such as the choice of an occupation, a set of values to believe in and live by, and the development of a sexual identity. The adolescent question is "Who am I?"

Role confusion is normal. It may be the reason why some adolescents' lives seem so chaotic. It also may explain why some adolescents are extremely self-conscious. Confusion is represented by childish behavior to avoid resolving conflicts and by being impulsive in decision making.

Psychology and You: Good Looks Are Overrated

Often our opinions of ourselves relate to our looks. Many people actually think that they are better looking than what others rate them. Also, any social advantages, such as popularity, seem to decline as people mature. This may be because plain people work harder to develop social skills, while their better-looking peers do not receive the automatic attention they once did. Having good looks is not the only way to earn self-respect. Researchers studied a group of boys from age 10 to early adulthood, finding that those with consistently high self-esteem were not necessarily the best looking. The most confident boys were the ones whose parents had set high standards yet showed respect for the boys' own decision making.

Readings and Case Studies in Psychology

Have students read the Chapter 4 Reading selection in *Readings and Case Studies in Psychology* and answer the questions that follow the reading.

TEACHER Tip

Point out that in contrast to the egocentrism of 2- to 7-year-olds, adolescents display what David Elkind calls *social egocentrism.* In this stage, teens overestimate their impact upon the immediate environment. A teen might feel invincible. An example is when a teen falls head over heels in love with someone right away and wants to quit school and get married.

Psychology and You

Use the following question to direct a class discussion after students have read the **Psychology and You** feature.

Ask: **Why do you think the study found that parents' high standards and respect for their son's decision-making ability were more important to self-esteem than good looks? Do you think a study conducted with females would have the same results? Why or why not?**

PSYCHOLOGY LAB EXPERIMENT

Piaget's Pendulum To illustrate thought changes during adolescence, have students compare the ability of teens and young children to complete the following activity. Hang a pendulum from the door of your classroom. Tell students that four factors can affect the swing of a pendulum: length of string, weight of pendulum, release point of pendulum, and force with which it is pushed. Have five teen participants each devise two plans: one to swing the pendulum rapidly, the other to swing it slowly. Next, repeat the process with five children who are 6 to 8 years old. **Ask:** **What differences do you note in the way younger children approach the problem? What differences in cognitive development (Piaget) exist between the two groups?**

L2 **BLOCK SCHEDULING**

Profiles In Psychology

Ask students to read the **Profiles In Psychology** feature and then discuss the following questions:

1. How did Erikson's upbringing affect his choice of a career? *(He did not feel that he belonged because he was mocked by Jewish peers for not looking like a Jew and by non-Jewish peers for his religion. His own experience seems to be a prime motivator for his interest in psychology.)*
2. How is Erikson's stages of development theory reflected in the quote? *(Erikson saw life as a process of continual development. At each stage, humans face different challenges. He proposes that children will be more at ease if their elders share their experiences in facing the demands of the various life stages.)*

FYI

Explain that Erik Erikson came out of a school known today as the *Neo-Freudians.* This is the name given to the theorists who expanded upon and revised psychoanalytic theory from the late 1930s to the early 1950s. Neo-Freudians disagreed with Freud's emphasis on instinctual energy and childhood sexuality. They looked instead for more complex human motivations, such as societal factors.

Profiles In Psychology

Erik Erikson

1902–1994

"Healthy children will not fear life if their elders have integrity enough not to fear death."

Born of Danish parents, Erikson never knew his father. Erik's father left his mother before he was even born. His mother married a German-Jewish pediatrician. Erikson felt that he did not belong. Mocked in synagogues because of his fair features and ostracized by non-Jews because of his faith, the development of an identity became one of the greatest concerns of Erikson's life.

Erikson traveled to Rome as an art student to study the works of Michelangelo, and this experience inspired him to study psychoanalysis with Anna Freud (Sigmund Freud's daughter). The success of therapy convinced Erikson to become an analyst.

Although Erikson never formally attained a degree in psychology, he taught at such prestigious institutions as Harvard and Yale. His work with the Sioux and Yurok Native American groups convinced Erikson that development is a lifelong process. His major contribution to the field of psychology was his identification of a life cycle consisting of eight distinct stages (see Chapter 3).

Marcia's View of the Identity Crisis

Erikson's theory finds support in the work of another psychologist, James Marcia. According to Marcia (1966), Erikson is correct in pointing to the existence of an adolescent identity crisis. That crisis arises because individuals must make commitments on such important matters as occupation, religion, and political orientation. Using the categories of "crisis" and "commitment," Marcia distinguished four attempts to achieve a sense of identity (see Figure 4.6): (1) *identity moratorium adolescents,* who are seriously considering the issues but have not made a commitment on any of the important matters facing them; (2) *identity foreclosure adolescents* have made a firm commitment about issues based not on their own choice but on the suggestion of others; (3) *identity confused or diffused adolescents,* who have not yet given any serious thought to making any decisions and have no clear sense of identity; and (4) *identity achievement adolescents,* who considered many possible identities and have freely committed themselves to occupations and other important life matters.

These categories must not be too rigidly interpreted. It is possible for an individual to make a transition from one category to another, and it is also possible for the same individual to belong to one category with respect to religious commitment and to another with respect to political orientation or occupational choice. Marcia's main contribution is in clarifying the sources and nature of the adolescent identity crisis.

Although Erikson and Marcia insist that all adolescents experience an identity crisis, not all psychologists agree. The term "crisis" suggests that adolescence is a time of nearly overwhelming stress. It also implies that the adolescent transition to maturity requires a radical break with childhood experience. As we noted earlier, many psychologists believe that

INTERDISCIPLINARY CONNECTIONS ACTIVITY

Literature Ask students to read *The Great Gatsby,* paying particular attention to Nick. As they read, have students write down the important events that occur and how Nick is affected by them. After they finish reading the story, challenge students to prepare a 2- to 3-page analysis of Nick's moral development from the beginning to the end of the book. **L3** **BLOCK SCHEDULING**

Figure 4.6 **Adolescent Identity Categories**

Progress in the search for one's identity can be divided into four categories. ***In which category would you place someone who is not actively concerned with his or her identity and is waiting until later to decide the issue?***

	Exploring identity issues	Not exploring identity issues yet
Decisions already made	Identity Achievement	Identity Foreclosure
Decisions not yet made	Identity Moratorium	Identity Diffusion

Source: Adapted from Kalat, 2005.

adolescence is not strife-ridden, but a smooth transition from one stage of life to the next—especially following a healthy childhood.

One of the reasons Erikson may have arrived at his view is that he focused his study on disturbed adolescents who sought clinical psychiatric treatment. When adolescents attending school are selected at random and studied, critics point out that most show no sign of crisis and appear to be progressing rather smoothly through adolescence (Haan & Day, 1974).

Reading Check What is the major criticism of Erikson's theory?

Social Learning View

Psychologists and social scientists seeking an alternative to Erikson's theory have offered several other explanations for adolescent identity formation. A.C. Peterson (1988), for example, argues that crisis is not the normal state of affairs for adolescents. When crises develop—as they do in a little more than 20 percent of all adolescent boys (Offer & Offer, 1975)—the cause is generally a change in the external circumstances of an individual's life rather than a biological factor. Thus, a divorce in the family or a new set of friends may trigger teenage rebellion and crisis, but no internal biological clock dictates those events.

Human development, in Albert Bandura's view, is one continuous process. At all stages, including adolescence, individuals develop by interacting with others. Because of Bandura's emphasis on interaction in understanding adolescence and all other phases of human development, his approach is usually referred to as the **social learning theory** of development (Bandura, 1977).

social learning theory: Bandura's view of human development; emphasizes interaction

Margaret Mead also stressed the importance of the social environment in adolescent identity formation. On the basis of her studies in Samoa (1973), for example, she concluded, like Bandura, that human development is more a continuous process than one marked by radical discontinuity. In that remote part of the world, adolescents are not expected to act any differently than they did as children or will be expected to act as adults. The reason is that children in Samoa are given a great

CHAPTER 4
Section 2, pages 101–108

Figure 4.6

Visual Instruction Discuss examples of teens' decisions, such as career, religion, or college choices.

Caption Answer Such individuals would be classified as identity diffusion adolescents.

Reading Check Answer The major criticism of Erikson's theory is that crisis is not the normal state of affairs for adolescents. Crises that do occur are most often triggered by external factors, such as a divorce or moving to a new school, rather than internal, identity upheaval.

3 ASSESS

Assign Section 2 Assessment as homework or as an in-class activity.

Section Quiz 4–2

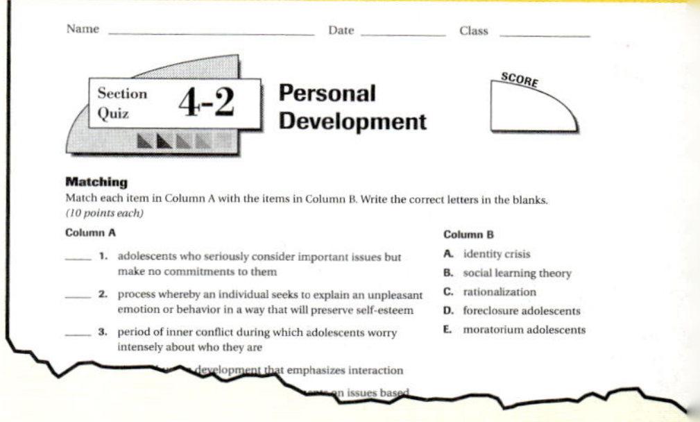
Name ____ Date ____ Class ____

Section Quiz 4-2 **Personal Development**

SCORE

Matching
Match each item in Column A with the items in Column B. Write the correct letters in the blanks. *(10 points each)*

Column A
____ 1. adolescents who seriously consider important issues but make no commitments to them
____ 2. process whereby an individual seeks to explain an unpleasant emotion or behavior in a way that will preserve self-esteem
____ 3. period of inner conflict during which adolescents worry intensely about who they are

Column B
A. identity crisis
B. social learning theory
C. rationalization
D. foreclosure adolescents
E. moratorium adolescents

EXTENDING THE CONTENT

Moral Development In a longitudinal study of adolescent moral development, Nancy Eisenberg of Arizona State University has found that moral reasoning does not necessarily progress in a straight line through stages. The study involved assessing the participants' responses to moral dilemmas over a 19-year period. She found that helpful and selfless responses tended to increase during early adolescence and then level off and decline somewhat during late adolescence. It seems that as adolescents approach adult responsibilities, they reexamine their values and reassess their moral choices.

Figure 4.7

Caption Answer Mead characterized adolescence as a natural progression from childhood to adulthood. During her observations of the children in Samoa, she discovered that Samoan children did not undergo abrupt identity crises with the onset of puberty.

Reteach

According to Erikson, adolescents face a crisis of identity formation versus identity confusion. Ask students to explain the difference between the two sides of this crisis.

Enrich

Divide the students into groups. Conduct a debate in which each group argues in support of one of the five theories presented in the section (Erikson, Marcia, Peterson, Bandura, and Mead).

4 CLOSE

Put two headings on the board: *Crisis* and *Continuous Process*. Have students classify examples of typical teenage events under one of the two headings.

Figure 4.7 Adolescence in Samoa

The Samoa that Mead saw is now gone. Once a place in which most young people came of age with relative ease, Samoa has become a place where young people experience great difficulty in terms of finding a place in their society. As a result, they currently have one of the highest suicide rates in the world. ***How did Mead characterize adolescence? Why did she characterize it this way?***

deal of responsibility. They do not suddenly go from being submissive in childhood to being dominant later in life. Mead also pointed out that in Samoa, as in other nonindustrial societies, children have gender roles similar to those of adults and therefore do not experience the onset of sexuality as an abrupt change or a traumatic experience. The identity crisis, then, is by no means a universal phenomenon.

Personality development in adolescence is a complex phenomenon. It involves not only how a person develops a sense of self, or identity, but how that person develops relationships with others and the skills used in social interactions. No one theory can do justice to all that is involved in the process of personality development. Erikson's emphasis on the adolescent's need for his or her own identity is an important contribution. In adolescence, self-esteem is influenced by the process of developing an identity. (Self-esteem refers to how much one likes oneself. Self-esteem is linked to feelings of self-worth, attractiveness, and social competence.) By focusing on the psychology of the individual, however, Erikson tended to ignore the influence of society. The studies of Bandura and Mead provide needed correctives. To arrive at a balanced picture of personality change and identity formation in adolescence, we must call upon all viewpoints.

SECTION 2 Assessment

1. **Review the Vocabulary** Describe the social learning theory.
2. **Visualize the Main Idea** Use a chart similar to the one below to describe the characteristics of each category of Marcia's identity theory.

Identity Status	Characteristics

3. **Recall Information** What is an example of rationalization and a reason it might occur?
4. **Think Critically** What factors may help adolescents in their search for an identity? How might adolescents discover occupations, religions, or political orientations that are right for them?
5. **Application Activity** Select one of Dr. David Elkind's adolescent problems and characterize that problem in a cartoon or fictional dialogue.

SECTION 2 Assessment Answers

1. The social learning theory states that human development is a continuous process that occurs as humans interact with others.
2. Charts should reflect an understanding of Marcia's identity theory.
3. Students' answers will vary. For example, a student who fails a test says that the test covered material that was not discussed in class.
4. Students' answers will vary. They may list support and respect from parents or other adults, manageable crises, and acceptance by peers.
5. Students' answers will vary. For example, a student could be shown working a math problem at the board and be thinking, "I can't believe everyone is staring at me. Did I forget to comb my hair?" to demonstrate self-consciousness.

SECTION 3 Social Development

Reader's Guide

■ **Main Idea**

Adolescents undergo many changes in their social relationships, adjusting to new relationships with parents and the influence of peers.

■ **Vocabulary**

- clique
- conformity
- anorexia nervosa
- bulimia nervosa

■ **Objectives**

- Describe the role of family and peers during adolescence.
- Discuss difficulties that some adolescents encounter.

EXPLORING PSYCHOLOGY

Peer Pressure

Consider the following situation: "You are with a couple of your best friends on Halloween. They're going to soap windows, but you're not sure whether you should or not. Your friends say you should, because there's no way you could get caught." What would you really do?

—adapted from *Developmental Psychology* by T.J. Berndt, 1979

The situation above was presented to participants from the third, sixth, ninth, and twelfth grades. The participants had to determine what they would do in the situation. The results demonstrated that conformity to peer pressure rose steadily from the third to the ninth grade, then declined with twelfth graders.

Adolescents experience various changes in their social relationships. No longer a child though not yet an adult, the teenager must find a new role in the family—one that parents are not always ready to accept. He or she must also adjust to new, often more intense relationships with peers.

THE ROLE OF THE FAMILY

Families in the United States have experienced marked changes in the past several decades. Prior to 1970, the typical American family had a wage-earning father working outside the home and a mother who worked

SECTION RESOURCES

Reproducible Masters

- Guided Reading Activity 4–3
- Vocabulary Activity 4–3
- Section Quiz 4–3

Transparencies

- Daily Focus Transparency 4–3

Multimedia

- *ExamView® Assessment Suite* CD-ROM
- Presentation Plus! Software

1 FOCUS

Section Objectives

1. Describe the role of family and peers during adolescence.
2. Discuss difficulties that some adolescents encounter.

BELLRINGER
Motivational Activity

Project Daily Focus Transparency 4–3 and have students answer the questions.

Available as blackline master

Daily Focus Transparency 4–3

Reader's Guide

Use the Reader's Guide to introduce concepts and vocabulary.

■ **Exploring Psychology**

Ask students to read the **Exploring Psychology** feature and then discuss the following question: **Why do you think conformity to peer pressure tends to decline from the ninth to the twelfth grade?**

■ **Vocabulary Precheck**

Have students write each vocabulary term on one side of an index card and its definition on the other side, then study their flash cards.

2 TEACH

L1 Discussion Write the following two headings on the board: *Family Influence* and *Peer Influence.* Create a list under each heading by asking students to brainstorm the way each of these socializing agents influences teen behavior. You might also ask students to indicate whether each item on the list is a positive or negative influence. Based on the list, ask students if the family or the peer group has more influence over teen development.

Reading Check Answer
During adolescence, the child learns to become independent of the family.

Guided Reading Activity 4–3

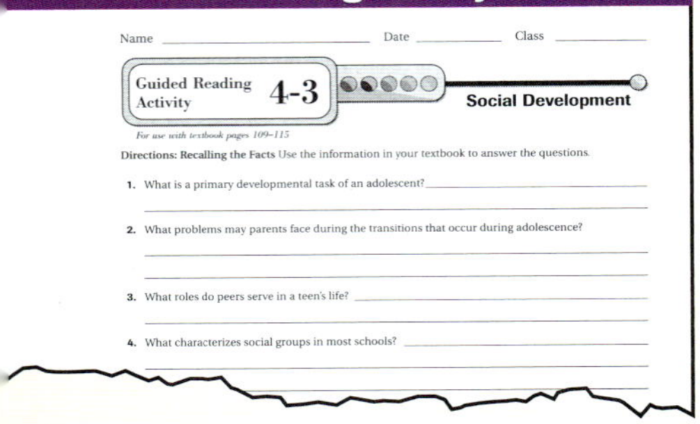
Name ______ Date ______ Class ______

Guided Reading Activity 4-3 — Social Development

For use with textbook pages 109–115

Directions: Recalling the Facts Use the information in your textbook to answer the questions.

1. What is a primary developmental task of an adolescent? ______
2. What problems may parents face during the transitions that occur during adolescence? ______
3. What roles do peers serve in a teen's life? ______
4. What characterizes social groups in most schools? ______

PSYCHOLOGY JOURNAL

Ask students to make a list of the ways in which their parents have been involved in their lives. Then have them make a list of the ways they would like them to be involved in their lives. **Ask: What can you do to bridge any gaps between the two lists?** ■

within the home. Now, almost half of all marriages end in divorce, more than half of all adult women are in the workforce, and the typical family has two wage earners.

Regardless of these changes, one of the principal developmental tasks for adolescents is becoming independent of their families. Unfortunately, the means of achieving this status are not always clear, either to the adolescents or to their parents. First, there are mixed feelings on both sides. Some parents have built their lifestyles around the family and are reluctant to let the child go. Such parents know they will soon have to find someone else on whom to shift their emotional dependence. Also, parents whose children are old enough to leave home sometimes have to wrestle with their own fears of advancing age. Many parents worry about whether their children are really ready to cope with the realities of life—worries shared by the adolescents themselves. At the same time that young people long to get out on their own and try themselves against the world, they worry about failing. This internal struggle is often mirrored in the adolescent's unpredictable behavior, which parents may interpret as "adolescent rebellion." Against this background of uncertainty, which is almost universal, there are various family styles of working toward autonomy.

Reading Check
How does the role of the family change during adolescence?

clique: a small, exclusive group of people within a larger group

More About...
Are Boys in Trouble?

Many researchers claim that today's boys are in trouble and it is time to pay attention to how we are raising them. Why? Let us just look at the numbers. Males die in greater numbers in infancy than females. Boys are far more likely than girls to be told they have learning disabilities, to be sent to the principal's office, to be suspended from high school, or to commit crimes. In adolescence boys kill themselves five times more often than girls do. In adulthood they are being jailed at increasing rates, abandoning families, and are more likely to be the victims of or commit violence.

Some psychologists seek to explain these numbers by proposing that the way we parent and educate boys does not allow them to fully develop the capacity for emotional depth and complexity. As a result, boys are less capable than girls of meeting the challenges of adolescence successfully. In effect, we are not training boys correctly. Their traditional survival qualities, such as physical strength and dominant personalities, no longer assure their survival or success.

THE ROLE OF PEERS

Adolescents can trust their peers not to treat them like children. Teenagers spend much of their time with friends—they need and use each other to define themselves. High schools are important as places for adolescents to get together, and they do get together in fairly predictable ways. Most schools contain easily recognizable and well-defined groups. These groups are arranged in a fairly rigid hierarchy—everyone knows who belongs to which group and what people in that group do with their time. Early in adolescence the groups are usually divided by sex, but later the sexes mix. Groups usually form along class lines. Some school activities bring teenagers of different social classes together, but it is the exception rather than the rule that middle-class and lower-class adolescents are close friends.

Besides class, what determines whether an adolescent will be accepted by a peer group? Many studies have shown that personal characteristics are very important. These studies indicate that popularity is very much based on good looks and personality. With both sexes, athletic ability is also an important factor. Today many peer groups adopt very distinct styles to express themselves.

Belonging to a **clique** (a group within a group) is very important to most adolescents and serves several

COOPERATIVE LEARNING ACTIVITY

Creating a Poster Organize the class into small groups. Ask each group to select one of the following issues as the topic for its poster: teen depression, teen suicide, anorexia nervosa, or bulimia nervosa. For the topic selected, the groups should research the causes, the incidence of occurrence, and the help available in your community for the problem. Ask students to use the research to create a poster that encourages someone who is struggling with the problem to seek appropriate help. **BLOCK SCHEDULING**

functions. Most obviously, perhaps, it fulfills the need for closeness with others. In addition, it gives the adolescent a means of defining himself or herself, a way of establishing an identity. The group does this by helping the individual achieve self-confidence, develop a sense of independence from family, clarify values, and experiment with new roles. For instance, members of cliques may imitate one another's clothing, speech, or hairstyles. By providing feedback, clique members not only help define who an individual is but also who he or she is not: group membership separates an adolescent from others who are not in his or her group.

Of course, there are drawbacks to this kind of social organization. One of the greatest is the fear of being disliked, which leads to **conformity**—the "glue" that holds the peer group together. A teenager's fear of wearing clothes that might set him or her apart from others is well known. Group pressures to conform, however, may also lead young people to do more serious things that run contrary to their better judgment.

Despite their tendency to encourage conformity, peer groups are not always the dominant influence in an adolescent's life. Both parents and peers exercise considerable influence in shaping adolescent behavior and attitudes. Peers tend to set the standards on such matters as fashion and taste in music. In addition, their advice on school-related issues may also be considered more reliable than parental counsel (Berndt, 1992).

When it comes to basic matters, however, involving marriage, religion, or educational plans, adolescents tend to accept their parents' beliefs and to follow their advice (Offer & Schonert-Reichl, 1992). Only in a few areas touching basic values—for example, drug use or sexual behavior—are there differences. Even here the differences are not fundamental and represent only a difference in the strength with which the same basic belief is held. For example, adolescents may have more liberal views on premarital sex than their parents do.

Reading Check Why do adolescents join cliques?

conformity: acting in accordance with some specified authority

Figure 4.8 The Rebellious Teen

Adolescence is often described as a time of children's rebellion against parents. This rebellion is usually aimed at the controls parents exercise over the adolescents' behavior. ***Who replaces parents as a source of emotional support for adolescents?***

For Better or For Worse reprinted by permission of United Feature Syndicate, Inc.

Reading Check Answer Adolescents join cliques to be close to others and to define themselves. Cliques may help adolescents achieve self-confidence, develop a sense of independence, clarify values, and experiment with new roles.

PSYCHOLOGY Update

Emotions and Biology The teen years often bring emotional turmoil. A study published in 1998 used MRI scans to compare the emotions of healthy 10- to 18-year-olds with those of healthy adults. The neuropsychologists looked for differences in activity in the amygdala and the frontal lobe. Teens showed a higher level of brain activity in the amygdala, which is the part of the brain associated with base instincts and "gut" reactions, while adults showed a higher level of brain activity in the frontal lobe, which is responsible for rational thinking and reasoning. Thus, the emotionally immature reasoning of adolescents appears to have a biological source.

Figure 4.8

Caption Answer Peers generally replace parents as a source of emotional support.

MEETING SPECIAL NEEDS

Learning Style: Auditory/Musical Tell students that many songwriters use periods of turmoil or stress in their lives as inspiration for their songs. Ask students to find a song that expresses the transition that takes place from childhood to adulthood or that describes the conflicts that may occur during the teenage years. Have them write down the title of the song, its writer, its performer, and the particular phrases in the lyrics that express the transition or conflict. Encourage students to share their findings with the class. **L2**

Refer to ***Inclusion for the High School Social Studies Classroom Strategies and Activities*** in the TCR for strategies for students with different learning styles.

(*)

Figure 4.9

Caption Answer Adolescents use their peers to define themselves and to find a place to fit in.

PSYCHOLOGY Online

Links and instructional guidelines can be found in the **Web Activity Lesson Plan** at glencoe.com.

Vocabulary Activity 4–3

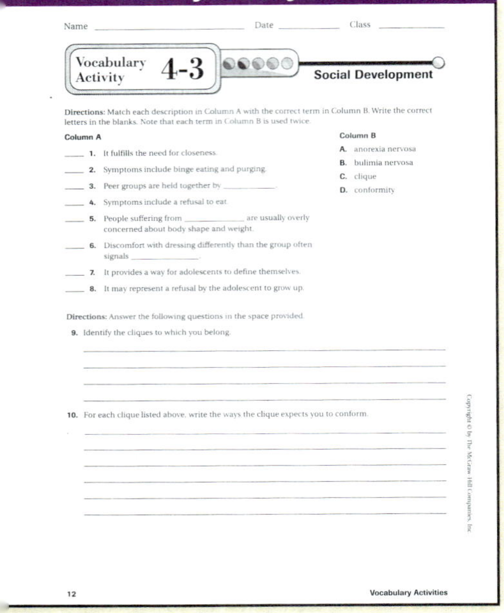
Name ______ Date ______ Class ______

Vocabulary Activity 4-3 — Social Development

Directions: Match each description in Column A with the correct term in Column B. Write the correct letters in the blanks. Note that each term in Column B is used twice.

Column A

____ **1.** It fulfills the need for closeness.
____ **2.** Symptoms include binge eating and purging.
____ **3.** Peer groups are held together by ______.
____ **4.** Symptoms include a refusal to eat.
____ **5.** People suffering from ______ are usually overly concerned about body shape and weight.
____ **6.** Discomfort with dressing differently than the group often signals ______.
____ **7.** It provides a way for adolescents to define themselves.
____ **8.** It may represent a refusal by the adolescent to grow up.

Column B

A. anorexia nervosa
B. bulimia nervosa
C. clique
D. conformity

Directions: Answer the following questions in the space provided.

9. Identify the cliques to which you belong.

10. For each clique listed above, write the ways the clique expects you to conform.

Copyright © by The McGraw-Hill Companies, Inc.

12 Vocabulary Activities

Readings and Case Studies in Psychology

Have students read the Chapter 4 Case Study selection in *Readings and Case Studies in Psychology* and answer the questions that follow the case study.

Figure 4.9 Peer Groups

As individuals progress from childhood to adolescence, peers become very important. ***Why are adolescents so heavily influenced by peers?***

Peer groups, then, do not pose a threat to parental authority. Even though parents spend less time with their adolescent children as the latter mature, their influence is still strong. Adolescents of both sexes tend to choose friends with values close to those of their parents. As a result, these peer groups are of immense help to the adolescent in making the transition from dependent child to independent adult. Thus, generational conflict is not nearly so pronounced as some researchers would have us believe.

On the other hand, psychologist Judith Rich Harris claims that peer groups, not parents, teach children how to behave in the world (Harris, 1998). So, the only influence parents are able to have over their children is by supplying the environment in which they meet peers. She argues that parents should live in a good neighborhood so their children associate with positive peers. Many psychologists passionately criticize Harris's theory. Critics claim that there is a very strong relationship between parenting styles and the social development of children and that the style is more important than the neighborhood.

DIFFICULTIES DURING ADOLESCENCE

As we have seen in this chapter, adolescence is a time of transition. There are many developmental tasks to be mastered, but adolescence is not distinct from other periods of life in this respect. As Erikson (1968) pointed out, every stage of life brings with it unique challenges that are specific to that stage, whether it is old age, early childhood, or adolescence.

Given the great array of profound changes the adolescent must cope with involving his or her mind, body, emotions, and social relationships, it is natural and normal that most adolescents should experience some temporary psychological difficulties. The great majority, however, adjusts fairly quickly. Although some studies show that mental illness and suicide are relatively rare among adolescents, the rates of both have at times been high. Between 1950 and 1990, for example, the teenage suicide rate quadrupled. Since then, the rate has been in steady decline. Suicide figures, however, may be underestimated because medical personnel sometimes label a death as an accident to protect the victim's family.

PSYCHOLOGY Online

Student Web Activity
Visit the *Understanding Psychology* Web site at glencoe.com and click on **Chapter 4—Student Web Activities** for an activity about adolescent development.

CRITICAL THINKING ACTIVITY

Identifying Central Issues Remind students that change is part of adolescence. Ask students to discover the signs that an adolescent's behavior is not just different but is dangerous. Research one of the following difficulties: depression, attempts at suicide or threats of suicide, drug use, alcohol use, eating disorders, attempts to run away, or teen pregnancy. Challenge students to use their research to develop a list of warning signs that indicate that the difficulty may be developing. Have students use the list to develop an informational pamphlet for teens and parents. **L2**

The illusion of invulnerability—"Others may get caught, but not me!"—is a part of adolescent egocentrism. This illusion may lead adolescents to do things with their peers they would not do alone. This troubled minority often "acts out" problems in one of several ways. Acts of juvenile delinquency—running away from home, teen pregnancies, alcohol and drug abuse, and underachievement at school—are typical (see Figure 4.10). Juveniles were involved in 15 percent of all violent crime arrests and 29 percent of all property crime arrests in the United States in 2003 (Snyder, 2005). Repeat offenders and the fact that many offenders are not caught make these data hard to interpret, though. Most juveniles generally outgrow these tendencies as they mature.

Unfortunately, troubled adolescents do not simply "outgrow" their problems but carry them into later life if they are not treated. Adults, therefore, should be concerned about troubled teenagers. It is important to note, however, that unusual behavior should be seen as a more intense form, or a more extreme degree, of normal behavior. It should be considered just a different kind of behavior. For example, teenagers who experiment with drugs—or even become drug abusers—need understanding. By not labeling the teenaged drug abuser "strange" or "abnormal," we can begin to understand his or her psychological needs.

Did You Know?

Reporting Suicides Publicizing teen suicides does not seem to prevent more suicides. In fact the opposite seems to occur—publicizing suicides seems to encourage more suicides. Psychologists are trying to understand why this happens.

Teenage Depression and Suicide

According to Kathleen McCoy (1982), the phenomenon of teenage depression is much more widespread than most parents or educators suspect. To many grownups who see adolescence as the best years of

Figure 4.10 Juvenile Arrests in the United States

Juvenile arrests for both violent crime and property crime decreased over the past decade. ***What factors contribute to juvenile delinquency?***

Types of crime	Number of juvenile arrests	Percent of total arrests	Percent change	
			1994-2003	1999-2003
Violent Crime	**92,300**	**4.2**	**-32**	**-9**
Murder	1,130	.1	-68	-18
Forcible rape	4,240	.2	-25	-11
Robbery	25,440	1.1	-43	-8
Aggravated assault	61,490	2.8	-26	-9
Property crime	**463,300**	**20.9**	**-38**	**-15**
Burglary	85,100	3.8	-40	-15
Larceny- theft	325,600	14.7	-35	-15
Motor vehicle theft	44,500	2.0	-52	-15
Arson	8,200	.4	-36	-12

L1 Demonstration Ask students—voluntarily—to dress in a manner that is totally different from their peer group. (For example, if baggy clothes are popular, dress in a well-tailored business suit.) Have students record the reactions they receive from peers and from adults. Ask students to share their results with the class. Based on the findings, what observations can students reach about the pressure to conform to one's social group? ELL

TEACHER Tip

Suicide is one of the leading causes of death for people between the ages of 15 and 24. Because of this, discussion of suicide is a particularly sensitive topic among teens. You might want to preview this part of the section by first exploring some of the support facilities for suicide within your community.

Figure 4.10

Visual Instruction Explain to students that the most successful programs for dealing with juvenile delinquency are ones that try to address potential problems early.

Caption Answer The primary factors are illusion of invulnerability and peers that are committing crimes.

PSYCHOLOGY LAB EXPERIMENT

Making Observations Have students work in pairs. Each pair will visit a public place where both teens and adults are likely to gather. For 30 minutes, students should observe the number of obvious cliques and answer the following questions for each: **What behaviors or outward appearances identify the clique? What is the age range of the members of each clique? Did you observe more teens or more adults in cliques?** Have students write a summary of their findings and create a bar graph that shows the number of teen cliques and the number of adult cliques that they observed. **L2** **BLOCK SCHEDULING**

CULTURAL CONNECTIONS

Historical and cross-cultural studies of eating disorders indicate that in societies that view the primary role of women as biological (procreation), the rates of anorexia are significantly lower than in societies that value women for their looks. For example, the incidence of anorexia in Arabic countries is less than in European countries.

Figure 4.11

Caption Answer Treatment involves a focus on weight gain and treatment of the psychological causes.

3 ASSESS

Assign Section 3 Assessment as homework or as an in-class activity.

Section Quiz 4–3

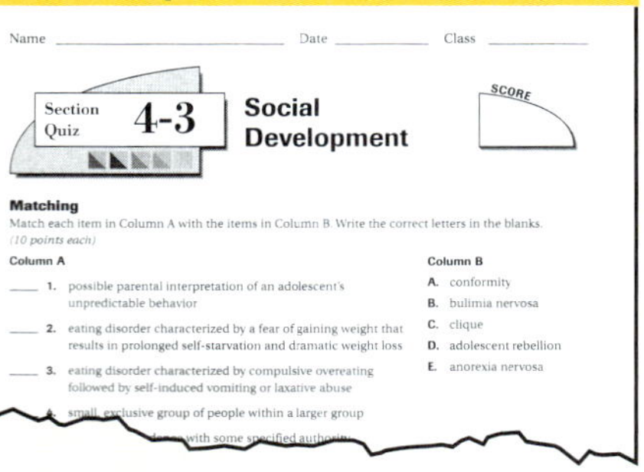
Name ______ Date ______ Class ______

Section Quiz 4-3 **Social Development** SCORE

Matching

Match each item in Column A with the items in Column B. Write the correct letters in the blanks. *(10 points each)*

Column A

____ **1.** possible parental interpretation of an adolescent's unpredictable behavior

____ **2.** eating disorder characterized by a fear of gaining weight that results in prolonged self-starvation and dramatic weight loss

____ **3.** eating disorder characterized by compulsive overeating followed by self-induced vomiting or laxative abuse

4. small, exclusive group of people within a larger group

with some specified authority

Column B

A. conformity
B. bulimia nervosa
C. clique
D. adolescent rebellion
E. anorexia nervosa

Reteach

Ask students to write a summary of the role of families and the role of peers in adolescents' lives.

life, depression and youth may seem incompatible. What events trigger depression in adolescents? One major event is the loss of a loved one through separation, family relocation, divorce, or death. The adolescent may experience grief, guilt, panic, and anger as a reaction. If the teenager is not able to express these feelings in a supportive atmosphere, depression may result.

Another form of loss that causes depression is the breakdown of the family unit, often as a result of separation and divorce. Family members may be in conflict with each other and thus unable to communicate well. Adolescents may be therefore deprived of the emotional support they need.

Unlike depressed adults, who usually look and feel sad or "down," depressed teenagers may appear to be extremely angry. They often engage in rebellious behavior such as truancy, running away, drinking, using drugs, or being sexually promiscuous. Often, depressed teenagers appear intensely hyperactive and frantic, traits that are frequently mistaken for normal behavior in teenagers. McCoy urges parents and educators to be aware of the warning signals of teenage depression and suicide. One warning signal is a change in the intensity and frequency of rebellious behavior. Others are withdrawal from friends, engaging in dangerous risk taking, talking about suicide, and excessive self-criticism. Frequently, the greatest danger of suicide occurs after a depression seems to be lifting.

The best way to deal with teenage depression is to communicate with the teenager about his or her problems. Sometimes a caring, listening parent or a responsive, sensitive friend can help the youth deal with his or her concerns. In other cases, parents and their teenage child may need to seek professional help. This is particularly true when few channels of communication are open.

anorexia nervosa: a serious eating disorder characterized by a fear of gaining weight that results in prolonged self-starvation and dramatic weight loss

Figure 4.11 Anorexia

Anorexia develops over time as a way of coping with emotional stress or pain, unhappiness, or other problems a person may have. ***How is anorexia nervosa treated?***

Eating Disorders

Eating disorders such as anorexia nervosa and bulimia nervosa affect many teenagers and young adults, especially females. Adolescents who develop eating disorders do not get the calories or the nutrition they need to grow. A serious eating disorder, **anorexia nervosa,** is characterized by refusing to eat and not maintaining weight. People suffering from this disorder have an intense fear of gaining weight or amassing fat. Anorexics have a distorted body

INTERDISCIPLINARY CONNECTIONS ACTIVITY

Cultural Life Tell students that *nuclear families* are the norm in industrialized societies like Europe and the United States. In other parts of the world, however, societies value *extended families* made of two or more generations. Assign students to research extended families in African nations such as Kenya or Asian nations such as China. Tell them to focus on child-rearing practices and the roles assigned to people in their teens. **Ask**: **How do you think parent-adolescent relationships might differ in extended families? What other stresses might develop within families?** Have students present their findings in oral reports to the class. **L2**

image—they see themselves as overweight and fat even though they are underweight and thin.

When faced with the pressures of adolescence, some people develop abnormal eating patterns. Some psychologists suggest that anorexia represents a female's refusal to grow up. Girls who develop anorexia typically miss menstrual cycles. Other psychologists propose that anorexia is an attempt by teenagers to assert control over their lives at a time when so much seems beyond their control. Treatment for anorexics involves a focus on encouraging weight gain and dealing with psychological problems. Another serious disorder, **bulimia nervosa,** is characterized by binge eating followed by purging—vomiting, using laxatives, or rigorous dieting and fasting—to eliminate the calories taken in during the binge. People suffering from bulimia nervosa are excessively concerned about body shape and weight. Bulimics usually engage in this behavior in private.

Some psychologists suggest that bulimia may result from a teen's feeling of alienation during adolescence or a need to find approval from others. Some bulimics also experience depression, anxiety, and mood swings. Treatment involves therapy and the use of antidepressant drugs.

Psychology and You: Culture and Body Image

"You've gained weight" is a traditional compliment in Fiji. Dinner guests in the South Pacific are supposed to eat as much as possible. A nicely rounded body is the norm for men and women. All that changed, though, with the arrival of TV. Now, girls in Fiji dream of looking like American stars on TV—skinny. In fact, eating disorders are more common in industrialized countries, suggesting that cultural factors play a major role in body image. Meanwhile, in Fiji, the percentage of girls with eating disorders has increased, and in a 1998 survey a high percentage of the girls stated that they had been on a diet. How does today's culture affect you? What is your ideal body image? Why?

bulimia nervosa: a serious eating disorder characterized by compulsive overeating usually followed by self-induced vomiting or abuse of laxatives

SECTION 3 Assessment

1. **Review the Vocabulary** What are the symptoms of anorexia nervosa and bulimia nervosa?
2. **Visualize the Main Idea** Using a graphic organizer similar to the one at right, identify and describe three difficulties that adolescents might encounter.

   Difficulty: → Causes: → Treatment:

3. **Recall Information** How does the influence of parents over their children change during adolescence?
4. **Think Critically** Why do adolescents form cliques? Do you think cliques serve a positive or negative purpose? Explain your answers.
5. **Application Activity** Create an informational pamphlet on a problem some teens encounter, such as eating disorders or depression. Include statistics and treatment suggestions.

Psychology and You

Use the following question to direct a class discussion after students have read the **Psychology and You** feature.

Ask: Why did American stars affect the way that girls from Fiji viewed their bodies?

Enrich

Ask students to create a hypothesis to explain why publicizing teen suicides seems to lead to more suicides rather than reducing the incidence of suicide.

4 CLOSE

Write the words *Conformity* and *Nonconformity* on the board. Ask students to give specific examples of behavior that indicates conformity and behavior that indicates nonconformity.

SECTION 3 Assessment Answers

1. Symptoms of anorexia nervosa include refusing to eat and not maintaining weight. Symptoms of bulimia nervosa include binge eating followed by purging to eliminate the calories taken in.
2. Graphic organizers should reflect an understanding of the difficulties adolescents may encounter. An understanding of the causes and treatments of these difficulties should also be apparent.
3. Parents' influence, especially over social situations, generally diminishes during adolescence. However, adolescents still want their parents' support, advice, and acceptance.
4. Students' answers will vary. Cliques may serve both positive and negative purposes. They allow an adolescent to grow socially and to form close friendships. Their negatives include blind conformity and rigid thinking.
5. Students' answers will vary. Evaluate the pamphlets based on the quality of research and the presentation of the information.

1 FOCUS

Section Objectives

1. Explain the difference between gender identity and gender role.
2. Describe gender differences in personality and cognitive abilities.

BELLRINGER
Motivational Activity

Project Daily Focus Transparency 4–4 and have students answer the questions.

Available as blackline master

Daily Focus Transparency 4–4

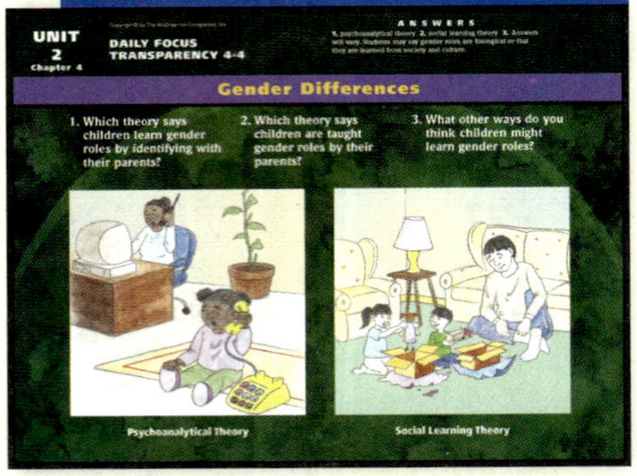

Reader's Guide

Use the Reader's Guide to introduce concepts and vocabulary.

Exploring Psychology

Ask students to read the **Exploring Psychology** feature and then discuss: **What differences have you experienced in the way males and females express emotions?**

Vocabulary Precheck

Have students divide each vocabulary term into smaller, recognizable parts. Ask them to define each of the smaller parts in their own words. Then have them read the Glossary definition of the term.

Use the **Vocabulary PuzzleMaker CD-ROM** to create crossword and word search puzzles.

SECTION 4 Gender Roles and Differences

Reader's Guide

Main Idea

Females and males have physical and psychological gender differences. Our beliefs about what we think it means to be male or female influence our behavior.

Vocabulary

- gender identity
- gender role
- gender stereotype
- androgynous
- gender schema

Objectives

- Explain the difference between gender identity and gender role.
- Describe gender differences in personality and cognitive abilities.

EXPLORING PSYCHOLOGY

Boys Will Be Boys . . .

On the Oceanside playground I watched four boys from Miss Bailey's classroom start to climb up the "dirt pile" at the edge of the grassy playing field. As they climbed and compared the gripping power of their shoes, Matt suggested that they have a "falling contest; see who can fall the farthest," which they proceeded to do. . . .

In gestures of intimacy that one rarely sees among boys, girls stroke or comb their friends' hair. They notice and comment on one another's physical appearance such as haircuts or clothes, and they borrow and wear one another's sweatshirts or sweaters.

—from *Gender Play: Girls and Boys in School* by Barrie Thorne, 1993

Many people just take for granted the differences between boys and girls, claiming that "boys will be boys," or something similar. Pick up a magazine, turn on the TV, or look outside your window—gender stereotypes are everywhere. Some parents dress baby girls in pink and boys in blue, give them gender-specific names, and expect them to act differently.

The first question asked of new parents is "Is the baby a boy or a girl?" Your gender greatly influences how you dress, move, work, and play. It can influence your thoughts and others' thoughts about you. Are there significant psychological differences between males and females? Do children learn gender identities or are they born different?

SECTION RESOURCES

Reproducible Masters

- Guided Reading Activity 4–4
- Vocabulary Activity 4–4
- Section Quiz 4–4

Transparencies

- Daily Focus Transparency 4–4

Multimedia

- Vocabulary PuzzleMaker CD-ROM
- *ExamView® Assessment Suite* CD-ROM
- Presentation Plus! Software

GENDER ROLES

Gender identity and gender roles are two different, though closely related, aspects of our sexual lives. **Gender identity** is one's physical and biological makeup. It is your awareness of being male or female. Thus, if one has a vagina, one's gender identity is female; if a penis, male. Gender identity includes genetic traits we have inherited and may include some gender-linked behaviors as well. Between the ages of 2 and 3, most children learn to label themselves as boys or girls. By the age of 5, most children have learned the thoughts, expectations, and behaviors that accompany their gender role (Biernat & Wortman, 1991).

A person's **gender role** is defined partly by genetic makeup but mainly by the society and culture in which the individual lives. The gender role is a standard of how a person with a given gender identity is supposed to behave and includes the traditional behaviors that society expects of people because they are male or female. For example, in the United States, men were traditionally viewed as dominant, competitive, and emotionally reserved; women were viewed as submissive, cooperative, and emotionally responsive. These traits were considered appropriate for the different sexes. Today young people have a much broader view of what is appropriate behavior for males and females.

Gender roles vary from one society to another, and they can change over time within a given society. Gender roles give social meaning to gender identity. However, not all societies agree on the roles the sexes should assume. Indeed, anthropologists have found that some societies reverse the roles that Americans traditionally give to men and women, while others assign to both sexes what we might consider masculine or feminine roles. Not only do gender roles vary among societies, but they also may change radically within a society, as we are witnessing today in the United States and Canada.

Sometimes gender roles become so rigid that they become **gender stereotypes.** Gender stereotypes are oversimplified or prejudiced opinions and attitudes concerning the way men or women should behave. These stereotypes—that men should be rugged and women sensitive—have their roots deep in a time in our history when a division of labor was necessary for survival. Today, however, modern technology and birth control have freed women from duties associated with child rearing and childbearing for a large part of their lives. Sharp gender-role divisions are no longer necessary or appropriate, especially in the labor force. New concepts of what it means to be masculine and feminine are more widely accepted.

Given these changing standards of acceptable gender roles, psychologist Sandra Bem argues that people should accept new **androgynous** roles—that is, roles that involve a flexible combination of traditionally male and female characteristics. She began her research by asking college students how desirable they considered various characteristics for a man and for a woman. Not surprisingly, she found that traits such as ambition, self-reliance, independence, and assertiveness were considered to be desirable for men. It was desirable for women to be affectionate, gentle, understanding, and sensitive to the needs of others.

gender identity: the sex group (masculine or feminine) to which an individual biologically belongs

gender role: the set of behaviors that society considers appropriate for each sex

gender stereotype: an oversimplified or distorted generalization about the characteristics of men and women

Reading Check How do gender roles differ from gender stereotypes?

androgynous: combining or blending traditionally male and female characteristics

2 TEACH

L1 Categorizing Data Ask students to think of the two most feminine and two most masculine people they know. Have each student make a list of the traits that led them to select these individuals. As a class, compile a master list of feminine and masculine characteristics on the board. Then write the following categories on the board: *Traits Defined by Biology/Genetics, Traits Traditionally Assigned by Society, Traits Assigned by U.S. Culture,* and *Nonstereotypical Traits* (i.e., traits that depart from the traditional norm). As a class, assign the items on the list of characteristics to one of these categories. ELL

Guided Reading Activity 4–4

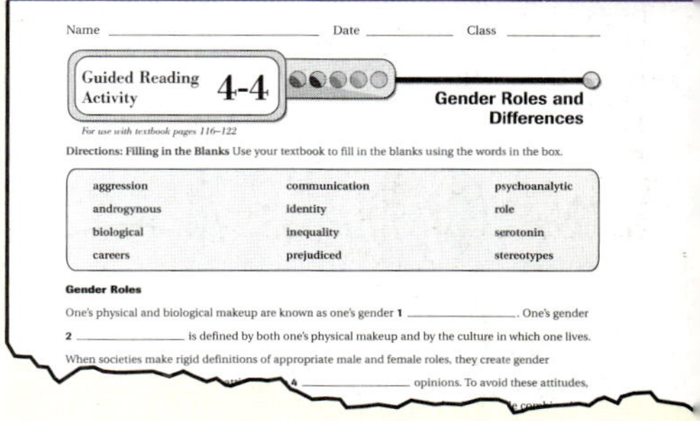
Name ______ Date ______ Class ______

Guided Reading Activity 4-4 — Gender Roles and Differences

For use with textbook pages 116–122

Directions: Filling in the Blanks Use your textbook to fill in the blanks using the words in the box.

aggression	communication	psychoanalytic
androgynous	identity	role
biological	inequality	serotonin
careers	prejudiced	stereotypes

Gender Roles

One's physical and biological makeup are known as one's gender 1 ______. One's gender 2 ______ is defined by both one's physical makeup and by the culture in which one lives. When societies make rigid definitions of appropriate male and female roles, they create gender

Reading Check Answer Gender roles are behaviors society considers appropriate for each gender. Gender stereotypes are oversimplified descriptions of male and female characteristics.

COOPERATIVE LEARNING ACTIVITY

Conducting an Interview Organize the class into small groups. Ask each group to identify someone working in a nontraditional job. Examples of nontraditional female jobs are plumbers, construction workers, and airline pilots. Examples of nontraditional male jobs are nurses, preschool teachers, and flight attendants. Each group should plan interview questions that explore how the person chose the job, what barriers they faced, what prejudices they have encountered, and what changes they have seen in the traditional role expectations since they have been working. Each group should prepare a 2- to 3-page report summarizing the interview and describing its conclusions about traditional and nontraditional roles in the workplace.
BLOCK SCHEDULING

Figure 4.12

Caption Answer Children can label themselves as male or female by the age of two or three.

Applying Psychology

Remind students that schemas are ways of organizing information. As a part of a culture, we tend to share similar experiences with people around us. As a result, cultural schemas arise. Psychological research indicates that American culture has a dominant gender schema. That is, we tend to emphasize gender roles and gender-role stereotyping. Assign students to visit a toy store and find examples of gender-role stereotyping. Have students share their findings with the class. As a class, discuss whether the emphasis on gender creates stereotypes that need not exist.

Psychology Journal

Ask students to write a description of themselves as though they were introducing themselves to a foreign pen pal. Students should review their descriptions and circle every word or phrase that describes their gender. Have them underline words or phrases that describe their talents, temperament, or values. ■

Figure 4.12 Gender Roles

Between the ages of 3 and 5, children gain ideas about which toys, clothes, or activities are appropriate for their gender. ***When do children start labeling themselves as male or female?***

These and other traits were then listed in a questionnaire called the Bem Sex Role Inventory. Bem asked people to rate how each of these traits applied to them on a scale from one (never or almost never true) to seven (always or almost always true). In one early report, Bem (1975) described the results for 1,500 Stanford undergraduates: about 50 percent stuck to traditional sex or gender roles (masculine males or feminine females), 15 percent were cross-sexed typed (women who described themselves in traditionally male terms or men who checked feminine adjectives), and 36 percent were considered androgynous, in that they checked off both male and female characteristics to describe themselves.

In later studies, Bem found that the people whose responses indicated androgynous preferences were indeed more flexible. Such women were able to be assertive when it was required, as could traditional males, but traditional females could not. Such people were also able to express warmth, playfulness, and concern, as could traditional females, but traditional males could not. In our complex world, Bem argues, androgyny should be our ideal: there is no room for an artificial split between our concepts of feminine and masculine roles.

Androgyny is becoming an accepted ideal in our culture. One consequence of this shift is that adolescents who are developing into adults have more choices in the way they define themselves in life. In some ways, this shift toward more freedom in gender roles has resulted in greater personal responsibility. No longer limited by rigid gender-role stereotypes, young people are challenged to define themselves according to their talents, temperaments, and values. At the same time, not all people accept the more androgynous gender roles. Older people, especially, may still be guided by traditional ideas about gender roles.

GENDER DIFFERENCES

Psychologists have found that most people do see differences between genders. Are these differences, though, real or imagined? Are these differences the result of cultural stereotypes, or do they show up in the actual behaviors of boys and girls?

Gender Differences in Personality

Are there differences between the sexes? Studies have found that besides the obvious physical differences, differences between males and females do exist. It is important to note that these differences, though, exist between groups of males and females. Individuals may or may not exhibit these differences.

One study (Mednick & Thomas, 1993) found that males are more confident than females, especially in academic areas or in tasks stereotyped as masculine, such as math and science. Even when they achieve the same

MEETING SPECIAL NEEDS

Learning Style: Intrapersonal Ask students to make a list of all the careers or professions in which they have some interest. Encourage them to list at least three different careers or professions and use the Internet to research gender questions. They should find answers to questions such as **How many people are employed in this field? What percentage are women? Men? Who are the best-known people in the career or profession? Are they primarily one gender?** Have students write a summary of each career or profession. **L2**

Refer to ***Inclusion for the High School Social Studies Classroom Strategies and Activities*** in the TCR for strategies for students with different learning styles.

grades as men, women perceive themselves as less competent than males. The self-confidence of females rises, though, when they perform tasks in which they receive clear and direct feedback on their performance, especially that which they complete alone.

Many studies have also found that aggression is one of the areas with the most significant differences between genders. (*Aggression* refers to hostile or destructive behavior.) Females engage in more verbal aggressive acts, while males participate in more physical aggression (Turner & Gervai, 1995). Some researchers propose that women also think differently about aggression (Kendrick, 1987). The women studied said they feel guilty or have more anxiety about the dangers involved in aggressive behavior.

Differences in aggressive behavior can be observed by watching children at play. Whereas males are more likely to use mock fighting and rough and tumble play, females tend to use indirect forms of aggression. This may include such things as talking about or rejecting, ignoring, or avoiding the target of aggression (Bjorkqvist, Lagerspetz, & Kaukianen, 1992).

What causes this physical aggression in boys? Starting at an early age, society encourages boys to be competitive and to settle conflicts through aggression. Evidence from studies of identical twins also indicates that men have lower levels of the neurotransmitter serotonin than women (Berman, Tracy, & Coccaro, 1997). Lower levels of serotonin have been associated with higher levels of aggression.

Another gender difference can often be detected in male and female communication styles. Although many popular stereotypes portray women as more talkative, studies have demonstrated that men actually talk more than women and interrupt women more while they are talking. Women talk more, though, when they have power in a relationship. Females are more likely to use *hedges* in speech, such as "kind of" or "you know." Women also use more *disclaimers*, such as "I may be wrong" or "I'm not sure." Finally, women use more *tag questions* at the end of sentences, such as "Okay?" (Lakoff, 1973; McMillan et al., 1977).

As far as nonverbal communication goes, women are more likely to show submission and warmth, whereas men display more dominance and status. More women than men, though, are sensitive to nonverbal cues (Briton & Hall, 1995).

Gender Differences in Cognitive Abilities

You may have heard someone claim that females are better than males at verbal skills, while males excel at spatial and mathematical skills. Janet Hyde and Marcia Linn (1988) examined 165 studies on verbal ability, finding that no measurable differences in verbal skills exist between males and females. If differences exist, they are relatively small. When researchers examined mathematical ability, they discovered no significant differences between male and female abilities.

Figure 4.13 Gender in the Media

The media often target specific genders using stereotypes in their advertisements. This may help children form their ideals of what it means to be a male or female. ***How might this doll advertisement reinforce gender stereotypes?***

CHAPTER 4
Section 4, pages 116–122

L1 Discussion Begin with the line from David Bowie's song *Rebel, Rebel:* "Your parents can't tell if you're a boy or a girl." Have a class discussion about the blur of gender among teenagers who adopt a nonsexed type look in clothing or appearance. **Ask: (1) How is nonsexed type appearance a form of social rebellion? (2) According to Sandra Bem, what are some of the traits of androgynous people? (3) Do you agree with Bem that "androgyny should be our ideal"? Why or why not?**

Vocabulary Activity 4–4

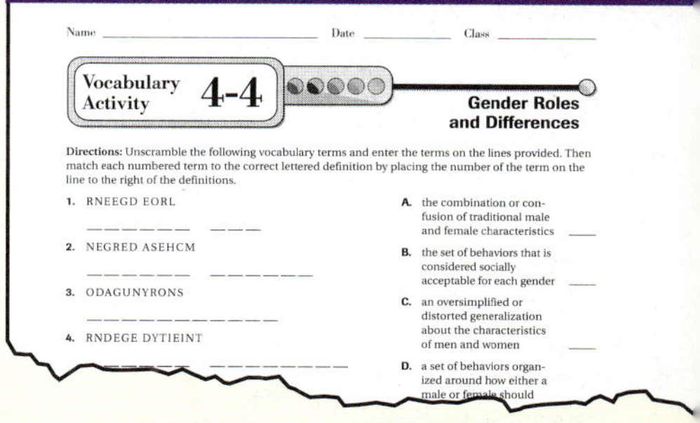

Name ______ Date ______ Class ______

Vocabulary Activity 4-4

Gender Roles and Differences

Directions: Unscramble the following vocabulary terms and enter the terms on the lines provided. Then match each numbered term to the correct lettered definition by placing the number of the term on the line to the right of the definitions.

1. RNEEGD EORL
2. NEGRED ASEHCM
3. ODAGUNYRONS
4. RNDEGE DYTIEINT

A. the combination or confusion of traditional male and female characteristics ____
B. the set of behaviors that is considered socially acceptable for each gender ____
C. an oversimplified or distorted generalization about the characteristics of men and women ____
D. a set of behaviors organized around how either a male or female should

Figure 4.13

Caption Answer This advertisement reinforces gender stereotypes by selling and glamorizing a doll that is dressed in very feminine clothes and wearing jewelry.

CRITICAL THINKING ACTIVITY

Making Generalizations Ask students to select a strong emotion such as anger or love. Have them draw a two-panel cartoon, one showing a male exhibiting the emotion and one showing a female exhibiting the same emotion. Display the cartoons and allow students time to view them. Discuss the gender differences in expressing emotions. **Ask: How do you think these behaviors are influenced by culture? How do you think genetic differences influence these behaviors? Do you think the expression of emotion varies among cultures? Students should provide examples in their answers. L2**

Figure 4.14

Caption Answer This cartoonist shows her opinion that some men are very practical, while some women are more sensitive and concerned about routine tasks such as shopping.

TEACHER Tip

Explain to students that the words *sex* and *gender* are often used interchangeably. Sex refers to the innate, biological differences that exist between males and females. Gender refers to the learned behaviors and psychological consequences that result from the biological differences.

Looking @ the Issues

Management and Gender Studies have found that female managers tend to be more results-oriented, while men tend to focus more on analysis and strategic planning. Female managers are consistently rated higher in empathy, people skills, and collaborative working skills. Male managers rate more highly on overall decision making, understanding of organization dynamics, and ability to perform financial analysis. **Ask: Do men and women have different management styles? How could personality differences explain these differing management styles? Do social role expectations explain, to some degree, the differences in management styles?**

Figure 4.14 Gender and Personality

Girls are often described as concerned, sensitive, and nurturing; boys are viewed as controlling, aggressive, and independent. ***How does this cartoon depict gender differences?***

When researchers examine specific topics and age trends, some differences do appear. For example, males and females perform about the same in problem solving until high school. At that point, males outperform females. Men also tend to do better than females on tests of spatial ability; however, women are better at tracking objects (see Figure 4.15).

In conclusion, there are very few cognitive differences between males and females. The studies mentioned above should not limit the participation of males and females in specific areas, or be used as a basis for discrimination. The studies fail to reflect individual differences of ability and do not reflect an individual's motivations, past history, and ambitions.

ORIGINS OF GENDER DIFFERENCES

How do differences in gender develop? How gender differences develop is one of the many questions that falls into the nature versus nurture issue. While some argue that differences between sexes are biological, others propose that we learn gender differences from our environment. Today most psychologists agree that nature and nurture interact to influence gender differences.

Biological Theory

The biological theory of gender role development emphasizes the role of anatomy, hormones, and brain organization. Supporters of this theory point out that regardless of what parents do, boys seem to prefer trucks, while girls prefer to play with dolls.

Supporters of this idea claim that differences in gender are the result of behaviors that evolved from early men and women. That is, men and women adopted certain behaviors throughout time in an attempt to

PSYCHOLOGY LAB EXPERIMENT

Making Observations Have students work in groups to conduct two types of observations. First, they should spend 30 minutes in a busy public place observing the way adults treat young boys and girls. Have students record behavior that reinforces or departs from traditional gender roles. Then, the group should spend 30 minutes observing interactions among male and female teenagers, recording the same types of behavior. The groups should prepare a report analyzing the behaviors noted during both observations to determine which was more prevalent—traditional or nontraditional gender roles. The analysis should also draw conclusions about any links between behavior taught to children and the behavior of teens. **L2** **BLOCK SCHEDULING**

survive. For example, men increased their chances of finding a mate and reproducing by adopting dominant and aggressive traits, while women increased their chances of raising children by being concerned, warm, and sensitive. Therefore, certain genetic or biological traits were formed in men and women (Archer, 1997).

Psychoanalytical Theory

According to Sigmund Freud, when a child identifies with a parent of the same sex, gender identity results. Little boys identify with their fathers, while girls identify with their mothers. This identification process occurs when children are between 3 and 5 years of age. Critics argue that identification seems to be the result, rather than the cause, of gender typing (Maccoby, 1992).

Social Learning Theory

The social learning theory emphasizes the role of social and cognitive processes on how we perceive, organize, and use information. For example, children learn their gender roles by observing and imitating models, such as their parents, friends, peers, and teachers. These models respond to and reward certain behaviors in boys and different behaviors in girls.

For example, parents may buy rugged toy trucks for boys and soft dolls for girls. Parents may punish a girl for being outspoken and reward her for completing household chores. Parents may encourage a boy's high ambitions and independence. In effect, these parents are rewarding or discouraging behaviors, depending on whether these behaviors match their views of traditional male and female gender roles.

Cognitive-Developmental Theory

The cognitive-developmental theory proposes that children acquire gender roles by interacting with their environment and thinking about those experiences. As they do this, children learn different sets of standards for male and female behavior (Bem, 1981).

To learn about gender, a child must first see himself or herself as male or female. Then the child begins to organize behavior around this

Figure 4.15 Test Yourself

Test A: Which two figures on the right are the same as the figure on the left? (Answers at bottom.)

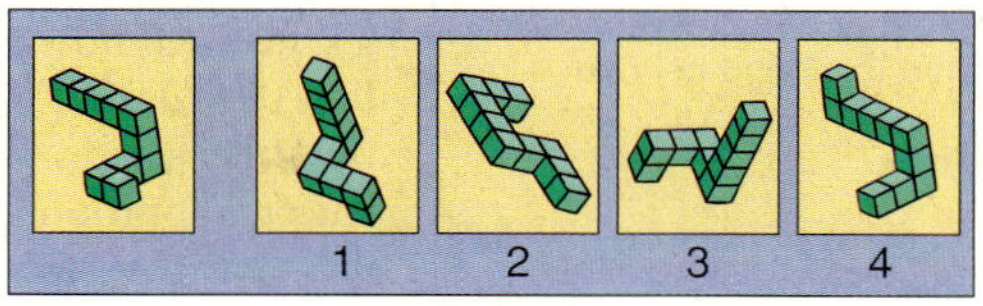

Test B: Cover the bottom box. Carefully study the top box for 1 minute. Then cover the top box, uncover the bottom box, and follow the instructions below.

Now note each item that remains in its original spot and each item that has been moved.

Source: Shepard & Metzler, 1971.

Answer to Test A: Figures 1 and 3 are the same as the figure on the left.

When it comes to spatial abilities, some argue that women are better than men at tracking objects and that men are better at forming "mental maps." In these tests, most men would find Test A easier, while most women find Test B easier. ***How might biological theories explain gender differences of spatial ability?***

L2 Classifying Information
Explain that psychologists are still researching the interplay between nature and nurture as it relates to gender identification. List the major theories that explain gender differences on the board. Display pictures from popular media showing males and females interacting in various ways. Ask students to use each of the theories to explain the male's or female's behavior.

Figure 4.15

Visual Instruction Tell students that the statements about the spatial ability of men and women are generalizations. They should not be used to limit the participation of males and females in certain activities.

Caption Answer Differences in spatial ability evolved from early men and women. Men needed to know the lay of the land to hunt and, therefore, developed a good sense of spatial ability.

3 ASSESS

Assign Section 4 Assessment as homework or as an in-class activity.

INTERDISCIPLINARY CONNECTIONS ACTIVITY

Sports Tell students that in 1972, Congress passed legislation known as Title IX, which was designed in part to give females greater access to athletic programs. Have students research how Title IX has been implemented at the high school and collegiate level. Research should focus on answering the following questions: **Has Title IX given women greater access to athletic programs? Has Title IX changed any stereotypes about women and sports? Has Title IX created any unintended inequities?** Based on the research, have students write a speech that answers the questions above and concludes with a section entitled "Where do we go from here?" **L2**

Section Quiz 4–4

Name ______________ Date ________ Class ________

Section Quiz 4-4 **Gender Roles and Differences** SCORE

Matching
Match each item in Column A with the items in Column B. Write the correct letters in the blanks. *(10 points each)*

Column A

____ 1. oversimplified generalization about the characteristics that belong to males and females
____ 2. the set of behaviors that a culture determines is appropriate for each gender
____ 3. a mental representation of behaviors organized around how either a male or a female should think and behave
____ 4. a flexible combination of traditional male and female roles
... which an individual biologically belongs

Column B

A. androgynous
B. gender identity
C. gender role
D. gender schema
E. gender stereotype

Reteach

Ask students to make a list of the differences in personality and cognitive abilities that they attribute to males and females.

Enrich

Ask students to write a short story about the experiences they would have if they took a job in a nontraditional field.

4 CLOSE

Bring several books intended for young children to class. Have students work in small groups to identify how gender roles are defined. Have volunteers from each group report their findings to the class. **Ask: How does the portrayal of male and female characters affect how children view male and female roles?**

gender schema: a set of behaviors organized around how either a male or female should think and behave

concept. The child may begin to acquire preferences consistent with his or her perceived gender. For example, a boy watches a football game and then engages in rough play with another boy. Eventually that boy forms a gender schema. A **gender schema** is a mental representation of behavior that helps a child organize and categorize behaviors. For instance, a girl develops a schema of how a female should act and then behaves in accordance with that schema. The girl begins to play with dolls when she perceives that this behavior fits in with her notion of what kinds of toys girls play with. When she acts appropriately with the schema, her self-confidence rises. When she fails to act in accordance with her schema, she feels inadequate.

CHANGING GENDER ROLES

The roles of women and men in society are changing. For example, before the 1960s in the United States, few women sought careers. Most women grew up expecting to marry and quit work to raise children. By the mid-1980s, though, this had changed. Most women had jobs outside the home. For women and men, work provides income, as well as a sense of accomplishment.

Despite the fact that more women are in the workforce, studies have shown that, in general, women do not advance as quickly as men and women occupy lower levels of leadership positions. Industrial/organizational psychologists propose that the inequality in the workplace may be the result of several factors. Companies may discriminate against women. Many women interrupt their careers for child care and in doing so miss opportunities for promotion and salary increases. Also, men and women may differ in their ambition. That is, women may have been taught by society to set different goals.

SECTION 4 Assessment

1. **Review the Vocabulary** What is a person's gender schema?
2. **Visualize the Main Idea** Using an organizer similar to the one below, list and characterize three theories explaining the origins of gender differences.

   Origins of Gender Differences
   I. ______________
   II. ______________

3. **Recall Information** According to the social learning theory, how do children learn gender roles?
4. **Think Critically** Why might many people disagree with or oppose biological theories of gender differences?
5. **Application Activity** Review a TV program, movie, Internet site, or advertisement. Analyze the gender roles portrayed, then answer the following question: What role do the media play in the development of gender stereotypes?

SECTION 4 Assessment Answers

1. A gender schema is one's mental picture of how males and females should think and behave.
2. Answers will vary. Answers may include Biological Theory, Psychoanalytical Theory, Social Learning Theory, or Cognitive-Developmental Theory.
3. Children learn gender roles from observing and imitating models, such as parents and teachers.
4. Students' answers will vary. Some opposition comes from those who theorize that gender roles are learned or that people can change or learn different gender roles.
5. Students' answers will vary. Students may cite examples in which the media is responsible for maintaining stereotypes. Students may also cite examples in which media has been specifically designed to eliminate gender stereotypes.

CHAPTER 4

Summary and Vocabulary

Adolescence is the transition period between childhood and adulthood—a period of learning adult roles.

Section 1 Physical and Sexual Development

Main Idea: All adolescents experience dramatic changes in their physical size, shape, and capacities, as well as biological development related to reproduction.

- In his theory of adolescence, G. Stanley Hall portrayed the adolescent as existing in a state of great storm and stress. Other psychologists and social scientists, such as Margaret Mead, regard adolescence as a relatively smooth continuous development out of childhood and into adulthood.
- The onset of puberty marks the end of childhood; both boys and girls experience a growth spurt just before puberty.
- The rate and pattern of sexual maturation varies so widely that it is difficult to apply norms or standards to puberty.

Section 2 Personal Development

Main Idea: The transition from childhood to adulthood involves changes in patterns of reasoning and moral thinking, as well as the development of one's identity.

- During adolescence, most people reach the stage of formal operations thinking in which thinking becomes abstract and less concrete.
- According to Erik Erikson, building an identity is a task that is unique to adolescence; most adolescents must go through an identity crisis, a time of inner conflict during which they worry intensely about their identities.

Section 3 Social Development

Main Idea: Adolescents undergo many changes in their social relationships, adjusting to new relationships with parents and the new influence of peers.

- One of the principal developmental tasks for adolescents is becoming independent of their families.
- Belonging to a peer group fulfills the need for closeness with others and gives the adolescent a means of establishing an identity.
- Parents and peers exercise influence in shaping adolescent behavior and attitudes.

Section 4 Gender Roles and Differences

Main Idea: Females and males have physical and psychological gender differences. Our beliefs about what we think it means to be male or female influence our behavior.

- During adolescence, individuals develop attitudes about gender and expectations about the gender role they will fill.
- Most psychologists agree that nature and nurture interact to influence gender differences.
- The roles of men and women in society are changing.

Chapter Vocabulary

initiation rites (p. 94)
puberty (p. 95)
menarche (p. 96)
spermarche (p. 96)
asynchrony (p. 96)
rationalization (p. 102)
identity crisis (p. 105)
social learning theory (p. 107)
clique (p. 110)
conformity (p. 111)
anorexia nervosa (p. 114)
bulimia nervosa (p. 115)
gender identity (p. 117)
gender role (p. 117)
gender stereotype (p. 117)
androgynous (p. 117)
gender schema (p. 122)

4 Summary and Vocabulary

Using the Chapter 4 Summary and Vocabulary

Use the Chapter 4 Summary and Vocabulary to preview, review, condense, or reteach the chapter.

Preview/Review

Use the Chapter Vocabulary list to help students review and study.

Activity Have students create a crossword puzzle using definitions or examples as the clues for the puzzle.

Vocabulary PuzzleMaker CD-ROM reinforces the vocabulary terms used in Chapter 4.

Condense

Have students read the Chapter 4 Summary.

Chapter 4 Guided Reading Activities

Reteach

Reteaching Activity 4

AUTHENTIC ASSESSMENT ACTIVITY

Creating a Collage Assign students to work individually or in pairs to design collages entitled "U.S. Teenagers Today." Collages may include objects, clippings, pictures, and any other items that students think capture the flavor of what it is like to be a teenager today. Set up a classroom display of the collages and have the students answer any questions about items they chose to include. **BLOCK SCHEDULING**

Refer to the ***Authentic Assessment*** booklet for additional activities and information about evaluating student performance.

PSYCHOLOGY Online

Have students visit the Web site at glencoe.com to review Chapter 4 and take the **Self-Check Quiz.**

GLENCOE TECHNOLOGY

PRESENTATION Plus! For a review of Chapter 4 content, see MindJogger Checkpoint on **Presentation Plus!**

Reviewing Vocabulary

1. g
2. c
3. e
4. j
5. a
6. f
7. b
8. d
9. i
10. h

Recalling Facts

1. Hall explained adolescence as representing a transition from beast to human, during which the person experiences great "storm and stress." Margaret Mead disagreed with this view and considered adolescence as a normal period of growth from childhood to adulthood. She theorized that the storm and stress is a cultural phenomenon.
2. She is referring to one's gender role.
3. Formal operations thinking is more abstract and allows adolescents to improve their problem-solving capabilities. They are able to contemplate the consequences of their actions and rationalize their behavior.
4. Erikson and Marcia: adolescents form their identities after experiencing identity crises, times of inner conflict; Bandura: individuals develop their identities by interacting with others; Mead: individuals develop their identities through social interaction.
5. The biological theory emphasizes the role of anatomy, hormones, brain organization, and evolutionary forces as the source of gender-role development.

Critical Thinking

1. Students' answers will vary. Students may be surprised by some of the similarities. Reasons for the differences include different points of view at different points in one's life.
2. Students' answers will vary. The most common responses will likely involve social development issues.
3. Students' answers will vary. Evaluate the student's ability to examine the issue from both points of view and reach a reasoned conclusion.
4. Students' answers will vary. Many students will support the identity crisis theory. As an extension, you could have students ask several adults if they experienced an identity crisis during their teen years.
5. Students' answers will vary. Cliques often form around shared interests, and it is these interests and the need to conform to the group that keep the groups together.

Psychology Projects

1. Answers will vary. Students should demonstrate how much advertising is geared to one's appearance.
2. Answers will vary. Topics may include clothing or appearance, vocabulary used, and behavior at social events.
3. Answers will vary. The montage should show how the traditional roles for male and female have changed over the years. Students should include examples of changes in family, social, and work roles.

CHAPTER 4 Assessment

PSYCHOLOGY Online

Self-Check Quiz
Visit the *Understanding Psychology* Web site at glencoe.com and click on **Chapter 4—Self-Check Quizzes** to prepare for the Chapter Test.

Reviewing Vocabulary

Choose the letter of the correct term or concept below to complete the sentence.

a. puberty
b. asynchrony
c. gender identity
d. gender role
e. identity crisis
f. social learning theory
g. clique
h. conformity
i. gender stereotypes
j. anorexia nervosa

1. Belonging to a(n) __________ is important to most adolescents and serves several functions.
2. A person's physical and biological makeup is his or her __________.
3. According to Erik Erikson, adolescents go through a(n) __________, a time of inner conflict in which they worry about their identities.
4. __________ is an eating disorder in which an individual refuses to eat and loses weight.
5. The biological event that marks the end of childhood is __________.
6. Albert Bandura's belief that individuals develop by interacting with others is referred to as the __________ of development.
7. Feet that are too large for the body is an example of __________, or the condition of uneven growth or maturation of bodily parts.
8. A person's __________ is the standard of how a person with a given gender identity is supposed to behave.
9. Oversimplified or prejudiced opinions and attitudes concerning the way men or women should behave are called __________.
10. An adolescent's fear of being set apart from others leads to __________ among peer group members.

Recalling Facts

1. Describe G. Stanley Hall's theory of adolescence. Does the research of Margaret Mead support his position? Explain.
2. When Sandra Bem discusses androgyny, is she talking about gender role or gender identity?
3. Explain what Jean Piaget means by *formal operations* thinking. How does this change in cognitive ability affect an adolescent?
4. Use a chart similar to the one below to explain the identity formation theory of each of the following: Erik Erikson, James Marcia, Albert Bandura, and Margaret Mead.

Psychologist/Social Scientist	Theory of Identity Formation

5. How does the biological theory of gender development explain the differences in gender?

Critical Thinking

1. Evaluating Information Write five words or phrases that, in your opinion, characterize adolescence. Then ask an adult to also write five words or phrases. What are the similarities and the differences? What are some reasons for the differences?
2. Analyzing Information Which of the developmental tasks of adolescence do you think is the most difficult? Explain your answer.
3. Demonstrating Reasoned Judgment Do you think an individual with an androgynous gender role is healthier than one with a traditional gender role? Explain your answer.
4. Making Inferences Erikson and Marcia insist that all adolescents experience an identity crisis. Do you agree? Explain your answer.
5. Synthesizing Information Identify three different cliques in your school. How would you characterize the people who belong to each group? What do you think keeps groups together?

CHAPTER 4 Assessment

Psychology Projects

1. **Physical and Sexual Development** It has often been said that American culture is preoccupied with youthfulness. Find as many examples as you can of this in newspapers, magazines, radio, television, and popular music. Pay particular attention to advertising that emphasizes the marketing of youthful values. Cut out examples as evidence and compile a bulletin-board display.
2. **Personal Development** Work with a partner to develop a skit of a situation that illustrates the conflict that Erik Erikson believes teenagers face in trying to be unique on the one hand and to fit in on the other hand. Present your skit to the class and discuss ways that teenagers can resolve this conflict.
3. **Gender Roles and Differences** Review magazines and newspapers from the past 50 years to find examples of traditional gender roles and nontraditional roles. Clip or photocopy your examples and display them in a montage titled "Gender Roles—The Last 50 Years." What do the pictures say about gender roles in this country in the past 50 years?

Technology Activity

During adolescence, young people begin to better understand abstract principles and often tend to become idealistic. Find out about issues that are facing your lawmakers today. Then find the e-mail addresses of your representatives and send an e-mail to them, expressing your views and your wishes for the way they should address the issues. Share any responses with the class.

Psychology Journal

Reread the journal entry that you wrote at the beginning of this chapter. Other social scientists have suggested that building an identity is a lifelong process and that changes to the identity occur throughout life. Write a journal entry that argues that building an identity is a lifelong process. Support your argument with evidence from the chapter as well as evidence from your own experience. Finally, reread both entries and write a short summary explaining whether you think one position is more valid than the other.

Building Skills

Interpreting a Graph Review the graphs below and then answer the questions that follow.

Practice and **assess** key social studies skills with **Glencoe Skillbuilder Interactive Workbook CD-ROM, Level 2.**

1. What is the major cause of death for people between the ages of 15 and 24?
2. How do the causes of death for the 15–24 age group compare to that of the 45–64 age group?
3. How do some of the thought processes of adolescents help explain the leading causes of death in young people?

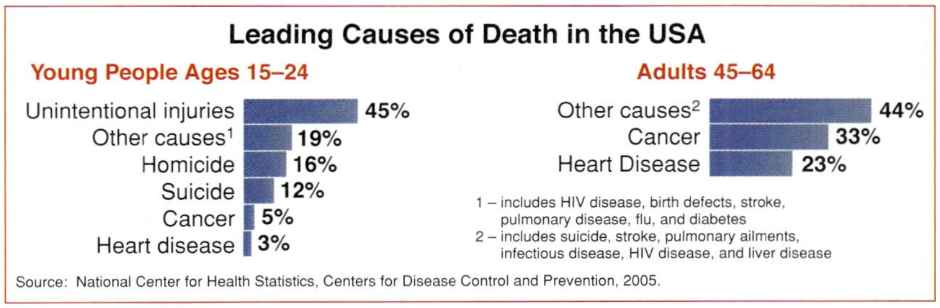

See the Skills Handbook, page 628, for an explanation of interpreting graphs.

Building Skills

1. unintentional injuries
2. The leading cause of death for the 15-24 age group is unintentional injuries, while the single (not combined) leading cause of death for the 45-64 age group is cancer.
3. The abstract thought processes of adolescents can often result in feelings of invulnerability, which lead to risk taking and self-destructive behavior.

GLENCOE TECHNOLOGY

CD-ROM

Glencoe Skillbuilder Interactive Workbook, Level 2

This interactive CD-ROM is designed to reinforce student mastery of essential social studies skills.

Chapter Bonus Test Question

This question may be used for extra credit on the Chapter Assessment.

Answer the following question:

I first described formal operations thinking—the thinking pattern that emerges during adolescence. Who am I?

Answer: Jean Piaget

Technology Activity

Students should analyze any e-mail responses they receive. Does the message indicate support for the student's position? Ask students to share their analyses of the responses they received.

Psychology Journal

Students' answers should show their ability to present a reasoned argument and to look at both sides of the issues.

Readings in Psychology

Block Schedule

This activity works well for a block-scheduling framework.

Reinforcing Vocabulary

Review the **Reader's Dictionary** terms with students to be sure they understand any unfamiliar items.

Background Information

About 90 percent of those suffering from anorexia nervosa are female. Bulimia nervosa also predominantly afflicts females. Although the incidence of eating disorders has increased sharply in the past few decades, they still affect a relatively small percentage of the population. About 1 in 100 women suffer from anorexia nervosa, and 3 in 100 women struggle with bulimia.

Since 1991, the percentage of boys diagnosed with eating disorders has increased from 5 percent of all sufferers to 10 percent. This alarming rate of increase is currently attributed to the fact that our culture now sets unrealistic standards for the male body shape and size.

TEACHER Tip

Explain how repeated portrayals of select body types, the kinds used in advertising, can lead viewers to automatically process such images as desirable. Such information processing can be overridden if additional information allows the viewer to reject the stereotype.

READINGS IN PSYCHOLOGY

Marya Hornbacher grew up in a comfortable, middle-class American home. At an early age, she remembers crying her heart out because she thought she was fat." By age nine, she was secretly bulimic; by age 15, anorexic. In this excerpt, taken from her memoirs *Wasted* (1998), Marya describes her illness.

Reader's Dictionary

virulence: extreme bitterness
cacophony: a harsh sound
belie: to show to be false or wrong

WASTED

BY MARYA HORNBACHER

I became bulimic at the age of nine, anorexic at the age of fifteen. I couldn't decide between the two and veered back and forth from one to the other until I was twenty, and now, at twenty-three, I am an interesting creature, an Eating Disorder Not Otherwise Specified. My weight has ranged over the past thirteen years from 135 pounds to 52, inching up and then plummeting back down. I have gotten "well," then "sick," then "well," then "sicker," and so on up to now; I am considered "moderately improved," "psychologically stabilized, behaviorally disordered," "prone to habitual relapse." I have been hospitalized six times, institutionalized once, had endless hours of therapy, been tested and observed and diagnosed and pigeonholed and poked and prodded and fed and weighed for so long that I have begun to feel like a laboratory rat. . . .

I am not here to spill my guts and tell you about how awful it's been, that my daddy was mean and my mother was mean and some kid called me Fatso in the third grade, because none of the above is true. I am not going to repeat, at length, how eating disorders are "about control," because we've all heard it. It's a buzzword, reductive, categorical, a tidy way of herding people into a mental quarantine and saying: *There*. . . . The question is really not *if* eating disorders are "neurotic" and indicate a glitch in the mind—even I would have a hard time justifying, rationally, the practice of starving oneself to death or feasting only to toss back the feast—but rather why; why this glitch, what flipped this switch, why so many of us? Why so easy a choice, this? Why now? Some toxin in the air? Some freak of nature that has turned women against their own bodies with a virulence unmatched in history, all of a sudden, with no cause? The individual does not exist outside of society. There are reasons why this is happening, and they do not lie in the mind alone.

This book is neither a tabloid tale of mysterious disease nor a testimony to a miracle cure. It's simply the story of one woman's travels to a darker side of reality, and her decision to make her way back. On her own terms.

My terms amount to cultural heresy. I had to say: I will eat what I want and look as I please and laugh as loud as I like and use the wrong fork and lick my knife. I had to learn strange and delicious lessons, lessons too few women learn: to love the thump of my steps, the implication of weight and presence and taking of space, to love my body's rebellious hungers, responses to touch, to understand myself as more than a brain attached to a bundle of bones. I have to ignore the cultural cacophony that singsongs all day long, Too much, too much, too much. . . .

ADDITIONAL READINGS ABOUT THE TOPIC

Claude-Pierre, P. (1999). *The Secret Language of Eating Disorders.* New York: Vintage Books.

Dosil, J. (2007). *Eating Disorders in Athletes.* New York: John Wiley and Sons.

Kotre, J., & Hall, E. (1990). *Seasons of Life: Our Dramatic Journey From Birth to Death.* Boston: Little Brown.

Levinkron, S. (1979). *The Best Little Girl in the World.* New York: Warner Books.

Wolf, N. (1992). *The Beauty Myth.* New York: Doubleday & Co., Inc.

I wrote this book because I believe some people will recognize themselves in it—eating disordered or not—and because I believe, perhaps naively, that they might be willing to change their own behavior, get help if they need it, entertain the notion that their bodies are acceptable, that they themselves are neither insufficient nor in excess. I wrote it because I disagree with much of what is generally believed about eating disorders, and wanted to put in my two cents, for whatever it's worth. I wrote it because people often dismiss eating disorders as manifestations of vanity, immaturity, madness. It is, in some ways, all of these things. But it is also an addiction. It is a response, albeit a rather twisted one, to a culture, a family, a self. I wrote this because I want to dispel two common and contradictory myths about eating disorders: that they are an insignificant problem, solved by a little therapy and a little pill and a pat on the head, a "stage" that "girls" go through—I know a girl whose psychiatrist told her that her bulimia was just part of "normal adolescent development"—and, conversely, that they must belie true insanity, that they only happen to "those people" whose brains are incurably flawed, that "those people" are hopelessly "sick."

An eating disorder is not usually a phase, and it is not necessarily indicative of madness. It is quite maddening, granted, not only for the loved ones of the eating disordered person but also for the person herself. It is, at the most basic level, a bundle of deadly contradictions: a desire for power that strips you of all power. A gesture of strength that divests you of all strength. A wish to prove that you need nothing, that you have no human hungers, which turns on itself and becomes a searing need for the hunger itself. It is an attempt to find an identity, but ultimately it strips you of any sense of yourself, save the sorry identity of "sick." It is a grotesque mockery of cultural standards of beauty that winds up mocking no one more than you. It is a protest against cultural stereotypes of women that in the end makes you seem the weakest, the most needy and neurotic of all women. It is the thing you believe is keeping you safe, alive, contained—and in the end, of course, you find it's doing quite the opposite. These contradictions begin to split a person in two. Body and mind fall apart from each other, and it is in this fissure that an eating disorder may flourish, in the silence that surrounds this confusion that an eating disorder may fester and thrive. . . .

There were numerous methods of self-destruction available to me, countless outlets that could have channeled my drive, perfectionism, ambition, and an excess of general intensity, millions of ways in which I could have responded to a culture that I found highly problematic. I did not choose those ways. I chose an eating disorder. I cannot help but think that, had I lived in a culture where "thinness" was not regarded as a strange state of grace, I might have sought out another means of attaining that grace, perhaps one that would not have so seriously damaged my body, and so radically distorted my sense of who I am.

Analyzing the Reading

1. Why did the author write this?
2. According to the author, how do eating disorders rob the sufferer of an identity?
3. **Critical Thinking** What underlying causes of her disorder does the author reveal?

ACTIVE READING STRATEGY

Explain to students that connecting means relating what they already know about a subject with what they are now reading about the subject. **Ask: What did you know about causes of anorexia and bulimia before reading this selection? What did you learn after reading this selection? Did reading this selection change your opinions about eating disorders? Explain.**

PSYCHOLOGY JOURNAL

Have students write a description of our cultural ideal for a male and a female. Then have them evaluate what important elements are missing from the culture's ideals. ■

FYI

At the other end of the spectrum are those who eat compulsively. Food controls their lives much like an addiction. Overeaters Anonymous, Inc., uses a program to treat compulsive eaters that is modeled on the 12-step program created by Alcoholics Anonymous.

Answers to Analyzing the Reading

1. She wrote it to help others recognize their destructive behaviors and help to motivate change. The author also wrote the book because she disagrees with much of what is generally believed about eating disorders, and she wanted to share her thoughts on the issue.
2. She describes it as a need for and a loss of power, strength, and control. She feels the desire to be thin, and thereby accepted, is so compelling that all other sense of self is lost. She describes the contradiction of becoming thin and "safe" while the body wastes away, leaving her with no identity except that of being "sick".
3. Answers will vary. Many causes are cited including vanity, immaturity, mental illness, addictive behavior, perfectionism, ambition, and a culture that sets unrealistic standards of what women should be.

Chapter 5 Resource Guide

SECTION RESOURCES

Daily Objectives	Reproducible Resources	Multimedia Resources
Section 1 **Adulthood** Describe the shifting priorities and outlooks on life that occur from adolescence throughout the remainder of life.	Guided Reading Activity 5–1 Vocabulary Activity 5–1 Section Quiz 5–1	Daily Focus Transparency 5–1 *ExamView® Assessment Suite* CD-ROM Presentation Plus! Software
Section 2 **Old Age** Discuss how our priorities and expectations change to match realities during old age.	Guided Reading Activity 5–2 Vocabulary Activity 5–2 Section Quiz 5–2	Daily Focus Transparency 5–2 *ExamView® Assessment Suite* CD-ROM Presentation Plus! Software
Section 3 **Dying and Death** Understand that most people face death by going through stages or an adjustment process.	Guided Reading Activity 5–3 Vocabulary Activity 5–3 Section Quiz 5–3	Daily Focus Transparency 5–3 Vocabulary PuzzleMaker CD-ROM *ExamView® Assessment Suite* CD-ROM Presentation Plus! Software

Blackline Master   CD-ROM   Transparency

Block Schedule

Activities that are particularly suited for use within the block-scheduling framework are identified throughout this chapter by the following designation: **BLOCK SCHEDULING**

KEY TO ABILITY LEVELS

Teaching strategies have been coded for varying learning styles and abilities.

L1 **BASIC** activities for all students
L2 **AVERAGE** activities for average to above-average students
L3 **CHALLENGING** activities for above-average students
ELL **ENGLISH LANGUAGE LEARNER** activities

Chapter 5 Resource Guide

Timesaving Tools

TeacherWorks™ All-In-One Planner and Resource Center

- **Interactive Teacher Edition** Access your Teacher Wraparound Edition and your classroom resources with a few easy clicks.
- **Interactive Lesson Planner** Planning has never been easier! Organize your week, month, semester, or year with all the lesson helps you need to make teaching creative, timely, and relevant.

Use Glencoe's **Presentation Plus!** multimedia teacher tool to easily present dynamic lessons that visually excite your students. Using Microsoft PowerPoint® you can customize the presentations to create your own personalized lessons.

Activity

From the Classroom of...

James F. Connington
Liberty High School
Liberty, SC

The Aging Process

Goal: To help students understand the aging process

Ask students to make four columns on a piece of paper. Label the columns "year," "self," "parents," and "grandparents." In the first column, they are to write the current year (for example, 2008). Below it they should continue the years in five-year increments, 2013, 2018. . . . In the second column, they should write their age; the third column is for the average age of their parents; and the fourth the average age of one set of grandparents. Next, students should determine their age for each year in the column to the left, then do the same for their parents and grandparents. A finished chart will show the ages of the student, his parents, and grandparents for the next 60 years. The following is an example of how the chart might look:

Year	Self	Parents	Grandparents
2008	15	42	67
2013	20	47	72
2018	25	52	77

Ask questions like **"When you are your parents' age, how old will they be?"** or **"When your grandparents are in their 80s how old will your parents be?"** This technique promotes discussion and understanding of the aging process without using artificial life-span designations, such as *people in their fifties,* which mean little to adolescents.

Psychology Online

Use our Web site for additional resources. All essential content is covered in the Student Edition.

You and your students can visit glencoe.com, the Web site companion to *Understanding Psychology*. This innovative integration of electronic and print media offers your students a wealth of opportunities. The student text directs students to the Web site for the following options:

- Chapter Overviews
- Student Web Activities
- Self-Check Quizzes

Answers are provided for you in the **Web Activity Lesson Plan.** Additional Web resources and Interactive Puzzles are also available.

Chapter 5 Resource Guide

Note: The following materials may be used when teaching Chapter 5. Section level support materials are shown at point of use in the margins of the Teacher Wraparound Edition.

TEACHING TRANSPARENCIES

Chapter 5
Concept Transparencies

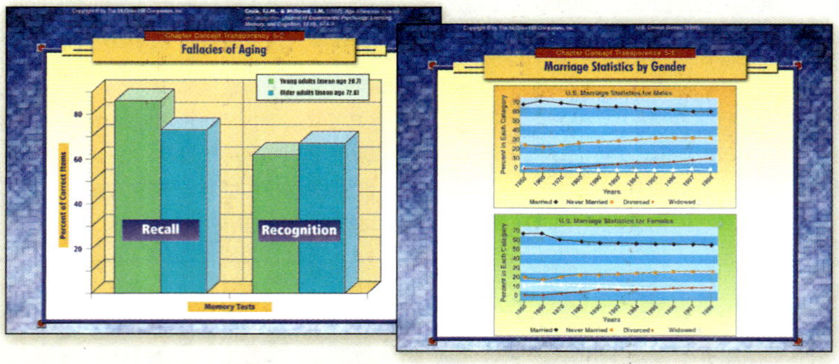

MULTIMEDIA

- Vocabulary PuzzleMaker CD-ROM
- *ExamView® Assessment Suite* CD-ROM
- TeacherWorks™ CD-ROM
- Glencoe Skillbuilder Interactive Workbook, Level 2
- Presentation Plus! Software

REVIEW AND REINFORCEMENT

Reteaching Activity 5

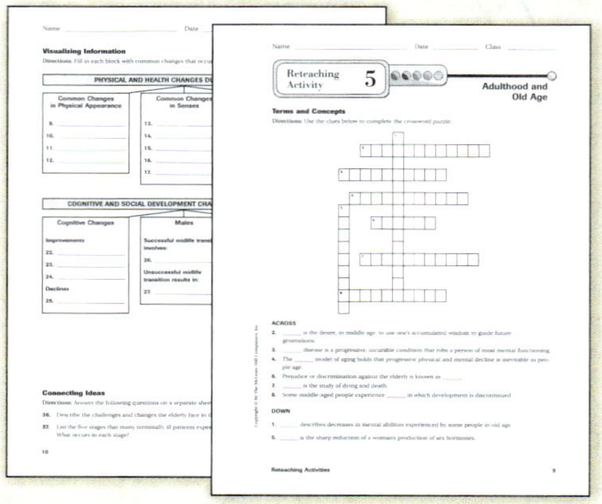

Graphic Organizer Activity 5

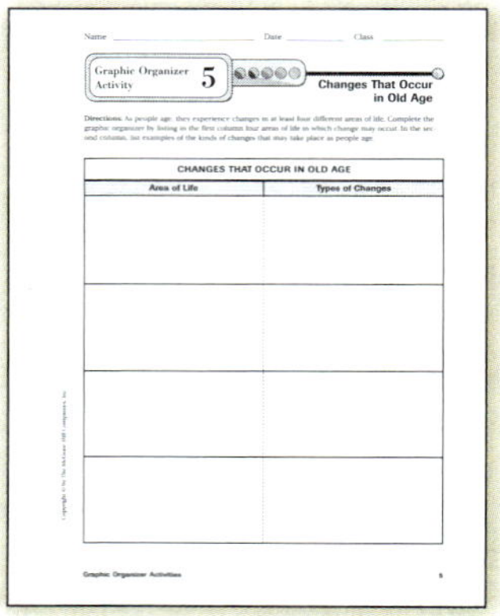

APPLICATION AND HANDS-ON

Psychology Projects 5–1 and 5–2

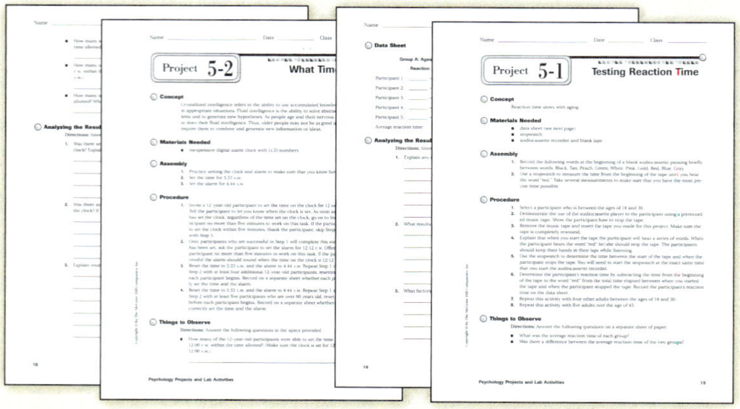

Application Activity 5

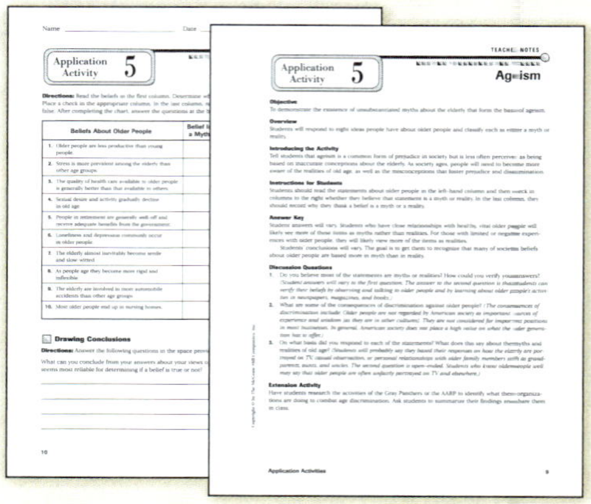

Chapter 5 Resource Guide

ASSESSMENT

Chapter 5 Test, Form A

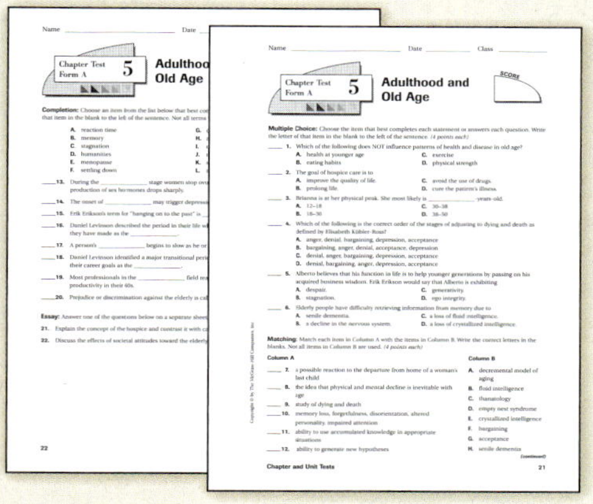

Chapter 5 Test, Form B

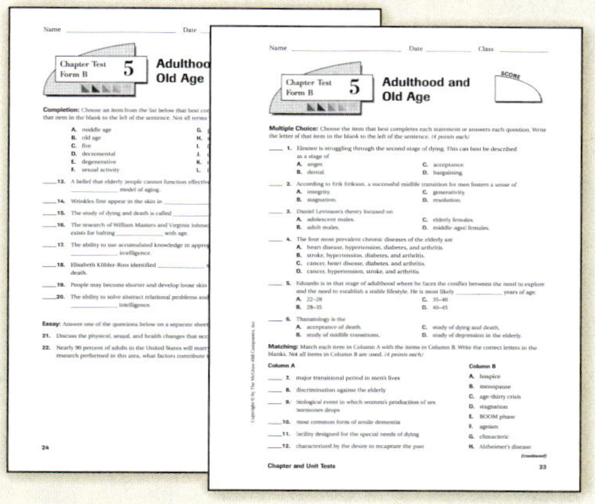

Authentic Assessment Activity 5

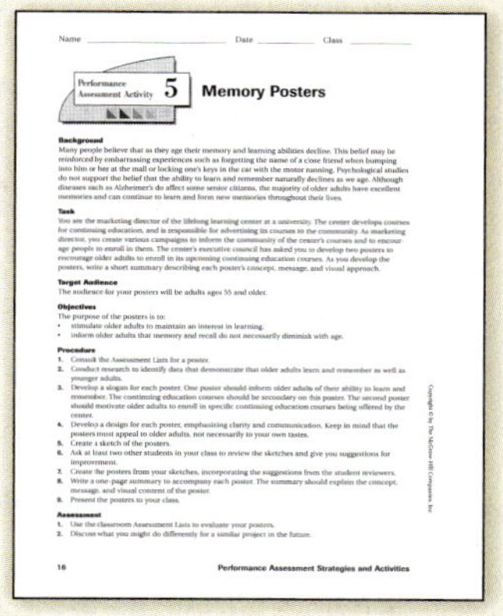

EXTENSION AND ENRICHMENT

Enrichment Activity 5

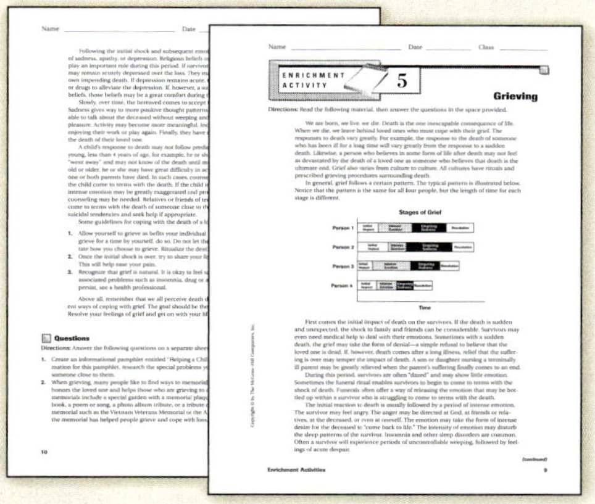

Critical Thinking Skills Activity 5

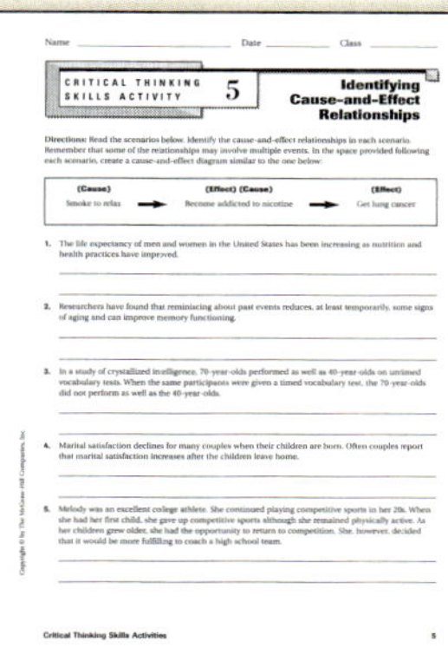

Psychology Reading 5

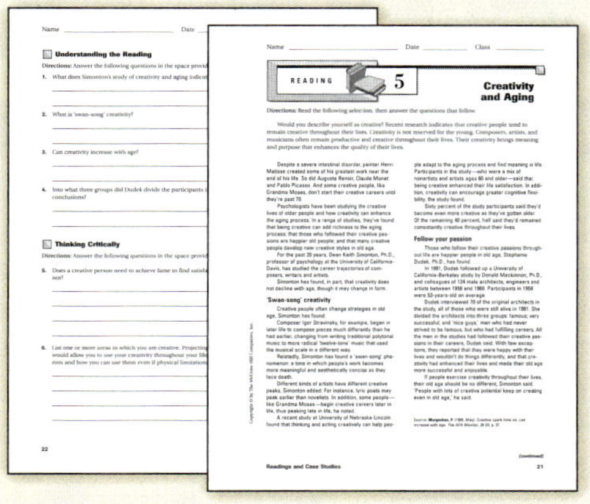

Psychology Case Study 5

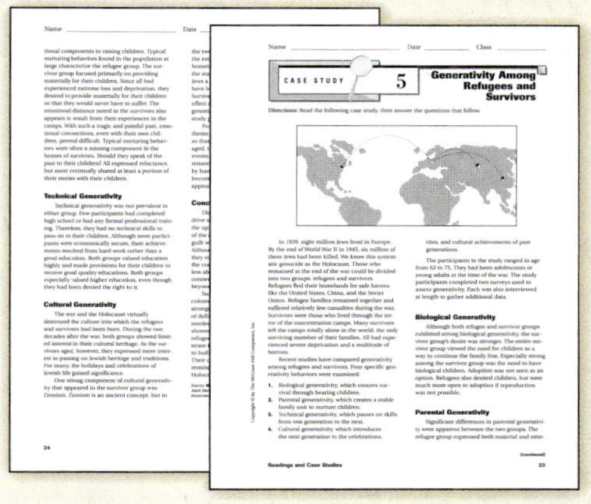

PSYCHOLOGY Online

Visit glencoe.com for a Chapter Overview for **Chapter 5—Adulthood and Old Age.**

GLENCOE TECHNOLOGY

PRESENTATION Plus! For a preview of Chapter 5 content, see MindJogger Checkpoint on **Presentation Plus!**

Psychology Journal

Ask students to list examples of adults who seem set in their ways or unwilling to try new things or risk new experiences to make changes.

This journal activity provides the basis for the Psychology Journal activity exercise in the Chapter Assessment. ■

CHAPTER 5 Adulthood and Old Age

Psychology Journal

You have probably heard the saying "You can't teach an old dog new tricks." In your journal, write whether you believe this saying is true, somewhat true, or false. ■

PSYCHOLOGY Online

Chapter Overview

Visit the *Understanding Psychology* Web site at glencoe.com and click on **Chapter 5—Chapter Overviews** to preview the chapter.

TWO-MINUTE LESSON LAUNCHER

Display at the front of the class pictures of people in various age groups. Have one of people in their 20s, one in their 30s, and so on. Ideally, the pictures should show people participating in a variety of activities and include well-known people in each age category. Place a piece of newsprint beneath each group of pictures. Divide the class into groups and assign each group one of the pictures. Have each group list the advantages and disadvantages of being in each age group. Leave the displays in place as you study the chapter. Encourage students to revise their lists as they learn more about adulthood and aging. Revisit the lists at the end of the chapter and discuss how their views of each age group have changed.

SECTION 1 Adulthood

Reader's Guide

Main Idea

Adulthood is a time of transition—it involves shifting priorities and outlooks on life from adolescence and throughout the remainder of life.

Vocabulary

- menopause
- generativity
- stagnation

Objectives

- Characterize the physical changes that take place during adulthood.
- Describe the social and emotional changes that occur during adulthood.

EXPLORING PSYCHOLOGY

Questions

I remember sitting in a restaurant in Nags Head, North Carolina, . . . A woman I barely knew came over to me. She shook my shoulder, got right in my face and said "Hey, hey. Did you just find out that life ain't fair? Hmmm?" All I could do was nod. I had lived to be forty years old. I was a child of an upper-middle-class family, blessed with good health, a good education, and endless possibilities. Now I was confronting age-old questions: "Where am I going with the rest of my life?" "Who am I?" I vaguely remembered asking these questions as a teenager but had forgotten the answers, if I ever knew them. After that I forgot to ask the questions.

—from *Awakening at Midlife* by Kathleen A. Brehony, 1996

Like the author above, many people face questions and adjustment in adulthood. What is adulthood like? For one thing, it is a period when opposite factors affect lives. There is change and sameness, success and failure, crisis and stability, joy and sadness. Adulthood can be a time when a person matures fully into what he or she is, or it can be a time when life closes in and what was once possibility is now limitation. How each of us reacts depends on our preparations, circumstances, and general outlook on life.

SECTION RESOURCES

Reproducible Masters

- Guided Reading Activity 5–1
- Vocabulary Activity 5–1
- Section Quiz 5–1

Transparencies

- Daily Focus Transparency 5–1

Multimedia

- *ExamView® Assessment Suite* CD-ROM
- Presentation Plus! Software

1 FOCUS

Section Objectives

1. Characterize the physical changes that take place during adulthood.
2. Describe the social and emotional changes that occur during adulthood.

BELLRINGER
Motivational Activity

Project Daily Focus Transparency 5–1 and have students answer the questions.

Available as blackline master

Daily Focus Transparency 5–1

Reader's Guide

Use the Reader's Guide to introduce concepts and vocabulary.

Exploring Psychology
Ask students to read the **Exploring Psychology** feature and then discuss: **Why do you think adolescents and adults in midlife ask the same question: "Who am I?"**

Vocabulary Precheck
Have students read the Glossary definition of each term. Ask them to restate each in their own words.

2 TEACH

L1 Making a Chart Have students work in small groups to design charts showing the similarities and differences between adolescence and old age. Column heads should include such things as *Physical Changes, Cognitive Development Tasks,* and *Social Development Tasks.* Based on the charts, **ask: What aspects of adjustment do the two stages have in common? What are the main differences? What, if any, strategies can adolescents and senior citizens use to deal with physical changes?** **BLOCK SCHEDULING**

Reading Check Answer Physical changes include the breakdown of muscles and fat, hair turning gray, skin becoming less elastic, wrinkles appearing, and sometimes the loss of weight and stature.

Guided Reading Activity 5–1

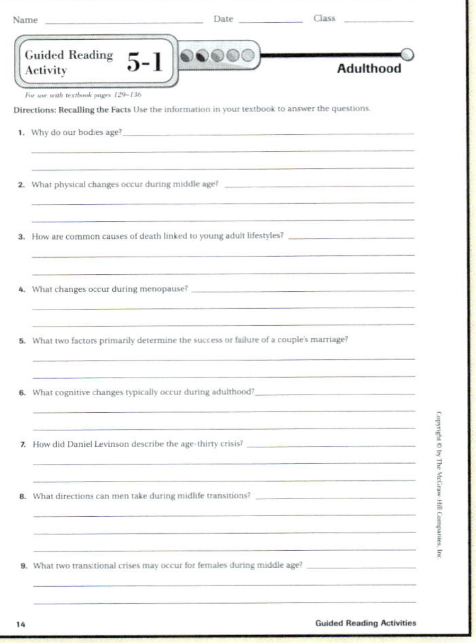
Name ________ Date ________ Class ________

Guided Reading Activity 5-1 — Adulthood

For use with textbook pages 129–136

Directions: Recalling the Facts Use the information in your textbook to answer the questions.

1. Why do our bodies age? ________
2. What physical changes occur during middle age? ________
3. How are common causes of death linked to young adult lifestyles? ________
4. What changes occur during menopause? ________
5. What two factors primarily determine the success or failure of a couple's marriage? ________
6. What cognitive changes typically occur during adulthood? ________
7. How did Daniel Levinson describe the age-thirty crisis? ________
8. What directions can men take during midlife transitions? ________
9. What two transitional crises may occur for females during middle age? ________

Copyright © by The McGraw-Hill Companies, Inc.

14 Guided Reading Activities

Reading Check What physical changes occur as we age?

PHYSICAL CHANGES

One theory of aging claims that our bodies age as a result of breakdowns in our bodies' cells. With time our bodies' cells become less able to repair themselves. Thus aging is the result of normal wear and tear on our bodies. Another theory says that our bodies age because our cells have preset biological clocks that limit the number of times cells can divide and multiply. As cells reach that limit, they begin to die, or the process of cell division occurs less accurately. Either way, aging occurs.

In general, young adults are at their physical peak between the ages of 18 and 30 (see Figure 5.1). This is the period when we are the strongest, healthiest, and have the quickest reflexes. For most adults, the process of physical decline is slow and gradual—not at all noticeable, even month to month. For example, a 20-year-old manages to carry four heavy bags of groceries, while a 40-year-old finds it easier to make two trips. What is lost physically may be replaced by experience. A 60-year-old racquetball player who is well versed in the game's strategies can compete with a faster, less experienced 30-year-old player.

In middle age, appearance changes. The hair starts to turn gray and perhaps to thin out. The skin becomes somewhat dry and inelastic, and wrinkles appear. In old age, muscles and fat built up over the years break down so that people often lose weight, become shorter, and develop more wrinkles, creases, and loose skin. Some physiological changes occur as we become older, while behavioral factors and lifestyles can affect psychological health.

The senses also change over time, requiring more and more stimulation. During their 40s, most people begin having difficulty seeing distant objects, adjusting to the dark, and focusing on printed pages, even if their eyesight has always been good. Many experience a gradual or sudden loss of hearing in their later years. In addition, reaction time slows. If an experimenter asks a young person and an older person to push a button when they see a light flash, the older person will take about 20 percent longer to do so.

Health Problems

Some of the changes we associate with growing older are the result of the natural processes of aging. Others result from diseases and from simple disuse and abuse. Good health reflects a life of making choices, which involve exercise, diet, and lifestyle. A person who eats sensibly, exercises, avoids cigarettes, drugs, and alcohol, and is not subjected to severe emotional stress will look and feel younger than someone who neglects his or her health.

More About...

The Cohort Effect

Suppose you were asked to measure the performance of trains at various points along a busy route. How would you go about it?

You might adopt a longitudinal approach. You would board a train and stay with it for its entire journey, recording your observations along the way. Alternatively, you might employ a cross-sectional strategy. You would ask observers stationed at key points to report on the performance of various trains that pass by.

Psychologists who study the behavior of people as they progress through adulthood and old age face a similar task. Since this journey can last decades, few researchers adopt a purely longitudinal approach. Instead, most conduct cross-sectional studies in which they can measure different age groups, or cohorts, together at one time.

However, people from different cohorts have different experiences in a number of important areas, including quality of education, nutrition, career opportunities, and social values. Their different backgrounds make it difficult to determine how age affects human abilities, attitudes, and even health.

COOPERATIVE LEARNING ACTIVITY

Role Playing Write each of Levinson's 10 stages on slips of paper. Have students draw a slip from a basket. Ask students to role-play a monologue in which they express the concerns, accomplishments, and frustrations of a man or woman at that stage of development. After each performance, ask the class to guess which stage was being portrayed. Ask students what elements of the monologue helped them identify the stage. **BLOCK SCHEDULING**

Three of the most common causes of death in later adulthood—heart disease, cancer, and cirrhosis of the liver—may be encouraged by the fast-moving lifestyle of young adults. Drug abuse—likely to peak in late adolescence or young adulthood and drop sharply after that—is a problem. Other factors contributing to early morbidity are inadequate diet and the effects of violence. Violent deaths may result from accidents, a tendency to push the physical limits, and a social environment that encourages risk taking among young adults (Miedzian, 1991). All three of these contributing factors are psychological, although they ultimately have biological consequences.

Figure 5.1 How Our Bodies Age

When young adults reach their 20s, they have reached the level of highest physical ability and capacity. ***What are some theories as to why our bodies age?***

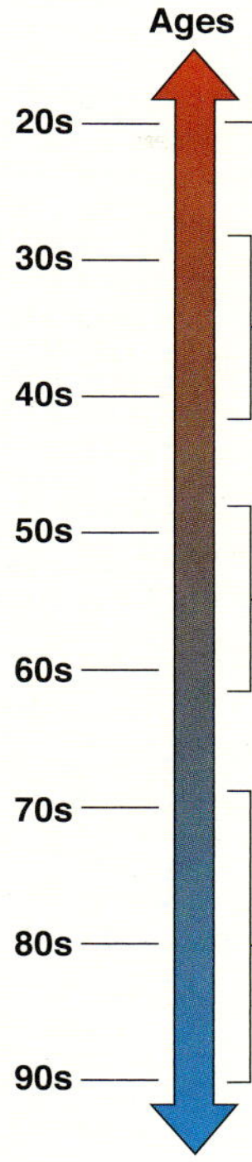

Early Adulthood: Most of us reach our peaks in our 20s. Our immune systems, senses, and mental skills operate at maximum efficiency.

Middle Adulthood: In our 30s and 40s, we may become less active and start to gain weight. By our late 40s, our heart rates, lung capacities, muscle strength, and eyesight slightly decrease.

Late Adulthood: In our 50s and 60s, we experience a gradual bone loss and a further decrease in lung output. Our skin wrinkles and our joints deteriorate. Sensory organs become less sensitive. Our hearts become less efficient.

Old Age: Our muscle strength, bone density, speed of nerve connections, and heart and lung output further decrease.

Menopause

Between the ages of 45 and 50, every woman experiences a stage called the *climacteric,* which represents all of the psychological and biological changes occurring at that time. A woman's production of sex hormones drops sharply—a biological event called **menopause.** The woman stops ovulating (producing eggs) and menstruating and therefore cannot conceive children. However, menopause does not cause any reduction in a woman's sexual drive or sexual enjoyment. Many women experience little or no discomfort during menopause. The irritability and severe depression some women experience during the climacteric, however, appear to have an emotional rather than physical origin.

menopause: the biological event in which a woman's production of sex hormones is sharply reduced

One study shows that the negative effects of menopause are greatly exaggerated. Women are also undergoing changes in roles and relationships at this time. Half of the women interviewed said they felt better, more confident, calmer, and freer after menopause than they had before. They no longer had to think about their periods or getting pregnant. They enjoyed sex as much as or more than they had before. A stable finding for many years has been women's uncertainty as to what to expect at menopause (Neugarten et al., 1963; Woods & Mitchell, 1999).

Figure 5.1

Visual Instruction Have students find information to compare the physical abilities and capacities of Olympic, college, professional, and senior athletes.

Caption Answer One theory is that our bodies age as a result of cell breakdown. Another theory proposes that we have a predetermined biological clock that controls when cells stop dividing and multiplying.

Looking @ the Issues

Sharing Information Although most psychologists do not prescribe drugs, it is increasingly important that psychologists discover what medications and alternative medicines their patients are taking. Some drugs, like Viagra, may have direct psychological effects. Other drugs that treat common afflictions like high blood pressure and diabetes can affect concentration, mood, alertness, and other facets of mental functioning. In addition to prescription drugs, over-the-counter substances like St. John's Wort may alter a person's mood. Use the following question to direct a class discussion. **Ask:** **Why might a patient be reluctant to share this type of information with his or her psychologist?**

MEETING SPECIAL NEEDS

Learning Style: Visual/Spatial Many artists paint self-portraits that show how they view themselves at various ages. Have students examine the self-portraits of a well-known artist over his or her lifespan. Artists who have painted multiple self-portraits include Rembrandt van Rijn and Vincent van Gogh. Ask students to write answers to the following questions as they view the self-portraits: **What physical changes do you see in these paintings? What conclusions can you draw about how the artist views the aging process? L1**

Refer to ***Inclusion for the High School Social Studies Classroom Strategies and Activities*** in the TCR for strategies for students with different learning styles.

Men do not go through any biological change equivalent to menopause. The number of sperm a man's body produces declines gradually over the years, but men have fathered children at an advanced age. It appears as if men generally go through psychological changes related to expectations about work, the death of parents, illness, and aging.

Marriage and Divorce

About 90 percent of adults in the United States will marry at some time in their lives. Forty to sixty percent of new marriages, though, end in divorce. What makes a marriage last? Researchers who have performed longitudinal studies on married couples have proposed that success or failure largely depends on two factors: how couples handle conflicts and how often couples share intimate and happy moments.

Although happily married couples seem to argue just as much as unhappy couples, they argue more constructively. They listen to each other and focus on solving the problem. They also show respect for each other's views. Unhealthy ways of dealing with conflict include ignoring or denying conflict, exaggerating issues, and having ugly verbal fights.

Sexual Behavior

Is there sex after 40? Studies have shown that sexual activity does not automatically decline with age. Indeed, as sex researchers William Masters and Virginia Johnson point out, there is no physiological reason for stopping sexual activity with advancing age (1970). Most older people who have an available partner maintain quite vigorous sex lives. Those who are inactive cite boredom with a partner of long standing, poor physical condition or illness (such as heart disease), or acceptance of the stereotype of loss of sex drive with aging (Mulligan & Moss, 1991).

Figure 5.2 Marriage

Many people, like this couple in India, marry in young adulthood. It is an Amish tradition for the father to adjust the height of this courting candle. His daughter must return from her date before the candle burns down to the first rung. ***How are conflicts resolved in happy marriages?***

COGNITIVE CHANGES

People are better at learning new skills and information, solving problems that require speed and coordination, and shifting from one problem-solving strategy to another in their mid-20s than they were in adolescence (Baltes & Schaie, 1977). These abilities are considered signs of intelligence and are among the skills that intelligence tests measure.

At one time many psychologists thought that intellectual development reached a peak in the mid-20s and then declined. The reason was that people do not score as high on intelligence

L1 Evaluating Stereotypes

Have students examine several issues of popular women's magazines. **Ask: To what extent do these magazines reinforce stereotypical attitudes about menopause and life after age 50? To what extent do they tear down these attitudes? Based on the magazine survey, how do you think the press might influence women's attitudes on aging?** ELL

PSYCHOLOGY JOURNAL

Ask students to poll adults they know on the health problems they are experiencing. They should find an adult to represent young adulthood, middle age, and old age. Have students record their findings in their journals. ■

TEACHER Tip

Explain that menopause was once viewed by women and much of society as an ending. Today many women view menopause as another transition in life, one that brings greater freedom—freedom from pregnancy and freedom to explore new directions.

Figure 5.2

Caption Answer Conflicts are resolved through listening and focusing on solving the problem. Happy couples respect each other's point of view.

CRITICAL THINKING ACTIVITY

Understanding Cause and Effect Some recent research indicates that the rate at which we age and the age we ultimately attain may be linked more to genetic programming than to behavior and the environment. Have students research attempts that are being made to slow down the aging process or to correct genetic factors that contribute to diseases such as breast cancer. Ask students to write a report on their findings. **L2**

tests in middle age as they did when they were younger—a cohort effect. Further investigation revealed that some parts of these tests measure speed, not intelligence (Bischof, 1969). An adult's reaction time begins to slow after a certain age. Intelligence tests usually penalized adults for this.

Even with a decline in speed, people continue to acquire information and to expand their vocabularies as they grow older. The ability to comprehend new material and to think flexibly improves with years and experience. This is particularly true if a person has had higher education, lives in a stimulating environment, and works in an intellectually demanding career. One researcher studied more than 700 individuals who were engaged in scholarship, science, or the arts. Although the patterns varied from profession to profession, most of the participants reached their peaks of creativity and productivity in their 40s (Dennis, 1966), but in the humanities, such as history, foreign languages, and literature, most reached their peaks later in their 60s.

Did You Know?

Arranged Marriages While most American couples marry for love, people in many other parts of the world follow the tradition of having marriages arranged. Arranged marriages often prove more lasting than ones based on love because the society usually disapproves of breaking up an arranged union. Some researchers also believe that the union lasts longer because each person enters the union without expectations of personal happiness. Such arranged marriages usually provide strong family ties and, therefore, support on both sides.

SOCIAL AND PERSONALITY DEVELOPMENT

An individual's basic character—his or her style of adapting to situations—is relatively stable over the years. Researchers are also convinced, however, that personality is flexible and capable of changing as an individual confronts new tasks. A number of researchers have given the same attitude and personality tests to individuals in late adolescence and again 10 or 15 years later. Many of the participants believed that they had changed dramatically, but the tests indicated that they had not. The degree of satisfaction they expressed about themselves and about life in general in their middle years was consistent with their earlier views. Confident young people remained confident; self-haters, self-hating; passive individuals, passive—unless something upsetting had happened to them, such as a sudden change in economic status (Kimmel, 1980).

Reading Check In what ways does intelligence increase as we grow older?

Despite the stability of character, people do face many changes in their lifetimes and adjust accordingly. Adults encounter new developmental tasks, just as adolescents do. They too must learn to cope with problems and deal with new situations. Learning the skills needed to cope with change seems to occur in stages for both adult males and females.

Levinson's Theory of Male Development

Daniel Levinson proposed a model of adult development for men (see Figure 5.3). Notice the similarity between Levinson's eras and the last three of the eight stages of Erikson's psychosocial theory, which was discussed in Chapter 3. Between these eras, Levinson identified important transition periods at ages 30, 40, 50, and 60 that last approximately 5 years.

Vocabulary Activity 5-1

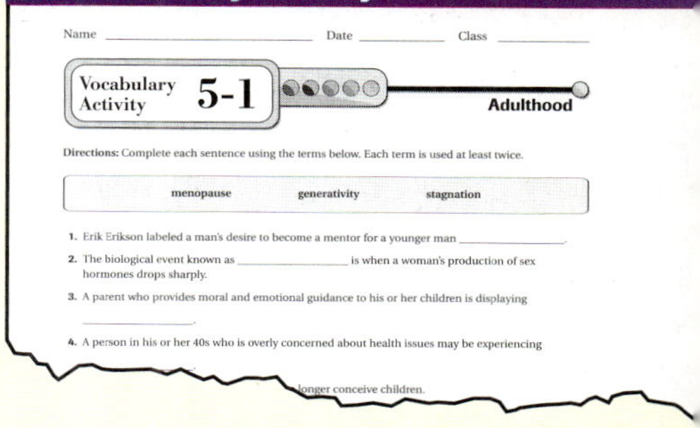

Reading Check Answer
As we grow older, our vocabularies continue to increase, as do our abilities to comprehend new material and think flexibly.

FYI

Males do not experience a sharp decline in hormone production during middle age. In men, the production of testosterone declines gradually with age.

Readings and Case Studies in Psychology
Have students read the Chapter 5 Case Study selection in *Readings and Case Studies in Psychology* and answer the questions that follow the case study.

PSYCHOLOGY LAB EXPERIMENT

Surveying Opinions Students will conduct a survey to compare opinions of teens and adults on political, social, and religious beliefs. Ask students to work in small groups to develop a survey to be given to adolescents and adults of middle or old age. Direct students to use a 5-point scale from Strongly Agree to Strongly Disagree. The survey should include 10 to 15 statements about beliefs. Give the students the following example: *People who burn the American flag are unpatriotic.* Have students make 20 copies of the survey and administer it to 10 teens and 10 middle-aged to older adults. The groups should then prepare a chart showing the results and a brief analysis of their findings. **L2**

Figure 5.3

Visual Instruction Ask students how Levinson's model challenges the attitude that adult life after age 30 is all downhill.

Caption Answer During the age-thirty crisis, men reexamine earlier commitments and may question the choices of marriage partner, career, and life goals.

TEACHER Tip

Stress that recent research on the aging process has fostered a new assumption about development: that personality is flexible and capable of change at every stage of life.

3 ASSESS

Assign Section 1 Assessment as homework or as an in-class activity.

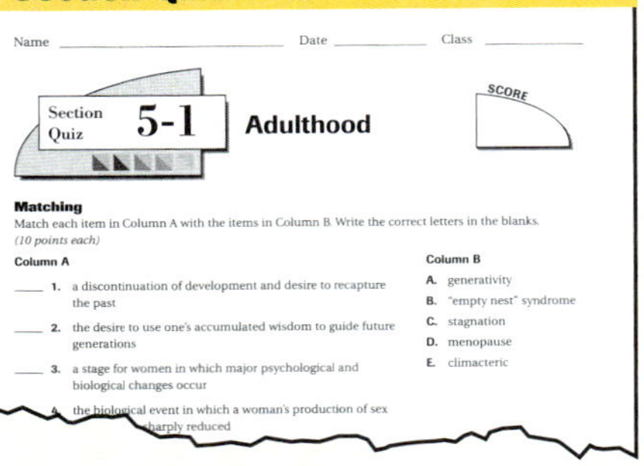
Section Quiz 5–1

Name ______ Date ______ Class ______

Section Quiz 5-1 **Adulthood** SCORE

Matching
Match each item in Column A with the items in Column B. Write the correct letters in the blanks. *(10 points each)*

Column A

____ 1. a discontinuation of development and desire to recapture the past

____ 2. the desire to use one's accumulated wisdom to guide future generations

____ 3. a stage for women in which major psychological and biological changes occur

4. the biological event in which a woman's production of sex ... sharply reduced

Column B

A. generativity
B. "empty nest" syndrome
C. stagnation
D. menopause
E. climacteric

Figure 5.3 Levinson's Theory of Male Development

This model shows the developmental sequence of a man's life that Levinson proposed. The scheme emphasizes that development is an ongoing process that requires continual adjustment. ***According to Levinson, what happens during the "age-thirty crisis"?***

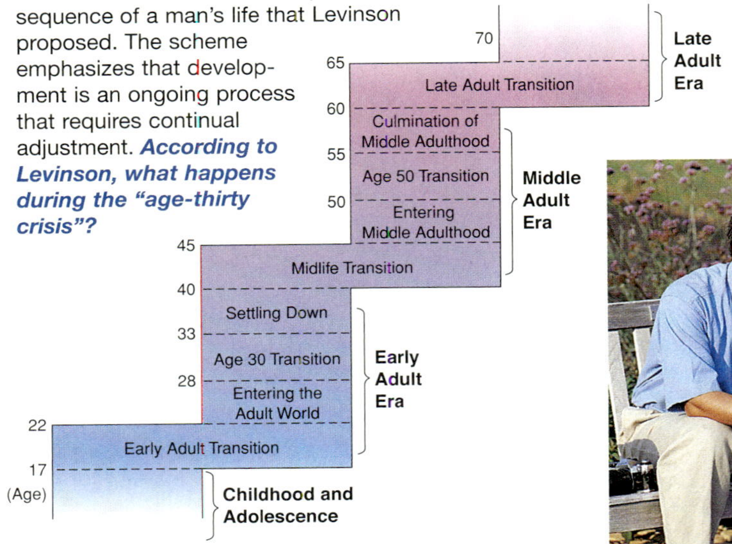

Entering the Adult World From about age 22 to age 28, the young man is considered, both by himself and by society, to be a novice in the adult world—not fully established as a man, but no longer an adolescent. During this time, he must attempt to resolve the conflict between the need to explore the options of the adult world and the need to establish a stable life structure.

The Age-Thirty Crisis Levinson's data reveal that the years between 28 and 30 are often a major transitional period. The thirtieth birthday can truly be a turning point; it could be called the "age-thirty crisis." During this transitional period, the tentative commitments that were made in the first life structure are reexamined, and many questions about the choices of marriage partner, career, and life goals are reopened, often in a painful way. The man feels that any parts of his life that are unsatisfying or incomplete must be attended to now, because it will soon be too late to make major changes.

Settling Down The questioning and searching that are part of the age-thirty crisis begin to be resolved as the second adult-life structure develops. Having probably made some firm choices about his career, family, and relationships, the man now begins actively carving out a niche in society, concentrating on what Levinson calls "making it" in the adult world.

Levinson found that near the end of the settling-down period, approximately between the ages of 36 and 40, there is a distinctive

INTERDISCIPLINARY CONNECTIONS ACTIVITY

Literature Have students locate and read the famous "All the world's a stage" speech from William Shakespeare's *As You Like It* (Act II, Scene vii), in which the cynical character Jacques describes the "seven ages" of humankind. Arrange for a volunteer to deliver the speech to the class using proper theatrical flourish and ask students to make note of what the seven ages are. Then have students compare Jacques's seven ages to the stages that Daniel Levinson proposed and to the physical, sexual, and intellectual changes described in this section. Point out that literature is often an excellent source of psychological insight. **L2**

BOOM phase—"becoming one's own man." Now it is time to become fully independent. During this period, the man strives to attain the seniority and position in the world that he identified as his ultimate goal at the beginning of the settling-down period.

The Midlife Transition At about age 40, the period of early adulthood comes to an end and the midlife transition begins. From about age 40 to age 45, the man begins again to ask questions, but now the questions concern the past as well as the future. He may ask: "What have I done with my life?" "What have I accomplished?" "What do I still wish to accomplish?" During this transition, he begins to develop yet another life structure that will predominate during the period of middle adulthood.

Often a successful midlife transition is accompanied by the man's becoming a mentor to a younger man. This event signals the attainment, in Erik Erikson's terms, of generativity. By **generativity,** Erikson means the desire to use one's wisdom to guide future generations—directly, as a parent, or indirectly. The opposite—**stagnation**—can also occur. Generativity or stagnation occurs for both men and women. An adult may choose to hang on to the past, perhaps by taking part in the same sports or hobbies. On the other hand, the same adult may become preoccupied with his health or bitter about the direction his life has taken.

Middle Adulthood The late 40s is a time when true adulthood can be achieved. The man who finds satisfactory solutions to his life's crises reaches a period of stability. He understands and tolerates others, and he displays a sensitivity and concern for other people as people. He is able to strike a balance between the need for friends and the need for privacy.

For the man who is not as fortunate, this period can be a time of extreme frustration and unhappiness. Instead of generativity, there is stagnation; instead of change and improvement, there is a mood of resignation to a bad situation. The job is only a job. The individual may feel cut off from family and friends, and the future holds no promise. By avoiding this life crisis, he is only inviting a later appearance of it, at age 50, with a more crushing force (Rogers, 1986). Keep in mind that Levinson's eras and transitions are based on averages from many individual interviews. Nobody's life is likely to match Levinson's divisions exactly.

Female Development

While there have been far more studies conducted among men than among women, some researchers have focused their attention on women's midlife development. While many men experience a crisis at midlife, married women at midlife may be facing fewer demands in their traditional task as mother. For many, this means greater personal freedom. As a result, they may be reentering the workforce, going back to college, or starting or renewing careers outside the home. Rather than a time of crisis, it is a time of opportunity for those who opted to have a family first. Evidence generally does not support the existence of a midlife crisis for most women in today's world (Berger, 2005).

PSYCHOLOGY Online

Student Web Activity
Visit the *Understanding Psychology* Web site at glencoe.com and click on **Chapter 5—Student Web Activities** for an activity about adult development.

generativity: the desire, in middle age, to use one's accumulated wisdom to guide future generations

stagnation: a discontinuation of development and a desire to recapture the past

PSYCHOLOGY Online

Links and instructional guidelines can be found in the **Web Activity Lesson Plan** at glencoe.com.

Reteach
Ask students to discuss which of the changes described in Levinson's model may arise from the individual's need for change and achievement. Then ask which may arise in response to the individual's environment.

EXTENDING THE CONTENT

Midlife Problems Marcelle Straatman, a human development specialist, lists four problems that many adults face during middle age: (1) choice anxiety is created by a fear of making poor choices, especially in view of one's own mortality; (2) lack of skills may arise if the person has not developed the mindset that learning is a continuous process; (3) lack of assurance arises when adults doubt themselves and do not have a strong support system from family and friends; and (4) inadequate information results from closing oneself to information and not taking full advantage of one's potential. **Ask: How similar are these to problems adolescents face? What can you conclude about maturity?**

CHAPTER 5

Section 1, pages 129–136

Quick Lab

Purpose Students will examine whether or not adult development is the same for men and women.

Process Skills Making generalizations, making comparisons, drawing conclusions

Teaching Strategies

- Review good interviewing techniques.
- Discuss the types of interview questions that may show differences in attitudes between males and females.

Analysis

1. Answers will vary. Men and women in middle age may have somewhat different views of work, family, and physical attractiveness.
2. Answers will vary. Some may note that broad generalizations are not possible with a small sample.

Enrich

Ask students to give examples of how generativity might manifest itself in a parent/child relationship. **Ask: How might a childless person fulfill the need for generativity?**

4 CLOSE

A number of factors influence social and personality development in later life, including gender, occupation, and ethnic or cultural background. Have students discuss how these factors as well as personal habits, interests, worries, lifestyle, and opportunities affect the adjustments that people make as they age.

Quick Lab

Do men and women go through the same stages of development?

The latest studies show that just as during adolescence, men and women also go through stages of development during adulthood. Are their experiences the same?

Procedure

1. Prepare a list of interview questions that address a person's attitudes about work, family relationships, and importance of physical attractiveness.
2. Arrange to interview, separately, a man and a woman who are middle-aged; explain the purpose of your interview to them.

Analysis

1. What differences in attitudes or feelings did you detect between the man and the woman?
2. Based on your interviews, do you think men and women go through different stages of adult development? Explain. As a class compare your conclusions.

See the Skills Handbook, page 622, for an explanation of designing an experiment.

The "Empty Nest" Syndrome A significant event in many women's lives is the departure from home of the last child. Contrary to popular belief, this event most likely is not traumatic. Most women enjoy greater freedom after their last child has left home. Both spouses reconnect and spend more time pursuing their own goals and interests. Fathers are more likely to experience children's departure negatively (Clay, 2003).

Of course, not all women experience the same sense of new freedom. Psychologists have found that a stable marriage makes a difference. If a woman has a warm relationship with her husband, she may find the adjustment easier because of his support. If the woman is widowed or divorced, the transition can be much more difficult but possibly more freeing.

Depression in Midlife Depression can affect people of all ages, but it is most common among middle-aged women. During the early years of a woman's life, she may derive a sense of personal worth from her roles of daughter, lover, wife, mother, and wage earner. These relationships change as children grow, parents die, or marriages fail. Some women begin to experience a sense of loss and personal worthlessness. The onset of menopause can trigger depression. Those who have defined themselves as childbearers may view themselves as useless. Other women welcome this time of life. Career women can draw a new sense of self-esteem from their work environment. Some women in their 50s find that the nature of their marriage changes when they no longer have to focus their attention on the needs of their children.

SECTION 1 Assessment

1. **Review the Vocabulary** What is menopause? What physical reactions does it cause?
2. **Visualize the Main Idea** Use a flowchart similar to the one below to summarize Levinson's theory of male development.

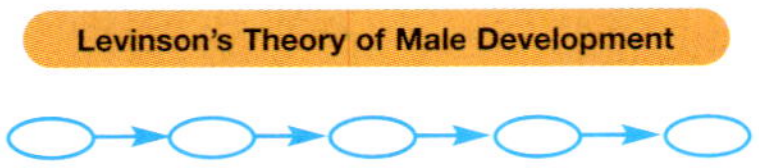

3. **Recall Information** How do generativity and stagnation affect a person's midlife transition?
4. **Think Critically** How do the intellectual abilities of young adults and older adults differ?
5. **Application Activity** Create a comparison chart of challenges faced by adults and adolescents. Include illustrations and real-life examples.

SECTION 1 Assessment Answers

1. the biological event in which a woman's production of sex hormones is sharply reduced; an end to ovulation and menstruation
2. Flowcharts should reflect an understanding of Levinson's theory of male development.
3. A person with opportunities to share wisdom with future generations will likely begin doing so during midlife transition. At the other end of the spectrum are those who choose to cling to the past. They are more likely to experience stagnation during midlife transition.
4. The intellectual abilities of young adults and older adults are similar, except that the vocabulary of older adults continues to expand, as does their ability to comprehend new material and to think flexibly.
5. Students' answers will vary. The chart should show both differences and similarities.

SECTION 2 Old Age

Reader's Guide

Main Idea

As we age, our priorities and expectations change to match realities, and we experience losses as well as gains.

Vocabulary

- decremental model of aging
- ageism
- senile dementia
- Alzheimer's disease

Objectives

- Identify changes that occur in health and life situation during old age.
- Summarize how people physically, mentally, and socially adjust to old age.

EXPLORING PSYCHOLOGY

Be Suspicious

Be suspicious if you are told ill health is what you can expect at your age. Remember the man of 104 who, when he complained of a stiff knee, was told, "After all, you can't expect to be agile," and replied, "My left knee's 104, too, and that doesn't hurt."

—from *Say Yes to Old Age: Developing a Positive Attitude Toward Aging* by Alex Comfort, 1990

Many people believe that experiencing problems in old age is inevitable. In one big-city newspaper, the photograph of a man celebrating his ninetieth birthday was placed on the obituary page. Is this only one newspaper editor's view on aging? Perhaps, but unfortunately, many people tend to regard old age as being just one step away from the grave. Indeed, some would rather die than grow old.

The fear of growing old is probably one of the most common fears in our society. We are surrounded with indications that aging and old age are negative—or at best something to ridicule. Birthday cards make light of aging; comedians joke about it. Advertisements urge us to trade in older products for the newer, faster model. We encourage older workers to retire—whether or not they want to retire—and replace them with younger people. Many do not even want to use the word *old* and instead refer to "golden agers" and "senior citizens."

SECTION RESOURCES

Reproducible Masters

- Guided Reading Activity 5–2
- Vocabulary Activity 5–2
- Section Quiz 5–2

Transparencies

- Daily Focus Transparency 5–2

Multimedia

- *ExamView® Assessment Suite* CD-ROM
- Presentation Plus! Software

1 FOCUS

Section Objectives

1. Identify changes that occur in health and life situation during old age.
2. Summarize how people physically, mentally, and socially adjust to old age.

BELLRINGER
Motivational Activity

Project Daily Focus Transparency 5–2 and have students answer the questions.

Available as blackline master

Daily Focus Transparency 5–2

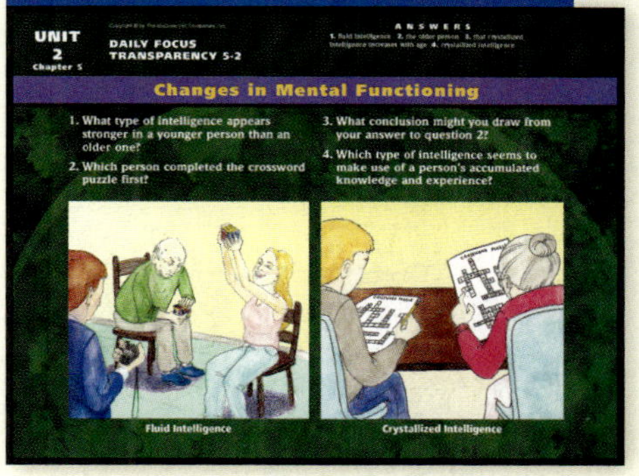

Reader's Guide

Use the Reader's Guide to introduce concepts and vocabulary.

Exploring Psychology

Ask students to read the **Exploring Psychology** feature and then discuss: **How can a positive attitude help during the aging process?**

Vocabulary Precheck

Have students read the Glossary definition of each term. Then challenge them to write a paragraph on old age that uses the terms.

2 TEACH

L1 Identifying Ageism Bring to class a collection of humorous birthday cards that deal with aging. Read them aloud to the class. **Ask: Which of the cards reveal attitudes based on a negative view of aging? Which cards use humor to underscore a positive view of aging?** Use this activity to provoke a discussion of how humor can sometimes be used to mask prejudice. ELL **BLOCK SCHEDULING**

Guided Reading Activity 5–2

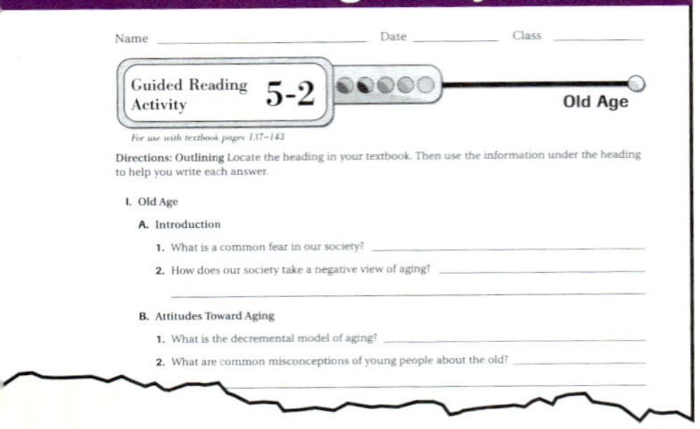
Name ______ Date ______ Class ______

Guided Reading Activity 5-2 — Old Age

For use with textbook pages 137–143

Directions: Outlining Locate the heading in your textbook. Then use the information under the heading to help you write each answer.

I. Old Age
  A. Introduction
    1. What is a common fear in our society? ______
    2. How does our society take a negative view of aging? ______
  B. Attitudes Toward Aging
    1. What is the decremental model of aging? ______
    2. What are common misconceptions of young people about the old? ______

Figure 5.4

Caption Answer The cartoonist views the process of aging as negative but does so with humor.

ATTITUDES TOWARD AGING

decremental model of aging: idea that progressive physical and mental decline are inevitable with age

ageism: prejudice or discrimination against the elderly

Many of our attitudes about aging are based on a **decremental model of aging,** which holds that progressive physical and mental decline is inevitable with age. In other words, chronological age is what makes people "old." In fact, there are great differences in physical condition among the elderly, depending on their genetic makeup and environment. Many of us know people who are 80 and look and act 50, and vice versa. The prevalence of the decremental view in our society can be explained in part by ignorance and a lack of contact with older people. The result is a climate of prejudice against the old. A researcher coined the word **ageism** to refer to this prejudice. As with racism and sexism, ageism feeds on myths rather than facts.

Young people tend to believe that the old suffer from poor health, live in poverty, and are frequent victims of crime. The elderly seldom see these as personal problems, though; interestingly, they tend to think of them as problems for other older people (Harris, 1978). Such beliefs, however, affect stereotypes of the elderly.

The notion that the aged withdraw from life and sit around doing nothing is also very common. This, too, is a false picture. There are many musicians and actors who are good examples of active older individuals, and many less well-known older people follow their lead. The majority of older Americans work or wish to work either for pay or as volunteers. Stereotypes perpetrate widespread misconceptions about older people.

One misconception is the notion that older people are inflexible or senile. Actually, rigidity is more a lifelong habit than a response to aging. The older person who is rigid probably was rigid as a young adult. Dementia (once called senility), which affects only 10 percent of the aged, usually results from disease rather than from the natural aging process.

Figure 5.4 Views of Growing Older

Despite the negative attitudes associated with growing older, many people find their forties, fifties, and older years rewarding periods of life. ***How does this cartoonist view the process of aging?***

COOPERATIVE LEARNING ACTIVITY

Writing a Profile Organize the class into small groups to write a profile of a person who has achieved a greater degree of success in old age than he or she did in younger years. The teams should research candidates for the profile. (Possible choices include poet William Carlos Williams, artists Georgia O'Keeffe or Grandma Moses, musician Pablo Casals, or everyday heroes of the students' own choosing.) Have each group discuss the various choices and select one. The team should write a 1- to 2-page profile of the person and, if possible, include a picture of the person and an example of the person's work. **BLOCK SCHEDULING**

CHANGES IN HEALTH

Physical strength and the senses decline about 1 percent a year through adulthood. Though most people over 65 consider themselves in good health, about 31 percent of American adults are obese (Centers for Disease Control and Prevention, 2005). Good health in adolescence and adult life carries over into old age. Eating habits and exercise influence patterns of health and disease. Today's emphasis on healthy lifestyles will also lead to physical wellness in old age.

All people, young and old, are subject to disease, though. About 35 percent of the elderly have at least one chronic disease (a permanent disability as opposed to an acute or temporary disability more common with younger people). The four most prevalent chronic diseases are heart disease, hypertension, diabetes, and arthritis. In general, the major causes of death among the old are heart disease, cancer, and strokes. Most older people, though, believe their health is good. Nearly 78 percent of noninstitutionalized adults aged 65 to 74 and 71 percent of those 75 and older rate their health as good (Centers for Disease Control and Prevention, 2005).

The quality of health care for the elderly remains by and large inferior to that of the general population. The reasons for this are numerous. The elderly in the lower socioeconomic class tend not to take care of themselves or to seek out treatment when needed. Some doctors may prefer to administer to younger patients with acute diseases rather than to older patients with long-term chronic conditions that can only be stabilized, not cured. Some doctors hold stereotypical views of the aged that can lead to misdiagnosis and improper treatment.

Some elderly people who are no longer able to care for themselves live with relatives. For others, there are institutions (but only about 4 percent of people 65 and older live in nursing homes). Too many of these nursing homes, however, have inadequate facilities. As more and more people each year reach late adulthood, it is crucial that there be a general overhaul of health care treatment for the elderly.

Figure 5.5 Living Long

A larger percentage of people in our society are living to more advanced ages. As a result, the elderly exert an increasing influence. ***How does a person's health change with age?***

CHANGES IN LIFE SITUATION

For younger people, transitions in life—graduation, marriage, parenthood—are usually positive and create a deeper involvement in life. In late adulthood, transitions—retirement, widowhood—are often negative and

Reading Check What major changes in life situation affect older people?

Figure 5.5

Caption Answer Physical strength and the sharpness of the five senses decline with age.

CURRICULUM CONNECTION

Health In recent years, various versions of the classic Olympic competition have been devised. In 2005, some 10,000 senior athletes competed in the U.S. Senior Olympics. The sports ranged from badminton and horseshoes to basketball and volleyball. Other countries hold their own version of the Senior Olympics. The purpose of Canada's Senior Games is "to promote participation by all seniors in an active and enjoyable lifestyle." Thus the Canada Senior Games are a means to an end—the promotion of activities for all seniors. Each event at the Canada Senior Games is composed of some combination of Physical Activity, Socialization, and/or Mental Stimulation.

Reading Check Answer Major changes facing older people include retirement, widowhood, reduced responsibilities, and increased isolation.

MEETING SPECIAL NEEDS

Learning Style: Interpersonal Arrange for students to volunteer a few hours over a couple of weeks at a senior citizen's center, nursing home, or other senior services program in your community. Students should keep a journal of their experiences and impressions, with a focus on uncovering any misconceptions in their attitudes toward the elderly. Students should prepare an oral report describing their experiences for the class and assessing changes in their attitudes toward the elderly. **L1** **BLOCK SCHEDULING**

Refer to ***Inclusion for the High School Social Studies Classroom Strategies and Activities*** in the TCR for strategies for students with different learning styles.

Psychology Journal

Ask students to select a misconception about old age. Have them write about a person they have encountered who tends to confirm that misconception. Then ask them to write about a person they have encountered who disproves the misconception. ■

Teacher Tip

Point out that such terms as *golden-ager* and *young at heart* are euphemisms—expressions meant to mask a harsher reality. Ask students to think of some other euphemisms connected with old age.

Applying Psychology

Driving has been called an American pastime. Except for people in a few large cities, most people use a personal car for nearly all their transportation needs. Most advocate groups claim that older drivers are more cautious and have fewer accidents. However, recent studies that factor in the number of miles driven indicate that drivers 75 years old and above are at a similar risk level to drivers 16–24 years old, who are considered high risk. **Ask: What factors should be considered in the decision to stop driving? What psychological factors affect a person's willingness to give up driving?**

reduce responsibilities and increase isolation. Perhaps the most devastating transition is the loss of a spouse. About 43 percent of women and 15 percent of men aged 65 and older are widowed. By the age of 75, nearly 22 percent of men and 6 out of 10 women are alone. Across the entire age spectrum, there are about four widows for every widower (U.S. Census Bureau, 2006). All too often, the person loses not just a spouse but the support of friends and family, who cannot cope with the widowed person's grief or feel threatened by the survivor's new status as a single person.

The symptoms of depression are very common in older adults. Many older people have suffered because of life challenges such as aging and loss of spouses and friends. Symptoms such as weight changes, feelings of worthlessness, extreme sadness, inability to concentrate, and thoughts of death and suicide are often cited. Depression is caused by many factors, such as genetic predisposition, family heritage, an unhealthy lifestyle, poor nutrition, lack of exercise, loneliness, and stress.

On the positive side, older people continue to learn and develop skills more than ever before. Some people attend night school, local adult education classes, or learn about computers. It has become clear that in older adults some abilities such as nonverbal tasks and problem solving may decline, but other abilities remain normal and some improve with age.

More About...

Growing Old

America's old people may not be given much respect because they often lack status. Many occupy the lower rungs of the economic ladder, though improvements in Medicare and Medicaid were offered in 2005 (Pear, 2006). In Japan that situation rarely develops because the able-bodied continue to work or to help their families in the home. In addition, they are guaranteed a minimum income, receive free annual health examinations, and are eligible for completely free medical care after age 70.

The Japanese also fully integrate the elderly into their daily lives. In Japan about 75 percent of the old live with their children, as opposed to only 25 percent in the United States. For those who do live alone, the Japanese have established programs to assure that they receive daily visits or calls. To encourage the active involvement of all older citizens in social activities, the government subsidizes Elders Clubs and sports programs. Through these programs the aged supply each other with mutual support.

CHANGES IN SEXUAL ACTIVITY

Just as young people tend to think sexual activity diminishes at midlife, they often believe it ceases altogether in old age. Yet the majority of people over the age of 65 continue to be interested in sex, and healthy partners enjoy sexual activity into their 70s and 80s. One psychologist commented that "Sexy young people mature into sexy middle-aged and elderly people" (Allgeier, 1983). As with so many human behaviors, the best predictor of future behavior is past behavior. For the elderly with an available partner, the frequency and regularity of sexual activities during earlier years are the best overall predictor of such activities in later years. The reasons some do not engage in sexual activity apparently are related to poor health or the death of a spouse, rather than to a lack of interest or to sexual physiology and functioning. Societal attitudes are another factor that discourages sexual expression by the elderly. Old people are not supposed to be interested in sex or be sexually active. Sexual relationships in old age—and even displays of affection—are often considered silly, improper, or even morally wrong.

People who grow old in this atmosphere may give up sexual activity because they are "supposed to." On a more personal level, older people often encounter opposition from family and friends if they want to remarry

CRITICAL THINKING ACTIVITY

Identifying Central Issues Assign students to develop a list of goals that they would like to achieve by each of the following ages: 30, 40, 50, 60, 70, and 80. Tell students to think of goals related to their personal relationships, education, choice of occupation, marriage, children, and health. Students should develop a time line identifying activities that will have to be performed or skills that will have to be developed in order to achieve these goals. Tell students that they should use the goals and time line to write a short personal essay identifying one preeminent goal they would like to accomplish during their lifetime and explain why it is important and how they will attempt to accomplish it. **L2**

after the death of a spouse. Children and family, too, find the idea of love and sex in old age ridiculous or even vaguely disgusting. A change in our ideas may enable a large segment of our population to continue to enjoy a guilt-free, healthy sex life in old age.

ADJUSTING TO OLD AGE

Many of the changes the elderly face make their adjustment to everyday life more difficult because they represent a loss of control over the environment. When older people are unable to maintain what they value most—good health, recognition in the community, visits from family and friends, privacy, leisure and work activities—the quality of their lives suffers dramatically, along with their self-image.

The loss of control is usually gradual, and it may involve both physical changes (becoming sick or disabled) and external circumstances (moving to a nursing home). Losing a husband is terrible enough, but the burden is only made worse by the further losses of friends and one's house. Those who experience a loss of control often develop a negative self-concept. They can regain a sense of control and a more positive self-image if they are helped to make the best of the options available to them. People with assertive personalities are often better at coping with life changes than more passive individuals because they are better able to demand and get the attention they need.

In order to help old people adjust, society must make some basic changes. Older people are beginning this process themselves by supporting organizations such as the AARP (American Association of Retired Persons). These groups speak out and lobby on social issues of importance to them. Since the population over 65 is constantly growing, social policy will have to take the elderly into consideration more and more (see Figure 5.6). Attitudes toward old people are already slowly changing. Eventually a time will come when old age will be considered the culmination of life, not simply the termination.

Psychology and You: Retirement and You

The average age in North America continues to creep upward. That is bad news for the smaller number of children being born and growing up now as they plan for their own retirement. Today's retirees can count on Social Security for funds—but will those funds be there when you retire? Social Security is not a personal retirement program; it is a tax-supported benefit. What workers pay in as a salary tax is paid right back out to today's retirees as a benefit.

As the number of older people increases and the number of people in the workforce does not, two things are happening. Social Security taxes are increasing, and full retirement benefits, formerly available at age 65, will not be available until age 67, by the time you retire. Today's workers—this means you—need to be finding other funding sources for their retirement.

CHANGES IN MENTAL FUNCTIONING

As people age, there are also changes in many of the mental functions they use, although there is much less decline in intelligence and memory than people think. If you compare measures of intellectual ability for a

Psychology and You

Use the following question to direct a class discussion after students have read the **Psychology and You** feature.

Ask: **What proposals are currently being considered by Congress to change the Social Security system? How will these changes affect you as you begin your working career? As you approach retirement age?**

Readings and Case Studies in Psychology

Have students review the Chapter 5 Reading selection in *Readings and Case Studies in Psychology* and answer the questions that follow the reading.

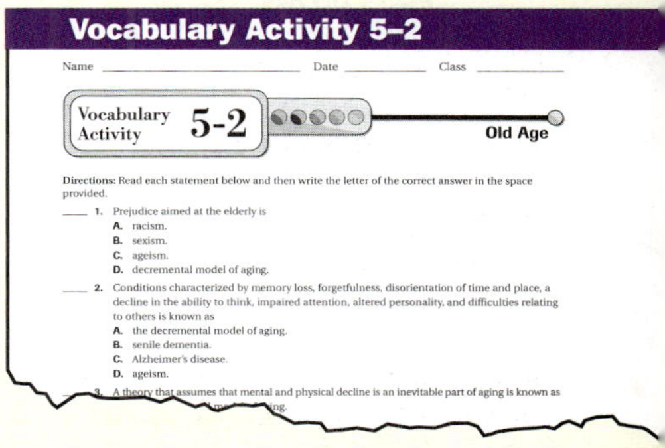

Vocabulary Activity 5–2

Name ______ Date ______ Class ______

Vocabulary Activity 5-2 — Old Age

Directions: Read each statement below and then write the letter of the correct answer in the space provided.

____ 1. Prejudice aimed at the elderly is
A. racism.
B. sexism.
C. ageism.
D. decremental model of aging.

____ 2. Conditions characterized by memory loss, forgetfulness, disorientation of time and place, a decline in the ability to think, impaired attention, altered personality, and difficulties relating to others is known as
A. the decremental model of aging.
B. senile dementia.
C. Alzheimer's disease.
D. ageism.

____ 3. A theory that assumes that mental and physical decline is an inevitable part of aging is known as

PSYCHOLOGY LAB EXPERIMENT

Crystallized Intelligence Tell students that this experiment will help them examine crystallized and fluid intelligence. Have students develop a vocabulary test similar to ones found in *Reader's Digest*. Encourage students to avoid words that are part of pop culture. They may want to use a dictionary to help them find words for the test. Students should arrange to give the vocabulary test to five people between the ages of 18 and 30 and five people over 55. Students should give each group of participants the same amount of time to complete the test. Have students chart the results of the two tests by age. **Ask:** **How do the results help you understand crystallized and fluid intelligence?** Have students summarize their findings in a short report. **L1** **BLOCK SCHEDULING**

Figure 5.6

Visual Instruction Have students use the current *Statistical Abstract of the United States* to gather information on changes in life expectancy for men and women in the United States since 1900. Students should use the data to create two line graphs.

Caption Answer People are living longer than ever before; life expectancy rates are higher in developed countries.

3 ASSESS

Assign Section 2 Assessment as homework or as an in-class activity.

Section Quiz 5–2

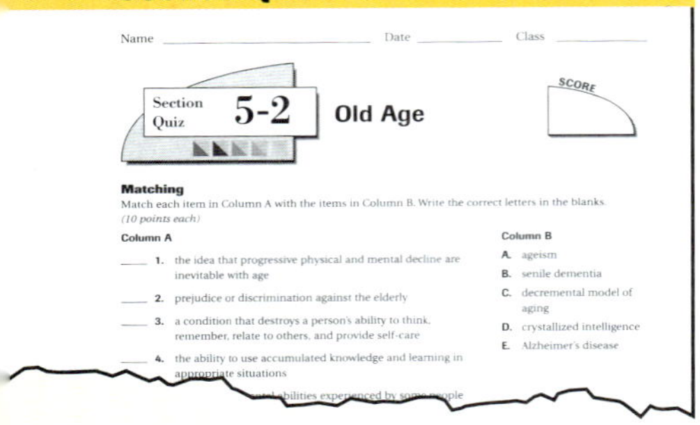
Name ______ Date ______ Class ______

Section Quiz 5-2 **Old Age**

SCORE

Matching
Match each item in Column A with the items in Column B. Write the correct letters in the blanks. *(10 points each)*

Column A

____ **1.** the idea that progressive physical and mental decline are inevitable with age

____ **2.** prejudice or discrimination against the elderly

____ **3.** a condition that destroys a person's ability to think, remember, relate to others, and provide self-care

____ **4.** the ability to use accumulated knowledge and learning in appropriate situations

Column B

A. ageism
B. senile dementia
C. decremental model of aging
D. crystallized intelligence
E. Alzheimer's disease

Reteach

Have students draw political cartoons that express with humor a common view of old age. Then ask students to write a short paragraph explaining why this view is correct or incorrect.

Figure 5.6 Percentage of Older Population

The number of elderly in the United States is rapidly growing. ***How have life expectancy rates changed since 1950?***

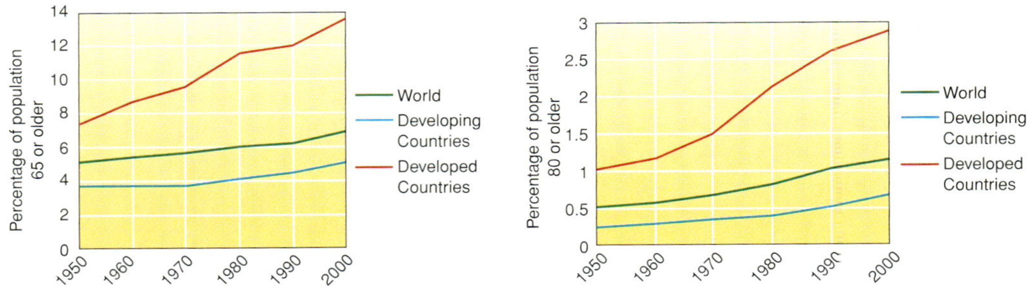

group of elderly people with similar measures for younger people, you might see a difference—namely that older people do not score as well on intellectual tests. However, the older group of people will most likely be less educated and less familiar with test taking than younger people. Furthermore, there are many different types of mental skills and abilities that combine to produce intellectual functioning, and these abilities do not develop at the same rate or time across the life span. Factors such as physical health, vision, hearing, coordination, the speed or timing of intelligence testing, and attitudes in the testing situation all affect intelligence test scores.

John Horn (1982) has proposed two types of intelligence: *crystallized* and *fluid* intelligence. Crystallized intelligence refers to the ability to use accumulated knowledge and learning in appropriate situations. This ability increases with age and experience. Fluid intelligence is the ability to solve abstract relational problems and to generate new hypotheses. This ability is not tied to schooling or education and gradually increases in development as the nervous system matures. As people age and their nervous systems decline, so does their fluid intelligence. Thus, older people may not be as good at problems that require them to combine and generate new ideas. A decline in the nervous system affects reaction time, visual motor flexibility, and memory (see Figure 5.7). Elderly people have difficulty retrieving information from memory. If they are asked to recognize a familiar name or object, they cannot do so as well as younger people.

Senile Dementia

senile dementia: decreases in mental abilities experienced by some people in old age

A small percentage of people develop senile dementia in old age. **Senile dementia** is a collective term that describes conditions characterized by memory loss, forgetfulness, disorientation of time and place, a decline in the ability to think, impaired attention, altered personality, and

INTERDISCIPLINARY CONNECTIONS ACTIVITY

Government Today many special-interest groups lobby Congress, the president, and other elected officials to support their particular positions. Ask students to research a special-interest group that lobbies on behalf of senior citizens, such as the AARP. Students may select this group or another group. The research should answer the following questions: **What current legislation are they attempting to influence? What positions do they hold on major social issues? What groups or individuals may oppose their positions? How do they finance their lobby efforts? What methods do they use to influence legislation?** Students should write a 2- to 3-page report discussing the findings of their research. **L2** 

difficulties in relating to others. Dementia has many causes—some forms are treatable, whereas others are not at this time.

Alzheimer's Disease The most common form of senile dementia is Alzheimer's disease. **Alzheimer's disease** is an affliction more commonly seen among the elderly. About 4.5 million people have this disease, and problems associated with it are the eighth leading cause of death among U.S. adults.

Alzheimer's is a neurological disease marked by a gradual deterioration of cognitive functioning. Early signs of the disease include frequent forgetting, poor judgment, increased irritability, and social withdrawal. Eventually Alzheimer's patients lose their ability to comprehend simple questions and to recognize friends and loved ones. Ultimately they require constant supervision and custodial care, often from trained professionals. Rarely do patients die from the disease itself, but their weakened state leaves them vulnerable to a variety of other potentially fatal problems.

The causes of Alzheimer's are complex and still not completely understood. Genetic susceptibility plays a role. Other causes may involve life events. At present there is no cure for the disease. Many patients and their caretakers (usually their families) are offered supportive therapy that helps them learn to accept the relentless progression of the disease and the limitations it imposes on its victims.

Figure 5.7 The Aging Brain

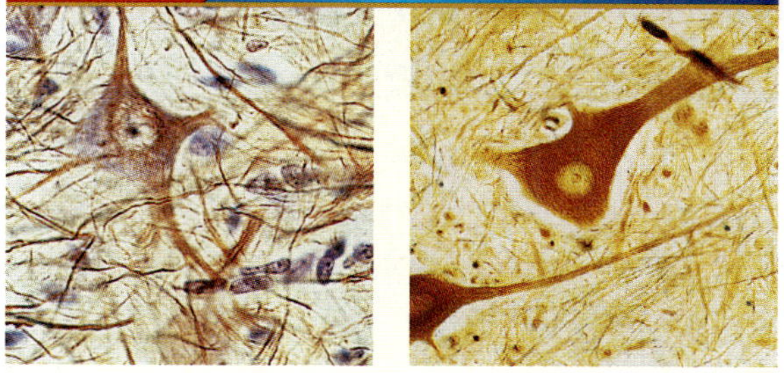

At left is a microscopic image of neurons (nerve cells) in the cerebellum (brain) of a young adult. At right is an image of neurons in an older adult. Notice that the branching of the dendrites decreases, reducing the connections between neurons. ***What effects do aging neuron connections have on older people?***

Alzheimer's disease: a condition that destroys a person's ability to think, remember, relate to others, and care for herself or himself

SECTION 2 Assessment

1. **Review the Vocabulary** Describe the decremental model of aging. Is this an accurate model of aging? Explain.
2. **Visualize the Main Idea** Use a graphic organizer similar to the one below to list and define the two types of intelligence.

3. **Recall Information** How do life transitions in late adulthood differ from those in early adulthood?
4. **Think Critically** How might a person differentiate between Alzheimer's disease and changes in mental processes as a result of aging?
5. **Application Activity** Create a "to-do" list that will help you successfully adjust to old age.

Figure 5.7

Caption Answer The aging neuron connections slow reaction time, visual motor flexibility, and memory.

Enrich

Like racism and sexism, ageism can have detrimental effects on people. Ask students to participate in a panel discussion analyzing the various elements of ageism in American society. Panelists should discuss how ageism is expressed and in what ways attitudes have changed or are changing.

4 CLOSE

Instruct students to prepare a two-column chart entitled "Opinions on Old Age." Have them label one column *Fiction* and the other column *Fact*. Have students fill in each column with as many items as possible that they discovered in reading this section.

SECTION 2 Assessment Answers

1. The model holds that progressive physical and mental decline is inevitable with age. More realistically, great differences do exist in these conditions depending on the genetic makeup and health of the elderly.
2. crystallized intelligence: the ability to use accumulated knowledge and learning; fluid intelligence: the ability to solve abstract problems and generate new hypotheses
3. In early adulthood, changes are positive and create a deeper involvement in life. In late adulthood, changes are likely to reduce responsibility and increase isolation.
4. Although all nervous systems decline with age, old people are generally still able to remain vital and live independently. People with Alzheimer's disease gradually lose cognitive functioning to the point that they lose their ability to comprehend simple commands and recognize loved ones and friends.
5. Students' answers will vary. Examples to include on the list are as follows: do eat a healthy diet, do get adequate exercise, do remain socially active, and do continue learning.

CHAPTER 5

Section 3, pages 144–147

1 FOCUS

Section Objectives

1. Identify the stages of dying.
2. Describe the services of hospices.

BELLRINGER
Motivational Activity

Project Daily Focus Transparency 5–3 and have students answer the questions.

Available as blackline master

Daily Focus Transparency 5–3

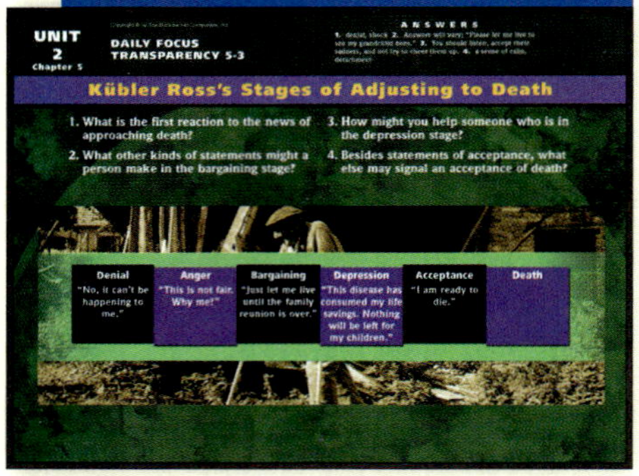

Reader's Guide

Use the Reader's Guide to introduce concepts and vocabulary.

■ **Exploring Psychology**

Ask students to read the **Exploring Psychology** feature and then discuss the following question: **What emotions and feelings is the poet expressing?**

■ **Vocabulary Precheck**

Have students read the Glossary definition of each vocabulary term. Then ask them to find the sources of these words and when they became part of our vocabulary.

Use the **Vocabulary PuzzleMaker CD-ROM** to create crossword and word search puzzles.

SECTION 3 Dying and Death

Reader's Guide

■ **Main Idea**

Death is inevitable. Most people face death by going through stages or an adjustment process.

■ **Vocabulary**

- thanatology
- hospice

■ **Objectives**

- Identify the stages of dying.
- Describe the services of hospices.

EXPLORING PSYCHOLOGY

Thinking About Death

Goodbye Papa, it's hard to die
When all the birds are singing in the sky
Now that the spring is in the air
Little kids are everywhere
Think of me and I'll be there.

—from "Seasons in the Sun" by Terry Jacks

Dying and death are popular subjects for many poets and songwriters. Why does death mystify us? Death is inevitable. Death is not just biological. When a person dies, there are legal, medical, psychological, and social aspects that need attention. It is not very easy to even define death anymore because there are medical advances that cloud this issue.

Biological death becomes entangled with social customs. These customs include cultural attitudes toward death, care of the dying, the place of death, and efforts to quicken or slow down the dying process. Death also has social aspects, including the disposal of the dead, mourning customs, and the role of the family. These social and cultural aspects of death are intertwined with our own thoughts and values about dying and death. Death may sound simple, but culturally it may be complex and confusing.

ADJUSTING TO DEATH

Once terminally ill patients have been informed of their condition, they must then cope with their approaching death. Elisabeth Kübler-Ross (1969) did some pioneering work on how the terminally ill react to their impending death. Her investigations made a major contribution in establishing **thanatology**—the study of dying and death. Based on interviews with 200 dying patients, she identified five stages of psychological

thanatology: the study of dying and death

SECTION RESOURCES

Reproducible Masters

- Guided Reading Activity 5–3
- Vocabulary Activity 5–3
- Section Quiz 5–3

Transparencies

- Daily Focus Transparency 5–3

Multimedia

- Vocabulary PuzzleMaker CD-ROM
- *ExamView*® *Assessment Suite* CD-ROM
- Presentation Plus! Software

adjustment. The first stage is *denial.* People's most common reaction to learning that they have a terminal illness is shock and numbness, followed by denial. They react by saying, "No, it can't be happening to me," or "I'll get another opinion." They may assert that the doctors are incompetent or the diagnosis mistaken. In extreme cases, people may refuse treatment and persist in going about business as usual. Most patients who use denial extensively throughout their illness are people who have become accustomed to coping with difficult life situations in this way. Indeed, the denial habit may contribute to the seriousness of a condition. For example, a person might refuse to seek medical attention at the onset of an illness, denying that it exists.

During the second stage, *anger,* the reaction of dying people is "Why me?" They feel anger—at fate, at the powers that be, at every person who comes into their life. At this stage, they are likely to alienate themselves from others, for no one can relieve the anger they feel at their shortened life span and lost chances.

During the stage of *bargaining,* people change their attitude and attempt to bargain with fate. For example, a woman may ask God for a certain amount of time in return for good behavior. She may promise a change of ways, even a dedication of her life to the church. She may announce that she is ready to settle for a less threatening form of the same illness and begin to bargain with the doctor over the diagnosis. For example, if she submits gracefully to some procedures, might she be rewarded by being spared the next stage of the illness? This stage is relatively short and is followed by the stage of *depression.*

During depression, dying people are aware of the losses they are incurring (for example, loss of body tissue, loss of job, loss of life savings). Also, they

Profiles In Psychology

Elisabeth Kübler-Ross

1926–2004

"If you have lived fully, then you have no regrets, because you have done the best you can. If you made lots of goofs—much better to have made lots of goofs than not to have lived at all."

As a young woman, Dr. Kübler-Ross visited a concentration camp in Maidanek, Germany, during World War II. There she spoke to a young Jewish woman who had just lost her entire family in a gas chamber. This woman was supposed to be the last one in the chamber, but there was not room, so she was spared. When Kübler-Ross asked how Nazi leader Adolf Hitler could commit such atrocities, the woman replied that there is a Hitler in every human. Kübler-Ross came to understand that depending on the circumstances, anyone could do horrible things.

After that experience Kübler-Ross sought to understand humans and human death. This eventually led her to develop a theory on the stages of dying. As a result of her studies, many people have been able to come to terms with death and help others die in peace.

2 TEACH

L1 Creating Lists Have students list the five stages of psychological adjustment that people who are dying make. Under each item on the list, have students write at least two statements that demonstrate the thinking of a person in that stage. **ELL** **PSY:** 14D

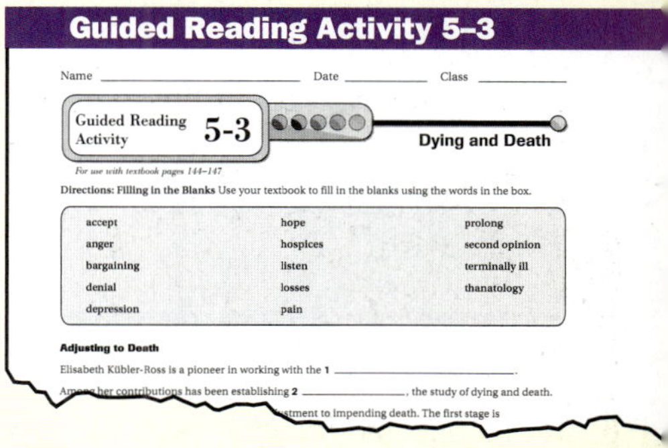
Guided Reading Activity 5–3

Name ______ Date ______ Class ______

Guided Reading Activity 5-3 — Dying and Death

For use with textbook pages 144–147

Directions: Filling in the Blanks Use your textbook to fill in the blanks using the words in the box.

accept	hope	prolong
anger	hospices	second opinion
bargaining	listen	terminally ill
denial	losses	thanatology
depression	pain	

Adjusting to Death

Elisabeth Kübler-Ross is a pioneer in working with the **1** ______.

Among her contributions has been establishing **2** ______, the study of dying and death.

...stment to impending death. The first stage is

Profiles In Psychology

Ask students to read the **Profiles In Psychology** feature and then discuss:

1. What did Kübler-Ross learn on a visit to the concentration camp in Maidanek, Germany? *(that, depending on the circumstances, anyone is capable of doing horrible things)*
2. What positive impact have her studies had on those who are facing their own deaths or helping someone who is dying? *(Her identification of the stages of dying helps people cope with their feelings about death and dying.)*

COOPERATIVE LEARNING ACTIVITY

Role Playing Organize the class into four groups. Ask the members of each group to imagine they are counseling the family of one of the following: an 80-year-old man who is dying of cancer; a 50-year-old woman who has suffered a stroke; a 30-year-old son who is dying of AIDS; and a 20-year-old daughter who is dying from injuries sustained in a car accident. Instruct members of each group to discuss their assigned situation and to determine the advice they might offer to the family to help the patient face death. Have each group role-play the counseling session. (If possible, suggest that students talk with social service and/or religious personnel who have experience in dealing with such heartbreaking situations.) **BLOCK SCHEDULING**

Reading Check Answer

Since individuals are unique, they may not experience all the stages or experience them in the same order.

Vocabulary Activity 5–3

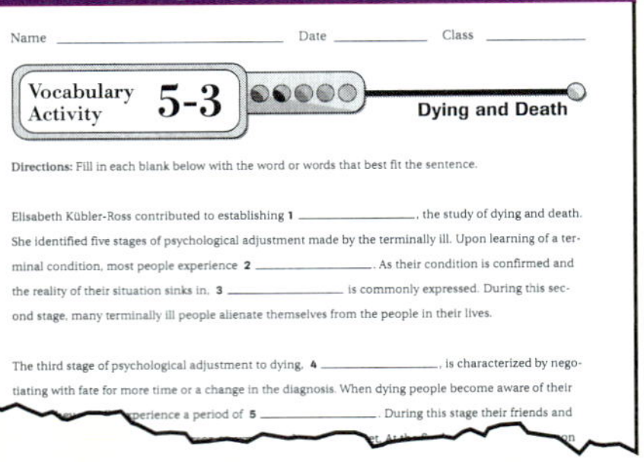
Name ________ Date ________ Class ________

Vocabulary Activity 5-3 Dying and Death

Directions: Fill in each blank below with the word or words that best fit the sentence.

Elisabeth Kübler-Ross contributed to establishing **1** ________, the study of dying and death. She identified five stages of psychological adjustment made by the terminally ill. Upon learning of a terminal condition, most people experience **2** ________. As their condition is confirmed and the reality of their situation sinks in, **3** ________ is commonly expressed. During this second stage, many terminally ill people alienate themselves from the people in their lives.

The third stage of psychological adjustment to dying, **4** ________, is characterized by negotiating with fate for more time or a change in the diagnosis. When dying people become aware of their ... experience a period of **5** ________. During this stage their friends and ...

Figure 5.8

Caption Answer At the funeral service, people may see the body, which may bring a sense of closure. Comfort provided by family and friends also helps with the acceptance of death.

3 ASSESS

Assign Section 3 Assessment as homework or as an in-class activity.

Section Quiz 5–3

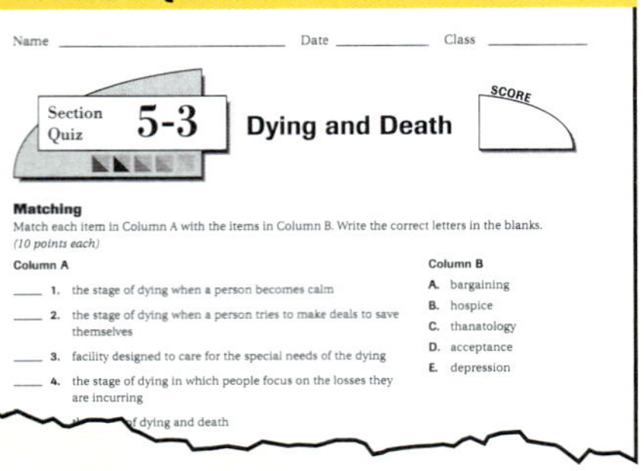
Name ________ Date ________ Class ________

Section Quiz 5-3 Dying and Death SCORE

Matching

Match each item in Column A with the items in Column B. Write the correct letters in the blanks. *(10 points each)*

Column A

____ **1.** the stage of dying when a person becomes calm

____ **2.** the stage of dying when a person tries to make deals to save themselves

____ **3.** facility designed to care for the special needs of the dying

____ **4.** the stage of dying in which people focus on the losses they are incurring

... of dying and death

Column B

A. bargaining
B. hospice
C. thanatology
D. acceptance
E. depression

are depressed about the loss that is to come: they are in the process of losing everybody and everything. Kübler-Ross suggests that it is helpful to allow such people to express their sadness and not to attempt to cover up the situation or force them to act cheerfully.

Finally, patients *accept* death. The struggle is over, and they experience a sense of calm. In some cases, the approach of death feels appropriate or peaceful. They seem to become detached intentionally so as to make death easier.

Not all terminal patients progress through the stages that Kübler-Ross describes. Some people may go through the stages but in different order, or they may repeat some stages. Critics note that individuals are unique and sometimes do not follow predictable patterns of behavior. For example, a person may die in the denial stages because he or she is psychologically unable to proceed beyond it or because the course of the illness does not grant the necessary time to do so. Kübler-Ross notes that patients do not limit their responses to any one stage; a depressed patient may have recurring bursts of anger. All patients preserve the hope that they may live after all. Camille Wortman and others have argued that Kübler-Ross's stages may simply identify the five most common styles of dealing with death, with no need to progress through stages.

Reading Check

Why do some people criticize Kübler-Ross's stages of dying?

Most people have trouble dealing with the thought of their own death, and they also find it difficult to deal with the death of others. What should we do when a loved one is approaching death? Like all people, dying people need respect, dignity, and self-confidence. Dying people need support and care. They require open communication about what is happening and help with legal and financial arrangements. What should we do after a loved one has died? Our society has developed certain standards that provide guidance on this point. For instance, in the 1800s, a widow or widower was expected to grieve for a long time. Today society encourages people to try to get back to their normal lives (Stroebe et al., 1992). How long a person grieves depends on the person who is grieving.

Figure 5.8 Burial Rites

The ceremonies associated with death in many cultures, like the Mexican culture, help people start to work through the grieving process. ***How might funeral ceremonies force people to confront and accept the death of a loved one?***

Hospices

Discussing death is one of the few taboos left in twenty-first century America. The breakdown of extended families and the rise of modern medicine have insulated most people in our society from death. Many people have no direct experience with death, and partly as a result, they are afraid to talk about it. In 1900 the average life span was less than 50 years, and most people died at home. Today, most Americans live until at least 78, and they die in nursing homes and hospitals. Machines can prolong existence long after a person has stopped living a normal life.

MEETING SPECIAL NEEDS

Learning Style: Naturalist Tell students that all cultures have various customs and rituals associated with death. One purpose of these customs is to help those who are living adjust emotionally and psychologically to loss. Ask students to interview adults, including a funeral home director, if possible, to learn about the customs and rituals surrounding death. Have students create a display that presents these customs and rituals and analyzes how they help those who are living adjust to loss. **L2** **BLOCK SCHEDULING**

Refer to ***Inclusion for the High School Social Studies Classroom Strategies and Activities*** in the TCR for strategies for students with different learning styles.

A movement to restore the dignity of dying revolves around the concept of the **hospice**—usually a special place where terminally ill people go to die. The hospice is designed to make the patient's surroundings pleasant and comfortable—less like a hospital and more like a home. Doctors in hospices do not try to prolong life but to improve the quality of life. A key component of hospice care is the use of tranquilizers and other drugs to ease discomfort and relieve pain. The patient in a hospice leads the most normal life he or she is able to do and is taken care of as much as possible by family members. If it can be arranged, a patient may choose to leave the hospice and die at home.

Another form of hospice service is becoming part of the mainstream of the health care system of the United States. This program features care for the elderly at home by visiting nurses, aides, physical therapists, chaplains, and social workers. Medicare now includes arrangements for providing and financing these hospice services. Many other insurance policies also include provisions for in-home hospice care and respite care. Growing rapidly in recent years, home-based hospice care is now a more frequently used service than inpatient hospice care in the United States.

Figure 5.9 **Hospice Care**

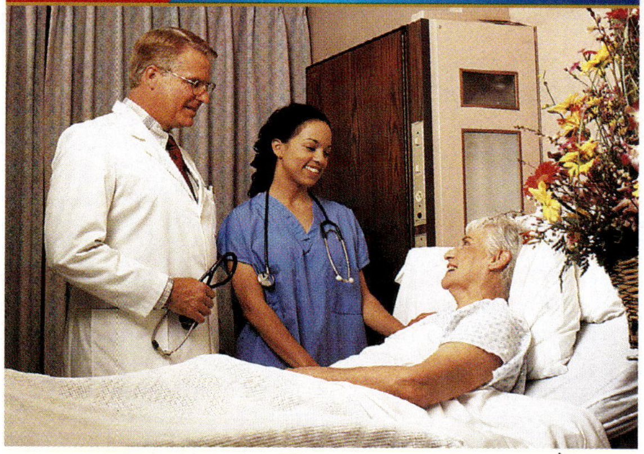

The staff of a hospice responds to the unique needs of the terminally ill by providing physical and emotional care. ***How does hospice care help a person die with dignity?***

hospice: a facility designed to care for the special needs of the dying

SECTION 3 Assessment

1. **Review the Vocabulary** Explain why thanatology is a subfield of psychology.
2. **Visualize the Main Idea** Using a diagram similar to the one below, list the most common reactions to dying.

3. **Recall Information** What do people go through during the denial stage of dying?
4. **Think Critically** Do you think that Kübler-Ross's stages of dying apply to other types of losses (such as in sports or a romantic breakup)? Explain.
5. **Application Activity** Research to find information on hospices and nursing homes. Evaluate the services these institutions provide and determine what services you would want if you needed to spend time in one of these places.

SECTION 3 Assessment Answers

1. Thanatology functions as a subfield of psychology because many of the issues related to dying and death involve the psychological adjustment to death.
2. 1. denial, 2. anger, 3. bargaining, 4. depression, and 5. acceptance
3. Denial is the first stage of psychological adjustment to dying and may include shock, numbness, refusal to believe diagnosis, search for second opinions, and, in some cases, refusal of treatment.
4. The psychological stages of dying may be relevant to other losses in life because there is a grieving process that most people experience when they lose something of value to them.
5. Students' answers will vary. They will most likely state that the quality of care is important, as is the need to treat people with respect and dignity.

Figure 5.9

Caption Answer It seeks to improve the quality of life and ease pain in a pleasant and comfortable surrounding.

Reteach

Write the five stages of psychological adjustment to death on the board. Ask students how they could be friends to a dying person in each of these stages.

Enrich

Have students find examples of poems or songs that express an emotional or psychological aspect of dying and death. Have them read aloud the poems or lyrics to the class.

4 CLOSE

Bring to class a brochure of services offered by a local hospice. Ask students to identify the services designed to assist in psychologically adjusting to death.

Going Further

Holland's Experiment With Euthanasia

Since 1984, euthanasia has rarely been prosecuted in Holland. In 1993 a law was passed in Holland that basically protects a doctor from prosecution for performing euthanasia under certain conditions.

The 1993 Burial Act requires the doctor to notify the local medical examiner that the death was a result of euthanasia. As long as all guidelines were followed, no prosecution will occur. Among the guidelines are that the person was suffering unbearably, that the decision was well reasoned, and that the doctor consulted with another physician for a second opinion.

The laws in Holland allow doctors to euthanize patients as young as 12. According to Holland's Justice Ministry, "For 12- to 15-year-olds, parental agreement is required, but in the case of a refusal by one of the parents, the request of a minor may be accepted if the doctor is convinced that this will mean avoiding serious suffering."

Discussing the Case Study

Ask: **Under what conditions, if any, should euthanasia be legal? What potential abuses could arise if euthanasia were legalized?** Use these questions to conduct a class debate.

Case Studies

Psychologically Able to Decide?

Period of Study: 1960–ongoing

Introduction: In April 1999, a Michigan court jury sentenced Dr. Jack Kevorkian, a pathologist, to 10 to 25 years in prison. The conviction was based on Kevorkian's role in the assisted suicide of a 52-year-old man who suffered from Lou Gehrig's disease.

Kevorkian provided his "patient" with lethal drugs. The doctor claimed he had used this "method" in about 130 other cases. Kevorkian argued that the assisted suicides he performed were methods of euthanasia. Euthanasia is allowing a terminally ill patient to die naturally without life support, or putting to death a person who suffers from an incurable disease (Rice, 2001). The Michigan jury that sentenced Kevorkian ruled that Kevorkian was guilty of murder because he had injected the lethal drugs directly into his patient. (The Lou Gehrig's disease sufferer was unable to take the drugs himself.)

The controversy surrounding Kevorkian and assisted suicide are the most well-known examples regarding not only euthanasia but also an individual's right to die. Opinions and feelings vary on this sensitive topic. For those who believe a terminally ill individual does have the right to die, it is important to determine if that person is psychologically able to make that final decision.

Hypothesis: How do you assess the psychological competence of a terminally ill person who desires death? This question must be resolved in a case-by-case manner and according to the varied laws of each state. Medical doctors and psychologists must rely on the information gathered from past and present cases of those who were granted permission by either physicians or the court system to terminate life-support systems.

Method: When a person is assessed for psychological competence, psychologists look for signs of depression, mental illness, and negative effects from any medication administered to them. If the terminally ill person does not show positive signs of these, the case is turned over to a physician, lawyer, court system, or any combination of these. From there, it is the legal decision of these authorities to allow the ill individual to follow through with the decision. This is the procedure used in adult cases. However, when the situation involves a child or teenager, the process is much more complex and emotionally difficult.

Results: Unfortunately experts cannot determine if a person who has opted to end life has made a psychologically sound decision. For this reason, among others, many people oppose the idea that a person can terminate his or her own life. Those who support euthanasia believe that it releases ill individuals from the pain and anguish their disease or condition has caused. They argue that it is unfair for others to grant or deny the choice of death because they have not experienced the pain and anguish of a terminally ill condition themselves.

Analyzing the Case Study

1. What is euthanasia? Why is it controversial?
2. Why was Dr. Kevorkian convicted of murder?
3. **Critical Thinking** How might you use Kübler-Ross's stages of dying to help you determine whether a person is psychologically able to terminate his or her life?

Answers for Analyzing the Case Study

1. Euthanasia is a deliberate termination of one's life with the assistance of someone else. It is controversial on religious and moral grounds, similar to the way suicide is. It is also controversial medically because of a doctor's position of trust and respect and oath to cause no harm.
2. Kevorkian administered the lethal dose of drugs to the individual.
3. Students' answers will vary. During denial people are unlikely to seek euthanasia. If experiencing anger or depression, a person may not be psychologically able to make a wise decision. If someone has accepted his or her own or another's impending death, he or she may be psychologically prepared to make a decision about euthanasia.

CHAPTER 5 Summary and Vocabulary

Much of people's fear of aging is rooted in stereotypes of what it means to grow older. The positive side of aging adult life is one of the best-kept secrets in our society.

Section 1 Adulthood

Main Idea: Adulthood is a time of transition—it involves shifting priorities and outlooks on life from adolescence and throughout the remainder of life.

- For most adults, the process of physical decline is slow and gradual.
- The adult years are a time when lifestyle may set the stage for problems that will show up then or in later life.
- Good physical and mental health seem to be the key factors affecting sexual activity in adulthood.
- The ability to comprehend new material and to think flexibly improves in early adulthood, and overall intelligence improves with age.
- An individual's basic character remains relatively stable throughout life.

Section 2 Old Age

Main Idea: As we age, our priorities and expectations change to match realities, and we experience losses as well as gains.

- The misbelief that progressive physical and mental decline is inevitable with age has resulted in a climate of prejudice against the old.
- The health of older people, for the most part, is related to their health when younger.
- In late adulthood, life transitions are often negative and reduce responsibilities and increase isolation.
- The frequency and regularity of sexual activities during earlier years is the best overall predictor of such activities in later years.
- Crystallized intelligence, or the ability to use accumulated knowledge and learning in appropriate situations, increases with age; fluid intelligence, or the ability to solve abstract relational problems and to generate new hypotheses, decreases with age.

Section 3 Dying and Death

Main Idea: Death is inevitable. Most people face death by going through stages or an adjustment process.

- Elisabeth Kübler-Ross identified five stages of psychological adjustment to death: denial, anger, bargaining, depression, and acceptance.
- A hospice is a special place where terminally ill people go to die; it is designed to make the patient's surroundings pleasant and comfortable.

Chapter Vocabulary

menopause (p. 131)
generativity (p. 135)
stagnation (p. 135)
decremental model of aging (p. 138)
ageism (p. 138)
senile dementia (p. 142)
Alzheimer's disease (p. 143)
thanatology (p. 144)
hospice (p. 147)

5 Summary and Vocabulary

Using the Chapter 5 Summary and Vocabulary

Use the Chapter 5 Summary and Vocabulary to preview, review, condense, or reteach the chapter.

Preview/Review

Use the Chapter Vocabulary list to help students review and study.

Activity Have students create a word search puzzle using definitions or examples as the clues for the puzzle.

Vocabulary PuzzleMaker CD-ROM reinforces the vocabulary terms used in Chapter 5.

Condense

Have students read the Chapter 5 Summary.

Chapter 5 Guided Reading Activities

Reteach

Reteaching Activity 5

AUTHENTIC ASSESSMENT ACTIVITY

Creating a Newsletter Tell students to imagine they are editors working on a newsletter for people entering middle and old age. Have them work in groups to design a 4-page edition entitled "So Now You're Over Forty." Instruct students to brainstorm a list of stories and features to be included. Topics should explore expert opinions on the physical, intellectual, social, and psychological changes that occur during middle and old age.

Refer to the ***Authentic Assessment*** booklet for additional activities and information about evaluating student performance.

CHAPTER 5 Assessment

PSYCHOLOGY Online

Self-Check Quiz
Visit the *Understanding Psychology* Web site at glencoe.com and click on **Chapter 5—Self-Check Quizzes** to prepare for the Chapter Test.

Reviewing Vocabulary

Choose the letter of the correct term or concept below to complete the sentence.

a. climacteric	**f.** ageism
b. menopause	**g.** senile dementia
c. generativity	**h.** Alzheimer's disease
d. stagnation	**i.** thanatology
e. decremental model of aging	**j.** hospice

1. During __________, a woman's production of sex hormones drops sharply.
2. The study of dying and death is __________.
3. Prejudice against the old is referred to as __________.
4. An adult who chooses to hang on to the past is experiencing __________.
5. __________ is a neurological disease marked by a gradual deterioration of cognitive functioning.
6. A(n) __________ is a special place where terminally ill people go to die.
7. Between the ages of 45 and 50, every woman experiences a stage called the __________, which represents all of the psychological and biological changes occurring at that time.
8. The desire to use one's wisdom to guide future generations is called __________.
9. According to a(n) __________, progressive physical and mental decline is inevitable with age.
10. __________ is characterized by memory loss, forgetfulness, disorientation of time and place, a decline in the ability to think, impaired attention, altered personality, and difficulties in relating to others.

Recalling Facts

1. Using a graphic organizer similar to the one below, identify three midlife issues faced by adult women.

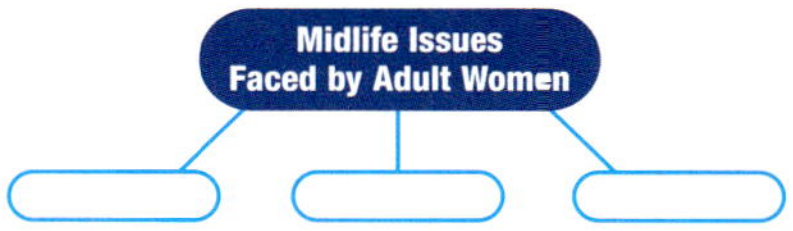

2. Describe how the "decremental model of aging" leads to ageism.
3. What is crystallized intelligence? What is fluid intelligence? Which type of intelligence increases with age?
4. List Kübler-Ross's five stages of psychological adjustment to death. What behaviors would you expect of someone at each stage?
5. What is a hospice designed to do? What types of people might live in a hospice?

Critical Thinking

1. **Making Inferences** Why do you think some men experience the age-thirty crisis? Do you think that some women might experience the age-thirty crisis? Explain.
2. **Analyzing Information** Do you think an individual's personality basically remains the same throughout the individual's life, or is it capable of change during adulthood? Explain your answer.
3. **Drawing Conclusions** Do you think that people of other cultures necessarily experience a "midlife crisis"? Why do you think so?
4. **Synthesizing Information** Dying and death have only recently become topics that are discussed openly. Given this growing openness, what changes do you see being made to make the adjustment to the prospect of dying less severe? What other changes do you think still need to be made?
5. **Demonstrating Reasoned Judgment** Some people believe that dying people should not be told they are dying. Do you agree? Why or why not?

5 Assessment

PSYCHOLOGY Online

Have students visit the Web site at glencoe.com to review Chapter 5 and take the **Self-Check Quiz.**

GLENCOE TECHNOLOGY

Presentation Plus! For a review of Chapter 5 content, see MindJogger Checkpoint on **Presentation Plus!**

Reviewing Vocabulary

1. b	**6.** j
2. i	**7.** a
3. f	**8.** c
4. d	**9.** e
5. h	**10.** g

Recalling Facts

1. menopause, empty-nest syndrome, and concerns over physical attractiveness
2. If one assumes that physical and mental decline are inevitable with age, then one makes automatic assumptions about the abilities of older people.
3. Crystallized intelligence is the ability to use one's accumulated knowledge and learning. Fluid intelligence refers to the ability to solve abstract problems and generate new hypotheses. Crystallized intelligence increases with age.
4. Denial: shock, disbelief, questioning doctor's diagnosis; anger: alienation from friends and family, overt anger; bargaining: attempts to make deals with fate, promises of changed behavior; depression: sadness, realization of losses that are occurring; acceptance: sense of calm, realization that the struggle is over
5. improve the quality of life for those who are near the end of life by relieving as much pain and suffering as possible; terminally ill patients, as well as patients with Alzheimer's disease and senile dementia

Critical Thinking

1. Students' answers will vary. Students may mention that men reexamine commitments made earlier in life with a view that changes must be made to make life more fulfilling. Some women may also experience the age-thirty crisis as they reexamine their career choices, partners, and so on.
2. Students' answers will vary. Most will likely say that one's basic personality and character is set by adulthood but that major events in the person's life can have some effect on personality.
3. Students' answers will vary. In less developed countries where the struggle for basic existence consumes much of a person's life, there may not be time or opportunity for a crisis.
4. Students' answers will vary. Many students will point to the increased services available through hospices as a way in which our society is making the adjustment easier.
5. Students' answers will vary. Most psychologists today believe that people have a right to know that they are dying. Increased openness and honesty is encouraged. Often the person suspects that he or she is dying, but if others will not acknowledge it, the person may be hindered in his or her psychological adjustment.

Building Skills

1. with a spouse
2. men; men generally have a shorter life span than women
3. Students may suggest that living with a spouse or relatives may provide continuity or social support while adjusting to the transitions of old age.

Building Skills

Interpreting Graphs Review the graphs, then answer the questions that follow.

Living Arrangements of Americans 65 and Older, 2003

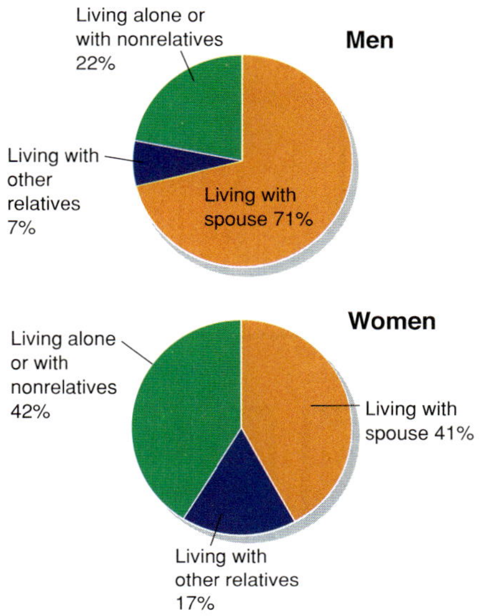

Source: U.S. Bureau of the Census, 2005.

1. With whom do most Americans 65 and older live?
2. Do more men or women of this age group live with a spouse? How can you explain this difference?
3. How might living arrangements affect a person's adjustment to old age?

Practice and **assess** key social studies skills with **Glencoe Skillbuilder Interactive Workbook CD-ROM, Level 2.**

See the Skills Handbook, page 628, for an explanation of interpreting graphs.

Psychology Projects

1. **Adulthood** Interview an adult who is more than 50 years old. Ask this person to describe himself or herself physically, socially, intellectually, and emotionally at the ages of 20, 30, 40, and 50. Before the interview, list specific questions that would provide this information. Ask which age was his or her favorite and why.
2. **Old Age** Explore the way that elderly adults are depicted in art and in the media. Bring in examples of art, literature, and newspaper or magazine articles that depict or describe the elderly. Present your findings to the class and explain whether they depict the elderly fairly.
3. **Dying and Death** Rituals surrounding death vary around the world. Research customs and rituals surrounding death in other countries or cultures. Present your findings in a pictorial essay.
4. **Aging and Society** With plastic surgery and cosmetics, many of the visible signs of aging can be camouflaged. Should men with gray hair dye their hair? Should women get face-lifts? Discuss the double-standard for aging men and women and its implications about the underlying values of society in a brief essay.

Technology Activity

Locate Web sites on the Internet that address issues of middle adulthood and late adulthood. (The Web site for the AARP is one such site.) Find out what kinds of information these sites offer. Evaluate the sites in terms of how they might benefit the lives of adults in middle and old age.

Psychology Journal

Reread the entry in your journal that you wrote about the saying "You can't teach an old dog new tricks." Think about this statement in light of adult development and learning. What evidence is there that this statement is incorrect? Using what you have learned, write an entry in your journal that presents evidence supporting both sides of the issue.

Technology Activity

Student evaluations should reference the wide variety of information available to older adults. They may classify the information as providing physical, social, and intellectual benefits.

Psychology Journal

Students' answers should show that they can argue both sides of the issue. The entries should include specific examples as well as a reasoned argument.

GLENCOE TECHNOLOGY

CD-ROM

Glencoe Skillbuilder Interactive Workbook, Level 2

This interactive CD-ROM is designed to reinforce student mastery of essential social studies skills.

Chapter Bonus Test Question

This question may be used for extra credit on the Chapter Assessment.

Answer the following question:

I am a Holocaust survivor who developed a theory on the stages of dying. Who am I?

Answer: Elisabeth Kübler-Ross

Psychology Projects

1. Answers will vary. Students may be surprised by the varied experiences of the person's life, as well as by the choice of a favorite age.
2. Answers will vary. Examples abound and, depending on the source, may show the traditionally stereotypic view of the decremental model of aging or the more open view of encouraging all adults to remain physically, mentally, and socially active throughout their lives.
3. Answers will vary. The pictorial essay should show a variety of cultural distinctions including the burial customs, the grieving process, and the ways in which the deceased are honored by the living.
4. Answers will vary. Students may discuss societal pressures to fight the signs of aging or advertising campaigns aimed at women and men to look young. Students should defend their arguments with evidence.

Unit 3 Planning Guide

National High School Psychology Standards

The national high school psychology standards identify what students in an introductory high school psychology course should learn. **The material covered in Unit 3 reflects content from two of the five content domains: *Cognitive* and *Biopsychological.*** To see a chapter-by-chapter correlation to the national standards, refer to the Teacher pages.

Content Domains for National High School Psychology Standards

Use this diagram to review the standards areas that are covered in Unit 3. Standards areas covered in this unit are highlighted in red in the diagram.

Methods
- Introduction and Research Methods

Sociocultural
- Individual Differences
- Personality and Assessment
- Psychological Disorders
- Treatment of Psychological Disorders
- Social and Cultural Dimensions of Behavior

Developmental
- Lifespan Development

Cognitive
- Learning
- Memory
- Thinking and Language
- States of Consciousness

Biopsychological
- Biological Bases of Behavior
- Sensation and Perception
- Motivation and Emotion
- Stress, Coping, and Health

BIBLIOGRAPHY

Readings for the Student

Bloom, F.E., Nelson, C.A., & Lazerson, A. (2005). *Brain, Mind, and Behavior.* New York: W.H. Freeman.

Newquist, H.P. (2005). *The Great Brain Book: An Inside Look at the Inside of Your Head.* New York: Scholastic.

Sacks, O. (1998). *The Man Who Mistook His Wife for a Hat: And Other Clinical Tales.* Boston, MA: Little Brown & Co.

Readings for the Teacher

Goldstein, E.B. (2006). *Sensation and Perception.* Boston, MA: Wadsworth/Thomson.

Howard, P.J. (2006). *The Owner's Manual for the Brain: Everyday Applications from Mind-Brain Research.* Austin, TX: Bard Press.

Watson J. (2005). *Essential Neuroscience.* Boston, MA: Blackwell Science.

Multimedia Resources

Internet. *Whole Brain Atlas.* www.med.harvard.edu/AANLIB/home.html

Videocassette. *Smithsonian World—the Doors of Perception.* (58 minutes). Smithsonian. The program explores our perceptions as filtered through human consciousness.

Unit 3 Resource Manager

Note: The following materials may be used when teaching Unit 3. Chapter level support materials can be found on the chapter resource pages.

GLENCOE'S ASSESSMENT ADVANTAGE

Use the following tools to easily assess student learning in a variety of ways:

- Authentic Assessment with Rubrics
- Section Quizzes, Chapter Tests, and Unit Tests
- glencoe.com
- SAT/SAT II Test Practice
- *ExamView® Assessment Suite* CD-ROM

APPLICATIONS AND HANDS-ON

Psychology Lab Activities 3–1, 3–2, and 3–3

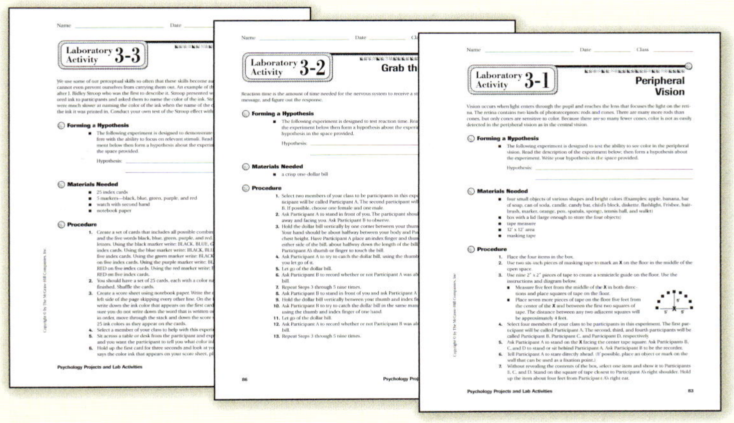
Laboratory Activity 3-3

Laboratory Activity 3-2 Grab th

Laboratory Activity 3-1 Peripheral Vision

ASSESSMENT

GLENCOE'S ASSESSMENT ADVANTAGE

Unit 3 Test, Form A

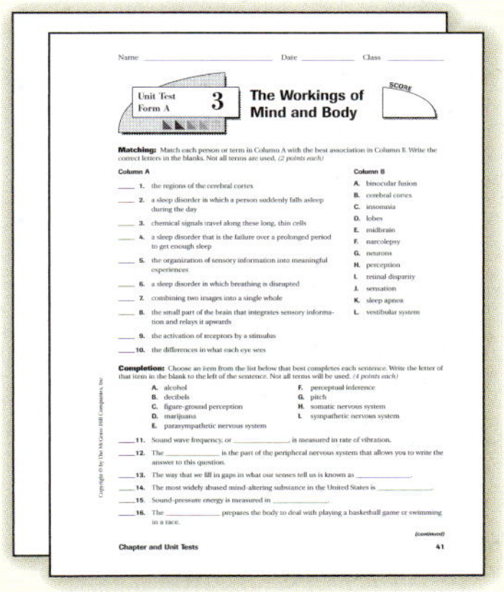
Unit Test Form A 3 The Workings of Mind and Body

Unit 3 Test, Form B

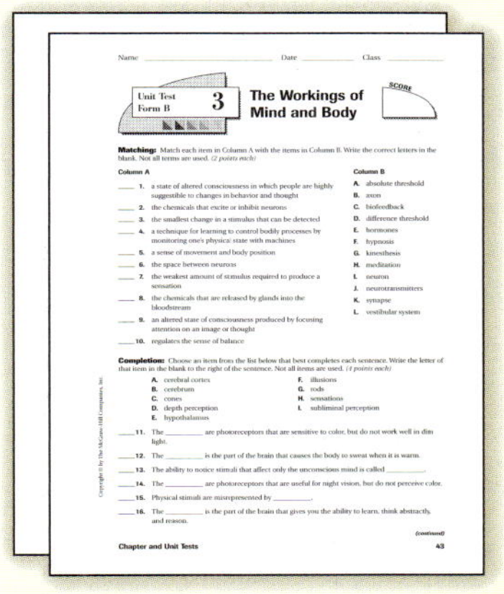
Unit Test Form B 3 The Workings of Mind and Body

PRESENTATION Plus!

Use Glencoe's ***Presentation Plus!*** multimedia teacher tool to easily present dynamic lessons that visually excite your students. Using Microsoft PowerPoint® you can customize the presentations to create your own personalized lessons.

Introducing
UNIT 3

Unit Overview

This unit explores the ways in which the brain and the body work together. **Chapter 6** describes how the nervous system, the endocrine system, and the environment affect the brain. **Chapter 7** explores altered states of consciousness. Sleep and sleep disorders are also introduced. **Chapter 8** examines sensation and perception. Sensory thresholds and the organization of perceptual information are explored.

Unit Objectives

After studying this unit, students will be able to:

1. Identify the structure and functions of the human brain.
2. Describe research into such techniques as biofeedback and meditation.
3. Outline the principles involved in perception.

UNIT 3

The Workings of Mind and Body

Contents

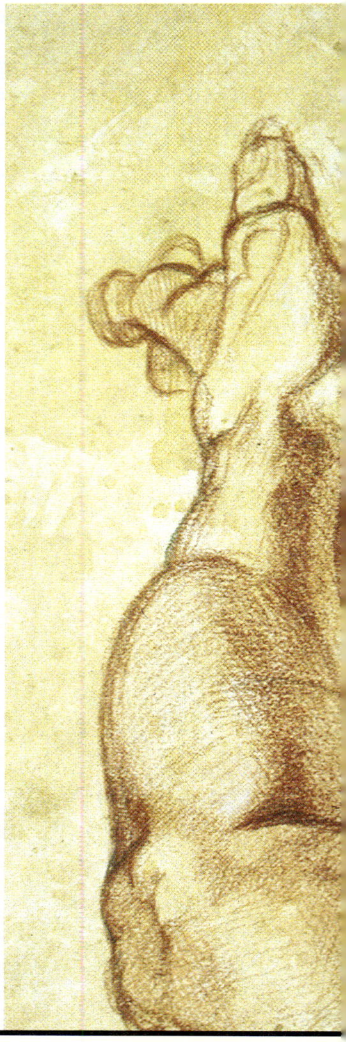

Sketch of the human brain and body ▶

EXTRA CREDIT PROJECT

Wall Charts Parts of Unit 3 connect human behavior with physiological processes. Assign groups of students to prepare a large anatomical wall chart showing the structure of key systems in the human body. Suggestions for the chart include the central nervous system, the brain (with labels as to localized function), the endocrine system, and the sense organs. Each group should prepare a short written report explaining the workings of the key system illustrated in its wall chart. Post these charts on the wall for reference throughout the unit. Some groups may want to add information to their charts as you work through Unit 3.

Why It's Important

Psychology is the study of what the nervous system does. The nervous system produced by your genes interacts with the environment to produce your behaviors. Your thoughts, emotions, memories, intelligence, and creativity are based on biological processes that take place within and between cells.

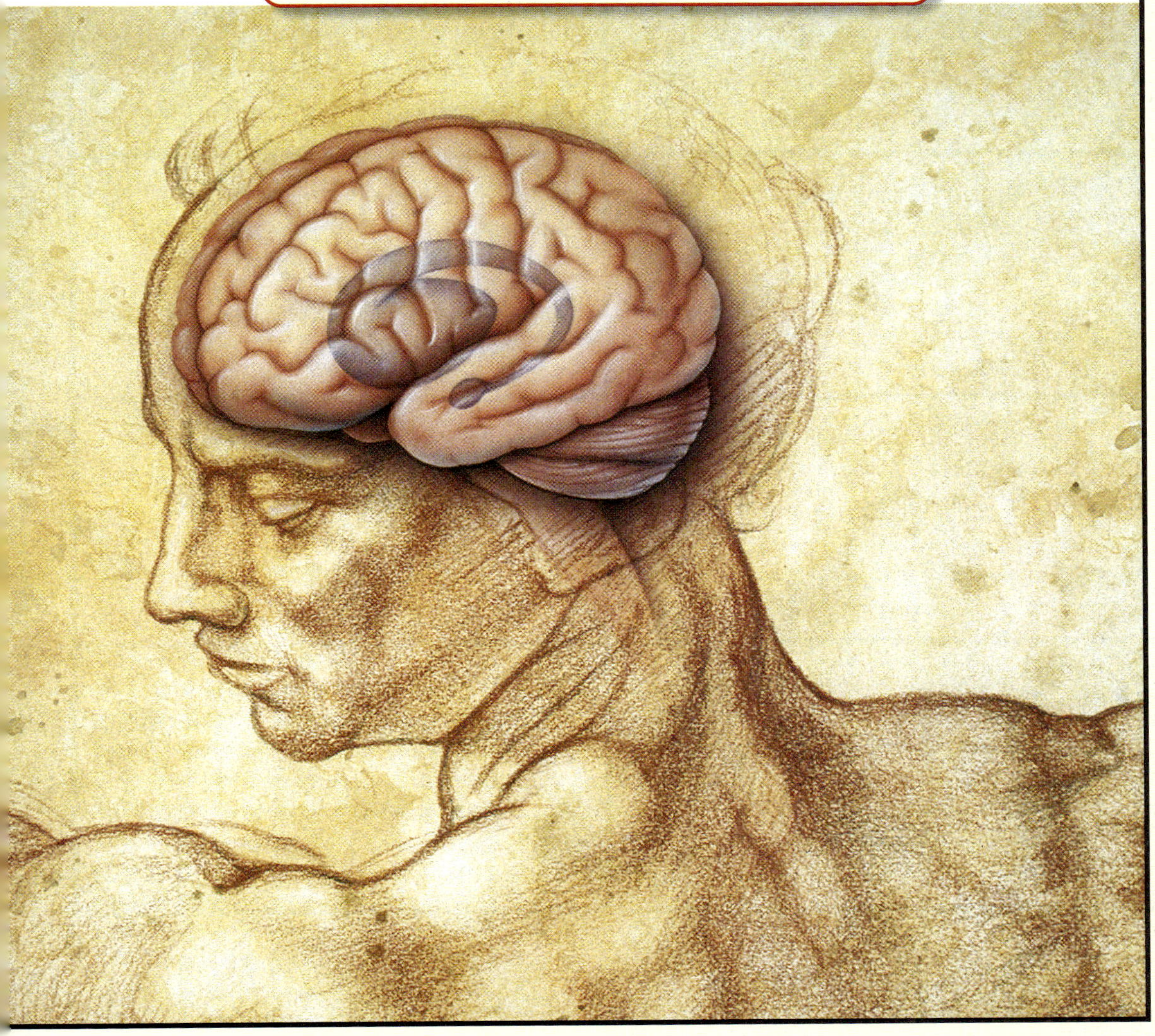

Psychology Fair Suggestion Box

Encourage students to get involved with a psychology fair. Here are some project suggestions for **Unit 3—The Workings of Mind and Body:**

- Research recent studies on the connection between the brain and behavior.
- Research new, natural approaches used to achieve altered states of consciousness.
- Explore how sleep disorders affect people and families.
- Examine how the human senses can be used to compensate for deficits in one of the other senses.
- Describe how illusionists deceive our senses.

Refer to ***Psychology Projects and Lab Activities*** in the TCR for help with organizing a psychology fair.

PSYCHOLOGY Online

Visit glencoe.com, the *Understanding Psychology* Web site, for Chapter Overviews, Student Web Activities, Interactive Puzzles, and Self-Check Quizzes for every chapter of the text.

PORTFOLIO PROJECT

Creating an Anthology Many exciting developments are occurring in the field of biopsychology. Have students work in small groups to create an anthology of articles about these developments. Ask students to find recent magazine or newspaper articles describing advances in the workings of the brain and in psychosurgery. Each group should create an anthology, which can be used for reference. Ask students to write one-paragraph summaries to accompany each article. These summaries should provide enough information to inform the reader of the subject, hypothesis, or theory being explored. **BLOCK SCHEDULING**

Chapter 6 Resource Guide

SECTION RESOURCES

Daily Objectives	Reproducible Resources	Multimedia Resources
Section 1 **The Nervous System: The Basic Structure** Understand that the nervous system helps us know how messages that are sent to and from the brain cause behavior.	Guided Reading Activity 6–1 Vocabulary Activity 6–1 Section Quiz 6–1	Daily Focus Transparency 6–1 *ExamView® Assessment Suite* CD-ROM Presentation Plus! Software
Section 2 **Studying the Brain** Discuss the many parts of the brain that work together to coordinate movement and stimulate thinking and emotions.	Guided Reading Activity 6–2 Vocabulary Activity 6–2 Section Quiz 6–2	Daily Focus Transparency 6–2 Vocabulary PuzzleMaker CD-ROM *ExamView® Assessment Suite* CD-ROM Presentation Plus! Software
Section 3 **The Endocrine System** Explain how the endocrine system controls and excites growth and affects emotions and behavior.	Guided Reading Activity 6–3 Vocabulary Activity 6–3 Section Quiz 6–3	Daily Focus Transparency 6–3 Vocabulary PuzzleMaker CD-ROM *ExamView® Assessment Suite* CD-ROM Presentation Plus! Software
Section 4 **Heredity and Environment** Identify heredity and environment and analyze how they affect your body and behavior.	Guided Reading Activity 6–4 Vocabulary Activity 6–4 Section Quiz 6–4	Daily Focus Transparency 6–4 Vocabulary PuzzleMaker CD-ROM *ExamView® Assessment Suite* CD-ROM Presentation Plus! Software

Blackline Master   CD-ROM   Transparency

Block Schedule

Activities that are particularly suited for use within the block-scheduling framework are identified throughout this chapter by the following designation: **BLOCK SCHEDULING**

KEY TO ABILITY LEVELS

Teaching strategies have been coded for varying learning styles and abilities.

L1 **BASIC** activities for all students
L2 **AVERAGE** activities for average to above-average students
L3 **CHALLENGING** activities for above-average students
ELL **ENGLISH LANGUAGE LEARNER** activities

Chapter 6 Resource Guide

Timesaving Tools

TeacherWorks™ All-In-One Planner and Resource Center

- **Interactive Teacher Edition** Access your Teacher Wraparound Edition and your classroom resources with a few easy clicks.
- **Interactive Lesson Planner** Planning has never been easier! Organize your week, month, semester, or year with all the lesson helps you need to make teaching creative, timely, and relevant.

Use Glencoe's **Presentation Plus!** multimedia teacher tool to easily present dynamic lessons that visually excite your students. Using Microsoft PowerPoint® you can customize the presentations to create your own personalized lessons.

Activity

From the Classroom of...

Susan Morton Hernandez
Morris Knolls High School
Rockaway, NJ

The Brain and Nervous System

Objective: To gain a better understanding of the location and function of the parts of the brain.

Materials: Teacher-designed chart (see below); clay/dough that dries on exposure to the air; plastic bags or plastic containers for storage between classes; masking tape to label containers

Procedure:

1. After discussing the structures and functions of the brain in class, send students home with a copy of the chart to be completed as homework. CHART NOTES: Design a 3-column chart, the far left column listing the structure, and the remaining columns titled "Location" and "Function."
2. The next day, supply students with a container of clay or dough.
3. Using their charts, students are to build a 3-dimensional cross section of the left side of the brain, making sure to include all the structures listed in their charts.
4. When students have completed their models, place them somewhere safe to dry overnight.
5. Conduct an assessment by writing each structure on a separate 3" x 5" index card. Have students select 5 different index cards and have them use their models to identify not only where the structure is, but what function it performs.

Psychology Online

Use our Web site for additional resources. All essential content is covered in the Student Edition.

You and your students can visit glencoe.com, the Web site companion to *Understanding Psychology*. This innovative integration of electronic and print media offers your students a wealth of opportunities. The student text directs students to the Web site for the following options:

- Chapter Overviews
- Student Web Activities
- Self-Check Quizzes

Answers are provided for you in the **Web Activity Lesson Plan.** Additional Web resources and Interactive Puzzles are also available.

Chapter 6 Resource Guide

Note: The following materials may be used when teaching Chapter 6. Section level support materials are shown at point of use in the margins of the Teacher Wraparound Edition.

TEACHING TRANSPARENCIES

Chapter 6 Concept Transparencies

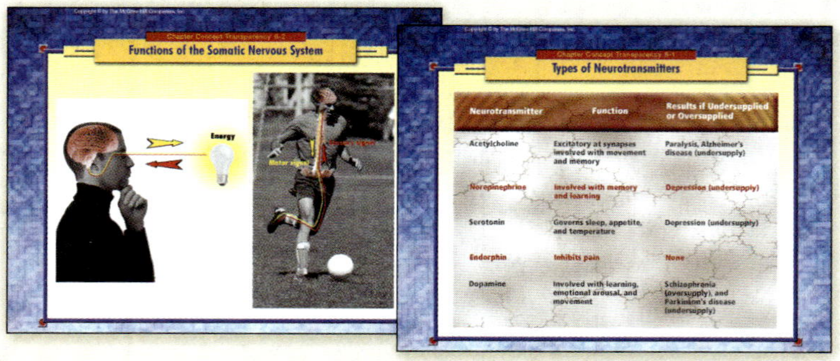

MULTIMEDIA

- Vocabulary PuzzleMaker CD-ROM
- *ExamView® Assessment Suite* CD-ROM
- TeacherWorks™ CD-ROM
- Glencoe Skillbuilder Interactive Workbook, Level 2
- Presentation Plus! Software

REVIEW AND REINFORCEMENT

Reteaching Activity 6

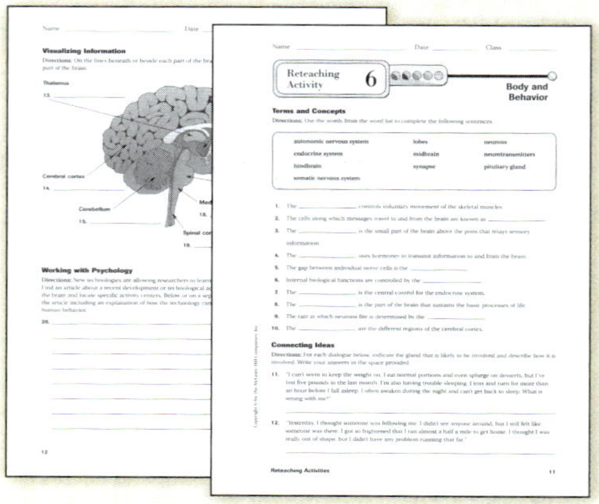

Graphic Organizer Activity 6

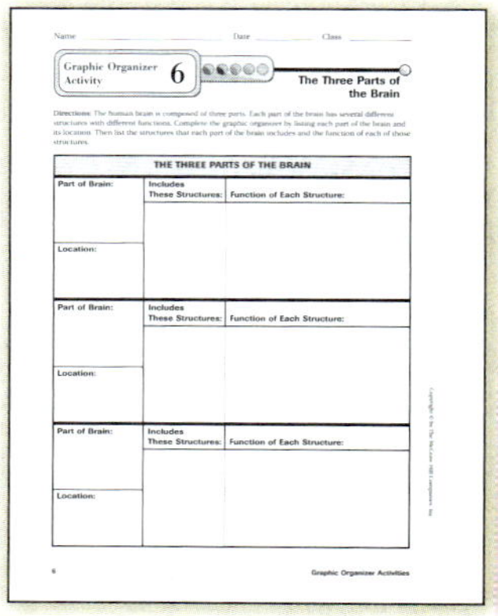

APPLICATION AND HANDS-ON

Psychology Projects 6–1 and 6–2

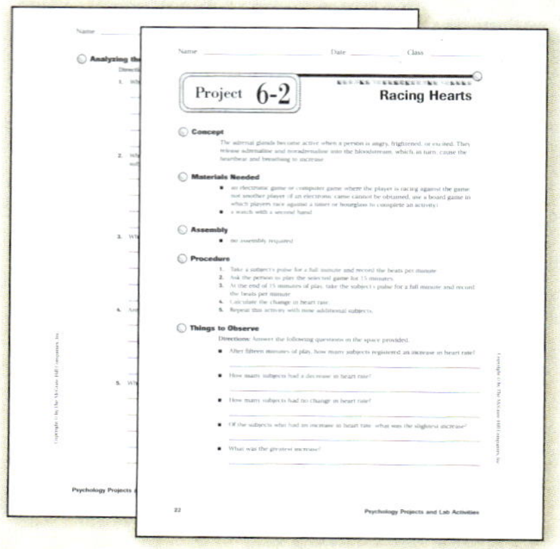

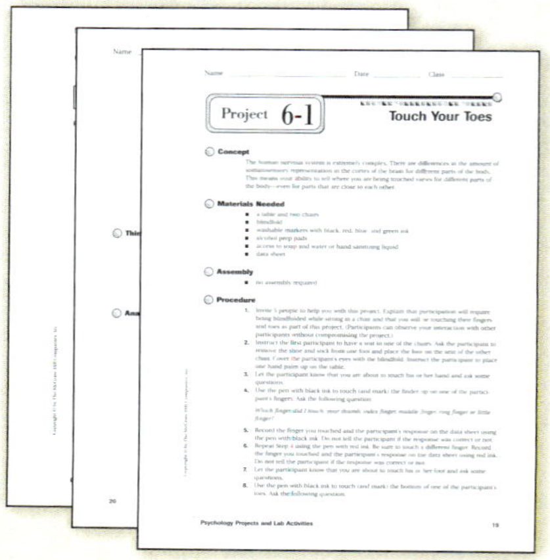

Application Activity 6

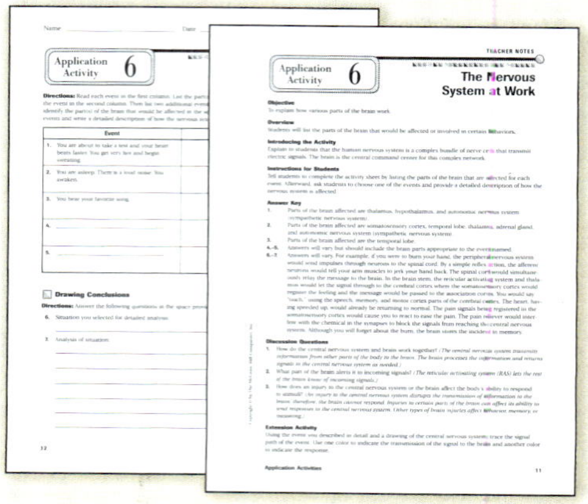

Chapter 6 Resource Guide

Glencoe's Assessment Advantage

ASSESSMENT

Chapter 6 Test, Form A

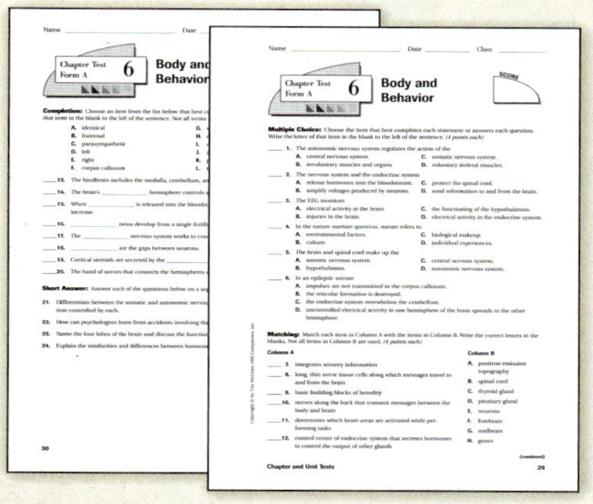

Chapter 6 Test, Form B

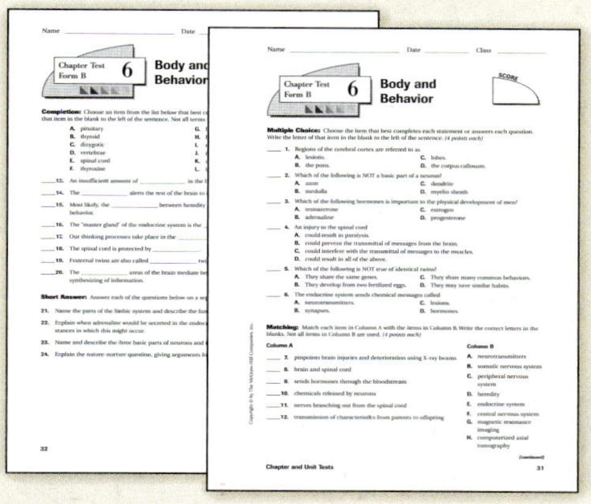

Authentic Assessment Activity 6

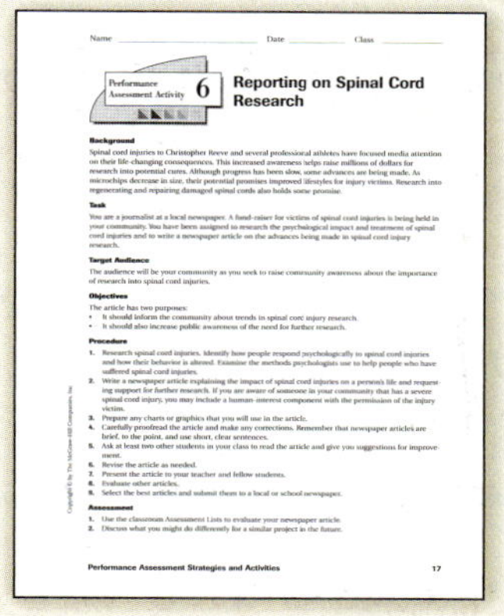

EXTENSION AND ENRICHMENT

Enrichment Activity 6

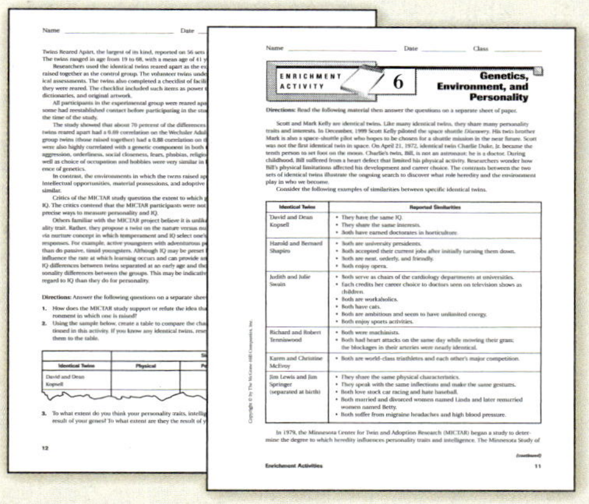

Critical Thinking Skills Activity 6

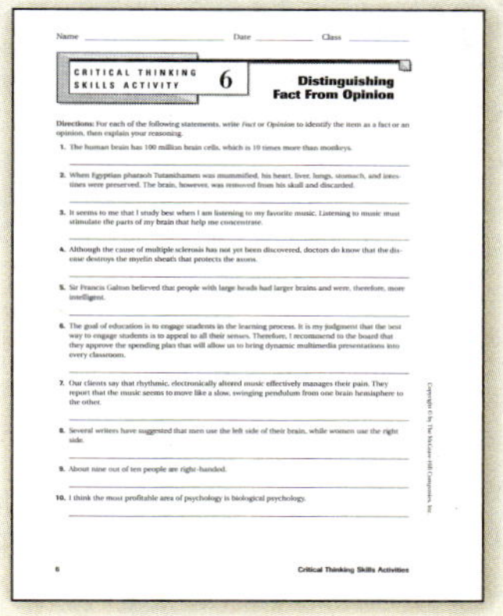

Psychology Reading 6

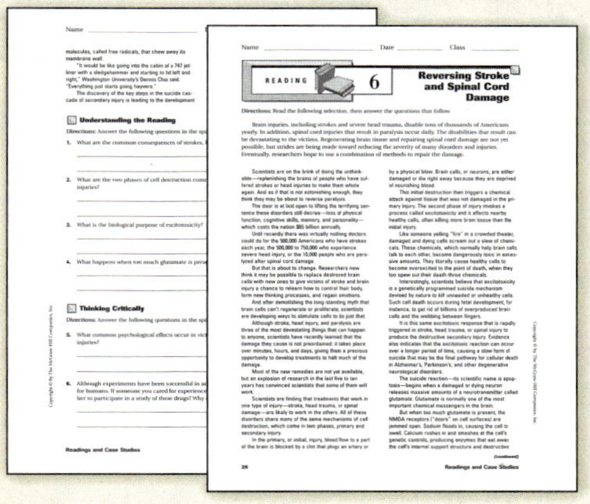

Psychology Case Study 6

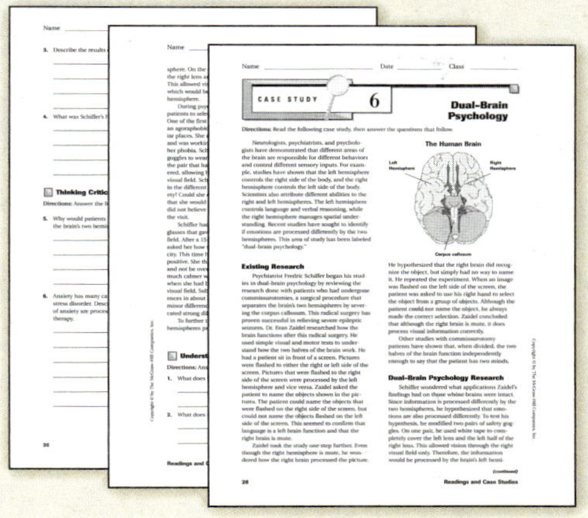

PSYCHOLOGY Online

Visit glencoe.com for a Chapter Overview for **Chapter 6—Body and Behavior.**

GLENCOE TECHNOLOGY

Presentation Plus! For a preview of Chapter 6 content, see MindJogger Checkpoint on **Presentation Plus!**

PSYCHOLOGY JOURNAL

Explain to students that all sensory information is processed by the brain. Have students use the computer analogy to explain the brain as the central processing unit of the body. Ask students to conjecture how our knowledge of the brain and its sensory processes was obtained.

This journal activity provides the basis for the Psychology Journal activity exercise in the Chapter Assessment. ■

CHAPTER 6

Body and Behavior

PSYCHOLOGY JOURNAL

Ask yourself why it is important for psychologists to study the brain and nervous system. Write your answer to this question in your journal and justify your response. ■

PSYCHOLOGY Online

Chapter Overview
Visit the *Understanding Psychology* Web site at glencoe.com and click on **Chapter 6—Chapter Overviews** to preview the chapter.

TWO-MINUTE LESSON LAUNCHER

Perform some sudden, unexpected action such as dropping a book on the floor. Ask students to describe their physical reactions to being startled. Ask them to brainstorm examples of how human behavior is affected by the functions of the body and by the genes with which people are born. List student responses on the board. **Ask: Are any of the behaviors named determined more by environment than by physical functions? If so, why?** Tell students that they will learn more about the relationship between the body and behavior in this chapter.

SECTION 1 The Nervous System: The Basic Structure

Reader's Guide

■ Main Idea
Learning about the nervous system helps us know how messages that are sent to and from the brain cause behavior.

■ Vocabulary
- central nervous system (CNS)
- spinal cord
- peripheral nervous system (PNS)
- neurons
- synapse
- neurotransmitters
- somatic nervous system (SNS)
- autonomic nervous system (ANS)

■ Objectives
- Identify the parts of the nervous system.
- Describe the functions of the nervous system.

EXPLORING PSYCHOLOGY

Have You Experienced the Runner's High?

It's almost like running is this great friend we both share . . . Anyway, that's what I'd like to talk to you about . . . running as a friend, a companion, a lover even . . . in other words, the relationship of running. "WHAT!?" many of you will be saying, "I thought that I was going to learn how to improve my 10k time." Go read *Runner's World* for that. You see, I don't view running as what I DO or who I AM, but as this thing, this force, that changes me over time. . . .

—from "Running and Me: A Love Story" by Joan Nesbit, 1999

Why does the writer above love running so much? One of the reasons may be that people who do a lot of running for exercise, especially long-distance running, often talk of an effect called a "runner's high." The longer they run, the more tired they get, of course; but at some point, the runners will "push through the wall" and "get their second wind." Why does this happen? Endorphins, which are neurotransmitters, produce the euphoria of a runner's high. As the body deals with a very physically stressful situation—running—the runner's body reacts to stress. So, in effect, running really does change you. In this section, you will learn how your nervous system can produce a runner's high.

SECTION RESOURCES

Reproducible Masters
- Guided Reading Activity 6–1
- Vocabulary Activity 6–1
- Section Quiz 6–1

Transparencies
- Daily Focus Transparency 6–1

Multimedia
- *ExamView® Assessment Suite* CD-ROM
- Presentation Plus! Software

1 FOCUS

Section Objectives
1. Identify the parts of the nervous system.
2. Describe the functions of the nervous system.

BELLRINGER
Motivational Activity

Project Daily Focus Transparency 6–1 and have students answer the questions.

Available as blackline master

Daily Focus Transparency 6–1

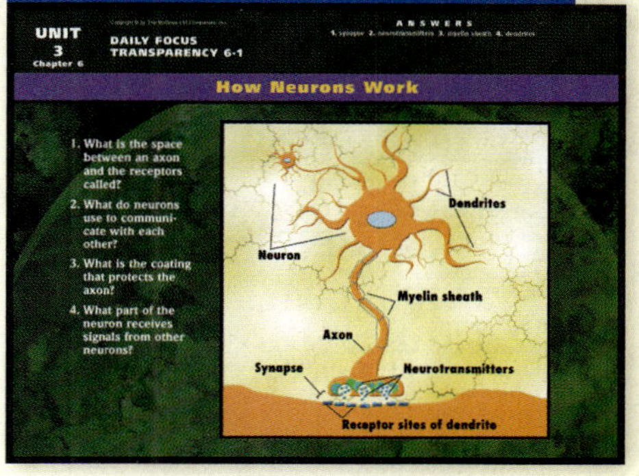

Reader's Guide

Use the Reader's Guide to introduce concepts and vocabulary.

■ Exploring Psychology
Ask students to read the **Exploring Psychology** feature and then discuss: **What other types of physically stressful situations may the human body encounter? How does the nervous system react?**

■ Vocabulary Precheck
Have students read the Glossary definition of each term. Provide them with a diagram of the central and peripheral nervous systems and ask them to label the diagram.

2 TEACH

L1 Demonstration **Ask:** **How can a neuron that fires according to the all-or-none principle relay different levels of stimulation?** After allowing time for students' ideas, explain that there are two means. First, an excitatory cell that is stimulated more heavily fires more rapidly. Second, if stimulation is heavy, a larger number of neurons will fire. To illustrate these concepts, apply the eraser end of a pencil to the skin. As pressure is increased, the level of pressure experienced increases. This is because the neurons are firing more rapidly and in greater number, sending pressure signals to the brain.

Guided Reading Activity 6–1

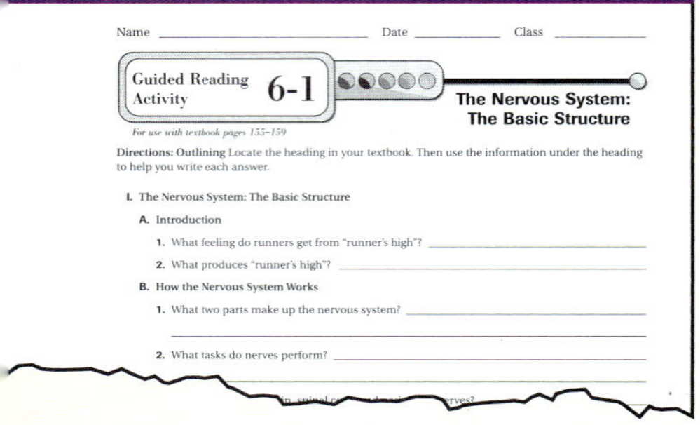
Name ______ Date ______ Class ______

Guided Reading Activity 6-1

The Nervous System: The Basic Structure

For use with textbook pages 155–159

Directions: Outlining Locate the heading in your textbook. Then use the information under the heading to help you write each answer.

I. The Nervous System: The Basic Structure

A. Introduction

1. What feeling do runners get from "runner's high"? ______
2. What produces "runner's high"? ______

B. How the Nervous System Works

1. What two parts make up the nervous system? ______
2. What tasks do nerves perform? ______

Figure 6.1

Visual Instruction Point out that the PNS connects the CNS to other parts of the body through 43 pairs of nerves that extend from the CNS.

Caption Answer the brain and the spinal cord

PSYCHOLOGY JOURNAL

Tell students to explain how neurons work using the metaphor of a relay race. ■

HOW THE NERVOUS SYSTEM WORKS

central nervous system (CNS): the brain and spinal cord

spinal cord: nerves that run up and down the length of the back and transmit most messages between the body and brain

peripheral nervous system (PNS): nerves branching beyond the spinal cord into the body

The nervous system is never at rest. There is always a job for it to do. Even when you are sleeping the nervous system is busy regulating your body functions. The nervous system controls your emotions, movements, thinking, and behavior–almost everything you do.

Structurally, the nervous system is divided into two parts—the **central nervous system [CNS]** (the brain and the **spinal cord**) and the **peripheral nervous system [PNS]** (the smaller branches of nerves that reach the other parts of the body) (see Figure 6.1). The nerves of the peripheral system conduct information from the bodily organs to the central nervous system and take information back to the organs. These nerves branch beyond the spinal column and are about as thick as a pencil. Those in the extremities, such as the fingertips, are invisibly small. All parts of the nervous system are protected in some way: the brain by the skull and several layers of sheathing, the spinal cord by the vertebrae, and the peripheral nerves by layers of sheathing. The bony protection of the spinal cord is vital. An injury to the spinal cord could prevent the transmittal of messages between the brain and the muscles, and could result in paralysis.

Figure 6.1 **The Nervous System**

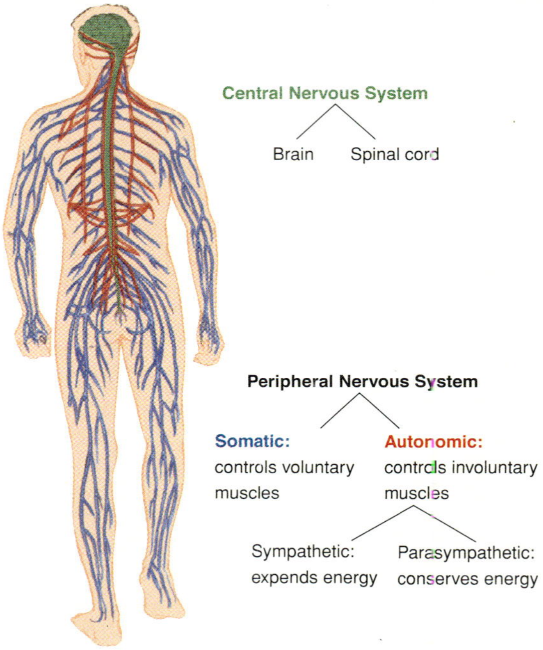

The nervous system is divided into two parts: the central nervous system (CNS) and the peripheral nervous system (PNS). ***What are the two main parts of the central nervous system?***

COOPERATIVE LEARNING ACTIVITY

Conducting Research Organize students into groups of four. Each group will research a different neurotransmitter. Encourage the group to make individual assignments to each member for a portion of the research. The research should focus on the types of neurotransmitters, how neurotransmitters were discovered, how they are transported, and how they can be deactivated or blocked. From the research, students should create a fact sheet with information and illustrations. Remind students that, during group work, roles will change. At times someone will be the leader and, at other times, a follower. In either role, the student should be a supportive group member.

Figure 6.2 Anatomy of Two Neurons

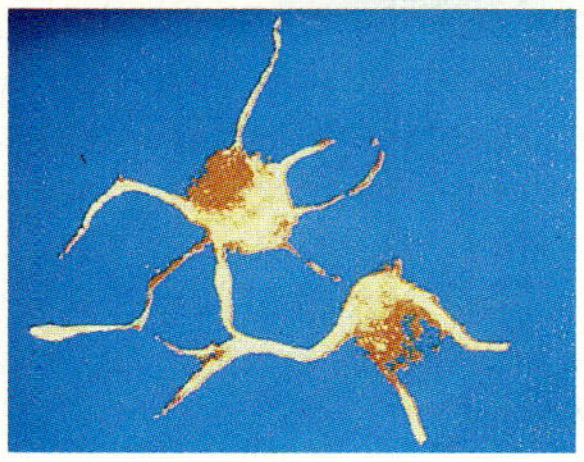

Photomicrograph of neurons

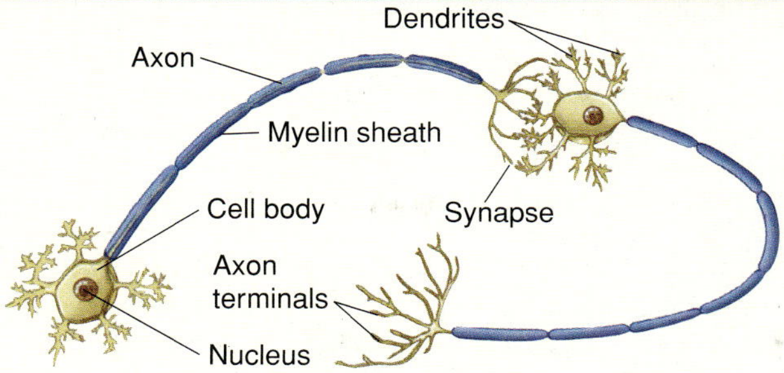

The human body contains billions of neurons. The neuron receives messages from other neurons via its dendrites. The messages are then transmitted down the axon and sent out through the axon terminals. The myelin sheath often is wrapped around the axon. ***What is the function of the dendrites?***

Neurons

Messages to and from the brain travel along the nerves, which are strings of long, thin cells called **neurons** (see Figure 6.2). Chemical-electrical signals travel down the neurons much as flame travels along a firecracker fuse. The main difference is that the neuron can fire (burn) over and over again, hundreds of times a minute.

Transmission between neurons, or nerve cells, occurs whenever the cells are stimulated past a minimum point and emit a signal. The neuron is said to fire in accord with the all-or-none principle, which states that when a neuron fires, it does so at full strength. If a neuron is not stimulated past the minimum, or threshold, level, it does not fire at all.

neurons: the long, thin cells of nerve tissue along which messages travel to and from the brain

Basic Parts of a Neuron Neurons have four basic parts: dendrites, the cell body (which contains the nucleus), an axon, and axon terminals. *Dendrites* are short, thin fibers that protrude from the cell body. Dendrites receive impulses, or messages, from other neurons and send them to the cell body. The single extended *axon* carries the impulses from the cell body toward the *axon terminals,* which release neurotransmitters to stimulate dendrites of the next neuron. Usually very short, axons can be several feet in length.

A white, fatty substance called the *myelin sheath* insulates and protects the axon for some neurons. In cases of multiple sclerosis, the myelin sheath is destroyed, and as a result, the behavior of the person is erratic and uncoordinated. The myelin sheath also speeds the transmission of impulses. Small fibers, called *axon terminals,* branch out at the end of the axon. Axon terminals are positioned opposite the dendrite of another neuron.

Reading Check What are the three basic parts of a neuron?

The Neuron Connection If you look closely at Figure 6.2, you can see that there is a space between the axon terminals of one neuron and the dendrites of another neuron. This space between neurons is called the **synapse.** The synapse is a junction or connection between the neurons (see Figure 6.3). A neuron transmits its impulses or message to another neuron across the

synapse: the gap that exists between individual nerve cells

MEETING SPECIAL NEEDS

Learning Style: Logical/Mathematical Have students select one of the following: autism, dyslexia, multiple sclerosis, Alzheimer's disease, Parkinson's disease, or Tourette's syndrome. Students should review current periodicals and the Internet for articles about brain or central nervous system research being done to identify the cause and possible cures to the disorder or problem. Have students write a 2- to 3-page paper about the current theories or hypotheses that may lead to treatments or cures. **L2**

Refer to ***Inclusion for the High School Social Studies Classroom Strategies and Activities*** in the TCR for strategies for students with different learning styles.

Figure 6.2

Visual Instruction Provide students with an unlabeled diagram of neurons. As you describe each part of the neuron, have students add labels.

Caption Answer The dendrites receive messages from other neurons and send them to the cell body.

Reading Check Answer the cell body, dendrites, and the axon

CURRICULUM CONNECTION

History In the late eighteenth century, Luigi Galvani discovered that severed frog legs would sometimes twitch during electrical storms when hung from metal hooks. This discovery led Galvani to experiment with the relationship between electrical impulses and muscle contractions. His discovery also led to the development of the first batteries.

TEACHER Tip

To illustrate the all-or-none principle of neurons, use the example of a sparkplug igniting the gaseous vapor in an engine cylinder. The piston within does nothing until the sparkplug fires, causing the vapor to explode.

CHAPTER 6

Section 1, pages 155–159

Figure 6.3

Visual Instruction Tell students that the synapse is less than one millionth of an inch wide. It is filled with fluid that transmits the chemicals from one neuron to another.

Caption Answer Neurons release neurotransmitters, which are received by the dendrite of another neuron. Efferent neurons carry signals from the brain to the glands and muscles.

Vocabulary Activity 6–1

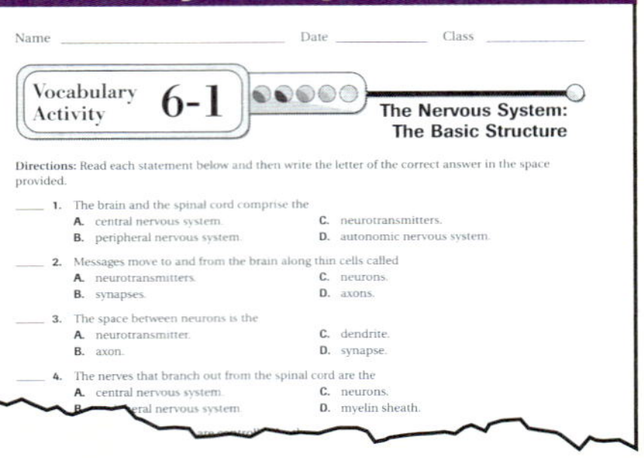
Name ____ Date ____ Class ____

Vocabulary Activity 6-1

The Nervous System: The Basic Structure

Directions: Read each statement below and then write the letter of the correct answer in the space provided.

____ 1. The brain and the spinal cord comprise the
A. central nervous system.
B. peripheral nervous system.
C. neurotransmitters.
D. autonomic nervous system.

____ 2. Messages move to and from the brain along thin cells called
A. neurotransmitters.
B. synapses.
C. neurons.
D. axons.

____ 3. The space between neurons is the
A. neurotransmitter.
B. axon.
C. dendrite.
D. synapse.

____ 4. The nerves that branch out from the spinal cord are the
A. central nervous system.
B. ...eral nervous system.
C. neurons.
D. myelin sheath.

3 ASSESS

Assign Section 1 Assessment as homework or as an in-class activity.

Section Quiz 6–1

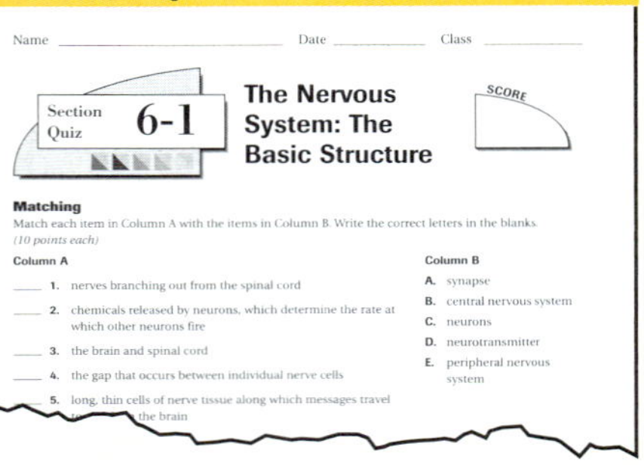
Name ____ Date ____ Class ____

Section Quiz 6-1

The Nervous System: The Basic Structure

SCORE

Matching

Match each item in Column A with the items in Column B. Write the correct letters in the blanks. *(10 points each)*

Column A

____ 1. nerves branching out from the spinal cord
____ 2. chemicals released by neurons, which determine the rate at which other neurons fire
____ 3. the brain and spinal cord
____ 4. the gap that occurs between individual nerve cells
____ 5. long, thin cells of nerve tissue along which messages travel ... the brain

Column B

A. synapse
B. central nervous system
C. neurons
D. neurotransmitter
E. peripheral nervous system

Reteach

Have students list examples of how the brain automatically controls the body's responses to external stimuli.

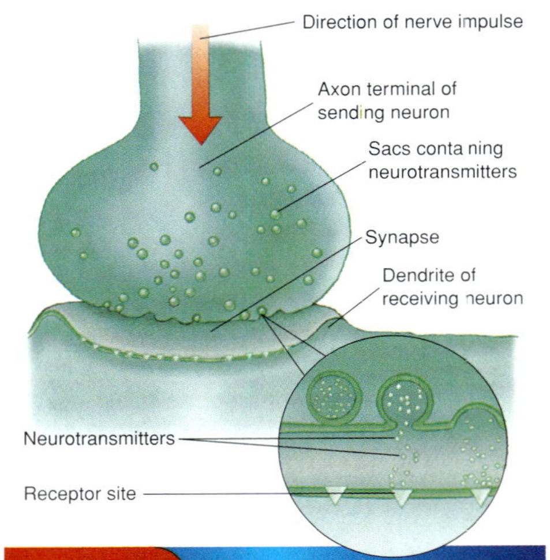

Figure 6.3 The Synapse

Neurons do not touch one another. Instead, a neuron sends its messages across a gap called a synapse by releasing neurotransmitters. These neurotransmitters are received by the dendrite of another neuron. ***How are neurons involved in sending a message to the brain to raise your arm to answer a question?***

synapse by releasing certain chemicals that are known as **neurotransmitters.** These neurotransmitters open chemical locks or excite the receptors. The neurotransmitters can excite the next neuron or stop it from transmitting (inhibition). With receptors only in the dendrites, the synapse allows signals to move in only one direction. There are many different neurotransmitters; for example, *norepinephrine* is involved with memory and learning, and *endorphin* inhibits pain. The oversupply or undersupply of certain neurotransmitters has been linked to certain diseases. For instance, an undersupply of *acetylcholine*, a neurotransmitter involved in movement and memory, is associated with paralysis and Alzheimer's disease. An over-supply of *dopamine*, involved in learning, emotional arousal, and movement, is linked to schizophrenia, while an undersupply is linked to Parkinson's disease. An undersupply of norepinephrine and *serotonin* may result in depression.

Neuron Activity The intensity of activity in each neuron depends on how many other neurons are acting on it. Each individual neuron is either ON or OFF, depending on whether most of the neurons acting on it are exciting it or inhibiting it. The actual destination of nerve impulses produced by an excited neuron, as they travel from one neuron to another, is limited by what tract in the nervous system they are on. Ascending tracts carry sensory impulses to the brain, and descending tracts carry motor impulses from the brain. There are different types of neurons. *Afferent* neurons, or sensory neurons, relay messages from the sense organs (including eye, ear, nose, and skin) to the brain. *Efferent* neurons, or motor neurons, send signals from the brain to the glands and muscles. *Interneurons* process signals, connecting only to other neurons, not to sensors or muscles.

neurotransmitters: the chemicals released by neurons, which determine the rate at which other neurons fire

Voluntary and Involuntary Activities

Some of the actions that your body makes in response to impulses from the nerves are voluntary acts, such as lifting your hand to turn a page (which actually involves many impulses to many muscles). Others are involuntary acts, such as changes in the heartbeat, in the blood pressure, or in the size of the pupils. The term **somatic nervous system (SNS)** refers to the part of the peripheral nervous system that controls voluntary activities. The term **autonomic nervous system (ANS)** refers to the part of the nervous system that controls involuntary activities, or those that ordinarily occur automatically, such as heartbeat, stomach activity, and so on.

The autonomic nervous system has two parts: the sympathetic and parasympathetic nervous systems. The sympathetic nervous system prepares the body for dealing with emergencies or strenuous activity. It

somatic nervous system (SNS): the part of the peripheral nervous system that controls voluntary movement of skeletal muscles

autonomic nervous system (ANS): the part of the peripheral nervous system that controls internal biological functions

CRITICAL THINKING ACTIVITY

Demonstrating Reasoned Judgment Point out that for centuries epileptics have been subject to discrimination because of their ailment and the way it affects their behavior. At one time, epileptics were believed to be possessed by evil spirits or presumed to be insane or unintelligent and therefore unfit for employment. Ask students to discuss how knowing the physiological causes of behavior might result in greater tolerance for those afflicted with epilepsy and similar ailments. (Students may want to contact the Epilepsy Foundation for additional information.) Students should summarize their thoughts in a written essay. **L2**

speeds up the heart to hasten the supply of oxygen and nutrients to body tissues. It constricts some arteries and relaxes others so that blood flows to the muscles, where it is most needed in emergencies and strenuous activity (such as running, thereby sometimes producing a runner's high). It increases the blood pressure and suspends some activities, such as digestion. In contrast, the parasympathetic nervous system works to conserve energy and to enhance the body's ability to recover from strenuous activity. It reduces the heart rate and blood pressure and helps bring the body back to its normal resting state.

All of this takes place automatically. Receptors are constantly receiving messages (hunger messages, the need to swallow or cough) that alert the autonomic nervous system to carry out routine activities. Imagine how difficult it would be if you had no autonomic nervous system and had to think about it every time your body needed to digest a sandwich or perspire.

Figure 6.4 Voluntary and Involuntary Activities

Climbing stairs is a voluntary activity. When the pupils of your eyes get smaller after they are exposed to brighter light, this is an involuntary activity. ***What other involuntary activities take place in your body?***

SECTION 1 Assessment

1. **Review the Vocabulary** List and describe the parts of the neuron.
2. **Visualize the Main Idea** In a diagram similar to the one below, list the divisions of the nervous system.

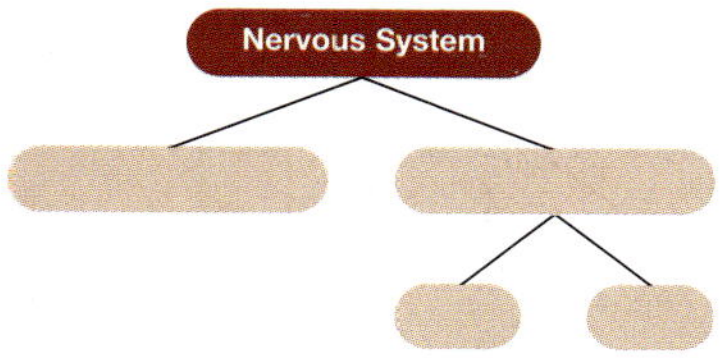

3. **Recall Information** What is the difference between afferent and efferent neurons? What are interneurons?
4. **Think Critically** Marty runs in marathons. Explain the functions of Marty's sympathetic and parasympathetic nervous systems during and after the race.
5. **Application Activity** Put your pen or pencil down and then pick it up again. Identify and describe the parts of the nervous system that caused those movements to happen.

SECTION 1 Assessment Answers

1. The cell body produces the energy needed to fuel neuron activity. The dendrites receive messages from other neurons and send them to the cell body. The axons carry impulses from the cell body toward the dendrites of another neuron.
2. Diagrams should reflect students' understanding of the nervous system.
3. Afferent neurons relay messages from the sense organs to the brain. Efferent neurons send signals from the brain to the glands and muscles. Interneurons process signals.
4. Students' answers should demonstrate an understanding of the sympathetic and parasympathetic nervous systems and their reactions to emergencies or strenuous activities.
5. Students' answers will vary. The elements to be included are afferent neurons (sight and skin), efferent neurons (signals to muscles in arm and hand to move, grasp, and raise the pencil), and neurotransmitters that send the signals.

Figure 6.4

Caption Answer Changes in your heartbeat and blood pressure are involuntary activities.

Enrich

Ask students to create a table showing the functions and the results of an under- or oversupply of the following neurotransmitters: acetylcholine, norepinephrine, serotonin, endorphin, and dopamine.

4 CLOSE

Revisit the **Exploring Psychology** feature at the beginning of the section. Have students use the information in this section to explain the runner's feeling of exhilaration.

1 FOCUS

Section Objectives

1. Identify the structure and functions of the human brain.
2. Discuss the different ways psychologists study the brain.

BELLRINGER
Motivational Activity

Project Daily Focus Transparency 6–2 and have students answer the questions.

Available as blackline master

Daily Focus Transparency 6–2

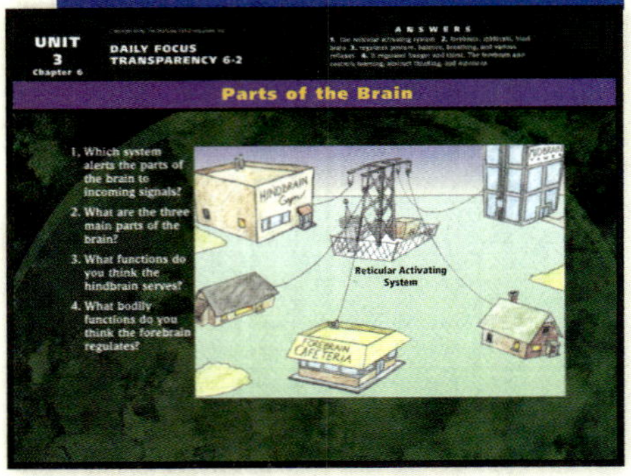

Reader's Guide

Use the Reader's Guide to introduce concepts and vocabulary.

■ Exploring Psychology

Ask students to read the **Exploring Psychology** feature and then discuss: **How did Hippocrates help change the notion that the brain, not the heart, was the source of thoughts and feelings?**

■ Vocabulary Precheck

Have students read the Glossary definition of each term. Then ask them to create a word search puzzle. Students should trade puzzles with a partner and complete the partner's word search.

Use the **Vocabulary PuzzleMaker CD-ROM** to create crossword and word search puzzles.

SECTION 2 Studying the Brain

Reader's Guide

■ Main Idea

There are many parts in the human brain that work together to coordinate movement and stimulate thinking and emotions.

■ Vocabulary

- hindbrain
- midbrain
- forebrain
- lobes
- electroencephalograph (EEG)
- computerized axial tomography (CT)
- positron emission tomography (PET)
- magnetic resonance imaging (MRI)

■ Objectives

- Identify the structure and functions of the human brain.
- Discuss the different ways psychologists study the brain.

EXPLORING PSYCHOLOGY

Origins of Thoughts

Early Greeks were not impressed with the brain. They suggested that the brain's main function was to cool the blood. They were much more impressed by the heart. They proposed that the heart was the source of feelings and thoughts. Hippocrates, however, observed the effect of head injuries on people's thoughts and actions and noted, "[F]rom the brain, and from the brain only, arise our pleasures, joys, laughter and jests, as well as our sorrows, pains, griefs and tears. Through it, in particular, we think, see, hear. . . . Eyes, ears, tongue, hands and feet act in accordance with the discernment [judgment] of the brain."

—adapted from *Psychology* by Peter Gray, 2006

Greek physician Hippocrates was right. In the 24 centuries since his observations, many attempts have been made to explain how the mass of soggy gray tissue known as the human brain could create the theory of relativity, the Sistine Chapel ceiling, and global warming. The mind, however, remains a mystery to itself.

THE THREE BRAINS

hindbrain: a part of the brain located at the rear base of the skull that is involved in the basic processes of life

The brain is composed of three parts: the hindbrain, midbrain, and forebrain (see Figure 6.5). The **hindbrain,** located at the rear base of the skull, is involved in the most basic processes of life. The hindbrain

SECTION RESOURCES

Reproducible Masters

- Guided Reading Activity 6–2
- Vocabulary Activity 6–2
- Section Quiz 6–2

Transparencies

- Daily Focus Transparency 6–2

Multimedia

- Vocabulary PuzzleMaker CD-ROM
- *ExamView® Assessment Suite* CD-ROM
- Presentation Plus! Software

includes the *cerebellum, medulla,* and the *pons.* The cerebellum, located behind the spinal cord, helps control posture, balance, and voluntary movements. The medulla controls breathing, heart rate, and a variety of reflexes, while the pons functions as a bridge between the spinal cord and the brain. The pons is also involved in producing chemicals the body needs for sleep.

The **midbrain** is a small part of the brain above the pons that arouses the brain, integrates sensory information, and relays it upward. The medulla and pons extend upward into the midbrain. The medulla, pons, and midbrain compose most of the brain stem, and the reticular activating system (RAS) spans across all these structures. The RAS serves to alert the rest of the brain to incoming signals and is involved in the sleep/wake cycle.

The **forebrain,** covering the brain's central core, includes the *thalamus,* which integrates sensory input. The thalamus is a relay station for all the information that travels to and from the cortex. All sensory information with the exception of smell enters the thalamus. All information from the eyes, ears, and skin enters the thalamus and then is sent to the appropriate areas in the cortex. Just below the thalamus is the *hypothalamus.* It controls functions such as hunger, thirst, and sexual behavior. It also controls the body's reactions to changes in temperature, so when we are warm, we begin to sweat, and when we are cold, we shiver.

The higher thinking processes—those that make us unique—are housed in the forebrain. The outer layer of the forebrain consists of the *cerebral cortex.* The inner layer is the *cerebrum.* The cerebral cortex and cerebrum surround the hindbrain and brain stem like the way a mushroom surrounds its stem. The cerebral cortex gives you the ability to learn and store complex and abstract information, and to project your thinking into the future. Your cerebral cortex allows you to see, read, and understand this sentence. The cortex, or bark, of the cerebrum is the site of your conscious thinking processes, yet it is less than one-fourth inch thick.

The *limbic system,* found in the core of the forebrain, is composed of a number of different structures in the brain that regulate our emotions and motivations. The limbic system includes the hypothalamus, amygdala, thalamus, and hippocampus. The amygdala controls violent

Figure 6.5 The Parts of the Brain

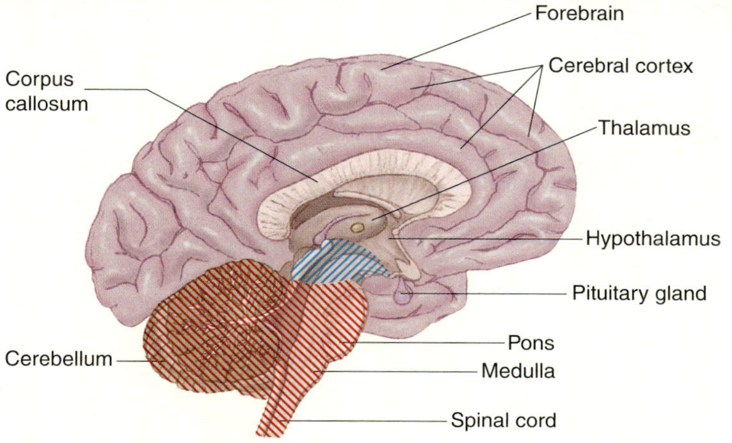

The brain is the largest, most complex part of the nervous system. ***What are the functions of the cerebellum?***

midbrain: a small part of the brain above the pons that arouses the brain, integrates sensory information, and relays it upward

forebrain: a part of the brain that covers the brain's central core, responsible for sensory and motor control and the processing of thinking and language

2 TEACH

L1 Demonstration Locate a model of the brain (one may be available in the school's biology lab). Review the structure of the brain with the class, and point out or have students name all the major parts. If available, bring brain models of other species as well so that students can compare brain size, parts, and functions of the human brain with those of other animals. Notice, for example, the declining size of the cortex in less sophisticated animals.

Figure 6.5

Visual Instruction Point out that about 80 percent of the brain's weight is made of the "new brain," the part of the brain associated with thinking and memory.

Caption Answer The cerebellum helps control posture, balance, and voluntary movements.

Guided Reading Activity 6-2

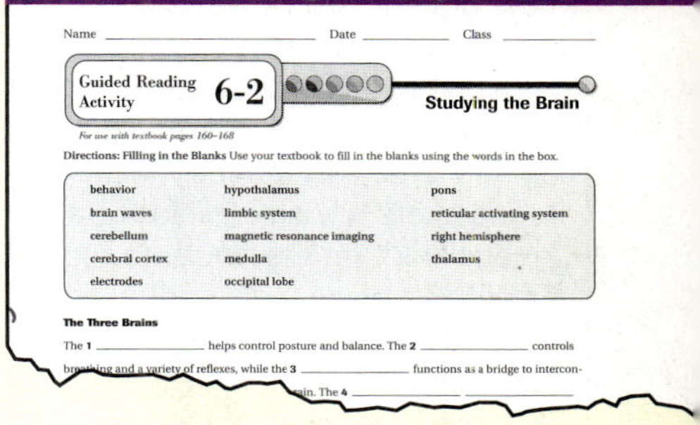
Name ______ Date ______ Class ______

Guided Reading Activity 6-2 Studying the Brain

For use with textbook pages 160–168

Directions: Filling in the Blanks Use your textbook to fill in the blanks using the words in the box.

behavior	hypothalamus	pons
brain waves	limbic system	reticular activating system
cerebellum	magnetic resonance imaging	right hemisphere
cerebral cortex	medulla	thalamus
electrodes	occipital lobe	

The Three Brains

The 1 ______ helps control posture and balance. The 2 ______ controls breathing and a variety of reflexes, while the 3 ______ functions as a bridge to intercon-

COOPERATIVE LEARNING ACTIVITY

Creating Illustrations Organize the class into small groups. Instruct each group to select a part of the brain and prepare an annotated illustration to present to the class. The illustration should convey the function of the particular part of the brain and how it interacts with other parts of the body. Encourage students to develop props, such as signs and other drawings, to aid their presentation. After each group has presented its illustration, have different groups collaborate to show how the various parts of the brain interact. **BLOCK SCHEDULING**

Reading Check Answer

The three parts of the brain are the hindbrain, midbrain, and forebrain.

Figure 6.6

Visual Instruction Provide students with a top view of the lobes of the brain. Have students identify the lobes and their effect on perception and behavior.

Caption Answer The motor cortex sends information to control body movement.

Looking @ the Issues

Dyslexia Dyslexia is a common reading disorder that is strongly linked to differences in brain function. For years, poor readers were labeled as lazy or slow. Today we recognize that dyslexics' brains function differently. Several recent studies indicate that dyslexics use more of their brain area to complete simple language tasks. Imaging techniques like PET scans and MRIs assist researchers in explaining how dyslexics' brains function. Researchers are also exploring a genetic link that may indicate that dyslexia is largely an inherited trait.

Ask students to predict how our increasing knowledge of the brain's functioning will change the way society views disorders like dyslexia. Also, instruct them to research current techniques used to help dyslexics learn to read.

Ask: **How will the current research likely affect the techniques used in the future to help dyslexics improve their reading skills?**

---

emotions such as rage and fear. The hippocampus is important in the formation of memories. If the hippocampus is damaged, it would be difficult to form new memories. Covering all these parts is the cerebrum.

Reading Check What are the three parts of the human brain?

lobes: the different regions into which the cerebral cortex is divided

The Lobes of the Brain

The cerebrum is really two hemispheres, or two sides. The cerebral hemispheres are connected by a band of fibers called the *corpus callosum.* Each cerebral hemisphere has deep grooves, some of which mark regions, or **lobes** (see Figure 6.6). The occipital lobe is where the visual signals are processed. Damage to this area can cause visual problems, even selective or total blindness. The parietal lobe is concerned with information from the senses from all over the body. The temporal lobe is concerned with hearing, memory, emotion, and speaking. The frontal lobe is concerned with organization, planning, and creative thinking.

The front of the parietal lobe receives information from the skin senses and from muscles. The number of touch sensors in a body part determines its sensitivity, and, along with the complexity of the part's movement, governs the amount of brain tissue associated with the part. The touch and movement of the hands, for example, involve more brain area than the more limited calves. The somatosensory cortex, at the back of the frontal lobe, receives information from the touch sensors. The motor cortex sends information to control body movement. The more sophisticated the movements (such as those used in speaking), the bigger the brain area involved in their control.

The association areas mediate between the other areas and do most of the synthesizing of information. For example, association areas turn sensory input into meaningful information. Different neurons are activated when we see different shapes and figures. The association areas arrange the incoming information into meaningful perceptions, such as the face of a friend or a favorite shirt.

Figure 6.6 The Cerebral Cortex

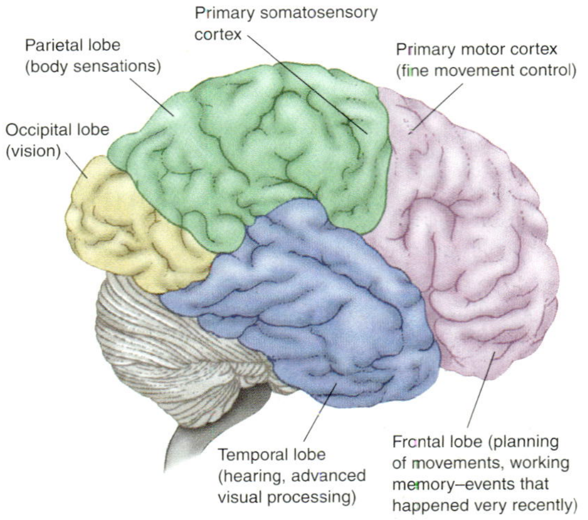

The functions of the cerebral cortex are not fully understood. Indicated here are some areas of behavioral importance. ***What is the function of the motor cortex?***

Left and Right Hemispheres There is much concern that information about properties of the left and right hemispheres is misinterpreted. Popular books have oversimplified the properties of the two hemispheres. In reality, the left and right sides complement and help each other, so be aware of this as we list the properties of each hemisphere. The two hemispheres in the cortex are roughly mirror images of each other. (Each of the four lobes is present in both hemispheres.) The corpus callosum carries messages back and forth

MEETING SPECIAL NEEDS

Learning Style: Kinesthetic Provide students with small Post-it Notes or other removable flags of different colors. Working with a model of the brain, have students use these flags to identify the three parts of the brain in one color, the lobes of the brain in another color, and the functions of the cerebral cortex in a third color. Before placing the flag, the student should write the part or function on the flag. Have students practice removing and replacing the flags from memory. **L1** **BLOCK SCHEDULING**

Refer to ***Inclusion for the High School Social Studies Classroom Strategies and Activities*** in the TCR for strategies for students with different learning styles.

Figure 6.7 Functions of the Brain's Hemispheres

The idea of whether we are "right-brained" or "left-brained" has been exaggerated. We constantly use both hemispheres of our brain, since each hemisphere is specialized for processing certain kinds of information. ***In what areas does the right hemisphere specialize?***

Front

Verbal: speaking, understanding language, reading, writing
Mathematical: adding, subtracting, multiplying, calculus, physics
Analytic: analyzing separate pieces that make up a whole

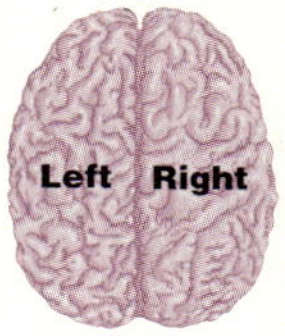

Nonverbal: understanding simple sentences and words
Spatial: solving spatial problems such as geometry, enjoying art
Holistic: combining parts that make up a whole

Back

between the two hemispheres to jointly control human functions. Each hemisphere is connected to one-half of the body in a crisscrossed fashion. The left hemisphere controls the movements of the right side of the body. For most people, the left side of the brain is where speech is located. The left side also is specialized for mathematical ability, calculation, and logic.

The right hemisphere controls the left side of the body. (Thus a stroke that causes damage to the right hemisphere will result in numbness or paralysis on the left side of the body.) The right hemisphere is more adept at visual and spatial relations. Putting together a puzzle requires spatial ability. Perceptual tasks seem to be processed primarily by the right hemisphere. The right side is better at recognizing patterns. Thus, music and art are better understood by the right hemisphere. Creativity and intuition are also found in the right hemisphere (see Figure 6.7) (Levy, 1985).

Split-Brain Operations In a normal brain, the two hemispheres communicate through the corpus callosum. Whatever occurs on one side is communicated to the other side. Some people have grand mal seizures, the most severe kind of seizure. Separating the brain hemispheres lessens the number and severity of the seizures (Kalat, 2006). As a result, the person has a split brain. The person has two brains that operate independently of each other. Since the corpus callosum is severed, there no longer is any communication between the hemispheres.

Many psychologists became interested in differences between the cerebral hemispheres when split-brain operations were tried on epileptics like Harriet Lees. For most of her life Lees's seizures were mild and could be controlled with drugs. However, at age 25 they began to get worse, and by 30 Lees was having as many as a dozen violent seizures a day. An epileptic seizure involves massive uncontrolled electrical activity that begins in either hemisphere and spreads across both. To enable Lees to live a normal life, she and the doctors decided to sever the corpus callosum so that seizures could not spread.

PSYCHOLOGY Online

Student Web Activity
Visit the *Understanding Psychology* Web site at glencoe.com and click on **Chapter 6—Student Web Activities** for an activity about biology and behavior.

Figure 6.7

Visual Instruction Explain to students that although much is known about left-brain and right-brain differences, most of the research was done with right-handed participants. Much less is known about the organization of the brains of left-handed individuals.

Caption Answer nonverbal, spatial, and holistic tasks

PSYCHOLOGY Online

Links and instructional guidelines can be found in the **Web Activity Lesson Plan** at glencoe.com.

Readings and Case Studies in Psychology

Have students read the Chapter 6 Reading selection in *Readings and Case Studies in Psychology* and answer the questions that follow the reading.

CRITICAL THINKING ACTIVITY

Demonstrating Reasoned Judgment Psychosurgery, usually a prefrontal lobotomy, has been performed many times as a way to alter psychopathic behavior. Its use among prisoners remains controversial not only because of the legal questions related to informed consent and effectiveness but also because of societal attitudes over the proper role of prisons. Are they intended to rehabilitate or to punish? If the former, are taxpayers morally obligated to fund expensive psychosurgical procedures that may rehabilitate prisoners? Ask students to take a stand on these issues by writing a persuasive essay in which they use psychological information to support their opinions. Also ask students to address the informed consent issue as it pertains to APA standards. **L2**

Profiles In Psychology

Ask students to read the **Profiles In Psychology** feature and then discuss the following questions:

1. What did Sperry's experiments demonstrate? *(how nerve cells connect to the central nervous system and how each hemisphere of the brain functions)*
2. What are the behavioral implications for split-brain research? *(Answers will vary. The research begins to help us understand the parts of the brain responsible for various human behaviors.)*

Vocabulary Activity 6–2

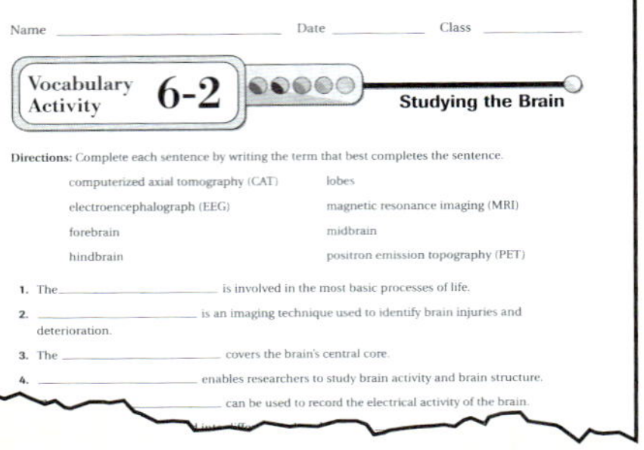
Name ______ Date ______ Class ______

Vocabulary Activity 6-2 Studying the Brain

Directions: Complete each sentence by writing the term that best completes the sentence.

computerized axial tomography (CAT)	lobes
electroencephalograph (EEG)	magnetic resonance imaging (MRI)
forebrain	midbrain
hindbrain	positron emission topography (PET)

1. The ______ is involved in the most basic processes of life.
2. ______ is an imaging technique used to identify brain injuries and deterioration.
3. The ______ covers the brain's central core.
4. ______ enables researchers to study brain activity and brain structure.

______ can be used to record the electrical activity of the brain.

Psychology Journal

Tell students to imagine that they had a severe disorder that doctors said could be relieved only through surgery to split the brain. Ask students to write a list of questions that they would want to have answered before they decided to have the surgery. ■

Profiles In Psychology

Roger Wolcott Sperry

1913–1994

"In other words, each hemisphere [of the brain] seems to have its own separate and private sensations; its own perceptions; its own concepts; and its own impulses to act. . . . Following surgery, each hemisphere also has thereafter its own separate chain of memories that are rendered inaccessible to the recall processes of the other."

Roger Sperry first became well-known in the specialized area of developmental neurobiology. He devised experiments that helped establish the means by which nerve cells become wired in particular ways in the central nervous system.

Sperry is probably best known for his pioneering split-brain research. In the 1950s and 1960s, Sperry devised a number of experiments to test the functions of each hemisphere of the brain. He argued that two separate hemispheres of consciousness could exist under one skull. Sperry pioneered the behavioral investigation of split-brain animals and humans. His experiments and techniques laid the groundwork for constructing a map of mental functions. In 1981 he became corecipient of the Nobel Prize for Physiology and Medicine for his investigation of brain functions.

Not only did the operation reduce the severity of seizures, but it also resulted in fewer seizures (Kalat, 2006). Psychologists were even more interested in the potential side effects of this operation. Despite the fact that patients who had this operation now had two functionally separate brains, they seemed remarkably normal. Researchers went on to develop a number of techniques to try to detect subtle effects of the split-brain operation.

If a man whose brain has been split holds a ball in his right hand, he would be able to say it is a ball. Place the ball in his left hand and he would not be able to say what it is. Information from the left hand is sent to the right hemisphere of the brain. Since the corpus callosum is severed, information cannot cross to the speech center in the left hemisphere.

Another experiment with split-brain patients involves tactile stimulation, or touch. In this experiment, objects are held in a designated hand but are blocked from the split-brain patient's view. Researchers project a word describing an object on a screen to either the right or left visual field. The patient's task is to find the object corresponding to the word they are shown. When words are presented for the right hemisphere to see, patients cannot say the word, but they can identify the object with their left hand touching it behind the screen.

To explore emotional reactions in split-brained individuals, researchers designed a test to incorporate emotional stimuli with objects in view. In one of these experiments, a picture of a nude person was flashed to either hemisphere. When researchers flashed the picture to the left hemisphere, the patient laughed and described what she saw. When

PSYCHOLOGY LAB EXPERIMENT

Protection From the Cold Have students research how the nervous system, the hypothalamus, and the cerebral cortex work to protect them from the cold. Have the students choose one of the following: walk outside without a coat when the temperature is below freezing; thrust their hand into a bucket of ice; or dip their bare feet into a cold bucket of water. Students should limit their exposure to one minute. Ask students to write down their immediate reactions to the cold and then answer the following questions: **What parts of your body were affected? How were they affected? How did your brain and central nervous system contribute to the reaction?** Students should prepare an oral report to present to the class. **L2**

the same was done to the right hemisphere, the patient said nothing, but her face became flush and she began to grin.

Research on split-brain patients has presented evidence that each hemisphere of the brain is unique with specialized functions and skills. Individuals who have had split-brain operations remained practically unchanged in intelligence, personality, and emotions.

HOW PSYCHOLOGISTS STUDY THE BRAIN

Mapping the brain's fissures and inner recesses has supplied scientists with fascinating information about the role of the brain in behavior. Psychologists who do this kind of research are called physiological psychologists, psychobiologists, or neuroscientists. Among the methods they use to explore the brain are recording, stimulating, lesioning, and imaging.

Recording

Electrodes are wires that can be inserted into the brain to record electrical activity in the brain. By inserting electrodes in the brain, it is possible to detect the minute electrical changes that occur when neurons fire. The wires are connected to electronic equipment that amplifies the tiny voltages produced by the firing neurons. Even single neurons can be monitored.

The electrical activity of whole areas of the brain can be recorded with an **electroencephalograph (EEG).** Wires from the EEG machine are attached to the scalp so that millions upon millions of neurons can be monitored at the same time (see Figure 6.8). Psychologists have observed that the overall electrical activity of the brain rises and falls rhythmically and that the pattern of the rhythm depends on whether a person is awake, drowsy, or asleep (as illustrated in Chapter 7). These rhythms, or brain waves, occur because the neurons in the brain tend to increase or decrease their amount of activity in unison.

Stimulation

Electrodes may be used to set off the firing of neurons as well as to record it. Brain surgeon Wilder Penfield stimulated the brains of his patients during surgery to determine what functions the various parts of the brain perform. In this way he could localize the malfunctioning part for which surgery was required, for example, for epilepsy. When Penfield applied a tiny electric current to points on the temporal lobe of the brain,

Quick Lab

Can you determine whether the left or right hemisphere of the brain is dominant?

The left hemisphere controls the movements of the right side of the body. This side of the brain is adept at language-related skills, mathematical ability, and logic. The right hemisphere controls the movements of the left side of the body. It is also the side that is more adept for creativity, intuition, and creative expressions such as art and music. Can you tell which side is dominant in people you know?

Procedure

1. Think about two of your friends or family members.
2. Compare them in terms of the areas that they seem to be most adept at—mathematics, logical thinking, musical ability, art, or speech.
3. Record your observations in a two-column chart.

Analysis

1. Based on your observations, which hemisphere seems to be dominant in each individual?

See the Skills Handbook, page 622, for an explanation of designing an experiment.

electroencephalograph (EEG): a machine used to record the electrical activity of large portions of the brain

Quick Lab

Purpose Students will examine the functions of the brain's hemispheres.

Process Skills Organizing information, relating cause and effect

Teaching Strategies

- Review which hemispheres are thought to be responsible for language, mathematical skills, logic, creativity, and intuition.
- Discuss the need for objectivity in making observations.

Analysis

1. Students' answers will vary. For those who are artistic, creative, or intuitive, students may indicate that their right hemisphere is dominant. For those who are logical or have good language skills, students may indicate that their left hemisphere is dominant.

PSYCHOLOGY Update

Computer Models The increasing power of the computer allows psychologists and other researchers to create neural network models, which are computer programs that seek to represent what a neuron does. The computer program is actually a series of computations that assumes that each neuron receives inputs from many others. By adding the inputs, any sum that exceeds a predetermined threshold results in an output. Researchers are beginning to use these models to explore such topics as attention, memory, and perception.

INTERDISCIPLINARY CONNECTIONS ACTIVITY

History Tell students that the pseudoscience of phrenology was an offshoot of scientific attempts to map the brain. Phrenologists believed that traits were localized in specific surface areas of the brain. Phrenology became a fad in the mid-1800s, and phrenological charts were even published for the presidential candidates in the 1860 election. Ask students to find out how phrenologists charted a person's personality. Encourage them to find an example of a phrenologist's chart. Have students exhibit their findings and discuss as a class why phrenology is a pseudoscience. **L2**

Figure 6.8

Caption Answer The activity rises and falls rhythmically. The pattern of the rhythm depends on a person's state—awake, drowsy, or asleep.

Readings and Case Studies in Psychology

Have students read the Chapter 6 Case Study selection in *Readings and Case Studies in Psychology* and answer the questions that follow the case study.

FYI

Recent studies have shown that men convicted of violent crimes are more likely to have abnormalities of their frontal lobes and their right hemispheres.

CULTURAL CONNECTIONS

Archaeology has found fossil evidence that most primitive tools were designed for right-handers. Research has shown that over time and across cultures, 9 out of 10 people are right-handed.

Figure 6.8 An EEG Machine

Scientists use an electroencephalograph (EEG) machine to measure brain waves. ***What have psychologists observed about the electrical activity of the brain?***

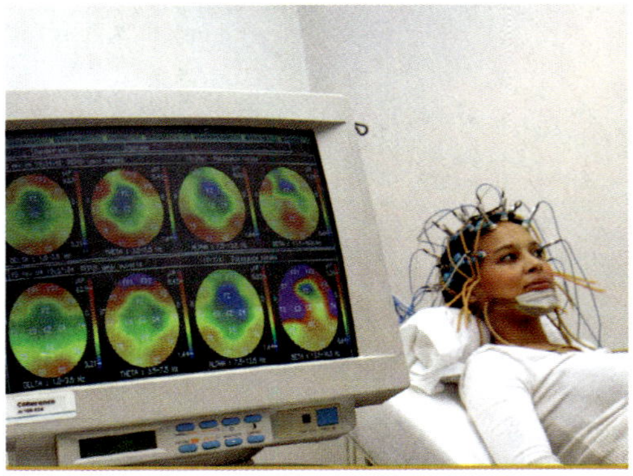

he could trigger whole memory sequences. During surgery, one woman heard a familiar song so clearly that she thought a record was being played in the operating room (Penfield & Rasmussen, 1950).

Stimulation techniques have aroused great medical interest. They have been used with terminal cancer patients to relieve them of intolerable pain without using drugs. A current delivered through electrodes implanted in certain areas of the brain may provide a sudden temporary relief (Delgado, 1969). Furthermore, some psychiatrists have experimented with similar methods to control violent emotional behavior in otherwise uncontrollable patients.

Lesions

Scientists sometimes create lesions by cutting or destroying part of an animal's brain. If the animal behaves differently after the operation, they assume that the destroyed brain area is involved with that type of behavior. For example, in one classic lesion study, two researchers removed a certain area of the temporal lobe from rhesus monkeys. Normally, these animals are fearful, aggressive, and vicious, but after the operation, they became less fearful and at the same time less violent (Klüver & Bucy, 1937). The implication was that this area of the brain controlled aggression. The relations revealed by this type of research are far more subtle and complex than people first believed.

Accidents

Psychologists can learn from the tragedies when some people suffer accidents. These accidents may involve the brain. Psychologists try to draw a connection between the damaged parts of the brain and a person's behavior. One such case involved an unusual accident in 1848. Phineas Gage was a respected railroad foreman who demonstrated restraint, good judgment, and the ability to work well with other men. His crew of men was about to explode some dynamite to clear a path for the railroad rails. As Gage filled a narrow hole with dynamite and tamped it down, it suddenly exploded. The tamping iron had caused a spark that ignited the dynamite. The tamping iron, which weighed over 13 pounds and was over 3 feet in length, shot into the air! It entered Gage's head right below the left eye, and it exited through the top of the skull.

Gage survived the accident, but his personality changed greatly. He became short-tempered, was difficult to be around, and often said inappropriate things. Gage lived for several years after the accident. In 1994 psychologists Hanna and Antonio Damasio examined Gage's skull using the newest methods available. They reported that the tamping iron had caused damage to parts of the frontal cortex. They found that damage to the frontal lobes prevents censoring of thoughts and ideas.

EXTENDING THE CONTENT

Techniques to Assess Brain Functioning In addition to PET scans, CT scans, and fMRIs, other techniques include:

- **Brain Electrical Activity Mapping (BEAM)** provides a computer-generated map of brain activity using colors to indicate different levels of activity.
- **Event-Related Potentials (ERP)** measure changes in patterns of brain activity in response to specific external stimuli.

Another unusual case took place in the nineteenth century. Dr. Paul Broca had a young patient who could only respond with hand gestures and the word "tan." Broca theorized that a part of the brain on the left side was destroyed, limiting the young man's communication processes. Many years later, researchers examined the young man's brain using modern methods. They discovered that Dr. Broca's theory was correct. The left side of the cortex, which is involved with the production of speech, was damaged. This area of the cortex is now known as Broca's area.

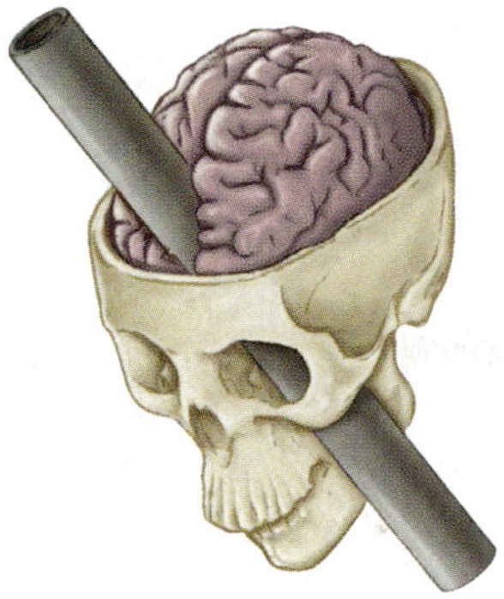

Path of tamping iron that passed entirely through Phineas Gage's skull

Images

Dr. Paul Broca uncovered the connection between the brain and speech. Researchers proved Dr. Broca's theory using PET scans. Today psychologists and medical researchers are using this and other sophisticated techniques, including CT scans and fMRI scans.

In the 1970s, **computerized axial tomography (CT)** scans were used to pinpoint injuries and other problems in brain deterioration. During a CT scan, a moving ring passes X-ray beams around and through a subject's head. Radiation is absorbed in different amounts depending on the density of the brain tissue. Computers measure the amount of radiation absorbed and transform this information into a three-dimensional view of the brain.

The **positron emission tomography (PET)** scan can capture a picture of the brain as different parts are being used. It involves injecting a slightly radioactive solution into the blood and then measuring the amount of radiation absorbed by blood cells. Active neurons absorb more radioactive solution than nonactive ones (see Figure 6.9). Researchers use the PET scan to see which areas are being activated while performing a task (Raichle, 1994). PET scans show activity in different areas of the brain when a person is thinking, speaking, and looking at objects. The scan changes when one is talking and when one is looking at a piece of art. These pictures change as the activity changes.

Another process, **magnetic resonance imaging**, or **MRI**, enables researchers to study both activity and brain structures (see Figure 6.10). It

computerized axial tomography (CT): an imaging technique used to study the brain to pinpoint injuries and brain deterioration

positron emission tomography (PET): an imaging technique used to see which brain areas are being activated while performing tasks

magnetic resonance imaging (MRI): a measuring technique used to study brain structure and activity

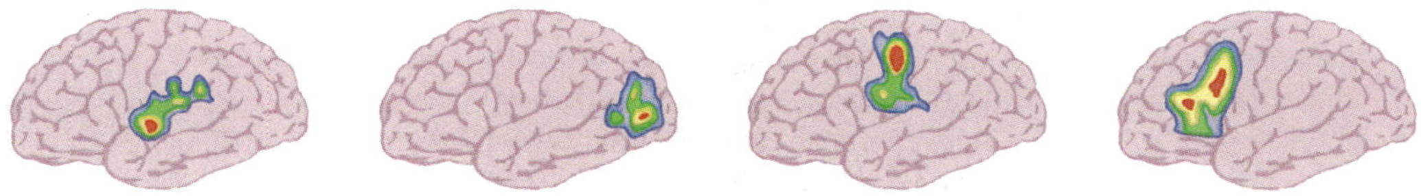

Hearing words | Seeing words | Reading words | Generating verbs

Figure 6.9 Brain Activity on a PET Scan

A computer transforms the different levels of absorption by neurons of radioactive solution into colors. Red and yellow indicate maximum activity of neurons, while blue and green indicate minimal activity. ***Why would psychologists use a PET scan?***

Figure 6.9

Visual Instruction Have students identify the various areas of the brain that show the most and least activity in these PET scans.

Caption Answer Psychologists use PET scans to identify the different areas of the brain that are active in performing tasks.

3 ASSESS

Assign Section 2 Assessment as homework or as an in-class activity.

Section Quiz 6–2

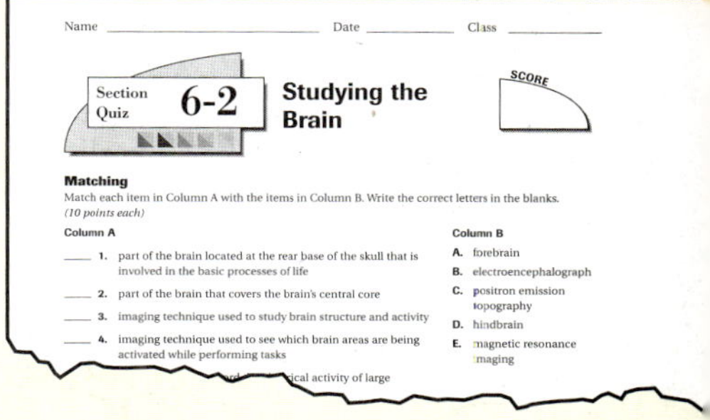

Name ______ Date ______ Class ______

Section Quiz 6-2 **Studying the Brain**

SCORE

Matching

Match each item in Column A with the items in Column B. Write the correct letters in the blanks. *(10 points each)*

Column A

____ 1. part of the brain located at the rear base of the skull that is involved in the basic processes of life

____ 2. part of the brain that covers the brain's central core

____ 3. imaging technique used to study brain structure and activity

____ 4. imaging technique used to see which brain areas are being activated while performing tasks

...ical activity of large

Column B

A. forebrain

B. electroencephalograph

C. positron emission topography

D. hindbrain

E. magnetic resonance imaging

EXTENDING THE CONTENT

Gender Differences and the Brain Researchers have long known that men's brains are slightly larger than women's brains. However, no research has proven that the size of the brain makes much difference in intelligence. There are, however, subtle differences in certain areas of the brains of males and females. Women tend to have stronger language skills, and men tend to have better spatial reasoning. The other specific differences occur in the areas of the hypothalamus that control reproduction, circadian rhythms, and mating behaviors.

Figure 6.10

Caption Answer MRIs allow researchers to study both the activity and structure of the brain by combining features of both CT and PET scans.

Reteach

List on the board the methods psychologists use to research the brain. Have students brainstorm the types of information that psychologists can learn from each method.

Enrich

Ask students to select a brain disorder or brain injury. Then ask them to research how the disorder or injury affects behavior.

4 CLOSE

As a class, discuss which of the methods for exploring the brain promises to yield the most practical benefits for treating human behavioral problems.

Figure 6.10 An MRI

Magnetic resonance imaging (MRI) studies the activities of the brain. ***Why does an MRI of the brain give a more thorough picture than a CT or PET scan would give?***

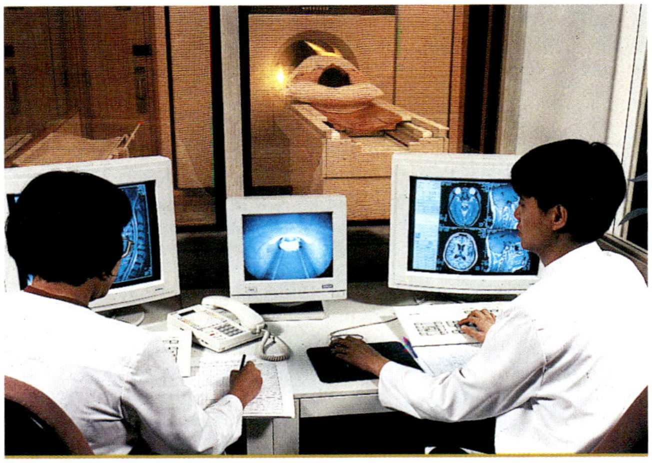

combines the features of both CT and PET scans. It involves passing nonharmful radio frequencies through the brain. A computer measures how these signals interact with brain cells and translates these signals into a detailed image of the brain. Researchers use MRIs to study the structure of the brain as well as to identify tumors or types of brain damage.

Researchers use a new technique of imaging, functional magnetic resonance imaging (fMRI), to directly observe both the functions of different structures of the brain and which structures participate in specific functions. The fMRI provides high-resolution reports of neural activity based on signals that are determined by blood oxygen level. The fMRI actually detects an increase in blood flow to the active structure of the brain. So, unlike the MRI, the fMRI does not require passing radio frequencies through the brain. With this new method of imaging, researchers have confirmed their hypotheses concerning the functions of areas such as the visual cortex, the motor cortex, and Broca's area of speech and language-related activities.

SECTION 2 Assessment

1. **Review the Vocabulary** List and describe the main functions of the lobes of the human brain.
2. **Visualize the Main Idea** In a diagram similar to the one below, list the parts of the brain.

Parts of the Human Brain

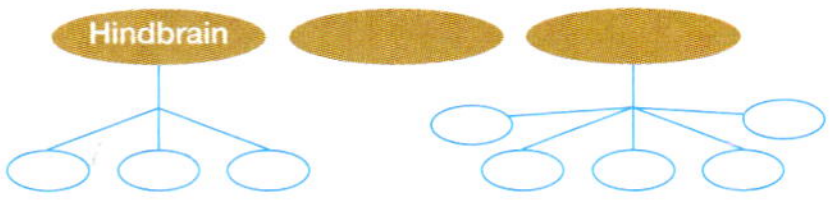

3. **Recall Information** What are the functions of the thalamus and hypothalamus?
4. **Think Critically** If a person suffers a traumatic head injury and then begins behaving differently, can we assume that brain damage is the reason for the personality change? Why or why not?
5. **Application Activity** A woman severely injured the right hemisphere of her brain. Create a scenario in which you describe two body functions that might be affected by the woman's injury.

SECTION 2 Assessment Answers

1. The occipital lobe is where visual signals are processed. The temporal lobes house hearing, memory, emotion, and speaking. The frontal lobes are concerned with organization, planning, and creative thinking. The parietal lobes are concerned with sensory information.
2. The hindbrain includes the cerebellum, medulla, and the pons. The midbrain integrates sensory information. The forebrain includes the thalamus, hypothalamus, cerebral cortex, corpus callosum, and pituitary gland.
3. The thalamus integrates all sensory information except smell. The hypothalamus controls basic biological needs.
4. A psychologist would not assume the brain is damaged, but would instead try to draw a connection between the damaged area and the person's behavior. The experience of trauma may also affect behavior.
5. Students' answers will vary. The woman will experience numbness or paralysis on the left side of her body and will lose some degree of movement and sensation.

Case Studies

One Person . . . Two Brains?

Period of Study: 1967

Introduction: Victoria had experienced intense epileptic seizures since she was six years old. Doctors placed Victoria on medication that prevented seizures for a period of time. However, after many years, the seizures returned with greater intensity. Weary and disgusted from living her life with the uncontrollable and agonizing seizures, Victoria decided it was time to seek a new treatment.

Doctors suggested and Victoria opted for a split-brain operation—an innovative procedure that has proved successful in treating patients with seizures. This operation involved opening the patient's skull and separating the two brain hemispheres by cutting the corpus callosum. Split-brain operations disrupt the major pathway between the brain hemispheres but leave each hemisphere functioning almost completely independently. The procedure prevents the spread of seizures from one hemisphere to the other. This reduces the chance of having a seizure or shortens the seizure if one does occur.

Upon completion of Victoria's split-brain operation, the time came to test her various brain functions that now involved nonconnected, independent hemispheres.

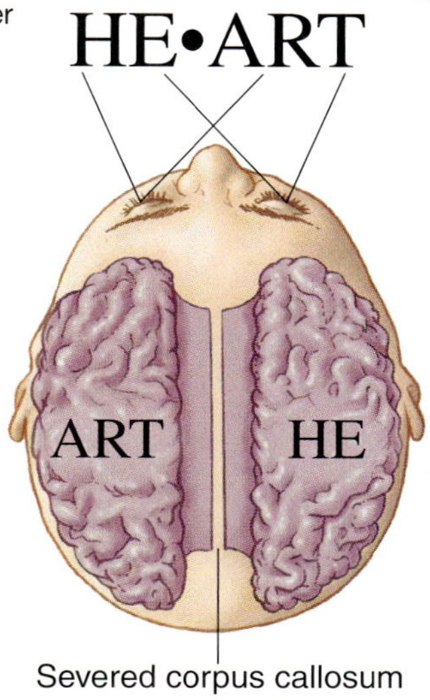

Hypothesis: Researchers wanted to explore the degree to which the two halves of the brain could communicate and function on their own after the operation.

Method: Researchers asked Victoria to stare at a black dot between the letters HE and ART. The information from each side of the black dot will be interpreted by the opposite hemisphere in Victoria's split brain. Victoria's right hemisphere will see HE and her left will only see ART (see diagram).

When Victoria was asked what she had seen, she reported to have seen the word ART. The word ART was projected to her left hemisphere, which contains the ability for speech. She did indeed see the word HE; however, the right hemisphere could not make Victoria say what she had seen. With her left hand, though, Victoria could point to a picture of a man, or HE. This indicated that her right hemisphere could understand the meaning of HE.

Results: Four months after Victoria's split-brain operation, she was alert and could easily remember and speak of past and present events in her life. Her reading, writing, and reasoning abilities were all intact. She could easily carry out everyday functions such as dressing, eating, and walking. Although the effects of her operation became apparent under special testing, they were not apparent in everyday life. Victoria, now free of her once-feared seizures, could live her life seizure-free, split-brained but unchanged.

Analyzing the Case Study

1. Why did Victoria choose to have a split-brain operation? What did the operation involve?
2. What questions did researchers set out to answer after Victoria's operation?
3. **Critical Thinking** What problems do you think Victoria might encounter in everyday life?

Going Further

Additional Experiments on Split-Brain Patients

Split-brain patients have provided psychologists with an excellent opportunity to explore how the brain's hemispheres operate. Each instance adds a little more to our knowledge of the brain.

In one experiment, a split-brain patient was blindfolded and a familiar object, such as a toothbrush, was placed in his left hand. When asked to name the item, the patient could not give it a name. When asked what the item was used for, the patient immediately began to brush his teeth. Researchers concluded that the patient knew what the item was, but his right brain had no language capability and therefore could not name it. When the patient was told to transfer the item to his right hand, he was immediately able to identify the item as a toothbrush.

Discussing the Case Study

Ask: How does split-brain surgery benefit both the patient and humans in general? Should split-brain surgery ever be performed on a person with no brain disorders? Encourage students to explain their reasoning.

Answers for Analyzing the Case Study

1. She wanted to relieve the seizures and be able to live a more normal life. The operation involved opening her skull and separating the hemispheres of her brain by cutting the corpus callosum. Victoria and her doctors realized that by cutting the major pathway between the two hemispheres, each hemisphere would function almost completely independently after the operation.
2. What functions can each hemisphere perform? What communication capability does each hemisphere have?
3. Answers will vary. Examples should focus on the problem of each hemisphere storing its own separate set of memories that are inaccessible to recall by the other. Examples could include conflicts in right-left brain communication, such as selecting something to eat, trying to pick up the selected item with one hand, or holding a conversation using only one hemisphere of the brain. Students should note that the effects of the operation are not so apparent in everyday life.

CHAPTER 6
Section 3, pages 170–173

1 FOCUS

Section Objectives

1. Describe the endocrine system.
2. Identify hormones and their function in the endocrine system.

BELLRINGER
Motivational Activity

Project Daily Focus Transparency 6–3 and have students answer the questions.

Available as blackline master

Daily Focus Transparency 6–3

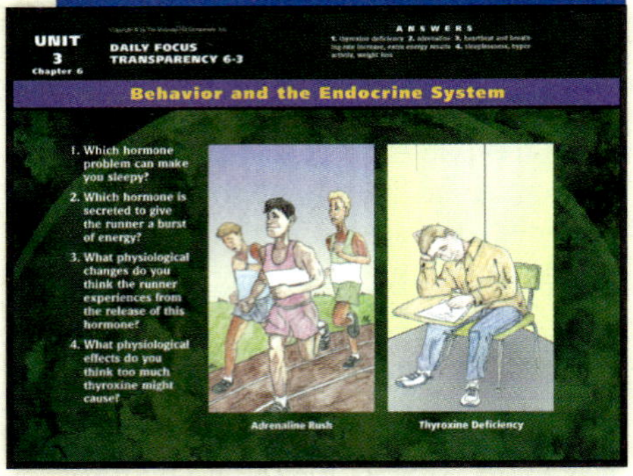

Reader's Guide

Use the Reader's Guide to introduce concepts and vocabulary.

■ **Exploring Psychology**
Ask students to read the **Exploring Psychology** feature and then discuss the following question: **How does adrenaline affect the body and the brain?**

■ **Vocabulary Precheck**
Have students read the Glossary definition of each term. Then ask students to rewrite each definition in their own words.

Use the **Vocabulary PuzzleMaker CD-ROM** to create crossword and word search puzzles.

SECTION 3 The Endocrine System

Reader's Guide

■ **Main Idea**
The endocrine system controls and excites growth and affects emotions and behavior in people.

■ **Vocabulary**
- endocrine system
- hormones
- pituitary gland

■ **Objectives**
- Describe the endocrine system.
- Identify hormones and their function in the endocrine system.

EXPLORING PSYCHOLOGY

Running With the Bulls

And then the gun goes off. I run up the cobblestone street. People are jogging at a moderate pace. There's no tremendous push for speed. . . . The second gun goes off—now people pick up the pace: the bulls have been released. . . . There's a sudden burst of speed, energy, panic, of bodies, and the bulls are in the ring. I high tail it to the perimeter, having heard too many tales of bulls going mad in the ring. . . . I caught up with Von and Don. I was just about to ask Don a question when I saw a bull charging Von. He stood frozen for a second, and at the last second jumped sideways in a crescent shape, as the bull missed him and tried to put his shoulder into Von. We ran up to him and he was five shades of white. . . .

—from "I Run With the Bulls" by **Mike Silva, 1995**

Every year in Pamplona, Spain, many people experience what some consider the ultimate "adrenaline rush." Fighting bulls and steers run through the town every morning of a nine-day fiesta. Hundreds of revelers literally run with the bulls. The bull-racing ritual is inhumane (more than 50 bulls are killed each day), and participants risk death if they should get gored by a bull. Why do people do it?

Many do it for the "rush." The rush comes from a hormone secreted by the endocrine system called adrenaline or epinephrine. The adrenal hormone declares an emergency situation to the body, requiring the body to become very active.

SECTION RESOURCES

Reproducible Masters
- Guided Reading Activity 6–3
- Vocabulary Activity 6–3
- Section Quiz 6–3

Transparencies
- Daily Focus Transparency 6–3

Multimedia
- Vocabulary PuzzleMaker CD-ROM
- *ExamView®* *Assessment Suite* CD-ROM
- Presentation Plus! Software

THE ENDOCRINE GLANDS

The nervous system is one of two communication systems for sending information to and from the brain. The second is the **endocrine system.** The endocrine system sends chemical messages, called hormones. The **hormones** are produced in the endocrine glands and are distributed by the blood and other body fluids. (The names and locations of these glands are shown in Figure 6.11.) Hormones circulate throughout the bloodstream but are properly received only at a specific site: the particular organ of the body that they influence. The endocrine glands are also called ductless glands because they release hormones directly into the bloodstream. In contrast, the duct glands release their contents through small holes, or ducts, onto the surface of the body or into the digestive system. Examples of duct glands are sweat glands, tear glands, and salivary glands.

Psychology and You: Do You Do This?

Human ethology is the study of human behavior as it naturally occurs. Basketball fans know that Michael Jordan stuck out his tongue when he attempted a difficult shot. Similarly, it has been found that expert billiard players stick out their tongues more often when making hard shots than when attempting relatively easy shots. According to ethologists, a tongue display acts as a nonverbal sign that interaction is not desired. For humans, the tongue displays seem to indicate that the person does not want to be interrupted because of the need to concentrate in a difficult situation.

Hormones have various effects on your behavior. They affect the growth of bodily structures such as muscles and bones, so they affect what you can do physically. Hormones affect your metabolic processes; that is, they can affect how much energy you have to perform actions. Some hormonal effects take place before you are born. Essentially all the physical differences between boys and girls are caused by a hormone called testosterone. Certain other hormones are secreted during stressful situations to prepare the body for action. Hormones also act in the brain to directly influence your moods and drives.

endocrine system: a chemical communication system, using hormones, by which messages are sent through the bloodstream

hormones: chemical substances that carry messages through the body in blood

Pituitary Gland

Directed by the hypothalamus, the **pituitary gland** acts as the master gland. The pituitary gland, located near the midbrain and the hypothalamus, secretes a large number of hormones, many of which control the output of hormones by other endocrine glands. The hypothalamus monitors the amount of hormones in the blood and sends out messages to correct imbalances.

What do these hormone messages tell the body to do? They carry messages to organs involved in regulating and storing nutrients so that despite changes in conditions outside the body, cell metabolism can continue on an even course. They also control growth and reproduction, including ovulation and lactation (milk production) in females.

pituitary gland: the center of control of the endocrine system that secretes a large number of hormones

Reading Check What is the function of the pituitary gland? The thyroid gland?

Thyroid Gland

The *thyroid gland* produces the hormone thyroxine. Thyroxine stimulates certain chemical reactions that are important for all tissues of the body. Too little thyroxine makes people feel lazy and lethargic—a

COOPERATIVE LEARNING ACTIVITY

Preparing an Oral Presentation Organize students into groups of four. Have each group select one of the endocrine glands mentioned in the text and do in-depth research for an oral report on that gland's connection to general health and behavior. Reports should include a description of the gland, its location, the hormones it secretes, the role it plays in the body, and an overview of the problems that may occur if it malfunctions. The group should also prepare appropriate visual aids including charts, drawings, and tables to be used during the report.

BLOCK SCHEDULING

2 TEACH

L1 Creating a Table Using Figure 6.11 as a basis, have students work in small groups to create a table listing the various glands of the endocrine system and explaining how they affect human behavior. Display completed tables in the classroom.

Guided Reading Activity 6–3

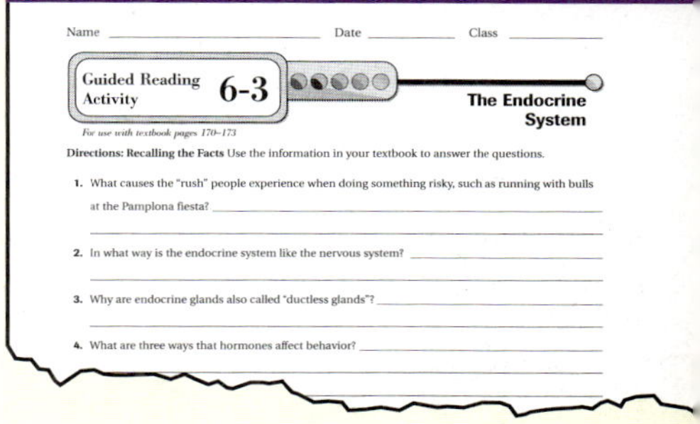
Name ______ Date ______ Class ______

Guided Reading Activity 6-3

The Endocrine System

For use with textbook pages 170–173

Directions: Recalling the Facts Use the information in your textbook to answer the questions.

1. What causes the "rush" people experience when doing something risky, such as running with bulls at the Pamplona fiesta? ______
2. In what way is the endocrine system like the nervous system? ______
3. Why are endocrine glands also called "ductless glands"? ______
4. What are three ways that hormones affect behavior? ______

Psychology and You

Use the following question to direct a class discussion after students have read the **Psychology and You** feature.

Ask: **Why may a tongue display indicate that a person is concentrating and does not want to be disturbed?**

Reading Check Answer The pituitary gland regulates the other endocrine glands by secreting hormones into the blood. The thyroid gland regulates metabolism.

CHAPTER 6
Section 3, pages 170–173

Figure 6.11

Visual Instruction Point out that scientists have discovered more than 30 different hormones in the human body.

Caption Answer The adrenal glands secrete hormones that help a person generate extra energy to handle a difficult situation.

Vocabulary Activity 6-3

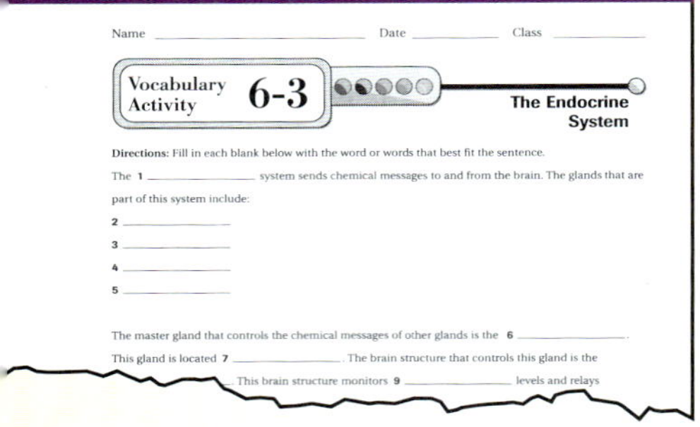
Name ____ Date ____ Class ____

Vocabulary Activity 6-3 The Endocrine System

Directions: Fill in each blank below with the word or words that best fit the sentence.

The 1 ________ system sends chemical messages to and from the brain. The glands that are part of this system include:

2 ________

3 ________

4 ________

5 ________

The master gland that controls the chemical messages of other glands is the 6 ________.

This gland is located 7 ________. The brain structure that controls this gland is the ________. This brain structure monitors 9 ________ levels and relays

3 ASSESS

Assign Section 3 Assessment as homework or as an in-class activity.

Section Quiz 6-3

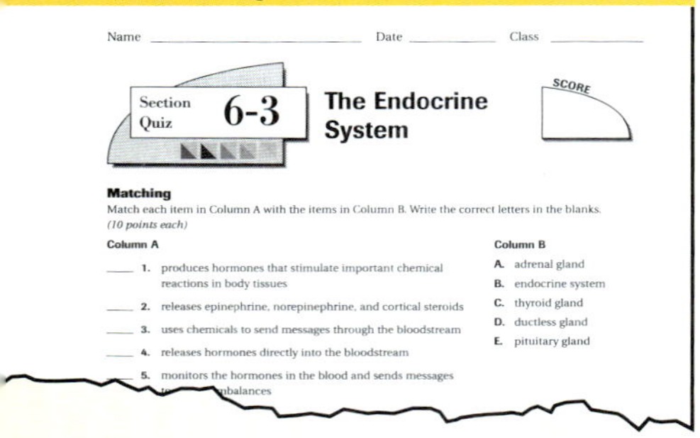
Name ____ Date ____ Class ____

Section Quiz 6-3 The Endocrine System SCORE

Matching

Match each item in Column A with the items in Column B. Write the correct letters in the blanks. (10 points each)

Column A	Column B
___ 1. produces hormones that stimulate important chemical reactions in body tissues	A. adrenal gland
___ 2. releases epinephrine, norepinephrine, and cortical steroids	B. endocrine system
___ 3. uses chemicals to send messages through the bloodstream	C. thyroid gland
___ 4. releases hormones directly into the bloodstream	D. ductless gland
___ 5. monitors the hormones in the blood and sends messages ... imbalances	E. pituitary gland

Reteach

List the following states on the board: fear, lethargy, anxiety, and arousal. Have students list the endocrine glands that would secrete hormones for each of these behaviors.

Figure 6.11 The Endocrine System

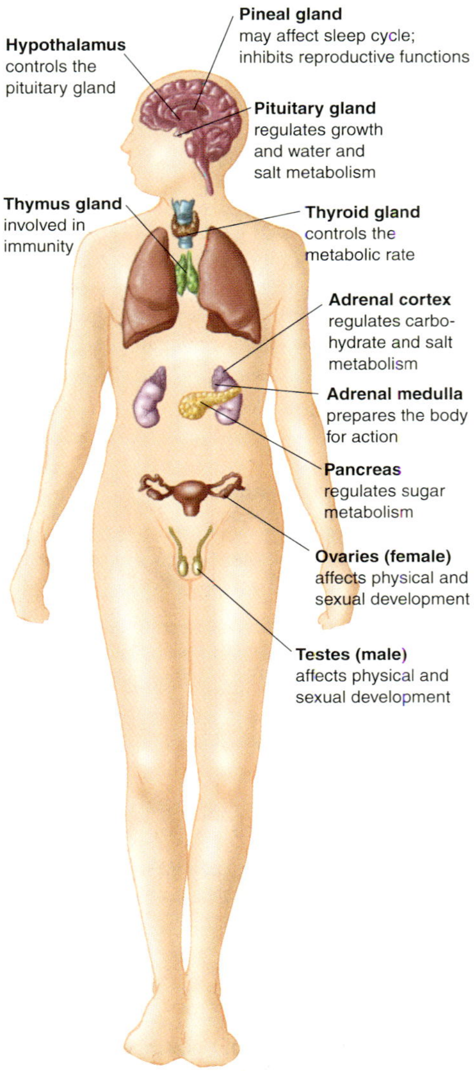

The endocrine system, which consists of ductless glands and the hormones they produce, works closely with the nervous system in regulating body functions. ***What is the function of the adrenal glands?***

condition known as hypothyroidism. Too much thyroxine may cause people to lose weight and sleep and to be overactive—a condition known as hyperthyroidism.

Adrenal Glands

The *adrenal glands* become active when a person is angry or frightened. They release epinephrine and norepinephrine (also called adrenaline and noradrenaline) into the bloodstream. These secretions cause the heartbeat and breathing to increase. They can heighten emotions, such as fear and anxiety. These secretions and other changes help a person generate the extra energy he or she needs to handle a difficult situation.

The adrenal glands also secrete cortical steroids. Cortical steroids help muscles develop and cause the liver to release stored sugar when the body requires extra energy for emergencies.

Sex Glands

There are two types of sex glands—*testes* in males and *ovaries* in females. Testes produce sperm and the male sex hormone *testosterone.* Low levels of testosterone are also found in females. Ovaries produce eggs and the female hormones *estrogen* and *progesterone,* although low levels of these hormones are also found in males.

Testosterone is important in the physical development of males, especially in the prenatal period and in adolescence. In the prenatal period, testosterone helps decide the sex of a fetus. In adolescence, testosterone is important for the growth of muscle and bone along with the growth of male sex characteristics.

Estrogen and progesterone are important in the development of female sex characteristics. These hormones also regulate the reproductive cycle of females. The levels of estrogen and progesterone vary throughout the menstrual cycle. These variances can cause premenstrual syndrome (PMS) in some women. PMS includes symptoms such as fatigue, irritability, and depression.

HORMONES VS. NEUROTRANSMITTERS

Both hormones and neurotransmitters work to affect the nervous system. In fact, the same chemical (such as norepinephrine) can be used as both a hormone and a neurotransmitter. So what is the difference between a hormone and a neurotransmitter?

MEETING SPECIAL NEEDS

Learning Style: Naturalist Have students research the problem of PCBs (polychlorinated biphenyls) and how they imitate natural hormones in both humans and animals. Ask them to use the information from their research to prepare a fact sheet and accompanying press release. The fact sheet should state the extent of the problem and provide sources to back up any claims. The press release should encourage people to write protest letters to manufacturers who release PCBs into the air or water. **L2** **BLOCK SCHEDULING**

Refer to ***Inclusion for the High School Social Studies Classroom Strategies and Activities*** in the TCR for strategies for students with different learning styles.

When a chemical is used as a neurotransmitter, it is released right beside the cell that it is to excite or inhibit. When a chemical is used as a hormone, it is released into the blood, which diffuses it throughout the body. For example, norepinephrine is a hormone when it is secreted into the blood by the adrenal glands. Norepinephrine is a neurotransmitter, though, when it is released by the sympathetic motor neurons of the peripheral nervous system.

Hormones and neurotransmitters appear to have a common evolutionary origin (Snyder, 1985). As multicellular organisms evolved, the system of communication among cells coordinated their actions so that all the cells of the organism could act as a unit. As organisms grew more complex, this communication system began to split into two more specialized communication systems. One, the nervous system, developed to send rapid and specific messages, while the other, involving the circulatory system, developed to send slow and widespread communication. In this second system, the chemical messengers evolved into hormones. Whereas neural messages can be measured in thousandths of a second, hormonal messages may take minutes to reach their destination and weeks or months to have their total effect.

Figure 6.12 An Adrenaline Rush

In the event of a life-threatening or highly stressful situation, the adrenal glands produce adrenaline to give people the necessary energy to cope. ***How does adrenaline affect emotions in people?***

SECTION 3 Assessment

1. **Review the Vocabulary** What are three ways that the endocrine system affects behavior?
2. **Visualize the Main Idea** In a chart similar to the one at right, identify the hormones produced by the glands and the functions of those hormones.
3. **Recall Information** How does the endocrine system differ from the nervous system?

Glands of the Endocrine System	
Gland	Hormone(s) released

4. **Think Critically** Explain what psychologists might learn about behavior by studying sex hormones.
5. **Application Activity** Describe a medical situation in which a psychologist would examine the thyroid gland. Describe the situation from the perspective of a patient.

SECTION 3 Assessment Answers

1. The endocrine system can heighten emotions, create symptoms of PMS, and make people feel lazy or be overactive.
2. Charts should reflect students' understanding of the endocrine system and its functions.
3. The nervous system sends chemical-electrical messages directly to the neuron of the cell it wishes to direct, creating rapid responses. The endocrine system secretes hormones (chemical messages) into the bloodstream to create slower but more widespread communication within the body.
4. Psychologists can learn differences between male and female physical growth, sexual development, rate of maturation, and their effects on PMS cycles in women.
5. Students' answers will vary. The patient may describe being constantly tired and having no energy even though he or she is eating properly and getting sufficient rest or being overactive and losing weight and sleep.

Figure 6.12

Caption Answer Adrenaline can heighten emotions such as fear and anxiety.

Enrich

Ask students to explain the major difference in how the nervous and endocrine systems work to help the brain monitor and control most human behavior.

4 CLOSE

Revisit the **Exploring Psychology** feature at the beginning of the section.

Ask: What happens to the endocrine system when the bulls are released?

1 FOCUS

Section Objectives

1. Give examples of the effects of heredity and environment on behavior.
2. Summarize research on the effects of heredity and environment on behavior.

BELLRINGER
Motivational Activity

Project Daily Focus Transparency 6–4 and have students answer the questions.

Available as blackline master

Daily Focus Transparency 6–4

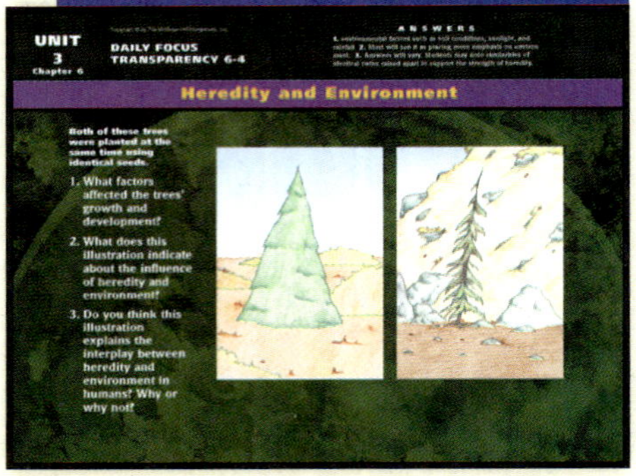

Reader's Guide

Use the Reader's Guide to introduce concepts and vocabulary.

■ **Exploring Psychology**
Ask students to read the **Exploring Psychology** feature and then discuss: **What is the most likely explanation for the girls' behavior?**

■ **Vocabulary Precheck**
Have students read the Glossary definition of each vocabulary term. Then have them write a paragraph that uses the terms and explains a theory of human behavior.

Use the **Vocabulary PuzzleMaker CD-ROM** to create crossword and word search puzzles.

SECTION 4 Heredity and Environment

Reader's Guide

■ **Main Idea**
Heredity is the transmission of characteristics from parents to children. Environment is the world around you. Heredity and environment affect your body and behavior.

■ **Vocabulary**
- heredity
- identical twins
- genes
- fraternal twins

■ **Objectives**
- Give examples of the effects of heredity and environment on behavior.
- Summarize research on the effects of heredity and environment on behavior.

EXPLORING PSYCHOLOGY

Nature or Nurture?

Two monozygotic [derived from the same egg] twin girls were separated at birth and placed in homes far apart. About four years later, researchers interviewed the adoptive parents of each girl. The parents of Shauna said, "She is a terrible eater—won't cooperate, stubborn, strong-willed. I can't get her to eat *anything* unless I put cinnamon on it." The parents of Ellen said, "Ellen is a lovely child—cooperative and outgoing." The researcher probed, asking, "How are her eating habits?" The response was: "Fantastic—she eats anything I put before her, as long as I put cinnamon on it!"

—from *Nature's Thumbprint: The New Genetics of Personality* by P.B. Neubauer and A. Neubauer, 1990

How much do genetic factors contribute to our behavior? How much do environmental factors? These questions have haunted psychologists for years. Some psychologists believe that genetics is like a flower, and the environment is like rain, soil, or fertilizer. Genes establish what you could be, and the environment defines the final product.

HEREDITY AND ENVIRONMENT

heredity: the genetic transmission of characteristics from parents to their offspring

People often argue about whether human behavior is instinctive (due to heredity) or learned (due to environment). **Heredity** is the genetic transmission of characteristics from parents to their offspring. Do people learn to be good athletes, or are they born that way? Do people learn to

SECTION RESOURCES

Reproducible Masters
- Guided Reading Activity 6–4
- Vocabulary Activity 6–4
- Section Quiz 6–4

Transparencies
- Daily Focus Transparency 6–4

Multimedia
- Vocabulary PuzzleMaker CD-ROM
- *ExamView® Assessment Suite* CD-ROM
- Presentation Plus! Software

do well in school, or are they born good at it? The reason for the intensity of the argument may be that many people assume that something learned can probably be changed, whereas something inborn will be difficult or impossible to change. The issue is not that simple, however. Inherited factors and environmental conditions always act together in complicated ways. Asking whether heredity or environment is responsible for something turns out to be like asking, "What makes a cake rise, baking powder or heat?" Obviously, an interaction of the two is responsible.

A Question of Nature vs. Nurture

The argument over the nature-nurture question has been going on for centuries. Nature refers to the characteristics that a person inherits—his or her biological makeup. Nurture refers to environmental factors, such as family, culture, education, and individual experiences. Sir Francis Galton became one of the first to preach the importance of nature in the modern era. In 1869 he published *Hereditary Genius,* a book in which he analyzed the families of over 1,000 eminent politicians, religious leaders, artists, and scholars. He found that success ran in families and concluded that heredity was the cause.

Many psychologists, however, have emphasized the importance of the environment. The tone was set by John Watson, the founder of behaviorism, who wrote in 1930: "Give me a dozen healthy infants, well-formed, and my own specified world to bring them up in and I'll guarantee to take any one at random and train him to become any type of specialist I might select—a doctor, lawyer, artist, merchant-chief, and, yes, even beggarman and thief, regardless of his talents, penchants, tendencies, abilities, vocations, and race of his ancestors" (Watson, 1930).

Reading Check What is heredity and how does it affect your behavior?

identical twins: twins who come from one fertilized egg; twins having the same heredity

genes: the basic building blocks of heredity

Genes and Behavior Genes are the basic units of heredity. They are reproduced and passed along from parent to child. All the effects that genes have on behavior occur through their role in building and modifying the physical structures of the body. Those structures must interact with their environment to produce behavior. For example, if your parents are musicians, you may have inherited a gene that influences your musical ability by contributing to brain development that analyzes sounds well.

Twin Studies

One way to find out whether a trait is inherited is to study twins. **Identical twins** develop from a single fertilized egg (thus, they are called monozygotic) and share the same **genes.** Genes are the basic building blocks of heredity (see Figure 6.13).

Figure 6.13 DNA and Genes

The molecules of DNA make up chromosomes that contain the codes for our biological makeup. ***What are genes?***

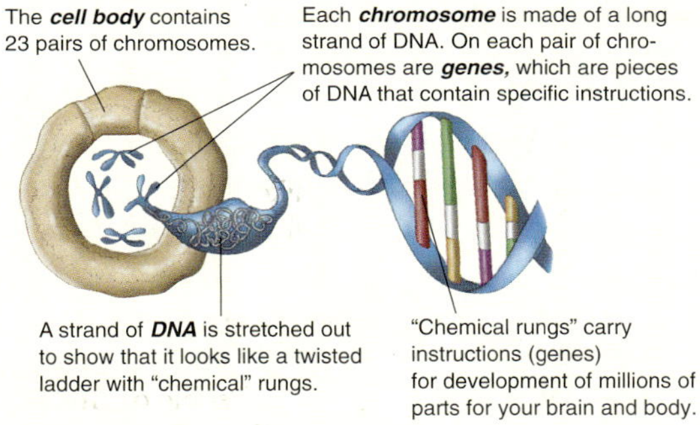

Source: Plotnik, 1999.

COOPERATIVE LEARNING ACTIVITY

Comparing Subjective Information Organize students into groups of four. Have each member in the group rate the traits listed below based on the influence of heredity and environment using a percentage rating system. For each trait, the total must equal 100 percent. For example, Intelligence: environment 60 percent; heredity 40 percent. Have the group chart each person's responses and then analyze similarities and differences among group members.

1. Body build
2. Intelligence
3. Personality
4. Mathematical ability
5. Baldness
6. Handedness
7. Height
8. Musical ability
9. Longevity

2 TEACH

Guided Reading Activity 6–4

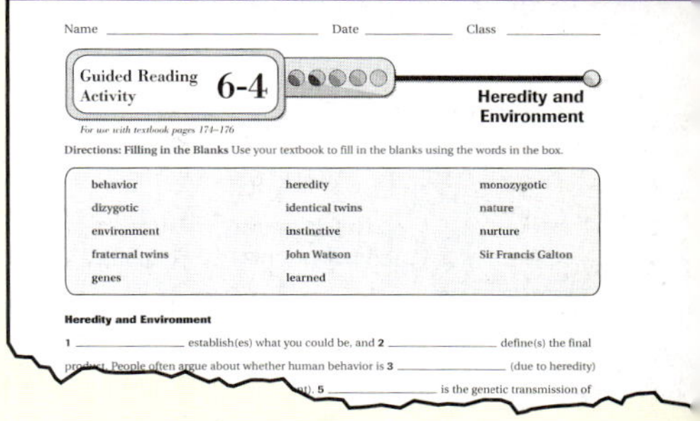
Name ____ Date ____ Class ____
Guided Reading Activity 6-4
Heredity and Environment
For use with textbook pages 174–176
Directions: Filling in the Blanks Use your textbook to fill in the blanks using the words in the box.

behavior	heredity	monozygotic
dizygotic	identical twins	nature
environment	instinctive	nurture
fraternal twins	John Watson	Sir Francis Galton
genes	learned	

Heredity and Environment
1 ____ establish(es) what you could be, and 2 ____ define(s) the final product. People often argue about whether human behavior is 3 ____ (due to heredity) ... 5 ____ is the genetic transmission of

Reading Check Answer the genetic transmission of characteristics; it acts with the environment to influence behavior

Vocabulary Activity 6–4

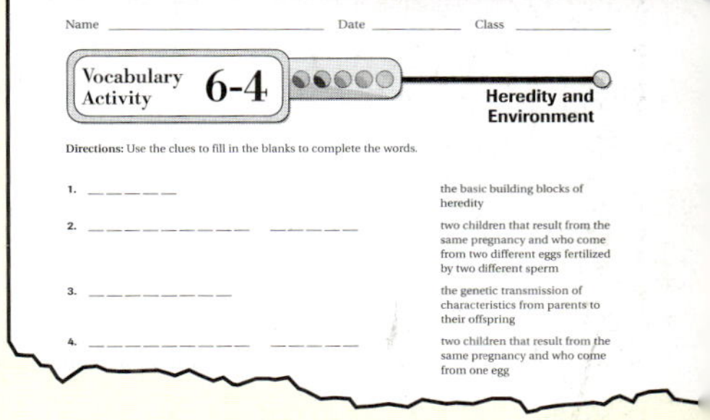
Name ____ Date ____ Class ____
Vocabulary Activity 6-4
Heredity and Environment
Directions: Use the clues to fill in the blanks to complete the words.
1. ____ the basic building blocks of heredity
2. ____ ____ two children that result from the same pregnancy and who come from two different eggs fertilized by two different sperm
3. ____ the genetic transmission of characteristics from parents to their offspring
4. ____ ____ two children that result from the same pregnancy and who come from one egg

Figure 6.13

Caption Answer the basic units of heredity

3 ASSESS

Assign Section 4 Assessment as homework or as an in-class activity.

CHAPTER 6
Section 4, pages 174–176

Figure 6.14

Caption Answer Psychologists question how much genetic factors and environmental factors each contribute to one's behavior.

Section Quiz 6–4

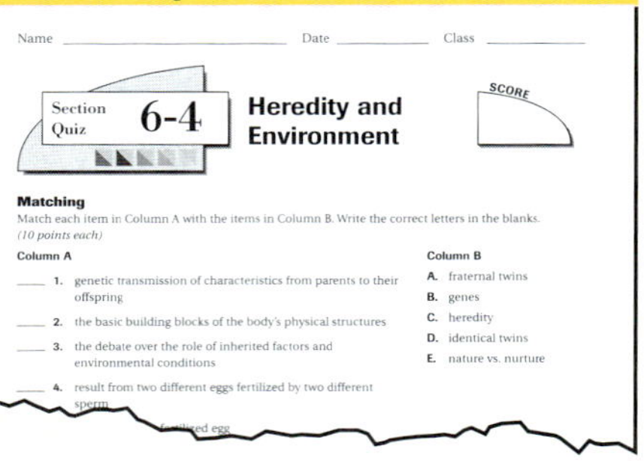
Name ______ Date ______ Class ______

Section Quiz 6-4 **Heredity and Environment** SCORE

Matching
Match each item in Column A with the items in Column B. Write the correct letters in the blanks. *(10 points each)*

Column A
____ 1. genetic transmission of characteristics from parents to their offspring
____ 2. the basic building blocks of the body's physical structures
____ 3. the debate over the role of inherited factors and environmental conditions
____ 4. result from two different eggs fertilized by two different sperm

Column B
A. fraternal twins
B. genes
C. heredity
D. identical twins
E. nature vs. nurture

Reteach
Have students summarize the various arguments made in the nature-nurture debate.

Enrich
Ask students to research current articles about the nature versus nurture debate. Ask them to write a one-page report summarizing current controversies on the subject.

4 CLOSE

With advances in genetic engineering, scientists may soon isolate the genes that are linked to certain behaviors.
Ask: **Would you favor being able to select the behavioral characteristics of your children? Explain.**

Figure 6.14 Identical Twins

Because identical twins share the same genes and most often the same environment, studying them is one way to find out whether a trait is inherited or learned. ***What do psychologists mean by the "nature-nurture question"?***

fraternal twins: twins who come from two different eggs fertilized by two different sperm

Fraternal twins develop from two fertilized eggs (thus, dizygotic), and their genes are not more similar than those of brothers or sisters.

Twins growing up in the same house share the same general environment, but identical twins also share the same genes. So, if identical twins who grow up together prove to be more alike on a specific trait than fraternal twins do, it probably means that genes are important for that trait.

Psychologists at the University of Minnesota have been studying identical twins who were separated at birth and reared in different environments (Holden, 1980). One of the researchers, Thomas Bouchard, reports that despite very different social, cultural, and economic backgrounds, the twins shared many common behaviors. For example, in one set of twins (both named Jim), both had done well in math and poorly in spelling while in school, both worked as deputy sheriffs, vacationed in Florida, gave identical names to their children and pets, bit their fingernails, had identical smoking and drinking patterns, and liked mechanical drawing and carpentry. These similarities and others suggest that heredity may contribute to behaviors that we normally associate with experience.

Many researchers now believe that many of the differences among people can be explained by considering heredity as well as experience. Contrary to popular belief, the influence of genes on behavior does not mean that nothing can be done to change the behavior. Although it is true that it is difficult and may be undesirable to change the genetic code that may direct behavior, it is possible to alter the environment in which the genes operate.

SECTION 4 Assessment

1. **Review the Vocabulary** Explain the difference between fraternal twins and identical twins.
2. **Visualize the Main Idea** In a diagram like the one below, explain how proponents of each view argue the nature-nurture debate.

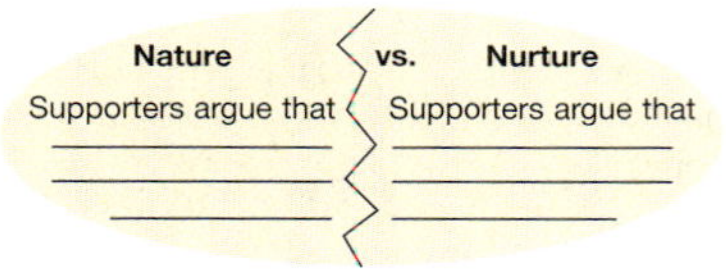

3. **Recall Information** What role do the genes play in influencing someone's behavior?
4. **Think Critically** Sue and Tracy are identical twins. Sue is good at drawing. Tracy is a starter on the basketball team. Explain what may cause differences in these twins.
5. **Application Activity** Describe a characteristic that you have. Explain whether you think this characteristic is hereditary or environmental.

SECTION 4 Assessment Answers

1. Identical twins have identical genetic makeup; fraternal twins come from two eggs and share no more genetic similarities than other siblings.
2. Nature supporters argue that a person's genetic makeup determines a person's behavior, whereas nurture supporters argue that a person's surroundings (environment) determine a person's character.
3. Genes build and modify structures of the body.
4. The difference is likely due to environmental factors that affected how the girls developed.
5. Students' answers will vary. Challenge students to select a nonphysical characteristic, such as athletic ability. Athletic ability is partially due to heredity since eye-hand coordination and body build have strong hereditary components. The environment's role in athletic ability may include age at which training occurred, availability of coaching, motivation, and nutrition.

CHAPTER 6 Summary and Vocabulary

Some psychologists (psychobiologists/neuroscientists) study how our behavior and psychological processes are connected to our biological processes. Our bodies and minds work together to create who we are.

Section 1 The Nervous System: The Basic Structure

Main Idea: Learning about the nervous system helps us know how messages that are sent to the brain cause behavior.

- The nervous system is divided into two parts: the central nervous system and the peripheral nervous system.
- Messages to and from the brain travel along the nerves.
- Nerve cells called neurons have three basic parts: the cell body, dendrites, and the axon.
- The somatic nervous system controls the body's voluntary activities, and the autonomic nervous system controls the body's involuntary activities.

Section 2 Studying the Brain

Main Idea: There are many parts in the human brain that work together to coordinate movement and stimulate thinking and emotions, resulting in behavior.

- The brain is made of three parts: the hindbrain, the midbrain, and the forebrain.
- The cortex of the brain is divided into the left and the right hemispheres; the left hemisphere controls the movements of the right side of the body, and the right hemisphere controls the movements of the left side of the body.
- Psychologists use recording, stimulation, lesions, and imaging to study the brain.

Section 3 The Endocrine System

Main Idea: The endocrine system controls and excites growth and affects emotions and behavior in people.

- The endocrine system, in addition to the nervous system, is a communication system for sending information to and from the brain.
- The endocrine system sends chemical messages, called hormones.

Section 4 Heredity and Environment

Main Idea: Heredity is the transmission of characteristics from parents to children. Environment is the world around you. Heredity and environment affect your body and behavior.

- Heredity is the genetic transmission of characteristics from parents to their offspring.
- Genes are the basic units of heredity; they are reproduced and passed along from parents to child.
- All the effects that genes have on behavior occur through their role in building and modifying the physical structures of the body.

Chapter Vocabulary

central nervous system (CNS) (p. 156)
spinal cord (p. 156)
peripheral nervous system (PNS) (p. 156)
neurons (p. 157)
synapse (p. 157)
neurotransmitters (p. 158)
somatic nervous system (SNS) (p. 158)
autonomic nervous system (ANS) (p. 158)
hindbrain (p. 160)
midbrain (p. 161)
forebrain (p. 161)
lobes (p. 162)
electroencephalograph (EEG) (p. 165)
computerized axial tomography (CT) (p. 167)
positron emission tomography (PET) (p. 167)
magnetic resonance imaging (MRI) (p. 167)
endocrine system (p. 171)
hormones (p. 171)
pituitary gland (p. 171)
heredity (p. 174)
identical twins (p. 175)
genes (p. 175)
fraternal twins (p. 176)

6 Summary and Vocabulary

Using the Chapter 6 Summary and Vocabulary

Use the Chapter 6 Summary and Vocabulary to preview, review, condense, or reteach the chapter.

Preview/Review

Use the Chapter Vocabulary list to help students review and study.

Activity Ask students to write an explanation of how the brain works through the nervous and endocrine systems to control body functions and behavior. Their explanations should include as many of the vocabulary terms as possible.

Vocabulary PuzzleMaker CD-ROM reinforces the vocabulary terms used in Chapter 6.

Condense

Have students read the Chapter 6 Summary.

Chapter 6 Guided Reading Activities

Reteach

Reteaching Activity 6

PERFORMANCE ASSESSMENT ACTIVITY

Writing a Research Proposal Organize students into small groups. Tell them to imagine they are research teams involved in studying the brain. Have them prepare a research proposal for a funding agency. The proposals should include a description of the team's goals and of the methods to be used in gathering the data—such as recording, stimulation, and lesioning. **BLOCK SCHEDULING**

Refer to the ***Authentic Assessment*** booklet for additional activities and information about evaluating student performance.

PSYCHOLOGY Online

Have students visit the Web site at glencoe.com to review Chapter 6 and take the **Self-Check Quiz.**

GLENCOE TECHNOLOGY

Presentation Plus!

For a review of Chapter 6 content, see MindJogger Checkpoint on **Presentation Plus!**

Reviewing Vocabulary

1. b	**6.** i
2. j	**7.** f
3. h	**8.** g
4. e	**9.** d
5. a	**10.** c

Recalling Facts

1. Messages travel along the nerves, which are strings of cells called neurons. Neurotransmitters are chemicals that carry the signal across the synapses between neurons or inhibit the neurons from transmitting.
2. occipital: processes visual signals; parietal: processes information from senses all over the body; temporal: regulates hearing, memory, emotion, and speech; frontal: concerned with organization, planning, and creative thinking
3. Four methods used to study the brain are recording, stimulation, lesioning, and imaging.
4. The messages are transmitted by hormones that circulate though the bloodstream to specific glands.
5. Identical twins share the same genes, while fraternal twins do not. Twins growing up in the same house share the same environment. Identical twins who grow up together share both environment and genes. If identical twins prove to be more alike on a specific trait than fraternal twins do, it probably means that genes are more important than environment for that trait.

Critical Thinking

1. If the autonomic nervous system did not regulate involuntary actions, we would spend most of our time and energy on the basic biological needs such as breathing, heart beating, and digestion.
2. A stroke that damages the frontal lobes would affect the person's ability to organize

CHAPTER 6

Assessment

PSYCHOLOGY Online

Self-Check Quiz

Visit the *Understanding Psychology* Web site at glencoe.com and click on **Chapter 6—Self-Check Quizzes** to prepare for the Chapter Test.

Reviewing Vocabulary

Choose the letter of the correct term or concept below to complete the sentence.

a. neurotransmitters	**f.** hindbrain
b. somatic nervous system	**g.** pituitary gland
c. autonomic nervous system	**h.** synapse
d. hormones	**i.** identical twins
e. midbrain	**j.** fraternal twins

1. The part of the nervous system that controls voluntary activities is the __________.
2. __________ develop from two fertilized eggs, and their genes are not more similar than those of brothers or sisters.
3. The space between neurons is called the __________.
4. The __________ is the part of the brain that integrates sensory information.
5. As a neuron transmits its message to another neuron across the synapse, it releases chemicals called __________.
6. __________ develop from a single fertilized egg and share the same genes.
7. Located at the rear base of the skull, the __________ is involved in the basic processes of life.
8. The __________ acts as the master gland of the body, controlling the output of hormones by other endocrine glands.
9. __________ are produced by endocrine glands and are distributed by the blood and other body fluids.
10. The part of the nervous system that controls involuntary activities is the __________.

Recalling Facts

1. Explain how messages travel to and from the brain through the nervous system.
2. Using a chart similar to the one below, describe the main function of each of the four lobes of the cerebral cortex.

Lobe	Main Function
Occipital	
Parietal	
Temporal	
Frontal	

3. Describe four methods used to study the brain.
4. How are the messages of the endocrine system transmitted throughout the body?
5. One way to find out whether a trait is inherited is to compare the behavior of identical and fraternal twins. Explain how this works.

Critical Thinking

1. **Analyzing Concepts** How would people's lives be different if the nervous system were not made of the somatic and the autonomic nervous systems? What if people had only a somatic nervous system?
2. **Synthesizing Information** Suppose a person suffers a stroke that causes damage to the frontal lobes. What aspects of the person's behavior would you expect to see change?
3. **Making Inferences** Provide an example of how the physiological reaction created by adrenaline is helpful in emergency situations.
4. **Applying Concepts** Do you think it is important for parents who wish to adopt a child to find out about the genetic makeup of the child? Why do you think so?
5. **Evaluating Information** Which aspects of your personality, your way of acting, and your appearance seem obviously the result of heredity? Which seem to be more related to your environmental upbringing? Which characteristics are definitely the result of an interaction between heredity and environment?

thoughts and solve problems. The personality of the person would also be altered.

3. The physiological reaction includes increased heart and breathing rates, a suspension of digestion, and other reactions that shift energy and focus to deal with the emergency situation.
4. Students' answers will vary. Some will say that a loving home environment is more important during the formative years than the genetic makeup of the child. Others will say that if the information can help them understand the challenges the child may face, the information would be worthwhile.
5. Students' answers will vary. Traits and characteristics common to several family members over several generations would indicate hereditary influences. Those common to family members living together but not common to those reared or living apart would indicate environmental influences. Athletic or musical abilities are the result of the interaction of heredity and environment.

Psychology Projects

1. Videos will vary. Have students decide the age of the children who will be viewing the video. The content, vocabulary, sentence length, and graphics used should be appropriate for the age of the children who will be viewing the video.

CHAPTER 6

Assessment

Psychology Projects

1. **The Nervous System: The Basic Structure** Working with two or three classmates, prepare a video that can be used to teach younger children how the brain and the nervous system work. You might consider making the video humorous to more easily gain the attention of younger children. Arrange to have children in lower grades view the video. Evaluate its effectiveness.
2. **Studying the Brain** Contact a hospital to find out more about the uses of CT scans, PET scans, and fMRIs. Find out under what circumstances each of the techniques would be used. Present your findings in a written report.
3. **The Endocrine System** Find out about problems that occur as a result of malfunctioning of parts of the endocrine system. Find out how such problems are treated and present your findings in an oral report.

Technology Activity

Scientists have recently gained greater insight into brain and neuron development in infants and young children. Search the Internet for information about this topic and about the implications the information has for parents and other caregivers. Summarize your findings in a brief report.

Psychology Journal

Much of what we know about the brain and its functioning has come from studies and experiments performed on animals. In your journal write an editorial explaining the reasons for your support of or opposition to using animals for psychological research. Be sure to include information on the American Psychological Association's stand on this issue.

Building Skills

Interpreting a Graph Researchers have found that the brains of patients with Alzheimer's disease have a large number of destroyed neurons in the part of the brain that is crucial for making memories permanent. These patients have also exhibited a loss of the neurotransmitter acetylcholine, resulting in memory difficulties. Review the graph and then answer the questions that follow.

1. According to the graph, how many people in the United States suffer from Alzheimer's disease?
2. How would you describe the projected number of cases of Alzheimer's by the year 2050?
3. What impact might the researchers' findings and the information in the graph have on the direction researchers might take to find a cure for the disease?

Practice and **assess** key social studies skills with **Glencoe Skillbuilder Interactive Workbook CD-ROM, Level 2.**

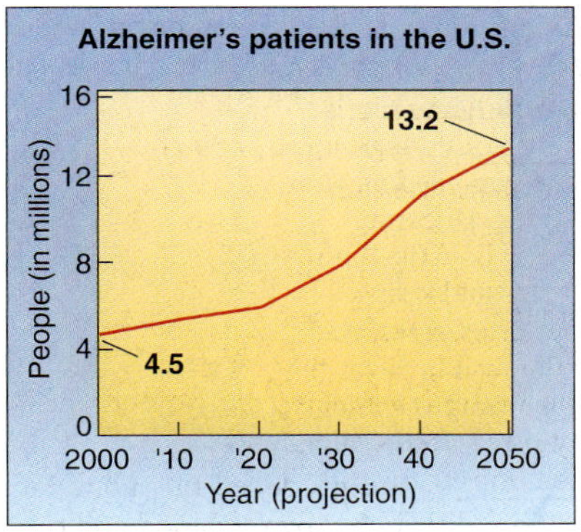

See the Skills Handbook, page 628, for an explanation of interpreting graphs.

Building Skills

1. about 4.5 million
2. a steady increase that nearly tripled in 50 years
3. As the incidence of Alzheimer's disease grows, researchers may attempt to find a cure involving acetylcholine as quickly as possible to help the millions afflicted with this disease.

GLENCOE TECHNOLOGY

CD-ROM

Glencoe Skillbuilder Interactive Workbook, Level 2

This interactive CD-ROM is designed to reinforce student mastery of essential social studies skills.

Chapter Bonus Test Question

This question may be used for extra credit on the Chapter Assessment.

Answer the following question:

I am a technique that records both brain activity and brain structures. What am I?

Answer: MRI (magnetic resonance imaging)

2. Reports will vary. Students may wish to divide their findings into uses that relate to (1) the brain and nervous system and (2) other parts of the body.
3. Students' reports will vary. Students may explore drug treatments, homeopathic treatments, and treatments that involve diet and exercise.

Technology Activity

Students should list the Internet sites. If students are having limited success finding useful sights, review basic search techniques to narrow the hits returned by the search engine. Students should provide brief summaries of several sites.

Psychology Journal

Students will take a stand on the issue of animal research. Support will likely focus around the benefit to humans of ethical animal research. Opposition will likely focus around the need to respect and treat animals in the same ways that we treat humans. Some students may oppose animal experiments with primates but accept the need for experiments with lower-level species. Students should support their opinions with evidence and logical arguments.

TIME REPORTS

Reader's Dictionary

Review the following terms with students to help them read and understand the article.

barrage: heavy, rapid outpouring
bequeathed: given or transmitted
eminently: highly or very
spawning: reproducing, especially in great numbers
slough: shed or discard dead cells and tissue
macaque: a genus of monkeys
paradigm: a model or framework used for theoretical purposes

CLICK HERE

TIME REPORTS

Visit **www.time.com/teach** for the complete text of this article, as well as related articles on the subject.

Block Schedule

This activity works well for a block-scheduling framework.

ACTIVE READING STRATEGY

Explain to students that pausing to review during reading improves comprehension. It also gives them an opportunity to revise or update their ideas about the purpose, main idea, and supporting details of the selection.

TIME REPORTS

LOTS OF ACTION IN THE MEMORY GAME

New experiments are prompting scientists to rethink their old ideas about how memories form—and why the process sometimes falters

By GEORGE JOHNSON

SCIENTISTS HAVE LONG BELIEVED that constructing memories is like playing with neurological Tinkertoys. Exposed to a barrage of sensations from the outside world, we snap together brain cells to form new patterns of electrical connections that stand for images, smells, touches and sounds.

The most unshakable part of this belief is that the neurons used to build these memory circuits are a depletable resource, like petroleum or gold. We are each bequeathed a finite number of cellular building blocks, and the supply gets smaller each year. That is certainly how it feels as memories blur with middle age and it gets harder and harder to learn new things. But like so many absolutes, this time-honored notion may have to be forgotten—or at least radically revised.

In the past year, a series of puzzling experiments has forced scientists to rethink this and other cherished assumptions about how memory works, reminding them how much they have to learn about one of the last great mysteries—how the brain keeps a record of our individual passage through life, allowing us to carry the past inside our head.

"The number of things we know now that we didn't know 10 years ago is not very large," laments Charles Stevens, a memory researcher at the Salk Institute in La Jolla, California. "In fact, in some ways we know less."

This much seems clear: the traces of memory—or engrams, as neuroscientists call them—are first forged deep inside the brain in an area called the hippocampus (after the Latin word for seahorse because of its arching shape). Acting as a kind of neurological scratch pad, the hippocampus stores the engrams temporarily until they are transferred somehow (perhaps during sleep) to permanent storage sites

CAPTURING MOMENTS . . .

MUSTARD OR KETCHUP? The memory of a Mark McGwire home run is likely to last longer than what you piled on your hot dog. Uncertain exactly how the brain creates and keeps memories, researchers do know it involves the hippocampus, which ultimately feeds memories to the cerebral cortex.

TIME Graphic by Lon Tweeten and Joe Zeff
Sources: *Understanding Psychology*, Robert S. Feldman; Dr. Charles Stevens, The Salk Institute

DIGITALLY MAN... IMAGE; MCGWIRE PHO... BY AMY SANC...

COOPERATIVE LEARNING ACTIVITY

Creating a Multimedia Presentation Organize the class into small groups. Ask the groups to select one of the following areas of the brain: corpus callosum, thalamus, hypothalamus, basal ganglia, cerebellum, pons, hippocampus, or amygdala. Each group will research the area of the brain, its functions, and the effects of damage on the person's behavior and abilities. Have the groups use their research to prepare a multimedia presentation about their chosen area of the brain. Remind students that multimedia means using more than one method to convey a message. **BLOCK SCHEDULING**

throughout the cerebral cortex. This area, located behind the forehead, is often described as the center of intelligence and perception. Here, as in the hippocampus, the information is thought to reside in the form of neurological scribbles, clusters of connected cells.

It has been considered almost gospel that these patterns are constructed from the supply of neurons that have been in place since birth. New memories, the story goes, don't require new neurons—just new ways of stringing the old ones together. Retrieving a memory is a matter of activating one of these circuits, coaxing the original stimulus back to life.

The picture appears eminently sensible. The billions of neurons in a single brain can be arranged in countless combinations, providing more than enough clusters to record even the richest life. If adult brains were cranking out new neurons as easily as skin and bone grow new cells, it would serve only to scramble memory's delicate filigree.

Studies with adult monkeys in the mid-1960s seemed to support the belief that the supply of neurons is fixed at birth. Hence the surprise when Elizabeth Gould and Charles Gross of Princeton University reported last year that the monkeys they studied seemed to be minting thousands of new neurons a day in the hippocampus of their brain. Even more jarring, Gould and Gross found evidence that a steady stream of the fresh cells may be continually migrating to the cerebral cortex.

No one is quite sure what to make of these findings. There had already been hints that spawning of brain cells, a process called neurogenesis, occurs in animals with more primitive nervous systems. For years, Fernando Nottebohm of Rockefeller University has been showing that canaries create a new batch of neurons every time they learn a song, then slough them off when it's time to change tunes.

But it was widely assumed that in mammals and especially primates (including the subset Homo sapiens), this wholesale manufacture of new brain parts had long ago been phased out by evolution. With a greater need to store memories for the long haul, these creatures would need to ensure that the engrams weren't disrupted by interloping new cells.

Not everyone found this argument convincing. (Surely birds had important things to remember too.) When neurogenesis was found to occur in people, the rationalizations began to take the tone of special pleading: there was no evidence that the new brain cells had anything to do with memory or that they did anything at all.

That may yet turn out to be the case with the neurons found by the Princeton lab. The mechanism Gould and her colleagues uncovered in macaque monkeys could be nothing more than a useless evolutionary leftover, a kind of neurological appendix. But if, as many suspect, the new neurons turn out to be actively involved with inscribing memories, the old paradigm is in for at least a minor tune-up—and maybe a complete overhaul. ■

—For the complete text of this article and related articles from TIME, please visit www.time.com/teach

ANALYZING THE ARTICLE

1. What assumptions did the Gould/Gross study challenge?
2. **CRITICAL THINKING** Recall an early-childhood event that made a strong impression on you. What do you remember seeing, hearing, tasting, smelling and touching?

Touch
The sun's heat activates sensory nerves, sending data to the cortex's **somatosensory area** for processing

Sound
The ear detects the roar of the crowd and relays it to the **primary auditory cortex** in the temporal lobe

Sight
The eye encodes the image of McGwire as nerve impulses and sends them to the **primary visual cortex**

Taste and Smell
Receptors in the nose pick up the flavor of the mustard and relay it to the **olfactory cortex**

... TO LAST A LIFETIME

Immediate memory
LESS THAN ONE MINUTE
Consisting of a brief flash of raw stimuli corresponding to the senses, it creates an image containing almost an exact replica of each stimulus. Unless transferred to short-term memory, however, the mental snapshot is quickly lost

Short-term memory
A FEW HOURS TO A WEEK
All the sensory information is then sent to the hippocampus where it is coordinated and organized. Over the next day, some parts of the snapshot begin to blur, while the more important details are moved to permanent storage

Long-term memory
PERMANENT
Some theorize that organization and repetition of the information cause it to be transferred and held in storage sites throughout the cerebral cortex. What is finally remembered is only a fraction of the original picture

TIME REPORTS

Questions for Discussion

Use the following questions for a class discussion after students have read the article.

1. Why might some memories be more enduring than others? *(Answers will vary. Students may indicate that some information is more important, that some stimuli are more salient, or that it is easier to remember information that is encountered or rehearsed frequently.)*
2. How might the brain respond to injury or trauma? *(Use this question to emphasize the shift from a rigid model of the brain to a malleable one. Following injury or trauma, some functions that are impaired can be recovered and relearned. Intact brain structures sometimes assume the functions of damaged ones, and neurons are able to form new connections.)*
3. Why are memories sometimes inaccurate? Give an example of a time your memory of an event differed from someone else's. *(Answers will vary. We often remember information that confirms our view of the world or that casts us in a positive light. At the same time, we may forget or avoid information that is disconcerting. Other theories examine the way in which memory is reconstructed and the role of interference.)*

ANSWERS TO ANALYZING THE ARTICLE

1. The Gould/Gross study challenged the assumption that primates can't make new neurons. In the traditional model of the brain, the number of neurons is fixed at birth, and it declines as we age. The Gould/Gross study suggested that primates make new neurons in the hippocampus; these neurons migrate to other areas of the brain.
2. Answers will vary. Encourage students to discuss the durability of each sensory impression. Discuss why some of these early childhood memories, such as the height of a playground slide or the depth of the pool's deep end, may seem exaggerated today.

Chapter 7 Resource Guide

SECTION RESOURCES

Daily Objectives	Reproducible Resources	Multimedia Resources
Section 1 **Sleep and Dreams** Discuss the four stages of sleep and the period of dreaming.	Guided Reading Activity 7–1 Vocabulary Activity 7–1 Section Quiz 7–1	Daily Focus Transparency 7–1 *ExamView® Assessment Suite* CD-ROM Presentation Plus! Software
Section 2 **Hypnosis, Biofeedback, and Meditation** Understand that hypnosis, biofeedback, and meditation are altered states of consciousness that can occur while we are awake.	Guided Reading Activity 7–2 Vocabulary Activity 7–2 Section Quiz 7–2	Daily Focus Transparency 7–2 *ExamView® Assessment Suite* CD-ROM Presentation Plus! Software
Section 3 **Drugs and Consciousness** Describe psychoactive drugs and how they interact with the central nervous system to alter consciousness.	Guided Reading Activity 7–3 Vocabulary Activity 7–3 Section Quiz 7–3	Daily Focus Transparency 7–3 *ExamView® Assessment Suite* CD-ROM Presentation Plus! Software

Blackline Master   CD-ROM   Transparency

Block Schedule

Activities that are particularly suited for use within the block-scheduling framework are identified throughout this chapter by the following designation: **BLOCK SCHEDULING**

KEY TO ABILITY LEVELS

Teaching strategies have been coded for varying learning styles and abilities.

L1 **BASIC** activities for all students

L2 **AVERAGE** activities for average to above-average students

L3 **CHALLENGING** activities for above-average students

ELL **ENGLISH LANGUAGE LEARNER** activities

Chapter 7 Resource Guide

Timesaving Tools

TeacherWorks™ All-In-One Planner and Resource Center

- **Interactive Teacher Edition** Access your Teacher Wraparound Edition and your classroom resources with a few easy clicks.
- **Interactive Lesson Planner** Planning has never been easier! Organize your week, month, semester, or year with all the lesson helps you need to make teaching creative, timely, and relevant.

Use Glencoe's **Presentation Plus!** multimedia teacher tool to easily present dynamic lessons that visually excite your students. Using Microsoft PowerPoint® you can customize the presentations to create your own personalized lessons.

Activity

From the Classroom of...

John Seiple
Lyons Township High School
LaGrange, IL

Substance Abuse Survey

Goal: Launch the discussion of drugs by having students fill out a survey.

Over the past seven years, the following survey has been reliable in that every class has ranked the "Commonly Used" substances low on the "Damaging" scale and vice versa. As a teacher, you must insist the students rank order the substances from 1 to 11.

Create a table similar to the model below that lists common illegal and legal drugs, alcoholic beverages, and tobacco products. Use 11 different substances. Allow space for the students to give a number ranking for "Most Commonly Used" and "Most Damaging."

Have students rank order the substances, from 1 to 11. For example, the substance ranked 1 would represent the most commonly used or most damaging substance. Tell them that there are no right or wrong answers. Remind them that this survey is anonymous and encourage them to answer truthfully.

Substance	Most Commonly Used	Most Damaging

Psychology Online

Use our Web site for additional resources. All essential content is covered in the Student Edition.

You and your students can visit glencoe.com, the Web site companion to *Understanding Psychology*. This innovative integration of electronic and print media offers your students a wealth of opportunities. The student text directs students to the Web site for the following options:

- Chapter Overviews
- Student Web Activities
- Self-Check Quizzes

Answers are provided for you in the **Web Activity Lesson Plan.** Additional Web resources and Interactive Puzzles are also available.

Chapter 7 Resource Guide

Note: The following materials may be used when teaching Chapter 7. Section level support materials are shown at point of use in the margins of the Teacher Wraparound Edition.

TEACHING TRANSPARENCIES

Chapter 7 Concept Transparencies

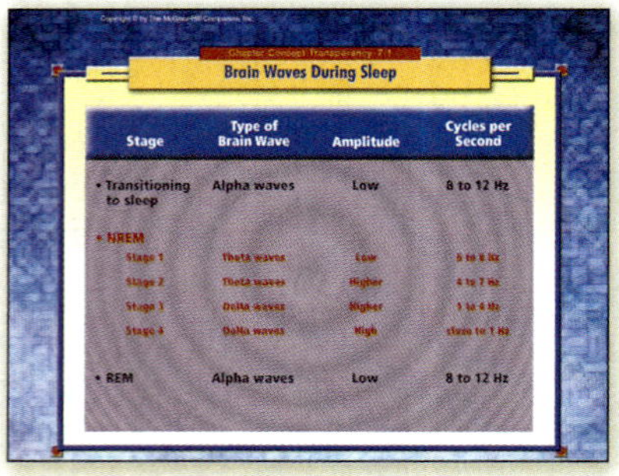

MULTIMEDIA

- **Vocabulary PuzzleMaker CD-ROM**
- ***ExamView*® *Assessment Suite* CD-ROM**
- **TeacherWorks™ CD-ROM**
- **Glencoe Skillbuilder Interactive Workbook, Level 2**
- **Presentation Plus! Software**

REVIEW AND REINFORCEMENT

Reteaching Activity 7

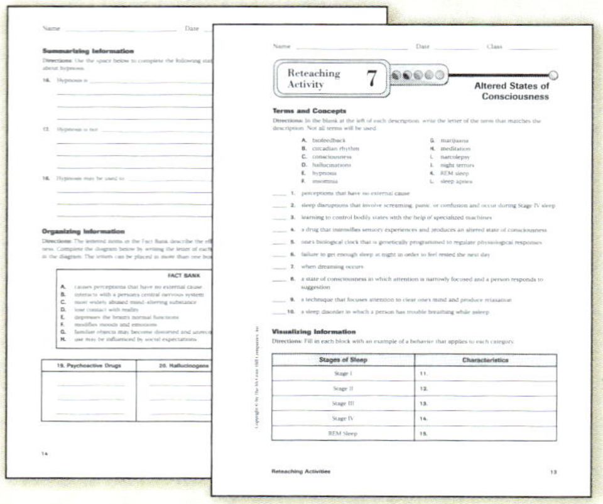

Graphic Organizer Activity 7

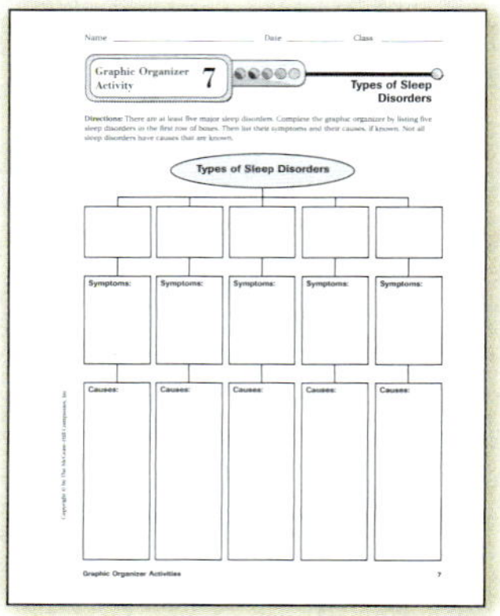

APPLICATION AND HANDS-ON

Psychology Projects 7–1 and 7–2

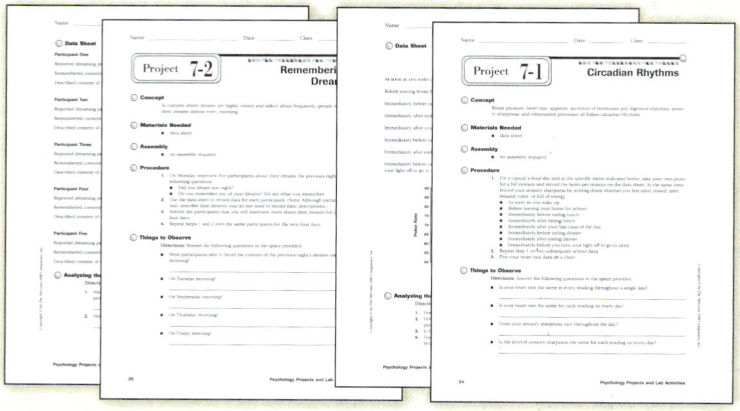

Application Activity 7

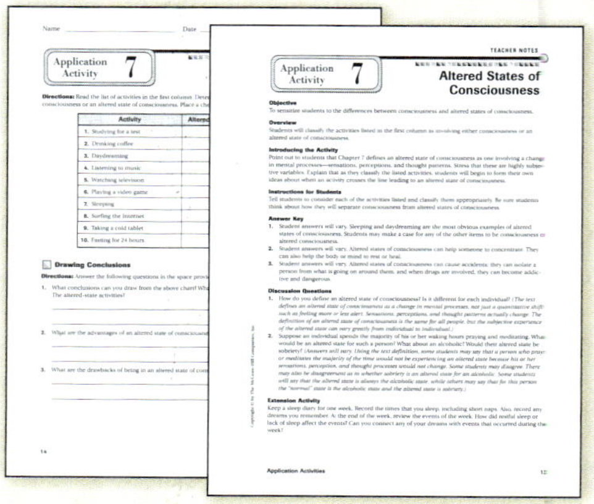

Chapter 7 Resource Guide

Glencoe's ASSESSMENT ADVANTAGE

ASSESSMENT

Chapter 7 Test, Form A

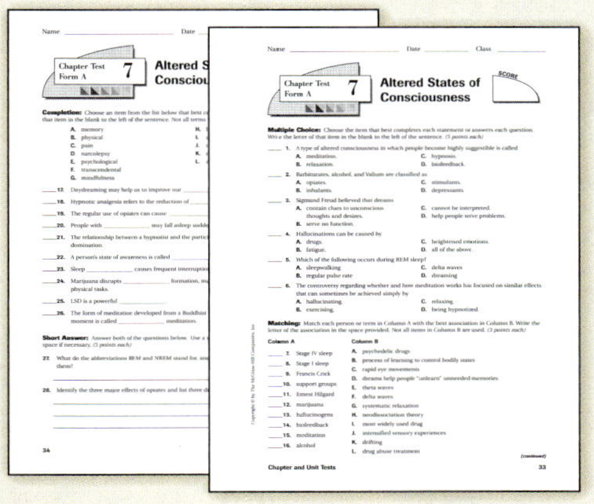

Chapter 7 Test, Form B

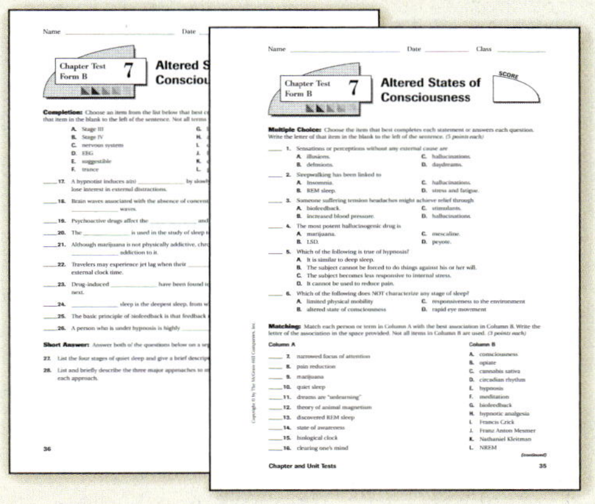

Authentic Assessment Activity 7

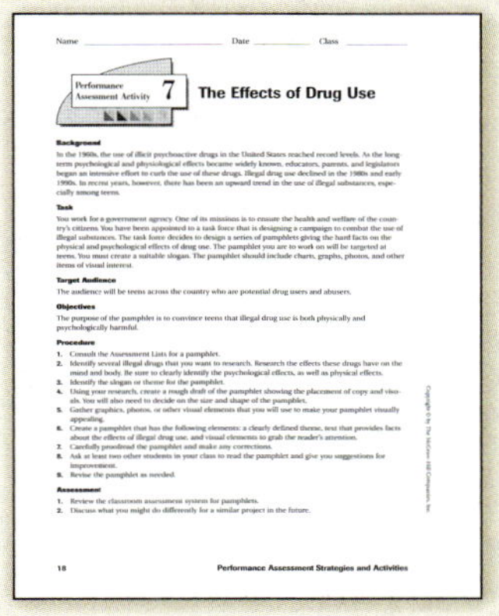

EXTENSION AND ENRICHMENT

Enrichment Activity 7

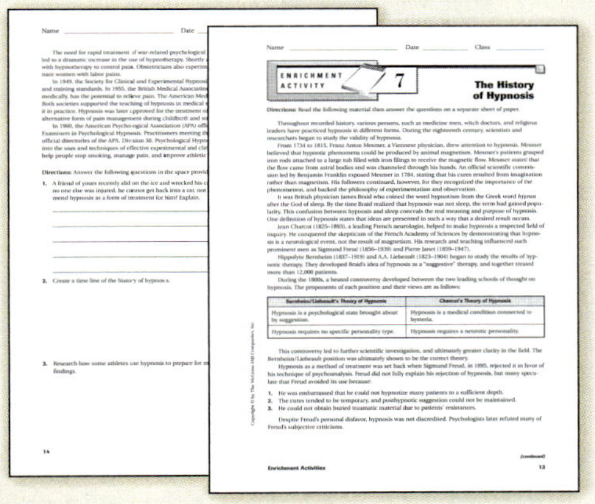

Critical Thinking Skills Activity 7

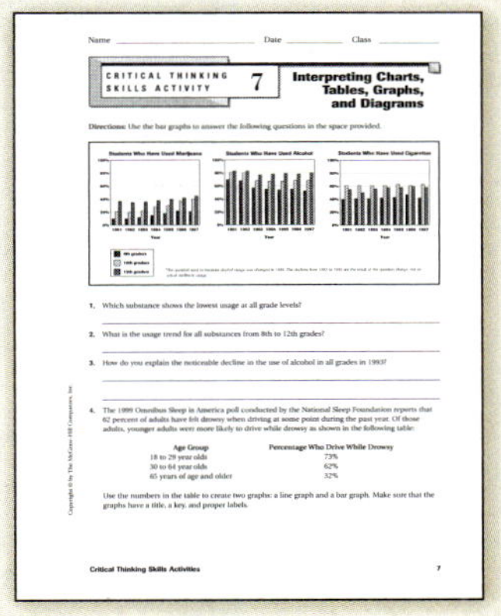

Psychology Reading 7

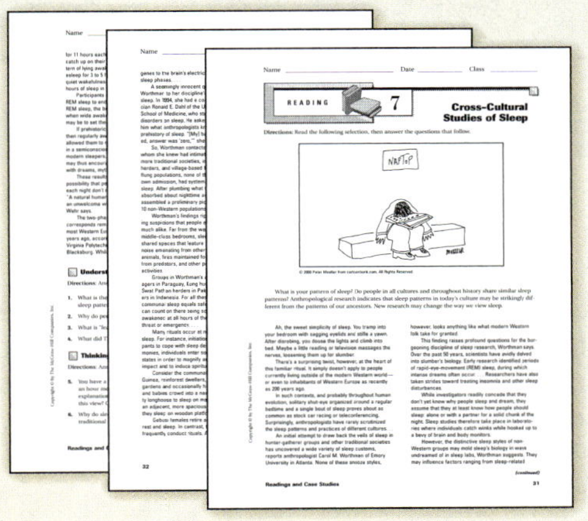

Psychology Case Study 7

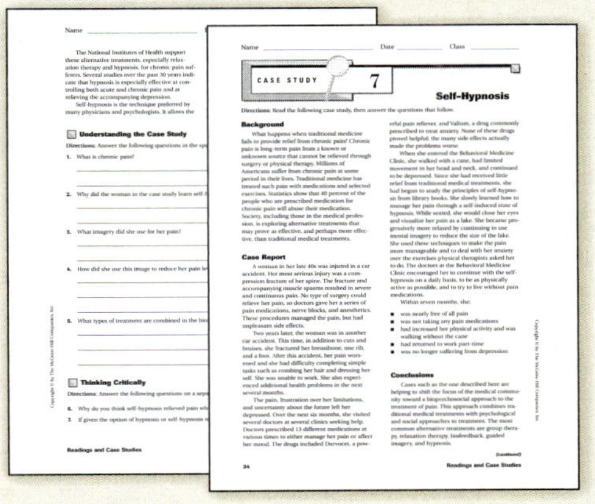

PSYCHOLOGY Online

Visit glencoe.com for a Chapter Overview for **Chapter 7—Altered States of Consciousness.**

GLENCOE TECHNOLOGY

For a preview of Chapter 7 content, see MindJogger Checkpoint on **Presentation Plus!**

PSYCHOLOGY JOURNAL

Explain that researchers are still exploring the reasons for sleep and dreaming. Challenge students to consider what would be lost and gained if the need for sleep were eliminated.

This journal activity provides the basis for the Psychology Journal activity exercise in the Chapter Assessment. ■

CHAPTER 7

Altered States of Consciousness

PSYCHOLOGY JOURNAL

What is the purpose of sleep? Do you think it would be possible or desirable to perfect a way to eliminate the need for sleep or dreams? Write a one-page essay in your journal answering these questions. ■

PSYCHOLOGY Online

Chapter Overview

Visit the *Understanding Psychology* Web site at glencoe.com and click on **Chapter 7—Chapter Overviews** to preview the chapter.

TWO-MINUTE LESSON LAUNCHER

Tell students to close their eyes and concentrate on listening to their own heartbeat for the next minute. After 30 seconds, quietly begin tapping a pencil on the desk. At the end of 60 seconds, ask how many students were able to hear their hearts beating. Then ask how many heard you tapping the pencil. Tell students that those who heard only their heartbeat and blocked out the tapping had entered a state of altered consciousness. Challenge students to brainstorm examples of altered states of consciousness *(daydreams, meditation, hypnosis, and so on)*. The ideas will be reviewed at the end of the chapter. Tell students that Chapter 7 will provide information to assess the accuracy of their speculations.

SECTION 1 Sleep and Dreams

Reader's Guide

Main Idea
Sleep—an essential state of consciousness—involves four stages and a period of dreaming.

Vocabulary
- consciousness
- REM sleep
- circadian rhythm
- insomnia
- sleep apnea
- narcolepsy
- nightmares
- night terrors
- sleepwalking

Objectives
- Describe the research related to sleep and dreams.
- List and discuss sleep disorders.

EXPLORING PSYCHOLOGY

Losing Sleep

In 1959 New York disk jockey Peter Tripp stayed awake for 200 hours to raise money for charity. . . . After about 50 hours, he started having mild hallucinations, seeing cobwebs in his shoes when there were none there and thinking that specks of dirt were bugs; by 100 hours, he became delirious and saw a doctor's tweed suit as a tangle of furry worms; at 120 he needed a stimulant to keep him awake. After 150 hours, he was disoriented, not knowing who or where he was, and he became paranoid—he backed against a wall, letting no one pass behind him; by 200 hours, his hallucinations had taken a sinister turn, and he thought a doctor trying to examine him was an undertaker come to bury him.

—from *The Human Mind Explained* edited by Susan A. Greenfield, 1996

How important is sleep to humans? Sleep is vital to mental health. Peter Tripp found out that if a person is deprived of sleep, he or she will have psychological symptoms (although not all people have symptoms as extreme as Tripp's). Most people think of sleep as a state of unconsciousness, punctuated by brief periods of dreaming. This is only partially correct. Sleep is a state of altered consciousness, characterized by certain patterns of brain activity and inactivity.

What is consciousness? **Consciousness** is a state of awareness. When we discuss altered states of consciousness, we mean that people can have different levels of awareness. Consciousness can range from

consciousness: a state of awareness, including a person's feelings, sensations, ideas, and perceptions

1 FOCUS

Section Objectives
1. Describe the research related to sleep and dreams.
2. List and discuss sleep disorders.

BELLRINGER
Motivational Activity

Project Daily Focus Transparency 7–1 and have students answer the questions.

Available as blackline master

Daily Focus Transparency 7–1

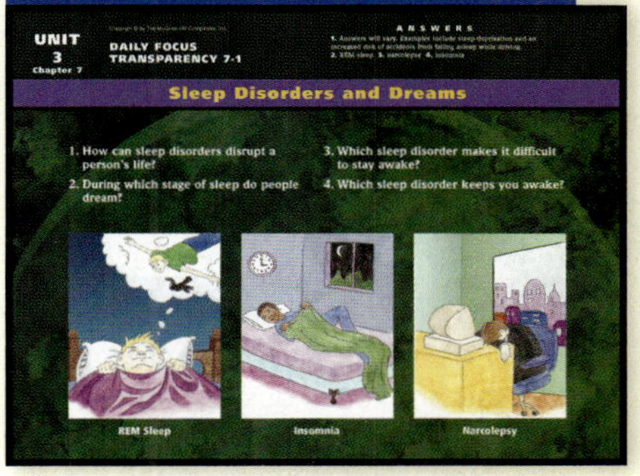

Reader's Guide

Use the Reader's Guide to introduce concepts and vocabulary.

Exploring Psychology
Ask students to read the **Exploring Psychology** feature and then discuss: **What does this feature tell you about the connection between sleep and the mind?**

Vocabulary Precheck
Have students read the Glossary definition of each vocabulary term. Then ask them to create a crossword puzzle from the terms, using the definitions as the clues.

SECTION RESOURCES

Reproducible Masters
- Guided Reading Activity 7–1
- Vocabulary Activity 7–1
- Section Quiz 7–1

Transparencies
- Daily Focus Transparency 7–1

Multimedia
- *ExamView® Assessment Suite* CD-ROM
- Presentation Plus! Software

2 TEACH

L1 Demonstration Conduct a session in which students sit in a darkened room for five minutes. During this time, direct students to be aware of their thoughts and bodily perceptions (such as the sound of a heartbeat). Challenge students to let go of every thought or physical sensation. Instead, they should try to focus on the pattern of their breathing—in, out, in, out.

End the session with the sound of a hand clap. Then slowly open the window shades or turn on a light. **Ask: How did the demonstration affect your mental processes? How were they different than during a routine five minute period? Would you describe these feelings as an altered state of consciousness?**

Figure 7.1

Visual Instruction One way to know that you are conscious is that you are aware of your own thoughts and surroundings. Consciousness, though, is a continuum, ranging from being totally aware and alert to being totally unaware and unresponsive.

Caption Answer Answers may include that a person draws upon information from the preconscious level while in conversation or while thinking about someone. Students should note that we use information from the preconscious level every day when we use what we already know—our knowledge and memories—to function normally.

alertness to nonalertness (see Figure 7.1). People who are fully aware with their attention focused on something are conscious of that something. A person who is not completely aware is in a different level of consciousness—an altered state of consciousness. Sleep illustrates an altered state of consciousness.

Although sleep is a major part of human and animal behavior, it has been extremely difficult to study until recently. A researcher cannot ask a sleeping person to report on the experience without first waking the person. The study of sleep was aided by the development of the electroencephalograph (EEG), a device that records the electrical activity of the brain.

WHY DO WE SLEEP?

We are not sure why people sleep. Sleep is characterized by unresponsiveness to the environment and usually limited physical mobility. Some people believe that sleep is restorative; it allows people to "charge up their batteries." These people believe that sleep is a time when the brain recovers from exhaustion and stress. Other people believe it is a type of primitive hibernation: we sleep to conserve energy. Some suggest that sleep is an adaptive process; that is, in earlier times sleep kept humans out of harm's way at night when humans would have been most vulnerable to animals with better night vision. Still other researchers believe we sleep to clear our minds of useless information. As a variation of this theory, some people believe we sleep to dream.

Figure 7.1 Freud's Levels of Consciousness

Sigmund Freud identified three levels of consciousness. In his approach to consciousness, he claimed that preconscious ideas are not in your awareness now, but you are able to recall them with some effort. Unconscious ideas are hidden and unretrievable. ***When would you use information from the preconscious level?***

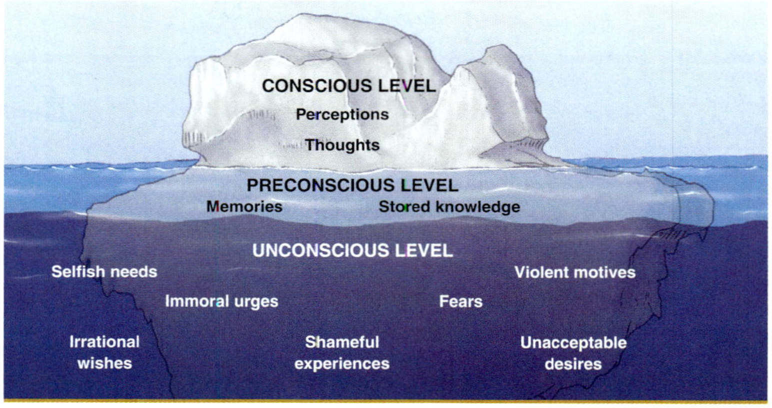

STAGES OF SLEEP

As you begin to fall asleep, your body temperature decreases, your pulse rate drops, and your breathing becomes slow and even. Gradually, your eyes close and your brain briefly shows alpha waves on the EEG, which are associated with the absence of concentrated thought and with relaxation (see Figure 7.2). Your body may twitch, your eyes roll, and brief visual images flash across your mind (although your eyelids are shut) as you enter Stage I sleep, the lightest level of sleep.

COOPERATIVE LEARNING ACTIVITY

Conducting Research Tell students that people who live farthest from the Equator may be affected by seasonal affective disorder (SAD). (The disorder is linked to a shortened period of daylight. People suffering from SAD may sleep for longer periods than they normally do.) Organize the students into groups of four to research SAD and how it affects people in various parts of the world. Each group should determine its cause, its physical and mental symptoms, and treatments that have been developed to lessen its effects. Research should also focus on the links between SAD and sleep. Each group should prepare a two-page report summarizing its findings. Encourage the groups to share their findings.

Early Stages

In Stage I sleep, your pulse slows a bit more and your muscles relax, but your breathing becomes uneven and your brain waves grow irregular. If you were awakened during this stage, you would report that you were "just drifting." This phase lasts for up to 10 minutes and is marked by the presence of theta waves, which are lower in amplitude and frequency than alpha waves. At this point, your brain waves occasionally shift from low-amplitude, high-frequency waves to high-amplitude, low-frequency waves—a pattern that indicates you have entered Stage II sleep. Your eyes roll slowly from side to side. Some 30 minutes later, you drift down into a deeper level of Stage III sleep, and large-amplitude delta waves begin to sweep your brain every second or so.

Figure 7.2 Patterns of Sleep

The top diagram shows the passage of a sleeper through the various stages of sleep over a seven-hour period. The bottom diagram shows the patterns of electrical activity (EEGs) in the brain that correspond to the various stages of sleep. The EEG pattern shown for being awake is one that occurs when a person is resting quietly with eyes closed.
How often during a night's sleep does a person reach Stage IV?

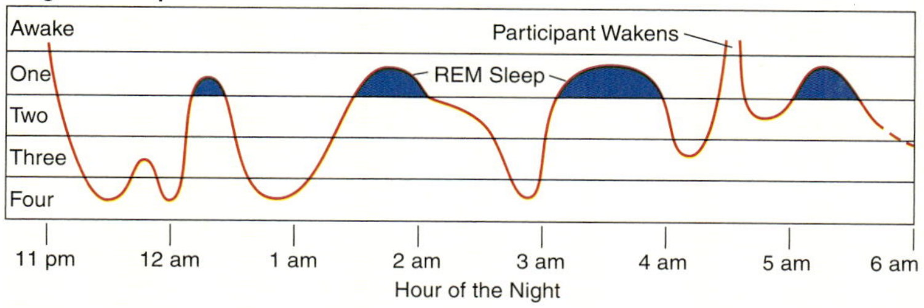

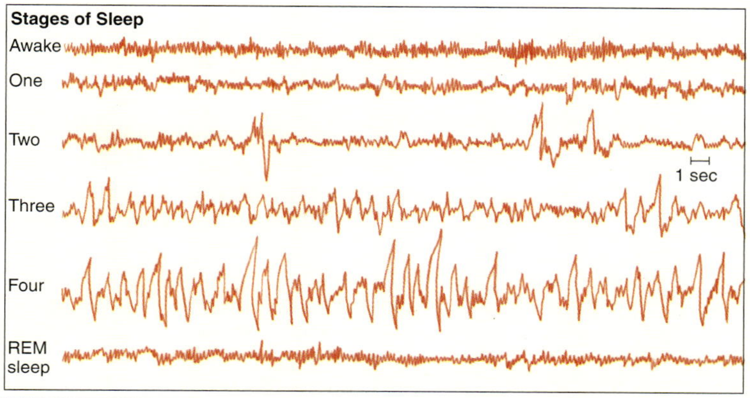

Later Stages

Stage IV is the deepest sleep of all, and it is difficult to waken a sleeper in this stage. Large, regular delta waves occurring more than 50 percent of the time indicate you are in a state of deep sleep. If you are awakened by a loud noise or sudden movement, you may feel disoriented. Talking out loud, sleepwalking, and bed-wetting—all of which may occur in this stage—leave no trace on the memory. Deep sleep is important to your physical and psychological well-being. Perhaps this is why people who are able to sleep only a few hours at a time descend rapidly into Stage IV and remain there for most of their nap.

On average a person spends 75 percent of sleep time in Stages I through IV. Once in Stage IV, something curious happens. While your muscles are even more relaxed than before, your eyes begin to move

Figure 7.2

Visual Instruction Have students create a chart summarizing the stages of sleep. Charts might include the following column heads: *Name of Stage, Physical State, Mental State,* and *Average Length of Stage.*

Caption Answer A person reaches Stage IV sleep four to five times a night.

Guided Reading Activity 7-1

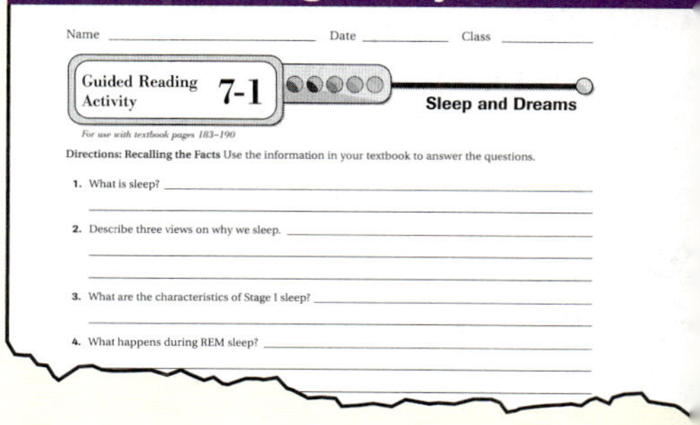
Name ______ Date ______ Class ______

Guided Reading Activity 7-1 — Sleep and Dreams

For use with textbook pages 183–190

Directions: Recalling the Facts Use the information in your textbook to answer the questions.

1. What is sleep? ______
2. Describe three views on why we sleep. ______
3. What are the characteristics of Stage I sleep? ______
4. What happens during REM sleep? ______

FYI

Prehistoric humans believed that the soul leaves the body during sleep. Ancient cultures worshiped gods they believed were responsible for sleep. The Greeks called such a deity Hypnos, and the Romans called him Somnus.

MEETING SPECIAL NEEDS

Learning Style: Logical/Mathematical Tell students that jet lag is a common ailment among long-distance travelers. Ask students to research what happens to the body when we travel to different time zones. Have students compare the effects of traveling by car and by jet across time zones. Ask students to explore whether there is a difference between flying east and flying west. Students should explain any differences. Finally, have students research and prepare a list of tips for travelers to minimize the effects of jet lag. **L2**

Refer to ***Inclusion for the High School Social Studies Classroom Strategies and Activities*** in the TCR for strategies for students with different learning styles.

PSYCHOLOGY JOURNAL

Ask students to chart the amount of sleep they receive each night over a two week period. At the beginning of each day, have the students record whether or not they feel they slept enough the previous night. At the end of 14 days, ask the students to use mean, median, and mode to evaluate their data. Then have them write a summary relating their numerical findings to their daily written evaluation. ■

Reading Check Answer

Stage IV sleep is the deepest form of sleep, in which brain waves exhibit delta wave patterns.

PSYCHOLOGY Update

REM Sleep and Dreaming REM sleep and dreaming are often considered synonymous. As psychologists continue to study the brain, they are discovering that the areas of the brain responsible for REM sleep and dreaming are not the same. REM sleep is caused by the secretion of acetylcholine in the pons, which is part of the brain stem. Dreaming seems to be located in the frontal lobes. One way in which psychologists have discovered the difference between the two activities is by studying accident victims. Those whose brain stems have not been damaged will still enter REM sleep, but they do not report any dream activity. Conversely, damage to the brain stem without accompanying damage to the frontal lobe results in dreams without REM sleep.

REM sleep: a stage of sleep characterized by rapid eye movements, a high level of brain activity, a deep relaxation of the muscles, and dreaming

rapidly. You have entered a more active type of sleep characterized by rapid eye movement. This is called **REM sleep.** Your pulse rate and breathing become irregular, and the levels of adrenal and sexual hormones in your blood rise—as if you were in the middle of an intensely emotional or physically demanding activity. Often, your face or fingers twitch and the large muscles in your arms and legs are paralyzed. Your brain now shows waves that closely resemble those of a person who is fully awake. For this reason, REM sleep is called active sleep. Stages I through IV are sometimes referred to as NREM (non-REM) or quiet sleep because of the absence of rapid eye movement. NREM sleep is accompanied by the slower pattern of brain waves. It is during REM sleep that almost all dreaming normally takes place.

REM sleep lasts from about 15 minutes (early at night) to 45 minutes (late at night), after which you retrace the descent to Stage IV. You go through this cycle every 90 minutes or so. Each time the period of Stage IV sleep decreases and the length of REM sleep increases, until you eventually wake up. At no point does your brain become totally inactive. REM sleep seems to serve psychological functions such as building efficient learning and memory processes.

Reading Check
What is Stage IV sleep?

HOW MUCH SLEEP?

Humans spend approximately one-third of their lives in sleep. The amount of sleep a person needs to function effectively varies considerably from individual to individual and from time to time within a person's life. Newborns spend an average of 16 hours a day sleeping, almost half of it in REM sleep. Sixteen-year-olds may spend as much as 10 to 11 hours asleep each night. Students in graduate school average 8 hours a night.

Men and women who are 70 years old or older may need only 5 hours of sleep. Adults average about 25 percent of their time in REM sleep and 75 percent in NREM sleep. Although the amount of sleep a person needs may vary, it does appear that everyone sleeps and that both types of sleep are important to normal functioning.

Have you ever noticed that there are certain times of the day when you are more alert or more tired? People seem to have an internal biological clock that regulates the sleep-wakefulness cycle. Blood pressure, heart rate, appetite, secretion of hormones and digestive enzymes, sensory sharpness, and elimination processes all follow circadian rhythms (Hrushesky, 1994). A **circadian rhythm** is a biological clock that is genetically programmed to regulate physiological responses within a time period of 24 or 25 hours. Circadian rhythms operate even when normal day and night cues are removed. For example, we usually standardize our sleep patterns according to the light of day and dark of night; yet experimenters who have lived for months at a time in the depths of a cave have still maintained a rhythm to their behaviors. Without any environmental cues, people maintained their circadian rhythms on about a 24- to 25-hour cycle. Researchers have determined

circadian rhythm: the rhythm of activity and inactivity lasting approximately one day

CRITICAL THINKING ACTIVITY

Identifying Central Issues Have students reread the section entitled "Dream Interpretation." **Ask:** **What was the central issue in the different views of dreams held by Freud and Kleitman?** *(whether dreams served a purpose)* Next, organize a debate on the following topic: *Resolved—Dreams hold no special meaning whatsoever; they are merely a jumble of events recalled by stimulated brain cells.* If possible, encourage students to do outside research in preparation for the debate. **L2**

that humans have a circadian cycle of approximately 24.18 hours (Czeisler et al., 1999).

Circadian rhythms do not control our sleep cycles; the environment and the 24-hour day control our cycles. Thus, when you miss sleep, this disruption becomes very apparent. Some travelers experience jet lag. This occurs when their internal circadian rhythms do not match the external clock time. For example, when you travel from New York to Moscow, your body is on a different time clock when you reach Moscow. You may feel tired and disoriented. What do you do to cure jet lag? It usually takes about one day for each hour of time change to reset your circadian clock.

SLEEP DISORDERS

Sleep is an active state essential for mental and physical restoration. Sometimes, though, we may have problems falling asleep or have problems during sleep. These sleep disorders may interfere with our quality of life and personal health, as well as endanger public safety because of their role in industrial or traffic accidents.

Insomnia

Everyone has had a sleepless night at one time or another—a night where nothing you do brings the calm, soothing peace you want. Some people have sleep problems like this all the time, and they rarely get more than an hour or two of uninterrupted sleep a night. **Insomnia**—a prolonged and usually abnormal inability to obtain adequate sleep—has many causes and takes many forms. Some people cannot sleep at night because of anxiety or depression. Overuse of alcohol or drugs can also cause insomnia.

insomnia: the failure to get enough sleep at night in order to feel rested the next day

Sleep Apnea

The sleep disorder **sleep apnea** causes frequent interruptions of breathing during sleep. One of the most common symptoms is a specific kind of snoring that may occur hundreds of times during the night. Each snoring episode lasts 10 to 15 seconds and ends suddenly, often with a physical movement of the entire body. A blockage of the breathing passages actually causes the snoring; during this time the victim is in fact choking—the flow of air to the lungs stops. The episode ends when low levels of oxygen or high levels of carbon dioxide in the blood trigger breathing reflexes.

sleep apnea: a sleep disorder in which a person has trouble breathing while asleep

Sleep apnea affects more than 12 million Americans, occurring most often among older people. People suffering from this disorder may feel listless, sleepy, and irritable during the day. Whereas insomnia is caused by mental stress, sleep apnea is usually caused by a physical problem that blocks the airway, such as enlarged tonsils, repeated infections in the throat or middle ear, or obesity. These conditions may cause the muscles at the base of the tongue to relax and sag repeatedly.

L1 Discussion Tell students that Alfred the Great (b. 849, King of Wessex, 871–899) recommended that a person work eight hours a day, play eight hours a day, and sleep the rest of the time. Request volunteers to explain how this advice compares to their own ideas on sleep (and life). Suppose students were psychologists who specialized in sleep patterns. **Ask: How would you respond to Alfred's recommendation?**

Vocabulary Activity 7-1

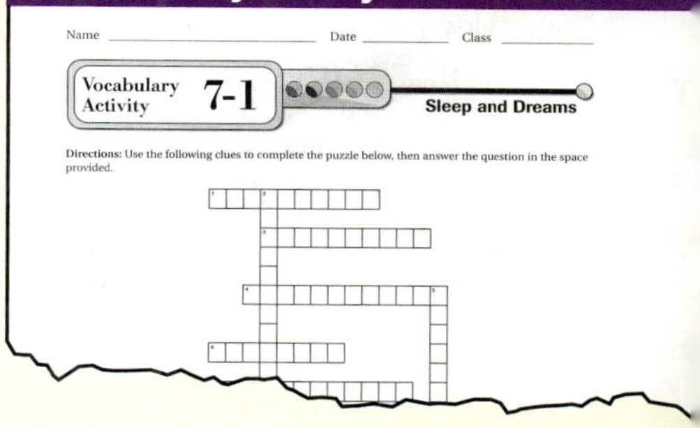
Name Date Class
Vocabulary Activity 7-1
Sleep and Dreams
Directions: Use the following clues to complete the puzzle below, then answer the question in the space provided.

Readings and Case Studies in Psychology
Have students read the Chapter 7 Reading selection in *Readings and Case Studies in Psychology* and answer the questions that follow the reading.

PSYCHOLOGY LAB EXPERIMENT

Dream Interpretation Give students a difficult brainteaser in sealed envelopes. Tell them to open the envelope and read the brainteaser right before they go to sleep. Tell students to keep a pencil and paper near their bedsides so that they can record any dreams they have as soon as they awaken. Discuss in class whether any of the dreams were related to the brainteaser and whether anyone came up with a solution to the brainteaser as a result of their dreams. **Ask: What do your findings lead you to conclude about the theories of why people dream? L1**

Applying Psychology

Ask students if they have ever suffered from insomnia. Tell them that if they have, they are in good company. Many famous people including Marilyn Monroe, Winston Churchill, and Napoleon Bonaparte suffered from insomnia. Marilyn Monroe suffered *onset insomnia,* which occurs when it takes more than 30 minutes to fall asleep. Winston Churchill experienced *maintenance insomnia,* which is characterized by awakening after a short period of sleep. Finally, Napoleon Bonaparte endured *early morning awakening,* in which he would awaken 30 to 60 minutes before he intended to arise. **Ask: What good sleep habits can help many people get a good night's sleep?**

TEACHER Tip

Remind students that the hypothalamus performs several functions, including a role in regulating the body's biological clock. The eyes send information about light and dark to the hypothalamus.

FYI

According to the Stanford University School of Medicine, more than 1 in 2,000 Americans are affected by narcolepsy. The condition is actually an attack of REM sleep. While drugs reduce the effects of narcolepsy, they cannot cure it.

narcolepsy: a condition characterized by suddenly falling asleep or feeling very sleepy during the day

nightmares: unpleasant dreams

night terrors: sleep disruptions that occur during Stage IV of sleep, involving screaming, panic, or confusion

sleepwalking: walking or carrying out behaviors while asleep

Narcolepsy

Another disorder, **narcolepsy,** is characterized by a permanent and overwhelming feeling of sleepiness and fatigue. Other symptoms include unusual sleep and dream patterns, such as dreamlike hallucinations or a feeling of temporary paralysis. People with narcolepsy may have sleep attacks throughout the day. The sleep attacks are accompanied by brief periods of REM sleep. Victims of narcolepsy may have difficulties in the area of work, leisure, and interpersonal relations and are prone to accidents because they have fallen asleep.

Nightmares and Night Terrors

Frightening dreams—**nightmares**—occur during the dream phase of REM sleep. A nightmare may frighten the sleeper, who will usually wake up with a vivid memory of a movielike dream. On the other hand, **night terrors** occur during Stage IV sleep (usually within an hour after going to bed). A night terror may last anywhere from five to twenty minutes and involve screaming, sweating, confusion, and a rapid heart rate. The person may suddenly awake from sleep or have a persistent fear that occurs at night. People usually have no memory of night terrors.

Sleepwalking and Sleep Talking

Sleepwalking is a disorder in which a person is partly, but not completely, awake during the night. That person may walk or do other things without any memory of doing so. Sleepwalking is a disorder associated with children, although some adults may sleepwalk. Most children who sleepwalk do not have emotional problems and will outgrow it. This disorder has been linked to stress, fatigue, and the use by adults of sedative medicines. Sleepwalking may also be inherited. It is usually harmless; however, it may become dangerous if sleepwalkers fall or otherwise injure themselves—their movements are often clumsy. It is neither dangerous nor necessary to awaken sleepwalkers.

Sleep talking is a common sleep disruption. Most people talk in their sleep more than they realize because they do not remember talking during sleep. Sleep talking can occur in either REM or NREM sleep. It can be a single word or a longer speech. Sometimes sleep talkers pause between sentences or phrases as if they are carrying on a conversation with someone else. You can even engage a sleep talker in a conversation sometimes. Like sleepwalking, sleep talking is harmless.

DREAMS

We call the mental activity that takes place during sleep dreaming. Everybody dreams, although most people are able to recall only a few, if any, of their dreams. (However, in cultures in which dreams are highly valued and talked about frequently, people remember their dreams almost every morning.) Sleep researchers sometimes make a point of waking study participants when they display REM during the night to ask

INTERDISCIPLINARY CONNECTIONS ACTIVITY

The Arts Tell students that a group of painters known as the *surrealists* believed that a dream could be transposed directly from the unconscious mind onto the canvas. Marcel Duchamp and his followers defined the movement as "pure psychic automatism...intended to express...the real process of thought." In creating their works, the surrealists borrowed heavily from the psychoanalysis started by Freud. Ask for volunteers to locate reproductions of surrealist paintings by artists such as Salvador Dali, Marc Chagall, Joan Miro, or Max Ernst. Show these works to the entire class. **Ask: What can you infer about the surrealist view of dreams? How does it match your own vision of dreams?** L2 ELL them about their dreams. The first few dreams are usually composed of vague thoughts left over from the day's activities. A participant may report that she was watching television, for example. As the night wears on, dreams become longer and more vivid and dramatic, especially dreams that take place during REM sleep. Because the amounts of time spent in REM sleep increase during the night, the last dream is likely to be the longest and the one people remember when they wake up. People, however, can rarely recall more than the last 15 minutes of a dream when they are awakened (Dement & Wolpert, 1958). Researchers have found that after people have been deprived of REM sleep, they subsequently increase the amount of time they spend in REM sleep. Thus, it appears that a certain amount of dreaming each night is necessary (Dement, 1976).

Figure 7.3 The Dream

Some researchers believe that when we sleep, electrical bursts occur that hit portions of the brain, firing off various memory circuits. The result? Dreams. Artist Jacob Lawrence created *Dreams No. 2* in 1965. ***What are other explanations for dreaming?***

The Content of Dreams

When people are awakened randomly during REM sleep and asked what they had just been dreaming, the reports generally are commonplace, even dull (Hall & Van de Castle, 1966). The dreams we remember and talk about "are more coherent, sexier, and generally more interesting" than those collected in systematic research (Webb, 1975).

Often we incorporate our everyday activities into our dreams. Researchers who have recorded the contents of thousands of dreams have found that most—even the late-night REM adventures—occur in such commonplace settings as living rooms, cars, and streets. Most dreams involve either strenuous recreational activities or passive events such as sitting and watching. A large percentage of the emotions experienced in dreams are negative or unpleasant—anxiety, anger, sadness, and so on. Contrary to popular belief, dreams do not occur in a split second; they correspond to a realistic time scale.

Some dreams are negative enough to be considered nightmares. Nightmares often have such a frightening quality that we awaken in the middle of them. The sense of dread in nightmares may be related to the intensity of brain activity and to the stimulation of those parts of the brain responsible for emotional reactions. The emotional reaction of dread may then influence the content of the dream.

Dream Interpretation

Dream interpretations have been discovered dating back to 5000 B.C. Sigmund Freud believed that no matter how simple or mundane, dreams may contain clues to thoughts the dreamer is afraid to acknowledge in his or her waking hours.

The Inuit people of North America, like Freud, believe that dreams contain hidden meanings. They believe that when dreaming, people enter the

Figure 7.3

Caption Answer Dreams are simply a stimulation of the brain cells; dreams allow us to resolve problems encountered during the day; dreams may be a way to perform mental housecleaning by getting rid of unneeded memories.

Looking @ the Issues

Sleep Deprivation Sleep deprivation is a contributing factor in about 550 traffic accidents per year. Sleep deprivation was a contributing factor in the Three Mile Island, Chernobyl, and Exxon Valdez accidents. Researcher Stanley Coren of the University of British Columbia has studied the effects of the change to daylight savings time. His research indicates that traffic accidents increase by 8 percent the Monday morning after daylight savings time begins. Correspondingly, traffic accidents decrease by about 8 percent the Monday after daylight savings time ends. **Ask: Do these correlations indicate a cause-and-effect relationship? What suggestions do you have for reducing the number of accidents the Monday after daylight savings time begins?**

3 ASSESS

Assign Section 1 Assessment as homework or as an in-class activity.

EXTENDING THE CONTENT

Lucid Dreaming A lucid dream is any dream you have in which you are aware that you are experiencing a dream. You realize at some point during the dream that what is occurring is not a real-life experience. Basically, your body is asleep and your mind is awake. Some scientists propose that the paralyzing effects of REM sleep may be the only thing keeping dreamers from actually performing the actions of their lucid dreams. Lucid dreaming is a skill some people can learn; it is an excellent way to control dreams in some way. Lucid dreams can be enjoyable experiences since you can, for instance, halt a nightmare, choose to fly, travel from country to country, or stand up to a bully.

Section Quiz 7-1

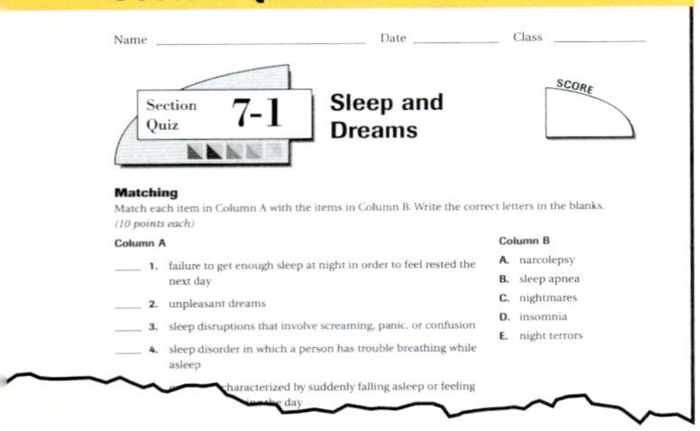
Name ______ Date ______ Class ______

Section Quiz 7-1 **Sleep and Dreams**

SCORE

Matching
Match each item in Column A with the items in Column B. Write the correct letters in the blanks.
(10 points each)

Column A	Column B
____ 1. failure to get enough sleep at night in order to feel rested the next day	A. narcolepsy
____ 2. unpleasant dreams	B. sleep apnea
____ 3. sleep disruptions that involve screaming, panic, or confusion	C. nightmares
____ 4. sleep disorder in which a person has trouble breathing while asleep	D. insomnia
... characterized by suddenly falling asleep or feeling ... the day	E. night terrors

Reteach

Ask students to create a chart of sleep disorders. The headings for the chart should include the following: *When It Occurs, What Causes It,* and *What Treatments Are Available.*

Enrich

Ask students to research techniques used to induce lucid dreaming (dreaming in which you are aware that you are dreaming). Have students try one of the methods and report on the effects to the class.

4 CLOSE

Have students conduct a panel discussion about the theories of why we dream. Have panelists represent the views of Freud, Kleitman, and Crick.

More About...

Freud on Dreams

Sigmund Freud was the first psychologist to study dreams thoroughly. He hypothesized that dreams express impulses and thoughts, often in highly symbolic form, that are unacceptable at the conscious level. Freud used the term *manifest content* to refer to the story line, images, and other perceptual aspects of dreams. Freud defined *latent content* as the hidden meaning of dreams that comes from the dreamer's unconscious wishes (Freud, 1965).

spiritual world where they interact with those who have passed away. These departed souls help the living reflect on some current or future event (Plotnik, 2005).

Some social scientists, however, are skeptical of dream interpretations. Nathaniel Kleitman, one of the pioneers who discovered REM sleep, wrote in 1960: "Dreaming may serve no function whatsoever." According to this view, the experience of a dream is simply an unimportant by-product of stimulating certain brain cells during sleep. Others argue that the common experience of feeling paralyzed in a dream simply means that brain cells that inhibit muscle activity were randomly stimulated (McCarley, 1978). One dream researcher advocates a problem-solving theory about dreaming (Cartwright, 1993). This theory proposes that dreaming allows people a chance to review and address some of the problems they faced during the day. One theorist, Francis Crick, believes that dreams are the brain's way of removing certain unneeded memories. In other words, dreams are a form of mental housecleaning. This mental housecleaning may be necessary because it is not useful to remember every single detail of your life.

Daydreams Daydreaming requires a low level of awareness and involves fantasizing, or idle but directed thinking, while we are awake. Usually we daydream when we are in situations that require little attention or when we are bored. Daydreaming serves useful purposes such as reminding us of or preparing us for events in our future. Daydreaming may also improve our creativity by generating thought processes. Some psychologists believe that daydreaming allows us to control our emotions.

SECTION 1 Assessment

1. **Review the Vocabulary** Describe the symptoms of insomnia, sleep apnea, narcolepsy, nightmares, night terrors, and sleepwalking.
2. **Visualize the Main Idea** Use a flowchart similar to the one below to list and describe the five stages of sleep.

3. **Recall Information** What is the difference between REM and NREM sleep? Which type lasts longer during a night's sleep?
4. **Think Critically** Why is sleep characterized as an *altered* state of consciousness? Why do you think we sleep?
5. **Application Activity** Create a Dream Diary. For one week attempt to remember and record your dreams. Then try to detect correlations between events in your life and your dreams.

SECTION 1 Assessment Answers

1. insomnia—the inability to sleep uninterrupted through the night; sleep apnea—a blockage of the breathing passageway during sleep; narcolepsy—permanent and overwhelming condition of sleepiness and fatigue; nightmares—awakening and remembering the vivid, fearful details of dreams; night terrors—dreams that may include screaming, sweating, confusion, and a rapid heart rate; sleepwalking—a partial awakening in which the person walks around without being consciously aware of it
2. Flowcharts should reflect students' understanding of the five stages of sleep.
3. REM sleep is characterized by rapid eye movement and twitching in the body's extremities. NREM sleep is a quiet sleep characterized by the absence of rapid eye movement. It lasts longer than REM sleep.
4. because the body is relaxed and unresponsive; Students' answers about why we sleep may vary.
5. Students' answers will vary. The diary should include correlations between life events and dreams.

SECTION 2 Hypnosis, Biofeedback, and Meditation

Reader's Guide

■ Main Idea

Hypnosis, biofeedback, and meditation are altered states of consciousness that can occur when we are awake.

■ Vocabulary

- hypnosis
- posthypnotic suggestion
- biofeedback
- meditation

■ Objectives

- Determine how hypnosis relates to consciousness.
- Describe research into such techniques as biofeedback and meditation.

EXPLORING PSYCHOLOGY

Not Feeling the Pain

Victor Rausch entered a hypnotic trance by focusing on Chopin's *Lush Nocturne in E-flat,* as it was played in the movie *The Eddy Duchin Story.* Rausch visualized scenes from the movie and wrapped his mind in appealing thoughts. Rausch's blood pressure and pulse rate remained steady for 75 minutes. During this 75 minutes Rausch was undergoing a gallbladder operation! He had refused the anesthetic, and during the surgery, he swears he felt no pain—just a little tugging. He even talked and joked with the surgical team during the procedure. After the surgery, he stood up and walked down the hall, riding the elevator to his hospital room.

—from "The Healing Power of Hypnosis" by Jean Callahan, 1997

Surgery without anesthesia may sound like a trick, but such operations have been performed by hypnotizing the patient. Although hypnosis still conjures up images of a circus magician saying, "You are getting sleepy, very sleepy . . . ," researchers are learning more about this mind-body connection. Doctors and therapists use hypnosis to help people quit smoking, lose weight, manage stress, overcome phobias, and diminish pain.

WHAT IS HYPNOSIS?

So what exactly is hypnosis? **Hypnosis** is a form of altered consciousness in which people become highly suggestible to changes in behavior and thought. By allowing the hypnotist to guide and direct them,

hypnosis: a state of consciousness resulting from a narrowed focus of attention and characterized by heightened suggestibility

SECTION RESOURCES

Reproducible Masters

- Guided Reading Activity 7–2
- Vocabulary Activity 7–2
- Section Quiz 7–2

Transparencies

- Daily Focus Transparency 7–2

Multimedia

- *ExamView® Assessment Suite* CD-ROM
- Presentation Plus! Software

1 FOCUS

Section Objectives

1. Determine how hypnosis relates to consciousness.
2. Describe research into such techniques as biofeedback and meditation.

BELLRINGER
Motivational Activity

Project Daily Focus Transparency 7–2 and have students answer the questions.

Available as blackline master

Daily Focus Transparency 7–2

Reader's Guide

Use the Reader's Guide to introduce concepts and vocabulary.

■ Exploring Psychology

Ask students to read the **Exploring Psychology** feature and then discuss: **How can hypnosis eliminate the pain involved in surgery?**

■ Vocabulary Precheck

Have students read the Glossary definitions. Ask them to restate the definitions in their own words.

2 TEACH

L1 Demonstration To illustrate the power of suggestion, request a team of students to conduct a "yawn poll." Have them start to yawn as they talk to friends or family. **Ask: How many times do you have to yawn before the other person also yawns? How many people are immune to the yawn?** Tell students to tally the results and report to the class. Use this experiment as a basis to explore the role of suggestion in hypnosis. ELL

Guided Reading Activity 7-2

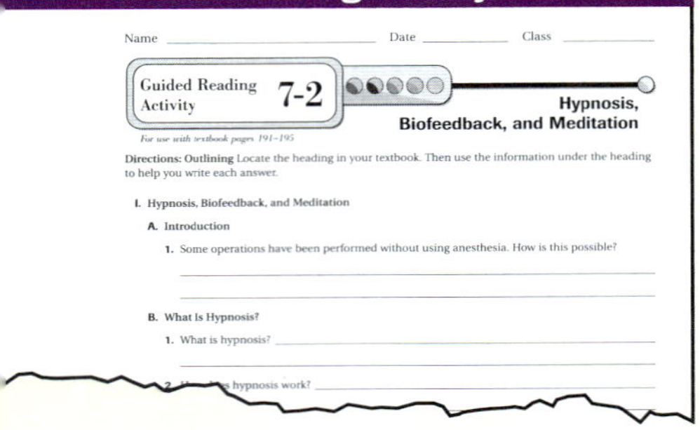
Name ______ Date ______ Class ______

Guided Reading Activity 7-2 — Hypnosis, Biofeedback, and Meditation

For use with textbook pages 191–195

Directions: Outlining Locate the heading in your textbook. Then use the information under the heading to help you write each answer.

I. Hypnosis, Biofeedback, and Meditation

A. Introduction

1. Some operations have been performed without using anesthesia. How is this possible?

B. What Is Hypnosis?

1. What is hypnosis?

2. How does hypnosis work?

Profiles In Psychology

Ask students to read the **Profiles In Psychology** feature and then discuss the following questions:

1. How did Mesmer treat his patients' medical problems? *(He passed a magnet over his patients' bodies while they were surrounded by iron fillings to redirect the flow of blood, nerve activity, and fluids.)*
2. What did he consider animal magnetism? *(He considered himself to be the magnet and the force he discharged to be animal magnetism.)*

Profiles In Psychology

Franz Anton Mesmer

1734–1815

"Truth is nothing but a path traced between errors."

Franz Anton Mesmer missed the narrow path of truth; he also missed the signs in his path that his science was faulty. Mesmer, however, became the first person to study and practice hypnosis. Mesmer believed that the human body is filled with a magnetic fluid that can become misaligned, causing illness. Realignment would restore health. Mesmer treated medical problems by placing his patients in a tub filled with water and iron filings; large iron rods protruded from the tub. Mesmer would then pass a magnet back and forth across the patient's body to redirect the flow of the blood, nerve activity, and fluids. Some of his patients reported dramatic results.

Later, Mesmer got rid of the magnet and used his own hand, claiming that he himself was the magnet. He called the force he discharged *animal magnetism*. Before Mesmer treated his patients, he told them to expect certain reactions, and his patients responded as anticipated. After his death, his followers called this healing technique "mesmerism" or "hypnotism." Although Mesmer was denounced as a fraud, and Mesmer's magnetic fluid was never proven to exist, he paved the way for studies relating to the readiness of some subjects to obey hypnotic suggestions and enter an altered state of consciousness.

people can be made conscious of things they are usually unaware of and unaware of things they usually notice. Participants may recall in vivid detail incidents they had forgotten or feel no pain when pricked with a needle. It happens in this way: At all times, certain sensations and thoughts are filtered out of our awareness. For example, as you read this sentence, you were probably not aware of the position of your feet until I called attention to that. By mentioning the position of your feet, your attention shifted to your feet—an area of your body that seconds before was outside your consciousness. Hypnosis shifts our perceptions in the same way.

Hypnosis does not put the participant to sleep, as many people believe. A hypnotic trance is quite different from sleep. In fact, participants become highly receptive and responsive to certain internal and external stimuli. They are able to focus their attention on one tiny aspect of reality and ignore all other inputs. The hypnotist induces a trance by slowly persuading a participant to relax and to lose interest in external distractions. Whether this takes a few minutes or much longer depends on the purpose of the hypnosis, the method of induction, and the participant's past experiences with hypnosis.

In an environment of trust, a participant with a rich imagination can become susceptible to the hypnotist's suggestions. Psychologists using hypnosis stress that the relationship between hypnotist and participant should involve cooperation, not domination. The participant is not under the hypnotist's control but can be convinced to do things he or she would not normally do. The person is simply cooperating with the hypnotist. Together they try to solve a problem or to learn more about

COOPERATIVE LEARNING ACTIVITY

Preparing a Grant Presentation Organize the class into four groups. Tell students that each group is competing with the others for a $400,000 grant to research altered states of consciousness. Each group should select one of the following altered states: sleep and dreams, hypnosis, biofeedback, or meditation. Their task is to prepare a presentation for the board awarding the grant. Each group's presentation should include a description of the altered state, reasons for studying it further, and a proposed research topic or project. Allow time for each group to deliver its presentation. If possible, have a panel of teachers select the grant winner.
BLOCK SCHEDULING

how the participant's mind works. Anyone can resist hypnosis by refusing to open his or her mind to the hypnotist. However, people under hypnosis can be induced to do things against their will. Mutual trust is important for hypnosis to be successful.

Theories of Hypnosis

Psychologists do not agree about the nature of hypnosis. Some, like Theodore Barber (1965), argue that hypnosis is not a special state of consciousness but simply the result of suggestibility. If people are just given instructions and told to try their hardest, they will be able to do anything that hypnotized people can do.

Others, like Ernest Hilgard (1986), believe that there is something special about the hypnotic state. People who are hypnotized are very suggestible; they go along with the hypnotist and do not initiate activities themselves; and they can more easily imagine and remember things. Hilgard believes that consciousness includes many different aspects that may become separated, or dissociated, during hypnosis. This view is called the neodissociation theory, which includes a "hidden observer"—a portion of the personality that watches and reports what happens to the hypnotized person.

Another explanation of hypnosis is based on the importance of suggestibility in the hypnotic induction (Green et al., 1998). According to some theorists (Sarbin & Coe, 1972, 1979), hypnotized people behave as they do because they have accepted the role of a hypnotized subject. We expect that hypnotized individuals will forget certain things when told or will recall forgotten material, and we play the role. Whether hypnosis is a special state of consciousness or not, it does reveal that people often have potential abilities that they do not use. Continued study may help us understand where these abilities come from and how to use them better.

Uses of Hypnosis

Although people have often seen hypnosis as a part of an entertainment act, it has serious uses in medical and therapeutic settings.

Hypnotists can suggest things for their participants to remember or forget when the trance is over. This is known as **posthypnotic suggestion.** For example, the hypnotist can suppress memory by suggesting that after the person is awakened, she will be unable to hear the word *psychology.* When she comes out of the trance, the participant

Reading Check What type of relationship is needed between a hypnotist and participant?

posthypnotic suggestion: a suggestion made during hypnosis that influences the participant's behavior afterward

Psychology and You: Hypnosis and Athletics

Olympic athletes use self-hypnosis to achieve peak performance. Many coaches and trainers realize the power of mental rehearsal before competition begins. Although self-hypnosis cannot turn an average soccer player into a world-class athlete, it can help you achieve your personal best. The next time you need a top performance, apply the following steps. Write a short summary of the event and the usefulness of self-hypnosis.

1. Relax. (If you have prepared physically for the upcoming challenge, relax and think about it.)
2. Set your short-term, specific, and achievable goals. (What is your objective?)
3. Concentrate, eliminate distractions, and visualize a peak performance.
4. Design a plan of action and mentally rehearse it by visualizing yourself performing to perfection.

Reading Check Answer The relationship between a hypnotist and a participant should be one of cooperation, not domination by the hypnotist.

Psychology and You

Use the following question to direct a class discussion after students have read the **Psychology and You** feature.

Ask: **To what other pursuits besides sports could these suggestions be applied?** *(musical or dance performances and giving a speech or presentation, for example)*

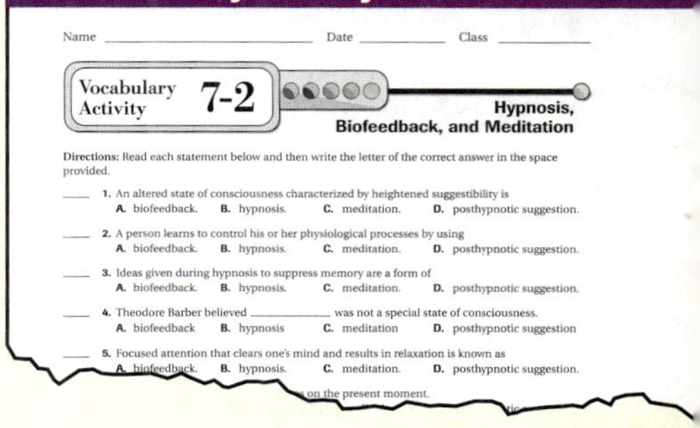
Vocabulary Activity 7-2

Name ______ Date ______ Class ______

Vocabulary Activity 7-2 — Hypnosis, Biofeedback, and Meditation

Directions: Read each statement below and then write the letter of the correct answer in the space provided.

____ 1. An altered state of consciousness characterized by heightened suggestibility is
A. biofeedback. B. hypnosis. C. meditation. D. posthypnotic suggestion.

____ 2. A person learns to control his or her physiological processes by using
A. biofeedback. B. hypnosis. C. meditation. D. posthypnotic suggestion.

____ 3. Ideas given during hypnosis to suppress memory are a form of
A. biofeedback. B. hypnosis. C. meditation. D. posthypnotic suggestion.

____ 4. Theodore Barber believed ______ was not a special state of consciousness.
A. biofeedback B. hypnosis C. meditation D. posthypnotic suggestion

____ 5. Focused attention that clears one's mind and results in relaxation is known as
A. biofeedback. B. hypnosis. C. meditation. D. posthypnotic suggestion.

on the present moment.

MEETING SPECIAL NEEDS

Learning Style: Visual/Spatial Assign students to prepare a series of illustrations to demonstrate how biofeedback could be used to treat migraine headaches. Have students use pictures or drawings of a biofeedback machine and of the human body. Tell them to use callouts on the human body to indicate the parts of the body that are altered using biofeedback. Tell students that their goal is to explain biofeedback in pictorial form. **L2 ELL BLOCK SCHEDULING**

Refer to ***Inclusion for the High School Social Studies Classroom Strategies and Activities*** in the TCR for strategies for students with different learning styles.

Quick Lab

Purpose Students will examine the power of suggestion.

Process Skills Identifying central issues, analyzing information

Teaching Strategies

- Review the procedures to be used.
- Recommend that students repeat the lab with a friend outside class. Have them read the directions to the friend and then observe the results.

Analysis

1. Answers will vary. Those who are suggestible will show a greater distance between hands than someone who is not suggestible.
2. Answers will vary. Reports should indicate the role of suggestibility in hypnosis.

3 ASSESS

Assign Section 2 Assessment as homework or as an in-class activity.

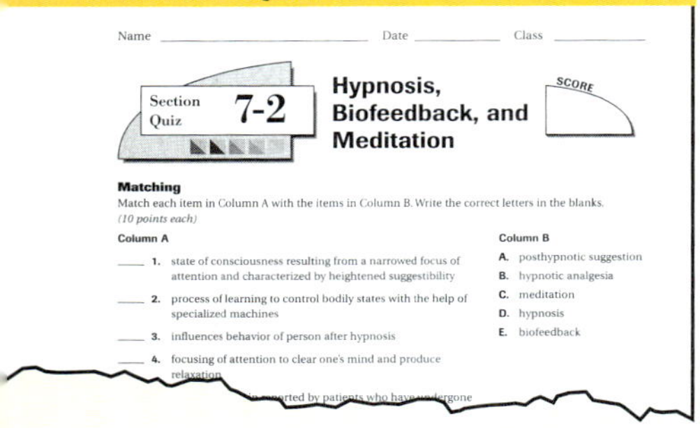
Section Quiz 7–2

Name ____________ Date ________ Class ________

Section Quiz 7-2 **Hypnosis, Biofeedback, and Meditation** SCORE

Matching
Match each item in Column A with the items in Column B. Write the correct letters in the blanks. *(10 points each)*

Column A

____ 1. state of consciousness resulting from a narrowed focus of attention and characterized by heightened suggestibility
____ 2. process of learning to control bodily states with the help of specialized machines
____ 3. influences behavior of person after hypnosis
____ 4. focusing of attention to clear one's mind and produce relaxation
...rted by patients who have undergone

Column B

A. posthypnotic suggestion
B. hypnotic analgesia
C. meditation
D. hypnosis
E. biofeedback

Reteach

Have students compare and contrast hypnosis, biofeedback, and meditation to answer the following: **What technology does each require? What effects does each have on the body? How is the mind affected by each?**

Quick Lab

Can you hypnotize yourself?

Sometimes just thinking of an action can result in producing that action—if you can imagine that action clearly enough.

Procedure

1. Stretch your arms in front of you, making sure the palms are facing each other at the same height and about two inches apart.
2. Close your eyes. Imagine that your right arm is getting heavier and heavier, while your left arm is getting lighter and lighter.
3. To help yourself, imagine that your right hand is holding a strap wrapped around several heavy books, while your left hand is holding a string tied to a helium balloon.

Analysis

1. After about a minute, open your eyes and see how far your hands have actually moved. Are they one or two inches or several inches apart?
2. Using what you have learned about hypnosis, explain the results in a brief report.

See the **Skills Handbook**, page 622, for an explanation of designing an experiment.

may report that some people around her are speaking strangely. They seem to leave out some words occasionally, especially when they are talking about topics involving the taboo word *psychology*. The participant is not aware that part of her consciousness has been instructed to block out that word. Memory can also be aided or enhanced through posthypnotic suggestion. Posthypnotic suggestion has been found to be particularly helpful in changing unwanted behaviors, such as smoking or overeating.

Hypnosis is sometimes used to reduce pain. *Hypnotic analgesia* refers to a reduction of pain reported by patients after they had undergone hypnosis. In these situations, the hypnotist works with the patient to reduce his or her anxiety and encourage relaxation. Therefore, a patient's perception of pain is reduced.

Therapists use hypnosis to help clients reveal their problems or gain insight into their lives. For example, hypnotherapists use hypnosis to allow their patients to think of their problems in a new way. Hypnosis, though, is not for all patients. Some fear the loss of control associated with hypnosis. Therapists often combine hypnosis with other therapies to help patients work through their problems.

BIOFEEDBACK

biofeedback: the process of learning to control bodily states with the help of machines monitoring the states to be controlled

A technique in which a person learns to control his or her internal physiological processes with the help of feedback is **biofeedback.** For example, you can be hooked up to a biofeedback machine so that a light goes on every time your heart rate goes over 80. You could then learn to keep your heart rate below 80 by trying to keep the light off.

Biofeedback has been used to teach people to control a wide variety of physiological responses, including brain waves (EEG), heart rate, blood pressure, skin temperature, and sweat-gland activity (Hassett, 1978). The basic principle of biofeedback is simple: feedback makes learning possible.

Biofeedback involves using machines to tell people about very subtle, moment-to-moment changes in the body. People can then experiment with different thoughts and feelings while they watch how each affects their bodies. In time, people can learn to change their physiological processes.

Some of the best-documented biofeedback cures involve special training in muscular control. Tension headaches often seem to result from constriction of the frontalis muscle in the forehead. Thomas Budzynski and others (1973) used biofeedback to teach people to relax this specific muscle. The practice went on for several weeks, while other people were

CRITICAL THINKING ACTIVITY

Understanding Cause and Effect Point out that one of the tools of meditation is known as a *koan*—a riddle or question that has no answer. Its purpose is to provoke concentration and self-control. To illustrate the use of a koan, challenge students to reflect on one of the following well-known examples. Tell them that there is no right or wrong answer.

- "What is the sound of one hand clapping?"
- "What did your face look like before your parents were born?"

Have students prepare a paper explaining how concentration on the koan helps induce an altered state of consciousness. The reports should include their own examples of a koan. **L2** given similar treatments without biofeedback. Only the biofeedback group improved significantly. Biofeedback used without drugs seems to help many people.

MEDITATION

When a person focuses his or her attention on an image or thought with the goal of clearing the mind and producing relaxation, or an inner peace, that person is practicing **meditation.** Meditation has been practiced in various parts of the world for thousands of years.

There are three major approaches to meditation. *Transcendental meditation* involves the mental repetition of a mantra, usually a Sanskrit phrase. The participant sits with eyes closed and meditates for 15 to 20 minutes twice a day. *Mindfulness meditation* was developed from a Buddhist tradition. This form of meditation focuses on the present moment. For example, the participant may move his or her focus through the body from the tips of the toes to the top of the head, while paying particular attention to areas that cause pain. *Breath meditation* is a concentration on one's respiration—the process of inhaling and exhaling.

Researchers generally agree that most people can benefit from the sort of systematic relaxation that meditation provides. Meditation has been found to help people lower blood pressure, heart rate, and respiration rate. The issue is not clear-cut, however. The people who benefit from meditation continue to practice it. Thus, the reported benefits may come from a biased, self-selected sample of successful practitioners. Other data suggest that while meditating, some people may actually be sleeping. If so, the reported benefits of meditation may result simply from relaxation.

meditation: the focusing of attention to clear one's mind and produce relaxation

A mandala is used to focus one's attention during meditation.

SECTION 2 Assessment

1. **Review the Vocabulary** Explain how a person can alter his or her consciousness by using meditation.
2. **Visualize the Main Idea** Using a diagram similar to the one below, list some explanations of hypnosis.

Explanations of Hypnosis		
1.	2.	3.

3. **Recall Information** What types of medical conditions could be helped through biofeedback?
4. **Think Critically** Why is it so important that the person being hypnotized trust his or her hypnotist?
5. **Application Activity** Try this meditation technique: (1) Take a few moments and form your lips into a half smile; (2) Hold this half smile for at least 10 minutes as you go about your ordinary activities. Did you notice a shift in how you acted and responded to others? Did others respond to you differently? Record and analyze your experiences.

CHAPTER 7
Section 2, pages 191–195

Enrich

Arrange for a hypnotist or someone well-versed in hypnosis to visit the class. Have the visitor explain the uses and techniques of hypnosis. Prior to the visit, assign students to formulate questions to ask the visitor. Have the class assess these questions for relevance. After the visit, instruct students to summarize how the visitor affected their opinion of hypnosis as a psychological tool.

4 CLOSE

Write the following two words on the board: *Sleep* and *Meditation.* Have students list the characteristics of each and then discuss how the two are similar and how they are different.

SECTION 2 Assessment Answers

1. A person focuses his or her attention on an object or sound to clear the mind and produce relaxation.
2. a result of suggestibility, not an altered consciousness; a separation or dissociation of the various aspects of consciousness; a role play in which one willingly plays the role of the hypnotized subject
3. Biofeedback can help a variety of stress-related ailments including high blood pressure and headaches. It can help control brain waves, skin temperature, sweat-gland activity, and heart rate.
4. Trust is important because anyone can resist hypnosis by refusing to open his or her mind to the hypnotist.
5. Students' answers will vary. Most will notice that others reacted to them positively, and many will respond that they began feeling more positive themselves.

Going Further

Biofeedback Training

Biofeedback requires people to learn various techniques like breathing and relaxation exercises. Typically, at least three to four training sessions are required to begin to realize the benefits. Once training is complete, the asthma sufferer will need to continue the exercises learned indefinitely.

A typical biofeedback session involves having the participant connected via wires to a computer. Electrodes are attached to different parts of the body that are targeted for measurement and modification, usually the head, hands, fingers, feet, or muscle areas. The signal transmitted from the electrodes to the computer provides immediate information through signals the asthma sufferer can see and/or hear about the levels of physiological activity.

The computer then indicates any changes in the activities of the participant's body that occur as a result of the relaxation and visualization techniques used during the session.

Discussing the Case Study

Ask: Do you think biofeedback will work for all asthma sufferers? Why or why not? Referring to the causes of asthma mentioned in the text, what other types of medical problems may be effectively treated using biofeedback?

Case Studies

A Breath of Fresh Air

Period of Study: Late 1970s to early 1980s

Introduction: Approximately 20 million people in the United States suffer from a chronic respiratory condition characterized by hypersensitivity, inflammation, and obstruction or narrowing of the airways. This condition is commonly known as asthma. An asthmatic person develops swollen airways lined with thick mucus. This causes the surrounding muscles to constrict, making it extremely difficult to breathe and sometimes leading to a life-threatening event. The occurrence of these symptoms is known as an asthmatic episode.

The causes of asthma are generally the results of allergic reactions, stress, endocrine changes, genetic makeup, and/or psychological traits. Those afflicted with asthma suffer from both gasping and irritating interruptions of their daily routine. Asthmatic individuals who choose to participate in aerobic sports of any kind must constantly monitor their breathing patterns. They must always be prepared to manage an oncoming episode.

For the past decade, medication in the form of an oral inhaler was the common way to treat an asthmatic episode. Researchers, however, are currently investigating a possible connection between halting an asthmatic episode and the use of biofeedback.

Hypothesis: Through the use of biofeedback, or gaining conscious control over an unconscious event, an asthma sufferer can gain control and relieve the tightening of the muscles that constrict airways.

Method: Recent studies have attempted to find the relationship between changes in muscular tension and breathing patterns in both asthmatic and nonasthmatic individuals. Researchers instructed participants to use deep breathing exercises while hooked up to biofeedback monitors. This allowed the participants to learn to control their heart rates during breathing cycles. The goal of this experiment was to control the muscle reflex that constricts airways during an asthmatic episode. Other types of biofeedback experiments were performed as well. No biofeedback machine was used for these experiments; instead, an important biofeedback "monitor"—a mirror—was used. The participant would perform the same type of breathing exercises in front of the mirror, thus monitoring muscle tension.

Results: Initial observation showed that the performance of these types of exercises might decrease asthma symptoms. Participants took lower dosages of medication, sometimes eliminating the medication entirely. Emergency room visits by participants involving asthmatic episodes decreased significantly. Overall, the benefits of biofeedback techniques used to control asthma are apparent. A number of questions regarding biofeedback techniques and asthma, however, remain unanswered. One such question involves researching long-term effects of these techniques. Because this research is relatively new, such questions may not be answered for years to come. These studies, though, may be the foundation for future therapies such as biofeedback to control migraine headaches, speech disorders, and blood pressure.

Analyzing the Case Study

1. What causes asthma?
2. Describe how participants monitored their physiological processes in the experiments.
3. **Critical Thinking** How did participants use biofeedback in the experiments? Why was it successful?

Answers for Analyzing the Case Study

1. Asthma is generally caused by allergic reactions, stress, endocrine changes, genetic makeup, or psychological traits.
2. They used biofeedback monitors, including mirrors, to learn to control their heart rates during breathing cycles and to learn to control the muscle reflex that constricts airways during an asthmatic episode.
3. They performed deep breathing exercises while hooked to monitors or using a mirror to look for signs of muscle tension. Participants learned to successfully control certain physiological processes. In the short-run, biofeedback reduced the use of medication and decreased the number of emergency room visits. The long-term effects are still not clear.

SECTION 3 Drugs and Consciousness

Reader's Guide

■ Main Idea

Psychoactive drugs interact with the central nervous system to alter consciousness.

■ Vocabulary

- psychoactive drugs
- marijuana
- hallucinations
- hallucinogens
- LSD

■ Objectives

- Describe the effects drugs have on consciousness.
- Define drug abuse.

EXPLORING PSYCHOLOGY

A Letter to Parents

Marijuana is the illegal drug most often used in this country. Since 1991, lifetime marijuana use has almost doubled among 8th- and 10th-grade students, and increased by a third among high school seniors. Our research shows that accompanying this upward pattern of use is a significant erosion in antidrug perceptions and knowledge among young people today. As the number of young people who use marijuana has increased, the number who view the drug as harmful has decreased. Among high school seniors surveyed in 2003, current marijuana use has increased by about 54 percent since 1991. The proportion of those seniors who believe regular use of marijuana is harmful has dropped by about 30 percent since 1991.

—from "Marijuana: Facts Parents Need to Know" by the National Institute on Drug Abuse, 2004

Marijuana use today starts at a young age, and potent forms of the drug are available. The National Institute on Drug Abuse (NIDA) warned parents in the letter above that marijuana is a serious threat—which they must talk to their children about. Marijuana is an example of a psychoactive drug. **Psychoactive drugs** interact with the central nervous system to alter a person's mood, perception, and behavior. These drugs range from stimulants like the caffeine in coffee and in cola drinks to depressants like alcohol to powerful hallucinogens like marijuana and LSD (see Figure 7.4).

psychoactive drugs: chemicals that affect the nervous system and result in altered consciousness

CHAPTER 7
Section 3, pages 197–202

1 FOCUS

Section Objectives

1. Describe the effects drugs have on consciousness.
2. Define drug abuse.

BELLRINGER
Motivational Activity

Project Daily Focus Transparency 7–3 and have students answer the questions.

Available as blackline master

Daily Focus Transparency 7–3

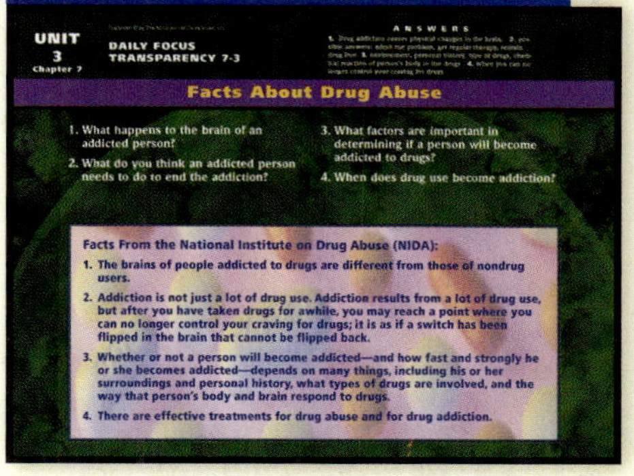

Reader's Guide

Use the Reader's Guide to introduce concepts and vocabulary.

■ Exploring Psychology
Ask students to read the **Exploring Psychology** feature. Ask: **What factors do you think have influenced the trend toward increased use of marijuana?**

■ Vocabulary Precheck
Have students read the Glossary definition of each term. Then ask them to work in pairs to quiz each other on the correct spelling and meaning of each term.

SECTION RESOURCES

Reproducible Masters

- Guided Reading Activity 7–3
- Vocabulary Activity 7–3
- Section Quiz 7–3

Transparencies

- Daily Focus Transparency 7–3

Multimedia

- *ExamView® Assessment Suite* CD-ROM
- Presentation Plus! Software

2 TEACH

L1 Identifying Cause and Effect Read aloud the following description of marijuana (cannabis) use written by J.R. Tinkleman (1975).

Initial effects of cannabis at low doses usually include euphoria, heightening of subjective sensory experiences, alterations in time sense, and the [feeling]...of a relaxed...passivity. With time,...these effects are intensified with impaired memory function, disturbed thought patterns, lapses of attention, and a...feeling of unfamiliarity.

Based on this quote, have students speculate on some of the physical causes of dependency upon marijuana. **Ask: What are some of the emotional and psychological effects of that dependency?**

Figure 7.4

Visual Instruction Point out to students the various effects on behavior for the drugs listed. Ask students which effects were different than what they had thought.

Caption Answer They relieve inhibitions and impair memory and judgment.

HOW DRUGS WORK

Like hormones, drugs are carried by the blood and taken up in target tissues in various parts of the body. Unlike hormones, though, drugs are taken into the body from the outside. People introduce drugs into their systems through routes that bring the drugs into contact with capillaries (the smallest blood vessels). From there, drugs are gradually absorbed into the blood. Then drug molecules act like neurotransmitters and hook onto the dendrites of neurons and send out their own chemical messages. For example, alcohol molecules may tell a nerve cell not to fire. As more and more cells cease firing, the alcohol user becomes slower and may eventually lose consciousness. LSD molecules may cause circuits in different areas of the brain to start firing together instead of separately, resulting in hallucinations.

MARIJUANA

marijuana: the dried leaves and flowers of Indian hemp *(Cannabis sativa)* that produce an altered state of consciousness when smoked or ingested

Marijuana, used as an intoxicant among Eastern cultures for centuries, is legally and morally acceptable in some societies, whereas alcohol is not. The sale and possession of marijuana is against the law in most states. Before 1960, marijuana use in the United States was common only

Figure 7.4 Some Psychoactive Drugs

Psychoactive drugs influence how we sense and perceive things and modify our moods, feelings, emotions, and thoughts. ***What effects do depressants produce?***

Drug Category	Effects on Behavior
Depressants Alcohol	Relaxant; relieve inhibitions; impair memory and judgment
Tranquilizers Barbiturates, benzodiazepines (Valium, Xanax)	Relieve anxiety; relax muscles; induce sleep
Opiates Morphine, heroin	Decrease pain; decrease attention to real world; unpleasant withdrawal effects as drug's effect wears off
Stimulants Caffeine, amphetamines, cocaine	Increase energy, alertness
Mixed Stimulant-Depressants Nicotine	Stimulate brain activity, but most smokers say cigarettes relax them
Distortion of Experience Marijuana (THC)	Intensifies sensory experiences; distorts perception of time; can relieve glaucoma, nausea; sometimes impairs learning, memory
Hallucinogens LSD, mescaline	Cause hallucinations, sensory distortions, and occasionally panic

COOPERATIVE LEARNING ACTIVITY

Creating Posters Organize the class into groups. Tell students that they have been chosen as part of a special presidential youth commission to develop materials for the war against drugs. Challenge each group to create a series of posters, brochures, and newspaper advertisements to discourage drug use among teenagers. Suggest that students contact local health organizations already involved in combating substance abuse for ideas. If possible, arrange to have the students display their posters throughout the building. **BLOCK SCHEDULING**

among members of certain subcultures. Marijuana use increased throughout the 1960s and most of the 1970s but then began to decline.

The active ingredient in marijuana is a complex molecule called tetrahydrocannabinol (THC), which occurs naturally in the common weed *Cannabis sativa,* or Indian hemp. Marijuana is made by drying the plant; hashish is a gummy powder made from the resin exuded by the flowering tops of the female plant. Both marijuana and hashish are usually smoked, but they can also be cooked with food and eaten.

The effects of the drug vary somewhat from person to person and also seem to depend on the setting in which the drug is taken and the user's past experience. The effects can be both pleasant and unpleasant. In general, though, many marijuana users report most sensory experiences seem greatly augmented—music sounds fuller, colors look brighter, smells are stronger, foods have stronger flavors, and other experiences are more intense than usual. Users may feel elated, the world may seem somehow more meaningful, and even the most ordinary events may take on an extraordinary significance. Marijuana is not a physically addictive drug, as heroin is, but people may become psychologically addicted, or dependent on the drug.

As many users of marijuana have discovered, the drug can instill or heighten a variety of unpleasant experiences. If a person is frightened, unhappy, or depressed to begin with, the chances are good that taking the drug will blow the negative feelings out of proportion so that the user's world, temporarily at least, becomes very upsetting. Cases have been reported in which marijuana appears to have helped bring on psychological disturbances in people who were already unstable before they used it.

Despite the obvious need for careful research on marijuana, the first controlled scientific studies of its effects did not appear until the late 1960s, scarcely anticipating its surge in popularity. Studies suggest that marijuana use is more damaging to the lungs than cigarette use. Although there is no direct evidence that marijuana use causes lung cancer, the tar and other chemicals in marijuana smoke are drawn deep into the lungs and held 20 to 40 seconds, adding to the drug's potential for hindering lung function (Ksir, Hart, & Ray, 2006).

Marijuana also disrupts memory formation, making it difficult to carry out mental and physical tasks (Lictman, Dimen, & Martin, 1995; Pope & Yurgelun-Todd, 1996). Some researchers believe that long-term use of the drug can lead to dependence (Stephens, Roffman, & Simpson, 1994). Research also showed that adults using marijuana scored lower than equal-IQ nonusers on a twelfth-grade academic achievement test (Block & Ghoneim, 1993).

HALLUCINATIONS

Perceptions that have no direct external cause—seeing, hearing, smelling, tasting, or feeling things that do not exist—are **hallucinations.** Hypnosis, meditation, certain drugs, withdrawal from a drug to which

PSYCHOLOGY Online

Student Web Activity
Visit the *Understanding Psychology* Web site at glencoe.com and click on **Chapter 7—Student Web Activities** for an activity about altered states of consciousness.

Reading Check How does marijuana use change a person's consciousness?

hallucinations: perceptions that have no direct external cause

MEETING SPECIAL NEEDS

Learning Style: Interpersonal Describe the following scenario to students: Imagine that a good friend has been having difficulty in school. This friend has become jittery, has lost weight, and has chronic insomnia. You also know that your friend is working part-time, helping care for a sick grandparent, and partying every weekend. Your friend finally admits to taking drugs just to cope. Yet when you attempt to encourage your friend to get help, he or she gets mad and storms away. Tell students to write their friend a letter to try to convince him or her to seek help. Have two students role-play the situation, attempting to resolve it using persuasion, compromise, and debate. **L2**

PSYCHOLOGY Online

Links and instructional guidelines can be found in the **Web Activity Lesson Plan** at glencoe.com.

Reading Check Answer Marijuana heightens the senses and impairs memory functions.

Guided Reading Activity 7-3

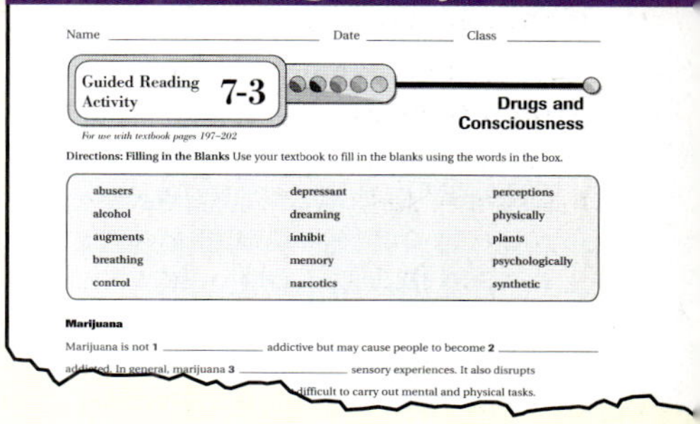
Name ______ Date ______ Class ______

Guided Reading Activity 7-3

Drugs and Consciousness

For use with textbook pages 197–202

Directions: Filling in the Blanks Use your textbook to fill in the blanks using the words in the box.

abusers	depressant	perceptions
alcohol	dreaming	physically
augments	inhibit	plants
breathing	memory	psychologically
control	narcotics	synthetic

Marijuana

Marijuana is not **1** ______ addictive but may cause people to become **2** ______ addicted. In general, marijuana **3** ______ sensory experiences. It also disrupts ... difficult to carry out mental and physical tasks.

PSYCHOLOGY JOURNAL

A regular user of marijuana offers you a ride home from school. The person states that smoking marijuana does not impair driving skill. Would you get in the car? Explain your answer. ■

CURRICULUM CONNECTION

History Prohibition was an effort in the late nineteenth century and early twentieth century to curb the use of alcohol in the United States. The Eighteenth Amendment to the Constitution was passed in 1919 and outlawed the sale of distilled spirits in the United States. Although alcohol consumption dropped drastically in the two years following the enactment, it began to rise again through the 1920s. One unintended consequence was a rise in crime as a strong black market for alcohol arose. In 1933 the Twenty-first Amendment to the Constitution repealed Prohibition, and the experiment outlawing a previously legal substance was declared a failure.

Figure 7.5

Caption Answer Hallucinations may be caused by hypnosis, meditation, certain drugs, drug withdrawal, or psychological breakdown.

one has become addicted, and psychological breakdown may produce hallucinations. Hallucinations can also occur under normal conditions. People hallucinate when they are dreaming and when they are deprived of the opportunity to sleep. Periods of high emotion, concentration, or fatigue may also produce false sensations and perceptions. For example, truck drivers on long hauls have been known to swerve suddenly to avoid stalled cars that do not exist. Even daydreams involve mild hallucinations.

Interestingly enough, it seems that hallucinations are very much alike from one person to the next. Soon after taking a drug that causes hallucinations, for example, people often see many geometric forms in a tunnel-like perspective. These forms float through the field of vision, combining with each other and duplicating themselves. While normal imagery is often in black and white, hallucinations are more likely to involve color.

One researcher (Seigel, 1977) traveled to Mexico's Sierra Madre to study the reactions of Huichol Native Americans who take peyote. He found that their hallucinations were much like those of American college students who took similar drugs. He believes that these reactions are similar because of the way such drugs affect the brain: portions of the brain that respond to incoming stimuli become disorganized, while the entire central nervous system is aroused.

hallucinogens: drugs that often produce hallucinations

LSD: a potent psychedelic drug that produces distortions of perception and thought

Figure 7.5 Isolation

In this cartoon by Roland B. Wilson, the lighthouse keeper has apparently become a little disturbed psychologically by his isolated life. His unconscious has produced a hallucinatory companion. ***What causes hallucinations?***

HALLUCINOGENS

So called because their main effect is to produce hallucinations, **hallucinogens** are found in plants that grow throughout the world. They have been used for their effects on consciousness since earliest human history (Schultes, 1976). These drugs are also called psychedelics because they create a loss of contact with reality. They can create a false body image and cause loss of self, dreamlike fantasies and hallucinations.

The best-known, most extensively studied, and most potent hallucinogen is **LSD** (lysergic acid diethylamide). In fact, it is one of the most powerful drugs known. LSD is a synthetic substance. A dose of a few millionths of a gram has a noticeable effect; an average dose of 100 to 300 micrograms produces an experiential state, called a trip, that lasts from 6 to 14 hours. To control such small doses, LSD is often dissolved into strips of paper or sugar cubes.

During an LSD trip, a person can experience any number of perceptions, often quite intense and rapidly changing. The person's expectations, mood, beliefs, and the circumstances under which he or she takes LSD can affect the experience, sometimes making it terrifying. Perceptual hallucinations are very common with LSD. Users may experience hallucinatory progressions in which simple geometric forms evolve into surrealistic impossibilities. The user may encounter such distortions that familiar objects become almost unrecognizable. A wall, for example, may seem to pulsate or breathe. One's

CRITICAL THINKING ACTIVITY

Analyzing Information Assign students to research nonchemical hallucinations such as those experienced in some Native American cultures. Tell them that an example is the sweat lodges used by the Lakota (Sioux). After an intense steam bath, sweat bathers are doused with icy cold water—much like the process in Scandinavian saunas. The bathers report euphoria more intense than any state induced by psychedelic drugs. Ask students to write a report on their findings. **L2**

senses, too, seem to intermingle; sounds may be seen and visual stimuli may be heard. A person may experience a dissociation of the self into one being who observes and another who feels. Distortions of time, either an acceleration or a slowing down, are also common. A single stimulus may become the focus of attention for hours, perceived as ever changing or newly beautiful and fascinating.

As measured by the ability to perform simple tasks, LSD impairs thinking, even though users may feel they are thinking more clearly and logically than ever before. Panic reactions are the most common of LSD's unpleasant side effects. Those who experience panic and later describe it often say that they felt trapped in the experience of panic and were afraid that they would never get out or that they would go mad. Use of LSD peaked in the 1960s. The likelihood of *flashback* experiences, even months after taking LSD, and public fears of chromosome damage—not confirmed by subsequent research—probably led to LSD's declining popularity (Ksir, Hart & Ray, 2006).

Figure 7.6 Just Say No

Many advertisements and programs aimed at kids, such as this one, warn of the dangers involved with drug use. ***What is the general treatment for those who abuse drugs?***

OPIATES

Opiates, usually called narcotics, include opium, morphine, and heroin. Opiates produce analgesia, or pain reduction; euphoria, which is sometimes described as a pleasurable state somewhere between awake and asleep; and constipation. Regular use of opiates can lead to physical addiction. An overdose of opiates results in a loss of control of breathing—the user then dies from respiratory failure.

ALCOHOL

The most widely used and abused mind-altering substance in the United States is alcohol. The consumption of alcohol is encouraged by advertisements and by social expectations and traditions. The immediate effect of alcohol is a general loosening of inhibitions. Despite its seeming stimulating effect, alcohol is actually a depressant that serves to inhibit the brain's normal functions. When people drink, they often act without the social restraint or self-control they normally apply to their behavior.

The effects of using alcohol depend on the amount and frequency of drinking and the drinker's body weight. As the amount consumed increases within a specific time, the drinker's ability to function diminishes. The person experiences slurred speech, blurred vision, and impaired judgment and memory. Permanent brain and liver damage and a change in personality can result from prolonged heavy use of alcohol.

Figure 7.6

Caption Answer Treatment includes admitting to a problem, entering a treatment program or therapy, and remaining drug free.

Vocabulary Activity 7-3

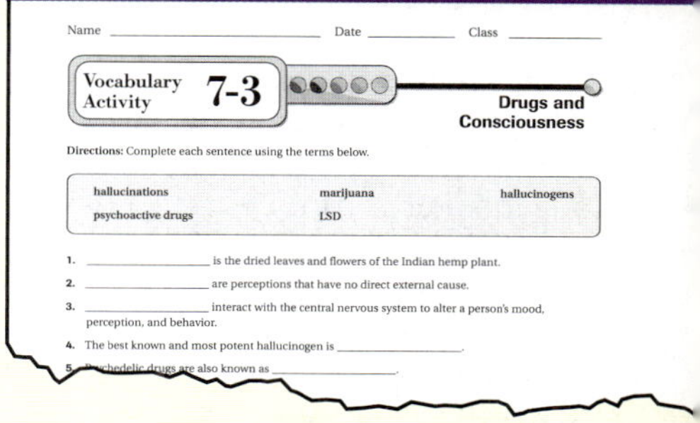
Name ______ Date ______ Class ______

Vocabulary Activity 7-3 — Drugs and Consciousness

Directions: Complete each sentence using the terms below.

hallucinations	marijuana	hallucinogens
psychoactive drugs	LSD	

1. ______ is the dried leaves and flowers of the Indian hemp plant.
2. ______ are perceptions that have no direct external cause.
3. ______ interact with the central nervous system to alter a person's mood, perception, and behavior.
4. The best known and most potent hallucinogen is ______.
5. Psychedelic drugs are also known as ______.

3 ASSESS

Assign Section 3 Assessment as homework or as an in-class activity.

Section Quiz 7-3

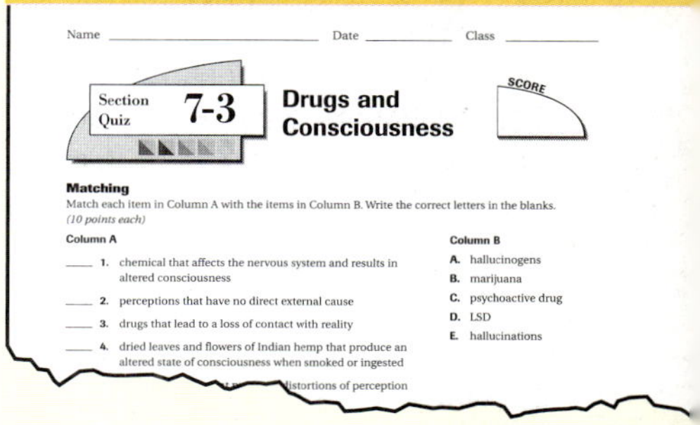
Name ______ Date ______ Class ______

Section Quiz 7-3 — Drugs and Consciousness — SCORE

Matching

Match each item in Column A with the items in Column B. Write the correct letters in the blanks. *(10 points each)*

Column A	Column B
____ 1. chemical that affects the nervous system and results in altered consciousness	A. hallucinogens
____ 2. perceptions that have no direct external cause	B. marijuana
____ 3. drugs that lead to a loss of contact with reality	C. psychoactive drug
____ 4. dried leaves and flowers of Indian hemp that produce an altered state of consciousness when smoked or ingested	D. LSD
...istortions of perception	E. hallucinations

PSYCHOLOGY LAB EXPERIMENT

Survey Tell students that national statistics indicate that the majority of high school students have tried alcohol or marijuana. Have students develop a confidential survey in which high school students are asked their age and the types of substances they have (a) tried and (b) use regularly. Substances should include alcohol, marijuana, tobacco, cocaine, and so on. Have students send out a schoolwide survey and create drop-off boxes for completed surveys throughout the school. Students should collect 25 samples of students' responses and chart the results by age and by substance and write an interpretation of the results. Based on the results, students should recommend a plan of action for the school. **L2**

Reading Check Answer

Hallucinogens alter mood states and perception. Alcohol loosens inhibitions and depresses the brain's normal functioning.

Reteach

List the drugs shown in Figure 7.4. Have each student vote for the five drugs that they consider to be the most dangerous. Tally the entire class's scores. Ask students why they believe these drugs are more dangerous than other drugs listed.

Enrich

Have students work in groups to research various drug treatment programs available in your area. Assign each group to select one treatment center or program and create a list of the types of therapy it uses and the types of drug problems it treats. Encourage students to attach any pamphlets or informational brochures to the list.

4 CLOSE

Direct students to assess their brainstorming list from the beginning of the chapter. (See the Two-Minute Lesson Launcher on page 182.) **Ask:** **What, if any, items would you delete from the list? What items would you add? What characteristics do altered states of consciousness have in common?**

Reading Check

How do hallucinogens and alcohol affect a person's consciousness?

Several studies suggested that not all of the early effects of drinking are the result of the alcohol alone; some are social effects. People expect to feel a certain way when they drink. In one study, men who were led to believe they were drinking alcohol when they were, in fact, drinking tonic water became more aggressive. They also felt more sexually aroused and were less anxious in social situations (Marlatt & Rohsenow, 1981).

DRUG ABUSE AND TREATMENT

Almost all of us have taken a psychoactive drug at some time—it may have been caffeine in a soda or a cup of tea. So at what point do we cross the line into drug abuse? Drug abusers are people who regularly use illegal drugs or excessively use legal drugs.

People abuse drugs for many reasons, such as to avoid boredom, to fit in with peers, to gain more self-confidence, to forget about problems, to relax, or simply to feel good. All of these reasons involve changing how people feel.

There are many risks associated with drug abuse, including danger of death or injury by overdose or accident, damage to health, legal consequences, and destructive behavior. The greatest risk associated with the abuse of psychoactive drugs, though, is loss of control. Although addiction does not occur immediately or automatically, drug abuse can turn into addiction—an overwhelming and compulsive desire to obtain and use drugs. Treatment for drug abuse usually involves the following steps:

1. The drug abuser must admit that he or she has a problem.
2. The drug abuser must enter a treatment program and/or get therapy.
3. The drug abuser must remain drug free. Many drug addicts are encouraged to join support groups to help them reduce drug use and fight off the temptation of returning to drugs. Many drug addicts suffer a relapse; that is, they return to using drugs. Support groups can be a powerful force in preventing that occurrence.

SECTION 3 Assessment

1. **Review the Vocabulary** How do psychoactive drugs affect consciousness? Describe the effects of marijuana and LSD.
2. **Visualize the Main Idea** Using a cause-and-effect diagram similar to the one below, describe the effects of three drugs on consciousness.

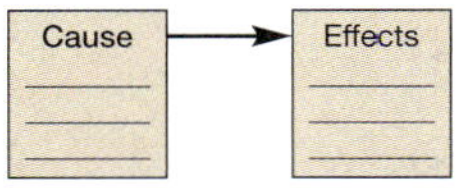

3. **Recall Information** When does drug use become drug abuse? Why do people abuse drugs?
4. **Think Critically** Do people use psychoactive drugs to increase or decrease their level of awareness? Explain.
5. **Application Activity** Design an antidrug advertisement for a billboard or magazine. Keep in mind the reasons people choose to abuse drugs when creating your ad.

SECTION 3 Assessment Answers

1. They alter mood, perceptions, and behavior. Marijuana heightens sensory experiences, gives feelings of elation, and may heighten unpleasant experiences. LSD users experience rapidly changing mood states, hallucinations, and an intermingling of senses. It impairs thinking and logic.
2. Students' answers will vary. Examples may include the following: alcohol—reduces inhibition, impairs memory and judgment; barbiturates—relieve anxiety, relax muscles, induce sleep; and morphine—reduces pain, decreases awareness of surrounding world.
3. Drug abuse is the regular use of illegal drugs or the excessive use of a legal drug. People may use drugs to avoid boredom, fit in with peers, gain self-confidence, forget problems, relax, or feel good.
4. Many claim that psychoactive drugs heighten their awareness, but in reality, they decrease the level of awareness by altering the state of consciousness.
5. Students' posters should clearly express one or more reasons that people abuse drugs.

CHAPTER 7

Summary and Vocabulary

Everything you think and feel is part of your conscious experience. An altered state of consciousness involves a change in mental processes, not just a quantitative shift (such as feeling more or less alert).

Section 1 Sleep and Dreams

Main Idea: Sleep—an essential state of consciousness—involves stages and periods of dreaming.

- Some researchers believe that sleep is restorative. Others believe sleep is a type of hibernation, necessary to conserve energy. Still others believe sleep clears the mind of useless information.
- There are several stages of sleep—from Stage I, the lightest level of sleep, to Stage IV, the deepest level of sleep. REM sleep is an active type of sleep characterized by rapid eye movement.
- Sometimes people have problems falling asleep or during sleep. Sleep disorders include insomnia, sleep apnea, narcolepsy, nightmares, night terrors, and sleepwalking.
- The mental activity that takes place during sleep is called dreaming.

Section 2 Hypnosis, Biofeedback, and Meditation

Main Idea: Hypnosis, biofeedback, and meditation are altered states of consciousness that can occur when we are awake.

- Hypnosis is a form of altered consciousness in which people become highly suggestible to changes in behavior and thought.
- Biofeedback has been used to teach people to control a wide variety of physiological responses.
- Studies have suggested that the regular practice of meditation is physically relaxing and can also lead to changes in behavior. Others argue that meditation is indistinguishable from regularly scheduled relaxation.

Section 3 Drugs and Consciousness

Main Idea: Psychoactive drugs interact with the central nervous system to alter consciousness.

- The effects of marijuana, a psychoactive drug, vary from person to person.
- Hallucinogens, whose main effect is to produce hallucinations, have been used for their effects on consciousness since earliest human history.
- LSD, a synthetic substance, is the most potent and most extensively studied hallucinogen.
- Alcohol is a depressant that serves to inhibit the brain's normal functions.
- Drug abusers are people who regularly use illegal drugs or excessively use legal drugs.

Chapter Vocabulary

consciousness (p. 183)
REM sleep (p. 186)
circadian rhythm (p. 186)
insomnia (p. 187)
sleep apnea (p. 187)
narcolepsy (p. 188)
nightmares (p. 188)
night terrors (p. 188)
sleepwalking (p. 188)
hypnosis (p. 191)
posthypnotic suggestion (p. 193)
biofeedback (p. 194)
meditation (p. 195)
psychoactive drugs (p. 197)
marijuana (p. 198)
hallucinations (p. 199)
hallucinogens (p. 200)
LSD (p. 200)

7 Summary and Vocabulary

Using the Chapter 7 Summary and Vocabulary

Use the Chapter 7 Summary and Vocabulary to preview, review, condense, or reteach the chapter.

Preview/Review

Use the Chapter Vocabulary list to help students review and study.

Activity Have students create flash cards with terms on one side and definitions on the other. Ask them to work in pairs with the flash cards to master the vocabulary terms.

Vocabulary PuzzleMaker CD-ROM reinforces the vocabulary terms used in Chapter 7.

Condense

Have students read the Chapter 7 Summary.

Chapter 7 Guided Reading Activities

Reteach

Reteaching Activity 7

PERFORMANCE ASSESSMENT ACTIVITY

Writing a Position Paper Explain that drug enforcement agencies have four tactics they can use to make a drug less available. Assign students to conduct research to find out about these tactics and which one(s) the government is currently using. Encourage students to investigate government sources, such as the Department of Justice and the Drug Enforcement Administration (DEA). Then have students write a 2- to 3-page paper stating their position on the following questions: **Which tactical plan is the government using? Should the government change drug enforcement plans or devote more effort and money to the current one?** Students should be able to support their positions.

PSYCHOLOGY Online

Have students visit the Web site at glencoe.com to review Chapter 7 and take the **Self-Check Quiz**.

GLENCOE TECHNOLOGY

PRESENTATION Plus!

For a review of Chapter 7 content, see MindJogger Checkpoint on **Presentation Plus!**

Reviewing Vocabulary

1. e
2. h
3. b
4. g
5. a
6. j
7. f
8. d
9. i
10. c

Recalling Facts

1. Adults spend about 25 percent of their time in REM sleep.
2. insomnia: ongoing problems with getting enough uninterrupted sleep; sleep apnea: a breathing problem that reduces the oxygen flow through the bloodstream and causes listlessness, sleepiness, and irritability; narcolepsy: a permanent and overwhelming feeling of fatigue and an inability to stay awake; nightmares: disturbance in REM sleep that causes the person to awaken with a vivid memory of the dream; sleepwalking: a partial awakening in which the person may perform daily activities without any memory of doing so; night terrors: sleep disruptions during Stage IV sleep involving screaming, panic, or confusion; sleep talking: harmless sleep disruption in which sleeper talks
3. Posthypnotic suggestion is a phenomenon in which the hypnotist suggests things that influence the participant's behavior after the trance is over.
4. Answers include reducing the effects of tension headaches, migraines, and asthma.
5. Alcohol is the most widely used and abused substance in the United States. The immediate effect of alcohol is the general loosening of inhibitions. It also impairs memory and judgment.

Critical Thinking

1. By breaking down the behavior into components, students will become more conscious of it. They will assess whether consciousness improves or hinders the action or the behavior being performed.
2. Freud believed that dreams contained clues to the unconscious mind and are full of hidden meanings. Kleitman theorized that dreaming did not have a specific purpose; it is simply a response to stimulation of brain cells during sleep. The problem-solving theory proposes that dreams allow people to review and address problems they faced during the day. Crick believes that dreams are the brain's way to unlearn or remove unneeded memories. Students' responses to the theory that they support will likely be based on their own experiences with dreams.
3. Students' answers will vary. Students who believe they are highly suggestible will believe they can be hypnotized. Those who prefer to always be in control will insist that hypnosis will not work on them.
4. Point out that some hallucinations are induced by fatigue or stress. Students' experiences and answers will vary.
5. Students' answers will vary. Many ads imply that drinking will make you the life of the party. While inhibitions may be lessened, you may also find that you are sleepy or extremely lethargic—hardly the energized partier often portrayed.

Psychology Projects

1. Answers will vary. Students' bar graphs may or may not follow the general patterns addressed in the text. As students hear the various presentations, ask them to make

CHAPTER 7 Assessment

PSYCHOLOGY Online

Self-Check Quiz
Visit the *Understanding Psychology* Web site at glencoe.com and click on **Chapter 7—Self-Check Quizzes** to prepare for the Chapter Test.

Reviewing Vocabulary

Choose the letter of the correct term or concept below to complete the sentence.

a. consciousness
b. insomnia
c. sleep apnea
d. narcolepsy
e. hypnosis
f. biofeedback
g. meditation
h. psychoactive drug
i. hallucinations
j. hallucinogens

1. __________ is a form of altered consciousness in which people become highly suggestible.
2. Marijuana is an example of a(n) __________, a drug that interacts with the central nervous system to alter a person's mood, perception, and behavior.
3. A prolonged and usually abnormal inability to obtain adequate sleep is called __________.
4. A person who focuses his or her attention on an image or thought with the goal of clearing the mind and producing relaxation is practicing __________.
5. A person's state of awareness is __________.
6. Substances such as LSD are called __________ because their main effect is to produce hallucinations.
7. A technique in which a person learns to control his or her internal physiological processes with the help of special machines is called __________.
8. A permanent and overwhelming feeling of sleepiness and fatigue is called __________.
9. __________ are perceptions that have no direct external cause.
10. __________ is a sleep disorder caused by a physical problem and results in frequent interruptions of breathing during sleep.

Recalling Facts

1. What percentage of sleep time do adults usually spend in REM sleep?
2. Using a chart similar to the one below, identify and describe six sleep disorders.

Sleep Disorder	Characteristics

3. Explain the phenomenon of posthypnotic suggestion.
4. List some health problems that biofeedback can potentially help.
5. What is the most widely used and abused mind-altering substance in the United States? How does it affect the user?

Critical Thinking

1. **Analyzing Concepts** Choose a behavior that you perform automatically and pay close attention to how you perform it. How does consciously thinking about the behavior affect your performance of it?
2. **Demonstrating Reasoned Judgment** Social scientists have varying ideas about the purpose and meaning of dreams. Review the various theories of social scientists presented in this chapter. Whose theory do you agree with the most? Why?
3. **Making Inferences** Do you think you could be hypnotized? Why or why not?
4. **Synthesizing Information** Have you ever hallucinated a sight or sound—perhaps when you were very tired or upset? What did you experience? Why do you suppose you created this particular hallucination?
5. **Making Comparisons** Look through magazines to find advertisements for alcoholic beverages. How do the ways that the advertisements portray drinking alcohol compare to the realities of drinking alcohol?

CHAPTER 7

Assessment

Psychology Projects

1. **Sleep and Dreams** Interview members of your family and friends to find out how many hours a night they sleep. Note their responses; then, as a class, record the results in a bar graph. What kinds of sleep patterns—in terms of age and gender—do you observe? Present your findings to the class in an oral report.
2. **Meditation** Meditation is an important part of some religions, such as Buddhism and Hinduism. Find out about the purpose of meditation in these religions and present your findings in a written report.
3. **Drugs and Consciousness** Research places in your community where a drug abuser can go for help. Locate the address, phone number, and the types of services offered in each place. Compile your findings in an informational pamphlet.
4. **Hypnosis** Contact a hypnotherapist and a stage hypnotist. Ask both: Is hypnosis an altered state of consciousness? What is the difference between a person's usual waking state and a hypnotic state? Do participants voluntarily agree to the hypnotist's suggestions? What applications of hypnosis do you recommend to people? Ask other questions to compare their views and uses of hypnosis. Report your findings to the class.

Technology Activity

Search the Internet to find out about various meditation techniques. Enter the term *meditation* to obtain a list of sites that actually provide techniques you can use to meditate. Try one or two of the techniques and report on their effectiveness to the class.

Psychology Journal

Many psychologists have theorized that by interpreting the content of our dreams, we can better understand our unconscious desires. Other social scientists have maintained a more commonplace view of dreams. Write a two-page essay in your journal that presents a case for both viewpoints. You may want to look for recent magazine articles on dreams. If possible, use a recent dream that you remember as an example to support one of the viewpoints.

Building Skills

Analyzing a Chart Review the chart below, then answer the questions that follow.

Percentage of 12th Graders Who Reported Ever Having Used Selected Drugs, 1994 to 2004

Year	Percentage Using Selected Drug			
	Marijuana	Cocaine	Alcohol	Cigarettes
1994	38.2	5.9	80.4	62.0
1995	41.7	6.0	80.7	64.2
1996	44.9	7.1	79.2	63.5
1997	49.6	8.7	81.7	65.4
1998	49.1	9.3	81.4	65.3
1999	49.7	9.8	80.0	64.6
2000	48.8	8.6	80.3	62.5
2001	49.0	8.2	79.7	61.0
2002	47.8	7.8	78.4	57.2
2003	46.1	7.7	76.6	53.7
2004	45.7	8.1	76.8	52.8

Source: University of Michigan, Survey Research Center, Institute for Social Research, Monitoring the Future Study, 1975–2004.

Practice and **assess** key social studies skills with **Glencoe Skillbuilder Interactive Workbook CD-ROM, Level 2.**

1. According to the table, which of the selected drugs are high school seniors most likely to use? Why do you think this is so?
2. In what year was marijuana use among high school seniors at its highest?
3. In what year was cocaine use among high school seniors at its lowest?
4. How did the percentage of seniors who smoked cigarettes change between 1994 and 2004? What factors might account for this?

See the Skills Handbook, page 628, for an explanation of interpreting charts.

Building Skills

1. alcohol; answers will vary
2. 1999
3. 1994
4. Cigarette use has gradually declined. The most likely factor is an increase in awareness campaigns focusing on the dangers of cigarettes. Also, an increase in positive peer pressure to abstain from cigarettes may play a part.

GLENCOE TECHNOLOGY

CD-ROM

Glencoe Skillbuilder Interactive Workbook, Level 2

This interactive CD-ROM is designed to reinforce student mastery of essential social studies skills.

Chapter Bonus Test Question

This question may be used for extra credit on the Chapter Assessment.

Answer the following question:

I am a low-level awareness that involves fantasizing or dreaming while you are awake. What am I?

Answer: daydreaming

generalizations about the sleep habits of their friends and family.

2. Answers will vary. Students will find the Internet useful in conducting the research. If possible, ask them to notice the differences among different sects of these religions.
3. Answers will vary. The pamphlet should be carefully proofread to make certain that all addresses and phone numbers are accurate. If possible, make the pamphlets available to students outside this class.
4. Work with students to help them identify appropriate people to contact. Students should prepare lists of questions prior to making the contact. Students should report answers to their questions by comparing the two views of hypnosis.

Technology Activity

Students can find a wealth of information about meditation on the Internet. Point out that anyone can post information to the Internet. However, that does not always make it accurate, wise, or useful.

Psychology Journal

Students' essays should present a well-reasoned case for both viewpoints. Evaluate students' ability to use examples, such as their own dreams, to create interest and support their reasoning.

Chapter 8 Resource Guide

SECTION RESOURCES

Daily Objectives	Reproducible Resources	Multimedia Resources
Section 1 **Sensation** Understand that sensations occur anytime a stimulus activates a receptor and that perceptions allow humans to react to their environment.	Guided Reading Activity 8–1 Vocabulary Activity 8–1 Section Quiz 8–1	Daily Focus Transparency 8–1 *ExamView® Assessment Suite* CD-ROM Presentation Plus! Software
Section 2 **The Senses** Describe how the sense organs are the receptors of sensations.	Guided Reading Activity 8–2 Vocabulary Activity 8–2 Section Quiz 8–2	Daily Focus Transparency 8–2 Vocabulary PuzzleMaker CD-ROM *ExamView® Assessment Suite* CD-ROM Presentation Plus! Software
Section 3 **Perception** Define perception as the way we interpret sensations and organize them into meaningful experiences.	Guided Reading Activity 8–3 Vocabulary Activity 8–3 Section Quiz 8–3	Daily Focus Transparency 8–3 Vocabulary PuzzleMaker CD-ROM *ExamView® Assessment Suite* CD-ROM Presentation Plus! Software

Blackline Master   CD-ROM   Transparency

Block Schedule

Activities that are particularly suited for use within the block-scheduling framework are identified throughout this chapter by the following designation: **BLOCK SCHEDULING**

KEY TO ABILITY LEVELS

Teaching strategies have been coded for varying learning styles and abilities.

- **L1 BASIC** activities for all students
- **L2 AVERAGE** activities for average to above-average students
- **L3 CHALLENGING** activities for above-average students
- **ELL ENGLISH LANGUAGE LEARNER** activities

Chapter 8 Resource Guide

Timesaving Tools

TeacherWorks™ All-In-One Planner and Resource Center

- **Interactive Teacher Edition** Access your Teacher Wraparound Edition and your classroom resources with a few easy clicks.
- **Interactive Lesson Planner** Planning has never been easier! Organize your week, month, semester, or year with all the lesson helps you need to make teaching creative, timely, and relevant.

Use Glencoe's **Presentation Plus!** multimedia teacher tool to easily present dynamic lessons that visually excite your students. Using Microsoft PowerPoint® you can customize the presentations to create your own personalized lessons.

Activity

From the Classroom of...

Parran H. Curry-Guy
North Education Center
Columbus, OH

Exploring the World of Senses

Goal
This activity can be used to help students use senses other than sight to experience the world around them.

Background
Students rarely consider how their experience of the world is affected by the coordination of their senses. When one of those senses is impaired, students can concentrate on what they experience through their other senses.

Activity
At the beginning of the study of sensation and perception, pair the students and have them take turns wearing a blindfold. The student who is not blindfolded leads the blindfolded student around the school building and grounds. The blindfolded student is directed to use the senses of hearing, smell, and touch to learn as much as possible about the building and grounds.

When all students have had the blindfold experience, they should discuss what they felt, what sounds they heard, and what smells they encountered. Students should also discuss how they felt about not having their sense of sight to guide them.

Psychology Online

Use our Web site for additional resources. All essential content is covered in the Student Edition.

You and your students can visit glencoe.com, the Web site companion to *Understanding Psychology.* This innovative integration of electronic and print media offers your students a wealth of opportunities. The student text directs students to the Web site for the following options:

- Chapter Overviews
- Student Web Activities
- Self-Check Quizzes

Answers are provided for you in the **Web Activity Lesson Plan**. Additional Web resources and Interactive Puzzles are also available.

Chapter 8 Resource Guide

Note: The following materials may be used when teaching Chapter 8. Section level support materials are shown at point of use in the margins of the Teacher Wraparound Edition.

TEACHING TRANSPARENCIES

Chapter 8
Concept Transparencies

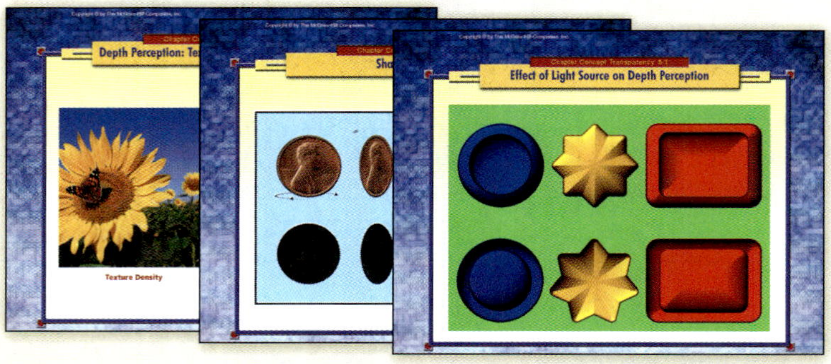

MULTIMEDIA

- **Vocabulary PuzzleMaker CD-ROM**
- ***ExamView® Assessment Suite* CD-ROM**
- **TeacherWorks™ CD-ROM**
- **Glencoe Skillbuilder Interactive Workbook, Level 2**
- **Presentation Plus! Software**

REVIEW AND REINFORCEMENT

Reteaching Activity 8

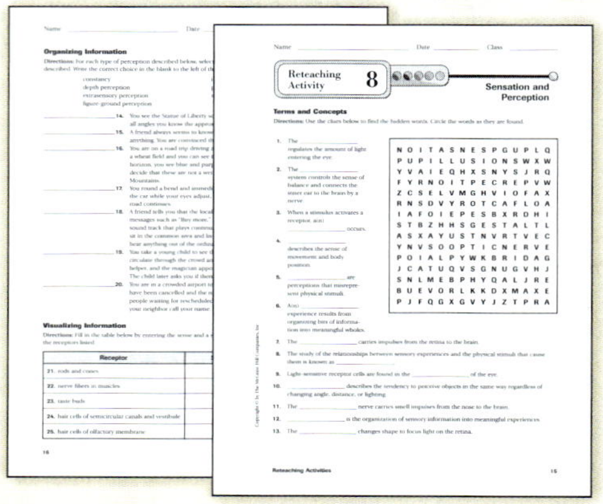

Graphic Organizer Activity 8

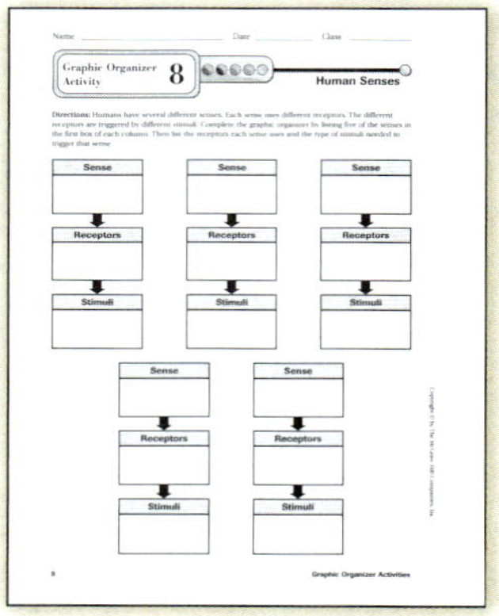

APPLICATION AND HANDS-ON

Psychology Project 8

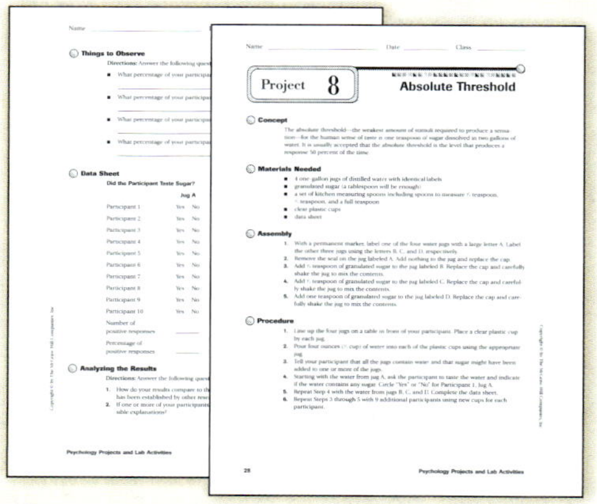

Application Activity 8

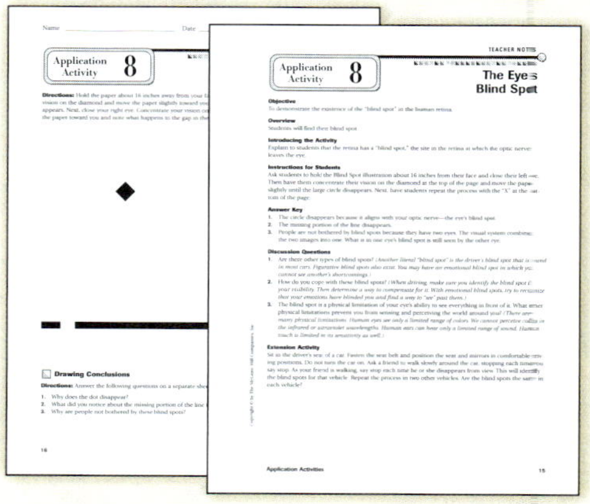

Chapter 8 Resource Guide

ASSESSMENT

GLENCOE'S ASSESSMENT ADVANTAGE

Chapter 8 Test, Form A

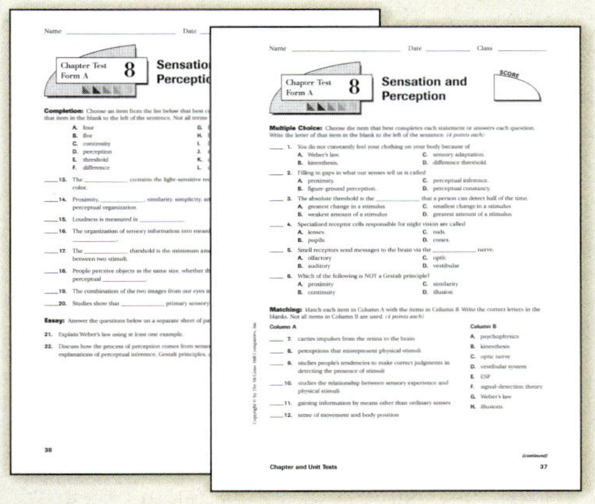
Chapter Test Form A 8 Sensation and Perception

Chapter 8 Test, Form B

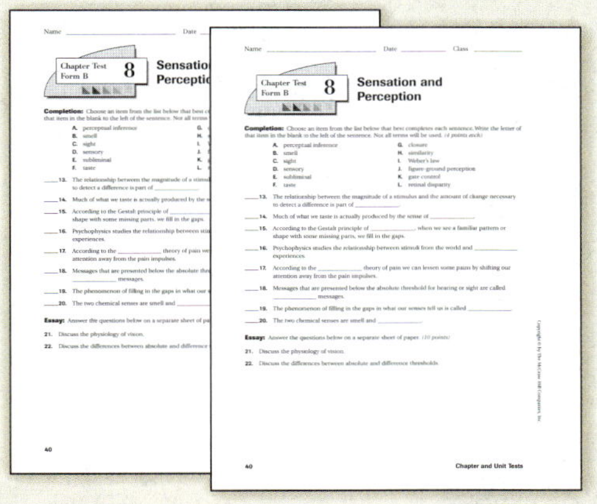
Chapter Test Form B 8 Sensation and Perception

Authentic Assessment Activity 8

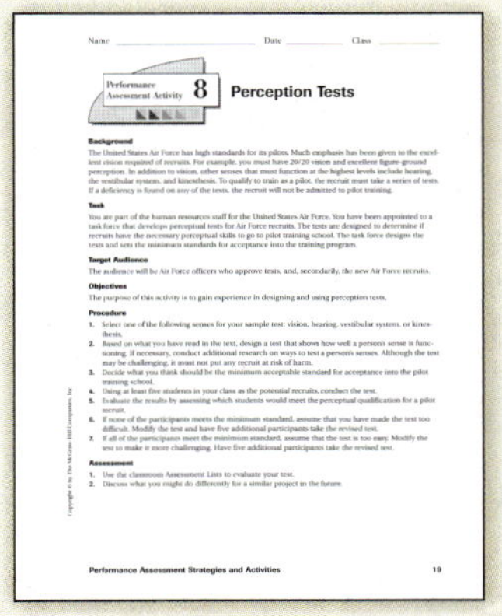
Performance Assessment Activity 8 Perception Tests

EXTENSION AND ENRICHMENT

Enrichment Activity 8

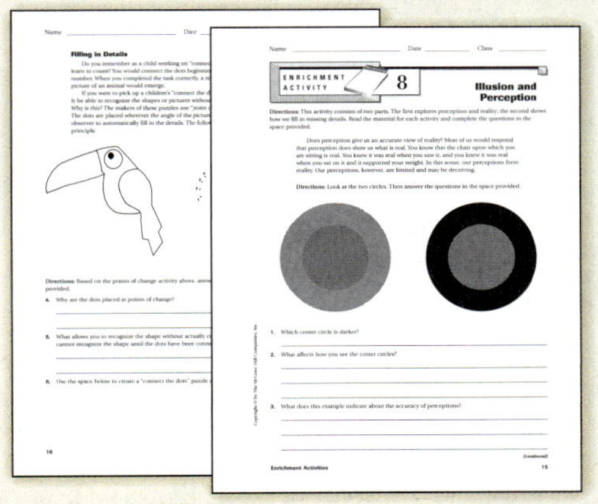
Enrichment Activity 8 Illusion and Perception

Critical Thinking Skills Activity 8

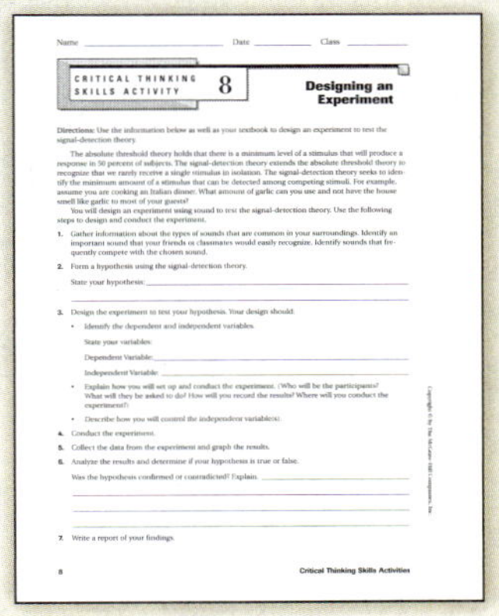
Critical Thinking Skills Activity 8 Designing an Experiment

Psychology Reading 8

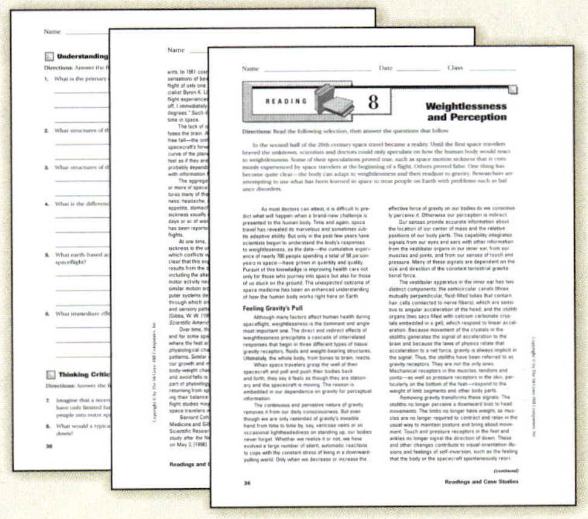
Reading 8 Weightlessness and Perception

Psychology Case Study 8

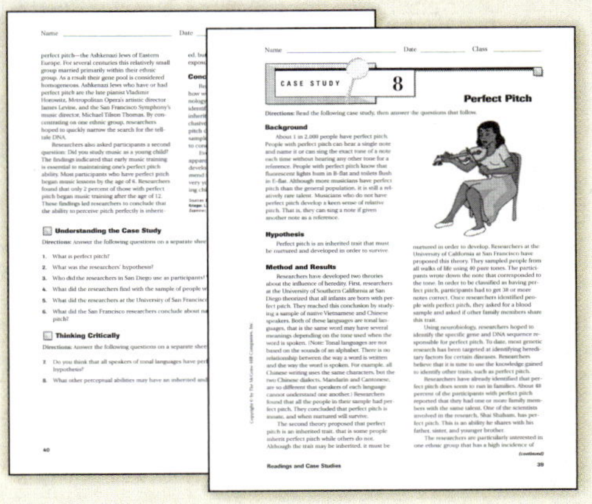
Case Study 8 Perfect Pitch

CHAPTER 8 *Introduction*

PSYCHOLOGY Online

Visit glencoe.com for a Chapter Overview for **Chapter 8—Sensation and Perception.**

GLENCOE TECHNOLOGY

Presentation Plus! For a preview of Chapter 8 content, see MindJogger Checkpoint on **Presentation Plus!**

PSYCHOLOGY JOURNAL

Ask students to consider what sounds are likely to catch their attention in a crowded, noisy environment. For example, would they be more likely to hear their own name, a name of a close friend or family member, or a scream for help? Have students write their observations in their journals.

This journal activity provides the basis for the Psychology Journal activity exercise in the Chapter Assessment. ■

CHAPTER 8

Sensation and Perception

PSYCHOLOGY Online

Chapter Overview
Visit the *Understanding Psychology* Web site at glencoe.com and click on **Chapter 8—Chapter Overviews** to preview the chapter.

PSYCHOLOGY JOURNAL

Were you ever in a crowded room and found yourself eavesdropping on another's conversation? In your journal, write down why you think this happened? ■

206

TWO-MINUTE LESSON LAUNCHER

Tell students that researchers have found that our experiences influence our perceptions. For example, people who live in urban environments that contain many angles and edges are more likely to be fooled by line-based optical illusions than people who live in rural, or open, spaces. Show students 2 or 3 photographs of people involved in various activities and settings. Ask students to write a short description of each scene. Then ask at least 5 volunteers to share their descriptions of each picture. Have the class compare the descriptions. Challenge students to explain how a group of people can look at the same picture and perceive it differently. Chapter 8 will help explain how people process sensory information.

SECTION 1 Sensation

Reader's Guide

Main Idea
Sensations occur anytime a stimulus activates a receptor. Perceptions allow humans to react to their environment.

Vocabulary
- sensation
- perception
- psychophysics
- absolute threshold
- difference threshold
- Weber's law
- signal-detection theory

Objectives
- Describe the field of study known as psychophysics.
- Define and discuss threshold, Weber's law, and signal detection.

EXPLORING PSYCHOLOGY

Discovering a New World

Helen Keller had been blind and deaf since she was two years old. For the next four years, Helen was "wild and unruly." Then when she was six, Anne Sullivan, a teacher, entered her life. Using the sense of touch as the link between their two worlds, Anne tried again and again, by spelling words into Helen's hand, to make Helen grasp the connection between words and the things they stood for. The breakthrough came one day as Anne spelled the word *water* into Helen's hand as water from a spout poured over it. "I stood still, my whole attention fixed upon the motions of her fingers," Helen remembered. "Suddenly I felt . . . a thrill of returning thought; and somehow the mystery of language was revealed to me."

—adapted from *ABC's of the Human Mind*, Reader's Digest, 1990

From that day forward, Helen "saw" the world in a new way. She discovered new ways to experience her world. "Occasionally, if I am very fortunate, I place my hand gently on a small tree and feel the happy quiver of a bird in full song." Helen had entered a world of sensations after she began organizing the stimuli in her world. Try it yourself.

In the next few seconds, something peculiar will start hap pening to the material youa rereading. Iti soft ennotre alized howcom plext hepro-ces sof rea ding is.

SECTION RESOURCES

Reproducible Masters
- Guided Reading Activity 8–1
- Vocabulary Activity 8–1
- Section Quiz 8–1

Transparencies
- Daily Focus Transparency 8–1

Multimedia
- *ExamView® Assessment Suite* CD-ROM
- Presentation Plus! Software

CHAPTER 8
Section 1, pages 207–213

1 FOCUS

Section Objectives
1. Describe the field of study known as psychophysics.
2. Define and discuss threshold, Weber's law, and signal detection.

BELLRINGER
Motivational Activity

Project Daily Focus Transparency 8–1 and have students answer the questions.

Available as blackline master

Daily Focus Transparency 8–1

Reader's Guide

Use the Reader's Guide to introduce concepts and vocabulary.

Exploring Psychology
Ask students to read the **Exploring Psychology** feature and then discuss: **What senses were unavailable to Helen Keller? How did she learn to compensate?**

Vocabulary Precheck
Have students read the Glossary definition of each term. Ask them to create flash cards with terms on one side and definitions on the other. Encourage students to work in pairs to master the terms.

2 TEACH

L1 Discussion Distribute copies of the following questions asked by James J. Gibson, one of the leading perception psychologists of the post–World War II era.

- Why do things look as they do?
- How do we see where we are in the environment?
- How do we see whether or not we are moving, and, if we are, where we are going?
- How do we see how to do things?

Organize the students into groups and tell them to imagine they are psychophysicists. **Ask: Based on information in the text, what tentative answers can you pose to each of these questions?** Have students share their findings with the class.
BLOCK SCHEDULING

Figure 8.1

Visual Instruction To reduce the effect of the illusion, have students cover half the illustration with their hand. The arcs remaining will not appear to spiral inward.

Caption Answer The combination of sensations and our past experiences result in a perception.

TEACHER Tip

To explain perception, divide the process of perception into its three basic components:
(1) translating a physical stimulus into the language of the nervous system (neural impulses);
(2) comprehending the basic components of the stimulus, such as shape, size, and color;
and (3) organizing the components into an understandable explanation.

As you can see, your success in gathering information from your environment, interpreting this information, and acting on it depends considerably on its being organized in ways you expect. In this chapter you will learn more about sensation and perception, both of which are necessary to gather and interpret information in our surroundings.

sensation: what occurs when a stimulus activates a receptor

perception: the organization of sensory information into meaningful experiences

psychophysics: the study of the relationships between sensory experiences and the physical stimuli that cause them

WHAT IS SENSATION?

The world is filled with physical changes—an alarm clock sounds; the flip of a switch fills a room with light; you stumble against a door; steam from a hot shower billows out into the bathroom, changing the temperature and clouding the mirror. Any aspect of or change in the environment to which an organism responds is called a *stimulus.* An alarm, an electric light, and an aching muscle are all stimuli for human beings.

A stimulus can be measured in many physical ways, including its size, duration, intensity, or wavelength. A **sensation** occurs anytime a stimulus activates one of your receptors. The sense organs detect physical changes in energy such as heat, light, sound, and physical pressure. The skin notes changes in heat and pressure, the eyes note changes in light, and the ears note changes in sound. Other sensory systems note the location and position of your body.

A sensation may be combined with other sensations and your past experience to yield a perception. A **perception** is the organization of sensory information into meaningful experiences (see Figure 8.1).

Figure 8.1 Fraser's Spiral

Fraser's spiral illustrates the difference between sensation and perception. Our perception of this figure is that of a spiral, but it is actually an illusion. Trace a circle carefully. Your finger will always come back to its starting point. ***How do we use sensation and perception together to understand our world?***

Psychologists are interested in the relationship between physical stimuli and sensory experiences. In vision, for example, the perception of color corresponds to the wavelength of the light, whereas brightness corresponds to the intensity of this stimulus.

What is the relationship between color and wavelength? How does changing a light's intensity affect your perception of its brightness? The psychological study of such questions is called **psychophysics.** The goal of psychophysics is to understand how stimuli from the world (such as frequency and intensity) affect the sensory experiences (such as pitch and loudness) produced by them.

THRESHOLD

In order to establish laws about how people sense the external world, psychologists first try to determine how much of a stimulus is necessary for a person to sense it at all. How much energy is required for someone to hear a sound or to see a light? How much of a scent must be in the room before one can smell it?

COOPERATIVE LEARNING ACTIVITY

Designing an Experiment Organize students into groups to test their own versions of the absolute thresholds listed in the text (page 209). Have each group select one of the senses and design an experiment to find an absolute threshold and to test the just noticeable difference for an increase or decrease in the intensity of a stimulus. The groups should state a hypothesis about the expected result. Then, they should conduct their experiment using the members of another group as the participants. The groups should analyze the results and state whether their findings validate the hypothesis. Encourage the groups to share their findings with the class.
BLOCK SCHEDULING

How much pressure must be applied to the skin before a person will feel it?

To answer such questions, a psychologist might set up the following experiment. First, a person (the participant) is placed in a dark room to dark-adapt. He is instructed to look at the wall and say "I see it" when he is able to detect a light. The psychologist then uses an extremely precise machine that can project a low-intensity beam of light against the wall.

The experimenter turns on the machine to its lowest light projection. The participant says nothing. The experimenter increases the light until finally the participant responds, "I see it." Then the experimenter begins another test in the opposite direction. He starts with a visible but faint light and decreases its intensity on each trial until the light seems to disappear. Many trials are completed and averaged. This procedure detects the **absolute threshold**—the weakest amount of a stimulus required to produce a sensation. The absolute threshold is the level of stimulus that is detected 50 percent of the time.

The absolute thresholds for the five senses in humans are the following: in vision—seeing a candle flame 30 miles away on a clear night; for hearing—hearing a watch ticking 20 feet away; for taste—tasting 1 teaspoon of sugar dissolved in 2 gallons of water; for smell—smelling 1 drop of perfume in a 3-room house; for touch—feeling a bee's wing falling a distance of 1 centimeter onto your cheek.

Profiles In Psychology

Gustav Theodor Fechner

1801–1887

"Imagine that you look at the sky through a tinted glass and pick out a cloud that is just noticeably different from the sky background. Now you use a much darker glass; the cloud does not vanish but is still just barely visible—because although the absolute levels of intensity are much lower through the darker glass, the ratio of intensities between cloud and sky has not changed."

Gustav Theodor Fechner started out as a young professor trying to demonstrate that every person, animal, and plant in the universe is composed of both matter and soul. He failed. At one point, in the midst of a depression, he painted his room black and remained in it day and night, seeing no one. When he finally emerged from his isolation, he walked through a garden, and the flowers looked brighter than he had ever seen them before.

On the morning of October 22, 1850, as Fechner lay in bed, a thought occurred to him. He arrived at the conclusion that a systemic relationship between bodily and mental experience could be demonstrated if a person were asked to report changes in sensations as a physical stimulus was varied. While testing these ideas, Fechner created the area of psychology known as psychophysics. Fechner's methods of sensory measurement inspired experimental research on the subject and revolutionized experimental psychology.

absolute threshold: the weakest amount of a stimulus that a person can detect half the time

Profiles In Psychology

Ask students to read the **Profiles In Psychology** feature and then discuss the following questions:

1. Why did the flowers look brighter after Fechner spent a long period in a room painted completely black? *(Fechner found that contrast in physical stimuli caused a variation in perception. The change, from an environment of near-total darkness to one of color, caused the colors to be perceived vividly, more so than when the observer's eyes were accustomed to light and color.)*
2. How did Fechner revolutionize experimental psychology? *(He used methods of sensory measurement to explain the way the mind perceives the outside world.)*

Guided Reading Activity 8-1

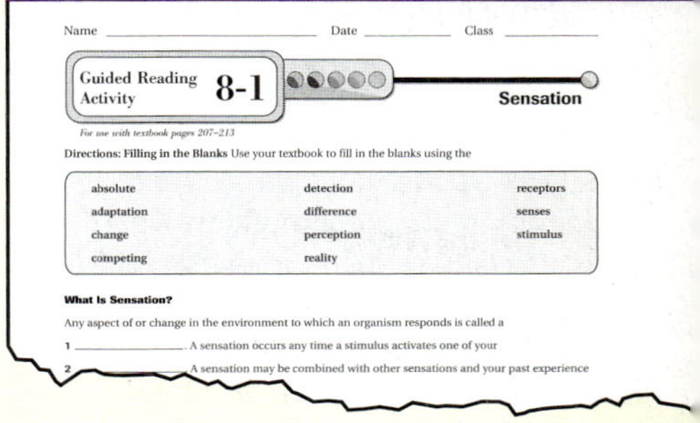

Name ______ Date ______ Class ______

Guided Reading Activity 8-1 — Sensation

Directions: Filling in the Blanks Use your textbook to fill in the blanks using the

absolute	detection	receptors
adaptation	difference	senses
change	perception	stimulus
competing	reality	

What Is Sensation?

Any aspect of or change in the environment to which an organism responds is called a

1. ______. A sensation occurs any time a stimulus activates one of your
2. ______. A sensation may be combined with other sensations and your past experience

MEETING SPECIAL NEEDS

Learning Style: Naturalist Tell students that the survival of many animals is dependent upon their senses. For example, deer have a heightened sense of smell that allows them to detect predators. Ask students to research the sensory skills of one of the following: hearing in dogs, dolphins, or bats; smell in lobsters, honeybees, or ants; or vision in predatory birds like hawks or owls. Ask students to write a one-page summary on how the animal uses the sense as a primary means of survival. **L2** **BLOCK SCHEDULING**

Refer to ***Inclusion for the High School Social Studies Classroom Strategies and Activities*** in the TCR for strategies for students with different learning styles.

Figure 8.2

Visual Instruction Have a class discussion about how the loss of each sense would limit a person's ability to perceive the world around him or her.

Caption Answer The vestibular sense, located in the inner ear, registers gravity and motion. It is our sense of balance.

Psychology Journal

Ask students to select one of the senses and write an essay about what life would be like without that sense. ■

Looking @ the Issues

Sensory Deprivation Tanks Sensory deprivation tanks, specifically flotation tanks, allow you to escape the constraints of gravity. Proponents claim that in the tank you can easily slip into altered states of consciousness. The release of endorphins into your bloodstream slows as sensory input diminishes. Roderick Borrie, Ph.D., recommends the flotation tank as the ideal way to recover from intense competition since stress is reduced, muscles are relaxed, and blood pressure and heart rate drop.

While short periods of sensory deprivation may be useful, long periods of deprivation decrease the brain's efficiency, may cause a partial loss of memory, lower IQ, and may result in hallucinations and personality changes. **Ask: Why are limited periods of deprivation useful? Why are long periods of deprivation harmful? Do you think that the effects of long-term deprivation can be reversed? Explain.**

Figure 8.2 The Human Senses

This chart lists the fundamental features that make up the human sensory system. ***What is our vestibular sense?***

Sense	Stimulus	Sense Organ	Receptor	Sensation
Sight	Light waves	Eye	Rods and cones of retina	Colors, patterns, textures, motion, depth in space
Hearing	Sound waves	Ear	Hair cells located in inner ear	Noises, tones
Skin sensations	External contact	Skin	Nerve endings in skin	Touch, pain, warmth, cold
Smell	Volatile substances	Nose	Hair cells of olfactory membrane	Odors (musky, flowery, burnt, minty)
Taste	Soluble substances	Tongue	Taste buds of tongue	Flavors (sweet, sour, salty, bitter)
Vestibular sense	Mechanical and gravitational forces	Inner ear	Hair cells of semicircular canals and vestibule	Spatial movement, gravitational pull
Kinesthesis	Body movement	Muscles, tendons, and joints	Nerve fibers in muscles, tendons, and joints	Movement and position of body parts

While these thresholds may seem impressive, we respond to very little of the sensory world. We cannot see X rays or microwaves. Dogs can hear a dog whistle, while we cannot. Humans hear only 20 percent of what a dolphin can hear. Some animals, such as bats and dolphins, have a superior sense of hearing. Other animals, such as hawks, have extremely sharp vision; still others, such as bloodhounds, possess a superior sense of smell. Humans sense a somewhat limited range of the physical phenomena in the everyday world.

SENSORY DIFFERENCES AND RATIOS

difference threshold: the smallest change in a physical stimulus that can be detected half the time

Another type of threshold is the **difference threshold.** The difference threshold refers to the minimum amount of difference a person can detect between two stimuli half the time. To return to our example of the person tested in a dark room, a psychologist would test for the difference threshold by gradually increasing the intensity of a visible light beam until the person says, "Yes, this is brighter than the light I just saw." With this technique, it is possible to identify the smallest increase in light intensity that is noticeable to the human eye.

A related concept is the *just noticeable difference,* or *JND.* This refers to the smallest increase or decrease in the intensity of a stimulus that a person is able to detect half the time. A particular sensory experience depends

CRITICAL THINKING ACTIVITY

Identifying Cause and Effect Tell students that *sensory deprivation* occurs whenever a person is denied use of one or more of his or her senses. Deprivation could be minor, such as when a person loses the sense of smell because of a cold. Or it could be serious, such as when someone is trapped in a cave or confined as a prisoner of war. Challenge students to brainstorm a list of situations that could qualify as sensory deprivation. Have them rank these from least serious to most serious. **Ask: What psychological effects could be caused by severe sensory deprivation? In the case of a prisoner of war, how might sensory deprivation further brainwashing? L2**

more on *changes* in the stimulus than on the absolute size or amount of the stimulus. For example, if you put a 3-pound package of food into an empty backpack, the perceived weight will be greatly increased. If you add the same amount to a backpack with a 100-pound weight in it, however, your perception of the weight will hardly increase at all. This is because the perception of the added weight reflects a proportional change, and 3 pounds does not provide much change in a 100-pound load.

This idea is known as **Weber's law:** the larger or stronger a stimulus, the larger the change required for a person to notice that anything has happened to it. By experimenting in this way with variations in sounds, temperatures, pressures, colors, tastes, and smells, psychologists are learning more about how each sense responds to change. Some senses produce huge increases in sensation in response to small increases in energy. For instance, the pain of an electric shock can be increased more than eight times by doubling the voltage. On the other hand, the intensity of a light must be increased many times to double its perceived brightness.

Some people are more sensitive to these changes than others. For example, people who can detect small differences in sensation work as food tasters, wine tasters, smell experts, perfume experts, and so on.

Quick Lab

Can you detect changes in stimuli?

What would it take for you to notice a difference in the weight of your backpack?

Procedure

1. Fill your backpack with materials so that it weighs 10 pounds, and put it on your back.
2. Assemble a collection of objects that weigh about 4 ounces (113 g) each, such as apples or oranges.
3. Ask a friend to insert the objects one at a time while you are seated, with the weight of your backpack off your back. Be sure you cannot see which object is being placed in the pack.

Analysis

1. After each object is placed in the pack, stand and report whether or not the backpack feels heavier.
2. Record the point at which you notice the difference in the weight of the pack.
3. Use the concept of difference threshold to explain your results.

See the Skills Handbook, page 622, for an explanation of designing an experiment.

SENSORY ADAPTATION

Psychologists have focused on people's responses to changes in stimuli because they have found that the senses are tuned to change. Senses are most responsive to increases and decreases, and to new events rather than to ongoing, unchanging stimulation. We are able to respond to changes in our environment because our senses have an ability to adapt, or adjust themselves, to a constant level of stimulation. They get used to a new level and respond only to deviations from it (see Figure 8.3).

A good example of this sensory adaptation is the increase in visual sensitivity that you experience after a short time in a darkened movie theater. At first you see only blackness, but after a while your eyes adapt to the new level, and you can see seats, faces, and so forth. Adaptation occurs for the other senses as well. Receptors in your skin adapt to the cold water when you go for a swim; disagreeable odors in a lab seem to disappear after a while; street noises cease to bother you after you have lived in a city for a time. Without sensory adaptation, you would feel the

Weber's law: the principle that for any change (Δs) in a stimulus to be detected, a constant proportion of that stimulus (s) must be added or subtracted

Reading Check According to Weber's law, how much must a strong stimulus change for a person to notice the change?

PSYCHOLOGY LAB EXPERIMENT

Signal-Detection Theory Choose a passage from a novel, textbook, or newspaper article. Then ask for six student volunteers. Ask the first participant to type the passage while given complete silence. Participants 2–6 will type the same passage while receiving one of the following distractions: someone humming, whistling, talking, laughing, and doing physical exercises. After all the participants have typed the passage, check the accuracy of their work. Tell students to compare the results. **Ask:** **How many mistakes did each participant make? Is there a connection between the number of mistakes and the level of distraction each participant received?** Ask students to summarize and relate their findings to signal-detection theory in a one-page report. **L2** **BLOCK SCHEDULING**

Quick Lab

Purpose Students will test difference thresholds and illustrate Weber's law.

Process Skills Understanding cause and effect, analyzing information

Teaching Strategies

- Review the procedures to be used.
- Recommend that students sit between trials so that a table supports the weight of their backpack. This will eliminate the bias that could be caused by the sound or shape of the items being placed in the backpack. Their friends should operate behind them, or the student should keep his or her eyes shut.

Analysis

1. Answers will vary. Students may have difficulty distinguishing when just a few lighter objects have been added. A difference in weight most likely will be noticed after several lighter objects are added.
2. Answers will vary. There may be more than one point at which the difference becomes noticeable, depending upon which items are placed in the pack.
3. Humans will notice a change in the total weight as it relates to the original weight of the backpack. Therefore, a 2-pound weight added to a 10-pound backpack will be more noticeable than an added weight of a 2-ounce piece of paper.

Reading Check Answer A strong stimulus will require a major increase or decrease to be noticeable.

Vocabulary Activity 8–1

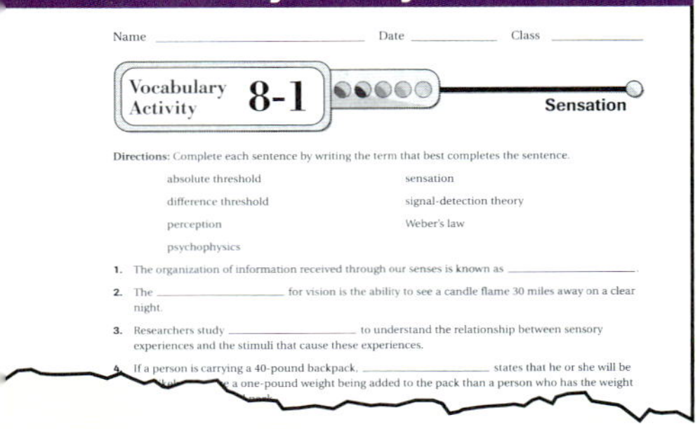
Name ______ Date ______ Class ______

Vocabulary Activity 8-1 — Sensation

Directions: Complete each sentence by writing the term that best completes the sentence.

absolute threshold · sensation · difference threshold · signal-detection theory · perception · Weber's law · psychophysics

1. The organization of information received through our senses is known as ______.
2. The ______ for vision is the ability to see a candle flame 30 miles away on a clear night.
3. Researchers study ______ to understand the relationship between sensory experiences and the stimuli that cause these experiences.
4. If a person is carrying a 40-pound backpack, ______ states that he or she will be

Figure 8.3

Visual Instruction Have students create a list of common sensory adaptations for each sense.

Caption Answer Sensory adaptation allows you to become accustomed to stimuli so that you do not feel constantly bombarded by the stimuli.

3 ASSESS

Assign Section 1 Assessment as homework or as an in-class activity.

Section Quiz 8–1

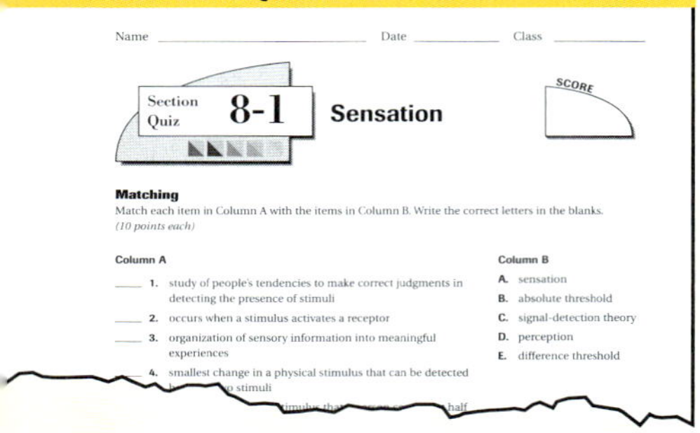
Name ______ Date ______ Class ______

Section Quiz 8-1 — Sensation

SCORE

Matching

Match each item in Column A with the items in Column B. Write the correct letters in the blanks. *(10 points each)*

Column A	Column B
____ 1. study of people's tendencies to make correct judgments in detecting the presence of stimuli	A. sensation
____ 2. occurs when a stimulus activates a receptor	B. absolute threshold
____ 3. organization of sensory information into meaningful experiences	C. signal-detection theory
____ 4. smallest change in a physical stimulus that can be detected	D. perception
	E. difference threshold

Reteach

Ask students to compare and contrast the just noticeable difference concept and the signal-detection theory. Ask students to explain the difference between a theory and a principle.

constant pressure of the clothes on your body, and other stimuli would seem to be bombarding all your senses at the same time.

Sensory adaptation allows us to notice differences in sensations and react to the challenges of different or changing stimuli. This principle is helpful when performing many activities, such as the work of police, security guards, and home inspectors. These people may notice minute changes and act appropriately.

SIGNAL-DETECTION THEORY

signal-detection theory: the study of people's tendencies to make correct judgments in detecting the presence of stimuli

There is no sharp boundary between stimuli that you can perceive and stimuli you cannot perceive. The **signal-detection theory** studies the relations between motivation, sensitivity, and decision making in detecting the presence or absence of a stimulus (Green & Swets, 1966). Detection thresholds involve recognizing some stimulus against a background of competing stimuli. A radar operator must be able to detect an airplane on a radar screen even when the plane's blip is faint and difficult to distinguish from blips caused by flocks of birds or bad weather, which can produce images that are like visual "noise." The radar operator's judgment will be influenced by many factors, and different operators appear to have different sensitivities to blips. Moreover, a specific individual's apparent sensitivity seems to fluctuate, depending on the situation. For example, a radar operator may be able to ignore other stimuli as long as she is motivated to keep focused, just as you may be motivated to complete your reading assignment no matter what distractions you encounter.

In studying the difficulties faced by radar operators, psychologists have reformulated the concept of absolute threshold to take into account the many factors that affect detection of minimal stimuli. As a result, signal-detection theory abandons the idea that there is a single true absolute threshold for a stimulus. Instead, it is based on the notion that the stimulus, here called a signal, must be detected in the presence of competing stimuli, which can interfere with detection of the signal.

Psychologists have identified two different types of processing stimuli, or signals. *Preattentive*

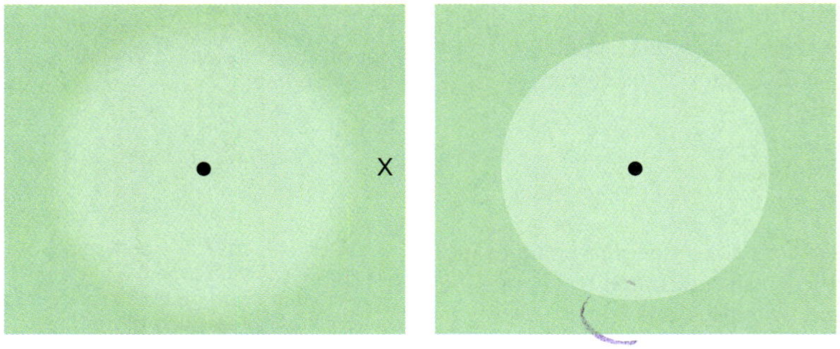

Figure 8.3 The Disappearing Circle

Sensation depends on change and contrast in the environment. Hold your hand over one eye and stare at the dot in the middle of the circle on the right. You should have no trouble maintaining the image of the circle. If you do the same with the circle on the left, however, the image will fade. The gradual change from light to dark does not provide enough contrast to keep the visual receptors in your eye firing at a steady rate. The circle reappears only if you close and reopen your eye or you shift your gaze to the X. **What is the purpose of sensory adaptation?**

INTERDISCIPLINARY CONNECTIONS ACTIVITY

The Media Tell students that psychologists usually apply Weber's law and sensory adaptation to one of the five senses, such as taste. **Ask:** **Do you think the same concept can be applied to the effects of the media upon behavior? For example, does the prevalence of violence on television make people less shocked by violence in general? Or does the use of disrespectful language make people less courteous in their day-to-day lives?** Assign students to find at least two magazine or newspaper articles on the subject and write summaries of the points made by the articles. **L2**

Figure 8.4 The Stroop Effect

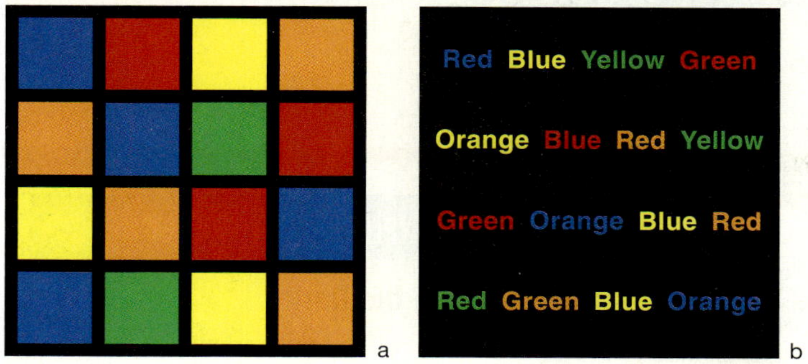

Try to name the colors of the boxes in *a* as fast as you can. Then try to read the words in *b* as fast as you can. Finally, try to name the colors of the words in *b* as fast as you can. You probably proceeded more slowly when naming the colors in *b*. ***Why was it more difficult to name the colors in b?***

process is a method for extracting information automatically and simultaneously when presented with stimuli. *Attentive process* is a procedure that considers only one part of the stimuli presented at a time. For example, when looking at Figure 8.4 *(b)*, the Stroop interference effect, preattentive, or automatic, processing acts as an interference. The tendency is to read the word instead of saying the color of the ink. Apparently people find it almost impossible not to read color names that appear before their eyes, because the name interferes with the response of naming the ink color when the two are different. In summary, we notice some things automatically in spite of distracting information. However, it requires more careful attention to notice other, less distinct items. This difference, though, is one of degree—all tasks require attention, but some require more attention than others.

SECTION 1 Assessment

1. **Review the Vocabulary** What is the difference between sensation and perception?
2. **Visualize the Main Idea** Complete the chart below by listing the five senses and their absolute thresholds.

Sense	Absolute Threshold
Sight	

3. **Recall Information** How does the signal-detection theory explain how you may be able to study while others are watching television in the same room?
4. **Think Critically** Why do you think we do not respond to all stimuli present in our environment?
5. **Application Activity** Place a watch or clock in an empty room. Move across the room to a point where you do not hear the ticking. Approach the clock one step at a time and mark the spot at which you first hear ticking. Repeat this experiment 10 times, alternately approaching and backing away. What are your conclusions? Write a brief analysis.

Figure 8.4

Visual Instruction Tell students that the Stroop effect illustrates how difficult it is to ignore some kinds of stimuli.

Caption Answer You were receiving two stimuli, the color and the word, which compete and slow you down when you try to name the color.

Enrich

Ask students to set up mini-experiments demonstrating Weber's law with various senses.

4 CLOSE

Discuss variations on the Stroop effect. **Ask: What would happen if you asked a four-year-old child who knew his colors but could not read to complete this activity? What if you tried this experiment with someone who did not speak English? What if you used noncolor words?**

SECTION 1 Assessment Answers

1. A sensation is the activation of a sensory receptor by a stimulus. A perception is the organization of sensation into meaningful experiences.
2. Sight: a candle flame from 30 miles away on a clear night; sound: a watch ticking 20 feet away; taste: 1 teaspoon of sugar dissolved in 2 gallons of water; smell: 1 drop of perfume in a 3-room house; and touch: a bee's wing falling 1 centimeter onto your cheek.
3. The signal-detection theory assumes that humans can choose what stimuli to attend to and block out other surrounding stimuli. Your motivations, sensitivity, and decision making affect your concentration.
4. Your body would be overloaded with stimuli if you tried to respond to them all. It would soon be unable to process more sensory information.
5. Students' answers will vary. Many will be able to hear the ticking from 20 feet or more if using a clock. If the background noise is kept constant, their results on the 10 trials should be similar. If the background noise changes, their results will likely be affected.

1 FOCUS

Section Objectives

1. Describe the nature and functioning of the sense organs.
2. Identify the skin and body senses and explain how they work.

BELLRINGER
Motivational Activity

Project Daily Focus Transparency 8–2 and have students answer the questions.

Available as blackline master

Daily Focus Transparency 8–2

Reader's Guide

Use the Reader's Guide to introduce concepts and vocabulary.

■ **Exploring Psychology**
Ask students to read the **Exploring Psychology** feature and then discuss the following question: **What is kinesthesis?**

■ **Vocabulary Precheck**
Have students read the Glossary definition of each vocabulary term. Then have them create a crossword puzzle using descriptions of the terms for the clues. Ask students to trade crossword puzzles and complete them.

Use the **Vocabulary PuzzleMaker Software** to create crossword and word search puzzles.

SECTION 2 The Senses

Reader's Guide

■ **Main Idea**
The sense organs—the eyes, ears, tongue, nose, skin, and others—are the receptors of sensations.

■ **Vocabulary**
- pupil
- lens
- retina
- optic nerve
- binocular fusion
- retinal disparity
- auditory nerve
- vestibular system
- olfactory nerve
- kinesthesis

■ **Objectives**
- Describe the nature and functioning of the sense organs.
- Identify the skin and body senses and explain how they work.

EXPLORING PSYCHOLOGY

Seeing in the Dark

Sit yourself in total darkness, a space so dark you cannot see your hand before your face. Now hold your hand before your face and move it from side to side. You see your hand in motion.

—from *A Second Way of Knowing: The Riddle of Human Perception* by Edmund Blair Bolles, 1991

Why did you see your hand moving even though it was totally dark while doing the experiment above? You have just experienced kinesthesis—one of the senses. Although people are thought to have five senses, there are actually more. In addition to vision, hearing, taste, smell, and touch, there are several skin senses and two internal senses: *vestibular* and *kinesthetic.*

Each type of sensory receptor takes some sort of external stimulus—light, chemical molecules, sound waves, and pressure—and converts it into a chemical-electrical message that can be transmitted by the nervous system and interpreted by the brain. So far, we know most about these processes in vision and hearing. The other senses have received less attention and are more mysterious in their functioning.

SECTION RESOURCES

Reproducible Masters
- Guided Reading Activity 8–2
- Vocabulary Activity 8–2
- Section Quiz 8–2

Transparencies
- Daily Focus Transparency 8–2

Multimedia
- Vocabulary PuzzleMaker CD-ROM
- *ExamView® Assessment Suite* CD-ROM
- Presentation Plus! Software

VISION

Vision is the most studied of all the senses, reflecting the high importance we place on our sense of sight. Vision provides us with a great deal of information about our environment and the objects in it—the sizes, shapes, and locations of things, and their textures, colors, and distances.

How does vision occur? Light enters the eye through the **pupil** (see Figure 8.5) and reaches the **lens,** a flexible structure that focuses light on the **retina.** The retina contains two types of light-sensitive receptor cells, or photoreceptors: *rods* and *cones.* These cells are responsible for changing light energy into neuronal impulses, which then travel along the **optic nerve** to the brain, where they are routed to the occipital lobe.

Cones require more light than rods before they begin to respond, and cones work best in daylight. Since rods are sensitive to much lower levels of light than cones, they are the basis for night vision. There are many more rods (75 to 150 million) than there are cones (6 to 7 million), but only cones are sensitive to color. Rods and cones can be compared to black-and-white and color film. Color film takes more light and thus works best in daylight, like our cones. Sensitive black-and-white film works not only in bright light but also in shadows, dim light, and other poor lighting conditions, just like our rods.

pupil: the opening in the iris that regulates the amount of light entering the eye

lens: a flexible, elastic, transparent structure in the eye that changes its shape to focus light on the retina

retina: the innermost coating of the back of the eye, containing the light-sensitive receptor cells

optic nerve: the nerve that carries impulses from the retina to the brain

Figure 8.5 The Human Eye

This cross section of the human eye shows the passage of light. Note that the retina receives an inverted image. ***What is the main function of the rods and cones?***

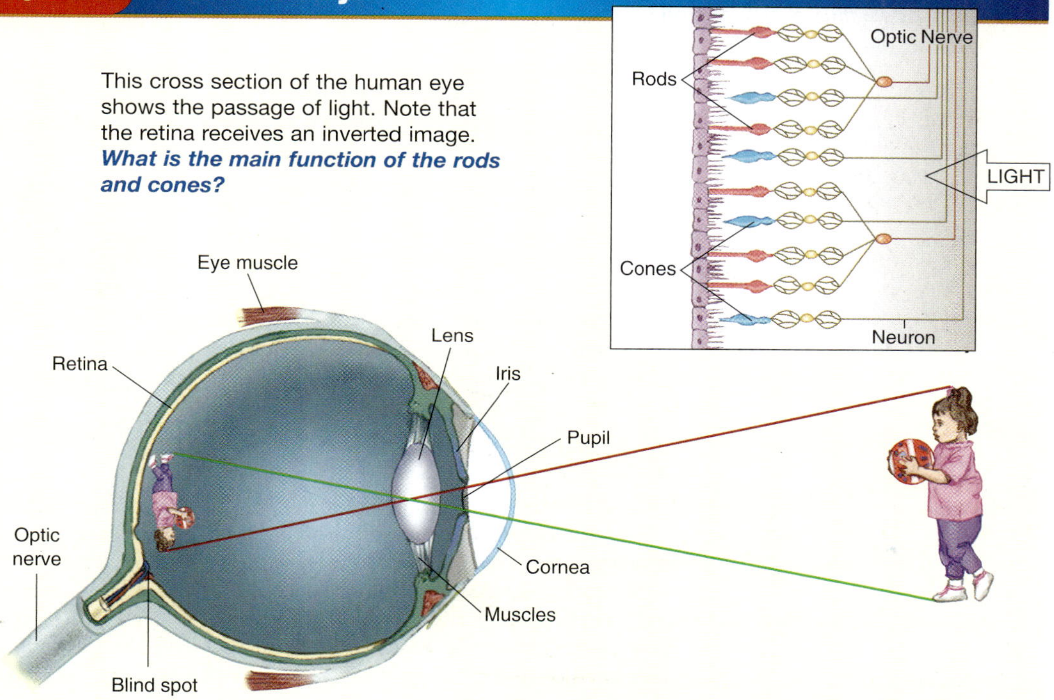

2 TEACH

L1 Demonstration To illustrate how rods and cones work, bring several pieces of brightly colored fabric or paper to class. Have students look at these materials in the normal classroom light. Then switch off the lights. **Ask: How has your sense of color diminished? What physiological factors account for this?** *(Cones need illumination to function. Rods are more sensitive to lower levels of light.)* ELL

Figure 8.5

Visual Instruction For you to see an object, such as a little girl with a ball, two things need to happen. First, your eyes gather and focus light into the retina. Then, the retina absorbs and transforms the light waves into impulses.

Caption Answer The rods and cones change light energy into chemical and neuronal impulses.

L1 Demonstration To illustrate one of the physical principles of color, you might repeat an experiment first conducted by Isaac Newton in 1704. Hold a prism up to sunlight and project a "rainbow" (spectrum) onto the classroom wall or a large white piece of paper. **Ask: Into what colors are the light rays refracted?** *(Newton devised the color wheel of primary and secondary colors: red, orange, yellow, green, blue, indigo, and violet.)*

COOPERATIVE LEARNING ACTIVITY

Building for Your Senses Tell students that some architects design buildings, parks, and memorials by considering the full range of sensory experience. Organize the class into small groups. Ask each group to select a public building or a place (for example, a park or monument). Have the groups visit the location and ask each group member to make a list of the sensory information he or she experiences. For example, what does the building look like, what does it feel like, what does it smell like, and what does it sound like? Have members of each group compare lists and create a summary of what sensory experiences the architect may have been attempting to convey. **BLOCK SCHEDULING**

PSYCHOLOGY and You

Use the following question to direct a class discussion after students have read the **Psychology and You** feature.

Ask: **In what other instances do people experience blind spots?**

Guided Reading Activity 8-2

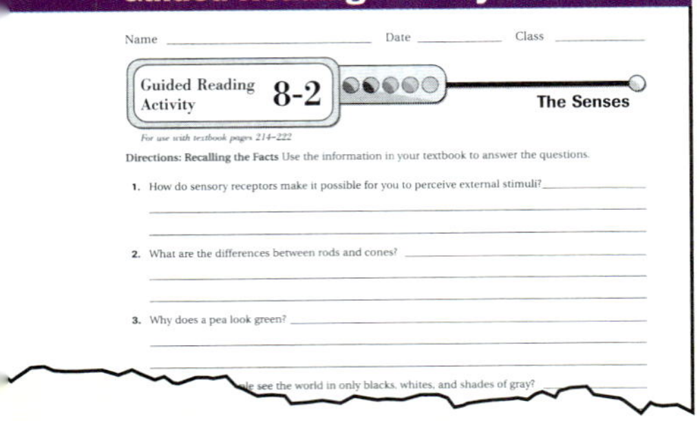
Name ______ Date ______ Class ______

Guided Reading Activity 8-2 — The Senses

For use with textbook pages 214–222

Directions: Recalling the Facts Use the information in your textbook to answer the questions.

1. How do sensory receptors make it possible for you to perceive external stimuli? ______
2. What are the differences between rods and cones? ______
3. Why does a pea look green? ______

...le see the world in only blacks, whites, and shades of gray? ______

CULTURAL CONNECTIONS

When the color preferences of college students in the United States, Kuwait, Iran, and Lebanon were studied, red and blue had the highest preference ranking for Americans only. Red and blue were the lowest-ranked color preferences in Kuwait. Green consistently ranked high among students from all four nations. Ask students to research other color preference studies among cultures and discuss their findings. Studies have been conducted comparing colors preferred by men and women, by religion, and by climate.

PSYCHOLOGY and You — Your Blind Spot

The point where the optic nerve exits the eye is the blind spot (see Figure 8.5). When light hits that point, the eye registers nothing because this area lacks photoreceptors—neurons that are sensitive to light. Find your blind spot by holding the diagram below about 3–4 inches (8–10 cm) away from your eyes.

Make sure the cross is on the right. Close your right eye and look directly at the cross with your left eye. Notice that you can also see the dot. Focus on the cross, but be aware of the dot as you slowly bring the diagram toward your face. The dot will disappear and then reappear as you bring the diagram toward your face. Now close your left eye and look directly at the dot with your right eye. This time the cross will disappear and reappear as you bring the diagram slowly toward your face. What has happened? When you hold the diagram so that the light from the dot falls on the blind spot, you cannot see the dot. This is your blind spot.

Light

Light is a form of electromagnetic radiation. Other forms of electromagnetic radiation include radio waves, microwaves, infrared radiation, ultraviolet rays, X rays, and gamma rays. All of these are known collectively as the electromagnetic spectrum (see Figure 8.6).

Visible light represents a small portion of the electromagnetic spectrum, which is composed of waves of different length and frequency. You can observe the wavelengths of visible light with a prism. Passing sunlight through a prism breaks the light into a rainbow of colors. Each of these colors is comprised of light of different wavelengths. While prisms transmit light, other objects absorb and reflect light. The object's color depends, in part, on the light that reaches our eyes. For example, a pea looks green because it reflects green light and absorbs other colors.

Color Deficiency

When some or all of a person's cones do not function properly, he or she is said to be color-deficient. There are several kinds of color deficiency, and most color-deficient people do see *some* colors (see Figure 8.7). For example, some people have trouble distinguishing between red and green. Fewer people have no trouble with red and green but cannot distinguish between yellow and blue. A very few people are totally color-deficient. They depend on their rods, so to them the world looks something like black-and-white television programs—nothing but blacks, whites, and shades of gray.

Color deficiency affects about 8 percent of American men and less than 1 percent of American women. It is a hereditary condition. This gene is carried in the genes of women whose vision is usually normal. These women pass the genes on to their sons, who are born color-deficient.

binocular fusion: the process of combining the images received from the two eyes into a single, fused image

retinal disparity: the differences between the images stimulating each eye

Binocular Fusion

Because we have two eyes, located about 2.5 inches (6.4 cm) apart, the visual system receives two images. Instead of seeing double, however, we see a single image—a composite of the views of two eyes. The combination of the two images into one is called **binocular fusion.**

Not only does the visual system receive two images but there is also a difference between the images on the retinas. This difference is called **retinal disparity.** You can easily observe retinal disparity by bringing an

MEETING SPECIAL NEEDS

Learning Style: Visual/Spatial Assign students to prepare one or more illustrations showing how one of the sense organs works. For example, students who select hearing should draw the structures of the human ear to show how sound is received and processed into nerve impulses. The illustration(s) should include a legend explaining the function of each part of the organ. **L1** **ELL** **BLOCK SCHEDULING**

Refer to ***Inclusion for the High School Social Studies Classroom Strategies and Activities*** in the TCR for strategies for students with different learning styles.

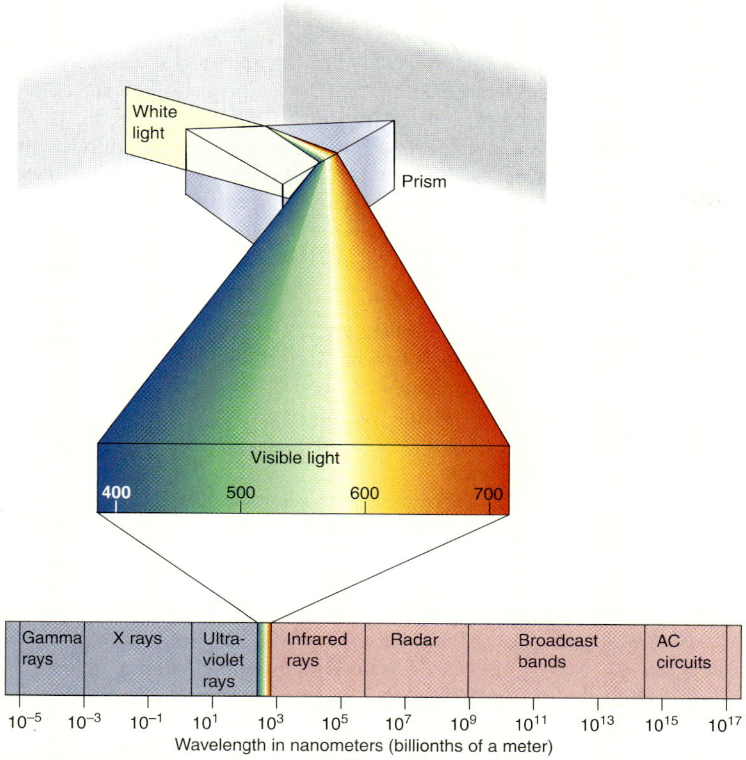

Figure 8.6 The Electromagnetic Spectrum

Light is the visible portion of the electromagnetic spectrum. When the wavelengths in white light are separated, the visual effect is an array of colors because different wavelengths are seen as different colors. ***Why are we able to see the wavelengths of the visible spectrum?***

object, such as an eraser, close to your eyes. Without moving it, look at the eraser first with one eye, then with the other. You will see a difference in the two images because of the different viewpoint each eye has. When you open both eyes, you will no longer see the difference but will instead see the object as solid and three-dimensional, if you have good binocular vision.

Retinal disparity is essential to your sense of depth perception. The brain interprets a large retinal disparity (a large difference between what the right eye and what the left eye are seeing) to mean that an object is nearby. The brain interprets a small retinal disparity (not much difference between the images the left and right eyes receive) to mean a distant object.

PSYCHOLOGY Online

Student Web Activity
Visit the *Understanding Psychology* Web site at glencoe.com and click on **Chapter 8—Student Web Activities** for an activity on sensation and perception.

Figure 8.6

Visual Instruction Point out the wide ranges of the electromagnetic spectrum that we cannot see. Ask students how humans use other portions of the electromagnetic spectrum *(creating X rays to detect broken bones, microwaves to cook food, radio waves to broadcast radio and television).*

Caption Answer These are the only wavelengths of light waves that the human eye can see. (Only these wavelengths excite the receptors in the human eye.)

FYI

Total color deficiency is the inability to see colors. Everything appears in shades of gray. This rare condition is known as monochromatism. Partial color deficiency, known as dichromatism, is the inability to distinguish one of the primary colors, usually red or green.

PSYCHOLOGY Online

Links and instructional guidelines can be found in the **Web Activity Lesson Plan** at glencoe.com.

CRITICAL THINKING ACTIVITY

Predicting Outcomes Tell students they will research how long it takes a person's eyes to adapt to the dark. Ask them to predict a person's behavior in the time between walking into a darkened room and his or her eyes adapting to the dark. Have students perform a naturalistic observation to see how closely their predictions match human behavior. Tell students to go early to a movie theater and take a seat near the back. Have them observe closely the behavior of those who enter the theater late, after the house lights are turned off. Students should write a one-page report stating their prediction and explaining how the observations supported the prediction or caused the student to reevaluate his or her prediction. **L2**

Figure 8.7

Visual Instruction Point out that color-deficient people learn to distinguish objects by brightness. The test on this page includes dots carefully equated for brightness. Therefore, the only way to see the number is by color. (Limitations of printing and classroom lighting may affect perception of these numbers.)

Caption Answer Color deficiency occurs when some or all of a person's cones do not function properly.

Readings and Case Studies in Psychology

Have students read the Chapter 8 Case Study selection in *Readings and Case Studies in Psychology* and answer the questions that follow the case study.

Figure 8.8

Visual Instruction Point out that one reason psychologists study illusions to such a great extent is that they reveal the built-in expectations of the perceptual system, thereby explaining its capacities and its limitations.

Caption Answer The flag will appear larger because the brain interprets the same image as large when it is far away and small when it is close.

PSYCHOLOGY JOURNAL

Ask students to cover one eye with an eye patch or gauze tape and walk around in familiar surroundings. **Ask:** **What differences do you notice?** Have them write a few paragraphs about their experiences. ■

Figure 8.7 Testing for Color Deficiency

Can you see numerals in the dot patterns that make up this figure? Those with normal vision will see a number, while those with red-green deficiency will see only random patches of color. ***What is the cause of color deficiency?***

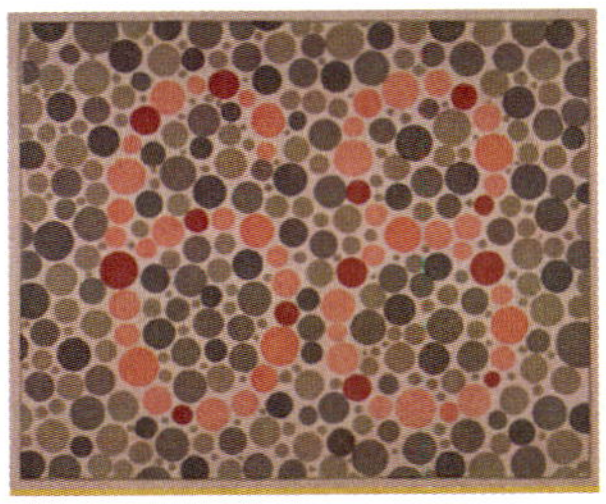

auditory nerve: the nerve that carries impulses from the inner ear to the brain, resulting in the perception of sound

Nearsightedness and Farsightedness Some of us are born with perfectly shaped eyeballs. These people have almost perfect vision. If your eyeball is a little too long, however, you are nearsighted. Objects are focused at a point slightly in front of the retina, so you can see objects that are near but distant objects seem blurry. If your eyeball is too short, you are farsighted. Objects are focused at a point slightly behind the retina, so you can see distant objects clearly but near objects appear blurry. Eyeglasses and contact lenses alter the focus of objects.

HEARING

Hearing depends on vibrations of the air, called sound waves. Sound waves from the air pass through various bones (see Figure 8.10) until they reach the inner ear, which contains tiny hairlike cells that move back and forth (much like a field of wheat waving in the wind). These hair cells change sound vibrations into neuronal signals that travel through the **auditory nerve** to the brain.

Loudness of sound is determined by the amplitude, or height, of sound waves. The higher the amplitude, the louder the sound. This strength, or sound-pressure energy, is measured in *decibels*. The sounds humans hear range upward from 0 decibels, just below the softest sound the human ear can detect, to about 140 decibels, which is roughly as loud as a jet plane taking off. Any sound over 110 decibels can damage hearing as can persistent sounds as low as 80 decibels. Any sound that is painful when you first hear it *will* damage your hearing if you hear it often enough. Figure 8.9 lists the decibel levels of some common sounds.

Pitch depends on sound-wave frequency, or the rate of the vibration of the medium through which the sound wave is transmitted. Low frequencies produce deep bass sounds, and high frequencies produce shrill squeaks. If you hear a sound composed of a combination of different frequencies, you can hear the separate pitches even though they occur simultaneously. For example, if you strike two keys of a piano at the same time, your ear can detect two distinct pitches.

Figure 8.8 A Changing Flag

Stare steadily at the lowest right-hand star for about 45 seconds. Then stare at the blank space to the left. You should see a negative afterimage of this figure. This occurs because the receptors for green, black, and yellow become fatigued or neuronal firing rates shift, allowing the complementary colors of each to predominate when you stare at the white paper. ***What happens when you shift your glance to a blank wall some distance away? Why?***

PSYCHOLOGY LAB EXPERIMENT

Location of Rods and Cones The outer part of the retina is covered exclusively by rods (no cones). To illustrate this, organize students into experimenters and participants. Give the experimenters red, blue, yellow, and green pencils. Tell participants to stare straight ahead at some fixed spot without moving their eyes. Then have experimenters stand behind the participants and move each pencil from the back toward the front of the participant's head. Have each participant say when he or she sees the pencil and when he or she can identify the color. Instruct experimenters to record the results for each color pencil. *(Students will see the pencil before the color. Also, because blue and yellow cones extend farther in the periphery, students should see these colors sooner.)* **L1** **ELL**

Sources of sounds can be located when your ears work together. When a noise occurs on your right, for example, the sound wave comes to both ears, but it reaches your right ear a fraction of a second before it reaches the left. It is also slightly louder in the right ear. These differences tell you from which direction it is coming.

The Pathway of Sound

The ear is designed to capture sound waves (see Figure 8.10). The outer ear receives sound waves, and the earflap directs the sounds down a short tube called the auditory canal. The vibration of air (the sound wave) causes air in the auditory canal to vibrate, which in turn causes the eardrum to vibrate.

The middle ear is an air-filled cavity. Its main structures are three tiny bones—the hammer, anvil, and stirrup. These bones are linked to the eardrum at one end and to the cochlea at the other end. When sound waves cause the eardrum to vibrate, these bones vibrate and push against the cochlea.

The cochlea makes up the inner ear. The cochlea is a bony tube that contains fluids and neurons. The pressure against the cochlea makes the liquid inside the cochlea move. Tiny hairs inside the cochlea pick up the motion. These hairs are attached to sensory cells. The sensory cells turn the sound vibrations into neuronal impulses. The auditory nerve carries these impulses to the brain. This neuronal input goes to the hearing areas of the cerebral cortex of the brain.

Deafness

There are two types of deafness. Conduction deafness occurs when anything hinders physical motion through the outer or middle ear or when the bones of the middle ear become rigid and cannot carry sounds inward. People with conduction deafness can usually be helped with a conventional hearing aid. A hearing aid picks up sound waves, changes them into magnified vibrations, and sends them to the inner ear. Sensorineural deafness occurs from damage to the cochlea, the hair cells, or the auditory neurons. People with complete sensorineural deafness cannot be helped with a conventional hearing aid, but may be helped with a special hearing aid called a cochlear implant. A cochlear implant is a miniature electronic device that is surgically implanted into the cochlea. The device changes sound waves into electrical signals. These signals are fed into the auditory nerve, which carries them to the brain. The brain then processes the sensory input.

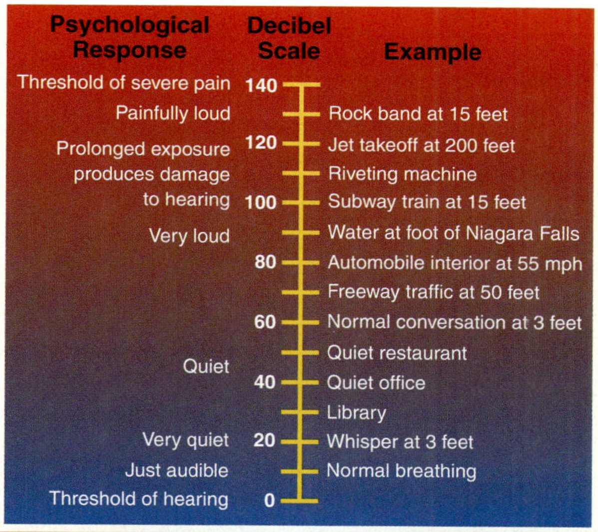

Figure 8.9 Decibel Levels

The loudness of a sound (its amplitude) is measured in decibels. Each increase of 10 decibels makes a sound 10 times louder. A normal conversation at 3 feet measures about 60 decibels, which is 10,000 times louder than a whisper of 20 decibels. Sound becomes painful at 130 decibels. ***What is the measurement in decibels of a subway train?***

Reading Check How does sound occur?

CHAPTER 8
Section 2, pages 214–222

Figure 8.9

Visual Instruction Tell students that about 20 million Americans are exposed every day to environmental noises loud enough to cause permanent hearing damage.

Caption Answer A subway train is measured at 100 decibels when it is 15 feet away.

PSYCHOLOGY Update

Sensory Dysfunction Recent studies suggest that many autistic children and adults have sensory dysfunction in one or more of their sensory systems including the hearing, vision, tactile, vestibular, or proprioceptive (internal) systems. Autistic children are often over- or underresponsive to sensory input. Specific treatment addressed to their sensory dysfunction can vastly improve their quality of life. For one autistic boy, three weeks of visual training reduced his retinal disparity and improved his eye-hand coordination.

Reading Check Answer
Sound occurs when vibrations in the air reach the hairlike cells in the inner ear, where the vibrations are turned into neuronal signals. These signals are carried to the brain by the auditory nerve, where the sensation is interpreted.

INTERDISCIPLINARY CONNECTIONS ACTIVITY

The Media Tell students that some filmmakers have attempted to create a sense of depth by filming scenes with two cameras, each taking pictures intended for a different eye. When these images are projected onto a screen, people see double unless they wear special 3-D (three-dimensional) glasses. These glasses allow each eye to view the image that was intended for it. Assign students to research the history of 3-D photography and movies or to explore how virtual reality uses 3-D concepts. **L2**

CHAPTER 8

Section 2, pages 214–222

Vocabulary Activity 8–2

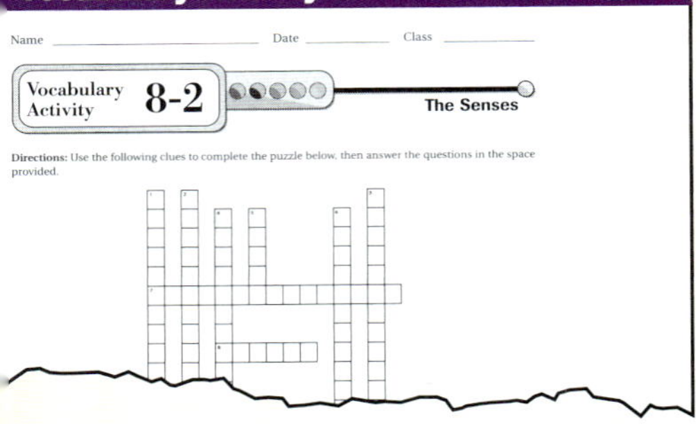
Name ______ Date ______ Class ______

Vocabulary Activity 8-2 The Senses

Directions: Use the following clues to complete the puzzle below, then answer the questions in the space provided.

Figure 8.10

Visual Instruction Discuss ways to include a hearing-impaired friend in students' daily activities. Suggest the following:

- Make sure you have your friend's attention before speaking.
- Maintain good eye contact with your friend when speaking.
- Speak and enunciate clearly.
- Use your normal speaking voice; do not shout.
- Ask for frequent feedback to make sure you are being understood.

Caption Answer The cochlea makes up the inner ear, where sound waves get translated into nerve impulses.

3 ASSESS

Assign Section 2 Assessment as homework or as an in-class activity.

BALANCE

vestibular system: three semicircular canals that provide the sense of balance, located in the inner ear and connected to the brain by a nerve

The body's sense of balance is regulated by the **vestibular system** inside the inner ear. Its prominent feature is the three *semicircular canals.* Hair cells project into the fluid within each of the canals. When you turn your head, these canals also move. Inertia causes the fluid in the canals to resist changes in motion, which bends receptor hair cells projecting into the fluid.

The stimuli for vestibular responses include movements such as spinning, falling, and tilting the body or head. Overstimulation of the vestibular sense by such movements can result in dizziness and motion sickness, as you probably have experienced by going on amusement-park rides. Although you are seldom directly aware of your sense of balance, in its absence you would be unable to stand or walk without stumbling or falling.

SMELL AND TASTE

olfactory nerve: the nerve that carries smell impulses from the nose to the brain

Smell and taste are known as the chemical senses because their receptors are sensitive to chemical molecules rather than to light energy or sound waves. For you to smell something, the appropriate gaseous molecules must come into contact with the smell receptors in your nose. These molecules enter your nose in vapors that reach a special membrane in the upper part of the nasal passages on which the smell receptors are located. These receptors send messages about smells through the **olfactory nerve** to the brain. For you to taste something, appropriate liquid chemicals must stimulate receptors in the taste buds on your tongue. Taste information is relayed to the brain along with data about the texture and temperature of the substance in your mouth (see Figure 8.11).

Studies show that four primary sensory experiences—sour, salty, bitter, and sweet—make up taste (Beebe-Center, 1949). The combining of taste, smell, and tactile sensations is known as *flavor.* Research suggests that a person can detect flavors anywhere on the tongue, using the taste buds pictured in Figure 8.11. There are people

Figure 8.10 The Human Ear

The earflap funnels sound waves down the ear canal to the eardrum. The bones of the middle ear pick up the vibrations and transmit them to the inner ear. ***What is the function of the cochlea?***

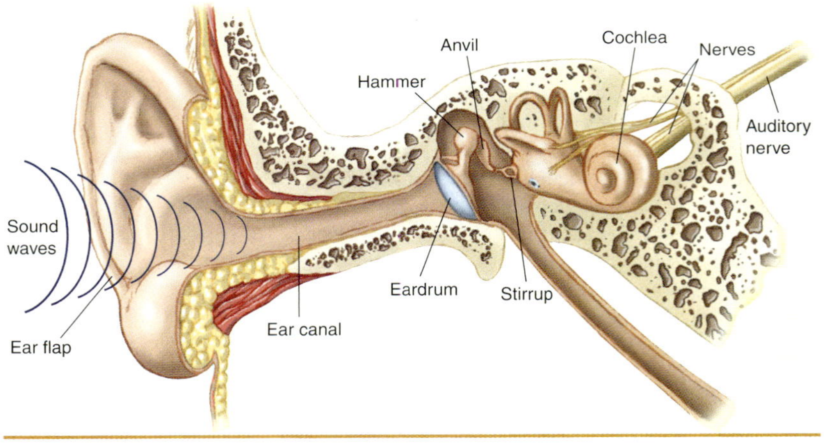

EXTENDING THE CONTENT

Environmental Psychologists Tell students that environmental psychologists focus on the relationships between people and their physical and social surroundings. They study such things as the effects of high-rise buildings on city dwellers. They also study the effects of noise pollution on human behavior. Environmental psychologists also consult with other specialists such as architects, urban planners, and sociologists. Encourage students to research the trends in environmental psychology.

who have greater taste sensitivities than others. So-called supertasters have two or more times the taste buds than nontasters, resulting in increased sensitivity to sweet, bitter, sour, and salty.

Much of what is referred to as taste is actually produced by the sense of smell. As people age, their sense of taste does not seem to decline. When older people complain that food does not taste as good as it once did, the reason usually is a loss of smell rather than a failing sense of taste (Bartoshuk, 1989). You have undoubtedly noticed that when your nose is blocked by a cold, foods usually taste bland.

Sensations of warmth, cold, and pressure also affect taste. Try to imagine eating cold chicken soup or drinking a hot soda. Now imagine the textural differences between a spoonful of pudding and a crunchy chocolate bar, and you will see how the texture and temperature of food influence taste.

The chemical senses seem to play a relatively unimportant role in human life when compared to their functions in lower animals. Insects, for example, often depend on smell to communicate with one another, especially in mating. In humans, smell and taste have become more a matter of pleasure rather than of survival.

THE SKIN SENSES

Receptors in the skin are responsible for providing the brain with at least four kinds of information about the environment: pressure, warmth, cold, and pain. Sensitivity to pressure varies from place to place in the skin. Some spots, such as your fingertips, are densely populated with receptors and are, therefore, highly sensitive. Other spots, such as the middle of your back or the back of your calf, contain relatively few receptors. Pressure sensations can serve as protection. For example, feeling the light pressure of an insect landing on your arm warns you of the danger of being stung.

Some skin receptors are particularly sensitive to hot or cold stimuli. To create a hot or cold sensation, a stimulus must have a temperature greater or less than the temperature of the skin in the sensing area. If you plunge your arm into a sink of warm water on a hot day, you will experience little or no sensation of its heat. If you put your arm in the same water on a cold day, however, the water will feel quite warm.

Many kinds of stimuli—scratches, punctures, pressure, heat, and cold—can produce pain. What they have in common is real or potential injury to bodily tissues. Pain makes it possible for you to prevent damage to your body; it is an emergency system that through your prior experience with pain demands immediate action.

Perceptions of Pain

Whereas other senses rely primarily on a single stimulus, pain results from many different stimuli. For example, pain can be caused by intense pressure, bright lights, loud noises, intense heat, and so on. There are two types of pain sensations—the sharp, localized pain you may feel immediately after an injury and the dull, generalized pain you may feel later.

Have you ever stubbed your toe and then rubbed it to reduce the pain? According to the *gate control theory of pain,* we can lessen some pains by shifting our attention away from the pain impulses or by sending other

Figure 8.11 The Human Tongue

When you chew, chemicals of the food mix with saliva and run down into trenches in your tongue. Once there, taste buds react to chemicals dissolved in saliva. ***How do the senses of taste and smell work together?***

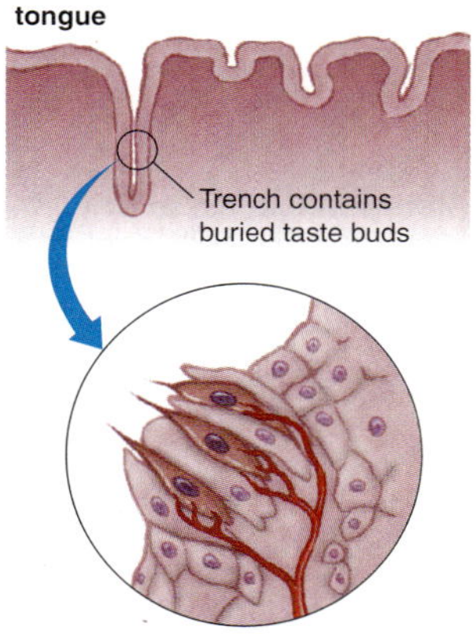

CHAPTER 8
Section 2, pages 214–222

Figure 8.11

Visual Instruction Tell students that on average people have about 9,000 taste buds on their tongues.

Caption Answer The receptors in your nasal passages and receptors in the taste buds work together to create the sensation we generally call taste.

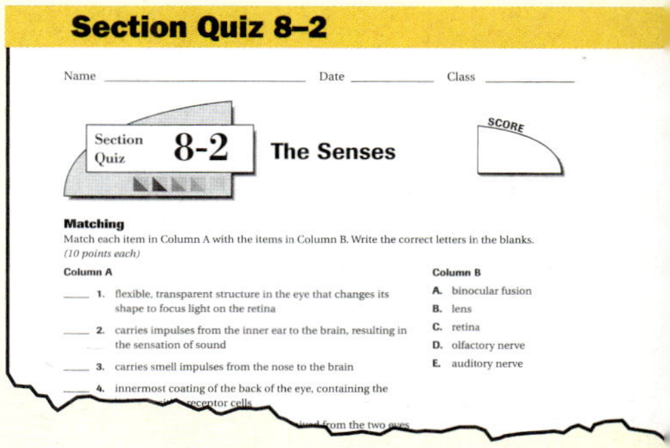
Section Quiz 8–2

Name ____ Date ____ Class ____

Section Quiz 8-2 The Senses

SCORE

Matching

Match each item in Column A with the items in Column B. Write the correct letters in the blanks. *(10 points each)*

Column A	Column B
____ 1. flexible, transparent structure in the eye that changes its shape to focus light on the retina	A. binocular fusion
____ 2. carries impulses from the inner ear to the brain, resulting in the sensation of sound	B. lens
____ 3. carries smell impulses from the nose to the brain	C. retina
____ 4. innermost coating of the back of the eye, containing the ... receptor cells	D. olfactory nerve
... from the two eyes	E. auditory nerve

Reteach

Have students create a table listing the senses, the organs responsible for the sensations, the stimuli to which each responds, and how the stimuli are translated into neural impulses.

EXTENDING THE CONTENT

The Senses of Smell and Taste Organize the class into groups of experimenters and participants. Have the participants blindfold themselves, while the experimenters give the participants something to taste, like a cookie, while holding a perfume-scented cloth or onion near the participants' noses. Ask the participants to describe the food's taste. After a few minutes, have the experimenters repeat the same taste test *without* holding anything up to the participants' noses. Have the participants again describe the food's taste. Compare the responses with the class as a whole. **Ask: Does this experiment prove or disprove the theory that much of what is referred to as taste is actually produced by the sense of smell? Explain. L1**

Psychology and You

Use the following question to direct a class discussion after students have read the **Psychology and You** feature.

Ask: **What other reactions between foods and drinks have you encountered?**

Enrich

Ask students to compare the ear and the eye. **Ask:** **Which structure in the ear is the optic nerve most like? To which structure in the eye can the cochlea be compared? Why?**

L1 Expressing Viewpoints

Recite these popular sayings to students:

- "Beauty is in the eye of the beholder."
- "Is your glass half empty or half full?"

Request volunteers to explain the meaning behind each of these sayings. *(Lead students to understand that both sayings emphasize that perception rests with the individual.)* Tell students that this chapter examines how and why we see the world as we do. It all starts with the senses. Tell students that in the next section you will discuss perception.

4 CLOSE

Now that students have studied the various sense organs, review the brain functions and to which areas of the brain the neuronal impulses for each sense are transmitted.

Psychology and You: Orange Juice and Toothpaste

Have you ever brushed your teeth and then had orange juice for breakfast? How did the orange juice taste? Usually the orange juice will taste bitter. Our taste buds have membranes that contain fatlike phospholipids, while toothpastes contain a detergent that breaks down fat and grease. So the toothpaste first assaults the membranes with its detergents, leaving them raw. Then chemicals in the toothpaste, such as formaldehyde, chalk, and saccharin, cause a sour taste when they mix with the citric and ascorbic acids of orange juice. Try eating artichokes, then drinking water. What does the water taste like?

signals to compete with the pain signals. This creates a sort of competition between nonpain and pain impulses. This bottleneck, or gate, limits the number of impulses that can be transmitted. Thus, by increasing nonpainful impulses (rubbing your toe), you decrease the pain impulses, and the sensation of pain is dulled.

The gate control theory of pain could explain how athletes are able to complete a game even though they have injured themselves. Although a soccer player may know that she has bruised her side, she may not feel the pain fully until the game is over and she has calmed down.

THE BODY SENSES

kinesthesis: the sense of movement and body position

The sense of movement and body position is **kinesthesis.** It cooperates with the vestibular and visual senses to maintain posture and balance. The sensation of kinesthesis comes from receptors in and near the muscles, tendons, and joints. When any movement occurs, these receptors immediately send messages to the brain. Without kinesthetic sensations, your movements would be jerky and uncoordinated. You could not walk without looking at your feet and complex physical activities, such as conducting surgery, piano playing, and acrobatics, would be impossible.

SECTION 2 Assessment

1. **Review the Vocabulary** What are the five basic senses? Describe two additional senses that humans have.
2. **Visualize the Main Idea** Use a flowchart similar to the one below to describe the pathway of sound.

The Pathway of Sound

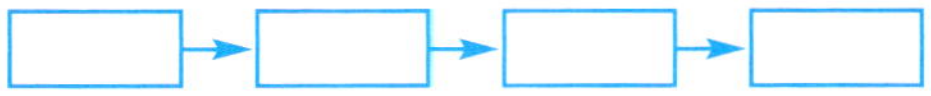

3. **Recall Information** What is the electromagnetic spectrum and why do we see only a portion of it?
4. **Think Critically** Why can we see steadily and read street signs even though we may be walking or running?
5. **Application Activity** Take a friend to a brightly lit area and then to a dimly lit area and notice how the size of his or her pupils change. How can you explain this?

SECTION 2 Assessment Answers

1. vision, hearing, taste, smell, and touch; the sense of balance (vestibular system) and sense of movement and body position (kinesthesis)
2. Outer ear receives sound waves. Earflap directs the sound down the auditory canal to the eardrum. The eardrum's vibration causes the bones in the middle ear to vibrate, pushing them against the cochlea. The hairs inside the cochlea have sensory cells that turn sound vibrations into neural impulses. The auditory nerve sends the impulses to the cerebral cortex of the brain.
3. The electromagnetic spectrum includes radio waves, microwaves, light, infrared radiation, ultraviolet rays, X rays, and gamma rays. The receptors in our eyes allow us to see only certain wavelengths.
4. The vestibular system regulates the body's sense of balance. The fluid in the semicircular canals moves as our bodies move, which allows our eyes to stay focused and keeps us from getting dizzy.
5. The pupil adjusts to let more or less light focus on the retina.

SECTION 3 # Perception

Reader's Guide

Main Idea

The way we interpret sensations and organize them into meaningful experiences is called perception.

Vocabulary

- Gestalt
- subliminal messages
- motion parallax
- constancy
- illusions
- extrasensory perception (ESP)

Objectives

- Outline the principles involved in perception.
- Describe how we learn to perceive and what illusions are.

EXPLORING PSYCHOLOGY

Trying to Catch a Fly

The frog's bug detector shows the rigidity of reflexive behavior. If you sever the frog's optic nerve, it will grow back together, and the bug detector will still work fine. If you sever the optic nerve and then rotate the frog's eye 180 degrees, the nerve will still heal and reestablish all the old connections; however, this time the results will not be so good. The bug detector does not know that everything has been rotated, so it miscomputes a bug's location. If the bug is high, the frog shoots its tongue low. If the bug is to the right, the tongue goes to the left. The frog never learns to compensate for the changed situation.

—from *A Second Way of Knowing: The Riddle of Human Perception* by Edmund Blair Bolles, 1991

The purpose of the excerpt above is to demonstrate to you how useful your powers of perception are. Perception goes beyond reflexive behavior and allows us to confront changes in our environment. Perceptual thinking is essential for us to adapt to change.

People do not usually experience a mass of colors, noises, temperatures, and pressures. Rather, we see cars and buildings, hear voices and music, and feel pencils, desks, and physical contact. We do not merely have sensory experiences; we perceive objects. The brain receives information from the senses and organizes and interprets it into meaningful experiences—unconsciously. This process is called perception.

SECTION RESOURCES

Reproducible Masters

- Guided Reading Activity 8–3
- Vocabulary Activity 8–3
- Section Quiz 8–3

Transparencies

- Daily Focus Transparency 8–3

Multimedia

- *ExamView® Assessment Suite* CD-ROM
- Presentation Plus! Software

1 FOCUS

Section Objectives

1. Outline the principles involved in perception.
2. Describe how we learn to perceive and what illusions are.

BELLRINGER
Motivational Activity

Project Daily Focus Transparency 8–3 and have students answer the questions.

Available as blackline master

Daily Focus Transparency 8–3

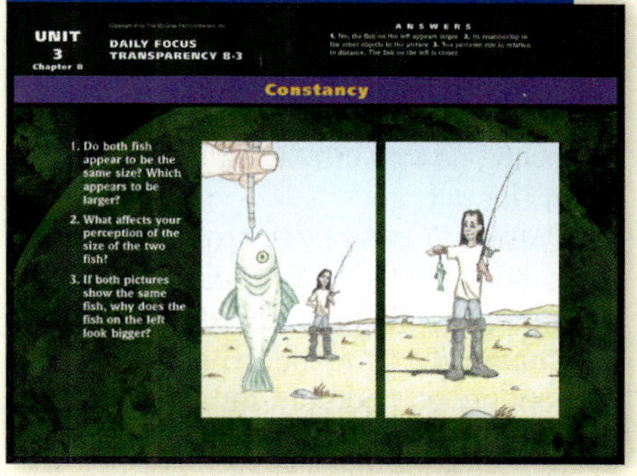

Reader's Guide

Use the Reader's Guide to introduce concepts and vocabulary.

Exploring Psychology
Ask students to read the **Exploring Psychology** feature and then discuss: **Where does perception occur: in the sensory organ, in the nerve, or in the brain?**

Vocabulary Precheck
Have students read the Glossary definition of each vocabulary term. Then ask them to scramble the words and provide a written clue. Ask pairs of students to trade lists and unscramble the words using the clues provided.

2 TEACH

L1 Discussion Encourage students to ponder the distinction between sensation and perception. **Ask:** **When a tree falls in the forest and no one is around to hear it, does it make a sound?** *(From a scientific point of view, the correct answer is no. Frequency [a physical event] influences pitch [an experience]. Likewise, amplitude influences loudness, and sound wave complexity influences timbre. The physical event occurs, but the psychological experience cannot occur if there is no experiencing organism present.)*

Figure 8.12

Visual Instruction Read aloud the following definitions of the five principles of Gestalt:

Closure: Tendency to group according to enclosed or completed figures rather than open or incomplete parts.
Continuity: Tendency to see smooth, continuous contours rather than discrete, disrupted shapes.
Proximity: Tendency to group together those elements that are close to each other.
Similarity: Tendency to group together those elements that are similar in appearance.
Simplicity: Tendency to perceive a pattern in the simplest, most organized manner—the foundation of Gestalt psychology.

Caption Answer We use them to help us group our sensations and fill in the gaps to make sense of the world.

PRINCIPLES OF PERCEPTUAL ORGANIZATION

Gestalt: the experience that comes from organizing bits and pieces of information into meaningful wholes

Through the process of perception, the brain is always trying to comprehend the confusion of stimuli that bombard the senses. The brain makes sense of the world by creating whole structures out of bits and pieces of information in the environment. Each whole that is organized by the brain is called a **Gestalt.** Here, the whole is more than the sum of the parts. (*Gestalt* is a German word meaning "pattern" or "configuration.")

Gestalt psychologists have tried to identify the principles the brain uses in constructing perceptions (Koffka, 1963). Some of the principles they have discovered are demonstrated in Figure 8.12. For example, people tend to see dots in patterns and groups. Principles that people use in organizing such patterns are *proximity, continuity, similarity, simplicity,* and *closure.* If the elements of the pattern are close to one another or are similar in appearance, they tend to be perceived as belonging to one another.

The Gestalt principles of organization help explain how we group our sensations and fill in gaps to make sense of our world. In music, for instance, you tend to group notes on the basis of their closeness, or proximity, to one another in time—you hear melodies, not single notes. Similarity and continuity are also important. They allow you to follow the

Figure 8.12 Gestalt Principles

Humans see patterns and groupings in their environment rather than disorganized arrays of bits and pieces. ***Why do we use the principles of organization illustrated here?***

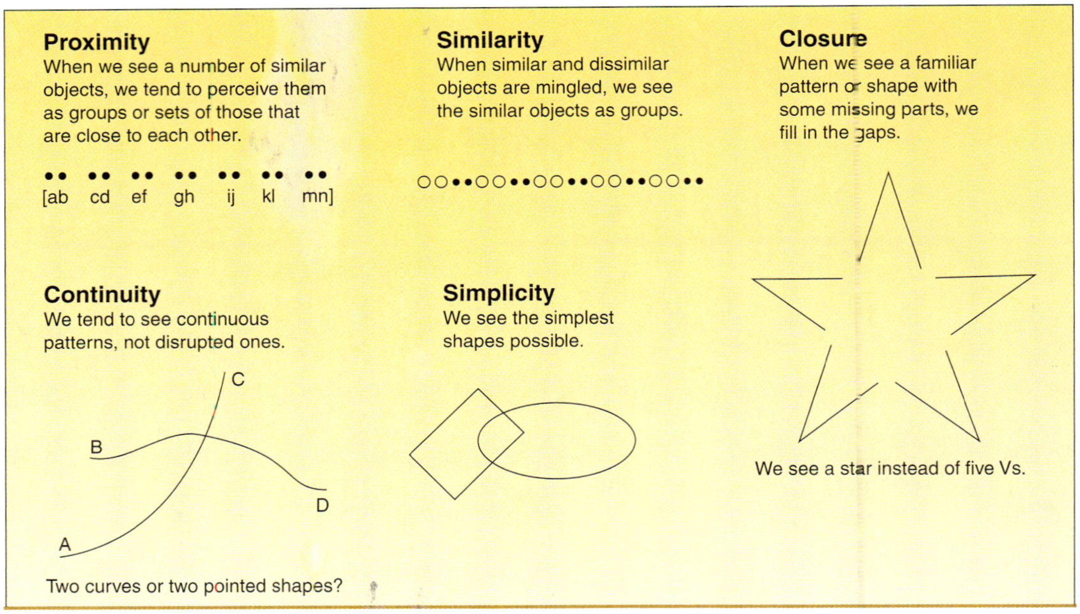

COOPERATIVE LEARNING ACTIVITY

Perception and Art Organize students into small groups. Assign each group one of the following artists: Michelangelo di Lodovico Buonarroti Simoni, Leonardo da Vinci, Rembrandt van Rijn, Hubert van Eyck, Peter Paul Rubens, Diego Rodríguez de Silva Velázquez, Michelangelo Merisi (Caravaggio), Édouard Manet, Georgia O'Keeffe, or Salvador Dalí. Explain that these masters painted in different styles and in different centuries. Ask each group to find one or more of the artist's paintings and study the use of perspective and other perceptual devices in his or her work. Have each group apply Gestalt principles and write a description of the artist's perceptual techniques that could be placed beside the original work in a museum.

sound of a particular voice or instrument even when many other sounds are occurring. Closure aids us in perceiving an object even though there may be gaps in what our senses pick up. The rule of simplicity states that we tend to perceive complex figures as divided into several simpler figures.

FIGURE-GROUND PERCEPTION

One form of perceptual organization is the division of experience into figure and ground (see Figure 8.13). Figure-ground perception is the ability to discriminate properly between a figure and its background. When you look at a three-dimensional object against the sky, you have no trouble distinguishing between the object and its background. Objects become the figure and stand out from the background. It is when something is two-dimensional, as in Figure 8.13, that you may have trouble telling the figure from the ground. Nevertheless, such figure-ground perceptions give clues as to the nature of perception. That we can perceive a single pattern in more than one way demonstrates that we are not passive receivers of stimuli.

Figure and ground are important in hearing as well as in vision. When you follow one person's voice at a noisy meeting, that voice is a figure and all other sounds become ground. Similarly, when you listen to a piece of music, a familiar theme may leap out at you: the melody becomes the figure, and the rest of the music merely background.

Did You Know?

Hearing Colors All of her life, a woman, finally diagnosed with synesthesia, had seen colors when she heard words or letters. She always saw yellow with hints of green when she heard the word *king*, for instance. *Synesthesia* is the mingling or swapping of sensory information in which stimulating one sense triggers conscious experience in another sense. People with synesthesia may experience spoken words as tastes or shapes, colors as smells, and touches as sounds. The condition occurs in about 1 in 25,000 people and may result from "crossed wires" in the sensory areas of the brain.

PERCEPTUAL INFERENCE

Often we have perceptions that are not based entirely on current sensory information. When you hear barking as you approach your house, you assume it is your dog—not a cat or a rhinoceros or even another dog. When you take a seat in a dark theater, you assume it is solid and will hold your weight even though you cannot see what supports the seat. When you are driving in a car and see in the distance that the road climbs up a steep hill then disappears over the top, you assume the road will continue over and down the hill, not come to an abrupt end just out of sight.

This phenomenon of filling in the gaps in what our senses tell us is known as *perceptual inference* (Gregory, 1970). Perceptual inference

Figure 8.13 What Is It?

What did you see the first time you looked at this illustration—a vase or two profiles? People invariably organize their experience into figure and ground. ***What does the fact that we perceive a single pattern more than one way demonstrate?***

CHAPTER 8
Section 3, pages 223–231

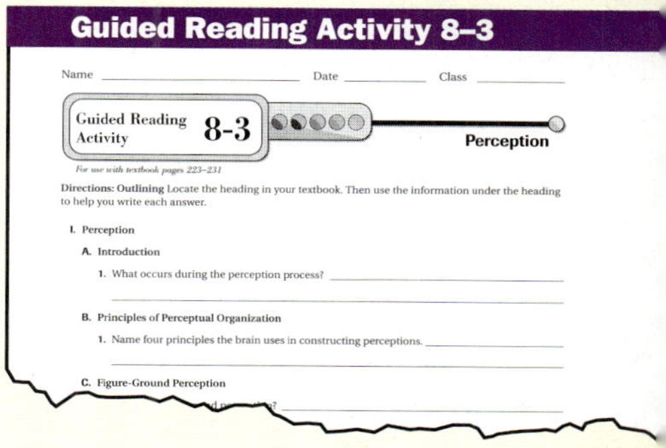
Guided Reading Activity 8–3

Name ______ Date ______ Class ______

Guided Reading Activity 8-3 — Perception

For use with textbook pages 223–231

Directions: Outlining Locate the heading in your textbook. Then use the information under the heading to help you write each answer.

I. Perception
  A. Introduction
    1. What occurs during the perception process? ______
  B. Principles of Perceptual Organization
    1. Name four principles the brain uses in constructing perceptions. ______
  C. Figure-Ground Perception

PSYCHOLOGY JOURNAL

Have students keep a log for 24 hours of the perceptual inferences they make. For example, they might hear the sound of the school bus before actually seeing it. Yet, based on past experience, they will perceive this auditory stimulus as a school bus. At the end of the 24-hour period, have students describe how perceptual inferences help people function more effectively. ■

Figure 8.13

Visual Instruction Point out that this is a classic example of the Gestalt principles in action.

Caption Answer It demonstrates that we do not receive stimuli passively and that the brain organizes and interprets stimuli.

MEETING SPECIAL NEEDS

Learning Style: Kinesthetic Explain that our perception of ourselves is based, in large part, on our mirror image, since this is the image we see most frequently. Tell students that Lewis Carroll, the author of *Alice in Wonderland*, was fascinated by words that appeared the same when viewed in a mirror. Have students print the following words in block, capital letters: BEECH, COOKBOOK, BOX. Then have them hold the paper in the mirror. The words will appear backwards. Next have them turn the paper upside down. The words are now readable. Ask students to think of other words that would look the same when turned upside down and viewed in a mirror. **L1** **ELL**

L2 Identifying Subliminal Messages Extend the discussion of subliminal perception by examining the following propaganda techniques:

- **Name Calling**—Using negative labels to discredit someone or something.
- **Glittering Generalities**—Broad statements that appeal to the emotions.
- **Card Stacking**—Slanting the facts.
- **Plain Folks**—Using folksy language.
- **Transfer**—Connecting a product with someone or something that is admired.
- **Bandwagon**—Appealing to people's desire to go along with the crowd.

Provide students with advertisements that use some of these techniques. **Ask: How do these ads influence perception? Why might people protest these techniques?**

Figure 8.14

Visual Instruction Point out to students that the O and the Qs share similar properties and so they are easier to group in the same set than the P.

Caption Answer The P is shaped very differently from the Qs.

Vocabulary Activity 8–3

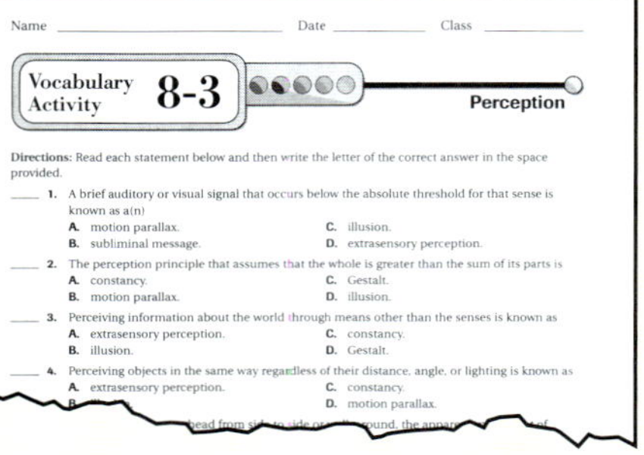
Name ______ Date ______ Class ______

Vocabulary Activity 8-3 Perception

Directions: Read each statement below and then write the letter of the correct answer in the space provided.

____ 1. A brief auditory or visual signal that occurs below the absolute threshold for that sense is known as a(n)
A. motion parallax. C. illusion.
B. subliminal message. D. extrasensory perception.

____ 2. The perception principle that assumes that the whole is greater than the sum of its parts is
A. constancy. C. Gestalt.
B. motion parallax. D. illusion.

____ 3. Perceiving information about the world through means other than the senses is known as
A. extrasensory perception. C. constancy.
B. illusion. D. Gestalt.

____ 4. Perceiving objects in the same way regardless of their distance, angle, or lighting is known as
A. extrasensory perception. C. constancy.
D. motion parallax.

This drawing seems to defy basic geometric laws.

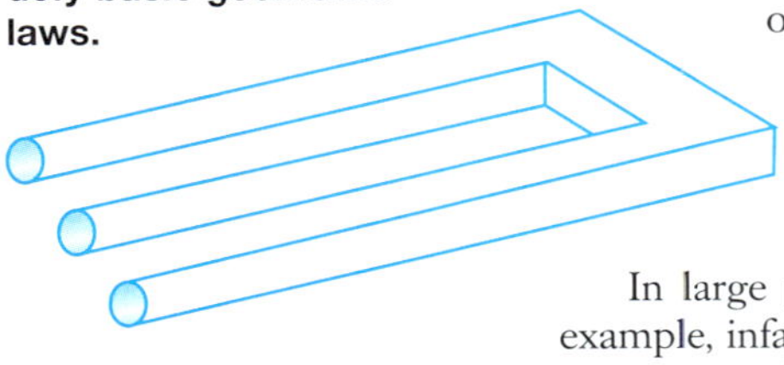

subliminal messages: brief auditory or visual messages that are presented below the absolute threshold

Figure 8.14 Pop-Out Features

Reality is a jumble of sensations and details. The letter *P* probably pops out to you. The *Q*s may also pop out, but not as much as the *P*. You may not have noticed the *O*, though. ***Why does the P pop out?***

QQQQQQQQ
QQQQQPQQ
QQOQQQQQ
QQQQQQQQ

is largely automatic and unconscious. We need only a few cues to inform us that a noise is our dog barking or that a seat is solid. Why? Because we have encountered these stimuli and objects in the past and know what to expect from them in the present. Perceptual inference, thus, often depends on experience. On the other hand, we are probably born with some of our ability to make perceptual inferences.

LEARNING TO PERCEIVE

In large part, perceiving is something that people *learn* to do. For example, infants under one month will smile at a nodding object the size of a human face, whether or not it has eyes, a nose or other human features. At about 20 weeks, however, a blank oval will not make most infants smile, but a drawing of a face or a mask will. The infant has learned to distinguish something that looks like a person from other objects. Infants 28 weeks and older are more likely to smile at a female than a male face. By 30 weeks, most infants smile more readily when they see a familiar face than when they see someone they do not know. It takes, however, 7 or 8 months for infants to learn to recognize different people (Ahrens, 1954).

Experiments with human beings have also shown that active involvement in one's environment is important for accurate perception. People who have been blind from birth and who have had their sight restored by an operation have visual sensations, but initially they cannot tell the difference between a square and a circle or see that a red cube is like a blue cube (Valvo, 1971). In fact, some had difficulty making such simple distinctions six months after their vision was restored.

Learning to perceive is influenced by our needs, beliefs, and expectations. When we want something, we are more likely to see it. Psychologists (Wispe & Drambarean, 1953) have demonstrated that hungry people are faster at identifying food-related words when words are flashed quickly in front of them. What we identify as truth may be twisted and reconstructed to fit our own belief systems. Previous experiences influence what we see (Lachman, 1996). For example, if you have always perceived all elderly women as honest, you might not even question the elderly woman at the next table when your wallet disappears in a restaurant, even if she is the most obvious suspect. This is called a perceptual set. This set prepares you to see what you want to see.

Subliminal Perception

In his 1957 book *The Hidden Persuaders,* Vance Packard divulged that advertisers were using a revolutionary breakthrough in marketing techniques—subliminal advertising. The word *subliminal* comes from the Latin: *sub* ("below") and *limen* (threshold). This concept used **subliminal messages,** which are brief auditory or visual messages presented below the absolute threshold so that there is less than a 50 percent chance that they will be perceived.

CRITICAL THINKING ACTIVITY

Understanding Cause and Effect Assign students to prepare an oral report on mirages—atmospheric optical illusions in which an observer sees a nonexistent body of water or an image of some distant object. Mirages project such a distinct image that they have even been photographed. Have students explain the scientific facts behind this natural illusion. Encourage them to include recorded images of mirages in their presentations. **L2**

One advertiser, James Vicary, falsely claimed that the words "Eat Popcorn" and "Drink Coke" had been flashed on a movie screen in a New Jersey theater on alternate nights for six weeks. Although the flashes were so brief (1/3000 of a second, once every five seconds) that none of the moviegoers even seemed to notice them, Vicary claimed that the sales of popcorn had risen 58 percent and Coke sales had risen 18 percent.

The public response to this announcement was long, loud, and hysterical. Congressional representatives called for FCC regulations, while several state legislatures passed laws banning subliminal ads. Eventually, Vicary admitted that the data from the movie theater experiment were false, and many people believe the experiment never really took place. However, public furor over the potential for abuse of subliminal advertising remained. In 1974, the FCC condemned subliminal advertising, regardless of its efficacy.

The idea for subliminal ads was a natural outgrowth of a long series of controversial studies on *subliminal perception*—the ability to notice stimuli that affect only the unconscious mind. Most of these earlier studies involved presenting verbal or visual material at intensities that were considered too low for people to perceive. A more critical look at the studies, however, revealed several flaws in the way they were designed and carried out. For example, no attempt was made to assess or control factors other than the subliminal message that might have influenced the purchase of Coke or popcorn. The temperature in the theater or the length of the movie might have contributed to the increase in sales. Unfortunately, the study was not presented in enough detail to be evaluated by scientists.

Even if it is possible for people to perceive information at very low levels of intensity, there is no clear evidence that these weak, often limited messages would be more powerful in influencing people than would conscious messages. Nevertheless, many people believe that subliminal advertising is powerful.

Figure 8.15 The Necker Cube

The Necker cube is an ambiguous figure. You can will yourself to see it as if you were looking down on it, with corner X closest to you, or as if you were looking up at it, with corner Y closest to you. ***How might you make this cube less ambiguous by adding details?***

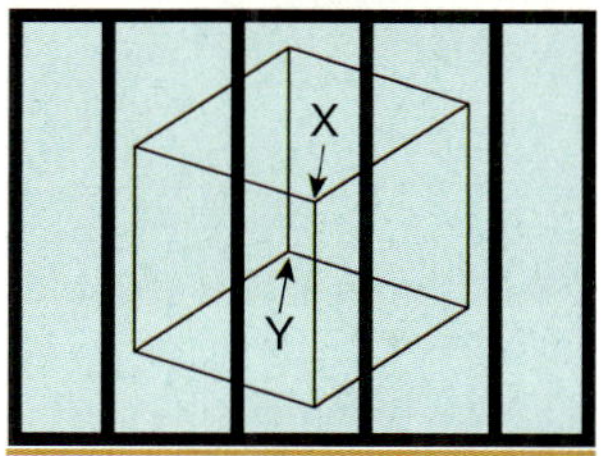

DEPTH PERCEPTION

Depth perception—the ability to recognize distances and three-dimensionality—develops in infancy. Psychologists have placed infants on large tables and found that they most likely will not crawl over the edge. From this observation, it is possible to infer that infants do have depth perception.

Monocular Depth Cues

People use many monocular depth cues to perceive distance and depth. *Monocular depth cues* are cues that can be used with a single eye. There are at least a half-dozen monocular cues external to us that we use. In the absence of any other cues, the size of an object—bigger is nearer—will be used. We use *relative height*—objects that appear farther away

Figure 8.15

Visual Instruction Point out the elementary features of a cube (lines, angles, patterns of light and dark, and color variations). Explain that these elementary features are combined into the perception of the whole image. Have students study the cube for a few moments and notice that even though the elementary features remain the same, the cube itself moves. Explain that this is not due to the image or the light source but to our interpretation (perception) of the image.

Caption Answer You can use shading to show back and front or top and bottom.

FYI

In 1990 Anthony Greenwald and his colleagues tested the power of suggestion by switching the labels on two subliminal tapes—one aimed at improving the memory, the other at improving self-esteem. At the end of one month, participants in the study reported an improvement in whatever area the label promised.

PSYCHOLOGY LAB EXPERIMENT

Depth Perception Have students work in pairs; one student will be called A, the other, B. Provide each pair with a drinking straw and a toothpick. Have A hold the straw parallel to the ground about two feet in front of B's face. Tell B to place the toothpick in the straw. Then tell B to cover his or her left eye and place the toothpick in the straw. Have B repeat the procedure with his or her right eye covered. Then have A and B reverse roles. **Ask:** **How does this experiment test depth perception? How is depth perceived differently using one eye (monocular vision) as opposed to both eyes (binocular vision)? L1 ELL** **BLOCK SCHEDULING**

Figure 8.16

Caption Answer You would see the mountains and distant sand dunes on different planes, perceiving that the mountains are farther away.

Applying Psychology

Ask students to collect samples of children's artwork. (Or arrange to get samples from an elementary school in your community.) Post the artwork around the room with labels indicating the children's ages. Tell students that many different developmental factors play a role in shaping children's art. In this case, however, students should focus on what the artwork reveals about children's perceptions of the environment. As a class, discuss the following questions: **What do proportional sizes, colors, and shapes tell about how children see the world? What stimuli capture the children's attention? How do the children depict depth, if at all?**

Reading Check Answer
Monocular cues can be perceived with only one eye, while binocular vision depends on the existence or movement of both eyes.

TEACHER Tip

Challenge students to explain why we perceive visual illusions. *(Sample answers: variations in the eye's visual sensory apparatus, interpretive errors made by the brain, previous learning experience)*

Figure 8.16 Monocular Cues

As you look down a long stretch of highway, the parallel sides of the road seem to converge. The expansive desert appears furrowed up close and smooth in the distance. ***How would you use the relative height cue to perceive the distance of the desert?***

from another object are higher on your plane of view. *Interposition,* or the overlapping of images, causes us to view the object we can see in its entirety to be closer than one whose outline is interrupted by another object. *Light and shadows* yield information about an object's shape and size. Brightly lit objects appear closer, while objects in shadows appear farther away. *Texture-density gradient* means that the farther removed an object is, the less detail we can identify (see Figure 8.16).

Another cue is **motion parallax**—the apparent movement of objects that occurs when you move your head from side to side or when you walk around. You can demonstrate motion parallax by looking toward two objects in the same line of vision, one near you and the other some distance away. If you move your head back and forth, the near object will seem to move more than the far object. In this way, motion parallax gives you clues as to which objects are closer than others.

motion parallax: the apparent movement of stationary objects relative to one another that occurs when the observer changes position

Another distance cue, *linear perspective,* is based on the fact that parallel lines converge when stretched into the distance (see Figure 8.16). For instance, when you look at a long stretch of road or railroad tracks, it appears that the sides of the road or the tracks converge on the horizon. A final related cue is *relative motion.* When you are riding in a car, for example, and look at distant mountains, the objects in a nearby field seem to be moving in the opposite direction to your movement. Yet, when you look at an animal in a nearby field, the mountains or land beyond the animal seem to be moving in the same direction you are.

Binocular Depth Cues

Binocular depth cues depend upon the existence or movement of both eyes. For example, *convergence* is the process by which your eyes turn inward to look at nearby objects. Another cue is the information provided by retinal disparity, as discussed earlier in the chapter. Because each of your eyes occupies a different position, each eye receives a slightly different image. That difference is *retinal disparity.* The brain interprets a large retinal disparity to mean a close object and a small retinal disparity to mean a distant object.

Reading Check
How do monocular and binocular depth cues differ?

INTERDISCIPLINARY CONNECTIONS ACTIVITY

The Arts To illustrate the ability to fill in gaps in what our senses tell us, organize a game of "Name That Tune." Ask students to bring in tapes or CDs of well-known songs. Instruct student DJs to play only one or two seconds of the music at a time. Record how many seconds into the song it takes before class members can guess the name of the song. Ask students to identify the auditory clues that provided them with their answers *(artist's voice, beat, lyrics, rhythm, instrumentation, and so on).* **L1**

CONSTANCY

When we have learned to perceive certain objects in our environment, we tend to see them in the same way, regardless of changing conditions. You probably judge the whiteness of the various portions of these pages to be fairly constant, even though you may have read the book under a wide range of lighting conditions. The light, angle of vision, distance, and, therefore, the image on the retina all change, but your perception of the object does not. Thus, despite changing physical conditions, people are able to perceive objects as the same by the processes of size, shape, brightness and color **constancy** (see Figure 8.17).

constancy: the tendency to perceive certain objects in the same way regardless of changing angle, distance, or lighting

An example of size constancy will illustrate how we have an automatic system for perceiving an object as being the same size whether it is far or near. A friend walking toward you does not seem to change into a giant even though the images inside your eyes become larger and larger as she approaches. To you, her appearance stays the same size because even though the size of your visual image is increasing, you are perceiving an additional piece of information: distance is decreasing. The enlarging eye image and the distance information combine to produce a perception of an approaching object that stays the same size.

Distance information compensates for the enlarging eye image to produce size constancy. If information about distance is eliminated, your perception of the size of the object begins to correspond to the actual size of the eye image. For example, it is difficult for most people to estimate the size of an airplane in the sky because they have little experience judging such huge sizes and distances. Pilots, however, can determine whether a flying plane is large and far away or small and close because they are experienced in estimating the sizes and distances of planes.

Through the wide middle range of brightness, and in a mix of many colors, reds are perceived as red, greens as green–color constancy. Similarly, across a wide range of light, from dawn's early light to dusk's fading light, the brightest shirt in a crowd will always be perceived the brightest–brightness constancy. With brightest light, colors fade to white; at dusk, they fade to gray or black.

illusions: perceptions that misrepresent physical stimuli

Figure 8.17 Shape Constancy

We perceive the opening door as being rectangular in shape, although our view of the shape of it changes as it opens. ***Why are perceptual constancies important to our understanding of the world?***

ILLUSIONS

Illusions are incorrect perceptions. Illusions can be useful in teaching us about how our sensory and perceptual systems work. Illusions are created when perceptual cues are distorted so that our brains cannot correctly interpret space, size, and depth cues. For example, look at the lines in Figure 8.18. Which lines in

TEACHER Tip

Discuss the role that light and shadow play in depth perception. Point out that the brain assumes light comes from above since our main source of light, the sun, shines down. Thus, when the bottom of an object is in shadow, we see it as projecting forward. On the other hand, when the top is in shadow, we view the object as being recessed.

Readings and Case Studies in Psychology

Have students read the Chapter 8 Reading selection in *Readings and Case Studies in Psychology* and answer the questions that follow the reading.

Figure 8.17

Visual Instruction Ask students to describe instances in which their eyes have played tricks on them. Encourage them to try to explain what caused the confusion.

Caption Answer They help our minds perceive objects in the same way despite the angle, distance, or lighting from which they are viewed.

EXTENDING THE CONTENT

Virtual Reality Ask students to describe examples they have seen of virtual reality headsets. If no student volunteers, tell students that they are odd-looking devices that completely cover a person's field of vision. To control movement during a virtual reality experiment, the participant wears special gloves or uses a joystick. Tell students that the reason for the headsets is to project differing images to the two eyes. The headset displays two separate images. When viewed at close proximity, both eyes see separate but overlapping images that help create the perception of depth.

Figure 8.18

Visual Instruction Tell students that in 1977, perceptual psychologist O.A. Favreau found that in nearly 20 textbooks the longer-looking line in the Müller-Lyer illusion was really longer. She then set out to see if the "Müller-Liar" illusion worked. Favreau drew two parallel lines 31 and 31.5 millimeters long. She placed the outward fins on the shorter line and the inward fins on the longer line. People perceived that the shorter line was longer, thus restoring the Müller-Lyer to its place in the history of psychology.

Caption Answer The brain interprets scenes using space, size, and depth cues. In illusions, these cues mislead the brain.

3 ASSESS

Assign Section 3 Assessment as homework or as an in-class activity.

Section Quiz 8–3

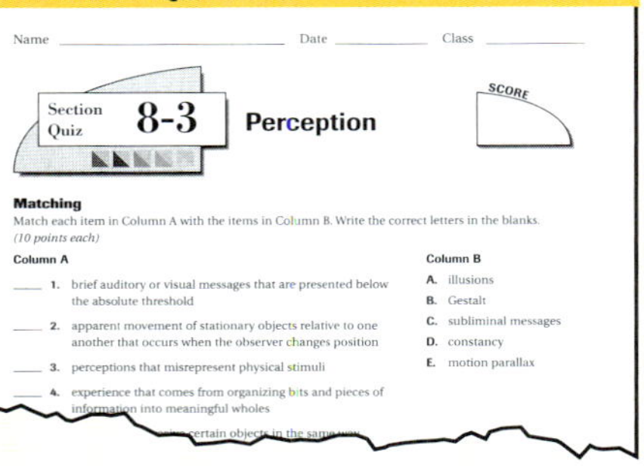
Name ______ Date ______ Class ______

Section Quiz 8-3 **Perception** SCORE

Matching
Match each item in Column A with the items in Column B. Write the correct letters in the blanks. *(10 points each)*

Column A

____ 1. brief auditory or visual messages that are presented below the absolute threshold
____ 2. apparent movement of stationary objects relative to one another that occurs when the observer changes position
____ 3. perceptions that misrepresent physical stimuli
____ 4. experience that comes from organizing bits and pieces of information into meaningful wholes

Column B

A. illusions
B. Gestalt
C. subliminal messages
D. constancy
E. motion parallax

Reteach

Assign students to write a paragraph explaining the difference between sensation and perception.

Figure 8.18 Lines of Different Lengths?

The Müller-Lyer illusion (a) and the Ponzo illusion (b) are depicted here. The lines between the arrowheads in (a) are exactly the same length, as are the heavy black lines in (b). Some psychologists believe that the reason the lines in (a) seem of different lengths is because they are interpreted as offering different cues to their distance from the viewer. The lines in (b) may appear to be different in length because the brain interprets this diagram as though it is from a scene such as that in (c). ***Why does the brain interpret scenes in certain ways?***

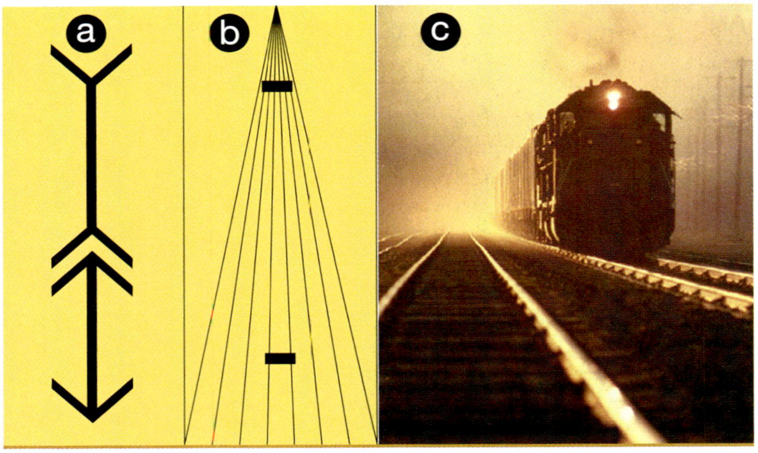

each set are longer? Measure the lengths of the pairs of lines with a ruler, then look again. Do the lines look as long now that you know they are the same? For most people, the answer is no.

A possible explanation of this type of illusion is that even though the patterns are two-dimensional, your brain treats them as three-dimensional. These illusions have features that usually indicate distance in three-dimensional space. The top line in Figure 8.18a, for example, can be thought of as the far corner of a room; the bottom line is like the near corner of the building. In Figure 8.18b and Figure 8.18c, the converging lines create the illusion of distance so that the lower bar looks nearer and shorter than the upper bar. This perceptual compensation seems to be unconscious and automatic.

Figure 8.19 shows two individuals in a room. Their sizes look dramatically different because you perceive the room as rectangular. In fact, the ceiling and walls are slanted so that the back wall is both shorter and closer on the right than on the left. Yet even when you know how this illusion was achieved, you still accept the peculiar difference in the sizes of the two people because the windows, walls, and ceiling appear rectangular. Your experience with rectangular rooms overrides your knowledge of how this trick is done.

EXTRASENSORY PERCEPTION

extrasensory perception (ESP): an ability to gain information by some means other than the ordinary senses

We are fascinated by things that cannot be seen, easily explained, or sometimes even verified, such as flying saucers, atoms, genes, and extrasensory perception. **Extrasensory perception (ESP)**—receiving information about the world through channels other than the normal senses—is a hotly debated topic. There are four types of ESP: (1) clairvoyance is perceiving objects or information without sensory input; (2) telepathy involves reading someone else's mind or transferring one's thoughts; 3) psychokinesis involves moving objects through purely mental effort;

EXTENDING THE CONTENT

ESP Assign students to research ESP using resources available in the library or on the Internet. Have them use their research to prepare a chart showing the different types of ESP experiences that they uncovered. Have them present this chart and an overview of opinions on ESP in an oral presentation to the class. After the class has heard the various presentations on ESP, ask volunteers to discuss whether they think parapsychology is a legitimate offshoot of psychology. **L2**

and (4) precognition is the ability to foretell events. Since the 1960s, James Randi, known as "The Amazing Randi," has campaigned against people who claim they have ESP. He has exposed many of these people as frauds.

Many people are convinced that ESP exists because of an intense personal experience that can never be scientifically validated. For instance, we all have some fears before traveling, and we imagine the worst: our plane will crash, our train will be derailed, or we will have an automobile accident. These events almost never happen, and we easily forget about our frightening premonitions. If the improbable should actually take place, however, our premonitions turn into compelling evidence for the existence of precognition. Such coincidences sometimes become widely publicized evidence supporting paranormal phenomena, and we may quickly forget all the occasions when our premonitions were completely wrong. If we are truly interested in validating the existence of ESP, though, we must keep track of the frequency of its failures as well as its successes.

Scientists have been investigating ESP since the 1900s. (Probably the most famous parapsychologist is J.B. Rhine.) Many scientists do not accept the results of experiments supporting ESP because the findings are highly unstable. One of the basic principles of scientific research is that one scientist should be able to replicate another scientist's results. Not only do different ESP experiments yield contradictory findings, but the same individual seems to show ESP on one day but not on the next. Perhaps the most telling argument against ESP is that when strict controls are used in an ESP experiment, there is little likelihood of demonstrating ESP. This is contrary to what one normally expects when trying to demonstrate a phenomenon using the scientific methods described in Chapter 2.

Figure 8.19 **A Strange Room**

The room, constructed by Adelbert Ames, changes depth cues to distort our perception. ***What makes this illusion work?***

SECTION 3 Assessment

1. **Review the Vocabulary** Describe the Gestalt principles of organization. How do these principles help us organize reality?

2. **Visualize the Main Idea** Use a graphic organizer similar to the one below to list and briefly describe monocular depth cues.

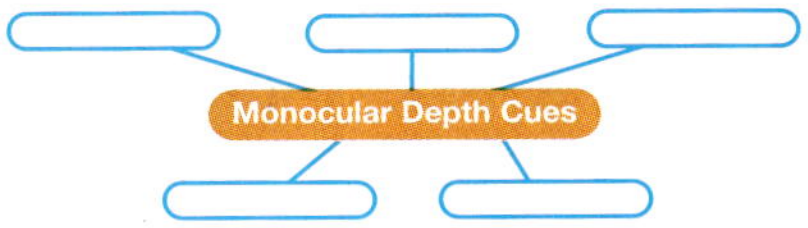

3. **Recall Information** What are the binocular depth cues? How do they help us judge reality?

4. **Think Critically** How do illusions demonstrate the difference between sensations and perceptions?

5. **Application Activity** Consider the following question: You have suddenly lost all perceptual constancies—what specific problems do you encounter? Create a scene—in the form of a play, narrative, or newspaper article—that illustrates a problem you might encounter.

SECTION 3 Assessment Answers

1. Gestalt principles of organization are proximity, similarity, closure, continuity, and simplicity. They help us organize perceptual information in a way that allows us to create a whole.
2. Students' answers should reflect an understanding of monocular depth cues.
3. Binocular depth cues depend on the existence or movement of both eyes. Convergence is when our eyes turn inward to view objects that are close. Large retinal disparity means the object is close; small retinal disparity means the object is farther away. These cues help us judge distance.
4. Sensations are the sensory input; perceptions are the sometimes inaccurate processing of the stimuli. The illusion is created when our brain misinterprets the sensory stimuli.
5. Students' answers will vary. Narratives should describe the difficulty in judging size and shape. People will appear to actually change size. The student will experience difficulty completing even simple tasks.

Figure 8.19

Caption Answer Answers will vary, but students should note that misinterpretations are caused by errors in visual processing and the way the brain interprets information. Our prior knowledge about the world and how we perceive it also causes errors.

Enrich

Have students write an essay entitled "Seeing Is Believing—or Is It?" from the point of view of a perceptual psychologist.

4 CLOSE

Have students write down five new things that they learned from this chapter. Tell them to complete this task without consulting their textbooks. Call on students to share their answers.

Going Further

Inattentional Blindness

Does perception occur when we are not paying attention? Recent studies in cognitive psychology suggest that we must be paying attention in order to perceive sensory stimuli. In one experiment, participants were shown a series of "+" signs, some with the horizontal bar longer and some with the vertical bar longer. As the signs were flashed on the screen, participants were asked to indicate which bar was longer.

After several trials, another object was shown on the screen at the same time. Objects that were placed away from the point where the + sign appeared were not noticed by 25 percent of the participants. When the + sign was moved to a new location and the distracting object was placed where the previous + sign had been, 75 percent of the participants did not see the distracting object.

These findings are simply a starting point in the research of attention and perception. The findings do, however, seem to indicate that what we perceive is largely affected by what we choose to pay attention to.

Discussing the Case Study

Ask: **Do you think that Kenge could learn size constancy if exposed to open spaces regularly? What reactions would you expect from Kenge's village when he explains the strange things he saw? Do you think Kenge and the other villagers simply did not pay attention to visual clues about distance and size constancy?**

Case Studies

Seeing Is Believing

Period of Study: Late 1950s and early 1960s

Introduction: In the late 1950s and early 1960s, an anthropologist, C.M. Turnbull, traveled to the Ituri Forest in the present-day country of the Democratic Republic of the Congo (formerly Zaire) to study the life and culture of the BaMbuti Pygmies. Turnbull traveled from one village to another. A 22-year-old man named Kenge from a local Pygmy village accompanied and assisted him. Kenge had spent all of his life living in the dense forests surrounding his village. He was accustomed to seeing only the images contained within the forests.

Hypothesis: Because Kenge had been isolated by the forests all of his life, the sight of new images would appear complex and confusing. The thick forests blocked the local villagers' view of distant objects such as animals, mountains, and the sun and moon on the horizon. Because Kenge had never seen these things, his perceptual development (in this case, *size constancy*, or the ability to perceive a familiar object as being the same size regardless of its distance from you) was limited. He understood only what he could see directly in front of him. The information collected from Turnbull's experience with Kenge raised the question of whether perceptual understanding is a learned ability or biological mechanism: a question of nature versus nurture.

Method: The discovery of Kenge's perceptual limitations took place when Turnbull and Kenge came to a clearing on the eastern edge of the Ituri Forest. At that point Kenge and Turnbull enjoyed a clear view of the Ruwenzori Mountains. Confused by the sight of the mountains, Kenge asked Turnbull if the mountains were hills or clouds. Turnbull explained that they were hills but much larger than any Kenge had seen before. Kenge agreed to ride with Turnbull to the mountains for further inspection. A passing thunderstorm obstructed the travelers' view and did not clear until the two reached the mountains. When Kenge peered up at the enormous mountain range, he was amazed.

As Turnbull and Kenge turned to leave, Kenge noticed a wide open plain on which stood a herd of buffalo. Kenge wanted to know what type of "insects" the buffalo were. Turnbull explained that the animals were not insects but buffalo. When the two arrived close to the herd of buffalo, Kenge now knew that the "insects" were buffalo all along, but he still could not understand why they had appeared to be so small.

Results: Turnbull's accounts support the idea that human perception develops (at least in the case of size constancy) as we use the environment around us, or by nurture. However, some research with infants supports the nature side of perception. For example, individuals who were blind at birth and later gained their sight were able to perceive figure-ground relationships. Are we born with certain perceptual abilities and not others, or is perception something we learn? In Kenge's case, perceptual ability was a learned phenomenon. Certain perceptual skills may be necessary for our survival. In Kenge's case, he did not need a wide range of size constancy to survive in the dense jungle.

Analyzing the Case Study

1. Why did some images seem confusing to Kenge?
2. According to Turnbull, how do we learn size constancy?
3. **Critical Thinking** Do you think that Kenge could adjust to life in your city or town? Explain the difficulties he might encounter.

Answers for Analyzing the Case Study

1. Kenge had been isolated from views of great distances his entire life. Since he lived in thick forests, Kenge had never experienced the view of distant objects. His brain had not stored information in memories about size constancy. Therefore, his brain did not know how to interpret the stimuli correctly. His perceptual development was limited.
2. According to Turnbull, size constancy is learned as we perceive the world around us. It is learned through experience.
3. Students' answers will vary. He might survive well in a large city like New York where the tall buildings fill the landscape and vistas are uncommon. Students may also argue that Kenge's perception will improve with experience.

CHAPTER 8

Summary and Vocabulary

People take in information through their senses. Through their senses they perceive the world around them.

Section 1 Sensation

Main Idea: Sensations initiate humans' understanding of their reality. Sensations occur anytime a stimulus activates a receptor.

- The absolute threshold is the weakest amount of a stimulus required to produce a perception; the difference threshold is the minimum amount of distinction a person can detect between two stimuli.
- Senses are most responsive to increases and decreases, rather than unchanging stimulation.
- Sensory adaptation allows people to notice differences in sensations and react to the challenges of different or changing stimuli.

Section 2 The Senses

Main Idea: The sense organs—the eyes, ears, tongue, nose, skin, and others—are the receptors of sensations.

- Vision provides people with a great deal of information about the environment and the objects in it.
- Hearing depends on vibrations of the air, called sound waves.
- The body's sense of balance is regulated by the vestibular system, adjacent to the inner ear.
- Smell and taste are known as the chemical senses because their receptors are sensitive to gaseous and liquid molecules respectively.
- Receptors in the skin are responsible for providing the brain with information about pressure, warmth, cold, and pain.
- Kinesthesis cooperates with the vestibular and visual senses to maintain our sense of movement and body position.

Section 3 Perception

Main Idea: The way we interpret sensations and organize them into meaningful experiences is called perception.

- The Gestalt principles of organization help explain how we group our sensations and fill in gaps to make sense of our world.
- Figure-ground perception is the ability to discriminate properly between figure and ground.
- Perceptual inference is the phenomenon of filling in the gaps in what our senses tell us.
- Learning to perceive is influenced by our needs, beliefs, and expectations.
- People use monocular depth cues and binocular depth cues to perceive distance and depth.
- Incorrect perceptions, created when perceptual cues are distorted, are called illusions.

Chapter Vocabulary

sensation (p. 208)
perception (p. 208)
psychophysics (p. 208)
absolute threshold (p. 209)
difference threshold (p. 210)
Weber's law (p. 211)
signal-detection theory (p. 212)
pupil (p. 215)
lens (p. 215)
retina (p. 215)
optic nerve (p. 215)
binocular fusion (p. 216)
retinal disparity (p. 216)
auditory nerve (p. 218)
vestibular system (p. 220)
olfactory nerve (p. 220)
kinesthesis (p. 222)
Gestalt (p. 224)
subliminal messages (p. 226)
motion parallax (p. 228)
constancy (p. 229)
illusions (p. 229)
extrasensory perception (ESP) (p. 230)

8

Summary and Vocabulary

Using the Chapter 8 Summary and Vocabulary

Use the Chapter 8 Summary and Vocabulary to preview, review, condense, or reteach the chapter.

Preview/Review

Use the Chapter Vocabulary list to help students review and study.

Activity Have students create a crossword puzzle using definitions or examples as the clues for the puzzle.

Vocabulary PuzzleMaker CD-ROM reinforces the vocabulary terms used in Chapter 8.

Condense

Have students read the Chapter 8 Summary.

Chapter 8 Guided Reading Activities

Reteach

Reteaching Activity 8

PERFORMANCE ASSESSMENT ACTIVITY

Writing a Pamphlet Many learning disabilities are, at least in part, the result of physical or perceptual problems, which may include dyslexia, autism, dyscalculia, dysgraphia, gross motor disabilities, fine motor disabilities, auditory sequencing problems, and dysnomia. Have students select one of these or other disabilities and design an informational pamphlet for parents whose children have just been diagnosed with the disorder. **BLOCK SCHEDULING**

Refer to the ***Authentic Assessment*** booklet for additional activities and information about evaluating student performance.

8 Assessment

PSYCHOLOGY Online

Have students visit the Web site at glencoe.com to review Chapter 8 and take the **Self-Check Quiz.**

GLENCOE TECHNOLOGY

PRESENTATION Plus! For a review of Chapter 8 content, see MindJogger Checkpoint on **Presentation Plus!**

Reviewing Vocabulary

1. f
2. b
3. d
4. j
5. h
6. e
7. a
8. i
9. c
10. g

Recalling Facts

1. A stimulus is any aspect of, or change in, the environment to which an organism responds. Examples include a light, a clock ticking in a quiet room, a pulled muscle, or a bolt of lightning.
2. Weber's law suggests that for any change (Δs) in a stimulus to be detected, a constant proportion of that stimulus (s) must be added or subtracted. In other words, in a larger sports arena, it would take a larger change, such as 100 lightbulbs burning out, for the observer to notice it.
3. The vestibular system is our sense of balance located in the inner ear. We need it to maintain balance.
4. Information includes warmth, cold, pain, and pressure.
5. It is the ability to discriminate properly a figure from the background around it. An example is when you hear your name spoken in a noisy room—you have discriminated the sound of your name from all the surrounding sounds.

Critical Thinking

1. Students' answers will vary. They should be able to clearly explain what the loss of the sense would do and how their lives would be affected. Students are most likely to mention vision and hearing.
2. Students' answers will vary. In daily life, color-deficient individuals may have difficulty matching socks after they have been laundered or creating matching outfits. Color-deficient individuals are not likely to become artists, fashion designers, or airline pilots.
3. The vestibular system controls balance, while kinesthesis is the sense of movement and body position. Both senses are needed, for example, when stepping off a train, subway, or other transportation.
4. Students' answers will vary. Some students may report feeling pressure or seeing colors. They may suggest a sense of vision from light energy left in the eye. They may also speculate that pressure causes the rods to send impulses to the brain.
5. Students' answers will vary. Students might mention the lack of choice in subliminal advertising. Students may also indicate that such messages seem to have little effect.

Psychology Projects

1. Most people will have difficulty identifying the taste of the food if they are smelling a stronger odor. Students should be able to explain the relationship between taste and smell.
2. Answers will vary. Lead students to understand how this experiment illustrates the principle of selective attention.
3. Students' experiments will vary but should show how sensory adaptation occurs.

CHAPTER 8 Assessment

PSYCHOLOGY Online

Self-Check Quiz
Visit the *Understanding Psychology* Web site at glencoe.com and click on **Chapter 8—Self-Check Quizzes** to prepare for the Chapter Test.

Reviewing Vocabulary

Choose the letter of the correct term or concept below to complete the sentence.

a. sensation
b. psychophysics
c. absolute threshold
d. difference threshold
e. binocular fusion
f. perception
g. vestibular system
h. kinesthesis
i. subliminal messages
j. illusions

1. The organization of sensory information into meaningful experiences is __________ .
2. The psychological study of questions such as the relationship between color and wavelength is called __________.
3. The minimum amount of difference a person can detect between two stimuli is the __________.
4. __________ are incorrect perceptions.
5. __________ is the sense of movement and body position.
6. The combination of two images into one is __________ .
7. A(n)__________ is created when a stimulus activates a receptor.
8. Advertisers sometimes use __________, which are brief auditory or visual stimuli presented below the absolute threshold so that there is less than a 50 percent chance that they will be perceived.
9. The weakest amount of stimuli required to produce a sensation is called the __________.
10. A body's sense of balance is regulated by the __________ connected to the inner ear.

Recalling Facts

1. Using a graphic organizer similar to the one below, define stimulus and give at least four examples of stimuli.

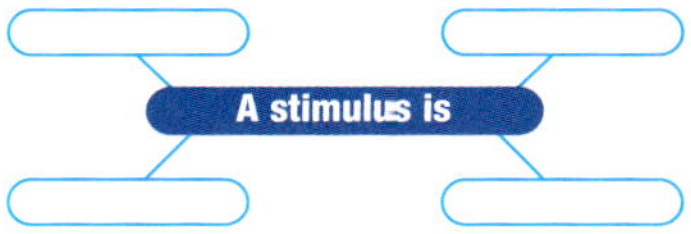

2. What is the psychological principle that explains why you are more likely to notice when a single lightbulb burns out in a room with three lamps than when a single lightbulb burns out in a sports arena?
3. What is our vestibular system? Why do we need it?
4. List four kinds of information we receive from our skin.
5. Define figure-ground perception and provide an example of it.

Critical Thinking

1. **Synthesizing Information** Which of the senses do you consider most important to you? Why do you think so?
2. **Making Inferences** How might being color-deficient affect your daily life? Your choice of career?
3. **Analyzing Concepts** What is the difference between vestibular sense and kinesthesis? In what situations are both senses needed?
4. **Analyzing Concepts** What sensation do you experience when you close your eyes and gently press on one of your eyeballs at the outer edge? How can you explain the visual experience in the absence of light rays?
5. **Evaluating Information** One of the objections to the use of subliminal advertising techniques is that they could be used to manipulate or influence large numbers of people without their knowing it. Do you think this is an important objection? Why or why not?

CHAPTER 8

Assessment

Psychology Projects

1. **The Senses** Peel a fresh potato and an apple. Have a friend close his eyes and smell a fresh onion while he takes a bite of each one. Can he tell which food is which without his sense of smell? Try this experiment with various people, using different foods that have similar textures. Report your findings in a chart. Explain the relationship between the senses of taste and smell.
2. **Perception** Watch a movie with your parents or grandparents. As soon as the film is over, ask each person to write a paragraph describing the last scene in the movie. Read each paragraph aloud. What was everyone's perception of the scene? How could you explain any differences?
3. **Sensation** Sensory adaptation refers to the ability of the senses to adjust themselves to a constant level of stimulation. Create a simple experiment to test for sensory adaptation. Ask a classmate to demonstrate the experiment.

Technology Activity

Search the Internet for information and examples of optical illusions. Present examples to your class and explain how the illusions were created.

Psychology Journal

1. Reread your journal entry about hearing another conversation in a crowded setting. Is your explanation still valid? If necessary, how would you change it?
2. Think about what it would be like if our senses did not have the limits they do. What visual problems might we have? What would we hear if our sense of hearing had a different range? Write answers to these questions in your journal.

Building Skills

Interpreting a Graph Review the graph, and then answer the questions that follow.

1. What three body parts are the least sensitive to touch?
2. Why are certain parts of the body more sensitive to touch than others?
3. How does the information in the graph help explain why people reading in Braille use their fingertips?

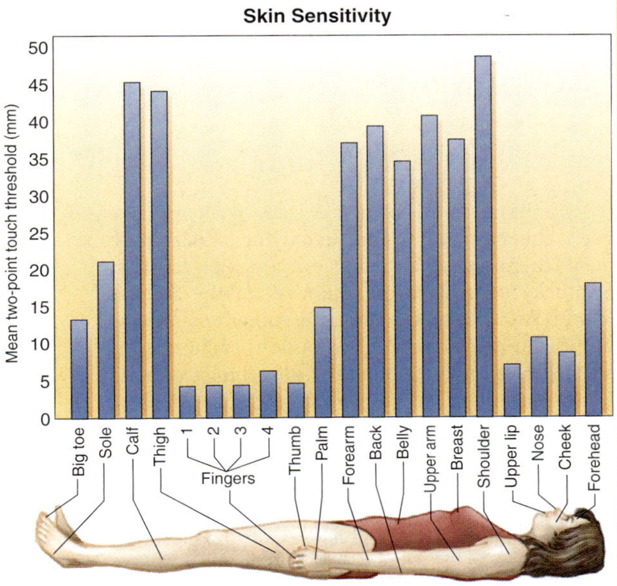

Practice and **assess** key social studies skills with **Glencoe Skillbuilder Interactive Workbook CD-ROM, Level 2.**

See the Skills Handbook, page 628, for an explanation of interpreting graphs.

Building Skills

1. shoulder, calf, and thigh
2. Sensitivity to touch varies because some places on the body have more receptors than others. Your fingertips, for example, have more receptors and are therefore more sensitive.
3. The graph shows that the fingertips are the most sensitive part of the body. The ability to sense the sometimes subtle changes in Braille is best achieved through the fingertips.

GLENCOE TECHNOLOGY

CD-ROM

Glencoe Skillbuilder Interactive Workbook, Level 2

This interactive CD-ROM is designed to reinforce student mastery of essential social studies skills.

Chapter Bonus Test Question

This question may be used for extra credit on the Chapter Assessment.

Answer the following question:

I am the theory that pain can be lessened by sending signals that compete with the pain signals. What am I?

Answer: gate control theory of pain

Technology Activity

Students can find a number of interesting illusions. Direct students to sites that generate stereograms. Ask how many students could perceive the hidden image.

Psychology Journal

1. Students' explanations should now reflect their understanding of figure-ground perception.
2. Students' answers will vary. Students may suggest scenarios in which our senses are overloaded by various stimuli, leading to indecisive or inaccurate responses to stimuli.

Readings in Psychology

Block Schedule

This activity works well for a block-scheduling framework.

Reinforcing Vocabulary

Review the **Reader's Dictionary** terms with students to be sure they understand any unfamiliar items.

Background Information

Does a person need experience to see (make sense of optical images)? Many people have addressed this question over the years. English philosopher John Locke considered the question in Book II of his *Essay Concerning Human Understanding* (1690). He decided that senses provided the mind with the simplest form of knowledge. He believed that repeated experience and reflection combined this knowledge to create "ideas" "before the mind."

The English surgeon William Cheselden put these considerations to the test in 1728 when he removed cataracts from the eyes of a 13-year-old boy who was born blind. Although the boy was highly intelligent, he experienced great difficulties with the simplest visual perceptions. For example, he had no concept of distance, space, or size. He was confused by the idea of a two-dimensional representation of the world. As Berkeley expected, the boy gradually learned to make sense of what he saw, but only if he was able to connect the visual experiences with tactile ones.

Readings in Psychology

How do we recognize an object we are seeing? The experience of Virgil, a 55-year-old man who regained his sight after being blind, raises questions about seeing and perception. Oliver Sacks, a physician, is known for writing case histories of neurological experiences. This account appeared in *The New Yorker* on May 10, 1993.

Reader's Dictionary

acute: severe

indolence: laziness or sloth

retina: the sensory membrane that lines the eye and functions as the instrument of vision

cataract: a clouding of the lens of the eye

incessant: continuing without interruption

coherence: being unified or understandable

agnostic: loss of ability to recognize familiar objects

To See and Not See

BY OLIVER SACKS

Virgil (nearly all the names in this account have been changed, and some identifying details have been disguised) was born on a small farm in Kentucky soon after the outbreak of the Second World War. He seemed normal enough as a baby, but (his mother thought) had poor eyesight even as a toddler, sometimes bumping into things, seemed not to see them. At the age of three, he became gravely ill with a triple illness—a meningitis or meningoencephalitis (inflammation of the brain and its membranes), polio, and cat-scratch fever. During this acute illness, he had convulsions, became virtually blind, paralyzed in the legs, partly paralyzed in his breathing, and, after ten days, fell into a coma.

He remained in a coma for two weeks. When he emerged from it, he seemed, according to his mother, "a different person" and "sort of dull inside"; he showed a curious indolence, nonchalance, passivity, seemed nothing at all like the spunky, mischievous boy he had been.

The strength in his legs came back over the next year, and his chest grew stronger, though never, perhaps, entirely normal. His vision also recovered significantly—but his retinas were now gravely damaged. Whether the retinal damage was caused wholly by his acute illness or perhaps partly by a congenital retinal degeneration was never clear.

In Virgil's sixth year, cataracts began to develop in both eyes, and it was evident that he was becoming functionally blind. That same year, he was sent to a school for the blind, and there he eventually learned to read Braille and to become adept with the use of a cane. . . .

Virgil graduated from the school, and when he was twenty, decided to leave Kentucky, to seek training, work, and a life of his own in a city in Oklahoma. He trained as a massage therapist, and soon found employment at a Y.M.C.A. He was obviously good at his job, and highly esteemed, and the Y was happy to keep him on its permanent staff and to provide a small house for him across the road, where he lived with a friend, also employed at the Y. Virgil had many clients—it is fascinating to hear the tactile detail with which he can describe them—and seemed to take a real pleasure and pride in his job. . . . Life was limited, but stable in its way.

Then, in 1991, he met Amy. . . . [Amy] saw Virgil stuck (as she perceived it) in a vegetative, dull life. . . . Restoring his sight [through surgery], she must have felt, would, like marriage, stir him from his indolent bachelor existence and provide them

ADDITIONAL READINGS ABOUT THE TOPIC

Deregowski, J.B. (1980). *Illusions, Patterns and Pictures: A Cross-Cultural Perspective.* London: Academic Press.

Edelman, S. (1999). *Representation and Recognition in Vision.* Cambridge, MA: MIT Press.

Gregory, R.L. (1997). *Eye and Brain: The Psychology of Seeing.* (5th ed). Princeton, NJ: Princeton University Press.

Kaufman, L. (2006). *Sight and Mind: An Introduction to Visual Perception.* New York: Oxford University Press.

both with a new life. . . . Virgil himself showed no preference in the matter; he seemed happy to go along with whatever they decided.

Finally, in mid-September, the day of the surgery came. Virgil's right eye had its cataract removed, and a new lens implant was inserted; then the eye was bandaged, as is customary, for twenty-four hours of recovery. The following day, the bandage was removed, and Virgil's eye was finally exposed, without cover, to the world. The moment of truth had come.

Or had it? The truth of the matter (as I pieced it together later), if less "miraculous" than Amy's journal suggested, was infinitely stranger. The dramatic moment stayed vacant, grew longer, sagged. No cry ("I can see!") burst from Virgil's lips. He seemed to be staring blankly, bewildered, without focusing, at the surgeon, who stood before him, still holding the bandages. Only when the surgeon spoke—saying "Well?"—did a look of recognition cross Virgil's face.

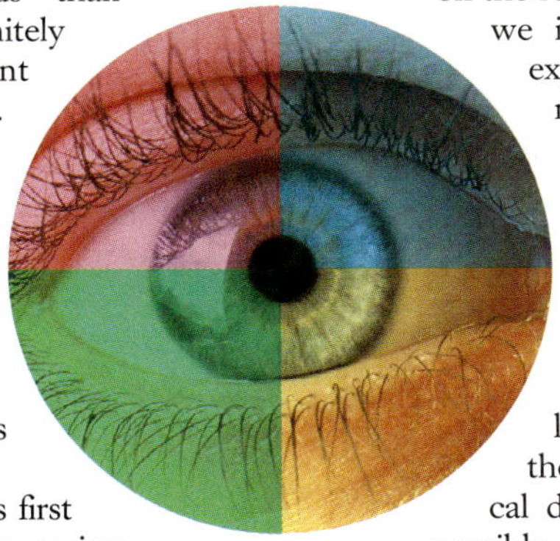

Virgil told me later that in this first moment he had no idea what he was seeing. There was light, there was movement, there was color, all mixed up, all meaningless, a blur. Then out of the blur came a voice that said, "Well?" Then, and only then, he said, did he finally realize that this chaos of light and shadow was a face—and, indeed, the face of his surgeon. . . .

The rest of us, born sighted, can scarcely imagine such confusion. For we, born with a full complement of senses, and correlating these, one with the other, create a sight world from the start, a world of visual objects and concepts and meanings. When we open our eyes each morning, it is upon a world we have spent a lifetime *learning* to see. We are not given the world: we make our world through incessant experience, categorization, memory, reconnection. But when Virgil opened his eye, after being blind for forty-five years—having had little more than an infant's visual experience, and this long forgotten—there were no visual memories to support a perception, there was no world of experience and meaning awaiting him. He saw, but what he saw had no coherence. His retina and optic nerve were active, transmitting impulses, but his brain could make no sense of them; he was, as neurologists say, agnostic.

Everyone, Virgil included, expected something simpler. A man opens his eyes, light enters, and falls on the retina: he sees. It is as simple as that, we imagine. And the surgeon's own experience, like that of most ophthalmologists, had been with the removal of cataracts from patients who had almost always lost their sight late in life—and such patients do indeed, if the surgery is successful, have a virtually immediate recovery of normal vision, for they have in no sense lost their ability to see. And so, though there had been a careful surgical discussion of the operation and of possible postsurgical complications, there was little discussion or preparation for the neurological and psychological difficulties that Virgil might encounter. . . .

On the day he returned home after the bandages were removed, his house and its contents were unintelligible to him, and he had to be led up the garden path, led through the house, led into each room, and introduced to each chair.

Analyzing the Reading

1. How did Virgil become blind?
2. Why didn't Virgil realize what he was seeing after his sight was regained?
3. **Critical Thinking** What psychological difficulties do you think Virgil encountered after regaining his sight?

ACTIVE READING STRATEGY

Explain to students that pausing to review during reading improves comprehension. It also gives them an opportunity to revise or update their ideas about the purpose, main idea, and supporting details of the selection.

PSYCHOLOGY JOURNAL

Virgil had no visual memories to support what he saw after his vision was restored. Ask students what strategies they would use to teach concepts of sight to someone who was blind. For example, how would they explain a rainbow to a blind person? ■

FYI

Perfect 20/20 vision is not the only requirement for military pilots. They must also have contrast sensitivity. For example, a pilot must exhibit the ability to see a white object moving across an expanse of snow.

Answers to Analyzing the Reading

1. Virgil was born with poor eyesight but became very sick at the age of three with a triple illness—meningitis, polio, and cat-scratch fever. At the age of six he developed cataracts, which made him functionally blind.
2. Virgil had no visual memories and experiences on which to base and compare visual images. His retina and optic nerve were transmitting impulses, but his brain could not make sense of them.
3. Answers will vary, but students should note that after regaining his sight, Virgil had problems perceiving the world—he had not learned to see. The world that he saw did not immediately make sense to him. Students may surmise that Virgil felt confused, depressed, or alienated.

Unit 4 Planning Guide

National High School Psychology Standards

The national high school psychology standards identify what students in an introductory high school psychology course should learn. **The material covered in Unit 4 reflects content from two of the five content domains: *Cognitive* and *Biopsychological*.** To see a chapter-by-chapter correlation to the national standards, refer to the Teacher pages.

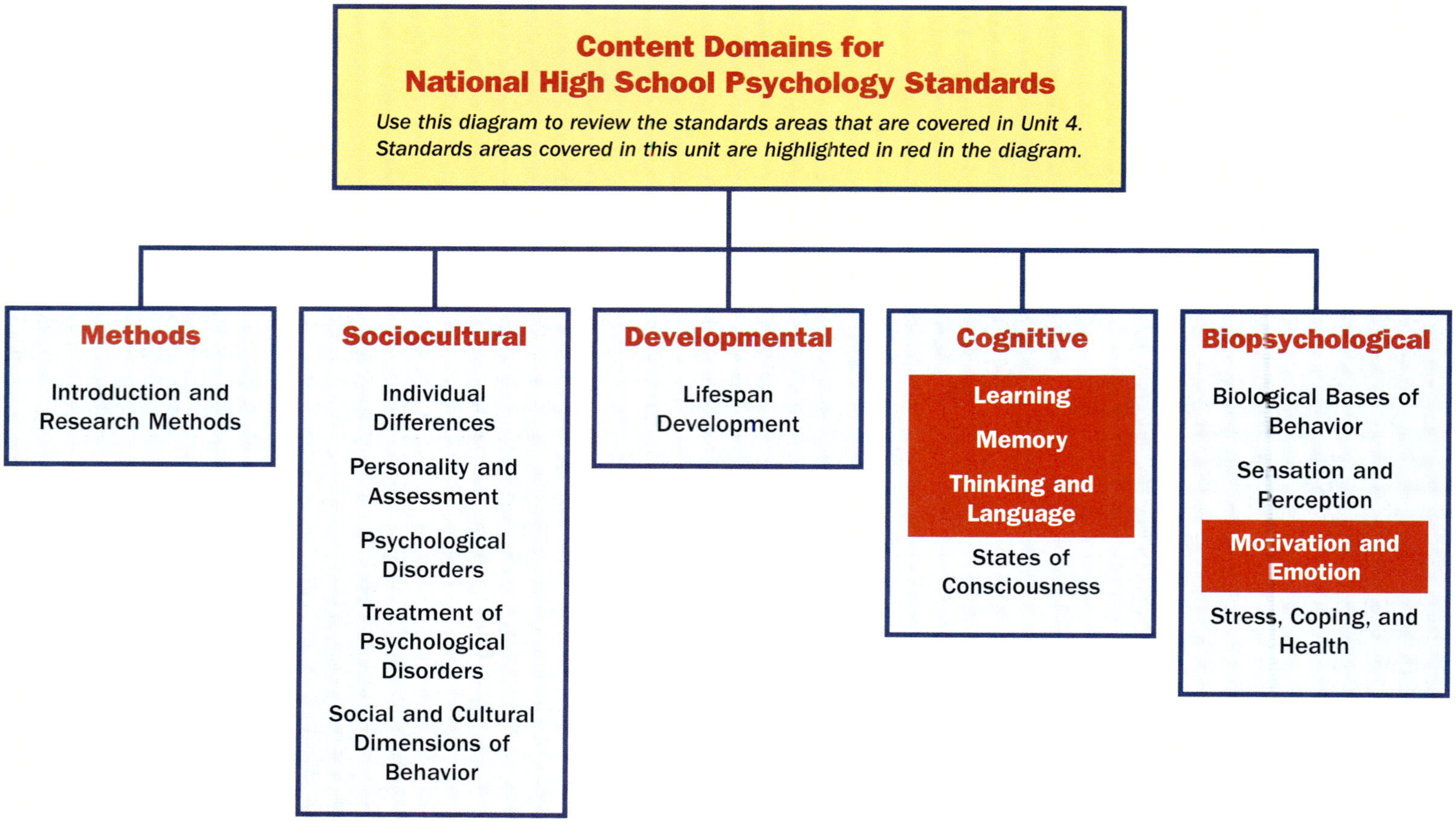

BIBLIOGRAPHY

Readings for the Student

Carpendale, J., & Lewis, C. (2006). *How Children Develop Social Understanding.* Malden, MA: Blackwell Publishing.

Lucas, B. (2006). *Boost Your Brain Power Week by Week.* London: Duncan Baird Publishers.

O'Donohue, W.T., and Ferguson, K.E. (2001). *The Psychology of B.F. Skinner.* Thousand Oaks, CA: Sage Publications.

Readings for the Teacher

Gluck, M.A. (2006). *Learning and Memory: From Brain to Behavior.* New York: Worth Publishers.

Martin, R.A. (2006). *The Psychology of Humor: An Integrative Approach.* San Diego, CA: Academic Press.

Uttl, B., Ohta, N., & Siegenthaler, A., eds. (2006). *Memory and Emotion: Interdisciplinary Perspectives.* Malden, MA: Blackwell Publishing.

Multimedia Resources

Videocassette. *A Conversation with B.F. Skinner* (23 minutes). McGraw-Hill Training Systems. In this video Skinner discusses the basic principles of behaviorism and the issues of control and freedom in human behavior.

Videocassette. *Learning and Memory* (60 minutes). Films Incorporated Educational. Shows the operation of memory in the learning process.

Unit 4 Resource Manager

Note: The following materials may be used when teaching Unit 4. Chapter level support materials can be found on the chapter resource pages.

GLENCOE'S ASSESSMENT ADVANTAGE

Use the following tools to easily assess student learning in a variety of ways:

- Authentic Assessment with Rubrics
- Section Quizzes, Chapter Tests, and Unit Tests
- glencoe.com
- SAT/SAT II Test Practice
- *ExamView® Assessment Suite* CD-ROM

APPLICATIONS AND HANDS-ON

Psychology Lab Activities 4–1, 4–2, 4–3

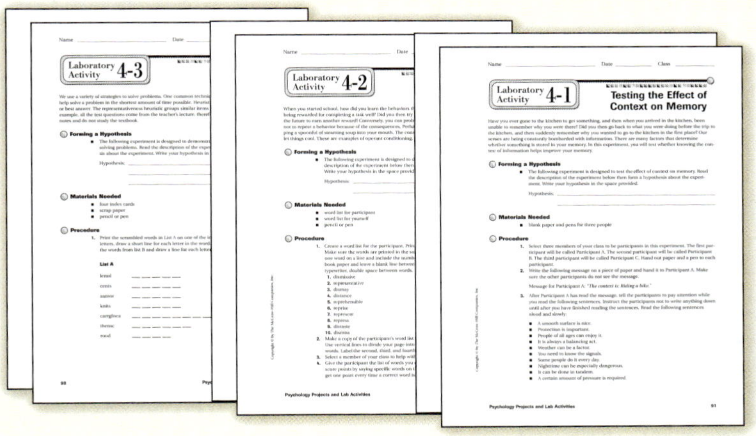
Laboratory Activity 4-3

Laboratory Activity 4-2

Laboratory Activity 4-1 Testing the Effect of Context on Memory

ASSESSMENT

GLENCOE'S ASSESSMENT ADVANTAGE

Unit 4 Test, Form A

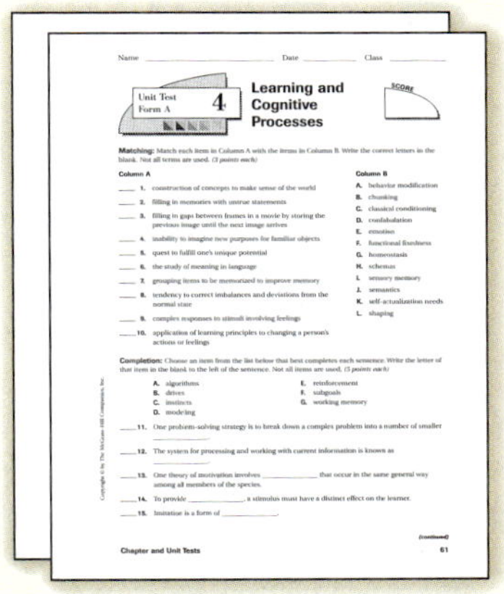
Unit Test Form A 4 Learning and Cognitive Processes

Unit 4 Test, Form B

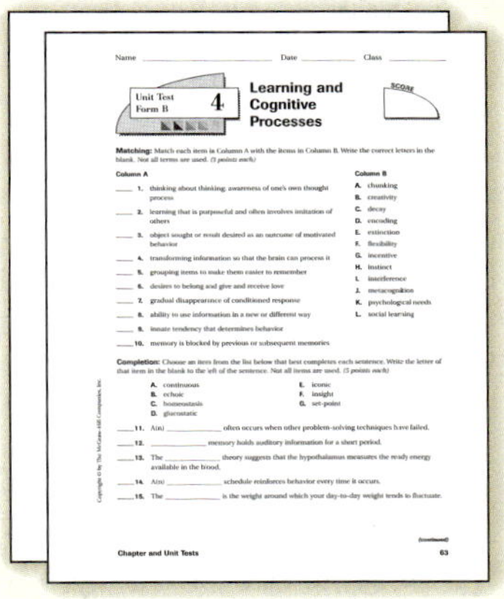
Unit Test Form B 4 Learning and Cognitive Processes

PRESENTATION Plus!

Use Glencoe's ***Presentation Plus!*** multimedia teacher tool to easily present dynamic lessons that visually excite your students. Using Microsoft PowerPoint® you can customize the presentations to create your own personalized lessons.

Introducing
UNIT 4

Unit Overview

This unit explores different learning techniques and processes. It explains how we summon unique thoughts and memories to help us perform day-to-day functions. **Chapter 9** examines three different types of learning—classical conditioning, operant conditioning, and social learning. It also illustrates how the principles of learning are applied to human and animal behavior through such techniques as reinforcement. **Chapter 10** investigates the ways in which people receive, process, store, retrieve, and analyze information. **Chapter 11** discusses problem solving, decision making, and reasoning processes. It also explores the relationship between language and human thought. **Chapter 12** looks at the physical and mental factors that cause people to act a specific way at a specific time. It also examines the theories explaining how and why people experience various emotions.

Unit Objectives

After studying this unit, students will be able to:

1. Describe the principles and techniques of classical and operant conditioning and social learning.
2. Explain the concepts of memory and information processing.
3. Identify the basic elements of language.
4. List reasons for the physiological and psychological factors associated with motivation and emotion.

UNIT 4

Learning and Cognitive Processes

Contents

A soccer player shoots for the goal.

EXTRA CREDIT PROJECT

Conducting an Interview Ask students to choose someone they know who has a particular skill that they would like to learn. Have students interview that person to find out how he or she acquired the skill and how long it took to reach current proficiency. Students should also find out what reinforcement the individual received while learning. For example, did the reinforcement come from another person or from completion of the task? Students should present their findings in brief oral reports to the class. **BLOCK SCHEDULING**

Why It's Important

Learning is involved in almost every phenomenon psychologists study and occurs in many different ways. Every individual uses learning techniques and processes and summons unique thoughts and memories to perform day-to-day functions.

PORTFOLIO PROJECT

Improving Cognitive Skills Explain to students that psychologists can help people use their minds as effectively as possible. Ask students to develop a plan that would help parents and educators teach elementary school students in the most effective manner. Students may wish to focus on a specific subject area, such as social studies or math. Encourage students to consider the following questions: **How can the principles of classical and operant conditioning and social learning be applied to specific learning situations? How do most children learn to solve problems, make decisions, and use language? Are these methods effective?** Students should present their plan in a report to the rest of the class.

Psychology Fair Suggestion Box

Encourage students to get involved with a psychology fair. Here are some project suggestions for **Unit 4—Learning and Cognitive Processes:**

- Research parents' influence on the behavior of their children, and vice versa.
- Demonstrate strategies for improving your memory.
- Explore the ways in which nondirected thinking is used by creative people.
- Analyze typical classroom situations in which the processes of modeling/imitation and vicarious reinforcement affect student behavior.
- Describe the role of positive and negative reinforcement in determining effort allocation.

Refer to ***Psychology Projects and Lab Activities*** in the TCR for help with organizing a psychology fair.

PSYCHOLOGY Online

Visit glencoe.com, the *Understanding Psychology* Web site, for Chapter Overviews, Student Web Activities, Interactive Puzzles, and Self-Check Quizzes for every chapter of the text.

Chapter 9 Resource Guide

SECTION RESOURCES

Daily Objectives	Reproducible Resources	Multimedia Resources
Section 1 **Classical Conditioning** Describe classical conditioning, the learning procedure in which associations are made between a neutral stimulus and an unconditioned stimulus.	Guided Reading Activity 9–1 Vocabulary Activity 9–1 Section Quiz 9–1	Daily Focus Transparency 9–1 *ExamView® Assessment Suite* CD-ROM Presentation Plus! Software
Section 2 **Operant Conditioning** Explain how operant conditioning occurs when the consequences that follow a behavior increase or decrease the likelihood of that behavior occurring again.	Guided Reading Activity 9–2 Vocabulary Activity 9–2 Section Quiz 9–2	Daily Focus Transparency 9–2 Vocabulary PuzzleMaker CD-ROM *ExamView® Assessment Suite* CD-ROM Presentation Plus! Software
Section 3 **Social Learning** Discuss how social learning involves people making decisions and acting upon the information available to them.	Guided Reading Activity 9–3 Vocabulary Activity 9–3 Section Quiz 9–3	Daily Focus Transparency 9–3 *ExamView® Assessment Suite* CD-ROM Presentation Plus! Software

Blackline Master CD-ROM Transparency

Block Schedule

Activities that are particularly suited for use within the block-scheduling framework are identified throughout this chapter by the following designation: **BLOCK SCHEDULING**

KEY TO ABILITY LEVELS

Teaching strategies have been coded for varying learning styles and abilities.

L1 **BASIC** activities for all students
L2 **AVERAGE** activities for average to above-average students
L3 **CHALLENGING** activities for above-average students
ELL **ENGLISH LANGUAGE LEARNER** activities

Chapter 9 Resource Guide

Timesaving Tools

TeacherWorks™ All-In-One Planner and Resource Center

- **Interactive Teacher Edition** Access your Teacher Wraparound Edition and your classroom resources with a few easy clicks.
- **Interactive Lesson Planner** Planning has never been easier! Organize your week, month, semester, or year with all the lesson helps you need to make teaching creative, timely, and relevant.

Use Glencoe's **Presentation Plus!** multimedia teacher tool to easily present dynamic lessons that visually excite your students. Using Microsoft PowerPoint® you can customize the presentations to create your own personalized lessons.

ACTIVITY

From the Classroom of...

Dale Kinney
Ralston High School
Omaha, NE

Just Like Pavlov's Dogs

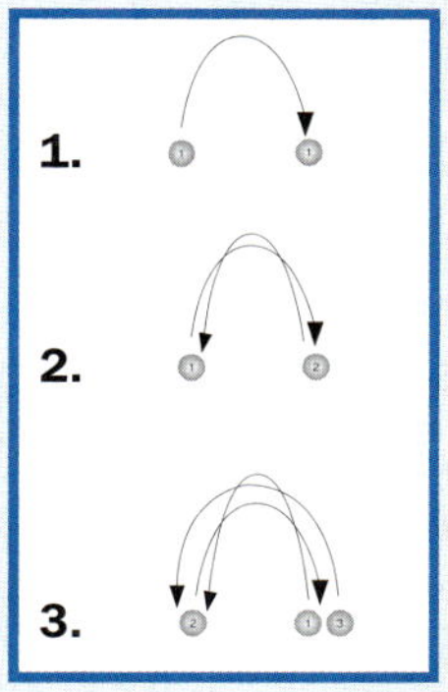

This activity helps students gain a better understanding of conditioning, shaping, positive and negative reinforcement, and modeling. Obtain tennis balls. You may ask your school's tennis coach or the manager of a racquet club. Have students toss one ball about three feet into the air, and catch it with the other hand (see diagram 1). Students should complete the toss with both hands, back and forth, using only one ball.

Then have students use two balls. They will throw one into the air and, when it reaches the apex, throw the other one into the air, making the balls crisscross as shown in diagram 2. Note how crucial timing is. Have students practice with two balls for a few minutes. Then have them add a third ball. Tell them that whichever hand holds two balls at the start is the hand that begins the sequence. Each hand alternates throwing a ball into the air as shown in diagram 3. Afterwards, ask the students to identify which aspects of the exercise acted as positive and negative reinforcements. Discuss how these elements affected persistence and how modeling enhanced the learning process.

PSYCHOLOGY Online

Use our Web site for additional resources. All essential content is covered in the Student Edition.

You and your students can visit glencoe.com, the Web site companion to *Understanding Psychology*. This innovative integration of electronic and print media offers your students a wealth of opportunities. The student text directs students to the Web site for the following options:

- Chapter Overviews
- Student Web Activities
- Self-Check Quizzes

Answers are provided for you in the **Web Activity Lesson Plan.** Additional Web resources and Interactive Puzzles are also available.

Chapter 9 Resource Guide

Note: The following materials may be used when teaching Chapter 9. Section level support materials are shown at point of use in the margins of the Teacher Wraparound Edition.

TEACHING TRANSPARENCIES

Chapter 9 Concept Transparencies

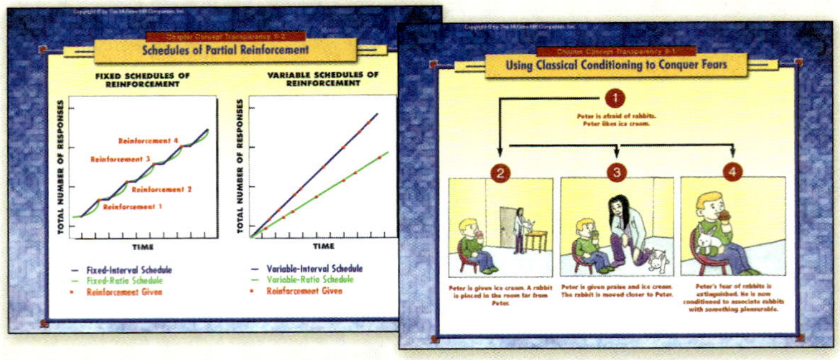

MULTIMEDIA

- **Vocabulary PuzzleMaker CD-ROM**
- ***ExamView® Assessment Suite* CD-ROM**
- **TeacherWorks™ CD-ROM**
- **Glencoe Skillbuilder Interactive Workbook, Level 2**
- **Presentation Plus! Software**

REVIEW AND REINFORCEMENT

Reteaching Activity 9

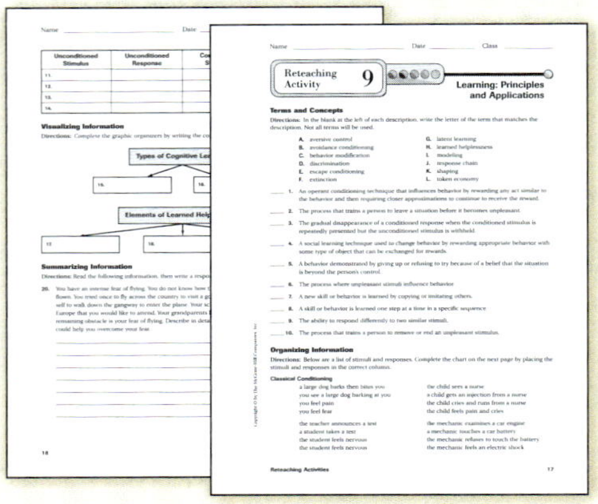

Graphic Organizer Activity 9

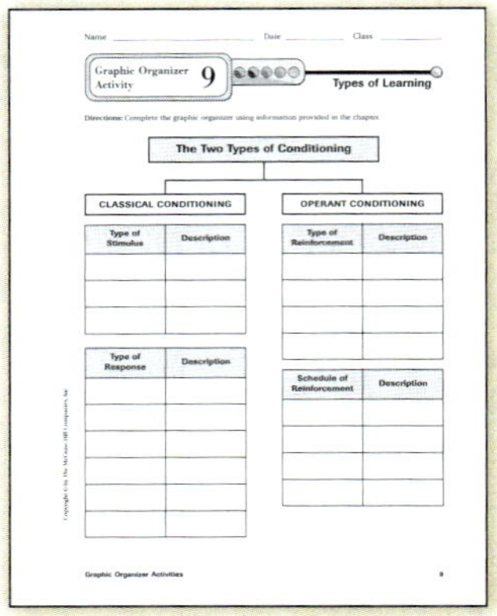

APPLICATION AND HANDS-ON

Psychology Projects 9–1 and 9–2

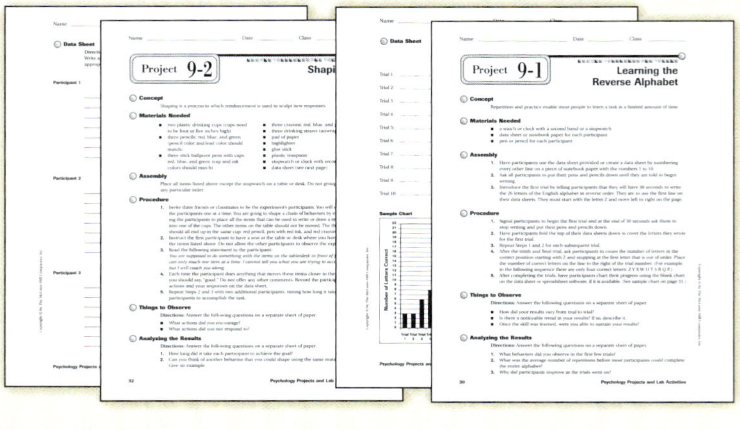

Application Activity 9

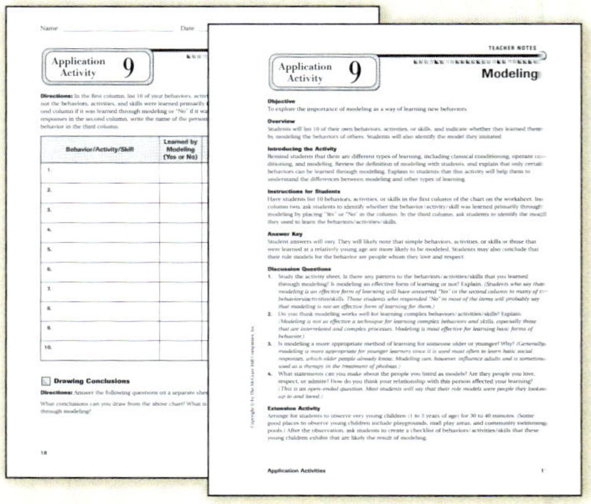

Chapter 9 Resource Guide

ASSESSMENT

Chapter 9 Test, Form A

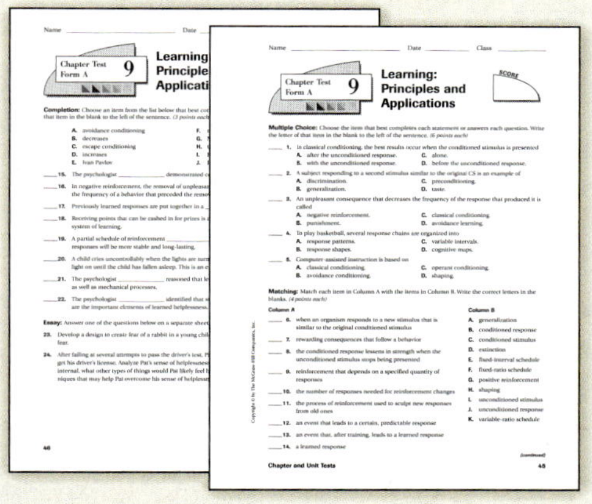

Chapter 9 Test, Form B

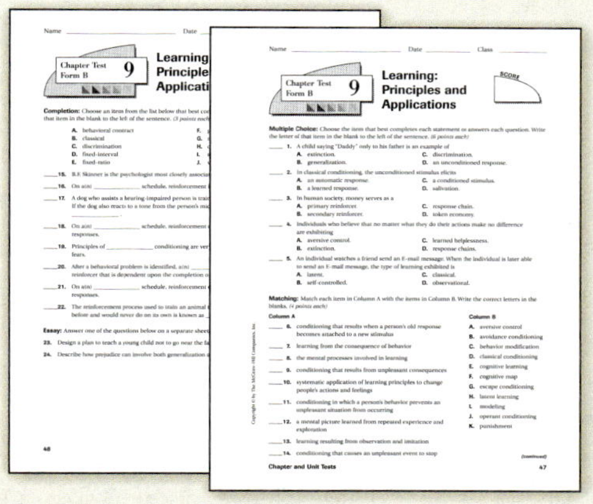

Authentic Assessment Activity 9

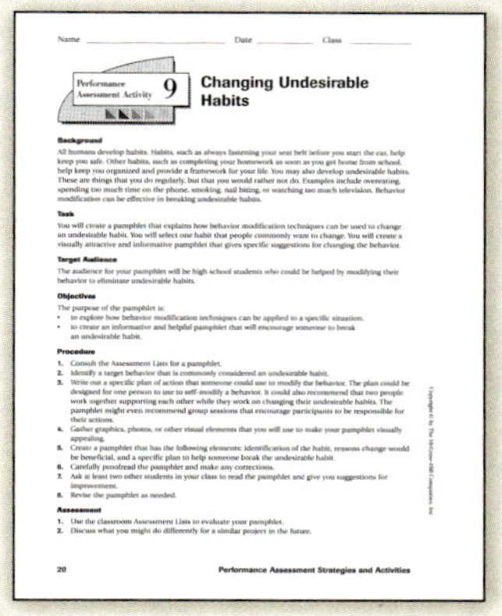

EXTENSION AND ENRICHMENT

Enrichment Activity 9

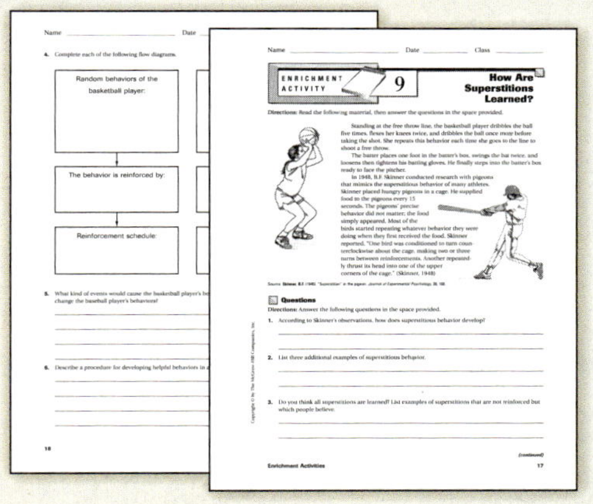

Critical Thinking Skills Activity 9

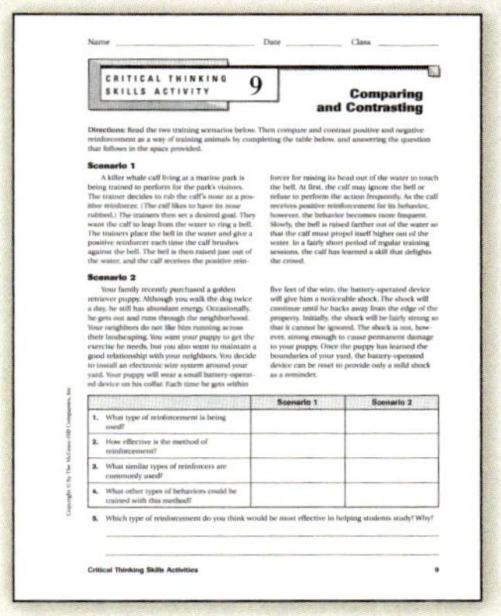

Psychology Reading 9

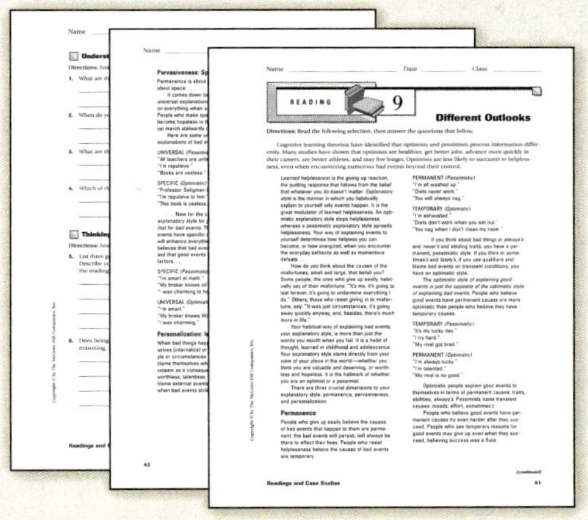

Psychology Case Study 9

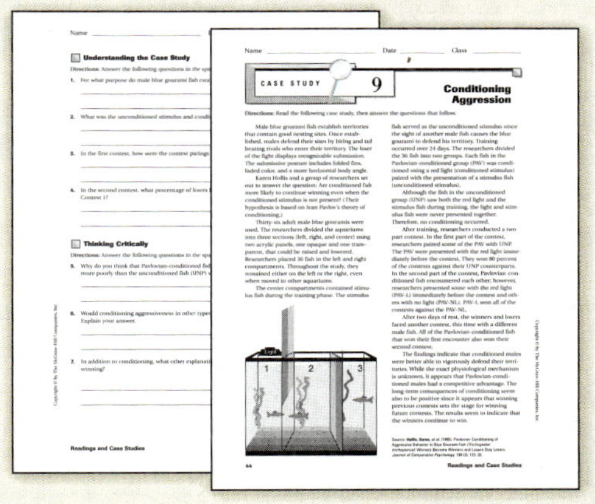

PSYCHOLOGY Online

Visit glencoe.com for a Chapter Overview for **Chapter 9—Learning: Principles and Applications.**

GLENCOE TECHNOLOGY

For a preview of Chapter 9 content, see MindJogger Checkpoint on **Presentation Plus!**

PSYCHOLOGY JOURNAL

Help students jog their memories by listing the various ways skills can be taught—verbal directions, demonstration, coaching, and so on.

This journal activity provides the basis for the Psychology Journal activity exercise in the Chapter Assessment. ■

CHAPTER 9

Learning: Principles and Applications

PSYCHOLOGY Online

Chapter Overview
Visit the *Understanding Psychology* Web site at glencoe.com and click on **Chapter 9—Chapter Overviews** to preview the chapter.

PSYCHOLOGY JOURNAL

Recall a situation in which you taught another person a skill or how to do a task. Write a brief account about it in your journal. Make sure to include a description of how reinforcement, punishment, or modeling was part of your teaching strategy. ■

240

TWO-MINUTE LESSON LAUNCHER

Albert Einstein did not begin to speak until he was three years old. His mastery of speech was so slow that his family feared he would never learn to talk. Thomas Edison had trouble with grammar and spelling; his writing was terrible even in his late teens. **Ask: How do we know that learning has occurred?** Discuss how learning is inferred by observing changes in performance. Point out that a psychologist can create a controlled situation that is conducive to learning and then objectively measure performance over time. List factors other than learning, such as emotion, motivation, and health, that can also influence performance.

SECTION 1 Classical Conditioning

Reader's Guide

■ **Main Idea**

People acquire certain behaviors through classical conditioning, a learning procedure in which associations are made between a neutral stimulus and an unconditioned stimulus.

■ **Vocabulary**

- classical conditioning
- neutral stimulus
- unconditioned stimulus (US)
- unconditioned response (UR)
- conditioned stimulus (CS)
- conditioned response (CR)
- generalization
- discrimination
- extinction

■ **Objectives**

- Describe the principles of classical conditioning.
- Outline the techniques of classical conditioning.

EXPLORING PSYCHOLOGY

Which Pen Would You Choose?

The researchers placed the participants in a room. In this room the participants first viewed purple pens. As the participants sat staring at the purple pens, pleasant music played in the background. Then the music stopped, and the purple pens were taken away. Suddenly green pens appeared. As the participants sat staring at the green pens, they heard unpleasant music in the background. Later, the researchers offered the pens to the participants. The participants could pick a purple or green pen. The participants overwhelmingly chose purple pens. Why?

—adapted from *The Story of Psychology* by Morton Hunt, 1993

Why did the participants choose purple pens over green in the experiment above? This experiment took place in 1982 and was based on a principle that is widely used today in television commercials. Pairing a product with pleasant sensations motivates consumers to make a choice without an awareness of why they made that choice.

The Russian physiologist Ivan Pavlov called what was taking place in similar situations *conditioning*. In **classical conditioning,** a person's or animal's old response becomes attached to a new stimulus. This is one example of learning. What is learning? *Learning* is a relatively permanent change in a behavioral tendency that results from experience.

classical conditioning: a learning procedure in which associations are made between a neutral stimulus and an unconditioned stimulus

SECTION RESOURCES

Reproducible Masters

- Guided Reading Activity 9–1
- Vocabulary Activity 9–1
- Section Quiz 9–1

Transparencies

- Daily Focus Transparency 9–1

Multimedia

- *ExamView® Assessment Suite* CD-ROM
- Presentation Plus! Software

1 FOCUS

Section Objectives

1. Describe the principles of classical conditioning.
2. Outline the techniques of classical conditioning.

BELLRINGER
Motivational Activity

Project Daily Focus Transparency 9–1 and have students answer the questions.

Available as blackline master

Daily Focus Transparency 9–1

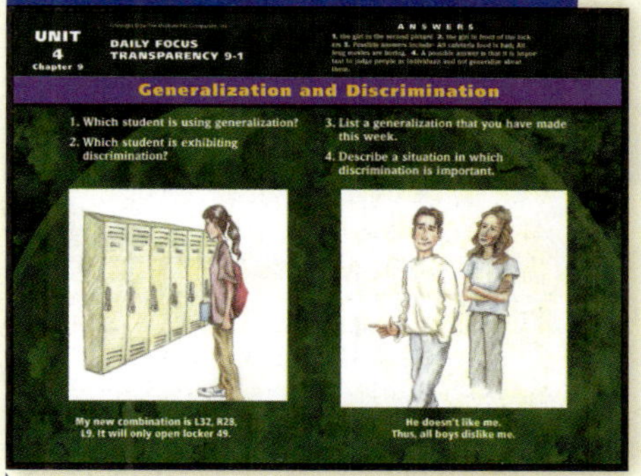

Reader's Guide

Use the Reader's Guide to introduce concepts and vocabulary.

■ **Exploring Psychology**
Ask students to read the **Exploring Psychology** feature and then discuss: **Why did the students choose the purple pens?**

■ **Vocabulary Precheck**
Have students read the Glossary definition of each term. Then ask them to restate each definition in their own words.

CHAPTER 9
Section 1, pages 241–248

2 TEACH

L1 Understanding Cause and Effect Organize students into small groups and ask each group to appoint a recorder. Next, direct the groups to review the pages on classical conditioning. Based on these pages, have students write a series of four or more statements that explain the cause-and-effect relationships between the different kinds of stimuli and responses. After the groups complete their statements, ask each recorder to report for the group. List the valid statements on the board. Discuss any invalid statements, and challenge students to correct these statements.

Guided Reading Activity 9-1

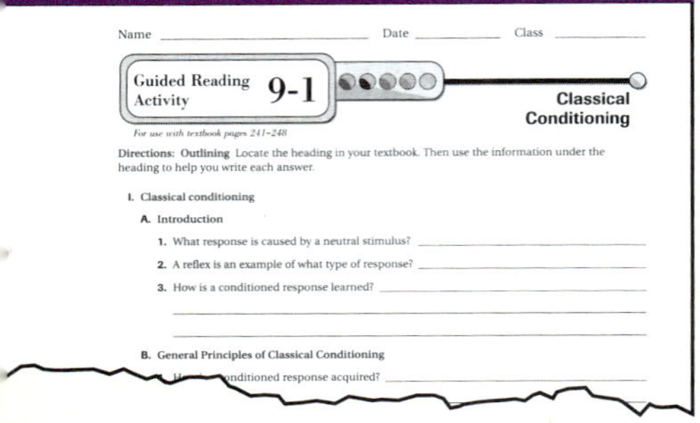
Name ______ Date ______ Class ______

Guided Reading Activity 9-1 — Classical Conditioning

For use with textbook pages 241–248

Directions: Outlining Locate the heading in your textbook. Then use the information under the heading to help you write each answer.

I. Classical conditioning
A. Introduction
1. What response is caused by a neutral stimulus? ______
2. A reflex is an example of what type of response? ______
3. How is a conditioned response learned? ______

B. General Principles of Classical Conditioning
...nditioned response acquired? ______

FYI

The concept of association can be traced back to the Greek philosopher Plato, who believed that learning largely relies on associating a new object with existing knowledge of related objects or concepts. Association is strongly linked to recollection or memory.

Pavlov's discovery of this type of learning—the principle of classical conditioning—was accidental. Around the turn of the twentieth century, Pavlov had been studying the process of digestion. Pavlov wanted to understand how a dog's stomach prepares to digest food when something is placed in its mouth. Then he noticed that the mere sight or smell of food was enough to start a hungry dog salivating. Pavlov became fascinated with how the dog anticipated the food and how salivation occurred before the food was presented, and he decided to investigate.

CLASSICAL CONDITIONING

Pavlov began his experiments by ringing a tuning fork and then immediately placing some meat powder on the dog's tongue. He chose the tuning fork because it was a **neutral stimulus**—that is, one that had nothing to do with the response to meat (salivation) prior to conditioning. After only a few times, the dog started salivating as soon as it heard the sound, even if the food was not placed in its mouth (see Figure 9.1). Pavlov demonstrated that a neutral stimulus (here, tuning fork or bell's ring) can cause a formerly unrelated response. This occurs if it is presented regularly just before the stimulus (here, food) that normally brings about that response (here, salivation).

Pavlov used the term *unconditioned* to refer to stimuli and to the automatic, involuntary responses they caused. Such responses include blushing, shivering, being startled, or salivating. In the experiment, food was the **unconditioned stimulus (US)**—an event that leads to a certain, predictable response usually without any previous training. Food normally causes salivation. A dog does not have to be taught to salivate when it smells meat. The salivation is an **unconditioned response (UR)**—a reaction that occurs naturally and automatically when the unconditioned stimulus is presented; in other words, a reflex.

Under normal conditions, the sound of a tuning fork would not cause salivation. The dog had to be taught, or conditioned, to associate this sound with food. An ordinarily neutral event that, after training, leads to a response such as salivation is termed a **conditioned stimulus (CS).** The salivation it causes is a **conditioned response (CR).** A conditioned response is learned. A wide variety of events may serve as conditioned stimuli for salivation—the sight of food, an experimenter entering the room, the sound of a tone, or a flash of light. A number of different reflex responses that occur automatically following an unconditioned stimulus (US) can be conditioned to occur following the correct conditioned stimulus (CS).

neutral stimulus: a stimulus that does not initially elicit any part of an unconditioned response

unconditioned stimulus (US): an event that elicits a certain predictable response typically without previous training

unconditioned response (UR): an organism's automatic (or natural) reaction to a stimulus

conditioned stimulus (CS): a once-neutral event that elicits a given response after a period of training in which it has been paired with (occurred just before) an unconditioned stimulus

conditioned response (CR): the learned reaction to a conditioned stimulus

GENERAL PRINCIPLES OF CLASSICAL CONDITIONING

Classical conditioning helps animals and humans adapt to the environment. It also helps humans and animals avoid danger. Psychologists have investigated why and in what circumstances classical conditioning occurs, leading to a greater understanding of the principles of classical conditioning.

COOPERATIVE LEARNING ACTIVITY

Creating Storyboards Organize the class into small groups to create storyboards that illustrate the steps in the classical conditioning experiment performed by Pavlov or some other experiment in classical conditioning. The storyboards should include both drawings (and other appropriate graphics) and captions that pertain to the three phases of classical conditioning: before, during, and after training. After the groups have presented their storyboards to the class, display their works in the classroom. **BLOCK SCHEDULING**

Figure 9.1 Classical Conditioning Experiment

Pavlov's students used this apparatus. The tube leading from the dog's mouth allowed saliva to be measured and recorded on the kymograph. ***What was the point of this experiment?***

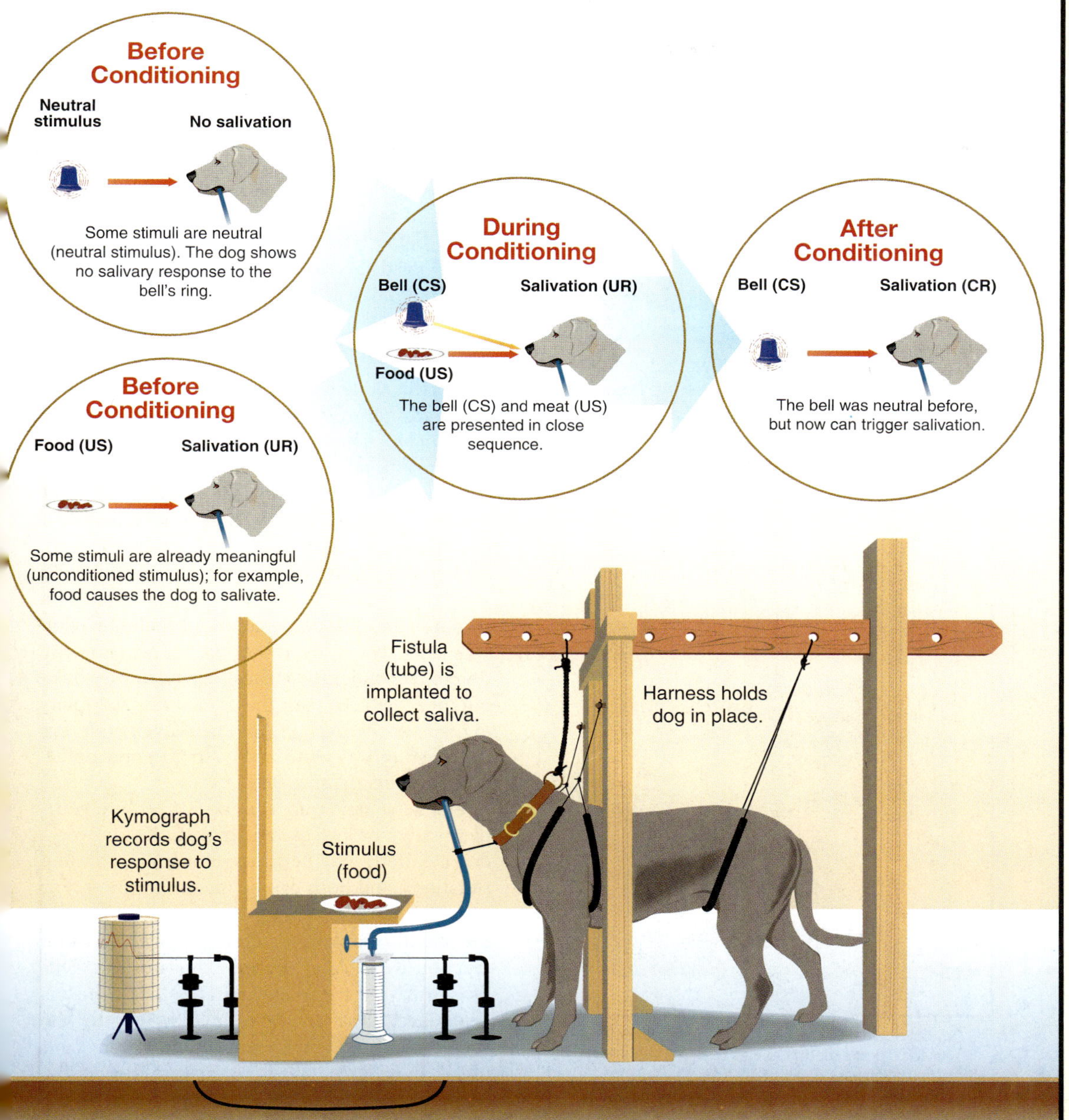

Figure 9.1

Visual Instruction Pavlov spent the first half of his career studying the digestive system. His keen observations led him to discover what he called "psychical secretion." Ask students what they think Pavlov might have meant by this.

Caption Answer that conditioning occurs when a neutral stimulus causes a formerly unrelated response

CURRICULUM CONNECTION

Biology Explain to students that the first time they hear a song they might have a strong emotional response to it. When the song loses its ability to produce that kind of response, they have become habituated to it. This is caused by a biological change in which there is a decrease in neurotransmitters, the chemicals that carry messages to the brain. The brain has learned to ignore the message. The routes the neurotransmitters had originally created to tell the brain about the song have weakened and become less important.

MEETING SPECIAL NEEDS

Learning Style: Intrapersonal Active learning tasks that involve students' own experiences and prior knowledge will help them better understand the principles and techniques involved in conditioning. In discussing the practical application of classical conditioning to human behavior, ask students to write a journal entry explaining step-by-step how they overcame an unwanted habit, such as tardiness or oversleeping. Have the students share any insights they gained about conditioning as a result of this activity. **L2**

Refer to ***Inclusion for the High School Social Studies Classroom Strategies and Activities*** in the TCR for strategies for students with different learning styles.

PSYCHOLOGY JOURNAL

Ask students to write in their journal about a personal fear. The written response will not be shared with the rest of the class. Encourage them to describe the experience of fear in as much detail as possible. Ask them to consider the origin of their fears—were they learned or are they instinctive? ■

TEACHER Tip

A good way to illustrate the process of extinction is to connect it with a discussion of taste aversions (pp. 246–247), which most students will have experienced. Ask volunteers to describe how they developed aversions to certain foods. If any students have overcome an aversion, ask them to describe the process.

Figure 9.2

Caption Answer The ringing bell is the neutral stimulus; attacking the cat is the CR.

Vocabulary Activity 9-1

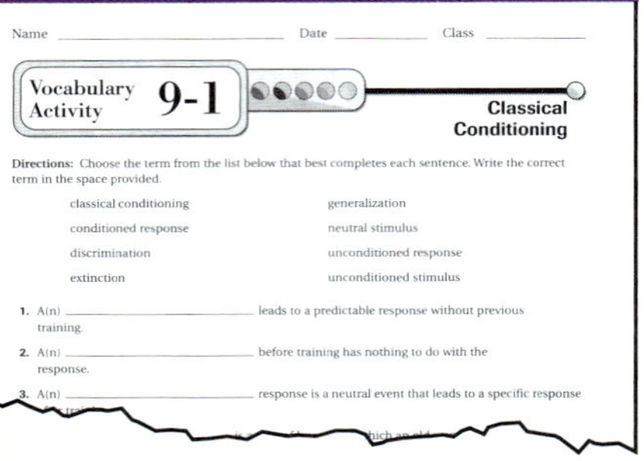
Name ______ Date ______ Class ______

Vocabulary Activity 9-1 Classical Conditioning

Directions: Choose the term from the list below that best completes each sentence. Write the correct term in the space provided.

classical conditioning, generalization, conditioned response, neutral stimulus, discrimination, unconditioned response, extinction, unconditioned stimulus

1. A(n) ______ leads to a predictable response without previous training.
2. A(n) ______ before training has nothing to do with the response.
3. A(n) ______ response is a neutral event that leads to a specific response

Acquisition

Acquisition of a classically conditioned response generally occurs gradually. With each pairing of the conditioned stimulus (CS) and the unconditioned stimulus (US), the conditioned response (CR)—or learned response—is strengthened. In Pavlov's experiment, the more frequently the tuning fork was paired with the food, the more often the tone brought about salivation—the conditioned response.

The timing of the association between the conditioned stimulus (the tone) and the unconditioned stimulus (food) also influences learning. Pavlov tried several different conditioning procedures in which he varied the time between presenting the conditioned stimulus and the unconditioned stimulus. He found that classical conditioning was most reliable and effective when the conditioned stimulus was presented just before the unconditioned stimulus. He found that presenting the conditioned stimulus (CS) about half a second before the unconditioned stimulus (US) would yield the strongest associations between the tuning fork and the meat.

generalization: responding similarly to a range of similar stimuli

discrimination: the ability to respond differently to similar but distinct stimuli

Figure 9.2 Pavlov's Research

The name of Pavlov is well-known in the field of psychology because of his pioneering research. ***In this cartoonist's depiction, what is the neutral stimulus? The CR?***

THE FAR SIDE By GARY LARSON

Unbeknownst to most students of psychology, Pavlov's first experiment was to ring a bell and cause his dog to attack Freud's cat.

Generalization and Discrimination

In the same set of experiments, Pavlov also explored the processes of *generalization* and *discrimination*. **Generalization** occurs when an animal responds to a second stimulus similar to the original CS without prior training with the second stimulus. When Pavlov conditioned a dog to salivate at the sight of a circle (the CS), he found that the dog would salivate when it saw an oval as well. The dog had generalized its response to include a similar stimulus. Pavlov was later able to do the opposite, teaching the dog to respond only to the circle by always pairing meat powder with the circle but never pairing it with the oval. Pavlov thus taught the dog **discrimination**—the ability to respond differently to different stimuli.

Generalization and discrimination are complementary processes and are part of your everyday life. Both may occur spontaneously in some situations, and both can be taught in others. For example, assume a friend has come to associate the sound of a dentist's drill (CS) with a fearful reaction (CR). After several exposures to a dentist's drill, your friend may find that he or she has generalized this uncomfortable feeling to the sound of other, nondental drills. Later, your friend may learn to discriminate between the sound of a dentist's drill and other drills.

CRITICAL THINKING ACTIVITY

Classifying Information To help students understand the principle of generalization, analyze the example of the dentist's drill on page 244. Discuss generalization by asking students to suggest other examples from their own experiences. Make a table with three columns on the board, and label the columns *Conditioned Stimulus, Conditioned Response,* and *Similar Stimulus.* Have students help you fill in the table by telling you what to put in each column for each example. **L1** **ELL**

Extinction and Spontaneous Recovery

A classically conditioned response, like any other behavior, is subject to change. Pavlov discovered that if he stopped presenting food after the sound of the tuning fork, the sound gradually lost its effect on the dog. After he repeatedly struck the tuning fork without giving food, the dog no longer associated the sound with the arrival of food—the sound of the tuning fork no longer caused the salivation response. Pavlov called this effect **extinction** because the CR had gradually died out.

Even though a classically conditioned response may be extinguished, this does not mean that the CR has been completely unlearned. If a rest period is given following extinction, the CR may reappear when the CS is presented again but not followed by a US. This *spontaneous recovery* does not bring the CR back to original strength, however. Pavlov's dogs produced much less saliva during spontaneous recovery than they did at the end of their original conditioning. Alternating lengthy rest periods and the tone without food caused more rapid loss of salivation each time and less recovery the next time the CS was presented.

A good example of extinction and spontaneous recovery can occur if you are involved in a car accident. Following the accident it may at first be difficult to drive again. You might even find it difficult to open the door and get into the car. As you approach the car, your hands begin to shake and your knees get shaky as well. Your heartbeat even increases as you get nearer. After a few days, opening the door and getting into the car do not bother you as much. Several months go by and the fears of the car and the accident have been extinguished. One day, several months later, as you begin to approach the car, your heart begins to race and your knees and hands begin to shake. You have had a spontaneous recovery of the fear reaction.

Profiles In Psychology

Ivan Petrovich Pavlov

1849–1936

"While you are experimenting, do not remain content with the surface of things. Don't become a mere recorder of facts, but try to penetrate the mystery of their origin."

Born in central Russia, Pavlov abandoned his family's hopes that he would become a priest, and instead pursued science. After receiving his doctoral degree from the University of St. Petersburg in 1897, he began performing his own research into digestion and blood circulation. The work that made Pavlov famous actually began as a study of digestion, for which he won the Nobel Prize in 1904. Pavlov discovered that salivation and the action of the stomach were closely linked to reflexes in the autonomic nervous system. By studying conditioned reflexes, it became possible to examine human behavior objectively, instead of resorting to subjective methods.

Pavlov distrusted the new science of psychiatry. He did think, though, that conditioned reflexes could explain the behavior of psychotic people. He believed that those who withdrew from the world may associate all stimuli with possible injury or threat.

extinction: the gradual disappearance of a conditioned response when the conditioned stimulus is repeatedly presented without the unconditioned stimulus

L2 Demonstrating Reasoned Judgment The principle of extinction is the basis for many psychological treatments aimed at alleviating irrational fears, or phobias. The psychologist systematically desensitizes the patient to the feared object or experience until the phobic response is extinguished. Ask students to design a program of steps by which a psychologist might extinguish an individual's fear of heights and develop a test by which the programs could be evaluated.

Profiles In Psychology

Ask students to read the **Profiles In Psychology** feature and then discuss the following questions:

1. How did Pavlov's research on digestion make him famous? *(He discovered that salivation and the action of the stomach were linked to conditioned reflexes in the autonomic nervous system. This allowed Pavlov to study human behavior objectively.)*
2. What did Pavlov believe about conditioned reflexes? *(that they could explain the behavior of psychotic people because those who withdrew from the world associated all stimuli with injury or threat)*

PSYCHOLOGY LAB EXPERIMENT

Classical Conditioning (This experiment works best if participants have light-colored eyes). Make sure the room is dark enough for the participant's eyes to dilate when the lamp is turned off, yet light enough to still observe pupil dilation. Explain this procedure to the experimenters: Sit at a table with a lamp. Place a glass of water and a spoon within reach. Turn off the lamp and observe how the participant's eyes adapt. Switch the light on. For the next 10 trials, tap the glass with the spoon immediately prior to turning off the lamp. On the 11th trial, tap the glass but leave the lamp on. Ask the experimenter to describe what happens to the participant's eyes in behavioral terms. Discuss with students the impact of Pavlov's classical conditioning experiments on current thinking in psychology. **L1**

CULTURAL CONNECTIONS

Canalization, the process in which people are conditioned to prefer one stimulus over another because they perceive that stimulus as more satisfying, differs from culture to culture. People in different cultures are conditioned to various preferences of food, color, and beauty. For example, most people in the United States do not consider insects to be edible, while other cultures may consider them a delicacy.

Reading Check Answer Taste aversions develop after a bad experience follows eating a particular food. People learn to associate the food with the negative experience.

PSYCHOLOGY Update

Taste aversions Many chemotherapy patients develop taste aversions to the last thing they ate before receiving treatment. Over the course of chemotherapy treatment, some patients develop taste aversions to foods they have always enjoyed. To avoid these taste aversions and the accompanying weight loss, chemotherapy patients are now given an odd tasting piece of candy immediately before treatment.

3 ASSESS

Assign Section 1 Assessment as homework or as an in-class activity.

CLASSICAL CONDITIONING AND HUMAN BEHAVIOR

John B. Watson and Rosalie Rayner (1920) used conditioning on a human infant in the case of Little Albert (see Case Studies, page 249). Watson questioned the role that conditioning played in the development of emotional responses in children. He and Rayner attempted to condition an 11-month-old infant named Albert to fear laboratory rats. At first Albert happily played with the rats. When Watson struck a steel bar with a hammer to produce a loud sound, Albert began to display a fear response. Eventually Albert showed fear each time he saw the rat even though the loud sound was not repeated. Although this demonstration is now viewed as unethical (because the researchers taught Little Albert to fear things that he previously had no fear of), it provided evidence that emotional responses can be classically conditioned in humans. In this case the US is the loud noise, the UR is fear, the CS is the rat, and the CR is fear.

Did You Know?

Classical Conditioning Have you ever noticed how movie directors use music in their movies? Did you ever hear a song and then think about either the movie it was from or the person you were with when you saw the movie? If so, you experienced classical conditioning. The music had become a "signal" that triggers memories and emotions. A conditioned emotion, such as fear, is a very difficult response to extinguish. It may trigger physical, cognitive, and emotional reactions.

Using the principle of classical conditioning, O. Hobart and Mollie Mowrer (1938) discovered a practical solution to the problem of bed-wetting. One reason bed-wetting occurs is that children do not wake up during the night to body signals that they have a full bladder. The Mowrers developed a device known as the *bell and pad.* It consists of two metallic sheets perforated with small holes and wired to a battery-run alarm. The thin, metal sheets—wrapped in insulation or padding—are placed under the child's bedsheets. When the sleeping child moistens the sheet with the first drops of urine, the circuit closes, causing the alarm to go off and wake the child. The child can then use the bathroom.

The alarm is the unconditioned stimulus that produces the unconditioned response of waking up. The sensation of a full bladder is the conditioned stimulus that, before conditioning, did not produce wakefulness. After several pairings of the full bladder (CS) and the alarm (US), the child is able to awaken to the sensation of a full bladder without the help of the alarm. This technique has proven to be a very effective way of treating bed-wetting problems.

Taste Aversions

Reading Check How do people develop taste aversions?

Suppose you go to a fancy restaurant. You decide to try an expensive appetizer you have never eaten, for instance, snails. Then suppose that, after dinner, you go to a concert and become violently ill. You will probably develop a taste aversion; you may never be able to look at another snail without becoming at least a little nauseated.

Your nausea reaction to snails is another example of classical conditioning. What makes this type of conditioning interesting to learning theorists is that when people or other animals become ill, they seem to decide, "It must have been something I ate," even if they have not eaten

INTERDISCIPLINARY CONNECTIONS ACTIVITY

History The English philosopher John Locke theorized that knowledge is not inborn but learned through experience. He reasoned that our observations and experiences supply our understanding of the world around us. In *An Essay Concerning Human Understanding,* Locke explained that our senses convey to the mind distinct perceptions of things according to the way the senses are affected. Ask students to use Locke's ideas to explain the process by which taste aversions are created. Encourage students to research Locke and his philosophy. Students should present a short written report describing the relationship between Locke's ideas and earlier and later theories of learning. **L3**

Figure 9.3 Examples of Common Conditioned Responses

If you have pets and feed them canned food, what happens when you use the can opener? The animals may come running even when you are opening a can of peas. ***Why do you feel distress at the mere sight of flashing police lights?***

CS	CR	US	UR
Dentist/ sound of drill	Tension	Drill	Tension
Product (soda pop)	Favorable feeling	Catchy jingle or slogan	Favorable feeling
Flashing police car lights	Distress	Speeding ticket	Distress

for several hours. It is unlikely that the concert hall in which you were sick will become the conditioned stimulus, nor will other stimuli from the restaurant—the wallpaper pattern or the type of china used. What is more, psychologists can even predict which part of your meal will be the CS—you will probably blame a new food. Thus, if you get sick after a meal of salad, steak, and snails, you will probably learn to hate snails, even if they are really not the cause of your illness.

John Garcia and R.A. Koelling (1966) first demonstrated this phenomenon with rats. The animals were placed in a cage with a tube containing flavored water. Whenever a rat took a drink, lights flashed and clicks sounded. Then, some of the rats were given an electric shock after they drank. All these rats showed traditional classical conditioning—the lights and the sounds became conditioned stimuli, and the rats tried to avoid them in order to avoid a shock. The other rats were not shocked but were injected with a drug that made them sick after they drank and the lights and sounds occurred. These rats developed an aversion not to the lights or the sounds but only to the taste of the flavored water.

This special relationship between food and illness was used in a study that made coyotes avoid sheep by giving them a drug to make them sick when they ate sheep (Gustavson et al., 1974). This application is important because sheep farmers in the western United States would like to eliminate the coyotes that threaten their flocks, while naturalists are opposed to killing the coyotes. If coyotes could be trained to hate the taste of sheep, they would rely on other foods and thus learn to coexist peacefully with sheep.

In summary, classical conditioning helps animals and humans predict what is going to happen. It provides information that may be helpful to their survival. Learning associated with classical conditioning may aid animals in finding food or help humans avoid pain or injury. For example, parents may condition an infant to avoid a danger such as electrical outlets by shouting "NO!" and startling the infant each time he approaches an outlet. The infant fears the shouts of the parents, and eventually the infant may fear the outlet even when the parents are not there.

PSYCHOLOGY Online

Student Web Activity Visit the *Understanding Psychology* Web site at glencoe.com and click on **Chapter 9—Student Web Activities** for an activity about learning.

Figure 9.3

Visual Instruction Point out that each of the examples in the chart demonstrates the same procedural pattern: An unconditioned stimulus (drill grinding teeth) elicits an unconditioned response (tension). The US becomes paired with a conditioned stimulus (sound of the drill). As the US and CS are paired, the conditioned response (tension) is learned.

Caption Answer The feeling of distress at the sight of flashing police lights is the result of classical conditioning. You may associate receiving a traffic ticket with flashing police lights.

PSYCHOLOGY Online

Links and instructional guidelines can be found in the **Web Activity Lesson Plan** at glencoe.com.

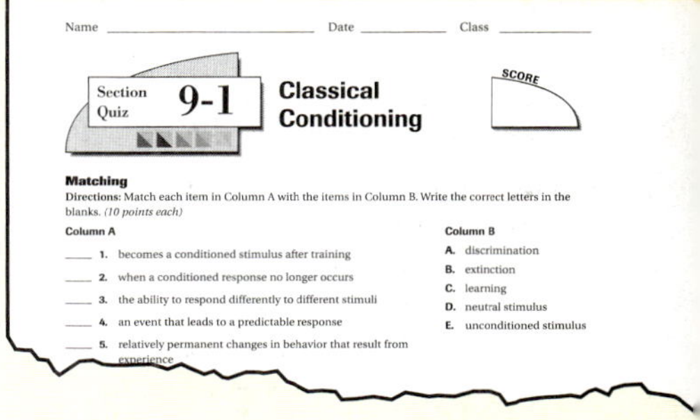
Section Quiz 9–1

Name ______ Date ______ Class ______

Section Quiz 9-1 **Classical Conditioning** SCORE

Matching

Directions: Match each item in Column A with the items in Column B. Write the correct letters in the blanks. *(10 points each)*

Column A

____ 1. becomes a conditioned stimulus after training
____ 2. when a conditioned response no longer occurs
____ 3. the ability to respond differently to different stimuli
____ 4. an event that leads to a predictable response
____ 5. relatively permanent changes in behavior that result from experience

Column B

A. discrimination
B. extinction
C. learning
D. neutral stimulus
E. unconditioned stimulus

EXTENDING THE CONTENT

Little Albert Students may wonder who Little Albert was and what eventually became of him. Albert was the son of an employee of the Phipps Clinic at Johns Hopkins University in Baltimore, where Watson and Rayner were conducting their experiments. Albert left their study when he was adopted by a family outside of Baltimore. Nothing of his subsequent history is known. If alive today, Albert would be in his eighties. You might ask students to speculate whether extinction eventually occurred in Albert's case or whether they think Albert may still have an inexplicable fear of furry white animals.

Figure 9.4

Visual Instruction Use the table to point out that the time at which the critical part of the conditioning occurs helps define the differences between classical and operant conditioning.

Caption Answer In classical conditioning, the learner responds to its environment, while in operant conditioning, the learner actively operates on its environment.

Reteach

Ask students to write a summary explaining how people and animals learn responses through classical conditioning.

Enrich

Divide the class into small groups. Ask each group to list five examples of classical conditioning in everyday life. Then have the groups exchange lists and identify the US, CS, UR, and CR for each example.

4 CLOSE

Ask students to make a list of daily habits and preferences and then explain how classical conditioning played a part in creating those habits and preferences.

Figure 9.4 **Classical Conditioning vs. Operant Conditioning**

Classical conditioning and operant conditioning both involve the establishment of relationships between two events. Classical conditioning and operant conditioning, though, use very different procedures to reach their goals. ***What role does the learner's environment play in each type of conditioning?***

Classical Conditioning	Operant Conditioning
1. Always a specific stimulus (US) that elicits the desired response	1. No identifiable stimulus; learner must first respond, then behavior is reinforced
2. US does not depend upon learner's response	2. Reinforcement depends upon learner's behavior
3. Environment elicits response from learner	3. Learner actively operates on its environment

Classical conditioning is an example of a behaviorist theory. *Behaviorism* is the attempt to understand behavior in terms of relationships between observable stimuli and observable responses. *Behaviorists* are psychologists who study only those behaviors that they can observe and measure. Behaviorists are not concerned with unobservable mental processes. They emphasize actions instead of thoughts. We will discuss another behaviorist learning theory, operant conditioning, in the next section. Classical conditioning is a process by which a stimulus that previously did not elicit a response comes to elicit a response after it is paired with a stimulus that naturally elicits a response. In contrast, operant conditioning is a process by which the consequences of a response affect the likelihood that the response will occur again (see Figure 9.4).

SECTION 1 Assessment

1. **Review the Vocabulary** What is the difference between a neutral stimulus and an unconditioned stimulus?
2. **Visualize the Main Idea** In a graphic organizer similar to the one below, describe the process of classical conditioning.

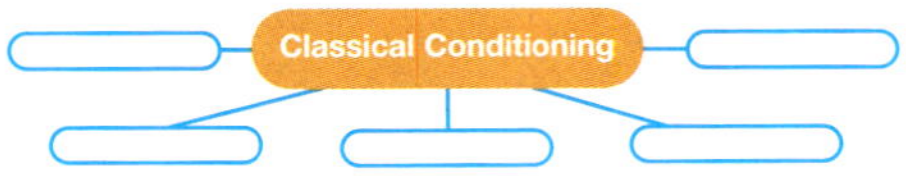

3. **Recall Information** How are generalization and discrimination related to classical conditioning?
4. **Think Critically** Under what conditions might a conditioned response become extinct?
5. **Application Activity** You have a friend who inhales noisily when standing next to you and then puffs air into your eye. You find that you now blink when you hear your friend inhale. Identify and decribe the neutral stimulus, the US, UR, CS, and CR in your behavior.

SECTION 1 Assessment Answers

1. A neutral stimulus does not initially elicit any part of the unconditioned response; an unconditioned stimulus elicits a certain predictable response typically without previous training.
2. The diagram should include: acquisition, generalization, discrimination, extinction, and spontaneous recovery.
3. When one responds to a stimulus similar to the conditioned stimulus, generalization has occurred. The ability to respond differently to different stimuli is discrimination.
4. when the participant no longer associates the conditioned stimulus with the unconditioned stimulus
5. neutral stimulus = puffing air into your eye; US = air puffed into your eye; UR = blinking; CS = your friend inhaling; CR = blinking

Case Studies

The Case of Little Albert

Period of Study: Winter, 1919–1920

Introduction: John B. Watson and Rosalie Rayner showed how conditioning could be used on a human infant. The study led to ethical questions on research with humans. From such research, Watson concluded that there are only a few instinctive reflexes in humans, among them, sucking, reaching, and grasping. In addition, infants have three innate emotional responses to stimuli: fear at hearing a loud sound or at suddenly being dropped; rage when arm or head movements are forcibly restrained; and love when stroked, rocked, gently patted, and the like.

Hypothesis: Most human behaviors and emotional reactions are built up of conditioned responses. (When an emotionally exciting object stimulates the subject simultaneously with an object not emotionally exciting, the latter object may in time arouse the same emotional reaction as the former object.)

Method: Watson and Rayner presented Albert (a well-adjusted 9-month-old) with many objects, including a rat, blocks, a rabbit, a dog, a monkey, masks with and without hair, cotton, wool, and burning newspapers. Albert showed no fear of any of these objects—they were all neutral stimuli for the fear response.

Watson and Rayner decided that, when Albert was 11 months old, they would attempt to condition him to fear rats. They began by placing a furry white rat in front of him. Albert would reach out to touch it, and each time he did, one of Watson's assistants would strike a metal bar with a hammer behind Albert. The first time the metal bar was struck, Albert fell forward and buried his head in a pillow. The next time he reached for the rat and the bar was struck, Albert began to whimper. The noise, the unconditioned stimulus, brought about a naturally unconditioned response, fear. After only a few such pairings, the rat became a *conditioned stimulus* that elicited a *conditioned response,* fear.

Five days after Watson and Rayner conditioned Albert to fear rats, they presented him with blocks, a rabbit, a rat, and a dog, each alone. They also showed him a number of other stimuli, including a Santa Claus mask. Albert reacted fearfully to all but the blocks. His conditioned fear response generalized to include the rabbit and all of the white furry objects he was shown, but not to any dissimilar toys.

Results: One of the most frequent criticisms of the experiment was that Watson and Rayner taught a well-adjusted child to be fearful. Apparently, the researchers knew at least one month ahead of time that Albert would be leaving the study, and yet they made no attempt to extinguish his conditioned fears (Harris, 1979). Psychologists today are unable to repeat the Little Albert study because of the ethical standards of the APA (see Chapter 2).

One of Watson's students, Mary Cover Jones (1924, 1974), developed an extinction procedure called counterconditioning to reduce people's existing fears. Peter was a boy who was extremely fearful of rabbits. Jones helped Peter eliminate his fear by pairing the feared object (the rabbit) with pleasant experiences, such as eating ice cream or receiving special attention.

Analyzing the Case Study

1. Did the results of Watson and Rayner's experiment support their hypothesis? Explain.
2. How did Albert's response become generalized?
3. **Critical Thinking** How were the principles of classical conditioning used to reduce Peter's fear of rabbits?

Going Further

Research With Human Participants: Ethical Principles

The Little Albert study led to questions related to research ethics. As a result, the American Psychological Association published a set of binding ethical principles that govern psychologists' research, revised (1992) as follows:

Planning research: Using recognized standards of competence and ethics, psychologists plan research so as to minimize the possibility of misleading results.

Responsibility: Psychologists are responsible for the dignity and welfare of participants.

Compliance with law and standards: Psychologists obey all state and federal laws and regulations.

Research responsibilities: Psychologists reach an agreement regarding the rights and responsibilities of both participants and researcher(s) before research is started.

Informed consent: When consent is required, psychologists obtain a signed informed consent before starting any research with a participant.

Deception in research: Deception is used only if no better alternative is available.

Discussing the Case Study

Ask: **Was it ethical for Watson and Rayner to teach a previously well-adjusted child to be fearful?** Have students explore this question in a class debate. Remind them to review the information above as well as consider the value of the research versus the negative impact of the methods used.

Answers for Analyzing the Case Study

1. Yes; Albert eventually became conditioned to fear any furry white object that resembled a rat. The white rat was used to elicit a conditioned response (fear) in Albert. Then other white furry objects were presented to him. His conditioned response generalized to include these objects as well as the rat.
2. Albert was conditioned specifically to fear rats, but his response extended to rabbits and other furry white objects that resembled rats.
3. A counter-conditioning procedure was used to reduce Peter's fear of rabbits. The feared object (rabbit) was paired with a pleasant experience, such as eating ice cream. Peter began to associate the rabbit with pleasant experiences.

CHAPTER 9

Section 2, pages 250–258

SECTION 2 Operant Conditioning

Reader's Guide

Main Idea

Operant conditioning occurs when the consequences that follow a behavior increase or decrease the likelihood of that behavior occurring again.

Vocabulary

- operant conditioning
- reinforcement
- primary reinforcer
- secondary reinforcer
- fixed-ratio schedule
- variable-ratio schedule
- fixed-interval schedule
- variable-interval schedule
- shaping
- response chain
- aversive control
- negative reinforcement
- escape conditioning
- avoidance conditioning

Objectives

- Outline the principles of operant conditioning.
- Describe applications of operant conditioning.

EXPLORING PSYCHOLOGY

Saved by a Theory

The therapists noted that the depressed woman did not eat; she was in critical danger of dying of starvation. What should they do? The woman did seem to enjoy visitors at the hospital and the TV set, radio, books and magazines, and flowers in her room. The therapists moved her into a room devoid of all these comforts, and put a light meal in front of her; if she ate anything at all, one of the comforts was temporarily restored. The therapists gradually withheld the rewards unless she continued to eat more. Her eating improved, she gained weight. Within months she was released from the hospital. A follow-up consultation with her 18 months later found her leading a normal life.

—from *The Story of Psychology* by Morton Hunt, 1993

Suppose your dog is wandering around the neighborhood, sniffing trees, checking garbage cans, looking for a squirrel to chase. A kind neighbor sees the dog and tosses a bone out the kitchen door to it. The next day, the dog is likely to stop at the same door on its rounds, if not go to it directly. Your neighbor produces another bone, and another the next day. Your dog becomes a regular visitor.

Both stories are examples of **operant conditioning**—that is, learning from the consequences of behavior. The term *operant* is used because

operant conditioning: learning in which a certain action is reinforced or punished, resulting in corresponding increases or decreases in occurrence

1 FOCUS

Section Objectives

1. Outline the principles of operant conditioning.
2. Describe applications of operant conditioning.

BELLRINGER
Motivational Activity

Project Daily Focus Transparency 9–2 and have students answer the questions.

Available as blackline master

Daily Focus Transparency 9–2

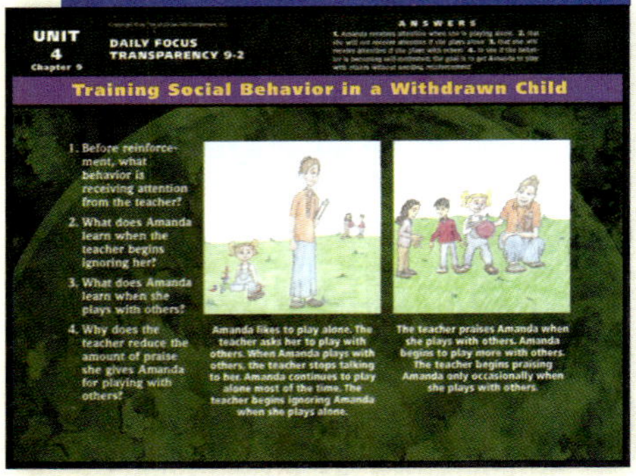

Reader's Guide

Use the Reader's Guide to introduce concepts and vocabulary.

Exploring Psychology

Ask students to read the **Exploring Psychology** feature and then discuss: **How did the therapists use the comforts to get the woman to eat?**

Vocabulary Precheck

Have students work with a partner to create a crossword puzzle using the vocabulary terms. Then have pairs of students exchange and complete puzzles.

Use the **Vocabulary PuzzleMaker CD-ROM** to create crossword and word search puzzles.

SECTION RESOURCES

Reproducible Masters

- Guided Reading Activity 9–2
- Vocabulary Activity 9–2
- Section Quiz 9–2

Transparencies

- Daily Focus Transparency 9–2

Multimedia

- Vocabulary PuzzleMaker CD-ROM
- *ExamView® Assessment Suite* CD-ROM
- Presentation Plus! Software

the subject (the depressed woman and the wandering dog in our examples) operates on or causes some change in the environment. This produces a result that influences whether the subject will operate or respond in the same way in the future. Depending on the effect of the operant behaviors, the learner will repeat or eliminate these behaviors to get rewards or avoid punishment.

How does operant conditioning differ from classical conditioning? One difference lies in how the experimenter conducts the experiment. In classical conditioning, the experimenter presents the CS and US independent of the participant's behavior. The UR is elicited. Reactions to the CS are then observed. In operant conditioning, the participant must engage in a behavior in order for the programmed outcome to occur. In other words, operant conditioning is the study of how voluntary behavior is affected by its consequences (see Figure 9.5).

REINFORCEMENT

Burrhus Frederic (B.F.) Skinner has been the psychologist most closely associated with operant conditioning. He believed that most behavior is influenced by a person's history of rewards and punishments. Skinner trained (or shaped) rats to respond to lights and sounds in a special enclosure called a Skinner box (see Figure 9.6). To conduct this experiment, a rat is placed inside the box. The rat must learn how to solve the problem of how to get food to appear in the cup. (This can be done by pressing a bar on the cage wall.) The rat first explores the box. When the rat moves toward the bar, the experimenter drops food into the cup. The food is important to the hungry rat. After the rat begins to approach the cup for food consistently, the experimenter begins to drop food into the cup only if the rat presses the bar. Eventually, when the rat is hungry it will press the bar to get food.

The food that appears in the cup is a reinforcer in this experiment. **Reinforcement** can be defined as a stimulus or event that increases the likelihood that the preceding behavior will be repeated. Whether or not a particular stimulus is a reinforcement depends on the effect the stimulus has on the learner. Examples of reinforcers that people usually respond to are social approval, money, and extra privileges.

Suppose you want to teach a dog to shake hands. One way would be to give the animal a treat every time it lifts its paw up to you. The treat is called a *positive reinforcer.* In this example, the dog will eventually learn to shake hands to get a reward.

Your dog will stop shaking hands when you forget to reward it for the trick. Extinction will occur because the reinforcement is withheld, but

Reading Check How is operant conditioning different from classical conditioning?

reinforcement: stimulus or event that follows a response and increases the likelihood that the response will be repeated

Figure 9.5 Operant Conditioning

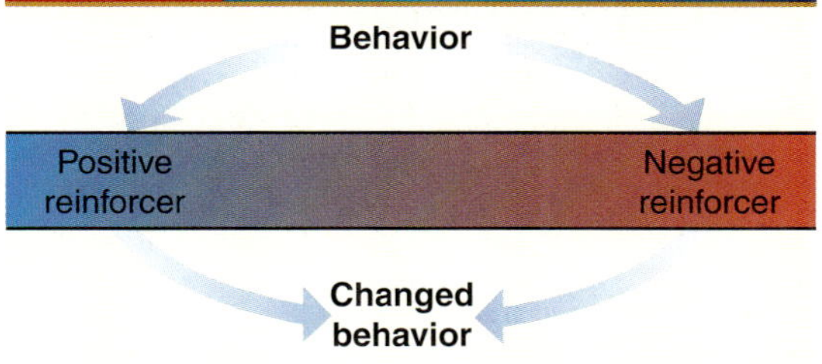

We do not just react to our environment, we behave in ways that seem designed to *produce* certain environmental changes. For example, I flip the light switch to illuminate a room. I say, "Please, pass the salt," to get the salt shaker. ***According to the diagram, what must happen for behavior to change?***

2 TEACH

L1 Evaluating Generalizations Read the following statement by B.F. Skinner to the class: "Everything we do and are is determined by our history of rewards and punishments." Ask students to evaluate this generalization and express their opinions. ELL

Guided Reading Activity 9-2

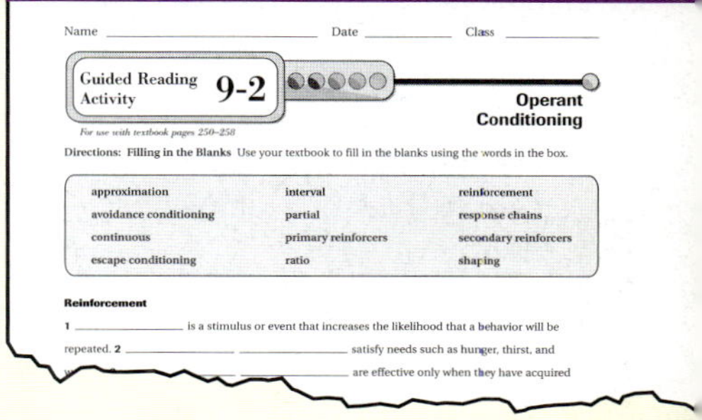
Name ______ Date ______ Class ______

Guided Reading Activity 9-2 — Operant Conditioning

For use with textbook pages 250–258

Directions: Filling in the Blanks Use your textbook to fill in the blanks using the words in the box.

approximation	interval	reinforcement
avoidance conditioning	partial	response chains
continuous	primary reinforcers	secondary reinforcers
escape conditioning	ratio	shaping

Reinforcement

1 ______ is a stimulus or event that increases the likelihood that a behavior will be repeated. 2 ______ ______ satisfy needs such as hunger, thirst, and ______ are effective only when they have acquired

Reading Check Answer Operant conditioning is the process of learning from consequences of behavior. Classical conditioning is the process in which a person's natural responses become attached to a new stimulus.

Figure 9.5

Visual Instruction Remind students that in operant conditioning, reinforcements are used to bring about a desired behavior.

Caption Answer Reinforcement must occur before there is a change in behavior.

COOPERATIVE LEARNING ACTIVITY

Identifying Schedules of Reinforcement Organize the class into four large groups, and assign each group one of the four partial schedules of reinforcement. Ask each group to think of examples of behaviors that are reinforced according to their schedule. Challenge them to think of as many examples as they can in a set period of time. Have each group share its examples with the rest of the class and then ask for additional examples from members of the other groups. Remind the students that during group work they will sometimes be leaders and other times followers, but at all times they should work to create a supportive group climate.

Figure 9.6

Caption Answer After a period of time, the rat presses on the lever to get food pellets. This repeated behavior shows that learning has occurred.

TEACHER Tip

In discussing reinforcement, make sure students understand the distinction between a primary reinforcer and a secondary reinforcer. Help students understand the difference by challenging them to think of examples of each.

FYI

Millions have read *Walden Two,* B.F. Skinner's best-known work. One small group created a community in Virginia based on the Walden Two model. Although what became known as the Twin Oak Community has survived, its members have long ago given up trying to shape behavior based on Skinner's reinforcement method.

Figure 9.6 A Skinner Box

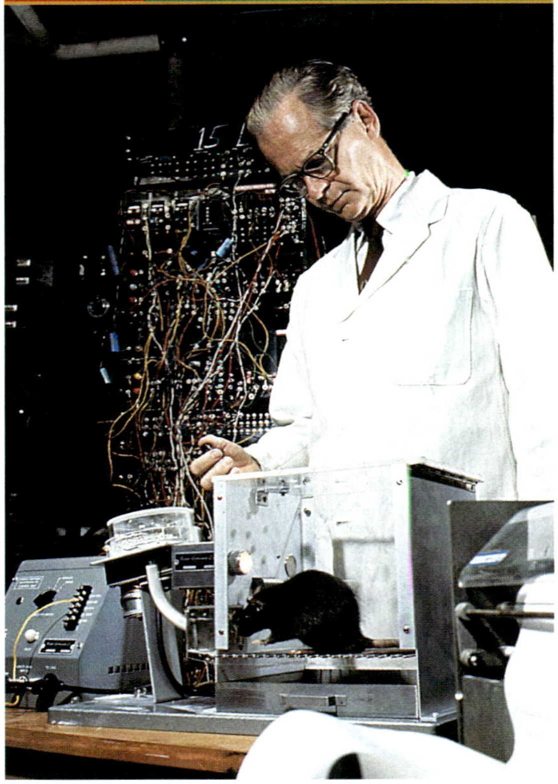

The Skinner box is a basic apparatus used to test theories of operant conditioning. When the rat presses the bar located on the side of the box, food is delivered to the cup. ***How does the rat display that learning has occurred?***

it will take a period of time. (Remember, in classical conditioning, extinction is the disappearance of a conditioned response when an unconditioned stimulus no longer follows a conditioned stimulus.) In fact, for a while after you stop rewarding the dog, it will probably become impatient, bark, and paw even more insistently than it did before, until it gives up shaking hands. Eventually the dog will try to shake hands again, indicating that spontaneous recovery has occurred.

Whereas positive reinforcement occurs when something the animal wants (a treat for the dog) is *added* after an action, negative reinforcement occurs when something unpleasant is *taken away* if the animal performs an action.

Primary and Secondary Reinforcers

Reinforcers come in many varieties. Some reinforcers are primary and some are secondary. A **primary reinforcer** is one that satisfies a biological need such as hunger, thirst, or sleep. A **secondary reinforcer** is one that has been paired with a primary reinforcer and through classical conditioning has acquired value and the ability to reinforce. With conditioning, almost any stimulus can acquire value and become a secondary reinforcer.

One experimenter (Wolfe, 1936) demonstrated this with chimpanzees. Poker chips have no value for chimps—they are not edible and they are not very much fun to play with. This experimenter, however, used operant and classical conditioning to teach chimps to value poker chips as much as humans value money. He provided the animals with a "Chimp-O-Mat" that dispensed peanuts or bananas, which are primary reinforcers. To obtain food, the chimps had to pull down on a heavily weighted bar to obtain poker chips, then insert the chips in a slot in the machine. With repetition, the poker chips became conditioned reinforcers. Their value was evident from the fact that the chimpanzees would work for them, save them, and sometimes try to steal them from one another.

Money is the best example of a secondary reinforcer in human society. You have learned that getting money is associated with buying food or material things. Other examples of secondary reinforcers would include praise, status, and prestige. All of these items are associated with a primary reinforcer and have acquired value, so they reinforce certain types of behavior when they are earned.

primary reinforcer: stimulus that is naturally rewarding, such as food or water

secondary reinforcer: stimulus such as money that becomes rewarding through its link with a primary reinforcer

MEETING SPECIAL NEEDS

Learning Style: Verbal/Linguistic We perform a wide range of operant behaviors every day. For example, operant conditioning is involved if your students study hard to earn good grades. Ask students to choose a specific task, skill, or behavior they would like to teach a young child. Ask them to write a detailed report explaining step-by-step how they would use operant conditioning concepts to teach the child the chosen task, skill, or behavior. Have students identify related antecedents, behavior, and consequences. **L2**

Refer to ***Inclusion for the High School Social Studies Classroom Strategies and Activities*** in the TCR for strategies for students with different learning styles.

SCHEDULES OF REINFORCEMENT

One important factor in operant conditioning is the timing and frequency of reinforcement. Behavior that is reinforced every time it occurs is said to be on a *continuous schedule* of reinforcement. You might suppose that behavior would best be maintained by reinforcing every response. However, when positive reinforcement occurs only intermittently, or on a *partial schedule,* the responses are generally more stable and last longer once they are learned. A person or animal that is continuously reinforced for a behavior tends to maintain that behavior only when the reinforcement is given. If the reinforcement stops, the behavior quickly undergoes extinction. For example, a rat learns to press a bar most rapidly when it receives food each time it does so. When the rat stops receiving food each time it presses the bar, however, it quickly stops its bar-pressing. Behaviors that are acquired on partial schedules of reinforcement are established more slowly but are more persistent. For example, a rat that is only sometimes rewarded with food for pressing a bar will continue to press even though no food appears. Rats and humans that are reinforced on partial schedules of reinforcement cannot always predict when the next reinforcement will occur, so they learn to be persistent.

Skinner discovered the strength of partial reinforcement when his apparatus kept breaking down. Skinner found that the rats kept responding even though they were reinforced randomly. In fact, the rats responded with even greater endurance.

Although intermittent reinforcement may be arranged in a number of ways, four basic methods, or schedules, have been studied in the laboratory (see Figure 9.7). Schedules of partial reinforcement may be based either on the *number* of correct responses that the animal makes between reinforcements (*ratio* schedule) or on the *amount of time* that elapses before reinforcement is given (*interval* schedule). In either case, reinforcement may appear on a *fixed,* or predictable, schedule or on a *variable,* or unpredictable, schedule. The four basic schedules result from the combination of these four possibilities. People and animals respond differently to each type.

- In a **fixed-ratio schedule,** reinforcement depends on a specified quantity of responses, such as rewarding every fourth response. The student who receives a good grade after completing a specified amount of work and the typist who is paid by the number of pages

Quick Lab

What reinforcement schedules operate in your classroom?
Do you think that students would do schoolwork if there were no grading system? What reinforcements would operate if grades were abolished?

Procedure

1. Identify the types of reinforcers that operate in your classroom.
2. Make a chart that lists the type of reinforcer (primary, secondary, positive, negative) and the classroom behavior it usually elicits.
3. Devise a system for your classroom that could replace the existing reinforcers with new ones (and achieve the same results).

Analysis

1. Describe how the new reinforcers operate.
2. Indicate what responses the new reinforcers are supposed to elicit.

See the Skills Handbook, page 622, for an explanation of designing an experiment.

fixed-ratio schedule: a pattern of reinforcement in which a specific number of correct responses is required before reinforcement can be obtained

CHAPTER 9
Section 2, pages 250–258

Quick Lab

Purpose Students will examine the reinforcement schedules used in the classroom.

Process Skills Organizing information, relating cause and effect

Teaching Strategies

- Review the four types of partial reinforcement schedules with students.
- Discuss the cause-and-effect relationships between reinforcement and behavior.

Analysis

1. Students will probably note that grades act as reinforcers for most students. An "A" grade is a positive and secondary reinforcer. Discomfort or fear of bad grades may serve as negative, secondary reinforcers.
2. Students' systems should properly label and describe the negative, positive, primary, and secondary reinforcers that will replace the current system. Students should propose how the system will operate and what reactions the responses will most likely elicit.

Vocabulary Activity 9–2

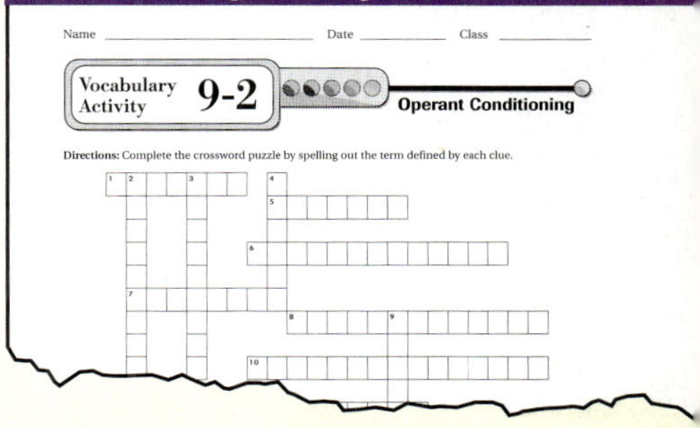

CRITICAL THINKING ACTIVITY

Predicting Outcomes Challenge students to use the concept of operant conditioning to predict and list some problems that could arise from applying the theory to humans. Encourage students to consider social, educational, and political arenas. For example, Joseph Stalin tried to control the behavior of others to advance his own ideas during his dictatorship in the former Soviet Union (mid-1920s–1953). Students should consider the following questions: **How could the ability to control learning using the concept of operant conditioning be abused? How might an individual's freedom of choice be influenced? How did Stalin use operant conditioning to ensure the outcome of given courses of action, such as obeying laws or paying taxes? L2**

L2 Discussing Reinforcers Ask for volunteers to provide examples of primary and secondary reinforcers. Stress that a reinforcer is very participant-specific. In other words, a stimulus that acts as a reinforcer for one participant might have no effect on another participant. Ask students to create a list in their journals that identifies which of the examples discussed they think would have an effect on them.

Figure 9.7

Visual Instruction Ask students to describe problems that might originate when working with a fixed-ratio schedule. Use the example of factory workers who are paid according to the number of items they produce, regardless of the time spent in producing them. Help students by pointing out the temptation to shortcut such a system.

Caption Answer A fixed-ratio schedule requires that reinforcement be given after a specified quantity of responses. In a fixed-interval schedule, the reinforcement is based on a fixed-time schedule.

PSYCHOLOGY JOURNAL

Have students record examples of fixed-interval and variable-interval scheduling from their own lives. Encourage them to analyze the effectiveness of the approach for each example and to consider whether another schedule of reinforcement might work better. ■

completed are on fixed-ratio schedules. People tend to work hard on fixed-ratio schedules. Another example would be dentists who get paid $150 for *each* cavity repaired or filled.

variable-ratio schedule: a pattern of reinforcement in which an unpredictable number of responses are required before reinforcement can be obtained

- A **variable-ratio schedule** does not require that a fixed or set number of responses be made for each reinforcement, as in the fixed-ratio schedule. Rather, the number of responses needed for a reinforcement changes from one reinforcer to the next. Slot machines are a good example of a variable-ratio schedule. They are set to pay off after a varying number of attempts at pulling the handle. Generally, animals on variable-ratio schedules of reinforcement tend to work or respond at a steady, high rate. Since the reinforcement is unpredictable, there is typically no pause after a reward because it is possible that a reward will occur on the very next response. Door-to-door salespeople and individuals who do telephone surveys are also operating on variable-ratio schedules since they never know how many doorbells they will have to ring or how many calls they will have to make before they make a sale or find someone who will answer the survey.

fixed-interval schedule: a pattern of reinforcement in which a specific amount of time must elapse before a response will elicit reinforcement

- On a **fixed-interval schedule,** the first correct response after a specified amount of time is reinforced. The time interval is always the same. Once animals gain experience with a fixed-interval reinforcement schedule, they adjust their response rates Since no reinforcement occurs for a period of time no matter what their behavior, they learn to stop responding immediately after reinforcement is given and then begin to respond again toward the end of the interval. The result is regular, recurring periods of inactivity followed by short bursts of responding, producing a "scalloped" response curve. Tests are often given on a fixed-interval schedule. It is likely that you will study feverishly the day before a test but study much less immediately afterwards.

	Ratio	Interval
Fixed schedules	**Fixed Ratio** (reinforcement after a fixed number of responses) • being paid for every 10 pizzas made • being ejected from a basketball game after five fouls	**Fixed Interval** (reinforcement of first response after a fixed amount of time has passed) • cramming for an exam • picking up your check from your part-time job
Variable schedules	**Variable Ratio** (reinforcement after varying number of responses) • playing a slot machine • sales commissions	**Variable Interval** (reinforcement of first response after varying amounts of time) • surprise (pop) quizzes in class • dialing a friend on the phone and getting a busy signal

Figure 9.7 Partial Schedules of Reinforcement

B.F. Skinner pointed out many examples of how schedules of reinforcement maintain and control different behaviors. The different schedules produce different response rates. ***How does a fixed-ratio schedule differ from a fixed-interval schedule of reinforcement?***

PSYCHOLOGY LAB EXPERIMENT

Avoidance Conditioning Organize students into groups of experimenters and participants. Explain that they will be conducting an experiment in both avoidance conditioning and classical conditioning. Ask the participant to sit at a table about two feet from the experimenter. The participant should then place his or her right hand on the table, palm down. Using a ruler, the experimenter should lightly tap the table every few seconds. Periodically, the ruler should be tapped twice against the table and pressed gently on the participant's knuckles. After a few repetitions of this procedure, the participant should begin to show avoidance responses by either withdrawing the hand after two taps or by anticipating them. **L1** ELL

- On a **variable-interval schedule,** the time at which the reinforcement is given changes. If you are trying to call a friend, but the line is busy, what do you do? You keep trying. The reinforcer will be gained the first time you dial after your friend has hung up, but you do not know when that is going to occur. The usual response rate on a variable-interval schedule is slow, but steady—slower than on any other schedule of partial reinforcement. In fact, your eagerness to reach your friend probably will determine roughly how often you try the phone again . . . and again.

In summary, ratio schedules are based on numbers of responses, while interval schedules are based on time. Responses are more resistant to extinction when reinforced on a variable rather than on a fixed schedule. To be most effective, however, the reinforcement must be consistent for the same type of behavior, although it may not occur each time the behavior does. The complexity of our behavior means that most reinforcers in human relationships are on a variable schedule. How people will react cannot always be predicted.

Figure 9.8 Clicker Training

Clicker training is a form of shaping. The trainer waits for the dog to sit on its own. The instant its rear goes down, the trainer hits the clicker (an audio signal) and the dog gets the treat. The clicker acts as an acoustical marker to tell the dog, "That's what I'm reinforcing." ***How might you use shaping to teach a dog to shake?***

SHAPING AND CHAINING

Operant conditioning is not limited to simple behaviors. When you acquire a skill such as knitting, photography, playing basketball, or talking persuasively, you learn more than just a single new stimulus-response relationship. You learn a large number of them, and you learn how to put them together into a large, smooth-flowing unit.

Shaping is a process in which reinforcement is used to sculpt new responses out of old ones. An experimenter can use this method to teach a rat to do something it has never done before and would never do if left to itself. He or she can shape it, for example, to raise a miniature flag. The rat is physically capable of standing on its hind legs and using its mouth to pull a miniature flag-raising cord, but at present it does not do so. The rat probably will not perform this unusual action by accident, so the experimenter begins by rewarding the rat for any action similar to the wanted responses, using reinforcement to produce closer and closer approximations of the desired behavior.

Imagine the rat roaming around on a table with the flag apparatus in the middle. The rat inspects everything and finally sniffs at the flagpole. The experimenter immediately reinforces this response by giving the rat a food pellet. Now the rat frequently sniffs the flagpole, hoping to get another pellet, but the experimenter waits until the rat lifts a paw before he gives it another reward. This process continues with the experimenter reinforcing close responses and then waiting for even closer ones. Eventually, the experimenter has the rat on its hind legs nibbling at the cord. Suddenly the rat seizes the cord in its teeth and yanks it.

variable-interval schedule: a pattern of reinforcement in which changing amounts of time must elapse before a response will obtain reinforcement

shaping: technique in which the desired behavior is "molded" by first rewarding any act similar to that behavior and then requiring ever-closer approximations to the desired behavior before giving the reward

L3 Analyzing Passages In 1928 John B. Watson and Rosalie Rayner published a best-selling book titled *Psychological Care of Infant and Child.* Read the following passage aloud:

There is a sensible way of treating children. Treat them as though they were young adults. Dress them, bathe them with care and circumspection. Let your behavior always be objective and kindly firm. Never hug or kiss them, never let them sit on your lap. If you must, kiss them on the forehead when they say goodnight. Shake hands with them in the morning. Give them a pat on the head if they make an extraordinary good job or a difficult task.

Ask: **What type of principles and techniques does this passage recommend to shape human behavior? What would children learn from such techniques? What are the strengths and shortcomings of this method?**

Figure 9.8

Caption Answer Wait for the dog to move its paw toward you or paw at you on its own. Then immediately hit the clicker and reward the dog with a treat. Repeat this process until the dog can shake on command.

INTERDISCIPLINARY CONNECTIONS ACTIVITY

Literature The Skinner box has its parallels in utopian literature. To help students make the connection, discuss the notion that a Skinner box is a complete, artificially controlled environment in which rewards and punishments can be delivered. An example is Aldous Huxley's *Brave New World.* In this novel, individuals are conditioned to think, act, feel, believe, and respond the way the government wants them to. Ask students to research synopses of various twentieth-century utopian novels in literary reference books. Then ask students to choose one novel and relate it to behaviorism, considering whether such fictions could ever occur. Students should discuss their findings in a written report. **L3**

Looking @ the Issues

Phobias A phobia is an intense fear of something that interferes with a person's daily life. In a class discussion, have students list common phobias or intense fears (i.e., fear of heights, fear of spiders, fear of flying, fear of enclosed places). Divide the class into groups of four or five. Ask each group to select a phobia and describe how shaping could be used to overcome the fear. The group should prepare a written list of steps to be used.

Figure 9.9

Caption Answer Students' answers may vary. Answers may include descriptions of the response chains necessary for learning to play the piano, learning to solve mathematical problems, or learning to ski.

CULTURAL CONNECTIONS

The Suzuki Method of music education was introduced in the 1950s by Japanese violinist Shinichi Suzuki. He believes that children can best learn to play an instrument by first observing others playing it, then imitating what they see. He compared learning to play an instrument to learning language skills. Using the Suzuki method, children as young as three or four become skilled musicians before they can read one note of music. Reading music is learned later, at about the same time that children learn to read words.

Immediately the rat is rewarded, and it begins pulling rapidly on the cord. A new response has been shaped. Shaping has been used to teach animals tricks. For example, if a television character points her finger to the ground and her dog immediately lies down, we need to remember that shaping was involved in the dog's behavior. If shaping is done properly, almost any animal can learn some unusual tricks.

Combining Responses: Chaining

In order to learn a skill, a person must be able to put various new responses together. Responses that follow one another in a sequence are combined into **response chains.** Each response produces the signal for the next one.

In learning, chains of responses are organized into larger *response patterns.* For example, the complex skill of swimming has three major chains that are combined to make up the whole swimming pattern—an arm-stroking chain, a breathing chain, and a leg-kicking chain (see Figure 9.9). After much practice, you no longer have to think about the different steps involved. The behavior takes on a rhythm of its own: the chains of responses flow naturally as soon as you dive into the water.

It is often necessary to learn simple responses before mastering the complex pattern. If you cannot hit a nail with a hammer, you certainly cannot build a house. Therefore, before a person can learn to perform a particular skill, he or she must learn all the lower skills that make the larger skill possible.

response chain: learned reactions that follow one another in sequence, each reaction producing the signal for the next

aversive control: process of influencing behavior by means of unpleasant stimuli

negative reinforcement: increasing the strength of a given response by removing or preventing a painful stimulus when the response occurs

AVERSIVE CONTROL

Reinforcement refers to anything that increases the frequency of an immediately preceding behavior. Aversive, or unpleasant, consequences influence much of our everyday behavior. **Aversive control** refers to this type of conditioning or learning. There are two ways in which unpleasant events can affect our behavior—as negative reinforcers or as punishers.

Figure 9.9 Swimming—A Response Chain

To learn to swim, you must first learn the arm stroke, then how to breathe properly, and finally how to kick your legs. ***What similar response chains can you describe that you would have to develop to learn other skills?***

Negative Reinforcement

In **negative reinforcement,** a painful or unpleasant stimulus is removed. The removal of unpleasant consequences increases the frequency of a behavior. It may help you to understand negative reinforcement if you remember that it *follows* and *negates,* or takes away, an aversive stimulus. B.F. Skinner provided this example:

EXTENDING THE CONTENT

Psychologists at Work People usually associate psychologists with therapists and similar counselors who offer advice to patients and clients. Point out to students that most of the psychologists whose studies are described in this chapter are *experimental psychologists.* These professionals perform most of their work in laboratories and adhere strictly to controlled scientific procedures. Unlike therapists, experimental psychologists are involved in "pure research" and do not immediately apply their knowledge beyond the laboratory. Such specialists generally hold doctoral degrees and are proficient in mathematics because they must be able to analyze the data they collect according to statistical procedures.

If walking with a stone in your shoe causes you to limp, removing the stone (negating it) allows you to walk without pain. Other examples of negative reinforcers are fear and experiencing disapproval of unwelcome behavior.

Two uses of negative reinforcement that psychologists have studied in detail are *escape conditioning* and *avoidance conditioning*. In **escape conditioning,** a person's behavior causes an unpleasant event to stop. Consider the case of a child who hates liver and is served it for dinner. She whines about the food and gags while eating it. At this point, her father removes the liver. The whining and gagging behavior has been thus negatively reinforced, and the child is likely to whine and gag in the future when given an unpleasant meal. This kind of learning is called escape conditioning because the behavior of the child allowed her to escape the liver meal.

escape conditioning: training of an organism to remove or terminate an unpleasant stimulus

In **avoidance conditioning,** the person's behavior has the effect of preventing an unpleasant situation from happening. In our example, if the child starts whining and gagging when the father removes the liver from the refrigerator to cook it, we would identify the situation as avoidance conditioning; the child avoided the unpleasant consequences by whining early enough. The reinforcer here is the reduction of the child's disgust—not having to eat liver.

avoidance conditioning: training of an organism to respond so as to prevent the occurrence of an unpleasant stimulus

Punishment

The most obvious form of aversive control is punishment. In punishment, an unpleasant consequence occurs and decreases the frequency of the behavior that produced it. Negative reinforcement and punishment operate in opposite ways. In negative reinforcement, escape or avoidance behavior is *repeated* and increases in frequency. In punishment, behavior that is punished decreases or is *not repeated*. If you want to stop a dog from pawing at you when it wants attention, you should loudly say, "NO!" and reprimand it when it paws at you. Such actions are called *punishers* (see Figure 9.10).

As with reinforcers, the events or actions that serve as punishers depend on their effect on the learner. For example, if a young child in a large family seeks extra attention from her parents, that child may misbehave. In response the parents punish the child by reprimanding her. The reprimands are meant to be punishers. The reprimands, however, may actually serve as reinforcers for a child who wants attention. Perhaps sending her to her room every time she misbehaved would have been an appropriate punisher; this unpleasant stimulus would have discouraged her from repeating the behavior.

Disadvantages of Punishment

Psychologists have found several disadvantages in using aversive stimuli (punishment) to change behavior. For one thing, aversive stimuli can produce unwanted side effects such as rage, aggression, and fear. Then, instead of having to change only one problem behavior, there may be two

CHAPTER 9

Section 2, pages 250–258

3 ASSESS

Assign Section 2 Assessment as homework or as an in-class activity.

Section Quiz 9–2

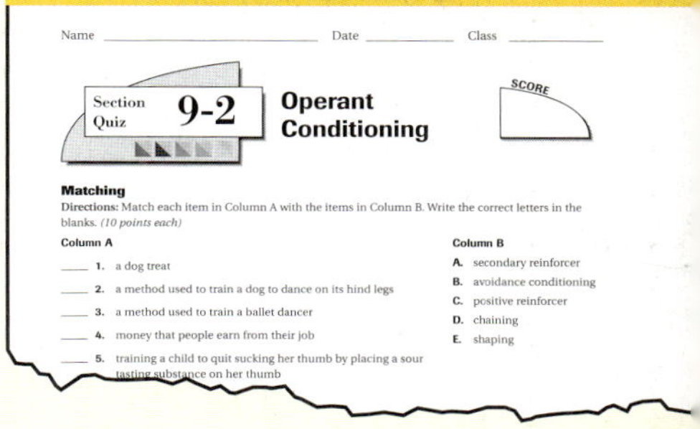
Name ______ Date ______ Class ______

Section Quiz 9-2 **Operant Conditioning**

SCORE

Matching

Directions: Match each item in Column A with the items in Column B. Write the correct letters in the blanks. *(10 points each)*

Column A

____ 1. a dog treat

____ 2. a method used to train a dog to dance on its hind legs

____ 3. a method used to train a ballet dancer

____ 4. money that people earn from their job

____ 5. training a child to quit sucking her thumb by placing a sour tasting substance on her thumb

Column B

A. secondary reinforcer

B. avoidance conditioning

C. positive reinforcer

D. chaining

E. shaping

Reteach

On the board, copy key statements from Section 2, but change them in some way to make the statements false. Ask students to write the statements correctly.

CRITICAL THINKING ACTIVITY

Understanding Cause and Effect A Skinner box uses food to reward a rat for pressing a bar. Does the type and amount of food matter? Ask students to conjecture how these two factors might affect experiment outcome. What role might they play during experiment replication, when other scientists attempt the same experiment? Discuss with students the difference between reliability and validity. Wanting to control all the variables in his behavior modification experiments with rats, Skinner convinced a manufacturer to develop food pellets of uniform size and composition. Today there are uniform food pellets for different types of animals. **L2**

Figure 9.10

Caption Answer Calvin's tumbles act as punishers for putting his pants on wrong. If Calvin learns to avoid putting on his pants wrong, he will walk without falling.

Enrich

Have students write an essay comparing classical conditioning and operant conditioning as ways of learning. Select students to read and discuss their essays.

4 CLOSE

Challenge students to brainstorm typical daily activities that are the result of some sort of conditioning. Record students' responses on the board and then ask them to identify the specific type of conditioning involved for each activity.

Figure 9.10 Aversive Stimuli

Punishment occurs when an unpleasant consequence following a behavior decreases the chances that the behavior will recur. ***How might Calvin's tumbles act as punishers?***

or more. For example, children whose parents rely on spanking to control disobedience may also have to deal with the problem of their children's increased aggressiveness toward other children.

A second problem with punishment is that people learn to avoid the person delivering the aversive consequences. Children learn to stay away from parents or teachers who often punish them. One consequence of this is that such parents and teachers have less opportunity to correct the children's inappropriate behavior. Also, punishment is likely to merely suppress, but not eliminate, such behavior. The punished behavior is likely to occur at some other time or in some other place.

Punishment alone does not teach appropriate and acceptable behavior. Without positive coaching and modeling, the child may never learn the correct behavior or understand what the parents think is the acceptable behavior in a given situation.

SECTION 2 Assessment

1. **Review the Vocabulary** Explain how the four schedules of partial reinforcement work.
2. **Visualize the Main Idea** In a chart similar to the one below, list four types of reinforcers and give an example of each.

Types of Reinforcers	Example

3. **Recall Information** What is the difference between escape conditioning and avoidance conditioning?
4. **Think Critically** How do positive and negative reinforcement affect a teenager's choice and purchase of clothes? Provide examples in your answer.
5. **Application Activity** Using principles of operant conditioning, design a plan to teach a puppy a new trick.

SECTION 2 Assessment Answers

1. Behavior is reinforced according to fixed or variable reinforcement schedules that are based on numbers of responses or times of responses.
2. Students should list examples for the four types of partial reinforcers.
3. Escape conditioning—training the subject to remove or terminate an unpleasant stimulus; avoidance conditioning—training the subject to respond so as to prevent the occurrence of an unpleasant stimulus
4. Answers will vary. Students may mention favorable or unfavorable peer, family, or social reactions and attention (including punitive responses from authority figures) as factors affecting the purchase.
5. Students' answers will vary, but principles of conditioning (shaping) should be used.

SECTION 3 Social Learning

Reader's Guide

Main Idea
Social learning, consisting of cognitive learning and modeling, involves how people make decisions and act upon the information available to them.

Vocabulary
- social learning
- cognitive learning
- cognitive map
- latent learning
- learned helplessness
- modeling
- behavior modification
- token economy

Objectives
- Cite the principles involved in cognitive learning and modeling.
- Identify the principles of learning used in behavior modification.

EXPLORING PSYCHOLOGY

Would You Treat Bobo This Way?

Children were told to play while in another part of the room an adult "model" aggressively "played" with a 5-foot inflated Bobo doll. The model laid the Bobo doll on its side, sat on it, and punched it repeatedly in the nose. The model then raised the Bobo doll, picked up a mallet and struck the doll on the head, then kicked the doll around the room. Following this experience, the youngsters were brought to a room that contained many attractive toys and the Bobo doll. The children exhibited a good deal of aggressive behavior toward the Bobo doll—behavior resembling that of the adult model.

—adapted from "Transmission of Aggression Through Imitation of Aggressive Models" by Albert Bandura, Dorothea Ross, and Sheila A. Ross, published in *Journal of Abnormal and Social Psychology*, 1961

Why did the children display such aggressive behavior? Albert Bandura performed the study above in 1961 to demonstrate that the children learned aggressive behaviors simply by watching a model perform these behaviors. The study illustrated the third type of learning, called **social learning.** Social learning theorists view learning as purposeful—going beyond mechanical responses to stimuli or reinforcement. The two types of social learning are cognitive learning and modeling.

social learning: process of altering behavior by observing and imitating the behavior of others

1 FOCUS

Section Objectives
1. Cite the principles involved in cognitive learning and modeling.
2. Identify the principles of learning used in behavior modification.

BELLRINGER
Motivational Activity

Project Daily Focus Transparency 9–3 and have students answer the questions.

Available as blackline master

Daily Focus Transparency 9–3

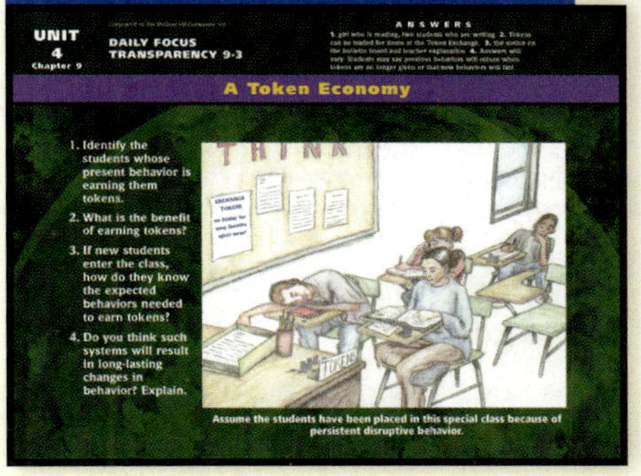

Reader's Guide
Use the Reader's Guide to introduce concepts and vocabulary.

Exploring Psychology
Ask students to read the **Exploring Psychology** feature and ask: **Why did children show aggressive behavior toward the Bobo doll?**

Vocabulary Precheck
Have students write each term on one side of an index card and its definition on the other side. Encourage them to master the terms by studying their flash cards.

SECTION RESOURCES

Reproducible Masters
- Guided Reading Activity 9–3
- Vocabulary Activity 9–3
- Section Quiz 9–3

Transparencies
- Daily Focus Transparency 9–3

Multimedia
- *ExamView® Assessment Suite* CD-ROM
- Presentation Plus! Software

2 TEACH

L1 Identifying Types of Learning Ask students to share a recently learned skill or item of information. After each student speaks, have the class discuss how the learning took place. What happened to make their understanding of the skill or information click into place? ELL

Figure 9.11

Caption Answer Answers will vary. The information (acquired through latent learning) about our surroundings, such as the location of a street or house, is used by humans every day as we make our way to school and work.

Guided Reading Activity 9–3

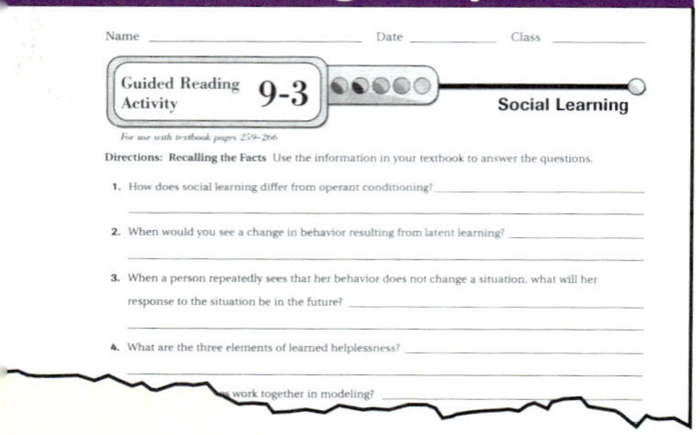
Name ______ Date ______ Class ______

Guided Reading Activity 9-3 — Social Learning

For use with textbook pages 259–266

Directions: Recalling the Facts Use the information in your textbook to answer the questions.

1. How does social learning differ from operant conditioning? ______
2. When would you see a change in behavior resulting from latent learning? ______
3. When a person repeatedly sees that her behavior does not change a situation, what will her response to the situation be in the future? ______
4. What are the three elements of learned helplessness? ______

PSYCHOLOGY Update

Latent Learning According to recent research, the elements that contribute to latent learning may begin in the early months of human life. Research at Rutgers University suggests that human infants can remember fairly detailed experiences and surroundings. In addition, University of Massachusetts psychologist Rachel Clifton found that infants could retrieve that memory as long as 18 months later.

"THEN, AS YOU CAN SEE, WE GIVE THEM SOME MULTIPLE CHOICE TESTS."

Figure 9.11 Mazes and Maps

This cartoonist exaggerates the cognitive learning capabilities of rats. ***In what ways do humans use information obtained from latent learning in daily life?***

COGNITIVE LEARNING

Cognitive learning focuses on how information is obtained, processed, and organized. Such learning is concerned with the *mental* processes involved in learning. Latent learning and learned helplessness are examples of cognitive learning.

Latent Learning and Cognitive Maps

In the 1930s, Edward Tolman argued that learning involved more than mechanical responses to stimuli; it involved mental processes. Tolman would place a rat in a maze and allow it to explore the maze without giving the rat any reinforcement, such as food. Then he would place food at the end of the maze and record which path the rat took to reach the food. The rat quickly learned to take the shortest route to the food. Next, Tolman blocked the shortest path to the food. The rat then followed the next shortest path to the food. Tolman believed that the rat had developed a **cognitive map** of the maze. A cognitive map is a mental picture of a place, such as the maze. The rats had developed a cognitive map of the maze when allowed to explore the maze on their own.

Tolman called the type of learning demonstrated by the rat **latent learning.** Latent learning is not demonstrated by an immediately observable change in behavior at the time of the learning. Although the learning typically occurs in the absence of a reinforcer, it may not be demonstrated until a reinforcer appears. For example, have you ever had to locate a building or street in a section of your city or town that you were unfamiliar with? You may have been through that section of town before and remembered details such as an unusual sign or large parking lot. Remembering these details may have helped you find the building or street you were looking for. You had learned some details without intending to do so.

cognitive learning: form of altering behavior that involves mental processes and may result from observation or imitation

cognitive map: a mental picture of spatial relationships or relationships between events

latent learning: alteration of a behavioral tendency that is not demonstrated by an immediate, observable change in behavior

Learned Helplessness

Psychologists have shown that general learning strategies can affect a person's relationship to the environment. For example, if a person has numerous experiences in which his or her actions have no effect, he or she may learn a general strategy of helplessness or laziness.

In the first stage of one study (Hiroto, 1974), one group of college students were able to turn off an unpleasant loud noise, while another group

COOPERATIVE LEARNING ACTIVITY

Creating a Wall Chart Have the class create a wall chart illustrating the three types of modeling described in this section. The first category should depict the type of behavior in which no learning occurs; the second should show examples of observational learning, such as a teacher demonstrating how to work a math problem; and the third should depict examples involving disinhibition, such as learning to overcome a fear of water by watching people frolicking in the waves. ELL BLOCK SCHEDULING had no control over the noise. Later, all were placed in a situation in which they merely had to move a lever to stop a similar noise. Only the ones who had control over the noise in the first place learned to turn it off. The others did not even try!

It is not hard to see how these results can apply to everyday situations. In order to be able to try hard and to be full of energy, people must learn that their actions *do* make a difference. If rewards come without effort, a person never learns to work (learned laziness). If pain comes no matter how hard one tries, a person gives up. This occurrence is called **learned helplessness.**

learned helplessness: condition in which repeated attempts to control a situation fail, resulting in the belief that the situation is uncontrollable

Martin Seligman believes that learned helplessness is one major cause of depression. He reasons that when people are unable to control events in their lives, they generally respond in one of the following ways: (1) they may be less motivated to act and thus stop trying; (2) they may experience a lowered sense of self-esteem and think negatively about themselves; or (3) they may feel depressed (see Figure 9.12).

Seligman identified three important elements of learned helplessness: *stability, globality,* and *internality.* Stability refers to the person's belief that the state of helplessness results from a permanent characteristic. For example, a student who fails a math test can decide that the problem is either temporary ("I did poorly on this math test because I was sick") or *stable* ("I never have done well on math tests and never will"). Similarly, the person can decide that the problem is either specific ("I'm no good at math tests") or *global* ("I'm just dumb"). Both stability and globality focus on the student—on *internal* reasons for failure. The student could have decided that the problem was external ("This was a bad math test") instead of internal. People who attribute an undesirable outcome to their own inadequacies will probably experience depression along with guilt and self-blame.

Figure 9.12 Learned Helplessness

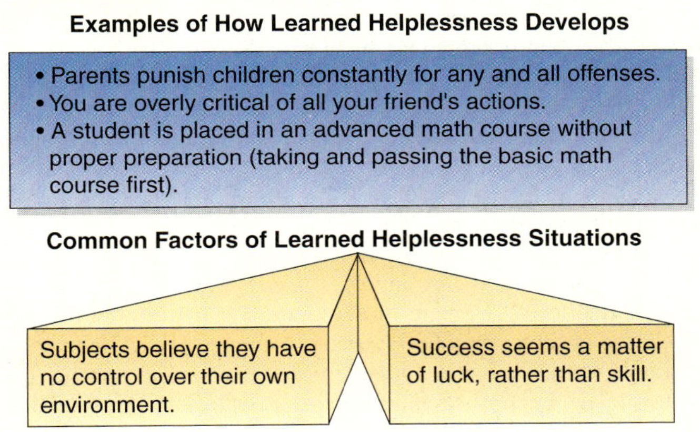

What happens when it is impossible for a learner to have an effect on the environment? What happens when a learner is punished and cannot escape the punishment? The learner may give up trying to learn. ***How can learned helplessness cause depression?***

CHAPTER 9

Section 3, pages 259–266

Figure 9.12

Visual Instruction Discuss with students how they felt on the first day of psychology class. Remind them of the class requirements and syllabus they were given. **Ask: How did you feel? Were you overwhelmed by the class requirements? How might these feelings relate to learned helplessness?**

Caption Answer Seligman believes that when people are unable to control events in their lives, they are less motivated to act and thus stop trying. As a result, they also may think badly about themselves and feel depressed.

FYI

The study habits that work most effectively for one person may not work well for someone else. It is even likely that the study habits that are effective for most girls will be different from the effective study habits of boys. There appears to be differences between the brains and thinking styles of girls and boys. This difference is not about intelligence or ability, but rather about approach. Boys tend to concentrate on one specific approach, while girls may address a problem from many angles.

MEETING SPECIAL NEEDS

Learning Style: Visual/Spatial Supply students with a list of locations with which they are all familiar, such as the school, library, neighborhood, and so on. Provide recall time, and then challenge students to draw their cognitive map of the site. Invite students to compare and contrast their maps with those of their classmates. **L1**

Refer to ***Inclusion for the High School Social Studies Classroom Strategies and Activities*** in the TCR for strategies for students with different learning styles.

CHAPTER 9

Section 3, pages 259–266

L2 Identifying Helplessness

Ask students to recall the last time that they had to wait in line for an unexpectedly long time. Have them write a description of the behaviors they observed in themselves while waiting in line. **Ask:** **Did anyone experience resignation or a feeling of helplessness? How did you cope with the feelings?**

Vocabulary Activity 9–3

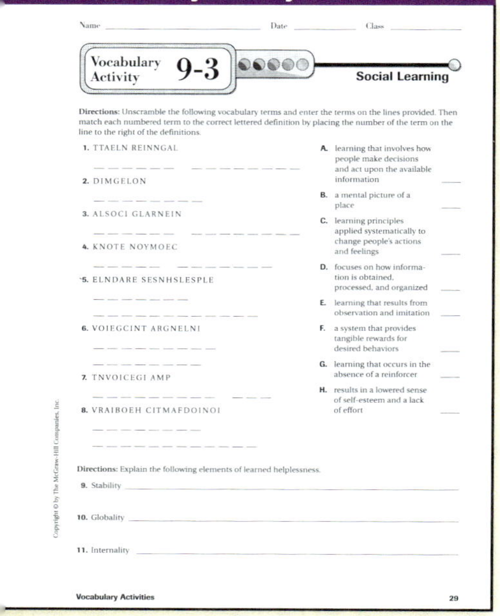
Name ______ Date ______ Class ______

Vocabulary Activity 9-3 — Social Learning

Directions: Unscramble the following vocabulary terms and enter the terms on the lines provided. Then match each numbered term to the correct lettered definition by placing the number of the term on the line to the right of the definitions.

1. TTAELN REINNGAL
2. DIMGELON
3. ALSOCI GLARNEIN
4. KNOTE NOYMOEC
5. ELNDARE SESNHSLESPLE
6. VOIEGCINT ARGNELNI
7. TNVOICEGI AMP
8. VRAIBOEH CITMAFDOINOI

A. learning that involves how people make decisions and act upon the available information ____
B. a mental picture of a place ____
C. learning principles applied systematically to change people's actions and feelings ____
D. focuses on how information is obtained, processed, and organized ____
E. learning that results from observation and imitation ____
F. a system that provides tangible rewards for desired behaviors ____
G. learning that occurs in the absence of a reinforcer ____
H. results in a lowered sense of self-esteem and a lack of effort ____

Directions: Explain the following elements of learned helplessness.

9. Stability ______
10. Globality ______
11. Internality ______

Vocabulary Activities 29

Reading Check Answer

In observational learning, an observer watches someone perform a behavior and is later able to reproduce it closely. In disinhibition, an observer watches someone else engage in a threatening activity without being punished and finds it easier to engage in that behavior later. Classroom examples will vary.

More About...

TV and Violence

Before you turn 18 years old, you probably will have witnessed 200,000 violent acts on TV. What effect does this have on you? Since the 1960s more than 3,000 studies have investigated the link between television violence and real violence.

A study released in 1998 (National Television Violence Study found that by watching violence on television, viewers risk the following results: (1) They learn to behave violently. (2) They become desensitized to violence. (3) They become more fearful of being attacked.

The study also found the following:

- 45 percent of the "bad" characters in violent TV programs go unpunished.
- 51 percent of the violent interactions on TV show no pain; 34 percent show unrealistically low levels of harm.
- 26 percent of violent scenes involve the use of guns.
- Only 3 percent of violent programs emphasize a nonviolent theme.
- Only 14 percent of violent scenes show blood and gore.
- 42 percent of violent scenes on TV involve humor.

modeling: learning by imitating others; copying behavior

Wall Chart

MODELING

The second type of social learning is **modeling.** When you go to a concert for the first time, you may be very hesitant about where to go, when to enter (especially if you are late), when to clap, how to get a better seat after the first intermission, and so on. So you observe others, follow them, and soon you are an "old hand." This illustrates a third type of learning—observation and imitation.

The general term for this kind of learning is *modeling.* It includes three different types of effects. In the simplest case—the first type of modeling—the behavior of others simply increases the chances that we will do the same thing. We clap when others do, look up at a building if everyone else is looking there, and copy the styles and verbal expressions of our peers. No learning occurs in this case, in the sense of acquiring new responses. We simply perform old responses that we otherwise might not be using at the time.

The second type of modeling is usually called *observational learning,* or imitation. In this sort of learning an observer watches someone perform a behavior and is later able to reproduce it closely, though the observer was unable to do this before observing the model. An example is watching someone else do an unfamiliar dance step and afterward being able to do the dance step yourself.

Have you ever noticed that some children seem to behave in a manner similar to their parents? Albert Bandura suggested that we watch models perform and then imitate the models' behavior. Bandura and his colleagues demonstrated observational learning by using a Bobo doll (see Exploring Psychology on page 259). The experimenters found that children were more likely to act aggressively after they had observed aggressive behavior.

Individual differences in personality may help to explain why people act differently when shown the same movie containing violent material. The American Psychological Association (APA) Commission on Violence and Youth (1993) reported that personal qualities do play a role. One child may learn that violence is right and another child may view violence as pitiful. Others have found that more aggressive children seek out violent television and are also more affected by it.

A third type of modeling involves *disinhibition.* When an observer watches someone else engage in a threatening activity without being punished, the observer may find it easier to engage in that behavior later. For example, someone with a snake phobia may watch another person handling snakes. Such observation may help alleviate the phobia. This procedure is used in clinical work as we will see in the chapter on therapies (Chapter 17).

Reading Check

How does observational learning differ from disinhibition? Give classroom examples.

CRITICAL THINKING ACTIVITY

Analyzing Information In an experiment on learned helplessness, Seligman found that animals that were unable to change their situation for long periods of time seemed unable or unwilling to change when the possibility was opened to them. Ask students to consider the following questions: **What implications do such experiments have for humans? Can you think of situations in your life in which you have experienced the effect of learned helplessness?** Have students present their findings and conclusions, perhaps in a panel-discussion format. **L2**

Figure 9.13 The Imitation of Others

Social learning theorists argue that much learning results from observing the behavior of others and from imagining the consequences of our own behavior. ***What behaviors might this child be learning?***

Inflated doll similar to Bobo doll

BEHAVIOR MODIFICATION

The term *behavior modification* often appears in magazine articles describing research on changing people's behavior through drugs, "mind control," or even brain surgery. In fact, it is none of these things. **Behavior modification** refers to the systematic application of learning principles (classical conditioning, operant conditioning, and social learning) to change people's actions and feelings. When you give your little brother a quarter to leave you alone, that is very much like behavior modification. Behavior modification involves a series of well-defined steps to change behavior. The success of each step is carefully evaluated to find the best solution for a given situation.

behavior modification: systematic application of learning principles to change people's actions and feelings

The behavior modifier usually begins by defining a problem in concrete terms. For example, Johnnie's mother might complain that her son is messy. If she used behavior modification to reform the child, she would first have to define "messy" in objective terms. For example, he does not make his bed in the morning, he drops his coat on the couch when he comes inside, and so on. She would not worry about where his bad habits come from. Rather, she would work out a system of rewards and punishments aimed at getting Johnnie to make his bed, hang up his coat, and do other straightening-up tasks.

Modeling, operant conditioning, and classical conditioning principles have been used in behavior modification. Classical conditioning principles are particularly useful in helping people to overcome fears, and we shall discuss them when we consider the problem of treating psychological disorders (Chapter 17). Modeling is often used to teach desired behaviors. In addition, as you will see in the following examples, operant conditioning principles have also been applied to everyday problems.

Computer-Assisted Instruction

Some instructors teach their students by a conversational method very similar to what computer-assisted instruction (CAI) is using today. CAI is a refinement of the concept of programmed instruction that was

CHAPTER 9

Section 3, pages 259–266

Figure 9.13

Caption Answer The child could be learning aggressive behavior. People who witness aggressive behavior learn that aggression is okay and are less likely to condemn it. Therefore, they may act more aggressively themselves.

Applying Psychology

Ask students to research some of the many techniques that psychologists have developed to help people learn self-control. Then ask each student to draw up a formal behavior contract (somewhat like a legal document) intended to help them overcome a simple behavioral problem, such as watching too much television or chronic tardiness. Tell students that they should check their contracts to be sure they include appropriate reinforcers and use successive approximations.

PSYCHOLOGY JOURNAL

Ask students to review their television and movie watching choices. Have them write a brief description explaining how the technologies of motion pictures and television may have influenced students' attitudes toward violence, weapons, language, personal development, and sex.

PSYCHOLOGY LAB EXPERIMENT

Token Economies Have students work together to develop a token economy for the classroom to improve student behavior. Students should come to an agreement on the specific behaviors that would be rewarded, the tokens that would be used, the real rewards for which the tokens could be exchanged, and a way to make the system financially self-sustaining. After students have finalized their system, have them implement it in the classroom for a set period of time. At the end of the trial period, students should discuss the changes they observed in students' behavior as a result of the token economy. Was it successful? Do they think it could be successful if used throughout the school? **L3**

L3 Computer-Aided Instruction Model Have a group of students who have access to a computer and presentation software such as PowerPoint® or HyperStudio® prepare a computer-aided instruction model that would help an elementary school child learn vocabulary words.

Psychology and You

Use the following question to direct a class discussion after students have read the **Psychology and You** feature.
Ask: **What other bad habits do people form by opting for immediate gratification even when it includes delayed punishment?**

Figure 9.14

Visual Instruction Tell students that Bandura believes that social learning can occur by exposure and imitation alone.

Caption Answer The environment acts as a reinforcer or punisher regarding behavior, motivations, beliefs, etc.

Create token economy

Psychology and You: How You Form Bad Habits

Do you procrastinate? For example, have you ever found yourself cramming for an important test the night before? Operant conditioning probably played a role in your bad habit of procrastination. You selected immediate positive reinforcement and delayed punishment. That is, you opted to spend your time doing something else, such as watching TV, instead of studying.

Procrastination provided the *immediate* reinforcement of giving you more leisure time. The punishment, lower grades or lack of sleep the day before the test, was *delayed.* Many bad habits are formed when people follow this pattern of immediate reinforcement and delayed punishment.

introduced by S.L. Pressey (1933) and refined by B.F. Skinner in the 1950s.

The essential concept of programmed instruction is based on operant conditioning. The material to be learned is broken down into simpler units called frames. Each time the student shows that she or he has learned the information in a frame, the student is given positive reinforcement in the form of new information, choices, or point rewards similar to those used in video games. Each question, or prompt, builds on information already mastered. The computer retains (as does the student) exactly what the learner understands on the basis of the student's answers to questions.

Several principles of learning are being applied in CAI. The student is learning complex material through a response chain. She or he is reinforced constantly. Knowledge is being shaped in a systematic and predictable way. The student is able to have a dialogue with the instructor on every point, which is often impossible for a class of students in a conventional setting.

token economy: conditioning in which desirable behavior is reinforced with valueless objects, which can be accumulated and exchanged for valued rewards

Token Economies

Psychologists tried an experiment with a group of troubled boys in Washington, D.C. In fact, the boys had been labeled "uneducable" and placed in the National Training School. The experimenters used what is known as a **token economy** to motivate the boys. The youngsters received points—or secondary reinforcers—for good grades on tests. They could cash in these points for such rewards as snacks or lounge privileges. A majority of the students showed a significant increase in IQ scores. The boys continued to improve in the months that followed, showing that they were, indeed, educable (Cohen & Filipczak, 1971). Similarly, behavioral programs to reduce prison violence reduce post-prison violence in the community (French et al., 2003).

In token economies, people are systematically paid to act appropriately. In the real world, behaviorists argue the rewards are just as real; they are simply less systematic. In overcrowded mental hospitals, for example, the only way some patients can get attention is by acting out. Overworked staff members simply

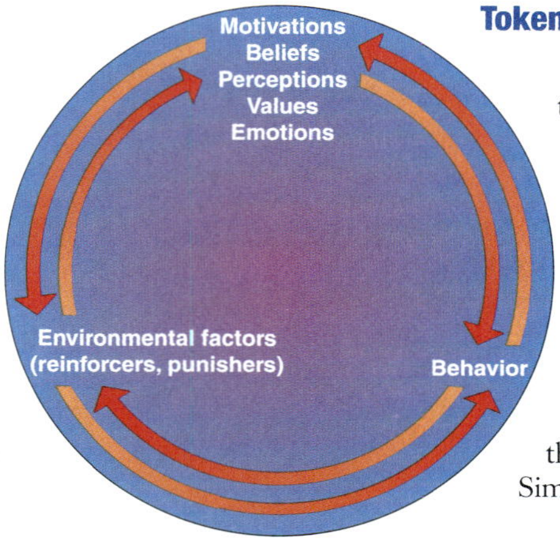

Figure 9.14 How Social Learning Works

Social learning theorists argue that much learning results from observing the behavior of others and from imagining the consequences of our own behavior. ***What role does the environment play in social learning?***

INTERDISCIPLINARY CONNECTIONS ACTIVITY

Government To help students make the connection, explain to students that although it is not always apparent, conditioning is at work in many areas of society. Ask students to investigate one of the following issues related to the United States government to identify the role of conditioning in each situation: political parties, senatorial courtesy, government lobbyists. Once students have chosen the issue they want to explore, have them focus on two lines of questioning: **(1) How has conditioning helped to create the current state of affairs that surround the issue? (2) How can new conditioning improve the current state of affairs within the issue?** Ask students to summarize their findings in short oral reports to the class. **L2**

do not have time to bother with people who are not causing trouble. Since attention from the staff is reinforcing for these patients, people are rewarded for undesirable behavior. By systematically rewarding only desirable behavior, token economies have improved conditions in prisons, mental hospitals, halfway houses, and classrooms.

Self-Control

One of the most important features in behavior modification is an emphasis on asking people to set up personal systems of rewards and punishments to shape their own thoughts and actions—this is a self-control program. As in any application of behavior modification, the first step in self-control is to define the problem. People who smoke too much would be encouraged to actually count how many cigarettes they smoked every hour of the day and note what kinds of situations led them to smoke. (After a meal? When talking to friends? Driving to work?) Similarly, people who have a very poor opinion of themselves would have to define the problem more concretely. They might begin by counting the number of self-deprecating remarks they make and thoughts they have. Researchers have found that just keeping track of behavior in this way often leads a person to start changing it.

The next step may be to set up a behavioral contract. A behavioral contract simply involves choosing a reinforcer (buying a new shirt, watching a favorite TV program) and making it depend on some less desirable but necessary act such as getting to work on time or washing the kitchen floor. One soda lover who had trouble studying decided

Figure 9.15 Improving Study Habits

Studying effectively is an active process. By using successive approximations (reading one more page each time you sit down to study) and positive reinforcements (rewarding yourself for productive studying), you can improve your study habits. The SQ4R and PQ4R methods are active methods of studying. ***How can you improve your own study habits?***

SQ4R Method	PQ4R Method
Survey the chapter. Read the headings. Read any summaries. Your goal is to get a general understanding of the chapter.	**Preview** the chapter by surveying general topics to be studied.
Question the material. Formulate questions about the material as if you were the instructor writing the test.	**Question** yourself by transforming heads into questions.
Read carefully and try to answer the questions you formulated. If you become distracted or tired, stop reading. Pick it up later.	**Read** the section or chapter carefully while trying to answer the questions you created.
Write down the answers to your questions. Sum up the information in your own words.	**Reflect** on the text as you are reading to try and understand it, think of examples, and relate to information about the topic that you already know.
Recite to yourself what you have read. Recall main headings and ideas. Be sure to put the material into your own words. Answer questions aloud.	**Recite** the information by answering your own questions aloud.
Review the material. Summarize the main points in the chapter. Answer the questions you have formulated.	**Review** the material by recalling and summarizing main points.

Figure 9.15

Visual Instruction After reviewing the tables, ask students to consider which method of studying has been most effective in their lives.

Caption Answer Students' answers may include some of the concepts discussed in this section.

TEACHER Tip

Make sure students understand that a token economy operates according to three principles:

1. The participant is reinforced with tokens for appropriate behavior.
2. The number of tokens is proportional to the requirements of the response.
3. The tokens may be cashed in for rewards.

3 ASSESS

Assign Section 3 Assessment as homework or as an in-class activity.

EXTENDING THE CONTENT

Token Economies Used in Teaching Head Start is a government-funded child development program for children from low-income families. One Head Start program used a token economy to help teach preschoolers to write. The tokens they earned could be exchanged for such things as food and movies. The study compared the results of the children who participated in the token economy with children who had not participated in it. The differences were dramatic. Children who participated in the token economy not only improved their skills, but their attitude toward school was much more positive.

Section Quiz 9–3

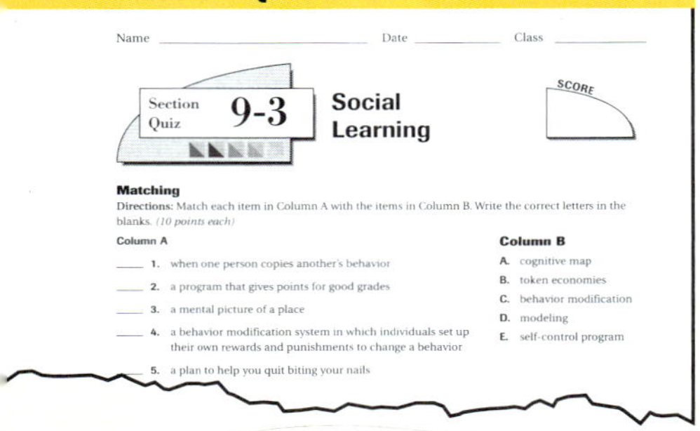

Name ______ Date ______ Class ______

Section Quiz 9-3 **Social Learning**

SCORE

Matching

Directions: Match each item in Column A with the items in Column B. Write the correct letters in the blanks. *(10 points each)*

Column A

____ 1. when one person copies another's behavior

____ 2. a program that gives points for good grades

____ 3. a mental picture of a place

____ 4. a behavior modification system in which individuals set up their own rewards and punishments to change a behavior

____ 5. a plan to help you quit biting your nails

Column B

A. cognitive map

B. token economies

C. behavior modification

D. modeling

E. self-control program

Reteach

Have students write 10 questions and answers about the content of Section 3. Select a number of students and use their questions to quiz the class.

Enrich

Ask students to create a poster that illustrates the two types of social learning.

4 CLOSE

Ask students to list the events in their daily lives they can associate with social learning.

that she would allow herself a soda only after she studied for half an hour. Her soda addiction remained strong, but her study time increased dramatically under this system.

Improving Your Study Habits

One psychologist designed a program to help students improve their study habits. A group of student volunteers were told to set a time when they would go to a small room in the library they had not used before. They were then to work only as long as they remained interested. As soon as they found themselves fidgeting, daydreaming, or becoming bored, they were to read one more page before they left.

The next day they were asked to repeat the same procedure, adding a second page to the amount they read between the time they decided to leave and the time they actually left the library. The third day they added a third page, and so on. Students who followed this procedure found that in time they were able to study more efficiently and for longer periods.

Why did this procedure work? Requiring students to leave as soon as they felt distracted helped to reduce the negative emotions associated with studying. Studying in a new place removed the conditioned aversive stimulus. Thus, aversive responses were not conditioned to the subject matter or the room, as they are when students force themselves to work. The procedure also made use of successive approximations. The students began by reading just one more page after they became bored and only gradually increased the assignment. In conclusion, it is important to note that classical and operant conditioning and social learning do not operate independently in our lives. All three forms of learning interact in a complex way to determine what and how we learn.

SECTION 3 Assessment

1. **Review the Vocabulary** How is a token economy an example of behavior modification?
2. **Visualize the Main Idea** In a diagram similar to the one below, identify three important elements of learned helplessness.

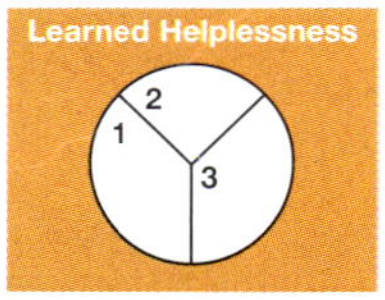

3. **Recall Information** How can you improve your study habits through conditioning?
4. **Think Critically** What principles of modeling should parents consider when rewarding and punishing their children? Provide reasons for your answer.
5. **Application Activity** Devise a plan of behavior modification (such as teaching your dog not to bark indoors or stopping your friend from knuckle cracking) by applying learning principles.

SECTION 3 Assessment Answers

1. A token economy reinforces desirable behavior in exchange for points or rewards.
2. Diagrams should include these elements: stability, globality, and internality.
3. Students' answers should include discussions of aversive stimuli, successive approximations, and positive reinforcement.
4. Parents should consider how and where children learn behaviors (simple modeling and observational learning); parents should also reward and punish consistently, so that disinhibition does not lead to poor behavior.
5. Students' plans should include applications of classical conditioning, operant conditioning, and social learning.

CHAPTER 9

Summary and Vocabulary

Learning is a relatively permanent change in a behavioral tendency that results from experience. Not all behaviors are acquired in the same way. Psychologists have studied three basic types of learning: classical conditioning, operant conditioning, and social learning.

Section 1 Classical Conditioning

Main Idea: People acquire certain behaviors through classical conditioning, a learning procedure in which associations are made between a neutral stimulus and a conditioned response.

- Ivan Pavlov discovered the principles of classical conditioning.
- The four elements involved in classical conditioning are US, UR, CS, and CR.
- Generalization and discrimination are complementary processes in which the participant responds to similar stimuli in the same manner or responds differently to dissimilar stimuli.
- A CR will sometimes reappear spontaneously after extinction in a process called spontaneous recovery.
- Classical conditioning may be used to affect human behavior, such as taste aversions and fears.

Section 2 Operant Conditioning

Main Idea: Operant conditioning occurs when the consequences that follow a behavior increase or decrease the likelihood of that behavior occurring again.

- Operant conditioning, as explained by B.F. Skinner, means that human behavior is influenced by one's history of rewards and punishments.
- Reinforcers (positive and negative, and primary and secondary) are stimuli that increase the likelihood that certain behaviors will be repeated.
- Behavior is reinforced according to continuous or partial reinforcement schedules that are based on numbers of responses or times of responses.
- Reinforcing responses that are increasingly similar to the desired behavior is a process called shaping.
- Punishments are stimuli that decrease the likelihood that certain behaviors will be repeated.

Section 3 Social Learning

Main Idea: Social learning, consisting of cognitive learning and modeling, involves how people make decisions and act upon the information available to them.

- Latent learning is not demonstrated by an immediately observable change in behavior at the time of learning.
- If people have numerous experiences in which their actions have no effect, they may learn a general strategy of learned helplessness.
- Modeling is a type of learning that occurs as the result of observation and imitation.
- Behavior modification uses learning principles to change people's actions or feelings.

Chapter Vocabulary

classical conditioning (p. 241)
neutral stimulus (p. 242)
unconditioned stimulus (US) (p. 242)
unconditioned response (UR) (p. 242)
conditioned stimulus (CS) (p. 242)
conditioned response (CR) (p. 242)
generalization (p. 244)
discrimination (p. 244)
extinction (p. 245)
operant conditioning (p. 250)
reinforcement (p. 251)
primary reinforcer (p. 252)
secondary reinforcer (p. 252)
fixed-ratio schedule (p. 253)
variable-ratio schedule (p. 254)
fixed-interval schedule (p. 254)
variable-interval schedule (p. 255)
shaping (p. 255)
response chain (p. 256)
aversive control (p. 256)
negative reinforcement (p. 256)
escape conditioning (p. 257)
avoidance conditioning (p. 257)
social learning (p. 259)
cognitive learning (p. 260)
cognitive map (p. 260)
latent learning (p. 260)
learned helplessness (p. 261)
modeling (p. 262)
behavior modification (p. 263)
token economy (p. 264)

9 Summary and Vocabulary

Using the Chapter 9 Summary and Vocabulary

Use the Chapter 9 Summary and Vocabulary to preview, review, condense, or reteach the chapter.

Preview/Review

Use the Chapter Vocabulary list to help students review and study.

Activity Have students create flash cards for each of the vocabulary terms in this chapter. Then encourage students to work in pairs, using the flash cards to quiz each other.

Vocabulary PuzzleMaker CD-ROM reinforces the vocabulary terms used in Chapter 9.

Condense

Have students read the Chapter 9 Summary.

Chapter 9 Guided Reading Activities

Reteach

Reteaching Activity 9

PERFORMANCE ASSESSMENT ACTIVITY

Creating a Course Outline Individuals may sometimes learn more about learning by teaching others. Provide opportunities for students to teach or tutor another individual or group in some subject area or skill. To focus their teaching experiences, have students prepare an outline for a course titled "The Many Ways of Learning." Students should design the course to cover the three main types of learning discussed in Chapter 9.

Refer to the ***Authentic Assessment*** booklet for additional activities and information about evaluating student performance.

9 Assessment

PSYCHOLOGY Online

Have students visit the Web site at glencoe.com to review Chapter 9 and take the **Self-Check Quiz**.

GLENCOE TECHNOLOGY

Presentation Plus!

For a review of Chapter 9 content, see MindJogger Checkpoint on **Presentation Plus!**

Reviewing Vocabulary

1. c
2. f
3. i
4. a
5. j
6. g
7. b
8. h
9. d
10. e

Recalling Facts

1. Learning takes place automatically in classical conditioning. In operant conditioning, one learns from one's behavior and its consequences.

2. Taste aversions develop after a bad experience with a particular food. If you become ill after eating a food, you will learn to stay away from that food for a long time.

3. fixed-ratio: depends on a specified quantity of responses; variable-ratio: occurs after unknown number of responses; fixed-interval: the first correct response after a specified amount of time is reinforced; variable-interval: the time at which reinforcement is given changes

4. classical conditioning: an old response becomes attached to a new stimulus; a stimulus that normally elicits a given response is repeatedly preceded by a neutral stimulus that eventually evokes a similar response when presented by itself; salivating when thinking of a favorite food; operant conditioning: learning from the consequences of behavior; a certain action is reinforced or punished, resulting in corresponding increases or decreases in the likelihood that similar actions will occur again; you study hard because it results in good grades; social learning: learning by watching and imitating others; people analyze events and make a decision before giving a response; children act violently after they have seen violence on television

CHAPTER 9 Assessment

PSYCHOLOGY Online

Self-Check Quiz
Visit the *Understanding Psychology* Web site at glencoe.com and click on **Chapter 9—Self-Check Quizzes** to prepare for the Chapter Test.

Reviewing Vocabulary

Choose the letter of the correct term or concept below to complete the sentence.

a. extinction
b. behavior modification
c. unconditioned stimulus
d. generalization
e. schedules
f. secondary
g. token economy
h. modeling
i. operant conditioning
j. escape conditioning

1. A stimulus that elicits a predictable response without training is called a(n) ________.

2. Money is an example of a(n) ________ reinforcer.

3. ________ is a type of learning based on the consequences of actions.

4. In conditioning, ________ results from the repeated performance of a response without reinforcement.

5. ________ is the process of removing an aversive stimulus after it has started.

6. In a(n) ________, people are rewarded for behaving in an appropriate manner with valueless objects.

7. ________ refers to the systematic application of learning principles to change people's actions and feelings.

8. When children imitate the behavior of their parents, they are practicing a form of learning called ________.

9. The tendency for a stimulus similar to the original conditioned stimulus to elicit a response similar to the conditioned response is called ______.

10. The various ways that reinforcers occur after a behavior has been elicited are referred to as ________.

Recalling Facts

1. What are the differences between classical and operant conditioning?

2. How do taste aversions develop?

3. What are the four partial schedules of reinforcement, and how do they differ?

4. Create three diagrams like the one below on your paper—one each for classical conditioning, operant conditioning, and social learning. Fill in each with the definition, how it works, and an example of that type of learning.

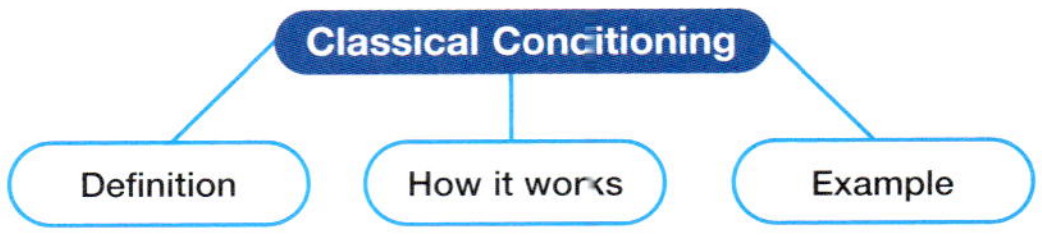

5. Name and describe the three different types of modeling.

Critical Thinking

1. Identifying Alternatives Which of the schedules of reinforcement do your instructors generally use in conducting their classes? How would your classes be different if they used the other schedules?

2. Applying Concepts Businesses often make use of conditioning techniques in their commercials. Think of specific examples of such advertising. Describe how the principles of conditioning are used in those advertisements.

3. Synthesizing Information How might a therapist help cigarette smokers quit smoking using classical conditioning techniques? Using operant conditioning techniques? Using social learning techniques?

4. Evaluating Information Is punishment an effective tool of learning? Describe the advantages or disadvantages of using punishment to teach a child a behavior.

5. Predicting Consequences How has technology made parenting more challenging? Provide examples to support your answer.

5. simplest form: the behavior of others simply increases the chances we will do the same thing; observational learning (imitation): watching someone perform a behavior and reproducing that same behavior later; disinhibition: watching someone else engage in a threatening activity without being punished makes it easier for one to engage in that same activity later

Critical Thinking

1. Be sure students start by analyzing the reinforcement schedule currently in use and then explain how their classes would be different under each of the other schedules.

2. Encourage students to bring clippings or videotapes of current ads to class for discussion. Students should be able to identify the types of conditioning used in each advertisement.

3. Answers will vary. Classical conditioning: the therapist might use a nauseating drug to make smoking unpleasant. Operant conditioning: the therapist might use a positive reinforcer to help the participant stop smoking. Social learning: the therapist could have the smoker observe and model the behavior of nonsmokers in social situations.

4. Students' answers should include examples to support or refute the idea of using punishment.

CHAPTER 9 Assessment

Psychology Projects

1. **Classical Conditioning** Select some particular task that you find difficult or unpleasant. Whenever you begin to work at this task, play one of your favorite tapes or CDs. Do this for two weeks and then analyze your reactions. Have your feelings toward the music become associated with the task? Do you find it easier to work and complete the task? Write a report that explains your findings in light of what you know about conditioning techniques.
2. **Operant Conditioning** Go to a public place where you can watch parents and children interacting. Watch a parent-child interaction long enough to identify an aversive stimulus the parent or child may be using to control behavior. What particular behavior of the child is the parent attempting to change? What particular behavior of the parent is the child attempting to change? Are they successful? Collect your observations and conclusions in a report.

Technology Activity

Use the Internet to locate the Web site of a self-help or support group at which self-control and other self-improvement techniques are taught. You should look for the following stages/techniques: definition of the problem, establishment of behavioral contracts, and application of reinforcers in a program of successive approximations. Evaluate the site and summarize your findings in a brief report.

Psychology Journal

Reread the journal entry in which you described your attempts to teach a skill or task. Did you use classical conditioning, operant conditioning, or social learning techniques? Make a new entry, describing and identifying your learning techniques. Explain why your teaching strategy was successful or unsuccessful.

Building Skills

Interpreting a Chart Review the chart of O. Hobart Mowrer's experiment to stop bed-wetting below. Then answer the questions that follow.

Practice and **assess** key social studies skills with **Glencoe Skillbuilder Interactive Workbook CD-ROM, Level 2.**

Mowrer's Experiment	*Stimulus*	*Response*
Before Conditioning	Full Bladder (neutral stimulus) Alarm (US)	No awakening Awakening (UR)
During Conditioning	Full Bladder (CS) paired with Alarm (US)	Awakening (UR)
After Conditioning	Full Bladder (CS)	Awakening (CR)

1. What happened in the above experiment? What things were paired to lead to awakening?
2. Explain how the CS, US, CR, and UR relate to the end result (awakening).
3. Which type of learning is displayed in this chart?

See the Skills Handbook, page 628, for an explanation of interpreting charts.

Assessment

Building Skills

1. Although a full bladder does not awaken the child, an alarm does. So an alarm (US) was paired with a full bladder, the neutral stimulus, to produce awakening (CR).
2. The alarm (US) led to an awakening (UR). A full bladder, the neutral stimulus, did not produce awakening. When the alarm (US) was paired with the full bladder (CS), awakening to the full bladder became the conditioned response (CR).
3. classical conditioning

GLENCOE TECHNOLOGY

CD-ROM
Glencoe Skillbuilder Interactive Workbook, Level 2

This interactive CD-ROM is designed to reinforce student mastery of essential social studies skills.

Chapter Bonus Test Question

This question may be used for extra credit on the Chapter Assessment.
Answer the following question:
I am a type of modeling. I occur when an observer sees another person engage in a threatening situation without experiencing negative consequences. The observer may find it easier to attempt that behavior. What am I?
Answer: disinhibition

5. Answers will vary. New technologies have increased children's access and exposure to various images, programs and recordings, making it more difficult to monitor what children are hearing or seeing. Students may mention that observational learning involves imitating behavior.

Psychology Projects

1. Answers will vary. Students should demonstrate an understanding of conditioning techniques.
2. Answers will vary. Students should identify positive and negative reinforcers and their effect on frequency of behavior. Students should demonstrate an understanding of operant conditioning techniques.

Technology Activity

Students' reports should include an evaluation as well as a summary of the self-help/support group site they chose. Encourage students to share the address of the Web sites they found.

Psychology Journal

Students' answers should express an understanding of the three types of learning discussed in Chapter 9.

TIME REPORTS

Reader's Dictionary

Review the following terms with students to help them read and understand the article.

neuron: nerve cells equipped to receive and transmit electrical signals
malleable: capable of being altered by outside forces or influences
dendrites: extensions from a nerve cell that receive signals from other neurons
axon: single, threadlike structure within a neuron that carries signals to other neurons
metabolism: chemical changes in living cells by which energy is provided for vital processes

CLICK HERE

TIME REPORTS

Visit **www.time.com/teach** for the complete text of this article, as well as related articles on the subject.

Block Schedule

This activity works well for a block-scheduling framework.

TIME REPORTS

Fertile Minds

From birth, a baby's brain cells proliferate wildly, making connections that may shape a lifetime of experience. The first three years are critical

By J. MADELEINE NASH

RAT-A-TAT-TAT. RAT-A-TAT-TAT. If scientists could eavesdrop on the brain of a human embryo 10, maybe 12 weeks after conception, they would hear an astonishing racket. Inside the womb, long before the earliest dreamy images flicker through the cortex, nerve cells in the developing brain crackle with purposeful activity. Like teenagers with telephones, cells in one neighborhood of the brain are calling friends in another, and these cells are calling their friends, and they keep calling one another over and over again, "almost," says neurobiologist Carla Shatz of the University of California, Berkeley, "as if they were autodialing."

But these neurons—as the long, wiry cells that carry electrical messages through the nervous system and the brain are called—are not transmitting signals in scattershot fashion. That would produce a featureless static, the sort of noise picked up by a radio tuned between stations. On the contrary, evidence is growing that the staccato bursts of electricity that form those distinctive rat-a-tat-tats arise from coordinated waves of neural activity, and that those pulsing waves, like currents shifting sand on the ocean floor, actually change the shape of the brain, carving mental circuits into patterns that over time will enable the newborn infant to perceive a father's voice, a mother's touch, a shiny mobile twirling over the crib.

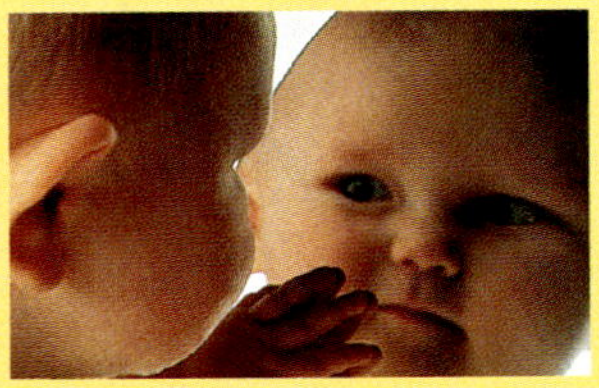

Wiring Vision

WHAT'S GOING ON Babies can see at birth, but not in fine-grained detail. They have not yet acquired the knack of focusing both eyes on a single object or developed more sophisticated visual skills like depth perception. They also lack hand-eye coordination.
WINDOW OF LEARNING Unless it is exercised early on, the visual system will not develop.

The finding that the electrical activity of brain cells changes the physical structure of the brain is breathtaking. For the rhythmic firing of neurons is no longer assumed to be a by-product of building the brain but essential to the process, and it begins well before birth. The brain begins working long before it is finished. And the same processes that wire the brain before birth also drive the explosion of learning that occurs immediately afterward.

At birth, a baby's brain contains 100 billion neurons. Also in place are a trillion glial cells which form a kind of honeycomb that protects and nourishes the neurons. But while the brain contains virtually all the nerve cells it will ever have, the pattern of wiring between them has yet to stabilize. Up to this point, says Shatz, "what the brain has done is lay out circuits that are its best guess about what's required for vision, for language, for whatever." And now it is up to neural activity—no longer spontaneous, but driven by sensory experiences—to take this rough blueprint and refine it.

During the first years of life, the brain undergoes a series of extraordinary changes. Starting shortly after birth, a baby's brain produces trillions more connections between neurons than it can possibly use. Then the brain eliminates connections, or synapses, that are seldom or never used. The excess synapses in a child's brain undergo a pruning, starting around the age of 10 or earlier, leaving behind a mind whose patterns of emotion and thought are unique.

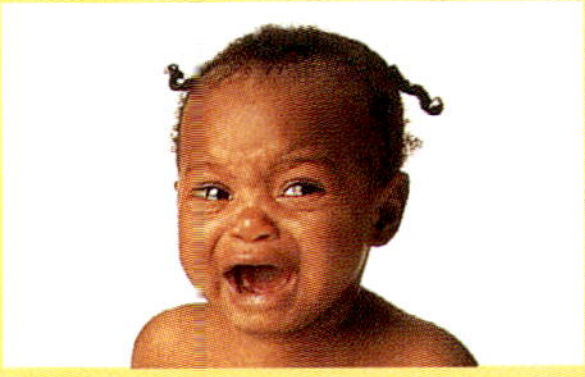

Wiring Feelings

WHAT'S GOING ON Among the first circuits the brain constructs are those that govern emotions. Around two months of age, the distress and contentment experienced by newborns start to evolve into more complex feelings: joy and sadness, pride and shame.
WINDOW OF LEARNING Emotions develop in increasingly complex layers.

FROM LEFT TO RIGHT: PENNY GENTIEU; JADE ALBERT; JADE ALBERT; PENNY GENTIEU

Deprived of a stimulating environment, a child's brain suffers. Researchers at Baylor College of Medicine, for example, have found that children who don't play much or are rarely touched develop brains 20% to 30% smaller than normal for their

COOPERATIVE LEARNING ACTIVITY

Conducting a Debate Divide the class into two groups. Have students use the information found in this article as well as information found through their own research to conduct a debate on one of the following positions: (1) New parents should be more "hands-on" with their children and less focused on their careers. (2) The government should invest more money into improving existing day-care programs. Each group should present a summary of its arguments after participating in the debate. **BLOCK SCHEDULING**

age. Lab animals provide another parallel. Not only do young rats reared in toy-strewn cages exhibit more complex behavior than rats confined to sterile, uninteresting boxes, researchers at the University of Illinois have found, but the brains of these rats contain as many as 25% more synapses per neuron. Rich experiences, in other words, really do produce rich brains.

The new insights into brain development have profound implications for parents and policymakers. In an age when mothers and fathers are increasingly pressed for time, the results coming out of the labs are likely to increase concerns about leaving very young children in the care of others. For the data underscore the importance of hands-on parenting, of finding the time to cuddle a baby, talk with a toddler and provide infants with stimulating experiences.

The new insights have infused new passion into the political debate over early education and day care. There is an urgent need, say child-development experts, for preschool programs designed to boost the brain power of kids born into impoverished households. Without such programs, they warn, the current drive to curtail welfare costs by pushing mothers with infants and toddlers into the work force may backfire. "There is a time scale to brain development, and the most important year is the first," notes Frank Newman, president of the Education Commission of the States. By three, a neglected child bears marks that are very difficult to erase.

But the new research offers hope as well. Scientists have found that the brain during the first years of life is so malleable that very young children who suffer strokes or injuries that wipe out an entire hemisphere can still mature into highly functional adults. Moreover, it is becoming clear that well-designed preschool programs can help many children overcome glaring deficits in their home environment. With appropriate therapy, say researchers, even serious disorders like dyslexia may be treatable. While inherited problems may place certain children at greater risk than others, says Dr. Harry Chugani, a neurologist at Wayne State University in Detroit, that is no excuse for ignoring the environment's power to remodel the brain. "We may not do much to change what happens before birth, but we can change what happens after a baby is born," he observes.

Strong evidence that activity changes the brain began accumulating in the 1970s. But only recently have researchers had tools powerful enough to reveal the precise mechanisms by which those changes are brought about. Neural activity triggers a biochemical cascade that reaches all the way to the nucleus of cells and the coils of DNA that encode specific genes. In fact, two of the genes affected by neural activity in embryonic fruit flies, neurobiologist Corey Goodman and his colleagues at Berkeley reported, are identical to those that other studies have linked to learning and memory. How thrilling, exclaims Goodman, that the snippets of DNA that embryos use to build their brains are the same ones that will later allow adult organisms to process and store new information.

As researchers explore the once hidden links between brain activity and brain structure, they are beginning to construct a sturdy bridge over the chasm that previously separated genes from the environment. Experts now agree that a baby does not come into the world as a genetically preprogrammed automaton or a blank slate, but arrives as something much more interesting. For this reason the debate that engaged countless generations of philosophers—whether nature or nurture calls the shots—no longer interests most scientists. They are much too busy chronicling the ways in which genes and the environment interact. "It's not a competition," says Dr. Stanley Greenspan, a psychiatrist at George Washington University. "It's a dance." ■

—For the complete text of this article and related articles from TIME, please visit www.time.com/teach

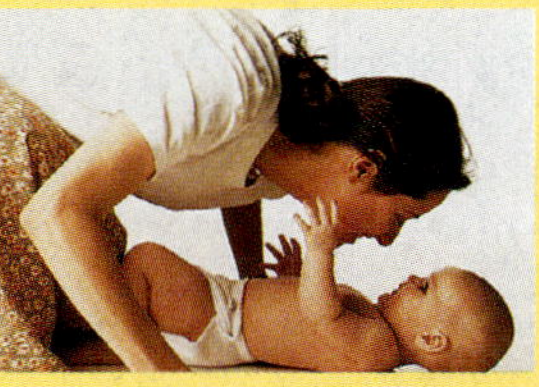

Wiring Language

WHAT'S GOING ON Even before birth, an infant tunes into the melody of its mother's voice. Over the next six years, its brain will set up the circuitry to decipher and reproduce the lyrics. A six-month-old can recognize the vowel sounds that are building blocks of speech.
WINDOW OF LEARNING Language skills, sharpest early on, grow throughout life.

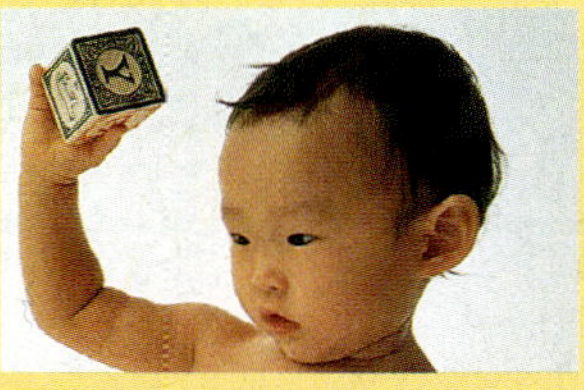

Wiring Movement

WHAT'S GOING ON At birth babies can move their limbs, but in a jerky, uncontrolled fashion. Over the next four years, the brain progressively refines the circuits for reaching, grabbing, sitting, crawling, walking and running.
WINDOW OF LEARNING Motor-skill development moves from gross to increasingly fine.

Analyzing the Article

1. What "discovery" does this article detail?
2. **CRITICAL THINKING** Do you agree that your "uniqueness" was developed in the first three years of your life? Why or why not?

TIME REPORTS

Active Reading Strategy

Explain to students that rereading a confusing part of a passage, and relating information to previous knowledge, might clarify their understanding. Explain that good readers often pause to reread, question, or think about what they have read.

Questions for Discussion

Use the following questions for a class discussion after students have read the article.

1. People often compare the human brain to a computer. How is a brain different from a computer? *(The brain begins working before it is finished being built; it runs continually; it can't be upgraded.)*
2. Why is providing a stimulating environment to humans in the first years of life so important? *(After the brain develops connections between neurons, it begins to eliminate the connections that are never used. If a baby is not stimulated, then many of the connections between neurons are eliminated.)*
3. Use Chapter 9 to review the importance of the environment in learning. Discuss why Dr. Greenspan describes brain development as a "dance" between genes and the environment. *(Genes and the environment interact to shape and develop an individual.)*

Answers to Analyzing the Article

1. Scientists have found growing evidence that the electrical activity of brain cells changes the physical structure of the brain. Such activity is said to begin about 10 to 12 weeks after conception. The mental circuits that are developed are carved into patterns that will, over time, enable the newborn infant to recognize a father's voice and a mother's touch.
2. Students' answers may vary, but students should be able to support their opinions.

Chapter 10 Resource Guide

SECTION RESOURCES

Daily Objectives	Reproducible Resources	Multimedia Resources
Section 1 **Taking in and Storing Information** Describe the three processes involved in memory: encoding, storage, and retrieval.	Guided Reading Activity 10–1 Vocabulary Activity 10–1 Section Quiz 10–1	Daily Focus Transparency 10–1 *ExamView® Assessment Suite* CD-ROM Presentation Plus! Software
Section 2 **Retrieving Information** Understand that stored memory can be retrieved by recognition, recall, and relearning.	Guided Reading Activity 10–2 Vocabulary Activity 10–2 Section Quiz 10–2	Daily Focus Transparency 10–2 Vocabulary PuzzleMaker CD-ROM *ExamView® Assessment Suite* CD-ROM Presentation Plus! Software

Blackline Master   CD-ROM   Transparency

Block Schedule

Activities that are particularly suited for use within the block-scheduling framework are identified throughout this chapter by the following designation: **BLOCK SCHEDULING**

KEY TO ABILITY LEVELS

Teaching strategies have been coded for varying learning styles and abilities.

L1 **BASIC** activities for all students
L2 **AVERAGE** activities for average to above-average students
L3 **CHALLENGING** activities for above-average students
ELL **ENGLISH LANGUAGE LEARNER** activities

Chapter 10 Resource Guide

Timesaving Tools

TeacherWorks™ All-In-One Planner and Resource Center

- **Interactive Teacher Edition** Access your Teacher Wraparound Edition and your classroom resources with a few easy clicks.
- **Interactive Lesson Planner** Planning has never been easier! Organize your week, month, semester, or year with all the lesson helps you need to make teaching creative, timely, and relevant.

Use Glencoe's **Presentation Plus!** multimedia teacher tool to easily present dynamic lessons that visually excite your students. Using Microsoft PowerPoint® you can customize the presentations to create your own personalized lessons.

Activity

From the Classroom of…

Stacy Brosier
Belvidere High School
Belvidere, IL

Proactive Interference

Materials: about 10 decks of standard playing cards

1. Before class, remove all jacks, queens, kings, and aces. You will end up with 10 packs of 36 cards.
2. Organize students into groups of three and give each group one pack of cards.
3. Students will divide the cards in various ways. The students who are not dividing the cards need to watch the behaviors of those who are. Give the following instructions to the students.

   The first person in each group will divide the packs and make two piles. Put the odd-numbered cards on the left and the even-numbered on the right. The person should then pick up the cards, shuffle them, and repeat the process by doing the opposite; place the even cards on the left and the odd on the right, shuffle. Then put the odd on the left and the even on the right, shuffle, and hand the pack to the next person in the group. Complete the task as quickly as possible.
4. Ask students what they observed. *(They should have noticed cards being put in the wrong piles and a slowing down of the students as they divide up the cards.)* Have students explain why those behaviors occurred. *(Proactive interference occurred when students got the sorting confused because they were remembering the previous way the cards were piled.)*

Psychology Online

Use our Web site for additional resources. All essential content is covered in the Student Edition.

You and your students can visit glencoe.com, the Web site companion to *Understanding Psychology*. This innovative integration of electronic and print media offers your students a wealth of opportunities. The student text directs students to the Web site for the following options:

- Chapter Overviews
- Student Web Activities
- Self-Check Quizzes

Answers are provided for you in the **Web Activity Lesson Plan**. Additional Web resources and Interactive Puzzles are also available.

Chapter 10 Resource Guide

Note: The following materials may be used when teaching Chapter 10. Section level support materials are shown at point of use in the margins of the Teacher Wraparound Edition.

TEACHING TRANSPARENCIES

Chapter 10
Concept Transparency

MULTIMEDIA

- **Vocabulary PuzzleMaker CD-ROM**
- ***ExamView® Assessment Suite* CD-ROM**
- **TeacherWorks™ CD-ROM**
- **Glencoe Skillbuilder Interactive Workbook, Level 2**
- **Presentation Plus! Software**

REVIEW AND REINFORCEMENT

Reteaching Activity 10

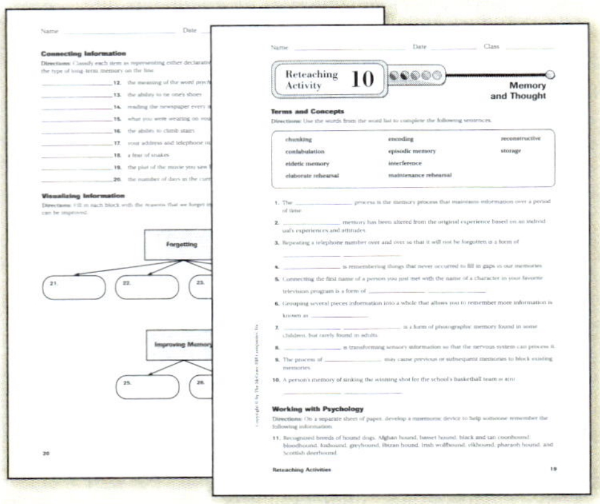
Reteaching Activity 10
Memory and Thought
Terms and Concepts
Working with Psychology

Graphic Organizer Activity 10

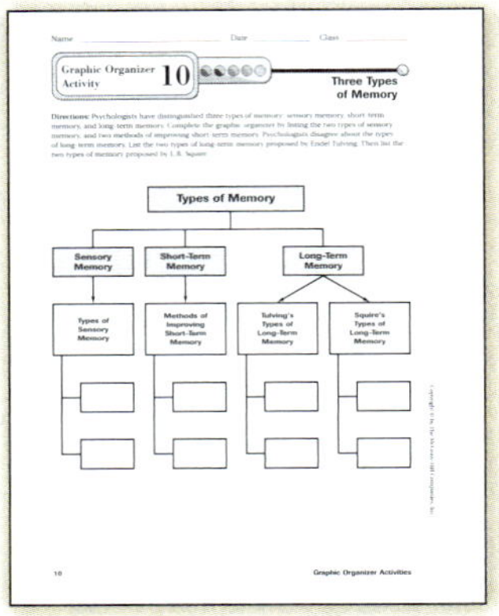
Graphic Organizer Activity 10
Three Types of Memory
Types of Memory
Sensory Memory
Short-Term Memory
Long-Term Memory

APPLICATION AND HANDS-ON

Psychology Projects 10–1 and 10–2

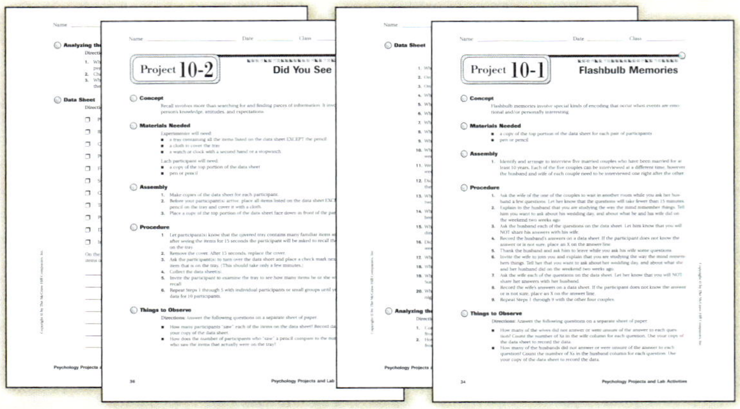
Project 10-2
Did You See
Project 10-1
Flashbulb Memories

Application Activity 10

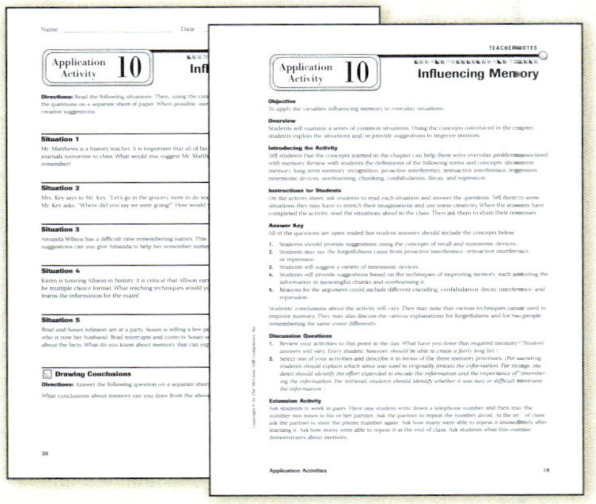
Application Activity 10
Influencing Memory

Chapter 10 Resource Guide

GLENCOE'S ASSESSMENT ADVANTAGE

ASSESSMENT

Chapter 10 Test, Form A

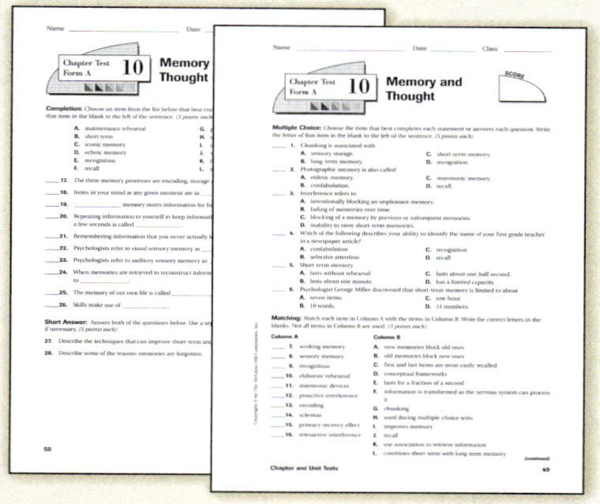

Chapter 10 Test, Form B

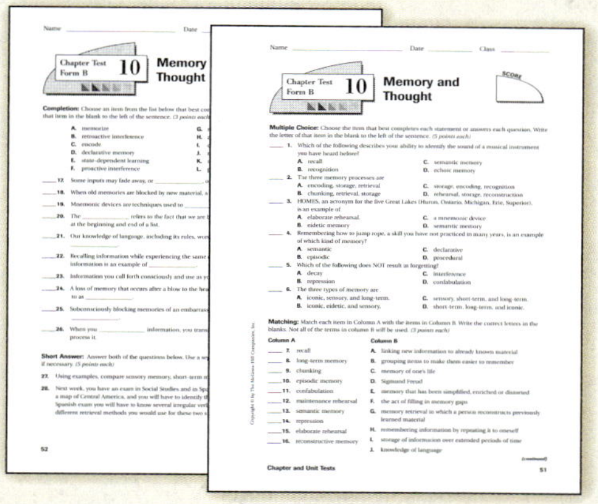

Authentic Assessment Activity 10

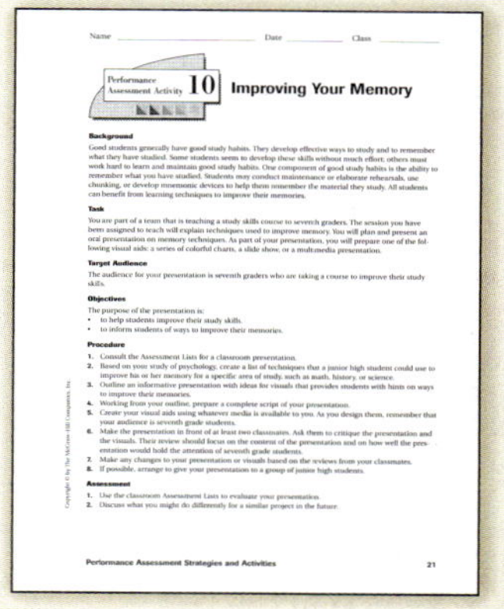

EXTENSION AND ENRICHMENT

Enrichment Activity 10

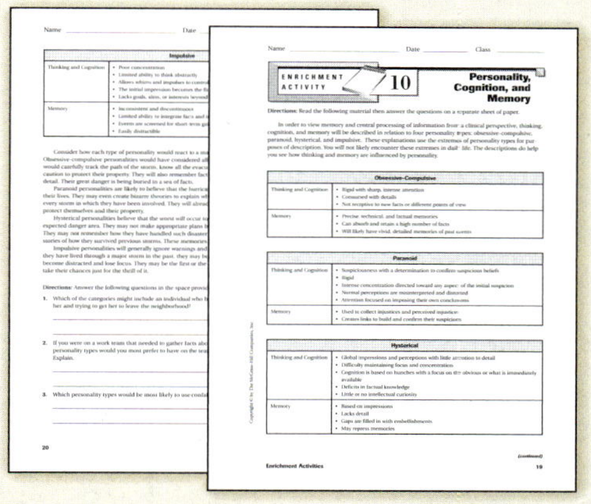

Critical Thinking Skills Activity 10

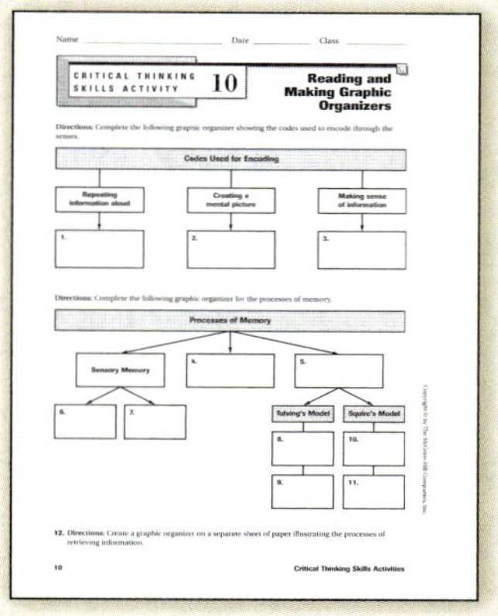

Psychology Reading 10

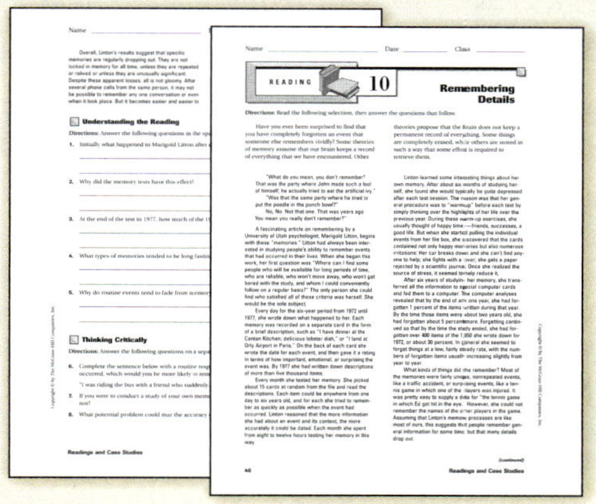

Psychology Case Study 10

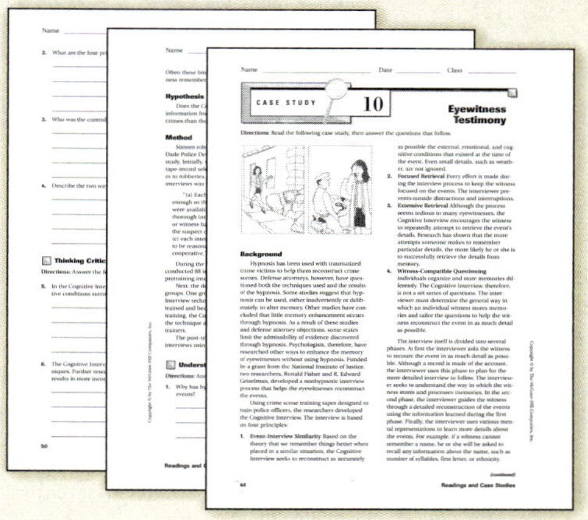

PSYCHOLOGY Online

Visit glencoe.com for a Chapter Overview for **Chapter 10—Memory and Thought.**

GLENCOE TECHNOLOGY

For a preview of Chapter 10 content, see MindJogger Checkpoint on **Presentation Plus!**

PSYCHOLOGY JOURNAL

Tell students to recall their earliest memories, including stories told by their families. Ask them to consider the roles such memories serve in shaping an individual's identity.

This journal activity provides the basis for the Psychology Journal activity exercise in the Chapter Assessment. ■

CHAPTER 10 Memory and Thought

PSYCHOLOGY JOURNAL

Think back to your childhood and recall your earliest memory. Describe this memory in your journal. ■

PSYCHOLOGY Online

Chapter Overview
Visit the *Understanding Psychology* Web site at glencoe.com and click on **Chapter 10—Chapter Overviews** to preview the chapter.

272

TWO-MINUTE LESSON LAUNCHER

Tell students that many people think that memory is an exact representation of what our senses perceive. However, when more than one eyewitness reports on the events surrounding an accident, their reports often contain significant differences. At a prearranged signal, arrange for a "stranger" to run into your class, take several items from your desk, and run back out laughing. Have students write a brief paragraph describing what they just witnessed, including a description of the "stranger." Then, have volunteers read their eyewitness accounts aloud. **Ask: What differences did you note among the descriptions? Why do these differences exist?** Finally, have the "stranger" reappear. Ask students to review their descriptions of the "stranger" and note any differences.

SECTION 1 Taking in and Storing Information

Reader's Guide

■ **Main Idea**

There are three processes involved in memory: encoding, storage, and retrieval.

■ **Vocabulary**

- memory
- encoding
- storage
- retrieval
- sensory memory
- short-term memory
- maintenance rehearsal
- chunking
- semantic memory
- episodic memory
- declarative memory
- procedural memory

■ **Objectives**

- Explain the three processes of memory.
- Describe the information-processing model of memory.

EXPLORING PSYCHOLOGY

A Life Without Memory

John Kingsley came to our attention in a shocking news story about an 83-year-old Alzheimer's patient who was found unattended in his wheelchair at a dog race track outside of Spokane, Washington. Attached to his chair was a note misidentifying him. John did not know who he was or how he got to the races. He could not help authorities find his family or his previous caregivers. John Kingsley, like many other patients during advanced stages of Alzheimer's disease, is alive, but without life. Without a memory of his past, or the ability to remember anything new, John's life is nothing but the existing moment.

—from *Psychology: Science, Behavior, and Life* by R.H. Ettinger, Robert L. Crooks, and Jean Stein, 1994

What would life without memory be like? Can you even imagine it? Consider all the material stored in your memory: your Social Security number, the capital of South Dakota, "The Star-Spangled Banner," your first love's phone number, the important generals of the Civil War, the starting lineup for the Boston Red Sox, your best friend in first grade, and so on. What kind of incredible filing system allows you to instantly recover a line from your favorite movie? How does all that information fit in your head?

SECTION RESOURCES

Reproducible Masters

- Guided Reading Activity 10–1
- Vocabulary Activity 10–1
- Section Quiz 10–1

Transparencies

- Daily Focus Transparency 10–1

Multimedia

- *ExamView® Assessment Suite* CD-ROM
- Presentation Plus! Software

1 FOCUS

Section Objectives

1. Explain the three processes of memory.
2. Describe the information-processing model of memory.

BELLRINGER
Motivational Activity

Project Daily Focus Transparency 10–1 and have students answer the questions.

Available as blackline master

Daily Focus Transparency 10–1

Reader's Guide

Use the Reader's Guide to introduce concepts and vocabulary.

■ **Exploring Psychology**

Ask students to read the **Exploring Psychology** feature. Then ask: **Which would be more frightening to you—not being able to remember the past or not being able to learn anything new? Why?**

■ **Vocabulary Precheck**

Have students write their best guess at the definition for each term. Then have them look up the terms in the Glossary to see how closely their definitions match.

2 TEACH

L1 Demonstration To illustrate sensory memory storage, completely darken the room for several minutes. While the lights are out, tape up a large block of black print, such as newsprint, on a white background. Tell students to look in the direction of the print as you flick on the lights for a second or less. **Ask: What part of the letter block did you recall when the lights went off again?** *(Some students may have seen a blur; others may have retained an image of the letters.)* Ask students to write a short paragraph explaining how this activity illustrates the storage of sensory memory.

Figure 10.1

Visual Instruction Point out that, like computers, our brains use electronic circuits to process information.

Caption Answer Encoding is the process of transforming information so that the nervous system can process it.

FYI

In addition to iconic and echoic memories, sensory memories are created by the other senses. They are known as haptic memory (touch), gustic memory (taste), and olfactic memory (smell).

THE PROCESSES OF MEMORY

memory: the input, storage, and retrieval of what has been learned or experienced

encoding: the transforming of information so the nervous system can process it

Memory is the input, storage, and retrieval of what has been learned or experienced. Who sings your favorite song? Who were your friends in eighth grade? To recall this information, you use one memory process, assuming two others occurred previously. (see Figure 10.1).

The first memory process is **encoding**—the transforming of information so that the nervous system can process it. Basically you use your senses—hearing, sight, touch, taste, temperature, and others—to encode and establish a memory. You use *acoustic codes* when you try to remember something by saying it out loud, or to yourself, repeatedly. For example, in trying to remember the notes that make up the spaces in the treble clef of a musical measure, you would repeat the letters "F," "A," "C," and "E." When you attempt to keep a mental picture of the letters, you are using *visual codes*. Another way you might try to remember the notes is by using *semantic codes*. In this way, you try to remember the letters by making sense of them. For example, if you wanted to remember the letters "F," "A," "C," "E," you might remember the word *face*. In this way, you have to remember only the word rather than the individual letters.

storage: the process by which information is maintained over a period of time

After information is encoded, it goes through the second memory process, **storage.** This is the process by which information is maintained over time. How much information is stored depends on how much effort was put into encoding the information and its importance. Information can be stored for a few seconds or for much longer.

retrieval: the process of obtaining information that has been stored in memory

The third memory process, **retrieval,** occurs when information is brought to mind from storage. The ease with which information can be retrieved depends on how efficiently it was encoded and stored (as well as on other factors, such as genetic background).

Figure 10.1 The Processes of Memory

Memory involves three processes. ***What does the first process of memory involve?***

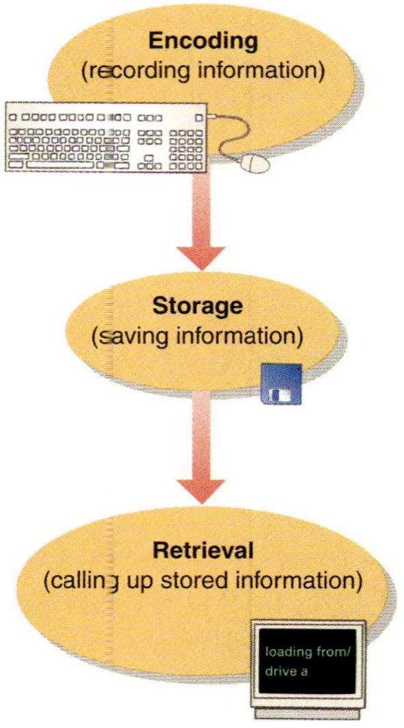

THREE STAGES OF MEMORY

Once the senses encode a memory in the brain, the brain must hold on to the input and store it for future reference. One model distinguishes three types of memory—sensory, short-term, and long-term—each of which has a different function and time span (see Figure 10.2).

Sensory Memory

sensory memory: very brief memory storage immediately following initial stimulation of a receptor

In **sensory memory,** the senses of sight and hearing (among other senses) are

COOPERATIVE LEARNING ACTIVITY

Creating Posters Organize students into groups to create posters explaining either the memory process (encoding, storage, and retrieval) or the three stages of memory (sensory, short-term, and long-term). Once the group has selected the topic for its poster, the team should brainstorm ways to create a visually interesting and informative poster. The posters may include drawings, photos, charts, or other eye-catching elements. The poster should have a title. Tell the groups that their goal should be to inform the viewer about the topic in one minute or less.

BLOCK SCHEDULING

able to hold an input for a fraction of a second before it disappears. For example, when you watch a motion picture, you do not notice the gaps between frames. The actions seem smooth because each frame is held in sensory storage until the next frame arrives.

George Sperling (1960) demonstrated this phenomenon in an ingenious experiment. He used a tachistoscope (a device that presents a picture for a very brief time) to present a group of letters and numbers to people for a twentieth of a second. Previous studies had shown that if you present a stimulus like this,

8	1	V	F
X	L	5	3
B	7	W	4

people will usually be able to tell you four or five of the items. Sperling believed that the stimulus created a visual image of the letters and that only a few could be read back before the image faded. Psychologists refer to this visual sensory memory as *iconic memory.* (Iconic memories hold visual information for up to a second.)

Sperling then told the participants in his experiment that after he flashed the letters on the tachistoscope screen, he would present a tone. Upon hearing a high tone, the participants were to tell him the top row; a medium tone, the middle row; and a low tone, the bottom row. Once people learned this system, they were indeed able to remember about 75 percent of any one row if asked to recall immediately. Thus, he proved that the participant retains a brief image of the whole picture so that he or she can still read off the items in the correct row after the picture has left the screen. Psychologists refer to auditory sensory memory as *echoic memory.* This is a type of sensory memory that holds auditory information for 1 or 2 seconds.

Sensory memory serves three functions. First, it prevents you from being overwhelmed. Every second of every day, you are bombarded with various incoming stimuli. If you had to pay attention to all of these stimuli—what you are immediately seeing, hearing, smelling, and feeling—you might easily feel overwhelmed. Since the information in sensory memory is short-lived, anything that you do not pay attention to vanishes in seconds. Second, sensory memory gives you some decision time. The information in sensory memory is there for only a few seconds—just long enough for you to decide whether it is worth paying attention to this information. If you choose to pay attention, the information is automatically

Figure 10.2 Stages of Memory

Psychologists often compare human memory to a computer; however, unlike a computer, people can never fill their long-term memories so full that there is no room left for storage. ***How do the capacities of sensory memory and short-term memory differ?***

	Sensory memory	Short-term memory	Long-term memory
Capacity	Virtually everything you see or hear at one instant	About 7 items in healthy adults	Vast; uncountable
Duration	Fraction of a second	Less than 20 seconds if not rehearsed	Perhaps a lifetime
Example	You see something for an instant, and then someone asks you to recall one detail	You look up a telephone number and rehearse it long enough to dial it	You remember the house where you lived when you were 7 years old

Reading Check What is the difference between iconic and echoic memory?

MEETING SPECIAL NEEDS

Learning Style: Auditory/Musical Memories, both painful and pleasant, are a common theme in music. Ask students to find examples of songs that focus on memories. Have them prepare an oral report, illustrated with relevant song lyrics, that assesses the most common memories recounted in popular music. The reports should include some information or explanation of why people hang on to such memories. **L2**

Refer to ***Inclusion for the High School Social Studies Classroom Strategies and Activities*** in the TCR for strategies for students with different learning styles.

Figure 10.2

Visual Instruction Explain that the path of memories resembles a roadmap. If you take a wrong turn, you end up at a dead end. Memory processing works the same way—the dead end is the process of forgetting.

Caption Answer Sensory memory is held only momentarily and includes virtually everything you perceive at any one moment. Short-term memory is short-lived and consists of about seven items for most adults.

Reading Check Answer Iconic memories are visual; echoic memories are auditory.

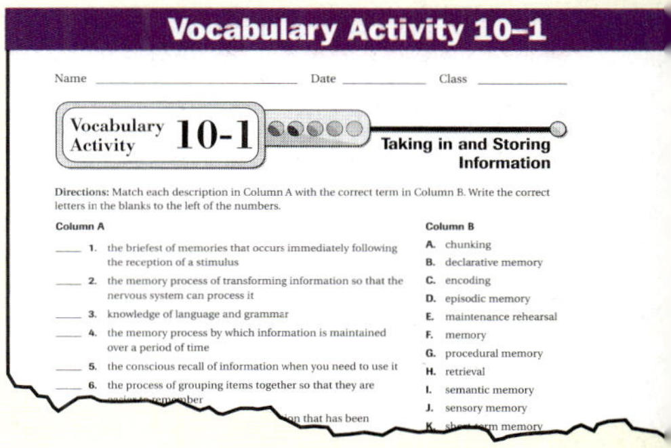
Vocabulary Activity 10–1

Name ______ Date ______ Class ______

Vocabulary Activity 10-1 Taking in and Storing Information

Directions: Match each description in Column A with the correct term in Column B. Write the correct letters in the blanks to the left of the numbers.

Column A	Column B
____ 1. the briefest of memories that occurs immediately following the reception of a stimulus	A. chunking
____ 2. the memory process of transforming information so that the nervous system can process it	B. declarative memory
____ 3. knowledge of language and grammar	C. encoding
____ 4. the memory process by which information is maintained over a period of time	D. episodic memory
____ 5. the conscious recall of information when you need to use it	E. maintenance rehearsal
____ 6. the process of grouping items together so that they are ...	F. memory
	G. procedural memory
	H. retrieval
	I. semantic memory
	J. sensory memory

CHAPTER 10

Section 1, pages 273–280

Guided Reading Activity 10–1

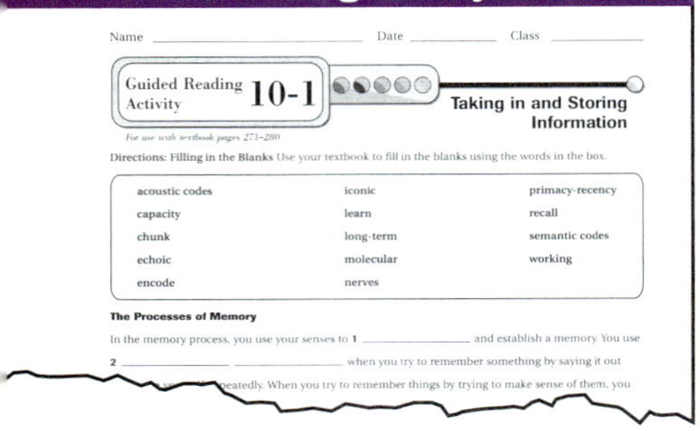
Name Date Class

Guided Reading Activity 10-1

Taking in and Storing Information

Directions: Filling in the Blanks Use your textbook to fill in the blanks using the words in the box.

acoustic codes	iconic	primacy-recency
capacity	learn	recall
chunk	long-term	semantic codes
echoic	molecular	working
encode	nerves	

The Processes of Memory

In the memory process, you use your senses to 1 ______ and establish a memory. You use 2 ______ when you try to remember something by saying it out ...eatedly. When you try to remember things by trying to make sense of them, you

Psychology Journal

Ask students to list examples of chunking that they have used in the last week. ■

Figure 10.3

Visual Instruction Tell students that in an experiment in 1979, fewer than half the participants were able to spot the genuine penny. A is the correct penny image.

Caption Answer You could use maintenance rehearsal techniques to memorize the look of the penny.

transferred to short-term memory. Finally, sensory memory allows for continuity and stability in your world. For instance, iconic memory makes images in your world smooth and continuous, whereas echoic memory lets you play back auditory information, giving you time to recognize sounds as words. The information held momentarily by the senses has not yet been narrowed down or analyzed. It is short-lived, temporary, and fragile. However, by the time information gets to the next stage—short-term memory—it has been analyzed, identified, and simplified so that it can be conveniently stored and handled for a longer time.

short-term memory: memory that is limited in capacity to about seven items and in duration by the subject's active rehearsal

maintenance rehearsal: a system for remembering that involves repeating information to oneself without attempting to find meaning in it

Short-Term Memory

The things you have in your conscious mind at any one moment are being held in **short-term memory.** Short-term memory does not necessarily involve paying close attention. You have probably had the experience of listening to someone only partially and then having that person accuse you of not paying attention. You deny it, and to prove your innocence, you repeat, word for word, the last words he or she said. You can do this because you are holding the words in short-term memory.

Maintenance Rehearsal To keep information in short-term memory for more than a few seconds, you usually have to repeat the information to yourself or out loud. This is what psychologists mean by **maintenance rehearsal.** When you look up a telephone number, for example, you can remember the seven digits long enough to dial them if you repeat them several times. If you are distracted or make a mistake in dialing, the chances are you will have to look up the number again. It has been lost from short-term memory. By using maintenance rehearsal (repeating the telephone number over and over again), you can keep the information longer in short-term memory.

Psychologists have measured short-term memory by seeing how long a participant can retain a piece of information without rehearsal. The experimenter shows the participant three letters, such as CPQ, followed by three numerals, such as 798, one second later. To prevent rehearsal, the participant has been instructed to start counting backward by threes and reporting the result in time with a metronome striking once per second. (A *metronome* is an instrument designed to mark exact time by a regularly repeated tick.) If the participant performs this task for only a short time, she or he will usually remember the letters. If kept from rehearsing for 18 seconds, however, recall will be no better than a random guess; the information is forgotten. Short-term memory lasts a bit less than 20 seconds without rehearsal.

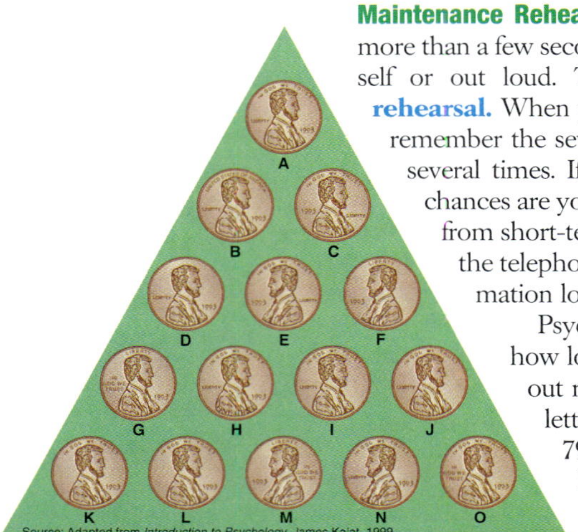

Source: Adapted from *Introduction to Psychology,* James Kalat, 1999.

Figure 10.3 Spot the Real Penny

Which is the genuine penny among the fakes? (Ask your teacher for the correct answer.) Even though you live in the United States and probably see hundreds of pennies a week, it is difficult to identify the real one. Mere repetition, such as seeing something over and over again, does not guarantee a strong memory. ***What could you do to remember exactly how a penny looks?***

Chunking Short-term memory is limited not only in its duration but also in its capacity. It can hold only about seven unrelated items. Suppose, for

CRITICAL THINKING ACTIVITY

Analyzing Information Ask students to consider the following analogies: "Memory encoding is like a photograph" or "Memory encoding is like a videotape." Ask students to use what they know about encoding to write a one-page paper supporting one of the two analogies. Have students select the analogy that seems closer to the actual encoding process. (Note: Students will need to consider the process used to prepare and view photographs and videotapes.) Students' responses will vary. The traditional view that encoding is like a photograph implies a series of individual events captured in isolation. A more complete understanding is that encoding is like a videotape, a continuous running series of events. **L3**

Figure 10.4 Using Short-Term Memory

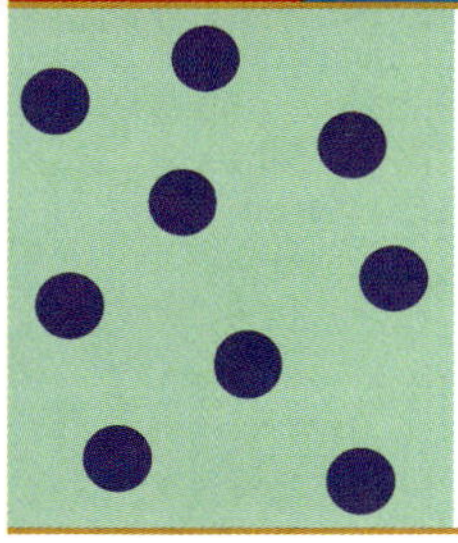

Glance quickly at the left figure in this pair, then look away. How many dots did you see? Now do the same with the right figure. You were probably surer and more accurate in your answer for the right figure. ***Why is this so?***

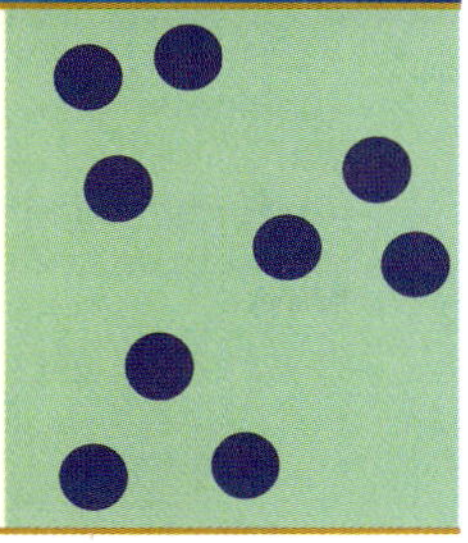

example, someone quickly reels off a series of numbers to you. You will be able to keep only about seven or eight of them in your immediate memory. Beyond that number, confusion about the numbers will set in. The same limit is there if the unrelated items are a random set of words. We may not notice this limit to our capacity because we usually do not have to store so many unrelated items in our immediate memory. Either the items are related (as when we listen to someone speak), or they are rehearsed and placed in long-term memory.

The most interesting aspect of this limit, discovered by George Miller (1956), is that it involves about seven items (plus or minus two items) of any kind. Each item may consist of a collection of many other items, but if they are all packaged into one chunk, then there is still only one item. Thus we can remember about seven unrelated sets of initials, such as COMSAT, HIV, SST, or the initials of our favorite radio stations, even though we could not remember all the letters separately. This is referred to as **chunking** because we have connected, or chunked, them together; in other words, HIV is one item, not three.

One of the tricks of memorizing a lot of information quickly is to chunk together the items as fast as they come in. If we connect items in groups, we have fewer to remember. For example, we remember new phone numbers in two or three chunks (555-6794 or 555-67-94) rather than as a string of seven digits (5-5-5-6-7-9-4). As Figure 10.4 illustrates, we use chunking to remember visual as well as verbal inputs.

Even with chunking, storage in short-term memory is only temporary. Information is available, generally, for less than 20 seconds and no more than 30 seconds, assuming no rehearsal has occurred. After that, it is part of the long-term memory, or it is lost. Short-term memory contains information that is of possible interest. Information worth holding on to must be rehearsed with the intent to learn in order to transfer it to long-term memory. Rehearsal without intent to learn yields no transfer, no memory.

The Primacy-Recency Effect Read the grocery list at the right. Immediately after reading this list, write down as many of the items as you can. Which terms did you remember? The *primacy-recency* effect refers to the fact that we are better able to recall information presented at the beginning and end of a list. Most likely, you remembered the first four

chunking: the process of grouping items to make them easier to remember

PSYCHOLOGY Online

Student Web Activity
Visit the *Understanding Psychology* Web site at glencoe.com and click on **Chapter 10—Student Web Activities** for an activity about memory.

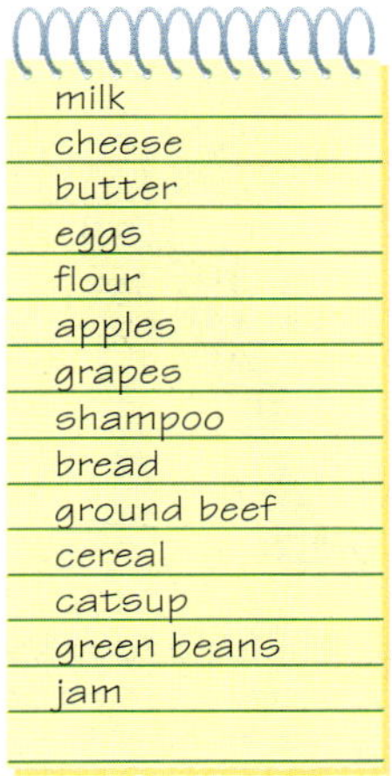

CHAPTER 10
Section 1, pages 273–280

Figure 10.4

Visual Instruction Ask students why this experiment is a demonstration of short-term memory *(because they will soon forget how many dots they saw in either figure).*

Caption Answer The organization of dots into chunks, or groups, makes it easier to process the information.

PSYCHOLOGY Online

Links and instructional guidelines can be found in the **Web Activity Lesson Plan** at glencoe.com.

TEACHER Tip

Challenge students to apply the chunking technique on their next exam. Ask them to report how helpful this technique was in helping them recall information during the test.

PSYCHOLOGY LAB EXPERIMENT

Memory Organize the class into groups of five. Have one student in each group act as the experimenter. The experimenter reads aloud a list of 10 two-digit numbers. After a 3-second pause, the experimenter asks the first student to write down the numbers. After 5 seconds, the second student is asked to write down the numbers. After 15 seconds, the third student is asked to write down the numbers. After 30 seconds, the fourth student is asked to write down the numbers. Have each group graph its results, recording time along the x-axis and number of items correctly recalled on the y-axis. **Ask: What conclusions can you draw about information storage? L1**

CHAPTER 10
Section 1, pages 273–280

L1 Demonstration Arrange for another teacher to stop in your room at the start of the class. Engage in a lively conversation for two or three minutes. Later near the end of class, have students write down everything that they recall about the incident—nature of the conversation, description of the visitor, and so on. Ask volunteers to share their recollections. **Ask: How does this demonstration illustrate the points made about the formation of long-term memories?**

Figure 10.5

Visual Instruction Without rehearsal, new information stays in short-term memory for less than 30 seconds.

Caption Answer Encoding occurs when the senses receive a stimulus and convert the sensation into neural impulses. It occurs to enter information from short-term memory into long-term memory.

PSYCHOLOGY Update

Memory and Language A recent study conducted by Susan Ellis Weismer and Julia Evans examined the correlation between working memory and language skills. They examined two groups of children. The experimental group had been diagnosed with a specific language impairment. The control group had normal language skills. The study found a significant correlation between working memory and language skills development. However, the study did not clearly identify whether a deficit in language skills caused poor performance on tests of working memory or whether a deficit in working memory impaired the development of language skills. *Source:* Weismer, S.E., & Evans J. (1999). An examination of verbal working memory capacity in children with specific language impairment. *Journal of Speech, Language and Hearing Research,* 42 (5), 1249–60.

Figure 10.5 Three Systems of Memory

The moment you pay attention to information in sensory memory, that information enters short-term memory. Then that information remains in short-term memory for a few seconds. If you rehearse that information, it stays; if you do not, it disappears. ***When does the process of encoding take place?***

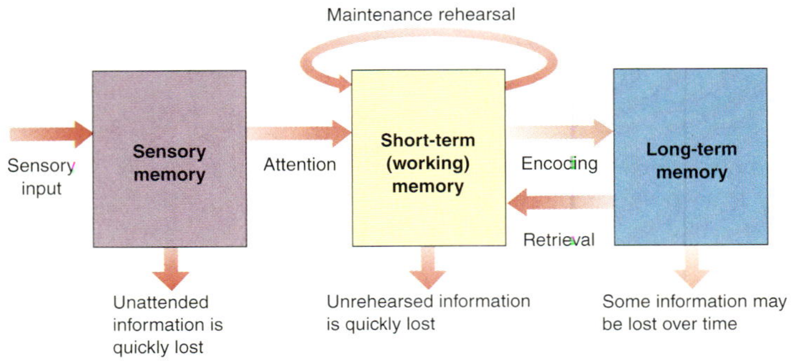

or five items in the list because you had more time to rehearse them. This is the *primacy effect.* You may have also recalled the last four or five items in the list because they were still accessible in short-term memory. This is the *recency effect.* However, you may have forgotten the middle items in the list. When trying to remember the middle items in a list, such as this one, your attention is split between trying to remember previous items and trying to rehearse new ones.

Working Memory Short-term memory is also called *working memory.* Working memory serves as a system for processing and working with current information. Working memory includes both short-term memory (events that just occurred) and information stored in long-term memory, now recalled for current information.

Long-Term Memory

Long-term memory refers to the storage of information over extended periods of time. Information is not stored like a piece of paper in a filing cabinet; it is stored according to categories or features. You reconstruct what you must recall when you need it. When you say a friend has a good memory, you probably mean he or she can recall a wide variety of information accurately. The capacity of long-term memory appears to be limitless. Long-term memory contains representations of countless facts, experiences, and sensations. You may not have thought of your childhood home for years, but you can probably still visualize it.

Long-term memory involves all the processes we have been describing. Suppose you go to see a play. As the actors say their lines, the sounds flow through your sensory storage. These words accumulate in short-term memory and form meaningful phrases and sentences.

Learning to perform activities requiring skills, such as in-line skating, is part of procedural memory.

INTERDISCIPLINARY CONNECTIONS ACTIVITY

Cultural Life Tell students that the *flashbulb memory phenomenon* centers around a specific, important, or surprising event. The memory is so vivid that it represents a mental snapshot. For people in the baby boom generation, the assassination of President John F. Kennedy is a flashbulb memory. Assign students to explore the effect of the Kennedy assassination on members of their parents' generation. Suggest that they read articles surrounding the death of his son, John F. Kennedy, Jr. Ask students to write a paper identifying evidence of the flashbulb memory phenomenon in the stories. **L2**

You attend to the action and changing scenery in much the same way. Together, they form chunks in your memory. An hour or two later, you will have forgotten all but the most striking lines, but you have stored the meaning of the lines and actions in long-term memory. The next day, you may be able to give a scene-by-scene description of the play. Throughout this process, the least important information is dropped and only the essentials are retained (see Figure 10.5). A month or two later, without much rehearsal, you may remember only a brief outline of the plot and perhaps a few particularly impressive moments. In time you may not remember anything about the play. Other, more recently stored items block access to earlier memories or may even replace them. Yet if you see the play again, you will probably recognize the lines of the play and anticipate the actions. Although it has become less accessible, elements of the play are still stored in long-term memory.

Did You Know?

Prosopagnosia Memory problems can sometimes take a surprising twist. One example is the peculiar condition known as *prosopagnosia,* in which the patient is unable to recognize familiar faces—even his or her own face. People who have this condition can still perceive other aspects of faces, however, such as whether a person's expression is happy or sad. This memory problem usually results from a stroke or head injury.

Types of Long-Term Memory For almost a century, the study of memory focused on how long information was stored for usage. Then a Canadian psychologist, Endel Tulving (1972), proposed that we have two types of memory. **Semantic memory** is our knowledge of language, including its rules, words, and meanings. We share that knowledge with other speakers of our language. **Episodic memory** is our memory of our own life, such as when you woke up this morning. Stored here are personal things where time of occurrence is important. Everyone's episodic memory is unique.

L.R. Squire (1987) proposed a related model of memory. **Declarative memory** involves both episodic and semantic memory. This is information you call forth consciously and use as you need it. **Procedural memory** does not require conscious recollection to have past learning or experiences impact our performance. One form of procedural memory involves *skills,* learned as we mature—including both complex skills such as swimming or driving a car and simple skills such as tying a tie. As we gain a skill, we gradually lose the ability to describe what we are doing. Other types of procedural memory, such as fear of bugs, include habits and things learned through classical conditioning.

semantic memory: knowledge of language, including its rules, words, and meanings

episodic memory: chronological retention of the events of one's life

declarative memory: stored knowledge that can be called forth consciously as needed

procedural memory: permanent storage of learned skills that does not require conscious recollection

MEMORY AND THE BRAIN

What happens in the brain when something is stored in long-term memory? The answers are highly controversial. There is growing evidence that physiological changes occur in the brain, but psychologists are only beginning to identify how and where memories are stored.

What physiological changes occur when we learn something? Some psychologists theorize a change in the neuronal structure of nerves occurs. Others contend that learning is based on molecular or chemical changes in the brain. The evidence is more and more clear that both sides are correct.

3 ASSESS

Assign Section 1 Assessment as homework or as an in-class activity.

Section Quiz 10–1

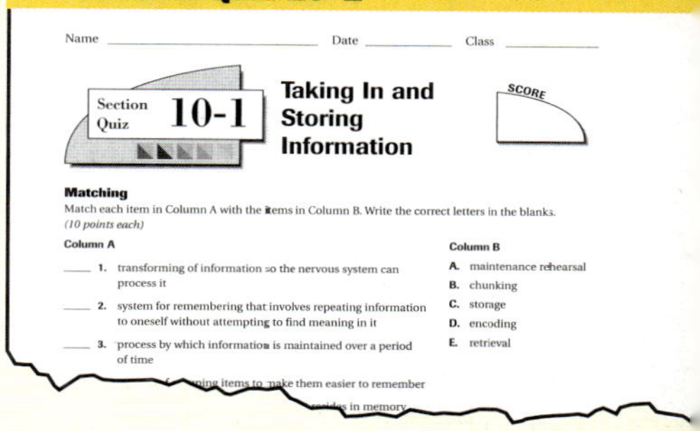
Name ______ Date ______ Class ______

Section Quiz 10-1 **Taking In and Storing Information** SCORE

Matching

Match each item in Column A with the items in Column B. Write the correct letters in the blanks. *(10 points each)*

Column A	Column B
____ 1. transforming of information so the nervous system can process it	A. maintenance rehearsal
____ 2. system for remembering that involves repeating information to oneself without attempting to find meaning in it	B. chunking
____ 3. process by which information is maintained over a period of time	C. storage
	D. encoding
	E. retrieval

Reteach

Illustrate chunking by creating an overhead transparency with a continuous line of characters. The characters should actually be acronyms such as CIA, MIA, and MTV. Give students 15 seconds to memorize the string. Have them write down what they remember. Repeat the process with the string of characters separated into the acronyms. **Ask:** **What does this tell us about the duration of short-term memory? What other short-term memory devices do you use?**

EXTENDING THE CONTENT

Types of Long-Term Memory As a class, brainstorm examples of the four main types of long-term memory: semantic memory, episodic memory, declarative memory, and procedural memory. Tell students that you want them to find existing pictures or take pictures to illustrate each of the four types of long-term memory. They can use the examples that were brainstormed for ideas. Assign students to assemble the photos with a written explanation of each type of long-term memory. **L2** **ELL**

CHAPTER 10
Section 1, pages 273–280

Figure 10.6

Visual Instruction Review the basic parts of the brain that were introduced in Chapter 6.

Caption Answer This memory would be a declarative memory and would involve the hippocampus, the amygdala, and the cortex.

Enrich
Write the following quote by Cicero, the Roman orator, on the board: "Memory is the treasury and guardian of all things." Ask students how important memory seemed to be to Cicero. Have students find other famous quotes about memory. **Ask: What do these quotes tell us about the function or purpose of memory?**

4 CLOSE

Ask students to draw a picture demonstrating the processes of memory (encoding, storage, and retrieval).

Figure 10.6 Memory Centers in the Brain

Researchers have identified the parts of the brain that are involved in memory. ***What parts of the brain are involved in remembering the date of a special event?***

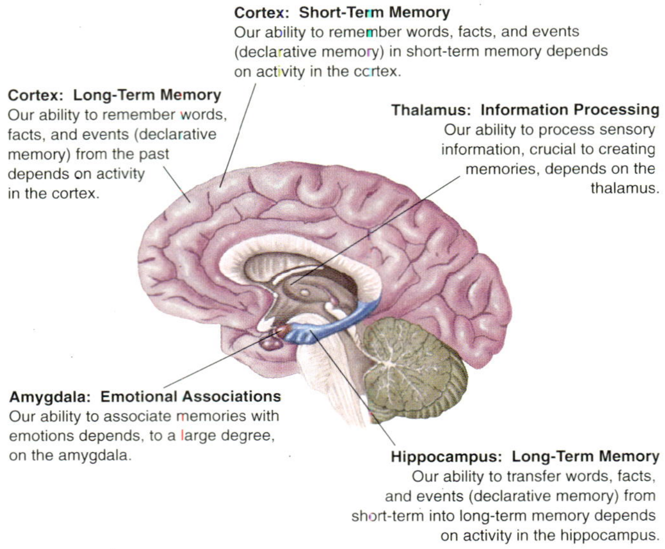

Source: Adapted from *Introduction to Psychology*, Rod Plotnik, 2005.

What changes occur depend on the level at which you are examining the changes that learning creates.

Where does learning occur? There is growing evidence that formation of procedural memories involves activity in an area of the brain called the *striatum*, deep in the front part of our cortex (see Figure 10.6). Declarative memories result from activity in the hippocampus and the amygdala (Mishkin, Saunders, & Murray, 1984).

It is not clear yet how individual nerve cells—called neurons—establish connections with one another when learning occurs. It is clear that a very complex chemical process precedes the formation of new connections between neurons. Some have credited increases in calcium. Others talk of decreased potassium flow. Processes as diverse as increased protein synthesis, heightened levels of glucose, and other biochemical processes are involved (Kalat, 2006). Exactly how it all fits together remains an active area of research.

SECTION 1 Assessment

1. **Review the Vocabulary** List and describe the processes of memory.
2. **Visualize the Main Idea** In a diagram similar to the one below, list the different stages of memory and write an example of each.

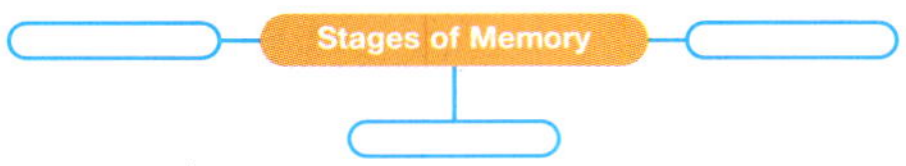

3. **Recall Information** What is the purpose of maintenance rehearsal? How does the process work?
4. **Think Critically** In what ways is your memory like a computer? In what ways is it different? Explain your responses.
5. **Application Activity** Create a skit that illustrates how you would perform activities such as swimming or bicycle riding if you did not have procedural memory. Share your skit.

SECTION 1 Assessment Answers

1. Encoding is the process of transforming sensory and other information so that the nervous system can receive it. Storage is the maintenance of the memory in the brain for a period of time. The period of time depends on the effort made to remember the information. Retrieval occurs when the information is brought to mind from storage.
2. Diagrams should reflect an understanding of the different stages of memory.
3. Maintenance rehearsal is the repetition of information so that it can be remembered. There is no attempt to find meaning in the information.
4. Memory and computers encode, process, and store information. Memory may store unlimited information in numerous categories, while a computer stores limited information in only one category, or file.
5. Students' answers will vary. The skits should demonstrate the relearning of the information each time the activity is attempted. No one could ever become proficient at the skill.

Case Studies

The Case of H.M.

Period of Study: 1953

Introduction: In 1953 a man, known by the initials H.M., underwent major surgery in an effort to cease or minimize the occurrence of epileptic seizures. The doctors chose to remove the hippocampus. Knowledge regarding the function of the hippocampus, however, was limited at that time.

The surgery proved quite effective in decreasing the frequency and severity of the seizures. In fact, preliminary tests showed that H.M.'s IQ had risen slightly because he now could better concentrate on tasks. As time passed, doctors detected an unforeseen and devastating result of the surgery—H.M. had lost the ability to store new long-term memories. Although he could remember events that occurred before the operation, H.M. could no longer retain information about events occurring after the surgery. Amazingly, he could still read, carry on conversations, and solve problems. He could recall information he learned five to ten minutes beforehand, but H.M.'s brain could not transfer that short-term information into long-term memory.

Hypothesis: The case of H.M. sparked many theories about the functions of the hippocampus region of the brain. One theory proposed that the transfer of short-term memory into long-term memory was fixed in the hippocampus region. H.M.'s memories before the operation remained mostly intact, but after the operation, there was no hippocampus region to which to transfer new memories—new information had nowhere to go and so could not be recalled at a later time.

Method: Doctors tested H.M. by presenting him with information, distracting him momentarily, and then asking him to recall the information first discussed. H.M. was unable to learn sequences of digits beyond the usual short-term memory span of seven digits. Likewise, H.M. could not recognize the photographs of people shown and described to him just a short time earlier.

Interestingly, H.M. demonstrated that he could learn difficult motor skills such as solving puzzles. Although H.M. clearly demonstrated skill in completing these activities, he reported never to have learned the activities. This implied that H.M. could learn new motor abilities even though he could not retain new long-term memories.

Results: The most apparent source of H.M.'s problem was a disruption in transferring short-term memory to long-term memory. This indicated that the hippocampus region is not involved with storing long-term memory, because recollection of presurgery events was intact. Thus, the hippocampus region of the brain *may be* the component involved in this memory transferring process but *definitely is* a pathway through which this information travels.

H.M. lived the rest of his life with the frustration of not remembering the current year, his age, or where he lived. He was placed in the care of a nursing home and had to be accompanied by someone everywhere he wanted to go. He needed constant reminders of what he was doing. He could not remember anything following the year 1953—the year of his surgery. Sadly, H.M. was literally "frozen in time."

Analyzing the Case Study

1. What type of surgery did H.M. have? Why?
2. What problems did H.M. encounter following the surgery? Why?
3. **Critical Thinking** If a virus suddenly destroyed your hippocampus, what effect would it have on your performance in school?

Going Further

Stress Hormones and Memory

Unlike other parts of the brain, the hippocampus continues to grow throughout your lifetime. Researchers are making efforts to boost the production of these brain cells.

Researchers are currently exploring links between stress hormones such as corticosteroids and memory loss. Studies in rats have shown that by blocking stress hormones, the production of brain cells in the hippocampus increased.

Since the body needs stress hormones, which are produced by the adrenal glands, it is not possible to remove these glands. Researchers, however, may be able to develop drugs to limit the production of the hormones and boost the production of brain cells.

Discussing the Case Study

Ask: **Why do you think H.M.'s existing memories were unaffected? What does the fact that he could still learn motor skills tell you about procedural memory?**

Answers for Analyzing the Case Study

1. H.M. had the hippocampus area of his brain removed in an attempt to stop, or at least minimize, the occurrence of epileptic seizures.
2. H.M. could not form new long-term memories. The hippocampus plays an important role in the formation of memories. It is not involved in storing long-term memory, but it does act as a pathway through which information travels.
3. Students' answers will vary. Students would not be able to pass tests on new material, although they would still be able to perform well on aptitude tests built on learning that had occurred before the virus destroyed the hippocampus.

1 FOCUS

Section Objectives

1. Identify several memory retrieval processes.
2. Explain the processes involved in forgetting.

BELLRINGER
Motivational Activity

Project Daily Focus Transparency 10–2 and have students answer the questions.

Available as blackline master

Daily Focus Transparency 10–2

Reader's Guide

Use the Reader's Guide to introduce concepts and vocabulary.

Exploring Psychology

Ask students to read the **Exploring Psychology** feature and then discuss: **Which ability would you prefer: to remember long strings of numbers or to remember everyday things like faces of friends and the location of your belongings? Why?**

Vocabulary Precheck

Have students read the Glossary definition. Then have them create a word search puzzle. Ask pairs of students to trade and complete puzzles.

Use the **Vocabulary PuzzleMaker CD-ROM** to create crossword and word search puzzles.

SECTION 2 Retrieving Information

Reader's Guide

Main Idea

Stored memory can be retrieved by recognition, recall, and relearning.

Vocabulary

- recognition
- recall
- reconstructive processes
- confabulation
- schemas
- eidetic memory
- decay
- interference
- elaborative rehearsal
- mnemonic devices

Objectives

- Identify several memory retrieval processes.
- Explain the processes involved in forgetting.

EXPLORING PSYCHOLOGY

What a Memory!

Rajan Mahadevan stood before the packed house of the International Congress on Yoga and Meditation. He recited, from memory, the first 30,000 digits of pi, which is often rounded off to two decimal points, or 3.14. He did not err until the 31,812th digit. This feat took 3 hours and 44 minutes and earned him a place in the *Guinness Book of World Records*. . . .

Rajan can repeat a string of 60 numbers after a single hearing, while most of us can repeat an average of about seven random numbers. Rajan is one of only a half-dozen people in the world known to have such gargantuan memory powers.

Despite Rajan's unbelievable ability to memorize numbers, he seems to be worse than average at recalling faces, and he constantly forgets where he put his keys.

—adapted from *Introduction to Psychology* by Rod Plotnik, 2005

The example above illustrates the brain's tremendous capacity for storing and retrieving information. Stored information is useless unless it can be retrieved from memory. Once you have forgotten to send a card for your mother's birthday, for example, it is not very consoling to prove that you have the date filed away in your brain. We have all experienced the acute embarrassment of being unable to remember a close friend's name. There are few things in life more frustrating than having a word "on the tip of your tongue" and not being able to remember it.

SECTION RESOURCES

Reproducible Masters

- Guided Reading Activity 10–2
- Vocabulary Activity 10–2
- Section Quiz 10–2

Transparencies

- Daily Focus Transparency 10–2

Multimedia

- Vocabulary PuzzleMaker CD-ROM
- *ExamView*® *Assessment Suite* CD-ROM
- Presentation Plus! Software

The problem of memory is to store many thousands of items in such a way that you can find the one you need when you need it. The solution to retrieval is organization. Because human memory is extraordinarily efficient, it must be extremely well organized. Psychologists do not yet know how it is organized, but they are studying the processes of retrieval for clues.

RECOGNITION

Human memory is organized in such a way as to make recognition quite easy—people can say with great accuracy whether or not something is familiar to them. If someone asked you the name of your first-grade teacher, for example, you might not remember it. Chances are, however, that you would recognize the name if you heard it. Similarly, a multiple choice test may bring out knowledge that a student might not be able to show on an essay test. The ability to recognize suggests that much more information is stored in memory than one might think.

The process of **recognition** provides insight into how information is stored in memory. We can recognize the sound of a particular musical instrument (say, a piano) no matter what tune is being played on it. We can also recognize a tune no matter what instrument is playing it. This pattern of recognition indicates that a single item of information may be indexed under several headings so that it can be reached in many ways. A person's features, for instance, may be linked to a large number of categories. The more categories the features are filed in, the more easily they can be retrieved, and the more likely you are to recognize someone.

Psychology and You: Remembering Classmates

Few of us will ever forget our high school days, but how many of us will remember the names and faces of our high school classmates 10, 20, 30, and even 40 years after graduation? According to one study, apparently more of us will than you might think.

To find out just how long our long-term memory is, researchers showed nearly 400 high school graduates, ranging in age from 17 to 74, pictures from their high school yearbooks. Here are the surprising results:

- Thirty-five years after graduation, people could identify the faces of 9 out of 10 of their classmates. The size of the high school made no difference in their response.
- Fifteen years after graduation, participants could recall 90 percent of their classmates' names.
- Name recall began to fade to between 70 and 80 percent by the time people reached their late 30s.
- Women generally had better memories for names and faces than men.

Researchers explain these amazing results by looking at the way we collect this information in the first place. Our storehouse of names and faces is built over our four-year high school careers, and continual repetition helps cement this knowledge in our memories for decades (Bahrick, Bahrick, & Wittinger, 1974; Kolata, 1993).

recognition: memory retrieval in which a person identifies an object, idea, or situation as one he or she has or has not experienced before

RECALL

More remarkable than the ability to recognize information is the ability to recall it. **Recall** is the active reconstruction of information. Just think about the amount of recall involved in a simple conversation. Each person uses hundreds of words involving all kinds of information, even though each word and bit of information must be retrieved separately from the storehouse of memory.

recall: memory retrieval in which a person reconstructs previously learned material

CHAPTER 10
Section 2, pages 282–288

2 TEACH

L1 Demonstration Ask students to bring in a picture of themselves when they were in elementary school (not baby pictures). Place the pictures on a poster board with a number beneath each picture. Give students time to fill in the names of as many people as they recognize. Have students identify their picture. **Ask: How well did you do? How did you recognize so many of your classmates when they have changed so much? What does this suggest about memory and recognition?** ELL

Psychology and You

Use the following question to direct a class discussion after students have read the **Psychology and You** feature.
Ask: Will you be likely to have the same recall ability with the people you work with on your first job? Why or why not?

Guided Reading Activity 10–2

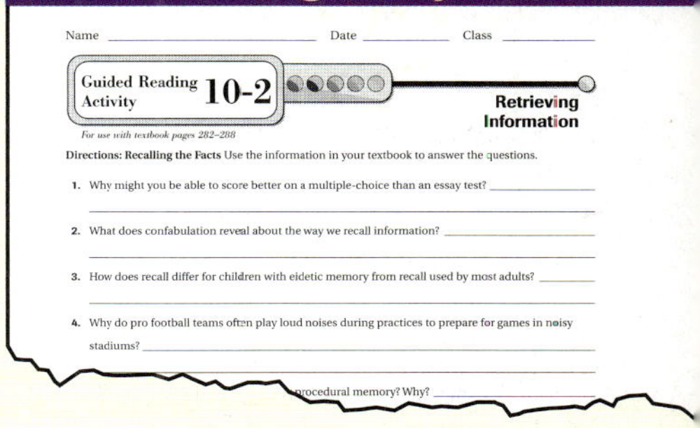
Name ______ Date ______ Class ______

Guided Reading Activity 10-2

Retrieving Information

For use with textbook pages 282–288

Directions: Recalling the Facts Use the information in your textbook to answer the questions.

1. Why might you be able to score better on a multiple-choice than an essay test? ______
2. What does confabulation reveal about the way we recall information? ______
3. How does recall differ for children with eidetic memory from recall used by most adults? ______
4. Why do pro football teams often play loud noises during practices to prepare for games in noisy stadiums? ______

procedural memory? Why? ______

COOPERATIVE LEARNING ACTIVITY

Testing Recall Organize students into small groups. Ask each group to create a short skit that shows an emotionally charged situation. Examples include the breakup of a boyfriend and girlfriend, a disagreement with a parent, or a minor traffic accident. If possible, have the groups videotape their skits. Ask the groups to prepare two series of questions about the events that happened. The point of the questions should be the same, but the adjectives used to describe the situation should be different. Ask the groups to show the video to two other groups and ask them to write answers to the questions that have been prepared. The groups should review the responses and see what differences in recall resulted from the way in which the questions were worded. **BLOCK SCHEDULING**

Applying **Psychology**

Ask your friends what brands of snack foods and health care products they prefer. Then ask them how they chose those particular brands. Psychologists have found that even though most people respond that it is the brand their parents use or the brand recommended by a friend, in reality they are likely to have been influenced by advertisements they have seen or heard. Often advertisers use subtle messages to suggest features or benefits of a product that are not a reality. Ask students to find examples of an implied or inferred benefit in a print advertisement.

FYI

People tend to forget more quickly information that does not correspond with their own images of themselves. As a person's self-image changes, so does the information he or she recalls about the past. This process is known as *autobiographical memory.*

PSYCHOLOGY JOURNAL

Ask students to compare their memories of an event with a friend who experienced the same event. Tell them to write down how their memories are similar and how they are different. Then ask students to explain the differences using the information they are learning in this chapter. ■

More About...

Eyewitness Testimony

One situation in which recognition is extremely important is in the courtroom. It is very convincing to a judge or jury when an eyewitness points to someone in the room and says, "He's the one who did it."

Elizabeth Loftus (1974) has shown that even after it had been proven that the eyesight of a witness was too poor for her to have seen a robber's face from where she stood at the scene of a robbery, the jury was still swayed by her testimony. Lawyers cite many cases of people falsely accused by eyewitnesses whose testimonies later proved to be inaccurate.

A person's memory of an event can be distorted in the process of remembering it. Shocking events, such as those involving violence, can disrupt our ability to form a strong memory. Without a strong, clear memory of the event, the eyewitness is more likely to incorporate after-the-fact information into the recall. Jurors should remember that the eye is not a camera, and recall is not videotape.

Recall involves more than searching for and finding pieces of information, however. It involves a person's knowledge, attitudes, and expectations. The brain is not like a video recorder that plays back episodes intact. Remembering is an active process guided by experience, knowledge, and cues we receive from the environment. Recall is influenced by **reconstructive processes.** Our memories may be altered or distorted, depending on our experiences, attitudes, and inferences from other information. One type of mistake is called **confabulation,** which is when a person "remembers" information that was never stored in memory. If our reconstruction of an event is incomplete, we fill in the gaps by making up what is missing. Sometimes we may be wrong without realizing it.

Occasionally our memories are reconstructed in terms of our **schemas.** These are conceptual frameworks we use to make sense of the world. They are sets of expectations about something that is based on our past experiences. Elizabeth Loftus and J.C. Palmer (1974) conducted a classic study on the roles that schemas play in memory reconstruction. Participants in this study watched a film of a two-car accident. They were then asked to fill out a questionnaire about the accident. One of the questions had four different versions. Some participants were asked, "About how fast were the two cars going when they *contacted* each other?" In the other versions of the questions, the words *hit, bumped,* or *smashed* were substituted for the word *contacted.* Participants given the question with the word *contacted* recalled a speed of 32 mph. Those given the word *hit* recalled a speed of 34 mph, those given the word *bumped* recalled 38 mph, and those given the word *smashed* recalled speeds of 41 mph. Therefore, the schemas people used—whether the cars contacted, hit, bumped, or smashed—affected the way they reconstructed the crash.

About 5 percent of all children do not seem to reconstruct memories actively. They have an **eidetic memory,** a form of photographic memory shared by few adults. Children with eidetic memory can recall very specific details from a picture, a page, or a scene briefly viewed. Photographic memory in adults is extremely rare. It involves the ability to form sharp visual images after examining a picture or page for a short time and then recalling the entire image later.

reconstructive processes: the alteration of a recalled memory that may be simplified, enriched, or distorted, depending on an individual's experiences, attitudes, or inferences

confabulation: the act of filling in memory gaps

schemas: conceptual frameworks a person uses to make sense of the world

eidetic memory: the ability to remember with great accuracy visual information on the basis of short-term exposure

State-Dependent Learning

Have you ever become upset at someone and while doing so remembered many past instances of when you were upset at the same person? This is an example of state-dependent learning. *State-dependent learning* occurs when you recall information easily when you are in the

MEETING SPECIAL NEEDS

Learning Style: Verbal/Linguistic Tell students that *loaded words* are terms or phrases packed with emotional and/or double meanings. For example, if you had witnessed a car accident and were asked what happened when the cars "smashed," you may answer differently than if you were asked what happened when the cars "came into contact." In this case, smashed is the loaded word. Have students find passages in their favorite novels that use loaded words. Ask them to reproduce three of these passages and write a 2- to 3-paragraph analysis of how these words help the reader recall the action or the point that the author was attempting to convey. **L3** **BLOCK SCHEDULING**

same physiological or emotional state or setting as you were when you originally encoded the information. This is why some people advise you to study for a test in the same classroom or setting in which you will take the test. Being in a certain physiological or emotional state serves as a cue to help you more easily recall stored information.

RELEARNING

While recognition and recall are measures of declarative memory, relearning is a measure of both declarative and procedural memory. Suppose you learned a poem as a child but have not rehearsed it in years. If you can relearn the poem with fewer recitations than someone with ability similar to yours, you are benefiting from your childhood learning.

FORGETTING

Everyone experiences a failure of memory from time to time. You are sure you have seen that person before but cannot remember exactly where. You have the word on the tip of your tongue, but. . . . When information that once entered long-term memory is unable to be retrieved, it is said to be forgotten. Forgetting may involve decay, interference, or repression.

Some inputs may fade away, or **decay,** over time. Items quickly decay in sensory storage and short-term memory, as indicated earlier. It is not certain, however, whether long-term memories can ever decay. We know that a blow to the head or electrical stimulation of certain parts of the

decay: fading away of memory over time

Profiles In Psychology

Elizabeth Loftus

1944–

"One of the things that we know about memory for very upsetting experiences, traumatic experiences, is that the memory does not work like a videotape recorder."

The work of Elizabeth Loftus has been in the forefront of a raging debate over memory. Loftus has spent much of her life gathering evidence that memory is extremely fragile and not always accurate. She has shown that eyewitness testimony is often unreliable and that false memories can be triggered merely by suggestion. The manner in which a person builds memories can be altered by information acquired after the original experience.

Her work is controversial because it raises doubts about the validity of repressed memories of repeated trauma, such as that of childhood abuse. Loftus has testified in hundreds of court cases, including the case of George Franklin. Franklin was sent to jail in 1990 for first-degree murder after his daughter Eileen recalled, 20 years later, that her father had killed her friend in 1969. Eileen had recounted the details of the murder to the police in amazing detail. Eileen's memory of the event, though, changed—matching media descriptions of it. Loftus noted that memory changes over time, and as more time passes, our memories become more distorted. Loftus believes that there exists a very real possibility that Eileen unconsciously created the memory as a result of guilt, anger, fear, and desperation connected to the childhood abuse she suffered at the hands of her father.

Profiles In Psychology

Ask students to read the **Profiles In Psychology** feature and then discuss the following questions:

1. Why does Loftus believe eyewitness testimony is often unreliable? *(Loftus believes that memory can be influenced both by suggestion and by future information.)*
2. How could the negation of repressed memories affect child abuse victims? *(For real victims, their memories may not be believed. However, for those who are falsely accused, their lives could be saved from devastation.)*

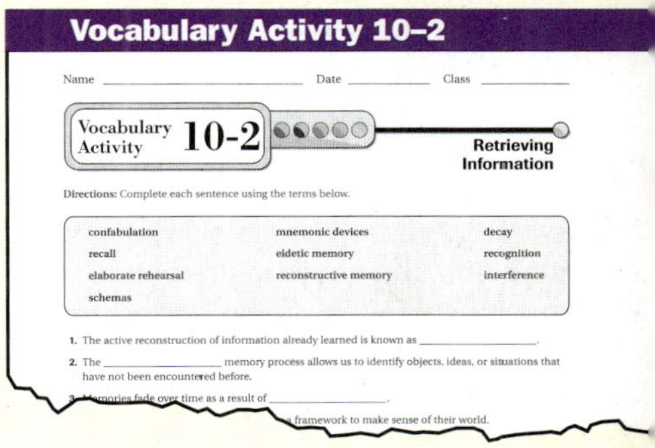
Vocabulary Activity 10–2

Name ____ Date ____ Class ____

Vocabulary Activity 10-2 Retrieving Information

Directions: Complete each sentence using the terms below.

confabulation	mnemonic devices	decay
recall	eidetic memory	recognition
elaborate rehearsal	reconstructive memory	interference
schemas		

1. The active reconstruction of information already learned is known as ____.
2. The ____ memory process allows us to identify objects, ideas, or situations that have not been encountered before.
3. Memories fade over time as a result of ____.

a framework to make sense of their world.

CRITICAL THINKING ACTIVITY

Demonstrating Reasoned Judgment Provide the following quote from William James to students: *Forgetting is as important as recollecting. . . . If we remembered everything, we should be as ill off as if we remembered nothing. It would take as long for us to recall a space of time as it took the original time to elapse, and we should never get ahead with our thinking.* Have students make a list of the functions of forgetting from James's perspective and from their own experiences. **L2**

Figure 10.7

Caption Answer Decay is the fading away of memory. Sensory and short-term memory decay. It is not known for sure whether long-term memories decay.

Readings and Case Studies in Psychology
Have students read the Chapter 10 Case Study selection in *Readings and Case Studies in Psychology* and answer the questions that follow the case study.

CULTURAL CONNECTIONS

Dutch chess master and psychologist Adrian de Groot wanted to know what separated a good chess player from a grand master. He reviewed the simultaneous displays and blindfold demonstrations that amaze onlookers. In simultaneous displays, grand masters take on several challengers at the same time. They move from board to board and make moves with seeming ease. In blindfold demonstrations, the grand master plays the game blindfolded, being told his or her opponent's moves. In his research, de Groot found that the primary difference between grand masters and good chess players is the ability to recall chess positions. Grand masters seem to have an almost instinctive recall of thousands of past chess moves.

3 ASSESS

Assign Section 2 Assessment as homework or as an in-class activity.

Figure 10.7 Memory Failure

You may experience memory failure because of decay, interference, or repression. ***What is decay?***

brain can cause loss of memory. The memories lost, however, are the most recent ones; older memories seem to remain. The fact that apparently forgotten information can be recovered through meditation, hypnosis, or brain stimulation suggests that at least some memories never decay. Rather, interference or repression causes people to lose track of them.

Interference refers to a memory being blocked or erased by previous or subsequent memories. This blocking is of two kinds: proactive and retroactive. In *proactive interference* an earlier memory blocks you from remembering later information. In *retroactive interference* a later memory or new information blocks you from remembering information learned earlier. Suppose you move to a new home. You now have to remember a new address and phone number. At first you may have trouble remembering them because the memory of your old address and phone number gets in the way (proactive interference). Later, you know the new information but have trouble remembering the old data (retroactive interference). It is important to note that proactive interference does not lead to retroactive interference; the two are separate concepts.

It may be that interference actually does erase some memories permanently. In other cases the old data have not been lost. The information is in your memory somewhere, if only you could find it. According to Sigmund Freud, sometimes blocking is no accident. A person may subconsciously block memories of an embarrassing or frightening experience. This kind of forgetting is called *repression*. The material still exists in the person's memory, but it has been made inaccessible because it is so disturbing.

interference: blockage of a memory by previous or subsequent memories or loss of a retrieval cue

Did You Know?

Flashbulb Memories Ask your friends where they were on September 11, 2001, when they found out that terrorists had attacked New York's World Trade Center. They will most likely remember in vivid detail. This ability is called "flashbulb memory." This type of memory usually involves events that are shocking or emotional. Scientists have concluded that flashbulb memories involve special kinds of encoding that occur when events are extreme and/or personal.

Amnesia

Some people also forget information due to amnesia. *Amnesia* is a loss of memory that may occur after a blow to the head or as a result of brain damage. Amnesia may also be the result of drug use or severe psychological stress.

Infant amnesia is the relative lack of early declarative memories. For example, why is it that we do not seem to remember much from when we were 2 or 3 years old? Although some children do form lasting memories, most memories from early childhood seem to fade away.

Psychologists have proposed several theories to explain infant amnesia. Freud thought that infant

PSYCHOLOGY LAB EXPERIMENT

Effect of Prompting Demonstrate the effect of prompting with the following activity. Bring a mix of 20 objects, both familiar and unfamiliar, into class in a bag. Record these items on a list jumbled among another 10 to 15 items. Quickly pull each of the items out of the bag and then put them back in the bag or somewhere out of the students' view. Then tell half the students to write down what they saw. Have the other half of the class circle the items they saw on a prepared list. Compare the results. **Ask: How does prompting improve the process of recall? How would prompting help improve such tasks as studying for tests?** *(Clue words could trigger the recall of information.)* **L1** ELL **BLOCK SCHEDULING**

memories are repressed because of the emotional traumas of infancy. Others believe that because infants do not yet understand language, their memories are nonverbal, whereas later memories are verbal (once language is learned). Still others claim that the hippocampus may not be mature enough in infancy to spark memories or that infants have not yet developed a sense of self to experience memories.

IMPROVING MEMORY

Techniques for improving memory are based on efficient organization of the things you learn and on chunking information into easily handled packages.

Meaningfulness and Association

As we discussed earlier, using repetition, or maintenance rehearsal, can help you remember for a short period of time. In this method, words are merely repeated with no attempt to find meaning. A more efficient way of remembering new information involves **elaborative rehearsal.** In this method, you relate the new information to what you already know. The more meaningful something is, the easier it will be to remember. For example, you would be more likely to remember the six letters DFIRNE if they were arranged to form the word FRIEND.

Similarly, you remember things more vividly if you associate them with things already stored in memory or with a strong emotional experience. The more categories a memory is indexed under, the more accessible it is. If an input is analyzed and indexed under many categories, each association can serve as a trigger for the memory. If you associate the new information with strong sensory experiences and a variety of other memories, any of these stimuli can trigger the memory. The more senses and experiences you use when trying to memorize something, the more likely it is that you will be able to retrieve it—a key to improving memory.

For similar reasons, a good way to protect a memory from interference is to overlearn it—to keep on rehearsing it even after you think you know it well. Another way to prevent interference while learning new material is to avoid studying similar material together. Instead of studying history right after political science, study biology in between. Still another method is to space out your learning. Trying to absorb large amounts of information at one sitting results in a great deal of interference. It is far more effective to study a little at a time—called *distributed practice.*

In addition, how you originally learn or remember something influences how readily you recall that information later. If a bit of information is associated with a highly emotional event or if you learned this bit of

Quick Lab

Can you improve your memory?

At one time or another we have all had to memorize items—a list of facts, telephone numbers, or a dialogue in a play. Are there ways to improve these memorization tasks?

Procedure

1. Give several friends and classmates the following list of numbers to memorize: 6, 9, 8, 11, 10, 13, 12, 15, 14, 17, 16, etc.
2. Tell some people to simply memorize the number sequence.
3. Tell others that there is an organizational principle behind the number sequence (which they are to discover) and to memorize the numbers with the aid of this principle. (The principle here is "plus 3, minus 1.")

Analysis

1. Which group was better at remembering the number sequence? Why do you think this is so? Write a brief analysis.

See the Skills Handbook, page 622, for an explanation of designing an experiment.

elaborative rehearsal: the linking of new information to material that is already known

CHAPTER 10
Section 2, pages 282–288

Quick Lab

Purpose Students will test techniques to improve memory.

Process Skills Demonstrating reasoned judgment

Teaching Strategies

- Review the procedures to be used.
- If people cannot identify the principle, recommend that students give them hints without telling them the principle.

Analysis

1. The group that understood the principle would be better at remembering the sequence because they could link numbers in a pattern.

Section Quiz 10–2

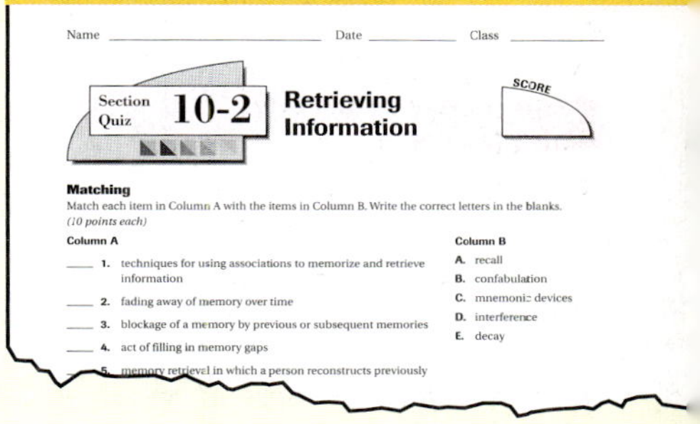
Name ______ Date ______ Class ______

Section Quiz 10-2 **Retrieving Information**

SCORE

Matching
Match each item in Column A with the items in Column B. Write the correct letters in the blanks. *(10 points each)*

Column A
____ 1. techniques for using associations to memorize and retrieve information
____ 2. fading away of memory over time
____ 3. blockage of a memory by previous or subsequent memories
____ 4. act of filling in memory gaps
____ 5. memory retrieval in which a person reconstructs previously

Column B
A. recall
B. confabulation
C. mnemonic devices
D. interference
E. decay

Reteach

Have students list ways in which they have used meaningfulness and association to help them remember the material covered in this psychology course.

INTERDISCIPLINARY CONNECTIONS ACTIVITY

The Arts Have students work individually or in groups to design a visual mnemonic to remember the artistic style of a famous artist important in art history. Examples might include the following: Mary Cassatt and impressionism, Roy Lichtenstein and pop art, Georges Seurat and pointillism. Suggest that students consult an art history book in the library for additional ideas. You might arrange for students to present their graphic learning devices to some of the world history classes in your school. **L2**

Psychology and You

Use the following question to direct a class discussion after students have read the **Psychology and You** feature.

Ask: Why might thinking about something else help you remember the information you were searching for?

Reading Check Answer Common mnemonic devices include using associations, forming mental pictures, and making up words, stories, and rhymes.

Enrich

Have students create mnemonic devices that they can use in their study of psychology.

4 CLOSE

Tell students that there is an ongoing debate about the validity of repressed memories. Explain to students what repressed memories are. Then ask them to review the material in the chapter and offer an opinion about repressed memories.

Psychology and You

On the Tip of Your Tongue

Have you ever tried to remember something but could not quite do so, saying, "I know it; it's on the tip of my tongue"? What you experienced is called the tip-of-the-tongue phenomenon. Later, in a different situation, the information you were looking for earlier comes to you. Why does this happen? In certain cases, maybe you encoded the information in your memory with insufficient retrieval cues and just cannot find an association to retrieve the memory. In other cases, the information may be blocked through interference. When you think about other things, the information pops back into your memory.

information in the absence of interference, you will more easily recall that information because of the strength of that memory.

Mnemonic Devices

Techniques for using associations to memorize information are called **mnemonic devices.** The ancient Greeks memorized speeches by mentally walking around their homes or neighborhoods and associating each line of a speech with a different spot—called the Method of Loci. Once they made the associations, they could recall the speech by mentally retracing their steps and picking up each line. The rhyme we use to recall the number of days in each month ("Thirty days has September") is a mnemonic device. In the phrase "Every Good Boy Does Fine," the first letters of the words are the same as the names of the musical notes on the lines of a staff (E, G, B, D, and F).

mnemonic devices: techniques for using associations to memorize and retrieve information

Another useful mnemonic device is to form mental pictures. Suppose you have trouble remembering the authors and titles of books or which artists belong to which schools of painting. To plant the fact in your mind that John Updike wrote *Rabbit, Run,* you might picture a RABBIT RUNning UP a DIKE. To remember that Picasso was a Cubist, picture someone attacking a giant CUBE with a PICKAX, which sounds like Picasso (Lorayne & Lucas, 1974). Mnemonic devices are not magical. Indeed, they involve extra work—making up words, stories, and so on. The very effort of trying to do this, however, may help you remember things.

Reading Check What are some common mnemonic devices?

SECTION 2 Assessment

1. **Review the Vocabulary** What is the difference between proactive and retroactive interference? Between maintenance and elaborative rehearsal?
2. **Visualize the Main Idea** In a graphic organizer similar to the one below, explain the three processes of memory retrieval.

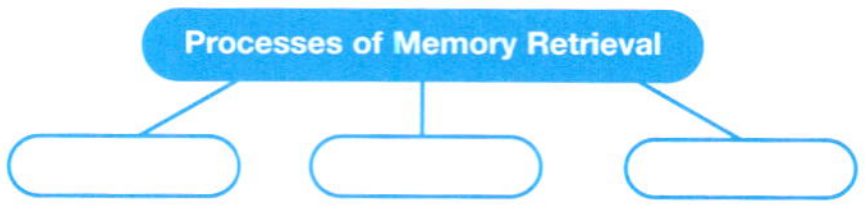

3. **Recall Information** What is state-dependent learning? How does it relate to studying and taking exams?
4. **Think Critically** What types of test questions do you prefer: those that require recall, such as essay questions, or those that require recognition, such as multiple choice questions? Why?
5. **Application Activity** Provide an example of a mnemonic device that helped you learn or remember something.

SECTION 2 Assessment Answers

1. Proactive interference results when an earlier memory blocks you from remembering later information. Retroactive interference occurs when newer information blocks you from remembering earlier information. Maintenance rehearsal is a system for remembering that involves repeating information to oneself. Elaborative rehearsal involves linking new information to material that is already known.
2. Graphic organizers should reflect students' understanding of recall, recognition, and eidetic memory.
3. State-dependent learning occurs when you are in the same physiological or emotional state or setting as you were when you originally encoded the information. You may have better recall on tests by studying in the room in which you will actually take the test.
4. Answers may vary. Most students will select recognition questions since the answer is provided for them.
5. Answers will vary. An example is "Thirty days has September, April, June, and November. All the rest have 31, except. . . ."

CHAPTER 10 Summary and Vocabulary

Memory is a complex mental process that allows us to recognize friends and family as well as to do things such as drive, speak a language, and play an instrument. Psychologists have sought to understand memory and to find ways to improve it.

Section 1 Taking in and Storing Information

Main Idea: There are three processes involved in memory: encoding, storage, and retrieval.

- During encoding, you use your senses to encode and establish a memory.
- Storage is the process by which information is maintained over a period of time.
- Retrieval occurs when information is brought to mind from storage.
- According to one theory, there are three types of memory—sensory, short-term, and long-term—each with a different purpose and time span.
- Although psychologists agree that some physiological changes occur in the brain when something is stored in long-term memory, they are only beginning to identify how and where memories are stored.

Section 2 Retrieving Information

Main Idea: Stored memory can be retrieved by recognition, recall, and relearning.

- Human memory is organized in such a way as to make recognition quite easy.
- Recall involves a person's knowledge, attitudes, and expectations.
- Recall seems to result from the reconstruction of the features of a memory from which the required information is extracted.
- People's memories are sometimes reconstructed in terms of their schemas.
- State-dependent learning aids recall only if you are in the same physiological or emotional state as you were when you originally encoded the information.
- Forgetting can be the result of decay, interference, or repression.
- Memory can be improved through meaningfulness, association, lack of interference, and degree of original learning.

Chapter Vocabulary

memory (p. 274)
encoding (p. 274)
storage (p. 274)
retrieval (p. 274)
sensory memory (p. 274)
short-term memory (p. 276)
maintenance rehearsal (p. 276)
chunking (p. 277)
semantic memory (p. 279)
episodic memory (p. 279)
declarative memory (p. 279)
procedural memory (p. 279)
recognition (p. 283)
recall (p. 283)
reconstructive processes (p. 284)
confabulation (p. 284)
schemas (p. 284)
eidetic memory (p. 284)
decay (p. 285)
interference (p. 286)
elaborative rehearsal (p. 287)
mnemonic devices (p. 288)

10 Summary and Vocabulary

Using the Chapter 10 Summary and Vocabulary

Use the Chapter 10 Summary and Vocabulary to preview, review, condense, or reteach the chapter.

Preview/Review

Use the Chapter Vocabulary list to help students review and study.

Activity Have students create flash cards with the term on one side and the definition on the other. Encourage them to work with another classmate to master the vocabulary terms.

Vocabulary PuzzleMaker CD-ROM reinforces the vocabulary terms used in Chapter 10.

Condense

Have students read the Chapter 10 Summary.

Chapter 10 Guided Reading Activities

Reteach

Reteaching Activity 10

PERFORMANCE ASSESSMENT ACTIVITY

Conducting a Survey Ask students to select a significant news event that has occurred since they started the school year. Create a brief survey that asks specific questions about the details of the event. (Students should research the event to make certain they know the facts.) Students should administer the survey to 10 friends or classmates and then analyze the results to identify examples of faulty recall. **BLOCK SCHEDULING**

Refer to the ***Authentic Assessment*** booklet for additional activities and information about evaluating student performance.

10 Assessment

PSYCHOLOGY Online

Have students visit the Web site at glencoe.com to review Chapter 10 and take the **Self-Check Quiz.**

GLENCOE TECHNOLOGY

Presentation Plus! For a review of Chapter 10 content, see MindJogger Checkpoint on **Presentation Plus!**

Reviewing Vocabulary

1. b	**6.** h
2. j	**7.** a
3. g	**8.** c
4. e	**9.** d
5. f	**10.** i

Recalling Facts

1. Acoustic codes are formed when you try to remember something by saying it aloud. Visual codes are attempts to keep mental pictures of information. Semantic codes use whole words to remember information.
2. Two storage strategies are rehearsal and chunking.
3. The primacy-recency effect means that we tend to remember items that fall at the beginning and end of a list.
4. The two types of interference are proactive interference and retroactive interference. In proactive interference, an earlier memory blocks you from remembering later information. In retroactive interference, a later memory or new information blocks you from remembering information learned earlier.
5. You can improve your memory by meaningfulness, association, lack of interference, degree of original learning, and use of mnemonic devices.

Critical Thinking

1. Students' answers will vary. Most students will mention chunking; some may mention mnemonic devices.
2. Students' answers will vary. Most students will note how much easier school would be because they would not have to spend as much time studying. Some students may also mention the annoyance of not being able to forget information that is not useful.
3. Students' answers will vary. Focus the discussion on the thought processes involved, such as the influence of mood upon recall and so on, rather than the details of the event.
4. Students' answers will vary. Students might mention the faulty nature of memory, confabulation, and other problems with recall that could affect a witness's memory of events.
5. Meaningfulness is one of the keys to improving memory. When teachers create situations in which learning is meaningful to students, they will remember what they have learned.

Psychology Projects

1. Information from neuroscientists and neuropsychologists is rapidly evolving. Make sure students use reliable sources for their information. Access to the Internet would be especially useful.
2. Answers will vary. Students may have very strong feelings about this subject. Challenge students to separate their feelings from the facts. The work of Elizabeth Loftus is highly readable and would be a good source of information.

CHAPTER 10 Assessment

PSYCHOLOGY Online

Self-Check Quiz
Visit the *Understanding Psychology* Web site at glencoe.com and click on **Chapter 10—Self-Check Quizzes** to prepare for the Chapter Test.

Reviewing Vocabulary

Choose the letter of the correct term or concept below to complete the sentence.

a. memory	**f.** recall
b. storage	**g.** confabulation
c. short-term memory	**h.** schemas
d. episodic memory	**i.** eidetic memory
e. procedural memory	**j.** elaborative rehearsal

1. __________ is the second memory process during which information is maintained passively over a sometimes extended period of time.
2. When you relate new information to what you already know you are practicing __________.
3. __________ is a mistake in memory during which a person recalls information that was never stored in memory.
4. The skills you develop when you learn how to swim become part of your __________.
5. The active reconstruction of information is called __________.
6. __________ are conceptual frameworks we use to make sense of the world.
7. __________ is the input, storage, and retrieval of what has been learned or experienced.
8. The things you have in your conscious mind at any one moment are held in your __________.
9. When you remember what you did on your vacation, you are experiencing __________.
10. A small percentage of children have a(n) __________, or photographic memory.

Recalling Facts

1. Using a graphic organizer similar to the one below, identify and describe the codes used to encode a memory.

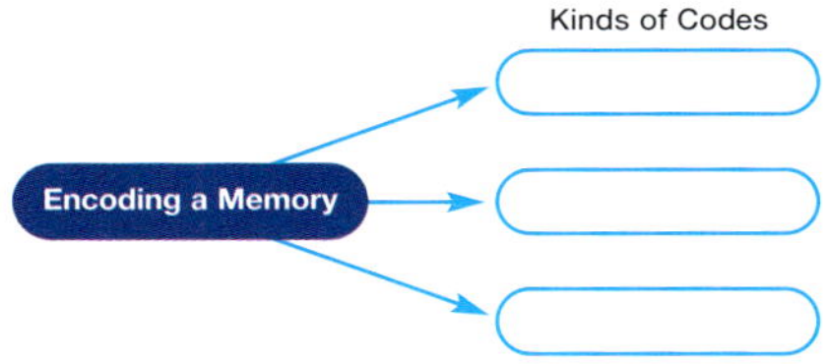

2. List two strategies for expanding the limits of short-term memory.
3. Describe the primacy-recency effect.
4. What are the two types of interference that block memory?
5. Describe five methods you can use to improve your memory.

Critical Thinking

1. **Evaluating Information** Explain what methods you use to memorize items such as lists or phone numbers. Which method do you find most effective? Why?
2. **Analyzing Information** How would having a photographic memory make your life different?
3. **Synthesizing Information** Try to remember what you did on your last birthday. As you probe your memory, verbalize the mental steps you are going through. What processes do you use to remember?
4. **Making Inferences** As a juror, what concerns might you have when hearing eyewitness testimony? Why?
5. **Applying Concepts** Why is it important for teachers to make learning meaningful to their students?

CHAPTER 10 Assessment

Psychology Projects

1. **Taking in and Storing Information** Research the latest findings about the workings of the brain in terms of memory. Share your findings in a written report. You might include diagrams in your report.
2. **Retrieving Information** Research the use of repressed memories in recent child abuse cases. Report the results of the cases and the effects of repressed memories on the outcomes.
3. **Approaches to Memory** Use this textbook and other sources to research several psychological approaches to memory, such as psychoanalytic, behavioral, humanistic, or cognitive. Summarize your findings in a chart.
4. **Recall** Pick several events that should produce flashbulb memories. Interview 10 people about their memories of the events, and identify similarities and differences in their remembrances.

Technology Activity

Search the Internet for Web sites that provide information to help you improve your memory. Several sites provide tips and techniques to help you remember a variety of facts, such as mathematical formulas. Explore and evaluate these sites, try out several tips for yourself, and then report your findings to the class.

Psychology Journal

Reread the journal entry you wrote about your earliest memory. Write an analysis explaining why you think this is your first memory and why it continues to stay in your mind. Explain whether any confabulation might be involved in this memory. Were other people involved? Is their recall of the memory consistent with the way you remember it? Explain.

Building Skills

Interpreting a Graph The graph below shows the results of an experiment in which the ability to remember names and faces of classmates by high school graduates was tested. In a recognition test, participants were asked to match yearbook pictures of classmates with their names. In a recall test, participants were shown yearbook pictures and asked to simply recall the names. Review the graph below, then answer the questions that follow.

Recognition and Recall Tests

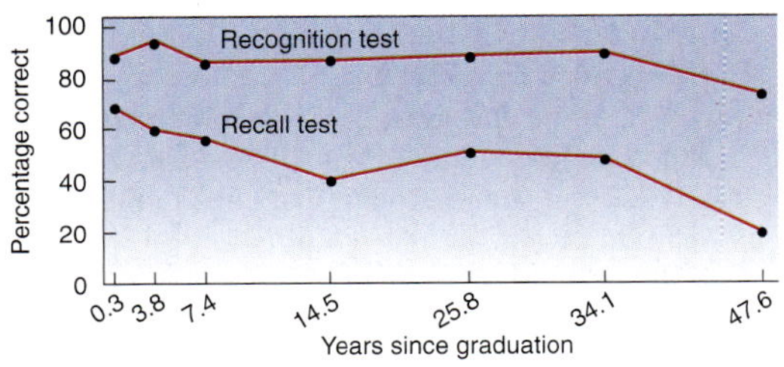

Source: Bahrick, Bahrick, & Wittinger, 1974.

Practice and **assess** key social studies skills with **Glencoe Skillbuilder Interactive Workbook CD-ROM, Level 2.**

1. Which group of participants was most able to recall the names of their classmates?
2. What percentage of participants recalled the names of their classmates 34 years after graduation? 47 years after graduation?
3. How did retrieving information using recall change over a period of 50 years?
4. What effect does time have on retrieving information when recall is used? When recognition is used?
5. When you remember past events and people, how accurate do you think your memory is? Explain.

See the Skills Handbook, page 628, for an explanation of interpreting graphs.

Building Skills

1. the group that took the recognition test
2. about 50 percent; about 20 percent
3. The percentage of people who correctly recalled information gradually decreased from about 70 percent to about 20 percent.
4. Time has a negative effect on retrieving information when recall is used. As time increases, the ability to correctly recall information decreases. Time does not seem to have as much of an effect on the ability to correctly retrieve information using recognition.
5. Students' answers will vary. Some students may realize the potential faultiness of their memories. Students may note that memories that are recalled may be less accurate than memories associated with the process of recognition.

GLENCOE TECHNOLOGY

CD-ROM

Glencoe Skillbuilder Interactive Workbook, Level 2

This interactive CD-ROM is designed to reinforce student mastery of essential social studies skills.

Chapter Bonus Test Question

This question may be used for extra credit on the Chapter Assessment.

Answer the following question:

I am the part of the brain that transfers words, facts, and events from short-term to long-term memory. What am I?

Answer: hippocampus

3. Answers will vary. Have students use the index of the book to find references to the various approaches in the text. Encourage students to use the Internet and reference books for their research.
4. Answers will vary. Students should choose events that are extreme and/or personal, as these are most likely to produce flashbulb memories.

Technology Activity

Students can find a number of sites. Have them search for interactive memory demonstrations that give immediate feedback. Ask students to share the Web sites they found with their classmates.

Psychology Journal

Students' explanations should now reflect their understanding of the potential faultiness of memories. Students may stubbornly hold on to their memory of the event even after finding out that another person who was present has a different memory. Students should be able to explain how their schemas affect their memories.

Readings in Psychology

Block Schedule

This activity works well for a block-scheduling framework.

Reinforcing Vocabulary

Review the **Reader's Dictionary** terms with students to be sure they understand any unfamiliar items.

Background Information

Have you ever awakened in a strange room? For a few seconds you have no explanation for where you are and why you are there. This describes daily existence for Henry. Without any long-term memory, each moment was entirely new.

Remarkably, Henry's ability to read, write, and comprehend were not impaired. Among his favorite activities was solving crossword puzzles. After spending considerable time solving a puzzle, he could be handed a fresh copy of the same puzzle, and he would have no memory of the clues or the words that fit those clues.

He also enjoyed watching television. He could follow the story lines, laugh at the jokes, and respond to the suspense. Of course, reruns did not bother him since he had no memory of ever having seen the episode.

READINGS IN PSYCHOLOGY

In 1953, doctors performed brain surgery on a man named Henry, also known as H.M. The doctors hoped to alleviate HenryÕ severe epileptic seizures by removing his hippocampus, where they believed the seizures originated. Although the surgery relieved Henry's seizures, he suffered severe memory problems. For years after the operation he cited the year as 1953 and could not encode new long-term memories, even though his existing long-term memories remained intact. Philip F. Hilts chronicled Henry's story in *Memory's Ghost*, published in 1995.

Reader's Dictionary

M.I.T.: Massachusetts Institute of Technology

hippocampus: a curved structure within the temporal lobe of the brain involved in transforming many kinds of short-term memories into permanent storage

MEMORY'S GHOST

BY PHILIP F. HILTS

We were out in the sun once, Henry in his wheelchair and I beside him, waiting for the taxi to take us for his brain scan. It was the usual changeable, disturbing weather of a Boston spring, but just now, it was bright and warm. "Great day!" I said. "And sunny!" As I said it, a shadow crossed the walk, and the sun dived into a cloud. Henry laughed. "Well, just as soon as you say it, it isn't!"

Across the street was a construction site. We watched at length; the crane—it must have been ten stories tall—swung out over the deep hole and back up to its bank, a huge bucket of gray muck gliding down. "I bet they are glad they don't have to haul that all the way up," said Henry. I glanced up the street for the taxi, and quickly Henry's gaze followed. He wasn't sure why we were looking there, and he studied me. My head was turning back to the construction, and Henry's gaze settled there again, too. He watches and listens for clues, for the implications of a question, for hints at what the subject is, how he should feel, and how he should answer. How else could he be more than like a dog, waiting expectantly at the door? I imagine him walking, always a little uncertain, but compelled to press ahead while around him is a blank fog. "And I moved forward," said poet W.S. Merwin, "because you must live forward, which is away from whatever it was that you had, though you think when you have it that it will stay with you forever."

I recall one of my visits to Henry. As he talked with Dr. Corkin, who had come to get him for tests, I observed in silence. When she approached, he looked up, blank at first. I could almost put words to passing expressions on his face: Ah, a face that seems familiar. To talk to me? Yes—she takes up my eyes.

"How are you, Henry?"

He groped a little, feeling just behind him for something. "Fine, I guess," he said, and smiled a little. Again he watched, expectantly.

"Do you know what we're going to do today?"

I felt him turn metaphorically to search for an answer. Then he shrugged. "I don't remember."

But then she handed him his walker. He can grasp it, flip out the legs, set it just ahead of himself, and lean up into it.

"Why do you use a walker, Henry, do you know?"

ADDITIONAL READINGS ABOUT THE TOPIC

Gazzaniga, M.S. (2000). *The Mind's Past.* University of California Press.

Restak, R.M. (1991). *The Brain Has a Mind of Its Own.* New York: Crown Trade Paperbacks.

Schacter, D.L. (1997). *Searching for Memory.* New York: HarperCollins.

Sweatt, J.D. (2003). *Mechanisms of Memory.* San Diego, CA: Academic Press.

A brief look into the fog. Nothing there. He looked down. "Well, it's my legs," he said. He quickly realized the humor in this too-obvious reply, and grinned.

Down the hall, he turned left, heading for the experiment room. How did his body know to go that way? Part of his brain has learned, though the other has not. The one that is supposed to keep track of what has been learned is missing.

At the plain gray table in the experiment room, Dr. Corkin asked, "Do you know where you are, Henry?"

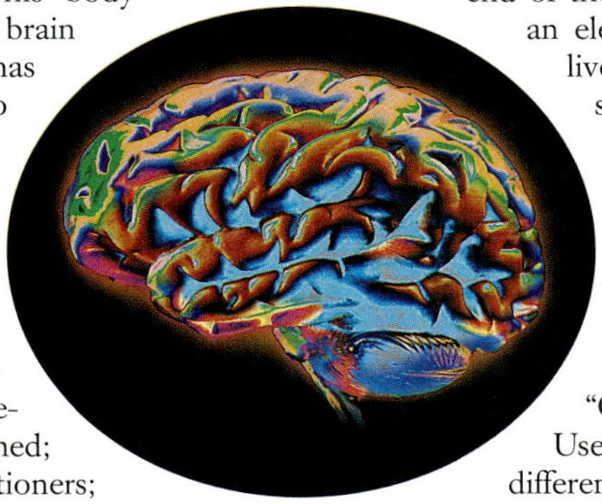

Again, he looked out into a fog. But here! There is something! "Well, at M.I.T.!" He beamed; he gathered a scrap for his questioners; he always likes to please. It has taken decades of travel to M.I.T. and frequent talk of the place for him to know that if he's being tested, this must be M.I.T.

Finally, as we stood out in the sun, the taxi arrived to take us across the Charles River. We bundled the awkward wheelchair in the trunk, him in the back seat, and we took the taxi over to Brigham and Women's Hospital where the magnetic resonance scanner awaited him. It is more than a device, it is the size of a room, and it is not pressed against the patient like an X-ray scope, but surrounds the patient as he is inserted *within* the machine.

Henry was a bit dubious about this, especially as he had to remove all metal objects from his person. That meant his belt, and he was shy removing it in front of the women researchers in the room. He was more chagrined after he removed it and everyone could see that there was a paper clip holding his trousers together.

I sat in the room with him, while everyone else retreated to another room, behind a large observation window. They spoke to Henry by microphone, trying to reassure him by tone of voice while they were in fact being distant and cold. And that noise! It was like being in a closet with a jackhammer operating in slow motion.

From all this crudeness issued, on the other end of the computing systems and wires, an elegant, flickering color image. A live image of his brain, slice by slice, as the imager moved backward through his brain taking images one plane at a time. When the imager reached Henry's temporal lobes and the place where his middle brain should be, the researcher at the panel let out a low gasp. "Oh! That's beautiful!" he said. Used to peering at subtle shading differences denoting massive tumors, he was now confronted with a huge black hole in the center of the brain, the first thing of its kind he had ever seen.

The series of images lead to measurements, recalculations, new guesses. There is, Dr. Corkin has discovered, a little more of the hippocampus present than was thought. But the other bits of middle brain linked to it, the parahippocampal gyrus, the entorhinal cortex, and the perirhinal cortex are all destroyed: they must be an important part of the "hippocampal" system of memory consolidation.

The pictures from within the dome of Henry's skull are a bit startling. Of course, we could have guessed what they might look like. But it is not the same to guess as to see the lovely textured images of the brain and then the black, ragged edges where tissue has been sucked out.

Analyzing the Reading

1. What types of things does Henry seem unable to recall?
2. Why does the researcher seem excited by Henry's brain scan?
3. **Critical Thinking** Why does the author compare Henry to a dog?

Active Reading Strategy

Suggest to students that if they are having trouble understanding part of the selection, they can use details provided by the writer to mentally walk through each step in the process being described to create a mental picture.

Psychology Journal

Have students write a list of normal, day-to-day activities they could not do if they had no long-term memory. ■

FYI

Jean Piaget believed until he was 15 years old that he could remember a day when he was 2 years old that someone had attempted to kidnap him. He could remember specific details of the event. When he was 15, the woman who had been his nurse confessed that she had made up the story. Piaget realized what he remembered was not the actual event but were the stories his nurse and others told him about the event.

Answers to Analyzing the Reading

1. He could not recall names, faces, places, plans, and simple directions. Henry does not recall what he was intending to do at any one moment.
2. The scan helps to identify with more precision the parts of Henry's brain that are missing. The researcher usually sees subtle differences in scans indicating tumors or other abnormalities. Henry's brain scan, though, shows a huge black hole—something the researcher has never before seen.
3. Since Henry cannot recall what he is doing from one moment to the next, he must watch the people around him and react to their clues about how to behave and respond. For example, if a companion turns his head to look to the left, Henry will turn his head to the left in an attempt to figure out what is going on.

Chapter 11 Resource Guide

SECTION RESOURCES

Daily Objectives	Reproducible Resources	Multimedia Resources
Section 1 **Thinking and Problem Solving** Understand that thinking involves changing and reorganizing the information stored in memory to create new or transformed information.	Blackline Master: Guided Reading Activity 11–1 Blackline Master: Vocabulary Activity 11–1 Blackline Master: Section Quiz 11–1	Transparency: Daily Focus Transparency 11–1 CD-ROM: *ExamView® Assessment Suite* CD-ROM CD-ROM: Presentation Plus! Software
Section 2 **Language** Explain how language and thought are closely related.	Blackline Master: Guided Reading Activity 11–2 Blackline Master: Vocabulary Activity 11–2 Blackline Master: Section Quiz 11–2	Transparency: Daily Focus Transparency 11–2 CD-ROM: Vocabulary PuzzleMaker CD-ROM CD-ROM: *ExamView® Assessment Suite* CD-ROM CD-ROM: Presentation Plus! Software

Blackline Master   CD-ROM   Transparency

Block Schedule

Activities that are particularly suited for use within the block-scheduling framework are identified throughout this chapter by the following designation: **BLOCK SCHEDULING**

KEY TO ABILITY LEVELS

Teaching strategies have been coded for varying learning styles and abilities.

- **L1** **BASIC** activities for all students
- **L2** **AVERAGE** activities for average to above-average students
- **L3** **CHALLENGING** activities for above-average students
- **ELL** **ENGLISH LANGUAGE LEARNER** activities

Chapter 11 Resource Guide

Timesaving Tools

TeacherWorks™ All-In-One Planner and Resource Center

- **Interactive Teacher Edition** Access your Teacher Wraparound Edition and your classroom resources with a few easy clicks.
- **Interactive Lesson Planner** Planning has never been easier! Organize your week, month, semester, or year with all the lesson helps you need to make teaching creative, timely, and relevant.

Use Glencoe's **Presentation Plus!** multimedia teacher tool to easily present dynamic lessons that visually excite your students. Using Microsoft PowerPoint® you can customize the presentations to create your own personalized lessons.

Activity

From the Classroom of...

Patrick Mattimore
South San Francisco High School
San Francisco, CA

The Gray Box

Purpose: To use critical thinking skills and metacognition

Materials Needed: A large, empty gray box

Procedure: Tell students that restructuring high schools is a major topic among school administrators. (Although that information is true, the rest of this story is fictional.) In 1998, a State Department of Education sponsored a statewide contest and awarded a $25,000 cash prize to the person who came up with the most innovative plan for a restructured high school. The Department of Education was so enamored with the winning entry that it built scale models for resale. Show students a gray box, and tell them that enclosed in the box are the model and plans that were purchased from the Department of Education. Tell students that they will ask you up to 20 yes/no questions to try to determine the exact structure and details of the school. After several minutes of questions and the yes/no responses, challenge students to guess at the structure. Then reveal the empty gray box to students.

Discussion: Ask students to reflect on their own thinking processes during the exercise (metacognition). How did they revise their thinking as a result of new information? How can asking the right (or the wrong) questions be useful in helping us think about problems, novel situations, and human behavior?

Psychology Online

Use our Web site for additional resources. All essential content is covered in the Student Edition.

You and your students can visit glencoe.com, the Web site companion to *Understanding Psychology*. This innovative integration of electronic and print media offers your students a wealth of opportunities. The student text directs students to the Web site for the following options:

- Chapter Overviews
- Student Web Activities
- Self-Check Quizzes

Answers are provided for you in the **Web Activity Lesson Plan**. Additional Web resources and Interactive Puzzles are also available.

Chapter 11 Resource Guide

Note: The following materials may be used when teaching Chapter 11. Section level support materials are shown at point of use in the margins of the Teacher Wraparound Edition.

TEACHING TRANSPARENCIES

Chapter 11
Concept Transparencies

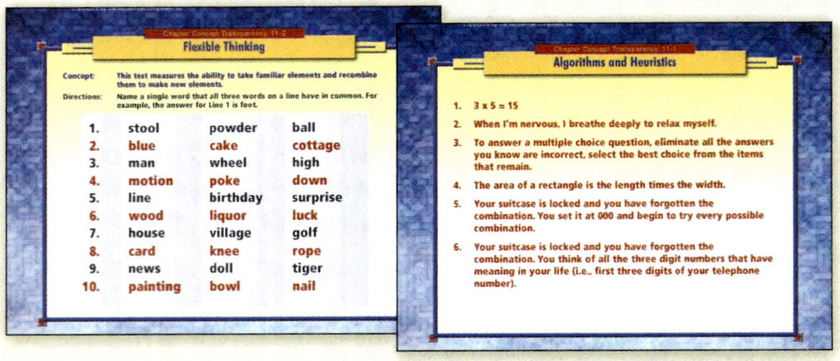

MULTIMEDIA

- **Vocabulary PuzzleMaker CD-ROM**
- ***ExamView® Assessment Suite* CD-ROM**
- **TeacherWorks™ CD-ROM**
- **Glencoe Skillbuilder Interactive Workbook, Level 2**
- **Presentation Plus! Software**

REVIEW AND REINFORCEMENT

Reteaching Activity 11

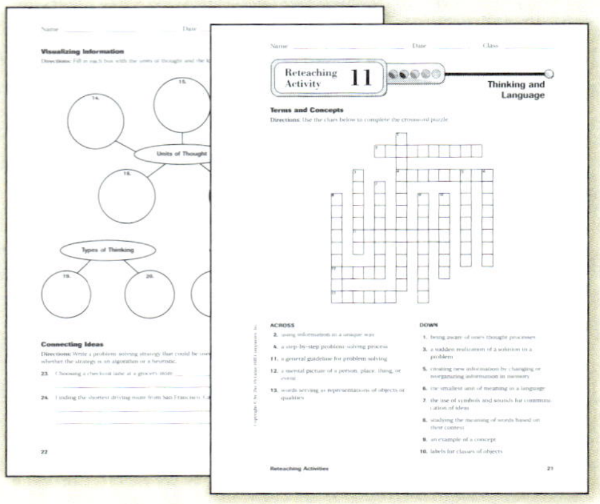

Graphic Organizer Activity 11

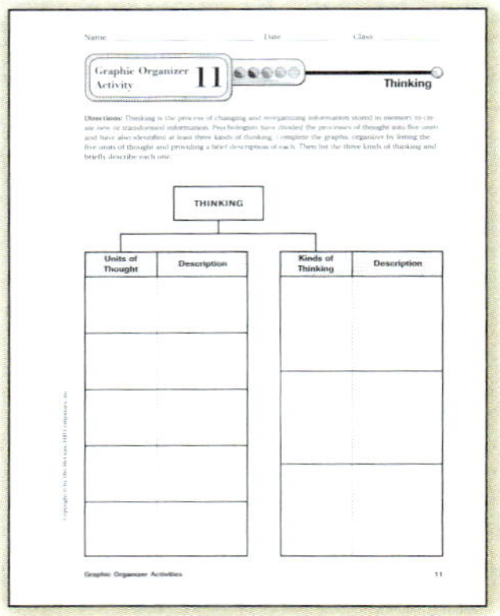

APPLICATION AND HANDS-ON

Psychology Projects 11–1 and 11–2

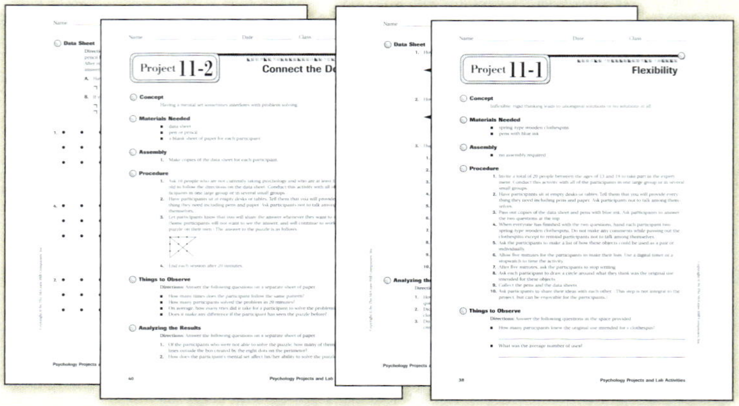

Application Activity 11

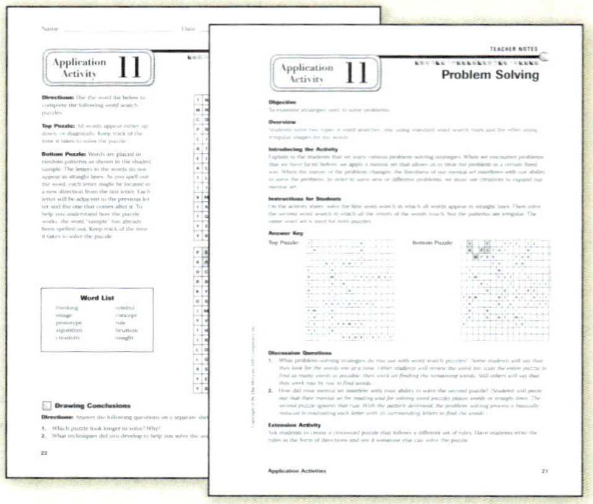

Chapter 11 Resource Guide

GLENCOE'S ASSESSMENT ADVANTAGE

ASSESSMENT

Chapter 11 Test, Form A

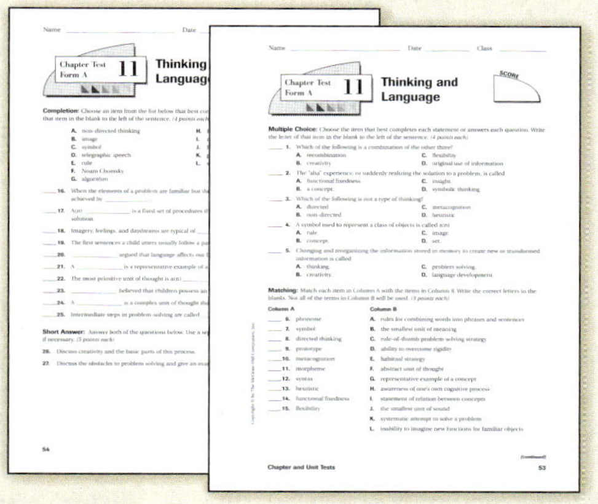
Chapter Test Form A 11 Thinking and Language

Chapter 11 Test, Form B

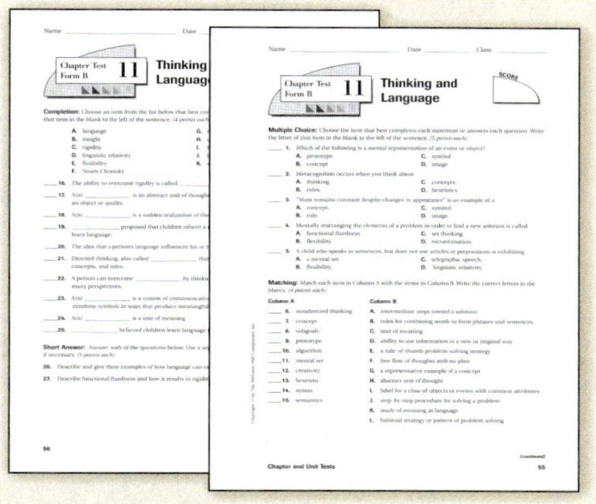
Chapter Test Form B 11 Thinking and Language

Authentic Assessment Activity 11

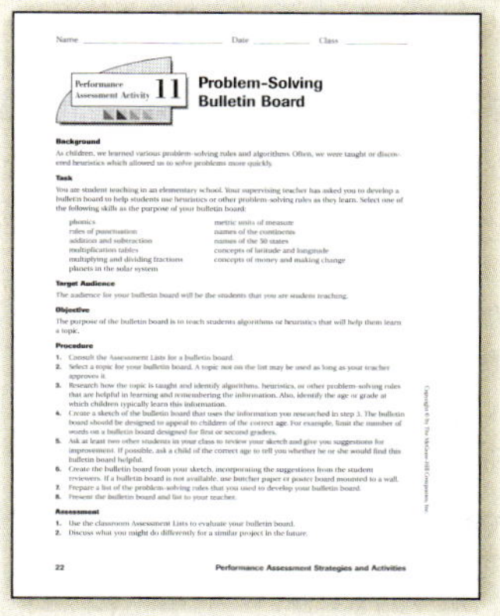
Performance Assessment Activity 11 Problem-Solving Bulletin Board

EXTENSION AND ENRICHMENT

Enrichment Activity 11

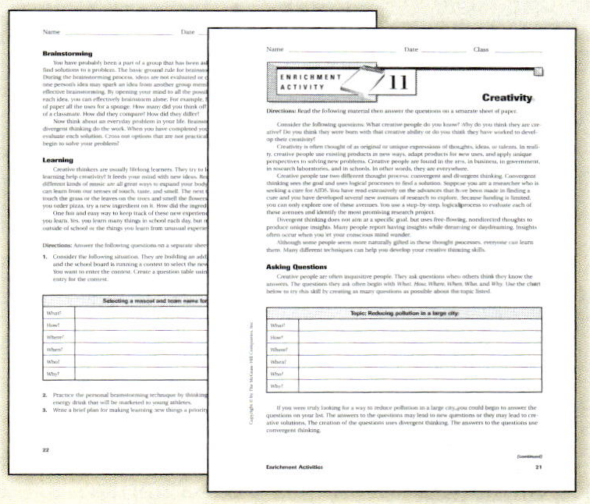
Enrichment Activity 11 Creativity

Critical Thinking Skills Activity 11

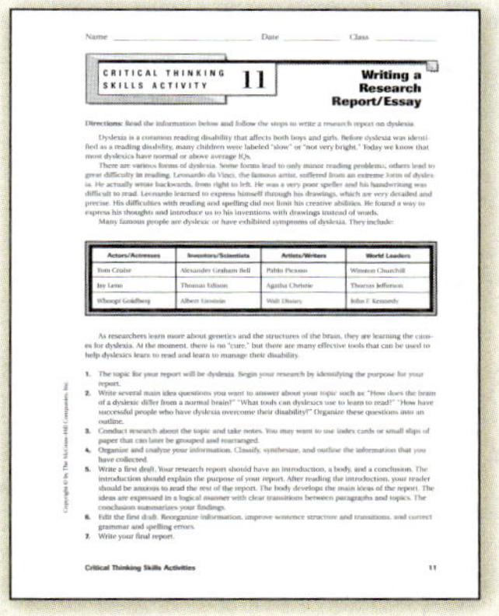
Critical Thinking Skills Activity 11 Writing a Research Report/Essay

Psychology Reading 11

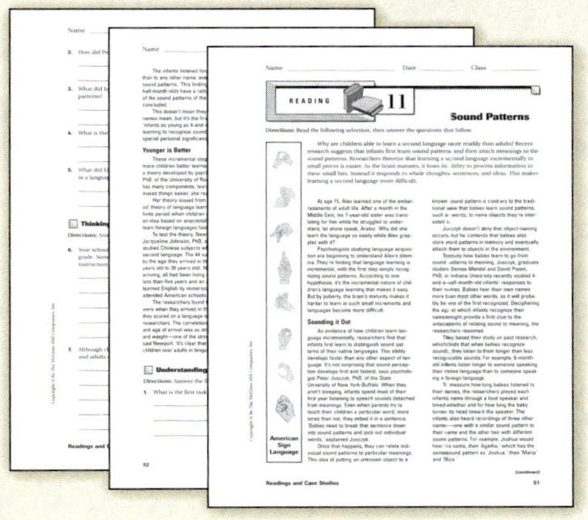
Reading 11 Sound Patterns

Psychology Case Study 11

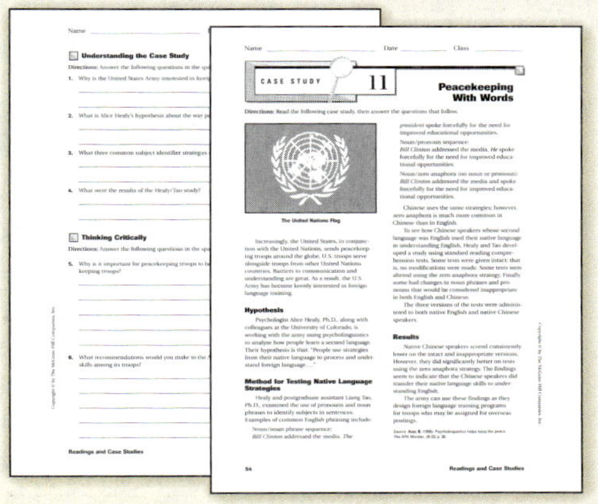
Case Study 11 Peacekeeping With Words

PSYCHOLOGY Online

Visit glencoe.com for a Chapter Overview for **Chapter 11—Thinking and Language.**

GLENCOE TECHNOLOGY

PRESENTATION Plus!

For a preview of Chapter 11 content, see MindJogger Checkpoint on **Presentation Plus!**

PSYCHOLOGY JOURNAL

Explain that the connection between language and higher-level thinking skills is well documented. We organize thought by language. Therefore, increasing your vocabulary will allow you to process more information.

This journal activity provides the basis for the Psychology Journal activity exercise in the Chapter Assessment. ■

CHAPTER 11 Thinking and Language

PSYCHOLOGY JOURNAL

In your journal, answer the following question: If you increase the size of your vocabulary, will you think better? Use past experiences to explain your answer. ■

PSYCHOLOGY Online

Chapter Overview
Visit the *Understanding Psychology* Web site at glencoe.com and click on **Chapter 11—Chapter Overviews** to preview the chapter.

294

TWO-MINUTE LESSON LAUNCHER

Creative people have the ability to think flexibly and develop many unique solutions. One test developed by J.P. Guilford to test creativity is to find unique uses for common, everyday objects. Give every student in the class a common, everyday object such as a glass, a paper clip, a pair of scissors, and so on. Randomly assign students to work in pairs. Tell them that they are to combine their items in some way to make a new object that serves some purpose. Ask volunteers to share their new invention. **Ask: How did you use creativity to make the new object? In what ways did you have to overcome set mental patterns to complete the assignment? What gave you the insight to complete the task?**

SECTION 1 Thinking and Problem Solving

Reader's Guide

■ Main Idea

Thinking involves changing and reorganizing the information stored in memory to create new or transformed information, such as creative problem-solving strategies.

■ Vocabulary

- thinking
- image
- symbol
- concept
- prototype
- rule
- metacognition
- algorithm
- heuristic
- mental set
- functional fixedness
- creativity
- flexibility
- recombination
- insight

■ Objectives

- Identify the units of thought and the kinds of thinking.
- Explain strategies for and obstacles to problem solving.

EXPLORING PSYCHOLOGY

A Radical Assumption

Historians often refer to "the Copernican revolution" as a milestone in the history of science. Copernicus was a careful and creative scientist who eventually solved a problem that others before him had failed to solve: how to account for the movement of the planets in the heavens. . . . Copernicus finally created a theory that nicely predicted the movements of the planets. To do so, however, he had to make a radical assumption. Prior to Copernicus, everyone had taken it for granted that the sun and the other planets revolve around the Earth, and indeed, it looks that way to the naked eye. Copernicus argued that, if one made this assumption, it would be impossible to predict with accuracy the movement of the planets. His theory began with an alternate assumption, namely, that the Earth and the other planets in our solar system revolve around the sun.

—from *The Ideal Problem Solver* by John D. Bransford and Barry S. Stein, 1984

Going beyond memory, how do we think? How do we solve problems? How do we create ideas? How did Copernicus come up with his idea? If storage and retrieval were the only processes we used to handle information, human beings would be little more than glorified cameras and VCRs. Yet we are capable of doing things with information that make the most complex computers seem simple by comparison. These processes—thinking and problem solving—are most impressive when they show originality or creativity.

SECTION RESOURCES

Reproducible Masters

- Guided Reading Activity 11–1
- Vocabulary Activity 11–1
- Section Quiz 11–1

Transparencies

- Daily Focus Transparency 11–1

Multimedia

- *ExamView® Assessment Suite* CD-ROM
- Presentation Plus! Software

1 FOCUS

Section Objectives

1. Identify the units of thought and the kinds of thinking.
2. Explain strategies for and obstacles to problem solving.

BELLRINGER
Motivational Activity

Project Daily Focus Transparency 11–1 and have students answer the questions.

Available as blackline master

Daily Focus Transparency 11–1

Reader's Guide

Use the Reader's Guide to introduce concepts and vocabulary.

■ Exploring Psychology

Ask students to read the **Exploring Psychology** feature. Then ask: **In what ways did Copernicus's assumption show creativity and originality? Why was it difficult for people to accept Copernicus's discoveries?**

■ Vocabulary Precheck

Have students create a matching puzzle by writing the terms in one column and the Glossary definitions in random order in a second column. Have pairs of students trade and complete puzzles.

2 TEACH

L1 Classifying Information Have students work in small groups to design a chart classifying examples of the five units of thought: images, symbols, concepts, prototypes, and rules. Encourage students to illustrate at least some of the entries. After students have shared their charts, point out that to complete this assignment, they used a critical thinking skill known as classification. **Ask: Is classification an example of directed or nondirected thinking?** ELL BLOCK SCHEDULING

TEACHER Tip

Tell students that concepts are stored in memory using complex networks. These are links that interrelate concepts. For example, food would be linked to meat, vegetables, and fruit. Networks have many branches. For example, asparagus, peas, and corn are linked to vegetables, which in turn are linked to food. Explain that researchers have discovered that knowing one word in a network allows other words in the network to be recalled more quickly.

Guided Reading Activity 11-1

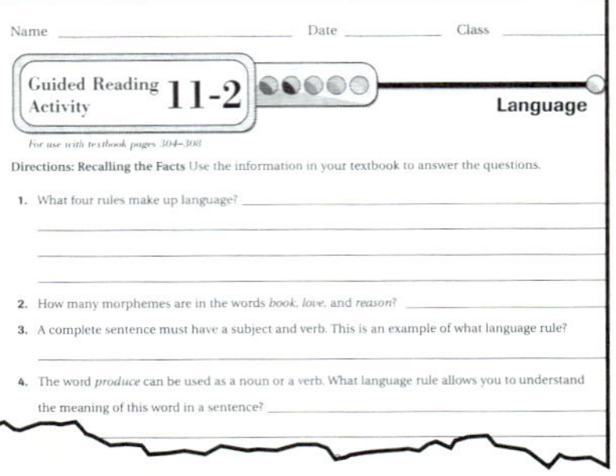
Name ______ Date ______ Class ______

Guided Reading Activity 11-2

Language

Directions: Recalling the Facts Use the information in your textbook to answer the questions.

1. What four rules make up language?
2. How many morphemes are in the words *book, love,* and *reason?*
3. A complete sentence must have a subject and verb. This is an example of what language rule?
4. The word *produce* can be used as a noun or a verb. What language rule allows you to understand the meaning of this word in a sentence?

THINKING

thinking: changing and reorganizing the information stored in memory to create new information

You may view **thinking** as changing and reorganizing the information stored in memory to create new or transformed information. By thinking, for example, humans are able to put together any combination of words from memory and create sentences never devised before, such as this one.

Units of Thought

image: a visual, mental representation of an event or object

The processes of thought depend on several devices, or units of thought: images, symbols, concepts, prototypes, and rules. One very basic unit of thought is an **image,** a visual, mental representation of a specific event or object. The representation is not usually an exact copy; rather, it contains only the highlights of the original. For example, if an adult tries to visualize a grandmother who died when he was seven, he would probably remember only a few details—perhaps the color of her hair or a piece of jewelry she wore—without a portrait or photo.

Imaging is an effective way to think about concepts. In 1971 two researchers (Shepard & Metzler) presented participants with 1,600 pairs of geometric images (see Figure 11.1). The researchers then asked the participants to determine if the objects in each pair were identical or different. The researchers discovered that the participants completed the task by rotating an image of one of the objects in their minds in an effort to see both patterns from the same perspective.

symbol: an abstract unit of thought that represents an object or quality; anything that stands for or represents something else

Another abstract unit of thought is a **symbol,** a sound, object, or design that represents an object or quality. The most common symbols in thinking are words; every word is a symbol that stands for something other than itself. An image represents a specific sight or sound, but a symbol may have a number of meanings. That symbols differ from the things they represent enables us to think about things that are not present, to consider the past and future, and to imagine things and situations that never will be or never were. Numbers, letters, punctuation marks, and icons are all familiar symbols of ideas that have no concrete existence.

concept: a label for a class of objects or events that have at least one attribute in common

When a symbol is used as a label for a class of objects or events with at least one common attribute—or for the attribute itself—it is called a **concept.** *Animals, music, liquid,* and *beautiful people* are examples of concepts based on the common attributes of the objects and experiences belonging to each category. Thus the concept *animal* separates a group of organisms from such things as automobiles, carrots, and Roquefort cheese. Concepts enable us to chunk large amounts of information. We do not have to treat every new piece of information as unique, since we already know something about the class of objects or experiences to which the new item belongs.

prototype: a representative example of a concept

When we think of a concept, we often think of a representative example of it. When you think of a vehicle, for example, you might picture a car or a truck. This representation is called a **prototype.** The prototype you picture may not be an example that you have actually experienced. Most often it simply is an example that has most of the characteristics of the particular concept.

COOPERATIVE LEARNING ACTIVITY

Encouraging Creativity Organize students into groups and ask the members of each group to imagine they are a team of child-care workers at a new learning center for young children. Challenge them to write a list of "Dos" and "Do Nots" on a poster titled "Creating Creativity." Next, assign students to develop a list of activities and/or games that might encourage creativity. Have a member from each group share its plan with the class. **BLOCK SCHEDULING**

A more complex unit of thought is a **rule,** a statement of a relation between concepts. The following are examples of rules: a person cannot be in two places at the same time; mass remains constant despite changes in appearance.

Images, symbols, concepts, prototypes, and rules are the building blocks of mental activity. They provide an economical and efficient way for people to represent reality, to manipulate and reorganize it, and to devise new ways of acting. For example, a person can think about pursuing several different careers, weigh their pros and cons, and decide which to pursue without having to try every one of them.

Kinds of Thinking

People think in several ways. *Directed thinking* is a systematic and logical attempt to reach a specific goal or answer, such as the solution to a math problem. This kind of thinking, also called *convergent thinking,* depends on symbols, concepts, and rules. Directed thinking is deliberate and purposeful. It is through directed thinking that we solve problems; formulate and follow rules; and set, work toward, and achieve goals.

In contrast, another type, called *nondirected* (or *divergent*) *thinking,* consists of a free flow of thoughts with no particular plan and depends more on images (see Figure 11.2).

Nondirected thinking is usually rich with imagery and feelings such as daydreams, fantasies, and reveries. People often engage in nondirected thought when they are relaxing or escaping from boredom or worry. This kind of thinking may provide unexpected insights into one's goals and beliefs. Scientists and artists say that some of their best ideas emerge from drifting thoughts that occur when they have set aside a problem for the moment.

A third type of thinking is **metacognition,** or thinking about thinking. When you tackle an algebra problem and cannot solve it, thinking about your strategy may cause you to change to another strategy.

PROBLEM SOLVING

One of the main functions of directed thinking is to solve problems—to bridge the gap mentally between a present situation and a desired goal. The gap may be between hunger and food, a column of figures and a

Figure 11.1 Using Imagery

Rotate pairs of images of the patterns below in your mind to make them match. Do the drawings in each pair represent the same object, or are they different objects? (Check with your teacher to find out which pairs match.) ***How do we use images when we are thinking about something?***

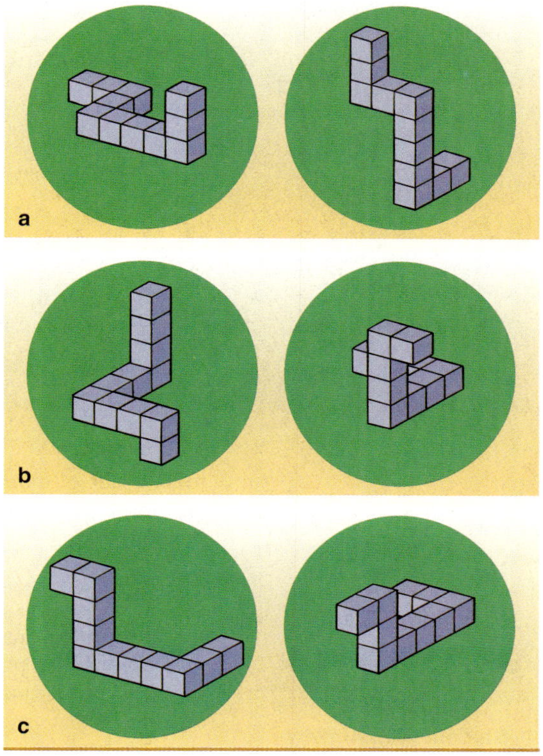

Reading Check What is the difference between a symbol and a concept? An image and a prototype?

rule: a statement of relation between concepts

metacognition: the awareness of or thinking about one's own cognitive processes

MEETING SPECIAL NEEDS

Learning Style: Logical/Mathematical Provide students with various types of paper-based puzzles or brainteasers. Students may work individually or in pairs to solve them, keeping a copy of each attempted solution. Direct students to use storyboards to record each attempt at a solution. For each attempt, have students write down the strategies or approaches used to solve the problem. **Ask:** **Did thinking about problem-solving strategies and approaches help you solve the puzzle more quickly? Explain. L2** **BLOCK SCHEDULING**

Refer to ***Inclusion for the High School Social Studies Classroom Strategies and Activities*** in the TCR for strategies for students with different learning styles.

Figure 11.1

Visual Instruction Explain to students that they must create mental images to solve this puzzle. Roger Shepard and Jacqueline Metzler used similar images in an experiment in 1971 and concluded that imagined vision (mental imagery) is very similar to real vision. Pairs (a) and (b) are the same objects, whereas the objects in (c) do not match.

Caption Answer We use images to represent events or objects. The images are not usually exact copies of the original.

Applying Psychology

Tell students that our boundaries for concepts can be fuzzy. Many items may be classified in more than one category. For example, visit a convenience store and survey the variety of beverages offered for sale. Which ones would you classify as soft drinks? Do you see any beverages that one person may think of as a soft drink and another think of as a fruit drink or some other category of beverage? Ask students to think of another concept that may have fuzzy boundaries and have them set up an experiment to test their theories.

Reading Check Answer A symbol is an abstract unit of thought that represents an object or quality, while a concept is a label for a class of objects that share at least one common attribute. An image is a visual, mental representation of an event or object, while a prototype is a representative example of a concept.

Figure 11.2

Visual Instruction Ask for a volunteer to read De Bono's problem aloud. Then challenge students to solve it in two minutes. Have class members share their answers.

Caption Answer People are most likely to engage in nondirected thinking when they are relaxing or trying to escape from stress or boredom.

PSYCHOLOGY Online

Links and instructional guidelines can be found in the **Web Activity Lesson Plan** at glencoe.com.

PSYCHOLOGY JOURNAL

Ask students to list examples of problem-solving techniques that they have learned. For each, students should write an example of the type of problem for which they would use the strategy. Ask them to illustrate the relationship between intermediate goals and terminal goals during problem solving. ■

Vocabulary Activity 11–1

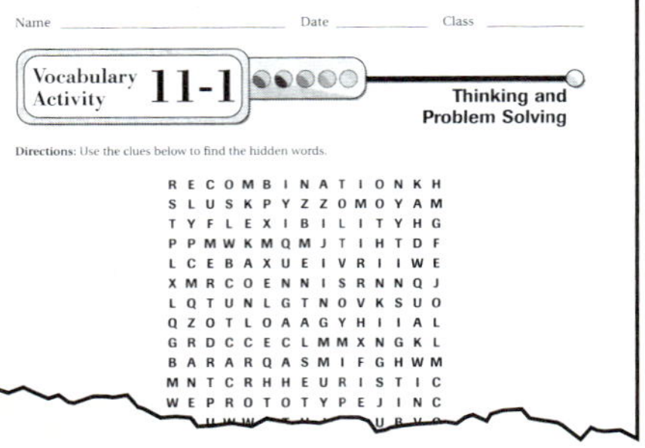

Name ______ Date ______ Class ______

Vocabulary Activity 11-1

Thinking and Problem Solving

Directions: Use the clues below to find the hidden words.

R	E	C	O	M	B	I	N	A	T	I	O	N	K	H
S	L	U	S	K	P	Y	Z	Z	O	M	O	Y	A	M
T	Y	F	L	E	X	I	B	I	L	I	T	Y	H	G
P	P	M	W	K	M	Q	M	J	T	I	H	T	D	F
L	C	E	B	A	X	U	E	I	V	R	I	I	W	E
X	M	R	C	O	E	N	N	I	S	R	N	N	Q	J
L	Q	T	U	N	L	G	T	N	O	V	K	S	U	O
Q	Z	O	T	L	O	A	A	G	Y	H	I	I	A	L
G	R	D	C	C	E	C	L	M	M	X	N	G	K	L
B	A	R	A	R	Q	A	S	M	I	F	G	H	W	M
M	N	T	C	R	H	H	E	U	R	I	S	T	I	C
W	E	P	R	O	T	O	T	Y	P	E	J	I	N	C

Figure 11.2 Directed vs. Nondirected Thinking

This problem was devised by psychologist Edward De Bono, who believes that conventional directed thinking is insufficient for solving new and unusual problems. His approach to problem solving requires use of nondirected thinking to generate new ways of looking at the problem situation. (The answer to this problem is provided in Figure 11.7.) ***When are people most likely to engage in nondirected thinking?***

total, a lack of money and bills to pay, or cancer and a cure. In all these examples, getting from the problem to the solution requires some directed thinking.

Strategies

Problem solving depends on the use of strategies, or specific methods for approaching problems. One strategy is to break down a complex problem into a number of smaller, more easily solved subgoals. *Subgoals* are intermediate steps toward a solution. For example, it is the end of the semester and your life is falling apart. You do not even have time to tie your shoelaces. You solve the problem by breaking it down into small pieces: studying for a science exam, finishing that overdue paper, canceling your dinner date, scheduling regular study breaks to maintain what is left of your sanity, and so forth.

For some problems, you may work backward from the goal you have set. Mystery writers often use this method: They decide how to end the story ("who did it") and then devise a plot leading to this conclusion.

Another problem may require you to examine various ways of reaching a desired goal. Suppose a woman needs to be in Chicago by 11 A.M. on July 7 for a business conference. She checks train departures and arrivals, airline schedules, and car-rental companies. The only train to Chicago that morning arrives at 5 A.M. (too early), and the first plane arrives at 11:30 A.M. (too late). So she decides to rent a car and drive.

PSYCHOLOGY Online

Student Web Activity
Visit the *Understanding Psychology* Web site at glencoe.com and click on **Chapter 11—Student Web Activities** for an activity on thinking and problem solving.

CRITICAL THINKING ACTIVITY

Synthesizing Information Request volunteers to play a game of charades for the class. Each volunteer should think of a phrase to act out through the use of gestures. Ask them to choose a category, such as movies or song titles, from which to pick their phrases. The rest of the class should use the techniques of memory retrieval—such as recall and recognition—to solve the problem of interpreting wordless communication. When the exercise is done, **ask:** **Did you devise a set of strategies to approach the charades? Did anyone experience a feeling of insight in figuring out the answer? L1 ELL**

To determine which strategy to use, most of us analyze the problem to see if it resembles a situation we have experienced in the past. A strategy that worked in the past is likely to work again. We tend to do things the way we have done them before, and often, we shy away from new situations that call for new strategies. The more unusual the problem, the more difficult it is to devise a strategy for dealing with it.

Algorithms An **algorithm** is a fixed set of procedures that, if followed correctly, will lead to a solution. Mathematical and scientific formulas are algorithms. For example, to find the product of 345 and 23, we multiply the numbers according to the rules of multiplication to get a correct answer of 7,935. To play chess or checkers, we follow algorithms, or a fixed set of rules.

algorithm: a step-by-step procedure for solving a problem

Heuristics While algorithms can be useful in finding solutions, they are a time-consuming method. People often use shortcuts to solve problems, and these shortcuts are called heuristics. **Heuristics** are experimental strategies, or rules of thumb, that simplify a problem, allowing one to solve problems quickly and easily (see Figure 11.3). For example, when watching the Wheel of Fortune game show, you might use what you already know about prefixes, suffixes, and roots of words to fill in the missing letters of a word or phrase. If a friend comes to you with a problem, your advice might include what has worked for you in the past.

heuristic: a rule-of-thumb problem-solving strategy

mental set: a habitual strategy or pattern of problem solving

Although heuristics allow us to make quick decisions, they can result in bad decisions because we make the decisions using shortcuts and sometimes ignore pertinent information.

Obstacles to Problem Solving

There are times when certain useful strategies become cemented into the problem-solving process. When a particular strategy becomes a habit, it is called a **mental set**—you are set to treat problems in a certain way. For example, a chess player may always attempt to control the four center squares of the chessboard. Whenever her opponent attacks, she responds by looking for ways to

Figure 11.3 Types of Heuristics

Heuristics are mental shortcuts. Although they are not rules that always provide the correct answers, they are strategies that experience has taught us to apply. ***What is the availability heuristic?***

1. **Availability Heuristic:** We rely on information that is more prominent or easily recalled and overlook information that is available but less prominent.
   Example: In the news, we see people winning the lottery all the time and overestimate our chances at winning it also.
2. **Representativeness Heuristic:** We tend to assume that if an item is similar to members of a particular category, it is probably a member of that category, too.
   Example: I have flipped a coin 10 times and it has landed on tails every time. The odds are it will land on heads this time. (The odds are 50–50, as they are for each coin toss.)
3. **Anchoring Heuristic:** We make decisions based on certain ideas, or standards, that are important to us.
   Example: In my family, everyone gets up by 8:00 A.M. every day, including weekends. I believe that only lazy people sleep past 8:00 A.M. (I formed a judgment about other people based on a standard in my family.)

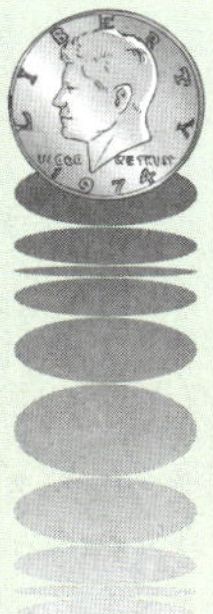

Figure 11.3

Visual Instruction Remind students that although heuristics are faster than algorithms, they are not always as reliable.

Caption Answer the mental shortcut we use when we rely on information that is more prominent or easily recalled and overlook information that is available but less prominent

CURRICULUM CONNECTION

Mathematics Write the following on the board:

1.	H	H	H	H	H	H
2.	H	T	T	H	T	H

Ask: What would you predict the next flip to be in each sequence? Most students will predict tails as the next flip for both. They are using a heuristic known as representativeness, in which they compare an event to a prototype. Students don't expect a coin toss to repeatedly turn up heads, so they predict tails for the next toss. According to probability rules, however, each flip is an independent action, meaning that there is a 50 percent chance for either outcome regardless of previous results. Thus, while representativeness can be useful, it can lead to illogical decisions.

PSYCHOLOGY LAB EXPERIMENT

Directed and Nondirected Thinking Use the following demonstration to determine if a person is a directed thinker. On a sheet of paper, have participants quickly write down the answer to these questions: **What is the color of snow?** *(white)* **What do cows drink?** *(The answer is "water," but a surprising number of people will say "milk.")* Explain to participants that directed thinkers may not answer the question spontaneously. Instead they will think it through and come up with the correct answer—water. Participants who respond with their first free association will probably say milk because they will link milk and white with cows. This is an example of nondirected thinking. **Ask: Which method of thinking do you think is most creative? Why? L1** **BLOCK SCHEDULING**

CHAPTER 11
Section 1, pages 295–302

Figure 11.4

Visual Instruction Have students draw nine dots on a separate sheet of paper. Ask them to work out the solution and put their pencils down when they have completed the activity. After one minute, provide the following hint: the lines can extend beyond the dots. Give students a few more minutes to complete the activity, then have a volunteer share the solution.

Caption Answer Our mental sets make us see the nine dots as a closed shape and we think that we must stay within its boundaries.

Figure 11.5

Visual Instruction Have students work in pairs, with one as the participant and the other the observer. The participant should talk through the process that he or she is performing to solve this problem. The observer should write down how the participant solved the problem.

Caption Answer Functional fixedness may prevent the participant from seeing the boxes as having functions other than holding candles and matches.

3 ASSESS

Assign Section 1 Assessment as homework or as an in-class activity.

Figure 11.4 Connecting the Dots

Connect all nine dots shown by drawing four straight lines without lifting your pencil from the paper or retracing any lines. (The answer appears in Figure 11.7.) ***How does following a mental set sometimes interfere with problem solving?***

regain control of those four squares. She has a set for this strategy. If this set helps her win, fine. Sometimes, however, a set interferes with problem solving, and then it is called rigidity. You probably know the old riddle "What is black, white, and read all over? A newspaper." When you say the riddle, the word *read* sounds like *red*, which is why some people cannot guess the answer. *Read* is heard as part of the black and white set—it is interpreted as being a color. If you asked, "What is black and white and read by people every day?" the correct answer would be obvious—and boring.

One form of set that can interfere with problem solving is **functional fixedness**—the inability to imagine new uses for familiar objects. In experiments on functional fixedness, people are asked to solve a problem that requires them to use a familiar object in an unfamiliar way (Duncker, 1945). Because they are set to use the object in the usual way, people tend to pay attention only to the features of the object that relate to its everyday use (see Figures 11.4 and 11.5). They respond in a rigid way.

Another type of rigidity occurs when a person makes a wrong assumption about a problem. In Figure 11.6, for example, the problem is to arrange the six matches into four equilateral triangles. Most people have trouble solving this puzzle because they falsely assume that they must stay within a two-dimensional figure.

People trying to solve the kind of problem described in the *Psychology and You* feature on page 301 experience a third kind of rigidity. Most people look for direct methods of solving problems and do not see solutions that require several intermediate steps.

Rigidity can be overcome if the person realizes that his or her strategy is not working and looks for other ways to approach the problem. The more familiar the situation, the more difficult this will be. Rigidity is less likely to occur with unusual problems. Many individuals are trained, through formal education, to think of only one way to do things. Rigidity can be overcome by thinking about—or being taught to think about—and analyzing situations from many perspectives.

functional fixedness: the inability to imagine new uses for familiar objects

creativity: the capacity to use information and/or abilities in new and original ways

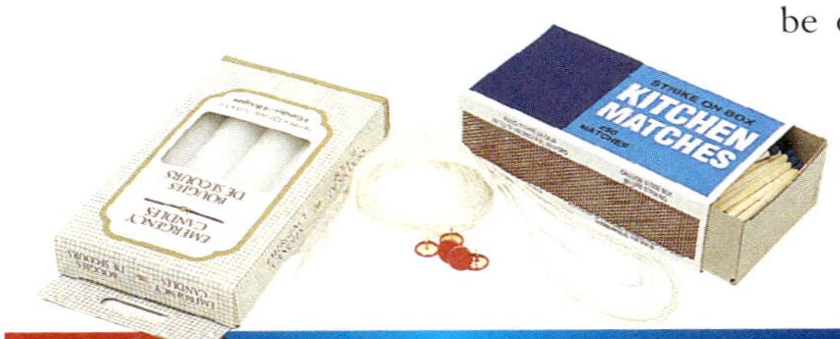

Figure 11.5 Overcoming Functional Fixedness

Given the materials pictured here, how would you go about mounting a candle vertically on a wooden wall in such a way that it can be lit? (The solution is presented in Figure 11.7.) ***How might functional fixedness make it difficult to solve this problem?***

CREATIVITY

The ability to use information in such a way that the result is somehow new, original, and meaningful is **creativity.** All problem solving requires some creativity. Certain ways of solving problems, however, are simply more brilliant or beautiful or efficient than others. Psychologists do not know exactly why some people are able to think more creatively than others, although they have identified some of the characteristics of creative thinking, including flexibility and the ability to recombine elements to achieve insight.

INTERDISCIPLINARY CONNECTIONS ACTIVITY

History Remind students of Copernicus's radical assumption. Assign them to research other famous inventors or geniuses. Examples include Marie Curie, Albert Einstein, Thomas Edison, or Henry Ford. Have students write a short biography that presents the original solution, idea, or invention developed by each person. Then have them assess some of the character traits that encouraged creativity in the individual. In a follow-up discussion, share the following statements from John Dryden ("Genius must be born, and never taught") and Thomas Edison ("Genius is 10 percent inspiration and 90 percent perspiration"). **Ask:** **In terms of psychology, which statement do you agree with? Which is more valid? L2** **BLOCK SCHEDULING**

Flexibility

The ability to overcome rigidity is **flexibility.** Psychologists have devised a number of ingenious tests to measure flexibility. In one test, psychologists ask people how many uses they can imagine for a single object, such as a brick or a paper clip. The more uses a person can devise, the more flexible he or she is said to be. Whether such tests actually measure creativity is debatable. Nevertheless, it is obvious that inflexible, rigid thinking leads to unoriginal solutions or no solutions at all.

Recombination

When the elements of a problem are familiar but the required solution is not, it may be achieved by **recombination,** a new mental arrangement of the elements. In football and basketball, for example, there are no new moves—only recombinations of old ones. Such recombination seems to be a vital part of creativity. Many creative people say that no truly great poem, no original invention, has ever been produced by someone who has not spent years studying his or her subject. The creative person is able to take the information that he or she and others have compiled and put it together in a totally new way. The brilliant philosopher and mathematician Sir Isaac Newton, who discovered the laws of motion, once said, "If I have seen further, it is by standing on the shoulders of giants." In other words, he was able to recombine the discoveries of the great scientists who had preceded him to uncover new and more far-reaching truths.

Insight

The sudden emergence of a solution by recombination of elements is called **insight.** Insight usually occurs when problems have proved resistant to all problem-solving efforts and strategies. The scientist, artist, or, in fact, anyone can reach a point of high frustration and temporarily abandon a task. Yet the recombination process seems to continue on an unconscious level. When the person is absorbed in some other activity, the answer seems to appear out of nowhere. This sudden insight has appropriately been called the "aha" experience.

Certain animals appear to experience this same cycle of frustration, temporary diversion (during which time the problem incubates), and then sudden insight. For example, Wolfgang Köhler (1976) placed a chimpanzee in a cage where a cluster of bananas was hung out of its reach. Also in the cage were several wooden boxes. At first the chimpanzee tried various unsuccessful ways of getting at the fruit. Finally it sat down, apparently giving up, and simply stared straight ahead for a while. Then suddenly it jumped up, piled three boxes on top of one another, climbed to the top of the pile, and grabbed the bananas.

Psychology and You

Solve This Problem

How would you go about solving this problem? A man and his two sons want to get across a river. The boat they have available can hold a maximum of only 200 pounds. The father weighs 200 pounds and the sons weigh 100 pounds each. How can all three people cross the river? (You'll find the answer in Figure 11.7.)

Figure 11.6 Overcoming Wrong Assumptions

Arrange these six matches so that they form four equilateral triangles. (The solution appears in Figure 11.7.) ***What are two characteristics of creative thinking?***

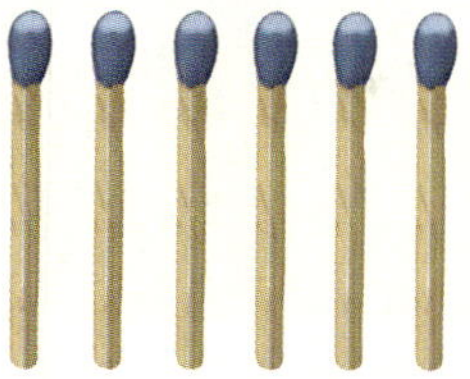

flexibility: the ability to overcome rigidity, to remain open to alternate strategies

recombination: rearranging the elements of a problem to arrive at an original solution

insight: the apparent sudden realization of the solution to a problem

CHAPTER 11
Section 1, pages 295–302

Figure 11.6

Visual Instruction Provide matches or sections of wooden sticks for students to manipulate into triangles.

Caption Answer Creative thinking requires flexibility and recombination.

Psychology and You

Use the following questions to direct a class discussion after students have read the **Psychology and You** feature.

Ask: **What creative processes did you use to solve this problem? How is this a good test of creativity?**

Section Quiz 11-1

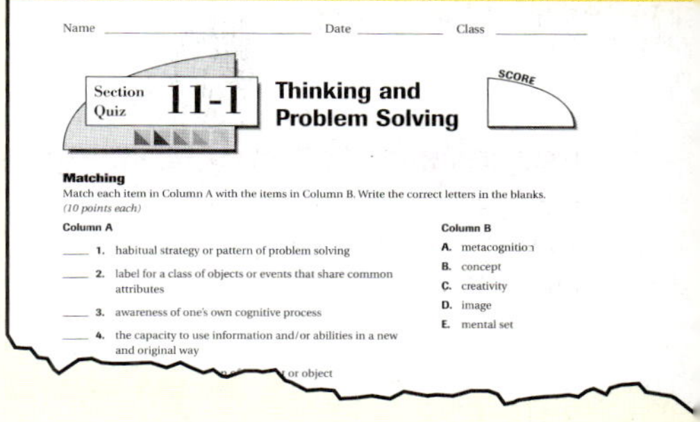

Name ______ Date ______ Class ______

Section Quiz 11-1 Thinking and Problem Solving

SCORE

Matching
Match each item in Column A with the items in Column B. Write the correct letters in the blanks.
(10 points each)

Column A

____ 1. habitual strategy or pattern of problem solving

____ 2. label for a class of objects or events that share common attributes

____ 3. awareness of one's own cognitive process

____ 4. the capacity to use information and/or abilities in a new and original way

Column B

A. metacognition
B. concept
C. creativity
D. image
E. mental set

EXTENDING THE CONTENT

Functional Fixedness Arrange two rulers and a number of distracter objects (such as a small ball, coins, and toy blocks) on a table. Using masking tape, create a border around the objects. Next to the table, place two desks so that there is approximately one and one-half feet beyond arm's length between them. Place a peg and a ring on one desk. Ask a volunteer to sit at the second desk. Give the student the following task: place the ring over the peg without leaving or moving the desk. The problem can be solved by using the tape border to connect the two rulers, which can then be used to complete the task. Explain that the activity demonstrates the concept of functional fixedness—the tape's function as a border inhibits its recognition as a potential tool. **L2** **ELL**

Figure 11.7

Visual Instruction Point out to students that the answers to Figures 11.2, 11.4, 11.5, 11.6, and the **Psychology and You** feature are included in Figure 11.7.

Reteach

Have students share instances when a solution to a seemingly unsolvable problem came out of nowhere. Ask students how the solution demonstrates insight.

Enrich

Write the following quote by Sidney Sugarman on the board: "Teach the young people how to think, not what to think." Ask students to write a one-page essay explaining the difference between learning how to think and learning what to think.

4 CLOSE

Assign groups of students to list common algorithms and heuristics that are used in different academic disciplines, such as mathematics, geography, history, and chemistry.

Figure 11.7 Answers to Pages 298, 300, and 301

page 298

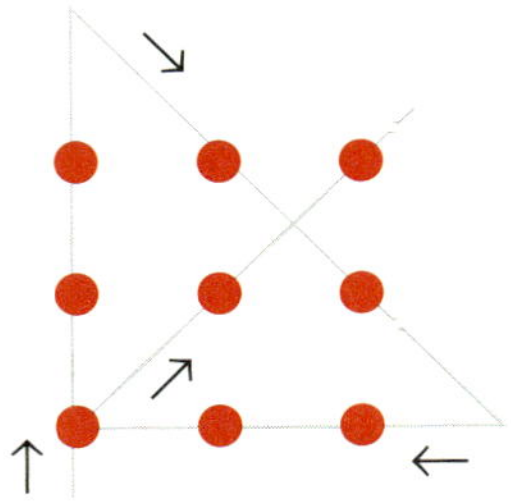

page 300

page 300

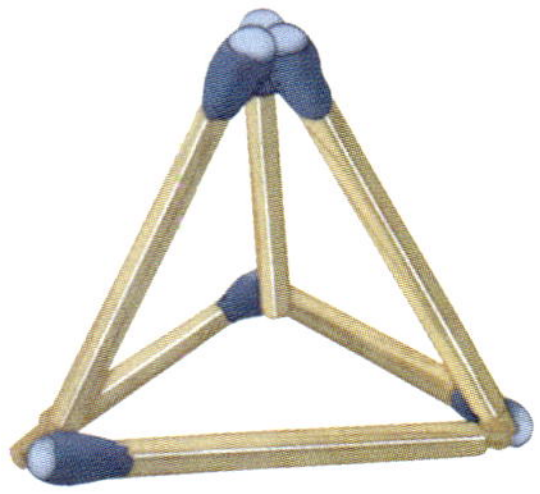

page 301

"F" represents "Father," and each "S" represents a "Son."

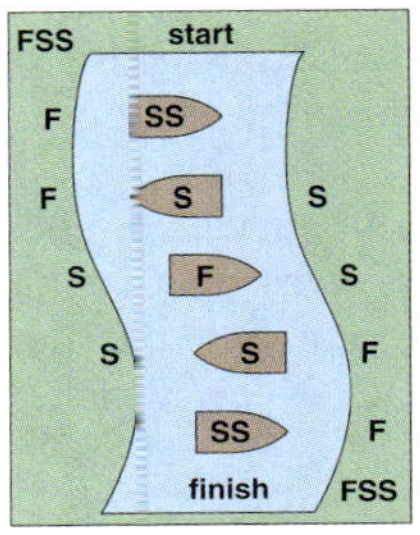

page 301

SECTION 1 Assessment

1. **Review the Vocabulary** Describe two obstacles to problem solving.
2. **Visualize the Main Idea** In a diagram similar to the one below, describe the characteristics of creative thinking.

Characteristics of Creative Thinking

3. **Recall Information** What is the difference between convergent and divergent thinking? Give specific examples.
4. **Think Critically** If you were a teacher, would you allow students to solve math problems using different approaches if they reached the same answer? Why?
5. **Application Activity** Focus on a favorite board game. Provide a written description of problem-solving techniques you would use to win the game. Compare your strategies with those of your classmates.

SECTION 1 Assessment Answers

1. A mental set is a strategy that has been used repeatedly and has become a habit. Functional fixedness is the inability to imagine new uses for objects.
2. Flexibility is the ability to overcome rigidity and functional fixedness. Recombination is the ability to group items in new and different ways. Insight is the apparent sudden realization of the solution to a problem.
3. Convergent thinking is a systematic, logical approach to problem solving that relies on symbols, concepts, and rules. Most people use convergent thinking to balance their checkbooks. Nondirected thinking involves free association of ideas in random order with no particular goal or plan. A person may create a layout for a new flower bed using nondirected thinking.
4. Teachers should allow different approaches as long as the approach does not lead to faulty thinking or incorrect solutions when applied to other types of problems.
5. Students' answers will vary. Recommend board games like Monopoly that involve some element of skill, not simply chance.

Case Studies

Checkmate

Period of Study: 1997

Introduction: On May 11, 1997, the final match of a rematch took place in the contemplative game of chess. The champion of the previous match, which had taken place a year earlier, was Garry Kasparov, a former scientist. Many consider Kasparov to be the best chess player to have ever lived. Kasparov's opponent was Deep Blue, a computer.

Hypothesis: The idea of a human versus a machine fascinated experts in a wide range of scientific studies. Most of them had the highest confidence in Kasparov's chances to defeat the computer for the second time. Psychologists believed that a computer preprogrammed with information of any kind would prove no match for the thought capacity and perceptions of the human mind. Even though Deep Blue was programmed to play the game of chess with perfection, a nonfeeling and nonthinking machine could not defeat the ability of the human mind to think abstractly. A machine could also not match the human mind's feelings of determination and desire.

Method: As we know, computers are not thinkers—they can only do what they are programmed to do. Deep Blue, however, has amazing capacities. It can consider 300 million possible chess moves per second. With each of these 300 million possibilities, Deep Blue is programmed to assess the situation these moves will put it in. The human brain can evaluate only a very small fraction of moves compared to what Deep Blue can do. The Deep Blue defeated by Kasparov the previous year was an earlier version of the 1997 model. A victory for Deep Blue could mean computers would not have to operate like a human brain to surpass it.

For his rematch with Deep Blue, Kasparov planned to copy his strategy from the previous year. This would involve using the early match (in a series of matches) to inspect the mighty computer for weaknesses and then to exploit those weaknesses (Anand, 1997).

Results: Deep Blue, the computer, defeated Kasparov. Experts explained that Kasparov's defeat was the result of comparing Deep Blue too much to the version he had played against the year before. The new and improved Deep Blue seemed to use moves that were very human-like. For every seemingly well-conceived move Kasparov made, the computer countered in devastating ways.

The time-consuming chess game robbed Kasparov of much of his concentration, whereas Deep Blue displayed no fatigue, frustration, or other human weaknesses. Now that psychologists know a human's mental capacity can be outmatched by a computer's programming, what assumptions can they make? Can a machine really prove to be more intelligent than the person who creates it? Do the physical limitations or the emotions of humans prevent us from using our full brain capacity? These questions and others like them may not be answered for years to come. This situation is new, and further testing in this area is needed to assess the issues accurately.

Analyzing the Case Study

1. Why was Kasparov favored to win the rematch?
2. What advantages did each opponent bring to the contest?
3. **Critical Thinking** Why were psychologists interested in the rematch between these two opponents?

Going Further

Kasparov vs. the World

In a unique chess match via the Internet that began in June 1999 and continued for several months, Kasparov squared off against all the players in the world who wanted to participate. A panel of grand masters suggested the world team's possible moves. An estimated 10,000 players worldwide then cast their votes on the world team's moves. The move that received the greatest number of votes was used. The game lasted four months, longer than most experts expected. Kasparov won the hard-fought battle, retaining the title of the world's greatest human chess player.

Discussing the Case Study

Ask: **What did psychologists learn from this match?** *(Psychologists learned that a computer can be programmed to defeat the human ability to think abstractly and creatively.)* **Do you think computers can be more intelligent than the humans who make them? In what ways?** *(In this scenario, computers can process more information and arrive at the best solution to a given set of problems. This computer would still require human programming to use its processing power in other ways.)* **What are the possible consequences to society if computers can be made more intelligent than humans?** *(Society may benefit if the intelligence is geared toward solving complex problems.)*

Answers for Analyzing the Case Study

1. Kasparov was believed to have greater thought power and creativity. Experts believed that a computer preprogrammed with information would prove no match for the abstract thought capacity and perceptions of the human mind. In addition, Kasparov had defeated a previous version of Deep Blue one year earlier.
2. Kasparov brought experience, ability to spot and exploit weaknesses, and passion. Deep Blue brought the capacity to process 300 million possible moves per second. Deep Blue also would not become fatigued or frustrated.
3. Psychologists wanted to know if computers could be more intelligent than their human makers. They also sought to understand how emotions and physical limitations affect human behavior.

1 FOCUS

Section Objectives

1. Explain the structure of language.
2. Describe how children develop language.

BELLRINGER
Motivational Activity

Project Daily Focus Transparency 11–2 and have students answer the questions.

Available as blackline master

Daily Focus Transparency 11–2

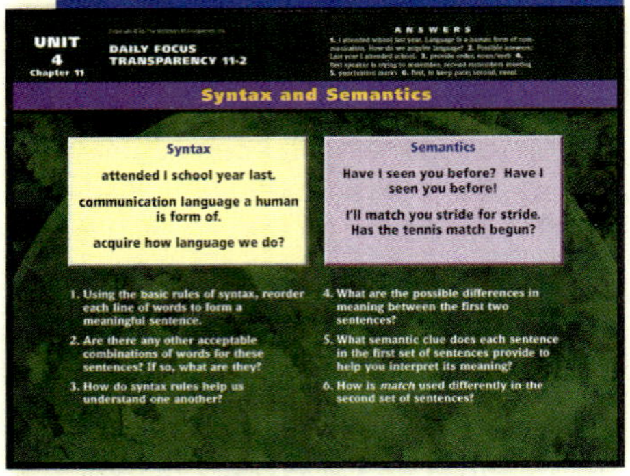

Reader's Guide

Use the Reader's Guide to introduce concepts and vocabulary.

Exploring Psychology

Ask students to read the **Exploring Psychology** feature and then discuss: **Why are the experiences of hearing your own language spoken so different from hearing another language spoken?**

Vocabulary Precheck

Have students read the Glossary definition of each word. Then have students create a list of at least three examples for each of the terms.

Use the **Vocabulary PuzzleMaker CD-ROM** to create crossword and word search puzzles.

SECTION 2 Language

Reader's Guide

Main Idea

Language and thought are closely related. Language requires the learning of a set of complex rules and symbols, yet most people have little difficulty learning their native language.

Vocabulary

- language
- phoneme
- morpheme
- syntax
- semantics

Objectives

- Explain the structure of language.
- Describe how children develop language.

EXPLORING PSYCHOLOGY

What Language Do You Understand?

Listen to someone speaking a language you do not know. You hear an unsung song, ever changing, rising and falling, occasionally illuminated by flashes of feeling. The sounds themselves are little more than vocal noises. If there are words, you cannot disentangle them; if there is a message, you cannot understand it. Interest evaporates. You might as well stare at a brick wall.

Now listen to a good friend. It is the same kind of vocalization, but you cannot hear it in the same way. The noises are there, but they are totally transparent. Your mind passes right through the sounds, through the words, through the sentences, and into the mind of your friend. Your experience is totally different.

—from *The Science of Words* by George A. Miller, 1991

Of all the things we do, nothing seems as complex and as important as understanding and speaking a language. We must learn thousands of words and a limited number of rules of grammar to make sense of those words to communicate and share ideas.

THE STRUCTURE OF LANGUAGE

language: the expression of ideas through symbols and sounds that are arranged according to rules

Do you ever talk to yourself? Some people talk to themselves when they are thinking or solving a problem. When we are talking or thinking, we are using language. What is language? **Language** is a system of

SECTION RESOURCES

Reproducible Masters

- Guided Reading Activity 11–2
- Vocabulary Activity 11–2
- Section Quiz 11–2

Transparencies

- Daily Focus Transparency 11–2

Multimedia

- Vocabulary PuzzleMaker CD-ROM
- *ExamView® Assessment Suite* CD-ROM
- Presentation Plus! Software

communication that involves using rules to make and combine symbols in ways that produce meaningful words and sentences. Language lets us communicate facts and ideas. It allows us to tell each other about the past, present, and future. We solve problems and make decisions based on learning that is transmitted through language. Language consists of three elements: phonemes (units of sound), morphemes (units of meaning), and syntax (units of organization). The study of meaning, or semantics, is the most complex aspect of language.

Phonemes

The smallest units of sound in human languages are **phonemes.** Phonemes can be represented by a single letter (such as consonants like *t* or vowels like *e*) or a combination of letters, such as *sh* (see Figure 11.8).

We can produce about 100 different recognizable sounds, but not all sounds are used in all languages. For instance, the English language uses about 43 sounds while some languages use as few as 15 sounds and others use as many as 85 sounds.

phoneme: an individual sound that is a basic structural element of language

Morphemes

A **morpheme** is the smallest unit of meaning (see Figure 11.8). It is made up of one or more phonemes. Morphemes can be a word, a letter (*s*), a prefix (*un-* in *uncertain*), or a suffix (*-ly* in *slowly*). For example, the words *book, love,* and *reason* are single morphemes, while *loves, relearn,* and *walked* have two morphemes (*love* and *-s, re-* and *learn, walk* and *-ed*).

morpheme: the smallest unit of meaning in a given language

Syntax

Syntax refers to rules for combining words into meaningful phrases or sentences to express thoughts that can be understood by others. For example, the following string of words probably does not make sense: "Boy small bike large rode." In English we follow grammatical rules, such as placing adjectives in front of nouns. If you applied these rules to the sentence above, it could read: "The small boy rode a large bike." Every language has these rules, although the rules differ from language to language.

syntax: language rules that govern how words can be combined to form meaningful phrases and sentences

Semantics

The study of meaning or extracting meaning from morphemes, words, sentences, and context is **semantics.** The same word can have different meanings. Consider the following sentences: "A mind is a terrible thing to waste. Do you mind if I sit next to you?" The word *mind* is understood differently in the two sentences. How did you

semantics: the study of meaning in language

Figure 11.8 Phonemes and Morphemes

The word *fearlessness* has nine phonemes and three morphemes. ***What is the difference between phonemes and morphemes?***

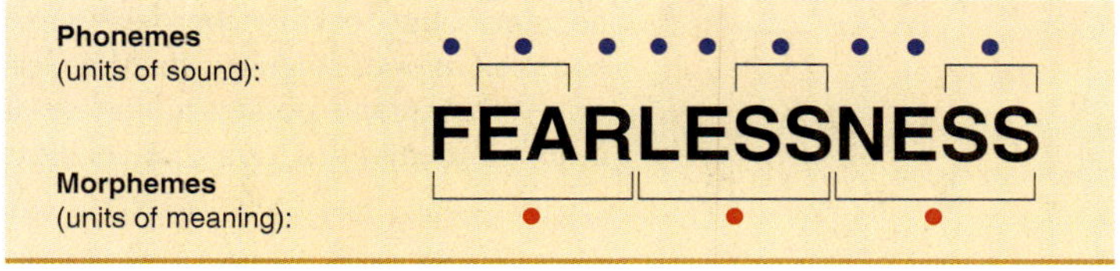

2 TEACH

L1 Discussion Place several declarative sentences in an illogical order on the board or on an overhead projector transparency. For example: (1) store I to meet a to friend went Judy and the. (2) oldest world the today Russia lives person in the in. Make sure that at least two of the sentences have more than one possible recombination. Have students write the possible logical sentences from the words. **Ask: What syntax rules did you use to determine the logical order? What differences in semantics can you identify among these sentences?** ELL

Guided Reading Activity 11–2

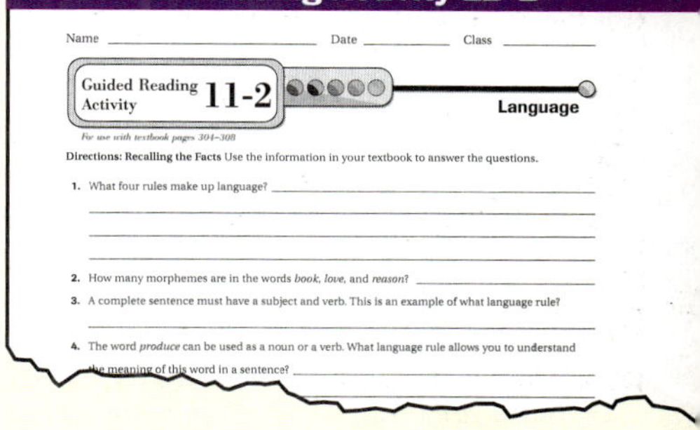
Name ______ Date ______ Class ______

Guided Reading Activity 11-2

Language

For use with textbook pages 304–308

Directions: Recalling the Facts Use the information in your textbook to answer the questions.

1. What four rules make up language? ______
2. How many morphemes are in the words *book, love,* and *reason*? ______
3. A complete sentence must have a subject and verb. This is an example of what language rule? ______
4. The word *produce* can be used as a noun or a verb. What language rule allows you to understand the meaning of this word in a sentence? ______

Figure 11.8

Visual Instruction Have students who are taking a foreign language share phonemes that are different from the phonemes in English.

Caption Answer A phoneme is only a sound; a morpheme has meaning.

COOPERATIVE LEARNING ACTIVITY

American Sign Language Organize students into small groups to prepare a multimedia presentation on American Sign Language (ASL). Tell students that ASL is the preferred method of communication in the hearing-impaired community. Explain that it does not use the same syntax as English. Suggest the following areas of research to find information needed for the presentation: history of signing; ASL grammar rules; differences between ASL and finger spelling; variations in signs based on region of the country, age, or ethnicity; and whether ASL should be considered a separate language. Encourage students to use any multimedia resources available in a creative and informative way.

CHAPTER 11
Section 2, pages 304–308

Profiles In Psychology

Ask students to read the **Profiles In Psychology** feature and then discuss the following questions:

1. What does Noam Chomsky think is inborn? *(the mechanism to learn the rules of language)*
2. Is the language-acquisition device (LAD) of an American the same as the LAD of a Spaniard? Explain. *(Yes, the mechanism is the same, but the language learned depends on the one that the infant hears spoken.)*

PSYCHOLOGY JOURNAL

Ask students to—if possible—find a letter, paper, or report that they wrote when they were in elementary school. Have them compare it to a similar document that they have written in the last year. Tell students to write an essay in their journal explaining how their writing has changed. They should consider the following questions: **Has the syntax changed? How do the changes reflect changes in your thinking and reasoning abilities?** ■

Readings and Case Studies in Psychology

Have students read the Chapter 11 Reading selection in *Readings and Case Studies in Psychology* and answer the questions that follow the reading.

Profiles In Psychology

Noam Chomsky

1928–

"[A] human being is a biological organism like any other. It's a biological organism with a very unique intellectual capacity that we are only barely beginning to understand. I think our intellectual capacities are very highly structured."

Avram Noam Chomsky created the idea of *transformational grammar.* Transformational grammar is a system for describing the rules that determine all the sentences that can possibly be formed in any language. Chomsky claims that each of us is born with brain structures that make it relatively easy to learn the rules of language. Chomsky called those innate brain structures the *language-acquisition device,* or *LAD.* The LAD includes inborn mechanisms that guide a person's learning of the unique rules of his or her native language.

know what the word *mind* means in each sentence? From your knowledge of semantics, you knew that in the first sentence *mind* was a noun, while in the second sentence it was a verb. Your knowledge of a word's meaning depends partly on context.

LANGUAGE DEVELOPMENT

For many years a debate over exactly how children learn language raged. B.F. Skinner believed that children learned language as a result of operant conditioning. When children utter sounds that are similar to adult speech patterns, their behavior is reinforced through smiles and extra attention; therefore, children repeat those sounds. Eventually children learn to produce speech. Critics state that children understand language before they speak—and before they receive any reinforcement. They also believe that children learn the rules of language before they receive any feedback on speaking correctly.

Some psychologists argue that children learn language through observation, exploration, and imitation. These social learning advocates point out that children use language to get attention, ask for help, or to gain other forms of social contact. Parents can stimulate language acquisition by responding to and encouraging language development. These psychologists believe that both innate and environmental factors play a part in how a child learns language.

Although Noam Chomsky believed that reinforcement and imitation do contribute to language development, he did not believe that all the complex rules of language could be learned that way. Chomsky (1957) theorized that infants possess an innate capacity for language; that is, children inherit a mental program that enables them to learn grammar.

MEETING SPECIAL NEEDS

Learning Style: Intrapersonal Assign students to write two letters to a good friend. Tell them that the letters are private and no one else will see them. In the first letter, the students should write about a recent event that was exciting or interesting. The second letter should be about the same event, but they should assume that things turned out badly. Tell them to compare the two letters and make a list of the words used in each letter that express emotion or feeling. The list should have two headings: *Positive* and *Negative*. Ask students to write one paragraph beneath the list expressing which letter was more difficult to compose and why. **L2**

BLOCK SCHEDULING

HOW LANGUAGE DEVELOPS

If Chomsky is right, then we would expect that all children go through similar stages of language development, no matter what culture or language group they belong to. Infants, in fact, do go through four stages of language development.

Beginning at birth, infants can cry and produce other sounds indicating distress. Around 2 months of age, infants begin to *coo.* Cooing refers to long, drawn-out sounds such as *oooh* or *eeeh.* At around 4 months of age, infants reach the first stage of language development and begin to *babble.* Babbling includes sounds found in all languages, such as *dadada* and *bababa.* When babbling, infants learn to control their vocal cords and to make, change, repeat, and imitate the sounds of their parents. At around 9 months of age, infants refine their babbling to increasingly include sounds that are part of their native language. Whereas in children who can hear, babbling is oral, deaf children babble by using hand signals. They repeat the same hand signals over and over again.

At around 12 months of age, infants begin to utter single words. They use these words to describe familiar objects and people, such as *da-da* or *doggie.* At this stage, children use single words to describe longer thoughts. For example, a child may say "da" to mean "Where is my father?" or "I want my father."

Toward the end of their second year, children place two words together to express an idea. Children may say "Milk gone" to indicate that the milk has spilled or "Me play" to mean "I want to play." This stage indicates that the child is beginning to learn the rules of grammar. The child's vocabulary has expanded to about 50 to 100 words and continues to expand rapidly, as was discussed in Chapter 3.

By age 2–3, children form sentences of several words. These first sentences follow a pattern called *telegraphic speech.* This is a pattern of speaking in which the child leaves out articles such as *the,* prepositions such as *with,* and parts of verbs. For example, a child may say, "I go park," to mean, "I am going to the park." By age 5, language development is largely complete, although vocabulary and sentence complexity continue to develop.

Psychology and You: Bilingualism

Bilingualism is the ability to speak and understand two languages. How do bilingual people, though, keep the two languages separate? They do not. Try this experiment. Say the ink color of the following words aloud.

YELLOW GREEN RED BLUE VERDE AZUL AMARILLO ROJO

If you speak only English, you probably had a little trouble with the first four and had less trouble with the last four. If you speak Spanish, though, you knew that *verde, azul, amarillo,* and *rojo* are the Spanish words for *green, blue, yellow,* and *red.* You had difficulty with all the items.

Although it takes children longer to master two languages rather than just one, bilingual people can express their thoughts in a wide variety of ways. Bilingual children also learn early that there are different ways of expressing the same idea.

Reading Check What is the nature versus nurture debate concerning the development of language?

CHAPTER 11
Section 2, pages 304–308

Vocabulary Activity 11–2

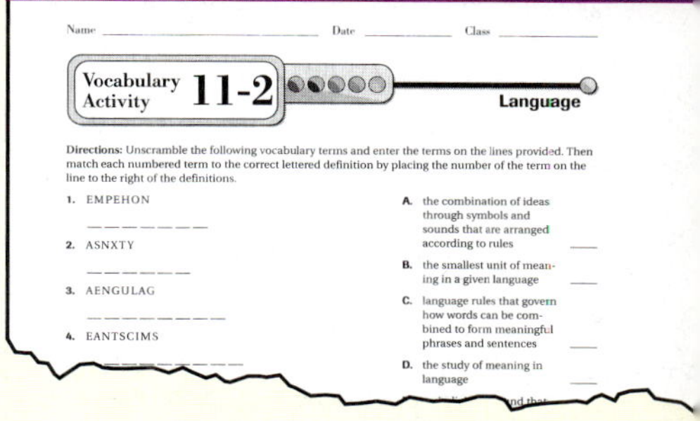
Name ______ Date ______ Class ______

Vocabulary Activity 11-2 — Language

Directions: Unscramble the following vocabulary terms and enter the terms on the lines provided. Then match each numbered term to the correct lettered definition by placing the number of the term on the line to the right of the definitions.

1. EMPEHON
2. ASNXTY
3. AENGULAG
4. EANTSCIMS

A. the combination of ideas through symbols and sounds that are arranged according to rules ___
B. the smallest unit of meaning in a given language ___
C. language rules that govern how words can be combined to form meaningful phrases and sentences ___
D. the study of meaning in language ___

Psychology and You

Use the following question to direct a class discussion after students have read the **Psychology and You** feature.

Ask: Why would someone who spoke Spanish have difficulty with some of the words?

Reading Check Answer The nurture argument assumes that we learn language through reinforcement. The nature argument assumes that the capacity for language is inborn.

3 ASSESS

Assign Section 2 Assessment as homework or as an in-class activity.

CRITICAL THINKING ACTIVITY

Distinguishing Fact From Opinion Have students use the Internet or the local library to review the studies that have been done on chimpanzees and their abilities to acquire language. From their research, students should answer the following questions: **What distinguishes language from communication? Have chimpanzees learned to communicate in a meaningful way? Have chimpanzees demonstrated an ability to learn language?** Ask students to write an essay that offers an answer to these questions. Students should include examples from the studies they research. Encourage students to share their research with the class. **L3**

CHAPTER 11

Section 2, pages 304–308

Section Quiz 11–2

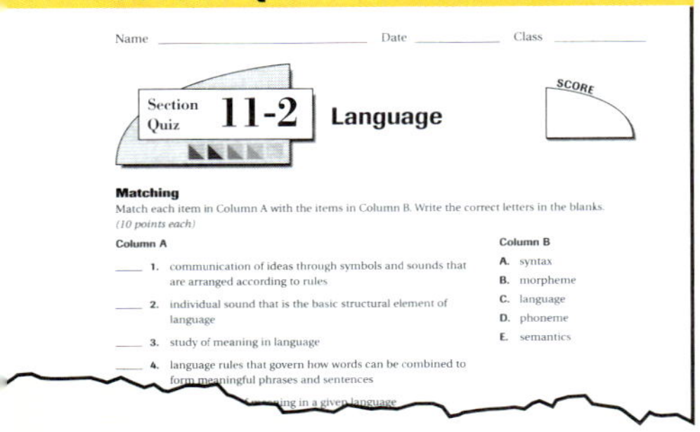
Name ______ Date ______ Class ______

Section Quiz 11-2 Language

SCORE

Matching

Match each item in Column A with the items in Column B. Write the correct letters in the blanks. *(10 points each)*

Column A

____ 1. communication of ideas through symbols and sounds that are arranged according to rules

____ 2. individual sound that is the basic structural element of language

____ 3. study of meaning in language

____ 4. language rules that govern how words can be combined to form meaningful phrases and sentences

Column B

A. syntax

B. morpheme

C. language

D. phoneme

E. semantics

Reteach

Tell students that context determines the meaning of the word. Ask for volunteers to use the word "square" as an adjective, a verb, an adverb, and a noun. Write each sentence on the board.

Enrich

Have students write an essay titled "Language Expresses My Values."

4 CLOSE

Have students draw a time line showing the progression of language development in children from birth through age 4.

DO ANIMALS LEARN LANGUAGE?

Animals communicate with one another. We have all seen dogs bark or growl at each other. Do animals, though, learn language? Language involves more than just communicating—it involves rules of grammar. It involves combining words or phrases into meaningful sentences. Although animals do not possess the ability to use grammatical rules, they have been taught to communicate with humans. (Refer to Chapter 3 for an in-depth discussion.)

GENDER AND CULTURAL DIFFERENCES

People use language to communicate their culture and express their ideas. Do people who speak different languages actually think differently from one another? Benjamin Whorf (1956) argued that language affects our basic perceptions of the physical world. Whorf used the term *linguistic relativity* to refer to the idea that language influences thoughts. For instance, consider the word *snow.* Whorf estimated that the Inuit have many words for snow (including separate words for damp snow, falling snow, and melting snow) because their survival depends upon traveling and living in snow. According to Whorf's theory, different terms for snow help the Inuit see the different types of snow as different. On the other hand, Whorf claimed that Americans have one word for snow. Critics have pointed out that Americans actually have many words for snow. Whorf's theory of linguistic relativity still claims supporters, but it is difficult to separate culture from language when studying the use of language and the perceptions it influences.

Does the English language express a particular value system? Some people argue that certain words in language create gender stereotypes. For example, a chairman may be a man or a woman. The use of pronouns also affects our thinking. Nurses, secretaries, and schoolteachers are often referred to as *she,* while doctors, engineers, and presidents are often referred to as *he.* Many organizations have instituted guidelines for the use of nonsexist language.

SECTION 2 Assessment

1. **Review the Vocabulary** How many phonemes are in the word "thoughtfully"? How many morphemes?
2. **Visualize the Main Idea** Using a flowchart similar to the one below, list the stages of language development.

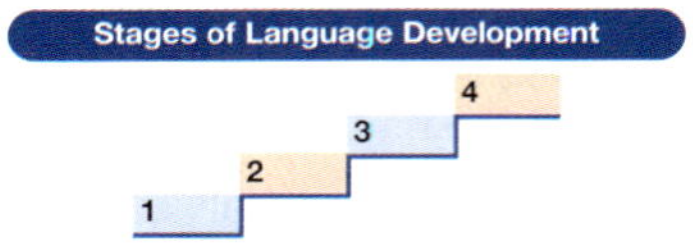

3. **Recall Information** How might we express gender values in our use of language?
4. **Think Critically** You have taught your pet parrot to speak perfect English and understand several commands. Have you taught it language? Explain.
5. **Application Activity** In ordinary English, there is no resemblance between the written appearance of a word and the idea for which it stands. Write the following words in such a way that the word illustrates the idea: war, empty, fly, kick, Mommy.

SECTION 2 Assessment Answers

1. 7 phonemes (th ough t f u ll y), 3 morphemes (thought ful ly)
2. (1) babble at about 4 months, (2) single words at around 1 year, (3) place two words together, (4) telegraphic speech in which words are omitted but meaning is clear at about 2 years of age.
3. Gender values are expressed by the use of male and female pronouns to refer to people in certain roles (nurse, she; doctor, he) and by use of gender-biased language such as chairman, salesman, and saleslady.
4. No, it is simply mimicking what it has been taught. For example, it cannot form new sentences from words it knows and it cannot use grammatical rules.
5. Students' answers will vary. Have students share their answers with the class and discuss the similarities and differences among the answers.

CHAPTER 11 Summary and Vocabulary

Solving problems, creating ideas, and expressing our ideas through language are some of the most important skills that we acquire in our lives.

Section 1 Thinking and Problem Solving

Main Idea: Thinking involves changing, reorganizing, and recombining the information stored in memory to create new or transformed information, such as creative problem-solving strategies.

- Thought depends on several processes or components: images, symbols, concepts, prototypes, and rules.
- There are several kinds of thinking: directed, or convergent, thinking; nondirected, or divergent, thinking; and metacognition.
- Problem solving depends upon the use of strategies or specific methods for approaching problems.
- People use algorithms, or fixed sets of procedures, and heuristics, or mental shortcuts, to solve problems.
- At times certain useful strategies become so cemented into the problem-solving process that they actually interfere with problem solving. When a particular strategy becomes a habit, it is called a mental set.
- Functional fixedness, or the inability to imagine new functions for familiar objects, can interfere with problem solving.
- Some characteristics of creative thinking include flexibility and the ability to recombine elements to achieve insight.

Section 2 Language

Main Idea: Language and thought are closely related. Language requires the learning of a set of complex rules and symbols, yet most people have little difficulty learning their native language.

- Language consists of three parts: phonemes, morphemes, and syntax.
- According to B.F. Skinner, children learn language as a result of operant conditioning.
- Noam Chomsky theorized that children inherit a mental program that enables them to learn grammar.
- Infants go through four stages of language development—babbling at around 4 months of age, uttering single words at around 12 months of age, placing words together to express ideas at around 2 years of age, and forming complex, compound sentences by 4 years of age.
- People use language to communicate their culture and express their ideas.

Chapter Vocabulary

thinking (p. 296)
image (p. 296)
symbol (p. 296)
concept (p. 296)
prototype (p. 296)
rule (p. 297)
metacognition (p. 297)
algorithm (p. 299)
heuristic (p. 299)
mental set (p. 299)
functional fixedness (p. 300)
creativity (p. 300)
flexibility (p. 301)
recombination (p. 301)
insight (p. 301)
language (p. 304)
phoneme (p. 305)
morpheme (p. 305)
syntax (p. 305)
semantics (p. 305)

11 Summary and Vocabulary

Using the Chapter 11 Summary and Vocabulary

Use the Chapter 11 Summary and Vocabulary to preview, review, condense, or reteach the chapter.

Preview/Review

Use the Chapter Vocabulary list to help students review and study.

Activity Have students create a matching game by placing the term on one card and an example of the term on another card. Ask students to trade games with a classmate and match all the terms with their examples.

Vocabulary PuzzleMaker CD-ROM reinforces the vocabulary terms used in Chapter 11.

Condense

Have students read the Chapter 11 Summary.

Chapter 11 Guided Reading Activities

Reteach

Reteaching Activity 11

PERFORMANCE ASSESSMENT ACTIVITY

Creating a New Product New products are invented by people who see a need and figure out a way to satisfy it. Brainstorm as a class various needs that students have. Have students work in groups and use this list to create a plan for a new or improved product. Tell them to keep a written record of how they selected the need and will create the product, showing how they used flexibility, recombination, or insight during the process. **BLOCK SCHEDULING**

Refer to the ***Authentic Assessment*** booklet for additional activities and information about evaluating student performance.

PSYCHOLOGY Online

Have students visit the Web site at glencoe.com to review Chapter 11 and take the **Self-Check Quiz**.

GLENCOE TECHNOLOGY

Presentation Plus!

For a review of Chapter 11 content, see MindJogger Checkpoint on **Presentation Plus!**

CHAPTER 11 Assessment

PSYCHOLOGY Online

Self-Check Quiz

Visit the *Understanding Psychology* Web site at glencoe.com and click on **Chapter 11—Self-Check Quizzes** to prepare for the Chapter Test.

Reviewing Vocabulary

Choose the letter of the correct term or concept below to complete the sentence.

a. prototype
b. algorithm
c. functional fixedness
d. insight
e. phonemes
f. syntax
g. semantics
h. mental set
i. thinking
j. metacognition

1. A(n) __________ is a fixed set of procedures that, if followed correctly, will lead to a solution.
2. __________ is the study of the meaning of words or phrases when they appear in sentences or contexts.
3. Changing or reorganizing the information stored in memory to create new or transformed information is __________.
4. A person experiences __________ when he or she comes upon a solution to a problem by creating a new mental arrangement of the elements of the problem.
5. The strategy of problem solving that you use over and over again is your ________.
6. __________ is a set of rules for combining words, phrases, and sentences to express thoughts that can be understood by others.
7. Thinking about thinking is called __________.
8. When you think of a car as an example of a vehicle, you are thinking of a(n) __________.
9. The smallest units of sound in the human language are called __________.
10. The inability to imagine new functions for familiar objects is called __________.

Recalling Facts

1. Define the five units of thought. Then list the five units of thought in order of increasing complexity.
2. What is creativity? What are the three characteristics of creative thinking? Give an example of one of the three characteristics.
3. Using a graphic organizer similar to the one below, identify and explain the structures of language.

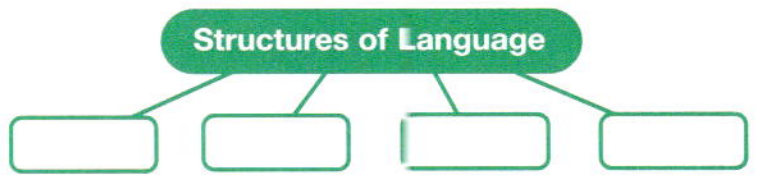

4. What are three strategies people often use to solve problems? Explain how you have used one of these strategies to solve a problem.
5. How did B.F. Skinner and Noam Chomsky differ in their ideas about how children learn language?

Critical Thinking

1. **Applying Concepts** Do you think using algorithms rather than heuristics is always the best way to solve problems? Why or why not?
2. **Making Inferences** What kind of thinking—directed or nondirected—do you think is required for creativity? Why do you think so?
3. **Analyzing Concepts** Based on what you have learned about language development, do you think all students in elementary school should be taught a foreign language? Why or why not?
4. **Synthesizing Information** According to the theory of linguistic relativity, a person's language influences his or her thoughts. Do you believe that bilingual people have more complex thought processes than people who speak only one language? Explain your answer.
5. **Demonstrating Reasoned Judgment** What theory of language development do you agree with the most? Why?

Reviewing Vocabulary

1. b	**6.** f
2. g	**7.** j
3. i	**8.** a
4. d	**9.** e
5. h	**10.** c

Recalling Facts

1. Images are mental representations of events or objects. Symbols are abstract units of thought that represent objects or qualities. Concepts are symbols used for classes of objects or events that share at least one common attribute. Prototypes are representative examples of concepts. Rules are statements of relations between concepts. In order of increasing complexity, the units of thought are image, symbol, concept, prototype, and rule.
2. Creativity is the ability to use information in new and original ways. Three characteristics of creative thinking are flexibility, recombination, and insight. Students' answers will vary.
3. Phonemes are the smallest units of sound. Morphemes are the smallest units of meaning. Syntax is the set of rules for expressing thoughts with words and sentences. Semantics is the meaning of words or phrases as they appear in context.
4. People solve problems by (1) breaking the problem into smaller, more easily solved subgoals, (2) using algorithms, and (3) using heuristics. Students' answers will vary but should demonstrate an understanding of problem-solving strategies.
5. Skinner believed that language developed as a result of reinforcement–through nurture. Chomsky believes that the ability to acquire language is innate and will develop naturally.

Critical Thinking

1. No one problem-solving strategy is appropriate for all situations. Algorithms are quite effective for some types of problems like multiplication. Heuristics may be more appropriate for solving problems quickly.
2. Students' answers will vary. Both types of thinking can be used in creativity. Students should support their viewpoints with examples from their own life or from the lives of others.
3. Students' answers will vary. Language development may be slowed by the introduction of a second language, but many will support the benefits of learning a second language. For example, bilingual people can express their thoughts in a wide variety of ways.
4. Students' answers will vary. In general, the larger one's vocabulary, the greater his or her thinking capacity. Bilingual individuals have a larger vocabulary and may have more complex thought processes.
5. Students' answers will vary. Those who support Skinner will likely point to experiences in which a child has responded to encouragement (reinforcement) from others. Those who support Chomsky will state that the pattern of language development appears much the same across languages, indicating an inborn brain structure that makes it easy to acquire language skills.

CHAPTER 11 Assessment

Psychology Projects

1. **Problem Solving** Suppose you wanted to put together a jigsaw puzzle. What are the problem-solving strategies you might use? Which one do you think would work best? Present your strategies in an illustrated "how-to" pamphlet for others to refer to.
2. **Language** Listen to the speech of a child between the ages of 2 and 4. Pay special attention to the child's language skills. Then write a report explaining what parts of language structure the child is exhibiting.
3. **Thinking** Ask 15 to 20 people to give you directions to a specific location, such as the school gym. Notice how they describe the directions (by using only words, creating a map, or using their hands). After they have finished, ask them to describe the mental imagery they used. In a brief report, summarize your findings.

Technology Activity

The Internet has several sites designed for parents of preschool children. Locate some of these sites to find out what suggestions parents can obtain to improve language development in their young children. Report and evaluate the suggestions in light of the information about language development you have learned in this chapter.

Psychology Journal

Consider how language shapes your thinking and how language and thought are integrated processes. Recall an episode in your life in which you used language (your communication skills) to solve an important problem. Describe the event and analyze why you were equipped to resolve this particular issue.

Building Skills

Interpreting a Graph Many factors contribute to a child's language development. Review the graph, then answer the questions that follow.

1. What does the graph illustrate?
2. What conclusion can you draw about the relationship of the number of words that a parent says to a child and the size of the child's vocabulary?
3. What theory of language development does the information in this graph best support?

Practice and **assess** key social studies skills with **Glencoe Skillbuilder Interactive Workbook CD-ROM, Level 2.**

See the Skills Handbook, page 628, for an explanation of interpreting graphs.

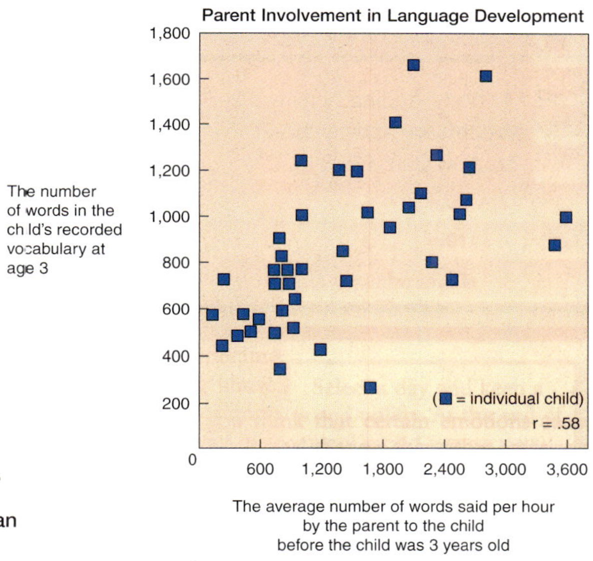

Source: Robert S. Feldman, *Understanding Psychology*, 1999.

Building Skills

1. It shows the relationship between the number of words said by a parent to a child and the child's vocabulary at age 3.
2. There is a positive relationship between the number of words a parent says to a child and the size of that child's vocabulary. Usually, the more words a child hears from the parent, the larger that child's vocabulary will be.
3. The information presented in this graph best supports B.F. Skinner's theory of language development. The child's vocabulary can be expanded through parental reinforcement.

GLENCOE TECHNOLOGY

CD-ROM

Glencoe Skillbuilder Interactive Workbook, Level 2

This interactive CD-ROM is designed to reinforce student mastery of essential social studies skills.

Chapter Bonus Test Question

This question may be used for extra credit on the Chapter Assessment.

Answer the following question:

I transmit learning and communicate facts and ideas. What am I?

Answer: language

Psychology Projects

1. Answers will vary. Students might mention associating puzzle pieces by color, shape, and so on.
2. Answers will vary. Students should note the use of telegraphic speech, incorrect grammar that follows logical rules, and the use of expressions that the children have mimicked from adults.
3. Answers will vary. The sample size of 15 should allow for a wide variety of responses. The reports should indicate the different ways that people express themselves.

Technology Activity

Students should find a wealth of information on the Web. By searching under "early childhood development," several of the search engines will respond with recommended sites. Some of these deal directly or indirectly with language development.

Psychology Journal

Answers will vary. Challenge students to think about how they would have solved the problem if the other people involved spoke a different language.

Chapter 12 Resource Guide

SECTION RESOURCES

Daily Objectives	Reproducible Resources	Multimedia Resources
Section 1 **Theories of Motivation** Explain motivation and why we experience it in different ways.	Guided Reading Activity 12–1 Vocabulary Activity 12–1 Section Quiz 12–1	Daily Focus Transparency 12–1 *ExamView® Assessment Suite* CD-ROM Presentation Plus! Software
Section 2 **Biological and Social Motives** Understand that biological needs are physiological requirements we must fulfill to survive, whereas social needs are learned through experience.	Guided Reading Activity 12–2 Vocabulary Activity 12–2 Section Quiz 12–2	Daily Focus Transparency 12–2 *ExamView® Assessment Suite* CD-ROM Presentation Plus! Software
Section 3 **Emotions** Describe the three parts of emotions—the physical, cognitive, and behavioral aspects.	Guided Reading Activity 12–3 Vocabulary Activity 12–3 Section Quiz 12–3	Daily Focus Transparency 12–3 Vocabulary PuzzleMaker CD-ROM *ExamView® Assessment Suite* CD-ROM Presentation Plus! Software

Blackline Master   CD-ROM   Transparency

Block Schedule

Activities that are particularly suited for use within the block-scheduling framework are identified throughout this chapter by the following designation: **BLOCK SCHEDULING**

KEY TO ABILITY LEVELS

Teaching strategies have been coded for varying learning styles and abilities.

- **L1** **BASIC** activities for all students
- **L2** **AVERAGE** activities for average to above-average students
- **L3** **CHALLENGING** activities for above-average students
- **ELL** **ENGLISH LANGUAGE LEARNER** activities

Chapter 12 Resource Guide

Timesaving Tools

TeacherWorks™ All-In-One Planner and Resource Center

- **Interactive Teacher Edition** Access your Teacher Wraparound Edition and your classroom resources with a few easy clicks.
- **Interactive Lesson Planner** Planning has never been easier! Organize your week, month, semester, or year with all the lesson helps you need to make teaching creative, timely, and relevant.

Use Glencoe's **Presentation Plus!** multimedia teacher tool to easily present dynamic lessons that visually excite your students. Using Microsoft PowerPoint® you can customize the presentations to create your own personalized lessons.

Activity

From the Classroom of...

Don Leach
George Washington High School
San Francisco, CA

Create an Ad

Purpose: To apply the major theories of motivation

Strategy: The students become industrial psychologists who have been hired to create an ad. Put the following choices on the board for teams of four students to choose from: new snack food, new perfume for both females and males, new kind of car, new kind of nonalcoholic drink, new line of clothing, new over-the-counter drug, new communication device, or Internet service. Instruct students to apply drive-reduction, incentive theory, or cognitive theory and create a product name, a slogan, and an image using photographs, video, or a skit. They must target a specific population. They will market test their ad on a sample population, the rest of the class. Have the teams write a report telling reasons they selected their product's name, slogan, and image, who their target population is, and what motivational theory(ies) they applied.

Have all groups present their products on the same day. Then hand out a market-test score sheet so that students can rate each product. Remove all references to the product from students' sight. The score sheet should ask students to remember the name, slogan, image, and motivational theory used for each product. A group's score is based on how well their classmates can remember the product information.

Psychology Online

Use our Web site for additional resources. All essential content is covered in the Student Edition.

You and your students can visit ____________, the Web site companion to *Understanding Psychology.* This innovative integration of electronic and print media offers your students a wealth of opportunities. The student text directs students to the Web site for the following options:

- Chapter Overviews
- Student Web Activities
- Self-Check Quizzes

Answers are provided for you in the **Web Activity Lesson Plan**. Additional Web resources and Interactive Puzzles are also available.

Chapter 12 Resource Guide

Note: The following materials may be used when teaching Chapter 12. Section level support materials are shown at point of use in the margins of the Teacher Wraparound Edition.

TEACHING TRANSPARENCIES

Chapter 12 Concept Transparencies

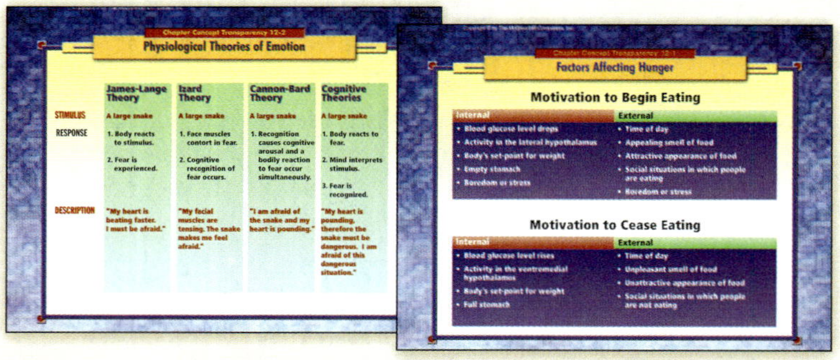

MULTIMEDIA

- Vocabulary PuzzleMaker CD-ROM
- *ExamView® Assessment Suite* CD-ROM
- TeacherWorks™ CD-ROM
- Glencoe Skillbuilder Interactive Workbook, Level 2
- Presentation Plus! Software

REVIEW AND REINFORCEMENT

Reteaching Activity 12

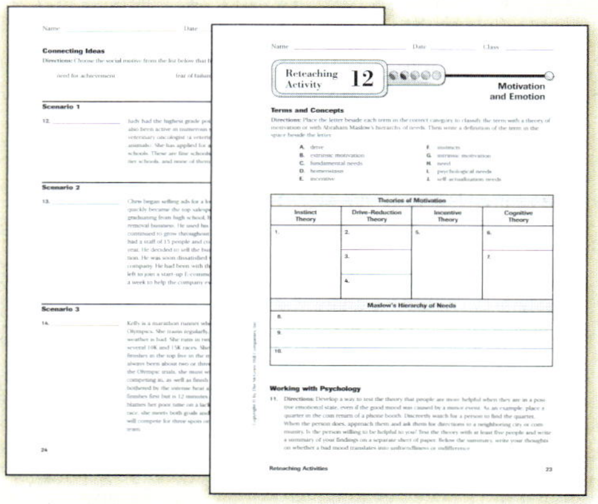

Graphic Organizer Activity 12

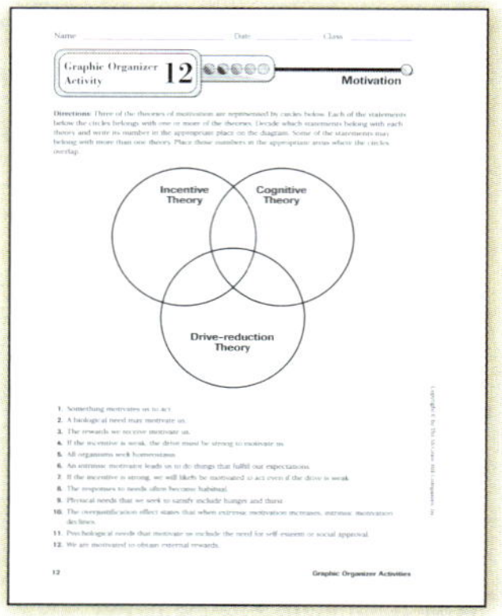

APPLICATION AND HANDS-ON

Psychology Project 12

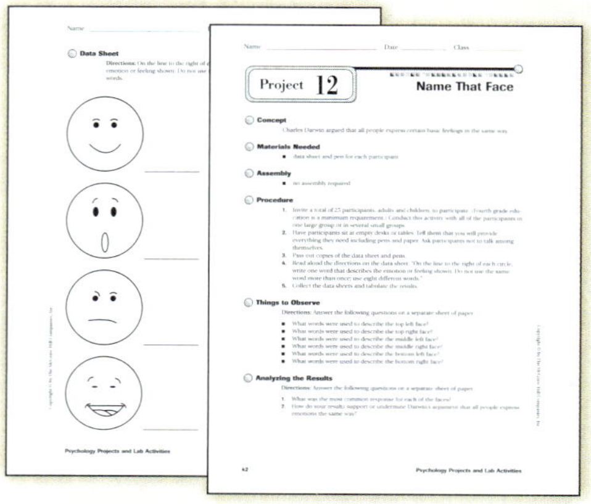

Application Activity 12

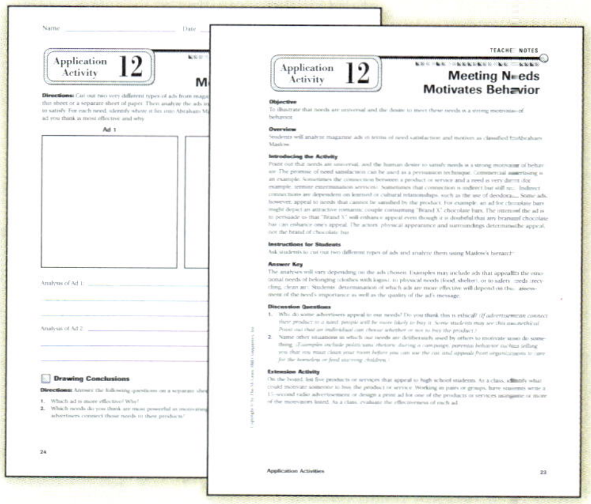

Chapter 12 Resource Guide

ASSESSMENT

GLENCOE'S ASSESSMENT ADVANTAGE

Chapter 12 Test, Form A

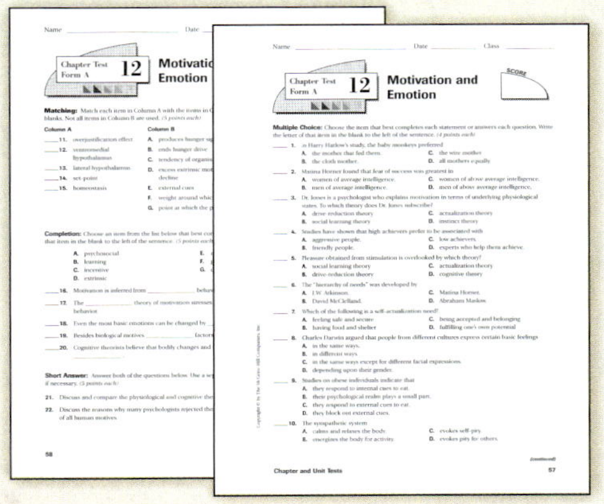
Chapter Test Form A 12 Motivation and Emotion

Chapter 12 Test, Form B

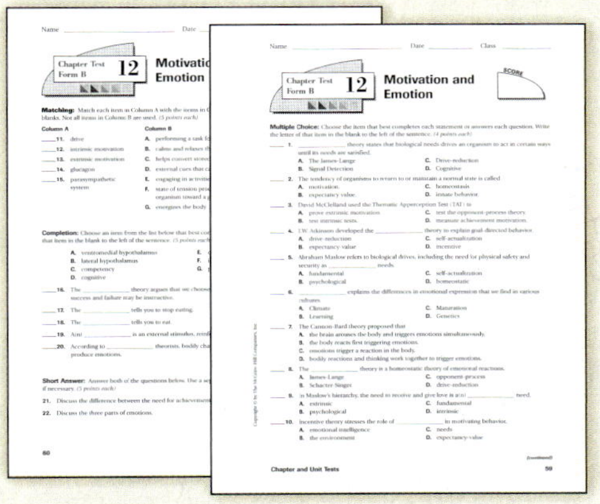
Chapter Test Form B 12 Motivation and Emotion

Authentic Assessment Activity 12

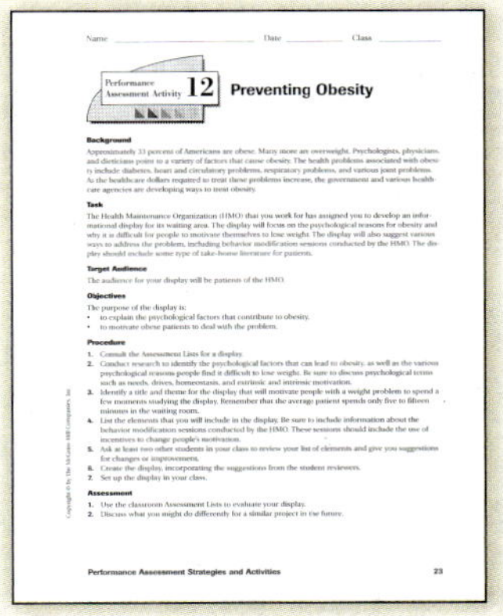
Performance Assessment Activity 12 Preventing Obesity

EXTENSION AND ENRICHMENT

Enrichment Activity 12

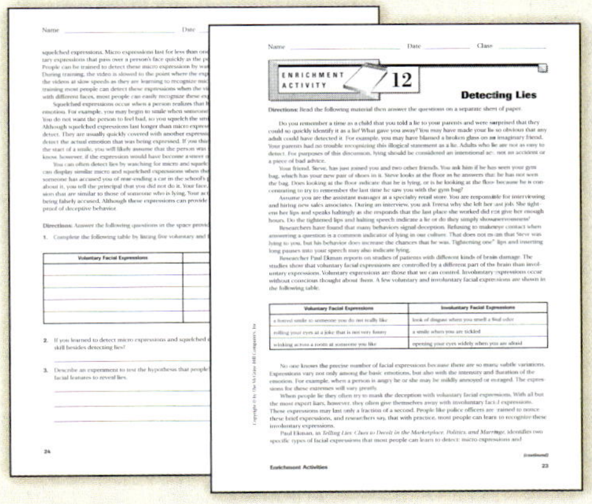
Enrichment Activity 12 Detecting Lies

Critical Thinking Skills Activity 12

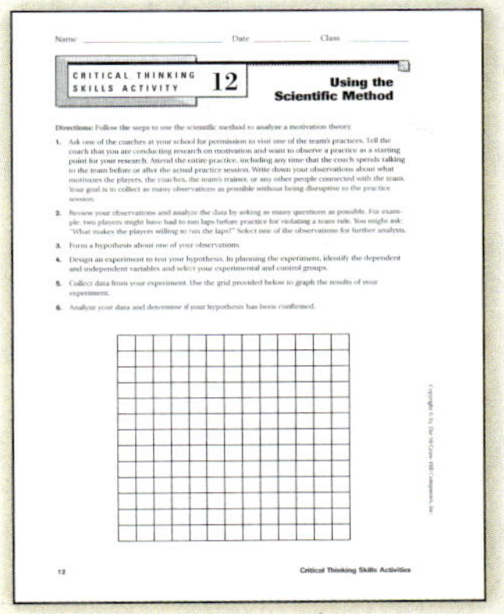
Critical Thinking Skills Activity 12 Using the Scientific Method

Psychology Reading 12

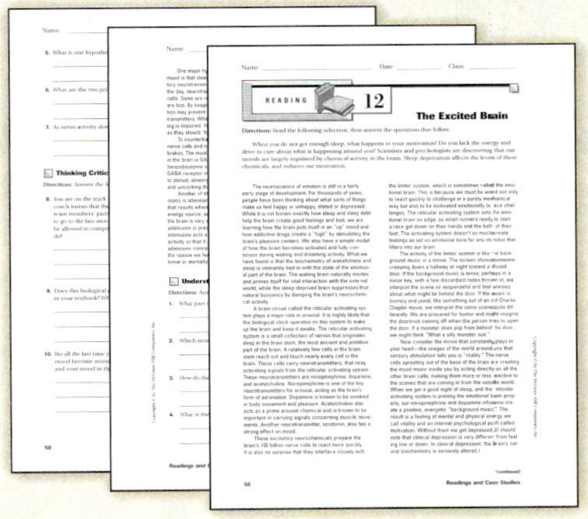
Reading 12 The Excited Brain

Psychology Case Study 12

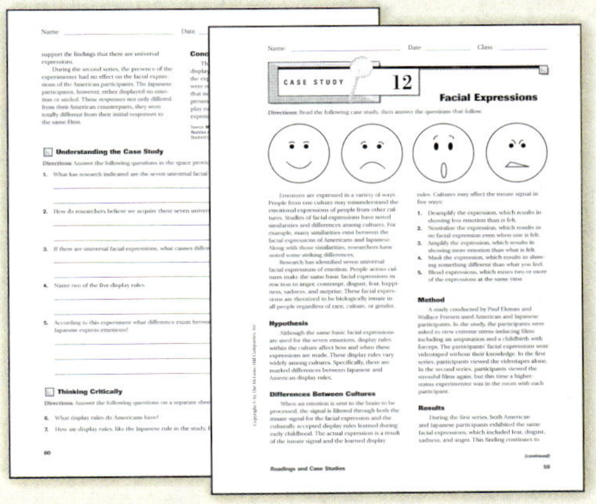
Case Study 12 Facial Expressions

CHAPTER 12 *Introduction*

PSYCHOLOGY Online

Visit ______________ for a Chapter Overview for **Chapter 12—Motivation and Emotion.**

GLENCOE TECHNOLOGY

PRESENTATION Plus!

For a preview of Chapter 12 content, see MindJogger Checkpoint on **Presentation Plus!**

PSYCHOLOGY JOURNAL

Explain to students that our concerns and future aspirations give us motivation to take action. They may also be the things in which we invest the greatest emotion.

This journal activity provides the basis for the Psychology Journal activity exercise in the Chapter Assessment. ■

CHAPTER 12

Motivation and Emotion

PSYCHOLOGY JOURNAL

Think about the present-day concerns and future aspirations that are most important to you. List 6 to 10 of them in any order in your journal. ■

PSYCHOLOGY Online

Chapter Overview
Visit the *Understanding Psychology* Web site at glencoe.com and click on **Chapter 12—Chapter Overviews** to preview the chapter.

312

TWO-MINUTE LESSON LAUNCHER

Remind students of one of the heroes of the 1996 Olympic games, Kerri Strug. After badly spraining her ankle minutes before, Kerri, in obvious pain, landed the vault that allowed the United States women's gymnastic team to win its first ever gold medal. Ask students what they think motivated Kerri to such heroics. Have students share other examples of people who have accomplished what seemed impossible because they were motivated to act. From the examples, have students make a list of the motives that drove these people to succeed.

SECTION 1 Theories of Motivation

Reader's Guide

Main Idea

Psychologists explain motivation and why we experience it in different ways through instinct, drive-reduction, incentive, and cognitive theories of motivation.

Vocabulary

- motivation
- instincts
- need
- drive
- homeostasis
- incentive
- extrinsic motivation
- intrinsic motivation

Objectives

- Describe four theories of motivation.
- Discuss the difference between intrinsic and extrinsic motivation.

EXPLORING PSYCHOLOGY

Don't Look Back

Willie Davis, the great defensive end at Green Bay . . . had given [another player] a kind of mental tip that he used to motivate himself. He had used it ever since a game the Packers lost against the Eagles back in the 1960s. As he left the field at the end of the game, Davis had turned around, the stands emptying, and he realized that he was leaving something on the field—namely, regrets that he had not given the extra effort, the extra push . . . and that he was going to have to live with that regret for the rest of his life because there was no way that he could recapture that moment. He made up his mind then that he would never again look back at a football field or even a day's effort at what he was doing with any sense of regret.

—from *The X Factor: A Quest for Excellence* by George Plimpton, 1995

Why did Davis play football so intensely? Why do people try to climb Mount Everest or cross the Atlantic in a balloon? Why do some people spend every waking moment memorizing batting averages, while others do not know the difference between the New York Yankees and the Toledo Mud Hens? As the song asks, why do fools fall in love?

SECTION RESOURCES

Reproducible Masters

- Guided Reading Activity 12–1
- Vocabulary Activity 12–1
- Section Quiz 12–1

Transparencies

- Daily Focus Transparency 12–1

Multimedia

- *ExamView® Assessment Suite* CD-ROM
- Presentation Plus! Software

1 FOCUS

Section Objectives

1. Describe four theories of motivation.
2. Discuss the difference between intrinsic and extrinsic motivation.

BELLRINGER
Motivational Activity

Project Daily Focus Transparency 12–1 and have students answer the questions.

Available as blackline master

Daily Focus Transparency 12–1

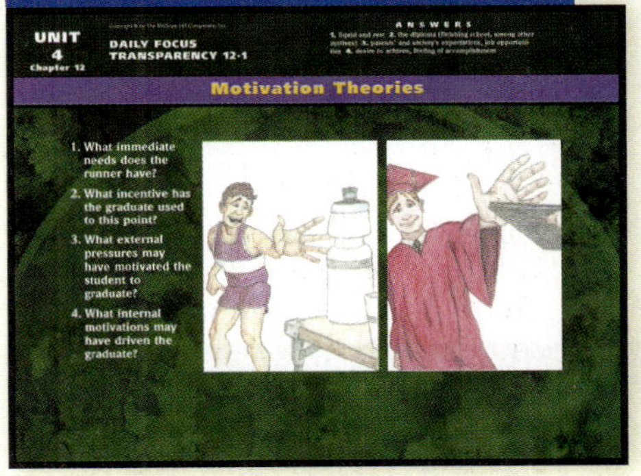

Reader's Guide

Use the Reader's Guide to introduce concepts and vocabulary.

Exploring Psychology

Ask students to read the **Exploring Psychology** feature and then discuss: **How does motivation help you go the extra mile or give extra effort?**

Vocabulary Precheck

Have students write each term on an index card. Then have them read the Glossary definition of each term. Next to the word on the index card, students should restate the definition in their own words.

2 TEACH

L1 Brainstorming Ask students to brainstorm a list of experiences that are naturally pleasurable but do not seem to reduce biological drives. To start the list, write "pausing to watch a beautiful sunset" on the board. **Ask:** **In what ways do the items on this list argue against the drive-reduction theory?** ELL

Psychology Journal

Ask students to record for one hour all the behaviors that they engage in. Remind them not to forget basic biological behaviors like eating or sleeping. Then have students classify each of these behaviors as either an instinct or a drive. ■

Guided Reading Activity 12-1

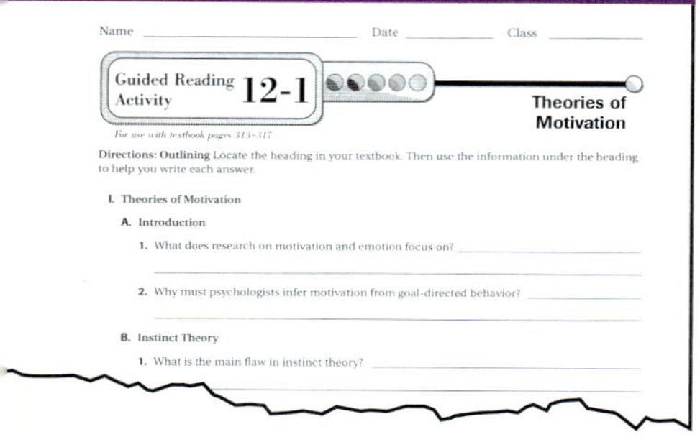
Name ______ Date ______ Class ______

Guided Reading Activity 12-1 — Theories of Motivation

For use with textbook pages 313–317

Directions: Outlining Locate the heading in your textbook. Then use the information under the heading to help you write each answer.

I. Theories of Motivation

A. Introduction

1. What does research on motivation and emotion focus on? ______

2. Why must psychologists infer motivation from goal-directed behavior? ______

B. Instinct Theory

1. What is the main flaw in instinct theory? ______

FYI

Instinct theorists would explain a child's making and throwing of snowballs as an instinct to play because it is a behavior engaged in by children around the world. Do other species share the same instinct? Japanese monkeys known as macaques also make snowballs. They carry them and roll them on the ground, but they never throw them.

motivation: an internal state that activates behavior and directs it toward a goal

Although all psychology is concerned with what people do and how they do it, research on motivation and emotion focuses on the underlying whys of behavior. **Motivation** includes the various psychological and physiological factors that cause us to act a certain way at a certain time.

We see Kristin studying all weekend while the rest of us hang out, and since we know she wants to go to law school, we conclude that she is motivated by her desire to get good grades. We see Mikko working after classes at a job he does not like, and since we know he wants to buy a car, we conclude that he is motivated to earn money for the car. Movies often have motives or emotions as their central theme. On the street, you hear words like *anger, fear, pain, starving,* and hundreds of others describing motives and emotions. Conceptions of motivation in psychology are in many ways similar to those expressed in everyday language. Because motivation cannot be observed directly, psychologists, like the rest of us, infer motivation from goal-directed behavior. Human behavior is energized by many motives that may originate from outside of us or inside of us.

Psychologists explain motivation and why we experience it in different ways. We will discuss instinct, drive-reduction, incentive, and cognitive theories of motivation.

INSTINCT THEORY

instincts: innate tendencies that determine behavior

In the 1900s, psychologist William McDougall (1908) proposed that humans were motivated by a variety of instincts. **Instincts** are natural or inherited tendencies of an organism to make a specific response to certain environmental stimuli without involving reason. Instincts occur in almost the same way among all members of a species. For example, salmon respond to instinctive urges to swim thousands of miles through ocean waters and up rivers to reach the exact spot in a gravel bed where they were spawned years earlier. Psychologist William James (1890) proposed that humans have instincts such as cleanliness, curiosity, parental love, sociability, and sympathy.

Eventually, though, psychologists realized a flaw in the instinct theory. Instincts do not explain behavior; they simply label behavior. Although some psychologists still study instinctual behaviors (now called fixed action patterns), they have focused on other theories to explain motivation.

DRIVE-REDUCTION THEORY

need: biological or psychological requirement of an organism

Something that motivates us moves us to action. The thing that motivates us starts with a **need** that leads to a drive. A need results from a lack of something desirable or useful. We have both physiological and psychological needs. We need oxygen and food to survive (physiological needs). We may also need self-esteem or social approval (psychological needs). We learn our psychological needs with practice; failing to fulfill some of them is not life-threatening.

COOPERATIVE LEARNING ACTIVITY

Exploring the Instinct Theory Organize the class into small groups. Have each group brainstorm a list of animal instincts. Give them an example such as migration patterns of monarch butterflies. Have each group select two animal instincts to research. The research should answer the following questions: *Do animals have instincts? What are they? Can instincts predict animal behavior?* Have the groups use their answers to these questions to compare instinctual behavior in animals to human behavior. **Ask:** **Do humans really have instincts? What are they? Can instincts predict human behavior? Can instincts *explain* human behavior?** *(Instincts only describe behavior.)*

A need produces a drive. A **drive** is an internal condition that can change over time and orients an individual toward a specific goal or goals. We have different drives with different goals. For example, hunger drives us to eat, curiosity drives us to find something out, and fatigue drives us to rest.

Drive-reduction theory emerged from the work of experimental psychologist Clark Hull (1943), who traced motivation back to basic physiological needs. According to Hull, when an organism is deprived of something it needs or wants (such as food or water), it becomes tense and agitated. To relieve this tension, it engages in more or less random activity. Thus biological needs *drive* an organism to act, and the organism strives to maintain homeostasis. **Homeostasis** is the tendency of the body to return to or maintain a balanced state.

Figure 12.1 Harlow's Monkeys

The monkeys in Harlow's study spent most of their time with the cloth mother even though they fed from the wire mother. ***What does this result indicate about motivation?***

If a behavior reduces a drive, the organism will begin to acquire a habit. That is, when the drive is again felt, the organism will tend first to try the same response. Habits channel drives in certain directions. In short, drive-reduction theory states that physiological needs drive an organism to act in either random or habitual ways. This drive continues until the organism's needs are satisfied and it returns to a preset optimal state.

drive: a state of tension produced by a need that motivates an organism toward a goal

homeostasis: the tendency of all organisms to correct imbalances and deviations from their normal state

Hull suggested that all human motives—from the desire to acquire property to striving for excellence and seeking affection or amusement—are extensions of basic biological needs. For example, people develop the need for social approval because as infants they were fed and cared for by a smiling mother or father. Gradually, through conditioning and generalization, the need for approval becomes important in itself. So, according to Hull, approval becomes a learned drive.

The results of subsequent experiments suggested, however, that Hull had overlooked some of the more important factors in human—and animal—motivation. According to drive-reduction theory, infants become attached to their mothers because mothers usually relieve such drives as hunger and thirst. Harry Harlow (1905-1981) and others doubted that this was the only, or even the main, source of an infant's love for its mother. Harlow took baby monkeys away from their mothers and put them alone in cages with two surrogate, or substitute, mothers made mostly of wire (see Figure 12.1). One of the wire mothers was equipped with a bottle. If the drive-reduction theory were correct, the monkeys would become attached to this figure because it was their only source of food. The other wire mother was covered with soft cloth but could not provide food to relieve hunger. In test after test, the baby monkeys preferred to cling to the cloth mother, particularly when strange, frightening objects were put into their cages (Harlow & Zimmerman, 1959).

Reading Check What is the difference between a need and a drive?

Some drive theorists overlooked the fact that some experiences (such as hugging something or someone soft) are inherently pleasurable.

CHAPTER 12

Section 1, pages 313–317

Figure 12.1

Caption Answer It indicates that other factors work in conjunction with drive reduction to influence behavior.

TEACHER Tip

To make certain that students understand homeostasis, list the following items on the board: *hunger, anger, cold,* and *alienation*. Then have students describe how homeostasis can be achieved in each of the situations listed.

Vocabulary Activity 12-1

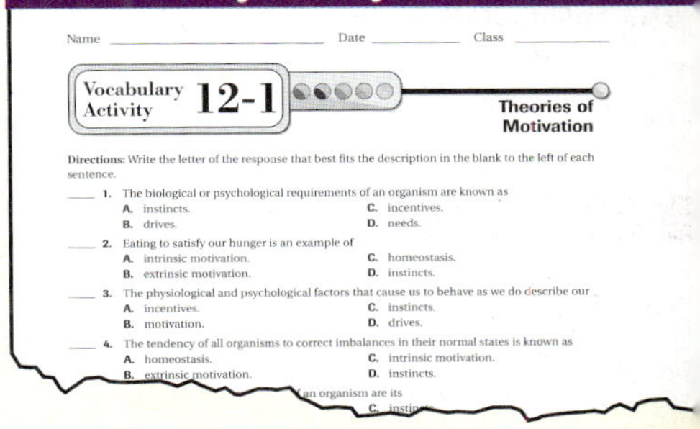

Name ______ Date ______ Class ______

Vocabulary Activity 12-1

Theories of Motivation

Directions: Write the letter of the response that best fits the description in the blank to the left of each sentence.

____ 1. The biological or psychological requirements of an organism are known as
A. instincts. C. incentives.
B. drives. D. needs.

____ 2. Eating to satisfy our hunger is an example of
A. intrinsic motivation. C. homeostasis.
B. extrinsic motivation. D. instincts.

____ 3. The physiological and psychological factors that cause us to behave as we do describe our
A. incentives. C. instincts.
B. motivation. D. drives.

____ 4. The tendency of all organisms to correct imbalances in their normal states is known as
A. homeostasis. C. intrinsic motivation.
B. extrinsic motivation. D. instincts.

Reading Check Answer A need is something required to sustain an organism physically or psychologically, while a drive is the tension caused by the need that motivates action.

MEETING SPECIAL NEEDS

Learning Style: Logical/Mathematical Explain to students that a continuum is a scale on which a category of items falls. Ask students to create a continuum with inherited or physiological motives at one end and social motives that are learned on the other end. Ask students to make a list of common motives for actions they perform. Then have them place each motive on the continuum. To get students started, provide the following examples: hunger and thirst are purely physiological motives and would fall at one end of the continuum. Achievement is a purely social motive and would fall at the other end. **L2** **BLOCK SCHEDULING**

CHAPTER 12

Section 1, pages 313–317

Quick Lab

Purpose Students will explore how advertising motivates behavior.

Process Skills Classifying information, making generalizations

Teaching Strategies

- Review the procedures to be used.
- Encourage students to find ads that represent all the theories of motivation presented in the text.

Analysis

1. Answers will vary. Advertisers appeal to basic instincts and drives. They may offer intrinsic or extrinsic motivations.
2. Answers will vary. For example, an ad for an expensive gold watch may appeal to the status that one will achieve by wearing such an expensive item. This can be paired with the incentive theory.
3. Answers will vary. In the case of the gold watch above, the product appeals to the desire for status or need for recognition.

3 ASSESS

Assign Section 1 Assessment as homework or as an in-class activity.

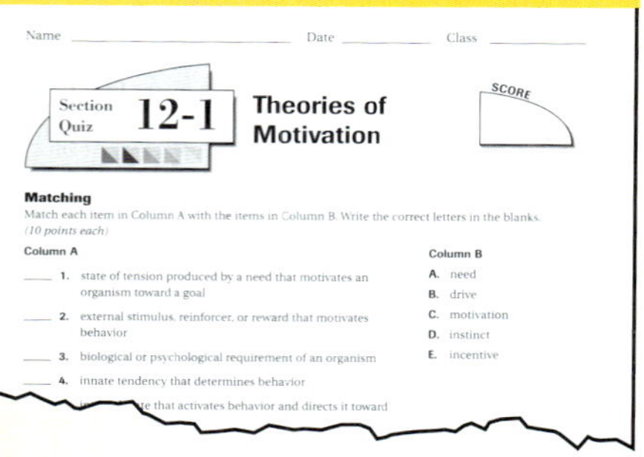
Section Quiz 12–1

Name ______ Date ______ Class ______

Section Quiz 12-1 Theories of Motivation

SCORE

Matching

Match each item in Column A with the items in Column B. Write the correct letters in the blanks. *(10 points each)*

Column A	Column B
____ 1. state of tension produced by a need that motivates an organism toward a goal	A. need
____ 2. external stimulus, reinforcer, or reward that motivates behavior	B. drive
____ 3. biological or psychological requirement of an organism	C. motivation
____ 4. innate tendency that determines behavior	D. instinct
...te that activates behavior and directs it toward	E. incentive

Quick Lab

How do advertisements "motivate" people to buy products?

Advertisers use a variety of techniques to appeal to consumers. Do any of these techniques appeal to human motivations?

Procedure

1. Find examples of various advertisements in magazines.
2. Record the kinds of items being advertised.
3. Focus on the way the advertisers promote the items.

Analysis

1. Describe how the advertisers appeal to consumers to buy the product.
2. Apply the method used to advertise the product to one of the theories of motivation discussed in the chapter.
3. How do the advertisements appeal to human motives? Present your analysis in a written report.

See the Skills Handbook, page 622, for an explanation of designing an experiment.

Although these experiences do not seem to reduce biological drives, they serve as incentives or goals for behavior. Also, sometimes we engage in activities that increase the tension we experience. For example, although you do not need or want extra anxieties, you may enjoy riding roller coasters or watching scary movies. These activities momentarily increase your anxiety and disrupt your homeostasis.

Many psychologists conclude that there could be no general theory of motivation of the type Hull suggested. There are many types of behavior that cannot be explained through deprivation.

INCENTIVE THEORY

The drive-reduction theory of motivation emphasizes the internal states of the organism; however, the incentive theory stresses the role of the environment in motivating behavior. Whereas a drive is something inside of us that causes us to act, our actions are directed toward a goal, or incentive. An **incentive** is the object we seek or the result we are trying to achieve through our motivated behavior. Incentives are also known as reinforcers, goals, and rewards. While drives push us to reduce needs, incentives pull us to obtain them. For example, hunger may cause us to walk to the cafeteria, but the incentive for our action is the sandwich we intend to eat.

Sometimes our drive (hunger) is so strong that we do not care if the incentive (sandwich) is weak. For example, if we are really hungry, we may eat a sandwich from the cafeteria even though we know that the cafeteria's sandwiches are not that tasty. However, if our drive (hunger) is weak, our incentive must be strong. For instance, you may be slightly hungry but really like peanut butter sandwiches, so you will eat one.

People are motivated to obtain positive incentives and to avoid negative incentives. For example, the incentive of food may draw you to the refrigerator. The cognitive expectations of humans also guide their behavior.

incentive: an external stimulus, reinforcer, or reward that motivates behavior

COGNITIVE THEORY

Cognitive psychologists seek to explain motivation by looking at forces inside and outside of us that energize us to move. They propose that we act in particular ways at particular times as a result of extrinsic and intrinsic motivations. **Extrinsic motivation** refers to engaging in activities to reduce biological needs or obtain incentives or external rewards. **Intrinsic motivation** refers to engaging in activities because those activities are personally rewarding or because engaging in them fulfills our beliefs or expectations. For example, if you spend hours and hours

extrinsic motivation: engaging in activities that either reduce biological needs or help us obtain external incentives

intrinsic motivation: engaging in activities because they are personally rewarding or because they fulfill our beliefs and expectations

CRITICAL THINKING ACTIVITY

Demonstrating Reasoned Judgment Ask students to consider how society and societal values affect the expression of competitiveness. Remind students to think about what motivates people to be competitive. Ask students to respond to the following questions in a 1- to 2-page paper. **What are the motivations behind competition in sports? In other arenas? Why is competitiveness accepted in some arenas, like sports, but rejected in others, like being first in line at the grocery store? Is competition constructive or destructive? When does competition cross the line and become a socially unacceptable form of aggression? L2**

playing basketball because you wish to excel at the sport, you are responding to intrinsic motivation. If you spend hours playing basketball because your parents want you to excel at the sport, you are responding to extrinsic motivation. However, if you play basketball just for the fun of it, you are playing because of intrinsic motivation.

In many instances, you engage in an activity because of both extrinsic and intrinsic motivations. For example, you may go out to dinner with your friends because you need to satisfy your hunger (an extrinsic motivation) and because you enjoy the taste of the restaurant's food and wish to socialize with your friends (intrinsic motivations). If you are motivated by both intrinsic and extrinsic motivations, do you perform more effectively or persistently at a task? Psychologists have proposed the *overjustification effect*: when people are given more extrinsic motivation than necessary to perform a task, their intrinsic motivation declines. Say, for example, you enjoy reading books. According to the overjustification effect, if someone started paying you to read books, you would enjoy reading books less. You might ask yourself, "Why am I doing this?" and answer, "It's not because I enjoy reading books; it's because I'm getting paid to do it." If you are suddenly paid less, you may start reading less. If you are no longer being paid to read books, you might lose all interest in the task.

Figure 12.2 **Incentive to Win**

The incentive theory explains that we engage in certain behaviors because we are motivated by high-value incentives such as praise, recognition, or awards. ***How are incentives different from drives?***

SECTION 1 Assessment

1. **Review the Vocabulary** What is the difference between extrinsic and intrinsic motivation?
2. **Visualize the Main Idea** Compare and contrast two theories of motivation by using a diagram similar to the one below.

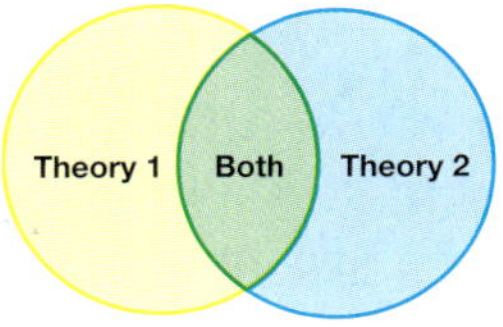

3. **Recall Information** Give an example of an instinct (fixed action pattern). Why are instincts unable to explain motivation adequately?
4. **Think Critically** Which theory of motivation might best explain why you work (or do not work) to get good grades? Explain.
5. **Application Activity** When you are motivated, three things are true: you are energized to engage in an activity, you focus your energies toward reaching a goal, and you have differing intensities of feelings about achieving your goal. Use the criteria above to describe two activities or behaviors you engaged in today.

SECTION 1 Assessment Answers

1. Extrinsic motivation satisfies a biological need or helps achieve an external incentive. Intrinsic motivation comes from within and fulfills our beliefs and expectations.
2. Answers will vary but should demonstrate an understanding of the theories of motivation in this section.
3. Curiosity may be considered a fixed action pattern. These instinctual behaviors simply label behaviors, but they offer no explanation of what motivated the behavior.
4. Students' answers will vary. They may select either the incentive, cognitive, or drive reduction theories. Answers should include examples.
5. Answers will vary. Examples of behaviors for which students may be highly motivated include studying for a test and saving money for a car. Common behaviors for which motivation may be low include getting to school on time and practicing your band instrument.

Figure 12.2

Caption Answer Drives are internal, while incentives are external.

Reteach

Write the following chain on the board: *event (food deprivation) → drive (hunger) → action (eating) → result (drive reduction)*. Have students complete other examples of this chain to better understand the drive-reduction theory.

Enrich

Ask students to make charts listing common incentives for the following types of people: student, salesperson, college graduate, couple getting married, and psychologist.

4 CLOSE

Have students make a list of positive incentives that many students seek and negative incentives that most students seek to avoid.

Going Further

Risk Homeostasis

Canadian psychologist Gerald Wilde has proposed a theory of risk homeostasis. In his book *Target Risk* he explains that things like antilock braking systems, airbags, seatbelt laws, traffic lights, and speed regulations do not have the intended effect. All of these efforts to protect people and reduce traffic casualties do not have the intended effect because, according to Wilde, they fail to influence people's willingness to take risks.

Wilde proposes that such measures actually encourage bad driving because people know that efforts are being made to keep them safe. He claims that people are willing to accept a certain amount of risk in return for real or perceived benefits. For example, people who feel safer in cars may drive faster. This, at least partially, offsets the benefits of the increased safety measures.

Discussing the Case Study

Ask: How can we learn to "listen" to the needs of our bodies for such things as food, warmth, and sleep?

Case Studies

A Balance for Living

Period of Study: 1940

Introduction: When you are driving a car for a long time, eventually the gas tank will need refueling. Many cars are built today with computer systems that can tell when many other things need our attention, such as changing the oil or simply closing a door that did not shut completely. It is important that we respond to these signals. The same can be said for human beings; we require maintenance for operating properly as well.

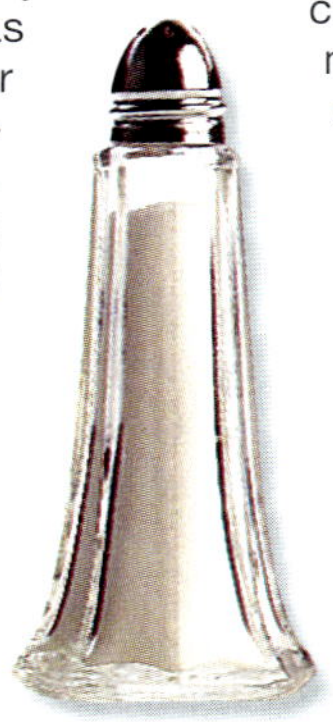

Like modern cars, humans also have a built-in computer. This computer is the human brain. The human body must keep in balance all of the particles and liquids that help maintain our organ systems and, together, keep us alive and well every day. This collective action is known as *homeostasis*. Homeostasis refers to a person's behavior and the corresponding actual physical need. For example, when a person is hungry, he eats. When he has completed a strenuous physical activity and becomes thirsty, he drinks.

In 1940 a one-year-old boy referred to as D.W. developed an odd craving for salt. His favorite foods included any items in which a major ingredient was salt. These foods included salted crackers, pretzels, and potato chips. Also, to the shock of his parents, D.W. would pour salt from the shaker directly into his mouth. When his parents denied him access to these salted edibles, D.W. would cry and throw tantrums until his parents gave in. As he developed a vocabulary, one of D.W.'s first words was indeed *salt*.

Hypothesis: At this time, doctors were not aware of any physiological need for a person, especially at this young age, to consume as much salt as D.W. demanded. The only possible explanation was that the young child just liked the taste of salt. The case of D.W. would eventually result in a number of both physiological and psychological hypotheses.

Method: D.W.'s parents placed him in a hospital setting where he could be checked by doctors because they believed there was more to this unusual situation than just a child's pleasure in tasting salt. The doctors planned to begin general physiological testing to check for chemical deficiencies, disease, or even mental disabilities. During this time—about two days—D.W. became excessively aggravated and enraged. His hospital diet did not include the sufficient amount of salt that D.W. had craved his whole life. Unfortunately, D.W. died only a short time after he entered the hospital and before the scheduled tests could be completed.

Results: An autopsy on D.W. revealed that his adrenal glands did not adequately supply his body with the amount of salt it needed. Although he was very young, D.W.'s body relayed to his brain that he needed to consume more salt to balance out his body systems. It is safe to believe that a child at that age could not understand what salt is or how it operates within the human body, yet somehow young D.W. knew that he did indeed need to have salt and he knew where to get it. This example demonstrates the important role homeostasis plays within the human body and the effect it has on the mind and behavior of a person to maintain various physiological balances.

Analyzing the Case Study

1. What is homeostasis? How does it affect behavior?
2. Why did D.W. crave salt?
3. **Critical Thinking** Recall a time when you experienced your body's own homeostasis in action. Describe the episode. How did you know what you needed?

Answers for Analyzing the Case Study

1. Homeostasis refers to the collective action of the human body to keep our organ systems alive and well and in a balanced state. The need for the body to be in homeostasis will motivate action to maintain it.
2. His adrenal glands did not adequately supply the amount of salt his body needed. He made up for this deficiency by eating large amounts of salt that his body craved.
3. Answers will vary. Common examples include being overheated after strenuous exercise and being extremely hungry after a fast. In these cases, heat and hunger motivated you to rest, cool down, and drink water or eat. With these actions, your body returned to a state of equilibrium.

SECTION 2

Biological and Social Motives

Reader's Guide

Main Idea

Much of life is spent trying to satisfy biological and social needs. Biological needs are physiological requirements that we must fulfill to survive, whereas social needs are those that are learned through experience.

Vocabulary

- lateral hypothalamus (LH)
- ventromedial hypothalamus (VMH)
- fundamental needs
- psychological needs
- self-actualization needs

Objectives

- Describe the biological and social needs of humans.
- Explain Maslow's hierarchy of needs.

EXPLORING PSYCHOLOGY

Why Do We Eat?

Many psychologists have noticed that rats often begin to eat and drink after being handled. For example, if you remove a number of rats from their cages, weigh them, and then return them to their cages, you will soon hear the crunching sound of food pellets being eaten. Two psychologists (Antelmen & Szechtman, 1975) reasoned that the handling, a form of mild stress, activated mechanisms involved in eating. So they devised a way of administering stress to the rats—pinching the rats' tails gently with a pair of padded pliers. The technique did indeed induce eating. Normal animals that were pinched twice a day gained more weight than nonpinched rats.

—adapted from *Psychology: The Science of Behavior* by Neil R. Carlson, 1984

Eating, as demonstrated above, serves both biological and psychological (social) needs. People spend much of their lives trying to satisfy biological and social needs. We choose what, how much, and when to eat because of both biological and social factors. Why is it, though, that some people seem more motivated than others when it comes to achieving something, such as a win in basketball or success at a job? Social needs, such as achievement, also influence our lives.

SECTION RESOURCES

Reproducible Masters

- Guided Reading Activity 12–2
- Vocabulary Activity 12–2
- Section Quiz 12–2

Transparencies

- Daily Focus Transparency 12–2

Multimedia

- *ExamView® Assessment Suite* CD-ROM
- Presentation Plus! Software

1 FOCUS

Section Objectives

1. Describe the biological and social needs of humans.
2. Explain Maslow's hierarchy of needs.

BELLRINGER
Motivational Activity

Project Daily Focus Transparency 12–2 and have students answer the questions.

Available as blackline master

Daily Focus Transparency 12–2

Reader's Guide

Use the Reader's Guide to introduce concepts and vocabulary.

Exploring Psychology

Ask students to read the **Exploring Psychology** feature and then discuss: **Does stress increase or decrease your appetite? Why do you think this is so?**

Vocabulary Precheck

Have students read the Glossary definitions of the vocabulary terms. Give students a picture of the brain showing the hypothalamus. Have them add labels to identify the two parts of the hypothalamus. Ask students to create a hierarchy of the needs and their definitions.

CHAPTER 12

Section 2, pages 319–327

2 TEACH

L1 Discussion Point out that much human behavior is obviously not related to primary reinforcers, such as thirst, hunger, or sex. Ask students why they think, for example, that a miser continues to hoard money even when there is no need to do so. Ask students to think of common behaviors of their own or of their peers that could be considered independent of the rewards that originally gave rise to those behaviors. Have them speculate on motivations for those behaviors. **BLOCK SCHEDULING**

Guided Reading Activity 12–2

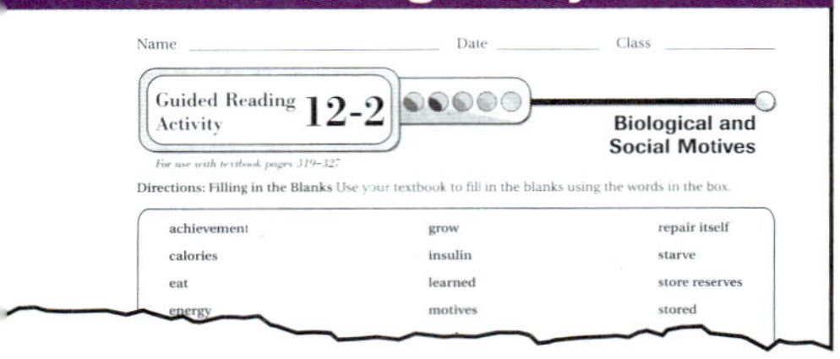
Name ______ Date ______ Class ______

Guided Reading Activity 12-2 Biological and Social Motives

For use with textbook pages 319–327

Directions: Filling in the Blanks Use your textbook to fill in the blanks using the words in the box.

achievement	grow	repair itself
calories	insulin	starve
eat	learned	store reserves
energy	motives	stored

Figure 12.3

Visual Instruction Have students add other needs to the chart, placing them where they fit on the list of needs.

Caption Answer We try to satisfy basic biological needs first.

PSYCHOLOGY JOURNAL

Tell students to keep a careful record of the times when they eat their meals and snacks. They should include both the starting and ending times. Have students identify any patterns that may indicate when their hypothalamus is signaling them to begin or cease eating. Also have students identify when psychosocial hunger factors may be at work. ■

Figure 12.3 Some Biological and Social Needs

Whereas biological needs are physiological requirements critical to our survival, we acquire social needs through experience and learning. ***Which needs do you think we try to satisfy first?***

Some Biological Needs	Some Social Needs
Food Water Oxygen Sleep Avoidance of pain	Need to excel Need for social bonds Need to nourish and protect others Need to influence or control others Need for orderliness Need for fun and relaxation

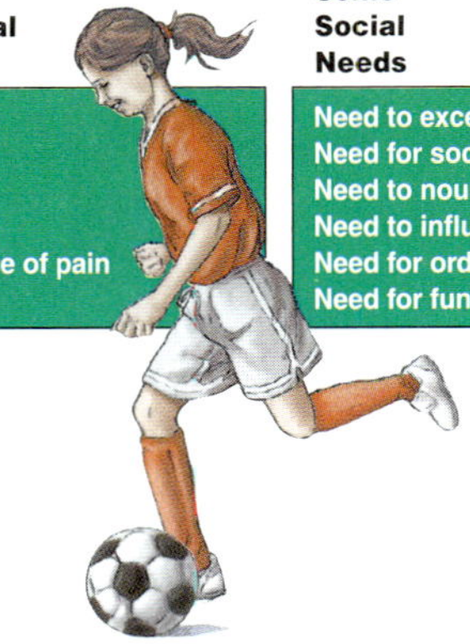

Source: Adapted from *Introduction to Psychology*, Plotnik, 1999.

BIOLOGICAL MOTIVES

Some behavior is determined by the internal, or physiological, state of the organism. Like other animals, human beings have certain survival needs. Our biological needs are critical to our survival and physical well-being (see Figure 12.3). The nervous system is constructed in such a way that dramatic variations in blood sugar, water, oxygen, salt, or essential vitamins lead to changes in behavior designed to return the body to a condition of chemical balance. The first part of this section discusses the role of such physiological factors in motivating behavior.

All organisms, including humans, have built-in regulating systems that work like thermostats to maintain such internal processes as body temperature, the level of sugar in the blood, and the production of hormones. When the level of thyroxine in the bloodstream is low, the pituitary gland secretes a thyroid-stimulating hormone, causing the thyroid gland to secrete more thyroxine. When the thyroxine level is high, the pituitary gland stops producing this hormone. Similarly, when your body temperature drops below a certain point, you start to shiver, certain blood vessels constrict, and blood is directed to the surface for heat. All these activities reduce heat loss and bring body temperature back to the correct level. If your body heat rises above a certain point, you start to sweat, certain blood vessels dilate, and evaporation cools you.

The tendency of all organisms to correct imbalances and deviations from their normal state is known as *homeostasis.* Several of the drives that motivate behavior are homeostatic—hunger, for example.

Hunger

What motivates you to seek food? Often you eat because the sight and smell of, say, pizza tempts you into a restaurant. Other times you eat out of habit because you always have lunch at 12:30 or to be sociable because a friend invites you out for a snack. Yet suppose you are working frantically to finish a term paper. You do not have any food, so you ignore the fact that it is dinnertime and you keep working. At some point your body will start to demand food. You may feel an aching sensation in your stomach. What produces this sensation? What makes you feel hungry?

Your body requires food to grow, to repair itself, and to store reserves. To what is it responding? If the portion of the hypothalamus called the **lateral hypothalamus (LH)** is stimulated with electrodes, a laboratory animal will begin eating, even if it has just finished a large meal. Conversely, if the LH is removed surgically, an animal will stop eating

lateral hypothalamus (LH): the part of the hypothalamus that produces hunger signals

COOPERATIVE LEARNING ACTIVITY

Creating a Television Commercial Organize students into small groups to create a television commercial for a household product. If possible, students should videotape the commercial. If this option is not available, the groups should create complete storyboards of their commercial. Explain that each group should establish roles for its members and make sure that everyone is involved. Tell the groups that the commercial should attempt to subtly persuade people that one or more of their needs will be satisfied if they buy the product. After the groups make their presentations, ask which needs the commercials were directed toward and how successful the commercials were in promising to satisfy those needs.

and eventually die of starvation if it is not fed artificially. Thus the LH provides the signals that tell you when to eat.

If a different portion of the hypothalamus called the **ventromedial hypothalamus (VMH)** is stimulated, an animal will slow down or stop eating altogether, even if it has been kept from food for a long period. If the VMH is removed, however, the animal will eat everything in sight until it becomes so obese it can hardly move (see Figure 12.4). This indicates that the VMH provides the signals that tell you when to stop eating. In addition, the hypothalamus responds to temperature—the LH signal is more active in cold temperatures, while the VMH signal is more active in warm temperatures.

ventromedial hypothalamus (VMH): the part of the hypothalamus that can cause one to stop eating

Other factors also influence your hunger. The *glucostatic theory* suggests that the hypothalamus monitors the amount of glucose, or ready energy, available in the blood. As the level of blood glucose entering cells drops, the LH fires to stimulate you to eat. At the same time, the pancreas releases *insulin* to convert the incoming calories into energy—whether to be consumed by active cells or converted into stored energy in the form of fat for use later. After your meal—as your blood glucose level drops—the pancreas secretes *glucagon,* which helps convert the stored energy back into useful energy. Current thinking holds that environmental factors such as habit and convenience often override hormonal and neural control of eating (Woods et al., 2003).

Another factor affecting eating is the *set-point*—the weight around which your day-to-day weight tends to fluctuate. Although your daily calorie intake and expenditure of energy vary, your body maintains a very stable weight over the long run.

Thus, the hypothalamus interprets at least three kinds of information—the amount of glucose entering the cells of your body, your set-point, and your body temperature. These determine whether or not the hypothalamus will contribute to causing you to eat.

Figure 12.4 When to Stop Eating

This obese rat has a damaged ventromedial hypothalamus and so overate until it weighed 1,080 grams—about eight times what a normal rat at this age weighs. ***How does the hypothalamus help determine whether you will eat or not?***

Hunger—Other Factors Besides the biological motives, other factors may be at work when you feel hungry or eat. These factors are sometimes called *psychosocial hunger factors.* These are external cues that can affect eating, such as where, when, and what we eat. Cues such as smell and the appearance of food can affect eating behavior. When other people are eating, we tend to eat more. You may also choose not to eat because of social pressures, such as trying to look like the thin models in magazines. Sometimes when we are bored or stressed, we eat more. You may eat popcorn when watching a movie because this is what you always do, or you may eat just because it is lunchtime.

Psychosocial factors have a huge impact on our eating habits and sometimes contribute to eating disorders, such as binge eating or eating when depressed.

Readings and Case Studies in Psychology

Have students read the Chapter 12 Reading selection in *Readings and Case Studies in Psychology* and answer the questions that follow the reading.

Cultural Connections

A study comparing various managerial characteristics of men and women from four cultures examined the correlation between the need for personal success and the fear of failure. It was found that in American culture, personal success is more highly valued than in Singapore, Japan, or India. In these cultures, social acceptance is much more highly valued than personal success. In American culture, the fear of failure rated high on the list of concerns. In the other three cultures, the fear of failure rated much lower.

Figure 12.4

Caption Answer The hypothalamus interprets information—including the glucose levels in your body, your set-point, and your body temperature—to determine whether you will eat.

MEETING SPECIAL NEEDS

Learning Style: Naturalist Assign students to watch young children as they are attempting to master some aspect of a sport or game. **Ask:** **What evidence can you observe to prove the competency theory that people choose moderately difficult tasks in which both successes and failures can be instructive?** Students should keep an accurate log of their observations. Ask students to report their findings in an oral report. **L2**

Refer to ***Inclusion for the High School Social Studies Classroom Strategies and Activities*** in the TCR for strategies for students with different learning styles.

CURRICULUM CONNECTION

Health Motivational sports psychologists have proposed a theory to improve the results and the enjoyment of participating in athletics at both a competitive and a recreational level. The theory shifts the focus away from the egocentric view of winning at all costs and toward a task-oriented view. The task-oriented view focuses on goal setting and achievement that moves athletes to the next level of skill and achievement. It does not remove motivation to win from the equation but simply shifts the emphasis to becoming driven to perform tasks at an increasingly higher level.

Reading Check Answer Obese people respond to external cues for food, while normal-weight people are guided by internal cues.

Figure 12.5

Visual Instruction Using Schachter's conclusions about obesity, ask students: **How can the high rates of obesity in America be explained?**

Caption Answer The percentage of overweight people ages 20 to 74 has increased steadily over time. Also, there are fewer overweight women than overweight men.

Obesity

There is a growing body of evidence that a person's weight is controlled by biological factors. There appears to be a genetic component that may predispose some people to obesity (Jackson et al., 1997; Montague et al., 1997). Overweight and obesity are determined by body mass index (BMI), a measure based on height and weight. Using the BMI measure, about 65 percent of American adults are overweight and about 31 percent are obese (see Figure 12.5).

Stanley Schachter (1971) and his colleagues at Columbia University conducted a number of ingenious studies that show that obese people respond to external cues—they eat not because they are hungry, but because they see something good to eat or their watches tell them it is time to eat.

To prove this, Schachter first set up a staged taste test in which people were asked to rate five kinds of crackers. The goal was to see how many crackers normal-weight and overweight people would eat. Each person, instructed to skip lunch, arrived hungry. Some were told that the taste test required a full stomach, and they were given as many roast beef sandwiches as they wanted. The rest stayed hungry. Schachter predicted that normal-weight people eat because they are hungry, while obese people eat whether they are hungry or not. This was true. People of normal weight ate more crackers than overweight people did when both groups were hungry and fewer crackers after they had eaten the roast beef.

In another study, Schachter put out a bowl of almonds that people could eat while they sat in a waiting room. Overweight people ate the nuts only when they did not have to take the shells off. Thus, again they ate simply because the food was there. People of normal weight were equally likely to try a few nuts whether they were shelled or not.

Reading Check What did Schachter conclude about the differences between overweight and normal-weight people?

In summary, Schachter argued that overweight people respond to external cues (for example, the smell of cookies hot from the oven), while normal-weight people respond to internal cues, such as the stomach signals of hunger. His work shows that even physiological needs like hunger are influenced by complex factors.

Other factors, such as an insufficient level of exercise, also contribute to obesity. Increasing your level of exercise can lead to weight loss, just as too little exercise in proportion to the amount of food you eat leads to weight gain. Anxiety and depression, on the other hand, are not causes of

Figure 12.5 Percentage of Overweight Americans

Overweight people face increased risk for heart disease, stroke, high blood pressure, clogged arteries, adult onset diabetes, and early death. ***What is the trend in weight gain in the United States?***

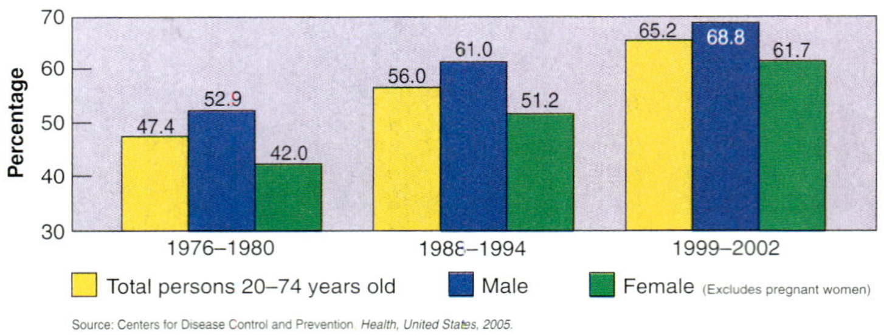

CRITICAL THINKING ACTIVITY

Demonstrating Reasoned Judgment Point out that homeostatic drives are ones that are controlled primarily by physiological processes over which an individual has little or no conscious control, such as the drive to quench a thirst. Nonhomeostatic drives, such as sexual behavior, fear, and aggression, are greatly influenced by social and psychological factors. To some extent they can be consciously controlled. Ask students to create a list of at least 10 nonhomeostatic behaviors. For each behavior listed, students should rate the degree of conscious control a person has over the behavior. **L2**

overeating. These conditions occur just as frequently among people of normal weight as among those who are overweight (Wadden & Stunkard, 1987).

SOCIAL MOTIVES

Many psychologists have concentrated their research on social motives rather than on the unlearned, biological motives we have been discussing. Social motives are learned from our interactions with other people.

Measuring the Need for Achievement

The achievement motive concerns the desire to set challenging goals and to persist in trying to reach those goals despite obstacles, frustrations, and setbacks. One reason the achievement motive has been so well researched is that David McClelland became interested in finding some quantitative way of measuring social motives (McClelland et al., 1953). His main tool for measuring achievement motivation was the Thematic Apperception Test (TAT). This test consists of a series of pictures. Participants are told to make up a story that describes what is happening in each picture. (Tests of this sort are called projective tests, and we will describe them in detail in Chapter 13.) At this point, it is only important to know that there are no right or wrong answers. Since the test questions are ambiguous, the answers must be created from the participant's own beliefs, motives, and attitudes. Each story is coded for certain kinds of themes. These themes are scored according to their relevance to various types of needs, such as achievement, that is, setting goals, competing, and overcoming obstacles.

Based on these tests, McClelland developed a scoring system for the TAT. For example, a story would be scored high in achievement imagery if the main character were concerned with standards of excellence and a high level of performance, with unique accomplishments (such as inventions and awards), or with the pursuit of a long-term career or goal. Coding has been refined to the point where trained coders agree about 90 percent of the time.

Participants register a high need for achievement if they display persistence on tasks or the ability to perform better on tasks, set challenging but realistic goals, compete with others to win, and are attracted to challenging tasks or careers.

Psychology and You

Genetics and Weight

Besides our individual set-points—the weight that our bodies strive to maintain throughout our lives—other genetic, or inherited, factors affect our weight. With a higher set-point we can store more fat. When we add weight, we add fat cells. When we lose weight, each cell gives up a little, emitting signals for more.

We also inherit different rates of metabolism. Your metabolism involves how efficiently your body breaks down food into energy and how quickly your body burns off calories. You may eat the same number of calories as your friend, but if you have a lower metabolic rate than your friend, you burn less fuel (calories) and are more likely to store excess food as fat. The problem is, as you lose weight, the efficiency of your digestive system increases, wringing more calories out of each bite.

Researchers have found weight-regulating genes that play a role in metabolism. One gene increases neuropeptide Y, a brain chemical that leads to increased eating (Gura, 1997). Another gene increases a person's metabolism (Warden, 1997).

Psychology and You

Use the following question to direct a class discussion after students have read the **Psychology and You** feature.
Explain that many health food supplements claim to boost metabolism. **Ask: Why do people want to boost metabolism? What ways exist to boost metabolism without taking nutritional supplements?**

Applying Psychology

Scouting organizations worldwide are well known for their badges and awards that encourage achievement. Have students research one of the national or international scouting organizations and write a report about the social motives used by these organizations.

Vocabulary Activity 12–2

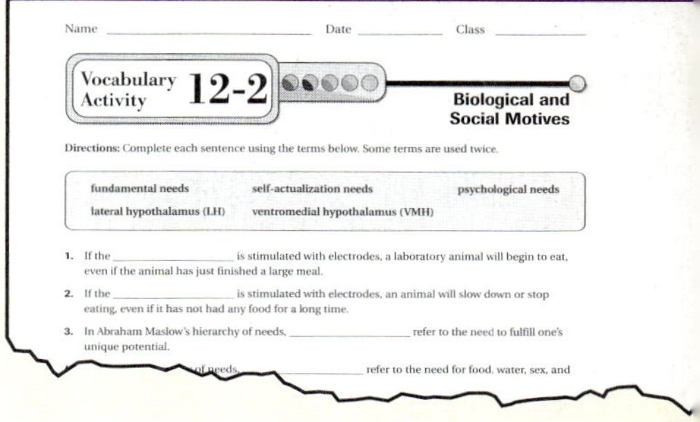
Name ______ Date ______ Class ______

Vocabulary Activity 12-2

Biological and Social Motives

Directions: Complete each sentence using the terms below. Some terms are used twice.

fundamental needs — self-actualization needs — psychological needs — lateral hypothalamus (LH) — ventromedial hypothalamus (VMH)

1. If the ______ is stimulated with electrodes, a laboratory animal will begin to eat, even if the animal has just finished a large meal.
2. If the ______ is stimulated with electrodes, an animal will slow down or stop eating, even if it has not had any food for a long time.
3. In Abraham Maslow's hierarchy of needs, ______ refer to the need to fulfill one's unique potential.

of needs, ______ refer to the need for food, water, sex, and

PSYCHOLOGY LAB EXPERIMENT

Testing a Hypothesis State the following hypothesis: adding extrinsic motivation to a task that has been performed well for its intrinsic motivation may lead to a drop in performance. Organize the class into small groups to test this hypothesis. The experiments should involve an experimental and a control group. The activity should be moderately challenging and can be timed and measured. At Stage 1, both groups perform the activity. At Stage 2, the experimental group is told that they will be paid $1 for every correct completion of the activity. At Stage 3, both groups are asked to complete the activity again, but neither group is rewarded. Ask students to chart and interpret their results. **L2**

L2 Discussion Point out that according to a study by John Atkinson and George Litwin, high achievers take moderate risks when asked to perform a task that will bring some form of reward or punishment. Subjects with a high fear of failure will either take little risk (ensuring success) or very great risk (making it almost impossible to succeed and thereby lowering anxiety). **Ask: Academically, how can you identify high and low achievers? Socially, what characterizes high and low achievers? Athletically, how are high and low achievers identified?**

PSYCHOLOGY Online

Links and instructional guidelines can be found in the **Web Activity Lesson Plan** at glencoe.com.

PSYCHOLOGY Update

Academic Dishonesty Academic dishonesty occurs at all levels of schooling. Research into the causes of cheating yields the following findings:

- 70 percent of high school students and 56 percent of middle school students have cheated on an exam in the past year.
- 90 percent believe that cheating is wrong.
- The primary cause of cheating is a fear of failure.

Schools and educators are using character education, honor codes, and clearly written integrity policies to combat cheating. Multiple versions of tests and classroom monitors are also used to combat academic dishonesty.

PSYCHOLOGY Online

Student Web Activity
Visit the *Understanding Psychology* Web site at glencoe.com and click on **Chapter 12—Student Web Activities** for an activity on motivation.

People who scored high and low in achievement on the TAT were compared in a variety of situations. McClelland followed up the careers of some students at Wesleyan University who had been tested with the TAT in 1947. He wanted to see which students had chosen entrepreneurial work—that is, work in which they had to initiate projects on their own. He found that 11 years after graduation, 83 percent of the entrepreneurs (business managers, insurance salespeople, real estate investors, consultants, and so on) had scored high in achievement, but only 21 percent of the nonentrepreneurs had scored that high (McClelland, 1965).

McClelland did not believe we should all train ourselves as high achievers. In fact, he said that such people are not always the most interesting and they are usually not artistically sensitive (McClelland & Harris, 1971). They would also be less likely to value intimacy in a relationship. Studies have shown that high achievers prefer to be associated with experts who will help them achieve, instead of with more friendly people.

Critics have claimed that using McClelland's TAT is not a reliable method of testing the need for achievement. They assert that TAT stories are difficult to score because different test-scorers may assign different importance to particular responses.

Fear of Failure While some people are motivated by a need for achievement, others may be motivated by a fear of failure. A person displays a fear of failure, for example, when he stops taking guitar lessons because improvement seems too difficult, or she decides not to try out for the baseball team because she probably cannot make it anyway. How does the fear of failure differ from the need for achievement? People display fear of failure when they choose easy tasks offering assured success or impossible tasks with no chance of success. For example, let us say that you have your choice of three puzzles to solve. The first puzzle is extremely easy, and you know that you can solve it. The second puzzle is more difficult, but it can be solved with effort. The third puzzle is extremely difficult, and you are certain it is impossible to solve. People with a strong need for achievement tend to choose the difficult but not impossible puzzle. People who choose the extremely easy puzzle, however, display a fear of failure. Choosing the third puzzle also shows a fear of failure because the person can blame failure on the difficulty of the task.

People who are motivated by the fear of failure often find excuses to explain their poor performances. They do this to maintain a good self-image. For example, a sprinter may explain her slow time in the race as a result of missed sleep. If you receive a poor grade on a test, you may claim that the test was biased. Although creating these types of excuses helps us maintain positive feelings about ourselves, it may also prevent us from taking responsibility for our own actions.

Fear of Success Matina Horner (1970, 1972) asked 89 men to write a story beginning with the line, "After first term finals, John finds himself at the top of his medical school class." Substituting the name Anne for John in the opening line, she also asked 90 women to write a story. Ninety

INTERDISCIPLINARY CONNECTIONS ACTIVITY

History Ask students to research a political or historical figure of their own choosing. The purpose of the research is to identify the motivations behind the individual's success or rise to power or prominence. Ask students to write a short informative essay explaining the individual's motivations in terms of one or more of the theories of motivation discussed in this section. Encourage students to share the results of their research with the class. If time permits, have a class discussion comparing and contrasting the motivations of the different individuals students researched. **L2**

percent of the men wrote success stories. However, more than 65 percent of the women predicted doom for Anne.

On the basis of this study, Horner identified another dimension of achievement motivation—the *fear of success.* Some people (like the females in Horner's study) are (or were) raised with the idea that being successful in all but a few careers is odd and unlikely. Thus, a woman who is a success in medicine, law, and other traditionally male occupations must be a failure as a woman. It might have been acceptable for Anne to pass her exams, but the fact that she did better than all the men in her class made the female participants anxious.

Horner discovered that bright women, who had a very real chance of achieving in their chosen fields, exhibited a stronger fear of success than did women who were average or slightly above average. Expecting success made them more likely to avoid it, despite the obvious advantages of a rewarding career. This seemed to confirm Horner's belief that success involves deep conflicts for some people.

Other researchers then set out to verify Horner's findings. They quickly found that the picture was more complicated than Horner's study suggested. For one thing, it is very difficult to define success. Being a mother might be quite satisfying for one woman but a sign of failure for someone who would have preferred a career outside the home. Also, it is often difficult to tell whether a person who does not try something is more afraid of success or failure.

Reading Check What is the motive to avoid success?

In the late 1960s, when Horner's study was conducted, medical school was still dominated by males. Likewise, nursing school was dominated by females. What if females write about males and vice versa? What if females or males write about males' success in a female-dominated occupation? Then we find both men and women write stories reflecting Horner's fear of success (Cherry & Deaux, 1978). Later, researchers analyzed 64 studies bearing on the issue that Horner had raised. Measured on a mean rate, 45 percent of the men expressed a fear of success, while 49 percent of the women did—a small difference (Paludi, 1984). So, fear of success is found in both men and women.

Other Theories J.W. Atkinson developed an *expectancy-value* theory to explain goal-directed behavior. *Expectancy* is your estimated likelihood of success, and *value* is simply what the goal is worth to you.

Others have argued instead for a *competency* theory. Too easy a task or too difficult a task means we do not learn anything about how competent we are. So, to prove and improve our competency, we choose moderately difficult tasks where both successes and failures may be instructive (Schneider, 1984).

For example, in one experiment in a ring-toss game, children could choose to stand 1 to 15 feet

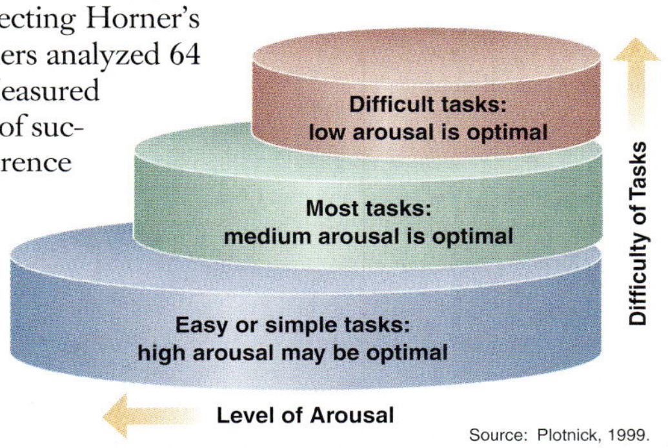

Figure 12.6 Your Performance

The Yerkes-Dodson law says that your performance on a task is an interaction between the level of physiological arousal and the difficulty of the task. So on difficult tasks, you do better if your arousal level is low. ***According to the Yerkes-Dodson law, what level of arousal would help you do well on an exam?***

TEACHER Tip

In discussing the competency theory, point out that studies indicate that people who score high in the need for achievement persist longer on difficult tasks—and do better—than most lower-scoring individuals. These individuals are also more likely to set challenging but realistic goals.

Reading Check Answer The fear of success is another dimension of achievement motivation in which some people are raised with the idea that being successful in all but a few careers is odd and unlikely, so they fear and avoid success.

Figure 12.6

Visual Instruction Ask students to provide examples of tasks that could be performed with low, medium, and high levels of physiological arousal.

Caption Answer A low to medium level of physiological arousal would help you do well on an exam.

EXTENDING THE CONTENT

Psychologists at Work Edwin Garrigues Boring once described all psychologists as falling into two groups—biotropes and sociotropes. Biotropes lean toward biology to explain behavior, while sociotropes lean toward sociology for explanations. As a branch of psychology, *social psychology* is the study of the behavior of individuals in a social context. Psychologists involved in this subdiscipline conduct research on such topics as worker performance, group dynamics, and group decision processes. Ask students to identify the psychologists mentioned in this chapter as biotropes or sociotropes.

Figure 12.7

Caption Answer People motivated by a fear of failure are likely to make excuses for their poor performance and do not try as hard or for as long as those who have a need for achievement.

3 ASSESS

Assign Section 2 Assessment as homework or as an in-class activity.

Section Quiz 12–2

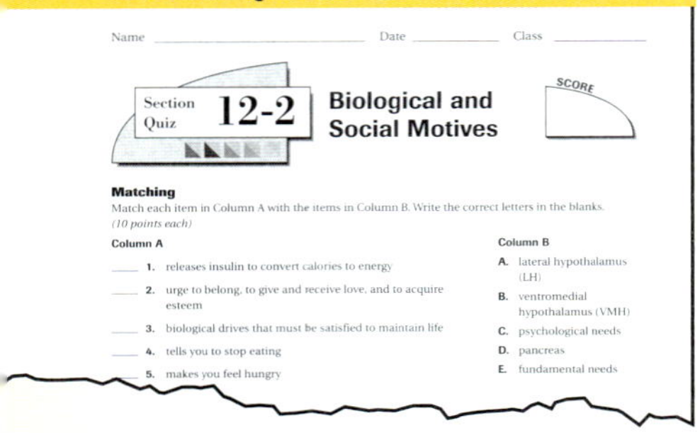
Name ______ Date ______ Class ______

Section Quiz 12-2 Biological and Social Motives

SCORE

Matching

Match each item in Column A with the items in Column B. Write the correct letters in the blanks. *(10 points each)*

Column A	Column B
____ 1. releases insulin to convert calories to energy	A. lateral hypothalamus (LH)
____ 2. urge to belong, to give and receive love, and to acquire esteem	B. ventromedial hypothalamus (VMH)
____ 3. biological drives that must be satisfied to maintain life	C. psychological needs
____ 4. tells you to stop eating	D. pancreas
____ 5. makes you feel hungry	E. fundamental needs

Reteach

List the various theories discussed in this section on one side of the board. List behaviors that are common to teenagers on the other side of the board. Ask students to select a behavior and identify how each theory would explain or classify the behavior. (Note that some behaviors cannot be explained by some theories.)

Figure 12.7 Lacking the Fear of Failure

Preschool children are very optimistic about their own abilities. They show great joy after successfully completing a task but rarely get discouraged by their failures. ***Why do people who are motivated by the fear of failure not perform as well as people who are motivated by the need for achievement?***

fundamental needs: biological drives that must be satisfied to maintain life

psychological needs: the urge to belong and to give and receive love, and the urge to acquire esteem

self-actualization needs: the pursuit of knowledge and beauty or whatever else is required for the realization of one's unique potential

away from the stake onto which they tried to toss rings as a group watched. Those with a high need for achievement were up to 10 times more likely to choose an intermediate distance from the stakes than to choose ridiculously easy or impossibly difficult distances (McClelland, 1958).

Maslow's Hierarchy of Needs

Abraham Maslow, one of the pioneers of humanistic psychology, believed that *all* human beings need to feel competent, to win approval and recognition, and to sense that they have achieved something. He placed achievement motivation in the context of a hierarchy of needs all people share (see Figure 12.8). Maslow proposed that after we satisfy needs at the bottom of the triangle, we advance up to the next level and seek to satisfy the needs at that level. If we are at a higher level and our basic needs (on a lower level) are not satisfied, we may come back down the hierarchy.

Maslow's scheme incorporates all the factors we have discussed so far in this chapter and goes a step further. He begins with biological drives, including the need for physical safety and security. He asserted that people have to satisfy these **fundamental needs** to live. If people are hungry, most of their activities will be motivated by the drive to acquire food, and their functioning on a higher level will be hindered.

The second level in Maslow's hierarchy consists of **psychological needs:** the need to belong and to give and receive love, and the need to acquire esteem through competence and achievement. Maslow suggested that these needs function in much the same way that biological needs do and that they can be filled only by an outside source. A lack of love or esteem makes people anxious and tense. There is a driven quality to their behavior. They may engage in random, desperate, and sometimes maladaptive activities to ease their tensions.

Self-actualization needs are at the top of Maslow's hierarchy. These may include the pursuit of knowledge and beauty or whatever else is required for the realization of one's unique potential. Maslow believed that although relatively few people reach this level, we all have these needs. To be creative in the way we conduct our lives and use our talents, we must first satisfy our fundamental and psychological needs. The satisfaction of these needs motivates us to seek self-actualization. Maslow thus added to motivation theory the idea that some needs take precedence over others and the suggestion that achieving one level of satisfaction releases new needs and motivations.

Other research does not support Maslow's conclusion that one need must be satisfied before another can be (Liebert & Spiegler, 1994). Christopher Columbus, for example, may have achieved self-actualization, but he certainly put his (and many others') need for safety at risk in

EXTENDING THE CONTENT

Maslow's Belongingness Need Dan McAdams identified two components of Maslow's belongingness need. The first is the need for affiliation, which is a desire to maintain social relationships. The strength of this need varies among people. Most people seek their own optimum level of social contact. The second component is a need for intimacy. This is satisfied by close relationships characterized by open communication. The strength of this need also varies among people.

opting to seek a new route to China. Would we not conclude that his need for esteem was dominant in his search? Also, some people do not seem interested in fulfilling higher needs, such as achievement, although their lower, biological needs or safety needs have been met.

These researchers are suggesting that perhaps Maslow identified types of needs that may operate in all of us, but there is no guarantee that the needs must be satisfied in order. Any one need may dominate at a particular time, even as the organism is seeking to respond to others among his or her dominant needs. A need may be dominant in any of us at a particular moment, without necessarily meaning the other needs are not present and influencing our behavior at some level.

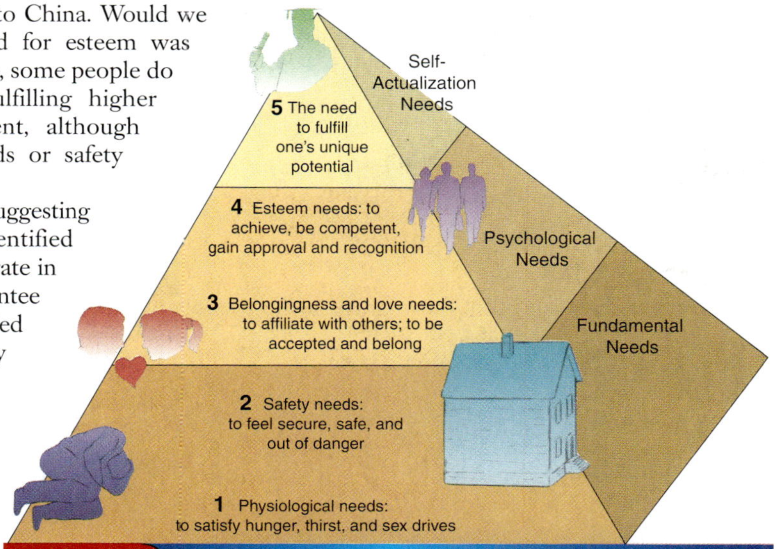

Figure 12.8 Maslow's Hierarchy of Needs

According to Maslow, only after satisfying the lower level of needs is a person free to progress to the ultimate need of self-actualization. ***Into what category in the hierarchy do biological needs fall?***

SECTION 2 Assessment

1. **Review the Vocabulary** Describe how fundamental, psychological, and self-actualization needs differ.
2. **Visualize the Main Idea** Use an organizer similar to the one below to list four motives associated with hunger.

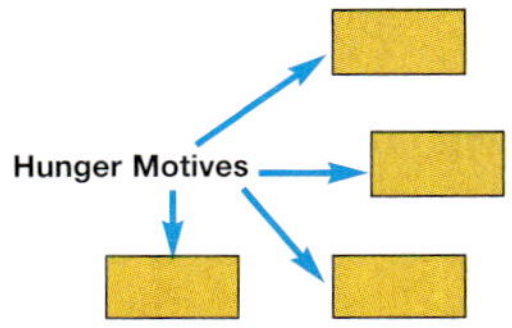

3. **Recall Information** What is the difference between the expectancy-value theory and the competency theory?
4. **Think Critically** What strategies would you offer to a friend who wanted to increase his or her need for achievement level? Explain why.
5. **Application Activity** Review Maslow's hierarchy of needs and analyze your life according to Maslow's scheme. Which groups of needs are frequently met? How do your needs—both fulfilled and unfulfilled—affect your thoughts and behaviors?

SECTION 2 Assessment Answers

1. fundamental needs: needs that must be met to sustain life; psychological needs: needs to belong, to give and receive love, and to acquire esteem; self-actualization needs: needs that allow us to reach our unique potential as humans
2. Answers will vary and may include (1) sight and smell of food, (2) habits, (3) physical sensation of hunger, and (4) level of glucose in the bloodstream
3. The expectancy-value theory explains behavior as the tradeoff between the likelihood of success and the value of the goal for which you are aiming. The competency theory suggests that we choose tasks or behaviors that are moderately difficult in order to learn how competent we are.
4. Your friend should set difficult yet realistic goals and exhibit persistence in achieving those goals.
5. Students' answers will vary. Most will say that their fundamental needs are frequently met and that they rarely give these needs much thought. Many will say that their psychological needs are regularly met.

Figure 12.8

Visual Instruction Point out that Maslow contended that the lower the need in the hierarchy, the more potent it becomes if unfulfilled. A person who is starving, for example, will show little regard for self-esteem.

Caption Answer Biological needs fall into the fundamental needs category.

Enrich

Ask students to list things that are important in their lives—either present-day concerns or future aspirations. When the lists are completed, have students evaluate the items in terms of Maslow's hierarchy and classify them by type of need.

4 CLOSE

Assign the various theories of motivation in this section to small groups. Each group should create a role play that demonstrates or explains the theory.

1 FOCUS

Section Objectives

1. Give examples of the physiological theories of emotion.
2. Explain the cognitive theorists' approach to the study of emotion.

BELLRINGER
Motivational Activity

Project Daily Focus Transparency 12–3 and have students answer the questions.

Available as blackline master

Daily Focus Transparency 12–3

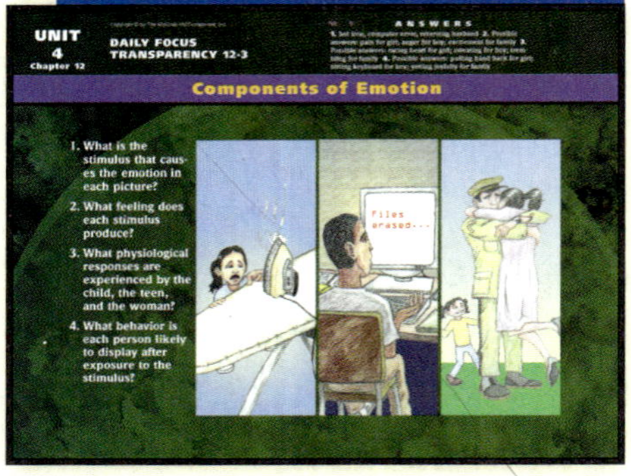

Reader's Guide

Use the Reader's Guide to introduce concepts and vocabulary.

■ **Exploring Psychology**
Ask students to read the **Exploring Psychology** feature and then discuss: **How does emotion affect your actions? What emotions can cause you to temporarily "lose your mind"?**

■ **Vocabulary Precheck**
Have students read the Glossary definition of *emotion*. Then ask them to make a list of emotions.

Use the **Vocabulary PuzzleMaker CD-ROM** to create crossword and word search puzzles.

SECTION 3 Emotions

Reader's Guide

■ **Main Idea**
All emotions consist of three parts—the physical, cognitive, and behavioral aspects. Theories of emotion propose that emotions result from physical changes and/or mental processes.

■ **Vocabulary**
- emotion

■ **Objectives**
- Give examples of the physiological theories of emotion.
- Explain the cognitive theorists' approach to the study of emotion.

EXPLORING PSYCHOLOGY

Victory!

The United States and China were locked in a scoreless tie. . . . The game—the Women's World Cup final—had come down to a single penalty kick. [Brandi] Chastain approached the ball and barely hesitated before drilling her shot perfectly into the upper right corner of the net. As frenzied fans in Pasadena, Calif.'s Rose Bowl roared, she whipped off her shirt and waved it at the crowd before being buried in celebration by a pile of her teammates. "I didn't hear any noise. I didn't look at the [Chinese goalkeeper]," she said of her shot. "As soon as the whistle blew, I just stepped up and hit it. I just kind of lost my mind."

—from *Newsweek*, July 19, 1999

What drove Brandi Chastain to perfect her soccer game? Why did she try so hard? How did she feel when she scored the winning goal? Was she tired, thirsty, excited, nervous, or happy? It is difficult to draw a clear line between motives and emotions. When a person needs food, the stomach contracts, the level of sugar in the blood drops, neural and endocrine systems are thrown slightly off balance, and taste buds become more sensitive. When a person is frightened, heart and breathing rates quicken, energy level rises, senses mobilize, and blood rushes away from the stomach to the brain and to the heart and other muscles. Of course, a poet might diagnose a pounding heart, loss of appetite, and heightened awareness of the moonlight and scented breezes

SECTION RESOURCES

Reproducible Masters
- Guided Reading Activity 12–3
- Vocabulary Activity 12–3
- Section Quiz 12–3

Transparencies
- Daily Focus Transparency 12–3

Multimedia
- Vocabulary PuzzleMaker CD-ROM
- *ExamView*® *Assessment Suite* CD-ROM
- Presentation Plus! Software

as love. Why, if all three involve identifiable physiological changes, do we call hunger a biological drive, and fear and love emotions?

It depends on whether we are describing the source of our behavior or the feelings associated with our behavior. When we want to emphasize the needs, desires, and mental calculations that lead to goal-directed behavior, we use the word *drive* or *motivation*. When we want to stress the feelings associated with these decisions and activities, we use the word *emotion* or *affect*.

Clearly, the two are intertwined. We frequently explain our motives in terms of emotions. Why did you walk out of the meeting? I was angry. Why do you go to so many parties? I enjoy meeting new people and love to dance. Why did you lend your notes to someone you do not particularly like? I felt guilty about talking behind his back.

As these examples demonstrate, emotions push and pull us in different directions. Sometimes emotions function like biological drives—our feelings energize us and make us pursue a goal. Which goal we pursue may be determined by our social learning experiences. Other times we do things because we think they will make us feel good; anticipated emotions are the incentive for our actions. Finally, emotions help us make decisions and communicate what is going on inside of us. As a result, others respond to our emotions and treat us accordingly.

Many psychologists talk about our *emotional intelligence.* This is the ability to perceive, imagine, and understand emotions and to use that information in decision making. We often need to make complicated decisions at work, in school, and with family and friends. The wrong decision can get us in trouble. Our emotional intelligence helps us gauge the situation and determine an appropriate action. For example, suppose you were talking with friends and wanted to tell a joke. Will your friends enjoy the joke, or will they think it is offensive? Judging the emotions involved in this social situation is a sign of your emotional intelligence.

EXPRESSING EMOTIONS

An **emotion** is a subjective feeling provoked by real or imagined objects or events that have high significance to the individual. Emotions result from four occurrences: (1) you must interpret some stimulus;

emotion: a set of complex reactions to stimuli involving subjective feelings, physiological arousal, and observable behavior

Figure 12.9 The Range of Emotions

Emotions are subjective feelings, so psychologists cannot agree on how many emotions exist or the exact impact of a specific emotion. ***How can you explain "avoidance behavior" and "approach behavior" indicated in this chart?***

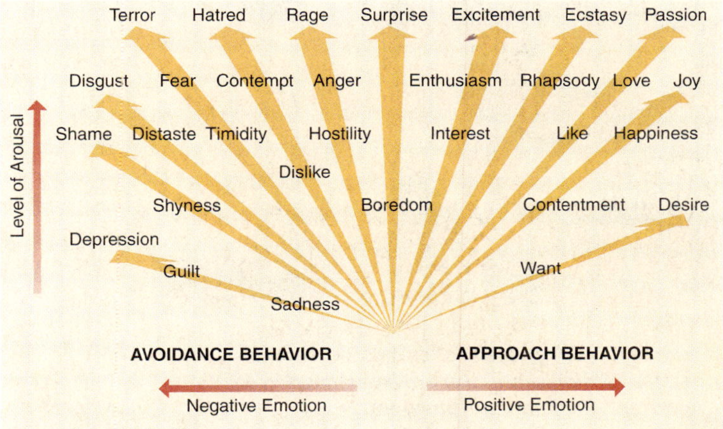

Source: Kissin, 1986.

CHAPTER 12
Section 3, pages 328–336

2 TEACH

L1 Evaluating a Generalization Charles Darwin believed that emotions develop because they have survival value. Have students discuss the validity of this generalization. **Ask: What are the survival values of emotions such as hate, anger, joy, love, fear, and empathy? If emotions are indeed linked to survival, do animals have emotions?**

Guided Reading Activity 12–3

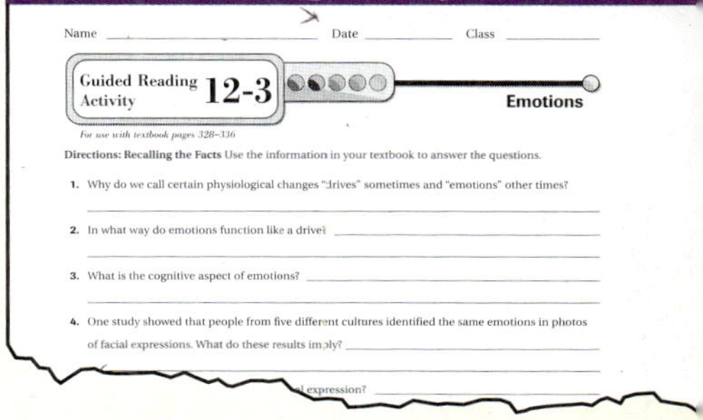

Name ________ Date ________ Class ________

Guided Reading Activity 12-3 — Emotions

For use with textbook pages 328–336

Directions: Recalling the Facts Use the information in your textbook to answer the questions.

1. Why do we call certain physiological changes "drives" sometimes and "emotions" other times?
2. In what way do emotions function like a drive?
3. What is the cognitive aspect of emotions?
4. One study showed that people from five different cultures identified the same emotions in photos of facial expressions. What do these results imply?

...l expression?

Figure 12.9

Visual Instruction Tell students that this chart is one psychologist's attempt to arrange emotions along two dimensions—positive and negative emotions and the level of physiological arousal involved.

Caption Answer Avoidance behavior represents negative emotion, which a person usually tries to evade. Approach behavior represents positive emotions, which are enjoyable and desired.

COOPERATIVE LEARNING ACTIVITY

Creating a Skit Explain to students that in late medieval times, morality plays became a popular form of drama. In these plays, the characters portrayed various virtues and vices battling for possession of a person's soul. Organize students into small groups to create a skit about emotion. Modeled after the morality plays, the groups' skits should show the central character's emotions coming to life and interacting in some sort of dramatic or comic situation. Have the groups present their skits to the rest of the class. **BLOCK SCHEDULING**

Readings and Case Studies in Psychology

Have students read the Chapter 12 Case Study selection in *Readings and Case Studies in Psychology* and answer the questions that follow the case study.

PSYCHOLOGY Update

Emotional Intelligence Recent studies indicate that the emotional intelligence of a company's executives affects the company's performance at all levels. For example, at PepsiCo, the divisions that exceeded their revenue targets were led by people who had strengths in most of the emotional intelligence competencies that have been identified by Daniel Goleman. The competencies include taking initiative, team leadership, and empathy. Conversely, those divisions that performed poorly were led by people who did not display emotional intelligence. Since emotional intelligence can be learned, some companies are providing training for their top executives.

PSYCHOLOGY JOURNAL

Tell students to write about a time when they knew what a friend was feeling just by looking at the friend's face. Ask students to analyze how they knew what their friends were feeling. ■

Figure 12.10

Caption Answer Students may suggest that the male on the left is expressing sadness, guilt, or timidity; the female on the right is displaying happiness, contentment, or self-satisfaction.

Did You Know?

Emotions and Decisions During surgery to remove a brain tumor, "Elliot" suffered damage to his prefrontal cortex (Damasio, 1994). After the surgery, Elliot reported feeling almost no emotions. He described his brain surgery and the following deterioration of his life with calm detachment. Along with the loss of emotions, though, Elliot lost his ability to make decisions. When given information, he could discuss probable outcomes of each decision he might make, but he could not actually make the decision. If he forced himself to make a decision, he soon abandoned his decision. As a result, Elliot could not maintain normal relationships with friends. This points to the fact that our emotions play a large role in our decision making.

(2) you have a subjective feeling, such as fear or happiness; (3) you experience physiological responses, such as an increased heart rate; and (4) you display an observable behavior, such as smiling or crying (Plotnik, 2005).

All emotions have three parts: the physical, the behavioral, and the cognitive parts. The physical aspect has to do with how the emotion affects the physical arousal of an individual. This level of arousal directs the body how to respond to the experienced emotion. The behavioral part is the outward expression of the emotion, such as body language, hand gestures, and the tone of a person's voice. The cognitive aspect concerns how we think about or interpret a situation, which affects our emotions. For example, if someone says hello, we interpret that person as being friendly, hostile, or mocking, which in turn affects our emotional response.

In *The Expression of the Emotions in Man and Animals* (1872), Charles Darwin argued that all people express certain basic feelings in the same ways. Without knowing a person's language, you can tell whether he or she is amused or infuriated just by looking at that person's face (see Figure 12.10). One group of researchers (Ekman, Friesen, & Ellsworth, 1972) selected a group of photographs they thought depicted surprise, anger, sadness, and happiness. They then showed the photographs to people from five different cultures and asked them to say what they believed the person in each photograph was feeling. The overwhelming majority of the participants identified the emotions as the researchers expected they would. Was this simply because they had met Americans—or at least seen American television shows and movies—and so learned how to read our facial expressions? Apparently not. A second study was conducted in a remote part of New Guinea with people who had relatively little contact with outsiders and virtually no exposure to mass media. They, too, were able to identify the emotions being expressed.

These studies imply that certain basic facial expressions are *innate*—that is, part of our biological inheritance. Observations of children who were born without sight and hearing lend support to this view. These youngsters could not have learned how to communicate feelings by observing other people. Still, they laugh like other children when they are happy, pout and frown to express

Figure 12.10 Facial Feedback

There are many specific inherited facial expressions that signal specific feelings or emotional states. ***Which emotions are expressed in these photos? Explain your answers.***

MEETING SPECIAL NEEDS

Learning Style: Verbal/Linguistic Lie detection continues to have its advocates and its detractors. Have students conduct research to determine to what extent the results of lie detector tests are admissible as evidence in courts of law. Based on the research, hold a debate on the following: *Resolved—Polygraphs should be admissible evidence in determining a defendant's guilt or innocence.* **L2** **BLOCK SCHEDULING**

Refer to ***Inclusion for the High School Social Studies Classroom Strategies and Activities*** in the TCR for strategies for students with different learning styles.

resentment, and clench their fists and teeth in anger (Goodenough, 1932).

Psychologist Carroll Izard and his colleagues (Trotter, 1983) developed a coding system for assessing emotional states in people. By noticing changes in different parts of the face, such as the eyebrows, eyes, and mouth, they have been able to identify 10 different emotional states. For example, anger is indicated when a person's eyebrows are sharply lowered and drawn together, and the eyes narrowed or squinted (see Figure 12.11). Another psychologist (Russell, 1994) studied the impact of emotions on facial structures in 11 cross-cultural studies. He concluded that there are universally recognized facial expressions of emotions.

Learning is an important factor in emotional expression. James Averill (1983) believes that many of our everyday emotional reactions are the result of social expectations and consequences. He believes that emotions are responses of the whole person and that we cannot separate an individual's physical or biological experience of emotions from that person's thoughts or actions associated with those emotions. We learn to express and experience emotions in the company of other people, and we learn that emotions can serve different social functions. Parents, for example, modify their children's emotions by responding angrily to some outbursts, by being sympathetic to others, and on occasion by ignoring their youngsters. In this way, children are taught which emotions are considered appropriate in different situations.

Learning explains the differences we find among cultures once we go beyond such basic expressions as laughing or crying. Children will imitate the expressions used by their parents or caregivers. Thus, emotions are universal, but the expression of them is limited by learning how to

Profiles In Psychology

Paul Ekman

1934–

"The face is the primary site for the display of emotions. Together with the voice, it may tell the listener how the speaker feels about what is being said . . ."

Paul Ekman claims that human faces express emotion in a universal way. That is, we all smile when we are happy and scowl when we are angry. Ekman did not always believe this, though. He once thought that facial expressions were learned and differed depending on our culture. Then Ekman traveled to Papua New Guinea and studied the Fores—an isolated group. He found that they grinned when they were happy and scowled when angry, just like we do.

Since then Ekman has developed the Facial Action Coding System (FACS), which organizes facial expressions into 46 separate movements, such as blinking, raising our brows, and pursing our lips. Ekman and other researchers used FACS to identify the facial characteristics of seven emotions: anger, fear, contempt, disgust, sadness, surprise, and happiness. Ekman claims that few of us (10 to 20 percent) can actually hide our true emotions. Despite our efforts, for example, to hide our disgust, some facial movements give us away.

CRITICAL THINKING ACTIVITY

Evaluating a Hypothesis After the students have read about the Schachter-Singer experiment (pages 333–334), instruct them to work in pairs or small groups to devise another scenario that might be used to test the validity of the theory. Students should consider the following question: **Do internal components of emotion affect a person differently, depending on his or her interpretation or perception of the social situation?** After each pair or group has presented its scenario to the class, ask the students to decide which scenario would be the best test of the theory. **L2**

Profiles In Psychology

Ask students to read the **Profiles In Psychology** feature and then discuss the following questions:

1. To whom does Ekman say the Facial Action Coding System applies? *(He believes the system can be applied to most people across many cultures.)*
2. How many people can truly disguise or hide their emotions? *(few; 10 to 20 percent)*
3. Even when we think we are hiding our emotions, what usually gives us away? *(Some subtle facial movement or a change in voice inflection often gives away our emotions.)*

CURRICULUM CONNECTION

Health At least three separate studies have shown that cancer patients who participate in social support groups live longer and have a better quality of life. Researchers believe the key to the social support groups is that they allow cancer patients to freely express their emotions. A trained leader who is often a cancer survivor usually facilitates such groups.

CHAPTER 12

Section 3, pages 328–336

Figure 12.11

Visual Instruction Tell students to try to go about 10 hours without expressing emotions. This is not only difficult, it can be agonizing. Emotions send powerful social signals about how you feel, help you adapt to situations, arouse you physiologically, and motivate many behaviors.

Caption Answer Students will probably select the triangular, diagonal, or straight-edged elements because they seem hard, uncompromising, and therefore frightening.

Looking @ the Issues

Computers and Emotions What if computers could "understand" your emotions and react accordingly? With the link between emotions and physiological changes well established, it may be possible to program computer chips to sense those physiological changes and interpret the emotion that is creating the changes. For example, you are running late to a meeting and find your anger building as you sit in a traffic jam. The computer chip that you are wearing senses the physiological changes, interprets the emotion, and automatically activates the car's stereo system to play calming music. **Ask:** **Would you want to wear a computer chip that could interpret your emotions? What potential uses and abuses do you see for this type of technology?**

Vocabulary Activity 12–3

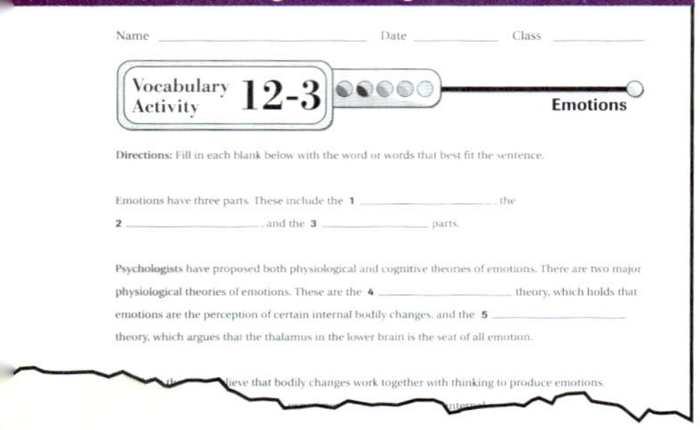
Name ______ Date ______ Class ______

Vocabulary Activity 12-3 — Emotions

Directions: Fill in each blank below with the word or words that best fit the sentence.

Emotions have three parts. These include the **1** ______, the **2** ______, and the **3** ______ parts.

Psychologists have proposed both physiological and cognitive theories of emotions. There are two major **physiological** theories of emotions. These are the **4** ______ theory, which holds that emotions are the perception of certain internal bodily changes, and the **5** ______ theory, which argues that the thalamus in the lower brain is the seat of all emotion.

...lieve that bodily changes work together with thinking to produce emotions.

Figure 12.11 **Threatening Elements**

When people from various cultures were asked to identify the threatening shapes in each pair, they consistently selected the triangular and diagonal elements. ***Which elements would you use to make a scary mask? Why?***

Mask making

express them. Children are taught—either directly or indirectly—which emotions are appropriate in certain circumstances. Children learn how to express these emotions at the appropriate times. In effect, children are learning an emotional culture. What these findings suggest is that all of us are born with the capacity for emotion and with certain basic forms of expression, but when, where, and how we express different feelings depend in large part on learning.

Analyzing facial expressions helps us to describe emotions, but it does not tell us where emotions come from. Some psychologists believe emotions derive from physical changes, while others believe that emotions result from mental processes.

Physiological Theories

Trying to figure out the cognitive, behavioral, and physical parts of emotions has led to several theories of emotions. In *Principles of Psychology*, a classic work published in 1890, William James attempted to summarize the best available literature on human behavior, motivations, and feelings. When it came to drawing up a catalog of human emotions, James gave up; he felt there were too many subtle variations. Yet he was struck by the fact that nearly every description of emotions he read emphasized bodily changes. We associate feelings with sudden increases or decreases in energy, muscle tension and relaxation, and sensations in the pits of our stomachs.

The James-Lange Theory After much thought, James concluded that we use the word *emotion* to describe our visceral, or gut, reactions to the things that take place around us. In other words, James (1890) believed that emotions are the perception of certain internal bodily changes.

> My theory . . . is that *the bodily changes follow directly the perception of the exciting fact, and that our feeling of the same changes as they occur IS the emotion.* Commonsense says, we lose our fortune, are sorry and weep; we meet a bear, are frightened and run; we are insulted by a rival, are angry and strike. . . . [T]he more rational statement is that we feel sorry because we cry, angry because we strike, afraid because we tremble. . . . Without the bodily states following on the perception, the latter would be . . . pale, colorless, destitute of emotional warmth.

Whereas other psychologists had assumed that emotions trigger bodily changes, James argued that bodily reactions form the basis of labeling and experiencing emotions. Because Carl Lange came to the same conclusion at about the same time, this position is known as the *James-Lange theory* (Lange & James, 1922). Carroll Izard's (1972) theory of emotions bears a striking resemblance to the James-Lange theory. He believed that our conscious experience of emotion results from the sensory feedback we receive from the muscles in our faces (see More About Facial Feedback Theory). You can check this out by noticing the difference in your emotional experience when you smile for two minutes as opposed to when you frown for two minutes. According to Izard's view, if you

PSYCHOLOGY LAB EXPERIMENT

Physiological Aspects of Emotion Ask students to find five participants to test the physiological aspects of emotions. Tell students to work with the participants one at a time. Have them tell the participant to tense the muscles in his or her upper body for 15 seconds. As they do, students should ask participants to pay careful attention to their bodily reactions and sensations and have them describe what they are experiencing. Students should then ask the participant to compare these reactions and sensations to any feelings they have while experiencing a particular emotion. Students should summarize their findings in a paragraph. **L1** **ELL** **BLOCK SCHEDULING**

continue to frown, you will experience an unpleasant emotion. Thus, we react to our physiological state and label it as sadness.

Critics of the James-Lange theory claim that different emotions such as anger, sadness, or fear are not necessarily associated with different physiological reactions. For example, anger and fear may cause the same bodily reactions. Therefore, James had it backwards—you do not run from trouble and then feel fear; you feel fear first and then run. Critics also allege that some complex emotions such as jealousy or love require much interpretation and thought on our part. The James-Lange theory leaves out the influence of cognition on emotions. Although physiological changes do not cause emotions, they may increase the intensity of the emotions that we feel. For instance, when we feel anger and our hearts race, that anger may be heightened by the way our body reacts to it.

The Cannon-Bard Theory In 1929 Walter B. Cannon published a summary of the evidence against the James-Lange theory. Cannon argued that the thalamus (part of the lower brain) is the seat of emotion—an idea Philip Bard (1934) expanded and refined. According to the *Cannon-Bard theory*, certain experiences activate the thalamus, and the thalamus sends messages to the cortex and to the other body organs. This theory states that the brain sends two reactions—arousal and experience of emotion. But one does not cause the other. Thus, when we use the word *emotion*, we are referring to the simultaneous burst of activity in the brain and gut reactions. In Cannon's words, "The peculiar quality of emotion is added to simple sensation when the thalamic processes are aroused" (1929). Later, more sophisticated experiments showed that the thalamus is not involved in emotional experience, but the hypothalamus is.

Cannon also emphasized the importance of physiological arousal in many different emotions. He was the first to describe the fight-or-flight reaction of the sympathetic nervous system that prepares us for an emergency. Some of the signs of physiological arousal are measured in one of the most famous applications of psychological knowledge—lie detection.

Cognitive Theories

Cognitive theorists believe that bodily changes and thinking work together to produce emotions. Physiological arousal is only half of the story. What you feel depends on how you interpret your symptoms. This, in turn, depends on labeling the physical arousal with an emotion to interpret our internal state.

The Schachter-Singer Experiment Stanley Schachter and Jerome Singer designed an experiment to explore this theory (1962). They told all their

More About...

Facial Feedback Theory

The facial feedback theory says that your brain interprets feedback from the movement of your facial muscles as different emotions (Ekman, 1984). For example, you see a dark shadow in the corner of your bedroom at night. You react by raising your eyebrows and widening your eyes. Your brain interprets these facial expressions as those associated with fear, and you feel fear.

Critics of this theory claim that although your facial expressions may influence your emotions, they do not cause your emotions. People whose facial muscles are paralyzed can experience emotions even though their facial muscles do not move (McIntosh, 1996). You can influence your mood, though, with your expressions. For instance, have you ever noticed that if you just smile, you feel a little happier?

Reading Check How does the Cannon-Bard theory differ from the James-Lange theory?

INTERDISCIPLINARY CONNECTIONS ACTIVITY

The Arts Assign students to find examples of modern abstract paintings—such as those by Mark Rothko, Jackson Pollock, and Helen Frankenthaler—that they feel express particular emotions through shape and color alone. If possible, display the examples in the classroom, and poll the students to see how many agree that the paintings express identifiable emotions. Ask students to name the emotion being depicted before finding out the painting's title. **L2** ELL

L2 Discussion In discussing cognitive theories, begin by having students review the dictionary definition of *cognition* (the process of knowing in the broadest sense). Emphasize that knowing what is going on within and around us affects physiological arousal. As an example, pose this scenario: Two fathers are videotaping a graduation ceremony. One knows that his daughter has been selected to receive a prestigious scholarship. The other does not know that his son has been selected as the other recipient of the scholarship. **Ask:** **Whose videotape is more likely to show a jolt at the moment his child's name is announced? Whose videotape is more likely to show evidence of shaking before the announcement? Why is this so?**

FYI

There is little evidence to suggest that men and women differ in their feeling of emotions. There is, however, research that indicates that women tend to express their emotions more freely and frequently than men.

Reading Check Answer The Cannon-Bard theory states that emotion is the result of the brain sending two simultaneous reactions, one dealing with physiological sensations and one to trigger emotion. These reactions are not linked in a cause-and-effect relationship. The James-Lange theory, on the other hand, stated that emotions are the perception of physiological changes.

L1 Understanding How Panic Spreads Ask students to use the Schachter-Singer experiment as a basis for explaining the way in which panic can run through a crowd. *(People who do not know the extent of a crisis might be inclined to take their cues from others who have begun to panic.)* Ask students to think of real-life situations in which unwarranted panic swept through a crowd. ELL

TEACHER Tip

Point out that the polygraph does not detect lying. Rather, it measures changes in a person's nervous system.

Reading Check Answer The environment influences our interpretation of the internal components of emotion and the way the emotion is expressed.

FYI

Centuries ago in some parts of Asia, officials used a form of lie detection based on the lessening of salivation under nervous stress. Suspects were ordered to fill their mouths with dry rice. The suspect who had the most difficult time spitting out the rice was judged the guilty party.

More About...

Lie Detection

Throughout time, people have tried to find a way to detect when others are lying. The polygraph is an instrument that records the arousal of the sympathetic nervous system, including blood pressure, heart rate, and breathing rate. The polygraph works under the assumption that people feel nervous when they lie, so their physiological reactions will give them away. How effective are polygraphs? Many innocent people become nervous when questioned and so appear to be lying.

The Guilty-Knowledge test, though, is a modified version of the polygraph test. The questioner asks more accurate questions—questions that could be threatening only to someone who knows the unpublicized facts of the crime. For example, instead of asking, "Did you rob the gas station?" the person is asked, "Was the gas station robbed at 6:00 P.M.? At midnight? With a gun? With a knife?" People who display heightened arousal in response to the correct answers are presumed guilty. This test identifies guilty people more accurately.

participants they were testing the effects of a vitamin on eyesight. In reality, most received an adrenaline injection. The *informed* group was told that the injection would make their hearts race and their bodies tremble (which was true). The *misinformed* group was told that the injection would make them numb. An *uninformed* group was not told anything about how their bodies would react to the shot. A *control* group received a neutral injection that did not produce any symptoms. Like the third group, these participants were not given any information about possible side effects.

After the injection, each participant was taken to a room to wait for the vision test. There they found another person who was actually part of the experiment. The participants thought the accomplice had had the same injection as theirs. Everyone completed the same questionnaire. As this happened, the accomplice applied the second independent variable. For half the participants he got happier and happier, eventually shooting the questionnaire into the wastebasket. For the other group of participants he got equally active but ever angrier, eventually throwing away the wadded-up questionnaire.

Participants from the first group, who had been told how the injection would affect them, watched the accomplice with mild amusement. So did participants who had received the neutral injection. However, those from the second and third groups, who either had an incorrect idea or no idea about the side effects, joined in with the accomplice. If he was euphoric, so were they; if he was angry, they became angry.

Reading Check According to Schachter, what role does the environment play in the emotions you experience?

What does this experiment demonstrate? Internal components of emotion (such as those adrenaline produces) affect a person differently, depending on his or her interpretation or perception of the social situation. When people cannot explain their physical reactions, they take cues from their environment. The accomplice provided cues. Yet when people knew that their hearts were beating faster because of the shot, they did not feel particularly happy or angry. The experiment also shows that internal changes are important—otherwise the participants from the neutral group would have acted in the same way as those from the misinformed groups. Perception and arousal *interact* to create emotions.

Critics of this theory point out that you do not need to first experience physiological arousal to feel an emotion. Sometimes you feel an emotion first, and then your body reacts. For example, you may let your brother use your computer. When you go to use your computer and see that all of your files have been destroyed, you get angry, and then your body reacts with anger. Critics also say that you use processes other than environmental cues to interpret your emotions. Your thoughts play a large role in appraising your emotions.

EXTENDING THE CONTENT

Emoticons When e-mail first became popular as a means of informal communication, clever e-mail users developed keyboard shortcuts to show various emotions. These became known as emoticons. They consist of standard keyboard characters and are read by tilting one's head to the left 90 degrees. On a blank acetate transparency, invite students to draw their favorite emoticon and label it with the emotion being expressed. Ask students to explain why emoticons are popular in informal e-mail messages. L1 ELL

Opponent-Process Theory Physiological processes clearly are controlled by homeostatic mechanisms that usually keep the body within certain narrow limits. Emotions can be as disabling as a salt imbalance to normal activity. Why would the body not develop a homeostatic mechanism to control the effects of extreme emotions? The body has sympathetic and parasympathetic systems. The sympathetic system energizes the body for activity, while the parasympathetic system calms and relaxes the body. The opponent-process theory states that these two systems act in concert to regulate and manipulate our emotions.

Psychologists Richard Solomon and John Corbit (1974) proposed the opponent-process theory—a homeostatic theory of emotional reactions based on classical conditioning. They proposed that the removal of a stimulus that excites one emotion causes a swing to an opposite emotion. If the external, emotion-arousing event is State A, the internal force is labeled State B (see Figure 12.13).

Suppose you meet someone on the first day of school, and from the start, you like each other. The two of you stun your English teacher with sharp questions and quick answers when challenged. Later, you share a wonderful lunch—both of you love the same four-topping pizza. An afternoon in the park was glorious, and doing homework assignments together is fun and easy. Then, later that day, your friend tells you that his or her family is moving to the coast—gone forever. You are annoyed . . . but let us face it, the next day you are back out looking for another special person (because little classical conditioning has occurred). The opponent-process theory would indicate that with this person you were subjected to State A, which aroused your emotions, but no State B had developed.

Now let us put a different slant on the ending. Your friend did not move away. You marry and enjoy a loving relationship and a long, healthy life together. One morning, however, your spouse dies. Your years together had produced a strong countering State B, which occurred anytime you were in the presence of your beloved. It kept your emotions near neutral and allowed you to get on with your daily activities. Yet now

Figure 12.12 Theories of Emotion

These theories of emotion differ depending on the relationship of physiological change and cognitive interpretation of emotion. ***What causes the emotion in each theory?***

James-Lange Theory

↓ You experience physiological changes.

↓ Your brain interprets the physiological changes.

↓ You feel a specific emotion.

↓ You demonstrate observable behavior.

Facial Feedback Theory

↓ The muscles in your face move to form an expression.

↓ Your brain interprets the muscle movement.

↓ You feel an emotion.

↓ You demonstrate observable behavior.

Cannon-Bard Theory

↓ Your experience activates the hypothalamus.

↓ This produces messages to the cerebral cortex and your body organs. The reacting organs activate sensory signals.

↓ Sensory signals combine with cortical message, yielding emotion.

Schachter-Singer Experiment

↓ You experience physiological arousal.

↓ You interpret (cognitively) environmental cues.

↓ You feel an emotion.

↓ You demonstrate observable behavior.

Figure 12.12

Visual Instruction Give students an emotion such as anger or fear and have them apply each theory to the emotion.

Caption Answer James-Lange—physiological change; facial feedback—movements in facial muscles in reaction to a stimulus are interpreted by brain; Cannon-Bard—the experience activates the hypothalamus to react and you experience the emotion at the same time; Schachter-Singer—an experience arouses you, and you interpret the environmental cues to feel the emotion.

3 ASSESS

Assign Section 3 Assessment as homework or as an in-class activity.

Section Quiz 12-3

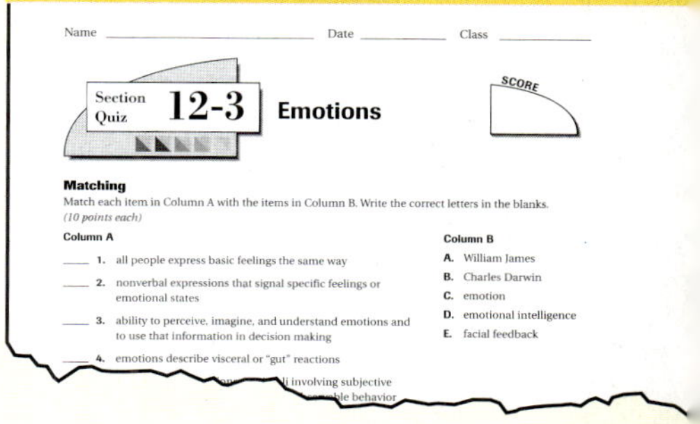
Name ______ Date ______ Class ______

Section Quiz 12-3 **Emotions**

SCORE

Matching

Match each item in Column A with the items in Column B. Write the correct letters in the blanks. *(10 points each)*

Column A

____ 1. all people express basic feelings the same way

____ 2. nonverbal expressions that signal specific feelings or emotional states

____ 3. ability to perceive, imagine, and understand emotions and to use that information in decision making

____ 4. emotions describe visceral or "gut" reactions

Column B

A. William James

B. Charles Darwin

C. emotion

D. emotional intelligence

E. facial feedback

EXTENDING THE CONTENT

Writing a Poem Ask students to write a before-and-after poem that illustrates the emotional shift that occurs in people as they move from State A to State B according to the opponent-process theory. Suggest the poem contain two stanzas—the first describing State A and the second describing State B. Emphasize that poems can be short and written in free-form, nonrhyming verse. Ask volunteers to read their poems aloud. **L2**

Figure 12.13

Caption Answer As the experience is repeated, the wide swings in emotion from State A to State B diminish. As the intensity of State A is reduced, that of State B is strengthened.

Reteach

Have students compare and contrast the physiological and cognitive theories of emotion. Students should create a Venn diagram to show the differences and similarities.

Enrich

Ask students to write a one-paragraph summary of the opponent-process theory and give one original example of how the theory operates.

4 CLOSE

Prepare a display of various facial expressions from pictures in magazines or pictures taken specifically for this section. Have students identify the emotion by interpreting the facial expressions.

Figure 12.13 Fear and Relief

According to the opponent-process theory, when the stimulus for one emotion is removed, you feel the opposite emotion. ***According to this theory, what happens when the experience is repeated many times?***

that your spouse is gone, you are left with only the incredibly depressing effects of the remaining classically conditioned State B. Have you ever had the misfortune of watching one of your grandparents lose the partner to whom he or she was deeply devoted?

The significance of this theory is that if the State A event is a terrifying one, such as your first parachute jump, it still predicts what will happen. Novice parachutists are terrified coming out of a plane but are wildly delighted when they return to the ground—they are subject to a brief, happy rebound. Experienced jumpers know that how they pack their chutes is crucial, how they coordinate during the fall is important, and it is important that they know how to land. The jump is eventually only a bit stressful—thanks to the positive, classically conditioned State B. They usually jump for the long-term satisfaction that is generated—again, thanks to the long-lasting, positive counter reaction to the now-absent State A—once the jump itself is completed.

In fact, other emotion researchers believe that emotion may play an important role in our survival as human beings and in our ability to achieve goals, precisely because it spurs us to action. Emotions and physical changes are intertwined. It will probably be many years before we understand all the complex ways in which the two interact in human behavior.

SECTION 3 Assessment

1. **Review the Vocabulary** What are the three parts of an emotion?
2. **Visualize the Main Idea** Use a flowchart similar to the one below to describe how the opponent-process theory works.

The Opponent-Process Theory

3. **Recall Information** What does it mean when psychologists say that certain facial expressions are *innate?*
4. **Think Critically** You are awakened by a loud noise in the middle of the night. You feel frightened and you start to tremble. According to the James-Lange theory, which came first—the fright or the trembling? According to Schachter and Singer's theory, which came first?
5. **Application Activity** Create a self-test to evaluate the presence and intensity of an emotion. For example, if you are testing for anger, you may create a checklist that includes the following: People tell you that you need to calm down. You feel tense much of the time. Give the self-test to several people and rate their responses.

SECTION 3 Assessment Answers

1. Emotions consist of (1) the physical, (2) the behavioral, and (3) the cognitive aspects.
2. stimulus perceived → State A emotion aroused → removal of stimulus → swing to State B, the opposite emotion
3. Psychologists have studied facial expressions across cultures and found that certain facial expressions are associated with the same emotion in the different cultures. Psychologists conclude that these expressions are inborn, or present at birth.
4. Both theories propose that the trembling preceded the fright. According to the James-Lange theory, the trembling caused your fright. According to the Schachter-Singer theory, you trembled, appraised environmental cues, and then felt fright.
5. Students' answers will vary. The self-tests should avoid using the word for the actual emotion that students are testing for. For extension, ask students if the differences in intensity of the expression of emotion indicate that two people experience emotions at different intensities.

CHAPTER 12 Summary and Vocabulary

The study of motivation and emotion focuses on the underlying why of behavior. Motivation refers to the physical and mental factors that cause us to act in a specific way when aroused. Emotion involves our subjective feelings, physical arousal, and external expressions in response to situations and events.

Section 1 Theories of Motivation

Main Idea: Psychologists explain motivation and why we experience it in different ways through instinct, drive-reduction, incentive, and cognitive theories of motivation.

- The instinct theory of motivation stresses that humans are motivated by a variety of instincts.
- The drive-reduction theory is based on the idea that all human motives are extensions of basic biological needs.
- The incentive theory stresses the role of the environment in motivating behavior.
- The cognitive theory proposes that motivation is influenced by forces both inside and outside individuals that energize them to move.

Section 2 Biological and Social Motives

Main Idea: Much of life is spent trying to satisfy biological and social needs. Biological needs are physiological requirements that we must fulfill to survive, whereas social needs are those that are learned through experience.

- Biological motives often involve organisms' need to correct imbalances and deviations from their normal state.
- The hypothalamus interprets three kinds of information—the amount of glucose entering a body's cells, an individual's set-point, and body temperature—to determine whether an individual will eat or not.
- Social motives are learned from people's interactions with other people.
- The achievement motive concerns the desire to set challenging goals and to persist in trying to reach those goals despite obstacles, frustrations, and setbacks.

Section 3 Emotions

Main Idea: All emotions consist of three parts—the physical, cognitive, and behavioral aspects. Theories of emotion propose that emotions result from physical changes and/or mental processes.

- An emotion is a subjective feeling provoked by real or imagined objects or events that have high significance to the individual.
- All emotions have three parts: the physical, the behavioral, and the cognitive parts.
- Some psychologists believe emotions derive from physical changes, while others believe that emotions result from mental processes.

Chapter Vocabulary

- motivation (p. 314)
- instincts (p. 314)
- need (p. 314)
- drive (p. 315)
- homeostasis (p. 315)
- incentive (p. 316)
- extrinsic motivation (p. 316)
- intrinsic motivation (p. 316)
- lateral hypothalamus (LH) (p. 320)
- ventromedial hypothalamus (VMH) (p. 321)
- fundamental needs (p. 326)
- psychological needs (p. 326)
- self-actualization needs (p. 326)
- emotion (p. 329)

12 Summary and Vocabulary

Using the Chapter 12 Summary and Vocabulary

Use the Chapter 12 Summary and Vocabulary to preview, review, condense, or reteach the chapter.

Preview/Review

Use the Chapter Vocabulary list to help students review and study.

Activity Have students create a word search puzzle using definitions or examples as the clues for the puzzle. Then ask pairs of students to exchange and complete each other's puzzles.

Vocabulary PuzzleMaker CD-ROM reinforces the vocabulary terms used in Chapter 12.

Condense

Have students read the Chapter 12 Summary.

Chapter 12 Guided Reading Activities

Reteach

Reteaching Activity 12

PERFORMANCE ASSESSMENT ACTIVITY

Photo Survey Organize the class into groups of 3 or 4 students. Then ask each group to find magazine photos of facial expressions for at least six different emotions. Tell students to mount the photos on separate, numbered sheets of paper. Have each group survey 20 people of different ages and genders. The group should give each participant a data sheet consisting of a space for their age and gender and lines numbered 1 through 6. Students should direct participants to complete the data sheet by identifying the emotion being expressed in each photo. Each group should analyze the data by age and gender, using charts and written explanations of their findings. Encourage the groups to compare their findings.

PSYCHOLOGY Online

Have students visit the Web site at glencoe.com to review Chapter 12 and take the **Self-Check Quiz**.

GLENCOE TECHNOLOGY

PRESENTATION Plus! For a review of Chapter 12 content, see MindJogger Checkpoint on **Presentation Plus!**

Reviewing Vocabulary

1. c	**6.** i
2. j	**7.** f
3. h	**8.** a
4. e	**9.** g
5. d	**10.** b

Recalling Facts

1. The drive-reduction theory emerged from the work of Clark Hull, an experimental psychologist who traced motivation back to basic physiological (biological) needs.
2. Extrinsic motivation satisfies a biological need or helps achieve an external incentive. Intrinsic motivation comes from within us and fulfills our beliefs and expectations.
3. McClelland uses the Thematic Apperception Test (TAT). The answers to this test are ambiguous and therefore must be created from the participant's own beliefs, motives, and attitudes. The test is scored according to the levels of achievement imagery.
4. physiological needs, safety, belongingness and love, esteem, and self-actualization
5. James-Lange: physiological changes experienced and brain interprets change → specific emotion felt → observable behavior is demonstrated; Cannon-Bard: stimulus experienced and hypothalamus activated → hypothalamus sends message to cerebral cortex and body's organs simultaneously → emotion is felt and body reacts at the same time.

Critical Thinking

1. Many students will start to crave bread. According to drive-reduction theory, since students are deprived of something they want, they may feel tense and seek to relieve that tension. Encourage students to consider how realistic dieting really is in light of the drive-reduction theory.
2. The incentive or cognitive theories, which stress the role of the environment in motivating our behavior. (Cognitive theory also includes internal drives.) Our actions are directed toward a goal or incentive. Some people engage in high-risk activities, such as sky-diving, because they want to experience the thrill and rush of excitement.
3. Students' answers will vary. Encourage students to consider the short-term and long-term consequences of the two motivators.
4. Students' answers will vary. The most likely factors are the sight and smell of the food and the habit of overeating at holiday meals.
5. Students should recognize the difference between feeling an emotion (internal process) and expressing an emotion (external evidence). There is no conclusive evidence that the feeling of emotion in terms of physiological responses varies significantly for men and women. Research, however, does indicate that women express emotion more readily than men.

CHAPTER 12 Assessment

PSYCHOLOGY Online

Self-Check Quiz
Visit the *Understanding Psychology* Web site at glencoe.com and click on **Chapter 12—Self-Check Quizzes** to prepare for the Chapter Test.

Reviewing Vocabulary

Choose the letter of the correct term or concept below to complete the sentence.

a. motivation	**f.** ventromedial hypothalamus (VMH)
b. need	**g.** fundamental needs
c. drive	**h.** psychological needs
d. incentive	**i.** self-actualization needs
e. lateral hypothalamus (LH)	**j.** emotion

1. An internal condition that orients an individual toward a specific goal is a(n) __________.
2. A(n) __________ is a subjective feeling provoked by real or imagined objects or events that have high significance to the individual.
3. The need to belong and to give and receive love are part of an individual's __________.
4. The __________ is the part of the brain that sends signals to tell you to eat.
5. The result an individual is trying to achieve through his or her motivated behavior is a(n) __________.
6. According to Maslow, needs such as the pursuit of knowledge and beauty are part of an individual's __________.
7. The __________ is the part of the brain that sends signals to tell you when you have had enough food.
8. __________ includes the various psychological and physiological factors that cause people to act a certain way at a certain time.
9. According to Maslow, __________ are the first level of needs that people have to satisfy.
10. A lack of something desirable or useful is a(n) __________.

Recalling Facts

1. Which theory of motivation suggests that all human motives are extensions of basic biological needs?
2. Explain the difference between extrinsic motivation and intrinsic motivation.
3. How does McClelland measure a person's need for achievement?
4. Describe the five levels of needs in Maslow's hierarchy.
5. Using diagrams similar to the ones below, identify the basic principles in the James-Lange theory and the Cannon-Bard theory of emotions.

Critical Thinking

1. **Evaluating Information** Try going without bread in your meals for several days a week. Do you find that you are beginning to think about bread more often? Are you becoming more aware of advertisements for bread? Compare your experience with the description of drive-reduction behavior in this chapter.
2. **Making Inferences** Which theory of motivation would best explain why some people engage in high-risk activities, such as sky-diving or mountain climbing?
3. **Demonstrating Reasoned Judgment** Cognitive psychologists believe that people behave in particular ways because of extrinsic motivation or intrinsic motivation. Which of the two do you think is the stronger motivator? Why do you think so?
4. **Synthesizing Information** What factors might account for overeating at holiday dinners, such as Thanksgiving?
5. **Applying Concepts** Using what you have learned about emotions in the chapter, respond to the following statement: Men feel fewer emotions than women.

CHAPTER 12

Assessment

Psychology Projects

1. **Theories of Motivation** Choose one of the following theories of motivation: the drive-reduction theory, the incentive theory, or the cognitive theory. Review each theory's explanation of motivation. Then work with a partner to create a skit that illustrates the basic premises of the theory you chose.
2. **Emotions** With a partner or as a group, select 10 emotions to express. Then play a variation of charades, with one person attempting to convey each of these emotions by facial expression alone. What emotions are harder to convey than others? Are there consistent differences in interpretation between individuals? How important do you think context (the social situation in which the facial expression occurs) is in perceiving other people's emotions? Summarize your group interaction.

Technology Activity

Use the Internet to find the latest research about motivation. Summarize your findings in a short paper, comparing the latest research results with the theories discussed in the chapter.

Psychology Journal

Analyze the list of concerns and aspirations you wrote in your journal. Evaluate these items in terms of Maslow's hierarchy of needs. In other words, classify the items in terms of fundamental needs, psychological needs, and self-actualization needs. In your journal, write a rationale for classifying the individual items as you did.

Building Skills

Interpreting a Chart In an experiment run by Paul Ekman, actors were hired to assume specific facial expressions that mirrored emotions. One group was told which facial muscles to contract, but they were not told to feel or express any particular emotion. Another group was asked to think of emotional experiences in their lives that produced the six emotions listed. The researchers then measured several physiological responses of both groups. Review the information in the chart, then answer the questions that follow.

Changes in Heart Rate and Skin Temperature for Six Emotions

Specific Emotion	Change in Heart Rate (beats/min.)	Changes in Skin Temperature (degrees C)
Anger	+8.0	+.16
Fear	+8.0	−.01
Distress	+6.5	+.01
Joy	+2.0	+.03
Surprise	+1.8	−.01
Disgust	−0.3	−.03

Source: Ekman, Levenson, & Friesen, 1983.

1. What emotions did the study address? What physiological changes were measured?
2. Which emotion seemed to have the greatest effect on physiology? The least effect?
3. Why do you think that certain emotions cause greater physiological changes than other emotions?

See the Skills Handbook, page 628, for an explanation of interpreting charts.

Practice and **assess** key social studies skills with **Glencoe Skillbuilder Interactive Workbook CD-ROM, Level 2.**

Building Skills

1. The study addressed the following emotions: anger, fear, distress, joy, surprise, and disgust. Changes in heart rate and skin temperature were measured.
2. Anger had the greatest effect and disgust the least effect.
3. Answers will vary, but students may mention that intense emotions, such as those dealing with threat assessment (fight or flight), cause greater physiological changes.

GLENCOE TECHNOLOGY

CD-ROM

Glencoe Skillbuilder Interactive Workbook, Level 2

This interactive CD-ROM is designed to reinforce student mastery of essential social studies skills.

Chapter Bonus Test Question

This question may be used for extra credit on the Chapter Assessment.

Answer the following question:

I am the weight around which your day-to-day weight tends to fluctuate. What am I?

Answer: set-point

Psychology Projects

1. Answers will vary. Students observing the skit should be able to quickly identify the theory being demonstrated.
2. Answers will vary. After completing this project, have a class discussion in which the partners or groups compare their findings.

Technology Activity

Students should be encouraged to list the different ways in which motivation theory is being applied. Examples of applications found on the Internet include employee motivation, improvements in health, and motivating athletes. Encourage students to share with the class the Web sites they found.

Psychology Journal

Answers will vary. Ask students which level of need was identified most frequently and why.

Unit 5 Planning Guide

National High School Psychology Standards

The national high school psychology standards identify what students in an introductory high school psychology course should learn. **The material covered in Unit 5 reflects content from one of the five content domains: *Sociocultural*.** To see a chapter-by-chapter correlation to the national standards, refer to the Teacher pages.

Content Domains for National High School Psychology Standards

Use this diagram to review the standards areas that are covered in Unit 5. Standards areas covered in this unit are highlighted in red in the diagram.

Methods
- Introduction and Research Methods

Sociocultural
- **Individual Differences**
- **Personality and Assessment**
- Psychological Disorders
- Treatment of Psychological Disorders
- Social and Cultural Dimensions of Behavior

Developmental
- Lifespan Development

Cognitive
- Learning
- Memory
- Thinking and Language
- States of Consciousness

Biopsychological
- Biological Bases of Behavior
- Sensation and Perception
- Motivation and Emotion
- Stress, Coping, and Health

BIBLIOGRAPHY

Readings for the Student

Kaplan, R.M., & Saccuzzo, D.P. (2004). *Psychological Testing: Principles, Applications, and Issues.* Boston, MA: Wadsworth/Thomson.

Sternberg, R.J. (2003). *Why Smart People Can Be So Stupid.* New Haven, CT: Yale University Press.

Readings for the Teacher

Hawkins, J., & Blakeslee, S. (2004). *On Intelligence.* New York: Times Books.

Sternberg, R.J., & Preiss, D.D. (2005). *Intelligence and Technology.* Mahwah, NJ: Lawrence Erlbaum Associates.

Multimedia Resources

Internet. www.act.org/research/briefs/index.html provides nontechnical research essays relating to the ACT.

Internet. www.personalitypage.com provides information about personality and sample personality tests.

Videocassette. *Intelligence—A Complex Concept* (28 minutes). McGraw-Hill Films. This video presents different concepts of intelligence and several kinds of tests for measuring intelligence.

Unit 5 Resource Manager

Note: The following materials may be used when teaching Unit 5. Chapter level support materials can be found on the chapter resource pages.

GLENCOE'S ASSESSMENT ADVANTAGE

Use the following tools to easily assess student learning in a variety of ways:

- Authentic Assessment with Rubrics
- Section Quizzes, Chapter Tests, and Unit Tests
- glencoe.com
- SAT/SAT II Test Practice
- *ExamView® Assessment Suite* CD-ROM

APPLICATIONS AND HANDS-ON

Psychology Lab Activity 5

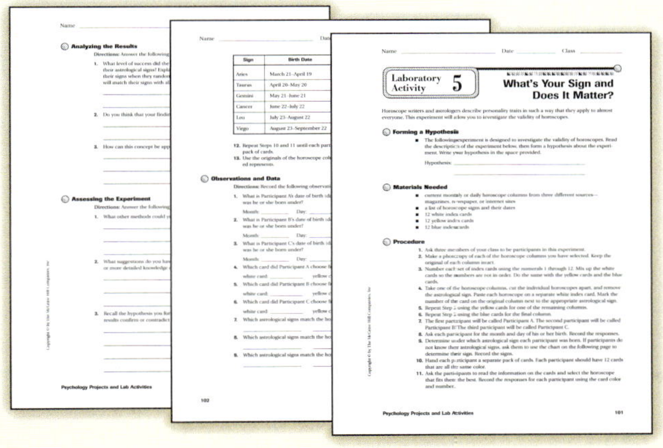
Laboratory Activity 5
What's Your Sign and Does It Matter?

ASSESSMENT

GLENCOE'S ASSESSMENT ADVANTAGE

Unit 5 Test, Form A

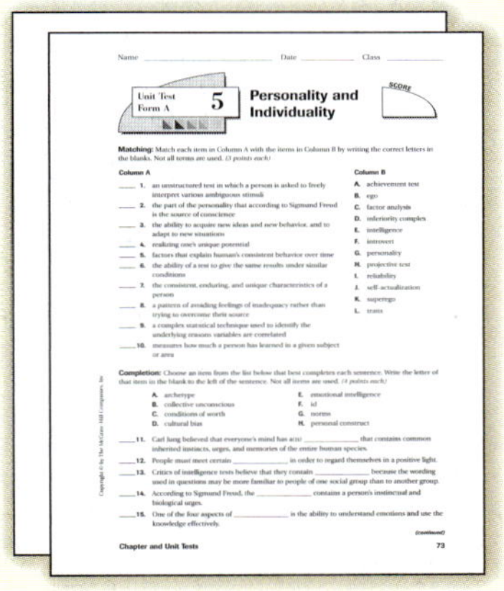
Unit Test Form A 5
Personality and Individuality

Unit 5 Test, Form B

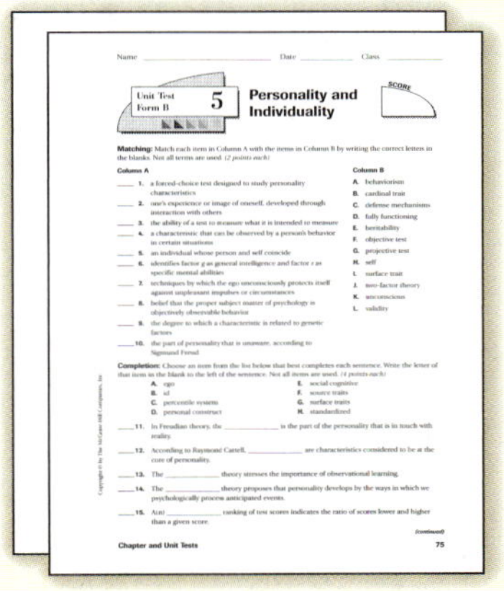
Unit Test Form B 5
Personality and Individuality

PRESENTATION Plus!

Use Glencoe's ***Presentation Plus!*** multimedia teacher tool to easily present dynamic lessons that visually excite your students. Using Microsoft PowerPoint® you can customize the presentations to create your own personalized lessons.

Introducing
UNIT 5

Unit Overview

This unit explores personality—why people act the way they do in specific situations—and individuality. **Chapter 13** investigates the characteristics of psychological tests and explores various types of psychological tests, including those that measure intelligence, achievement, abilities, interests, and personality. **Chapter 14** explores the theories of personality that have been developed by the different schools of psychology.

Unit Objectives

After studying this unit, students will be able to:

1. Describe the characteristics of good psychological tests.
2. List the major schools of personality theory.

UNIT 5

Personality and Individuality

Contents

Personality on display

EXTRA CREDIT PROJECT

Conducting a Survey Ask students to survey a representative group of students from each of the grades within your school (at least 10 students per grade) about their understanding of the word "intelligent." Suggest that students use the following incomplete sentence as a survey tool. "I consider a person intelligent if he/she __________." Have students sort through responses to identify and categorize the traits named. Ask students to identify any common measures of intelligence identified by the participants. Instruct students to reexamine these findings after the completion of Unit 5.

Why It's Important

Throughout time people have proposed different theories to explain the development of human personality. In the seventeenth century, Thomas Hobbes argued that all humans are inherently selfish. In the eighteenth century, Jean-Jacques Rousseau claimed that humans are basically good. Which is it? What makes us who we are?

Psychology Fair Suggestion Box

Encourage students to get involved with a psychology fair. Here are some project suggestions for **Unit 5—Personality and Individuality:**

- Research and evaluate modern criticisms of Freud's psychoanalytic theory.
- Explore the various types of intelligence.
- Research alternative views of intelligence and methods of testing intelligence.
- Investigate different personality testing strategies.

Refer to ***Psychology Projects and Lab Activities*** in the TCR for help with organizing a psychology fair.

PSYCHOLOGY Online

Visit glencoe.com, the *Understanding Psychology* Web site, for Chapter Overviews, Student Web Activities, Interactive Puzzles, and Self-Check Quizzes for every chapter of the text.

PORTFOLIO PROJECT

Creating an Oral Presentation Explain to students that the view of what constitutes intelligence has expanded. Tell them that many parents of young children do not know about the various types of intelligence that are recognized by educators. Assign students to use either L.L. Thurstone's or Howard Gardner's theories of intelligence to create an oral presentation for an elementary school PTA/PTO meeting. The purpose of the presentation is to present a broader definition of intelligence and explain the programs that the school uses to encourage various expressions of intelligence. The students should prepare either visual aids to be used during the presentation or a fact sheet that can be handed out to parents.

Chapter 13 Resource Guide

SECTION RESOURCES

Daily Objectives	Reproducible Resources	Multimedia Resources
Section 1 **Characteristics of Psychological Tests** Examine the characteristics that make a psychological test useful: reliability, validity, and standardization.	Guided Reading Activity 13–1 Vocabulary Activity 13–1 Section Quiz 13–1	Daily Focus Transparency 13–1 *ExamView® Assessment Suite* CD-ROM Presentation Plus! Software
Section 2 **Intelligence Testing** Explore the ways in which IQ tests are used to measure intelligence and explain the various theories of what constitutes intelligence.	Guided Reading Activity 13–2 Vocabulary Activity 13–2 Section Quiz 13–2	Daily Focus Transparency 13–2 Vocabulary PuzzleMaker CD-ROM *ExamView® Assessment Suite* CD-ROM Presentation Plus! Software
Section 3 **Measuring Achievement, Abilities, and Interests** Describe the various tests psychologists have developed to assess special abilities and experiences.	Guided Reading Activity 13–3 Vocabulary Activity 13–3 Section Quiz 13–3	Daily Focus Transparency 13–3 *ExamView® Assessment Suite* CD-ROM Presentation Plus! Software
Section 4 **Personality Testing** Explain how personality tests are used to assess personality characteristics and identify problems.	Guided Reading Activity 13–4 Vocabulary Activity 13–4 Section Quiz 13–4	Daily Focus Transparency 13–4 *ExamView® Assessment Suite* CD-ROM Presentation Plus! Software

Blackline Master CD-ROM Transparency

Block Schedule

Activities that are particularly suited for use within the block-scheduling framework are identified throughout this chapter by the following designation: **BLOCK SCHEDULING**

KEY TO ABILITY LEVELS

Teaching strategies have been coded for varying learning styles and abilities.

L1 **BASIC** activities for all students

L2 **AVERAGE** activities for average to above-average students

L3 **CHALLENGING** activities for above-average students

ELL **ENGLISH LANGUAGE LEARNER** activities

Chapter 13 Resource Guide

Timesaving Tools

TeacherWorks™ All-In-One Planner and Resource Center

- **Interactive Teacher Edition** Access your Teacher Wraparound Edition and your classroom resources with a few easy clicks.
- **Interactive Lesson Planner** Planning has never been easier! Organize your week, month, semester, or year with all the lesson helps you need to make teaching creative, timely, and relevant.

Use Glencoe's **Presentation Plus!** multimedia teacher tool to easily present dynamic lessons that visually excite your students. Using Microsoft PowerPoint® you can customize the presentations to create your own personalized lessons.

Activity

From the Classroom of...

Doug Terry
Columbus High School
Columbus, NE

Honesty Test

To introduce students to personality tests, tell them that this test is just for fun. They will grade it themselves and will not have to share the results. The test generates good class discussion about the fairness of objective tests.

The test should consist of two parts. For Part A, create a series of 15 yes/no questions such as: "Would you tell your boss if you know of another employee stealing from the company?" "Is shoplifting the same as stealing?" For Part B, create five multiple choice questions about the students' own behavior related to honesty and dishonesty. For example, "I have stolen . . . (A) only when I had the chance; (B) only when I really needed something; (C) but it was a mistake I would never repeat; (D) never." "Calling in sick as a means of getting some extra time off is something . . . (A) I have a right to do; (B) everybody does; (C) I would do only as a last resort to get time off; (D) dishonest."

You may also include the following bonus question: "Do you think the government should make it legal for a person to steal from a company that pays low wages?"

Create a scoring system that rewards students for giving the honest response. For example, give five points for the honest response and no points for the dishonest response. Set up a ranking system that allows students to rank themselves as always honest, usually honest, and so on.

Psychology Online

Use our Web site for additional resources. All essential content is covered in the Student Edition.

You and your students can visit glencoe.com, the Web site companion to *Understanding Psychology*. This innovative integration of electronic and print media offers your students a wealth of opportunities. The student text directs students to the Web site for the following options:

- Chapter Overviews
- Student Web Activities
- Self-Check Quizzes

Answers are provided for you in the **Web Activity Lesson Plan**. Additional Web resources and Interactive Puzzles are also available.

Chapter 13 Resource Guide

Note: The following materials may be used when teaching Chapter 13. Section level support materials are shown at point of use in the margins of the Teacher Wraparound Edition.

TEACHING TRANSPARENCIES

Chapter 13
Concept Transparencies

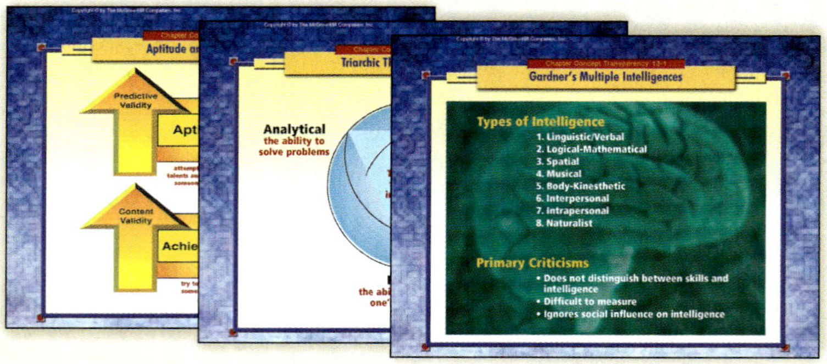

MULTIMEDIA

- Vocabulary PuzzleMaker CD-ROM
- *ExamView® Assessment Suite* CD-ROM
- TeacherWorks™ CD-ROM
- Glencoe Skillbuilder Interactive Workbook, Level 2
- Presentation Plus! Software

REVIEW AND REINFORCEMENT

Reteaching Activity 13

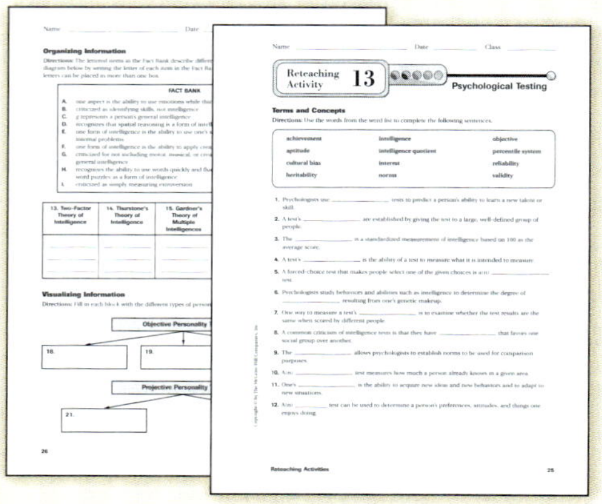

Graphic Organizer Activity 13

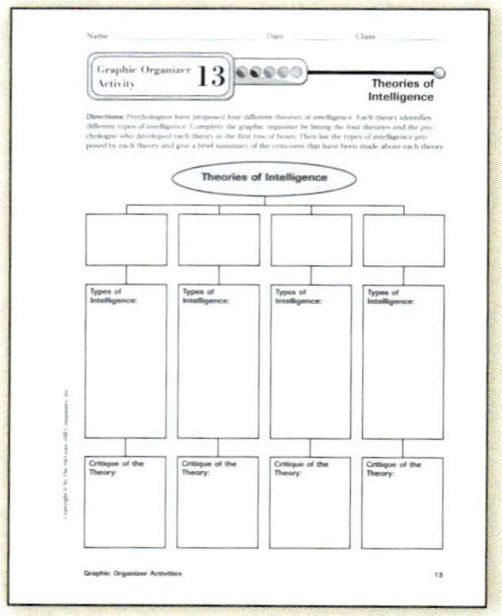

APPLICATION AND HANDS-ON

Psychology Projects 13–1 and 13–2

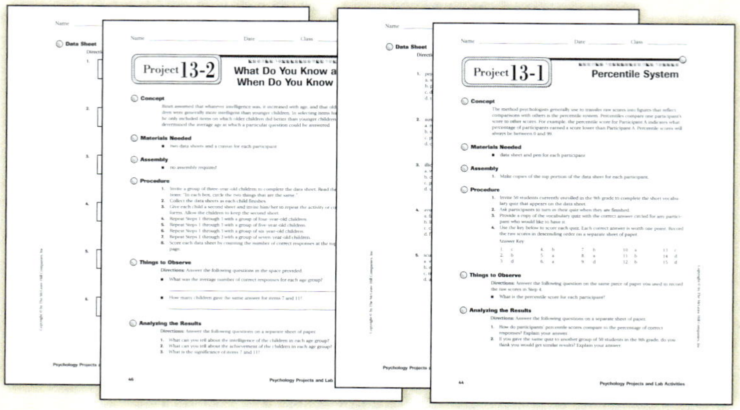

Application Activity 13

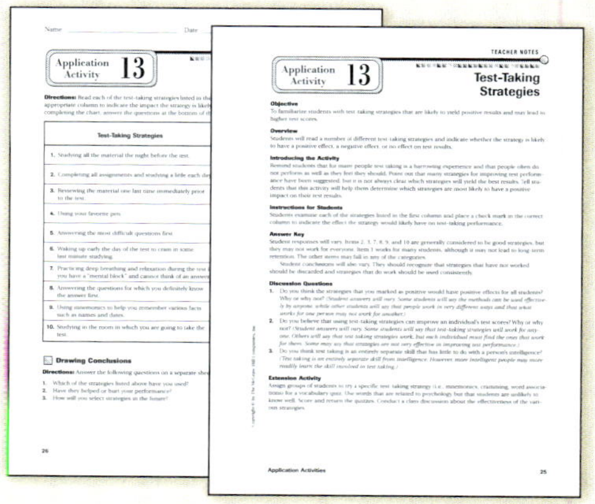

Chapter 13 Resource Guide

ASSESSMENT

Chapter 13 Test, Form A

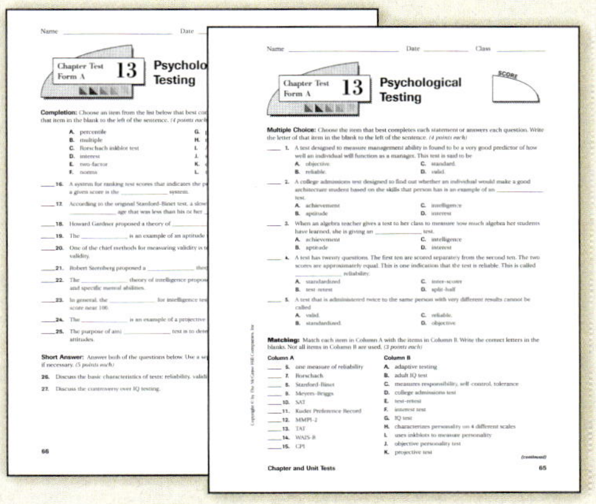

Chapter 13 Test, Form B

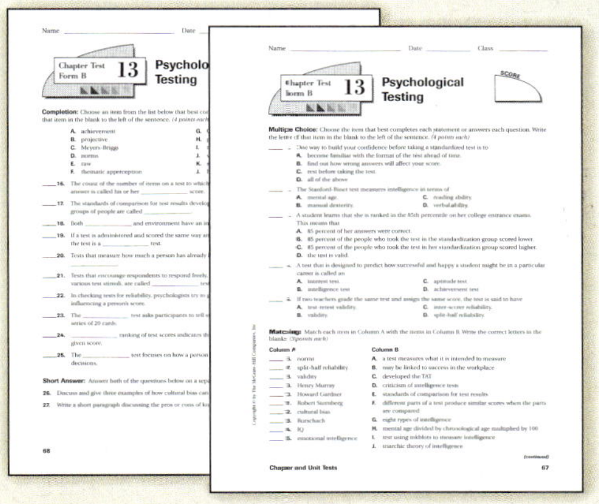

Authentic Assessment Activity 13

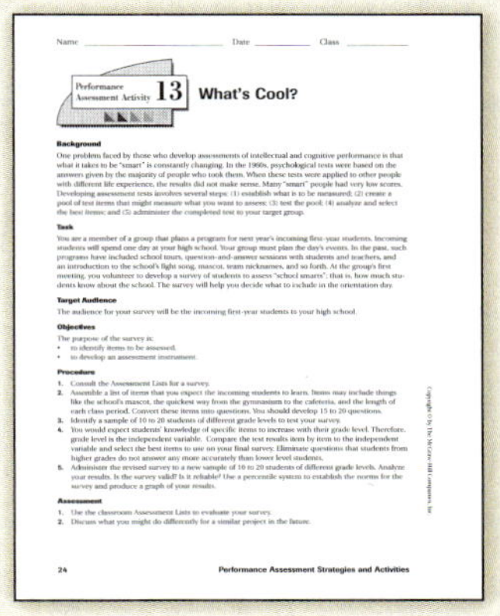

EXTENSION AND ENRICHMENT

Enrichment Activity 13

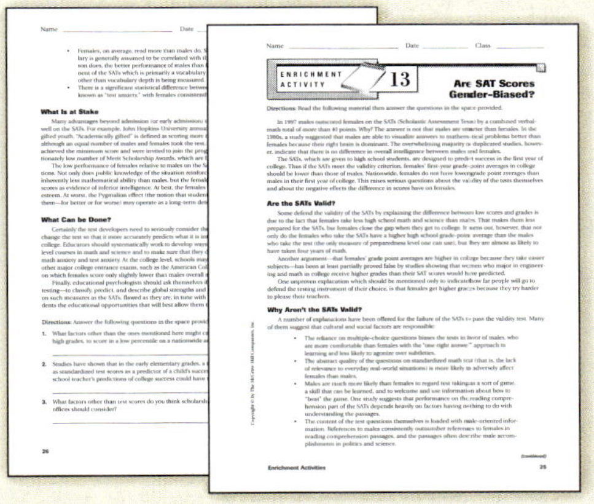

Critical Thinking Skills Activity 13

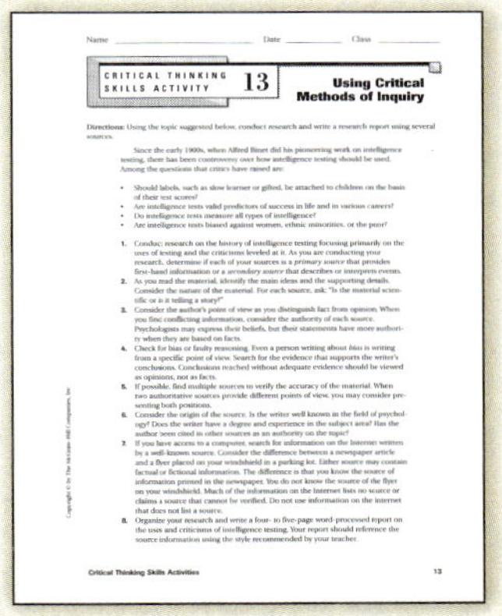

Psychology Reading 13

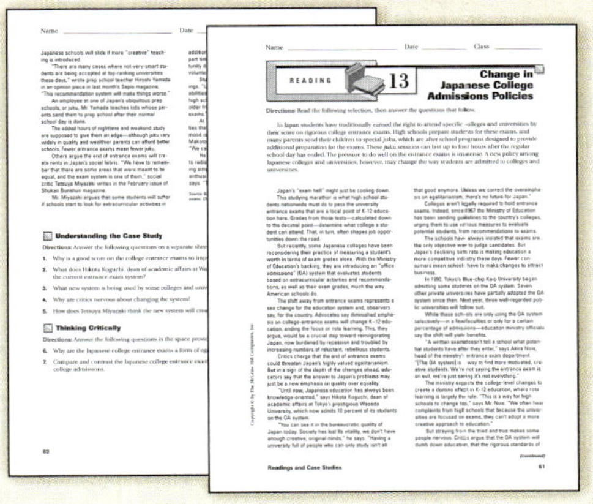

Psychology Case Study 13

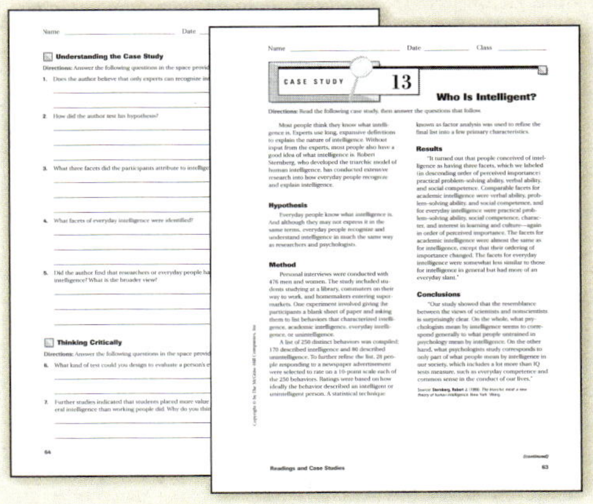

PSYCHOLOGY Online

Visit glencoe.com for a Chapter Overview for **Chapter 13—Psychological Testing.**

GLENCOE TECHNOLOGY

PRESENTATION Plus!

For a preview of Chapter 13 content, see MindJogger Checkpoint on **Presentation Plus!**

PSYCHOLOGY JOURNAL

Help students identify the characteristics desirable in a good teacher by generating a list of abilities, personality traits, and achievements.

This journal activity provides the basis for the Psychology Journal activity exercise in the Chapter Assessment. ■

CHAPTER 13

Psychological Testing

PSYCHOLOGY JOURNAL

Suppose you were asked to select the best person to be your teacher from among a group of applicants. How would you go about making the selection? Write your answer in your journal. ■

PSYCHOLOGY Online

Chapter Overview
Visit the *Understanding Psychology* Web site at glencoe.com and click on **Chapter 13—Chapter Overviews** to preview the chapter.

TWO-MINUTE LESSON LAUNCHER

Tell students that finding the right person for a job is a challenge for managers. In addition to needing the right set of skills, today's workplaces need people with the right personality for the job. Increasingly, companies are using personality tests to help make hiring decisions. Companies may use standard tests like the Myers-Briggs Type Indicator Test or may spend $2,500 to $3,000 per test to have customized tests designed. **Ask: Have you ever worked with someone who was not right for the job? What made him or her wrong for the job? Would a personality test have helped identify people who were better suited for the job? Have you ever considered what type of job would suit your personality? Explain.**

SECTION 1 Characteristics of Psychological Tests

Reader's Guide

■ Main Idea

To be useful, tests have to be standardized and exhibit reliability and validity.

■ Vocabulary

- reliability
- validity
- percentile system
- norms

■ Objectives

- Identify three ways of measuring reliability.
- Explain test standardization and how test validity is assessed.

EXPLORING PSYCHOLOGY

Not Fair!

I vividly remember my first genuine IQ test. I was 17 at the time. The youth director at my church was in graduate school, working on an advanced degree in psychology, and as part of a course in intelligence testing, he was required to administer an IQ test to several subjects. I was one of his selected "volunteers," although I was also a friend. I remember wondering later about whether or not he had given me an unfair advantage on the test. He often responded to my asking for clarification by going into great detail while explaining a particular kind of question. I wondered if my score would be comparable to that of another person who was tested by someone who was not so generous about clarifying items.

—from *Psychology: Science, Behavior, and Life* by Robert L. Crooks and Jean Stein, 1988

All psychological tests have one characteristic that makes them both fascinating and remarkably practical—they try to make it possible to find out a great deal about a person in a short time. Tests can be useful in predicting how well a person might do in a particular career; in assessing an individual's desires, interests, and attitudes; and in revealing psychological problems. One virtue of standardized tests is that they can provide comparable data about many individuals. Tests can show how an individual compares to others. Further,

SECTION RESOURCES

Reproducible Masters

- Guided Reading Activity 13–1
- Vocabulary Activity 13–1
- Section Quiz 13–1

Transparencies

- Daily Focus Transparency 13–1

Multimedia

- *ExamView® Assessment Suite* CD-ROM
- Presentation Plus! Software

1 FOCUS

Section Objectives

1. Identify three ways of measuring reliability.
2. Explain test standardization and how test validity is assessed.

BELLRINGER
Motivational Activity

Project Daily Focus Transparency 13–1 and have students answer the questions.

Available as blackline master

Daily Focus Transparency 13–1

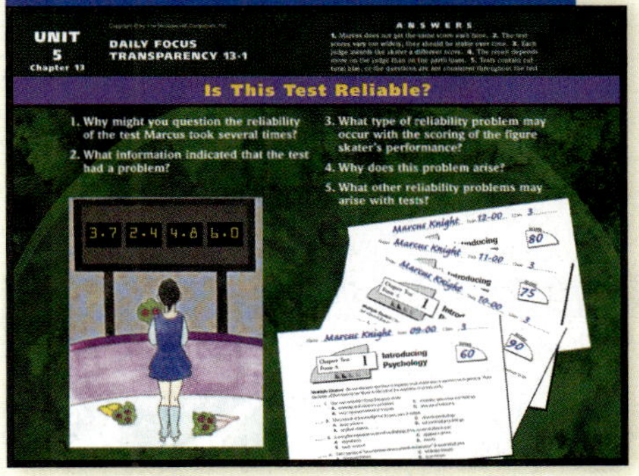

Reader's Guide

Use the Reader's Guide to introduce concepts and vocabulary.

■ Exploring Psychology

Ask students to read the **Exploring Psychology** feature. Then ask: **Do you think the clarifications offered by the friend affected the results of the test? Explain.**

■ Vocabulary Precheck

Have students read the Glossary definition of each vocabulary term. Then ask them to restate each definition in their own words.

CHAPTER 13
Section 1, pages 343–347

2 TEACH

L1 Discussion Explain that people often place a great deal of faith in what psychologists tell them—particularly in what psychological tests tell them. Point out that issues sometimes arise when the results of a test may affect a person's future because the test results are used to point a person in a specific direction. Suppose a woman shows a high mechanical aptitude. She then chooses to become an aviation specialist without adequately exploring other career options. **Ask: Is this a misuse of testing? Why or why not?** Challenge students to cite what they consider to be potential examples of test misuse or abuse. Remind students that test results are tools for measuring and predicting human behavior. They are not intended as an end in themselves. ELL

Guided Reading Activity 13–1

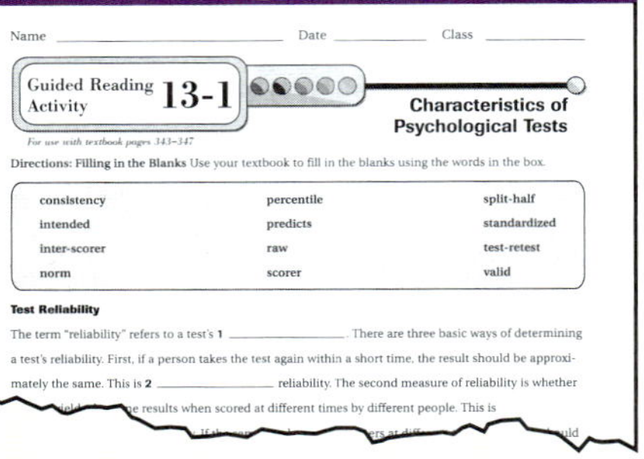
Name ______ Date ______ Class ______

Guided Reading Activity 13-1 — Characteristics of Psychological Tests

For use with textbook pages 343–347

Directions: Filling in the Blanks Use your textbook to fill in the blanks using the words in the box.

consistency	percentile	split-half
intended	predicts	standardized
inter-scorer	raw	test-retest
norm	scorer	valid

Test Reliability

The term "reliability" refers to a test's **1** ______. There are three basic ways of determining a test's reliability. First, if a person takes the test again within a short time, the result should be approximately the same. This is **2** ______ reliability. The second measure of reliability is whether ... results when scored at different times by different people. This is

Figure 13.1

Caption Answer You can use measures of reliability and validity to judge a test's usefulness.

psychologists can use some tests to help people understand things about themselves more clearly. Using tests to predict behavior can be controversial. It is important to keep in mind what the test is measuring.

One of the great dangers of testing is that we tend to forget that tests are merely tools for measuring and predicting human behavior. We start to think of test results (for example, an IQ) as an end in itself. The justification for using a test to make decisions about a person's future depends on whether a decision based on test scores would be fairer and more accurate than one based on other criteria. The fairness and usefulness of a test depend on reliability, validity, and standardization.

TEST RELIABILITY

reliability: the ability of a test to give the same results under similar conditions

The term **reliability** refers to a test's consistency—its ability to yield the same result under a variety of similar circumstances. There are three basic ways of determining a test's reliability. First, if a person retakes the test or takes a similar test within a short time after the first testing, does he or she receive approximately the same score? If, for example, you take a mechanical aptitude test three times in the space of six months and score 65 in January, a perfect score of 90 in March, and 70 in June, then the test is unreliable because it does not produce a measurement that is stable over time. The scores vary too much. This is assessing the measure's *test-retest* reliability (see Figure 13.2).

The second measure of reliability is whether the test yields the same results when scored at different times by different people. If both your teacher and another teacher critique an essay test that you have taken, and one gives you a B while the other gives you a D, then you have reason to complain about the test's reliability. The score you receive depends more on the grader than on you. This is called *interscorer* reliability. If the same teacher grades papers at different times, he or she may score the same essay differently. This is *scorer* reliability. On a reliable test, your score would be the same no matter who graded it and when it was graded.

One final way of determining a test's reliability is to randomly divide the test items in half and score each half separately. The two scores should be approximately the same. This is called *split-half* reliability. If a test is supposed to measure one quality in a person—for example, reading comprehension or mathematical ability—it should not have some sections on which the person scores high and others on which he or she scores low.

Figure 13.1 Taking Psychological Tests

Americans rely heavily on psychological testing because such tests promise to reveal a great deal about a person in a very short time. ***How can you judge the fairness and usefulness of a test?***

COOPERATIVE LEARNING ACTIVITY

Designing a Test Organize the class into small groups to identify the types of tests that should be used to screen candidates for a job as a firefighter. If possible, obtain a copy of the job requirements for a firefighter in your town or city. Have each group write its ideas on an overhead transparency. For example, a group may include a reading comprehension section on its test. Have each group present its overhead transparency to the class. Lead a discussion about the validity of each item listed. Then tell students that a court has held that reading and math skills are not critical to the job of firefighter; therefore, a test that included these sections was ruled discriminatory. Ask students if they agree or disagree with this ruling. **BLOCK SCHEDULING**

In checking tests for reliability, psychologists try to prevent variables from influencing a person's score. All kinds of irrelevant matters can interfere with a test. No test can screen out all interferences, but a highly reliable test can eliminate a good part of them.

TEST VALIDITY

A test may be reliable but still not valid. **Validity** is the ability of a test to measure what it is intended to measure (see Figure 13.3). For example, a test that consists primarily of Spanish vocabulary lists will not measure ability for engineering. A history test will not measure general learning ability. A test you take in physical education class may not measure your knowledge of grammar, or a math test that asks questions that were not covered in class does not measure what you learned in class.

Determining the validity of a test is more complex than assessing its reliability. One of the chief methods for measuring validity is to find out how well a test predicts performance—its *predictive* validity. For example, a group of psychologists designs a test to measure management ability. They ask questions about management systems, attitudes toward employees, and other relevant information. Will the people who score high on this test really make good managers?

Suppose the test makers decide that a good way to check the validity of the test is to find out how much a manager's staff improves in productivity in one year. If the staffs of those equally skilled managers who scored high on the test improve more than the staffs of those managers who scored low on the test, the test may be considered valid. Corporations may then adopt it as one tool to use in deciding whom to hire as managers, assuming the test is also valid for their situations.

What if managers who are good at raising productivity are poor at decision making? It may be that this test measures talent for improving productivity, not general management ability. This is the kind of difficulty psychologists encounter in trying to assess the validity of a test. As the example shows, nothing can be said about a test's validity unless the purpose of the test is absolutely clear.

STANDARDIZATION

Tests must be *standardized*. Standardization refers to two things. First, standardized tests must be administered and scored the same way every time. Test administrators are trained to follow the same procedures and

Figure 13.2 Judging Reliability

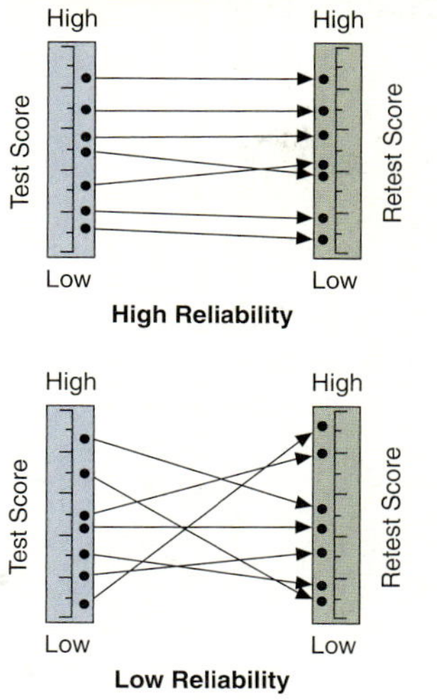

On the left, the test scores obtained by seven individuals are ordered on a scale. On the right, the corresponding scores on a second version of the same test, given at a later time, are ordered. In the upper diagram, the two sets of scores correspond very closely—meaning the test is highly reliable. ***What is meant by saying a test is reliable?***

validity: the ability of a test to measure what it is intended to measure

CHAPTER 13

Section 1, pages 343–347

Figure 13.2

Visual Instruction Point out that time is an important factor in determining test reliability. The two tests must be administered within a short time of each other.

Caption Answer A reliable test yields the same result under similar conditions.

PSYCHOLOGY JOURNAL

Ask students to review the tests they have taken in the last few weeks and answer the following questions. **Would the test pass a check for interscorer and split-half reliability? Can a test that does not meet the goals for reliability still be valid?** ■

Vocabulary Activity 13–1

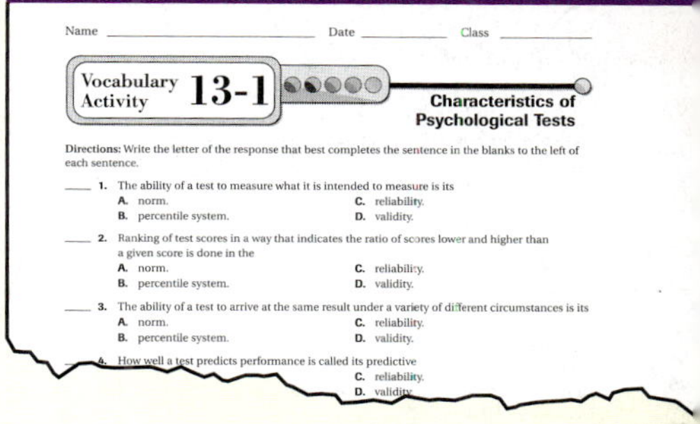
Name ________ Date ________ Class ________

Vocabulary Activity 13-1

Characteristics of Psychological Tests

Directions: Write the letter of the response that best completes the sentence in the blanks to the left of each sentence.

____ **1.** The ability of a test to measure what it is intended to measure is its
A. norm. **C.** reliability.
B. percentile system. **D.** validity.

____ **2.** Ranking of test scores in a way that indicates the ratio of scores lower and higher than a given score is done in the
A. norm. **C.** reliability.
B. percentile system. **D.** validity.

____ **3.** The ability of a test to arrive at the same result under a variety of different circumstances is its
A. norm. **C.** reliability.
B. percentile system. **D.** validity.

____ **4.** How well a test predicts performance is called its predictive
C. reliability.
D. validity.

MEETING SPECIAL NEEDS

Learning Style: Logical/Mathematical Give students anonymous test scores from last year's class tests. Provide the scores by student, giving all the test scores for students 1 through 10. Tell students to examine the scores of each student. **Ask: What conclusion can you reach about whether the tests were reliable; that is, did each student generally get the same letter grade on each test or were the scores all over the place? Why? What reasons other than unreliable tests may account for differences? L1**

Refer to ***Inclusion for the High School Social Studies Classroom Strategies and Activities*** in the TCR for strategies for students with different learning styles.

Figure 13.3

Visual Instruction Point out that at one time some scientists (Alfred Binet among them) tried to prove a correlation between head size and intelligence.

Caption Answer A valid test is one that has the ability to measure what it is intended to measure.

Reading Check Answer
A raw score does not indicate where the student ranks among all the students who took the same test.

3 ASSESS

Assign Section 1 Assessment as homework or as an in-class activity.

Section Quiz 13–1

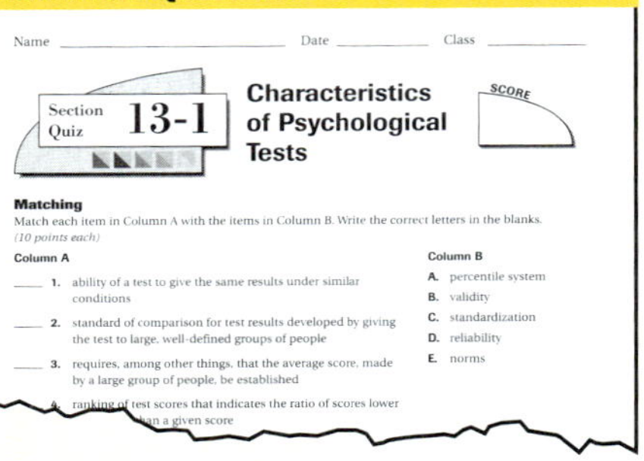
Name ______ Date ______ Class ______

Section Quiz 13-1 **Characteristics of Psychological Tests** SCORE

Matching
Match each item in Column A with the items in Column B. Write the correct letters in the blanks. *(10 points each)*

Column A	Column B
____ 1. ability of a test to give the same results under similar conditions	A. percentile system
____ 2. standard of comparison for test results developed by giving the test to large, well-defined groups of people	B. validity
____ 3. requires, among other things, that the average score, made by a large group of people, be established	C. standardization
4. ranking of test scores that indicates the ratio of scores lower ... than a given score	D. reliability
	E. norms

Reteach

Tell students they have been assigned to develop a test for a psychology course. Ask students to describe the type of test that they would design if validity were the only consideration.

Figure 13.3 Judging Validity

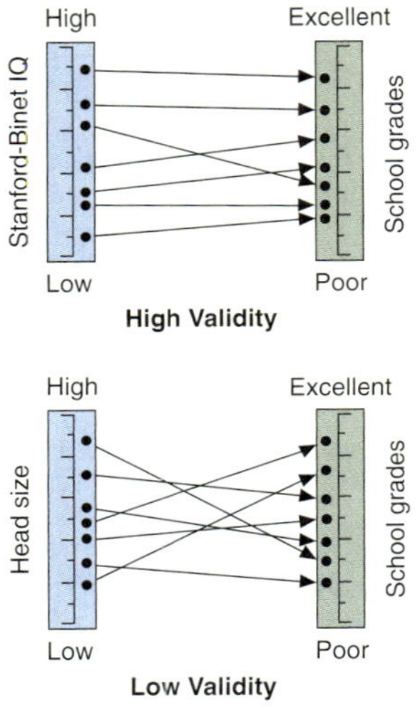

The upper diagram represents the result of comparing the Stanford-Binet Intelligence Scale scores with school grades. The lower diagram represents the comparison of scores on the head size test of intelligence with school grades. (The head size test is simply measuring the size of a student's head.) ***What defines a valid test?***

to ask the same questions the same way. If test administrators give instructions in an inconsistent manner or provide hints, errors in assessing the test taker would result. Second, standardization refers to establishing the norm, or average score, made by a large group of people.

Establishing Norms

Once a test result is obtained, the examiner must translate the score into something useful. Suppose a child answers 32 of 50 questions on a vocabulary test correctly. What does this score mean? If the test is reliable and valid, it means that the child can be expected to understand a certain percentage of the words in a book at the reading level being tested. In other words, the score predicts how the child will perform at a given level.

Yet a raw score does not tell us where the child stands in relation to other children at his or her age and grade level. If most children answered 45 or more questions correctly, 32 is a low score. If most answered only 20 questions correctly, however, 32 is a very high score.

When psychologists design a test to be used in a variety of settings, they usually set up a scale for comparison by establishing norms. This is usually done by transforming raw test scores into a **percentile system,** which resembles what is called grading on the curve. In the percentile system, the scores actually achieved on the test are placed in order, ranging from the highest to the lowest. Each score is then compared with this list and assigned a percentile according to the percentage of scores that fall at or below this point. For example, if half the children in the above example scored 32 or below, then a score of 32 is at the 50th percentile. If 32 were the top score, it would be at the 100th percentile. In the example given in Figure 13.4, a score of 32 puts the child in the 75th percentile, because only 25 percent of the children tested achieved a higher score.

percentile system: ranking of test scores that indicates the ratio of scores lower and higher than a given score

Reading Check Why must raw scores be transformed into percentiles?

In order to make such comparisons, the test is given first to a large representative sample of the group to be measured—for example, sixth graders or army privates. Percentiles are then established on the basis of the scores achieved by this standardization group. These percentiles are called the test's **norms.** Most of the intelligence, aptitude, and personality tests you will encounter have been provided with norms in this way. Your percentile on an aptitude test, such as the Scholastic Assessment Test (SAT), reflects your standing among people of your age and grade who have taken these exams.

norms: standard of comparison for test results developed by giving the test to large, well-defined groups of people

CRITICAL THINKING ACTIVITY

Demonstrating Reasoned Judgment Tell students that since the 1980s, many businesses have routinely administered integrity tests, such as lie-detector examinations, to their employees. Employers point to statistics that claim that United States businesses lose billions of dollars each year to employee theft. Labor organizations, however, complain that integrity tests are neither reliable nor valid. They claim that many honest people have been ruined by the potentially false scoring of these tests. Ask students to write a persuasive paper taking either the position of the employer or the position of the labor unions. **L2**

You should remember, however, that norms are not really standards, although a norm group is sometimes misleadingly referred to as a standardization group. Norms refer only to what has been found to be average for a particular group. If John can read at the 50th percentile level, that does not mean that he has met some absolute standard for ability to read. It means only that he reads better than half the population and worse than the other half in his particular group.

In summary, when you take a test and obtain your score, you should consider the following questions in evaluating the results. (1) Do you think that if you took the same test again, you would receive a similar score? (2) Does your performance on this test reflect your usual performance in the subject? (3) If you were to compare your score with those of your classmates, would it reflect your general standing within that group?

Figure 13.4 Establishing Percentiles

The range of possible raw scores on a test is shown in relation to an idealized curve that indicates the proportion of people who achieved each score. The vertical lines indicate percentiles, or proportions of the curve below certain points. Thus, the line indicated as the 1st percentile is the line below which only 1 percent of the curve lies. ***How do psychologists establish a scale for comparing test results?***

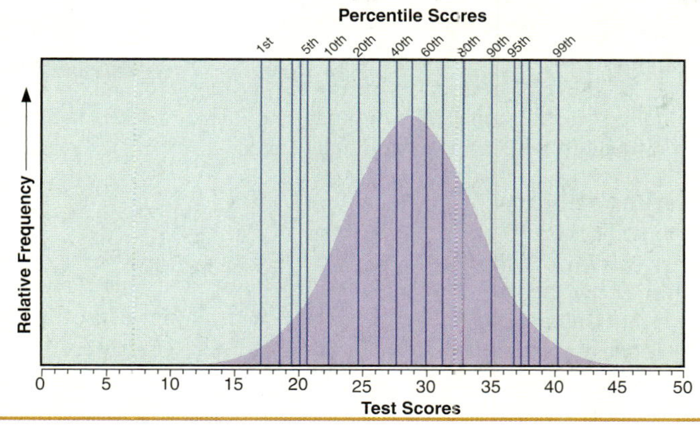

SECTION 1 Assessment

1. **Review the Vocabulary** What is meant when we ask about the reliability or validity of a test?
2. **Visualize the Main Idea** Using a diagram similar to the one below, identify three measures of a test's reliability.

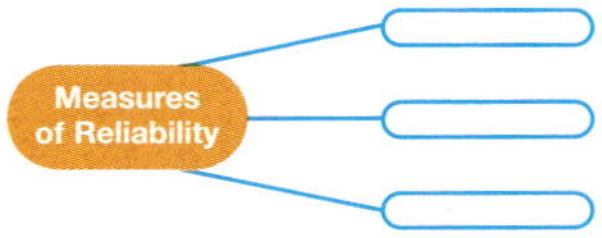

3. **Recall Information** What does it mean if a test is standardized? Why do we standardize tests?
4. **Think Critically** Do you think an intelligence test would be a valid test for measuring a person's knowledge of a foreign language? Explain.
5. **Application Activity** Ask a teacher for an anonymous listing of all the scores on a recent test. Using the information in this section, establish the percentiles for the test scores.

CHAPTER 13
Section 1, pages 343–347

Figure 13.4

Visual Instruction Ask students to determine what score would put a person in the 50th percentile *(29)*, the 90th percentile *(35)*, and so on.

Caption Answer They might use the percentile system.

Enrich

Ask students to list types of tests. Then have them create a table with the types of tests listed vertically and the various tests of reliability and validity listed horizontally. For each test, students should fill in the cells of the table with the words *high* or *low* to describe the reliability and validity of the tests.

4 CLOSE

Ask students to write an explanation of percentile ranking. Have a student share his or her answer. Then ask other students to add to or modify the explanation.

SECTION 1 Assessment Answers

1. Reliability refers to a test's consistency over time and across test takers. Validity refers to a test's ability to assess what it was designed to assess.
2. Test-retest reliability measures the test's ability to produce a measurement (score) that is stable over time. Interscorer reliability refers to the test's ability to yield the same results when scored at different times by different people. Split-half reliability is measured by dividing the test in half and scoring each half separately. The two scores should be approximately the same.
3. Standardized tests are administered and scored the same way each time and norms have been established. Tests are standardized to prevent errors in assessing test results.
4. No, an intelligence test does not relate specifically to knowledge of or ability to learn a foreign language.
5. Students' answers will vary. If students have access to an electronic spreadsheet, the scores can be entered and the percentile rankings calculated automatically.

1 FOCUS

Section Objectives

1. Explain the various views of intelligence.
2. Identify two kinds of IQ tests.

BELLRINGER
Motivational Activity

Project Daily Focus Transparency 13–2 and have students answer the questions.

Also available as blackline master

Daily Focus Transparency 13–2

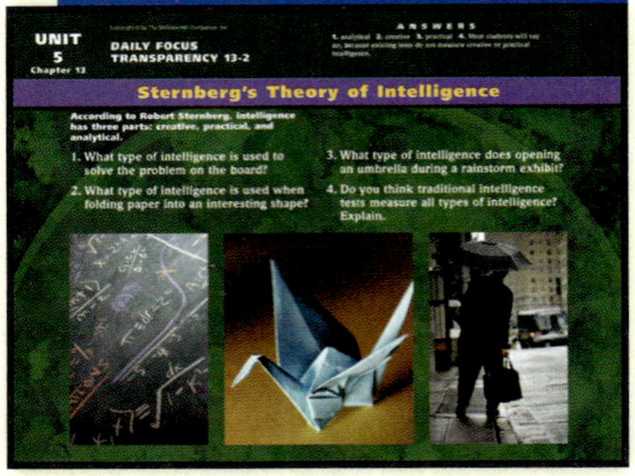

Reader's Guide

Use the Reader's Guide to introduce concepts and vocabulary.

Exploring Psychology

Ask students to read the **Exploring Psychology** feature. Ask: **How would you describe the intelligence exhibited by the Trukese?**

Vocabulary Precheck

Have students read the definitions of the vocabulary terms. Then have them create flash cards with the term on one side and the definition on the other. Encourage students to use the flash cards to study.

Use the **Vocabulary PuzzleMaker CD-ROM** to create crossword and word search puzzles.

SECTION 2 Intelligence Testing

Reader's Guide

Main Idea

Several IQ tests are used to measure intelligence, although there are many views about what constitutes intelligence.

Vocabulary

- intelligence
- two-factor theory
- triarchic theory
- emotional intelligence
- intelligence quotient (IQ)
- heritability
- cultural bias

Objectives

- Explain the various views of intelligence.
- Identify two kinds of IQ tests.

EXPLORING PSYCHOLOGY

Is This Intelligence?

It is typical for members of the Trukese, a small tribe in the South Pacific, to sail a hundred miles in open ocean waters. Although their destination may be just a small dot of land less than a mile wide, the Trukese are able to sail unerringly toward it without the aid of compass, chronometer, sextant, or any of the other sailing tools that are indispensable to modern western navigation. They are able to sail accurately, even when prevailing winds do not allow a direct approach. . . .

How are the Trukese able to navigate so effectively? If you ask them, they could not explain it.

—from *Understanding Psychology* by Robert S. Feldman, 2002

Trukese intelligence

Trukese navigation abilities point out the difficulty in coming to grips with what is meant by intelligence. Some might say that the inability of the Trukese to explain their sailing techniques is a sign of unintelligent behavior. It is hard to accuse the Trukese of being unintelligent, though. They sail successfully through the open ocean waters every day.

VIEWS OF INTELLIGENCE

Psychologists do not agree on the meaning of the word *intelligence.* Most believe that **intelligence** is the ability to acquire new ideas and new behavior and to adapt to new situations. Others believe that

SECTION RESOURCES

Reproducible Masters

- Guided Reading Activity 13–2
- Vocabulary Activity 13–2
- Section Quiz 13–2

Transparencies

- Daily Focus Transparency 13–2

Multimedia

- Vocabulary PuzzleMaker CD-ROM
- *ExamView® Assessment Suite* CD-ROM
- Presentation Plus! Software

intelligence is what allows you to do well on intelligence tests and in school. The concept, however, continues to be difficult to pin down. Over the years, psychologists have presented several different views of intelligence.

Figure 13.5 Thurstone's Seven Primary Mental Abilities

Theory	Main Ideas
Verbal comprehension	ability to understand the meaning of words, concepts, and ideas
Numerical ability	ability to use numbers quickly to compute answers to problems
Spatial relations	ability to visualize and manipulate patterns and forms in space
Perceptual speed	ability to grasp perceptual details quickly and accurately and to determine similarities and differences between stimuli
Word fluency	ability to use words quickly and fluently in performing such tasks as rhyming, solving anagrams, and doing crossword puzzles
Memory	ability to recall information such as lists of words, mathematical formulas, and definitions
Inductive reasoning	ability to derive general rules and principles from presented information

Thurstone's theory of intelligence did not include the idea of a general intelligence. ***How does Thurstone's theory compare to Gardner's theory?***

Two-Factor Theory of Intelligence

British psychologist Charles Spearman proposed his **two-factor theory** of intelligence in 1904. According to Spearman's theory, two factors contribute to a person's intelligence. The first factor, *g*, represents a person's general intelligence. This involves a person's ability to perform complex mental work, such as problem solving. A second factor, *s*, represents a person's specific mental abilities, such as verbal or math skills. Spearman believed that every individual had a certain level of general intelligence.

Critics argue that *g* does not measure many other kinds of mental abilities such as motor, musical, or creative abilities. These critics argue that intelligence cannot be reduced to just *g* and expressed by a single IQ score.

intelligence: the ability to acquire new ideas and new behavior, and to adapt to new situations

two-factor theory: proposes that a person's intelligence is composed of a general ability level and specific mental abilities

Thurstone's Theory of Intelligence

A major opponent of Spearman's theory was L.L. Thurstone (1938). After testing a large number of people on more than 50 different ability tests, Thurstone concluded that there was no evidence for the general intelligence that Spearman had identified. Instead, Thurstone proposed that intelligence is composed of seven primary mental abilities (see Figure 13.5). He believed that a person's intelligence needed to be a measurement of all seven mental abilities and not just a measurement of one factor.

Gardner's Theory of Multiple Intelligences

Psychologist Howard Gardner (1983, 1999) rejected the traditional idea of intelligence as primarily the ability to think logically. He believes this view is inadequate because it omits many important skills. Gardner argues for a broader perspective that includes eight types of intelligence (see Figure 13.6). Seven types of intelligence are: (1) verbal ability;

Reading Check How did Thurstone's definition of intelligence differ from Spearman's?

COOPERATIVE LEARNING ACTIVITY

Funding for Head Start Organize the class into small groups. Have each group research the federally funded child care program, Head Start, initiated by President Lyndon Johnson in 1964. Research areas should include original purpose, benefits of environmental intervention for preschool children, comparison of test scores between children who have been in Head Start and those of similar socioeconomic background who have not, and the future direction of the program. Have each group prepare a funding request to be presented orally to the Ways and Means Committee of the House of Representatives. The group's funding request should reflect its view on whether the program should be expanded or reduced.

2 TEACH

L1 Evaluating Concepts Tell students that many people who have not done well in school have made great intellectual or artistic contributions. Conversely, many who have scored very high on intelligence tests have gone on to lead unproductive lives. **Ask: What does the word *intelligence* mean to you? What relation do you think exists between the following: (1) intelligence and success, (2) intelligence and creativity, and (3) intelligence and empathy toward others?**

Figure 13.5

Visual Instruction Tell students that Thurstone's work has influenced modern IQ tests that produce not one but several scores, each for a different mental ability.

Caption Answer Thurstone's theory relates intelligence primarily to the ability to think logically. Gardner's theory takes a broader perspective of intelligence.

Reading Check Answer Thurstone disagreed with the notion that there is one factor known as general intelligence. He defined intelligence using seven primary mental abilities.

Profiles In Psychology

Ask students to read the **Profiles In Psychology** feature and then discuss the following questions:

1. What are the criticisms of Gardner's theory? *(Critics claim that his theory is weak and that students should not be used as guinea pigs to test a weak theory. Verbal and math skills are still required to be successful in life.)*
2. How do teachers implement Gardner's theory in the classroom? *(They teach the same topic using many different approaches that allow students to demonstrate their strengths in learning through one or more methods.)*

Readings and Case Studies in Psychology

Have students read the Chapter 13 Case Study selection in *Readings and Case Studies in Psychology* and answer the questions that follow the case study.

Guided Reading Activity 13–2

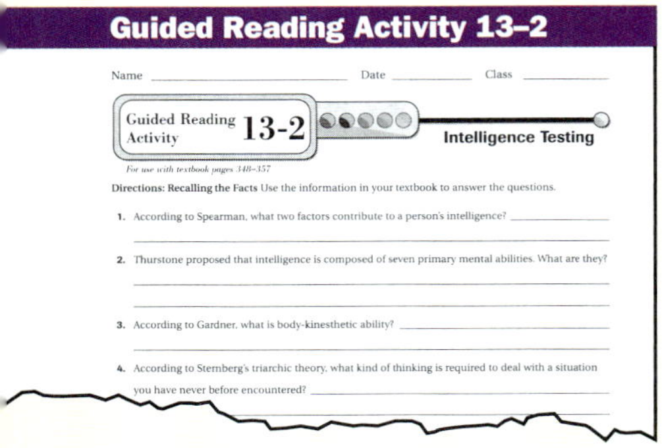
Name ______ Date ______ Class ______

Guided Reading Activity 13-2 — Intelligence Testing

For use with textbook pages 348–357

Directions: Recalling the Facts Use the information in your textbook to answer the questions.

1. According to Spearman, what two factors contribute to a person's intelligence? ______
2. Thurstone proposed that intelligence is composed of seven primary mental abilities. What are they? ______
3. According to Gardner, what is body-kinesthetic ability? ______
4. According to Sternberg's triarchic theory, what kind of thinking is required to deal with a situation you have never before encountered? ______

Profiles In Psychology

Howard Gardner

1943–

"I'm sure there are lots of different intelligences. I'm sure an educational approach that pays attention to this is going to be more effective than one that denies it."

Many parents and teachers have embraced Howard Gardner's idea of multiple intelligences. Critics, though, doubt that the multiple intelligences theory should be implemented in the classroom. Critics argue that although Gardner's theory has helped teachers appreciate the many talents of students, the theory is weak. The danger lies in wasting precious school time.

In the classroom, teachers usually implement Gardner's theory by attacking a concept from many different perspectives or viewpoints. For example, to teach kids about the oceans, teachers have them write about cleaning a fish, draw a sea creature, role-play a sea creature, use diagrams to compare and contrast ships, and so forth (Collins, 1998).

Again, critics argue that although a teacher may tap into a child's strongest intelligence by using various instructional approaches, that child must still rely on verbal and math skills to succeed in higher education and a career. Gardner's theory has yet to be stringently tested. Gardner himself claims, "We are not yet certain of the goodness of the idea of multiple intelligences."

(2) logical-mathematical reasoning skills; (3) spatial ability, or the ability to find your way around an environment and to form mental images of it; (4) musical ability, or the ability to create and perceive pitch and rhythm patterns; (5) body-kinesthetic ability, or skill at fine motor movements required for tasks such as gem cutting, surgery, and athletics; (6) interpersonal skills, involving understanding the feelings of others; and (7) intrapersonal skills, or knowledge of oneself. Gardner later added an eighth intelligence—naturalist intelligence. Naturalist intelligence is a person's ability to identify and classify patterns in nature. Gardner (1999) has considered, but seems less certain about, a ninth intelligence, which concerns the experience of existence.

Gardner's research on the results of brain disease convinced him that humans possess these eight different and often unrelated intellectual capacities, or intelligences. Moreover, he argues that the biological organization of the brain affects one's strength in each of the eight areas.

Critics of Gardner's theory argue that some of what Gardner called "intelligence" are really skills. For instance, someone with exceptional musical abilities or body-kinesthetic abilities is really just talented. These critics claim that intelligence and talent (or skill) are two different things.

Sternberg's Theory of Intelligence

triarchic theory: proposes that a person's intelligence involves analytical, creative, and practical thinking skills

Robert Sternberg (1985) proposed a **triarchic theory,** or three-part theory, of intelligence. Sternberg proposed that intelligence can be divided into three ways of processing information. The first way is using *analytical* thinking skills, or the ability to solve problems. These kinds of skills are the

MEETING SPECIAL NEEDS

Learning Style: Verbal/Linguistic Tell students that Walter Lippmann, a political journalist in the early part of the twentieth century, once contended that IQ tests can be turned into "an engine of cruelty." Assign students to research Walter Lippmann's reasons for making this accusation. Ask students to write a speech defending or attacking Lippmann's view. If possible, allow volunteers to present their speeches to the class. **L2**

Refer to ***Inclusion for the High School Social Studies Classroom Strategies and Activities*** in the TCR for strategies for students with different learning styles.

Figure 13.6 Gardner's Multiple Intelligences

Gardner proposed that each person has numerous and unrelated intelligences. He points out that a person can be outstanding in some intelligences and not in others. ***What is the difference between interpersonal and intrapersonal intelligence?***

Intelligence	Description	Example
Linguistic/Verbal	ability to utilize language	skill at learning, using, and understanding languages
Logical-Mathematical	ability to process and compute logical problems and equations	skill at solving algebra problems
Spatial	ability to comprehend shapes and images in three dimensions	skill at putting puzzles together or molding sculptures
Musical	ability to perform and compose music	skills at performing and comprehending music
Body-Kinesthetic	ability to perceive and control movement, balance, agility, grace	sense of how one's body should act and react in a physically demanding situation
Interpersonal	ability to interact with and understand others and to interpret their behavior	skill at gauging others' moods and motivations
Intrapersonal	ability to understand and sense oneself	skill at using self-esteem, self-enhancement, and strength of character to solve internal problems
Naturalist	ability to identify and classify patterns and relationships in natural surroundings	skill at distinguishing differences among large numbers of similar objects

ones that are traditionally measured on intelligence tests. The second way is applying *creative* thinking to solving problems and dealing with new situations. The third is using *practical* thinking skills to help adjust to and cope with one's environment. Sternberg's ideas stress the point that traditional intelligence tests do not measure and assess intelligences found in everyday life. Like Gardner's theory, though, Sternberg's theory makes it difficult to measure intelligence, at least with traditional types of measurements.

Emotional Intelligence

Another type of intelligence is called **emotional intelligence**. It is related to Gardner's concepts of interpersonal and intrapersonal intelligences and has been discussed in the popular press. Emotional intelligence has four major aspects (Mayer & Salovey, 1997):

- The ability to perceive and express emotions accurately and appropriately
- The ability to use emotions while thinking
- The ability to understand emotions and use the knowledge effectively
- The ability to regulate one's emotions to promote personal growth

emotional intelligence: interpersonal and intrapersonal abilities needed to understand and use knowledge of emotions effectively

CHAPTER 13
Section 2, pages 348–357

Applying Psychology

Ask students to find three pictures of males and three of females. In each group of three, one person should look frightened, stressed, or angry; one should look happy or excited; and one should have a neutral look. Tell them to show five participants the three pictures that match his or her gender. Then have them ask the participants to put themselves in the place of the person in the picture and describe what is happening. The student should write down any of the participants' words or phrases that express emotion. **Ask:** **What types of emotional words or phrases did the participants use? What conclusions can you draw about each participant's emotional intelligence? Was this a valid test of emotional intelligence? Why or why not?**

Figure 13.6

Visual Instruction Tell students that Gardner studied seven people, including Sigmund Freud and Mohandas Gandhi, when creating his theory. Most of the people that Gardner studied struggled to have their creative ideas accepted.

Caption Answer Interpersonal intelligence refers to the ability to interact with others. Intrapersonal intelligence refers to the ability to accurately perceive oneself.

CRITICAL THINKING ACTIVITY

Synthesizing Information Have students create a graphic organizer that shows the various types of intelligence identified by Charles Spearman, L.L. Thurstone, Howard Gardner, and Robert Sternberg. After creating the graphic organizers, have students summarize the similarities and differences among the four theories in one to two paragraphs. **L2**

PSYCHOLOGY Online

Links and instructional guidelines can be found in the **Web Activity Lesson Plan** at glencoe.com.

PSYCHOLOGY JOURNAL

Ask students to write their reaction to the following statement: "Intelligence tests don't measure ability; they measure developed ability." ■

CULTURAL CONNECTIONS

The Chinese used aptitude tests as civil service exams more than 4,000 years ago. The first modern tests were devised by European Sir Francis Galton. His techniques, used at the World Fair in Chicago in 1883 and the International Health Exhibition in London in 1884, do not resemble the tests used today. His test included measuring muscle strength, the size of people's heads, reaction time, various thresholds, and so on. From his tests, he proposed that intelligence was completely inherited.

Readings and Case Studies in Psychology

Have students read the Chapter 13 Reading selection in *Readings and Case Studies in Psychology* and answer the questions that follow the reading.

This view of intelligence has intrigued many psychologists. Major proponents of this view have linked emotional intelligence to success in the workplace. Some psychologists, however, argue that emotional intelligence is simply a measurement of extraversion. More research needs to be done to confirm this theory of intelligence (see TIME Reports, p. 372).

THE DEVELOPMENT OF INTELLIGENCE TESTS

Among the most widely used and widely disputed tests in the United States and Canada today are those that are designed to measure intelligence in terms of an IQ score. Alfred Binet, a French psychologist, worked with Theodore Simon to develop a useful intelligence test. In 1904 Binet was asked by the Paris school authorities to devise a means of picking out "slow learners" so they could be placed in special classes from which they might better profit. Binet was unable to define intelligence, but he believed it was complex. He thought it was reflected in the things children do—making common-sense judgments, telling the meanings of words, and solving problems and puzzles. Binet also assumed that whatever intelligence was, it increased with age. That is, older children had more intelligence than younger children. Therefore, in selecting items for his test, he included only items on which older children did better than younger children.

By asking the same questions of many children, Binet determined the average age at which a particular question could be answered. For example, he discovered that certain questions could be answered by most 12-year-olds but not by most 11-year-olds. If a child of 11, or even 9, could answer these questions, he or she was said to have a mental age of 12. If a child of 12 could answer the 9-year-old-level questions but not the questions for 10-year-olds and 11-year-olds, he or she was said to have a mental age of 9. Thus a slow learner was one who had a mental age that was less than his or her chronological age.

PSYCHOLOGY Online

Student Web Activity
Visit the *Understanding Psychology* Web site at glencoe.com and click on **Chapter 13—Student Web Activities** for an activity on intelligence testing.

The Stanford-Binet Intelligence Scale

Binet's intelligence test has been revised many times since he developed it. The Binet test currently used in the United States is a revision created at Vanderbilt University—the Stanford-Binet Intelligence Scale (Roid, 2003). The Stanford-Binet, like the original test, groups test items by age level. Although used mainly with school-aged children and young adults, the test can now be used with participants from age 3 to 85+ and includes tasks from defining words to explaining events in daily life. Participants are tested one at a time. Examiners must carry out standardized instructions while putting the person at ease, getting him to pay attention, and encouraging him to try as hard as he can (see Figure 13.7).

intelligence quotient (IQ): standardized measure of intelligence based on a scale in which 100 is average

The **IQ,** or **intelligence quotient,** was originally computed by dividing a child's mental age (the average age of those who also received the same score as that child) by chronological (actual) age and multiplying by 100.

$$IQ = \frac{\text{Mental Age}}{\text{Chronological Age}} \times 100$$

PSYCHOLOGY LAB EXPERIMENT

Test Development Ask students to work in pairs or small groups to devise a test for one of Gardner's types of intelligence. The test should be able to be scored with a reasonable degree of interscorer reliability. The scores should also be quantifiable. For example, students may use vocabulary tests to assess linguistic/verbal intelligence. Have the students administer the test to at least 20 people and then score the test and create a percentile ranking from the samples. Ask students to write an assessment of the validity of the test based on their results. Encourage students to share their findings with the rest of the class. **L2** **BLOCK SCHEDULING**

So an 8-year-old child who scored at the mental age of 8 would have an IQ of 100. Although the basic principles behind the calculation of IQ remain, scores are figured in a slightly different manner today. Researchers assign a score of 100 to the average performance at any given age. Then, IQ values are assigned to all the other test scores for this age group. If you have an IQ of 100, for example, this means that 50 percent of the test takers who are your age performed worse than you. In addition, test scores for several abilities are now reported instead of one general score, but the test is no longer widely used (Vernon, 1987). Instead, the Otis-Lennon Ability Test is often used. This test seeks to measure the cognitive abilities that are related to a student's ability to learn and succeed in school. It does this by assessing a student's verbal and nonverbal reasoning abilities.

The Wechsler Tests

Three frequently used intelligence tests are the revised versions of the Wechsler Adult Intelligence Scale, or WAIS-III (Wechsler, 1997), for adults aged 16 to 89; the Wechsler Intelligence Scale for Children, or WISC-IV (Wechsler, 2003), for children 6 to 16+ years old; and the Wechsler Preschool and Primary Scale of Intelligence, or WPPSI-III, for children 2 to 6 years old.

In addition to yielding one overall score, the Wechsler tests yield percentile scores in several areas—vocabulary, information, arithmetic, picture arrangement, and so on (see Figure 13.8). These ratings are used to compute separate IQ scores for verbal and performance abilities. This type of scoring provides a more detailed picture of the individual's strengths and weaknesses than a single score does.

THE USES AND MEANING OF IQ SCORES

In general, the norms for intelligence tests are established in such a way that most people score near 100 (see Figure 13.9). This means that about 95 percent of people score between 70 and 130. Only a little more than 2 percent score at or above 130. These people are in at least the 97th percentile. Those who score below 70 have traditionally been classified as mentally handicapped. More specific categories include mildly handicapped, but educable (55–69); moderately handicapped, but trainable (40–54); severely handicapped (25–39); and profoundly handicapped (below 25).

Figure 13.7 Typical Items on the Stanford-Binet Test

An examiner has built a tower of blocks (top) and has told the child, "You make one like this."

Why is age important in administering and scoring the Stanford-Binet test?

Age	Sample Test Item
4	"Why do people live in houses?" "Birds fly in the air; fish swim in the ____."
8	"What should you do if you find a lost puppy?" "Stephanie can't write today because she twisted her ankle. What is wrong with that?"
12	"What does *regret* mean?" "Here is a picture. Can you tell me what is wrong with it?"

CHAPTER 13

Section 2, pages 348–357

FYI

Anne Anastasi was the third woman to be elected president of the American Psychological Association. Among her major contributions to psychology are the validity concepts of psychological testing. She defined validity as "what the test measures and how well it does so." The basic categories of validity that she identified are content, predictive, concurrent, and construct. Many of her concepts are still used today.

Figure 13.7

Caption Answer The test is scored by comparing mental and chronological ages.

Possible answers to test items: People live in houses to stay warm. Fish swim in the water. You should tell an adult and help find its owner. She does not use her ankle to write. *Regret* means being sorry for something you did or said.

Vocabulary Activity 13–2

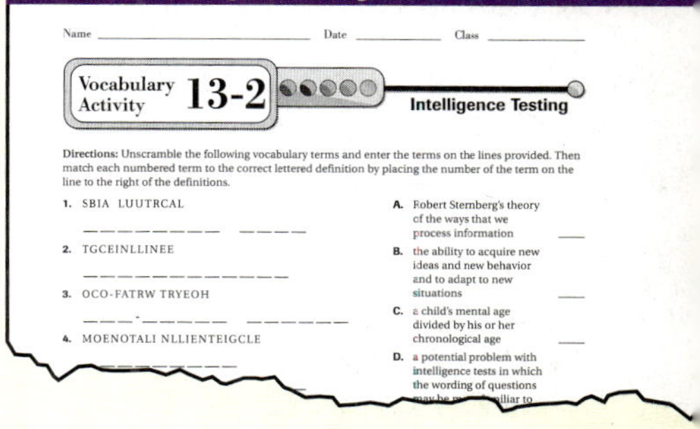
Name ____ Date ____ Class ____

Vocabulary Activity 13-2

Intelligence Testing

Directions: Unscramble the following vocabulary terms and enter the terms on the lines provided. Then match each numbered term to the correct lettered definition by placing the number of the term on the line to the right of the definitions.

1. SBIA LUUTRCAL
2. TGCEINLLINEE
3. OCO-FATRW TRYEOH
4. MOENOTALI NLLIENTEIGCLE

A. Robert Sternberg's theory of the ways that we process information ____
B. the ability to acquire new ideas and new behavior and to adapt to new situations ____
C. a child's mental age divided by his or her chronological age ____
D. a potential problem with intelligence tests in which the wording of questions

INTERDISCIPLINARY CONNECTIONS ACTIVITY

Mathematics Psychologists must often be expert mathematicians in order to draw statistical conclusions from the raw data that they collect. Ask students to review the formula for calculating the intelligence quotient, found on page 352 of the text. Have students create at least five problems using various mental and chronological ages. Then have them trade their problems with another student. Each student should solve the problems to calculate the IQ. After students have completed the problems, ask them to write a short summary describing the relationship between the mental and chronological age and the resulting IQ in each problem.

Figure 13.8

Visual Instruction Explain that the Wechsler tests place more emphasis on performance than the Stanford-Binet does, so less verbally oriented people are not as likely to be put at a disadvantage.

Caption Answer The Wechsler tests are designed for adults, school-aged children, and preschool children and measure separate IQ scores for verbal and performance abilities. The Stanford-Binet test computes a single IQ figure.

Answers to sample test questions:

- July 4
- 5¢
- to mock or jeer
- They are articles of clothing.
- 751829
- the fourth wheel
- The most logical order is right picture, left picture, and center picture.
- The block design is created by rearranging the blocks to create the design shown.

CURRICULUM CONNECTION

The Law Two legal cases challenged the use of intelligence tests on the basis of cultural bias. In United States circuit court cases *Larry P.* v. *Riles* (1979) and *P.A.S.E.* v. *Hannon* (1980), parents of African American children claimed that their children had been placed in classes for the mentally retarded based solely on culturally biased IQ tests. The judges in these two cases reached opposite opinions. One found the tests to be culturally biased, while the other found the tests to be valid and nondiscriminatory.

Figure 13.8 Sample Items on the Wechsler Tests

These test items are similar to those included in the various Wechsler intelligence scales. (Not all test items and scales are included here.) ***How do the Wechsler tests compare to the Stanford-Binet Intelligence test?***

VERBAL SCALE	EXAMPLE
Information	What day of the year is Independence Day?
Arithmetic	If eggs cost $.60 a dozen, what does one egg cost?
Vocabulary	Tell me the meaning of *scoff.*
Similarities	In what way are hats and shoes alike?
Digit Span	Listen carefully, and when I am through, say the numbers right after me. 7 5 1 8 2 9

PERFORMANCE SCALE	EXAMPLE
Picture Completion	What part is missing from this picture?

Picture Arrangement	Arrange the panels to make a meaningful story.

Block Design	Put the blocks together to make this picture.

What do these scores mean? What do the tests measure? IQ scores seem to be most useful when related to school achievement; they are quite accurate in predicting which people will do well in schools, colleges, and universities. Critics of IQ testing do not question this predictive ability. They do wonder, however, whether such tests actually measure intelligence. As stated earlier, most psychologists agree that intelligence is the ability to acquire new ideas and new behavior and to adapt to new situations. Is success in school or the ability to take a test a real indication of such ability? Generally, IQ tests measure the ability to solve certain types of problems. Yet they do not directly measure the ability to pose

EXTENDING THE CONTENT

Mental Level vs. Mental Age When Alfred Binet and his assistant, Theodore Simon, devised their intelligence tests, they often referred to *mental level*. However, when the American testers translated Binet's writings, they used the term *mental age* instead. This term, introduced by Wilhelm Stern along with *intelligence quotient* (IQ), implied an ordered progression of development. To Binet, mental age represented something fixed and unchangeable, while mental level emphasized that a child's intelligence could change. Binet also opposed the idea of IQ, because he felt that representing human intelligence in a single number was misleading.

those problems or to question the validity of problems posed by others (Hoffman, 1962). This is only part of the reason why IQ testing is so controversial.

Psychology and You — **Your IQ**

Can we say that you do well in school because you have a high IQ? Consider this: a baseball player has a low batting average. A fan explains that the player does not get a lot of hits because he has a low batting average. Is this statement true? No, that baseball player has a low batting average because he does not get a lot of hits. In the same way, we cannot say that a student does poorly in school because he has a low IQ score. IQ tests measure the same skills that schoolwork requires. An IQ score measures performance; it does not explain it.

CONTROVERSY OVER IQ TESTING

Much of the debate about IQ testing centers around the following issues: do genetic differences or environmental inequalities cause two people to receive different scores on intelligence tests? The question of cultural bias in intelligence tests has also been controversial.

Nature vs. Nurture

A technique researchers use to help determine whether genetics or environment affects scores on intelligence tests is studying the results of testing of people with varying degrees of genetic relationship. In regard to intelligence, researchers have found a high degree of **heritability**—

heritability: the degree to which a characteristic is related to inherited genetic factors

Figure 13.9 **Distribution of IQ Scores**

This normal curve displays intelligence as measured by the Stanford-Binet and Wechsler tests. The mean IQ score is 100; the standard deviation is 15. ***What percentage of people score at least 145 on IQ tests?***

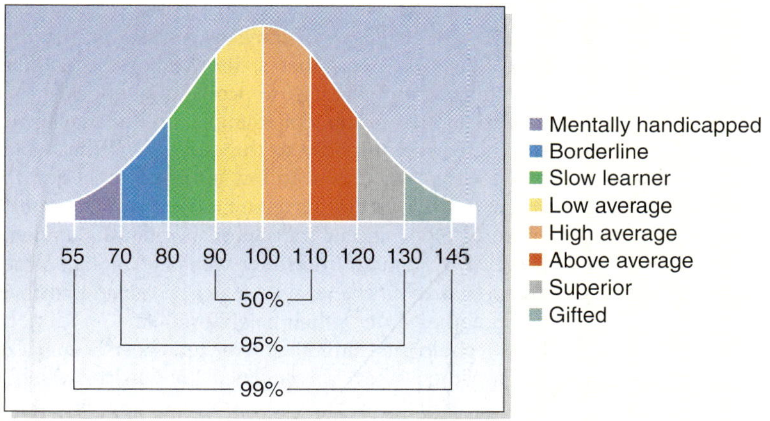

Psychology and You

Use the following question to direct a class discussion after students have read the **Psychology and You** feature.

Ask: Is IQ a good predictor of success in school? Why do you think this is so?

Looking @ the Issues

Cultural Literacy In his book, *What Every American Needs to Know,* E.D. Hirsch argues that one of the keys to success is an understanding of the predominant culture. He called such knowledge *cultural literacy.* Cultural literacy includes common events and language shared by members of the culture. The basic facts of science, politics, literature, art, history, entertainment, sports, and geography are all part of what Hirsch means by cultural literacy. **Ask: Who determines what should be included in tests of cultural literacy? How do such tests exclude groups who do not speak the "cultural language"?**

Figure 13.9

Visual Instruction Tell students that most IQ tests are designed to have a mean of 100 and a standard deviation of 15.

Caption Answer only about .5 percent

EXTENDING THE CONTENT

Cultural Bias Henry H. Goddard played a part in one of psychology's sorrier episodes. Goddard set up a program in which a staff administered psychological tests to immigrants arriving at Ellis Island. In 1917, Goddard reported that 80 percent of the Hungarians, 79 percent of the Italians, and 87 percent of the Russians tested were feebleminded. He based these conclusions on tests with questions such as "What is Crisco?" and "Who is Christy Mathewson?" *(a pitcher for the New York Giants).* Today, we recognize these tests as culturally biased. At the time, however, Congress used such "scientific" evidence to back the restrictive immigration laws of 1924.

3 ASSESS

Assign Section 2 Assessment as homework or as an in-class activity.

Section Quiz 13–2

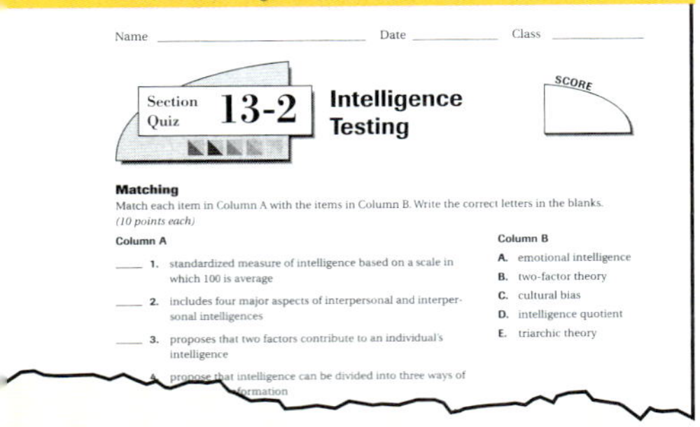
Name ________ Date ________ Class ________

Section Quiz 13-2 **Intelligence Testing**

SCORE

Matching

Match each item in Column A with the items in Column B. Write the correct letters in the blanks. *(10 points each)*

Column A

____ **1.** standardized measure of intelligence based on a scale in which 100 is average

____ **2.** includes four major aspects of interpersonal and interpersonal intelligences

____ **3.** proposes that two factors contribute to an individual's intelligence

4. propose that intelligence can be divided into three ways of ...formation

Column B

A. emotional intelligence
B. two-factor theory
C. cultural bias
D. intelligence quotient
E. triarchic theory

Reteach

Have students revisit the **Exploring Psychology** feature at the beginning of this section. **Ask: Based on what you have learned about intelligence, do you consider the Trukese to be intelligent? Whose theory of intelligence best identifies intelligence?**

a measure of the degree to which a characteristic is related to inherited genetic factors. They found that as genetic relationship increases, say, from parent and child to identical twins, the similarity of IQ also increases.

The best way to study the effects of nature and nurture is to study identical twins who have been separated at birth and raised in different environments. Dr. Tom Bouchard has studied more than 100 sets of twins who were raised apart from one another. Bouchard concluded that IQ is affected by genetic factors—a conclusion supported by the discovery of a specific gene for human intelligence (Plomin, 1997). Bouchard believes 70 percent of IQ variance can be attributed to heredity, but others (Plomin et al., 1994) found the hereditary estimate to be only 52 percent.

Regarding environment, studies show that brothers and/or sisters raised in the same environment are more likely to have similar IQs than siblings raised apart. Environment, therefore, does impact IQs.

Some researchers study the effects of the environment on IQ factors by focusing on preschool programs, such as Head Start, that expose economically disadvantaged youths to enriching experiences. Some studies show that quality preschool programs help raise IQs initially, but the increase begins to fade after some years. Participating children, however, are less likely to be in special education classes, less likely to be held back, and more likely to graduate from high school than are children without such preschool experiences (Zigler, Styfco, & Gilman, 1993). Each year of school missed may drop a person's IQ as much as 5 points (Ceci, 1991). The richness of the home environment, the quality of food, and the number of brothers and sisters in the family all affect IQ.

Both heredity and environment have an impact on intelligence. Advances in behavioral genetics research continue to refine results on the contributions that heredity and experience have on IQ. It remains clear that these two factors are both contributing and interact in their effects.

cultural bias: an aspect of an intelligence test in which the wording used in questions may be more familiar to people of one social group than to another group

Cultural Bias

A major criticism of intelligence tests is that they have a **cultural bias**—that is, the wording used in questions may be more familiar to people of one social group than to another group. For example, on one intelligence test the correct response to the question, "What would you do if you were sent to buy a loaf of bread and the grocer said he did not have any more?" was "try another store." A significant proportion of minority students, however, responded that they would go home. When questioned about the answer, many explained that there was no other store in their neighborhood.

Psychologists admit that some tests have been biased because they assess accumulated knowledge, which is dependent on a child's environment and opportunities in that environment. As a consequence, efforts have been

More About...

Family Size and IQ

The classic study of family size and IQ was conducted in the Netherlands. It was based on the military examinations of more than 386,000 Dutch people. Researchers found that the brightest children came from the smallest families and had few, if any, brothers and sisters when they were born. Thus, the first-born child in a family of two was usually brighter than the last child in a family of 10. The differences in IQ, however, from one birth-order position to another average only about one-quarter point.

The effects of family size on intelligence may be explained by the impact of a houseful of children on the home environment. Larger families increase the amount of time a child spends with other children and decrease the amount of parental attention he or she receives. When this happens, development of intelligence has been known to suffer (Zajonc & Markus, 1976), but interpersonal skills may improve.

PSYCHOLOGY LAB EXPERIMENT

Questionnaire Explain that various groups have raised questions about the validity and reliability of personality inventories and intelligence tests used in education, business, and courts of law. Have students work in pairs to design a questionnaire that asks for people's opinions about the use of these tests in making such decisions as college admissions, hiring and promotion of employees, and as evidence in court cases. The questions should be designed to allow participants to answer in a range from *Strongly Disagree* to *Strongly Agree*. Have the pairs of students give the questionnaire to at least 20 people of various ages. Ask the class to combine their results and show their findings in a chart. **Ask: What conclusions can you draw about people's reactions to these tests? L2**

made to make the tests less biased (see Figure 13.10). However, it is unlikely that a test will ever be developed that will be completely free of cultural bias. All tests are based on the assumptions of a particular culture.

Figure 13.10 The Dove Counterbalance Intelligence Test

In the 1960s, psychologist Adrian Dove developed the Counterbalance Intelligence Test to stress that cultural background can influence performance on an intelligence test. ***What characteristics would a test without cultural bias have?***

1. "T-Bone Walker" got famous for playing what?
   a. Trombone
   b. Piano
   c. "T-Flute"
   d. Guitar
   e. "Hamɔone"
2. Who did "Stagger Lee" kill (in the famous blues legend)?
   a. His mother
   b. Frankie
   c. Johnny
   d. His girlfriend
   e. Billy
3. If you throw the dice and "7" is showing on top, what is facing down?
   a. "seven"
   b. "snake eyes"
   c. "boxcars"
   d. "little Joes"
   e. "eleven"
4. "You've got to get up early in the morning if you want to ________."
   a. catch the worms
   b. be healthy, wealthy, and wise
   c. try to fool me
   d. fare well
   e. be the first one on the street
5. Many people say that "Juneteenth" (June 19) should be made a legal holiday because this was the day when ________.
   a. the slaves were freed in the USA
   b. the slaves were freed in Texas
   c. the slaves were freed in Jamaica
   d. the slaves were freed in California
   e. Martin Luther King was born
   f. Booker T. Washington died

SECTION 2 Assessment

1. **Review the Vocabulary** What are the two-factor and triarchic theories of intelligence?
2. **Visualize the Main Idea** Using a chart similar to the one below, describe how the two major tests of intelligence are scored.

Name of Test	How Scored
Stanford-Binet	
Wechsler tests	

3. **Recall Information** What are Gardner's eight types of intelligence?
4. **Think Critically** Which has the greatest effect on intelligence—nature or nurture? Explain.
5. **Application Activity** Develop a list of criteria that you think are essential in determining intelligence. Compare your list with your classmates' lists and together create a class list.

SECTION 2 Assessment Answers

1. The two-factor theory identifies a general intelligence, *g* factor, and a second factor, *s*, that represents a person's specific abilities. The triarchic theory identifies three parts to intelligence: analytical thinking, creative thinking, and practical thinking.
2. Stanford-Binet: Mental age/Chronological age x 100; Wechsler: an overall score and percentile scores in vocabulary, information, arithmetic, picture arrangement, and so on.
3. verbal/linguistic, logical-mathematical, spatial, musical, body-kinesthetic, interpersonal, intrapersonal, and naturalist
4. Students' answers will vary. Heredity likely determines a basic range for intelligence, but nurture affects where in that range a person falls.
5. Students' answers will vary. It is likely that students will take a broad view of the abilities that contribute to intelligence. Their lists are likely to be similar to Gardner's multiple intelligences.

Figure 13.10

Visual Instruction Explain that Adrian Dove intentionally designed questions to be culturally biased against middle-class whites. **Ask: How successful was Dove in this task? What was Dove's motivation?** *(to prove that standard intelligence tests lacked validity because of pro-white cultural bias)*

Caption Answer Such tests would avoid test questions that could be answered by members of only one cultural or socioeconomic background.

Answers to test:
1. d
2. e
3. a
4. c
5. b

Enrich
Have students research Gardner's latest writings on intelligence. Then ask students to prepare an oral report explaining how Gardner's theory has evolved.

4 CLOSE

List Gardner's eight types of intelligence on the board. Ask students to give examples of people they know who appear to exhibit high levels of intelligence in each of Gardner's seven intelligence categories. Ask students to explain how they identified the people they chose.

Going Further

Updated Versions of WAIS

The Psychological Corporation is the business that markets the WAIS, as well as many other psychological testing instruments.

The most recent product developments include the WAIS-III. The third edition of the test has been rigorously tested for validity and standardization. It reflects the age and abilities of today's population. The published norms for the test have been expanded so that it is now useful to people up to 89 years of age.

In older test takers, the WAIS-III is often paired with the WMS-III, which tests memory. The WMS-III can be used with 16- to 89-year-olds. It tests immediate memory, which is recall of information just learned; delayed memory, which is the ability to remember things 25 to 35 minutes after learning; and working memory. These two tests have been co-normed so that the relationship between intellectual functioning and memory can be examined.

Discussing the Case Study

Ask: **Why are psychologists asked to give psychological tests to various parties in legal cases?** Have students find other examples of expert testimony from a psychologist that played a major role in a case's outcome.

Case Studies

WAIS-R: *Is It Reliable?*

Period of Study: Withheld

Introduction: What happens when the results of psychological testing cross over into another field? This situation takes place numerous times within the judicial system. It is common for psychologists to be called in on a court case to assess the competency and ability of certain individuals to play key roles in the case. Psychologists, in most of these cases, use tests measuring intelligence levels. The judicial system correlates intelligence level with the ability of an individual to take part in a legal proceeding. In these instances, the validity of the tests used is assumed. However, reliability is equally critical. Psychological tests can be administered to an individual to gain certain results. If these results are not consistent with a repeat testing, the original results are meaningless.

In a trial involving the alleged statutory rape of a 22-year-old woman, psychological testing played a vital role in the outcome. Even though the victim was of legal age, prosecutors filed charges of force or threatening of force to commit a sexual act, stating that the alleged victim was incapable of giving meaningful consent because of a mental disability. Prosecutors called in a psychologist to perform testing on the victim using the Wechsler-Adult Intelligence Scale-Revised test, or WAIS-R. This specific intelligence test is highly useful for measuring conditions of mental handicap in individuals.

The results of the first test indicated the woman had an IQ below 70, demonstrating significant, but not clear, signs of possible mental handicap. The defense attorney demanded a repeat test be performed.

Hypothesis: The prosecuting team expected the test results to prove the reliability of the respected WAIS-R. They knew the test clearly measured what it is supposed to measure; thus, they wanted to see consistent results. The defending team, however, wanted to see inconsistencies in the test scores of the 22-year-old woman in the hopes the defendant would be set free. Because the WAIS-R holds much prestige within the psychological field, it seemed most likely that results would resemble that of the first test.

Method: The psychologist who administered the WAIS-R informed the court that the odds were against a substantial rise in the IQ of the woman. The psychologist, however, also informed the court that pressure and stress surrounding the trial could have played a major impact on how the woman scored on the first test. With this second scenario weighing heavily on the minds of the prosecution, the psychologist presented the woman with the WAIS-R once again.

Results: On the second WAIS-R test, the woman scored only one point higher than her score the first time. The psychological test proved reliable.

As mentioned, the factors of validity and reliability are highly valuable in studying and testing psychological hypotheses. These two concepts proved equally important in deciding the fate of a man accused in a court of law. The concept of reliability paved the way for a man to be found guilty of rape and sentenced to 15 years in prison.

Analyzing the Case Study

1. Why was the WAIS-R used in this instance?
2. Why did the defense on this case want the alleged victim to retake the test?
3. **Critical Thinking** What might significantly different results on the WAIS-R have meant in this case?

Answers for Analyzing the Case Study

1. The WAIS-R is considered an excellent instrument for identifying conditions of mental handicap. Prosecutors wanted to show that the victim was incapable of giving meaningful consent to sexual relations because of a mental disability. They wanted to prove the accused was guilty of statutory rape.
2. The defense wanted to attack the reliability of the test. They were hoping to see inconsistencies in the test scores of the woman, which would mean the defendant could be set free.
3. Since the test indicated borderline mental handicap, if its reliability could be questioned, the defense could contend that the victim was capable of consent.

SECTION 3

Measuring Achievement, Abilities, and Interests

Reader's Guide

Main Idea

Psychologists have developed tests to assess special abilities and experiences.

Vocabulary

- aptitude test
- achievement test
- interest inventory

Objectives

- Identify the most widely used aptitude tests, achievement tests, and interest inventories.
- Explain the application of aptitude tests, achievement tests, and interest inventories.

EXPLORING PSYCHOLOGY

What Are Your Interests?

Breathless, Vin dashed into the chemistry lab, "Sorry I'm late, Mrs. Baker," he told his instructor. "I was helping Mr. Eads plant marigolds around the flagpole."

Mrs. Baker sighed patiently. "I'm glad to give you extra help, Vin, but try to be on time."

"Sorry," Vin repeated. "I guess I have more fun in a garden than I do in chem lab."

Mrs. Baker smiled in surprise. "You like to garden? A garden *is* a chemistry lab."

Now Vin looked surprised. "It is?"

"Sure," Mrs. Baker replied. "Making food from sunlight, drawing nutrients from soil—these are chemical processes. . . ."

—from *Shaping Your Future* by Eddye Eubanks, Connie R. Sasse, and Linda R. Glosson, 2000

Vin views digging in the garden as fun, not work. What subject fascinates you? What career should you choose? What are your interests and aptitudes? Which subject most motivates you to learn more? Intelligence tests are designed to measure a person's overall ability to solve problems that involve symbols such as words, numbers, and pictures. Psychologists have developed other tests to assess special abilities and experiences. These include aptitude tests, achievement tests, and interest inventories.

SECTION RESOURCES

Reproducible Masters

- Guided Reading Activity 13–3
- Vocabulary Activity 13–3
- Section Quiz 13–3

Transparencies

- Daily Focus Transparency 13–3

Multimedia

- *ExamView® Assessment Suite* CD-ROM
- Presentation Plus! Software

1 FOCUS

Section Objectives

1. Identify the most widely used aptitude tests, achievement tests, and interest inventories.
2. Explain the application of aptitude tests, achievement tests, and interest inventories.

BELLRINGER
Motivational Activity

Project Daily Focus Transparency 13–3 and have students answer the questions.

Available as blackline master

Daily Focus Transparency 13–3

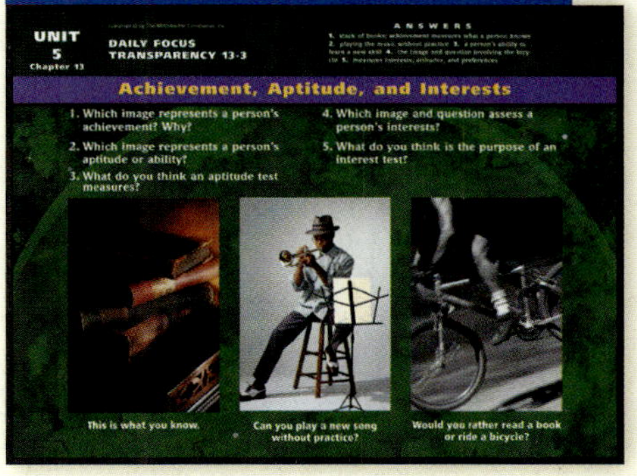

Reader's Guide

Use the Reader's Guide to introduce concepts and vocabulary.

Exploring Psychology

Ask students to read the **Exploring Psychology** feature. Ask: **What interests you? How can you relate those interests to things you would like to do as an adult?**

Vocabulary Precheck

Have students read the Glossary definition of each type of test. Ask them to create a table that lists the types of test, their definitions, and examples of the tests.

2 TEACH

L1 Applying Concepts Ask students to explain the difference between *predictive validity* and *content validity*. **Ask: To which kind of test does each term apply?** *(Aptitude tests are predictive of how well a person can learn a new skill. Achievement tests measure how well a person has mastered content knowledge.)*

Figure 13.11

Visual Instruction Ask: Which question took the longest for you to solve? Why? *(probably 3, it involves both verbal comprehension and mathematical calculation)*

Caption Answer Aptitude tests identify talents and predict how well people can learn a new skill.

Test answers are:

1. c and b **2.** a and d
3. d **4.** c

Guided Reading Activity 13-3

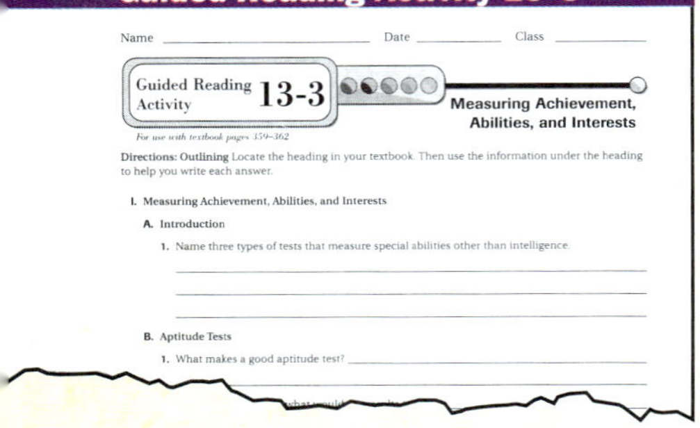
Name ______ Date ______ Class ______

Guided Reading Activity 13-3 — Measuring Achievement, Abilities, and Interests

For use with textbook pages 359–362

Directions: Outlining Locate the heading in your textbook. Then use the information under the heading to help you write each answer.

I. Measuring Achievement, Abilities, and Interests

A. Introduction

1. Name three types of tests that measure special abilities other than intelligence.

B. Aptitude Tests

1. What makes a good aptitude test? ______

Figure 13.12

Caption Answer They measure what a student has already learned.

Figure 13.11 The GATB

Samples of items from the GATB testing verbal skills, mathematical skills, and manual skills are shown here. ***What is the purpose of an aptitude test?***

1. Which two words have the same meaning?
   (a) open (b) happy
   (c) glad (d) green
2. Which two words have the opposite meaning?
   (a) old (b) dry
   (c) cold (d) young
3. A man works 8 hours a day, 40 hours a week. He earns $1.40 an hour. How much does he earn each week?
   (a) $40.00 (b) $50.60
   (c) $44.60 (d) $56.00
4. At the left is a drawing of a flat piece of metal. Which object at the right can be made from this piece of metal?

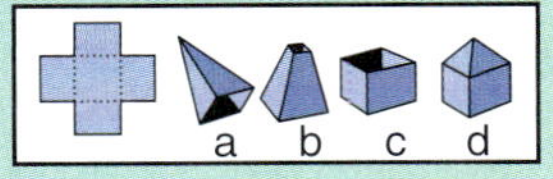

APTITUDE TESTS

Aptitude tests attempt to discover a person's talents and to predict how well he or she will be able to learn a new skill. They are assessed primarily in terms of their *predictive validity*. Two such tests are the Differential Aptitude Test (DATE) and the General Aptitude Test Battery (GATB). The GATB is the most widely used of these tests (see Figure 13.11). Actually, the GATB comprises nine different tests, ranging from vocabulary to manual dexterity. Test results are used to determine whether a person shows promise for each of a large number of occupations. In addition to the GATB, there are aptitude tests in music, language, art, mathematics, and other special fields.

The SAT and the American College Test (ACT) are general aptitude tests. These tests were designed to predict a student's success in college. The best predictor of how a student will do in college is how he or she did in high school. However, grading standards differ among high schools. So, combined with high school grades, the SAT is a fairly good predictor of student success in college.

Figure 13.12 Medical Aptitude

The Law School Admissions Test (LSAT) and the Medical College Admissions Test (MCAT) help predict how well a student will do in law school and medical school. ***How do tests like the SAT, LSAT, and MCAT also measure achievement?***

ACHIEVEMENT TESTS

Whereas aptitude tests are designed to predict how well a person will be able to learn a new skill, **achievement tests** are designed to measure how much a person has already learned in a particular area. Such tests not only enable an instructor to assess a student's knowledge, but they also help students assess their progress for themselves. They are validated in terms of their *content validity*, or how well they measure students' mastery of a set of knowledge.

The distinction between achievement and aptitude tests has become somewhat blurred. What psychologists had thought were tests of aptitude—defined as *innate* ability or talent—turned out to measure experience as well, so that in part they were achievement tests. On the other hand, achievement tests often turned out to be the best predictors of many kinds of occupational abilities, so that they were in some sense aptitude tests. Because of this overlap, the distinction between the two types of tests rests more on purpose and validation than on

COOPERATIVE LEARNING ACTIVITY

Scholastic Assessment Tests The Scholastic Assessment Test (SAT) has become a rite of passage for more than 1 million students planning to attend college each year. To investigate the institutionalization of the SATs, request groups of students to study college catalogs in the guidance office or library. Students should consider the following: **Of the total number of catalogs reviewed, how many requested submission of SAT scores? What were the mean verbal and math scores requested?** Suppose students refused to take the SAT. How do they think their decision might limit college choices? Hypothetically, do students think colleges would turn down a straight-A student who did not take the SAT? Why or why not?

content. If a test is used to predict future ability, it is considered an aptitude test; if it is used to assess what a person already knows, it is an achievement test.

Computers are often used to administer achievement tests. One method is called *adaptive testing* (Van der Linden & Glas, 2000). In a standard test, everyone gets the same questions in the same order. With adaptive testing, however, the computer changes the question difficulty as it adapts the test to your performance. If you answer several problems correctly, the computer challenges you with harder problems. If you miss a question, the computer follows it with an easier problem.

This process enables the computer to identify your ability by finding the difficulty level where you answer most, but not all, of the problems correctly. Adaptive testing is more accurate than standard testing, especially when test takers are either very high or very low in ability.

Computers can also adapt tests to include more problems in areas where your answers are frequently wrong. This procedure is called *adaptive instruction* (Kasschau, 2000). By increasing the questions posed on topics you are missing, the computer reinforces more careful studying in areas least understood (Ray, 2004).

Quick Lab

Do interest inventories help determine a career?

Interest inventories are used as predictors of how likely an individual completing the inventory will enjoy and succeed in a profession.

Procedure

1. Choose a profession that you might be interested in pursuing and find information about its requirements and responsibilities.
2. Develop a series of questions that would address and assess a person's interest in the particular profession.
3. Administer the inventory to classmates.

Analysis

1. Determine whether the responses indicate an interest in the profession you chose.
2. After you make your determination, ask those who took the inventory if a career in the profession you chose is something they might enjoy.
3. How would you evaluate your inventory in terms of its predictive value?

See the Skills Handbook, page 622, for an explanation of designing an experiment.

INTEREST INVENTORIES

The instruments for measuring interests are fundamentally different from the instruments for measuring abilities. Answers to questions on an intelligence test indicate whether a person can, in fact, do certain kinds of thinking and solve certain kinds of problems. There are right and wrong answers. The answers to questions on an interest or a personality test, however, are not scored as right or wrong. The question in this type of testing is not, "How much can you do?" or "How much do you know?" but, "What are you like?" or "What do you like?"

The essential purpose of an **interest inventory** is to determine a person's preferences, attitudes, and interests. Most interest inventories compare the person's responses to the responses given by people in clearly defined groups, such as professions or occupations. The more a person's interest patterns correspond to those of people in a particular occupation, the more likely that person is to enjoy and succeed in that profession.

For example, when constructing the widely used Campbell Interest and Skill Survey (Campbell, 1992), psychologists compared the responses of people who are successfully employed in different occupations to the responses of people in general. Suppose most engineers said they liked

aptitude test: estimates the probability that a person will be successful in learning a specific new skill

achievement test: measures how much a person has learned in a given subject or area

interest inventory: measures a person's preferences and attitudes in a wide variety of activities to identify areas of likely success

Reading Check Why is the SAT considered an aptitude test?

CHAPTER 13
Section 3, pages 359–362

Quick Lab

Purpose Students will examine the usefulness of interest inventories.

Process Skills Demonstrating reasoned judgment, designing an experiment

Teaching Strategies

- Provide students with resources to explore their favorite career.
- Remind students to pay close attention to the wording of the questions they use.

Analysis

1. Answers will vary. Encourage students to use a large enough sample that at least one person will indicate an interest in the particular profession.
2. Answers will vary.
3. Answers will vary. Many students will find that the inventory was not valid.

Vocabulary Activity 13–3

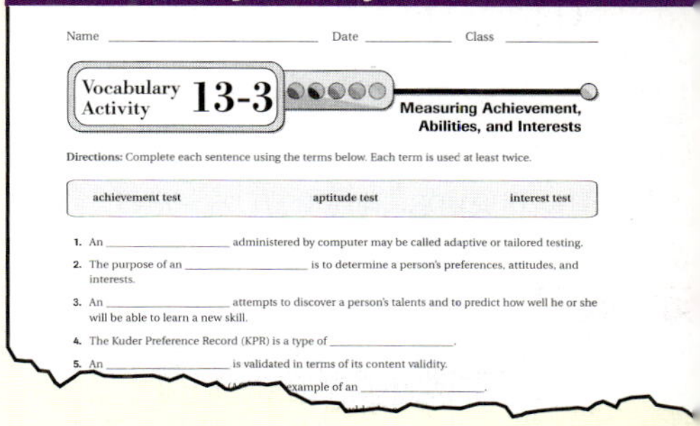
Name ____ Date ____ Class ____

Vocabulary Activity 13-3 — Measuring Achievement, Abilities, and Interests

Directions: Complete each sentence using the terms below. Each term is used at least twice.

achievement test — aptitude test — interest test

1. An ____ administered by computer may be called adaptive or tailored testing.
2. The purpose of an ____ is to determine a person's preferences, attitudes, and interests.
3. An ____ attempts to discover a person's talents and to predict how well he or she will be able to learn a new skill.
4. The Kuder Preference Record (KPR) is a type of ____.
5. An ____ is validated in terms of its content validity.

Reading Check Answer

The SAT assesses a person's talent and predicts how well he or she will learn new skills.

3 ASSESS

Assign Section 3 Assessment as homework or as an in-class activity.

MEETING SPECIAL NEEDS

Learning Style: Naturalist Challenge students to act as investigative reporters. Their assignment is to write an informative news story on the use of tests by employers in your community. Request volunteers to contact as many employers as possible. Have them ask the following questions: (1) Are tests part of the application process? If so, to what extent are they used in making hiring decisions? (2) Are tests used after hiring to determine promotions, reassignments, or pay raises? (3) What retraining do you offer employees who do poorly on a test? After students have compiled their data, have them write their news stories for class distribution.

L2 **BLOCK SCHEDULING**

CHAPTER 13

Section 3, pages 359–362

Figure 13.13

Caption Answer a person's preferences, attitudes, and interests

Section Quiz 13–3

Name ____________ Date ________ Class ________

Section Quiz 13-3

Measuring Achievement, Abilities, and Interests

SCORE

Matching

Match each item in Column A with the items in Column B. Write the correct letters in the blanks. *(10 points each)*

Column A

____ 1. order of questions is changed by computer as it tailors the test to the individual's performance

____ 2. innate ability or talent

____ 3. estimates the probability that a person will be successful in learning a specific new skill

____ 4. measures a person's preferences, attitudes, and interests in certain activities

Column B

A. achievement test

B. interest test

C. aptitude test

D. adaptive test

E. aptitude

Reteach

Have students write one question for each type of test in this section. Collect the questions. Randomly read the questions aloud and have the class categorize the question as belonging to an aptitude test, achievement test, or interest inventory.

Enrich

Have students research and report on the ongoing campaign of some inner-city schools to raise their students' SAT or ACT scores.

4 CLOSE

Ask students to create a list showing the three types of tests, giving an example of each, and explaining when each would be used.

Figure 13.13 The KPR

Shown are items from the Kuder Preference Record (KPR). The individual taking the test chooses from among three possible activities the one he or she would most like to do and the one he or she would least like to do. ***What is the Kuder Preference Record designed to measure?***

	Most		Least
G. Read a love story	○	G.	○
H. Read a mystery	○	H.	○
I. Read science fiction	○	I.	○
J. Visit an art gallery	○	J.	○
K. Browse in a library	○	K.	○
L. Visit a museum	○	L.	○
M. Collect autographs	○	M.	○
N. Collect coins	○	N.	○
O. Collect butterflies	○	O.	○
P. Watch television	○	P.	○
Q. Go for a walk	○	Q.	○
R. Listen to music	○	R.	○

the idea of becoming astronomers but would not be interested in a coaching job, whereas people in general were evenly divided on these (and other) questions. A person who responded as the engineers did would rank high on the scale of interest in engineering. The Kuder Preference Record, part of which is shown in Figure 13.13, is based on the same principle.

The purpose of these measures is to help people find the career that is right for them. It is important to note that although interest inventories can be of great value to people who are undecided about the career path they should take, they provide only one source of information. Along with interests, a student's abilities should be taken into account. A person should not make an important decision, such as that of career, on the basis of a single test or inventory.

SECTION 3 Assessment

1. **Review the Vocabulary** Write a short paragraph explaining what aptitude, achievement tests, and interest inventories are designed to measure.
2. **Visualize the Main Idea** Using a diagram similar to the one below, identify why an individual might take an aptitude, achievement, or interest inventory.

	Why would someone take this test?
Aptitude test	
Achievement test	
Interest inventory	

3. **Recall Information** What is the content validity of a test? What is the predictive validity of a test?
4. **Think Critically** Do you think a person should base his or her career choice on the results of an interest test? Explain your answer.
5. **Application Activity** Choose a favorite sport or hobby. Devise a short aptitude test that you think would help predict how well an individual would be able to learn the skills needed for the sport or hobby you chose.

SECTION 3 Assessment Answers

1. Aptitude tests can be used to help a person discover his or her talents and to predict the ability of a person to learn a new skill. Achievement tests measure how much a person has already learned in the area being tested. Interest inventories assess a person's preferences, attitudes, and interests.
2. Aptitude test—career direction; achievement test—demonstrate the body of knowledge that has been learned; interest inventory—categorize likes and preferences to help determine career direction
3. Content validity refers to the test's ability to measure correctly the body of knowledge the participant has already learned; predictive validity refers to the test's ability to assess the person's likely success.
4. Students' answers will vary. Career choices should not be made based on one set of tests; it can, however, provide direction to narrow down one's career choices.
5. Students' answers will vary. Encourage students to determine the skills required for the sport or hobby.

SECTION 4 Personality Testing

Reader's Guide

■ **Main Idea**

Personality tests are used to assess an individual's characteristics and to identify problems.

■ **Vocabulary**

- personality test
- objective test
- projective test

■ **Objectives**

- Identify the most widely used personality tests.
- Describe the use of personality tests.

EXPLORING PSYCHOLOGY

Why Do You Have Your Personality?

What makes people different from one another? The ancient Greeks thought the answer had something to do with the four basic body fluids or humors: blood, phlegm, black bile, and yellow bile. According to the Greek physician Hippocrates (460–371 B.C.), there were four possible personality types. *Sanguine* individuals had an abundance of blood: they tended to be cheerful, optimistic, and active. *Phlegmatic* people were listless, sluggish, and tired because they had too much phlegm. Sad, brooding *melancholic* temperaments resulted from too much black bile, and *choleric* (easy to anger) personalities resulted from an excess of yellow bile.

—from *Psychology: Science, Behavior, and Life* by R.H. Ettinger, Robert L. Crooks, and Jean Stein, 1994

Hippocrates' adjectives survive today in the words we use to describe personality types. The explanations for what causes personality differences, though, have changed dramatically. Psychologists and psychiatrists use **personality tests** to assess an individual's characteristics and to identify problems and psychological disorders, as well as to predict how a person might behave in the future. Some of these tests are objective tests, while others are projective tests.

personality test: assesses an individual's characteristics and identifies problems

SECTION RESOURCES

Reproducible Masters

- Guided Reading Activity 13–4
- Vocabulary Activity 13–4
- Section Quiz 13–4

Transparencies

- Daily Focus Transparency 13–4

Multimedia

- *ExamView® Assessment Suite* CD-ROM
- Presentation Plus! Software

1 FOCUS

Section Objectives

1. Identify the most widely used personality tests.
2. Describe the use of personality tests.

BELLRINGER
Motivational Activity

Project Daily Focus Transparency 13–4 and have students answer the questions.

Available as blackline master

Daily Focus Transparency 13–4

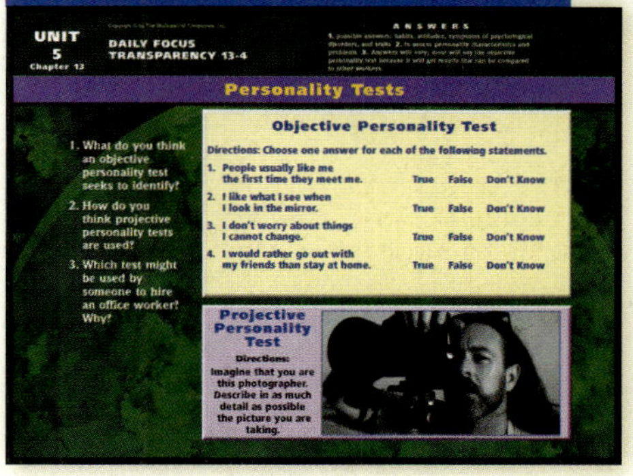

Reader's Guide

Use the Reader's Guide to introduce concepts and vocabulary.

■ **Exploring Psychology**

Ask students to read the **Exploring Psychology** feature. Then ask: **What do you think determines a person's personality?**

■ **Vocabulary Precheck**

Have students write their best guess at a definition for each vocabulary term. Then have them read the Glossary definition. Ask them to revise their written definition to reflect what they learned.

2 TEACH

L1 Making a Chart Have groups of students create charts for either objective or projective personality tests. Each chart should state the purpose of such tests, list examples of such tests, explain who is qualified to give the tests, and list the reasons these tests are used. Challenge students to conduct research for any additional information that would be helpful to understanding the two types of tests.
BLOCK SCHEDULING

Guided Reading Activity 13–4

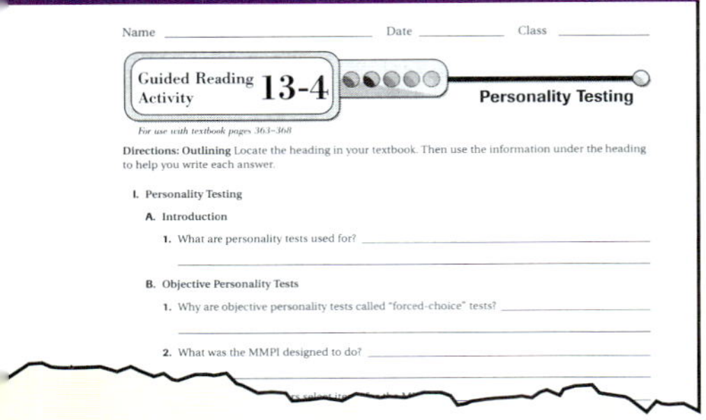
Name ______ Date ______ Class ______

Guided Reading Activity 13-4 — Personality Testing

For use with textbook pages 363–368

Directions: Outlining Locate the heading in your textbook. Then use the information under the heading to help you write each answer.

I. Personality Testing
A. Introduction
1. What are personality tests used for? ______
B. Objective Personality Tests
1. Why are objective personality tests called "forced-choice" tests? ______
2. What was the MMPI designed to do? ______

TEACHER Tip

Point out to students the ethical dangers associated with psychological tests. Mention that a fine line exists between the legitimate use of tests to weed out unsuitable candidates and their misuse that results in discrimination against whole classes or groups of people.

OBJECTIVE PERSONALITY TESTS

objective test: a limited- or forced-choice test in which a person must select one of several answers

Some of the most widely used personality tests are based on simple pencil-and-paper responses. **Objective tests** are usually constructed in a limited- or forced-choice format; that is, a person must select one of a small number of possible responses, and a specific scoring key is created.

The MMPI

One of the most widely used tests for general personality assessment is the Minnesota Multiphasic Personality Inventory (MMPI). (The MMPI was revised, updated, and published in 1990. The new version is called MMPI-2.) Like other personality tests, the MMPI-2 has no right or wrong answers. The test consists of 567 statements to which a person can respond *true, false,* or *cannot say.* Some examples of test statements are: I like tall women; I wake up tired most mornings; I am envied by most people; and I often feel a tingling in my fingers.

The items on the MMPI-2 reveal habits, fears, delusions, sexual attitudes, and symptoms of psychological disorders. Psychologists originally developed the test to help diagnose psychiatric disorders. Although the statements that relate to a given characteristic (such as depression) are scattered throughout the test, the answers can be pulled out and organized into a single depression scale or scoring key. There are 10 such clinical scales to the MMPI (see Figure 13.14). In scoring the MMPI, a psychologist looks for patterns of responses, not a high or low score on one or all of the scales. This is because the test items do not, by themselves, identify personality types; the pattern of scale scores does so.

In creating the original MMPI, the test makers did not try to think up statements that would identify depression, anxiety, and so forth. Rather, they invented a wide range of statements about all sorts of topics and gave the test to groups of people already known to be well adjusted, depressed, anxious, and so on. They retained for the test those questions that discriminated among these groups—questions, for example, that people suffering from depression almost always answered differently from other groups (Hathaway & McKinley, 1940). As a result, many of the items on the test may cause critics to question the test's face validity. For example, if you answer *false* to "I attend religious services frequently," you will score one point on the depression scale. This and other items like it were included simply because more depressed people than nondepressed people answer *false* to this item.

One of the ways in which the MMPI-2 identifies individuals who give inaccurate responses is that an untrue response to one statement may be caught by the rephrasing of the same question at a later point.

Did You Know?

The Validity of Horoscopes How can astrologers and horoscopes accurately describe you and your life? Horoscope writers and astrologers actually describe your personality traits in such a way that they apply to almost everyone. They use what is called the *Barnum principle.* Named after circus owner P.T. Barnum, it is a method of naming general traits, not specific traits. This means horoscopes lack validity, an essential factor in any good personality test. Because horoscopes are aimed at applying to everyone, they do not measure what they are supposed to measure—individual personality traits (Plotnik, 2005).

COOPERATIVE LEARNING ACTIVITY

Building Design Organize the class into small groups. Ask the members of each group to imagine that they are architects hired by the Educational Testing Service. The group's goal is to draft a plan creating the ideal testing environment. You might want to discuss with students the concept of an ideal testing environment before they begin. Offer the students the option of presenting their ideas in writing, drawings, or a combination of forms. Call on a member from each group to present the group's plan to the class as a whole. Remind the students that during group work they will sometimes be leaders and other times followers, but at all times they should work to create a supportive group climate.

Figure 13.14 MMPI Scales

The MMPI is a true-false self-questionnaire that is designed to assess major patterns of personality and emotional disorders. Clinical scales identify the specific areas whose content includes references to a specific disorder. Validity scales assess whether the test taker was lying or faking answers. ***Why is the MMPI considered an objective test?***

Clinical Scales	High score indicates that the test taker:
Hs–Hypochondriasis	expresses stress in physical terms
D–Depression	experiences depression and hopelessness
Hy–Conversion Hysteria	expresses emotion without insight
Pd–Psychopathic Deviate	is maladaptive and fights authority
Mf–Masculinity-Feminity	rejects, confuses, or questions traditional gender roles
Pa–Paranoia	has a tendency to misinterpret others' motives
Pt–Psychasthenia	worries obsessively
Sc–Schizophrenia	has a situational problem, not necessarily schizophrenia
Ma–Hypomania	has too much energy and is unable to get anything done
Si–Social Introversion	is withdrawn
Validity Scales	
?–Question	Corresponds with the number of items left unanswered
L–Lie	Some individuals fail to truthfully mark items and describe someone whom they envision as having a perfect personality
F–Infrequency	Some individuals are unwilling to cooperate with the test instructions and mark items in a random manner; others exaggerate their difficulties to get special attention
K–Correction	Some individuals deny certain characteristics about themselves and their families and so slant their answers to hide something

The subject of thousands of studies, the MMPI has been one of the most frequently used psychological tests (Lubin, Larsen, & Matarazzo, 1984). The MMPI-2 includes revisions aimed at modernizing the language, removing sexist terms or phrases, and adding items reflecting current issues such as Type A personalities, alcohol abuse, drug abuse, eating disorders, and suicide. The test can also differentiate common demeanors such as extraversion-introversion and assertiveness. Most psychologists believe that scores on the MMPI-2 should be supplemented and confirmed with interviews and observation for proper diagnosis. The test is best for diagnosing extreme cases of psychological disorders.

Figure 13.14

Visual Instruction Explain that the MMPI was first developed in the 1930s and 1940s and was intended for use by clinical and counseling psychologists to help diagnose psychological disorders.

Caption Answer The MMPI is a forced-choice questionnaire.

PSYCHOLOGY JOURNAL

Ask students to use the basic descriptions of personality discussed in the **Exploring Psychology** feature to describe their personality type. ■

MEETING SPECIAL NEEDS

Learning Style: Interpersonal Explain that the Thematic Apperception Test (TAT) is a projective test in which the test taker projects his or her thoughts onto the people in the picture. Have students find or stage photos of the following: (1) a person opening a door and entering a room with a suitcase in his hand; (2) a man and a woman in formal attire engaged in a conversation; and (3) a man looking in a window from outside a house. Have students write a paragraph about what is going on in each picture and what the characters are thinking. Collect the responses and share some of the responses anonymously. **Ask: Can you identify the gender of the writer? What, if anything, do the stories reveal about the writers? L2**

CHAPTER 13

Section 4, pages 363–368

Reading Check Answer

The MMPI can be used to identify symptoms of psychological disorders, habits, fears, delusions, and sexual attitudes.

Vocabulary Activity 13–4

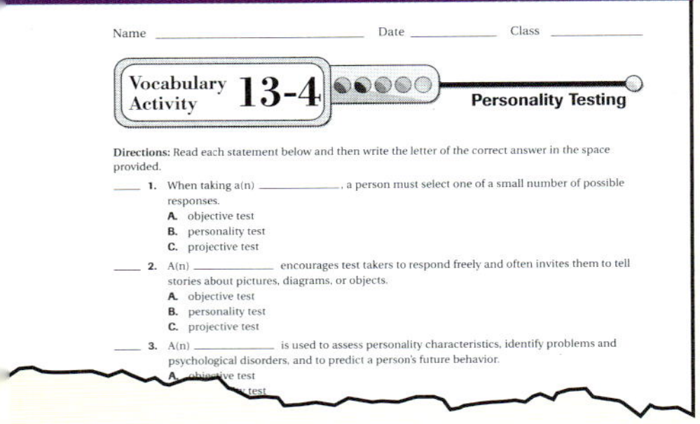
Name ______ Date ______ Class ______

Vocabulary Activity 13-4 Personality Testing

Directions: Read each statement below and then write the letter of the correct answer in the space provided.

____ **1.** When taking a(n) ______, a person must select one of a small number of possible responses.
A. objective test
B. personality test
C. projective test

____ **2.** A(n) ______ encourages test takers to respond freely and often invites them to tell stories about pictures, diagrams, or objects.
A. objective test
B. personality test
C. projective test

____ **3.** A(n) ______ is used to assess personality characteristics, identify problems and psychological disorders, and to predict a person's future behavior.
A. objective test

Figure 13.15

Caption Answer Projective tests are open-ended examinations that invite people to tell stories about pictures, diagrams, and objects.

Looking @ the Issues

Personality Testing at Work A headline in a Denver, Colorado, newspaper claimed that industrial/organizational psychology, including personality testing, could "take the guesswork out of hiring." **Ask: What dangers do you see in basing hiring decisions on personality tests? How good a predictor is a test like Myers-Briggs on the likelihood of finding the right person for the job?**

Reading Check What is the purpose of the MMPI?

The CPI

The California Psychological Inventory (CPI) is similar to the MMPI but is developed for more general use. Even though it uses some of the same questions, it does not have any of the questions that reveal psychiatric illnesses (Gough, 1987). It measures traits such as responsibility, self-control, and tolerance. The CPI is used to predict things like adjustment to stress, leadership, and job success. Although it is known to be fairly valid and reliable, the CPI can prove faulty for an individual. The test results may point out that the individual has a problem when that individual really does not. Like all personality tests, the CPI is useful for general screening and in locating individuals who may need help. If an individual's scores indicate that a problem exists, though, the test should be followed by one-on-one discussion with a counselor or psychologist for further investigation.

The Myers-Briggs Test

Another popular personality test is the Myers-Briggs Test (MBTI). The test focuses on how a person takes in information, makes decisions, and approaches day-to-day tasks. This test characterizes personality on four different scales—extraversion vs. introversion, intuition vs. sensing, feeling vs. thinking, and judging vs. perceiving.

For example, an extravert prefers engaging in activities involving other people, whereas an introvert enjoys solitude. Sensing and intuition refer to the contrast between using senses primarily in a practical way ("I have to see it to believe it") or believing something without knowing exactly why. In the thinking and feeling contrast, thinking is more logical, whereas feeling involves using a personal, values-oriented way of responding to events and people. Finally, in the judging vs. perceiving contrast, those who prefer judgment tend to have a more organized and structured manner, while those who prefer using perceptive abilities are more flexible.

The creators of the MBTI believe that each person's personality is a combination of these characteristics. Your personality type influences your communication style, how you carry out personal relationships, your work style, as well as other lifestyle choices. The purpose of the test is to offer test takers an evaluation of their personalities so that they may better understand how they relate to others and how others relate to them. With this knowledge, the creators of the test hope to help people live more productive, rewarding lives. Businesses may use this test to make better decisions about whom to hire and promote. Students can use this test to optimize the match between their learning style and the teaching style of their instructor.

projective test: an unstructured test in which a person is asked to respond freely, giving his or her own interpretation of various ambiguous stimuli

Figure 13.15 Taking the Rorschach Test

In interpreting a person's responses to the ink blots on the Rorschach test, as much attention may be paid to the style of the responses as to their content. ***What are projective tests?***

PROJECTIVE PERSONALITY TESTS

Unlike objective tests, **projective tests** encourage test takers to respond freely, giving their own interpretations of various test stimuli. These tests are open-ended examinations that invite people to tell stories about pictures, diagrams, or objects. The idea is that the test material has no established meaning, so the story a person tells must say something

CRITICAL THINKING ACTIVITY

Demonstrating Reasoned Judgment Tell students that many people have faith in the results of psychological tests because the tests purport to be based on scientific principles. In other words, people believe tests can measure such things as intelligence, achievement, and personality types in much the same way that a thermometer can measure temperature. Have students write a newspaper article exposing the fallacy of this type of reasoning. **L2**

about his or her needs, wishes, fears, and other aspects of personality. In other words, the test taker will project his or her feelings, perspectives, and attitudes onto the test items.

The Rorschach Inkblot Test

Perhaps the best-known and most widely discussed projective measure is the Rorschach inkblot test, developed by Swiss psychiatrist Hermann Rorschach in 1921. Rorschach created 10 cards with inkblot designs and a system for interpreting responses (see Figure 13.15). After 10 years of researching responses to thousands of ink blots, he chose 10 specific ones that elicited emotional responses in people. Five of the blots are black and gray on a white background; two have red splotches plus black and gray; and three cards have a mixture of different colors.

To administer the test, a psychologist hands the ink blots one by one to the test taker, asking the person to say what he sees. The person might say that a certain area represents an airplane or an animal's head. In a second round, the psychologist asks certain general questions in an attempt to discover what aspects of the ink blot determined the person's response. There are no right or wrong answers. The psychologist may keep a record of things the test taker does, such as what he says he sees, where and how he holds the cards, and the length of time he pauses before answering.

The theory underlying the test is that anything that someone does or says will reveal an aspect of that person's personality. There are several systems for scoring Rorschach responses. Some are very specific; for example, according to one system, a person who mentions human movement more often than color in the ink blots is probably introverted, while an extrovert will mention color more than movement. Other systems are far more intuitive—for example, noting whether the test taker is open or hostile. Many researchers have criticized the Rorschach, charging that the scoring systems are neither reliable nor valid and that the results often depend on the psychologist's expectations. The test, though, continues to be used by therapists as an introduction to therapy.

The TAT

The second most widely used projective measure was developed by Henry Murray (1943). The Thematic Apperception Test (TAT) consists of a series of 20 cards containing pictures of vague but suggestive situations (see Figure 13.16). The individual is asked to tell a story about the picture, indicating how the situation shown on the card developed, what the characters are thinking and feeling, and how it will end. The TAT is used to urge clients to speak freely about their problems (see Chapter 12 for more on the TAT).

As with the Rorschach, there are many different scoring systems for the TAT. The interpreter usually focuses on the themes that emerge from the story and the needs of the main characters: Are they aggressive? Do they seem to have needs for achievement, love, or sex? Are they being attacked or criticized by another person, or are they receiving affection and comfort? The responses are used to assess the motivation and personality characteristics of the individual taking the test. The test can also be used to assess the personality problems of individuals.

Figure 13.16 Taking the TAT

A person taking the TAT would be shown a picture such as this one and asked to make up a story about it. ***What does the TAT assess?***

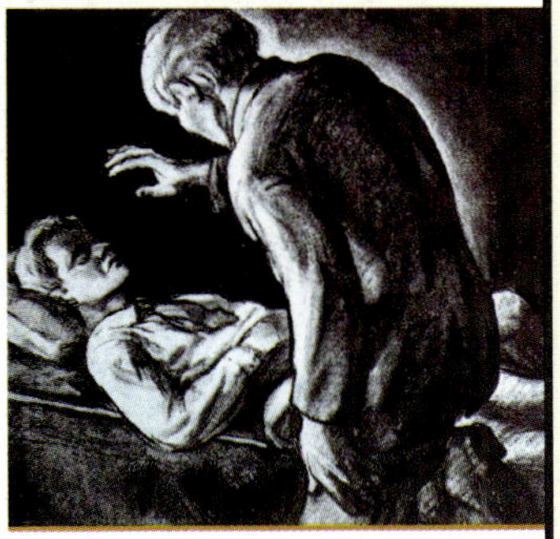

Figure 13.16

Caption Answer The TAT is used to help clients speak freely about their feelings and problems. It assesses a client's motivation and personality characteristics.

3 ASSESS

Assign Section 4 Assessment as homework or as an in-class activity.

Section Quiz 13–4

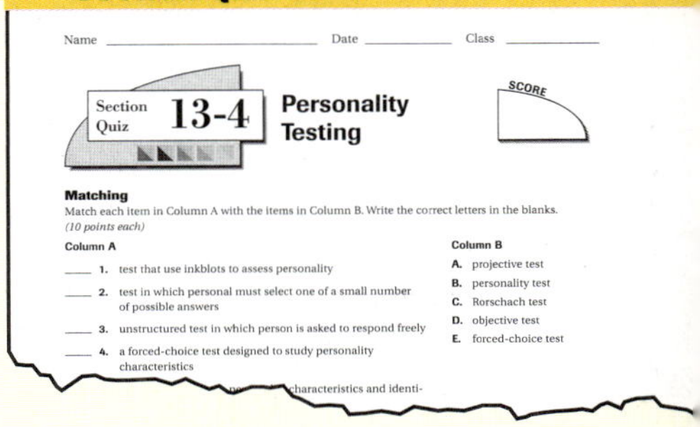
Name ______ Date ______ Class ______

Section Quiz 13-4 **Personality Testing**

SCORE

Matching
Match each item in Column A with the items in Column B. Write the correct letters in the blanks. *(10 points each)*

Column A
____ **1.** test that use inkblots to assess personality
____ **2.** test in which personal must select one of a small number of possible answers
____ **3.** unstructured test in which person is asked to respond freely
____ **4.** a forced-choice test designed to study personality characteristics
characteristics and identi-

Column B
A. projective test
B. personality test
C. Rorschach test
D. objective test
E. forced-choice test

Reteach

Have each student draw a Venn diagram to compare the MMPI and the CPI. Remind students to list the similarities between the tests in the part of the circles that overlap.

PSYCHOLOGY LAB EXPERIMENT

Evaluating Projective Testing Evaluate the use of projective testing by having students make their own ink blots in class. Provide students with drawing paper and watercolor paints. Tell them to produce some in color and some in black and white. Choose 10 that you will show to all of your psychology students. Instruct students to write down their responses to these blots. After exploring these interpretations, have students write an essay evaluating the pros and cons of projective testing as a measurement of personality. **L2**
BLOCK SCHEDULING

Figure 13.17

Visual Instruction Ask students to explain how poor preparation can lead to test anxiety. Then ask them to create a list of tips for improving test preparedness.

Caption Answer A behaviorist would focus on changing the person's actual behaviors that have led to the test anxiety. For example, a behaviorist might use a series of positive reinforcements to reward the person for studying (setting priorities, selecting a proper study area, establishing a study time, and increasing total study time).

Enrich
Have students research the Keirsey Temperament Sorter, which extends the Myers-Briggs categories to define four basic types of temperaments: Guardians, Artisans, Idealists, and Rationals.

4 CLOSE

Ask students to rate the MMPI, CPI, Rorschach, and TAT tests for reliability and validity. They should use rating scales from high to low.

Figure 13.17 Approaches to Reducing Test Anxiety

Many people worry about taking any kind of test. When someone comes to a psychologist complaining of test anxiety, the psychologist may approach the problem in a variety of ways, depending on his or her theoretical orientation. ***How would a behaviorist attempt to reduce testing anxiety?***

Approach	Solution
Biological (focus on physiological arousal, i.e. sweaty palms)	Reduce anxiety through stress-reducing activities
Cognitive (focus on thinking/excessive worrying)	Channel worry into studying
Behavioral (focus on actual behaviors)	Increase study time by selecting a good place to study, rewarding yourself for studying, keeping a record of your study time, establishing priorities, specifying time for specific tasks
Psychoanalytic (focus on personality problems that underlie bad study habits)	Work to change personality characteristics, such as procrastination
Humanistic (focus on conscious beliefs and perceptions)	Teachers work with students so that students develop feelings of competence and reach their full potential
Sociocultural (focus on influence of culture and ethnicity)	Students from different cultures have different values and resources; work to understand differences and similarities

Source: Adapted from Plotnik, 2005.

It is important to note that personality tests, as with aptitude, achievement, interest, and intelligence tests, are just one tool that a psychologist can use to evaluate a person's psychological state. A conscientious psychologist should pair testing with other evidence gained through interviews and observation before drawing any conclusions or making any diagnoses.

SECTION 4 Assessment

1. **Review the Vocabulary** What is the difference between objective and projective tests?
2. **Visualize the Main Idea** Using a chart similar to the one below, identify the characteristics of the Rorschach inkblot test and the Thematic Apperception Test (TAT).

Name of Test	Characteristics
Rorschach test	
Thematic Apperception Test	

3. **Recall Information** How does the CPI differ from the MMPI? How does the CPI differ from the Myers-Briggs test?
4. **Think Critically** What are the advantages and disadvantages of using objective personality tests versus projective personality tests?
5. **Application Activity** Choose two personality traits. Develop several test questions that you think would assess these traits. Discuss and evaluate your questions with your classmates.

SECTION 4 Assessment Answers

1. Objective personality tests force participants to select an answer among the various choices. Projective tests are open-ended and allow the participant to formulate his or her own responses.
2. The information in students' charts should demonstrate an understanding of the Rorschach test and the TAT.
3. Unlike the MMPI, the CPI does not have any of the questions that reveal psychological illnesses. The CPI measures traits such as responsibility, self-control, and tolerance. The Myers-Briggs test characterizes personality on four different scales.
4. Objective personality tests are more reliable because interscorer reliability is much higher. They can also identify personality disorders more specifically than projective tests. The primary disadvantage is that they force people to make a choice when none of the options may truly reflect the person's personality.
5. Students' answers will vary. Recommend that students review the Myers-Briggs trait pairs as they are developing the questions.

CHAPTER 13 Summary and Vocabulary

Tests evaluate academic performance and measure mental abilities or personality characteristics. The usefulness of a test depends upon how well it is constructed and the extent to which scores are related to actual performance.

Section 1 Characteristics of Psychological Tests

Main Idea: To be useful, tests have to exhibit reliability, validity, and standardization.

- There are three basic ways of determining a test's reliability: test-retest, scorer or interscorer, and split-half reliability.
- One of the chief methods for measuring validity is to find out how well a test predicts performance.
- Tests have to be standardized; they must be administered and scored the same way every time, and they must have established norms.

Section 2 Intelligence Testing

Main Idea: Several IQ tests are used to measure intelligence, although there are many views about what constitutes intelligence.

- Charles Spearman proposed that two factors contributed to a person's intelligence.
- L.L. Thurstone proposed that intelligence is composed of seven primary mental abilities.
- Howard Gardner proposed that there are eight types of intelligence.
- Two major intelligence tests are the Stanford-Binet and the Wechsler tests.
- Much of the debate about IQ testing is over how genetic differences and environmental inequalities affect performance.

Section 3 Measuring Achievement, Abilities, and Interests

Main Idea: Psychologists have developed tests to assess special abilities and experiences.

- Aptitude tests are used to identify a person's talents and to predict how well he or she will be able to learn a new skill.
- Achievement tests are designed to measure how much a person has already learned in a particular area.
- Interest inventories are used to determine a person's preferences, attitudes, and interests.

Section 4 Personality Testing

Main Idea: Personality tests are used to assess personality characteristics and to identify problems.

- Personality tests can be objective or projective.
- One of the most widely used objective personality tests is the Minnesota Multiphasic Personality Inventory (MMPI-2).
- The two major projective personality tests are the Rorschach inkblot test and the Thematic Apperception Test (TAT).

Chapter Vocabulary

reliability (p. 344)
validity (p. 345)
percentile system (p. 346)
norms (p. 346)
intelligence (p. 348)
two-factor theory (p. 349)
triarchic theory (p. 350)
emotional intelligence (p. 351)
intelligence quotient (IQ) (p. 352)
heritability (p. 355)
cultural bias (p. 356)
aptitude test (p. 360)
achievement test (p. 360)
interest inventory (p. 361)
personality test (p. 363)
objective test (p. 364)
projective test (p. 366)

13 Summary and Vocabulary

Using the Chapter 13 Summary and Vocabulary

Use the Chapter 13 Summary and Vocabulary to preview, review, condense, or reteach the chapter.

Preview/Review

Use the Chapter Vocabulary list to help students review and study.

Activity Have students make a list of terms that belong under each of the following categories: theories of intelligence, controversies in psychological testing, and types of tests.

Vocabulary PuzzleMaker CD-Rom reinforces the vocabulary terms used in Chapter 13.

Condense

Have students read the Chapter 13 Summary.

Chapter 13 Guided Reading Activities

Reteach

Reteaching Activity 13

PERFORMANCE ASSESSMENT ACTIVITY

Creating a Chart Ask students to imagine that they are the authors or editors of this textbook. **Ask:** **What kind of chart do you think would help students gain an overview of all the different kinds of tests discussed in this chapter?** Have students work independently or in small groups to design a chart summarizing the nature and purpose of IQ, aptitude, achievement, interest, and personality tests. **BLOCK SCHEDULING**

Refer to the ***Authentic Assessment*** booklet for additional activities and information about evaluating student performance.

PSYCHOLOGY Online

Have students visit the Web site at glencoe.com to review Chapter 13 and take the **Self-Check Quiz**.

GLENCOE TECHNOLOGY

Presentation Plus!

For a review of Chapter 13 content, see MindJogger Checkpoint on **Presentation Plus!**

Reviewing Vocabulary

1. c	**6.** h
2. a	**7.** b
3. g	**8.** f
4. e	**9.** d
5. j	**10.** i

Recalling Facts

1. Validity is the ability of a test to measure what it is intended to measure. One way of determining validity is to find out how well a test predicts future performance.
2. Norms are standards of comparison for test results. Norms are percentiles established on the basis of the scores achieved by a large representative sample of the group to be tested.
3. Thurstone claimed intelligence is composed of seven primary mental abilities and that measurement of intelligence should involve all seven factors. Gardner rejected the traditional idea that intelligence is primarily the ability to think logically. He has identified eight types of intelligence that include thinking ability but extend to such areas as musical ability, body-kinesthetic abilities, and intrapersonal skills. Sternberg introduced a triarchic model of intelligence that identified three ways of processing information—analytical, creative, and practical.
4. Aptitude tests, such as the SAT, are designed to predict how well a person will learn a new skill. Achievement tests, such as final exams, are designed to measure how much a person already knows about a given subject.
5. Objective personality tests, such as the MMPI, require the individual to select one answer from a small number of given choices; they usually have only one method of scoring. Projective personality tests, such as the TAT, consist of open-ended questions to which individuals respond freely; they often have several possible methods of scoring.

Critical Thinking

1. Answers will vary, but should include evaluative references to all three models.
2. Answers will vary. Ask students to volunteer their own definitions of intelligence. Once intelligence has been fully defined, have students list criteria and methods.
3. Answers will vary. Such tests would not be valid over the long run. People's feelings about their life or their work vary widely over time due to changing circumstances.
4. Answers will vary. If psychologists are given consistent training in their use, a reasonable degree of accuracy can be assumed. The scoring cannot be fully standardized, but a psychologist can be reasonably consistent in his or her assessments over time.
5. Answers will vary. Encourage students to explore the difference between using tests to identify unsuitable candidates and using tests to discriminate against specific classes or categories of people.

CHAPTER 13 Assessment

PSYCHOLOGY Online

Self-Check Quiz
Visit the *Understanding Psychology* Web site at glencoe.com and click on **Chapter 13—Self-Check Quizzes** to prepare for the Chapter Test.

Reviewing Vocabulary

Choose the letter of the correct term or concept below to complete the sentence.

a. validity	**f.** emotional intelligence
b. reliability	**g.** heritability
c. norms	**h.** cultural bias
d. intelligence	**i.** objective
e. triarchic theory	**j.** projective

1. A test's __________ are the percentiles established on the basis of the scores achieved by a standardization group.
2. The ability of a test to measure what it is intended to measure is its __________.
3. Researchers often investigate __________, a measure of the degree to which a characteristic is related to genetic factors.
4. The __________ of intelligence proposes that intelligence involves analytical, creative, and practical thinking skills.
5. In a(n) __________ test, a person is asked to give his or her own interpretations of various test stimuli.
6. __________ occurs when the wording used in questions may be more familiar to people of one cultural group than to another.
7. The ability of a test to yield the same result under a variety of different circumstances is its __________.
8. A person's __________ is related to concepts of interpersonal and intrapersonal intelligences.
9. __________ is the ability to acquire new ideas and new behavior and to adapt to new situations.
10. In a(n) __________ test, a person must select one of a small number of possible responses.

Recalling Facts

1. What is the validity of a test? How is the validity of a test determined?
2. Explain what norms are. How are norms established?
3. Using a chart similar to the one below, explain the following views of intelligence: Thurstone's, Gardner's, and Sternberg's.

Theory	View of Intelligence
L.L. Thurstone	
Howard Gardner	
Robert Sternberg	

4. Explain the difference between an aptitude test and an achievement test. Give an example of each type of test.
5. What are the two basic types of personality tests? What are some of the differences between the types? Give an example of each test.

Critical Thinking

1. **Demonstrating Reasoned Judgment** Which theory of intelligence discussed in the chapter do you agree with the most? Give reasons for your choice.
2. **Synthesizing Information** If you were asked to rate people on an intelligence scale of your own making, what criteria would you use and how would you make your decisions? What roles would memory, creativity, and emotional maturity play in your scale?
3. **Evaluating Information** Only a few tests have been used to predict how happy people will be with their lives or how successful they will be in their careers. Explain why you think this may be the case.
4. **Making Inferences** How accurate do you think the scoring for projective tests is? Can the scoring for these kinds of tests be standardized? Explain.
5. **Applying Concepts** Do you think personality tests should be used by employers to make decisions about hiring employees? Explain.

CHAPTER 13 Assessment

Psychology Projects

1. **Characteristics of Psychological Tests** Ask one of your academic teachers if you can spend some time after class talking about how he or she makes up a test. How does the teacher decide the number and type of questions? Does the teacher consider the validity or reliability of the test? How is the test scored? Present your findings in a written report.
2. **Intelligence Testing** Research various intelligence tests. Determine the criteria used to measure intelligence. Report your findings in a chart.
3. **Achievement and Personality Tests** In recent years, controversies have surrounded the use of achievement tests and personality tests. Research newspapers and magazines to find articles that explain these controversies. Summarize them in a short paper. Include your opinion of the arguments involved.
4. **Personality Testing** Contact the human resources department of a business in your community. Find out what criteria the company uses for hiring employees. Specifically, find out if the company uses personality tests or interviews to help in the hiring and what kinds of tests are used. Report your findings in a presentation.

Technology Activity

In recent years, take-at-home computerized IQ tests have become increasingly popular. Search the Internet to find examples of these kinds of tests. Also, find out about intelligence tests offered on CD-ROMs that parents can administer to their children. Evaluate the pros and cons of using these kinds of intelligence tests.

Psychology Journal

Reread your journal entry about selecting the best teaching prospect from among a group of applicants. Devise a test to use in your assessment. Consider and list in your journal the behaviors you most want to evaluate in the applicants.

Building Skills

Identifying Cause-and-Effect Relationships Review the cartoon below, then answer the questions that follow.

THE FAR SIDE By GARY LARSON

"Freeze!. . .Okay, now. . .Whose the brains of this outfit?"

1. Which person shown in the cartoon is the "brains of this outfit"?
2. How does this cartoonist illustrate the characters' intellects?
3. What assumptions are being made by the cartoonist?

See the Skills Handbook, page 624, for an explanation of identifying cause-and-effect relationships.

Practice and **assess** key social studies skills with **Glencoe Skillbuilder Interactive Workbook CD-ROM, Level 2.**

Building Skills

1. the man on the right with cards in his hands
2. The cartoonist tries to illustrate personality traits in the physical traits of each character.
3. Answers will vary. Students may suggest the "head size" view of intelligence, multiple intelligences, or emotional intelligence. Students should defend their opinions.

GLENCOE TECHNOLOGY

CD-ROM

Glencoe Skillbuilder Interactive Workbook, Level 2

This interactive CD-ROM is designed to reinforce student mastery of essential social studies skills.

Chapter Bonus Test Question

This question may be used for extra credit on the Chapter Assessment.

Answer the following question:

We are the two major controversies surrounding intelligence testing. What are we?

Answer: degree of heritability (nature vs. nurture) and cultural bias

Psychology Projects

1. Answers will vary. Encourage students to look for ways that teachers build reliability and validity into their tests. Also, have students compare the body of knowledge being taught to the type of tests given.
2. Answers will vary. Encourage students to compare the types of intelligence measured by each test and the range of people to whom the tests can be accurately administered.
3. Answers will vary. Their opinions should be well reasoned and state a firm position.
4. Answers will vary. Encourage students to identify all the elements that go into the hiring decision. Ask them to determine which elements are used to narrow the field of candidates and which are used to identify the one person best suited for the job.

Technology Activity

Students should focus their evaluation on the validity and reliability of these tests. Students should consider the following: Are all tests that claim to be IQ tests really testing intelligence? How do various tests appear to define intelligence?

Psychology Journal

Students' answers should express their understanding of the different types of testing instruments introduced in Chapter 13.

TIME REPORTS

Reader's Dictionary

Review the following terms with students to help them read and understand the article.

gratification: pleasure
emotional intelligence: how the mind processes feelings; the ability of a person to understand his or her feelings
buoyant: cheerful, having a positive outlook
resilient: ability to adjust or overcome trouble
quaint: old-fashioned or unfamiliar
neuroscientists: scientists who study the nerves and nervous tissue and their relation to behavior and learning
evolutionists: those who support the theory that species of living things change over long periods of time.
neocortex: the portion of the cerebral cortex seen at the surface (only found in mammals); responsible for many complex functions.

CLICK HERE

TIME REPORTS

Visit **www.time.com/teach** for the complete text of this article, as well as related articles on the subject.

Block Schedule

This activity works well for a block-scheduling framework.

TIME REPORTS

The EQ Factor

New research suggests that emotions, not IQ, may be the true measure of human intelligence

By NANCY GIBBS

IT TURNS OUT THAT A SCIENTIST CAN see the future by watching four-year-olds interact with a marshmallow. The researcher invites the children, one by one, into a plain room and begins the gentle torment. You can have this marshmallow right now, he says. But if you wait while I run an errand, you can have two marshmallows when I get back. And then he leaves.

Some children grab for the treat the minute he's out the door. Some last a few minutes before they give in. But others are determined to wait. They cover their eyes; they put their heads down; they sing to themselves; they try to play games or even fall asleep. When the researcher returns, he gives these children their hard-earned marshmallows. And then, science waits for them to grow up.

By the time the children reach high school, something remarkable has happened. A survey of the children's parents and teachers found that those who as four-year-olds had the fortitude to hold out for the second marshmallow generally grew up to be better adjusted, more popular, adventurous, confident and dependable teenagers. The children who gave in to temptation early on were more likely to be lonely, easily frustrated and stubborn. They buckled under stress and shied away from challenges. And when some of the students in the two groups took the Scholastic Aptitude Test, the kids who had held out longer scored an average of 210 points higher.

When we think of brilliance we see Einstein, deep-eyed, woolly haired, a thinking machine with skin and mismatched socks. High achievers, we imagine, were wired for greatness from birth. But then you have to wonder why, over time, natural talent seems to ignite in some people and dim in others. This is where the marshmallows come in. It seems that the ability to delay gratification is a master skill, a triumph of the reasoning brain over the impulsive one. It is a sign, in short, of emotional intelligence. And it doesn't show up on an IQ test.

For most of this century, scientists have worshipped the hardware of the brain and the software of the mind; the messy powers of the heart were left to the poets. But cognitive theory could simply not explain the questions we wonder about most: why some people just seem to have a gift for living well; why the smartest kid in the class will probably not end up the richest; why we like some people virtually on sight and distrust others; why some people remain buoyant in the face of troubles that would sink a less resilient soul. What qualities of the mind or spirit, in short, determine who succeeds?

The phrase "emotional intelligence" was coined by Yale psychologist Peter Salovey and the University of New Hampshire's John Mayer five years ago to describe qualities like understanding one's own feelings, empathy for the feelings of others and "the regulation of emotion in a way that enhances living." Their notion, handily shortened to EQ, is the subject of a new book, *Emotional Intelligence.* Author Daniel Goleman has brought together a decade's worth of behavioral research into how the mind processes feelings. His goal, he announces on the cover, is to redefine what it means to be smart. His thesis: when it comes to predicting people's success, brainpower as measured by IQ and standardized achievement tests may actually matter less than the qualities of mind once thought of as "character" before the word began to sound quaint.

"You don't want to take an average of your emotional skill," argues Harvard psychology professor Jerome Kagan, a pioneer in child-development research. "That's what wrong with the concept of intelligence for

SEYMOUR CHWAST/PUSHPIN GROUP INC

mental skills too. Some people handle anger well but can't handle fear. Some people can't take joy. So each emotion has to be viewed differently."

EQ is not the opposite of IQ. Some people are blessed with a lot of both, some with little of either. What researchers have been trying to understand is how they complement each other; how one's ability to handle stress, for instance, affects the ability to concentrate and put intelligence to use. Among the ingredients for success, researchers now generally agree

COOPERATIVE LEARNING ACTIVITY

Experiment Organize the class into small groups. Assign each group an age range of children, such as 3- to 4-year-olds. Tell each group to design an experiment similar to the marshmallow experiment in the reading. Have the group recruit five participants from their assigned age group. Have group members talk briefly with each participant before conducting the experiment. Ask group members to predict each child's behavior. Then have the groups conduct the experiment and analyze the results in a brief report. Have a class discussion about what this experiment indicates about EQ. **Ask:** **How well were you able to predict the results from talking with the participants before the experiment? Does age play a role in EQ? Does gender play a role in EQ?** **BLOCK SCHEDULING**

that IQ counts for about 20%; the rest depends on everything from class to luck to the neural pathways that have developed in the brain over millions of years of human evolution.

It is actually the neuroscientists and evolutionists who do the best job of explaining the reasons behind the most unreasonable behavior. In the past decade or so, scientists have learned enough about the brain to make judgments about where emotion comes from and why we need it. Primitive emotional responses held the keys to survival: fear drives the blood into the large muscles, making it easier to run; surprise triggers the eyebrows to rise, allowing the eyes to gather more information about an unexpected event. Disgust wrinkles up the face and closes the nostrils to keep out foul smells.

Emotional life grows out of an area of the brain called the limbic system, specifically the amygdala, whence come delight and disgust and fear and anger. Millions of years ago, the neocortex was added on, enabling humans to plan, learn and remember. Lust grows from the limbic system; love, from the neocortex. Animals like reptiles that have no neocortex cannot experience anything like maternal love; this is why baby snakes have to hide to avoid being eaten by their parents. Humans, with their capacity for love, will protect their offspring, allowing the brains of the young time to develop. The more connections between the limbic system and the neocortex, the more emotional responses are possible.

Without these emotional reflexes, rarely conscious but often terribly powerful, we would scarcely be able to function. "Most decisions we make have a vast number of possible outcomes, and any attempt to analyze all of them would never end," says University of Iowa neurologist Antonio Damasio, author of *Descartes' Error: Emotion, Reason and the Human Brain.* "I'd ask you to lunch tomorrow, and when the appointed time arrived, you'd still be thinking about whether you should come." What tips the balance, Damasio contends, is our unconscious assigning of emotional values to some of those choices. Whether we experience a somatic response—a gut feeling of dread or a giddy sense of elation—emotions are helping to limit the field in any choice we have to make. If the prospect of lunch with a neurologist is unnerving or distasteful, Damasio suggests, the invitee will conveniently remember a previous engagement.

When Damasio worked with patients in whom the connection between emotional brain and neocortex had been severed because of damage to the brain, he discovered how central that hidden pathway is to how we live our lives. People who had lost that linkage were just as smart, but their lives often fell apart nonetheless. They could not make decisions because they didn't know how they felt about their choices. They couldn't react to warnings or anger in other people. If they made a mistake, like a bad investment, they felt no regret or shame and so were bound to repeat it.

How much happier would we be, how much more successful as individuals and civil as a society, if we were more alert to the importance of emotional intelligence and more adept at teaching it? From kindergartens to business schools to corporations across the country, people are taking seriously the idea that a little more time spent on the "touchy-feely" skills so often derided may in fact pay rich dividends.

The problem may be that there is an ingredient missing. Emotional skills are morally neutral. Just as a genius could use his intellect either to cure cancer or engineer a deadly virus, someone with great empathic insight could use it to inspire colleagues or exploit them. Without a moral compass to guide people in how to employ their gifts, emotional intelligence can be used for good or evil. Columbia University psychologist Walter Mischel, who invented the marshmallow test, observes that the knack for delaying gratification that makes a child one marshmallow richer can help him become a better citizen or—just as easily—an even more brilliant criminal. Given the passionate arguments that are raging over moral instruction in this country, it is no wonder Goleman chose to focus more on neutral emotional skills than on the values that should govern their use. That's another book—and another debate. ■

—For the complete text of this article and related articles from TIME, please visit www.time.com/teach

Analyzing the Article

1. What is the purpose of the marshmallow test? How does it demonstrate EQ?
2. **CRITICAL THINKING** Is EQ the same as morality? How are they related? Do you think you can teach EQ to children?

Answers to Analyzing the Article

1. It is designed to see if young children can delay gratification. The ability to delay gratification is a triumph of the reasoning brain over the impulsive one. It is a sign of emotional intelligence.

2. No, emotional skills are morally neutral. Emotional intelligence can work with moral values to create great good, but without moral values, it can be used to do great harm. EQ might be enhanced through training.

TIME REPORTS

Active Reading Strategy

Suggest to students that if they are having trouble understanding part of the selection, they can use details provided by the writer to mentally walk through each step in the process being described to create a mental picture.

Questions for Discussion

Use the following questions for a class discussion after students have read the article.

1. What link does the author mention between those who delayed gratification on the marshmallow test and academic achievement? *(Those who were able to delay gratification as young children scored much higher on the SATs when they were teenagers.)*
2. What parts of the brain work together to allow for mature emotional responses? *(Emotional life grows out of the amygdala in the limbic system and the neocortex. The more connections between the limbic system and the neocortex, the more emotional responses are possible.)*
3. Why does the author say that we need emotional reflexes? *(to allow us to make decisions by unconsciously eliminating many of the choices)*

Chapter 14 Resource Guide

SECTION RESOURCES

Daily Objectives	Reproducible Resources	Multimedia Resources
Section 1 **Purposes of Personality Theories** Explore how personality theories provide a way of organizing the many characteristics that people have.	Guided Reading Activity 14–1 Vocabulary Activity 14–1 Section Quiz 14–1	Daily Focus Transparency 14–1 *ExamView® Assessment Suite* CD-ROM Presentation Plus! Software
Section 2 **Psychoanalytic Theories** Describe the three components of Freud's psychoanalytic theory: the id, the ego, and the superego.	Guided Reading Activity 14–2 Vocabulary Activity 14–2 Section Quiz 14–2	Daily Focus Transparency 14–2 Vocabulary PuzzleMaker CD-ROM *ExamView® Assessment Suite* CD-ROM Presentation Plus! Software
Section 3 **Learning Theories** Determine how behaviorists think some aspects of personality are learned.	Guided Reading Activity 14–3 Vocabulary Activity 14–3 Section Quiz 14–3	Daily Focus Transparency 14–3 *ExamView® Assessment Suite* CD-ROM Presentation Plus! Software
Section 4 **Humanistic and Cognitive Theories** Explore how the positive aspects of human nature are emphasized by the humanistic and cognitive theories.	Guided Reading Activity 14–4 Vocabulary Activity 14–4 Section Quiz 14–4	Daily Focus Transparency 14–4 *ExamView® Assessment Suite* CD-ROM Presentation Plus! Software
Section 5 **Trait Theories** Explain how trait theorists account for the consistency of behavior in different situations.	Guided Reading Activity 14–5 Vocabulary Activity 14–5 Section Quiz 14–5	Daily Focus Transparency 14–5 Vocabulary PuzzleMaker CD-ROM *ExamView® Assessment Suite* CD-ROM Presentation Plus! Software

Block Schedule

Activities that are particularly suited for use within the block-scheduling framework are identified throughout this chapter by the following designation: **BLOCK SCHEDULING**

Blackline Master

CD-ROM

Transparency

Chapter 14 Resource Guide

Timesaving Tools

TeacherWorks™ All-In-One Planner and Resource Center

- **Interactive Teacher Edition** Access your Teacher Wraparound Edition and your classroom resources with a few easy clicks.
- **Interactive Lesson Planner** Planning has never been easier! Organize your week, month, semester, or year with all the lesson helps you need to make teaching creative, timely, and relevant.

Use Glencoe's **Presentation Plus!** multimedia teacher tool to easily present dynamic lessons that visually excite your students. Using Microsoft PowerPoint® you can customize the presentations to create your own personalized lessons.

Activity

From the Classroom of...

Shannon Rice
Sickles High School
Tampa, FL

Theories of Personality

Time Required: 1 class period

When learning about the major theories of personality, this activity will help students remember which psychologist is responsible for which theory.

In groups of four, students are to create a "character collage" of an assigned psychologist (e.g., Freud, Skinner, James, Watson, Erikson, Bandura). The teacher can provide key words and concepts, or the students can research this information. On chart paper, the students will draw a caricature of the psychologist (for example, exaggerating Freud's beard and cigar) and create a collage around the picture filled with words and pictures illustrating key components of the theory. Students are assigned different tasks: two researchers, one graphic artist, and one project designer.

Psychology Online

Use our Web site for additional resources. All essential content is covered in the Student Edition.

You and your students can visit glencoe.com, the Web site companion to *Understanding Psychology*. This innovative integration of electronic and print media offers your students a wealth of opportunities. The student text directs students to the Web site for the following options:

- Chapter Overviews
- Student Web Activities
- Self-Check Quizzes

Answers are provided for you in the **Web Activity Lesson Plan**. Additional Web resources and Interactive Puzzles are also available.

KEY TO ABILITY LEVELS

Teaching strategies have been coded for varying learning styles and abilities.

- **L1** **BASIC** activities for all students
- **L2** **AVERAGE** activities for average to above-average students
- **L3** **CHALLENGING** activities for above-average students
- **ELL** **ENGLISH LANGUAGE LEARNER** activities

Chapter 14 Resource Guide

Note: The following materials may be used when teaching Chapter 14. Section level support materials are shown at point of use in the margins of the Teacher Wraparound Edition.

TEACHING TRANSPARENCIES

Chapter 14 Concept Transparencies

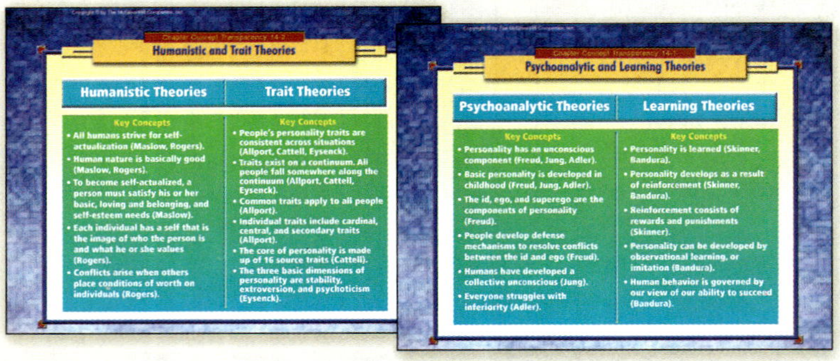

MULTIMEDIA

- Vocabulary PuzzleMaker CD-ROM
- *ExamView® Assessment Suite* CD-ROM
- TeacherWorks™ CD-ROM
- Glencoe Skillbuilder Interactive Workbook, Level 2
- Presentation Plus! Software

REVIEW AND REINFORCEMENT

Reteaching Activity 14

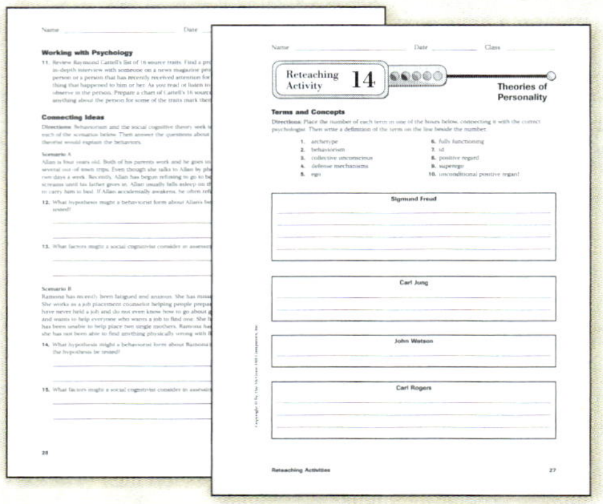

Graphic Organizer Activity 14

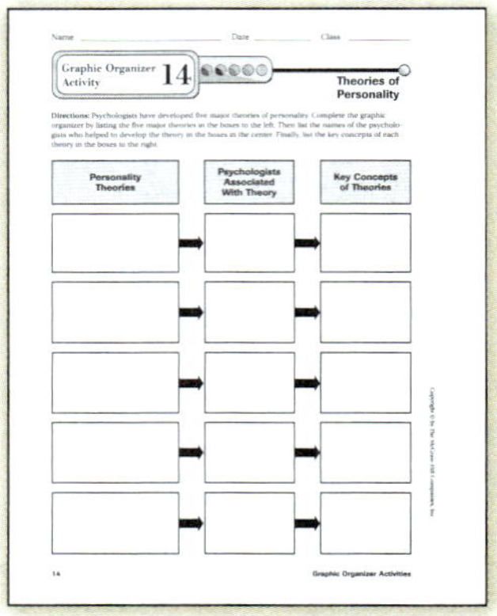

APPLICATION AND HANDS-ON

Psychology Projects 14-1 and 14-2

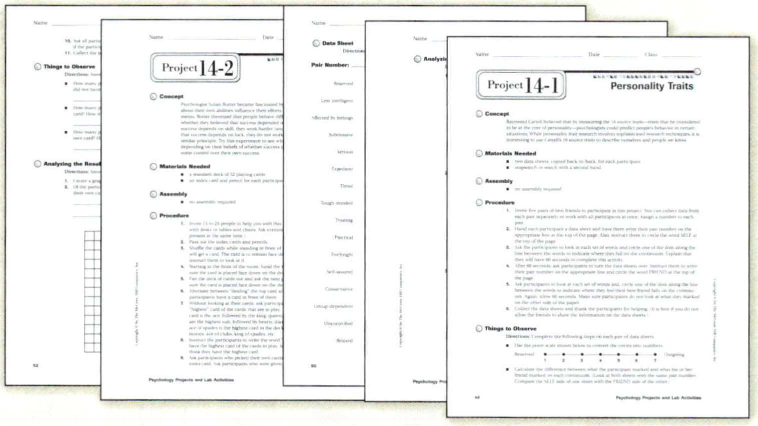

Application Activity 14

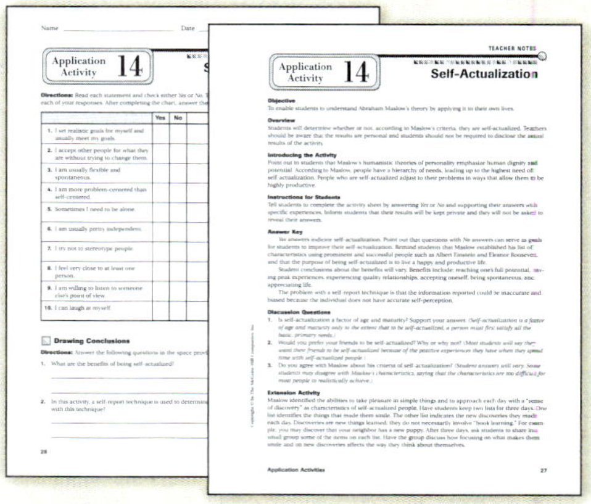

Chapter 14 Resource Guide

ASSESSMENT

Chapter 14 Test, Form A

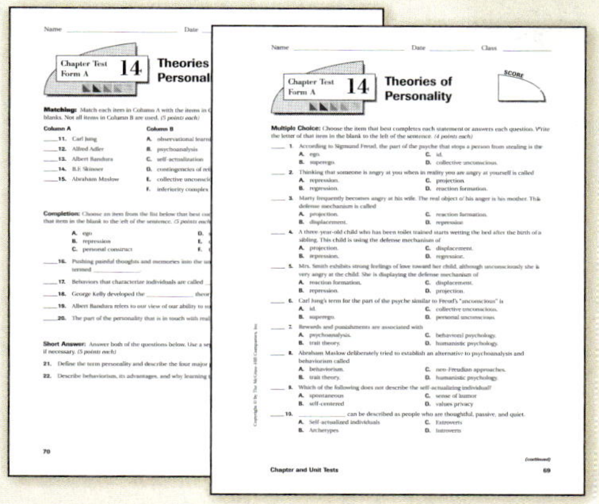

Chapter 14 Test, Form B

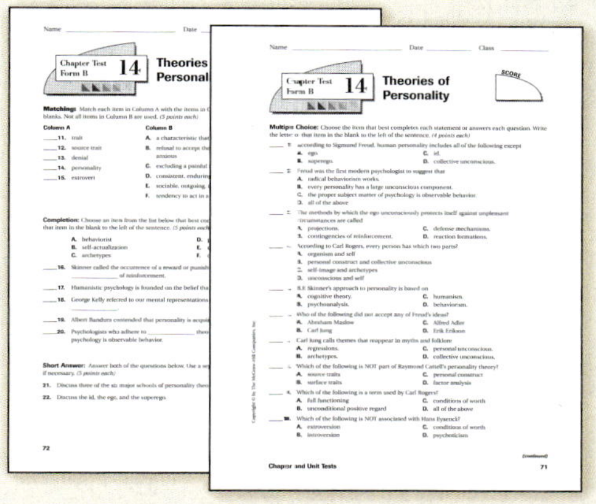

Authentic Assessment Activity 14

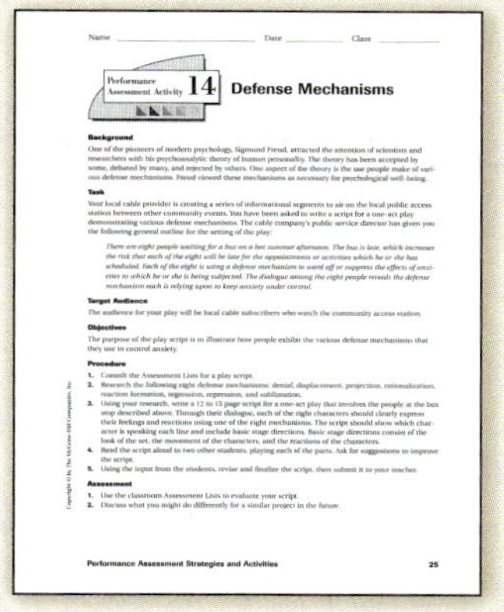

EXTENSION AND ENRICHMENT

Enrichment Activity 14

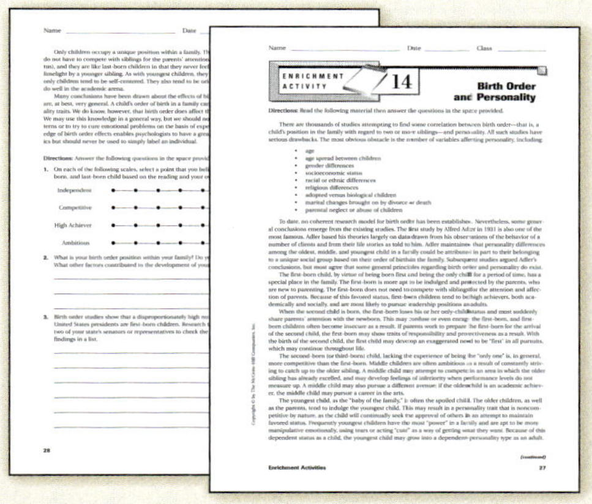

Critical Thinking Skills Activity 14

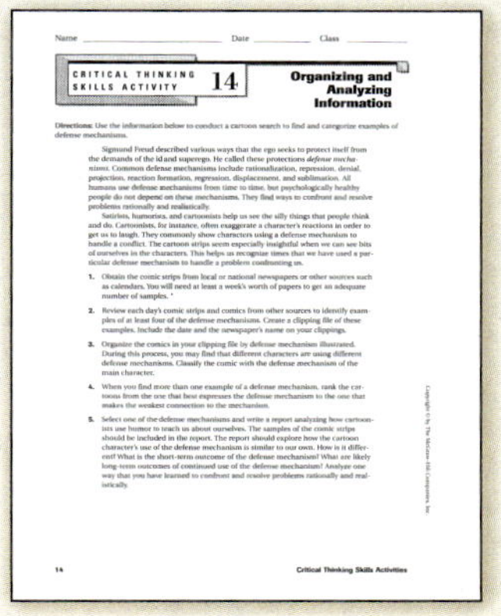

Psychology Reading 14

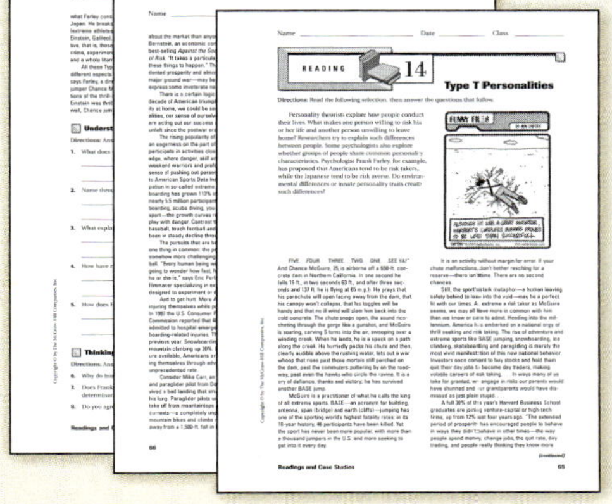

Psychology Case Study 14

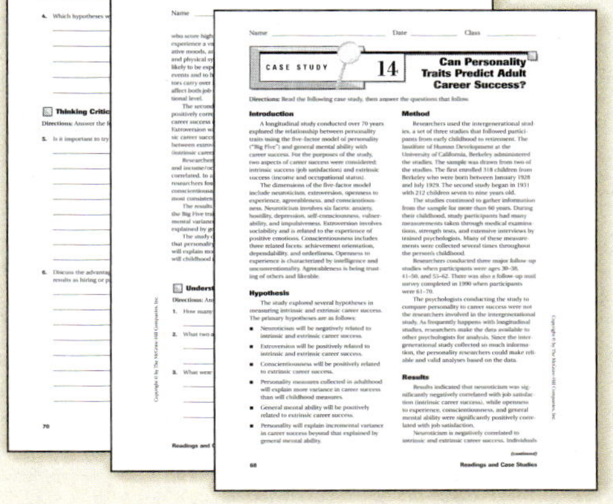

PSYCHOLOGY Online

Visit glencoe.com for a Chapter Overview for **Chapter 14—Theories of Personality.**

GLENCOE TECHNOLOGY

For a preview of Chapter 14 content, see MindJogger Checkpoint on **Presentation Plus!**

PSYCHOLOGY JOURNAL

Explain to students that humans interact differently with one another in different types of social settings. Encourage students to note these differences and the different types of responses from others.

This journal activity provides the basis for the Psychology Journal activity exercise in the Chapter Assessment. ■

CHAPTER 14

Theories of Personality

PSYCHOLOGY JOURNAL

Think of a person you have had a chance to observe in a variety of social settings. Write an entry in your journal describing that person's way of interacting with people. How do others respond to this person? How does this person influence others? How do they influence him or her? ■

PSYCHOLOGY Online

Chapter Overview
Visit the *Understanding Psychology* Web site at glencoe.com and click on **Chapter 14—Chapter Overviews** to preview the chapter.

374

TWO-MINUTE LESSON LAUNCHER

Share the following help-wanted ad with the class: *Wanted: Sales Manager. Established self-starter willing to accept responsibility for expanding business. Ability with creative staffing solutions and commitment to highest-quality services highly desired. The ideal candidate will be a team player with successful sales and interpersonal skills. College degree required.* **Ask: What type of personality traits does this ad request? Why might these traits be useful for a sales manager?** Tell students that they will learn more about personality and trait theories as they study Chapter 14.

SECTION 1 Purposes of Personality Theories

Reader's Guide

Main Idea
Personality theories provide a way of organizing the many characteristics that people have.

Vocabulary
- personality

Objectives
- Describe the major purposes of personality theories.
- List the major schools of personality theory.

EXPLORING PSYCHOLOGY

It's in the Personality

Shelly and Deirdre both failed their semester examinations in psychology, but they reacted in very different ways. When Shelly saw her grade, she felt sick to her stomach and had to fight back tears. She rushed home, and shut herself up in her room to lie in bed, stare at the ceiling, and feel inadequate. Deirdre, on the other hand, was all bluster. She ran to the cafeteria to join her friends and make loud jokes about the stupid questions on the test.

—from *Understanding Psychology,* Richard A. Kasschau, 1995

Why did Shelly and Deirdre act so differently in similar situations? There is something inside people that makes them think, feel, and act differently, and that something inside is what we mean by *personality*. When psychologists talk about aspects of personality, most agree that **personality** consists of the consistent, enduring, and unique characteristics of a person.

personality: the consistent, enduring, and unique characteristics of a person

PURPOSES OF THEORIES

The first purpose of personality theories is to provide a way of organizing the many characteristics you know about yourself and other people. You know people may be outgoing or shy, bossy or meek, quick-tempered or calm, witty or dull, fun-loving or gloomy, industrious or lazy. These words describe general ways of behaving that characterize an individual. Personality theorists try to determine whether certain traits go

SECTION RESOURCES

Reproducible Masters
- Guided Reading Activity 14–1
- Vocabulary Activity 14–1
- Section Quiz 14–1

Transparencies
- Daily Focus Transparency 14–1

Multimedia
- *ExamView® Assessment Suite* CD-ROM
- Presentation Plus! Software

1 FOCUS

Section Objectives
1. Describe the major purposes of personality theories.
2. List the major schools of personality theory.

BELLRINGER
Motivational Activity

Project Daily Focus Transparency 14–1 and have students answer the questions.

Available as blackline master

Daily Focus Transparency 14–1

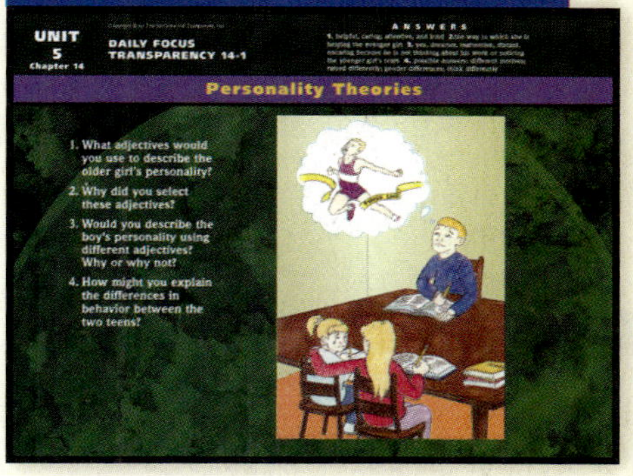

Reader's Guide

Use the Reader's Guide to introduce concepts and vocabulary.

Exploring Psychology
Ask students to read the **Exploring Psychology** feature. Then discuss: **What personality differences are apparent in the way the two teens reacted?**

Vocabulary Precheck
Have students read the Glossary definition of *personality.* Write the word and definition on the board. Then ask students to describe their own personality by writing at least 20 characteristics of themselves that are consistent and enduring.

2 TEACH

Guided Reading Activity 14-1

Name ______ Date ______ Class ______

Guided Reading Activity 14-1 — Purposes of Personality Theories

For use with textbook pages 375–377

Directions: Outlining Locate the heading in your textbook. Then use the information under the heading to help you write each answer.

I. Purposes of Personality Theories
A. Introduction
1. What is the "something" inside people that makes them think, feel, and act differently from one another? ______
B. Purpose of Personality Theories
1. What do all personality theorists look for? ______
2. What are three ways that theorists might try to explain the differences among individuals? ______

Reading Check Answer in terms of motives or how experiences shape personality

Figure 14.1

Caption Answer They organize characteristics about people, explain differences, explain how people conduct their lives, and determine how life can be improved.

Vocabulary Activity 14-1

Name ______ Date ______ Class ______

Vocabulary Activity 14-1 — Purposes of Personality Theories

Directions: Fill in each blank below with the word or words that best fit the sentence.

That "something inside" people that makes them think, feel, and act differently is what we mean by **1** ______. Personality consists of the **2** ______, **3** ______ and **4** ______ characteristics of a person.

The first purpose of **5** ______ is to provide a way of organizing the many characteristics you know about yourself and other people. A second purpose is to explain the differences among **6** ______. A third purpose is to explore how people **7** ______ their lives. A fourth purpose of personality theories is to determine how life ______

3 ASSESS

Assign Section 1 Assessment as homework or as an in-class activity.

Section Quiz 14-1

Name ______ Date ______ Class ______

Section Quiz 14-1 — Purposes of Personality Theories — SCORE

Matching
Match each item in Column A with the items in Column B. Write the correct letters in the blanks. (10 points each)

Column A	Column B
___ 1. studied the way rewards and punishments shape our actions	A. Sigmund Freud
___ 2. examined the impact of observational learning on personality	B. Abraham Maslow
___ 3. stressed human growth potential	C. Gordon Allport
___ 4. emphasized the importance of unconscious motivations	D. B.F. Skinner
___ 5. emphasized the importance of understanding personality characteristics	E. social learning theorists

together, why a person has some traits and not others, and why a person might exhibit different traits in different situations. There is a good deal of disagreement among theorists as to which traits are significant. Nevertheless, all theorists look to discover patterns in the ways people behave.

A second purpose of any personality theory is to explain the differences among individuals. In so doing, theorists probe beneath the surface. Some theorists might explain different behaviors in terms of motives. Others might try to find out how motives were established in the first place. Still other theorists might seek less obvious causes for individual differences, arguing, for example, that the roots of these differences could be traced back to childhood conflicts.

A third goal of personality theory is to explain how people conduct their lives. It is no accident that most personality theorists began as psychotherapists. In working with people who had difficulty coping with everyday problems, psychotherapists inevitably developed ideas about what it takes to live a relatively happy, untroubled life. Personality theorists try to explain why problems arise and why they are more difficult for some people to manage than for others.

In addition, the fourth purpose of personality theorists is to determine how life can be improved. It seems obvious that some people are dissatisfied with themselves, their parents, their husbands, wives, or children, or their home lives. People resign themselves to unrewarding jobs, and there is a widespread feeling that much is wrong with society and the world. Almost everyone recognizes that we need to grow and change, both individually and collectively. But what are the proper goals of growth and change? How can we cope with the inevitable conflicts of life?

Psychologists interested in personality attempt to answer these questions with systematic theories about human behavior. These theories are used to guide research. Research, in turn, can test how well a theory explains behavior. Thus, formal personality theories are attempts to make ideas about why people act in certain ways more scientific by stating them precisely and testing them systematically.

Reading Check How might psychologists explain differences in personalities?

Figure 14.1 Personality

Psychologists who study personality explore whatever it is that makes one person think, feel, and act differently from another. ***What are the purposes of personality theories?***

MAJOR SCHOOLS OF PERSONALITY THEORY

Psychology is a young discipline, and the development and testing of personality theories are still gaining sophistication. There are now many conflicting theories of personality, each with positive and negative aspects. Discussing both sides of various theories helps invigorate the discussion about personality.

In this chapter, we will describe major schools of thought among personality theorists. Psychoanalytic theories, developed by Sigmund Freud and his followers, emphasize the importance of motives hidden in the unconscious. B.F. Skinner and the behaviorists study the way rewards and punishments shape our actions. Social learning theories examine the impact of observational learning on personality. Cognitive

COOPERATIVE LEARNING ACTIVITY

Researching Historical Figures Read aloud the following quote of Henry David Thoreau: *If a man does not keep pace with his companions, perhaps it is because he hears a different drummer. Let him step to the music which he hears, however measured or far away.* As a class, discuss Thoreau's meaning. **Ask:** **About what type of person was Thoreau writing? How might a team player view such a person?** Organize students into small groups to identify and research historical figures that "marched to the beat of a different drummer." Have the groups prepare an oral presentation about the personality of the chosen figure. **BLOCK SCHEDULING**

Figure 14.2 Characteristics of Personality

In psychology, personality refers to the essential characteristics of a person. Cathy Guisewite, a cartoonist, has given personality characteristics to an animal—a dog. ***What factors do you think are influencing the personality of the dog in this cartoon?***

theorists focus on how our thoughts, perceptions, and feelings shape our personalities. Humanistic theorists, like Abraham Maslow and Carl Rogers, stress one's potential for growth, such as creativity and spontaneity. Finally, trait theorists, like Gordon Allport and Hans Eysenck, emphasize the importance of understanding basic personality characteristics such as friendliness and aggression.

Each of the theories we will discuss has a different image of human nature. What they have in common is a concern with understanding the differences among people.

SECTION 1 Assessment

1. **Review the Vocabulary** Write your own definition of *personality.* How does your definition compare to the textbook's definition?
2. **Visualize the Main Idea** Use a graphic organizer similar to the one below to list the purposes of personality theories.

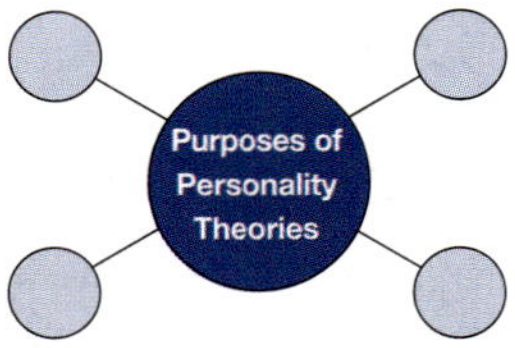

3. **Recall Information** What are the major schools of personality, and how do they differ?
4. **Think Critically** Do you think that you choose your own behaviors freely, or do you believe that your current behaviors are determined by previous behaviors and events? Explain.
5. **Application Activity** Work with a small group of students and take turns recalling some early memories. Jot down those memories, and discuss the following question: Do these early memories relate to your present personality?

SECTION 1 Assessment Answers

1. Answers will vary. Personality describes the consistent, enduring, and unique characteristics of a person.
2. The purposes are to organize the characteristics that describe people, to explain the differences among individuals, to explain how people conduct their lives, and to determine how life can be improved.
3. psychoanalytic (emphasizes hidden motives), behavioral (examines how rewards and punishments shape personality), social learning (examines the impact of observational learning on personality), cognitive (focuses on how our thoughts, perceptions, and feelings shape our personalities), humanistic (stresses one's human potential), and trait (emphasizes the importance of understanding basic personality characteristics)
4. Students' answers will vary. Encourage students to provide specific examples to support their positions.
5. Students' answers will vary. Tell students that they do not need to share memories that are painful or private.

Figure 14.2

Caption Answer Possible answers: desperation, her environment, and her desire to have a home

Reteach

Write a list of common personality characteristics on the board. Ask students to fill in the opposite characteristic.

Enrich

Have students list personality characteristics they believe are important to living a happy life.

4 CLOSE

Make a chart listing the major personality theories. Have students make columns listing the major psychologist(s) associated with the theory and the basic tenets of the theory.

1 FOCUS

Section Objectives

1. Explain Sigmund Freud's structural concepts of personality.
2. Describe Carl Jung's theory of personality.

BELLRINGER
Motivational Activity

Project Daily Focus Transparency 14–2 and have students answer the questions.

Available as blackline master

Daily Focus Transparency 14–2

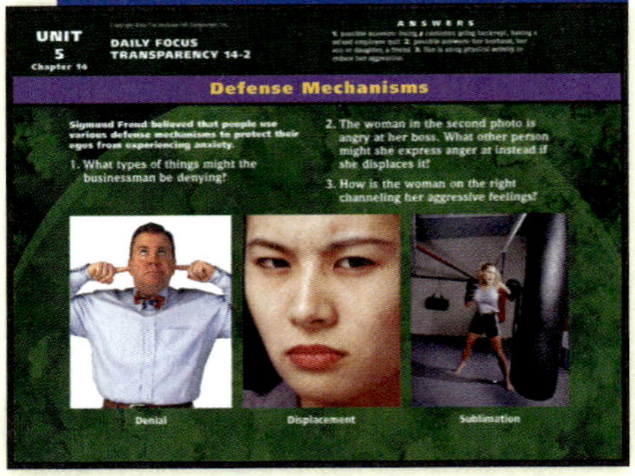

Reader's Guide

Use the Reader's Guide to introduce concepts and vocabulary.

Exploring Psychology

Ask students to read the **Exploring Psychology** feature. Then ask: **Do you agree that all "Freudian slips" are expressions of unconscious desires? Why or why not?**

Vocabulary Precheck

Have students read the Glossary definitions of the vocabulary terms. Ask them to create a word search puzzle using all the terms. They should provide clues to the terms using the definitions of the terms. Have students trade their puzzles with each other to complete.

Use the **Vocabulary PuzzleMaker CD-ROM** to create crossword and word search puzzles.

SECTION 2 Psychoanalytic Theories

Reader's Guide

Main Idea

Freud's psychoanalytic theory proposes that personality is made up of three components: the id, ego, and superego.

Vocabulary

- unconscious
- id
- ego
- superego
- defense mechanisms
- collective unconscious
- archetype
- inferiority complex

Objectives

- Explain Sigmund Freud's structural concepts of personality.
- Describe Carl Jung's theory of personality.

EXPLORING PSYCHOLOGY

Just a Slip

One of my colleagues was lecturing on the importance of regular health care. She said, "It is important to visit a veterinarian for regular checkups." According to Freud, mistakes like substituting *veterinarian* for *physician* are not accidental but rather "intentional" ways of expressing unconscious desires.

As it turns out, my colleague, who is in very good health, was having serious doubts about her relationship with a person who happened to be a veterinarian.

—from *Introduction to Psychology* by Rod Plotnik, 2005

Journal Topic: Choose a time when this happened to you.

Slips in speaking are common. People usually laugh at them, even if they are meaningful; sometimes, however, they are disturbing. Everyone has made a remark that hurt a friend and has later asked himself, "Why did I say that? I didn't mean it." Yet, when he thinks about it, he may realize that he was angry at his friend and wanted to get back at him.

SIGMUND FREUD AND THE UNCONSCIOUS

It was Sigmund Freud who first suggested that the little slips that people make, the things they mishear, and the odd misunderstandings they have are not really mistakes at all. Freud believed there was something

SECTION RESOURCES

Reproducible Masters

- Guided Reading Activity 14–2
- Vocabulary Activity 14–2
- Section Quiz 14–2

Transparencies

- Daily Focus Transparency 14–2

Multimedia

- Vocabulary PuzzleMaker CD-ROM
- *ExamView® Assessment Suite* CD-ROM
- Presentation Plus! Software

behind these mistakes, even though people claimed they were just accidental and quickly corrected themselves. Similarly, when he listened to people describe their dreams, he believed the dreams had some unconscious meaning, even though the people who dreamed them did not know what they meant.

Freud was a neurologist who practiced in Vienna in the late 1800s and early 1900s. Although he specialized in nervous disorders, many people talked to him about their private lives, conflicts, fears, and desires. He concluded that the most powerful influences on human personality are things outside our conscious awareness with no physiological basis.

Freud was the first modern psychologist to suggest that every personality has a large **unconscious,** or unaware, component. For Freud, experiences include feelings and thoughts as well as actual events. Freud believed that many of our experiences, particularly the painful episodes of childhood, are not forgotten but are stored in the unconscious. Although we may not consciously recall these experiences, they continue to influence our behavior. Freud believed that unconscious motives and the feelings people experience as children have an enormous impact on adult personality and behavior. Between the unconscious and the conscious is the *preconscious*—thoughts that can be recalled with relatively little effort. These thoughts consist of information just below the surface of awareness. Preconscious thoughts may include memories of recent events, recollections of friends, and simple facts–anything we can recall.

PSYCHOLOGY Online

Student Web Activity Visit the *Understanding Psychology* Web site at glencoe.com and click on **Chapter 14—Student Web Activities** for an activity on theories of personality.

unconscious: the part of the mind that contains material of which we are unaware but that strongly influences conscious processes and behaviors

THE ID, EGO, AND SUPEREGO

Freud explained human personality by saying that it was a kind of energy system, like a steam engine or an electric dynamo. The energy in personality comes from two kinds of powerful instincts—the life instincts and the death instincts. Freud theorized that all of life moves toward death and that the desire for a final end shows up in human personality as destructiveness and aggression. It is important to remember, however, that *life* instincts were more important in Freud's theory and he saw them primarily as erotic or pleasure-seeking urges. By 1923, Freud had described what became known as the structural concepts of the personality: id, ego, and superego (see Figure 14.3). Freud introduced them as a model of how the mind works. In other words, the id, ego, and superego are not actual parts of the brain; instead, they explain how the mind functions and how the instinctual energies are organized and regulated.

In Freud's theory, the **id** is the reservoir or container of the instinctual and biological urges. At birth, all your energy is invested in the id, responding unconsciously to inborn instinctive urges for food and water. The id

id: the part of the unconscious personality that contains our needs, drives, instincts, and repressed material

Figure 14.3 Freud's Model

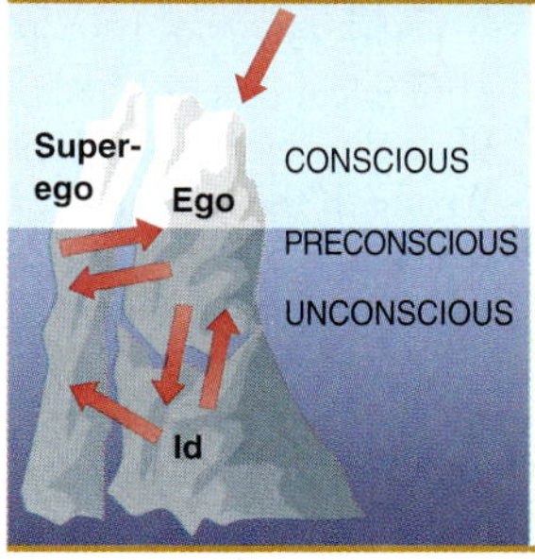

The ego tries to balance the demands of the id and the superego and the realities of the world. These interactions and conflicts are represented by arrows in the figure. ***Which of these components is the source of guilt feelings?***

2 TEACH

L1 Creative Writing Propose a decision-making scenario, such as the following, to the class:

You are on an overnight hike with a group of friends when a rainstorm suddenly hits. Everyone's food is destroyed in the downpour except one friend who wrapped her food in a plastic stuff sack. As night arrives, you are very hungry. You notice that your friend has wandered away from her backpack. Part of you wants to steal her food—you need it to have energy to finish the hike. Another part of you says the action is morally wrong. What will you do?

Challenge students to prepare a three-part dialogue in which the id, ego, and superego argue and resolve this moral dilemma. Request volunteers to read their dialogues to the class.

PSYCHOLOGY Online

Links and instructional guidelines can be found in the **Web Activity Lesson Plan** at glencoe.com.

Figure 14.3

Visual Instruction Make sure that students understand that Freud did not view the id, ego, and superego as separate entities or physical divisions of the brain. Instead, Freud used these as labels for strong psychological forces or motivations.

Caption Answer the superego

COOPERATIVE LEARNING ACTIVITY

Writing and Performing a Skit Organize the class into groups of three or four. Assign each group one of the defensive mechanisms described in the text. Direct the groups to write a skit illustrating the defense mechanism in action. Ask each group to present its skit to the class. After students present their skits, have other groups discuss the positive and negative effects of the defense mechanism on the characters involved. **BLOCK SCHEDULING**

Guided Reading Activity 14-2

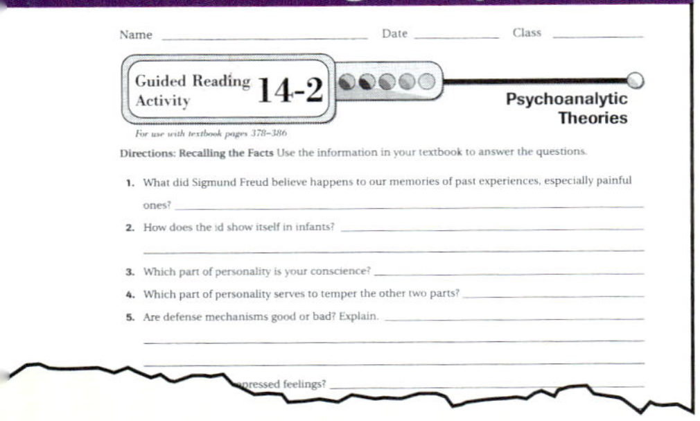
Name ____ Date ____ Class ____

Guided Reading Activity 14-2

Psychoanalytic Theories

For use with textbook pages 378–386

Directions: Recalling the Facts Use the information in your textbook to answer the questions.

1. What did Sigmund Freud believe happens to our memories of past experiences, especially painful ones?
2. How does the id show itself in infants?
3. Which part of personality is your conscience?
4. Which part of personality serves to temper the other two parts?
5. Are defense mechanisms good or bad? Explain.

...pressed feelings?

TEACHER Tip

Review Freud's theory of the stages of personality development discussed in Chapter 3. Consider assigning a student to prepare a mock news "recap," similar to those used in sports reporting.

CURRICULUM CONNECTION

History Explain that the study of history includes a subfield known as psychohistory. Psychohistory studies historical motivation using the insights of modern psychotherapy and the research methodology of history. Psychohistory strives to understand the origin of social and political behavior in individuals and among nations. One area of research applies personality theories to major figures from the past. Among those who have been studied are Napoleon Bonaparte, Adolf Hitler, and Richard Nixon.

is the lustful, impulsive, fun, or drive-ridden part of the unconscious. The demand of Sesame Street's Cookie Monster—"Me want cookie!"—is pure id. It operates in terms of what Freud called the *pleasure principle,* seeking immediate gratification of desires, regardless of the consequences. Doing something that may hurt someone's feelings, lying, and having fun are examples of the id's influence.

ego: the part of the personality that is in touch with reality and strives to meet the demands of the id and the superego in socially acceptable ways

The personality process that is mostly conscious is called the **ego.** Gradually forming during the second and third years of life and driven by psychic energy borrowed from the id, the ego is the rational, thoughtful personality process that operates in terms of Freud's *reality principle.* If, for example, a person is hungry, the id might drive her to seek immediate satisfaction by dreaming of food or by eating all the available food at once instead of keeping some of it for later. The ego would recognize that the body needs real food and that it will continue to need food. It would use the id's energy to urge preserving some of the food available now and looking for ways of finding more.

superego: the part of the personality that is the source of conscience and counteracts the socially undesirable impulses of the id

Suppose you thought of stealing the desired food from someone else. The **superego,** which represents the learning and incorporation of your primary caretaker's ideals, is the part of the personality that would stop you. The id represents what the person wants to do, the ego plans what she can do, and the superego advocates what she should do. It is the moral part of the personality, the source of conscience and of high ideals that can be said to operate in terms of a *moral principle.* The superego can also create conflicts and problems. It is sometimes overly harsh, like a very strict parent. Hence, it is the source of guilt feelings, which come from deviations from what it defines as right—better known as the conscience, or internalized values of the parents.

The id and the superego frequently come into conflict with each other. Because neither is concerned with reality, they may both come into conflict with the outside world as well. Freud saw the ego as the part of the person that must satisfy the demands of the id without offending the superego. If the id is not satisfied, the person feels an intolerable tension of longing or anger or desire. If the superego is not obeyed, the person feels guilty and inferior. If outside reality is ignored, the person suffers such outcomes as starvation or dislike by other people.

DEFENSE MECHANISMS

defense mechanisms: certain specific means by which the ego unconsciously protects itself against unpleasant impulses or circumstances

The ego's job is so difficult that all people unconsciously resort to psychological defenses. Rather than face intense frustration, conflict, or feelings of unworthiness, people deceive themselves into believing nothing is wrong. If the demands of the id and the ego cannot be resolved, it may be necessary to distort reality. Freud called these techniques **defense mechanisms** because they defend the ego from experiencing anxiety about failing in its tasks (see Figure 14.5). Freud believed that these defense mechanisms stem from the unconscious part of the ego. They ordinarily become conscious to the individual only during a form of psychotherapy called psychoanalysis—and then only with great difficulty.

MEETING SPECIAL NEEDS

Learning Style: Logical/Mathematical Tell students that the traditional view of only children has been that they are spoiled and self-centered. This view held that only children did not relate well in social situations and were overly dependent on their parents. Although more recent studies contradict this view, society still largely accepts the notion that only children are spoiled and selfish. Challenge students to use Freud's personality parts (id, ego, and superego) to explain the traditional view of only children. For example, ask students to describe the dominant personality part in only children. **L2** **BLOCK SCHEDULING**

To some degree, defense mechanisms are necessary for psychological well-being. They relieve intolerable confusion and stress, help people weather intense emotional crises, and give individuals time to work out problems they might not be able to solve if they allowed themselves to feel all the pressures at work within them. However, if a person resorts to defense mechanisms all of the time, he will avoid facing and solving his problems realistically. A few of the defense mechanisms Freud identified are discussed below.

Reading Check According to Freud, why do people create defense mechanisms?

Rationalization

If you explained your poor performance on your last math test by saying, "The test questions were bad; they didn't make sense," rather than admitting that you did not study for the test, you practiced *rationalization.* Rationalization involves making up acceptable excuses for behaviors that cause us to feel anxious.

Repression

When a person has painful memories and unacceptable thoughts and motives that cause the ego too much anxiety, she may push those thoughts or urges out of consciousness down into the unconscious. This process is called *repression.* The person simply pushes the disturbing thoughts and memories out of awareness without ever realizing it. For example, a grown woman whose father is meddling in her life may have the impulse to say, "I hate you, Dad." The woman may feel so anxious and afraid about having such an impulse that she unconsciously will come to believe that what she feels is not hatred. She replaces the feeling with apathy. She says, "I don't hate you. I have no special feelings at all about you." Nevertheless, the feelings of anger and hostility remain in the unconscious and may show themselves in cutting remarks, sarcastic jokes, slips of the tongue, or dreams.

Figure 14.4 Freudian Slip

Freudian slips are mistakes or slips of the tongue that we make in everyday speech. Freud believed that these slips reflect our unconscious thoughts or wishes. ***What is the Freudian slip that this speaker makes?***

Why you should always stick to the script.

Denial

You are in *denial* if you refuse to accept the reality of something that makes you anxious. For example, it is a stormy and frightening night, and the local television and radio announcers are advising citizens to take cover and observe the tornado warnings in effect. David does not believe that his town will get hit (he is in denial) and is severely injured after failing to heed the warnings.

Projection

Another way the ego avoids anxiety is to believe that impulses coming from within are really coming from other people. For example, a boy who is extremely jealous of his girlfriend but does not

CHAPTER 14
Section 2, pages 378–386

Reading Check Answer to defend their ego from experiencing anxiety attacks about their failures; to avoid facing intense frustration, conflict, or feelings of unworthiness

PSYCHOLOGY JOURNAL

Assign students to write about an example from their own experiences in which they have used one of the defense mechanisms. Also ask them to write about the consequences of using the defense mechanism. ■

Figure 14.4

Caption Answer The speaker inadvertently uses the phrase "heavy turnout," a slip of the tongue that could be taken as an (unintended) insult by the audience of obese people.

CULTURAL CONNECTIONS

Freud lived and worked during the Victorian era. The era is named for Great Britain's Queen Victoria, who ruled from 1837 to 1901. During her reign, Great Britain developed a worldwide empire. Her reign also saw a shift in values, with emphasis placed on proper dress and behavior. Male-female interactions became ritualized. Public displays of affection were highly frowned on; sex was never discussed openly. Freud's theories sharply contrasted with the mores of the time. He identified societal values as the reason why people repressed their feelings, especially concerning sexual desires.

CRITICAL THINKING ACTIVITY

Analyzing Information Assign students to keep a private log of conflicts they encounter each day. Emphasize that the diaries will not be collected. At the end of the day, students should pretend they are Freudian psychologists. After each entry in the log, they should analyze which Freudian principle was most operative in resolving the conflict. Was it (1) interaction between the id and superego, or (2) a defense mechanism? If a defense mechanism was used, students should attempt to name it. At the end of the week, tell students to prepare a list of the methods of conflict resolution used during the week. **L2**

CHAPTER 14
Section 2, pages 378–386

Figure 14.5

Visual Instruction Introduce the defense mechanism of *sublimation (redirecting a forbidden or socially unacceptable desire into a socially acceptable desire).* Ask students to explain how this term fits the definition of a *defense mechanism*? *(an ego defense against unacceptable behavior)*

Caption Answer They relieve confusion, help individuals get through emotional troubles, and provide time to resolve problems.

Vocabulary Activity 14–2

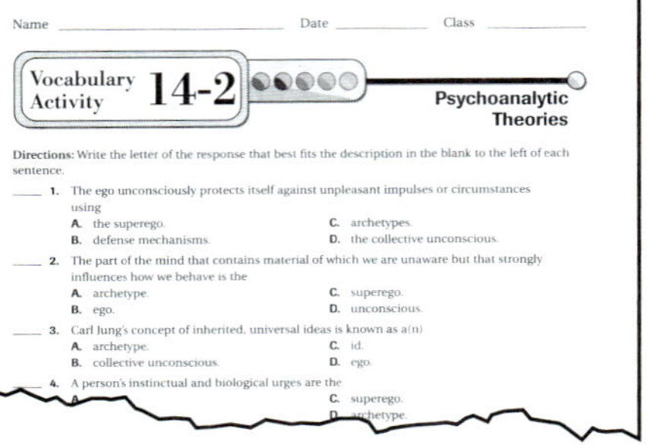
Name ______ Date ______ Class ______

Vocabulary Activity 14-2

Psychoanalytic Theories

Directions: Write the letter of the response that best fits the description in the blank to the left of each sentence.

____ **1.** The ego unconsciously protects itself against unpleasant impulses or circumstances using
A. the superego. **C.** archetypes.
B. defense mechanisms. **D.** the collective unconscious.

____ **2.** The part of the mind that contains material of which we are unaware but that strongly influences how we behave is the
A. archetype. **C.** superego.
B. ego. **D.** unconscious.

____ **3.** Carl Jung's concept of inherited, universal ideas is known as a(n)
A. archetype. **C.** id.
B. collective unconscious. **D.** ego.

____ **4.** A person's instinctual and biological urges are the
C. superego.
D. archetype.

PSYCHOLOGY Update

Narcissism Many psychiatrists believe that the root cause of many personality disorders is narcissism. Although all personality disorders are not mental illnesses, they can be greatly disabling. It is estimated that 60 to 70 percent of all prison inmates have some form of personality disorder. Freud did not think that psychoanalysis could effectively treat people with narcissistic personality disorders. However, modern psychoanalysts, beginning with Hyman Spotnitz in the 1940s, have found effective ways to transfer the narcissistic tendencies and treat patients successfully.

Figure 14.5 Defense Mechanisms

Projection refers to a person seeing attributes of his own personality in others. Repression is shown by a woman who is not only restraining a monstrous impulse but also trying to conceal from herself that she is doing so. The displacement of a widow's love for her lost husband onto her pets is another defense mechanism. ***In what ways are defense mechanisms helpful?***

Projection: a person believes that impulses really coming from within himself are coming from other people. (He is jealous of his girlfriend but claims that she's the one who is jealous.)

Displacement: a widow transfers her love for her late husband to her cats.

Repression: a person pushes painful memories or anxiety out of her consciousness; a person denies or forgets what is disturbing her.

want to admit to himself that he is threatened by her independence may claim, "I'm not jealous—she's the one who's always asking where I've been, who that girl was I was talking to. She's the one who's jealous." This mechanism is called *projection* because inner feelings are thrown, or projected, outside the self and assigned to others. If a person thinks, for example, that others dislike him when in reality he dislikes himself, he is said to be projecting. This is a common mechanism, which you may have used yourself from time to time.

Reaction Formation

Reaction formation involves replacing an unacceptable feeling or urge with an opposite one. For example, a divorced father may resent having his child for the weekend. Unconsciously, he believes it is terribly wrong for a father to react that way, so he showers the child with expressions of love, toys, and exciting trips. A woman who finds her powerful ambitions unacceptable may play the role of a weak, helpless, passive female who

PSYCHOLOGY LAB EXPERIMENT

Causes of Sibling Rivalry Have students work in small groups to design and conduct a survey about causes and solutions for sibling rivalry. Tell students that their participants should be eight to ten years old. Have students design a short survey to discover the frequency and length of disagreements among siblings, the reasons for the disagreements, and the ways disagreements are resolved. Each group will administer the survey to at least 10 children. Ask the groups to analyze the results and present their findings using graphs. The groups should then compare and compile final graphs. As a class, discuss the results in terms of Freud's personality theory and ideas on conflict resolution. **L2**

wants nothing more than to please the men in her life—unconsciously covering up her true feelings. Have you ever put on a front and acted strong and confident when you were really scared?

Regression

Regression means going back to an earlier and less mature pattern of behavior. When a person is under severe pressure, he may start acting in ways that helped him in the past. For example, he may throw a temper tantrum, make faces, cry loudly, or revert to eating and sleeping all the time the way he did as a small child. If you have ever been tempted to stick out your lower lip and pout when you know that you should really accept that you cannot have your own way, you have experienced regression.

Displacement

Displacement occurs when you cannot take out your anger on the source of your frustrations, so you displace it or take it out on a less powerful person. For example, if you wanted to hit your father but were afraid to, you might hit your little brother instead. Your poor brother gets slapped around partly because he reminds you of your father and partly because he is not as likely to hit back.

Sublimation

Sublimation refers to redirecting a forbidden desire into a socially acceptable desire. For example, you may be so frustrated by your friend's arrogant attitude that you work extra hard at soccer practice, pushing yourself to your physical limits. You have channeled your aggressive feelings into physical activities.

EVALUATING FREUD'S CONTRIBUTION

The recognition of the tremendous forces that exist in human personality and the difficulty of controlling and handling them were Freud's great contributions to understanding human life. After Freud, it became easier to understand why human life contains so much conflict. It is a matter, Freud thought, of a savage individual coming to terms with the rules of society. The id is the savage part, and the superego is the representative of society. In a healthy person, the ego (the "I") is strong enough to handle the struggle (Hall, 1954).

Freud was also the first psychologist to claim that infancy and childhood are critical times for forming a person's basic character structure. In his theory of psychosexual development, Freud reasoned that a child goes through five stages of development—oral, anal, phallic, latency, and genital. Conflicts arise in each of

More About...

Birth Order

Are you either the oldest child in the family or the youngest? Does this affect your personality? Frank Sulloway (1996) studied birth-order effects on personalities, coming up with the following characteristics:

- Firstborns are interested in preserving the status quo; later-borns are more open to new experiences and ideas.
- Firstborns are usually more responsible, achievement-oriented, and organized than those born later.
- Later-borns are usually more agreeable than firstborns.
- Firstborns are more jealous and fearful than later-borns.
- Firstborns have more assertive and dominant personalities but may not be as sociable as later-borns.

It is important to note that Sulloway's research focused on middle- to upper-class people in Western cultures and therefore may not apply to other cultures. Sulloway's research also is generalized, meaning it may not apply to every individual or every family.

L1 Developing Vocabulary

As you are discussing defense mechanisms, have students give working definitions for the following terms–*id, ego,* and *superego*. Have the students apply these terms to each of Freud's defense mechanisms. Ask students to explain how the interactions and conflicts among the id, ego, and superego generate each type of defense mechanism.

Ask: How do defense mechanisms help people? *(They relieve psychological confusion and stress, allowing people to cope with life).* **What are some negative aspects of defense mechanisms?** *(They are distortions of reality; the underlying problem may remain unresolved)* ELL

CURRICULUM CONNECTION

The Arts The modern word *personality* comes from the Latin term *personare*. The expression meant literally to "speak through" and referred to masks that ancient actors held in front of their faces during plays. By the time of the Renaissance, the word had evolved into *personality* and referred to the person behind the mask—the actor.

INTERDISCIPLINARY CONNECTIONS ACTIVITY

The Media Review the Cookie Monster's id behavior with the class. Then assign students to view several episodes of *Sesame Street* or one of the *Sesame Street* movies. **Ask: What examples of the *pleasure principle, reality principle,* and *moral principle* can you identify in the puppets' personalities?** *(Sometimes the Cookie Monster's superego kicks in; for example, with the words "Me sorry.")* Ask volunteers to write and perform a puppet show giving their puppets unique personalities. If students think puppet shows are silly, remind them that child psychologists often use puppets to help children express their feelings. L2

Figure 14.6

Caption Answer It is the part of the mind that contains inherited instincts, urges, and memories common to all people.

Looking @ the Issues

Basic Anxiety and Hostility Karen Horney wrote the following in *The Neurotic Personality in Our Time* (1937): "The typical conflict leading to anxiety in a child is that between dependency on the parents . . . and hostile impulses against the parents. Hostility may be aroused in a child in many ways: by the parents' lack of respect for him; by unreasonable demands and prohibitions, by injustice; by unreliability; by suppression of criticism; by the parents dominating him and ascribing these tendencies to love. . . . If a child, in addition to being dependent on his parents, is grossly or subtly intimidated by them and hence feels that any expression of hostile impulses against them endangers his security, then the existence of such hostile impulses is bound to create anxiety. . . . The resulting picture may look exactly like what Freud describes as the Oedipus complex: passionate clinging to one parent and jealousy toward the other or toward anyone interfering with the claim of exclusive possession. . . . *But the dynamic structure of these attachments is entirely different from what Freud conceives as the Oedipus complex. They are an early manifestation of neurotic* [anxiety-based] *conflicts rather than a primarily sexual phenomenon.*" **Ask:** **According to Horney, how is Freud wrong?** *(Whereas Freud considers conflict in childhood as arising from purely sexual motives, Horney sees the conflict as based on the child's anxiety about being dependent on the parents.)*

the stages. Freud claimed that a child's personality largely developed in the first five years, during which the child went through the first three stages of development. That child's personality became the result of how the child dealt with the conflicts that arose in each stage of development. Freud believed that personality was well formed by the time the child entered school and that subsequent growth consisted of elaborating this basic structure. Freud was the first person to demonstrate how the personality develops in a person. (Review Chapter 3 for a more detailed discussion of Freud's stages of development.)

Freud was also the first person to propose a unified theory to understand and explain human behavior. No other theory has been more complete, complex, or controversial. Some psychologists treat Freud's writings as a sacred text. At the other extreme, many have accused Freud of being unscientific by proposing a theory too complex to be tested. Freud's theories continue to be debated. Although not widely practiced now, psychoanalysis was the predecessor of all later personality theories, which were either extensions of Freud's work or reactions against it.

IN FREUD'S FOOTSTEPS

Freud's revolutionary ideas attracted many followers who ultimately disagreed with him, and a number of these psychoanalysts developed important theories of their own.

Carl Jung

collective unconscious: the part of the mind that contains inherited instincts, urges, and memories common to all people

archetype: an inherited idea, based on the experiences of one's ancestors, which shapes one's perception of the world

At one time, Carl Jung (1875–1961) was Freud's closest associate. When Freud and Jung started to argue about psychoanalytic theory, though, their personal relationship became strained. They stopped speaking to each other entirely a mere seven years after they met.

Jung disagreed with Freud on two major points. First, he took a more positive view of human nature, believing that people try to develop their potential as well as handle their instinctual urges. Second, he distinguished between the personal unconscious, which was similar to Freud's idea of the unconscious, and the **collective unconscious,** which is a storehouse of instincts, urges, and memories of the entire human species throughout history. He called these inherited, universal ideas **archetypes.** The same archetypes are present in every person. They reflect the common experiences of humanity regarding mothers, fathers, nature, war, and so on (see Figure 14.7).

Figure 14.6 Carl Jung

Carl G. Jung was one of the most mystical and metaphysical of the pioneer theorists. ***What is the collective unconscious?***

Jung went on to identify the archetypes by studying dreams and visions, paintings, poetry, folk stories, myths, and religions. He found that the same themes—the archetypes—appear again and again. He found that many cultures share certain myths, dreams, religious beliefs, and symbols separated by time. For example, the story of Jack and the Beanstalk is essentially the same as the story of

EXTENDING THE CONTENT

Criticism of Psychoanalysis Tell students that the practice of psychoanalysis, a type of therapy based on Freud's ideas, is on the decline in the United States. It has faced at least three criticisms. First, some claim that psychoanalysis does not help people, the patients being no better off after psychoanalysis than before. Many psychologists and psychiatrists disagree with this criticism. The second criticism is that interpretations by psychoanalysts cannot be disproved. In purely scientific terms, this criticism is generally true. The third is an economic criticism. Because psychoanalysis takes so much time, it is very costly. This means it is a treatment method unavailable to most people.

David and Goliath. Both tell how a small, weak, good person triumphs over a big, strong, bad person. Jung believed such stories are common and easy to understand because the situations they describe have occurred over and over again in human history and have been stored as archetypes in the unconscious of every human being (Jung, 1963). Jung argued that these archetypes influence our thoughts and feelings and help us build the foundation of our personalities. For example, one archetype is our sense of self. Our sense of self gives us direction and provides a sense of completeness. We use the concepts in our personal unconscious and collective unconscious to develop our personalities. We fit our personalities to these concepts. In the process of fitting our personalities to these beliefs, we may hide our real feelings and our real personalities, though.

Figure 14.7 Archetypes

According to Jung's theory, Superman can be considered an archetype of a hero and of goodness. ***What are archetypes?***

Alfred Adler

Like Jung, Alfred Adler (1870–1937) was an associate of Freud who left his teacher in the early part of the twentieth century to develop his own approach to personality theory. Adler believed that the driving force in people's lives is a desire to overcome their feelings of inferiority. Classic examples are Demosthenes, who overcame a speech impediment by practicing speaking with pebbles in his mouth and became the greatest orator of ancient Greece; Napoleon, a short man who conquered Europe in the early 1800s; and Glenn Cunningham, an Olympic runner who, as a child, lost his toes in a fire and had to plead with doctors who wanted to amputate his legs because they thought he would never be able to use them again.

Everyone struggles with inferiority, said Adler. He describes a person who continually tries to compensate for his weakness and avoid feelings of inadequacy as having an **inferiority complex.** Children first feel inferior because they are so little and so dependent on adults. Gradually they learn to do the things that older people can do. The satisfaction that comes from such simple acts as walking or learning to use a spoon sets up a pattern of overcoming inadequacies, a pattern that persists throughout life. Adler called these patterns *lifestyles.*

inferiority complex: a pattern of avoiding feelings of inadequacy rather than trying to overcome their source

Adler believed that the way parents treat their children influences the styles of life they choose. Overpampering, in which the parents attempt to satisfy the child's every whim, tends to produce a self-centered person who has little regard for others and who expects everyone else to do what he or she wants. On the other hand, the child who is neglected by his or her parents may seek revenge by becoming an angry, hostile person. Both the pampered and the neglected child tend to grow into adults who lack confidence in their ability to meet the demands of life. Ideally, said Adler, a child should learn self-reliance and courage from the father and generosity and a feeling for others from the mother (Adler, 1959). Adler believed that all humans are motivated by social urges and that each person is a social being with a unique personality.

Figure 14.7

Caption Answer Jung's term for inherited, universal ideas that shape our perceptions

TEACHER Tip

Freud considered the concept of repression as the cornerstone of his whole system. Explain to students that to unlock repression, a psychoanalyst "shrinks" a patient back to childhood. The nickname "shrink," for psychiatrists and psychologists, is derived from this process. Ask what stereotyped views of therapists are created by the nickname.

3 ASSESS

Assign Section 2 Assessment as homework or as an in-class activity.

Section Quiz 14–2

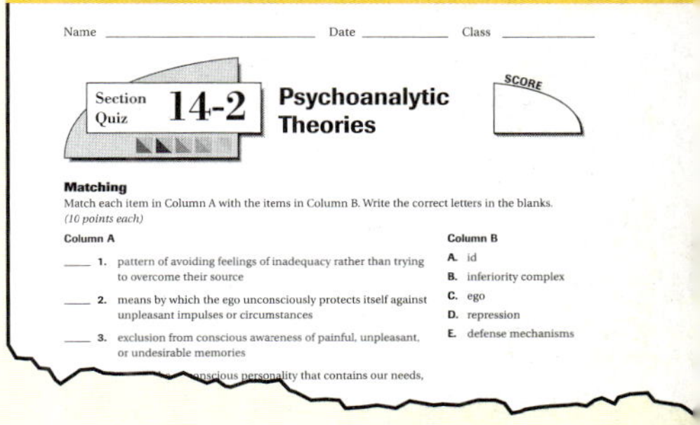
Name ______ Date ______ Class ______

Section Quiz 14-2 Psychoanalytic Theories

SCORE

Matching

Match each item in Column A with the items in Column B. Write the correct letters in the blanks. *(10 points each)*

Column A	Column B
___ 1. pattern of avoiding feelings of inadequacy rather than trying to overcome their source	A. id
___ 2. means by which the ego unconsciously protects itself against unpleasant impulses or circumstances	B. inferiority complex
___ 3. exclusion from conscious awareness of painful, unpleasant, or undesirable memories	C. ego
	D. repression
	E. defense mechanisms

EXTENDING THE CONTENT

Psychologists at Work The human personality has always intrigued philosophers and laypersons. Pseudosciences such as astrology, physiognomy, and Galen's humoral theory of temperament are all early examples of efforts to explain human behavior. In the post-Freudian era, psychologists have applied the tools of science to generate new, more complicated theories of personality. Today, personality psychologists present survey data to support their views. They also formulate and/or use tests as methods of measurement (see Chapter 13). Training includes advanced work in psychological theory, as well as courses in statistics and evaluative testing.

Figure 14.8

Caption Answer Adler believed the primary driving force in people's lives is the need to overcome feelings of inferiority. Freud believed that a person's unconscious is the primary driving force.

Reteach

List characters from popular television shows on the board. Have students identify whether the character operates primarily on Freud's pleasure, reality, or moral principles.

Enrich

Challenge students to explore the stories told to children of various cultures. **Ask:** **What similar themes or archetypes run through them?**

4 CLOSE

Divide students into pairs. Give them a stressful situation in which people might use a defense mechanism. Have each student select one of the defense mechanisms. Ask the pairs to role-play what might occur when two people are using defense mechanisms to resolve a problem or relieve stress.

Figure 14.8 Finding Individual Fulfillment

According to Adler, each person creates a plan—a lifestyle—for achieving superiority. The lifestyle of this Buddhist monk differs from that of Bill Gates. Each may have a different path to fulfillment. ***How does Adler's theory differ from Freud's?***

Other Theorists

Although Jung and Adler were the first figures to break with Freud, many others have followed. Erich Fromm's (1900–1980) theory centered around the need to belong and the loneliness that freedom can bring. Karen Horney (1885–1952) stressed the importance of basic anxiety, which a child feels because she is helpless, and basic hostility, a resentment of one's parents that generally accompanies this anxiety. She also disagreed with Freud on several basic beliefs. Horney believed that if a child is raised in an atmosphere of love and security, that child could avoid Freud's psychosexual parent-child conflict.

Erik Erikson (1902–1994) accepted Freud's basic theory, but he outlined eight psychosocial stages (described in Chapter 3) that every person goes through from birth to old age and that describe the importance of interacting with other people. These and other neo-Freudians have helped keep psychoanalytic theory alive and debated (Friman et al., 1993).

SECTION 2 Assessment

1. **Review the Vocabulary** Explain how the id, ego, and superego work together in a person.
2. **Visualize the Main Idea** Using a diagram similar to the one below, describe the basic views of personality of the following psychoanalysts: Carl Jung, Alfred Adler, and Sigmund Freud.

Psychoanalyst	Views of Personality

3. **Recall Information** What is the difference between personal unconscious and collective unconscious? How does the unconscious affect our personalities?
4. **Think Critically** What part of a personality—id, ego, or superego—do you think is the most important? Explain your answer.
5. **Application Activity** Create a cartoon that illustrates the use of one of the defense mechanisms discussed in this section.

SECTION 2 Assessment Answers

1. The id seeks to meet human instinctual and biological urges; the superego is the source of conscience and seeks to inhibit socially undesirable impulses; the ego is reality based and attempts to balance the demands of the id within the constraints imposed by the superego.
2. Students' diagrams should demonstrate an understanding of the views of Jung, Adler, and Freud.
3. The personal unconscious is the unique part of everyone that contains information of which we are unaware but which influences our conscious actions. The collective unconscious was identified by Jung as the part of the mind that contains inherited instincts, urges, and memories. Freud believed that unconscious motives and the feelings people experience as children have a great impact on personality.
4. Students' answers will vary. Encourage students to explore how the various parts influence one another.
5. Students' answers will vary. Encourage students to trace their favorite cartoon characters and assign different words to them.

SECTION 3 Learning Theories

Reader's Guide

Main Idea
Behaviorists are interested in how aspects of personality are learned.

Vocabulary
- behaviorism
- contingencies of reinforcement

Objectives
- Describe Skinner's concept of personality.
- Explain Bandura's social cognitive theory of personality.

EXPLORING PSYCHOLOGY

Responding to Oppression

There is such a thing as the freedom of exhaustion. Some people are so worn down by the yoke of oppression that they give up. A few years ago in the slum areas of Atlanta, a Negro guitarist used to sing almost daily: "Been down so long that down don't bother me." This is the type of negative freedom and resignation that often engulfs the life of the oppressed.

But this is not the way out. To accept passively an unjust system is to cooperate with that system; thereby the oppressed become as evil as the oppressor. . . .

—from *Stride Toward Freedom: The Montgomery Story* by Martin Luther King, Jr., 1963

In the excerpt above, Martin Luther King, Jr., described the behavior of some African Americans in the 1950s. King, a leader in the struggle for civil rights, observed this behavior and looked to the environment to see what was causing it. King recognized that an oppressive system maintained these behaviors. Like King, behaviorists look to the environment to see what is reinforcing behavior.

American psychology has long been dominated by the study of human and animal learning. John Watson believed that the proper subject matter of psychology ought to be observable behavior. He believed that if it could not be seen, then it could not be studied. His beliefs led to the study of behavior and what is called **behaviorism.** Behaviorists believe that as individuals differ in their learning experiences, they acquire different behaviors and, hence, different personalities.

behaviorism: belief that the proper subject matter of psychology is objectively observable behavior—and nothing else

SECTION RESOURCES

Reproducible Masters
- Guided Reading Activity 14–3
- Vocabulary Activity 14–3
- Section Quiz 14–3

Transparencies
- Daily Focus Transparency 14–3

Multimedia
- *ExamView® Assessment Suite* CD-ROM
- Presentation Plus! Software

1 FOCUS

Section Objectives
1. Describe Skinner's concept of personality.
2. Explain Bandura's social cognitive theory of personality.

BELLRINGER
Motivational Activity

Project Daily Focus Transparency 14–3 and have students answer the questions.

Available as blackline master

Daily Focus Transparency 14–3

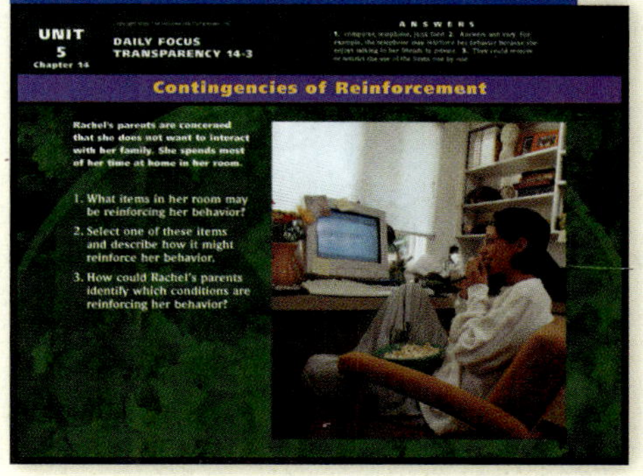

Reader's Guide

Use the Reader's Guide to introduce concepts and vocabulary.

Exploring Psychology
Ask students to read the **Exploring Psychology** feature and then discuss: **How are our personalities affected by what our environment teaches us?**

Vocabulary Precheck
Have students write a description of what they think each term might mean. Then have them read the Glossary definition and compare their descriptions.

2 TEACH

L1 Debate Organize students into two panels to debate the following question: **Is human behavior determined from within or without?** One panel, led by Sigmund Freud, will argue the "within" position. The other panel, led by B.F. Skinner, will argue the "without" position. Then have students decide what, if any, middle ground can be found between the two theories. **BLOCK SCHEDULING**

Figure 14.9

Caption Answer Behavior is motivated by reinforcement.

Guided Reading Activity 14–3

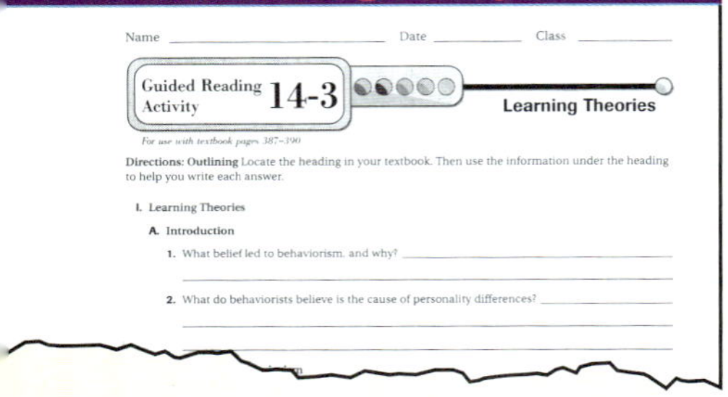
Name ______ Date ______ Class ______

Guided Reading Activity 14-3

Learning Theories

For use with textbook pages 387–390

Directions: Outlining Locate the heading in your textbook. Then use the information under the heading to help you write each answer.

I. Learning Theories

A. Introduction

1. What belief led to behaviorism, and why? ______

2. What do behaviorists believe is the cause of personality differences? ______

Reading Check Answer by examining the contingencies of reinforcement

PSYCHOLOGY JOURNAL

Tell students to write about a time when their behavior was influenced by the behavior of a friend or a family member. ■

Figure 14.9 B.F. Skinner's Box

Skinner devised a box to test the observable behavior of rats. ***According to Skinner, what motivates behavior?***

"IF WE DIDN'T DO SO WELL IN THE EASY BOX, THEY WOULDN'T HAVE GIVEN US THIS COMPLICATED BOX."

B.F. SKINNER: BEHAVIORISM

Although his behaviorism was not proposed as a theory of personality, B.F. Skinner had a major impact on personality theory. Skinner saw no need for a general concept of personality structure. He focused instead on precisely what causes a person to act in a specific way. It is a very pragmatic approach, one that is less concerned with understanding behavior than with predicting it and controlling it. He was interested in how aspects of one's personality are learned. (See Chapter 9 for more discussion of behaviorism.)

Consider the case of Ruben, a college sophomore who has been rather depressed lately. Sigmund Freud would likely seek the roots of Ruben's unhappiness in events in his childhood. Skinner's approach is more direct. First, Skinner would reject the vague label *depressed.* Instead, he would ask exactly how Ruben behaves. The answer may be that Ruben spends most of the day in his room, cuts all his classes, rarely smiles or laughs, and makes little effort to talk to anyone.

contingencies of reinforcement: the occurrence of rewards or punishments following particular behaviors

Skinner would try to uncover the **contingencies of reinforcement.** What conditions are reinforcing these behaviors? What rewards does Ruben receive for never leaving his room? One hypothesis is that Ruben's girlfriend Brandi has unintentionally reinforced this behavior by spending a lot of time with him, trying to cheer him up. Perhaps she did not pay enough attention to Ruben before he was depressed. Note that Skinner's approach immediately suggests a hypothesis that can be proved true or false. If paying attention to Ruben encourages his depression, then ignoring him should decrease the likelihood of this behavior. Brandi, therefore, might try ignoring Ruben for a few days. If he then starts leaving his room, which she should reinforce, she has discovered the contingencies of reinforcement that govern Ruben's behavior. If he does not leave his room, she will know that the hypothesis is wrong, and she can try something else. Perhaps Ruben is glued to the television in his room all day and has become a game show addict. Take away the television, and you will find out whether that is the reinforcer.

Reading Check How do behaviorists study personality?

At first, behaviorism may seem to imply that Ruben is somehow faking his depression so that he can watch game shows or see more of his girlfriend. Skinner does not make this assumption. Ruben may be entirely unaware of the rewards that are shaping his behavior. In any case, Ruben's feelings are beside the point. What matters is not what is going on inside Ruben's head but how he is behaving. The point is to specify his behavior and then find out what causes (reinforces) it.

COOPERATIVE LEARNING ACTIVITY

Role-Play About Social Learning Organize students into small groups. Explain to the groups that they will create a role-play situation in which one or more participants uses various methods of reinforcement to mold the behavior of another person. For example, a teacher may use reinforcement to alter classroom behavior. Have students present their plays. Then, use each play to discuss Skinner's contingencies of reinforcement and Bandura's theory of social learning. **BLOCK SCHEDULING**

Skinner's approach has become very popular among psychologists, partly because it is so action-oriented. Followers of Skinner's work have applied the techniques to a wide range of behaviors, from teaching pigeons to play table tennis to teaching severely mentally challenged people to dress themselves and take part in simple activities once believed beyond their abilities. Therapies have also been devised to help people with specific behavioral problems, such as phobias and obsessive-compulsive behavior.

Other human behavior, too, can be changed using rewards and punishments. The success of behaviorists with most people has been limited, however, partly because our reinforcers are so complex. To behaviorists, behavior in general is a combination of specific behaviors that have been reinforced, or learned. To change behavior, you change the reinforcer.

Psychology and You: What Is Your Locus of Control?

Julian Rotter wrote the first book describing the social cognitive approach to personality. Rotter argued that a person's behavior depends not only on objective, situational factors but also on that person's subjective beliefs. Our *locus of control* refers to our beliefs about how much control we have over certain situations. If you believe that you do have control over situations, you have an *internal* locus of control. If you think that your fate is determined by forces beyond your control, you have an *external* locus of control. People with an internal locus of control are, on average, less anxious and more content with life than those with an external locus of control.

To find a person's locus of control, a psychologist might ask the person if he believes the following:

1. In the long run, people get what they deserve.
2. Most tests are fair if a student is prepared.
3. Many times, tests are so unfair that studying is wasted energy.
4. It is better to make decisions and take action than to trust fate.

ALBERT BANDURA: SOCIAL COGNITIVE THEORY

Skinner emphasized reinforcement in his description of how personalities develop. Albert Bandura and his colleague Richard Walters (1963), however, argued that personality is acquired not only by direct reinforcement of behavior but also by observational learning, or imitation. As you remember from Chapter 9, in *observational learning* an individual acquires a new behavior by watching the actions of other people. For example, to teach a child how to hit a baseball with a bat, you could hand the child the bat and ball and reinforce him every time he used the bat and ball correctly. However, you would probably demonstrate the correct way to hold the bat and swing at the ball instead because this way the child would acquire the behavior more quickly. Bandura and Walters believed that much of a young child's individual behavior and personality is acquired by exposure to specific everyday models.

In Bandura's view, people direct their own behavior by their choice of models. In part, when your parents object to the company you keep, they are trying to change the models you use. The most effective models are those who are the most similar to and most admired by the observer. Thus, you are more likely to learn new behaviors from friends of your choosing than from friends your parents choose for you.

Psychology and You

Use the following question to direct a class discussion after students have read the **Psychology and You** feature.
Ask: **Which of the four questions identifies people with an internal locus of control?** *(2, 4)* **With an external locus of control?** *(1, 3)*

Vocabulary Activity 14–3

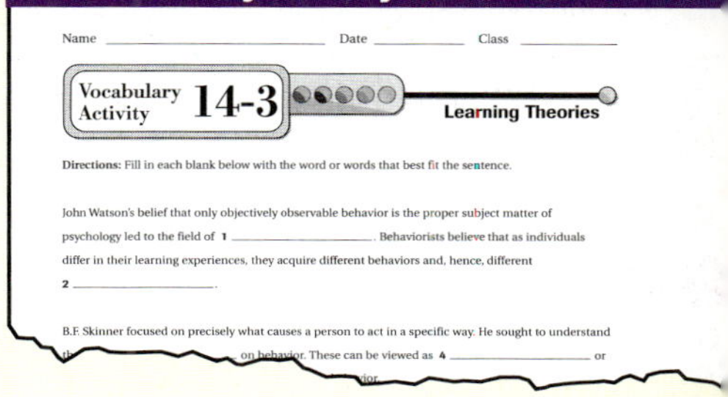
Name ____________ Date ________ Class ________

Vocabulary Activity 14-3 Learning Theories

Directions: Fill in each blank below with the word or words that best fit the sentence.

John Watson's belief that only objectively observable behavior is the proper subject matter of psychology led to the field of **1** ____________. Behaviorists believe that as individuals differ in their learning experiences, they acquire different behaviors and, hence, different **2** ____________.

B.F. Skinner focused on precisely what causes a person to act in a specific way. He sought to understand th… on behavior. These can be viewed as **4** ____________ or …vior.

3 ASSESS

Assign Section 3 Assessment as homework or as an in-class activity.

Section Quiz 14–3

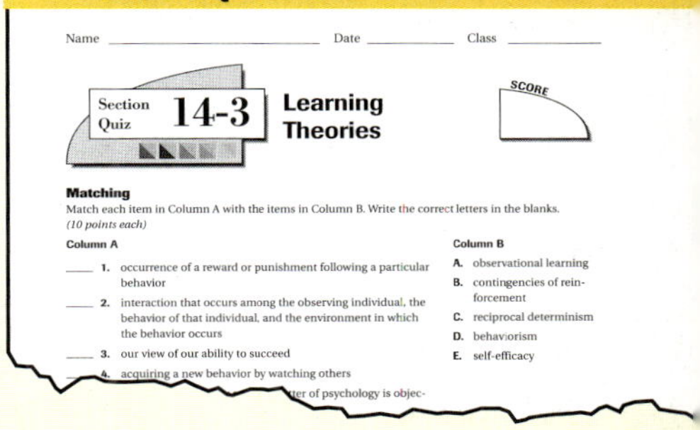
Name ____________ Date ________ Class ________

Section Quiz 14-3 Learning Theories

SCORE

Matching
Match each item in Column A with the items in Column B. Write the correct letters in the blanks. *(10 points each)*

Column A

____ **1.** occurrence of a reward or punishment following a particular behavior
____ **2.** interaction that occurs among the observing individual, the behavior of that individual, and the environment in which the behavior occurs
____ **3.** our view of our ability to succeed
____ **4.** acquiring a new behavior by watching others
…ter of psychology is objec-

Column B

A. observational learning
B. contingencies of reinforcement
C. reciprocal determinism
D. behaviorism
E. self-efficacy

MEETING SPECIAL NEEDS

Learning Style: Interpersonal Have students select one of the following topics: contingencies of reinforcement, observational learning, or reciprocal determinism. For the chosen topic, students should draw a cartoon that illustrates the appropriate learning theory. Ask students to distribute their cartoons to at least five classmates to read and determine which learning theory is being illustrated. **L2** **BLOCK SCHEDULING**

Refer to ***Inclusion for the High School Social Studies Classroom Strategies and Activities*** in the TCR for strategies for students with different learning styles.

Figure 14.10

Visual Instruction Given the importance of observation to the social learning theory, ask students to prioritize the influence of each of the three forces.

Caption Answer our beliefs, expectations, values, intentions, social roles, and emotional and biological makeup

Reteach

Reexamine the **Exploring Psychology** feature. Ask students to explain what Skinner and Bandura contributed to our understanding of why oppressed people may become resigned to their situations.

Enrich

Ask students to write an essay applying the social learning theory to the impact of constant reporting of violence by the media. Students should include suggested media guidelines for reporting such incidents.

4 CLOSE

Have students prepare a "recap" of the learning theories in a news highlight style.

Figure 14.10 Bandura's Social Cognitive Theory

According to Bandura's theory, a person's personality is shaped by an interaction among three forces—cognitive factors, behaviors, and environmental factors. ***What are the cognitive factors?***

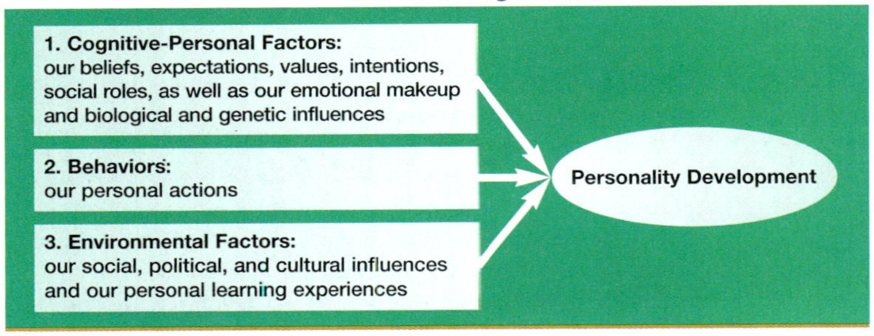

Bandura has made significant contributions to the development of behavioral theories of personality. His social cognitive theory (1986) recognizes the interaction called *reciprocal determinism* that occurs among the observing individual, the behavior of that individual, and the environment in which the behavior occurs (see Figure 14.10). One important concept that governs our behavior is our view of our ability to succeed, which Bandura called *self-efficacy*. You decide whether to go on a date by assessing the environment—the weather, your parents' current state of mind, your potential date's recent behaviors—the effects of your own past behavior, and your long-term past successes and failures. This leads to the development of an expectancy of success. As the behavior unfolds, you also develop *outcome expectations* (Bandura, 1997). As long as they remain positive, you will keep trying.

Whereas psychoanalytic theories emphasize the influence of childhood experiences, irrational thoughts, and unconscious forces, the advantage of learning theories of personality is that they focus on concrete actions that can be tested and measured. However, critics argue that the learning theories do not explain personality, nor do they give enough attention to the influence of genetic factors, emotions, and childhood experiences on personality.

SECTION 3 Assessment

1. **Review the Vocabulary** According to behaviorism, what is the proper subject matter of psychology? How does this relate to the study of personality?
2. **Visualize the Main Idea** Using a diagram similar to the one below, compare and contrast the following theories of behavior: behaviorism and social cognition.

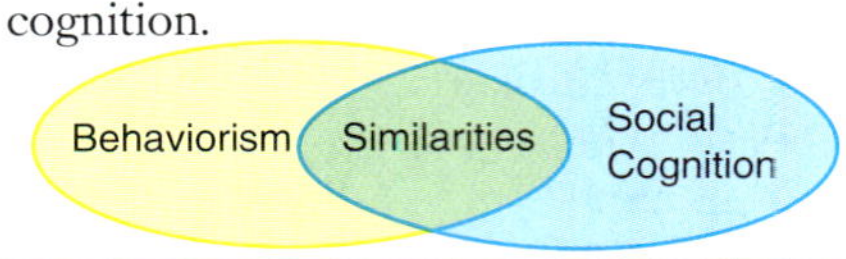

3. **Recall Information** Why do you think people have different personalities? How would behaviorists explain the differences?
4. **Think Critically** How would behaviorists and social learning theorists explain a person's persistence in becoming an accomplished tennis player?
5. **Application Activity** Choose a behavior of a younger sibling or of a friend that you would like to see change. Suggest a way to do so, using reinforcers to change the particular behavior.

SECTION 3 Assessment Answers

1. Psychology should study only observable behavior. Behaviorism demonstrates the influence of the environment on personalities.
2. Diagrams should reflect students' understanding of the behaviorist and social cognitive theories of behavior.
3. According to the learning theories, we have different personalities because we have different experiences in life. Different behaviors have been reinforced in different ways, and we have used different models for modeling our behavior. Behaviorists would suggest that different people experienced different reinforcements.
4. Behaviorists would assume that the drive to succeed in tennis has been reinforced in a variety of tangible and intangible ways. The social cognitive theorists would credit a mix of cognitive factors such as expectations and intentions and environmental factors such as the influence of people the tennis player respects.
5. Students' answers will vary. Students may want to review the material in Chapter 9.

SECTION 4

Humanistic and Cognitive Theories

Reader's Guide

Main Idea

Humanistic and cognitive theories of personality stress the positive aspects of human nature.

Vocabulary

- humanistic psychology
- self-actualization
- self
- positive regard
- conditions of worth
- unconditional positive regard
- fully functioning

Objectives

- Explain Maslow's idea of self-actualization.
- Describe Carl Rogers's view of human behavior.

EXPLORING PSYCHOLOGY

Changing a Nation

Jackie Robinson had to be bigger than life. He had to be bigger than the Brooklyn teammates who got up a petition to keep him off the ball club, bigger than the pitchers who threw at him or the base runners who dug their spikes into his shin, bigger than the bench jockeys who hollered for him to carry their bags and shine their shoes, bigger than the so-called fans who mocked him with mops on their heads and wrote him death threats. . . . Somehow, though, Jackie had the strength to suppress his instincts, to sacrifice his pride for his people's. It was an incredible act of selflessness that brought the races closer together than ever before and shaped the dreams of an entire generation.

—from "Jackie Robinson" by Henry Aaron in *TIME* magazine, June 14, 1999

In 1947 life in America was one of segregation. There were separate schools for African Americans and whites, separate restaurants, separate hotels, separate drinking fountains, and even separate baseball leagues—that is, until Jackie Robinson began playing for the Brooklyn Dodgers. Robinson played the game passionately and, despite colossal obstacles, changed the face of baseball. His experience shows the impact that believing in one's own abilities can have on personal success. The idea that individuals' perceptions of themselves can become their reality is part of the humanistic and cognitive theories of personality.

SECTION RESOURCES

Reproducible Masters

- Guided Reading Activity 14–4
- Vocabulary Activity 14–4
- Section Quiz 14–4

Transparencies

- Daily Focus Transparency 14–4

Multimedia

- *ExamView® Assessment Suite* CD-ROM
- Presentation Plus! Software

1 FOCUS

Section Objectives

1. Explain Maslow's idea of self-actualization.
2. Describe Carl Rogers's view of human behavior.

BELLRINGER
Motivational Activity

Project Daily Focus Transparency 14–4 and have students answer the questions.

Available as blackline master

Daily Focus Transparency 14–4

Reader's Guide

Use the Reader's Guide to introduce concepts and vocabulary.

Exploring Psychology

Ask students to read the **Exploring Psychology** feature. Then ask: **What drove Jackie Robinson to take such a big risk? Did Robinson fulfill his potential? Why or why not?**

Vocabulary Precheck

Have students read the Glossary definitions of the terms and create a matching game with terms on one card and definitions on another card, matching the terms and their definitions.

2 TEACH

L1 Making Posters Write the following statement on the board: *To thine own self be true.* **Ask: How would humanistic psychologists likely view this statement?** *(as a reflection of the human urge for self-actualization)* Working individually, assign students to draw posters illustrating this concept as it applies to them. Display the posters around the room. ELL **BLOCK SCHEDULING**

Looking @ the Issues

Humanism Tell students that Maslow began his career as a behavioral psychologist. He became a humanistic psychologist after the birth of his first child. Of the experience, he wrote: "I was stunned by the mystery and by the sense of not really being in control. I felt small and weak and feeble before all this. I'd say anyone who had a baby couldn't be a behaviorist." Ask students to discuss why the birth of his child would turn him away from behaviorism and toward humanism.

Figure 14.11

Caption Answer Despite all the personal risks and insults he endured, Robinson broke the color barrier in baseball, became a symbol for athletes of color, and excelled at his chosen endeavor, thereby realizing his own unique potential.

HUMANISTIC PSYCHOLOGY

humanistic psychology: a school of psychology that emphasizes personal growth and the achievement of maximum potential by each unique individual

self-actualization: the humanist term for realizing one's unique potential

Humanistic psychology may be viewed as a rebellion against the rather negative, pessimistic view of human nature that dominated personality theory in the early 1900s. Psychoanalysts emphasized the struggle to control primitive, instinctual urges on the one hand and to come to terms with the demands of the superego, or conscience, on the other. The behaviorists, too, saw human behavior in mechanistic terms: our actions are shaped by rewards and punishments. Humanistic psychologists object to both approaches on the grounds that they demean human beings—Freud by emphasizing irrational and destructive instincts, Skinner by emphasizing only external causes of behavior. In contrast, the humanists stress our ability to create and live by personal standards and perceptions.

Humanistic psychology is founded on the belief that all human beings strive for **self-actualization**—that is, the realization of our potentialities as unique human beings. Self-actualization involves an openness to a wide range of experiences, an awareness of and respect for one's own and other people's uniqueness, accepting the responsibilities of freedom and commitment, a desire to become more and more authentic or true to oneself, and an ability to grow.

Figure 14.11 An American First

Jackie Robinson was the first African American to play in major league baseball and became a hero to millions. ***How does Jackie Robinson's life reflect the humanist ideal of self-actualization?***

ABRAHAM MASLOW: GROWTH AND SELF-ACTUALIZATION

Abraham Maslow (1908–1970) became one of the guiding spirits of the humanistic movement in psychology. He deliberately set out to create what he called "a third force in psychology" as an alternative to psychoanalysis and behaviorism. Maslow tried to base his theory of personality on studies of healthy, creative, self-actualizing people who fully utilize their talents and potential rather than on studies of disturbed individuals.

When Maslow decided to study the most productive individuals he could find—in history as well as in his social and professional circles—he broke new ground. Psychotherapists developed the theories of personality discussed earlier after years of working with people who could not cope with everyday frustrations and conflicts. In contrast, Maslow was curious about people who not only coped with everyday problems effectively but who also created exceptional lives for themselves, people like Abraham Lincoln, Albert Einstein, and Eleanor Roosevelt.

Maslow found that although these people sometimes had great emotional difficulties, they adjusted in ways that allowed them to become

COOPERATIVE LEARNING ACTIVITY

Creating a Pamphlet Discuss the meaning of the expression "tough love" with the class *(taking strong measures—including leaving a person to his or her own destructive behavior—to bring about change).* Organize students into small groups. Ask the groups to consider the following questions: **How do you think Maslow and other humanists might view "tough love"? What, if any, alternatives might they suggest? Which approach do you think works best in curbing potentially destructive behavior?** Have students create a pamphlet that their peers could use to help a friend who has a drinking problem or other potentially destructive behavioral problem.

highly productive. Maslow also found that self-actualized individuals share a number of traits (see Figure 14.12). First, they perceive reality accurately, unlike most people who, because of prejudices and wishful thinking, perceive it rather inaccurately. Self-actualized people also accept themselves, other people, and their environments more readily than most people do. Without realizing it, most of us project our hopes and fears onto the world around us. We deny our own shortcomings and try to rationalize or change things we do not like about ourselves. Self-actualizing individuals accept themselves as they are.

Figure 14.12 Characteristics of Self-Actualized People

Maslow proposed the concept of a self-actualized personality, which identifies a person with high productivity and enjoyment of life. ***Do you think any person can develop a self-actualized personality, regardless of his or her social or economic status? Explain.***

They are realistically oriented.
They accept themselves, other people, and the natural world for what they are.
They have a great deal of spontaneity.
They are problem-centered rather than self-centered.
They have an air of detachment and a need for privacy.
They are autonomous and independent.
Their appreciation of people and things is fresh rather than stereotyped.
Most of them have had profound mystical or spiritual experiences, although not necessarily religious in character.
They identify with humanity.
Their intimate relationships with a few specially loved people tend to be profound and deeply emotional rather than superficial.
Their values and attitudes are democratic.
They do not confuse means with ends.
Their sense of humor is philosophical rather than hostile.
They have a great fund of creativeness.
They resist conformity to the culture.
They transcend the environment rather than just coping with it.

Source: Abraham Maslow, *Motivation and Personality,* New York: Harper & Row, 1970.

CHAPTER 14
Section 4, pages 391–397

Guided Reading Activity 14-4

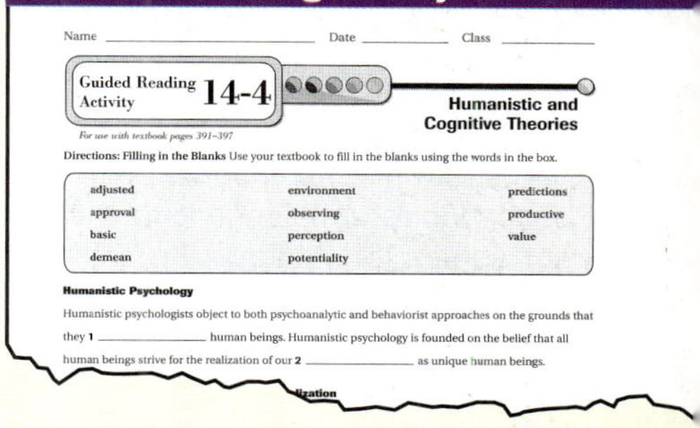
Name ______ Date ______ Class ______

Guided Reading Activity 14-4 — Humanistic and Cognitive Theories

For use with textbook pages 391–397

Directions: Filling in the Blanks Use your textbook to fill in the blanks using the words in the box.

adjusted	environment	predictions
approval	observing	productive
basic	perception	value
demean	potentiality	

Humanistic Psychology

Humanistic psychologists object to both psychoanalytic and behaviorist approaches on the grounds that they 1 ______ human beings. Humanistic psychology is founded on the belief that all human beings strive for the realization of our 2 ______ as unique human beings.

Figure 14.12

Visual Instruction To make certain students understand the terminology used in the table, ask them to provide an example that demonstrates each item. The examples may be real or fictitious.

Caption Answer Answers will vary. Famous examples of people who achieved self-actualization without necessarily having secure economic status are Mohandas Gandhi, Nelson Mandela, Mother Teresa, and Daw Aung San Suu Kyi, the Nobel Peace Prize winner from Myanmar.

PSYCHOLOGY JOURNAL

Have students consider the description of a self-actualized person. Then have them write the name of a person they know who they consider to have achieved self-actualization and explain why they believe the person to be self-actualized. ■

MEETING SPECIAL NEEDS

Learning Style: Intrapersonal Review Carl Rogers's ideas on self-image. Then have students complete the following statement: *My greatest potential as a person lies in my skill/ability/talent to* ________. Tell students to list as many examples of potential as possible. Have them ask friends and family members for suggestions as well. Based on the list and on Rogers's definition of positive self-worth, have students write a description of themselves. **L2**

BLOCK SCHEDULING

Refer to ***Inclusion for the High School Social Studies Classroom Strategies and Activities*** in the TCR for strategies for students with different learning styles.

Looking @ the Issues

Enhancing Self-Esteem Tell students that a key component of education today is enhancing the self-esteem of students. Psychologists have long believed that students with high self-esteem will achieve more. But how do you measure self-esteem? The Behavioral Academic Self-Esteem (BASE) Scale was developed by Stanley Coopersmith and Ragnar Gilberts in 1982. It seeks to measure self-esteem by categorizing behavior in five areas: student initiative, social attention, success/failure, social attraction, and self-confidence. Some of the specific assessments include a willingness to undertake new tasks, an ability to make decisions, an ability to talk in class as appropriate, and a capacity to accept correction without overreacting. **Ask: Do you think these assessments are important to self-esteem? What other assessments do you consider important in measuring self-esteem? How do you think self-esteem influences academic achievement?**

Figure 14.13

Caption Answer Possible answers include he accepts himself as he is, is secure, has a sense of humor, is spontaneous, appreciates simple things.

TEACHER Tip

Explain that the humanistic theory focuses on human potential. It stands in opposition to Freud's emphasis on unconscious factors beyond an individual's control. It is also a reaction to the mechanical nature of behaviorism.

Because they are secure in themselves, self-actualized individuals are more problem-centered than self-centered. They are able to focus on tasks in a way that people concerned about maintaining and protecting their self-image cannot. They are more likely to base decisions on ethical principles rather than on calculations of the possible costs or benefits to themselves. They have a strong sense of identity with other human beings, and they have a strong sense of humor but laugh with people, not at them.

Maslow also found that self-actualized people are exceptionally spontaneous. They do not try to be anything other than themselves, and they know themselves well enough to maintain their integrity in the face of opposition, unpopularity, and rejection. They are autonomous. They value privacy and frequently seek out solitude. This is not to say that they are detached or aloof; rather than trying to be popular, they focus on deep, loving relationships with the few people to whom they are truly close.

Finally, the people Maslow studied had a rare ability to appreciate even the simplest things. They approached their lives with a sense of discovery that made each day a new day. They rarely felt bored or uninterested. Given to moments of intense joy and satisfaction, or peak experiences, they enjoyed life itself. Maslow believed this to be both a cause and an effect of their creativity and originality (Maslow, 1970).

Maslow believed that to become self-actualized, a person must first satisfy his or her basic, primary needs—for food and shelter, physical safety, love and belonging, and self-esteem. Of course, to some extent the ability to satisfy these needs is often beyond our control. Still, no amount of wealth, talent, or beauty can totally shield someone from frustration and disappointment. All people have to adjust to maintain themselves and to grow.

Many psychologists have criticized Maslow's work. His claim that human nature is good, for example, has been called an intrusion of subjective values into what should be a neutral science. The levels of specific needs, such as physical contact comfort, discussed in Chapter 12, have not been defined (Feist, 1985). His study of self-actualizing people has been criticized because the sample was chosen on the basis of Maslow's own subjective criteria. How can one identify self-actualized people without knowing the characteristics of such people? But then, if one knows these characteristics to begin with, what sense does it make to list them as if they were the results of an empirical study?

Figure 14.13 Proclaiming Your Self-Worth

You can progress toward self-actualization after you have developed a sense of self-esteem, or self-worth. ***What traits associated with Maslow's definition of a self-actualized person does Charlie Brown display?***

CRITICAL THINKING ACTIVITY

Synthesizing Information Working individually or in pairs, have students review Lawrence Kohlberg's levels of moral development described in Chapter 4. Ask students to consider the following: **Using the theory of human development, at what stage would you place the self-actualized person described by Maslow?** *(probably Stage 6)* **What items in Figure 14.12 support your choice?** *(Answers will vary. Three examples of Stage 6 thinking include "They do not confuse means with ends." "They resist conformity to the culture." "They transcend the environment rather than just trying to cope with it.")* **L2**

CARL ROGERS: SELF THEORY

Carl Rogers (1902–1987) called the people he counseled "clients," not "patients." The word *patient* implies illness, a negative label that Rogers rejected. As a therapist, Rogers was primarily concerned with the path to self-actualization, or "full functioning," as he called it. Rogers believed that many people suffer from a conflict between what they value in themselves and what they believe other people value in them. There are two sides or parts to every person. Rogers believed that each person is constantly struggling to become more and more complete and perfect. Anything that furthers this end is good—the person wants to become everything he or she can possibly be. Different people have different potentialities, but every person wants to realize these potentialities, to make them real, whatever they are. Whatever you can do, you want to do—and do as well as possible. This optimism about human nature is the essence of humanism.

Profiles In Psychology

Carl Rogers

1902–1987

"[T]he client knows what hurts, what directions to go, what problems are crucial, what experiences have been buried."

Carl Rogers is best known for his role in the development of counseling. Rogers believed that therapy should focus on present problems—psychologists should not dwell on the past and the causes of present problems. Rogers believed that people are basically good and can solve their own problems once they realize that they can.

Rogers started out by rejecting two principles. He first began studying to become a minister, but then he started to doubt that the religious approach was the most effective way of helping people. Then, while training to become a psychoanalyst, Rogers realized that psychoanalysts focused on gaining insight into the causes of a patient's problems. Rogers rejected this approach, finally creating his client-centered approach. Rogers used his approach to help clients better understand their subjective experiences and then work to change their own subjective views of themselves, the world, and other people.

Rogers was also a teacher. He advocated one-on-one approaches to teaching. He saw the role of the teacher as one who creates an environment for engagement; that is, the teacher inspires an exploratory atmosphere in which students seek answers to problems.

Each individual also has what Rogers called a **self.** The self is essentially your image of who you are and what you value—in yourself, in other people, in life in general. The self is something you acquire gradually over the years by observing how other people react to you. You want approval or **positive regard.** You ask yourself, "How does she see me?" If the answer is "She loves me. She likes what I am and what I do," then you begin to develop positive regard for yourself.

Yet often this does not happen. In other words, she places conditions on her love: *If* you do what she wants, she likes you. Young and impressionable, you accept these verdicts and incorporate **conditions of worth**

self: one's experience or image of oneself, developed through interaction with others

positive regard: viewing oneself in a favorable light due to supportive feedback received from interaction with others

conditions of worth: the conditions a person must meet in order to regard himself or herself positively

Profiles In Psychology

Ask students to read the **Profiles In Psychology** feature and then discuss the following questions:

1. For what is Carl Rogers best-known? *(his role in the development of counseling)*
2. What two approaches did he reject? *(religion as an approach to helping people and psychoanalysis with its focus on the causes of problems)*
3. How did he describe the role of the teacher? *(as someone who creates an environment of exploration and excitement about learning)*

FYI

Have you ever heard your parents say, "You're acting just like your mother (or father)"? Some psychobiologists study how genetic, or inherited, traits shape our personalities. Although genetic factors do not set our behavior, they do interact with environmental factors to influence our behavior. For example, psychobiologists have found that identical twins (siblings that share the same genes) share many identical personality characteristics.

PSYCHOLOGY LAB EXPERIMENT

Examining Your Motivations Explain that *peak performance* is one key to Maslow's theory. Peak performance is a moment when all your personal powers, gratitude, and sense of fulfillment unite. Ask students to complete the following writing assignment using Maslow's own instructions: *I would like you to think of the most wonderful experiences of your life;...perhaps from being in love, or from listening to music or suddenly 'being hit' by a book or painting, or some great creative moment. First list these. And then try to tell me how you feel in such acute moments, how you feel differently from the way you feel at other times, how you are at the moment a different person.* **Ask: How does each experience described fit Maslow's definition of self-actualization? L2** **BLOCK SCHEDULING**

Reading Check Answer

The self is your image of who you are and what you value in yourself, in others, and in life.

Vocabulary Activity 14–4

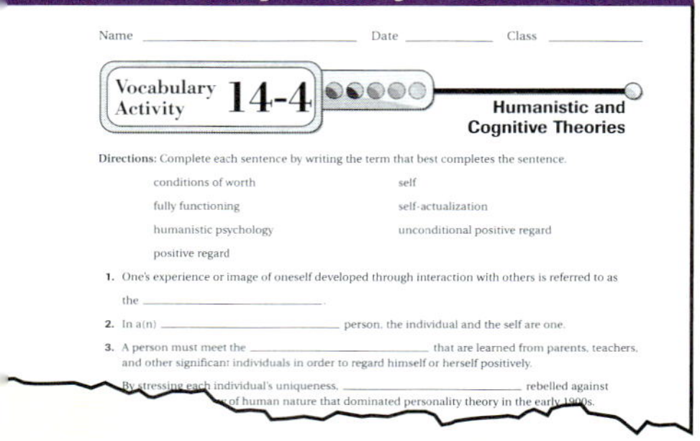
Name ______ Date ______ Class ______

Vocabulary Activity 14-4

Humanistic and Cognitive Theories

Directions: Complete each sentence by writing the term that best completes the sentence.

conditions of worth — self
fully functioning — self-actualization
humanistic psychology — unconditional positive regard
positive regard

1. One's experience or image of oneself developed through interaction with others is referred to as the ______.
2. In a(n) ______ person, the individual and the self are one.
3. A person must meet the ______ that are learned from parents, teachers, and other significant individuals in order to regard himself or herself positively.

3 ASSESS

Assign Section 4 Assessment as homework or as an in-class activity.

Section Quiz 14–4

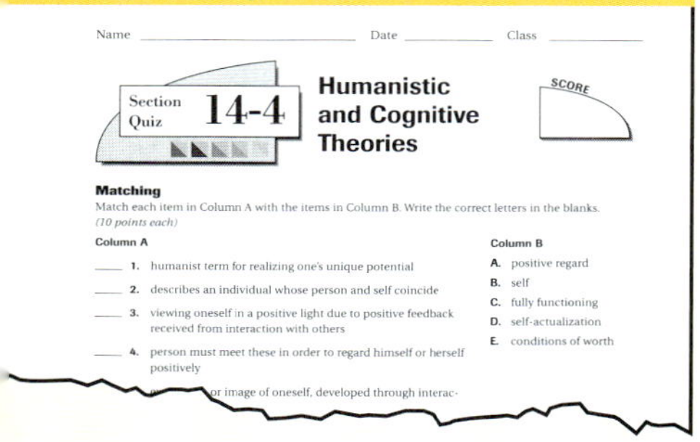
Name ______ Date ______ Class ______

Section Quiz 14-4

Humanistic and Cognitive Theories

SCORE

Matching

Match each item in Column A with the items in Column B. Write the correct letters in the blanks. *(10 points each)*

Column A

____ 1. humanist term for realizing one's unique potential
____ 2. describes an individual whose person and self coincide
____ 3. viewing oneself in a positive light due to positive feedback received from interaction with others
____ 4. person must meet these in order to regard himself or herself positively

Column B

A. positive regard
B. self
C. fully functioning
D. self-actualization
E. conditions of worth

Reteach

Write each of the major concepts of Carl Rogers's theory on the board. Have students define the terms and explain the connections between the concepts.

Reading Check

What is the "self" as Rogers defines it?

unconditional positive regard: the perception that individuals' significant others value them for what they are, which leads the individuals to grant themselves the same favorable opinion or view

fully functioning: an individual whose person and self coincide

into yourself. You begin to see yourself as good and worthy only if you act in certain ways. You have learned from your parents and from other people who are significant to you that unless you meet certain conditions, you will not be loved.

Rogers's work as a therapist convinced him that people cope with conditions of worth by rejecting or denying parts of their person that do not fit their self-concept. For example, if your mother grew cold and distant whenever you became angry, you learned to deny yourself the right to express or perhaps even feel anger. In effect, you are cutting off a part of your whole being; you are allowing yourself to experience and express only part of what you are.

The greater the gap between the self and the person, the more limited and defensive a person becomes. Rogers believed the cure for this situation—and the way to prevent it from ever developing—is **unconditional positive regard.** If significant others (parents, friends, a mate) convey the feeling that they value you for what you are in your entirety, you will gradually learn to grant yourself the same unconditional positive regard. The need to limit yourself declines or never develops in the first place. You will be able to accept your person and become open to *all* your feelings, thoughts, and experiences—and hence to other people. This is what Rogers meant by **fully functioning.** The person and the self are one. The individual is free to develop all of his or her potentialities. Like Maslow and other humanistic psychologists, Rogers believed that self-regard and regard for others go together and that the human potential for good and self-fulfillment outweighs the potential for evil and despair (Rogers, 1951, 1961, 1980).

Humanistic approaches to personality emphasize that life is a conscious experience—that is, we freely choose how we spend our lives. Our conscious experience, though, is private and subjective. Critics argue that the humanistic theories cannot be tested. These theories describe behavior rather than explain it. Humanists themselves argue that each individual is unique, and therefore their theories cannot predict behavior.

More About...

Culture and Personality

As you read this chapter, you should realize that the personality theories presented here do not apply to all humans. The observations on which these theories are based center primarily on studies of people in North America and Western Europe. Those studied, then, represent only a minority of the humans on Earth. People in non-Western cultures may look at themselves differently. For instance, such a person may not view herself as a separate entity from her family or community. Concepts such as internal locus of control, self-efficacy, and optimism may have different meanings depending on one's culture. In one study of Asian Americans, for example, those who expressed pessimism about their abilities performed better at solving problems than those who expressed optimism (Chang, 1996). In studies of Caucasian Americans, just the opposite results occurred—an optimistic belief in one's abilities correlates positively with problem solving.

COGNITIVE THEORY

Cognitive theory is based on analysis of our own perceptions, thoughts, and feelings. George Kelly (1905–1967) based his *personal construct theory* on an analysis of our perception of ourselves and our environment. In Kelly's view, our personality consists of our thoughts about ourselves, including our biases, errors, mistakes, and false conclusions.

Kelly's fundamental idea is that our "processes are psychologically channelized by the ways in which (each of us) anticipates events" (Kelly, 1958). He thought

INTERDISCIPLINARY CONNECTIONS ACTIVITY

History Have students select a historical figure who achieved much without having the apparent advantages of birth, social standing, or wealth. Have them research the figure and create a display entitled "You Can Make a Difference," highlighting the person's achievements in terms of Maslow's characteristics of self-actualization. If possible, exhibit the best of the displays in places where other students in the school can be inspired by the achievements of these historical figures. **L2**

these processes were channeled because our response options are limited by the organization of the network of our potential responses. Our individuality comes from the unique manner in which we organize our personal constructs–our schemas–our mental representations of people, events, and concepts.

Expanding on Kelly's work, psychiatrist Aaron T. Beck (1921-) noted his clients' tendency to think negatively–anticipating the worst–and maintain irrational thought processes. Beck developed a theory that would concentrate on turning negative thoughts into constructive ones by challenging clients' fundamentally flawed thought processes. Beck's intent was to help the client develop ways to explain his or her problems as related to the environment rather than automatically assuming they were personality flaws. Finally, a rational analysis would be conducted to develop new, different strategies for the experiences that previously had yielded negative conclusions from flawed thinking (Beck & Rush, 1989; Beck, 1995).

Some aspects of cognitive theory are moving closer to traditional behavioral theories of personality. However, the modern cognitive theories, in contrast to behavioral theory, maintain a more positive, optimistic view of our personality.

Figure 14.14 I'm OK—You're OK

Rogers proposed that people should relate to one another with unconditional positive regard. ***What is unconditional positive regard?***

SECTION 4 Assessment

1. **Review the Vocabulary** What is self-actualization? How does one achieve it?
2. **Visualize the Main Idea** Using a diagram similar to the one below, illustrate the steps an individual needs to take to be fully functioning, according to Rogers's theory.

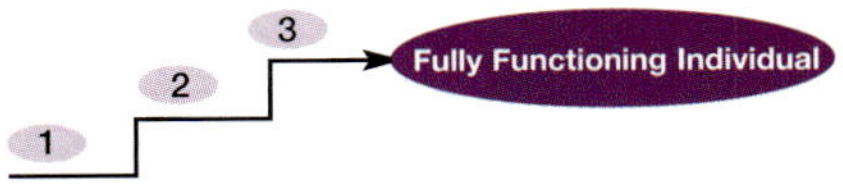

3. **Recall Information** How do conditions of worth influence your personality, according to Rogers?
4. **Think Critically** Do you think unconditional positive regard is important for healthy personality development? Why or why not?
5. **Application Activity** Think of a close friend, family member, or one of your heroes. Using the information in Figure 14.12, evaluate which traits of self-actualized individuals he or she shares.

Figure 14.14

Caption Answer the perception that significant people in your life value you for what you are, allowing you to share the same view of yourself

Enrich

Assign students to debate the following: *Resolved—That human beings have little free will in determining the shape of their personalities.* Appoint some students to argue the *pro* position using examples of behaviorist and psychoanalytic theories as evidence. Direct others to argue the *con* position using the ideas and experiments of Carl Rogers.

4 CLOSE

Divide students into groups. Assign each group one of the following: Abraham Maslow, Carl Rogers, George Kelly. Have each group create a table describing the theorists' lives, work, and major contributions to psychology.

SECTION 4 Assessment Answers

1. It is the realization of one's unique potential as a human being; openness to many experiences, awareness of and respect for one's own and other people's uniqueness, accepting the responsibilities of freedom and commitment, a desire to become truer to oneself, an ability to grow
2. Diagrams should reflect students' understanding of Rogers's theory and what it takes to be a fully functioning individual.
3. You redefine your personality by the conditions of worth imposed by those you respect, even if that means rejecting parts of yourself.
4. Students' answers will vary. Encourage students to consider the connection between acceptance and self concept.
5. Students' answers will vary. Encourage students to consider how their heroes' self-actualized characteristics influence the respect the students have for them.

1 FOCUS

Section Objectives

1. Explain the main features of trait personality.
2. Describe Allport's, Cattell's, and Eysenck's theories of personality.

BELLRINGER
Motivational Activity

Project Daily Focus Transparency 14–5 and have students answer the questions.

Available as blackline master

5Daily Focus Transparency 14–5

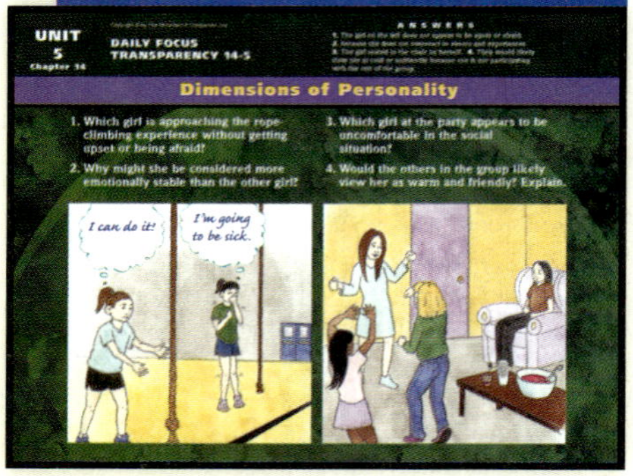

Reader's Guide

Use the Reader's Guide to introduce concepts and vocabulary.

Exploring Psychology

Ask students to read the **Exploring Psychology** feature. Then ask: **What words do you use to describe your friends to other friends? Are these traits accurate descriptions of the person's personality?**

Vocabulary Precheck

Have students read the Glossary definition of *trait* and then write down their best guess at the definitions of the remaining terms. Students should check their definitions against the Glossary.

Use the **Vocabulary PuzzleMaker CD-ROM** to create crossword and word search puzzles.

SECTION 5 Trait Theories

Reader's Guide

Main Idea

Trait theorists believe that character traits account for consistency of behavior in different situations.

Vocabulary

- trait
- cardinal trait
- factor analysis
- surface trait
- source trait
- extravert
- introvert

Objectives

- Explain the main features of trait personality.
- Describe Allport's, Cattell's, and Eysenck's theories of personality.

EXPLORING PSYCHOLOGY

Characteristics of Personality

"Tell me about Nelson," said Johnetta.

"Oh, he's just terrific. He's the friendliest guy I know—goes out of his way to be nice to everyone. He hardly ever gets mad. He's just so even-tempered, no matter what's happening. And he's really smart, too. About the only thing I don't like is that he's always in such a hurry to get things done. He seems to have boundless energy, much more than I have."

"He sounds great to me, especially in comparison to Rico," replied Johnetta. "He is so self-centered and arrogant it drives me crazy. I sometimes wonder why I ever started going out with him."

—from *Understanding Psychology* by Robert S. Feldman, 2005

trait: a tendency to react to a situation in a way that remains stable over time

Terms such as *nice, smart,* and *arrogant* refer to personality traits. Some theorists have argued that studying such traits in detail is the best approach to solving the puzzle of human behavior.

A **trait** is "any relatively enduring way in which one individual differs from another" (Guilford, 1959). A trait, then, is a predisposition to respond in a certain way in many different kinds of situations—in a dentist's office, at a party, or in a classroom. More than any other personality theorists, trait theorists emphasize and try to explain the consistency of a normal, healthy individual's behavior in different situations.

SECTION RESOURCES

Reproducible Masters

- Guided Reading Activity 14–5
- Vocabulary Activity 14–5
- Section Quiz 14–5

Transparencies

- Daily Focus Transparency 14–5

Multimedia

- Vocabulary PuzzleMaker CD-ROM
- *ExamView*® Assessment Suite CD-ROM
- Presentation Plus! Software

WHAT IS THE TRAIT THEORY OF PERSONALITY?

Trait theorists generally make two basic assumptions about these underlying sources of consistency. First, every trait applies to all people. For example, everyone can be classified as more or less dependent. Second, these descriptions can be quantified. We might, for example, establish a scale on which an extremely independent person scores 1, while a very dependent person scores 10.

Thus, every trait can be used to describe people. Aggressiveness, for example, is measured on a continuum; a few people are extremely aggressive or extremely unaggressive, and most of us fall somewhere in the middle. We understand people by specifying their traits, and we use traits to predict people's future behavior.

Trait theorists go beyond this kind of common-sense analysis, however, to try to discover the underlying sources of the consistency of human behavior. What is the best way to describe the common features of someone's behavior? Is he friendly, or socially aggressive, or interested in people, or self-confident, or something else? What underlying trait best explains his behavior?

Most (but not all) trait theorists believe that a few basic traits are central for all people. An underlying trait of self-confidence, for example, might be used to explain more superficial characteristics like social aggressiveness and dependency. If this were true, it would mean that a person would be dependent because he or she lacked self-confidence. Psychologists who accept this approach set out on their theoretical search for basic traits with very few assumptions.

This is very different from the starting point of other personality theorists we have considered. Freud, for example, began with a well-defined theory of instincts. When he observed that some people were stingy, he set out to explain this in terms of his theory. Trait theorists would not start by trying to understand stinginess. Rather, they would try to determine whether stinginess was a trait. That is, they would try to find out whether people who were stingy in one type of situation were also stingy in others. Then they might ask whether stinginess is a sign of a more basic trait like possessiveness: Is the stingy person also very possessive in relationships? Thus, the first and foremost question for the trait theorists is, "What behaviors go together?"

"That's Mr. Brock. He didn't have a happy New Year, a happy Valentine's Day, a happy St. Patrick's Day, a happy Easter, a happy Father's Day, a happy Halloween, a happy Thanksgiving, or a merry Christmas. He did have, however, a safe and sane Fourth of July."

Figure 14.15 Personality Traits

This cartoon highlights personality traits. Often we describe a person's personality in terms of traits. ***Which personality traits does this cartoon emphasize?***

Reading Check How does trait theory differ from psychoanalytic theories of personality?

2 TEACH

L1 Describing Traits Read aloud the definition of *trait* from the text. As a class, make a list of common traits on the board. Prepare on newsprint or poster board the headings: *Surface Trait* and *Source Trait*. Post these headings. Have students classify the traits that have been listed on the board by transferring items to the appropriate list. Note that some traits could be listed under both headings. ELL

Figure 14.15

Caption Answer Students may suggest unhappy, reserved, serious, or tough-minded.

Reading Check Answer Psychoanalytic theories attempt to explain behavior. The trait theory seeks to define and describe traits, assuming that all traits are present in all people.

FYI

Studies of identical twins reared together or apart have led many psychologists to the conclusion that personality traits are about 50 to 60 percent inherited, meaning that traits have some physiological basis.

COOPERATIVE LEARNING ACTIVITY

Identifying Central Issues Read aloud the following quotes.

- *The face is the image of the soul.* (Cicero)
- *I am not much in fear of these fat, sleek fellows, but rather those pale, thin ones.* (Julius Caesar)
- *Cassius hath a lean and hungry look; he thinks too much: such men are dangerous.* (from *Julius Caesar,* by William Shakespeare)

Ask: **Upon what basis are each of these personality judgments based?** *(physical appearance)* **To what extent do people still judge personality by physical types? What are the limitations of this attitude?** **L2**

CHAPTER 14

Section 5, pages 398–403

Guided Reading Activity 14–5

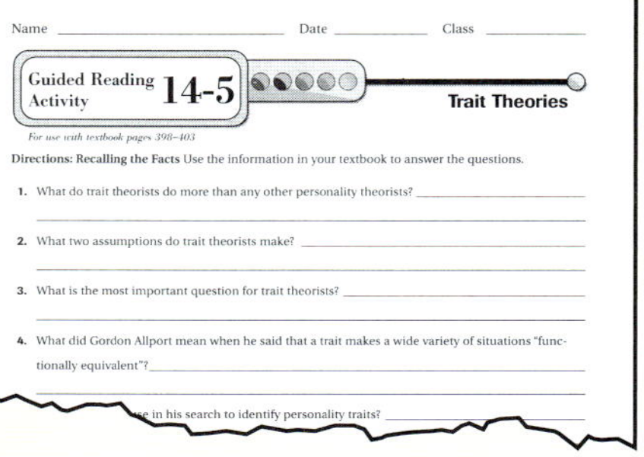
Name ______ Date ______ Class ______

Guided Reading Activity 14-5 — Trait Theories

Directions: Recalling the Facts Use the information in your textbook to answer the questions.

1. What do trait theorists do more than any other personality theorists? ______
2. What two assumptions do trait theorists make? ______
3. What is the most important question for trait theorists? ______
4. What did Gordon Allport mean when he said that a trait makes a wide variety of situations "functionally equivalent"? ______

PSYCHOLOGY JOURNAL

Have students consider their own traits and make a list of items that describe their central traits and their secondary traits. ■

Readings and Case Studies in Psychology

Have students read the Chapter 14 Reading selection in *Readings and Case Studies in Psychology* and answer the questions that follow the reading.

Figure 14.16

Visual Instruction Ask each student to orally define one or two of these source trait descriptions. Allow students to look up the words, if necessary, in order to refine their definitions.

Caption Answer He believed psychologists could predict people's behavior in certain situations.

3 tab book

Shutter fold

GORDON ALLPORT: IDENTIFYING TRAITS

Gordon W. Allport (1897–1967) was an influential psychologist in his day. A trait, Allport said, makes a wide variety of situations "functionally equivalent"; that is, a person's traits will be consistent in different situations. Allport, along with H.S. Odbert, probed an English dictionary, searching for words that described personality traits. They found almost 18,000 such words. They then narrowed the list by grouping synonyms and keeping just one word for each cluster of synonyms. Assuming any important personality trait is reflected in language, if Allport's team found words such as *honesty* and *dishonesty*, each was assigned to a separate cluster with similar contrasting words. Allport defined common traits as those that apply to everyone and individual traits as those that apply more to a specific person.

cardinal trait: a characteristic or feature that is so pervasive the person is almost identified with it

Allport described three kinds of individual traits. A **cardinal trait** is one that is so pervasive that the person is almost identified with that trait. An example would be Scrooge, who is identified as stingy and coldhearted in Charles Dickens's tale *A Christmas Carol.* A *central trait* makes us predictable (she's assertive; he's a flirt) in most situations. *Secondary traits,* such as our preferences in food and music, are least important to Allport and have a less consistent influence on us.

An example of an individual trait is found in Allport's book *Letters from Jenny* (1965), which consists of hundreds of letters that a woman whom Allport calls Jenny Masterson wrote to a friend (see Readings in Psychology, p. 408). Jenny reveals herself in these letters, which she wrote between the ages of 58 and 70, as a complex and fiercely independent woman. In his preface to the book, Allport wrote:

> [The] fascination of the Letters lies in their challenge to the reader (whether psychologist or layman) to "explain" Jenny—if he can. Why does an intelligent lady behave so persistently in a self-defeating manner?

Allport's own attempt to understand Jenny began with a search for the underlying traits that would explain the consistency of her behavior.

Figure 14.16 Cattell's Sixteen Source Traits

Cattell used his sixteen source traits to develop a personality questionnaire, which was used to measure the traits in an individual. Each trait is listed as a pair of opposites on a continuum. ***What did Cattell believe measuring the source traits could predict?***

Reserved	⟷	Outgoing
Less intelligent	⟷	More intelligent
Affected by feelings	⟷	Emotionally stable
Submissive	⟷	Dominant
Serious	⟷	Happy-go-lucky
Expedient	⟷	Conscientious
Timid	⟷	Venturesome
Tough-minded	⟷	Sensitive
Trusting	⟷	Suspicious
Practical	⟷	Imaginative
Forthright	⟷	Shrewd
Self-assured	⟷	Apprehensive
Conservative	⟷	Experimenting
Group-dependent	⟷	Self-sufficient
Uncontrolled	⟷	Controlled
Relaxed	⟷	Tense

MEETING SPECIAL NEEDS

Learning Style: Kinesthetic Have students construct an abacus-type scale for personality traits using Eysenck's three basic dimensions of personality. The scale should have anchors at each end representing the two extremes. Between the anchors, secure metal, twine, or other sturdy material on which beads can be strung. Use 10 beads for each dimension. All the beads at one end would indicate that someone is at the extreme on that dimension. Have students use the scales to describe their personalities using Eysenck's three dimensions. **L2** **BLOCK SCHEDULING**

RAYMOND CATTELL: SIXTEEN TRAIT THEORY

More recent theorists have concentrated on what Allport called *common traits,* which they try to quantify in a precise, scientific manner. Their primary tool in this task has been **factor analysis,** a sophisticated mathematical technique that describes the extent to which different personality variables are related.

Using Allport's list of traits, Raymond Cattell (1905–1998) proposed that characteristics that can be observed in certain situations make up 46 traits, called **surface traits,** of observable behavior. These traits make up behavior that is based on people's perceptions of personality. Using further factor analyses, Cattell found that certain surface traits seem to occur in clusters. Cattell further researched what these clusters had in common. This analysis resulted in 16 **source traits**—traits that he considered to be at the core of personality (see Figure 14.16). Cattell believed that by measuring these traits, psychologists could predict people's behavior in certain situations.

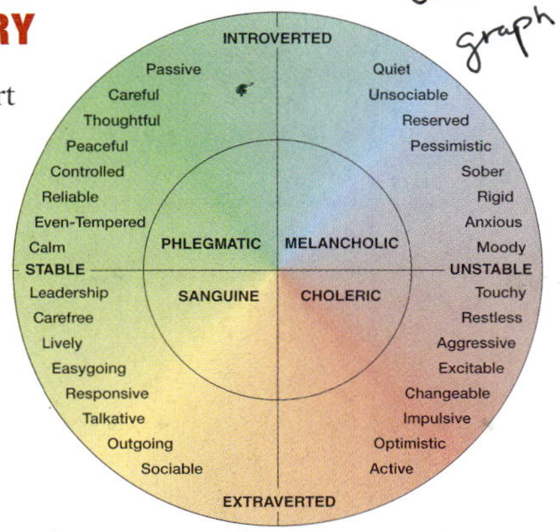

Figure 14.17 Eysenck's Personality Table

Eysenck hypothesized that introverted people share a number of traits, while extraverted people share the opposite traits. Eysenck's theory is similar to Galen's ancient theory for four temperaments (see the Case Study on page 23). ***What traits would an extraverted and stable (sanguine) person exhibit?***

HANS EYSENCK: DIMENSIONS OF PERSONALITY

Using factor analysis of personality data, Hans Eysenck (1916–), an English psychologist, concluded that there are two basic dimensions of personality (see Figure 14.17). The first dimension, *stability versus instability,* refers to the degree to which people have control over their feelings. At the emotionally stable end of the personality spectrum is a person who is easygoing, relaxed, well-adjusted, and even-tempered. At the anxiety-dominated end of the spectrum is the moody, anxious, and restless person.

Eysenck's second dimension was actually identified years earlier by Carl Jung as *extraversion versus introversion.* **Extraverts** are sociable, outgoing, active, lively people. They enjoy parties and seek excitement. On the other end of the dimension are **introverts,** who are more thoughtful, reserved, passive, unsociable, and quiet.

Years after he identified the first two dimensions, Eysenck added a third, *psychoticism.* At one end of this dimension are self-centered, hostile, and aggressive people, who act without much thought. Individuals at the other end of this dimension have what Freud might label high superego. They tend to be socially sensitive, high on caring and empathy, and easy people with whom to work (Eysenck, 1970, 1990).

THE ROBUST FIVE

Over the years, trait theorists have devised a number of ways to measure personality. Each involves a different number of traits or factors. Trait psychologists have shown that five traits appear repeatedly in

factor analysis: a complex statistical technique used to identify the underlying reasons variables are correlated

surface trait: a stable characteristic that can be observed in certain situations

source trait: a stable characteristic that can be considered to be at the core of personality

extravert: an outgoing, active person who directs his or her energies and interests toward other people and things

introvert: a reserved, withdrawn person who is preoccupied with his or her inner thoughts and feelings

Figure 14.17

Visual Instruction Discuss the relationship between Eysenck's personality dimensions and Galen's four temperaments. For example, Eysenck's extraverted, unstable type is similar to Galen's choleric type.

Caption Answer leadership, carefree, lively, easygoing, responsive, talkative, outgoing, sociable

FYI

Introverts tend to be motivated from within and are more oriented toward reflection and ideas. Extraverts tend to direct their attention outward and gain their motivation from outside sources. They also tend to look for meaning outside themselves.

Vocabulary Activity 14–5

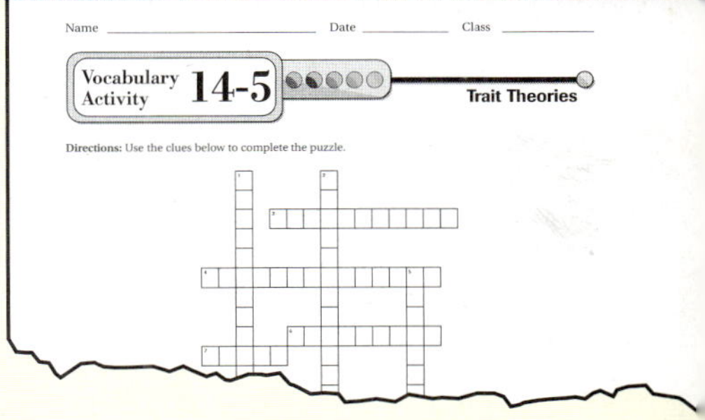

CRITICAL THINKING ACTIVITY

Allport's Functional Autonomy Tell students that Gordon Allport did not believe that a person's past was of great significance. He used the term *functional autonomy* to describe his belief. For example, Allport would state that it does not matter why you wanted to become a good student; it only matters that you are one now. Have students make a list of a half dozen of their personality traits. Ask students to consider past events that may have influenced these traits. Have students write a short summary of these events next to the trait in question. Now, ask students to debate the question: **From this point on in your life, what determines your behavior, past experiences or current personality traits? L2** BLOCK SCHEDULING

CHAPTER 14

Section 5, pages 398–403

Quick Lab

Purpose Students will explore how personality traits may be viewed differently.

Process Skills Designing an experiment, classifying information

Teaching Strategies

- Review the procedures to be used.
- Participants should understand what the terms *introversion* and *extraversion* mean.

Analysis

1. Answers will vary. Most students will note that these traits are opposite extremes and that most people a little of both.
2. Answers will vary. Students may note that the way we think about ourselves cannot be observed by others and that our actions do not always match our feelings or our view of ourselves.

3 ASSESS

Assign Section 5 Assessment as homework or as an in-class activity.

Section Quiz 14–5

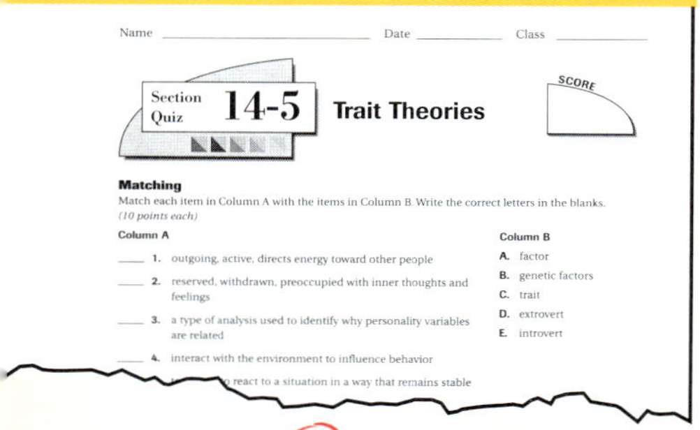
Name ______ Date ______ Class ______

Section Quiz 14-5 **Trait Theories** SCORE

Matching

Match each item in Column A with the items in Column B. Write the correct letters in the blanks. *(10 points each)*

Column A	Column B
____ 1. outgoing, active, directs energy toward other people	A. factor
____ 2. reserved, withdrawn, preoccupied with inner thoughts and feelings	B. genetic factors
____ 3. a type of analysis used to identify why personality variables are related	C. trait
____ 4. interact with the environment to influence behavior	D. extrovert
... react to a situation in a way that remains stable	E. introvert

Reteach

Have students select one of their favorite movie or television characters and rate that character using the five robust factors. Ask volunteers to share their descriptions with the class without naming the character. See if the class can guess the character based on the description.

Quick Lab

Do we see ourselves as others see us?

Some personality theorists talk about extraversion versus introversion as being a basic part of personality. Do people exhibit these traits in all situations? Are these traits easily identified?

Procedure

1. Choose five people (family members, friends, or acquaintances) and observe their behavior in several situations.
2. Record your observations by classifying each person as extraverted, introverted, or a combination of both.
3. Ask the five people whether they would consider themselves extraverted or introverted, and then record their responses.

Analysis

1. What do your results tell you about extraversion and introversion as personality traits? Are people extraverted or introverted in all situations all the time?
2. What do your results tell you about people's own perceptions of their personality versus the perceptions of others? What might account for any differences?

See the **Skills Handbook**, page 622, for an explanation of designing an experiment.

different research studies. Often called the "five robust factors," or "the big five," they are:

- *Extraversion,* which is associated with warmth, talkativeness, and being energetic. The opposite of this dimension is introversion, meaning being quiet or reserved.
- *Agreeableness,* which involves being sympathetic to others, kind, and trusting; the opposite is cruel and nontrusting.
- *Conscientiousness,* which identifies individuals who are dutiful, dedicated to completing tasks, organized, and responsible.
- *Openness to experience,* which describes people who are open-minded and willing to try intellectual experiences, new ideas, or creative experiences.
- *Emotional stability,* which identifies individuals who experience things relatively easily and without getting upset. The opposite is neuroticism—a tendency to experience unpleasant emotions a great deal of the time. (John, 1990; Costa, McCrae, & Dye, 1991)

Think of each big-five trait as a continuum. Each trait has many related traits. For example, conscientiousness at one end includes being responsible and dependable. On the other end, though, it involves being impulsive or careless.

Trait theorists assume that traits are relatively fixed, or unchanging. The advantage of trait theories is that by identifying a person's personality traits, that person's behavior can be predicted. However, critics argue that trait theories describe personality rather than explain it. Trait theorists cannot explain or predict behaviors across different situations. For example, a person may be quiet and reserved in class but outgoing and wild at a party. Why? Critics of trait theories propose that personality is an interaction between a person's traits and the effects of being in a particular situation. For example, whereas most theories of personality consider the person as an individual, some psychologists regard personality as a function of a person's social environment. One of the first of these thinkers was Harry Stack Sullivan (1892–1949).

Sullivan's ideas have been organized into a two-dimensional model. One dimension is power, which ranges from dominance at one end of the scale to submissiveness at the other. The second dimension is friendliness, which ranges from friendliness to hostility. Most behaviors can be described as a combination of these two dimensions. For example, helpfulness is a combination of dominance and friendliness, while trust is a combination of submissiveness and friendliness.

PSYCHOLOGY LAB EXPERIMENT

Which Are You? Share the following descriptions with the class. *Extravert:* (1) needs and likes to be with people; (2) energizes self through interaction with others; (3) needs and wants many friends; (4) interested in what is happening in the external world; (5) tends to be expressive; (6) tolerates criticism well; and (7) eager to jump into new situations. *Introvert:* (1) needs to have "space" (territorial); (2) energizes self by being alone; (3) limits friendships; (4) interested in internal reactions; (5) tends to be hesitant to express ideas/feelings; (6) takes criticism personally; and (7) often reluctant to jump into new situations. **Ask:** **According to these trait descriptions, are you an extravert or an introvert? Or does it depend upon the situation you are in? Explain. L2**

Figure 14.18 Theories of Personality

Theories of personality are used to organize personality characteristics, explain differences among individuals, explore how people conduct their lives, and determine how life can be improved. ***Which theory do you think best describes your personality? Explain.***

Theory	Main Ideas
Behaviorist Theories	focus on the way rewards and punishment shape our actions
Social Learning Theories	cognitive-personal factors, our behaviors, and environmental factors interact to shape our personalities
Psychoanalytic Theories	emphasize the importance of early childhood experiences, repressed thoughts, and conflict between conscious and unconscious forces
Cognitive Theories	our analysis of our own perceptions, thoughts, and feelings shape our personalities
Humanistic Theories	emphasize our capacity for personal growth, development of our full potential, and freedom to make choices
Trait Theories	focus on identifying, measuring, and classifying similarities and differences in personality characteristics or traits

Researchers also noticed that a person's actions tend to elicit specific responses from other people. A behavior and its most likely response are said to be complementary. For example, most people will respond to a request for help (trusting) by offering advice (helping), regardless of how helpful they are as individuals. Thus, many behaviors result not simply from a person's personality but also from that person's social environment.

SECTION 5 Assessment

1. **Review the Vocabulary** What is the difference between cardinal and central traits? Between surface and source traits?
2. **Visualize the Main Idea** Using a diagram similar to the one below, list the traits that make up each of Eysenck's three dimensions of personality.

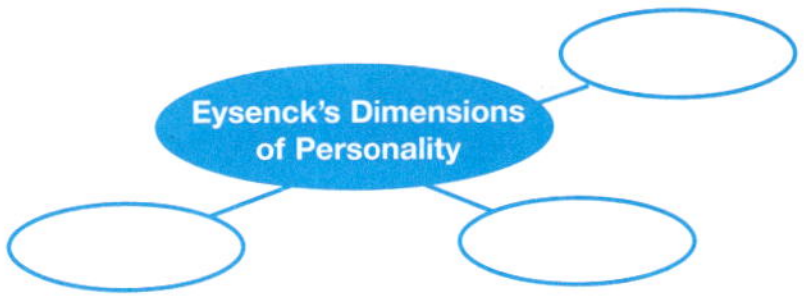

3. **Recall Information** What is the importance of common traits in Cattell's theory? What are Cattell's source traits?
4. **Think Critically** Do the five factors of personality in the five robust factors describe you? If not, what other characteristics would you want to add?
5. **Application Activity** Choose a character in a movie or television show you have recently seen. Describe the character in terms of the personality dimensions proposed by one of the trait theorists discussed in this section.

SECTION 5 Assessment Answers

1. A central trait is a characteristic that best describes a person, while a cardinal trait is so all-encompassing that it becomes an identifier for the person. Surface traits are characteristics that can be observed in certain situations. Source traits are characteristics considered to be at the core of the personality.
2. stability vs. instability, extraversion vs. introversion, and psychoticism vs. empathetic (socially sensitive)
3. Common traits are traits shared by all people. Source traits are the major traits that define one's personality and can be used to predict behavior.
4. Students' answers will vary. These will describe large parts of students' personalities, but students may identify other dimensions they consider important.
5. Students' answers will vary. Encourage students to select characters that have been well-developed by the writers. Challenge students to give specific examples of the character's personality dimensions.

Figure 14.18

Visual Instruction Assign students to provide a summary of one of the personality theories presented here.

Caption Answer Answers will vary. Students are likely to choose trait theories because they provide clear descriptions of personality, without attempting to explain personality.

Enrich

Assign pairs of students to observe people in a busy, public place such as a mall or park. Have them identify extraverts and introverts by simple observation. **Ask:** **What behaviors did you use to identify someone as an introvert or an extravert?**

4 CLOSE

Have students review literary characters they have studied to associate cardinal traits with characters in literature. For example, Peter Pan may be associated with being carefree and Scrooge with being stingy.

Going Further

Personality and Psychology

People differ from one another in many obvious ways. Psychologists interested in personality study the differences and similarities among people. They ask if characteristics of human nature are shared among all peoples. They study patterns and dimensions of personality and identify individual differences. These psychologists look for biological and environmental factors that influence personality. About half of our personality is attributed to genetics. The other half is influenced by social, ethnic, and cultural components.

Personality research extends to examining cognitive abilities, interpersonal styles, and how emotions are expressed. The research seeks to find useful models to measure personality traits and degrees of differences among people. The research centers on three questions:

1. How do people differ?
2. Can differences in one situation be used to predict differences in other situations?
3. How can theories of personality differences be tested and measured?

By answering these questions, personality theorists seek to clearly distinguish personality disorders from individual differences.

Discussing the Case Study

Ask: **What is a personality disorder? Why was Dan's personality disorder difficult to diagnose?**

Case Studies

Personality Disorder

Period of Study: 1967

Introduction: An actor and radio disc jockey, Dan was highly successful in his professional roles, which required an entertaining and extremely outspoken personality. Although Dan had to maintain these personality traits at work, sometimes traces of those traits leaked out into his private life. In one situation while Dan and a friend dined at a restaurant, Dan explicitly and loudly complained about the condition of the food. In actuality, according to Dan's friend, the food was fine—there was no valid reason for Dan's public display.

Dan's friend, psychologist Elton McNeil, described Dan's reactions as inappropriate. When McNeil asked Dan why he had acted that way, Dan said he did it because "he wanted to show how gutless the rest of the world is." Dan then said acting like that separates the classy people from the ordinary and that the next time he eats at that restaurant, he will be treated well. Concerned by his friend's statements, McNeil asked Dan if he felt guilty at all about treating his fellow human beings that way. Dan's answer was, "Who cares?"

Hypothesis: For those of us who are familiar with actors and radio disc jockeys, we know that their jobs require straightforward and sometimes confrontational behavior. An excess of these traits, though, can prove to be too much for healthy functioning in life.

Method: McNeil encouraged his friend to take part in some sort of counseling or therapy. Dan agreed. During a therapy session, Dan disclosed:

> I can remember the first time in my life when I began to suspect I was a little different from most people. When I was in high school my best friend got leukemia and died and I went to his funeral. Everybody else was crying and feeling sorry for themselves and as they were praying to get him into heaven, I suddenly realized that I wasn't feeling anything at all. He was a nice guy but what the hell. That night I thought about it some more and found that I wouldn't miss my mother and father if they died and that I wasn't too nuts about my brothers and sisters for that matter. I figured there wasn't anybody I really cared for but, then, I didn't need any of them anyway so I rolled over and went to sleep. (Davison & Neale, 2001)

Results: This description detailing the absence of emotion clearly indicated the possibility of a personality disorder. The *Diagnostic and Statistical Manual of Mental Disorders, Fourth Edition (DSM-IV)* defines a personality disorder as an enduring pattern of inner experience and behavior that differs significantly from the individual's culture, is extensive and inflexible, has an onset in adolescence or early adulthood, is stable over time, and leads to distress or impairment. An individual with a personality disorder is often capable of functioning normally in society, including holding a job, maintaining some personal relationships, and, on some occasions, showing signs of emotions. This is what makes discovering a personality disorder so difficult.

Dan's unusual behavior may have gone unnoticed for so long because his occupations required a person to behave a certain way. Unfortunately, it is not always easy to actually know if a person is acting out a role or displaying his or her own personality traits. In Dan's case, his role was his personality.

Analyzing the Case Study

1. Why did McNeil encourage Dan to enter therapy?
2. Why do psychologists consider Dan's behavior a disorder rather than just a personality type?
3. **Critical Thinking** Does everyone's personality change depending on the role they are playing (for instance, as student, friend, son, or daughter)? Explain.

Answers for Analyzing the Case Study

1. He encouraged Dan to enter therapy to deal with personality issues and behaviors that were affecting how Dan related to those around him. He questioned Dan's lack of emotions for other people.
2. Dan's behavior varied significantly from the accepted cultural norm and led to an impairment in his relationships with others. Dan's absence of emotion clearly pointed to the presence of a personality disorder. Like many people with a personality disorder, Dan was able to function in society, including holding a job, maintaining some personal relationships, and showing some emotions.
3. One's basic personality does not change; however, one's behavior may change to fit the situation. Certain personality traits may be more obvious in certain situations.

CHAPTER 14 Summary and Vocabulary

Psychologists have proposed various theories of personality. The theories attempt to help explain similarities and to provide reasons for differences in personality.

Section 1 Purposes of Personality Theories

Main Idea: Personality theories provide a way of organizing the many characteristics that people have.

- Personality theorists try to organize traits by similarities and differences, explore how people cope with life situations, and how people grow and change.

Section 2 Psychoanalytic Theories

Main Idea: Freud's psychoanalytic theory proposes that personality is made up of three components: the id, ego, and superego.

- Sigmund Freud believed that every personality has an unconscious component and that childhood experiences, even if not consciously recalled, continue to influence people's behaviors.
- The id, ego, and superego explain how the mind functions and how instinctual energies are regulated.

Section 3 Learning Theories

Main Idea: Behaviorists are interested in how aspects of personality are learned.

- Behaviorists believe that as individuals differ in their learning experiences, they acquire different behaviors and different personalities.
- Albert Bandura believed that personality is acquired not only by reinforcement but also by observational learning.

Section 4 Humanistic and Cognitive Theories

Main Idea: Humanistic and cognitive theories of personality stress the positive aspects of human nature.

- Humanistic psychology is founded on the belief that all human beings strive for self-actualization.
- Carl Rogers believed that many people suffer from a conflict between what they value in themselves and what they believe other people value in them.

Section 5 Trait Theories

Main Idea: Trait theorists believe that character traits account for consistency of behavior in different situations.

- Trait theorists believe we understand people by specifying their traits, and we use traits to predict people's future behavior.
- Gordon W. Allport defined common traits as those that apply to everyone and individual traits as those that apply more to a specific person.

Chapter Vocabulary

personality (p. 375)
unconscious (p. 379)
id (p. 379)
ego (p. 380)
superego (p. 380)
defense mechanisms (p. 380)
collective unconscious (p. 384)
archetype (p. 384)
inferiority complex (p. 385)
behaviorism (p. 387)
contingencies of reinforcement (p. 388)
humanistic psychology (p. 392)
self-actualization (p. 392)
self (p. 395)
positive regard (p. 395)
conditions of worth (p. 395)
unconditional positive regard (p. 396)
fully functioning (p. 396)
trait (p. 398)
cardinal trait (p. 400)
factor analysis (p. 401)
surface trait (p. 401)
source trait (p. 401)
extravert (p. 401)
introvert (p. 401)

14 Summary and Vocabulary

Using the Chapter 14 Summary and Vocabulary

Use the Chapter 14 Summary and Vocabulary to preview, review, condense, or reteach the chapter.

Preview/Review

Use the Chapter Vocabulary list to help students review and study.

Activity Ask students to write the vocabulary terms on index cards or pieces of paper. Have them write the definition on the opposite side. Ask students to select those terms that are related to one of the personality theories. Then have them group the terms with the correct personality theory.

Vocabulary PuzzleMaker CD-ROM reinforces the vocabulary terms used in Chapter 14.

Condense

Have students read the Chapter 14 Summary.

Chapter 14 Guided Reading Activities

Reteach

Reteaching Activity 14

PERFORMANCE ASSESSMENT ACTIVITY

Personality Masks Tell students that *personality* is derived from the Latin word *persona*—the term used to describe the masks worn in Greek theater. Roman actors adapted these masks, and they are still used today to identify the range of emotions portrayed in theater. Have students work in small groups to design at least four paper masks that convey particular personality types, or *personas*. Encourage students to think in relatively simple terms such as shy, angry, happy, and so on. Have the groups see if the rest of the class can identify each mask's personality trait. Ask students to select what they consider the two most important facial features used to convey the *persona*. **BLOCK SCHEDULING**

CHAPTER 14

Assessment

PSYCHOLOGY Online

Self-Check Quiz
Visit the *Understanding Psychology* Web site at glencoe.com and click on **Chapter 14—Self-Check Quizzes** to prepare for the Chapter Test.

Reviewing Vocabulary

Choose the letter of the correct term or concept below to complete the sentence.

a. personality
b. contingencies of reinforcement
c. trait
d. defense mechanism
e. inferiority complex
f. self-actualization
g. positive regard
h. conditions of worth
i. extravert
j. introvert

1. People who continuously try to compensate for their weakness and avoid feelings of inadequacy have a(n) __________.
2. A(n)__________ is a person who is reserved, passive, and unsociable.
3. A(n)__________ is a tendency to react the same way to different situations.
4. According to Carl Rogers, people require __________, or approval, from other people in order to acquire a self.
5. Events that maintain certain behaviors are called __________.
6. __________ is composed of the consistent, enduring, and unique characteristics of a person.
7. When a person deceives herself into thinking nothing is wrong instead of facing intense conflict, she is using a(n)__________.
8. A(n)__________ is a person who is outgoing and lively.
9. According to humanistic psychologists, all people strive for __________, or the realization of their potentialities as unique human beings.
10. __________ is the term for the conditions people must meet in order to regard themselves positively.

Recalling Facts

1. Using a graphic organizer similar to the one below, list the "five robust factors" of personality.

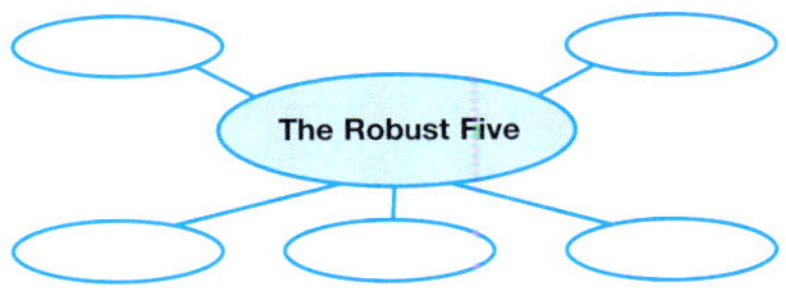

2. How did Bandura and Walters believe personality is acquired?
3. What technique might you be using if you think a teacher is angry at you because he or she gave a difficult test, when in reality the teacher actually is not angry?
4. According to Rogers, what situation creates a gap between the person and the self?
5. What are the two basic assumptions behind trait theories?

Critical Thinking

1. **Synthesizing Information** Imagine that you have a friend who is failing several subjects in school, does little homework, and fails to study for tests. Based on your knowledge of personality theories, how would Skinner explain your friend's behavior? How would Bandura explain the behavior?
2. **Making Inferences** What would life be like if people had only an id? An ego? A superego?
3. **Analyzing Concepts** Recall *Freudian slips* you have seen or heard. Write them down and try to determine the reasons for each slip.
4. **Applying Concepts** List the qualities and traits that you think comprise the self-actualized person.
5. **Demonstrating Reasoned Judgment** Some opponents of the humanistic theory of personality have criticized it for promoting the "me first" approach to living. They believe that the theory encourages selfishness. Do you agree with these critics? Why or why not?

14 Assessment

PSYCHOLOGY Online

Have students visit the Web site at glencoe.com to review Chapter 14 and take the **Self-Check Quiz**.

GLENCOE TECHNOLOGY

Presentation Plus!

For a review of Chapter 14 content, see MindJogger Checkpoint on **Presentation Plus!**

Reviewing Vocabulary

1. e
2. j
3. c
4. g
5. b
6. a
7. d
8. i
9. f
10. h

Recalling Facts

1. Extraversion is associated with warmth, talkativeness, and being energetic. Agreeableness involves being sympathetic, kind, and trusting to others. Individuals who are conscientious are dutiful, dedicated, organized, and responsible. People who are open-minded are willing to try new ideas and experiences. *Emotionally stable* are the words used to describe someone who experiences things relatively easily.
2. They believed personality is acquired by observational learning or imitation as well as by direct reinforcement.
3. You would be using the defense mechanisms of regression, projection, or rationalization.
4. According to Rogers, placing conditions of worth on an individual creates a gap between the person and the self.
5. The two basic assumptions are that every trait applies to all people and that these trait descriptions can be quantified.

Critical Thinking

1. Skinner would assume that your friend's behavior is being reinforced. He would recommend discovering and changing the contingencies of reinforcement. Bandura would suggest that your friend may have lowered his or her expectations to the point that he or she has given up trying.
2. Answers will vary. Students' answers should reflect an understanding of the three Freudian components.
3. Answers will vary. Students should mention how unconscious thoughts slip through to the surface.
4. Again, answers will vary; but they should coincide with the traits described on Maslow's list.
5. Answers should include examples representing key concepts from the humanistic viewpoint as well as arguments against it.

Psychology Projects

1. Encourage students to explore the full range of their personalities. You might explore whether the collages depict the social "I," the private "me," or a combination of both.
2. Ask volunteers to share their ideas by explaining the myth or fairy tale and identifying the archetypes. As a class, discuss how these archetypes represent common human experiences or traits.
3. Descriptions will vary along with the theory and person chosen. The goal is to apply the theory as a tool of analysis.

CHAPTER 14

Assessment

Psychology Projects

1. **Purposes of Personality Theories** Create a collage that depicts your personality, using pictures and words from magazines and newspapers. Display your collage in class and explain which theory discussed best describes your personality.
2. **Psychoanalytic Theories** Archetypes are evident in many myths and fairy tales. Choose a myth or fairy tale and identify the archetypes in it and the common experiences of humanity that these archetypes reflect.
3. **Trait Theories** Select a newspaper or news magazine article that describes the activities or accomplishments of a person—for example, a popular sports figure, politician, or businessperson. Then select one of the trait theories of personality to describe the person's behavior and outlook on life. You may have to go beyond the material in the article to make a convincing argument for the theory you have selected. Present your description in a report.

Technology Activity

There are various personality tests available on the Internet. Locate the Web sites of these tests. Report on the aspects of personality that these tests address and evaluate how well they do so. Share the Web addresses you found with the class.

Psychology Journal

1. Analyze the entry in your journal you wrote at the beginning of the study of this chapter. Now write another entry answering these questions: Does the person change behavior depending on the setting? What would you say are important reinforcers for this person? Explain your observations using a behavioral model of personality.
2. In your journal, describe the theory of personality that is most appealing to you. Which seems to make the most sense? Why?

Building Skills

Identifying Cause-and-Effect Relationships Review the cartoon, then answer the questions that follow.

1. What does "Robert's facade" refer to?
2. What aspect of Freud's psychoanalytic theory of personality is reflected in the cartoon?
3. How might a behaviorist explain Robert's behavior?
4. How might a trait theorist describe Robert's behavior?
5. How might a humanistic psychologist, such as Carl Rogers, explain Robert's behavior?

"We have to go now. Robert's façade is beginning to crumble."

Practice and **assess** key social studies skills with **Glencoe Skillbuilder Interactive Workbook CD-ROM, Level 2.**

See the Skills Handbook, page 624, for an explanation of identifying cause-and-effect relationships.

Building Skills

1. *Facade* refers to a false or superficial appearance. In this case, *facade* may refer to Robert's behavior or "act" in this social situation.
2. Answers may suggest that Robert's unconscious motives or desires are surfacing.
3. A behaviorist may propose that certain contingencies of reinforcement or expectations are influencing Robert's behavior.
4. A trait theorist would identify the traits that make up Robert's behavior, such as seriousness and tenseness, and study Robert's behavior and personality across different situations.
5. Carl Rogers would study Robert's struggle and his obstacles to becoming a fully functioning individual. He may say that Robert is experiencing a gap between person and self.

GLENCOE TECHNOLOGY

CD-ROM

Glencoe Skillbuilder Interactive Workbook, Level 2

This interactive CD-ROM is designed to reinforce student mastery of essential social studies skills.

Chapter Bonus Test Question

This question may be used for extra credit on the Chapter Assessment.

Answer the following question:

A person steps outside and is struck by a cold wind. The person returns to the house and puts on a coat. Which of Freud's principles is at work? Which personality process was at work?

Answer: reality principle; ego

Technology Activity

Students should be encouraged to compare several personality tests. Remind them that many of these tests would not meet the standards of reliability and validity described in Chapter 13.

Psychology Journal

1. Answers will vary. Remind students that changes in behavior do not indicate changes in personality. The behavioral model would explain differences in terms of reinforcements received or imitation of the behavior of others.
2. Encourage students to make reasoned arguments supporting their choices.

Readings in Psychology

Block Schedule

This activity works well for a block-scheduling framework.

Reinforcing Vocabulary

Review the Reader's Dictionary terms with students to be sure they understand any unfamiliar items.

Background Information

Gordon Allport focused on the obvious elements of personality, not worrying about the unconscious. His early tests of personality traits involved giving people situations and having them select their most likely response. Allport found that people exhibit similar traits in a variety of situations. For example, if a person is generous when he or she encounters a homeless person, he or she is also likely to be generous when inheriting a large sum of money.

Allport used the dictionary to identify a list of personality traits and descriptions. He eventually narrowed his list to 4,500 traits and 200 groups of traits. This list proved too extensive to use for studying personality traits. Researchers like Raymond Cattell narrowed the list to more manageable numbers. Cattell grouped personality traits into 16 trait dimensions. He used these 16 trait dimensions to predict people's behavior in certain situations.

Readings in Psychology

Psychologist Gordon Allport presents the letters of Jenny Gove Masterson (and others) as an intense case study of personality. JennyÕs letters trace a life of frustration and defeat. Between the ages of 58 and 70, Jenny wrote a series of 301 letters to Glenn and Isabel, two young friends. The letters dramatically illustrate her relationship with her son Ross. Jenny tells of her interests, hates, fears, and conflicts. These letters have led many psychologists and students to seek to explain Jenny's behavior and her personality.

Reader's Dictionary

philanderer: one who has many love affairs

enigma: a mystery

LETTERS FROM JENNY

EDITED AND INTERPRETED BY GORDON W. ALLPORT

Friday, April 19/29

Dear Glenn:

I'm afraid that I am quite a nuisance in shoving my affairs on Isabel and you, but when you remember the compact we made that time I was in Chicago, and all your care over me since, you will pardon. You are my only confidant.

My motive in telling you all this is not to gossip, or backbite, but because I know that when *I* drop out Ross will lie to you and make it appear that things were quite different with us. . . .

The chances are that Ross and I are again near the parting of the ways. He has never cared anything at all for me since he adopted, and was adopted by, the old philanderer. It is as well for him to try his luck again in matrimony—he can then take his other wife to visit his "Beloved Mother" his "B.M." as he did the first one, and they can all be happy together.

I have truly a noble son—an honor to his College, his friends, his family. And all for what? Can it be possible all this is merely for the sake of co-habiting with a woman who sells her body to the highest bidder?

Oh! If he would only settle down for 2 or 3 years and get a footing in business and not always belong to the "floating" population. He is not so very old yet altho' he has squandered 10 precious years. What in the world is the matter, Glenn dear?

I am not a charming person—not beautiful—not clever, but what of that? I carried him in my body for 9 mos. was good to him for many years (you know that) altho' he says I wasn't—that it was all *selfishness* on my part—but even granting all that to be so—I am still *his* Mother. Oh! what is it that's so wrong?

Be patient with me—I try you sadly—but I'm *alone,* and it's awful to be in the dark, and be alone.

I sincerely hope you are all well.

Jenny

P.S. *Do not* write to Ross about me. You would mean all right, of course, but Ross would be very angry, and resent it dreadfully. He says you don't "live"—don't know what "life" is—sometimes I think he is a little "off" and might kill me—he resents your having helped me, and my gratitude to Isabel and you.

ADDITIONAL READINGS ABOUT THE TOPIC

Axline, V. (1964). *Dibs in Search of Self.* New York: Ballantine.

Harary, K., & Donahue, E. (1994). *Who Do You Think You Are? Explore Your Many-Sided Self with the Berkeley Personality Profile.* San Francisco: Harper.

Heatherton, T.F., & Weinberger, J.L. (Eds.) (1997). *Can Personality Change?* American Psychological Association.

Wiggins, J.S. (Ed.) (1996). *The Five-Factor Model of Personality: Theoretical Perspectives.* Guilford Press.

Excerpts from a letter written by Ross to Glenn:

April 21, 1929

Your last letter was the one about Mother. I appreciate your interest and your desire to help me that I might help her. And yet, in a word, your letter merely emphasized my own feeling of frustration and futility. I'm afraid there is little one can do, or that I can do, to be a comfort and service of any real or lasting pleasure.

Mother has entrenched herself behind truths, half-truths, and utter fabrications concerning my limitations as the ideal son, and there is no dislodging her. No amount of even demonstrating my presence will change her constant reiteration that I am entirely bad and have cast her off in her old age. . . . Day and night, Mother recites her own good deeds to her family, her friends, her husband, her son, and how each in turn failed to pay her back. . . .

From Isabel [27 years after Jenny's death]

Dear Mr. Editor:

It is now twenty-seven years since Jenny Masterson died. You have asked me to re-read her Letters addressed to Glenn and myself, and in this perspective to make comments and interpretations concerning her tortured life.

Her Letters bring back many memories, but even in the perspective of years I cannot pretend to discover the key to her nature. Our relationship to her was essentially "neutral." We took pains not to become too deeply involved, but we always answered her communications and tried to help her in emergencies.

Her behavior, like the Letters, was intense, dramatic, and sometimes "hard to take." But to us her nature posed a challenge to understanding. What made her so intense, so vivid, so difficult? Even now her communications arouse in me a sense of the enigma of her personality as well as sympathy for her predicament. . . .

So we know that early in her life Jenny showed some of the factors evident in the Letters: her aloneness, her intense individuality and dramatization, her temper and tendency to quarrel. She was a puzzle to her family, and socially a problem long before we knew her. But to me the enigma is *how* she came to be such a problem to herself as well as to others. . . .

This self-defeating formula was with her from early years. At the age of 70 she is "the same only more so.". . .

Analyzing the Reading

1. What personality traits does Jenny display?
2. How does Ross view his mother?
3. **Critical Thinking** Isabel writes that Jenny's personality did not change as she aged, but became more difficult. Do you think that it is possible for a person to change his or her personality? Explain.

Readings in Psychology

Active Reading Strategy

Explain to students that pausing to review during reading improves comprehension. It also gives them an opportunity to revise or update their ideas about the purpose, main idea, and supporting details of the selection.

Psychology Journal

Have students write a letter to a psychologist describing someone whose actions and personality they do not understand. ■

Teacher Tip

Remind students that one goal of psychologists is to influence the behavior of their clients. For a person like Jenny, a clinical or counseling psychologist could help her change her destructive behaviors. Of course, Jenny would first have to desire to make changes in her life.

Answers to Analyzing the Reading

1. Answers will vary. Traits may include anxious, insecure, emotional, self-pitying, irritable, rude, and rigid.
2. He views her as a difficult person whose ideal he cannot live up to. Students may note that Ross feels frustrated because he believes there is little he can do to change how his mother feels and acts toward him. Ross feels that his mother has deluded herself and will not change her perceptions of him.
3. Answers will vary. Most researchers view personality as relatively set by the time we reach adulthood. Encourage students to explain their reasoning by using examples.

Unit 6 Planning Guide

National High School Psychology Standards

The national high school psychology standards identify what students in an introductory high school psychology course should learn. **The material covered in Unit 6 reflects content from two of the five content domains: *Biopsychological* and *Sociocultural.*** To see a chapter-by-chapter correlation to the national standards, refer to the Teacher pages.

Content Domains for National High School Psychology Standards

Use this diagram to review the standards areas that are covered in Unit 6. Standards areas covered in this unit are highlighted in red in the diagram.

Methods
- Introduction and Research Methods

Sociocultural
- Individual Differences
- **Personality and Assessment**
- **Psychological Disorders**
- **Treatment of Psychological Disorders**
- Social and Cultural Dimensions of Behavior

Developmental
- Lifespan Development

Cognitive
- Learning
- Memory
- Thinking and Language
- States of Consciousness

Biopsychological
- Biological Bases of Behavior
- Sensation and Perception
- Motivation and Emotion
- **Stress, Coping, and Health**

BIBLIOGRAPHY

Readings for the Student

Frank, A.W. (2002). *At the Will of the Body: Reflections on Illness.* Boston: Houghton Mifflin.

Green, H. (1984). *I Never Promised You a Rose Garden.* New York: New American Library.

Lazarus, R.S. (2006). *Stress and Emotion: A New Synthesis.* New York: Springer.

Sheehan, S. (1983). *Is There No Place on Earth for Me?* Boston: Houghton Mifflin.

Readings for the Teacher

Bergin, A., & Garfield, S. (2003). *Handbook of Psychotherapy and Behavior Change.* New York: John Wiley & Sons.

Frances, A., & Ross, R. (2001). *DSM-IV-TR Case Studies: A Clinical Guide to Differential Diagnosis.* Washington, DC: American Psychiatric Association.

Meyer, R.G. (2005). *Case Studies in Abnormal Behavior.* New York: Allyn & Bacon.

Multimedia Resources

Videocassette. *Handling Stress Today and Tomorrow* (30 minutes). A Cambridge Educational Production. This video helps students identify situations that cause stress and how to manage pressure.

Videocassette. *Multiple Personalities* (30 minutes). Ambrose Video. This video explores dissociative identity disorder and how child abuse causes it.

Unit 6 Resource Manager

Note: The following materials may be used when teaching Unit 6. Chapter level support materials can be found on the chapter resource pages.

GLENCOE'S ASSESSMENT ADVANTAGE

Use the following tools to easily assess student learning in a variety of ways:

- Authentic Assessment with Rubrics
- Section Quizzes, Chapter Tests, and Unit Tests
- glencoe.com
- SAT/SAT II Test Practice
- *ExamView® Assessment Suite* CD-ROM

APPLICATIONS AND HANDS-ON

Psychology Lab Activity 6

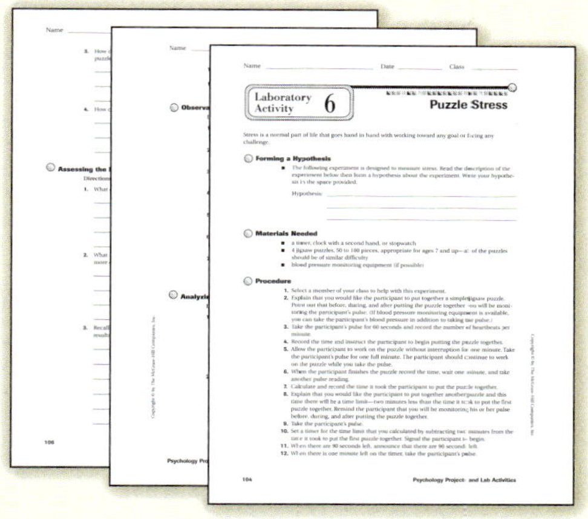

ASSESSMENT

GLENCOE'S ASSESSMENT ADVANTAGE

Unit 6 Test, Form A

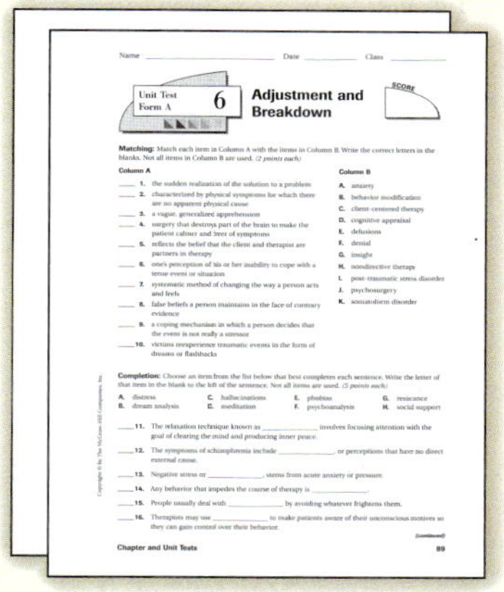

Unit 6 Test, Form B

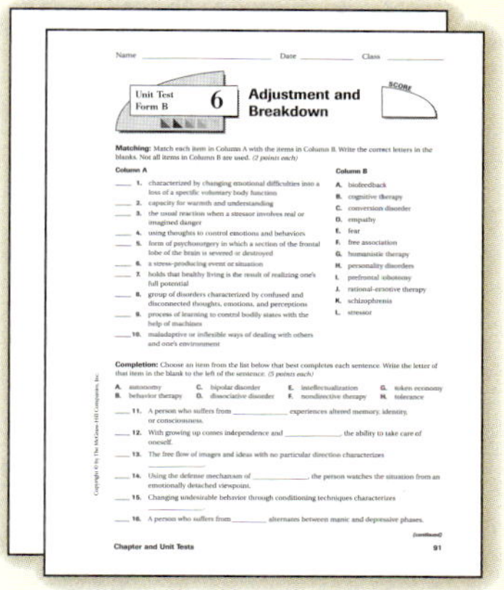

PRESENTATION Plus!

Use Glencoe's ***Presentation Plus!*** multimedia teacher tool to easily present dynamic lessons that visually excite your students. Using Microsoft PowerPoint® you can customize the presentations to create your own personalized lessons.

Introducing
UNIT 6

Unit Overview

This unit explores mental health, adjustment, and breakdown. It introduces several aspects of physical and psychological health. **Chapter 15** investigates the sources of stress, reactions to stress, and ways to cope with stress. **Chapter 16** explores how normal behavior becomes abnormal. Common types of psychological disorders are also discussed. **Chapter 17** discusses the various therapies available to treat psychological disorders.

Unit Objectives

After studying this unit, students will be able to:

1. Identify the various sources of stress.
2. Define psychological disorders.
3. Describe psychotherapy and its goals.

UNIT 6

Adjustment and Breakdown

Contents

Theater masks

EXTRA CREDIT PROJECT

Writing a Dialogue As students read the unit, ask them to explore the stresses that are common at different ages. For example, they could choose to look at the stresses of being newly married or they could look at the elderly and the stress of having one's spouse die. For the situation selected, have students consider the components and the likely causes of stress. Then have students write a dialogue between a client and a therapist on their first meeting. Tell them to begin the dialogue by having the client describe what has brought him or her to see the therapist. Also, tell them to end the dialogue by having the therapist describe types of therapy that may be helpful to the person.

Why It's Important

How are you supposed to live successfully day to day? One way to do so is by adjusting to the society in which you live. Whether you live in the city or country, you must adapt to your environment and the challenges it presents. Psychologists who study adjustment—the process of adapting to and actively shaping one's environment—try to understand why some people handle the experiences of life while others fail.

Psychology Fair Suggestion Box

Encourage students to get involved with a psychology fair. Here are some project suggestions for **Unit 6—Adjustment and Breakdown:**

- Explore coping mechanisms in dealing with stress.
- Research schizophrenia or a mood disorder.
- Describe one of the approaches to therapy.

Refer to ***Psychology Projects and Lab Activities*** in the TCR for help with organizing a psychology fair.

PSYCHOLOGY *Online*

Visit glencoe.com, the *Understanding Psychology* Web site, for Chapter Overviews, Student Web Activities, Interactive Puzzles, and Self-Check Quizzes for every chapter of the text.

PORTFOLIO PROJECT

Creating a Display Ask students to select one of the psychological disorders discussed in Chapter 16. During the study of this unit, have students create a display that could be used in a mental health clinic to inform people about the nature of the disorder, its causes and possible treatment options. The display should be both informative and visually appealing. Provide time for students to work on their displays throughout the study of Unit 6. **BLOCK SCHEDULING**

Chapter 15 Resource Guide

SECTION RESOURCES

Daily Objectives	Reproducible Resources	Multimedia Resources
Section 1 **Sources of Stress** Explain how stress results from our perceptions of demands placed upon us and our evaluations of situations we encounter.	Guided Reading Activity 15–1 Vocabulary Activity 15–1 Section Quiz 15–1	Daily Focus Transparency 15–1 *ExamView® Assessment Suite* CD-ROM Presentation Plus! Software
Section 2 **Reactions to Stress** Describe the beneficial and harmful reactions people have to stress.	Guided Reading Activity 15–2 Vocabulary Activity 15–2 Section Quiz 15–2	Daily Focus Transparency 15–2 Vocabulary PuzzleMaker CD-ROM *ExamView® Assessment Suite* CD-ROM Presentation Plus! Software
Section 3 **Coping with Stress** Explore the defensive and active coping strategies that people use to deal with stress.	Guided Reading Activity 15–3 Vocabulary Activity 15–3 Section Quiz 15–3	Daily Focus Transparency 15–3 Vocabulary PuzzleMaker CD-ROM *ExamView® Assessment Suite* CD-ROM Presentation Plus! Software
Section 4 **Stress in Your Life** Describe how college and work can lead to stress.	Guided Reading Activity 15–4 Vocabulary Activity 15–4 Section Quiz 15–4	Daily Focus Transparency 15–4 *ExamView® Assessment Suite* CD-ROM Presentation Plus! Software

Blackline Master CD-ROM Transparency

Block Schedule

Activities that are particularly suited for use within the block-scheduling framework are identified throughout this chapter by the following designation: **BLOCK SCHEDULING**

KEY TO ABILITY LEVELS

Teaching strategies have been coded for varying learning styles and abilities.

- **L1 BASIC** activities for all students
- **L2 AVERAGE** activities for average to above-average students
- **L3 CHALLENGING** activities for above-average students
- **ELL ENGLISH LANGUAGE LEARNER** activities

Chapter 15 Resource Guide

Timesaving Tools

TeacherWorks™ All-In-One Planner and Resource Center

- **Interactive Teacher Edition** Access your Teacher Wraparound Edition and your classroom resources with a few easy clicks.
- **Interactive Lesson Planner** Planning has never been easier! Organize your week, month, semester, or year with all the lesson helps you need to make teaching creative, timely, and relevant.

Use Glencoe's **Presentation Plus!** multimedia teacher tool to easily present dynamic lessons that visually excite your students. Using Microsoft PowerPoint® you can customize the presentations to create your own personalized lessons.

Activity

From the Classroom of...

Dean Hermes
Williston High School
Williston, ND

Is It Possible To Die From Grief?

Ask students the following question: **Is it possible to die from grief? Take a minute to think about it and write your response.**

While students are thinking about the question, have someone planted in the classroom release a blood-chilling scream.

Tell students to forget the original question and write how they reacted to the scream. Ask them to discuss how the sympathetic nervous system reacted and how the parasympathetic nervous system worked to calm them down after the event. Have them relate the experience to the fight-or-flight response. As a class, discuss students' reactions.

Psychology Online

Use our Web site for additional resources. All essential content is covered in the Student Edition.

You and your students can visit glencoe.com, the Web site companion to *Understanding Psychology*. This innovative integration of electronic and print media offers your students a wealth of opportunities. The student text directs students to the Web site for the following options:

- Chapter Overviews
- Student Web Activities
- Self-Check Quizzes

Answers are provided for you in the **Web Activity Lesson Plan**. Additional Web resources and Interactive Puzzles are also available.

Chapter 15 Resource Guide

Note: The following materials may be used when teaching Chapter 15. Section level support materials are shown at point of use in the margins of the Teacher Wraparound Edition.

TEACHING TRANSPARENCIES

Chapter 15
Concept Transparencies

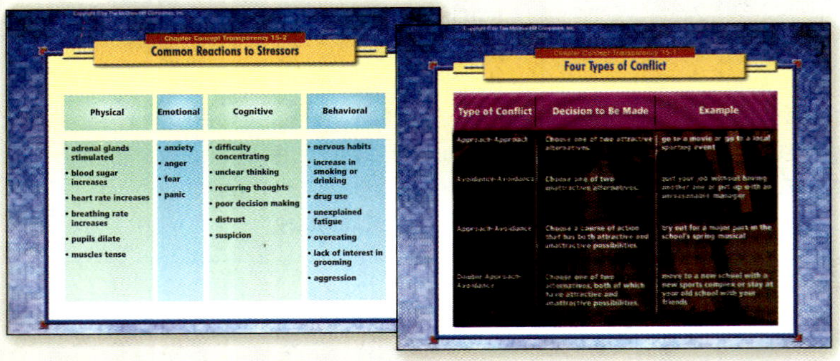

MULTIMEDIA

- **Vocabulary PuzzleMaker CD-ROM**
- ***ExamView® Assessment Suite* CD-ROM**
- **TeacherWorks™ CD-ROM**
- **Glencoe Skillbuilder Interactive Workbook, Level 2**
- **Presentation Plus! Software**

REVIEW AND REINFORCEMENT

Reteaching Activity 15

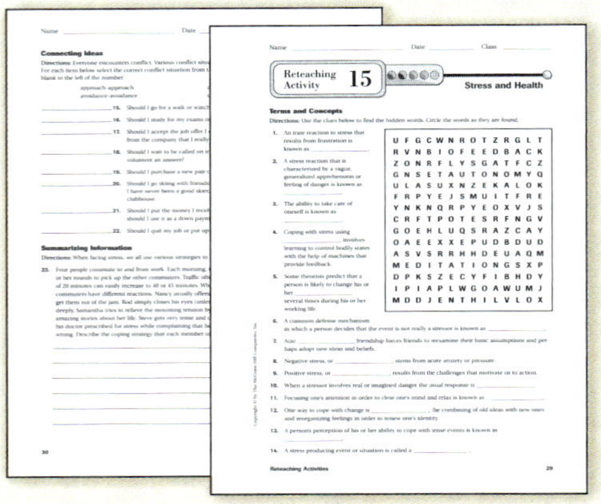

Graphic Organizer Activity 15

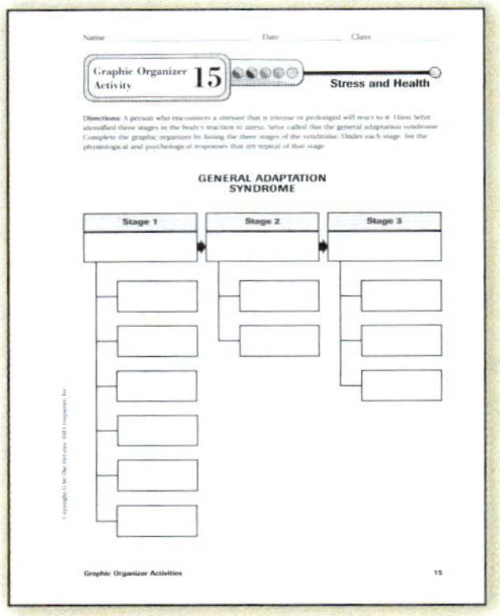

APPLICATION AND HANDS-ON

Psychology Project 15

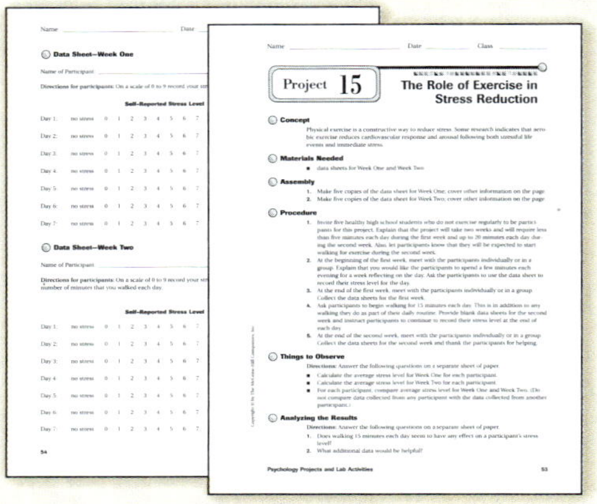

Application Activity 15

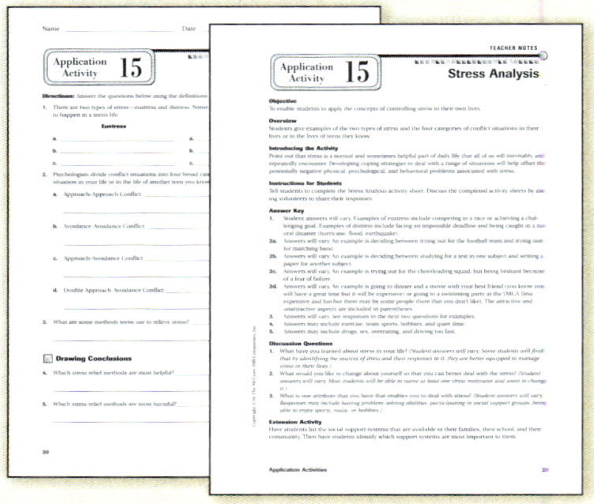

Chapter 15 Resource Guide

GLENCOE'S ASSESSMENT ADVANTAGE

ASSESSMENT

Chapter 15 Test, Form A

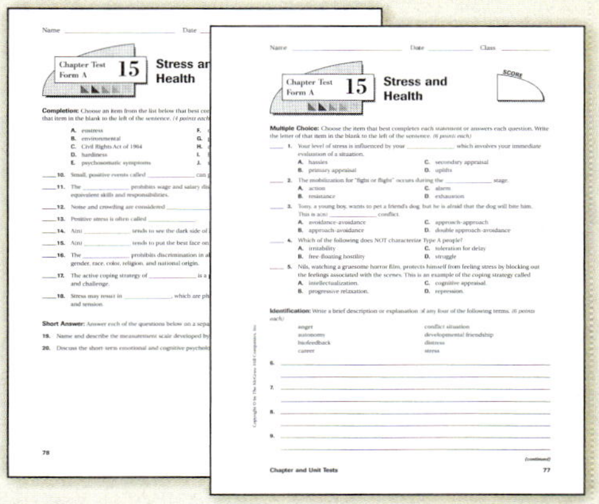

Chapter 15 Test, Form B

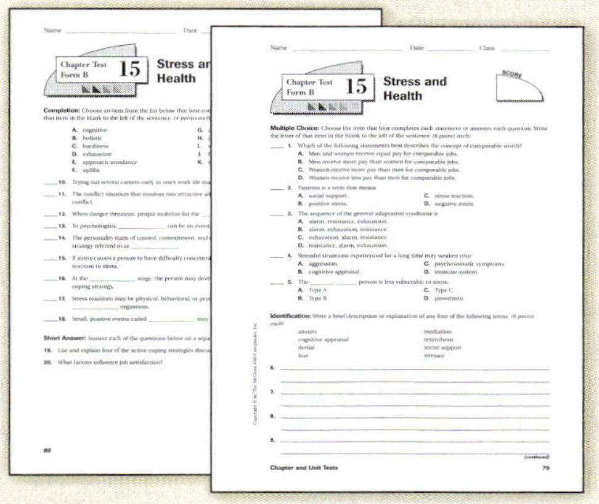

Authentic Assessment Activity 15

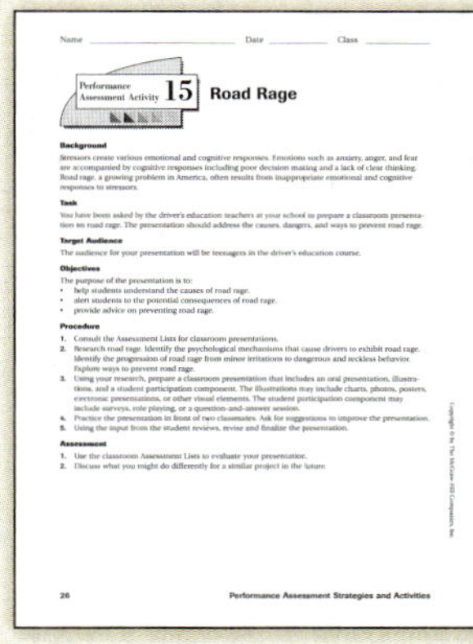

EXTENSION AND ENRICHMENT

Enrichment Activity 15

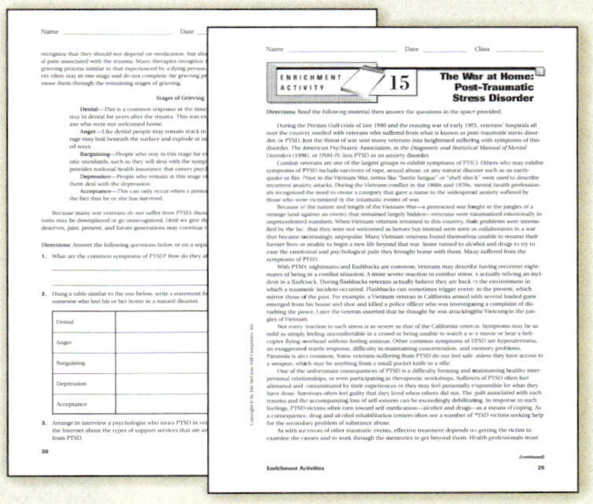

Critical Thinking Skills Activity 15

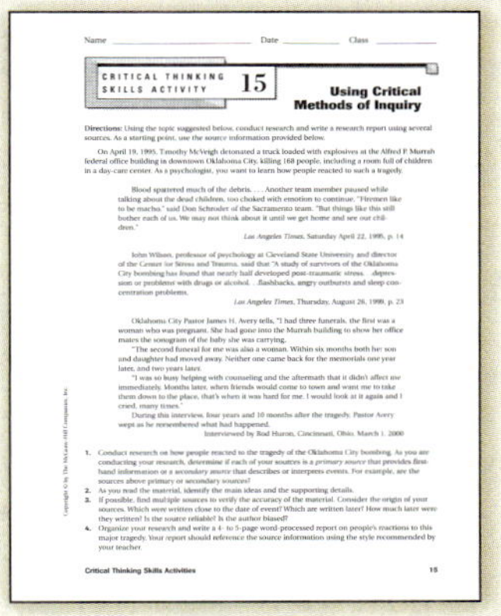

Psychology Reading 15

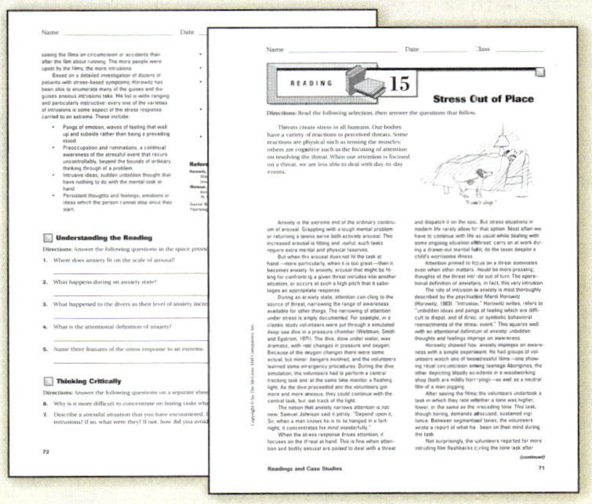

Psychology Case Study 15

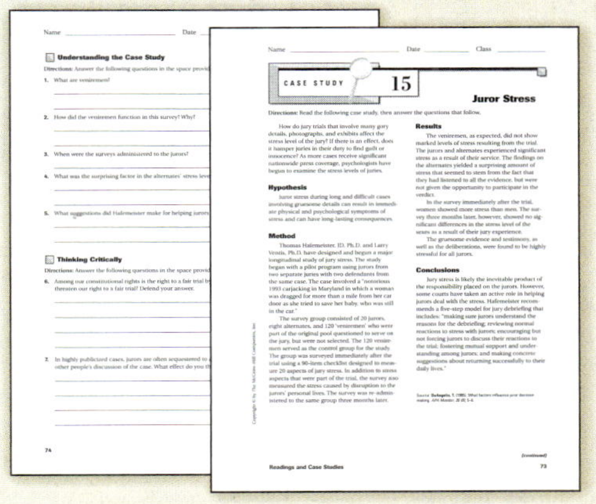

PSYCHOLOGY Online

Visit glencoe.com for a Chapter Overview for **Chapter 15—Stress and Health.**

GLENCOE TECHNOLOGY

For a preview of Chapter 15 content, see MindJogger Checkpoint on **Presentation Plus!**

PSYCHOLOGY JOURNAL

Explain that there are times that everyone feels stressed. As a class, discuss times when many students feel stressed about the same experience.

This journal activity provides the basis for the Psychology Journal activity exercise in the Chapter Assessment. ■

CHAPTER 15

Stress and Health

PSYCHOLOGY JOURNAL

What are the major sources of stress in school? Can you pinpoint specific occasions, times, and events when many students feel stressed? Answer these questions in your journal. ■

PSYCHOLOGY Online

Chapter Overview
Visit the *Understanding Psychology* Web site at glencoe.com and click on **Chapter 15—Chapter Overviews** to preview the chapter.

412

TWO-MINUTE LESSON LAUNCHER

Engage the students in a topic that is sure to get them arguing, such as "Schools could save money by dropping sports." After a short but spirited discussion, ask the students to find their pulses. Ask them to keep track of the beats as you count off 15 seconds. Have them record the number. Turn off the lights and tell students that they are to spend the next minute breathing deeply and focusing on relaxing all their muscles. When the minute has passed, repeat the pulse test. Ask students to compare the rates.

SECTION 1 Sources of Stress

Reader's Guide

Main Idea

Stress results from our perceptions of demands placed upon us and our evaluations of situations we encounter.

Vocabulary

- stress
- stressor
- stress reaction
- distress
- eustress
- conflict situation

Objectives

- Define stress.
- Identify various sources of stress.

EXPLORING PSYCHOLOGY

Mental Tension

Brandon, an ambitious high school junior, fails his final exam in French; he is terrified that his chances of getting into college have been ruined, and a day or two later he develops an unsightly rash. Juanita, Brandon's classmate, learns that her parents cannot afford to pay her tuition for her first year of college; her friends wonder why she has suddenly become so bad-tempered. Angela gets her first leading role in a high school play; while running to call her boyfriend, she realizes that she cannot remember his phone number.

—from *Understanding Psychology*, Richard A. Kasschau, 1995

Brandon, Juanita, and Angela may all suffer from the effects of stress. What exactly is stress? There are many definitions, and even researchers in the field use the term in several ways. To some psychologists, stress is an *event* that produces tension or worry. Others describe it as a person's physical or psychological *response* to such an event. Still other researchers regard stress as a person's *perception* of the event. A slight variation on these ideas is the definition that will be used in this chapter. **Stress** is the anxious or threatening feeling resulting from our appraisal of a situation and our reaction to demands placed upon us.

stress: a person's reaction to his or her inability to cope with a certain tense event or situation

SECTION RESOURCES

Reproducible Masters

- Guided Reading Activity 15–1
- Vocabulary Activity 15–1
- Section Quiz 15–1

Transparencies

- Daily Focus Transparency 15–1

Multimedia

- *ExamView® Assessment Suite* CD-ROM
- Presentation Plus! Software

1 FOCUS

Section Objectives

1. Define stress.
2. Identify various sources of stress.

BELLRINGER
Motivational Activity

Project Daily Focus Transparency 15–1 and have students answer the questions.

Available as blackline master

Daily Focus Transparency 15–1

Reader's Guide

Use the Reader's Guide to introduce concepts and vocabulary.

Exploring Psychology

Ask students to read the **Exploring Psychology** feature and then discuss the following question: **How can stress affect us physically, mentally, and emotionally?**

Vocabulary Precheck

Have students read the Glossary definition of *stress*. Then have them write their best guesses at the meanings of the other terms in this section. Students should look up the remaining words and compare the Glossary definition with their own definition.

2 TEACH

L1 Sources of Stress Ask students to write down on a sheet of paper five common stressors in their daily lives. Tell them not to put their names on the papers. Collect the lists and randomly record some of the stressors on the board. **Ask:** **What do you consider to be the *most* serious stressful events or situations? Why?**

Guided Reading Activity 15–1

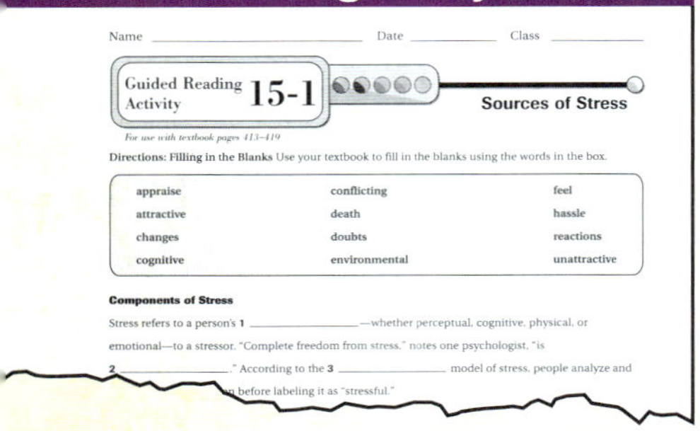
Name ____ Date ____ Class ____

Guided Reading Activity 15-1 — Sources of Stress

For use with textbook pages 413–419

Directions: Filling in the Blanks Use your textbook to fill in the blanks using the words in the box.

appraise	conflicting	feel
attractive	death	hassle
changes	doubts	reactions
cognitive	environmental	unattractive

Components of Stress

Stress refers to a person's **1** ____—whether perceptual, cognitive, physical, or emotional—to a stressor. "Complete freedom from stress," notes one psychologist, "is **2** ____." According to the **3** ____ model of stress, people analyze and ... before labeling it as "stressful."

Figure 15.1

Caption Answer a person's appraisal of a situation and that person's reactions to the demands placed upon him or her

stressor: a stress-producing event or situation

stress reaction: the body's response to a stressor

distress: stress that stems from acute anxiety or pressure

eustress: positive stress, which results from motivating strivings and challenges

conflict situation: when a person must choose between two or more options that tend to result from opposing motives

COMPONENTS OF STRESS

To refer to the stress-producing event or situation, we shall use the term **stressor.** It is important to note that an event that is a stressor for one person may not be for another. For example, traveling in an airplane may be a stressor for someone who has never flown but not for a flight attendant. Stress, then, will be used to refer to a person's reactions—whether perceptual, cognitive, physical, or emotional—to a stressor. To discuss the body's observable response to a stressor, we shall use the term **stress reaction.**

Many people think of stress only as a condition to be avoided. Canadian researcher Hans Selye (1907–1982), however, distinguished between two types of stress. Negative stress, or **distress,** stems from acute anxiety or pressure and can take a harsh toll on the mind and body. Positive stress, or **eustress,** results from the strivings and challenges that are the spice of life (Selye & Cherry, 1978; Selye, 1982).

Stress is a normal, even essential, part of life that goes hand in hand with working toward any goal or facing any challenge. In fact, as athletes gearing up for a game or students cramming for an exam can testify, stress can spur us on to greater effectiveness and achievement in some situations. In addition, whether we like it or not, we cannot escape stress; "Complete freedom from stress," notes one psychologist (Selye, 1974), "is death." We can, however, learn to cope with stress so that it makes our lives interesting without overwhelming us.

There is another component of stress. Richard Lazarus (1993) believes that how a person perceives and evaluates an event makes a difference. This is called the cognitive model of stress. People analyze and then evaluate a situation before it is labeled as stressful. For example, maybe you have accidentally cut your finger and did not realize it at the time. Only when you looked at the cut did you evaluate the situation as dangerous.

Figure 15.1 Suffering From Stress

Most of us have experienced a headache, upset stomach, muscle tension, or sleeplessness as a result of feeling stressed. ***What causes stress?***

CONFLICT SITUATIONS

In our daily lives, we often have to evaluate situations and then make difficult decisions between two or more options—for example, going to a movie with friends or staying home to study for tomorrow's exam. These alternatives tend to result from conflicting motives—say, the desire to socialize versus the desire to do well in school—and they are major sources of stress. These choices create **conflict situations** (Miller, 1944), and they fall into four broad categories (see Figure 15.2).

In an *approach-approach conflict,* the individual must choose between *two attractive alternatives.* For example, a high school senior has been accepted at two excellent colleges, and she must decide which

COOPERATIVE LEARNING ACTIVITY

Conflict Charts Organize the class into small groups. Assign each group a stressful situation that teens may encounter. Examples may include getting their first part-time job, learning to drive, quitting a job, or having their best friend move to a different state. Ask each group to create a chart showing how the situation may affect the following aspects of their lives: personal finances, relationship with parents, relationships with siblings, relationships with friends, involvement in activities, and grades in school. **BLOCK SCHEDULING**

Figure 15.2 Types of Conflict Situations

Conflict situations cause stress because you must give up something you want to get or face something you wish to avoid. ***How is the double approach-avoidance conflict different from the approach-avoidance conflict?***

Approach-Approach	Avoidance-Avoidance	Approach-Avoidance	Double Approach-Avoidance
You must choose between two attractive options.	You must choose between two disagreeable options.	You find yourself in a situation that has both enjoyable and disagreeable consequences.	You must choose between multiple options, each of which has pleasurable and disagreeable aspects.
Do I want to go to the concert or ballgame on Saturday?	Should I stay up all night studying for my physics or math final?	Should I ask him to go to the party with me? (He may say yes, or he may say no.)	Should I stay home and wait for my girlfriend to call me, or should I just go out with my friends?

one to attend. Such a "conflict" is generally easy to resolve. The student in this situation will find some reason to attend one college rather than the other—perhaps better climate or more courses in her intended major field. An approach-approach conflict is a conflict in name only. It does not produce a great deal of stress, because both choices are satisfying.

An *avoidance-avoidance conflict* occurs when an individual confronts *two unattractive alternatives*. Consider the case of a college graduate unable to find a job after many months of searching. She is finally offered a position that has no future and does not pay well. Should she accept it, or should she continue to look for something better? Either course of action will be frustrating, and there is usually a high level of indecision and stress. The young woman in this example may decide that one option is the "lesser of two evils," or she may try to escape the decision—for instance, by registering with a temporary-employment agency until she finds a more satisfactory job.

An individual who wants to do something but has fears or doubts or is repulsed by it at the same time is experiencing an *approach-avoidance conflict*. For example, a man wants to ask for a raise, but he is afraid he will be fired if he does. In cases like this, the degree of stress depends on the intensity of the desire or of the perceived threat. Resolution of this type of conflict often is very difficult and depends generally on the person's finding added reasons to choose one alternative over the other. The man in this example may learn that his boss thinks his work has been excellent; therefore, he feels there is little risk of being fired if he asks for more money.

Probably the most common conflict situation is a *double approach-avoidance conflict* in which the individual must choose between *two or more alternatives, each of which has attractive and unattractive aspects*. To use a simple illustration, a young woman working in Chicago cannot decide

Figure 15.2

Visual Instruction Ask students to provide their own examples of each type of conflict.

Caption Answer Double approach-avoidance involves choosing between two or more alternatives, each of which have pleasant and unpleasant aspects. An approach-avoidance situation has both pleasant and unpleasant options.

TEACHER Tip

Share with students the following sayings that describe conflict situations and have students identify the type of conflict.

1. Six of one, half dozen of the other.
2. Caught between a rock and a hard place.
3. You can't have your cake and eat it too.

FYI

Experts recommend several techniques that allow supervisors to create positive stress (eustress) in the workplace. Among the recommendations are to match the employee to the task, give authority and responsibility in equal measure, make certain the task is clearly understood, and provide regular reviews of employees' progress.

MEETING SPECIAL NEEDS

Learning Style: Logical/Mathematical Explain to students the difference between distress and eustress. Then ask them to list as many items as possible that create distress or eustress in their lives. Ask students to categorize the types of stress using the following categories: social stressors, environmental stressors, biological stressors, and psychological stressors. Then have students write a paragraph summarizing their lists. **L2** **BLOCK SCHEDULING**

Refer to ***Inclusion for the High School Social Studies Classroom Strategies and Activities*** in the TCR for strategies for students with different learning styles.

PSYCHOLOGY JOURNAL

Ask students to think of a stressful event that occurred in their lives within the last week. Have them write a paragraph describing their primary and secondary appraisals of the situation. ■

Vocabulary Activity 15–1

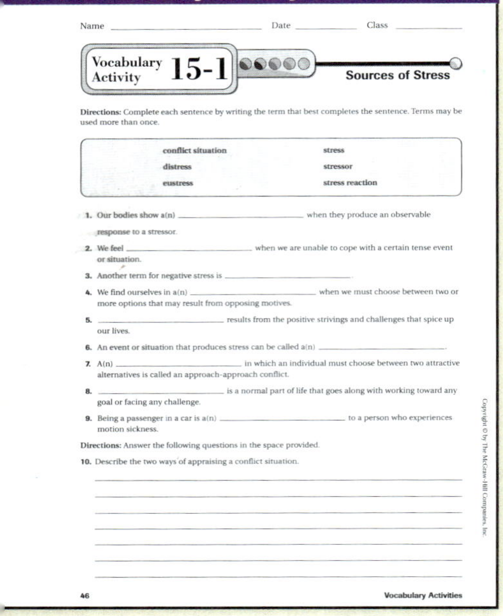

Name ____________ Date ________ Class ________

Vocabulary Activity 15-1 Sources of Stress

Directions: Complete each sentence by writing the term that best completes the sentence. Terms may be used more than once.

conflict situation	stress
distress	stressor
eustress	stress reaction

1. Our bodies show a(n) ____________ when they produce an observable response to a stressor.
2. We feel ____________ when we are unable to cope with a certain tense event or situation.
3. Another term for negative stress is ____________.
4. We find ourselves in a(n) ____________ when we must choose between two or more options that may result from opposing motives.
5. ____________ results from the positive strivings and challenges that spice up our lives.
6. An event or situation that produces stress can be called a(n) ____________.
7. A(n) ____________ in which an individual must choose between two attractive alternatives is called an approach-approach conflict.
8. ____________ is a normal part of life that goes along with working toward any goal or facing any challenge.
9. Being a passenger in a car is a(n) ____________ to a person who experiences motion sickness.

Directions: Answer the following questions in the space provided.

10. Describe the two ways of appraising a conflict situation.

46 **Vocabulary Activities**

Reading Check Answer

A primary appraisal is our immediate evaluation of a situation. A secondary appraisal involves our decision on how to deal with a potentially stressful situation.

whether to spend her vacation in Paris or at her parents' home in North Carolina. She has never been to Paris, but the airfare and hotel bills will be more than she can really afford. Visiting her parents will be inexpensive and relaxing but not very exciting. As in an approach-avoidance conflict, the degree of stress generated depends on the intensity of the attractions and repulsions.

Appraising a Situation

Why is it that some people view a situation, such as looking for a parking space, as stressful while others do not? The level of stress you feel depends on how you appraise the situation. *Primary appraisal* refers to our immediate evaluation of a situation. For instance, can we meet the demands of this situation? Does this situation present us with more challenges than we think we can handle? There are three ways you can appraise a situation—as irrelevant, positive, or negative. For example, if your teacher suddenly announces a pop quiz, you may feel okay about the situation. You think you know the material, and your teacher does not give difficult quizzes. You may look forward to pop quizzes and feel positive about the situation because you know the material on the quiz and are assured of a good grade. You may also evaluate the situation as a negative one—you have not looked at your notes in days. In this last example, you feel stressed.

A *secondary appraisal* involves deciding how to deal with a potentially stressful situation. At this point an individual appraises the situation and then decides on a coping strategy. We will discuss coping strategies in Section 3.

Reading Check What is the difference between a primary and secondary appraisal?

ENVIRONMENTAL STRESSORS

Environmental conditions such as noise may cause stress on the job, and these factors can have similar effects on the public at large. In fact, surveys have shown that Americans regard noise as one of the foremost irritants in their lives. Noise is particularly aggravating when it is loud, irregular, or uncontrollable. Constant exposure to unpleasant noise levels can lead to hearing loss and can interfere with learning. One study found that third and fourth graders in the flight path of a major airport showed significant increases in blood pressure and stress hormones, such as cortisol, compared to those without noise (Evans et al, 1998). People exposed to excessive noise at work have reported more headaches, nausea, and moodiness than others.

It was long assumed that crowding was an environmental stressor. Indeed, most people dislike certain high-density situations and can feel stress when other people get too close. Studies on crowding have found a relationship between high-rise apartments with many crowded people and aggression. Crowding itself,

Did You Know?

Personal Space The subway system in Tokyo hires people to push more people onto the subways during rush hours. It is an accepted part of Japanese culture to be able to function effectively within a small personal space. People in Middle Eastern societies also tend to have markedly small personal spaces compared to North Americans. As a result, they stand much closer in a conversation than is comfortable for most natives of the United States or Canada.

CRITICAL THINKING ACTIVITY

Making Comparisons Tell students that all the items on the Social Readjustment Rating Scale have two things in common. They all involve stress, and they also involve change of some sort. Ask the students to consider the values of the numbers on the SRS scale. How were the numbers compiled? *(They are averages.)* Does each life event have the same stress level for every person? *(No, each event affects people in varying degrees.)* What accounts for these differences? *(Each person has slightly different experiences and perceptions.)* Ask students to describe how expectation (outlook) affects the intensity of life events. **Ask: In your experience, are people who dislike change better equipped to cope with stress than people who claim to welcome change in their lives?** Assign students to write an essay expressing their views. **L2**

Figure 15.3 The Social Readjustment Rating Scale

Rank	Life Event	Mean Value	Rank	Life Event	Mean Value
1	Death of spouse	100	23	Son or daughter leaving home	29
2	Divorce	73	24	Trouble with in-laws	29
3	Marital separation	65	25	Outstanding personal achievement	28
4	Jail term	63	26	Spouse begin or stop work	26
5	Death of close family member	63	27	Begin or end school	26
6	Personal injury or illness	53	28	Change in living conditions	25
7	Marriage	50	29	Revision of personal habits	24
8	Fired at work	47	30	Trouble with boss	23
9	Marital reconciliation	45	31	Change in work hours or conditions	20
10	Retirement	45	32	Change in residence	20
11	Change in health of family member	44	33	Change in schools	20
12	Pregnancy	40	34	Change in recreation	19
13	Sex difficulties	39	35	Change in church activities	19
14	Gain of new family member	39	36	Change in social activities	18
15	Business readjustment	39	37	Mortgage or loans less than $10,000	17
16	Change in financial state	38	38	Change in sleeping habits	16
17	Death of close friend	37	39	Change in number of family get-togethers	15
18	Change to different line of work	36	40	Change in eating habits	15
19	Change in number of arguments with spouse	35	41	Vacation	13
20	Mortgage over $10,000	31	42	Christmas	12
21	Foreclosure of mortgage or loan	30	43	Minor violations of the law	11
22	Change in responsibilities at work	29			

Reprinted with permission from T.H. Holmes and R.H. Rahe, "The Social Readjustment Rating Scale," *Journal of Psychosomatic Research*, 1967, Table 3, p. 216. © 1967, Pergamon Press Ltd.

The SRRS lists 43 items that require individuals to make the most changes in their lives. Each number (mean value) refers to the expected impact that event would have on one's life. To obtain your score, add the numbers associated with each event you experienced in the past year. The total number reflects how much life change you have experienced. ***Which of the life events have the greatest impact on an individual?***

however, is not the problem. The problems occur not when you are crowded but when you *feel* crowded (Taylor, 1991).

Jonathan Freedman (1975) has concluded that the effects of crowding depend on the situation. If the situation is pleasant, crowding makes people feel better; if the situation is unpleasant, crowding makes them feel worse. In other words, being packed together *intensifies* people's reactions, but it does not *create* them.

Life Changes and Stress

Major life changes—marriage, serious illness, a new job, moving away, and a death in the family—are important sources of stress. Common to most of these events is the separation of an individual from familiar friends,

Figure 15.3

Visual Instruction Have students identify all the life events listed in the table that have occurred in their lives in the past three months. Then have them add up their scores. Ask students if they think the rating scale is valid.

Caption Answer death of a spouse

PSYCHOLOGY Update

Stress of Caregiving A recent study published in the *Journal of the American Medical Association* found that providing long-term care for a spouse creates stress and reduces the longevity of the caregiver. Researchers studied spouses between the ages of 66 and 96. About 48 percent of the study group reported that they provided extensive care to their spouse. The study found that spouses who were providing care and experiencing stress had mortality risks that were 63 percent higher than spouses who were not caregivers. The study concluded that support systems for caregivers are needed.

PSYCHOLOGY LAB EXPERIMENT

Measuring Risk for Stress Students will develop a survey to measure an individual's risk for stress. Have students work in small groups to develop a brief survey of seven to ten items that can help determine if someone is at risk for stress. Items may include such things as: "Do you get frustrated easily?" "Do you often feel left out or alone?" Have the group give the test to 25 participants and chart the results. Each group should share its results with the class. Remind the students that during group work they will sometimes be leaders and other times followers, but at all times they should work to create a supportive group climate. **L2**

Quick Lab

Purpose Students will identify stressful events in the lives of teens.

Process Skills Understanding cause and effect

Teaching Strategies

- Discuss the cause-and-effect relationships between stress and physical health.

Analysis

1. Answers will depend on the input from the participants.
2. Answers will vary. Ask students to analyze and compare their results to the SRRS developed by Holmes and Rahe.

3 ASSESS

Assign Section 1 Assessment as homework or as an in-class activity.

Section Quiz 15–1

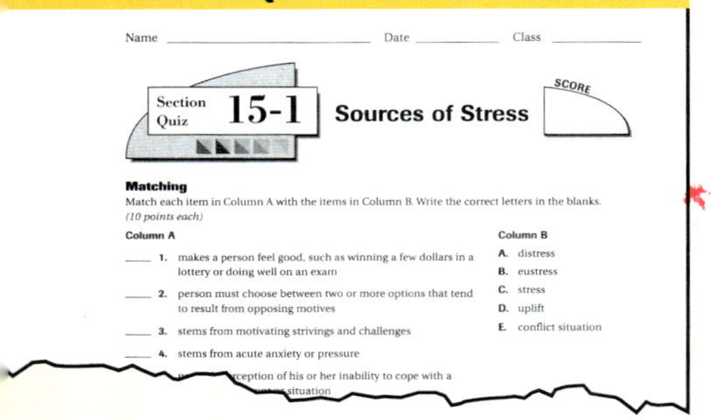
Name ______ Date ______ Class ______

Section Quiz 15-1 **Sources of Stress** SCORE

Matching
Match each item in Column A with the items in Column B. Write the correct letters in the blanks. *(10 points each)*

Column A
____ 1. makes a person feel good, such as winning a few dollars in a lottery or doing well on an exam
____ 2. person must choose between two or more options that tend to result from opposing motives
____ 3. stems from motivating strivings and challenges
____ 4. stems from acute anxiety or pressure

Column B
A. distress
B. eustress
C. stress
D. uplift
E. conflict situation

Reteach

Organize students into groups of four. Have each group list and describe examples of the four conflict situations. Have groups trade their examples and identify the conflict situations described.

Quick Lab

What stresses teenagers?

The SRRS lists events considered stressful for adults. Assume your job is to develop a similar scale for teenagers. In what ways would your scale be different?

Procedure

1. First, develop a list of life events that you deem stressful to teenagers and rank them from 1 to 20, with 20 being the most stressful. Assign each event a value based on how much adjustment the event requires.
2. Provide a copy of your list to several friends and ask them to circle the events that they have experienced in the past year.
3. Ask each person to indicate any illnesses they have had in the past year.

Analysis

1. For each person, add up the values for the events they have circled. Note the illnesses they recorded.
2. Does your rating scale show any relationship between stressful events that teenagers face and illnesses they experience? Explain.

See the Skills Handbook, page 622, for an explanation of designing an experiment.

relations, or colleagues. Even marriage—a positive change—may involve breaking free from many longstanding ties.

Many stress researchers have concentrated on these life changes to determine how much stress they are likely to cause. Two of the foremost life-change researchers are Thomas H. Holmes and Richard H. Rahe (1967), who developed a scale to measure the effects of 43 common events, ranging from the death of a spouse to going on a vacation. Holmes and Rahe asked a cross section of the population to rate each of these events on a scale of 1 to 100, with marriage assigned a value of 50, on the basis of how much adjustment the event required. The figures they obtained form the basis of their Social Readjustment Rating Scale (SRRS), which is shown in Figure 15.3. Please note that the SRRS was created in 1967 using males. It is also important to note that one life change can trigger others, thus greatly increasing the level of stress. Marriage, for example, may be accompanied by a change in financial status, a change in living conditions, and a change in residence—collectively much more stressful than any one source listed in Figure 15.3.

Rahe (1975) administered this scale to thousands of naval officers and enlisted men and found that the higher a man's score, the more likely he was to become physically ill. Men with scores below 150 tended to remain healthy, while about 70 percent of those with scores over 300 became sick. There are problems, however. Some of the items on the SRRS may result from illness, rather than cause it (Brett et al., 1990). For air traffic controllers, higher traffic volume and lower visual clarity lead to increased mood and health complaints (Repetti, 1993). Several studies suggest there is only a small relationship between stressful life events and illness (Brett et al., 1990). The scale also fails to measure stress caused by ongoing situations such as racism, poverty, and ignored daily hassles.

Hassles

In addition to the impact that major stressful events such as a divorce or a death in the family can have, psychologists have studied the effects that relatively minor, day-to-day stressors have on health. These more common stressors are called *hassles.* Examples of hassles include losing your car keys, being caught in a crowded elevator with a smoker, or being late for work or school because you were stuck in traffic (see Figure 15.4). Research has found a connection between hassles and health problems. It may be that hassles gradually weaken the body's

INTERDISCIPLINARY CONNECTIONS ACTIVITY

The Arts Have students write a short story, poem, or song developed around one or more of the life changes listed in the Holmes-Rahe Social Readjustment Rating Scale. Tell students that they should focus on the themes of *change* and *readjustment.* Their works should depict the various kinds of stress reactions that are involved in major life events. Ask for volunteers to read or perform their finished work in class. If your school has a literary magazine, suggest that students submit their works for publication. **L2**

defense system, making it harder to fight off potential health problems.

It has also been suggested that small, positive events, called *uplifts*, can protect against stress. Uplifts are things that make a person feel good, such as winning a tough chess match, going out to lunch with a good friend, or doing well on a semester exam. Some psychologists claim that uplifts can have the opposite effect of hassles; they can reduce stress and protect a person's health.

Figure 15.4 Some Daily Hassles

We face frustrations every day—these are the daily hassles of life. ***How can we combat the effects of hassles?***

- Household duties (cleaning, cooking, shopping)
- Concerns about health
- Time pressures (not enough time to get something done)
- Environmental hassles (noise, pollution, crime)
- Financial hassles (paying bills, saving for the future)
- Worries about your job
- Concerns about your future
- Inner hassles (feelings of low self-esteem or loneliness)

Source: Lazarus et al., 1985.

Every one of us faces many daily hassles—traffic, arguments, car trouble, and so on. Could it be that the primary effects of stress are the accumulation of little things that just constantly seem to hassle us (Weinberger, Hiner, & Tierney, 1987)? Seventy-five married couples recorded their everyday hassles, and it turned out that those with more hassles had significantly more health problems such as sore throats and headaches, which they experienced later (DeLongis, Folkman, & Lazarus, 1988).

SECTION 1 Assessment

1. **Review the Vocabulary** What is the difference between eustress and distress? Should stress always be avoided? Explain.
2. **Visualize the Main Idea** Use a chart similar to the one below to list examples of the different conflict situations.

Conflict Situation	Example
Approach-approach conflict	

3. **Recall Information** Why are life changes sources of stress? What are other sources of stress?
4. **Think Critically** Many people have criticized the SRRS. Can you think of a better way to measure stress? Explain.
5. **Application Activity** Select a day and keep a log of your daily hassles and uplifts. At the end of the day analyze your general mood—were you in a bad or good mood? Did your hassles outnumber your uplifts? Briefly outline a strategy by which you pay more attention to uplifts and brighten your mood.

Figure 15.4

Visual Instruction Remind students that hassles can result in feelings of tension, nervousness, worry, and sadness.

Caption Answer by making sure we have uplifts, or small positive events, in our lives

Enrich

Ask students to explore how personal space variations among cultures can create stress. Have them write a paragraph that expresses how a person who is used to much personal space feels when the space is invaded. Then ask them to write a paragraph from the point of view of the person who is used to little personal space.

4 CLOSE

Place the following headings on the board: *Environmental Stressors, Life Change Stressors,* and *Hassles.* Have students list stressful events that could be classified under each heading. Discuss any disagreements between classifications.

SECTION 1 Assessment Answers

1. Distress results from acute anxiety or pressure. Eustress is positive stress that motivates and challenges us. No; stress is a necessary ingredient in life. It helps us work toward a goal or face a challenge.
2. Examples will vary. The most difficult situations to describe are approach-avoidance and double approach-avoidance.
3. Life changes usually involve the separation of an individual from familiar friends and family. Breaking these longstanding and comfortable ties often causes stress. Environmental conditions such as noise and crowding can also cause stress.
4. Students' answers will vary. Biophysiological measurements would be more quantifiable and provide more precise measures.
5. Students' answers will vary. Plans to focus on uplifts may involve keeping a "Good News" list on which a person records all the uplifts. The person can review the list throughout the day.

CHAPTER 15
Section 2, pages 420–429

1 FOCUS

Section Objectives

1. Give examples of the psychological, physical, and behavioral reactions to stress.
2. Identify stages of the stress reaction.

BELLRINGER
Motivational Activity

Project Daily Focus Transparency 15–2 and have students answer the questions.

Available as blackline master

Daily Focus Transparency 15–2

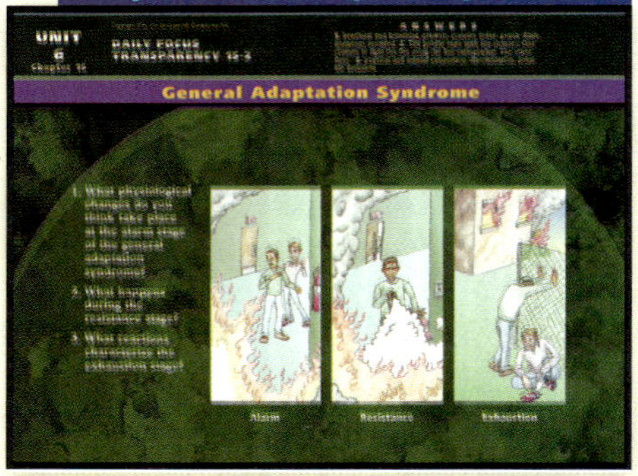

Reader's Guide

Use the Reader's Guide to introduce concepts and vocabulary.

Exploring Psychology
Ask students to read the **Exploring Psychology** feature. Then ask: **What stress did Joel encounter? How did he deal with his stress?**

Vocabulary Precheck
Have students read the definitions of the terms. Ask them to create flash cards with the term on one side and the definition on the other. Students should use the flash cards to study the terms.

Use the **Vocabulary PuzzleMaker CD-ROM** to create crossword and word search puzzles.

SECTION 2 Reactions to Stress

Reader's Guide

Main Idea
People react differently to life's stressors. These reactions may be beneficial or harmful.

Vocabulary
- anxiety
- anger
- fear
- social support

Objectives
- Give examples of the psychological, physical, and behavioral reactions to stress.
- Identify stages of the stress reaction.

EXPLORING PSYCHOLOGY

Beating the Odds

As a child, Joel Block couldn't reconcile who he knew he was with how he was perceived by his teachers.

"Every week, tests were given," he says. "The students were seated for the rest of the week according to their grades. I vied with another boy for the most weeks in The Dummy Row at the back. I remember vividly when he spit across the room at the 100 percent papers posted on the wall. The teacher yelled at him. He threw a chair in her direction and walked out. He never came back, so I held the record for the longest stay in The Dummy Row."

—from *Resiliency: How to Bounce Back* by Tessa Albert Warschaw and Dee Barlow, 1995

A person who encounters a stressor that is intense or prolonged will react to it. There is a wide variety of stress reactions, and their effects range from beneficial to harmful. Joel encountered stress throughout his educational career. Faced with sitting in "The Dummy Row" and not performing well on exams, Joel probably reacted in various ways—acting out, pouting, and feeling bad. Eventually (in college) Joel discovered he had a natural aptitude for psychology. He became a straight-A student and earned a Ph.D. in psychology. His reactions to stress may have changed from negative to positive ones.

Many of the physiological responses to stress are inborn methods that probably evolved to cope with stress effectively. In addition, many responses to stress are automatic. Just as the body reacts to a cut by producing new tissue, it has methods to heal the wounds of stress—crying, for example.

SECTION RESOURCES

Reproducible Masters
- Guided Reading Activity 15–2
- Vocabulary Activity 15–2
- Section Quiz 15–2

Transparencies
- Daily Focus Transparency 15–2

Multimedia
- Vocabulary PuzzleMaker CD-ROM
- *ExamView®* *Assessment Suite* CD-ROM
- Presentation Plus! Software

Coping mechanisms that worked for our remote ancestors are not necessarily successful in our modern technological society. Human beings are often slow to give up anything that is well established. We are more likely to depend solely on these ancient stress responses than to make conscious attempts to modify them or adopt others that we now know are more appropriate to our modern lifestyle.

The ways in which different people react to stress vary considerably; each person's response is the product of many factors. Stress reactions may be physical, psychological, or behavioral, but these categories are not clear-cut. The human body is a *holistic* (integrated) organism, and our physical well-being affects how we think and behave. For example, poor mental health can trigger physical illness or psychological illness.

FIGHT-OR-FLIGHT RESPONSE

Regardless of the stressor, the body reacts with immediate arousal. The adrenal glands are stimulated to produce: (a) hormones that increase the amount of blood sugar for extra energy; and (b) adrenaline, which causes rapid heartbeat and breathing and enables the body to use energy more quickly. These responses are designed to prepare a person for self-defense and are often called the *fight-or-flight response.* Wild animals experience the fight-or-flight response in reaction to attacks (see Figure 15.5). This response is needed for survival. Although you do not need to fight wild animals, the fight-or-flight response prepares you in the same way to face potentially dangerous situations. However, if stress persists for a long time, the body's resources are used up. The person becomes exhausted and, in extreme cases, dies.

Figure 15.5 **Fight-or-Flight Reaction**

When an animal senses possible danger, its endocrine system directs great sources of energy to its muscles and brain, preparing the creature for rapid action. You react the same way. ***How is stress necessary for survival?***

GENERAL ADAPTATION SYNDROME

Hans Selye (1956, 1976) identified three stages in the body's stress reaction: alarm, resistance, and exhaustion. Selye called this the *general adaptation syndrome.* In the *alarm* stage, the body mobilizes its fight-or-flight defenses; heartbeat and breathing quicken, muscles tense, the pupils dilate, and hormones that sustain these reactions are secreted. The person becomes exceptionally alert and sensitive to stimuli in the environment and tries to keep a firm grip on his or her emotions. For example, a hiker who confronts a rattlesnake on a mountain trail freezes in his tracks, is suddenly aware of every sound around him, and tries not to panic. If the alarm reaction is insufficient to deal with the stressor, the person may develop symptoms such as anxiety.

In the *resistance* stage, the person often finds means to cope with the stressor and to ward off, superficially at least, adverse reactions. Thus an isolated high-mountain hiker, caught off guard by a sudden blizzard, can use his knowledge

2 TEACH (*)

L1 Applying Concepts Write the following stages of the body's stress reaction on the board: *Alarm, Resistance*, and *Exhaustion*. Then have students pick one of the life events listed on the Social Readjustment Rating Scale in Figure 15.3. Assign students to work individually or in small groups to write a scenario in which a fictitious character goes through one or all of these stages. (Tell students that it is appropriate to use humor.) Request volunteers to read their scenarios aloud. Ask students to identify the stages of stress reaction exemplified by the stories.

Guided Reading Activity 15–2

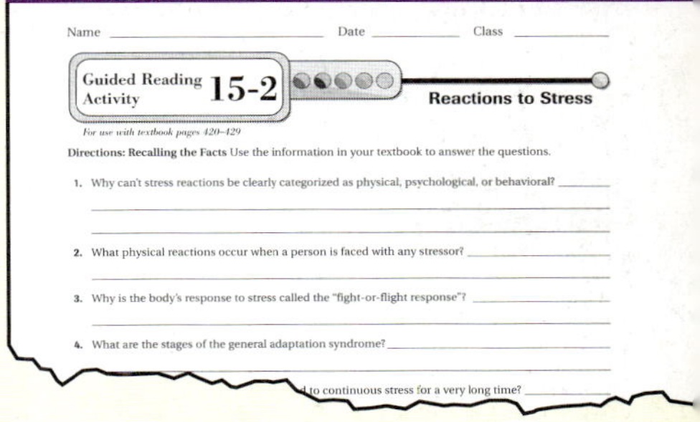

Name ____ Date ____ Class ____

Guided Reading Activity 15-2 — Reactions to Stress

For use with textbook pages 420–429

Directions: Recalling the Facts Use the information in your textbook to answer the questions.

1. Why can't stress reactions be clearly categorized as physical, psychological, or behavioral? ____
2. What physical reactions occur when a person is faced with any stressor? ____
3. Why is the body's response to stress called the "fight-or-flight response"? ____
4. What are the stages of the general adaptation syndrome? ____

...to continuous stress for a very long time? ____

Figure 15.5

Caption Answer Stress prepares you to face potentially dangerous situations.

COOPERATIVE LEARNING ACTIVITY

Creating a Poster Organize the class into small groups. Have each group select a high-stress job such as air traffic controller, firefighter, police officer, or medical resident. The groups should identify the sources of job stress and design a poster that can be displayed on the job site to warn workers of the health hazards of stress. Posters can be informative, inspirational, or humorous. **BLOCK SCHEDULING**

Figure 15.6

Caption Answer A person finds ways to cope with the stressor and fight off harmful reactions, at least temporarily.

Looking @ the Issues

Benefits of Stress Studies show that there can be long-term benefits of stress. In one study of people who experienced frequent illness, subjects were found to be more empathetic and more able to tolerate uncertainty. Stressful situations also require people to learn ways to manage the stress. In the process of resolving the stressful situations, they gain confidence in their abilities. This confidence can benefit people later as they encounter other stressful situations. **Ask:** **Do you think the long-term benefits of stress outweigh the short-term struggles? What would likely happen to someone who did not learn to successfully manage stressful situations?**

Readings and Case Studies in Psychology

Have students read the Chapter 15 Case Study selection in *Readings and Case Studies in Psychology* and answer the questions that follow the case study.

Figure 15.6 Stressful Situations

Our reactions to various events depend on our personalities and on the severity of the event itself. The family facing the destruction of their home, the high school senior waiting for her college admissions interview, and the man coping with a terminal illness are all experiencing various levels of stress. ***What happens during the resistance stage of stress?***

of the mountains to shelter himself. When his food runs out, though, all of his activities gradually deplete his internal reserves. At this stage, the person may suffer psychosomatic symptoms, which result from strain that he pretends is nonexistent. (Psychosomatic symptoms are real, physical symptoms that are caused by stress or tension.)

If exposure to the stressor continues, the individual reaches the stage of *exhaustion.* At this point, the adrenal and other glands involved in the fight-or-flight response have been taxed to their limit and become unable to secrete hormones. The individual reaches the breaking point. He or she becomes exhausted and disoriented and may develop delusions—of persecution, for example—in an effort to retain some type of coping strategy. The problem is that the very responses that were good for immediate resistance to stress, such as reducing digestion and boosting blood pressure, are detrimental in the long run. Some investigators have found that assembly-line workers in repetitive jobs over which they exercise very little control are likely to show the effects of stress. It is not surprising that the corporate executives running the company, who can control their own destiny to some degree, are less likely to show such stress (Karasek & Theorell, 1990). Farmers with high control over their work show very low susceptibility to chronic heart disease (Thelin, 1998).

EMOTIONAL AND COGNITIVE RESPONSES

anxiety: a vague, generalized apprehension or feeling of danger

anger: the irate reaction likely to result from frustration

fear: the usual reaction when a stressor involves real or imagined danger

Short-term psychological stress reactions may be either emotional or cognitive. The most common response to a sudden and powerful stressor is **anxiety,** which is a feeling of an imminent but unclear threat. An employee whose boss passes by in the hall without saying hello may develop anxiety about her future on the job. **Anger** is likely to result from frustration. A student who does not make the lacrosse team may fly into a rage when he puts his favorite CD in the player and it skips. **Fear** is usually the reaction when a stressor involves real danger—a fire, for example. Fear directs the individual to withdraw or flee, but in severe cases he or she may panic and be unable to act. Common examples of short-term emotional stress reactions are overreacting to minor irritations, getting

MEETING SPECIAL NEEDS

Learning Style: Verbal/Linguistic Read aloud the following excerpt from a *New York Times* editorial titled "Stress, Cops and Suicide" (12/1/93):

Few [police officers] *share details of their workday with their families for fear of frightening them. Inhabitants of a world where toughness is prized, even fewer feel free to reveal emotional fragility to their colleagues, let alone their superiors. . . . In killing themselves police officers may be, quite simply, relieving a stress about which they find it impossible to talk.*

Ask students to imagine that they are the police commissioner of New York City. Ask them to write a proposal for a program they would institute to curb suicides among police officers. **L2**

BLOCK SCHEDULING

no joy from daily pleasures, and doubting one's own abilities, while feeling tense, short-tempered, and more anxious.

Cognitive reactions to stress include difficulty in concentrating or thinking clearly, recurring thoughts, and poor decision making. A student who must give an oral presentation may worry about it but find himself unable to prepare for it. Another student wants to surprise her father with the news that she has been admitted to her first-choice college, but she cannot recall where his office is. Another type of cognitive stress reaction is unjustified suspicion or distrust of others.

Continued frustration can lead to burnout. People feel *burned out* when they feel they are incapable of doing their job well and they are physically worn out and emotionally exhausted from giving too much time or energy to a project while not receiving sufficient gratification. Prolonged stress, such as burnout, in combination with other factors, adversely affects mental health. It does not necessarily cause mental illness, but it may contribute to the severity of mental illness. There is an increased likelihood of developing a psychological disorder following a major life change, for example. Among those who attempt suicide and those with depression or anxiety-based disorders, there seems to be quite a definite link between stress and subsequent symptoms.

In Chapter 16, we will discuss a psychological disorder called *post-traumatic stress disorder*. This is a condition in which a person who has experienced a traumatic event feels severe and long-lasting aftereffects. This disorder is common among veterans of military combat and survivors of acts of terrorism, natural disasters such as floods and tornadoes, other catastrophes such as plane crashes, and human aggression such as rape and assault (see Figure 15.7). The event that triggers

Profiles In Psychology

Deepak Chopra

1947–

"By quieting the mind which then quiets the body and the less turbulent the body is, the more the self-repair, healing mechanisms get amplified."

Dr. Deepak Chopra is a major figure in the trend of holistic healing. *Holistic healing* refers to the idea that a person's mind and body are not independent matters; they function together as a unit. Instead of prescribing drugs to heal patients, Chopra believes that healing is a process that involves integrating the mind and the body.

A writer of both fiction and nonfiction, Chopra argues that what we think and feel can actually change our biology. He believes that by finding an inner peace and by relieving the stress of living, we can become healthy in mind and body.

Chopra blends Western medicine with the techniques of an ancient health care called Ayurveda. The basic idea behind Ayurveda is that a person's physical health is achieved through the integration of body, mind, and spirit. Chopra is a popular writer and adviser because he helps many people get past the hassles of daily existence and find pleasure in life.

Profiles In Psychology

Ask students to read the **Profiles In Psychology** feature and then discuss the following questions:

1. What is holistic healing? *(It refers to the idea that a person's mind and body function together as a unit. By integrating the mind and the body, healing can occur.)*
2. What does Chopra recommend as the means to achieve a healthy mind and body? *(He believes that what we think and feel affect our biology. By finding inner peace and relieving the stress in our lives, we can have a healthy mind and body.)*
3. What is Ayurveda? *(the techniques of an ancient health care based on the idea that physical health can be achieved by integrating the body, mind, and spirit)*

Psychology Journal

Ask students to write about a time when they felt burned out. Have them answer the following questions: **What did you do to recover from the feeling? What are you doing to avoid burnout in the future?** ■

CRITICAL THINKING ACTIVITY

Identifying Cause and Effect Ask students to list major problems and/or life changes they have confronted during the past few years. Next, have them organize these events into a time line. When the time lines are done, have students recall periods of physical illness over the same time span. Direct them to record these illnesses on the time line in red. Instruct students to identify correlations between life events and periods of physical illness. **Ask: Does a correlation exist between life changes or problems and experiencing physical illness? Does a cause-and-effect relationship exist between the two? Explain. L2**

the disorder overwhelms a person's normal sense of reality and ability to cope. The high stress levels associated with this disorder could result in a range of psychosomatic symptoms, such as insomnia, high blood pressure, and stomach problems.

BEHAVIORAL REACTIONS

There are many short-term behavioral changes that result from stress. A person may develop nervous habits (trembling or pacing, for example), gulp meals, smoke or drink more, take drugs, or feel tired for no reason. That person may develop a shaky voice, tremors, or strained expressions. There may be changes in his or her posture. He or she may temporarily lose interest in eating, grooming, bathing, and so on. Aggression toward family members is another way some people react to stress.

Some behavioral reactions are positive, however. In a tornado, for example, some people will risk their lives to save or help others. Such stressors often create attitudes of cooperation that override individual differences and disagreements.

Escape is another behavioral stress reaction, and it is often the best way to deal with frustration. For example, a woman who is on a bus that is caught in snarled traffic may get off and walk to her destination.

Figure 15.7 How Will This Affect Them?

In 2005, the destructive forces of Hurricane Katrina devastated the city of New Orleans. Many survivors may suffer from the effects of post-traumatic stress disorder. ***What is post-traumatic stress disorder, and whom does it affect?***

PSYCHOLOGY LAB EXPERIMENT

Demonstration of Stress To demonstrate how unexpected behavior can become a stressor in group situations, conduct the following experiment: At some time during class, stop what you are doing. Sit thoughtfully at your desk, perhaps exhibiting a facial expression indicative of some sort of distress. Do not respond to any questions the students may have. After a few minutes, ask them how they felt. **Ask:** **Did you experience an increase in stress and any accompanying physical reactions (such as nervousness or fear)?** If so, tell them that their bodies were reacting to the first of Selye's three stages—alarm. **L2** **ELL**

CURRICULUM CONNECTION

Health Treatment for post-traumatic stress disorder (PTSD) should begin as soon as symptoms appear. Common treatments include support groups, behavior therapy, and antianxiety drugs or antidepressants. The goal of treatment is to reduce the symptoms by encouraging the person to finish grieving. Support groups can be especially useful as they allow a person to express his or her feelings to people who have had similar experiences. Many sufferers of PTSD must be treated for depression or substance abuse before psychological problems can be effectively addressed.

Vocabulary Activity 15–2

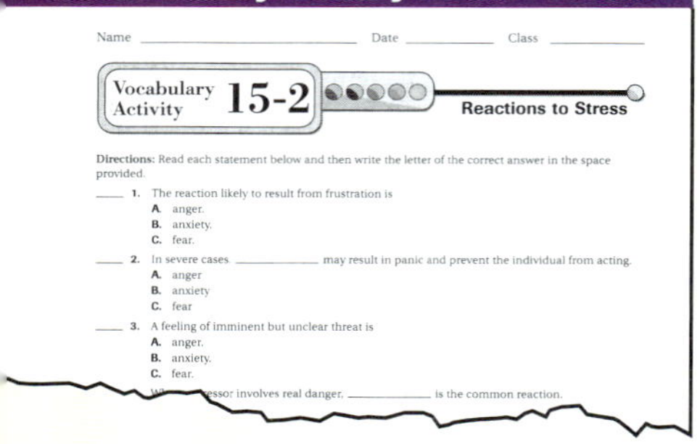
Name ______________ Date ________ Class ________

Vocabulary Activity 15-2 Reactions to Stress

Directions: Read each statement below and then write the letter of the correct answer in the space provided.

____ 1. The reaction likely to result from frustration is
A. anger.
B. anxiety.
C. fear.

____ 2. In severe cases ________ may result in panic and prevent the individual from acting.
A. anger
B. anxiety
C. fear

____ 3. A feeling of imminent but unclear threat is
A. anger.
B. anxiety.
C. fear.

...essor involves real danger, ________ is the common reaction.

Figure 15.7

Caption Answer Post-traumatic stress disorder (PTSD) is a condition in which a person who has experienced a traumatic event suffers severe and long-lasting aftereffects. The disorder is common among military combat survivors, survivors of natural disasters, and survivors of human aggression.

Figure 15.8 **The Fight-or-Flight Response**

Our fight-or-flight response is triggered by potentially dangerous or stressful situations, such as a scare in the middle of the night or giving a speech in public. As soon as you feel threatened, your body prepares itself for action. ***Why do our pupils dilate during the fight-or-flight reaction? Why do our muscles tense?***

1. You appraise a situation as physically or psychologically threatening.

2. Your thoughts activate the hypothalamus (in the brain). The hypothalamus stimulates the pituitary gland to secrete ACTH (adrenocorticotropic hormone)—a stress-fighting hormone. The hypothalamus also activates the sympathetic division of the autonomic nervous system.

3. The sympathetic nervous system stimulates a variety of physical responses to prepare the body for the stressful situation—this is the fight-or-flight response. (The parasympathetic nervous system later returns the body to its normal state.)

Fight-or-Flight Response

- heart rate increases
- blood pressure increases
- respiration becomes rapid and shallow
- liver releases stores of glycogen, raising blood sugar level
- digestive system shuts down and blood reroutes to muscles
- pupils dilate
- hair stands up on end
- excitatory hormones secreted (epinephrine and norepinephrine)
- muscles tense

While many people can endure great amounts of stress without marked behavioral responses, others may be seriously affected. Severe stress can be significant to the development of escapist personality styles—alcoholism, drug addiction, chronic unemployment, and attempted suicide, for example. Stress has also been noted as a contributing cause of aggressive personalities, delinquency, and criminal behavior.

PHYSICAL REACTIONS

Why do the daily hassles of life and major life changes sometimes make people ill? Your thoughts and emotions can produce physiological changes in your body. For example, some people develop *psychosomatic symptoms* as a result of stress. As mentioned earlier, psychosomatic symptoms are real, physical symptoms that are caused by stress or tension. They can include headaches, stomachaches, and muscle pains.

The physiological fight-or-flight response—accelerated heart rate and so on—is the body's immediate reaction to stress. This response is geared to prepare human beings to fight or run from an enemy such as a

L1 Making a Chart Assign groups of students to design a chart comparing the following categories: *Emotional and Cognitive Responses, Behavioral Reactions,* and *Physical Reactions.* Direct the groups to complete the charts from information in the text. ELL

Figure 15.8

Visual Instruction Explain to students that in nature, when an animal wins the battle or runs away, special chemicals are sent through the body to return the body's organ systems to their original state.

Caption Answer Pupils dilate to allow in more light. This enables us to see more of our surroundings. Our muscles tense to help us prepare for a physical challenge.

TEACHER Tip

Tell students that the study of the relationship between psychological factors and the immune system has given rise to a specialty known as *psychoneuroimmunology.* Investigators in this field suggest that mental imagery can alter the workings of the immune system. Positive images, such as seeing oneself recovering or imagining a powerful army of white blood cells vanquishing invading germs, may help the immune system in fighting disease.

INTERDISCIPLINARY CONNECTIONS ACTIVITY

Health Have students work in small groups to prepare an oral presentation about one of the major chronic diseases that have been linked to stress: peptic ulcers, hypertension, and certain kinds of asthma, arthritis, and heart disease. Students should research and describe the symptoms as well as the methods of diagnosis and treatment of each disorder. Encourage students to include visual aids in their presentations to the class. **L2**

CHAPTER 15
Section 2, pages 420–429

Figure 15.9

Caption Answer If your body is constantly involved in a fight-or-flight response, the immune system becomes suppressed and you become more susceptible to disease and infection.

Cultural Connections

The Christmas holiday season in America creates stress in many people's lives. The holiday season can bring people together, but it also causes some people deep psychological stress. Holiday stress can drive people to drink too much, eat too much, eat the wrong foods, keep unusual hours, stifle feelings, alter their routines, and generally fail to take care of themselves. Therapists' recommendations for coping with holiday stress are as follows:

1. Set realistic expectations.
2. Be willing to say no to avoid overcommitment of your time and your finances.
3. Look for positive things to do and avoid people who criticize everything and everybody.
4. If loneliness is a struggle for you, get involved in something that is meaningful to you. Helping others is a great way to tackle loneliness.
5. Make time to have fun.
6. Be forgiving and tolerant.

Figure 15.9 Attacking Pathogens

An immune system cell attacks a foreign invader—a bacteria cell. When the immune system is not suppressed by stress, for instance, it destroys pathogens that enter the body. ***What effect does the fight-or-flight response have on your immune system?***

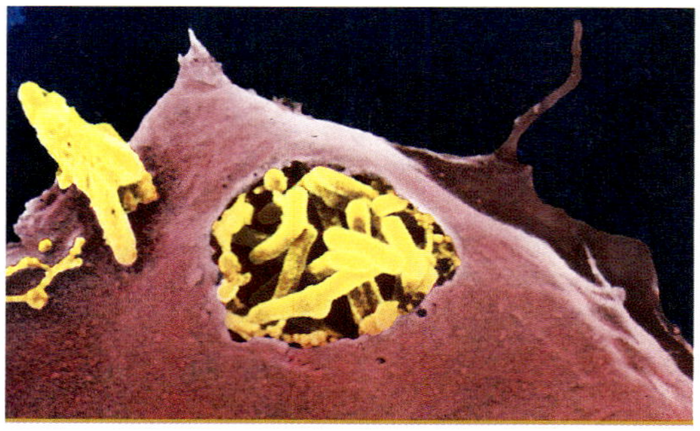

savage animal or band of warriors, and it was probably useful earlier in human history. We cannot deal with most modern stressors—a financial problem, for instance—in this manner, and physical responses to stress are now generally inappropriate. In fact, prolonged physical arousal from almost any stress can cause health problems, including difficulty in breathing, insomnia, migraine headaches, urinary and bowel irregularities, muscle aches, sweating, and dryness of mouth.

Stress is certainly a contributing cause of illness. We have already discussed the study by Rahe (1975) that linked low scores on the Holmes-Rahe scale to reports of good health for the following year, while high scores were linked with becoming sick in the following year.

Emotional stress clearly is related to such illnesses as peptic ulcers, hypertension, certain kinds of arthritis, asthma, and heart disease. Those who work in high-stress occupations may pay a high price. Air-traffic controllers, for example, juggle the lives of hundreds of people on air routes where a minor error can mean mass death. They are said to suffer from the highest incidence of peptic ulcers of any professional group (Cobb & Rose, 1973). Further, controllers at busy, high-stress airports have more ulcers than those at low-stress airports (Ballieux, 1984). Similarly, a student may come down with the flu on the day before a big exam. Stress weakens; illness may follow.

Stress can be at least partly responsible for almost *any* disease, as shown by the scope of illness associated with high Holmes-Rahe scores. Stress can contribute to disease in several ways. Sometimes it can be the direct cause of illness. A migraine headache, for example, is usually a physical reaction to stress. Stress may also contribute indirectly to illness. It reduces our resistance to infectious disease by tampering with the immune defense system (O'Leary, 1990). The **immune system** is your body's natural defense system against infection.

immune system: the body's natural defense system against infection

Have you ever caught a cold right in the middle of final exams week? Why did this happen? When you experience stressful situations for a long period of time, it decreases your immune system's ability to cope. Your body is constantly exposed to millions of pathogens (disease-causing bacteria or viruses). When these pathogens enter your body, they attack your body cells and use these cells to grow and multiply. The end result is an infection. Most of the time your body manages to stay free of infection because of the immune system. However, recall the third stage of Selye's general adaptation syndrome—exhaustion. When your body is continually involved in the fight-or-flight response, it reaches the breaking point. You become exhausted, and the immune system is suppressed. Your body becomes more susceptible to the diseases and infections caused by the pathogens that continually assault it.

EXTENDING THE CONTENT

Stress in Health Care Workers A recent study conducted by Dr. Ashley Weinberg and Dr. Francis Creed in Great Britain has found that health care workers, as a group, experience high levels of work-related stress as well as high levels of home-related stress. At work, the stress seems to be created by a lack of support from managers and difficulty balancing patients' needs with the time consuming, mundane aspects of the job (such as completing paperwork). At home, health care workers experience high rates of marital problems, problems with other relationships, and a high incidence of psychiatric disorders. When planning programs to reduce stress levels, both the work and home environments of health care workers should be considered.

FACTORS INFLUENCING REACTIONS TO STRESS

People's reactions to stress vary considerably. These reactions help people meet challenges in life, but they may also determine the amount of stress one feels.

Personality Differences

In some cases, an individual's personality may make him or her more vulnerable to stress. Some psychologists have suggested that people who exhibit a behavior pattern they call Type A are very likely to have coronary artery disease, often followed by heart attacks, in their thirties and forties. Those who do not have this pattern (Type B people) almost never have heart attacks before the age of 70 (Friedman & Rosenman, 1974).

Whereas Type B people are generally relaxed, patient, and do not easily become angry, the Type A person's body is in a chronic state of stress with an almost constant flow of adrenaline into the bloodstream. This adrenaline apparently interacts with cholesterol or other chemical agents to block the coronary arteries that lead to the heart. It may be that high levels of adrenaline prevent the normal chemical breakdown of cholesterol in the blood.

Reading Check What is a Type A personality?

Type A people are always prepared for fight or flight. They have a great deal of free-floating hostility, that is, anger that has no real object or focus. They are extremely irritable, and one of the things that irritates Type A people most is delay of any kind. They become impatient waiting in line, tend to move and eat rapidly, often try to do two or three things at once (such as reading while eating), and feel guilty when they are not actively doing something. They are also extremely competitive. In short, Type A people are always struggling—with time, other people, or both. Note that this describes an extreme version of the Type A personality. Most people respond to the world with Type A behavior at times, but they are not in a constant state of stress. It is important to note that psychologists disagree about both the definition of Type A personality and its relation to heart disease.

Another personality trait that can affect the strength of a stress reaction is emotional expressiveness. Some research suggests that people who neither express nor admit to strong feelings of despair,

Psychology and You

Road Rage

You may have witnessed road rage, or the inability to handle frustrations while driving. Going beyond aggressive driving, road rage involves a desire to retaliate and punish another driver. It may result in criminal behavior, such as violence or threatened violence. Psychologists believe road rage reflects a driver's anger and lack of self-control (Rathbone & Huckabee, 1999). It has become a national epidemic, with at least 218 people killed and 12,610 injured as a result of road rage between 1990 and 1996 (AAA Foundation for Traffic Safety, 1997).

What should you do to avoid road rage?

- Do not retaliate against another driver.
- Before you react to another driver, consider if this episode is worth risking your life.
- Be polite and courteous, even when others are not.
- If you are harassed by another driver and being followed, go to the nearest police station.
- Slow down and relax.
- Allow enough travel time.
- Remember that although you cannot control the behavior of other drivers, you can control your own behavior. Be calm and drive safely.

Reading Check Answer
Type A personalities are always prepared for fight or flight. They have a great deal of hostility, may be irritable, and cannot tolerate delays. They feel guilty when they are not doing something.

Psychology and You

Use the following question to direct a class discussion after students have read the **Psychology and You** feature.
Ask: **Have you ever witnessed road rage?** Ask students to describe the incident. **Which of these suggestions could have been useful in preventing or reducing the impact of the incident you described?**

FYI

Social psychologists have identified an important holistic connection between stress and physical health. For example, divorced and widowed people are more likely to have a weakened immune system than married people, making them prone to disease.

EXTENDING THE CONTENT

Loneliness Studies have shown that loneliness contributes to the severity of stress and the onset of stress-related diseases. Read the following quote aloud: "If I'm such a legend, then why am I so lonely? Let me tell you, legends are all very well if you've got somebody around who loves you." (Judy Garland) Have a class discussion about who can be affected by loneliness and how. Also discuss how social support can overcome loneliness. **L2**

Figure 15.10

Caption Answer People have stronger reactions to stressors that are beyond their control than to stressors that are within their control. People are better able to cope with stressors that are within their control.

3 ASSESS

Assign Section 2 Assessment as homework or as an in-class activity.

Section Quiz 15–2

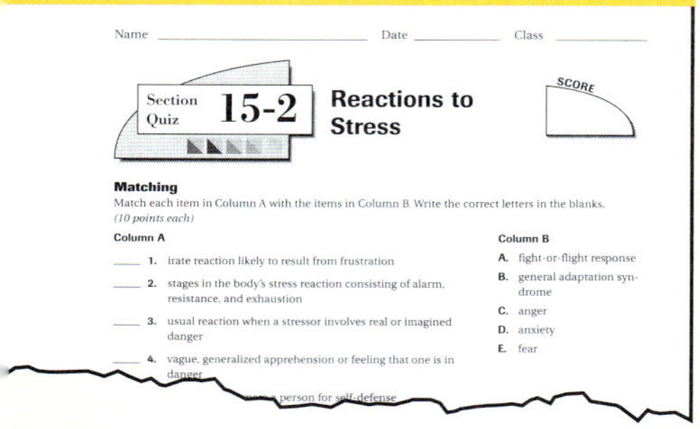
Name ______ Date ______ Class ______

Section Quiz 15-2 **Reactions to Stress**

SCORE

Matching
Match each item in Column A with the items in Column B. Write the correct letters in the blanks. *(10 points each)*

Column A	Column B
____ 1. irate reaction likely to result from frustration	A. fight-or-flight response
____ 2. stages in the body's stress reaction consisting of alarm, resistance, and exhaustion	B. general adaptation syndrome
____ 3. usual reaction when a stressor involves real or imagined danger	C. anger
____ 4. vague, generalized apprehension or feeling that one is in danger	D. anxiety
	E. fear

Reteach

Ask students to describe a stressful situation that is common among teens. Write the situation on the board. Beneath it make four headings for the ways that social groups provide support. Have students list specific things that support can provide in the situation.

depression, and anger are more likely to develop cancer than those who can give vent to their emotions. Some investigators have proposed a cancer-prone behavior pattern. People who deny their negative emotions tend to express feelings less freely, show a high tendency toward social conformity, and have a greater risk of getting cancer (Baltrusch, Stangel, & Titze, 1991). Negative life events such as those measured by the Holmes and Rahe scale do seem to be related to an increased likelihood of cancer in later life (Forsen, 1991).

social support: information that leads someone to believe that he or she is cared for, loved, respected, and part of a network of communication and mutual obligation

Perceived Control Over Stressors

The accepted view today is that physical disorders are more likely when we do not have control over stressors. Most evidence to support this theory comes from experiments on animals. J.M. Weiss (1972), for example, gave two groups of rats identical electric shocks. In one group, a rat could avoid the shock by touching its nose to a panel, while the other group had no control over the shocks. The group that could regulate the shocks developed far fewer ulcers than those that could not.

Subsequent experiments showed that feedback is also an important factor. Animals that responded to avoid shock and then heard a tone to signal that they had done the right thing suffered fewer ulcers than those that responded to avoid the shock but were given no feedback.

Weiss (1971) found that lack of feedback could harm human beings as well. His research showed that people develop ulcers when they have to make large numbers of responses but receive no feedback about their effectiveness.

So, in general, people prefer to have predictable stress over unpredictable stress. For example, when you know that a teacher has certain preferences in grading essay questions, it makes writing the paper a little easier. If you do not have any idea how the teacher plans to grade the essay, the writing is much harder. In one study (Matthews et al., 1989), psychologists exposed people to predictable and unpredictable noise, concluding that people may prefer predictable noise because it allows us to prepare and thus cope better. Our physical and psychological well-being is profoundly influenced by the degree to which we feel a sense of control over our lives (Sapolsky, 2004).

Figure 15.10 Stressful Jobs

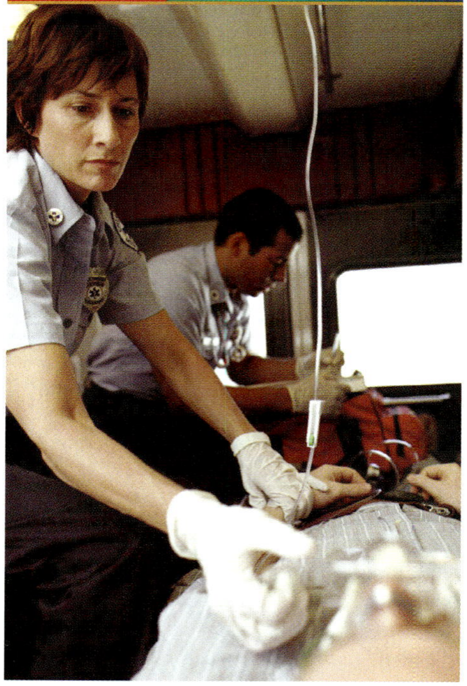

Some work, such as air traffic control, construction, and rescue operations, involves stress because of the job itself. People in these fields must deal with stress over which they have no control. ***How does your perceived control over stressors affect your stress levels?***

Social Support

Much research has pointed to the importance of social support in helping people work to decrease the effects of stressful situations. Social support can buffer an individual from the effects of stress. Sidney Cobb (1976) has defined **social support** as information that leads someone to believe that he or she is cared for, loved,

PSYCHOLOGY LAB EXPERIMENT

Type A Personalities Tell students that they will take a brief quiz to determine if they have a Type A personality. Ask the following questions and have students answer "yes" or "no" on a piece of paper. **(1) Are you continually aware of time? (2) Are you always in a rush? (3) Do you lose your patience when things take too long? (4) Do you always try to do more than one thing at the same time? (5) Do you tend to use nervous gestures to emphasize your point? (6) Do you evaluate your life in terms of how much you accomplish rather than what you accomplish?** Tell students that if they answered "yes" to most of these questions, it may be time to slow down and relax. **L1 ELL**

respected, and part of a network of communication and mutual obligation. He has found that social support can reduce both the likelihood and the severity of stress-related diseases—a finding often replicated (Cohen, 1988). Social support benefits have been documented for cancer, crowding, military combat, natural disasters, and AIDS.

Social groups seem to offer at least four kinds of support. First, *emotional* support involves concerned listening, which forms a basis for offering affection and concern and bolstering the stressed person's self-confidence. Second, *appraisal* support is interactive. The listener feeds back information and probing questions to the stressed person as an aid in sorting out, understanding, and planning to deal with the sources of the stress. *Informational* support emerges from appraisal support. Here the stressed person responds to what he or she has learned and evaluates the manner in which he or she is dealing with stressors. Finally, *instrumental* support represents active, positive support in the form of direct help such as money or living quarters. Yet there is evidence that some friends, despite the best intentions, may be more of a strain than a help in a crisis (Rook, 1990).

Some sources of social support can be especially helpful. Studies of male blue-collar workers have reported that social support from wives and supervisors counteracted the health consequences of stress more effectively than did support from coworkers, friends, or relatives.

More About...

Gender Differences and Stress

Who has higher stress levels—men or women? Women in the United States are more likely than men to live in poverty, to experience discrimination, and to be sexually or physically abused. Also, some psychologists argue that the traditional roles of women as primary caretakers and wives place them in positions in which anxiety and depression are more likely. For example, mothers are often made to feel responsible for events that they have little control over, such as the illness of a child or accidents in the home. Taking a job outside the home often reduces psychological stress for women. Studies show that as more and more women take jobs outside the home, the stress and anxiety experienced by the genders is becoming equalized (Kessler & McRae, 1981).

Enrich

Have students write an essay titled "Stress Yesterday, Today and Tomorrow." The essay should compare stress today with stress 100 years ago and stress 100 years from now. Ask students to consider the environmental changes that have occurred in the past 100 years and those that they foresee for the future.

4 CLOSE

As a class, brainstorm a list of the common fight-or-flight scenarios. Organize students into groups. Have the groups select one of the scenarios and make a chart describing the emotional, cognitive, behavioral, and physical reactions that are likely to occur if the situation is resolved and the stress is relieved after a relatively brief period of time.

SECTION 2 Assessment

1. **Review the Vocabulary** How does social support reduce stress?

General Adaptation Syndrome

2. **Visualize the Main Idea** Use a graphic organizer similar to the one above to describe the stages of the general adaptation syndrome.

3. **Recall Information** What is the fight-or-flight response? Why is it necessary for animals? For humans?

4. **Think Critically** Would you feel more stressed about a scheduled exam or a pop quiz? Why?

5. **Application Activity** Measure a friend's heart rate. Then have the person think of a terrifying situation. Did the heart rate increase? Choose another person and measure his or her heart rate. Have the person think of a peaceful, calming situation. Did the heart rate decrease? Summarize your findings.

SECTION 2 Assessment Answers

1. by allowing the person to feel cared for, loved, respected, and part of a network of support
2. Students should describe the alarm, resistance, and exhaustion stages.
3. It is the response to stress in which you will either stand firm and resolve the situation or flee from it. For animals, it aids in survival. They will fight weaker opponents and flee from stronger opponents. For humans, it also aids in survival by helping us face or flee threatening situations.
4. a pop quiz because you had no advance notice; you feel you have more control with a scheduled exam.
5. Students' answers will vary. The heart rate increases when a terrifying situation is considered because the person is exhibiting the fight-or-flight response. A calming situation should not raise stress or cause an increase in heart rate. Thinking about a calming situation may actually reduce your current level of stress.

1 FOCUS

Section Objectives

1. Explain defensive strategies of coping with stress.
2. Describe active strategies of coping with stress.

BELLRINGER
Motivational Activity

Project Daily Focus Transparency 15–3 and have students answer the questions.

Available as blackline master

Daily Focus Transparency 15–3

Reader's Guide

Use the Reader's Guide to introduce concepts and vocabulary.

Exploring Psychology

Ask students to read the **Exploring Psychology** feature. Then ask: **How is our level of stress affected by our outlook on the situation?**

Vocabulary Precheck

Have students create a crossword puzzle using the vocabulary terms from this section. They should use the definitions as the clues. Then have pairs of students trade and complete puzzles.

Use the **Vocabulary PuzzleMaker CD-ROM** to create crossword and word search puzzles.

SECTION 3 Coping With Stress

Reader's Guide

Main Idea

People deal with stress by employing defensive and active coping strategies.

Vocabulary

- cognitive appraisal
- denial
- intellectualization
- progressive relaxation
- meditation
- biofeedback

Objectives

- Explain defensive strategies of coping with stress.
- Describe active strategies of coping with stress.

EXPLORING PSYCHOLOGY

How Do You View Life?

There were two women who had rose gardens. One would awaken every morning, look out into the garden and groan: "Oh, there are so many weeds in my garden. It is going to take me forever to get rid of them!"

The other woman calmly put on her gardening gloves and hummed to herself as she methodically removed the weeds surrounding her roses.

"Oh, my beautiful roses," she said. "How lovely you look and smell!"

—from *Natural Stress-Busters for the Whole Family* by Lynn Allison, 1993

Stress, like those weeds in the women's rose gardens, can spring up and choke you—if you let it. Stress can smother your enjoyment of life and make you miserable. If you focus on the positive, however—the delightful blooming roses—the weeds need not be a source of stress but instead may be merely obstacles to overcome. Coping with stress is an attempt to gain control over a part of one's life. It is an attempt to master, control, reduce, and tolerate the stressors in one's life. People cope with stress in many ways. There is not just one way that is best for all people in all situations. People also have individualized coping styles. People know what works best for them. They have come to rely on what has worked in the past. What is your way of handling difficult situations?

Coping strategies may not always be healthy ways to adapt. Sometimes when we are under stress, we act in ways that are not in our best interests. There are methods that people use that hurt or harm others. These are known as maladaptive ways of coping.

SECTION RESOURCES

Reproducible Masters

- Guided Reading Activity 15–3
- Vocabulary Activity 15–3
- Section Quiz 15–3

Transparencies

- Daily Focus Transparency 15–3

Multimedia

- Vocabulary PuzzleMaker CD-ROM
- *ExamView® Assessment Suite* CD-ROM
- Presentation Plus! Software

PSYCHOLOGICAL COPING STRATEGIES

Our interpretation or evaluation of an event—a process psychologists call **cognitive appraisal**—helps determine its stress impact. For example, suppose you have a huge exam scheduled for next week. The way you appraise—or evaluate—the situation will determine the level of stress you feel. If you appraise the situation as a challenge that you can meet, you have positive feelings and your stress level is reduced. If you think of the situation as a threat, however, your negative feelings will increase your stress level. Drugs can affect cognitive appraisal. For example, drinking may help convince a man who has been fired that his troubles are not serious or that he will enjoy unemployment or that getting drunk is the best solution for the time being.

cognitive appraisal: the interpretation of an event that helps determine its stress impact

Defensive Coping Strategies

We can also try to influence our cognitive appraisals by means of defensive coping strategies, and stress reactions are more likely to occur when these strategies fail. Common defense mechanisms are **denial,** in which a person decides that the event is not really a stressor, and **intellectualization,** in which the person watches and analyzes the situation from an emotionally detached standpoint.

denial: a coping mechanism in which a person decides that the event is not really a stressor

intellectualization: a coping mechanism in which the person analyzes a situation from an emotionally detached viewpoint

Figure 15.11 Types of Coping Strategies

The two major ways that people deal with stress are by either focusing on it and trying to reduce it or ignoring the stress completely. ***Which of the strategies listed here involve an active attempt to reduce stress?***

Coping strategy	*Example*
Active coping	I take additional action to try to get rid of the problem.
Planning	I come up with a strategy about what to do.
Suppression of competing activities	I put aside other activities to concentrate on this.
Restraint coping	I force myself to wait for the right time to do something.
Seeking social support	I talk to someone about how I feel.
Positive reinterpretation and growth	I look for the good in what is happening.
Acceptance	I learn to live with it.
Turning to religion	I seek God's help.
Venting of emotions	I get upset and let my emotions out.
Denial	I refuse to believe that it has happened.
Behavioral disengagement	I give up the attempt to get what I want.
Mental disengagement	I turn to work or other substitute activities to take my mind off things.
Alcohol-drug disengagement	I drink alcohol or take drugs to think about it less.

COOPERATIVE LEARNING ACTIVITY

Role Playing Pass out 3" x 5" cards to the class, and ask each student to describe one stressful situation. Collect the cards, and divide the class into groups of four or five. Give each group one of the cards. Try to select situations that are clearly different from one another. Ask the groups to develop a play of the situation described on the card. Tell them to end the play right at the most stressful moment. (Someone in the group can call "Cut.") Brainstorm with the class constructive and destructive ways to complete the play. Remind the students that during group work they will sometimes be leaders and other times followers; but at all times they should work to create a supportive group climate. **BLOCK SCHEDULING**

2 TEACH

L1 Designing a Biofeedback System As a class, brainstorm ways in which stress is generally felt. To start the discussion, write *increased pulse* on the board. Under this topic, make a list of stress-causing events. Discuss the impact technology may have in creating such a system. After the list has been made, organize students into groups of four to design a biofeedback system that would help people recognize and control stress levels. Give the groups one restriction: the system must be portable. (Note: Students need only describe the system.)

Guided Reading Activity 15–3

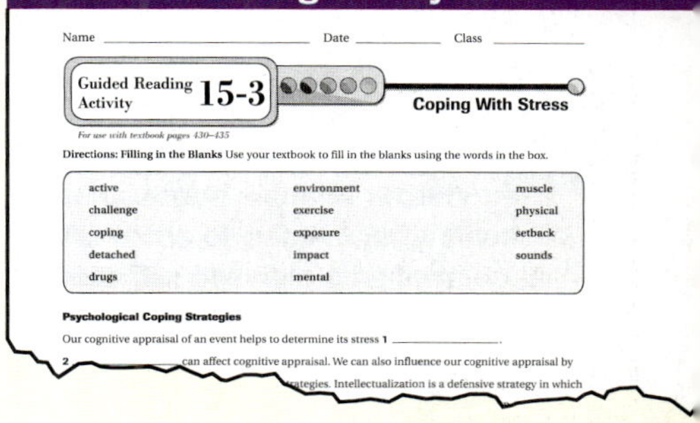
Name ________ Date ________ Class ________

Guided Reading Activity 15-3 — Coping With Stress

For use with textbook pages 430–435

Directions: Filling in the Blanks Use your textbook to fill in the blanks using the words in the box.

active	environment	muscle
challenge	exercise	physical
coping	exposure	setback
detached	impact	sounds
drugs	mental	

Psychological Coping Strategies

Our cognitive appraisal of an event helps to determine its stress **1** ________.

2 ________ can affect cognitive appraisal. We can also influence our cognitive appraisal by ...rategies. Intellectualization is a defensive strategy in which

Figure 15.11

Visual Instruction Discuss the possible long-term consequences of selecting one type of coping strategy. Ask students to identify times when each of the strategies would be appropriate.

Caption Answer active coping, planning, suppression of competing activities, seeking social support, turning to religion, positive reinterpretation and growth

CHAPTER 15

Section 3, pages 430–435

PSYCHOLOGY Online

Links and instructional guidelines can be found in the **Web Activity Lesson Plan** at glencoe.com.

Vocabulary Activity 15–3

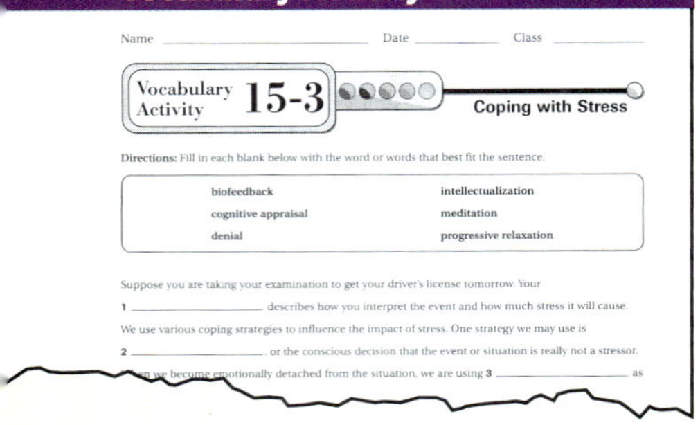
Name ______ Date ______ Class ______

Vocabulary Activity 15-3 Coping with Stress

Directions: Fill in each blank below with the word or words that best fit the sentence.

biofeedback	intellectualization
cognitive appraisal	meditation
denial	progressive relaxation

Suppose you are taking your examination to get your driver's license tomorrow. Your 1 ______ describes how you interpret the event and how much stress it will cause. We use various coping strategies to influence the impact of stress. One strategy we may use is 2 ______, or the conscious decision that the event or situation is really not a stressor. ...en we become emotionally detached from the situation, we are using 3 ______ as

PSYCHOLOGY JOURNAL

Assign students to write an assessment of the coping strategies they have used to deal with stressful situations in the past month. Challenge students to find alternatives for any strategies that are destructive. ■

Readings and Case Studies in Psychology

Have students read the Chapter 15 Reading selection in *Readings and Case Studies in Psychology* and answer the questions that follow the reading.

PSYCHOLOGY Online

Student Web Activity

Visit the *Understanding Psychology* Web site at glencoe.com and click on **Chapter 15—Student Web Activities** for an activity about stress.

Both denial and intellectualization can prevent physical reactions to stress. In one study (Lazarus et al., 1965), three groups of participants viewed a film that showed gruesome accidents at a sawmill. One group was told that the injuries were not real but were staged by the actors (denial). A second group was advised that they were seeing an educational film about the importance of safety measures (intellectualization). The third group was told nothing. The levels of physical reaction were lower in the first two groups than in the third. Thus, if a person does not evaluate an event or situation as stressful, a stress reaction will not occur. Yet that is really failing to deal with what could be a legitimate stressor (Holahan & Moos, 1985).

Active Coping Strategies

By appraising a situation as a challenge and not a threat, we can adopt an active coping strategy for dealing with stress (see Figure 15.11). Active coping strategies involve changing our environment or modifying a situation to remove stressors or reduce the level of stress.

Hardiness Some people acquire personality traits that are, in effect, active coping strategies. *Hardiness* refers to the personality traits of control, commitment, and challenge that help us reduce the stress we feel. *Control* involves feeling that we have the ability to affect the outcome of the situation. *Commitment* refers to establishing and pursuing our goals, while *challenge* means that we actively confront and solve problems instead of feeling threatened and powerless because of them. For instance, you may demonstrate hardiness if, when confronted with the assignment of giving a speech in public, you approach the assignment as a positive experience (challenge), believe that you can prepare and give a good speech (control), and prepare for and practice your speech (commitment).

Controlling Stressful Situations There are several ways in which we can control our exposure to stressful events and thereby reduce levels of stress. As noted earlier, escape or withdrawal, when possible, can be an effective coping strategy. A young woman who is not enjoying herself at a party, for example, can leave. When avoiding an event is not practical, controlling its timing may be helpful; you can try to space out stress-producing events. A couple who is planning to have a baby in the summer, for instance, may postpone looking for a new house.

Problem Solving Sometimes neither avoiding nor spacing events is possible. A high school senior may face a deadline for a college application and an important exam on the same day. In cases like this, problem solving or confronting the matter head-on can be the best way to cope. Regarding frustrations or conflicts as problems to be solved means the situation becomes a positive challenge rather than a negative setback. Problem solving involves a rational analysis of the situation that will lead to an appropriate decision. The student in our example may map out the remaining days and allocate specific times to work on the application and other times to study for the test. He may also decide that he can gain

MEETING SPECIAL NEEDS

Learning Style: Visual/Spatial Have students find or take pictures of people who are using the various coping strategies discussed in this section. Have students use the pictures to create an interactive display in which a person can match the pictures with a definition of the coping strategies being displayed. The display should include an answer key. **L2** ELL

BLOCK SCHEDULING

Refer to ***Inclusion for the High School Social Studies Classroom Strategies and Activities*** in the TCR for strategies for students with different learning styles.

more time for these activities by skipping band practice or postponing a date. Problem solving is a very healthy strategy that tends to develop flexibility and to sharpen insights and attention to detail.

Explanatory Style Martin Seligman (1991) describes two very different styles of thinking. The *optimist* typically puts the best face on any set of events. Following a loss, an optimistic quarterback will suggest, "What's done is done. Start thinking about next week!" The *pessimist* always sees the dark side. After becoming ill and missing the senior prom, the pessimist will say, "This always happens to me! I never get to. . . ." Seligman studied baseball players, grouping them as optimists or pessimists from their quotes in the sports pages. He found that the pessimists were much more likely to die at a younger age.

Figure 15.12 **Irrational Assumptions That Can Cause Stress**

Irrational Assumptions	Constructive Alternative
1. Everyone must approve of what I do.	I should concentrate on my own self-respect.
2. I must do everything to perfection.	I am imperfect; I have limitations, and that's okay.
3. Things must be the way I want them to be.	There are some situations that I cannot control. It's better to concentrate on matters that I can control.
4. Unhappiness is inevitable.	Unhappiness is the result of how I look at things.
5. I need someone stronger than I am to rely on.	I must rely on myself and act independently when necessary.
6. The world should be fair and just.	Although I can try to be fair and just in my behavior, sometimes the world is not fair.
7. I should worry about dangerous and fearsome things.	I realize that I can face what I consider fearful and try to render it nondangerous.
8. There's always a perfect solution out there that I should find.	Life is filled with probability and chance. I can enjoy life even though sometimes no perfect solution to a problem exists.
9. I should not question authorities or social beliefs.	It's better to evaluate situations and beliefs for myself.
10. It's better to avoid difficult and stressful situations.	There is no "easy way out"; I need to face my problems and work on solutions.

Source: Ellis, 1986.

Some people hold self-defeating, irrational beliefs that cause stress and prevent them from adequately adjusting to life's challenges. ***How might recognizing your irrational assumptions help you better cope with stress?***

Applying **Psychology**

Explain that in our busy society, time management has become the source of a great deal of stress. People fill their days with so many activities that they must hurry from one task to the next. As they do, they find themselves becoming more and more stressed. Ask students to try the following suggestions for three full days and then write a summary of the results.

1. Set realistic expectations of what you can accomplish each day.
2. Try living in the present; getting the most out of each moment.
3. Take at least 30 minutes each day to relax, meditate, or otherwise free your mind of all distractions (no television).
4. Simplify your life in some measurable way.

Figure 15.12

Visual Instruction Have students read the irrational assumptions and select one or two that they have used at some point in their lives. Challenge students to use the constructive alternative the next time they are tempted to make the irrational assumption.

Caption Answer By recognizing the irrational assumptions, a person can begin to shift his or her thinking toward a more constructive alternative.

CRITICAL THINKING ACTIVITY

Synthesizing Information Remind students that in Chapter 14, they were introduced to Carl Jung's concept of archetypes, or inherited universal ideas. Ask students to select at least three of the active coping strategies and identify an archetype from fiction or real life that symbolizes the strategy. An archetype for acceptance would be Charlie Brown. Have students create a chart that lists the coping strategy, their selected archetype, and a one-paragraph explanation of why this person or character is an archetype for that coping strategy. **L3**

CHAPTER 15
Section 3, pages 430–435

Figure 15.13

Visual Instruction Ask students to describe imaginary, stressful situations and possible reactions using this summary model.

Caption Answer A person may react to stress on physiological, behavioral, emotional, and/or cognitive levels. Examples may include: physiological—increased energy or tiredness; behavioral—developing nervous habits or attitudes that override individual differences and allow for cooperation, emotional—anger or the satisfaction of meeting a challenge; cognitive—poor decision making or a sudden clarity of thinking.

3 ASSESS

Assign Section 3 Assessment as homework or as an in-class activity.

Section Quiz 15–3

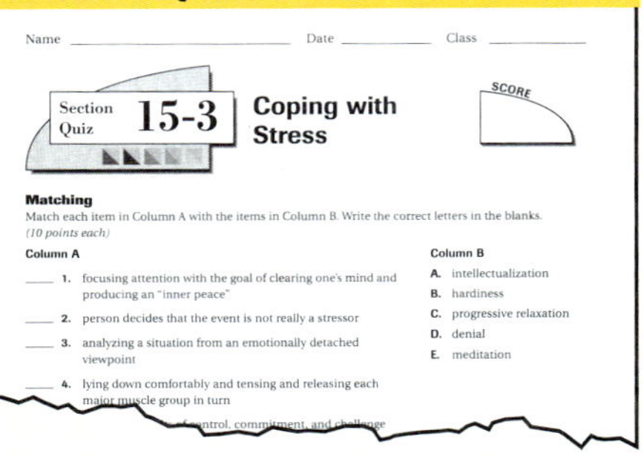
Name ______ Date ______ Class ______

Section Quiz 15-3 **Coping with Stress**

SCORE

Matching
Match each item in Column A with the items in Column B. Write the correct letters in the blanks.
(10 points each)

Column A
____ 1. focusing attention with the goal of clearing one's mind and producing an "inner peace"
____ 2. person decides that the event is not really a stressor
____ 3. analyzing a situation from an emotionally detached viewpoint
____ 4. lying down comfortably and tensing and releasing each major muscle group in turn

Column B
A. intellectualization
B. hardiness
C. progressive relaxation
D. denial
E. meditation

Reteach
Give pairs of students stressful situations to role-play. Have each pair develop a play showing a defensive and an active coping strategy.

progressive relaxation: lying down comfortably and tensing and releasing the tension in each major muscle group in turn

meditation: a focusing of attention with the goal of clearing one's mind and producing an "inner peace"

biofeedback: the process of learning to control bodily states by monitoring the states to be controlled

Relaxation Many techniques of relaxation have been developed especially to cope with stress. More than half a century ago, Dr. Edmond Jacobson devised a method called **progressive relaxation** to reduce muscle tension. This involves lying down comfortably and learning how to tense and then relax each major muscle group in turn. Jacobson later added exercises for mental relaxation in which a person conjures up images and then lets them go. This is known as **meditation** and is a relaxation technique that has been shown to counteract both physical and psychological responses to stress (see Chapter 7). Experienced meditators quickly reach an alpha-wave mental state related to that of Stage I sleep and are able to resume their activities feeling refreshed.

Biofeedback As explained in Chapter 7, **biofeedback** is a technique for bringing specific body processes, such as blood pressure and muscle tension, under a person's conscious control. The participant is hooked up to an electronic device that measures the process he or she wants to regulate and plays that process back in the form of either sounds or visual patterns. This feedback enables many, although not all, people to learn to control various bodily responses. Biofeedback has been used most successfully to train tense people to relax.

Figure 15.13 Stress: A Summary Model

Your evaluation of a situation interacts with the stressor and what you perceive to be the available resources to determine how you react to the stressor. You respond to stress on several levels. ***What are the levels of possible reactions to stress? Give an example for each level.***

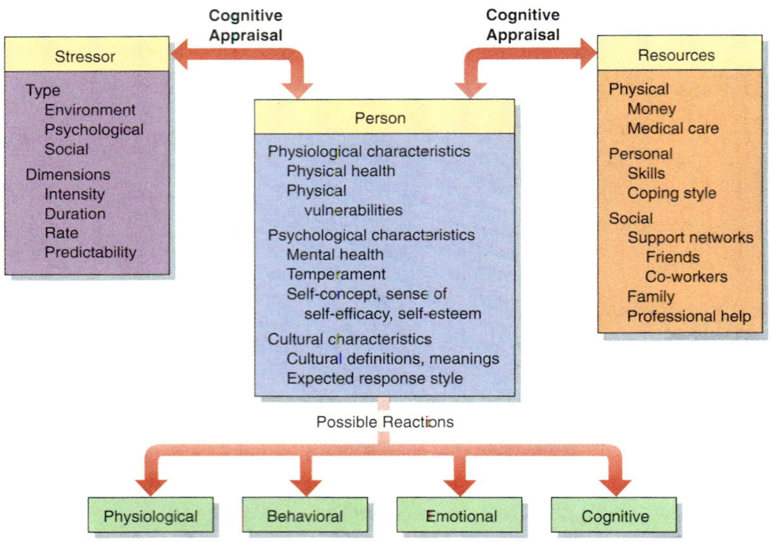

Source: Adapted from Gerrig and Zimbardo, 2005.

Humor Stress management experts often advise clients to try to maintain a sense of humor during difficult situations. Laughing actually releases the tension of pent-up feelings and can help you keep a proper perspective of the situation. In fact, people often resort to humor in very stressful situations. For example, a person may break out in hysterical laughter during the trying times following the death of a loved one. This laughter helps the individual deal with the intense emotional pain of a loss.

Exercise Physical exercise is another constructive way to reduce stress. It stimulates and provides

PSYCHOLOGY LAB EXPERIMENT

Progressive Relaxation Demonstrate progressive relaxation techniques by asking volunteers to lie on a mat on the floor and follow your directions. **(1) Feet:** Point feet straight out and curl toes tightly. Release and relax. **(2) Legs:** Keeping legs straight, lift feet off floor 10 inches. Relax. **(3) Stomach and chest:** Take a deep breath and tighten stomach muscles as you hold your breath. Push shoulders back and hold as you exhale slowly. Relax. **(4) Arms:** Tighten arm muscles as you move hands toward arms. Relax. **(5) Face and neck:** Smile broadly, tighten neck muscles, push eyebrows up and tighten. Relax. Ask volunteers to describe how they feel. **Ask:** **When would you be most likely to use progressive relaxation techniques? L1 ELL**

an outlet for physical arousal, and it may burn off stress hormones. Continuous rhythmic exercise—running or swimming, for example—is not only effective against stress but also ideal for respiratory and cardiovascular fitness. David Holmes and colleagues have performed experiments that indicate aerobic exercise reduces cardiovascular response and arousal following both stressful life events and immediate stress (Roth & Holmes, 1987; Holmes & Roth, 1988).

Support Groups and Professional Help We have discussed the positive role that social support plays in reducing stress. Groups that operate beyond ordinary personal networks, including Alcoholics Anonymous, Weight Watchers, and crisis prevention centers, can help people with specific stress-related problems. Professionals such as psychologists, doctors, social workers, and ministers can also be consulted.

Training A new, unfamiliar, or dangerous situation can be stressful because we are unsure we can deal with it. Training to prepare for such a situation can ease the stress. For instance, a person who is nervous about going to a friend's country club because she does not play tennis might take a few tennis lessons. Exposure to moderate stressors in a relatively safe but challenging environment allows a person to gain experience and confidence in coping.

Improving Interpersonal Skills Much of the stress we undergo results from interpersonal relations. Developing skills in dealing with others—family, friends, and coworkers—is thus one of the best ways to manage stress. There are several advantages to being able to interact well with others—increased self-confidence and self-esteem, less chance of loneliness or interpersonal conflict, and development of social support systems.

Reading Check How can the use of humor reduce stress?

SECTION 3 Assessment

1. **Review the Vocabulary** How does your cognitive appraisal of an event determine your stress level?
2. **Visualize the Main Idea** Use a graphic organizer similar to the one below to list several active coping strategies for dealing with stress.

Active Coping Strategies

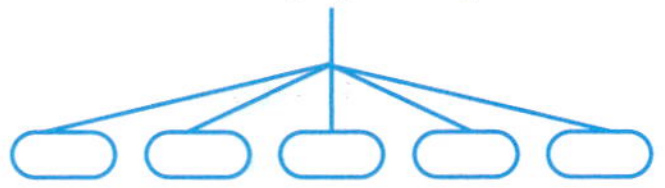

3. **Recall Information** How do people use denial and intellectualization to cope with stress?
4. **Think Critically** Why would writing about a stressful experience help you better cope with it?
5. **Application Activity** Think of a stressful situation that you have recently experienced. How did you cope with it? Describe and analyze your coping mechanism as a psychologist would in a brief report.

Reading Check Answer Humor reduces stress by releasing tension and by helping you maintain a proper perspective.

Enrich

Tell students that people who lost loved ones to the AIDS epidemic created the AIDS Memorial Quilt. It is made of more than 44,000 panels. Each panel is 3 feet by 6 feet—the approximate size of a human grave. The Quilt continues to grow and reflects the sorrow, anger, love, and hope of those who create it. **Ask: How does the Quilt reflect an active coping strategy?**

4 CLOSE

Have students prepare a list of the coping strategies they plan to employ during the next round of midterm or final exams.

SECTION 3 Assessment Answers

1. Your positive or negative feelings about a stressful event or situation help determine the impact of the stress on your life.
2. Students' graphic organizers may include the following: hardiness, controlling stressful situations, problem solving, positive explanatory style, relaxation, biofeedback, humor, exercise, support groups/professional help, training, and improving interpersonal skills.
3. When people use denial they refuse to acknowledge the existence of the stress-causing situation. People use intellectualization to create an emotional detachment between themselves and the situation.
4. Students' answers will vary. Writing could help you explore possible solutions to a problem or it could allow you to look at the situation from multiple perspectives to find a positive solution.
5. Students' answers will vary. Encourage students to use the language of psychologists as they write their reports.

Going Further

Stress and Immunity Studies

In an ongoing study of stress and immunity in breast cancer patients, researcher Barbara Andersen of The Ohio State University compared patients who participated in support groups and other types of stress intervention programs with those who did not. She tested patients four and eight months after surgery and found that those who participated in stress intervention programs had significantly lower levels of the stress hormone cortisol. Such hormones suppress the immune system, making the patient more susceptible to disease. (Lower levels of cortisol are, therefore, beneficial for the patient.)

Study participants also showed significantly higher levels of mucin, an antibody that has been linked to both the severity and the progression of breast cancer.

Discussing the Case Study

Ask: **Why do illusions seem to help people cope with serious illness? How did illusions improve the lives and health of the experimental groups?**

Case Studies

The Illusion of Stress

Period of Study: 1983, 1988

Introduction: In psychology, the term *illusions* is usually considered to be related to a psychosis, or a major psychological disorder in which a person's ability to think, respond emotionally, remember, communicate, or interpret reality is noticeably impaired. Although everyone experiences some perceptual illusions, those diagnosed with a schizophrenic-type disorder often experience bizarre illusions, hallucinations, or delusions. However, Shelley Taylor in 1983 and Taylor with Jonathon Brown in 1988 discovered that illusions might actually promote healthy living. These illusions are voluntary, unlike those associated with schizophrenia. Individuals use illusions to maintain optimistic, hopeful outlooks on situations that otherwise could cause an unhealthy amount of stress. Illusions such as these work for cancer sufferers, AIDS patients, individuals with physical injuries or mental disabilities, and people suffering from other serious illnesses.

Hypothesis: Taylor described illusions as beliefs that were based on "an overly optimistic view of the facts or that had no factual basis at all" (1983). Her hypothesis stated that women suffering from breast cancer who had illusions, by her definition, would cope better with stress from disfiguring surgeries, painful treatments, and the possibilities of death than would the same women who did not have these illusions. The women who would have illusions would benefit from placing themselves in hopeful situations. In addition to studying women with breast cancer, Taylor and Brown researched the illusion hypothesis further by expanding the population studied in 1988.

Method: Taylor conducted a two-year study on women diagnosed with breast cancer. Five years later, Taylor and Brown conducted their research. Both studies consisted of a control group who did not use optimistic illusions and an experimental group of those individuals who did. Once Taylor and Brown established the two groups, they assessed the emotions the participants displayed concerning their conditions, expectations for the future, how they maintained social relationships during their illnesses, and other measures focusing on self-esteem.

Results: Taylor and Brown found that the participants who used illusions to maintain an optimistic view were cheerful, had more friends, and were usually more persistent, creative, and productive than those without such positive illusions (Morris & Maisto, 2005). The positive outlooks these people hold create confidence and the motivation to pursue their interests. Thus, according to Taylor and Brown's findings, the use of illusions can reduce the occurrence of stress in situations that may otherwise be extremely stressful.

Extreme caution, though, should be taken when a person uses illusions. As mentioned earlier, illusions are often associated with psychological disorders. Not everyone can separate reality from fantasy. Some people who may use illusions by Taylor's definition could become fixed in their fantasies and lose the capability of returning to the real world. The use of illusions to reduce or eliminate stress not only requires a vivid imagination but also a strong mind.

Analyzing the Case Study

1. How is the use of illusions related to stress?
2. How did Taylor and Brown test their hypothesis?
3. **Critical Thinking** When do you think the use of illusions crosses the line from healthy to unhealthy living?

Answers for Analyzing the Case Study

1. Illusions can reduce stress by allowing people to focus on overly optimistic outcomes. Illusions allow people to place themselves in hopeful situations and, therefore, reduce the stress they feel.
2. They compared the emotions displayed by women with breast cancer who used optimistic illusions with those who did not use optimistic illusions.
3. Answers will vary. The use of illusions becomes unhealthy when they become substitutes for reality.

SECTION 4 Stress in Your Life

Reader's Guide

Main Idea

For many people, college and work involve adjustment and stress.

Vocabulary

- autonomy
- developmental friendship
- resynthesis
- career
- comparable worth

Objectives

- Identify some of the issues related to adjustment to college life.
- Describe issues related to starting a first job.

EXPLORING PSYCHOLOGY

Are You Ready for Independence?

I thought when I was a senior [in high school] that I was really independent. You know what I mean: I kept my own schedule, had a job and car, decided when I needed to do homework or not. But you and Dad were always there to back me up. If I didn't know how to do something, I could walk into the kitchen and ask you. Now I have to figure everything out by myself. *That's* independence.

—from *Almost Grown: Launching Your Child From High School to College* by Patricia Pasick, 1998

The quotation above is what a first-year college student at Tufts University told his mother during parents' weekend. Families do not stay together forever. Children grow up and leave home to set up new households and start their own families. This period of life signifies a major life change for both teens and parents. This life change involves dealing with stress.

Growing up involves gaining a sense of **autonomy**—the ability to take care of oneself—and independence. Each person learns to make decisions, develop a value system, be responsible, and to care for himself or herself. Growing up is a process that starts long before an individual leaves home to live as a self-sufficient adult. Yet ultimately, it means separating from the family, both physically and emotionally.

autonomy: ability to take care of oneself and make one's own decisions

CHOOSING COLLEGE

For millions of young Americans, college is one of the first big steps toward this separation. As college students individuals are freer than they ever have been or may ever be again. This can be a personally liberating

SECTION RESOURCES

Reproducible Masters

- Guided Reading Activity 15–4
- Vocabulary Activity 15–4
- Section Quiz 15–4

Transparencies

- Daily Focus Transparency 15–4

Multimedia

- *ExamView® Assessment Suite* CD-ROM
- Presentation Plus! Software

1 FOCUS

Section Objectives

1. Identify some of the issues related to adjustment to college life.
2. Describe issues related to starting a first job.

BELLRINGER
Motivational Activity

Project Daily Focus Transparency 15–4 and have students answer the questions.

Available as blackline master.

Daily Focus Transparency 15–4

Reader's Guide

Use the Reader's Guide to introduce concepts and vocabulary.

Exploring Psychology

Ask students to read the **Exploring Psychology** feature and then discuss the following question: **How does stress change as levels of responsibility change?**

Vocabulary Precheck

Have students write their best guess at a definition for each vocabulary term. Then have them read the definition from the Glossary. Students should revise their written definitions as necessary.

CHAPTER 15
Section 4, pages 437–442

2 TEACH

L1 Research Assign students to conduct brief interviews with at least one person in each of the following age groups: 8–12, 13–18, 19–25, 26–35, 36–45, 46–55, and 56 and over. Ask the students to find out what the interviewees' greatest stressors are and what, if anything, they do to manage stress. Have the class construct a chart comparing stressors and coping mechanisms in each age group. **Ask: What conclusions can you draw about age-related stress? Do the causes of stress change with age? If so, how? What, if any, changes took place in the coping mechanisms used by the interviewees?**

Reading Check Answer It may require moving, changing friends, and dealing with new people, situations, and choices. In addition, the student may need to evaluate abilities, motives, needs, and aspirations.

TEACHER Tip

Students often have unrealistic expectations of adult life. The research activity above should help students realize the kinds of stresses faced by adults and the ways that adults cope with stress in their lives.

and stimulating experience, but it also requires adjustment. The emotional upheaval many first-year college students feel has been called "college shock."

Peter Madison (1969) spent nearly 10 years collecting data on how several hundred students adjusted to college. Each student provided a detailed life history and kept a weekly journal. Madison had classmates write descriptions of some of the students, and he tested and retested some at various points in their college careers.

Madison found that many students approach college with high, and often unrealistic, aspirations. For example, Bridget wanted to be an astronomer. She liked the idea of being different, and she considered astronomy an elite and adventuresome field, but she did not know how many long, hard, unadventuresome hours she would have to spend studying mathematics to fulfill her dream. Keith planned to become a physician for what he described as humanitarian reasons. He had never thought about working in a hospital or watching people sicken and die, though.

These two students, like many others, based their goals on fantasy. They did not have the experience to make realistic choices or the maturity to evaluate their own motives and needs. Their experiences during the first semesters of college led them to change both their minds and their images of themselves.

Sources of Change

Reading Check What adjustments does going to college require?

How does going to college stimulate change? First, college may challenge the identity a student has established in high school. A top high school student may go to a top college. Nearly everyone there is as bright and competitive as she is. Within a matter of weeks the student's identity as a star pupil has evaporated, and she may have to struggle to get average grades. Young people who excelled in sports, drama, or student politics may have similar experiences. The high school student-body president discovers two other high school presidents in his dormitory alone.

Second, whether students come from small towns or big cities, they are likely to encounter greater diversity in college than they ever have before—diversity in religious and ethnic backgrounds, family income levels, and attitudes. A student who develops a close relationship with another, then discovers that the person holds beliefs or engages in behavior he or she has always considered immoral, may be badly shaken. You are faced with a choice—abandon deeply held values or give up an important friendship. Madison (1969) calls close relationships between people who force each other to reexamine their basic assumptions **developmental friendships.** He found that developmental friendships in particular and student culture in general have more impact on college students than professors do.

developmental friendship: friends force one another to reexamine their basic assumptions and perhaps adopt new ideas and beliefs

However, if instructors and assigned books clarify thoughts that have been brewing in a student's mind, they can make all the difference. This was true of Keith. Keith did extremely well in the courses required for a pre-med student, but he found he enjoyed his literature and philosophy classes far more. He began reading avidly. He felt as if each of the authors had deliberately set out to put all his self-doubts into words. In time Keith

COOPERATIVE LEARNING ACTIVITY

Coping With Everyday Stress Tell students they will be creating general public service announcements on how to deal with stress. Organize the class into small production teams. Ask each group to develop a videotape (or a storyboard) for a public service announcement titled "Surviving Stress." The focus of the announcement should be on coping with everyday stress, such as the types of stress encountered in the workplace. **BLOCK SCHEDULING**

realized that his interest in medicine was superficial. He had decided to become a doctor because it was a respected profession that would give him status, security, and a good income—and would guarantee his parents' love. The self-image Keith had brought to college was completely changed.

Coping With Change Madison found that students cope with the stress of going to college in several different ways. Some focus more narrowly when their goals are threatened by internal or external change. They redouble their efforts to succeed in the field they have chosen and avoid people and situations that might bring their doubts to the surface. Troy, for example, stayed with a chemical-engineering program for three years, despite a growing interest in social science. By the time he realized that engineering was not the field for him, it was too late to change majors. He got the degree but left college with no idea where he was heading.

Others avoid confronting doubt by frittering away their time, going through the motions of attending college but detaching themselves emotionally. Some students manage to keep their options open until they have enough information and experience to make a choice. Madison calls this third method of coping **resynthesis.** For most students this involves a period of indecision, doubt, and anxiety. The student tries to combine the new and old, temporarily abandons the original goal, retreats, heads in another direction, retreats again, and finally reorganizes his or her feelings and efforts around an emerging identity.

Figure 15.14 Experiencing Diversity

Going to college means orienting oneself to different faces, personalities, and living habits. ***How can experiencing different personalities and issues at college help a person develop his or her own identity?***

resynthesis: combining old ideas with new ones and reorganizing feelings in order to renew one's identity

WORKING

Graduating from college or high school involves thinking about and finding your first job and your career. But what is work? For one person work means loading 70,000 pounds on a five-axle truck, driving alone for several hours a day, perhaps for several days, with only a few stops for food and fuel, talk, relief, and sleep. While alone in the cab, tension is constant; it is hard to brake a truck suddenly while carrying thousands of pounds, so the driver must always think ahead. The work is wearing, yet the odd hours and independence are enjoyable.

For another person work means spending eight or nine hours a day at an advertising agency, dealing with clients and supervising commercial writers. This person earns good money, spends a great deal of time talking with people, and has plenty of opportunities to exercise his or her talents as a manager. All three are positive aspects of the job. Yet this person must also deal with deadlines and worry about whether millions of dollars' worth of ads will sell the products or not—and, subconsciously, whether it is worth the effort if they do.

MEETING SPECIAL NEEDS

Learning Style: Kinesthetic Ask students to research the best types of physical exercise to reduce stress. Have students use their research to develop a set of recommended exercises to reduce everyday types of stress. Ask students to try the exercises for a week and see if stress levels decrease. Stress levels may be measured by pulse or heart rate or by subjective measures such as how well they sleep or how they feel. Students should then develop a fact sheet to explain the exercise program. **L2** **BLOCK SCHEDULING**

Refer to ***Inclusion for the High School Social Studies Classroom Strategies and Activities*** in the TCR for strategies for students with different learning styles.

Figure 15.14

Caption Answer Challenges to one's values, beliefs, and assumptions through different personalities and issues force a person to examine the things that are most important to him or her and to make life choices.

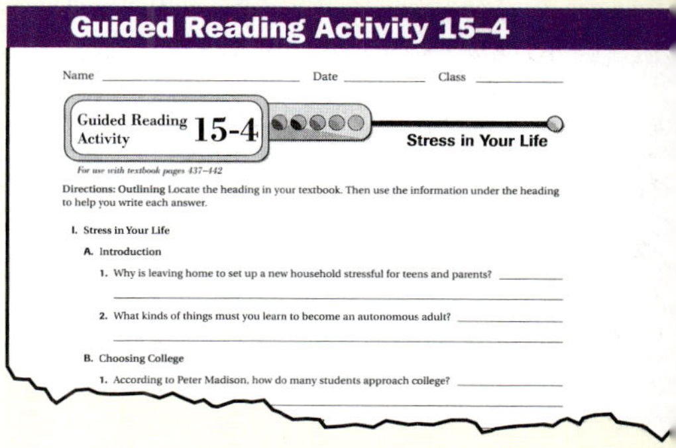

Guided Reading Activity 15–4

Name ______ Date ______ Class ______

Guided Reading Activity 15-4 Stress in Your Life

For use with textbook pages 437–442

Directions: Outlining Locate the heading in your textbook. Then use the information under the heading to help you write each answer.

I. Stress in Your Life
A. Introduction
1. Why is leaving home to set up a new household stressful for teens and parents? ______
2. What kinds of things must you learn to become an autonomous adult? ______
B. Choosing College
1. According to Peter Madison, how do many students approach college? ______

PSYCHOLOGY JOURNAL

Ask students to write about the stresses they have experienced at their places of employment. If the student is not currently employed, ask him or her to write about the workplace stresses that parents mention. ■

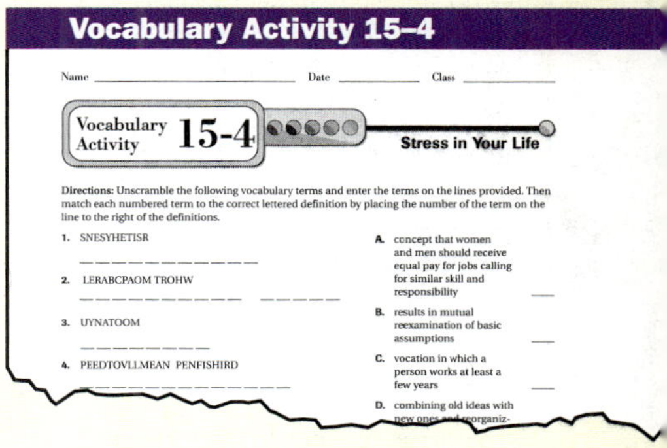

Vocabulary Activity 15–4

Name ______ Date ______ Class ______

Vocabulary Activity 15-4 Stress in Your Life

Directions: Unscramble the following vocabulary terms and enter the terms on the lines provided. Then match each numbered term to the correct lettered definition by placing the number of the term on the line to the right of the definitions.

1. SNESYHETISR ______
2. LERABCPAOM TROHW ______ ______
3. UYNATOOM ______
4. PEEDTOVLLMEAN PENFISHIRD ______

A. concept that women and men should receive equal pay for jobs calling for similar skill and responsibility ___
B. results in mutual reexamination of basic assumptions ___
C. vocation in which a person works at least a few years ___
D. combining old ideas with new ones and reorganiz-

Figure 15.15

Caption Answer A report submitted for a grade stands on its own without having to sell the idea to anyone. A quality report will not be rejected because of its ideas. At work, a report will be analyzed and discussed by team members and managers. It may be revised, usurped, or rejected not because of the quality of the work but because the ideas presented do not fit in some way with the organization. Also, whereas you receive immediate and specific feedback in the form of a grade on a class report, you may receive no feedback, little feedback, or mixed feedback on a report submitted at work.

Looking @ the Issues

Wasting Money At various times, we all waste money. Sometimes we think that we are buying just the right thing with our money. But, when we look back on the purchase, we view it as a waste of money. Other times, we know almost immediately that we have wasted our money. For example, we purchase a movie ticket and hate the movie. **Ask: How does wasting money create stress in your life? What are different ways that money can be wasted?** *(Examples include impulse buying, wasteful living, overpaying, buying on credit and paying too much interest, and buying the latest fad items.)* **Do these different ways to waste money create different levels of stress? Explain.**

Figure 15.15 Adjusting to Work

Entering the world of work can cause excitement, but it may also lead to disappointment. ***How might submitting a report at work be different from submitting a report in class for a grade?***

Dilbert reprinted by permission of United Feature Syndicate, Inc.

For a third person work means training severely disabled children to use their muscles to grasp a spoon, to gesture in sign language, and perhaps to take a few steps. The job is often depressing and frustrating, but there are also moments of intense per-sonal satisfaction when a child makes progress. The point is that each person's work experience is different and each person reacts differently to a job as a result of his or her own personality.

Work Satisfaction and Dissatisfaction

Industrial/organizational psychologists explore what factors contribute to job satisfaction. This research is important because low job satisfaction is associated with high rates of employee absenteeism and turnover, which leads to lower productivity. Job satisfaction is simply the attitude a worker has toward his or her job.

Some workers may seek high salaries, pleasant working conditions, and low-pressure jobs, while others may be concerned only with finding personal fulfillment at work. Most workers, however, have both economic and personal goals. One study (Quinn et al., 1971) identified five major sources of work satisfaction.

1. *Resources:* The worker feels that he or she has enough available resources—help, supplies, and equipment—to do the job well.
2. *Financial reward:* The job pays well, offers good fringe benefits, and is secure.
3. *Challenge:* The job is interesting and enables the worker to use his or her special talents and abilities.
4. *Relations with coworkers:* The worker is on good terms professionally and socially with colleagues.
5. *Comfort:* Working conditions and related factors—hours, travel to and from the job, work environment, and so on—are attractive.

Changing Careers

career: a vocation in which a person works at least a few years

Some theorists predict that in the future, people will change their **career**—a vocation in which a person works at least a few years—several times in their lifetimes. People today live longer than ever before, and so they have a longer work life. It is not uncommon for a person to retire from one job at the age of 60 or 65, then embark on a new career as a real-estate

CRITICAL THINKING ACTIVITY

Identifying Central Issues Conduct a brief interview with three people who have recently started new jobs. Ask them about the adjustments they have had to make in their day-to-day lives as a result of this new job. Compare the interviews and identify the similarities and differences between the adjustments of the three people. **Ask: Were any adjustments mentioned by all three interviewees? Were the interviewees working full-time jobs? If so, how do you think this influenced their responses? If not, what differences did you note between the full-time and part-time workers in terms of the adjustments they have made? L2**

agent, travel broker, writer, or consultant. Some employers have early-retirement programs that allow people at a relatively young age to leave jobs with partial pay. Alumni of these programs have been especially good candidates for subsequent careers. Many women also split their careers by stepping out of the job market to raise children, then reentering the working world for a second full career.

As we have seen, people want work that is psychologically as well as financially rewarding. If a person is unhappy at a job, changing careers may provide the answer. Job shopping, or trying out several careers, is most common among people who have recently entered the labor force and are still trying to get a feel for the work that suits them best. Across all ages, however, worker satisfaction is affected by the availability of other jobs. Research indicates that during periods when jobs are hard to find, workers tolerate more dissatisfaction with their present job (Carsten & Spector, 1987).

Does this mean you should forget about career training, since you probably will not stick with your first job? Not at all. You should acquire as many abilities and interests as you can—in and out of school. You should work to develop your interpersonal skills, and you should look at change as desirable and challenging. In these ways, more occupations will be open to you, and your chances of employment will be better.

Did You Know?

Enjoying Work Most people enjoy their work more if it is complex rather than simple, varied rather than routine, and not closely supervised by someone else. Most workers enjoy making many choices throughout the workday.

Comparable Worth

Consider the following two cases. Tonya is employed as a day-care supervisor for a state government. To qualify for this job, she needed three years of experience as well as college credit. In her job, she is responsible for not only the care and well-being of the children but also the supervision of several subordinates. Trent, also a state worker, is in charge of a storeroom and is responsible for supplying goods to various departments in his building as well as supervising several subordinates. To qualify for his job, Trent needed four years of experience. In terms of actual job demands, Trent's and Tonya's jobs might seem to be quite comparable. However, Trent is paid more than Tonya, despite Tonya's job requiring college credit.

In theory, jobs of comparable training, skill, and importance should be compensated at the same rate—this is **comparable worth.** In practice, however, the market value of many jobs traditionally held by females is considerably lower than that of comparable jobs traditionally held by males. Moreover, men and women are not evenly distributed among the various occupations (see Figure 15.16). Men have tended toward higher-paid occupations, while women have tended (or been encouraged) toward lower-paid occupations. Overall, women face a considerable gap between their income and that received by men.

Many groups have been working to achieve equal pay for comparable work. The National Organization for Women has made the upgrading of traditionally female jobs one of its highest priorities. Labor unions have also

Reading Check What is comparable worth? Why is it important?

comparable worth: the concept that women and men should receive equal pay for jobs calling for comparable skill and responsibility

CHAPTER 15
Section 4, pages 437–442

Reading Check Answer
Comparable worth is the idea that jobs of comparable training, skill, and importance should be compensated at the same rate. Comparable worth is an important issue because, overall, women face a considerable gap between their income and that received by men.

3 ASSESS

Assign Section 4 Assessment as homework or as an in-class activity.

Section Quiz 15–4

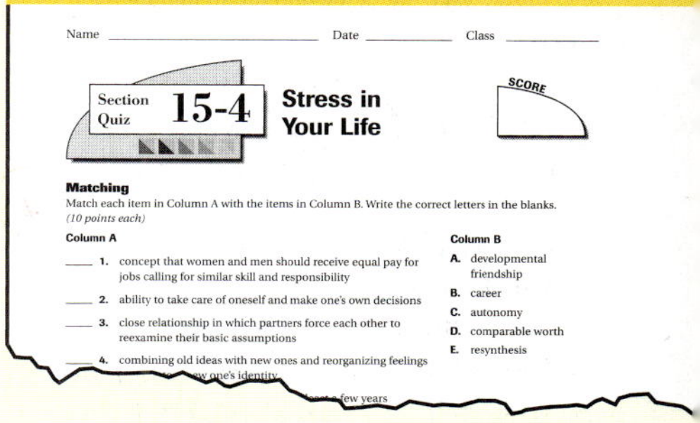
Name ____ Date ____ Class ____

Section Quiz 15-4 Stress in Your Life

SCORE

Matching
Match each item in Column A with the items in Column B. Write the correct letters in the blanks. *(10 points each)*

Column A

____ 1. concept that women and men should receive equal pay for jobs calling for similar skill and responsibility

____ 2. ability to take care of oneself and make one's own decisions

____ 3. close relationship in which partners force each other to reexamine their basic assumptions

____ 4. combining old ideas with new ones and reorganizing feelings

Column B

A. developmental friendship

B. career

C. autonomy

D. comparable worth

E. resynthesis

Reteach
Have a class discussion about the value of developing as many abilities as possible while training for a career. Discuss the advantages of having a diversity of job skills, given the temporary nature of many careers.

PSYCHOLOGY LAB EXPERIMENT

Job Satisfaction and Stress Have students work in pairs to develop a questionnaire to test the hypothesis that as job satisfaction increases, job stress decreases. The questionnaire should ask indirect questions about job satisfaction, such as "Do you receive adequate recognition for the work you do?" The questionnaire should also ask indirect questions about job stress, such as "Do you spend a lot of time outside work worrying about what you left undone?" The questions for job stress and job satisfaction should be randomly mixed. The questionnaire should include a space for the participant's job title. Students should have at least 10 people who work full-time complete the questionnaire. Have students analyze their results and prepare a job satisfaction chart for each participant. **L2**

CHAPTER 15
Section 4, pages 437–442

Figure 15.16

Visual Instruction Ask students to use the graph to answer the following question: **Which occupation(s) has about the same number of men and women?** *(sales occupations)*

Caption Answer Most men work in the construction trades and crafts. Most women work as health service workers.

Enrich

Have students prepare a chart or table showing men's and women's median wages over the last 30 years. **Ask: What changes have taken place? What has caused these changes?**

4 CLOSE

Ask students to write their goals for the next five years. Ask them what plans they have for education and work. Ask students to evaluate their progress. Then ask what their stress level was while they were writing their goals. **Ask: Does thinking about and planning for the future create stress? How do you plan to manage that stress?**

Figure 15.16 Distribution of Male and Female Workers by Occupation

One of the reasons for differences in pay between the genders is that men and women are not evenly distributed among occupations. If men tend to cluster in higher-paid occupations and if women tend to cluster in lower-paid occupations the average pay of men and women will differ. ***What are typical occupations for men? For women?***

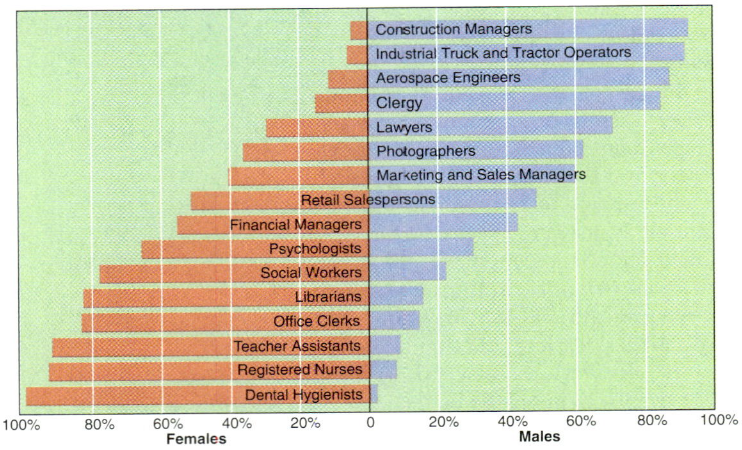

Source: U.S. Bureau of Labor Statistics, 2005.

been addressing the issue of pay equity. Congress passed two major laws to prevent discrimination and income discrepancies between men and women. The Equal Pay Act of 1963 prohibits wage and salary discrimination for jobs that require equivalent skills and responsibilities. The Civil Rights Act of 1964 prohibits discrimination in all areas of employment on the basis of gender, race, color, religion, and national origin. It may seem surprising that such laws are necessary. For economic reasons, though, many employers are unwilling to raise salaries, especially if they are able to find workers who will accept the low wages that they do offer. Workers face a hard choice: strike or accept a low wage to feed their family.

SECTION 4 Assessment

1. **Review the Vocabulary** Explain how going to college involves autonomy.
2. **Visualize the Main Idea** Use a diagram similar to the one below to identify five sources of work satisfaction.

3. **Recall Information** Why do developmental friendships have so much impact on a person?
4. **Think Critically** How do you think job satisfaction and productivity are related? Does good worker performance occur as a result of high job satisfaction, or is high job satisfaction a result of good worker performance? Explain your answers.
5. **Application Activity** Your future happiness in the world of work depends on factors like what you are doing, where you work, who you work with, and why you are working there. Use these factors to create a list of jobs or careers that might suit you. Explain your choices.

SECTION 4 Assessment Answers

1. For many people, college is the first time that they live on their own, out of their parents' home. It is also a time when most life choices are left up to the student.
2. resources, financial reward, challenge, relations with coworkers, comfort
3. Developmental friendships force people to reexamine their beliefs, values, and assumptions and may result in people adopting new values, beliefs, and goals.
4. Job satisfaction and productivity are highly correlated, especially when people at work are primarily motivated by extrinsic rewards. Challenge students to consider how knowing that you have done your job well, even if it is not a challenging job, can result in a high level of job satisfaction.
5. Students' answers will vary. Ask students to examine which of these factors are most important to them. For example, some people strongly desire to settle in one place. They may be willing to trade off other factors for a job that will not involve transfers to other cities.

CHAPTER 15

Summary and Vocabulary

Although all people experience stress at some point in their lives, how they react to it varies from individual to individual. People also use various techniques to cope with stress in their lives.

Section 1 Sources of Stress

Main Idea: Stress results from our perceptions of demands placed upon us and our evaluations of situations we encounter.

- Stress is a normal part of life that goes hand in hand with working toward any goal or facing any challenge.
- Making difficult decisions between two or more options results in conflicting motives and is a major source of stress.
- Major life changes are important sources of stress.

Section 2 Reactions to Stress

Main Idea: People react differently to life's stressors. These reactions may be beneficial or harmful.

- The body reacts to stress with the fight-or-flight response. This prepares the individual to either face potentially dangerous situations or escape them.
- The general adaptation syndrome identifies three stages in the body's stress reaction: alarm, resistance, and exhaustion.
- How people react to stress depends on their personality type, their perception of control over stressors, and the social support they receive.

Section 3 Coping With Stress

Main Idea: People deal with stress by employing defensive and active coping strategies.

- A person's interpretation and evaluation of an event helps determine its stress impact.
- Common defense mechanisms used to cope with stress are denial and intellectualization.
- Active coping strategies involve changing the environment or modifying a situation to remove stressors or reduce the level of stress.

Section 4 Stress in Your Life

Main Idea: For many people, college and work involve stress and adjustment.

- Attending college stimulates change in many students.
- Students find several ways of coping with the stress of going to college.
- Job satisfaction is simply the attitude a worker has toward his or her job.
- Overall, women face a considerable gap between their income and that received by men.

Chapter Vocabulary

stress (p. 413)
stressor (p. 414)
stress reaction (p. 414)
distress (p. 414)
eustress (p. 414)
conflict situation (p. 414)
anxiety (p. 422)
anger (p. 422)
fear (p. 422)
immune system (p. 426)
social support (p. 428)
cognitive appraisal (p. 431)
denial (p. 431)
intellectualization (p. 431)
progressive relaxation (p. 434)
meditation (p. 434)
biofeedback (p. 434)
autonomy (p. 437)
developmental friendship (p. 438)
resynthesis (p. 439)
career (p. 440)
comparable worth (p. 441)

15 Summary and Vocabulary

Using the Chapter 15 Summary and Vocabulary

Use the Chapter 15 Summary and Vocabulary to preview, review, condense, or reteach the chapter.

Preview/Review

Use the Chapter Vocabulary list to help students review and study.

Activity Have students create a word search puzzle using definitions or examples as the clues for the puzzle. Then have pairs of students exchange and complete each other's puzzles.

Vocabulary PuzzleMaker CD-ROM reinforces the vocabulary terms used in Chapter 15.

Condense

Have students read the Chapter 15 Summary.

Chapter 15 Guided Reading Activities

Reteach

Reteaching Activity 15

PERFORMANCE ASSESSMENT ACTIVITY

Creating a Pamphlet Tell students that they are employed in the Student Services department of a large university. They have been assigned to create a pamphlet that will be sent to all new students. The pamphlet will discuss stress and change. It should inform students of the typical stresses involved in adjusting to campus life. The pamphlet can use words, photos, drawings, charts, or tables to convey the message. **BLOCK SCHEDULING**

Refer to the ***Authentic Assessment*** booklet for additional activities and information about evaluating student performance.

PSYCHOLOGY Online

Have students visit the Web site at glencoe.com to review Chapter 15 and take the **Self-Check Quiz**.

GLENCOE TECHNOLOGY

Presentation Plus! For a review of Chapter 15 content, see MindJogger Checkpoint on **Presentation Plus!**

Reviewing Vocabulary

1. e	**6.** f
2. i	**7.** d
3. c	**8.** j
4. h	**9.** b
5. a	**10.** g

Recalling Facts

1. The most common conflict situation is double approach-avoidance conflict. It can be resolved by finding new factors that make one option more (or less) preferable, by finding a third alternative, or by choosing one of the alternatives.
2. Social groups offer (1) emotional support involving concerned listening and bolstering one's self-confidence; (2) appraisal support in which the group helps the person analyze the stressful situation; (3) instrumental support that provides direct, tangible help such as financial assistance, food, or temporary shelter; and (4) informational support, which emerges from appraisal support and helps the person evaluate the way he or she is dealing with stress.
3. Two techniques are progressive relaxation and meditation. Progressive relaxation reduces muscle tension and relaxes the mind as the body is relaxed. Meditation is focused thinking that creates a state similar to Stage I sleep and relieves both physical and psychological stress.
4. Students' identities are challenged as they encounter a greater diversity of people, attitudes, and values. Students experience independence and build developmental friendships. The emotional upheaval of moving to a new place and meeting new people can be stressful. College is often a change from life as students know it.
5. In the short term, stress can give you the physical energy needed to meet a challenge. If stress is not relieved, however, it can result in exhaustion and disease. Stress is a major contributor to peptic ulcers, hypertension, certain kinds of arthritis, asthma, and heart disease. Stress also suppresses the immune system, contributing to a variety of illnesses.

Critical Thinking

1. Answers will vary. Most students will see stress as a reaction to events. The effects that stress produces will vary among people because of their perceptions of an event.
2. Answers will vary. Have students identify the personality traits that make one more or less susceptible to the effects of stress. Stress suppresses the immune system, which inhibits the body's ability to fight disease.
3. Answers will vary. With defensive coping strategies, the stress is seen as a threat. People using active coping strategies treat stress as a challenge. In the long term, active coping strategies are more effective for dealing with ongoing sources of stress. However, defensive strategies may be effective for certain types of stress.
4. Answers will vary. Encourage students to think of college life as a positive transition from adolescence to adulthood.
5. Answers will vary. Encourage students with work experience to share their thoughts with the rest of the class.

CHAPTER 15 Assessment

PSYCHOLOGY Online

Self-Check Quiz
Visit the *Understanding Psychology* Web site at glencoe.com and click on **Chapter 15—Self-Check Quizzes** to prepare for the Chapter Test.

Reviewing Vocabulary

Choose the letter of the correct term or concept below to complete the sentence.

a. stressor	**f.** social support
b. stress reaction	**g.** cognitive appraisal
c. distress	**h.** progressive relaxation
d. eustress	**i.** autonomy
e. anxiety	**j.** comparable worth

1. __________ is a feeling of imminent but unclear threat.
2. People who are able to take care of themselves have gained a sense of __________.
3. Negative stress is called __________.
4. __________ is a technique used to reduce muscle tension.
5. A stress-producing event or situation is called the __________.
6. Information that leads an individual to believe that he or she is cared for, loved, and respected is called __________.
7. Positive stress is called __________.
8. The concept that jobs of comparable training, skill, and importance should be compensated at the same rate is called __________.
9. The body's observable response to a stress-producing event is called __________.
10. The process of interpreting and evaluating an event is called __________.

Recalling Facts

1. What is probably the most common conflict situation, and in what ways can this conflict be resolved?
2. Using a graphic organizer similar to the one below, identify and explain the four kinds of support that social groups offer for reducing stress.

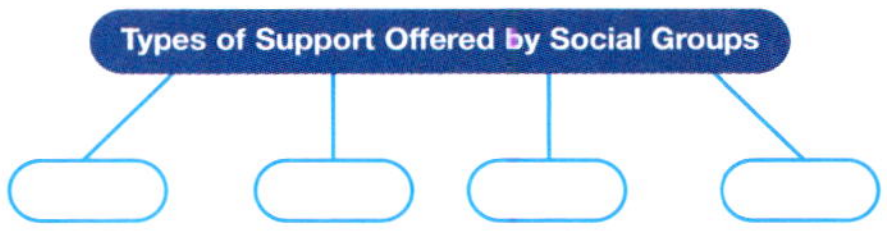

3. What are two relaxation techniques that can be used for coping with stress? How do they work?
4. List at least two of the new experiences and challenges that a student faces when entering college. How might these new experiences cause stress?
5. How can stress impact you physically? How does stress affect the immune system?

Critical Thinking

1. **Analyzing Concepts** As you have learned, some psychologists believe that stress is an event that produces worry. Others believe that stress is an individual's response to such an event. Still others believe stress is an individual's perception of the event. Which definition of stress do you agree with? Why?
2. **Synthesizing Information** Do you think all individuals are equally susceptible to stress-related illnesses? Are some people better able to cope with stress than others? What does this say about stress as a *cause* of illness? Explain.
3. **Evaluating Information** Two kinds of coping strategies are defensive coping strategies and active coping strategies. What is the difference between these coping strategies? Which of the two do you think is more effective in helping an individual cope with stress? Why do you think so?
4. **Making Inferences** Do you think increasing autonomy can create positive or negative feelings in a college student? Why do you think so?
5. **Demonstrating Reasoned Judgment** Which of the five major sources of job satisfaction do you think is the most essential? Why do you think so?

CHAPTER 15

Assessment

Psychology Projects

1. **Sources of Stress** Work with a partner to create a skit that illustrates each of the four conflict situations: approach-approach, avoidance-avoidance, approach-avoidance, and double approach-avoidance. Present your skit to the class and have your classmates identify the conflict situation you are demonstrating.
2. **Reactions to Stress** Find recent magazine articles about the latest research in the connection between stress and illness. Find out how stress contributes to the development of certain diseases. Report your findings in an oral report.
3. **Coping With Stress** Find out about various support groups and professional help available in your community (for illnesses, causes, etc.). You might look through your local phone book, contact a local hospital, or contact your local government offices for information. Identify the groups and help available and explain how they can help an individual cope with stress. Present your findings in an informational pamphlet.

Technology Activity

The Internet provides many sites regarding jobs and careers. Find several of these sites. What kinds of information do they provide? Do any of these sites offer advice for dealing with stress in the workplace or during a job hunt? Create a report with your findings. Include the addresses of the sites you found in your report.

Psychology Journal

Reread the journal entry you made at the beginning of the chapter. Next, consider these questions: Do students seem more stressed prior to tests or exams? Can you discover any common elements among these sources of stress? What might be done to alleviate stress in school? Would stress be reduced or eliminated if there were no grades? What if there were no tests? What would school be like without stress? Should stress in school be eliminated? Write your answers to these questions in your journal.

Building Skills

Interpreting a Graph Review the graph, then answer the questions that follow.

1. What are the three phases of the general adaptation syndrome?
2. In what phases might a person become most vulnerable to catching a cold? Why?
3. From the information contained in this graph, explain why people with stressful occupations might be prone to developing serious illnesses.

Phases of Selye's General Adaptation Syndrome

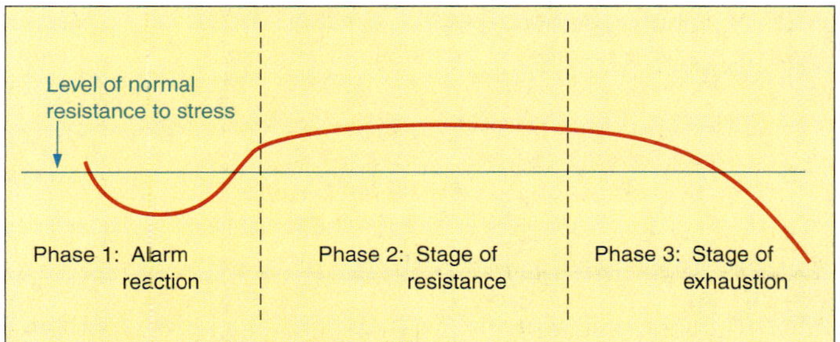

Source: Adapted from *The Stress of Life*, Selye, 1956.

Practice and **assess** key social studies skills with **Glencoe Skillbuilder Interactive Workbook CD-ROM, Level 2.**

See the Skills Handbook, page 628, for an explanation of interpreting graphs.

Building Skills

1. alarm, resistance, exhaustion
2. Phase 3 (exhaustion), because the body's immune system is weak due to lack of rest
3. People with stressful occupations are often exposed to stress for long periods of time. When this occurs, the body reaches its breaking point and becomes exhausted. The immune system is weakened and makes the body more susceptible to illness.

GLENCOE TECHNOLOGY

CD-ROM

Glencoe Skillbuilder Interactive Workbook, Level 2

This interactive CD-ROM is designed to reinforce student mastery of essential social studies skills.

Chapter Bonus Test Question

This question may be used for extra credit on the Chapter Assessment.

Answer the following question:

I am small, positive events that make people feel good and protect against the effects of stress. What am I?

Answer: uplifts

Psychology Projects

1. Skits may show four different situations or variations on one basic situation. Encourage students to use examples that teens typically encounter.
2. The reports should cite all source information. Have students look critically at who conducted the research.
3. Encourage students to gather as much information as possible. You may want to categorize the information by age categories, for example, help available for children, teens, families, and senior citizens.

Technology Activity

Students may also want to explore how to post a resume on the Web. Encourage students to share their findings with the class.

Psychology Journal

Students' answers should express their own stresses and how the information in the chapter is helping them learn to cope.

Chapter 16 Resource Guide

SECTION RESOURCES		
Daily Objectives	**Reproducible Resources**	**Multimedia Resources**
Section 1 **What Are Psychological Disorders?** Explore how psychologists draw the line between normal and abnormal behavior by looking at deviance, adjustment, and psychological health.	Blackline Master: Guided Reading Activity 16–1 Blackline Master: Vocabulary Activity 16–1 Blackline Master: Section Quiz 16–1	Transparency: Daily Focus Transparency 16–1 CD-ROM: *ExamView® Assessment Suite* CD-ROM CD-ROM: Presentation Plus! Software
Section 2 **Anxiety Disorders** Describe how anxiety disorders are marked by excessive fear, caution, and attempts to avoid anxiety.	Blackline Master: Guided Reading Activity 16–2 Blackline Master: Vocabulary Activity 16–2 Blackline Master: Section Quiz 16–2	Transparency: Daily Focus Transparency 16–2 CD-ROM: *ExamView® Assessment Suite* CD-ROM CD-ROM: Presentation Plus! Software
Section 3 **Somatoform and Dissociative Disorders** Explain how dealing with anxiety and stress can bring about somatoform and dissociative disorders in some people.	Blackline Master: Guided Reading Activity 16–3 Blackline Master: Vocabulary Activity 16–3 Blackline Master: Section Quiz 16–3	Transparency: Daily Focus Transparency 16–3 CD-ROM: Vocabulary PuzzleMaker CD-ROM CD-ROM: *ExamView® Assessment Suite* CD-ROM CD-ROM: Presentation Plus! Software
Section 4 **Schizophrenia and Mood Disorders** Explain how schizophrenia involves confused and disordered thoughts, and mood disorders involve disturbances in the experience and expressions of depression.	Blackline Master: Guided Reading Activity 16–4 Blackline Master: Vocabulary Activity 16–4 Blackline Master: Section Quiz 16–4	Transparency: Daily Focus Transparency 16–4 CD-ROM: *ExamView® Assessment Suite* CD-ROM CD-ROM: Presentation Plus! Software
Section 5 **Personality Disorders and Drug Addiction** Determine how personality disorders and drug addiction prohibit normal relationships and normal functioning.	Blackline Master: Guided Reading Activity 16–5 Blackline Master: Vocabulary Activity 16–5 Blackline Master: Section Quiz 16–5	Transparency: Daily Focus Transparency 16–5 CD-ROM: Vocabulary PuzzleMaker CD-ROM CD-ROM: *ExamView® Assessment Suite* CD-ROM CD-ROM: Presentation Plus! Software

Blackline Master   CD-ROM   Transparency

Chapter 16 Resource Guide

Timesaving Tools

TeacherWorks™ All-In-One Planner and Resource Center

- **Interactive Teacher Edition** Access your Teacher Wraparound Edition and your classroom resources with a few easy clicks.
- **Interactive Lesson Planner** Planning has never been easier! Organize your week, month, semester, or year with all the lesson helps you need to make teaching creative, timely, and relevant.

Use Glencoe's **Presentation Plus!** multimedia teacher tool to easily present dynamic lessons that visually excite your students. Using Microsoft PowerPoint® you can customize the presentations to create your own personalized lessons.

Activity

From the Classroom of...

Jerry Agner
Marion Harding High School
Marion, OH

Psychological Disorders

Students will complete a brief case study of an individual whom they consider "abnormal" and who has appeared on the cover of a national newsmagazine. Students must select one of the approaches to defining abnormality and use it to explain why and what is the abnormal behavior exhibited by the individual.

Psychology Online

Use our Web site for additional resources. All essential content is covered in the Student Edition.

You and your students can visit glencoe.com, the Web site companion to *Understanding Psychology*. This innovative integration of electronic and print media offers your students a wealth of opportunities. The student text directs students to the Web site for the following options:

- Chapter Overviews
- Student Web Activities
- Self-Check Quizzes

Answers are provided for you in the **Web Activity Lesson Plan**. Additional Web resources and Interactive Puzzles are also available.

KEY TO ABILITY LEVELS

Teaching strategies have been coded for varying learning styles and abilities.

L1 **BASIC** activities for all students
L2 **AVERAGE** activities for average to above-average students
L3 **CHALLENGING** activities for above-average students
ELL **ENGLISH LANGUAGE LEARNER** activities

Block Schedule

Activities that are particularly suited for use within the block-scheduling framework are identified throughout this chapter by the following designation: **BLOCK SCHEDULING**

Chapter 16 Resource Guide

Note: The following materials may be used when teaching Chapter 16. Section level support materials are shown at point of use in the margins of the Teacher Wraparound Edition.

TEACHING TRANSPARENCIES

Chapter 16
Concept Transparencies

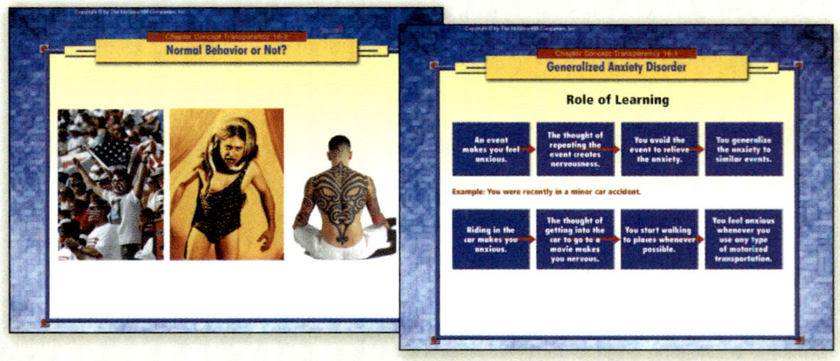

MULTIMEDIA

- **Vocabulary PuzzleMaker CD-ROM**
- ***ExamView® Assessment Suite* CD-ROM**
- **TeacherWorks™ CD-ROM**
- **Glencoe Skillbuilder Interactive Workbook, Level 2**
- **Presentation Plus! Software**

REVIEW AND REINFORCEMENT

Reteaching Activity 16

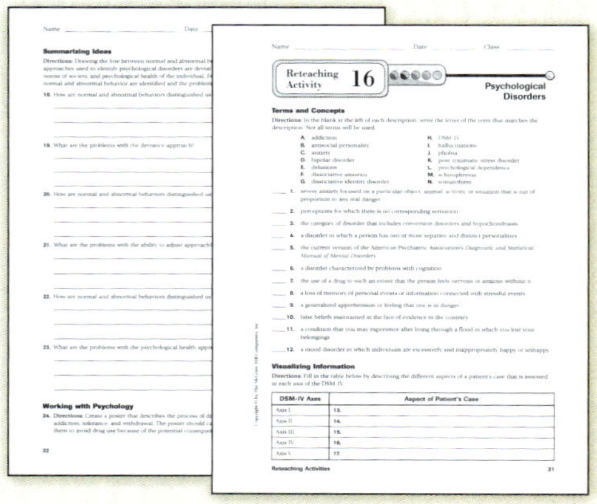

Graphic Organizer Activity 16

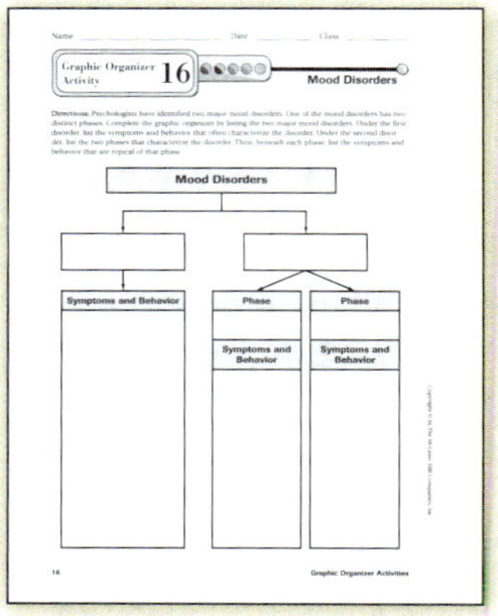

APPLICATION AND HANDS-ON

Psychology Project 16

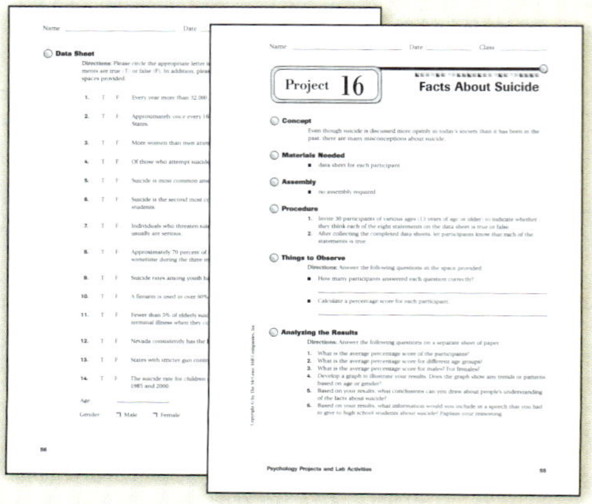

Application Activity 16

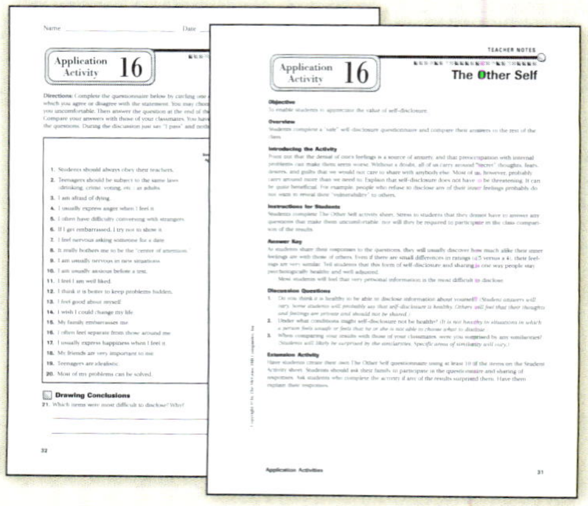

Chapter 16 Resource Guide

Glencoe's Assessment Advantage

ASSESSMENT

Chapter 16 Test, Form A

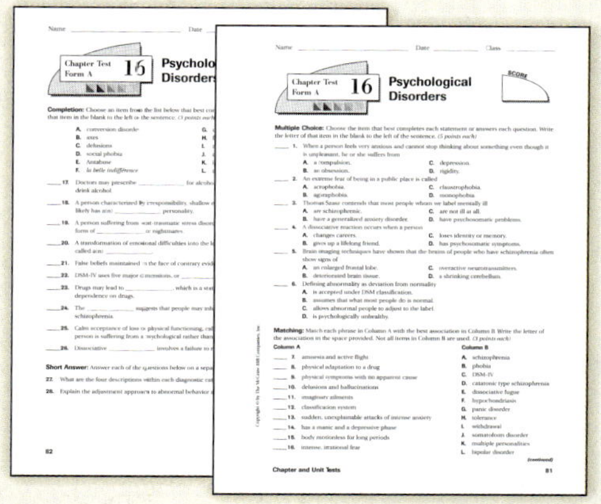

Chapter 16 Test, Form B

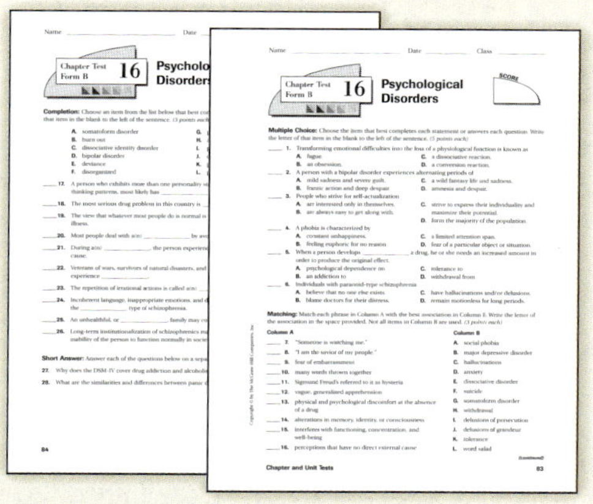

Authentic Assessment Activity 16

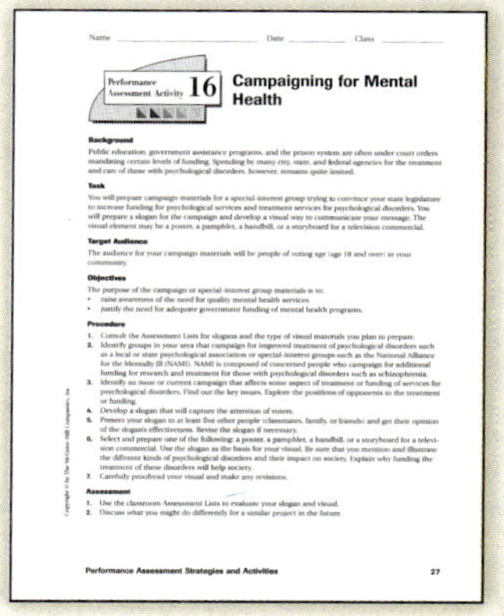

EXTENSION AND ENRICHMENT

Enrichment Activity 16

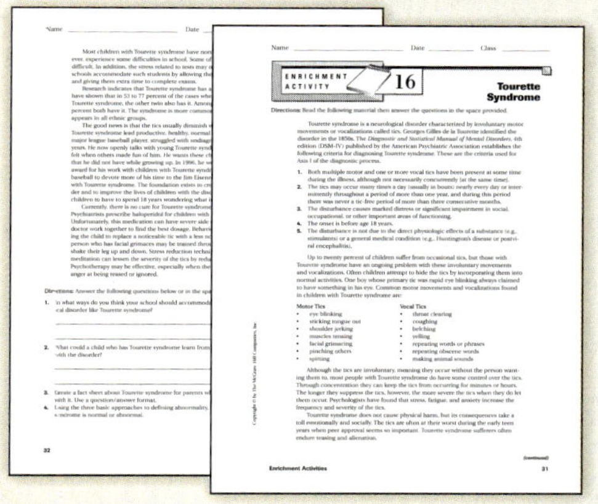

Critical Thinking Skills Activity 16

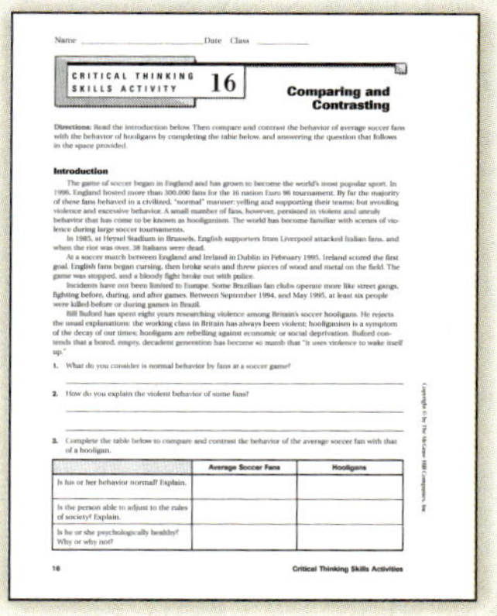

Psychology Reading 16

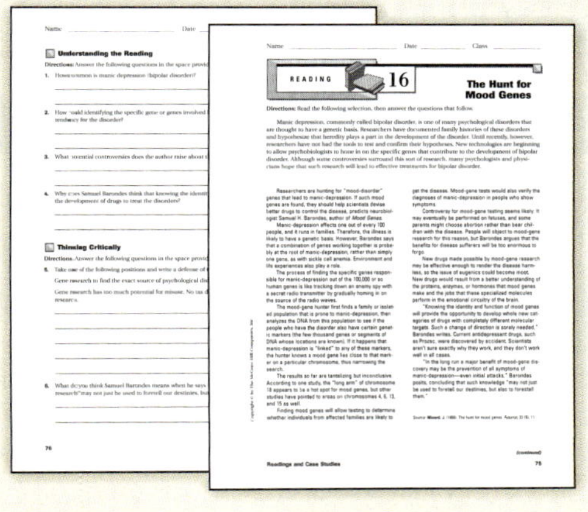

Psychology Case Study 16

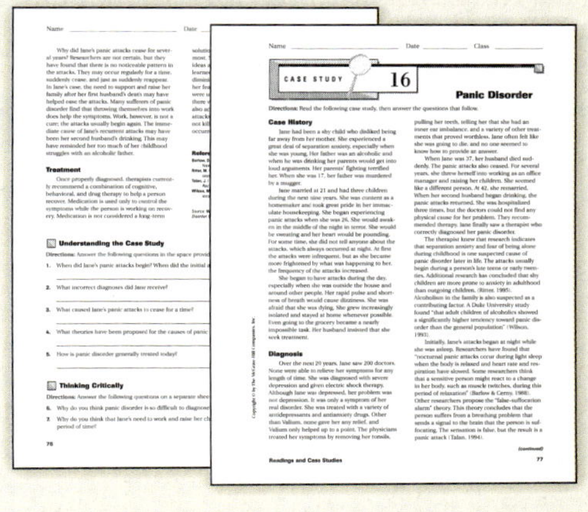

PSYCHOLOGY Online

Visit glencoe.com for a Chapter Overview for **Chapter 16—Psychological Disorders.**

GLENCOE TECHNOLOGY

Presentation Plus! For a preview of Chapter 16 content, see MindJogger Checkpoint on **Presentation Plus!**

PSYCHOLOGY JOURNAL

Review the various definitions of Glossary terms in this chapter. Ask students to distinguish between intense fears that have a cause and irrational fears.

This journal activity provides the basis for the Psychology Journal activity exercise in the Chapter Assessment. ■

CHAPTER 16 Psychological Disorders

PSYCHOLOGY JOURNAL

What is a phobia? Write your own working definition in your journal. Then describe some specific phobia that you have heard of. ■

PSYCHOLOGY Online

Chapter Overview
Visit the *Understanding Psychology* Web site at glencoe.com and click on **Chapter 16—Chapter Overviews** to preview the chapter.

TWO-MINUTE LESSON LAUNCHER

Read students the following hypothetical situation: A woman previously diagnosed with a psychological disorder was caught on videotape stealing a police car. The police officers used restraint, even after she threatened them with what appeared to be a weapon, and took her into custody unharmed. After the incident, her husband appealed to lawmakers to change the law that allows someone who has been diagnosed with a psychological disorder to refuse treatment. The woman's family believed that the incident could have been avoided if they had been allowed to admit her for psychiatric care. **Ask: Should the laws be changed? Under what circumstances should someone's caregivers be able to force treatment?**

SECTION 1

What Are Psychological Disorders?

Reader's Guide

Main Idea

Psychologists draw the line between normal and abnormal behavior in practice by looking at various attempts to define abnormal behavior, adjustments, and psychological health.

Vocabulary

- DSM-IV

Objectives

- Define psychological disorder.
- Distinguish between the concepts of normality and abnormality.

EXPLORING PSYCHOLOGY

Normal or Not?

A man living in the Ozark Mountains has a vision in which God speaks to him. He begins preaching to his relatives and neighbors, and soon he has the whole town in a state of religious fervor. People say he has a "calling." His reputation as a prophet and healer spreads, and in time he is drawing large audiences everywhere he goes. However, when he ventures into St. Louis and attempts to hold a prayer meeting, blocking traffic on a main street at rush hour, he is arrested. He tells the policemen about his conversations with God, and they hurry him off to the nearest mental hospital.

—from *Understanding Psychology,* Richard A. Kasschau, 1995

Who is right? The prophet or the police officers? It is often difficult to draw a line between normal and abnormal behavior. Behavior that some people consider normal seems abnormal to others. Many believe that having visions and hearing voices are important parts of a religious experience. Other people believe these are symptoms of a psychological disorder. The man in the example above was interviewed by psychiatrists, diagnosed as paranoid schizophrenic, and hospitalized. Had he stayed home, people would have continued to see him as perfectly normal—even popular.

SECTION RESOURCES

Reproducible Masters

- Guided Reading Activity 16–1
- Vocabulary Activity 16–1
- Section Quiz 16–1

Transparencies

- Daily Focus Transparency 16–1

Multimedia

- *ExamView® Assessment Suite* CD-ROM
- Presentation Plus! Software

1 FOCUS

Section Objectives

1. Define psychological disorder.
2. Distinguish between the concepts of normality and abnormality.

BELLRINGER
Motivational Activity

Project Daily Focus Transparency 16–1 and have students answer the questions.

Available as blackline master

Daily Focus Transparency 16–1

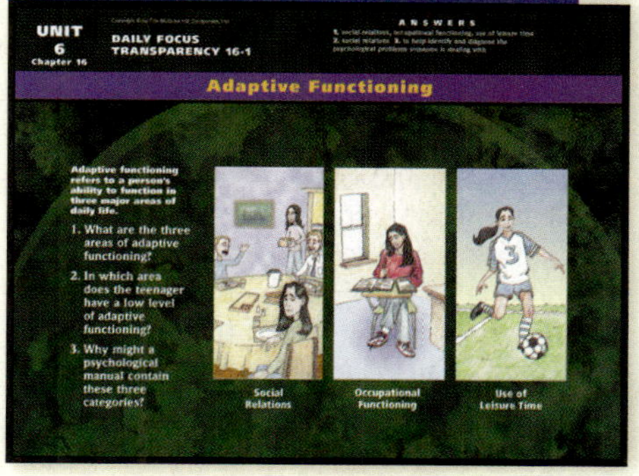

Reader's Guide

Use the Reader's Guide to introduce concepts and vocabulary.

Exploring Psychology

Ask students to read the **Exploring Psychology** feature and then discuss: **How can a person be viewed as normal in one community and abnormal in another?**

Vocabulary Precheck

Have students define the term psychological disorders. Then have them describe the five major dimensions of a person's mental functioning as defined by the American Psychiatric Association.

2 TEACH

L1 Defining Abnormal Behavior Brainstorm as a class examples of what students consider to be "normal" adolescent behavior. List these items on the board. Then ask students to imagine the following settings: (1) a rural village in India, (2) a presidential inauguration, (3) a funeral, and (4) a courtyard in the city of Beijing, China. **Ask: Which of the behaviors named would be "abnormal" in each of these settings? Why?** Use this activity to emphasize that defining "normal" is not simple. It depends upon such variables as behavioral setting, cultural perspective, public expectations, and so on.

Figure 16.1

Caption Answer Adjustment distinguishes those who are able to function physically, emotionally, and socially in society from those who cannot. People who fail to adjust may exhibit abnormal behavior.

Guided Reading Activity 16–1

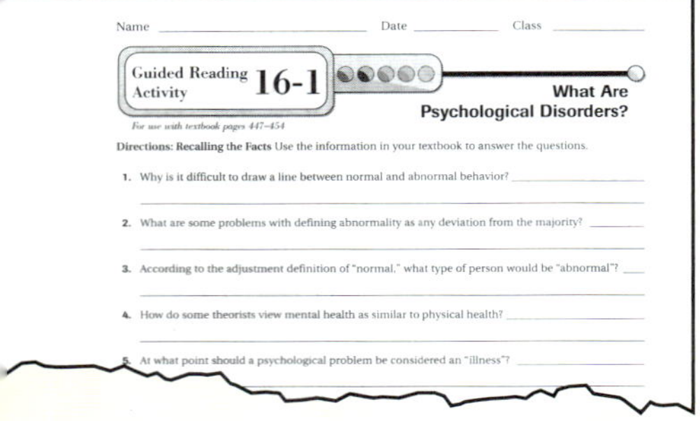
Name ______ Date ______ Class ______

Guided Reading Activity 16-1

What Are Psychological Disorders?

For use with textbook pages 447–454

Directions: Recalling the Facts Use the information in your textbook to answer the questions.

1. Why is it difficult to draw a line between normal and abnormal behavior? ______
2. What are some problems with defining abnormality as any deviation from the majority? ______
3. According to the adjustment definition of "normal," what type of person would be "abnormal"? ______
4. How do some theorists view mental health as similar to physical health? ______
5. At what point should a psychological problem be considered an "illness"? ______

Figure 16.1 Defining Behavior

This person is obviously suffering, but is her behavior abnormal? The abnormality of her behavior would depend on whether other elements of a psychological disorder are present. ***Why is adjustment an important way to distinguish normal behavior from abnormal behavior?***

DEFINING AND IDENTIFYING PSYCHOLOGICAL DISORDERS

In our example, the man was classified as mentally troubled because his behavior was so different from what others felt was normal under the circumstances. Yet the fact that a person is different does not necessarily mean that he or she is suffering from a mental illness. Indeed, going along with the crowd may at times be self-destructive. Most readers—and most psychologists—would agree that a teenager who uses cocaine because nearly everyone in his social circle does has problems.

How, then, do psychologists distinguish the normal from the abnormal? There are a number of ways to define abnormality, none of which is entirely satisfactory. We will look at the most popular ways of drawing the line between normal and abnormal in terms of deviance, adjustment, and psychological health. Then we will look at the application of these principles in legal definitions of abnormality. Finally, we will consider the criticism that in all these models people are arbitrarily labeled mentally ill.

Deviation From Normality

One approach to defining abnormality is to say that whatever most people do is normal. Abnormality, then, is any deviation from the average or from the majority. It is normal to bathe periodically, to express grief at the death of a loved one, and to wear warm clothes when going out in the cold, because most people do so. Because very few people take 10 showers a day, laugh when a loved one dies, or wear bathing suits in the snow, those who do so may be considered abnormal.

The deviance approach, however, as commonly used as it is, has serious limitations. If most people cheat on their income-tax returns, are honest taxpayers abnormal? If most people are noncreative, was Shakespeare abnormal? Different cultural norms must also be taken into consideration (see Figure 16.2). Because the majority is not always right or best, the deviance approach to defining abnormality is not by itself a useful standard.

Did You Know?

Hysteria Sometimes a lack of knowledge leads to nonsensical explanations for psychological phenomena. For example, the term *hysteria* comes from the Greek word for "uterus." The ancient Greeks diagnosed women with mental disorders by using a theory that the womb somehow moved around the body, occupying different positions. This "wandering of the uterus" theory led to characterizing any highly emotional behavior as hysteria. In the Middle Ages, the wandering uterus theory was used to explain demonic possession and led to persecutions of women for witchcraft.

COOPERATIVE LEARNING ACTIVITY

Distinguishing Normal From Abnormal Organize students into three small groups. Assign each group one of the three ways described in the text to distinguish between normal and abnormal behavior: deviations from normality, adjustment, or psychological health. Each group should prepare a defense of its assigned approach for distinguishing between normal and abnormal behavior. The defense should include examples of how the approach defines normal and abnormal. The groups should prepare an oral presentation with visual aids and demonstrations.

BLOCK SCHEDULING

Adjustment

Another way to distinguish normal from abnormal people is to say that normal people are able to get along in the world—physically, emotionally, and socially. They can feed and clothe themselves, work, find friends, and live by the rules of society. By this definition, abnormal people are the ones who fail to *adjust*. They may be so unhappy that they refuse to eat or so lethargic that they cannot hold a job. They may experience so much anxiety in relationships with others that they end up avoiding people, living in a lonely world of their own. However, not all people with psychological disorders are violent, destructive, or isolated. Sometimes, a person's behavior may only seem normal. Also, behavior that is socially acceptable in one society may not be acceptable in another. Again, the cultural context of a behavior must also be taken into consideration.

Psychological Health

The terms *mental illness* and *mental health* imply that psychological disturbance or abnormality is like a physical sickness—such as the flu or tuberculosis. Although many psychologists think that mental illness is different from physical illness, the idea remains that there is some ideal way for people to function psychologically, just as there is an ideal way for people to function physically. Some psychologists believe that the normal or healthy person would be one who is functioning ideally or who is at least striving toward ideal functioning. Personality theorists such as Carl Jung and Abraham Maslow (see Chapter 14) have tried to describe this striving process, which is often referred to as *self-actualization*. According to this line of thinking, to be normal or healthy involves full acceptance and expression of one's own individuality and humanness.

One problem with this approach to defining abnormality is that it is difficult to

Figure 16.2 Is This Normal?

What we consider normal and abnormal behavior depends on the context of the behavior. Here two men in Michoacán State, Mexico, display cultural dance masks. ***Why must you consider the cultural context of a behavior when determining whether the behavior is abnormal?***

TEACHER Tip

Students may tend to see every example of abnormal behavior in themselves or in others as a sign of a psychological disorder. Tell students that most people experience maladaptive behavior at different points in their lives. Explain that psychological disorders are distinguished by long periods of abnormal behavior, the inability to function over the long term, and disruptive behavior that has no connection to reality or to rationality.

FYI

Forty million Americans between the ages of 15 and 54 experience some kind of mental disorder.

Figure 16.2

Caption Answer Definitions of normal and abnormal behavior vary among cultures. For example, going into a trance may be seen as abnormal in U.S. culture but as normal in Native American culture.

MEETING SPECIAL NEEDS

Learning Style: Logical/Mathematical Tell students that the insanity defense has long been a source of controversy. For example, why was John Hinckley able to use the insanity defense, but Jeffrey Dahmer was found to be sane? Have students research "diminished capacity" as a defense. Ask them to prepare a written essay defending or opposing the diminished capacity defense. The essay should include a clear definition of diminished capacity and examples of attempts to use the defense. **L2**

Refer to ***Inclusion for the High School Social Studies Classroom Strategies and Activities*** in the TCR for strategies for students with different learning styles.

L1 Discussion Have students suggest social conditions that might encourage—or even necessitate—adaptive behaviors that would otherwise be considered improper, criminal, neurotic, or psychotic. Examples include hostage situations, acts of terrorism, natural disasters, and wars. Point out that many people require or seek counseling after involvement in such incidents. Ask students to describe the adaptive behaviors that might be employed in these situations.

PSYCHOLOGY JOURNAL

Ask students to examine Thomas Szasz's argument that the mentally ill simply have "problems in living." Then have students write a paragraph agreeing with Szasz's point of view and a second paragraph disagreeing with his point of view. ■

PSYCHOLOGY Update

Help for Primary Care Physicians

In the current U.S. health care system, many people are required by their health insurers to see a primary care physician first. The primary care physician makes an initial diagnosis and can refer patients to specialists. Since most primary care physicians are not psychiatrists, the DSM-IV-PC has been developed. It helps primary care physicians make the basic diagnosis needed to refer patients to the proper specialists. It uses the same basic approach as the DSM-IV but is limited to the most common disorders and simplifies the diagnosis procedure.

determine whether or not a person is doing a good job of actualizing himself or herself. How can you tell when a person is doing his or her best? What are the signs that he or she is losing the struggle? Answers to such questions often are arbitrary.

That definitions of abnormality are somewhat arbitrary has led some theorists to conclude that labeling a person as mentally ill simply because his or her behavior is odd is a mistake as well as cruel and irresponsible. The foremost spokesperson of this point of view is American psychiatrist Thomas Szasz (1984).

Szasz argued that most of the people whom we call mentally ill are not ill at all. They simply have "problems in living" that cause serious conflicts with the world around them. Yet instead of dealing with the patients' conflicts as things that deserve attention and respect, psychiatrists simply label them as sick and shunt them off to hospitals. Society's norms remain unchallenged, and psychiatrists remain in a comfortable position of authority. The ones who lose are the patients, who by being labeled abnormal are deprived both of responsibility for their behavior and of their dignity as human beings. As a result, Szasz claimed, the patients' problems intensify. Szasz's position, however, is a minority stand. Most psychologists and psychiatrists would agree that a person who claims to be God or Napoleon is truly abnormal and disturbed.

The fact that it is difficult to define abnormality does not mean that such a thing does not exist. What it does mean is that we should be very cautious about judging a person to be mentally ill just because he or she acts in a way that we cannot understand. It should also be kept in mind that mild psychological disorders are common. It is only when a psychological problem becomes severe enough to disrupt everyday life that it is thought of as an abnormality or illness.

More About...

The Insanity Defense

When John Hinckley was tried for shooting President Ronald Reagan in 1981, he was found "not guilty by reason of insanity." This raised public concerns about the legal definition of sanity.

In this case, not guilty did not mean that Hinckley did not commit the crime; it meant that he could not tell right from wrong or could not control his behavior because of a psychological disorder. Therefore, he could not be held criminally responsible for his behavior.

The terms *sane* and *insane* are legal terms. Psychological research has identified so many disorders of varying degrees that *insane* is too simplistic a term for a person with a psychological disorder. In fact, many people with psychological disorders are classified as sane under current legal standards.

People found not guilty by reason of insanity are not simply released; they are confined for treatment in special hospitals. Studies show that people found not guilty by reason of insanity are held for at least as long as people found guilty and sent to prison for similar crimes (American Psychiatric Association, 1993). After the Hinckley insanity defense, many states created review boards to oversee the treatment provided to those who have been found not guilty by reason of insanity.

THE PROBLEM OF CLASSIFICATION

For years psychiatrists have been trying to devise a logical and useful method for classifying emotional disorders. This task is difficult, because psychological problems do not lend themselves to the same sort of categorizing that physical illnesses do. The causes and symptoms of psychological disturbances and breakdowns and the cures for those breakdowns are rarely obvious or clear-cut.

All of the major classification schemes have accepted the medical model; they assume that abnormal behavior can be described in the same manner as

CRITICAL THINKING ACTIVITY

Classifying Information Assign students to work in pairs or in small groups to research the lives of assassins and would-be assassins. Choices include John Wilkes Booth, Charles Guiteau, Lee Harvey Oswald, James Earl Ray, Sirhan Sirhan, "Squeaky" Fromme, and Mark David Chapman. Tell students to focus on family/environmental backgrounds, personality profiles, and stated motives behind the shootings. **Ask: Did these individuals have any of the above aspects in common? Did any of the figures fit the definition of criminally insane? (A criminally insane person is a person who should not be held responsible for his or her acts because of mental disease or defect.) Explain.** Have students present their findings in oral reports. **L2**

any physical illness. The physician diagnoses a specific disease when a person has certain symptoms.

In 1952 the American Psychiatric Association agreed upon a system for classifying abnormal symptoms, which it published in the *Diagnostic and Statistical Manual of Mental Disorders,* or DSM. This book has been revised four times as the DSM-II (1968), DSM-III (1980), and DSM-III-Revised (1987). The most recent comprehensive revision, the **DSM-IV,** was published in 1994 and a minor text revision, DSM-IV-TR, in 2000.

A major change occurred in the shifts from DSM-II to DSM-III-R. Before 1980, the two most commonly used diagnostic distinctions were *neurosis* and *psychosis.* Although these terms have been replaced by more specific ones, they still are used by many psychologists. However, the conditions originally identified under neurosis and psychosis have been expanded into more detailed categories, including anxiety disorders, somatoform disorders, dissociative disorders, mood disorders, and schizophrenia.

Profiles In Psychology

Abraham Maslow

1908–1970

"Human life will never be understood unless its highest aspirations are taken into account."

One of the founders of humanistic psychology, Abraham Maslow spent his life developing theories that shaped counseling, education, social work, theology, marketing, and management. Early in his career, Maslow upset behaviorists by contradicting their theories of motivation and personality. If you recall, behaviorists propose that individuals learn new behaviors by responding to environmental stimuli that reward or punish their behaviors. Maslow emphasized that each individual has freedom in directing his or her own future. Maslow believed that individuals could achieve personal growth and self-fulfillment.

Maslow developed a theory of motivation that describes an individual's hierarchy of needs (see Chapter 12). Individuals progress from filling basic, biological needs to the highest social needs of what Maslow called self-actualization—the fulfillment of one's greatest human potential. Individuals organize their lives around these needs, trying to fulfill the needs at each level. If needs are not fulfilled at any level, conflict results. Attention to these needs, then, is a method to resolve psychological conflict.

DSM-IV: the fifth version of the American Psychiatric Association's *Diagnostic and Statistical Manual of Mental Disorders*

DSM-IV: New Ways to Categorize Mental Illness

Within each diagnostic category of the DSM-IV, the following descriptions are included:

1. *essential features*—characteristics that define the disorder;
2. *associated features*—additional features that are usually present;
3. information on *differential diagnosis*—that is, how to distinguish this disorder from other disorders with which it might be confused; and

PSYCHOLOGY LAB EXPERIMENT

Reactions to Abnormal Behavior Tell students that they will conduct a brief experiment to identify reactions to abnormal behaviors. Divide students into three groups. Assign each group one of the following behaviors: (1) Shake the hand of a friend, but hold on much longer than usual, (2) Make direct eye contact with someone on the bus or in the cafeteria, and prolong the gaze for 15 to 20 seconds, (3) Respond to a greeting such as "How are you?" with "Why do you want to know?" Tell students that each group member should complete the experiment, sometime during the day, and immediately write down the reactions he or she received. Have each group compile a list of the reactions that were used to indicate that students were acting abnormally. **L1** **BLOCK SCHEDULING**

Profiles In Psychology

Ask students to read the **Profiles In Psychology** feature and then discuss the following questions:

1. Why did Maslow upset behaviorists? *(He contradicted their theories with the belief that individuals had freedom to choose their actions, that they did not simply respond to rewards and punishments meted out by their environments.)*
2. How did Maslow describe human motivation? *(He described it as a hierarchy of needs from basic biological needs to self-actualization.)*
3. How did Maslow believe psychological conflicts were resolved? *(by attending to the unfulfilled needs of individuals)*

CULTURAL CONNECTIONS

In ancient times, Egyptians and Babylonians believed that mental illness was due primarily to evil spirits. Archaeologists frequently find evidence of a practice known as trephination, which involved drilling an opening in the skull to let evil spirits escape.

Vocabulary Activity 16–1

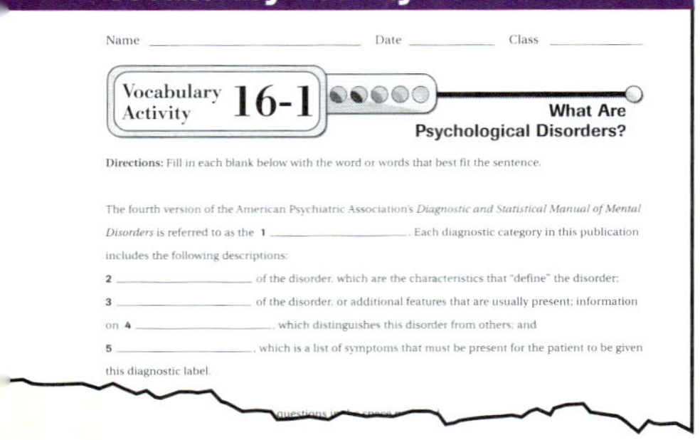
Name ____________ Date ________ Class ________

Vocabulary Activity 16-1

What Are Psychological Disorders?

Directions: Fill in each blank below with the word or words that best fit the sentence.

The fourth version of the American Psychiatric Association's *Diagnostic and Statistical Manual of Mental Disorders* is referred to as the **1** ____________. Each diagnostic category in this publication includes the following descriptions:
2 ____________ of the disorder, which are the characteristics that "define" the disorder;
3 ____________ of the disorder, or additional features that are usually present; information on **4** ____________, which distinguishes this disorder from others; and
5 ____________, which is a list of symptoms that must be present for the patient to be given this diagnostic label.

FYI

The phrase "mad as a hatter" became widely used because hatmakers suffered from tremors, slurred speech, and confusion. Scientists discovered that this condition was caused by mercury-laden vapors inhaled by the hatmakers while they worked on felt hats.

Figure 16.3

Visual Instruction Ask students to make a list of the words in the chart they don't understand. Then have them look up the words and write their definitions.

Caption Answer These are disorders in which people have trouble controlling desires that others usually restrain, such as excessive gambling or kleptomania.

4. *diagnostic criteria*—a list of symptoms, taken from the lists of essential and associated features, that must be present for the patient to be given a particular diagnostic label.

These more precise diagnostic criteria reduce the chances that the same patient will be classified as schizophrenic by one doctor and manic depressive by another. Because researchers often rely on diagnostic labels to study underlying factors that may cause disorders, it is especially important for their work that patients with similar symptoms be classified in the same diagnostic category.

The DSM-IV also recognizes the complexity of classifying people on the basis of mental disorders. Often a person may exhibit more than one disorder or may be experiencing other stresses that complicate the diagnosis. In early classification systems, it was difficult to give a patient more than one label. The DSM-III-R and now the DSM-IV have overcome this

Figure 16.3 **DSM-IV—Major Psychological Disorders of Axis I**

Individual cases of psychological disorders are diagnosed on the five axes of the DSM-IV. Axis I classifies symptoms into categories. ***What are impulse control disorders?***

Disorders usually first diagnosed in infancy, childhood, or adolescence	Includes disorders typically arising before adolescence, including attention deficit disorders, mental retardation, and stuttering
Delirium, dementia, and other cognitive disorders	Includes disorders of perceptual, memory, and thought distortion that stem from damage to the brain, such as Alzheimer's disease
Substance-related disorders	Includes maladaptive use of alcohol and drugs
Schizophrenia and other psychotic disorders	Characterizes types of schizophrenia and psychotic disorders by symptoms
Mood disorders	Includes disorders characterized by emotional disturbance, such as depression and bipolar disorder
Anxiety disorders	Includes disorders characterized by signs of anxiety, such as panic disorders and phobias
Somatoform disorders	Includes disorders characterized by somatic symptoms that resemble physical illnesses, such as conversion disorder and hypochondriasis
Dissociative disorders	Includes disorders that are characterized by sudden and temporary changes in memory, consciousness, identity, and behavior, such as dissociative identity disorder
Sexual and gender-identity disorders	Includes preferences for unusual acts to achieve sexual arousal and sexual dysfunctions
Eating disorders	Includes disorders such as anorexia nervosa and bulimia nervosa
Sleep disorders	Includes disorders associated with sleep, such as insomnia and sleepwalking
Impulse control disorders	Includes disorders characterized by a tendency to act on impulses that others usually inhibit, such as to gamble excessively or steal

Source: DSM-IV, American Psychiatric Association, 1994.

INTERDISCIPLINARY CONNECTIONS ACTIVITY

The Media As a class, discuss the debate over whether song lyrics, video games, Internet sites, television shows, and movies cause or contribute to deviant behavior in people. **Ask: When, if ever, should materials be censored? Who should decide whether material is suitable for young children and teens?** Organize students into two groups to debate the following issue: *Resolved—That freedom of speech and the press extend to all forms of expression.* **L2**
BLOCK SCHEDULING

Figure 16.4 **PET Scans**

The biological roots of abnormal behavior include genetic factors and occurrences that can lead to abnormal brain development. From left to right, these PET scans show a normal human brain, a brain tumor, and a bra n aneurysm. ***Which axis of the DSM-IV describes the medical conditions of psychological disorders?***

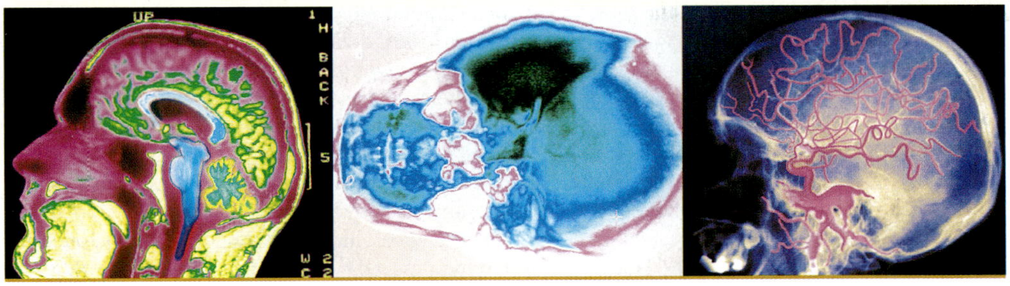

problem by using five major dimensions, or *axes,* to describe a person's mental functicning. Each axis reflects a different aspect of a patient's case.

Axis I is used to classify current symptoms into explicitly defined categories. These categories range from disorders that are usually first evident in infancy, childhood, or adolescence (such as conduct disorders) to substance-use disorders (such as alcoholism) to schizophrenia. Figure 16.3 shows a listing of major Axis I categories.

Axis II is used to describe developmental disorders and long-standing personality disorders or maladaptive traits such as compulsiveness, over-dependency, or aggressiveness. Axis II is also used to describe specific developmental disorders for children, adolescents, and, in some cases, adults. Examples of developmental problems that would be classified under Axis II are language disorders, reading or writing difficulties, mental retardation, autism, and speech problems.

It is possible for an individual to have a disorder on both Axis I and Axis II. For example, an adult may have a major depression noted on Axis I and a compulsive personality disorder noted on Axis II. A child may have a conduct disorder noted on Axis I and a developmental language disorder on Axis II. In other cases, a person may be seeking treatment primarily for a condition noted on Axis I or Axis II only. The use of both Axes I and II permits multiple diagnoses and allows the clinician flexibility in making provisional diagnoses when there is not enough information available to make a firm diagnosis.

Axis III is used to describe physical disorders or general medical conditions that are potentially relevant to understanding or caring for the person. In some cases, a physical disorder such as brain damage or a chemical imbalance may be causing the syndrome diagnosed on either Axis I or II.

Reading Check How does the DSM-IV categorize psychological disorders?

Did You Know?

Neurosis In DSM-II, neurosis was used to describe a variety of anxiety-based disorders. Today, these disorders are identified individually in DSM-IV as mood disorders, anxiety disorders, somatoform disorders, and dissociative disorders. Although anxiety-based behaviors are still sometimes described as neurotic, the term *neurosis* is no longer used to identify any psychological disorder.

Figure 16.4

Caption Answer Axis III describes physical disorders or medical conditions that are potentially relevant to managing or understanding the patient.

Reading Check Answer
The DSM-IV categorizes psychological disorders by describing the five major dimensions of a person's mental functioning.

Readings and Case Studies in Psychology
Have students read the Chapter 16 Case Study selection in *Readings and Case Studies in Psychology* and answer the questions that follow the case study.

3 ASSESS

Assign Section 1 Assessment as homework or as an in-class activity.

Section Quiz 16–1

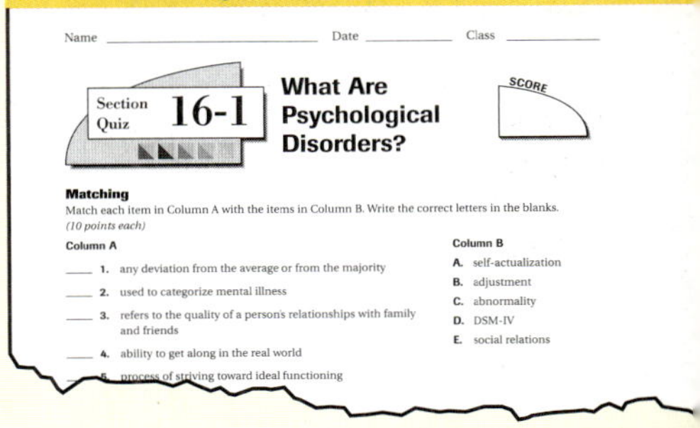
Name ______ Date ______ Class ______

Section Quiz 16-1 **What Are Psychological Disorders?**

SCORE

Matching
Match each item in Column A with the items in Column B. Write the correct letters in the blanks. *(10 points each)*

Column A	Column B
____ 1. any deviation from the average or from the majority	A. self-actualization
____ 2. used to categorize mental illness	B. adjustment
____ 3. refers to the quality of a person's relationships with family and friends	C. abnormality
____ 4. ability to get along in the real world	D. DSM-IV
____ 5. process of striving toward ideal functioning	E. social relations

EXTENDING THE CONTENT

Additional Material on Szasz Some claim that Thomas Szasz's theories ignore PET scans and additional neurological evidence of schizophrenia and other psychological disorders. Szasz argues that the links between PET scan irregularities and psychological disorders have not proven a cause-and-effect relationship. That is, no one has yet proved that psychological disorders are caused by irregularities in the brain. It may be that medication or poor treatment result in changes in the brain. He further argues that even if a cause-and-effect relationship is proved, people should be labeled as having brain diseases, not mental illnesses.

PSYCHOLOGY Online

Links and instructional guidelines can be found in the **Web Activity Lesson Plan** at glencoe.com.

Reteach

Review the three common approaches used to distinguish between normal and abnormal behavior. Then have students analyze the man in the **Exploring Psychology** feature on page 447 using each of the three approaches.

Enrich

Point out the loose use of the word *crazy* in everyday language. Ask students to cite some of the *crazy* behaviors of celebrities. Then ask students if they consider any of these people to have a psychological disorder. Have them defend their responses.

4 CLOSE

Have students make charts listing the five dimensions of mental functioning and the aspect of a person's functioning that is identified by each axis of the DSM-IV.

PSYCHOLOGY Online

Student Web Activity
Visit the *Understanding Psychology* Web site at glencoe.com and click on **Chapter 16—Student Web Activities** for an activity on psychological disorders.

Axis IV is a measurement of the current stress level at which the person is functioning. The rating of stressors (such as death of a spouse or loss of a job) is based on what the person has experienced within the past year. The prognosis may be better for a disorder that develops following a severe stressor than for one that develops after no stressor or a minimal stressor.

Axis V is used to describe the highest level of adaptive functioning present within the past year. Adaptive functioning refers to three major areas: social relations, occupational functioning, and the person's use of leisure time. *Social relations* refer to the quality of a person's relationships with family and friends. *Occupational functioning* involves functioning as a worker, student, or homemaker and the quality of the work accomplished. *Use of leisure time* includes recreational activities or hobbies and the degree of involvement and pleasure a person has in them.

This five-part diagnosis may be extremely helpful to researchers trying to discover connections among psychological disorders and other factors such as stress and physical illness. Although it is helpful, the DSM-IV labels a person, which may have negative influences on that person in the long run. When the label of a mental disorder is applied, it can reduce that person's sense of responsibility for his/her own actions. It also affects how others, including mental health professionals, regard that person. Experiments have demonstrated that labels affect how others view someone. In one experiment, grade-school boys behaved in a more critical manner toward other boys if they had been led to believe that those other boys had a psychological disorder, such as attention deficit disorder (Harris et al., 1992). It is important to note that many people develop a disorder listed in the DSM-IV at some point in their life. Of course, many of these incidences are temporary. In effect, many people who qualify for a disorder as diagnosed according to the DSM-IV are not very different from anyone else.

SECTION 1 Assessment

1. **Review the Vocabulary** What is the DSM-IV? How do psychologists use it?
2. **Visualize the Main Idea** Using a diagram similar to the one below, identify and describe three approaches psychologists use to identify psychological disorders.

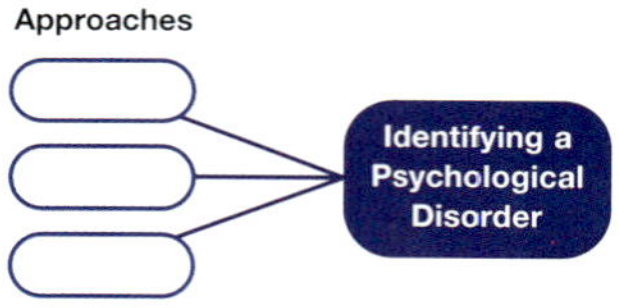

3. **Recall Information** What are the advantages and disadvantages of categorizing people by the DSM-IV?
4. **Think Critically** Many people suffer from mild psychological disorders. When do you think it is necessary for a person to seek help?
5. **Application Activity** Come up with your own definitions of normal and abnormal behavior. Explain how they differ from the descriptions in this section and why you defined them the way you did.

SECTION 1 Assessment Answers

1. the fourth version of the American Psychiatric Association's Diagnostic and Statistical Manual of Mental Disorders; to classify abnormal symptoms as a part of diagnosing psychological disorders
2. Students' diagrams should reflect an understanding of the approaches used to distinguish normal and abnormal behavior.
3. Advantages—more precise diagnostic criteria, recognizes the complexity of identifying and classifying psychological disorders, allows multiple psychological disorders to be identified, recognizes differences in severity of psychological disorders and ability to function in everyday life. Disadvantages—labels may become permanently affixed to a person.
4. Students' answers will vary. Explain that seeking help when the symptoms are relatively mild may help people with psychological disorders continue to function relatively well in everyday life.
5. Students' answers will vary. Challenge students to recognize stereotypes in their definitions.

SECTION 2

Anxiety Disorders

Reader's Guide

Main Idea

Anxiety disorders are marked by excessive fear, caution, and attempts to avoid anxiety.

Vocabulary

- anxiety
- phobia
- panic disorder
- post-traumatic stress disorder

Objectives

- Identify the behavioral patterns that psychologists label as anxiety disorders.
- Explain what causes anxiety disorders.

EXPLORING PSYCHOLOGY

Normal Anxiety or Not?

If you are walking down the street and a large dog runs at you barking, it's perfectly normal to be afraid. However, if you get anxious if a dog appears on the TV you're watching, that's a disorder. If a student gets up to give a speech in class and finds that his hands are trembling and his throat is dry, that's normal anxiety. If a student runs out of the room crying when called on to speak or faints while giving a speech, that isn't normal.

—from the files of Judith R. Levine, SUNY Farmingdale

Anxiety is a general state of dread or uneasiness that a person feels in response to a real or imagined danger. People suffering from anxiety disorders feel anxiety but not just normal anxiety. They suffer from anxiety that is out of proportion to the situation provoking it. This intense anxiety may interfere with normal functioning in everyday life. Anxiety disorders are the most common type of mental illness in the United States, affecting 40 million Americans annually (NIMH, 2006). These disorders share certain characteristics, including feelings of anxiety and personal inadequacy and an avoidance of dealing with problems. People with anxiety disorders often have unrealistic images of themselves. People who are deeply anxious seem unable to free themselves of recurring worries and fears. Their emotional problems may be expressed in constant worrying, sudden mood swings, or a variety of physical symptoms (for example, headaches, sweating, muscle tightness, weakness, and fatigue).

Anxious people often have difficulty forming stable and satisfying relationships. Even though their behavior may be self-defeating and ineffective in solving problems, those driven by anxiety often refuse to give up their behaviors in favor of more effective ways of dealing with anxiety. In

1 FOCUS

Section Objectives

1. Identify the behavioral patterns that psychologists label as anxiety disorders.
2. Explain what causes anxiety disorders.

BELLRINGER
Motivational Activity

Project Daily Focus Transparency 16–2 and have students answer the questions.

Available as blackline master

Daily Focus Transparency 16–2

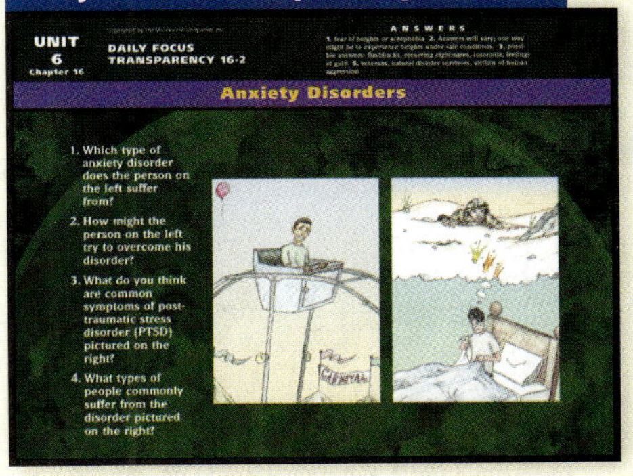

Reader's Guide

Use the Reader's Guide to introduce concepts and vocabulary.

Exploring Psychology

Ask students to read the **Exploring Psychology** feature and then discuss: **From this description, how would you distinguish between anxiety and phobia?**

Vocabulary Precheck

Have students read the Glossary definitions of the terms. Then have them write two paragraphs: one comparing and contrasting *anxiety* and *phobia* and the other explaining the symptoms of the two disorders.

SECTION RESOURCES

Reproducible Masters

- Guided Reading Activity 16–2
- Vocabulary Activity 16–2
- Section Quiz 16–2

Transparencies

- Daily Focus Transparency 16–2

Multimedia

- *ExamView® Assessment Suite* CD-ROM
- Presentation Plus! Software

2 TEACH

L1 Discussion Students are usually anxious to try to "diagnose" psychological disorders. Tell students that one way to learn about different psychological disorders is to read case studies or case reports and identify the psychological disorder the person is experiencing. Find an example of a brief case report of someone suffering from panic attacks, a phobia, or post-traumatic stress disorder. After reading aloud the report, conduct a class discussion to identify the precise disorder. After the class has selected a diagnosis, read the case conclusions to let students know if they have analyzed the case correctly. **BLOCK SCHEDULING**

Guided Reading Activity 16–2

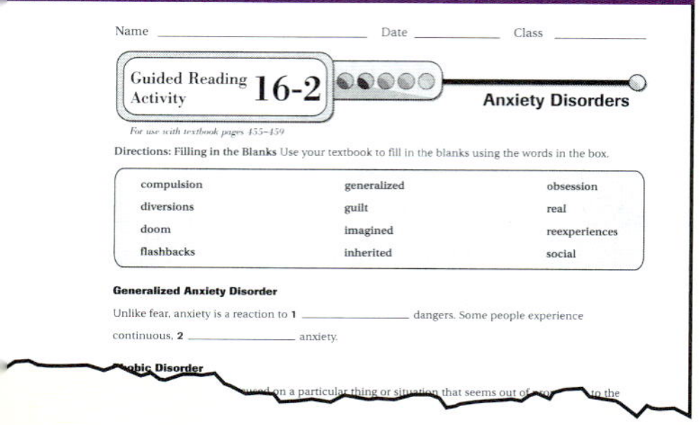
Name ______ Date ______ Class ______

Guided Reading Activity 16-2 — Anxiety Disorders

Directions: Filling in the Blanks Use your textbook to fill in the blanks using the words in the box.

compulsion	generalized	obsession
diversions	guilt	real
doom	imagined	reexperiences
flashbacks	inherited	social

Generalized Anxiety Disorder

Unlike fear, anxiety is a reaction to **1** ______ dangers. Some people experience continuous, **2** ______ anxiety.

Phobic Disorder

Figure 16.5

Caption Answer They experience physical symptoms such as muscular tension, inability to relax, poor appetite, indigestion, and poor sleep habits. They also have trouble dealing with others and fulfilling responsibilities.

PSYCHOLOGY JOURNAL

Ask students to write about a time in which the same thought kept recurring. Have them explain how they overcame the thought or the situations underlying it. ■

the DSM-IV, the anxiety disorders discussed include generalized anxiety disorder, phobic disorder, panic disorder, obsessive-compulsive disorder, and post-traumatic stress disorder.

GENERALIZED ANXIETY DISORDER

anxiety: a vague, generalized apprehension or feeling that one is in danger

phobia: an intense and irrational fear of a particular object or situation

Once in a while, everyone feels nervous for reasons he or she cannot explain, but a severely anxious person almost always feels this way. **Anxiety** is a generalized apprehension—a vague feeling that one is in danger. This anxiety potentially could blossom into full-fledged panic attacks, which may include choking sensations, chest pain, dizziness, trembling, and hot flashes. Unlike fear, which is a reaction to real and identifiable threats, anxiety is a reaction to vague or imagined dangers.

Some people experience a continuous, generalized anxiety. Fearing unknown and unforeseen circumstances, they are unable to make decisions or enjoy life. They may become so preoccupied with their internal problems that they neglect their social relationships. People who experience generalized anxiety often have trouble dealing with their family and friends and fulfilling their responsibilities, and this adds to their anxiety. They are trapped in a vicious cycle. The more they worry, the more difficulty they have; the more difficulty they have, the more they worry.

Figure 16.5 Normal Anxiety

Many situations may cause temporary anxiety or tension. Anxiety becomes a problem only when it interferes with your ability to cope with everyday life. ***What are some characteristics of people who suffer from anxiety disorders?***

Often the experience of generalized anxiety is accompanied by physical symptoms such as muscular tension, an inability to relax, a furrowed brow, and a strained face. Poor appetite, indigestion, diarrhea, and frequent urination are also common. Because anxious people are in a constant state of apprehension, they may have difficulty sleeping or, once asleep, may wake up suddenly in the night. As a result, they may feel tired when they wake up in the morning.

Why are some people so anxious? Some theorists stress the role of learning in producing anxiety. If a man feels very anxious on a date, for example, even the thought of another date may make him nervous, so he learns to avoid having dates and therefore never has a chance to unlearn the anxiety. His anxiety may then generalize to other situations and become a worse problem.

Other research suggests that anxiety disorders may be partly inherited. Environmental factors, such as unpredictable traumatic experiences in childhood, may also predispose someone to developing an anxiety disorder. Such a disorder usually occurs following a major life change, such as getting a job or having a baby. The uncertainties of modern life also may help explain the high incidence of generalized anxiety.

PHOBIC DISORDER

When severe anxiety is focused on a particular object, animal, activity, or situation that seems out of proportion to the real dangers involved, it is called a phobic disorder, or **phobia.** Phobias

COOPERATIVE LEARNING ACTIVITY

Creating a Poster Organize the class into groups of three or four. Assign each group a phobia such as the following: acrophobia, aerophobia, agoraphobia, amaxophobia, astraphobia, gephyrophobia, herpetophobia, microphobia, neophobia, nyctophobia, thanatophobia, and xenophobia. Tell each group to define the phobia and design a visual representation of the phobia on a poster. The posters can be displayed around the room to help students remember the names of various types of phobias. Remind the students that during group work they will sometimes be leaders and other times followers, but at all times they should work to create a supportive group climate. **BLOCK SCHEDULING**

Figure 16.6 Phobias

Some people's lives are consumed by inappropriate fears. These fears interfere with normal, everyday life. These people are suffering from a phobia. ***What is the fear of flying called?***

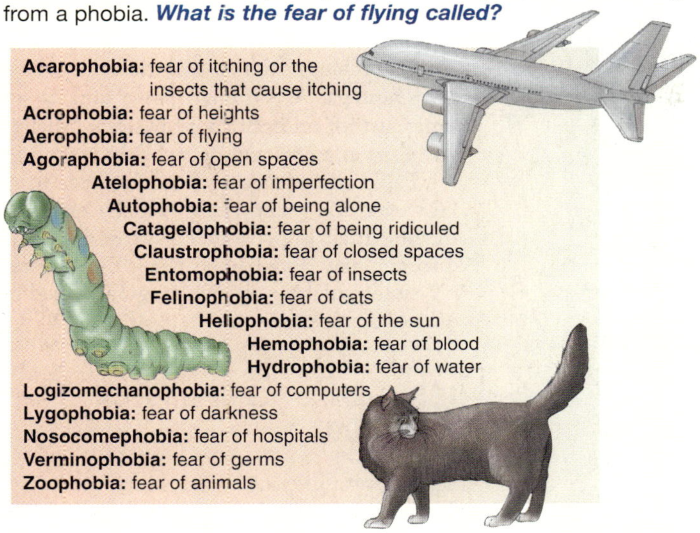

may be classified as specific phobias, social phobias, and agoraphobia. A *specific phobia* can focus on almost anything, including high places (acrophobia), enclosed spaces (claustrophobia), and darkness (nyctophobia) (see Figure 16.6). Victims of *social phobias* fear that they will embarrass themselves in a public place or a social setting. Perhaps the most common specific fear is of speaking in public, but others include eating in public, using public restrooms, meeting strangers, and going on a first date.

Phobic individuals develop elaborate plans to avoid the situations they fear. For example, people suffering from an extreme fear of being in a public place *(agoraphobia)* may stop going to movies or shopping in large, busy stores. Some reach the point where they will not leave their houses at all because that is the only place they feel safe.

Phobias range in intensity from mild to extremely severe. Most people deal with phobias by avoiding the thing that frightens them. Thus the phobias are learned and maintained by the reinforcing effects of avoidance, which reduces anxiety but not the phobia. One form of treatment for phobias involves providing the phobic person with opportunities to experience the feared object under conditions in which he or she feels safe.

PANIC DISORDER

Another kind of anxiety disorder is **panic disorder.** (*Panic* is a feeling of sudden, helpless terror, such as the overwhelming fright one might experience when cornered by a predator.) During a panic attack, a victim

panic disorder: an extreme anxiety that manifests itself in the form of panic attacks

CHAPTER 16
Section 2, pages 455–459

Figure 16.6

Caption Answer The fear of flying is aerophobia.

Vocabulary Activity 16–2

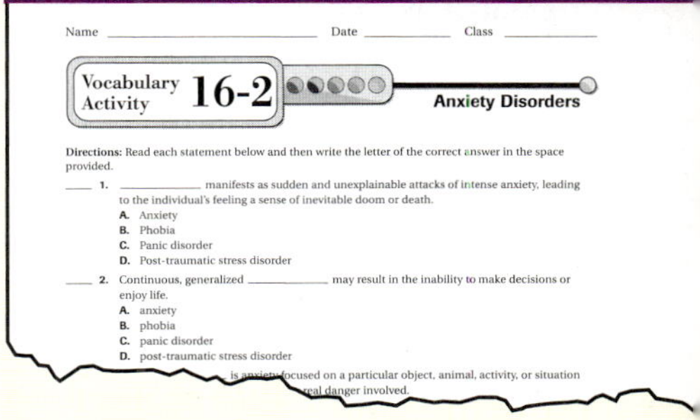
Name ____ Date ____ Class ____

Vocabulary Activity 16-2 Anxiety Disorders

Directions: Read each statement below and then write the letter of the correct answer in the space provided.

____ **1.** ____ manifests as sudden and unexplainable attacks of intense anxiety, leading to the individual's feeling a sense of inevitable doom or death.
A. Anxiety
B. Phobia
C. Panic disorder
D. Post-traumatic stress disorder

____ **2.** Continuous, generalized ____ may result in the inability to make decisions or enjoy life.
A. anxiety
B. phobia
C. panic disorder
D. post-traumatic stress disorder

3 ASSESS

Assign Section 2 Assessment as homework or as an in-class activity.

Section Quiz 16–2

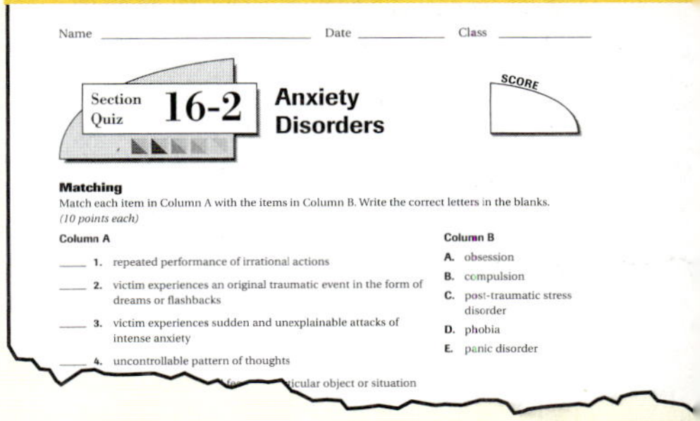
Name ____ Date ____ Class ____

Section Quiz 16-2 Anxiety Disorders — SCORE

Matching
Match each item in Column A with the items in Column B. Write the correct letters in the blanks.
(10 points each)

Column A
____ **1.** repeated performance of irrational actions
____ **2.** victim experiences an original traumatic event in the form of dreams or flashbacks
____ **3.** victim experiences sudden and unexplainable attacks of intense anxiety
____ **4.** uncontrollable pattern of thoughts

Column B
A. obsession
B. compulsion
C. post-traumatic stress disorder
D. phobia
E. panic disorder

MEETING SPECIAL NEEDS

Learning Style: Intrapersonal Have students write an autobiographical or fictitious story about an event or situation that created anxiety in a person's life. The story should describe the situation or event; explain the person's specific physical, emotional, and psychological reaction; and describe the resolution of the situation or event and the way in which the anxiety was relieved. Encourage students who like to draw to include illustrations with the story. **L2**
BLOCK SCHEDULING

Refer to ***Inclusion for the High School Social Studies Classroom Strategies and Activities*** in the TCR for strategies for students with different learning styles.

CHAPTER 16
Section 2, pages 455–459

Quick Lab

Purpose Students will explore fears that are most common among teenagers.

Process Skills Analyzing information

Teaching Strategies
- Review the procedures to be used.
- Remind students that the information they collect should be kept confidential.

Analysis
1. Results will vary. Encourage students to use various types of graphs to better understand the data collected.
2. Answers will vary. Many students will be surprised by the similarities between the responses of classmates and adults. Encourage students to compare similar situations such as a fear of taking exams and a fear of job interviews.

Reading Check Answer
A panic attack is a sudden, unexplainable attack of severe anxiety that causes feelings of doom or impending death and may include physical symptoms such as dizziness or chest pains.

Reteach
List the five disorders discussed in this section on separate sections of the board. Beneath each, place the headings *Symptoms* and *Causes*. Ask volunteers to list the symptoms and causes of each disorder.

Quick Lab

What fears are most common among teenagers?

Although most people do not experience severe phobias, many do experience mild fears. Find out what fears your classmates experience or have experienced.

Procedure
1. Prepare a list identifying some objects, animals, activities, or situations that are feared.
2. Distribute the list among your friends, classmates, and the adults you know.
3. Direct them to check the items on the list that identify a fear that they have; encourage them to write a fear they have that does not appear on the list.
4. Tally the responses.

Analysis
1. Record the results in a chart or graph, differentiating responses of the teenagers from those of the adults.
2. Determine the most common fears. What reasons can you provide for the similarities or the differences between the two groups?

See the Skills Handbook, page 622, for an explanation of designing an experiment.

Reading Check
What is a panic attack?

experiences sudden and unexplainable attacks of intense anxiety, leading the individual to feel a sense of inevitable doom or even the fear that he or she is about to die. Although symptoms of panic disorder differ from individual to individual, they may include a sense of smothering, choking, or difficulty breathing; faintness or dizziness; nausea; and chest pains. Although panic attacks sometimes last for an hour or more, they usually last just a few minutes and occur without warning.

Panic disorder may be inherited, in part. However, the panic victim usually experiences the first attack shortly after a stressful event. The disorder may also be the result of interpreting physiological arousal, such as an increased heart rate, as disastrous.

OBSESSIVE-COMPULSIVE DISORDER

A person suffering from acute anxiety may think the same thoughts over and over. Such an uncontrollable pattern of thoughts is called *obsession*. A person also may repeatedly perform coping behaviors, called *compulsions*. A person with an anxiety-based disorder may experience both these agonies together—a condition called *obsessive-compulsive disorder*.

A compulsive person may feel compelled to wash his hands 20 or 30 times a day or to avoid stepping on cracks in the sidewalk when he goes out. An obsessive person may be unable to rid herself of unpleasant thoughts about death or of a recurring impulse to make obscene remarks in public. The obsessive-compulsive may wash her hands continually *and* torment herself with thoughts of obscene behavior.

Everyone has obsessions and compulsions. Love might be described as an obsession, as might a hobby that occupies most of a person's spare time. Striving to do something perfectly is often considered to be a compulsion. If the person who is deeply engrossed in a hobby or who aims for perfection enjoys this intense absorption and can still function effectively, he or she usually is not considered disabled by anxiety. Psychologists consider it a problem only when such thoughts and activities interfere with what a person wants and needs to do. Someone who spends so much time double-checking every detail of her work that she can never finish a job is considered more anxious than conscientious.

Why do people develop obsessions and compulsions? Perhaps it is because they serve as diversions from a person's real fears and their origins and thus may reduce anxiety somewhat. In addition, compulsions provide a disturbed person with the evidence that she is doing something

CRITICAL THINKING ACTIVITY

Identifying Central Issues Share with students a case report describing a person who seems to have a panic disorder or an obsessive-compulsive disorder. Remind students how we use schemas to classify and make sense of information. Organize students into small groups and have them identify the disorder and then discuss possible causes of the disorder. Have the groups present their findings to the class. **Ask:** **How does your schema about psychological disorders help you identify the person's disorder? Would your findings be different if you were operating under Freud's schema? If you were operating under a schema that believed that demon possession was the primary cause of mental disorders, how would your analysis of the person's behavior change?**

well, even if it is only avoiding the cracks on a sidewalk. Obsessive-compulsive disorder does run in families, so there may be a possible genetic basis. Although most people with obsessive-compulsive disorder realize that their thoughts and actions are irrational, they feel unable to stop them.

POST-TRAUMATIC STRESS DISORDER

Post-traumatic stress disorder is a condition in which a person who has experienced a traumatic event feels severe and long-lasting aftereffects. This disorder is common among veterans of military combat and survivors of acts of terrorism, natural disasters such as floods or tornadoes, other catastrophes such as plane crashes, and human aggression such as rape and assault. The event that triggers the disorder overwhelms a person's sense of reality and ability to cope. The disorder may begin immediately after the occurrence of the traumatic event or it may develop later. Typical symptoms include involuntary flashbacks or recurring nightmares during which the victim reexperiences the ordeal, often followed by insomnia and feelings of guilt. Post-traumatic stress disorder can be extremely long-lasting. Studies show that survivors of Nazi concentration camps and soldiers returning from war may display symptoms decades after the traumatic event. Not everyone who experiences a traumatic event, though, develops post-traumatic stress disorder. People who are exposed repeatedly or over a long period of time to distressing conditions are more likely to develop the disorder. Social support, as discussed in Chapter 15, may protect a victim of trauma from the psychological aftereffects.

Figure 16.7 Trauma and Stress

Estimates suggest that about 18 percent of the American soldiers who fought in the Iraq War will develop post-traumatic stress disorder. ***How might war cause someone to develop this disorder?***

post-traumatic stress disorder: disorder in which victims of traumatic events experience the original event in the form of dreams or flashbacks

SECTION 2 Assessment

1. **Review the Vocabulary** Explain how excessive anxiety may lead to phobias or panic disorders.
2. **Visualize the Main Idea** Using a diagram similar to the one below, list five symptoms of generalized anxiety disorder.

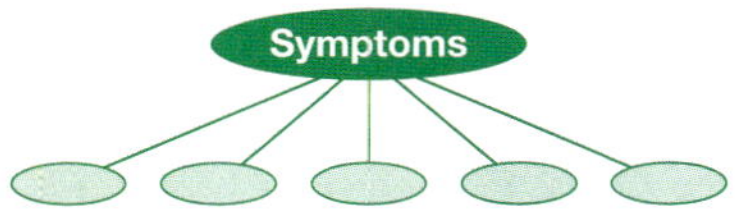

3. **Recall Information** What is anxiety? When is it normal? Abnormal?
4. **Think Critically** How would you differentiate between someone who is simply a perfectionist and someone who is suffering from obsessive-compulsive disorder?
5. **Application Activity** Interview a doctor or nurse who deals with war veterans (such as at your local vets center). Ask the professional to list the symptoms of post-traumatic stress disorder. Summarize your findings.

Figure 16.7

Caption Answer The events of war, such as losing loved ones, seeing the wounded and the dead, undergoing attacks, experiencing extreme fear, and so on, are traumatic events that can have a long-lasting impact on its victims.

Enrich

Ask each student to bring an example from literature or movies of a phobic disorder, panic disorder, obsessive-compulsive disorder, or post-traumatic stress disorder to share with the class.

4 CLOSE

Bring to class pictures from newspapers or newsmagazines showing recent traumatic events. Have students describe signs of anxiety seen on the faces of people. As a class, discuss the possible long-term consequences of experiencing traumatic events.

SECTION 2 Assessment Answers

1. Excessive anxiety relating to a particular object, activity, or situation may result in a phobia. In a panic disorder, a sudden attack of intense anxiety may cause a person to experience an overwhelming sense of doom and death.
2. a vague feeling of danger; a fear of the unknown that prevents one from making decisions; difficulty with social relationships; physical symptoms; and sleep disturbances
3. Anxiety is a vague, generalized apprehension or feeling that one is in danger. It is normal when it does not prevent someone from leading a normal life and abnormal when it inhibits the ability to maintain good social relationships or manifests itself with physical symptoms.
4. Striving for perfection becomes a problem only when such thoughts and activities interfere with what a person wants and needs to do in everyday life.
5. Students' answers will vary. Often we associate post-traumatic stress disorder only with Vietnam veterans. Encourage students to find out other names that have been used for the disorder in earlier wars.

1 FOCUS

Section Objectives

1. Identify the behavioral patterns that psychologists label as somatoform disorders.
2. Describe the symptoms of dissociative disorders.

BELLRINGER
Motivational Activity

Project Daily Focus Transparency 16–3 and have students answer the questions.

Available as blackline master

Daily Focus Transparency 16–3

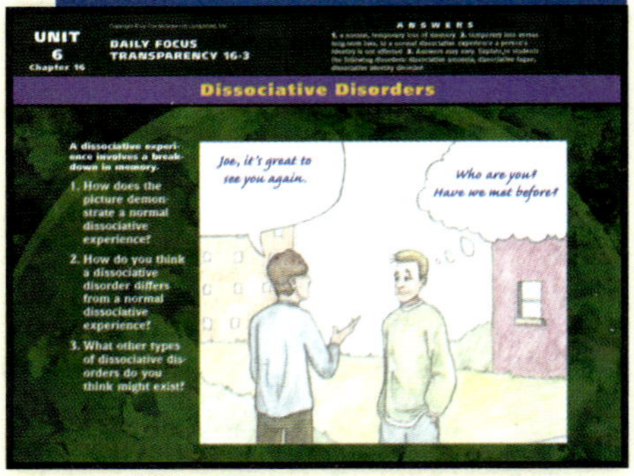

Reader's Guide

Use the Reader's Guide to introduce concepts and vocabulary.

Exploring Psychology

Ask students to read the **Exploring Psychology** feature. Then ask: **How can psychological distress manifest itself with physical symptoms?**

Vocabulary Precheck

Have students read the Glossary definitions of the terms. Then have them create a crossword puzzle using the definitions as the clues. Have pairs of students trade and complete each other's puzzles.

Use the **Vocabulary PuzzleMaker CD-ROM** to create crossword and word search puzzles.

SECTION 3 Somatoform and Dissociative Disorders

Reader's Guide

Main Idea

The inability to deal with anxiety and stress can lead to somatoform and dissociative disorders.

Vocabulary

- somatoform disorder
- conversion disorder
- dissociative disorder
- dissociative amnesia
- dissociative fugue
- dissociative identity disorder

Objectives

- Identify the behavioral patterns that psychologists label as somatoform disorders.
- Describe the symptoms of dissociative disorders.

EXPLORING PSYCHOLOGY

Why Can't the Prince Walk?

There is an ancient Persian legend about a physician named Rhazes who was called into the palace for the purpose of diagnosing and treating a young prince. Apparently, the prince could not walk. After the usual examination of the day, Rhazes determined that there was nothing wrong with the prince's legs, at least not physically. With little more than a hunch, Rhazes set out to treat what may be the first recorded case of conversion. In doing so, he took a risk: Rhazes unexpectedly walked into the prince's bathroom brandishing a dagger and threatened to kill him. Upon seeing him, "the startled prince abruptly fled, leaving his clothes, his dignity, his symptom, and undoubtedly part of his self-esteem behind."

—from *The Neuroses* by H.P. Laughlin, 1967

The prince in the excerpt above suffered from a somatoform disorder. These disorders are characterized by physical symptoms brought about by psychological distress. Today psychologists treat somatoform disorders with less drastic techniques. Psychologists may challenge conversion patients, attempting to force them out of the symptoms. It is important to note that the prince did not consciously fake his symptoms to avoid pressure or work; it is likely that he honestly could not move his legs. Psychologists must take this into account when treating such disorders.

SECTION RESOURCES

Reproducible Masters

- Guided Reading Activity 16–3
- Vocabulary Activity 16–3
- Section Quiz 16–3

Transparencies

- Daily Focus Transparency 16–3

Multimedia

- Vocabulary PuzzleMaker CD-ROM
- *ExamView*® *Assessment Suite* CD-ROM
- Presentation Plus! Software

SOMATOFORM DISORDERS

Anxiety can create a wide variety of physical symptoms for which no physical cause is apparent. This phenomenon is known as a **somatoform disorder,** or hysteria. The term *hysteria* was more commonly used in Sigmund Freud's time to refer to unexplainable fainting, paralysis, or deafness. Today the term *somatoform disorder* is preferred. Two of the major types of somatoform disorders that psychologists identify are *conversion disorders* and *hypochondriasis.*

somatoform disorder: a condition in which there is no apparent physical cause

Conversion Disorders

A **conversion disorder** is the conversion of emotional difficulties into the loss of a specific physiological function. While the loss of functioning is real, no actual physical damage is present. Many people occasionally experience mild conversion disorders, such as when someone is so frightened he or she cannot move, but a conversion disorder is not simply a brief loss of functioning due to fright. It persists.

conversion disorder: changing emotional difficulties into a loss of a specific voluntary body function

A conversion disorder results in a real and prolonged handicap; the person literally cannot feel anything in his left hand, move his legs, or exercise some other normal physical function. For example, a man might wake up one morning and find himself paralyzed from the waist down. The normal reaction to this would be panic. However, he might accept the loss of function with relative calm, called *la belle indifférence.* This calmness is one sign that a person is suffering from a psychological rather than a physiological problem. Most psychologists believe that people suffering from conversion disorders unconsciously invent physical symptoms to gain freedom from unbearable conflict. For example, a woman who lives in terror of blurting out things that she does not want to say may lose the power of speech. This resolves the conflict about speaking. Conversion disorders are comparatively rare.

Hypochondriasis

Conversion disorders must be distinguished from *hypochondriasis,* in which a person who is in good health becomes preoccupied with imaginary ailments. The hypochondriac spends a lot of time looking for signs of serious illness and often misinterprets minor aches, pains, bruises, or bumps as early signs of a fatal illness. Despite negative results in medical tests and physical

Figure 16.8 Avoiding Happiness

Some people may accuse those suffering from hypochondriasis of faking their illness (and preventing their own happiness). These people, though, do not fake their symptoms; they unrealistically interpret normal aches and pains as symptoms of more serious illnesses. ***How does hypochondriasis differ from a conversion disorder?***

Peanuts reprinted by permission of United Feature Syndicate, Inc.

COOPERATIVE LEARNING ACTIVITY

Conducting Research Organize students into five groups. Explain to the groups that they will be researching a disorder and finding examples of real people throughout history who have suffered from the disorder. For example, there is considerable evidence that Charles Darwin suffered from hypochondriasis. Assign each group one of the following disorders: conversion, hypochondriasis, dissociative amnesia, dissociative fugue, and dissociative identity disorder. Each group should conduct research and prepare a display about the disorder and include information about one or more people who have suffered from, or were believed to suffer from, the disorder. **BLOCK SCHEDULING**

2 TEACH

L1 Movie and Book Synopsis
Arrange for several students to watch *The Secret Garden.* Ask several other students to read the book by Frances Burnett on which the movie is based. Tell the students to focus on how the character Colin, who suffers from hypochondriasis, is treated by those around him. Ask each student to prepare a synopsis of the plot and of the character Colin. Have students present their synopses in class. As a class, discuss the various ways in which society treats those suffering from hypochondriasis and other somatoform disorders.

Guided Reading Activity 16–3

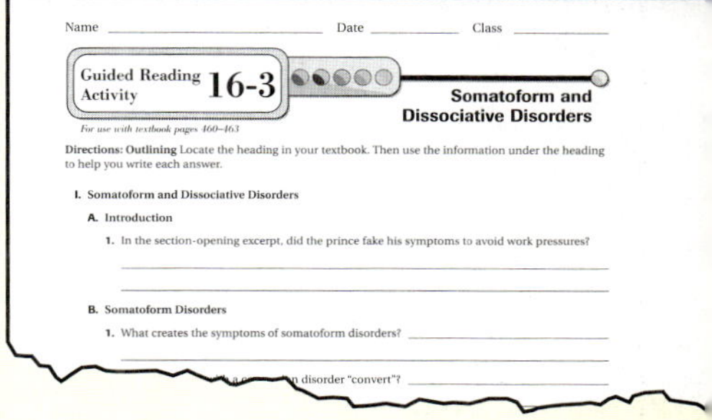
Name ______ Date ______ Class ______

Guided Reading Activity 16-3

Somatoform and Dissociative Disorders

For use with textbook pages 460–463

Directions: Outlining Locate the heading in your textbook. Then use the information under the heading to help you write each answer.

I. Somatoform and Dissociative Disorders

A. Introduction

1. In the section-opening excerpt, did the prince fake his symptoms to avoid work pressures?

B. Somatoform Disorders

1. What creates the symptoms of somatoform disorders?

disorder "convert"?

Figure 16.8

Caption Answer A person with hypochondriasis becomes preoccupied with imaginary ailments even though he or she is healthy. In conversion disorders, actual physiological difficulties result from psychological or emotional problems.

CHAPTER 16

Section 3, pages 460–463

PSYCHOLOGY JOURNAL

Ask students to write about a dissociative experience that they have had. ■

Vocabulary Activity 16–3

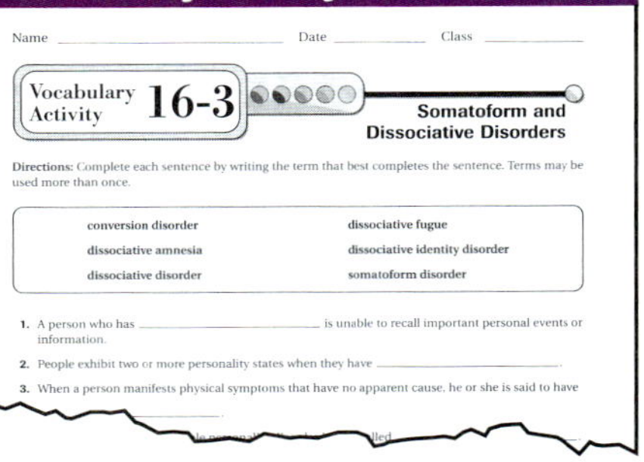
Name ____________ Date ________ Class ________

Vocabulary Activity 16-3

Somatoform and Dissociative Disorders

Directions: Complete each sentence by writing the term that best completes the sentence. Terms may be used more than once.

conversion disorder	dissociative fugue
dissociative amnesia	dissociative identity disorder
dissociative disorder	somatoform disorder

1. A person who has ____________ is unable to recall important personal events or information.
2. People exhibit two or more personality states when they have ____________.
3. When a person manifests physical symptoms that have no apparent cause, he or she is said to have

Reading Check Answer

The difference is that in a dissociative fugue, the person unexpectedly leaves his or her current surroundings.

3 ASSESS

Assign Section 3 Assessment as homework or as an in-class activity.

Section Quiz 16–3

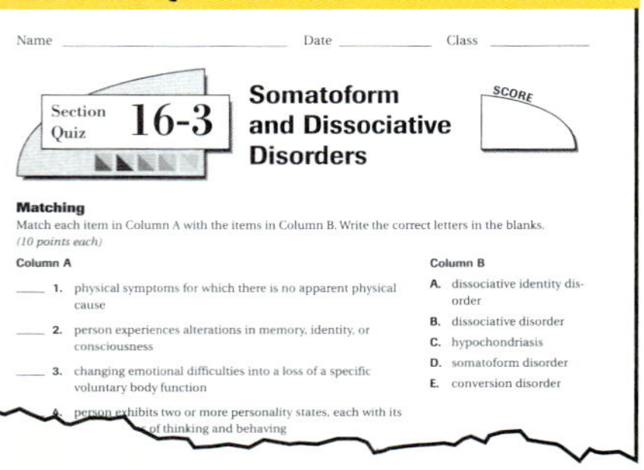
Name ____________ Date ________ Class ________

Section Quiz 16-3

Somatoform and Dissociative Disorders

SCORE

Matching

Match each item in Column A with the items in Column B. Write the correct letters in the blanks. *(10 points each)*

Column A	Column B
____ 1. physical symptoms for which there is no apparent physical cause	A. dissociative identity disorder
____ 2. person experiences alterations in memory, identity, or consciousness	B. dissociative disorder
____ 3. changing emotional difficulties into a loss of a specific voluntary body function	C. hypochondriasis
4. person exhibits two or more personality states, each with its ... of thinking and behaving	D. somatoform disorder
	E. conversion disorder

evaluations, the hypochondriac typically continues to believe that a disease or malfunction exists. Hypochondriasis occurs mainly during young adulthood and is equally common in men and women. According to psychoanalytic theory, hypochondriasis, like conversion, occurs when an individual represses emotions and then expresses them symbolically in physical symptoms.

DISSOCIATIVE DISORDERS

dissociative disorder: a disorder in which a person experiences alterations in memory, identity, or consciousness

You have probably had the experience of being lost in a daydream and failing to notice your friend calling your name. This is a normal dissociative experience. A **dissociative disorder** involves a more significant breakdown in a person's normal conscious experience, such as a loss of memory or identity. These psychological phenomena fascinate many people, so we hear a good deal about amnesia and multiple personalities. Actually, they are very rare.

dissociative amnesia: the inability to recall important personal events or information; is usually associated with stressful events

Memory loss that has no biological explanation, or **dissociative amnesia,** may be an attempt to escape from problems by blotting them out completely. Amnesiacs remember how to speak and usually retain a fund of general knowledge, but they may not know who they are, where they live and work, or who their family is. This amnesia should be distinguished from other losses of memory that result from physical brain damage, normal forgetting, or drug abuse. Dissociative amnesia most often results from a traumatic event, such as witnessing a terrible accident.

dissociative fugue: a dissociative disorder in which a person suddenly and unexpectedly travels away from home or work and is unable to recall the past

In **dissociative fugue,** another type of dissociative reaction, amnesia is coupled with active flight to a different environment. For example, a woman may suddenly disappear and wake up three days later in a restaurant 200 miles from home. If she is not treated, she may actually establish a new identity—assume a new name, marry, take a job, and so forth—in a new place. She may repress all knowledge of a previous life. A fugue state may last for days or for decades. However long it lasts, the individual, when she comes out of it, will have no memory of what happened in the interim. Fugue, then, is a sort of traveling amnesia, and it probably serves the same psychological function as dissociative amnesia, that is, escape from unbearable conflict or anxiety.

dissociative identity disorder: a person exhibits two or more personality states, each with its own patterns of thinking and behaving

In **dissociative identity disorder** (previously known as multiple personality disorder), a third type of dissociative disorder, someone seems to have two or more distinct identities, each with its own way of thinking and behaving. These different personality states may take control at different times.

Eve White, a young woman who sought psychiatric treatment for severe headaches and blackouts, has become a famous example. Eve White was a conscientious, self-controlled, rather shy person. However, during one of her therapy sessions, her expression—and her personality—suddenly changed. Eve Black, as she now called herself, was childlike, fun-loving, and irresponsible—the opposite of the woman who originally walked into the psychiatrist's office. Eve Black was conscious of

Reading Check

How is dissociative amnesia different from dissociative fugue?

MEETING SPECIAL NEEDS

Learning Style: Logical/Mathematical Have students research the case of Kenneth Bianchi, known as the Hillside Strangler, who terrorized Los Angeles in the late 1970s. Encourage students to discover how he tried to use multiple personality disorder, now known as dissociative identity disorder, to escape conviction and how psychiatrist Martin Orne was able to prove that Ken was faking his claim. Ask students to present their findings to the class as if presenting evidence to a jury. **L3** **BLOCK SCHEDULING**

Refer to ***Inclusion for the High School Social Studies Classroom Strategies and Activities*** in the TCR for strategies for students with different learning styles.

Eve White's existence but considered her a separate person. Eve White did not know about Eve Black, however, and neither was she conscious of Jane, a third personality that emerged during the course of therapy. (This case served as the basis for the film *The Three Faces of Eve*.) Some psychologists believe that this dividing up of the personality is the result of the individual's effort to escape from a part of the self that he or she fears. The secret self then emerges in the form of a separate personality. Dissociative identity disorder is extremely rare.

Eve's real name is Chris Costner Sizemore, and she published a book, *I'm Eve* (Sizemore & Pittillo, 1977), many years later, explaining that Eve ultimately had 22 separate personalities. Her case is often confused with Sybil, a woman whose 16 personalities were also described in a book and a film. While cases like Eve and Sybil are fascinating, they are extremely rare and very controversial.

People diagnosed with this disorder usually suffered severe physical, psychological, or sexual abuse during childhood. Individuals with dissociative disorders have learned to dissociate themselves from such stressful events by selectively forgetting them, thereby reducing the anxiety they feel.

Figure 16.9 The Personalities of Eve

Chris Sizemore (Eve) was able to overcome her disorder through therapy. She created this painting to symbolize the personalities present within her when she began therapy. ***What causes dissociative identity disorder?***

SECTION 3 Assessment

1. **Review the Vocabulary** Define and describe three dissociative disorders. Explain how these disorders differ from one another.
2. **Visualize the Main Idea** Use a graphic organizer similar to the one below to list dissociative disorders.

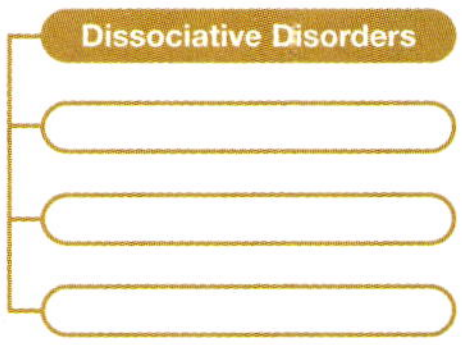

3. **Recall Information** What is the difference between a conversion disorder and hypochondriasis?
4. **Think Critically** Besides anxiety, how might you realize that you are suffering from a somatoform or dissociative disorder?
5. **Application Activity** As a class or in groups, arrange an appointment with a clinical psychologist, nurse, physician, or counseling psychologist. Question this person regarding the most common psychological problems young people face. Report your findings to the class.

SECTION 3 Assessment Answers

1. Dissociative amnesia is the inability to recall important personal events and information. In dissociative fugue, the person unexpectedly leaves his or her home or work and is unable to recall the past. Dissociative identity disorder causes a person to exhibit two or more separate personalities.
2. dissociative amnesia, dissociative fugue, and dissociative identity disorder
3. In a conversion disorder, physiological symptoms such as partial paralysis are caused by emotional difficulties. Hypochondriasis is a disorder in which a healthy person imagines various ailments.
4. Dissociative disorders could be recognized by "waking up" some place that is unfamiliar or having someone accuse you of actions taken for which you have no memory. Somatoform disorders may be recognized by unexplainable physical ailments.
5. Students' answers will vary. Encourage students to find interesting and innovative ways to share their findings.

Figure 16.9

Caption Answer The disorder is usually caused by severe childhood trauma such as physical, psychological, or sexual abuse.

Reteach

Have the class brainstorm common dissociative experiences. Ask students to compare and contrast these experiences to the various dissociative disorders discussed in the text.

Enrich

Have students research Chris Sizemore's life. Ask them to search for details regarding her childhood, personalities, and treatment.

4 CLOSE

Have students write an "Unsolved Mysteries" style story involving dissociative fugue disorder. Select the best of these stories and have the student-writer read the story aloud.

Going Further

Munchausen's by Proxy

In 1994, Kathleen Bush was lauded in a White House ceremony by First Lady Hillary Clinton as an outstanding example of a mother with a very sick child and no medical insurance.

Less than two years later, Kathleen Bush was arrested for child abuse. Her daughter, Jennifer, then 8 years old, had been hospitalized more than 200 times and had undergone 40 operations. Some accused her of having a disorder known as Munchausen's by Proxy, which is the creation of physical symptoms in one's child. The parent, usually the mother, appears to be seeking attention and sympathy from family, friends, and physicians. In this case, Kathleen Bush was accused of poisoning and infecting her daughter. Her daughter was put in protective custody by the state and improved rapidly after being removed from her mother's care.

Discussing the Case Study

Ask: What caused Goodman to suspect Munchausen's? What types of things do patients do to convince physicians that their symptoms are real? What evidence do they tend to leave of their deceit?

Case Studies

Munchausen's Syndrome

Period of Study: 1994

Introduction: In 1994 a physician consulted psychiatrist Berney Goodman regarding the condition of a patient who seemingly had a rare bowel condition—the patient vomited every time she ate. Together they diagnosed the patient with bowel paralysis. Goodman himself wanted to examine the patient. From the start, the patient refused to cooperate with Goodman. Goodman discovered that the patient had low blood pressure. This, though, did not correspond with the diagnosis of bowel paralysis.

Hypothesis: Goodman suspected that the patient suffered from *Munchausen's Syndrome*. Those who suffer from the ailment have developed great sensitivity to emotional pain and will use any methods possible to avoid feeling it. These methods are quite extreme and often deadly. The sufferers often attempt to hospitalize themselves with self-defined or self-induced symptoms. Their ultimate goal is to have the physician take extraordinary measures to save their life.

Method: After further investigation, Goodman discovered that the patient was secretly taking diuretics to produce the symptoms associated with bowel paralysis. His suspicions had been correct. A Munchausen's patient might complain of a variety of symptoms. A physician, though, has trouble finding these symptoms when examining the patient. Patients have added sugar to samples of urine, suggesting the presence of diabetes. They have visited dermatologists with rashes, sores, and lesions with no medical explanation but used sandpaper, chemical irritants, or excessive heat to make these symptoms appear. Munchausen's patients have swallowed corrosive substances, eroding the lining of their stomachs and throats to produce vomiting.

Munchausen's patients are not limited to displaying physical symptoms—they also imitate psychiatric disorders. Overdosing on psychoactive drugs to induce delusions and hallucinations is common for them. Patients may use techniques of persuasion to try to influence the physician to perform thorough medical investigations.

Although Munchausen's patients can puzzle and deceive physicians, they have a tendency to hide their methods poorly. Syringes are left lying around, they do not conceal pills neatly, and they allow themselves to be observed during their symptom-causing routines. These scenarios result in most diagnoses.

Results: Describing how Munchausen's Syndrome sufferers behave is much easier than explaining why. Some leads suggest that either all-caring or all-rejecting parental relationships are experienced and then re-created by the patient. They seem to invite their physicians into an all-nurturing relationship, and at other times they despise their physicians and create an all-rejecting relationship.

The difficulty in discovering and diagnosing Munchausen's Syndrome led to the absence of a clear-cut definition in the DSM-IV. Because of this, it is extremely difficult to treat those who are affected.

Analyzing the Case Study

1. What is Munchausen's Syndrome?
2. What are some possible causes of Munchausen's Syndrome?
3. **Critical Thinking** Why might a physician or psychologist suspect that someone is suffering from Munchausen's Syndrome? What is the danger in misdiagnosing this disorder?

Answers for Analyzing the Case Study

1. It is a serious disorder in which people will go to extreme lengths to avoid emotional pain. They may create both physical and psychological symptoms to have a physician take care of them.
2. A possible cause may be an all-caring or all-rejecting parental relationship that the person attempts to re-create with the physician.
3. A physician may suspect the presence of this disorder when a person seeks treatment but refuses to fully cooperate with the physicians or psychiatrists. It may also be suspected when there are a series of self-defined or self-induced symptoms for which the person attempts to be admitted to the hospital. However, Munchausen's patients have a tendency to hide their methods poorly, and they often allow themselves to be observed during their symptom-causing routines. If the disorder is diagnosed but is not really present, the person may not be treated for actual ailments. If the disorder is missed, the person may permanently injure himself or herself.

SECTION 4

Schizophrenia and Mood Disorders

Reader's Guide

Main Idea
Schizophrenia involves disordered thoughts. Mood disorders involve disturbances in the experience and expressions of depression.

Vocabulary
- schizophrenia
- delusions
- hallucinations
- major depressive disorder
- bipolar disorder

Objectives
- Describe the disorder of schizophrenia.
- Describe several theories that try to explain mood disorders.

EXPLORING PSYCHOLOGY

Word Salad

A woman was delighted to receive a letter from her son abroad, but distraught when she read it: "Dear mother . . . I am writing on paper. The pen I am using is from a factory called Perry and Co. The factory is in England. The city of London is in England. I know this from my school days. Then I always liked geography. My last teacher in that subject was Professor August A. He was a man with black eyes. There are also blue and grey eyes and other sorts too. I have heard it said that snakes have green eyes. All people have eyes. There are some, too, who are blind."

—from *The Human Mind Explained*, edited by Susan A. Greenfield, 1996

The man who wrote this letter later was diagnosed with schizophrenia. Sufferers of schizophrenia often have difficulty using language to communicate. They seem to go from one phrase to another by random association. This confused language may result because schizophrenia affects the working memory, which is used to form sentences. A person with schizophrenia will not remember the beginning of a sentence and thus finishes it with an unrelated thought. Schizophrenia is often misunderstood.

We can understand depression, and most of us have experienced anxiety. In addition, we can appreciate how people with these problems strive to overcome them as best they can. An individual with schizophrenia, however, who withdraws from normal life and whose distorted perceptions and behavior reach an irrational, fantastic, fear-laden, unimaginable

SECTION RESOURCES

Reproducible Masters
- Guided Reading Activity 16–4
- Vocabulary Activity 16–4
- Section Quiz 16–4

Transparencies
- Daily Focus Transparency 16–4

Multimedia
- *ExamView® Assessment Suite* CD-ROM
- Presentation Plus! Software

1 FOCUS

Section Objectives
1. Describe the disorder of schizophrenia.
2. Describe several theories that try to explain mood disorders.

BELLRINGER
Motivational Activity

Project Daily Focus Transparency 16–4 and have students answer the questions.

Available as blackline master

Daily Focus Transparency 16–4

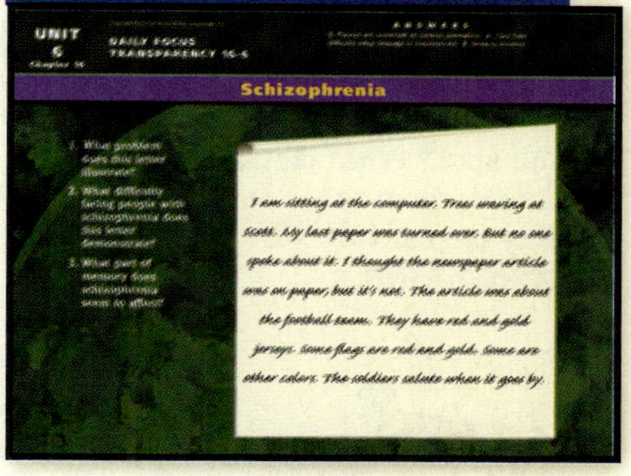

Reader's Guide

Use the Reader's Guide to introduce concepts and vocabulary.

Exploring Psychology
Ask students to read the **Exploring Psychology** feature. Then ask: **How does this letter show the man's difficulty in communicating?**

Vocabulary Precheck
Have students read the Glossary definitions of the terms. Then have them create flash cards with the terms on one side and definitions on the other to help them learn the terms.

2 TEACH

L1 Analyzing a Quote Tell students that the term *schizophrenia* was devised by Swiss psychiatrist Eugen Bleuler in 1908. Prior to that time, it had been called *dementia praecox*. Read aloud Bleuler's explanation of the term's origin.

I call the dementia praecox "schizophrenia" from the Greek words schizein, *meaning "to split," and* phren, *meaning "mind" because the "splitting" of the different psychic functions is one of its most important characteristics. For the sake of convenience, I use the word in the singular although it is apparent that the group includes several diseases.*

Ask: **How closely does Bleuler's description of schizophrenia match the description in the text? What similarities and differences can you spot? What distinguishes schizophrenia from other mood and personality disorders?** **BLOCK SCHEDULING**

FYI

In March 1997, the world was shocked by the mass suicide of Marshall Applewhite and 38 followers of the Heaven's Gate cult. Psychologists identify Applewhite and many other cult leaders as schizophrenic. Many of his followers had borderline personalities.

Readings and Case Studies in Psychology

Have students read the Chapter 16 Reading selection in *Readings and Case Studies in Psychology* and answer the questions that follow the reading.

schizophrenia: a group of disorders characterized by confused and disconnected thoughts, emotions, and perceptions

delusions: false beliefs that a person maintains in the face of contrary evidence

hallucinations: perceptions that have no direct external cause

level, does so in ways that are difficult to understand. Yet, psychologists are making progress in furthering our understanding of schizophrenia—the most complex and severe psychological problem we encounter.

WHAT IS SCHIZOPHRENIA?

While the disorders discussed thus far are primarily problems of emotion, schizophrenia is a problem of cognition, but it also involves emotion, perception, and motor functions. Schizophrenia affects about 1 percent of people worldwide, including 2.4 million Americans (National Institute of Mental Health, 2005), but the odds increase if schizophrenia is already in the family. What distinguishes this disorder from other types of psychological disturbance? **Schizophrenia** involves confused and disordered thoughts and perceptions. With schizophrenia, a person's thought processes are somewhat disturbed, and the person has lost contact with reality to a considerable extent. One expert has noted that someone with depression or severe anxiety problems dreams in an unreal way about life, while a person with schizophrenia lives life as an unreal dream. Schizophrenia is not a single problem; it has no single cause or cure. Rather, it is a collection of symptoms that indicates an individual has serious difficulty trying to meet the demands of life.

Suppose a psychiatrist is interviewing a patient who has just been admitted to a hospital. The individual demonstrates a wide assortment of symptoms. He is intensely excited, expresses extreme hostility toward members of his family, and at the same time claims that he loves them, showing conflicting feelings. One minute he is extremely aggressive, questioning the psychiatrist's motives and even threatening her. The next minute he withdraws and acts as if he does not hear anything she says. Then he begins talking again. "Naturally," he says, "I am growing my father's hair." Although all of the person's other behavior indicates psychological problems, this last statement would be the diagnostic bell ringer. It reveals that the man is living in a private, disordered reality.

Many individuals with schizophrenia experience **delusions**—false beliefs maintained in the face of contrary evidence—and **hallucinations**—perceptions in the absence of corresponding sensation. For example, a person with schizophrenia may perceive a voice when, in fact, there is no sound present. A person with schizophrenia may show a number of other symptoms as well. One is *incoherence,* or a marked decline in thought processes. The language of someone with schizophrenia may be sped up; sometimes, it is described as "word salad"—lots of words thrown together. Another symptom is

More About...

Autism

Schizophrenia and autism involve neurons in specialized areas of the brain. In autism, errors in the final stages of brain development affect the amygdala, limbic system, and possibly the cerebellum. These regions are related to language, information processing, and the emotional coloration of those processes (Ciaranello, 2001).

Obvious to the parents in haunting ways soon after birth, *infantile autism* causes children to differ from normal children in three ways. First, children with autism do not respond to other people. If you pick up an autistic child, he or she is stiff or limp; the child will not cling to you as normal children will. Second, an autistic child is very slow in developing language and communication skills. By age 5 or 6, they may simply repeat what has been said, a condition called *echolalia*. Third, autistic children are very limited in their interests and behavior. They may abuse themselves or repeat a simple hand motion for hours without ceasing.

Explaining autism's cause has been difficult. Learning-based and psychoanalytic attempts have failed. It is clear that genetics play a role (see Chapter 6; Ciaranello, 2001); an inborn defect may interact with later environmental or biological events (Carson & Butcher, 1992) to produce autism.

COOPERATIVE LEARNING ACTIVITY

Making a Chart Organize students into small groups. Have each group construct a chart comparing the various theories of schizophrenia. The column heads should be named for each of the theories. The row titles should include *Description of Theory, Supporting Evidence, Limitations of Theory,* and any other pertinent areas that the group can identify. Conduct a class discussion in which the groups share their charts. **Ask:** **Based on the information presented, what generalizations can you form about the causes of schizophrenia?** **BLOCK SCHEDULING**

disturbances of affect, or emotions that are inappropriate for the circumstances. In addition, an individual with schizophrenia may display severe *deterioration in normal movement,* which may occur as slowed movement, nonmovement, or as highly agitated behavior. Another symptom is a marked *decline in previous levels of functioning;* for example, a sharp dropoff in productivity at work. Yet another symptom is *diverted attention,* perhaps brought about by cognitive flooding, as if the person is unable to focus his or her attention.

Figure 16.10 Paranoia

A male patient diagnosed with schizophrenia with paranoid tendencies created this painting. It displays the symbolism of watchful eyes, grasping hands, and the self as subject matter. ***How is the paranoid type of schizophrenia characterized?***

TYPES OF SCHIZOPHRENIA

Psychologists classify schizophrenia into several subtypes. One, the *paranoid type,* involves hallucinations and delusions, including *grandeur:* "I am the savior of my people;" or *persecution:* "Someone is always watching me" (see Figure 16.10). People with the *catatonic type* may remain motionless for long periods, exhibiting a waxy flexibility in which limbs in unusual positions may take a long time to return to a resting, relaxed position—exactly as if melting a wax statue (see Figure 16.11). Symptoms of the *disorganized type* include incoherent language, inappropriate emotions, giggling for no apparent reason, generally disorganized motor behavior, and hallucinations and delusions. Another form of schizophrenia is the *remission type.* This diagnostic label is applied to anyone whose symptoms are completely gone or still exist but are not severe enough to have earned a diagnosis of schizophrenia in the first place. The expectation is that symptoms will return, so the schizophrenia is simply viewed as in remission. It is sometimes difficult to differentiate between types of schizophrenia because some symptoms are shared by all types. The *undifferentiated type* encompasses the basic symptoms of schizophrenia, such as deterioration of daily functioning, hallucinations, delusions, inappropriate emotions, and thought disorders.

Schizophrenia is a very complex condition, and treatment is long-term and usually requires hospitalization. Long-term institutionalization sometimes leads to a patient who is *burned out*—one who is unlikely to function normally in society. Schizophrenia may go into remission, in which the symptoms disappear and the person seems quite normal, but according to the DSM-IV, adjustment tends to deteriorate between successive episodes of

CHAPTER 16

Section 4, pages 465–473

Figure 16.10

Caption Answer The paranoid type of schizophrenia is characterized by hallucinations and delusions.

TEACHER Tip

Provide concrete examples of each of the common symptoms of schizophrenia. Discuss the problems that may result from each of these symptoms.

Guided Reading Activity 16–4

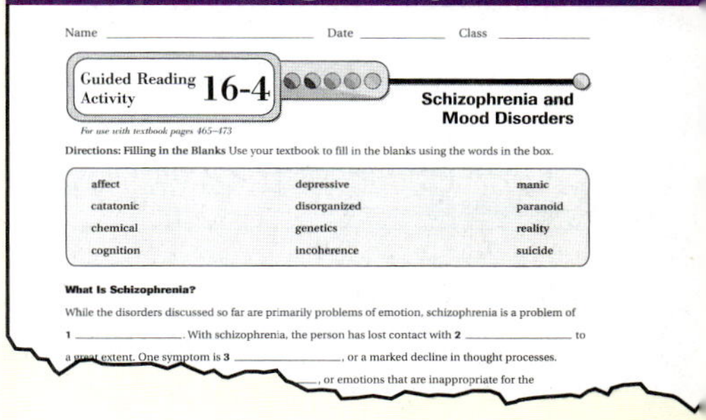
Name ______ Date ______ Class ______

Guided Reading Activity 16-4 — Schizophrenia and Mood Disorders

For use with textbook pages 465–473

Directions: Filling in the Blanks Use your textbook to fill in the blanks using the words in the box.

affect	depressive	manic
catatonic	disorganized	paranoid
chemical	genetics	reality
cognition	incoherence	suicide

What Is Schizophrenia?

While the disorders discussed so far are primarily problems of emotion, schizophrenia is a problem of 1 ______. With schizophrenia, the person has lost contact with 2 ______ to a great extent. One symptom is 3 ______, or a marked decline in thought processes. ______, or emotions that are inappropriate for the

PSYCHOLOGY JOURNAL

After reading the various theories of the causes of schizophrenia, have each student write a short explanation for a friend whose brother has just been diagnosed with schizophrenia, describing the causes of the disorder. ■

MEETING SPECIAL NEEDS

Learning Style: Logical/Mathematical Tell students that the cause of schizophrenia is somewhat related to heredity. Ask students to compare the increased risk of developing schizophrenia if the following relation has experienced schizophrenia: identical twins, fraternal twins, child of two schizophrenic parents, child of one schizophrenic parent, and sibling. Have students use the data provided in the text on page 468 and present their findings in graphical form. Encourage students to use creative visuals in their graphs. **L2**

Refer to ***Inclusion for the High School Social Studies Classroom Strategies and Activities*** in the TCR for strategies for students with different learning styles.

CHAPTER 16

Section 4, pages 465–473

Looking @ the Issues

Effects of Diagnosis on Treatment In the early 1970s, David Rosenhan and seven other researchers became pseudopatients at psychiatric hospitals. All were admitted to hospitals after complaining of hearing disembodied voices and were diagnosed as schizophrenic. Stays in the hospital ranged from one week to two months. After admission, none exhibited any abnormal behaviors, yet none of the hospital staff ever recognized them as normal. Interestingly, many of the patients in the hospitals suspected that the pseudopatients did not belong. **Ask:** **What does this research study indicate about the effect of diagnosis on how a person is treated? How can a diagnosis become a self-fulfilling prophecy?**

Figure 16.11

Caption Answer Schizophrenia is treatable; that is, it can often be brought under control with medication, but it is not curable.

Vocabulary Activity 16–4

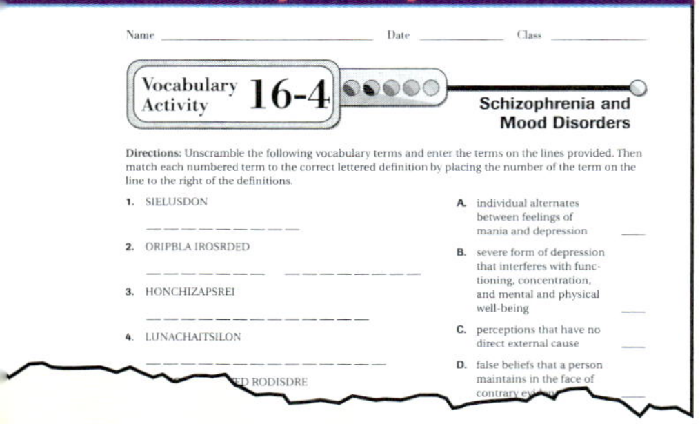
Name ______ Date ______ Class ______

Vocabulary Activity 16-4

Schizophrenia and Mood Disorders

Directions: Unscramble the following vocabulary terms and enter the terms on the lines provided. Then match each numbered term to the correct lettered definition by placing the number of the term on the line to the right of the definitions.

1. SIELUSDON
2. ORIPBLA IROSRDED
3. HONCHIZAPSREI
4. LUNACHAITSILON

...D RODISDRE

A. individual alternates between feelings of mania and depression ___

B. severe form of depression that interferes with functioning, concentration, and mental and physical well-being ___

C. perceptions that have no direct external cause ___

D. false beliefs that a person maintains in the face of contrary ev... ___

Did You Know?

Split Personality The term *schizophrenia* comes from Greek for "split personality." Schizophrenia does not refer to split personalities such as dissociative identity disorder, though. Schizophrenia involves a split between the intellectual and emotional parts of a single personality.

the reappearance of symptoms. Although recovery from schizophrenia is possible, no real cure for schizophrenia exists, and once an individual is diagnosed with schizophrenia, he or she may never escape from it.

CAUSES OF SCHIZOPHRENIA

What is the actual cause of schizophrenia? There are many theories, and just as certainly, there is disagreement among practitioners. In all likelihood, the ultimate cause is an interaction of environmental, genetic, and biochemical factors.

Biological Influences

Genetics is almost certainly involved in causing schizophrenia. One psychologist (Gottesman, 1991) summarized the results of more than 35 studies conducted in Western Europe from 1920 to 1987. As confirmed by others, he found that there is a 1 percent likelihood that anyone in the general population will develop schizophrenia. These odds, however, increase to 10 percent if schizophrenia is already in the family. Yet, even among identical twins, if one twin develops schizophrenia, only 48 percent of the twin's siblings will develop it. Schizophrenia is likely caused by a combination of genetic, epigenetic (factors that affect a cell but not its DNA), and environmental factors (Hanson & Gottesman, 2005) (see Figure 16.12).

Figure 16.11 Catatonic Type

A person suffering from the catatonic type of schizophrenia can hold an unusual position for long periods of time. ***Is schizophrenia curable?***

Researchers have studied children born into families where either parent or a parent's sibling was diagnosed with schizophrenia. Across several studies, if one or more siblings are diagnosed with schizophrenia, other children in the family will later be diagnosed with the condition less than 2 percent of the time. That probability rises to 5.5 percent if a parent or sibling is diagnosed (Mortensen, et al., 1999). Even where both parents were later diagnosed as having schizophrenia, about 50 percent of the children show no signs of schizophrenia. In summary, these studies show that psychologists cannot specify the exact contribution hereditary factors make to schizophrenia (Carson & Sanislow, 1992).

Biochemistry and Physiology

The proper working of the brain depends on the presence of right amounts of many chemicals, from oxygen to proteins. Some psychologists believe that psychosis is due largely to chemical imbalances in the brain. According to some theorists, occasionally people are born with a nervous system that gets aroused very easily and takes a long time to return to normal. Such people might be particularly likely to get upset when they are stressed.

CRITICAL THINKING ACTIVITY

Identifying Central Issues Have students research the struggle with schizophrenia experienced by one of the following well-known people: John Nash, mathematician and Nobel Prize winner; Lionel Aldridge, defensive end for the Green Bay Packers; Peter Green, guitarist for the band Fleetwood Mac; Syd Barrett, lead guitarist with Pink Floyd; or Vaclav Nijinsky, Russian dancer. Ask students to write a short story describing the person's battle with schizophrenia. **L1**

Figure 16.12 The Genain Quadruplets

In 1930 four identical girls were born. By high school, people had labeled the girls as somehow different. By the time they were young adults, all four were diagnosed with schizophrenia. ***From this case, what can psychologists infer about the causes of schizophrenia?***

Chemical problems may also be involved in the occurrence of schizophrenia. A number of researchers believe that the basic problem in schizophrenia is that too much or too little of certain chemicals has upset the brain's mechanisms for processing information, perhaps interfering with normal synaptic transmission.

The *dopamine hypothesis* suggests that an excess of dopamine at selected synapses is related to a diagnosis of schizophrenia. One psychologist (Carlsson, 1988) notes that correlational studies are not enough to demonstrate a direct role for dopamine in schizophrenia. It seems likely that chemicals play a role, but it is hard to tell whether these chemicals are the cause of schizophrenia or the result of it. Symptoms of schizophrenia may even be caused by the fact that people with schizophrenia tend to live in hospitals, where they get little exercise, eat institutional food, and are usually given daily doses of tranquilizers. Living under such conditions, anyone might develop chemical imbalances and abnormal behavior.

The use of CT and fMRI scans (see Chapter 6) has led to the discovery that the brains of people with schizophrenia often show signs of deteriorated brain tissue (Pearlson et al., 1989). One consistent result is that women who at some time develop schizophrenia are likely to have difficult pregnancies and difficulties giving birth. Obesity prior to pregnancy, infection during the second trimester (Wyatt & Susser, 2000), and oxygen deprivation to the fetus (Cannon et al., 2000) are correlated with children developing schizophrenia. The exact role of the environment in fostering schizophrenia is unclear, but it is involved.

Figure 16.12

Caption Answer There is no one cause of schizophrenia; genetics is almost certainly involved. However, one may inherit a disposition toward schizophrenia that develops due to exposure to environmental factors.

CULTURAL CONNECTIONS

Researchers at the Institute for Basic Psychiatry Research at the Aarhus University Hospital in Denmark analyzed 2,669 people diagnosed with schizophrenia. They examined several risk factors including family history of mental illness, time of the year that the people were born, and where the people lived during their childhoods. The study confirmed that a family history of schizophrenia was the primary risk factor. The study also found that those born in February and March and those living in urban environments ran a higher risk of developing schizophrenia. Researchers concluded that the time and place factors lend support to the viral theory of schizophrenia. This theory states that prenatal viruses may affect certain aspects of brain development. These changes to the brain may be the cause of the onset of schizophrenia later in life. A more controversial study suggests viral infections experienced by adults may trigger some cases of schizophrenia. Researchers reported that, "Viruses are more abundant in winter and are more likely to spread in crowded urban environments." *Source:* Talan, J. (1999, February 25) New schizophrenia risks found. *Newsday,* A24.

PSYCHOLOGY LAB EXPERIMENT

Conducting a Survey Tell students that many people have stereotypical ideas about people suffering from various psychological disorders. Have students work in small groups to develop a survey about people's attitudes about either schizophrenia or bipolar disorder. The surveys should consist of a series of statements with which people can agree or disagree. Each statement should include a rating scale from Strongly Agree to Strongly Disagree. Give students the following example: "A person with schizophrenia is incapable of holding a position of responsibility." Each group should administer the survey to at least 20 people of various age groups. Ask the groups to analyze the data and present their findings using tables and graphs. **L2** **BLOCK SCHEDULING**

L2 Analyzing a Quote Read aloud the following quote from Martin Seligman.

People become depressed when their explanatory style is internal ('I'm to blame'), stable ('I'll always be this way'), and global ('Nothing I do turns out right.'). . . .

Ask: How does Seligman believe that depressed people see themselves? *(as the cause of all problems; as unable to change or succeed)* **According to the theory of learned helplessness, how do such individuals see the external world?** *(as beyond their control)*

PSYCHOLOGY Update

Bipolar Disorder A study published in the May 1999 issue of the *Archives of General Psychiatry* indicates that omega-3 fatty acids found in fish oil may relieve the symptoms of bipolar disorder. The study involved a small sample of people being treated for bipolar disorder at the Brigham and Women's Hospital in Boston, Massachusetts. Researchers acknowledge that further research using larger samples is needed before a theory can be proposed.

Family and Interactions

From Freud onward, it has been tempting to blame the family situation in childhood for problems that develop during adulthood. Paul Meehl (1962, 1989) suggested that bad experiences during childhood are not enough, in and of themselves, to lead to schizophrenia; being part of a *pathogenic,* or unhealthful, family may contribute to problems in the adult years.

Studies show that families of individuals who later develop schizophrenia are often on the verge of falling apart. Another frequent finding is that family members organize themselves around—or in spite of—the very unusual, demanding, or maladaptive behavior of one member of the family. Communication, too, often seems disorganized in the early family life of people who later develop schizophrenia.

In Summary Which of these theories is correct? At this point, psychologists do not know. It may be that each is partially true. Perhaps people who inherit a tendency toward psychological disorders react more strongly to stressful situations than others would. The *diathesis-stress hypothesis* states that an individual may have inherited a predisposition toward schizophrenia. For schizophrenia to develop, however, that person must be exposed to an environment with certain stressors, such as bad family experiences, before the schizophrenia will develop. Explaining the causes of schizophrenia is perhaps the most complex research problem psychologists face.

MOOD DISORDERS

We all experience mood swings. Sometimes we are happy or elated, while at other times we feel dejected, miserable, or depressed. Yet even when we are discouraged, most of us still feel we can control our emotions and that these feelings will pass.

Occasional depression is a common experience. In some people, however, these moods are more intense and tend to last for longer periods. These individuals often get the sense that their depression will go on forever and that there is nothing they can do to change it. As a result, their emotions hamper their ability to function effectively or to seek help for their disorder. In extreme cases, a mood may cause individuals to lose touch with reality or seriously threaten their health or lives.

Major Depressive Disorder

major depressive disorder: severe form of lowered mood in which a person experiences feelings of worthlessness and diminished pleasure or interest in many activities

Individuals suffering from **major depressive disorder** spend at least two weeks feeling depressed, sad, anxious, fatigued, and agitated, experiencing a reduced ability to function and interact with others. The depression ranges from mild feelings of uneasiness, sadness, and apathy to intense suicidal despair. To be diagnosed as depression, these feelings cannot be attributed to bereavement (the loss of a loved one). This disorder is marked by at least four of the following symptoms: problems with eating, sleeping, thinking, concentrating, or decision making; lacking energy; thinking about suicide; and feeling worthless or guilty (American Psychiatric Association, 1994).

INTERDISCIPLINARY CONNECTIONS ACTIVITY

The Arts Have students research some famous figures in the arts who suffered from bouts of depression. Choices could include Vincent van Gogh, Robert Schumann, Hector Berlioz, William Styron, and Gustav Mahler. Ask students to write case studies of one of these figures for an abnormal psychology text. Have students read their case studies aloud to the class. **L2**

Bipolar Disorder

One type of mood disorder is **bipolar disorder,** in which individuals are excessively and inappropriately happy or unhappy. These reactions may take the form of high elation, hopeless depression, or an alternation between the two.

In the *manic phase,* a person experiences elation, extreme confusion, distractibility, and racing thoughts. Often the person has an exaggerated sense of self-esteem and engages in irresponsible behavior, such as shopping sprees or insulting remarks. As an example, consider the following behavior:

> On admission she slapped the nurse, addressed the house physician as God, made the sign of the cross, and laughed loudly when she was asked to don the hospital garb. This she promptly tore to shreds. . . . She sang at the top of her voice, screamed through the window, and leered at the patients promenading in the recreation yard. (Karnash, 1945)

Often, this state is not as easy to detect as some others because the person seems to be in touch with reality and blessed with an unending sense of optimism. During a manic episode, a person may behave as if he or she needs less sleep, and the activity level typically increases, as does the loudness and the frequency with which he or she speaks.

In the *depressive phase,* the individual is overcome by feelings of failure, sinfulness, worthlessness, and despair. In contrast to the optimism and high activity of a manic-type reaction, a depressive-type reaction is marked by lethargy, despair, and unresponsiveness. The behavior of someone who is depressed in a bipolar disorder is essentially the same as someone with a major depressive disorder (Perris, 1982), as in the following case:

> The patient lay in bed, immobile, with a dull, depressed expression on his face. His eyes were sunken and downcast. Even when spoken to, he would not raise his eyes to look at the speaker. Usually he did not respond at all to questions, but sometimes, after apparently great effort, he would mumble something about the "Scourge of God." (Morris & Maisto, 2005)

In some cases, a patient will alternate between frantic action and motionless despair. Some people experience occasional episodes of a manic-type or depressive-type reaction, separated by long intervals of relatively normal behavior. Others exhibit almost no normal behavior, cycling instead from periods of manic-type reactions to equally intense depressive-type reactions. Some theorists have speculated that the manic periods serve as an attempt to ward off the underlying hopelessness of the depressive periods. Others believe that mania can be traced to the same biochemical disorder responsible for depression.

Figure 16.13 Down in the Dumps

This scene expresses the emptiness and bleakness that a depressed person feels. ***When does depression become a psychological disorder?***

bipolar disorder: disorder in which an individual alternates between feelings of mania (euphoria) and depression

Reading Check What is the difference between a major depressive disorder and a bipolar disorder?

EXTENDING THE CONTENT

Postpartum Depression Tell students that postpartum depression is a relatively common depressive disorder that occurs among new mothers within three to four weeks after the birth of a child. Its symptoms are similar to other depressive disorders, plus it often includes anxiety about harm coming to the new baby. One possible explanation for the onset of depression after delivery of a child is the wide hormonal swings that occur as the mother's body readjusts to its nonpregnant state. Episodes of postpartum depression increase the risk for developing other types of depressive disorders.

Figure 16.13

Caption Answer Depression becomes a psychological disorder when the depressive mood is very intense, interferes with normal functioning, and lasts for more than two weeks.

Applying Psychology

Mental illnesses have been a common topic for films. Have students view one pair of the following films:

Bipolar disorder: *Blue Sky* (1994) and *A Fine Madness* (1966) or *Mr. Jones* (1991) and *The Snake Pit* (1947)
Schizophrenia: *Awakenings* (1990) and *Possessed* (1947)

After viewing the films, have students write an essay comparing and contrasting the treatment of the characters and society's view of the disorder.

Reading Check Answer Bipolar disorder is characterized by wide mood swings between depression and euphoria. Major depressive disorder is characterized by severe depression that interferes with normal functioning.

CHAPTER 16
Section 4, pages 465–473

Figure 16.14

Visual Instruction Ask students to analyze the statistics in terms of Seligman's theory of learned helplessness. For example, **ask: How does the theory explain the high incidence of suicide among people aged 75–84?**

Caption Answer ages 75–84; males

3 ASSESS

Assign Section 4 Assessment as homework or as an in-class activity.

Section Quiz 16–4

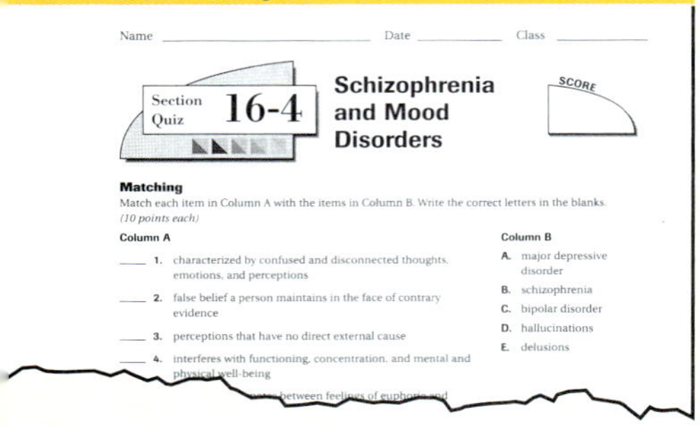
Name ______ Date ______ Class ______

Section Quiz 16-4 Schizophrenia and Mood Disorders SCORE

Matching
Match each item in Column A with the items in Column B. Write the correct letters in the blanks. (10 points each)

Column A	Column B
___ 1. characterized by confused and disconnected thoughts, emotions, and perceptions	A. major depressive disorder
___ 2. false belief a person maintains in the face of contrary evidence	B. schizophrenia
___ 3. perceptions that have no direct external cause	C. bipolar disorder
___ 4. interferes with functioning, concentration, and mental and physical well-being	D. hallucinations
	E. delusions

Reteach

Explore in a class discussion how the diathesis-stress hypothesis includes the various theories of the causes of schizophrenia.

Figure 16.14 Suicide Rates

Suicide rates vary according to age and gender. ***Which age group has the highest suicide rate? Which gender has the highest suicide rate?***

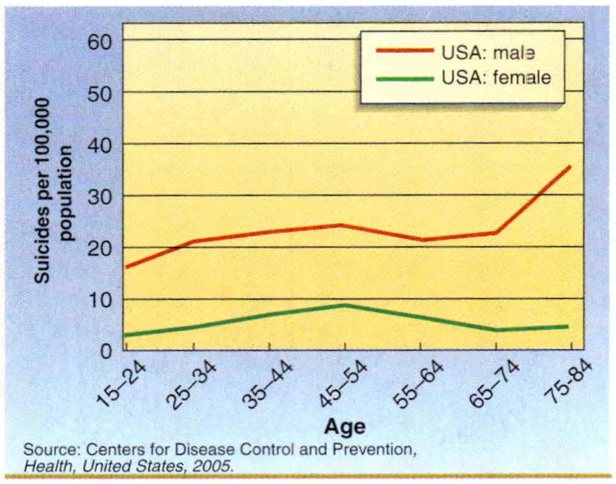

Source: Centers for Disease Control and Prevention, *Health, United States, 2005.*

Seasonal Affective Disorder

Many of us may feel a tinge of sadness when looking at a mid-February landscape of dull grays and browns. However, there are people who develop a deep depression in the midst of winter. These people are victims of *seasonal affective disorder,* or *SAD.* Throughout the winter they struggle with depression; their spirits lift only with the coming of spring. (People may also suffer annual depressions during the summer.) People suffering from SAD tend to sleep and eat excessively during their depressed periods.

Researchers have proposed that the hormone melatonin may play a role. The less light available (in winter), the more melatonin is secreted by the brain's pineal gland. A higher level of melatonin in their blood levels may cause some people to suffer from SAD. Researchers do not know why higher levels of melatonin lead to SAD in some people and not in others. Many SAD sufferers can be treated by sitting under bright fluorescent lights during the evening or early morning hours.

Explaining Mood Disorders

Psychological factors underlying mood disorders include certain personality traits (such as self-esteem), amount of social support, and the ability to deal with stressful situations. The cognitive theories of Aaron Beck and Martin Seligman have often served as the basis for research on depression. Beck (1983) believes that depressed people draw illogical conclusions about themselves; they blame themselves for normal problems and consider every minor failure a catastrophe. As described in Chapter 9, Martin Seligman (1975) believes that depression is caused by a feeling of learned helplessness. The depressed person learns to believe that he has no control over events in his life and that it is useless even to try.

Psychologists developed theories to provide a physiological or biological explanation of depression. Researchers are currently searching for the neurotransmitters (such as serotonin and noradrenaline) that cause mood disorders. They are also looking at genetic factors and faulty brain structure and function as possible causes. Many causes of depression may result from an interaction of biological and psychological factors.

More About...

Depression and Gender

After adolescence, women are about twice as likely as men to experience major depression. Why? One possibility is that hormonal changes occurring as a result of pregnancy lead to depression. In fact, some women go through postpartum depression shortly after giving birth. Some psychologists believe that the numbers are high for female depression simply because more women report their depression and seek help. Other psychologists believe that men may simply distract themselves when experiencing depression. For example, a man might go play basketball and not think about his feelings.

Suicide and Depression

Not all people who commit suicide are depressed, and not all depressed people attempt suicide. Many depressives, though, do think about suicide, and

EXTENDING THE CONTENT

Simple Schizophrenia Tell students that simple schizophrenia often first appears in the teenage years. It also tends to strike more males than females. Ask students to research the symptoms, suspected causes, and treatment of simple schizophrenia. Encourage students to interview professionals who are familiar with the disorder. Have students prepare a mock news report, including role-played interviews with professionals. If possible, have students videotape their news report for "broadcast" in the classroom.

some of them translate these thoughts into action.

People may take their lives for any number of reasons. It may be to escape from physical or emotional pain—perhaps a terminal illness or the loneliness of old age. It might be an effort to end the torment of unacceptable feelings, to punish themselves for wrongs they think they have committed, or to punish others who have not perceived their needs (Mintz, 1968). In many cases we simply do not know why the suicide occurred.

Statistics show, however, that every year more than 30,000 Americans end their lives—about 1 every 20 minutes. More women than men attempt suicide, but more men than women succeed (see Figure 16.14). Suicide is common among the elderly but also ranks as the fourth most common cause of death among adults between the ages of 18 and 65. Contrary to popular belief, people who threaten suicide or make an unsuccessful attempt usually *are* serious. Studies show that about 70 percent of people who kill themselves had threatened to do so within the three months preceding the suicide, and an unsuccessful attempt is often a trial run (American Foundation for Suicide Prevention, 2006).

Psychology and You: What Should You Do?

If you suspect someone you know is thinking about suicide, what should you do? Treat him (or her) like a normal human being. (Meanwhile, contact a professional psychologist or trusted teacher on how to guide your own behavior.) Do not assume that you will upset him—just talk to him. Do not be afraid to ask him about his thoughts (even suicidal ones). Listen to him—he might be relieved to have someone just listen. Urge him to get professional help. Most cities have suicide prevention hot lines.

SECTION 4 Assessment

1. **Review the Vocabulary** Define schizophrenia and list five symptoms of the disorder.
2. **Visualize the Main Idea** Use a graphic organizer similar to the one below to identify types of schizophrenia.

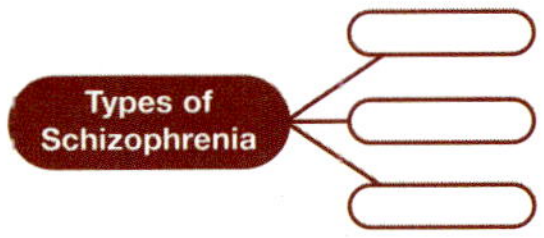

3. **Recall Information** What is the diathesis-stress hypothesis? How does it explain the development of schizophrenia?
4. **Think Critically** Recall the last time you failed or did not do well at something. What kind of explanation did you offer for your failure? Was this explanation pessimistic or optimistic? Explain. How did your explanation affect your mood or feelings?
5. **Application Activity** Schizophrenia often is misunderstood. Research facts about schizophrenia or the life of someone who has been diagnosed with schizophrenia and share this information with the class. As a class discuss and correct the false impressions about schizophrenia that you hold.

SECTION 4 Assessment Answers

1. Schizophrenia is a group of disorders characterized by confused and disconnected thoughts, emotions, and perceptions. Symptoms include delusions, hallucinations, incoherence, disturbances of affect, deterioration in normal movement, decline in previous levels of functioning, and diverted attention.
2. Types of schizophrenia are paranoid types, disorganized type, remission type, undifferentiated type, and catatonic type.
3. It theorizes that an individual may have inherited a predisposition toward schizophrenia that will only develop if exposed to certain stressors.
4. Students' answers will vary. Encourage students to explore the differences between a pessimistic and an optimistic outlook.
5. Students' answers will vary. Ask students what stereotypes they may have held about schizophrenia that have been challenged during their study of this section of the text.

Psychology and You

Use the following question to direct a class discussion after students have read the **Psychology and You** feature.

Ask: **How can allowing a person to talk about his or her feelings help that person overcome suicidal thoughts?**

Enrich

Challenge students to research the types of therapies used to assist people with major depressive disorder. Have students write a short paper summarizing their findings.

4 CLOSE

Draw a spiral on the board. Ask students to brainstorm ways in which the spiral describes mood disorders.

1 FOCUS

Section Objectives

1. Describe how personality disorders differ from other psychological disorders.
2. Explain how drug abuse is a psychological problem.

BELLRINGER
Motivational Activity

Project Daily Focus Transparency 16–5 and have students answer the questions.

Available as blackline master

Daily Focus Transparency 16–5

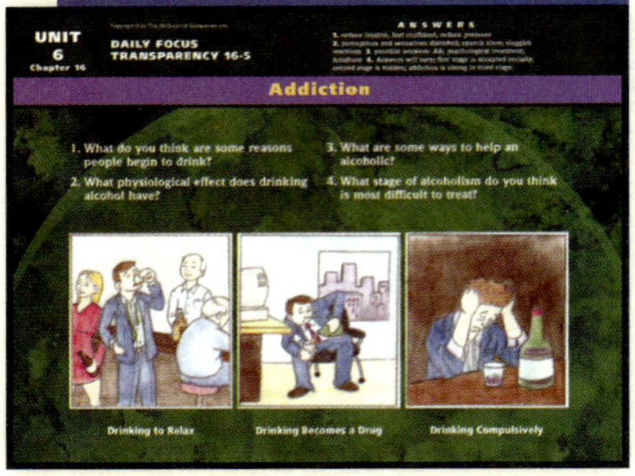

Reader's Guide

Use the Reader's Guide to introduce concepts and vocabulary.

Exploring Psychology
Ask students to read the **Exploring Psychology** feature and then discuss: **What shocks you the most about Gilmore's description of his crimes? Why?**

Vocabulary Precheck
Ask students to write down their best guess at the definition of the vocabulary terms. Then have them check their definitions against the Glossary. Ask students how well they did.

Use the **Vocabulary PuzzleMaker CD-ROM** to create crossword and word search puzzles.

SECTION 5

Personality Disorders and Drug Addiction

Reader's Guide

Main Idea
Personality disorders and drug addiction prohibit normal relationships and normal functioning.

Vocabulary
- personality disorders
- antisocial personality
- psychological dependence
- addiction
- tolerance
- withdrawal

Objectives
- Describe how personality disorders differ from other psychological disorders.
- Explain how drug abuse is a psychological problem.

EXPLORING PSYCHOLOGY

Aimless Crime

On October 7, 1976, Gary Gilmore was sentenced to death by a Utah court after a seemingly purposeless crime spree, and on January 16, 1977, he became the first person to be executed in the United States since 1966. . . . Gilmore had been released from prison only six months earlier, after serving time for armed robbery. . . . Gilmore himself described the next events: "I pulled up near a gas station. I told the service station guy to give me all of his money. I then took him to the bathroom and told him to kneel down and then I shot him in the head twice. The guy didn't give me any trouble but I just felt like I had to do it."

The very next morning, Gilmore left his car at another service station. . . . "I went in and told the guy to give me the money. . . . [T]hen I shot him. . . ."

—from *Abnormal Psychology*, 4th edition, by Martin E.P. Seligman, Elaine F. Walker, and David L. Rosenhan, 2001

Gary Gilmore's crimes are an example of crime without understandable motives. During a psychiatric interview, Gilmore observed, "I don't remember any real emotional event in all my life. . . . When you're in the joint, you stay pretty even all the time. . . . I'm not really excitable you know. I don't get emotional" (Rosenhan & Seligman, 1984). For Gilmore, emotions and social rules did not constrain his behavior. This lack of constraint is a sign of a personality disorder, specifically an antisocial personality disorder.

SECTION RESOURCES

Reproducible Masters
- Guided Reading Activity 16–5
- Vocabulary Activity 16–5
- Section Quiz 16–5

Transparencies
- Daily Focus Transparency 16–5

Multimedia
- Vocabulary PuzzleMaker CD-ROM
- *ExamView® Assessment Suite* CD-ROM
- Presentation Plus! Software

PERSONALITY DISORDERS

Personality disorders are different from the problems we have been discussing. People with personality disorders generally do not suffer from acute anxiety nor do they behave in bizarre, incomprehensible ways. Psychologists consider these people to have a disorder because they seem unable to establish meaningful relationships with other people, to assume social responsibilities, or to adapt to their social environment. This diagnostic category includes a wide range of self-defeating personality patterns, from painfully shy, lonely types to vain, pushy show-offs (see Figure 16.15). In this section we focus on people with **antisocial personalities**, who in the past were referred to as sociopaths or psychopaths.

personality disorders: maladaptive or inflexible ways of dealing with others and one's environment

antisocial personality: a personality disorder characterized by irresponsibility, shallow emotions, and lack of conscience

Antisocial Personality

Individuals with antisocial personalities exhibit a persistent disregard for and violation of others' rights. They treat people as objects—as things to be used for gratification and to be cast aside coldly when no longer wanted. Intolerant of everyday frustrations and unable to save or plan or wait, they live for the moment. Seeking thrills is their major occupation. If they should injure other people along the way or break social rules, they do not seem to feel any shame or guilt. Getting caught does not seem to rattle them, either. No matter how many times they are reprimanded, punished, or jailed, they never learn how to stay out of trouble. They simply do not profit from experience.

Many individuals with antisocial personalities can get away with destructive behavior because they are intelligent, entertaining, and able to feign emotions they do not feel. They win affection and confidence from

Figure 16.15 Types of Personality Disorders

An individual with a personality disorder displays an inflexible, long-standing, and maladaptive way of dealing with the environment and other people. ***What are the characteristics of an individual with a paranoid personality disorder?***

Disorder	Characteristics
Antisocial	displays pattern of disregarding and violating the rights of others without feeling remorse
Dependent	displays pattern of submissiveness and excessive need to be taken care of
Histrionic	displays excessive emotions; excessively seeks attention
Obsessive-Compulsive	has an intense interest in being orderly, having control, and achieving perfection
Paranoid	distrusts others; perceives others as having evil motives
Schizotypal	feels intense discomfort in close relationships; has distorted thinking and eccentric behavior

nar bar

2 TEACH

L1 Forming Conclusions Assign students to compile pictures of teenagers whose appearance or behavior may be interpreted as antisocial by some adults. Have students present these pictures, pointing out the details that led them to select each item. **Ask: As teenagers, do you view these same pictures as antisocial? Why or why not?** Based on this exercise, challenge students to form conclusions on differences between adult and adolescent definitions of antisocial behavior. ELL

CULTURAL CONNECTIONS

The prevalence of antisocial personality disorder is approximately 3 to 4 percent in the United States, Canada, Australia, and New Zealand. However, the rate in Taiwan is only 0.5 percent. Psychologists speculate that a culture emphasizing close family ties may be responsible for the lower incidence in Taiwan. Further research is needed to confirm this hypothesis.

Figure 16.15

Visual Instruction Have students describe how people with each of these disorders would have difficulty with everyday living.

Caption Answer The person distrusts others and perceives others as having evil motives.

COOPERATIVE LEARNING ACTIVITY

Creative Writing Tell students that many soap opera writers take psychology courses to get tips on character development. Organize students into small groups. Challenge each group to write an episode of an imaginary soap opera-type television program in which an established character—or a new character—grapples with a personality disorder. Encourage students to act out these episodes for the whole class. **Ask: What disorder did this episode address? What behavior characteristics serve as "diagnostic bell ringers"?** **BLOCK SCHEDULING**

Reading Check Answer

People with personality disorders do not exhibit anxiety or other strong emotional symptoms.

Guided Reading Activity 16–5

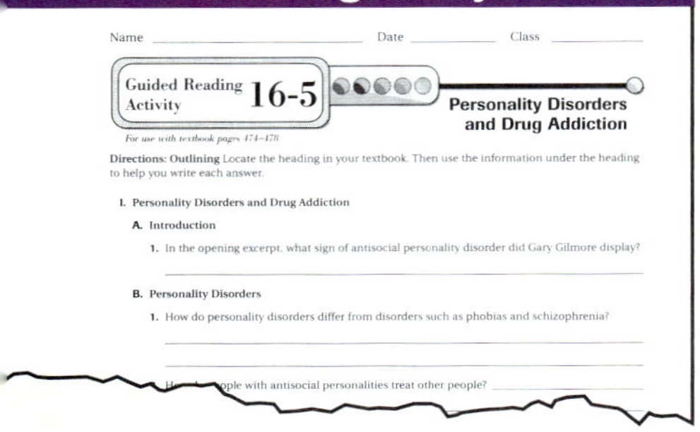
Name ______ Date ______ Class ______

Guided Reading Activity 16-5

Personality Disorders and Drug Addiction

For use with textbook pages 474–478

Directions: Outlining Locate the heading in your textbook. Then use the information under the heading to help you write each answer.

I. Personality Disorders and Drug Addiction

A. Introduction

1. In the opening excerpt, what sign of antisocial personality disorder did Gary Gilmore display?

B. Personality Disorders

1. How do personality disorders differ from disorders such as phobias and schizophrenia?

PSYCHOLOGY JOURNAL *

Have students write a description of a television or movie character who exhibits one of the personality disorders described in the text. ■

Vocabulary Activity 16–5

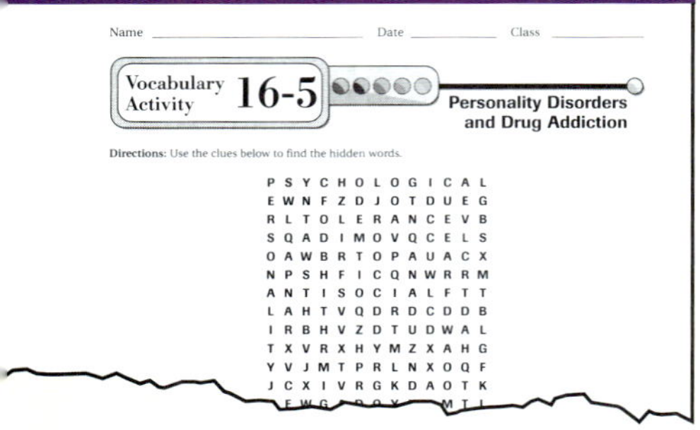
Name ______ Date ______ Class ______

Vocabulary Activity 16-5

Personality Disorders and Drug Addiction

Directions: Use the clues below to find the hidden words.

P	S	Y	C	H	O	L	O	G	I	C	A	L
E	W	N	F	Z	D	J	O	T	D	U	E	G
R	L	T	O	L	E	R	A	N	C	E	V	B
S	Q	A	D	I	M	O	V	Q	C	E	L	S
O	A	W	B	R	T	O	P	A	U	A	C	X
N	P	S	H	F	I	C	Q	N	W	R	R	M
A	N	T	I	S	O	C	I	A	L	F	T	T
L	A	H	T	V	Q	D	R	D	C	D	D	B
I	R	B	H	V	Z	D	T	U	D	W	A	L
T	X	V	R	X	H	Y	M	Z	X	A	H	G
Y	V	J	M	T	P	R	L	N	X	O	Q	F
J	C	X	I	V	R	G	K	D	A	O	T	K

TEACHER Tip

Tell students that one in four children in the United States is exposed to family alcoholism or alcohol abuse before age 18. Inform students that Alateen groups offer support to children of alcoholics. If possible, make information available to students from your local Alcoholics Anonymous group about Alateen groups.

others of whom they then take advantage. If caught, these individuals will either spin a fantastic lie or simply insist, with wide-eyed sincerity, that their intentions were utterly pure. Guilt and anxiety have no place in the antisocial personality.

Reading Check How are personality disorders different from anxiety disorders?

For example, Hugh Johnson was caught after defrauding people out of thousands of dollars in 64 separate swindles. Researchers reported the following when they asked Johnson why he had victimized so many people: "He replied with some heat that he never took more from a person than the person could afford to lose, and further, that he was only reducing the likelihood that other more dangerous criminals would use force to achieve the same ends" (Nathan & Harris, 1975).

How do psychologists explain such a lack of ordinary human decency? According to one theory, individuals with antisocial personalities have simply imitated their own antisocial parents. Other theories point to lack of discipline or inconsistent discipline or other problems during childhood. Finally, some researchers believe that these individuals have a dysfunction of the nervous system. Psychologists are still investigating the relationship between genes and antisocial behavior. While most of us get very nervous when we do something that we have been punished for in the past, those with antisocial personalities never seem to learn to anticipate punishment and remain calm while committing antisocial acts.

DRUG ADDICTION

In American society, drug abuse has become a major psychological problem. Millions of Americans depend so heavily on drugs that they hurt themselves physically, socially, and psychologically. For these reasons, drug addiction and alcoholism are covered in the DSM-IV.

psychological dependence: use of a drug to such an extent that a person feels nervous and anxious without it

Abuse of drugs invariably involves **psychological dependence.** Users come to depend so much on the feeling of well-being they obtain from the drug that they feel compelled to continue using it. People can become psychologically dependent on a wide variety of drugs, including alcohol, caffeine, nicotine (in cigarettes), cocaine, marijuana, and amphetamines. When deprived of the drug, a psychologically dependent person becomes restless, irritable, and uneasy.

addiction: a pattern of drug abuse characterized by an overwhelming and compulsive desire to obtain and use the drug

In addition to psychological dependence, drugs can lead to physiological **addiction.** A person is addicted when his system has become so used to the drug that the drugged state becomes the body's normal state. If the drug is not in the body, the person experiences extreme physical discomfort as he would if he were deprived of oxygen or water.

tolerance: physical adaptation to a drug so that a person needs an increased amount in order to produce the original effect

Just as dependence causes a psychological need for the drug, addiction causes a physical need. Furthermore, once a person is addicted to a drug, he develops **tolerance;** that is, his body becomes so accustomed to the drug that he has to keep increasing his dosage to obtain the high achieved with smaller doses. With certain sleeping pills, for example, a person can rapidly develop a tolerance for up to 16 times the original dose. Further, an addict must have his drug to

MEETING SPECIAL NEEDS

Learning Style: Verbal/Linguistic Explain that psychologists do not fully understand the causes of personality disorders. Ask students to research the genetic, psychodynamic, and social theories of causation for antisocial personality disorders. Have students also suggest childhood symptoms that may signal development of antisocial personality disorders. Tell students to use their research to write a newsmagazine-style report on antisocial personality disorders.

L2 **BLOCK SCHEDULING**

Refer to ***Inclusion for the High School Social Studies Classroom Strategies and Activities*** in the TCR for strategies for students with different learning styles.

retain what little physical and psychological balance he has left. If he does not get it, he is likely to go through the dreaded experience of withdrawal.

Withdrawal is a state of physical and psychological upset during which the body and the mind revolt against and finally get used to the absence of the drug. Withdrawal symptoms vary from person to person and from drug to drug. They range from a mild case of nausea and the shakes to hallucinations, convulsions, coma, and death.

withdrawal: the symptoms that occur after a person discontinues the use of a drug to which he or she has become addicted

Alcoholism

This country's most serious drug problem is alcoholism. In American society, consumption of alcohol often begins at an early age. Researchers estimate that nearly 77 percent of all high school seniors have consumed alcohol at some point in their lifetimes and that 48 percent of seniors have consumed it within the past month—down from 54 percent in 1991. Approximately 44 percent of all students entering high school have tried alcohol. An estimated 29 percent report having consumed five or more drinks in a row within the past two weeks, and nearly 3 percent of graduating seniors are drinking alcohol daily (Monitoring the Future, 2005). About 24 percent of the drivers' deaths in automobile and motorcycle accidents each year can be traced to alcohol. Excessive alcohol use is the third leading lifestyle-related cause of death in the United States. The cost in human suffering to the alcoholic, as well as to his or her family, is impossible to measure.

In small doses, alcohol is often called a social drug. The first psychological function that it slows down is our inhibitions. Two drinks can make a person relaxed, talkative, playful, even giggly. It is for this reason that many people consider alcohol a stimulant, when it is really a depressant.

As the number of drinks increases, problems multiply. One by one, the person's psychological and physiological functions begin to shut down. Perceptions and sensations become distorted, and behavior may become obnoxious. The person begins to stumble and weave, speech becomes slurred, and reactions, to a stop sign, for example, become sluggish or disappear. If enough alcohol accumulates in the body, it leads to unconsciousness and, in some cases, coma and death. It all depends on how much and how rapidly alcohol enters the bloodstream, which, in turn, depend on a person's weight, body chemistry, how much he or she drinks and how quickly, and his or her past experience with drinking.

Alcohol can produce psychological dependence, tolerance, and physiological dependence. One researcher (Jellinek, 1960) outlined four stages of a Disease Model of Alcoholism. In Stage I, the individual drinks and relaxation encourages more drinking. In Stage II, secret drinking occurs, with blackouts and no memory of drinking. Stage III features rationalization to justify the drinking, and Stage IV shows impaired thinking and compulsive drinking. The disease model is no longer favored. Other

Figure 16.16 Alcohol Abuse

Alcohol abuse is responsible for the deaths of approximately 75,000 Americans each year. ***When does alcohol use become a problem?***

Figure 16.16

Caption Answer Alcohol use becomes a problem when it produces psychological dependence, tolerance, and addiction.

3 ASSESS

Assign Section 5 Assessment as homework or as an in-class activity.

Section Quiz 16–5

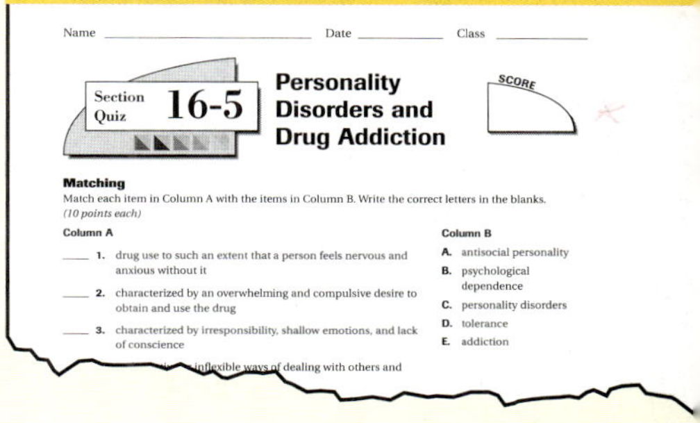

Name ______ Date ______ Class ______

Section Quiz 16-5 **Personality Disorders and Drug Addiction**

SCORE

Matching

Match each item in Column A with the items in Column B. Write the correct letters in the blanks. *(10 points each)*

Column A

____ 1. drug use to such an extent that a person feels nervous and anxious without it

____ 2. characterized by an overwhelming and compulsive desire to obtain and use the drug

____ 3. characterized by irresponsibility, shallow emotions, and lack of conscience

inflexible ways of dealing with others and

Column B

A. antisocial personality
B. psychological dependence
C. personality disorders
D. tolerance
E. addiction

CRITICAL THINKING ACTIVITY

Distinguishing Fact From Opinion Tell students that many psychologists say drug addiction is a disease. The law says drug use is a crime. Others, including psychologist Thomas Szasz, believe drug use should be decriminalized. Have students conduct research to prepare for a debate on the following topic: *Resolved—That drug use should be decriminalized.* **L2**

CHAPTER 16
Section 5, pages 474–478

Figure 16.17

Caption Answer Treatment may include helping a person through withdrawal, prescribing drugs, using psychotherapy, and group therapy such as Alcoholics Anonymous.

Reteach

Review the definition of *personality disorders*. Have the class list personality patterns that fit the definition. Discuss the types of problems that each personality type might have in dealing with people in social and family settings.

*** Enrich**

Have students prepare a fact sheet about drug or alcohol abuse. The sheet should inform readers of the signs of addiction and the dangers of drug and alcohol use.

4 CLOSE

Ask students to compare Raymond Cattell's 16 personality source traits in Chapter 14 (Figure 14.16, page 400) with the personality disorders listed in Figure 16.15, page 475.

Figure 16.17 Effects of Alcohol Use

As a person consumes more and more alcohol, psychological and physiological functions begin to shut down, as shown in these handwriting samples. ***How do you treat alcoholism?***

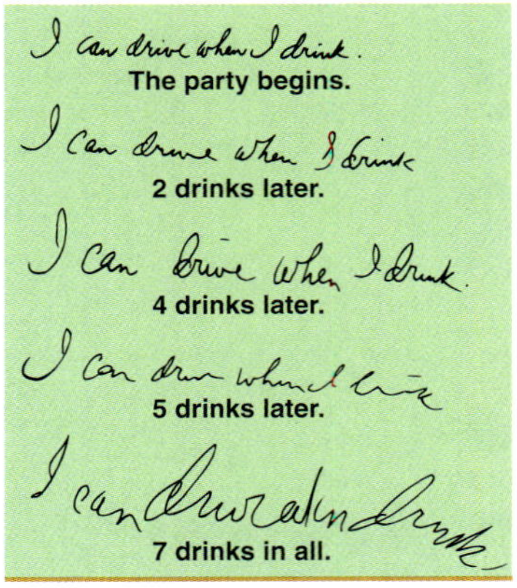

researchers have noted that if alcoholism is a disease, how many among those who never decide to drink would "catch" the "disease"? Those supporting an Adaptive Model suggest that choosing to drink is a voluntary process influenced by alcoholism as a response to individual psychological and environmental factors. Those with a former substance abuse problem have no problem because they choose not to (Alexander, 1990).

Alcoholism may develop from both environmental and genetic factors. A person's risk of becoming an alcoholic is three to four times higher if a member of the family is an alcoholic. Children of alcoholic parents may also be raised in an atmosphere of distrust, overdependence, and stress, which contributes to the possible development of alcoholism.

The first step in treating the alcoholic is to help her through the violent withdrawal, called *delirium tremens*, typical of alcohol addiction and then to try to make her healthier. She may be given a variety of treatments, from drugs to psychotherapy. Alcoholics Anonymous (AA), an organization for alcoholics run by people who have had a drinking problem in the past, has been more successful than most organizations. Some alcoholics must turn to medical treatment. Some doctors prescribe *Antabuse* to alcoholics. Antabuse, or disulfiram, is a chemical that blocks the conversion of acetaldehyde to acetic acid (O'Farrell et al., 1995). (Ordinarily, the liver converts alcohol into acetaldehyde, a toxic substance, and then converts acetaldehyde into acetic acid, a harmless substance.) When alcoholics take a daily Antabuse pill, they become violently sick if they have a drink of alcohol. The threat of the violent sickness may become an effective prevention. There is, however, no certain cure for alcoholism. One problem is that our society tends to encourage social drinking and to tolerate the first stage of alcoholism.

SECTION 5 Assessment

1. **Review the Vocabulary** How are addiction, tolerance, and withdrawal related to drug abuse?
2. **Visualize the Main Idea** Use an outline similar to the one below to list characteristics of an antisocial personality.

   I. Characteristics of an Antisocial Personality
   A. ______________________
   B. ______________________

3. **Recall Information** What are the four stages of alcoholism? How does the Adaptive Model explain drinking?
4. **Think Critically** How do personality disorders differ from other psychological disorders?
5. **Application Activity** Create a questionnaire for teens to help them determine when drinking alcohol becomes a problem.

SECTION 5 Assessment Answers

1. Addiction is a physiological dependence on drugs. Tolerance is a physical adaptation to a drug. Withdrawal is the psychological and physical symptoms that result when use of a drug is discontinued.
2. Characteristics of an antisocial personality include a pattern of remorseless disregard and violation of others' rights, treating people as objects, intolerance of everyday frustrations, and living for the moment.
3. The stages are (1) drinking relaxes the person and encourages more drinking; (2) the person believes he or she has to hide the drinking; (3) the person rationalizes the drinking to justify it; and (4) the person displays impaired thinking and drinks compulsively.
4. People with personality disorders do not suffer anxiety or bizarre behavior. Their problems involve the inability to establish and maintain meaningful social relationships or adapt to their social environment.
5. Students' answers will vary. Encourage students to select very conservative definitions of problem drinking.

CHAPTER 16 Summary and Vocabulary

When people's psychological processes break down, they can no longer function on a daily basis.

Section 1 What Are Psychological Disorders?

Main Idea: Psychologists draw the line between normal and abnormal behavior by looking at deviance, adjustment, and psychological health.

- One approach to defining abnormality is to say that whatever most people do is normal and any deviation from the majority is abnormal.
- Abnormality can be viewed as an inability to adjust to getting along in the world—physically, emotionally, and socially.
- No single, accepted definition of abnormal behavior exists.
- Psychiatrists use the DSM-IV to help them classify psychological disorders.

Section 2 Anxiety Disorders

Main Idea: Anxiety disorders are marked by excessive fear, caution, and avoidance.

- Generalized anxiety is often accompanied by physical symptoms.
- Other anxiety disorders include phobic, obsessive-compulsive, post-traumatic stress, and panic disorders.

Section 3 Somatoform and Dissociative Disorders

Main Idea: Failing to deal with anxiety can lead to somatoform and dissociative disorders.

- Somatoform disorders are psychological problems in which symptoms are focused on the body.
- Dissociative disorders involve a breakdown in a person's normal conscious experience.

Section 4 Schizophrenia and Mood Disorders

Main Idea: Schizophrenia involves disordered thoughts. Mood disorders involve disturbances in the experience and expressions of depression.

- Schizophrenia is a collection of symptoms relating to impairments in cognition, emotion, perception, and motor movement.
- Psychologists have classified several types of schizophrenia.
- Types of mood disorders are major depressive disorder, bipolar disorder, and seasonal affective disorder.

Section 5 Personality Disorders and Drug Addiction

Main Idea: Personality disorders and drug addiction prohibit normal relationships and normal functioning.

- People with personality disorders seem unable to establish meaningful relationships with other people or to adapt to their social environment.
- Abuse of drugs often involves psychological dependence, addiction, tolerance, and sometimes withdrawal.

Chapter Vocabulary

DSM-IV (p. 451)
anxiety (p. 456)
phobia (p. 456)
panic disorder (p. 457)
post-traumatic stress disorder (p. 459)
somatoform disorder (p. 461)
conversion disorder (p. 461)
dissociative disorder (p. 462)
dissociative amnesia (p. 462)
dissociative fugue (p. 462)
dissociative identity disorder (p. 462)
schizophrenia (p. 466)
delusions (p. 466)
hallucinations (p. 466)
major depressive disorder (p. 470)
bipolar disorder (p. 471)
personality disorders (p. 475)
antisocial personality (p. 475)
psychological dependence (p. 476)
addiction (p. 476)
tolerance (p. 476)
withdrawal (p. 477)

16 Summary and Vocabulary

Using the Chapter 16 Summary and Vocabulary

Use the Chapter 16 Summary and Vocabulary to preview, review, condense, or reteach the chapter.

Preview/Review

Use the Chapter Vocabulary list to help students review and study.

Activity Have students create a crossword puzzle using definitions or examples as the clues for the puzzle. Then have pairs of students exchange and complete each other's puzzles.

Vocabulary PuzzleMaker CD-ROM reinforces the vocabulary terms used in Chapter 16.

Condense

Have students read the Chapter 16 Summary.

Chapter 16 Guided Reading Activities

Reteach

Reteaching Activity 16

PERFORMANCE ASSESSMENT ACTIVITY

Creating a Notebook Have students work in pairs to collect newspaper articles about abnormal human behaviors. Direct them to mount each article onto a separate sheet of paper. Below the article, students should identify the category (or categories) of abnormal behavior that it exemplifies. For example, a report on drunk driving would illustrate addiction or alcoholism. Challenge students to find articles on at least five different abnormal behaviors. Have students compile these articles in a binder.

Refer to the ***Authentic Assessment*** booklet for additional activities and information about evaluating student performance.

PSYCHOLOGY Online

Have students visit the Web site at glencoe.com to review Chapter 16 and take the **Self-Check Quiz**.

GLENCOE TECHNOLOGY

PRESENTATION Plus! For a review of Chapter 16 content, see MindJogger Checkpoint on **Presentation Plus!**

Reviewing Vocabulary

1. b	**6.** h
2. f	**7.** e
3. d	**8.** g
4. a	**9.** c
5. j	**10.** i

Recalling Facts

1. The DSM-IV is less vague than the DSM-II. The conditions originally identified under neurosis and psychosis have been expanded into more detailed categories. Anxiety disorders, somatoform disorders, dissociative disorders, mood disorders, and schizophrenia are now included.
2. Symptoms associated with anxiety include muscular tension, inability to relax, furrowed brow, strained face, poor appetite, indigestion, diarrhea, frequent urination, and difficulty sleeping. Learned behavior, physiological factors, and suppression of unconscious desires are causes of anxiety.
3. A dissociative fugue is a reaction in which amnesia is coupled with active flight to a different environment. It serves as an escape from unbearable fear or anxiety. A dissociative fugue involves a different location and life apart from the prior life.
4. inherited predisposition, chemical imbalance in the brain, long-term exposure to unhealthy family life
5. irresponsible, immature, emotionally shallow, thrill-seeking

Critical Thinking

1. Answers will vary. Point out the subjective/cultural influences on the definition of psychological disorders.
2. Respect student privacy. Request volunteers to share their examples and ways of coping.
3. Answers will vary but should focus on the downward spiral and self-fulfilling prophecies that people suffering from major depressive disorder face.
4. Encourage students to reexamine the various theories of what causes schizophrenia. Student answers should reflect an understanding that schizophrenia involves a loss of contact with reality so that a person with schizophrenia is not able to talk his or her way through a problem.
5. Encourage students to gather information from AA or other treatment programs. Students should mention the roles of physical addiction and psychological dependence in the risk of a relapse.

Psychology Projects

1. Encourage students to explore how increased medical knowledge has helped change the view of the causes and treatments of psychological disorders.
2. Select the most informative pamphlets to reproduce and make available to students in your school.
3. Encourage students to reference specific examples of how his paintings showed the progression of the disorder.
4. Suggest that students focus their questions on treatment programs specifically designed for various age groups, especially teens.

CHAPTER 16 Assessment

PSYCHOLOGY Online

Self-Check Quiz

Visit the *Understanding Psychology* Web site at glencoe.com and click on **Chapter 16—Self-Check Quizzes** to prepare for the Chapter Test.

Reviewing Vocabulary

Choose the letter of the correct term or concept below to complete the sentence.

a. DSM-IV	**f.** bipolar disorder
b. phobia	**g.** delusions
c. anxiety	**h.** hallucinations
d. post-traumatic stress disorder	**i.** antisocial personality
e. somatoform disorder	**j.** withdrawal

1. An extreme fear of crowds is an example of a(n) __________.
2. A mood disorder in which individuals are excessively and inappropriately happy or unhappy is called a(n) __________.
3. A person who experiences severe and long-lasting aftereffects of a traumatic event is suffering from __________.
4. The __________ is a standard system for classifying abnormal behavior.
5. During __________, an addicted person's body and mind revolt against and finally get used to the absence of a drug.
6. __________ are perceptions in the absence of corresponding sensations.
7. A psychological disorder in which there is no apparent physical cause for certain physical symptoms is known as a(n) __________.
8. People suffering from schizophrenia sometimes experience __________, or false beliefs maintained in the face of contrary evidence.
9. A person who is experiencing a generalized apprehension is suffering from __________.
10. People with a(n) __________ are generally irresponsible and immature.

Recalling Facts

1. In what way does the system psychologists currently use to classify abnormal behavior differ from the one that preceded it?
2. Describe the symptoms associated with anxiety. Give two explanations for the occurrence of anxiety.
3. What is a dissociative fugue? What psychological function might it serve? How does it differ from dissociative amnesia?
4. Use a diagram similar to the one below to list and explain three possible causes of schizophrenia.

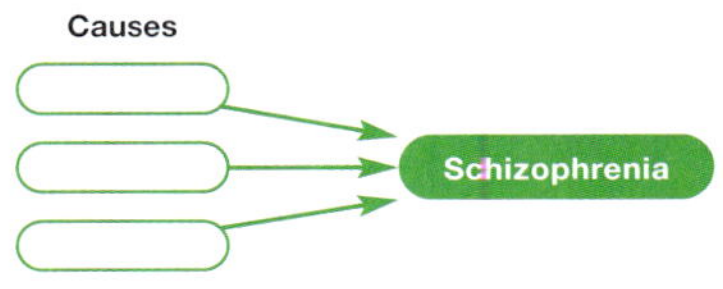

5. How would you describe someone who is classified as having an antisocial personality disorder?

Critical Thinking

1. **Synthesizing Information** Develop your own definition of *psychological disorder*. Is your definition free of social values, or are values a necessary part of such a definition? Explain.
2. **Analyzing Information** Consider times you have experienced a general apprehension and try to list the particular settings or situations in which you are most likely to feel this way. How do you cope with your anxiety?
3. **Applying Concepts** Why do you think it can be difficult for people suffering from major depressive disorder to take action to overcome the disorder?
4. **Making Inferences** Why might using drugs to treat schizophrenia be more effective than psychotherapy?
5. **Synthesizing Information** Why do you think people who have been treated for alcohol or drug abuse run the risk of a relapse?

CHAPTER 16

Assessment

Psychology Projects

1. **What Are Psychological Disorders?** Find out how psychological disorders were viewed in the past. You might focus on the views of ancient Greeks and of Europeans during the Middle Ages. Find out what were thought to be the causes of certain psychological disorders and how people with these disorders were treated. Summarize your findings in a brief report.
2. **Anxiety Disorders** Research magazine articles about programs available to help people combat certain phobias. For example, you might find out about classes that airlines provide to help people overcome their fear of flying. Summarize your findings in an informational pamphlet. Use standard grammar, spelling, sentence structure, and punctuation.
3. **Mood Disorders** The artist Vincent van Gogh suffered from a mood disorder. Find out how his disorder affected his work. You might provide examples of paintings that were created when he was psychologically healthy and those that were created when he was suffering from the disorder. Create a biography of 1–5 pages that details your findings.
4. **Personality Disorders and Drug Addiction** Contact a drug rehabilitation center for information about drug treatment programs in your community. If possible, have a qualified person from the center address the class about the kinds of treatment programs available. You might prepare a list of questions in advance to ask the speaker.

Technology Activity

Locate Web sites on the Internet about some of the psychological disorders discussed in this chapter, such as anxiety disorders or mood disorders. Find out about the latest methods of diagnosing and treating these disorders. Present your findings in a written report.

Psychology Journal

Read the working definition that you wrote in your journal at the start of Chapter 16. Revise the definition based on your study of the chapter, and write a paragraph describing a specific phobia.

Building Skills

Interpreting a Graph Review the graph at right, then answer the questions that follow.

1. According to the graph, what is the most common anxiety disorder reported in the United States?
2. What percentage of the United States population reports any anxiety disorder?
3. Do you think that suffering from an anxiety disorder is a common occurrence? Explain.

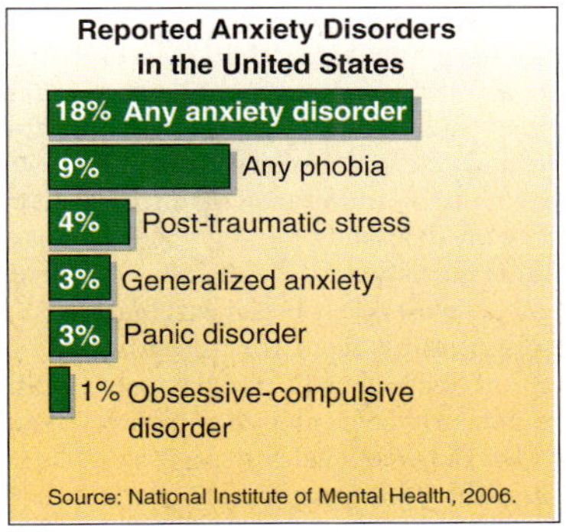

See the Skills Handbook, page 628, for an explanation of interpreting graphs.

Practice and **assess** key social studies skills with **Glencoe Skillbuilder Interactive Workbook CD-ROM, Level 2.**

Building Skills

1. post-traumatic stress
2. 18%
3. Since the graph shows that nearly 1 out of 5 people have suffered from an anxiety disorder, it is a relatively common occurrence.

GLENCOE TECHNOLOGY

CD-ROM

Glencoe Skillbuilder Interactive Workbook, Level 2

This interactive CD-ROM is designed to reinforce student mastery of essential social studies skills.

Chapter Bonus Test Question

This question may be used for extra credit on the Chapter Assessment.

Answer the following question:

I am one of the five major dimensions used by the DSM-IV that describes the highest level of functioning experienced during the past year. What am I?

Answer: Axis V

Technology Activity

Encourage students to concentrate on sites that address diagnosis and treatment. You may want to have students prepare a list of sites that they found most useful and can be used as references for other students.

Psychology Journal

Answers will vary. Have volunteers share their paragraphs without naming the phobia. Then have the rest of the class identify the phobia that is being described.

TIME REPORTS

Reader's Dictionary

Review the following terms with students to help them read and understand the article.

psyche: spirit or mind, especially the core of thoughts and emotion
epicenter: center or focus of an event
exponential: expanding at a rapid, increasing rate
triage: sorting and prioritizing patients so that medical resources have maximum benefit
cascade: fall or occur in stages

CLICK HERE

TIME REPORTS

Visit **www.time.com/teach** for the complete text of this article, as well as related articles on the subject.

Block Schedule

This activity works well for a block-scheduling framework.

TIME REPORTS

Attack on the Spirit

Shock waves from the terrorist blasts shook the nation's psyche. How do we recover?

By JEFFREY KLUGER

MOLLY GALO HAD GROWN accustomed to getting up at 3 a.m. to nurse her infant son. The tender moments in the quiet house were good for both mother and baby. But she won't do it anymore—at least not alone. Molly's husband Matt works on the 75th floor of Chicago's Sears Tower, "an obvious target" for terrorists, she says. Now when she gets up in the middle of the night, she gets Matt up with her. "I need company," says Galo. "I don't want to be alone with my thoughts." She now also insists that her husband always keep his cell phone on.

There can be an odd, exponential geometry to trauma. Lose a single person in an accident, and the lives of five or six more people are rocked. If the original death toll is higher, the shock waves may extend across an entire state. And when the number of fatalities reaches the thousands, the very mental health of the nation can be shaken.

As rescue workers began weighing the destruction from the terrorist attacks of September 11, psychologists were similarly beginning to estimate just what the emotional cost might be. Around the country, normally well-adjusted people have found themselves jumping at shadows, avoiding crowds, giving in to little rituals (take the subway to work but the bus home in the evening) that provide not a jot of real protection but somehow offer them an irrational reassurance that if another plane comes screaming out of the sky, maybe it won't be coming for them or their loved ones.

Some people will easily shake the jumpiness, but others may not—and therein could lie a quiet national crisis. Unlike cockpit recorders and buried bodies, damaged psyches often require a long time to reveal themselves. The longer they take to appear, the longer they will take to heal. "We need a systematic approach to triage not only physical problems but also emotional ones," says Dr. Robert Pynoos, director of the trauma and psychiatry program at UCLA.

Of the three places that were hit by the hijacked planes, New York City suffered by far the greatest emotional damage. As soon as the scope of the disaster became clear, grief counselors went on duty in hospitals and emergency centers around the city. The most severely shaken people were those who had been in or around the World Trade Center and survived the explosions.

Just as hard to soothe, though for different reasons, were the people one step away from the disaster—the tens of thousands of relatives of people missing or killed. At Manhattan's 69th Regiment Armory, family members waited in lines for hours to scan lists of victims treated at emergency rooms or identified as dead, looking for a familiar name. When they found nothing—as most did—they filled out a seven-page form describing the missing person with details that included hair color, length of fingernails and even earrings and shoes. Some brought strands of hair plucked from loved ones' brushes, hoping that if survival was out of the question, DNA identification would at least make death a tolerable certainty.

It's this kind of clutching at strands of hope that helps define the early stages of grief and shock. In most cases the grieving move on, following familiar steps that include anger, depression and, finally, acceptance. The September 11 blasts, however, may have ripped out that recovery route. "A woman kisses her husband goodbye, and the next thing she sees, the whole building falls down," says psychiatrist Marvin Lipkowitz of

ROBERT STOLARIK—GAMMA PRESSE FOR TIME

AFTERSHOCKS

The mental fallout may spread, but there are ways to control the damage

WHAT TO EXPECT

- Fear and anxiety
- Difficulty sleeping or nightmares
- Inability to concentrate
- Irritability
- Nervousness at sudden noises
- Inability to shake disturbing images of the tragedy

482 TIME, September 24, 2001

COOPERATIVE LEARNING ACTIVITY

Creating a Display Organize the class into small groups. Have each group select a national or local organization that provides services to trauma victims. Tell the groups to contact the organizations to request information about the services they provide. Have students identify the physical, financial, and psychological support services offered by the organization. Ask the groups to prepare a display for their organization showing the specific ways that the organization has helped with recent traumas. The displays should also include profiles of some of the people the organization employs to help trauma victims. **BLOCK SCHEDULING**

PATRICK WITTY

ONE STEP AWAY

As they fled, people who witnessed the buildings' collapse were stunned by the sight.

STEVE LISS FOR TIME

DISTANT RIPPLES

Those farther away who only read about the events or saw them on TV felt the anguish too.

HOW TO COPE

- Talk with friends and family members about your feelings of fear, grief, anger and irritability
- Volunteer to assist victims and their families
- Avoid making important decisions, but gradually return to as many routine activities as possible

WHEN TO SEEK HELP

All the symptoms at left are normal responses to extraordinary events like the Sept. 11 terrorist attack. Ordinarily, they dissipate over one to two weeks. If the number and intensity of the symptoms continue, they may signal post-traumatic stress disorder and require professional help. When begun early, treatment is extremely effective.

Maimonides Medical Center in Brooklyn. "There's a limit to what the mind can take."

If people who were touched by the devastation may be reaching that limit, it's possible that people living in other parts of the country may be moving close enough to glimpse it. The repeated slow-motion images of the towers swooning and buckling, the shots of victims tarred and feathered with blood and dust, the very ordinariness of the workday exploding into a doomsday may exact a psychological toll as people wonder whether the same fate will be visited on them too.

The physical symptoms that cascade from the brain when it is infected by fear are familiar—sweaty palms, jumpiness, accelerated heartbeat, sleeplessness. Long after the immediate danger has passed, anything that calls the trauma to mind—a picture of the New York skyline shorn of its two largest shapes; the sight of an airplane gliding by overhead—can give rise to the same symptoms. All too often, the most obvious coping mechanism, if only in the short run, is simple avoidance.

Happily, most experts don't expect the edginess to last. People who lost a loved one will naturally need a long period of grieving to recover. But others could move on fairly quickly. The acute anxiety that follows a trauma typically lasts one to three weeks before the feeling fades. It's only after three months elapse and the symptoms persist that true post-traumatic stress disorder [PTSD] sets in.

PTSD has been around as long as human traumas have, but it's only recently that experts have truly understood it. People with PTSD suffer repeated nightmares and flashbacks. They may sometimes feel emotionally flattened and at other times be given to outbursts. Left alone, PTSD can become completely disabling. But treatment with a trained therapist can be marvelously straightforward. Reliving the experiences in a controlled way—by talking about them, calling them up and laying them bare—strips them of their power to harm. Gradual exposure to the things that trigger anxiety—elevators, skyscrapers, airplanes—can also help. In some cases, so may antidepressants.

There's no way of knowing who will develop full-blown PTSD in the wake of the recent violence, and early indicators provide conflicting clues. A TIME/CNN poll taken two days after the attacks showed that 34% of Americans will change some aspect of their lives in response to the tragedies. While that also means that more than 60% won't, some people wonder how honest the respondents were being. The public has made a great show of declaring that no terrorist is going to make Americans alter the way they live. And while such swagger has served us well in the past, this time it may simply be discouraging us from admitting how downright scared we are. Doing so could be a vital step toward recovery. ■

—For the complete text of this article and related articles from TIME, please visit www.time.com/teach

ANALYZING THE ARTICLE

1. "Damaged psyches often require a long time to reveal themselves," writes TIME's Jeffrey Kluger. What does this mean?
2. **CRITICAL THINKING** Do you think it's better to maintain or to change one's routine in response to tragedy? Explain.

ACTIVE READING STRATEGY

Encourage students to react to what they read. **Ask:** **How did the selection make you feel? Did you enjoy the selection? Did you learn anything? What surprised you about the selection?**

Questions for Discussion

Use the following questions for a class discussion after students have read the article.

1. How does media coverage affect people who are far away from the epicenter of a tragedy? *(Media coverage exposes many more people to the event. Encourage students to discuss the consequences of this. For example, more people may experience different levels of stress or psychological harm, but there is also more support and assistance for the victims.)*
2. How might a tragedy or trauma affect people with pre-existing psychological disorders, such as depression or addiction? *(Answers will vary. Encourage students to discuss whether or not such stress could exacerbate the pre-existing conditions.)*
3. Why might someone refer to terrorism as a form of psychological warfare? *(Terrorism is designed to create fear and uncertainty in the survivors of an attack.)*

ANSWERS TO ANALYZING THE ARTICLE

1. Answers will vary. Psychological injuries can be repressed more effectively than physical injuries. Additionally, some students may say that a certain number of psychological symptoms are normal in the wake of trauma. It's only after time passes and the symptoms of stress remain that the depth of the trauma is revealed. Other students may speculate that psychological damage can be latent, revealing itself under later stress.
2. Answers will vary. Some students may indicate that maintaining a routine is comforting and shows strength in the face of adversity; others may feel change is smart because it increases safety and removes people from everyday stimuli that remind them of the tragedy.

Chapter 17 Resource Guide

SECTION RESOURCES

Daily Objectives	Reproducible Resources	Multimedia Resources
Section 1 **What Is Psychotherapy?** Describe psychotherapy and how it is the general term for several approaches used to treat psychological disorders.	Guided Reading Activity 17–1 Vocabulary Activity 17–1 Section Quiz 17–1	Daily Focus Transparency 17–1 *ExamView® Assessment Suite* CD-ROM Presentation Plus! Software
Section 2 **Psychoanalysis and Humanistic Therapy** Explain how psychoanalysis is an analysis of the conscious and unconscious mind based on the theories of Sigmund Freud, while humanistic therapy is designed to help people reach their full potential.	Guided Reading Activity 17–2 Vocabulary Activity 17–2 Section Quiz 17–2	Daily Focus Transparency 17–2 *ExamView® Assessment Suite* CD-ROM Presentation Plus! Software
Section 3 **Cognitive and Behavior Therapies** Describe how cognitive and behavior therapies help clients develop new ways of thinking and behaving.	Guided Reading Activity 17–3 Vocabulary Activity 17–3 Section Quiz 17–3	Daily Focus Transparency 17–3 *ExamView® Assessment Suite* CD-ROM Presentation Plus! Software
Section 4 **Biological Approaches to Treatment** Explain how biological approaches to treatment rely on methods such as medication, electric shock therapy, and surgery to help clients.	Guided Reading Activity 17–4 Vocabulary Activity 17–4 Section Quiz 17–4	Daily Focus Transparency 17–4 Vocabulary PuzzleMaker CD-ROM *ExamView® Assessment Suite* CD-ROM Presentation Plus! Software

Blackline Master CD-ROM Transparency

Block Schedule

Activities that are particularly suited for use within the block-scheduling framework are identified throughout this chapter by the following designation: **BLOCK SCHEDULING**

Chapter 17 Resource Guide

Timesaving Tools

TeacherWorks™ All-In-One Planner and Resource Center

- **Interactive Teacher Edition** Access your Teacher Wraparound Edition and your classroom resources with a few easy clicks.
- **Interactive Lesson Planner** Planning has never been easier! Organize your week, month, semester, or year with all the lesson helps you need to make teaching creative, timely, and relevant.

Use Glencoe's **Presentation Plus!** multimedia teacher tool to easily present dynamic lessons that visually excite your students. Using Microsoft PowerPoint® you can customize the presentations to create your own personalized lessons.

Activity

From the Classroom of...

Cindy Giglio
Kelly High School
Beaumont, TX

Attitudes About Therapy

Purpose: To examine what people in your community think about therapy

Tell students that they will be developing and administering a survey to find out about people's attitudes regarding the use of therapy to treat psychological problems. As a class, brainstorm a series of statements that would help you learn about people's attitudes concerning therapy. To begin the discussion, give students the following examples: "Therapy only works if the client really wants it to." "It is better to treat psychological disorders with drugs, rather than therapy."

From the brainstormed list, have the class select 15 statements to include in a survey. Have students prepare the survey form. At the top of the form, include a place for participants to specify their gender and age range. For each statement, participants should be able to select from a range of five responses: Strongly Agree, Somewhat Agree, Neither Agree nor Disagree, Somewhat Disagree, and Strongly Disagree. Reproduce enough forms so that every student can gather five samples.

Students should compile the results for the class and prepare a graphical analysis of the data. Discuss with the class the trends they found in their results. Ask questions such as: "What general attitudes about therapy are apparent?" "How does a person's age affect his or her attitude?" "How does a person's gender affect his or her attitude?"

Psychology Online

Use our Web site for additional resources. All essential content is covered in the Student Edition.

You and your students can visit glencoe.com, the Web site companion to *Understanding Psychology*. This innovative integration of electronic and print media offers your students a wealth of opportunities. The student text directs students to the Web site for the following options:

- Chapter Overviews
- Student Web Activities
- Self-Check Quizzes

Answers are provided for you in the **Web Activity Lesson Plan**. Additional Web resources and Interactive Puzzles are also available.

KEY TO ABILITY LEVELS

Teaching strategies have been coded for varying learning styles and abilities.

- **L1** **BASIC** activities for all students
- **L2** **AVERAGE** activities for average to above-average students
- **L3** **CHALLENGING** activities for above-average students
- **ELL** **ENGLISH LANGUAGE LEARNER** activities

Chapter 17 Resource Guide

Note: The following materials may be used when teaching Chapter 17. Section level support materials are shown at point of use in the margins of the Teacher Wraparound Edition.

TEACHING TRANSPARENCIES

Chapter 17 Concept Transparencies

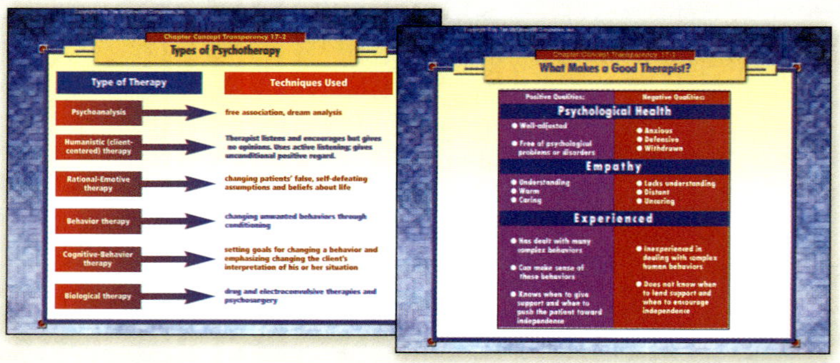

MULTIMEDIA

- Vocabulary PuzzleMaker CD-ROM
- *ExamView® Assessment Suite* CD-ROM
- TeacherWorks™ CD-ROM
- Glencoe Skillbuilder Interactive Workbook, Level 2
- Presentation Plus! Software

REVIEW AND REINFORCEMENT

Reteaching Activity 17

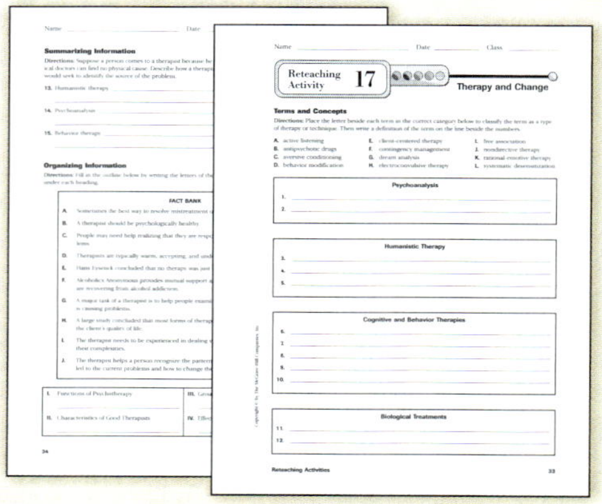

Graphic Organizer Activity 17

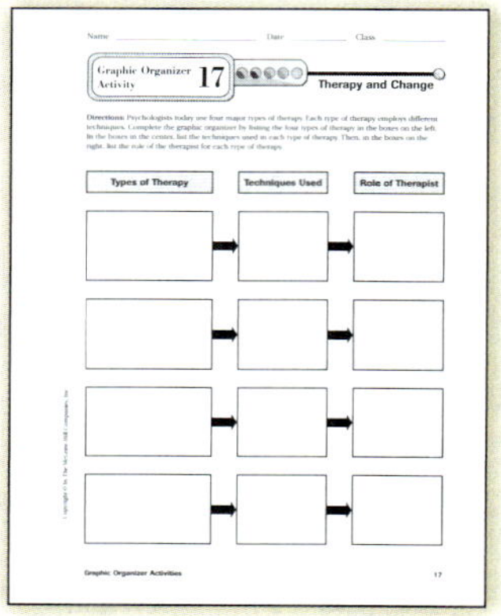

APPLICATION AND HANDS-ON

Psychology Project 17

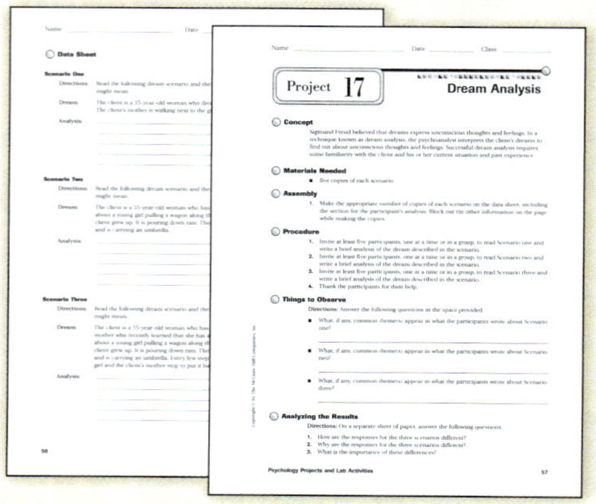

Application Activity 17

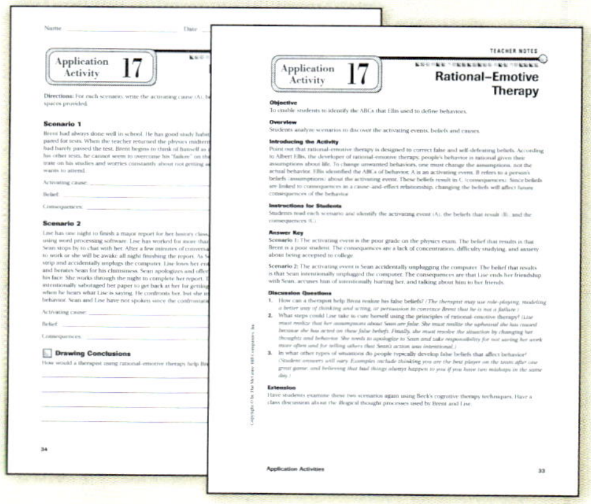

Chapter 17 Resource Guide

ASSESSMENT

Glencoe's Assessment Advantage

Chapter 17 Test, Form A

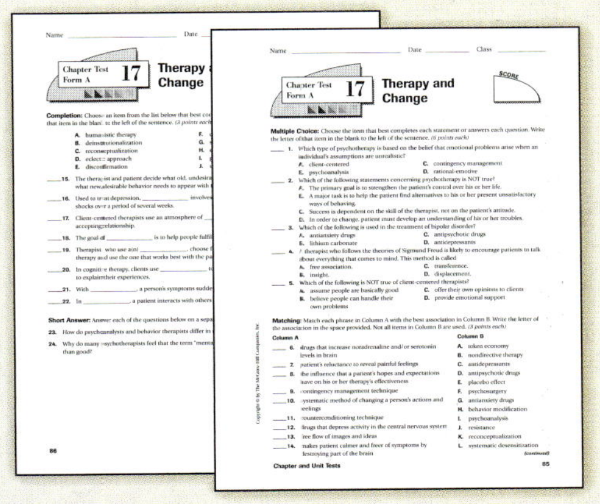
Chapter Test Form A 17 Therapy and Change

Chapter 17 Test, Form B

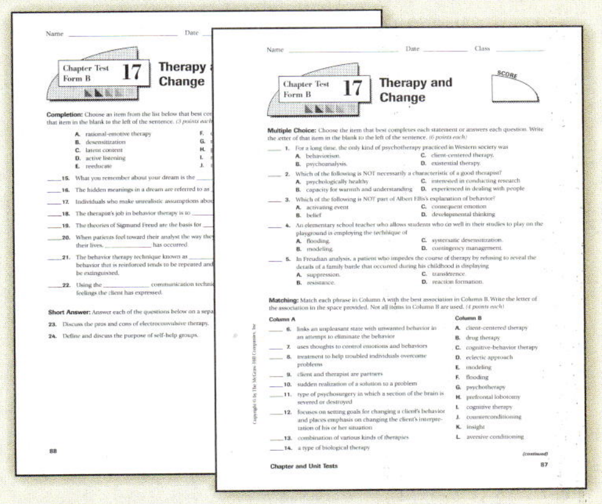
Chapter Test Form B 17 Therapy and Change

Authentic Assessment Activity 17

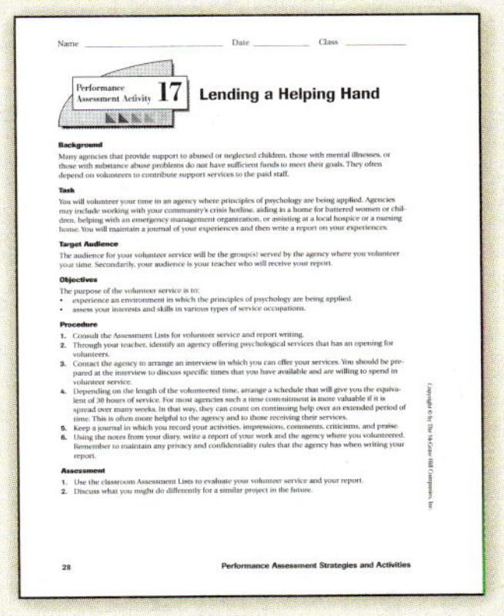
Performance Assessment Activity 17 Lending a Helping Hand

EXTENSION AND ENRICHMENT

Enrichment Activity 17

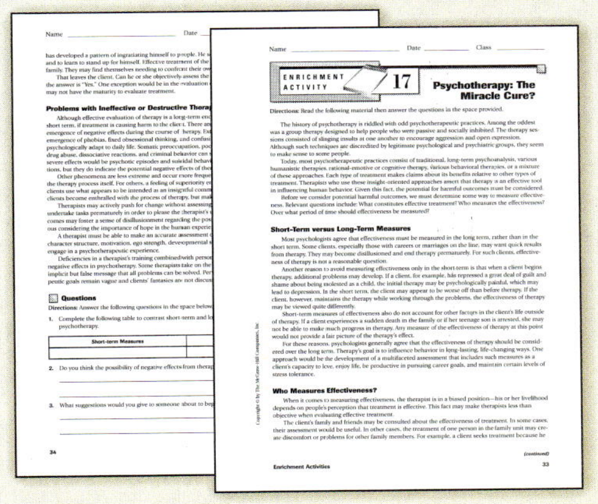
Enrichment Activity 17 Psychotherapy: The Miracle Cure?

Critical Thinking Skills Activity 17

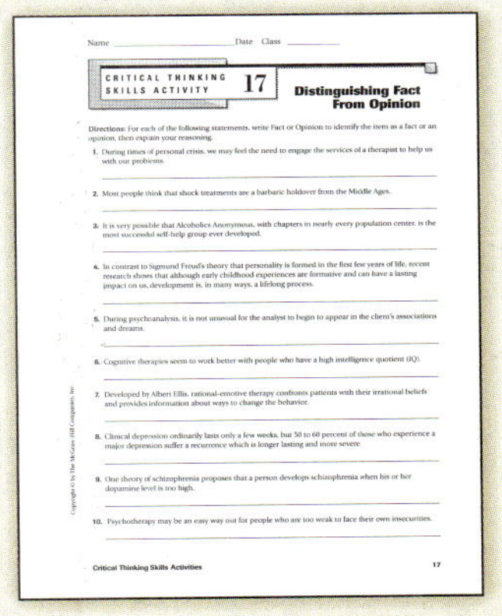
Critical Thinking Skills Activity 17 Distinguishing Fact From Opinion

Psychology Reading 17

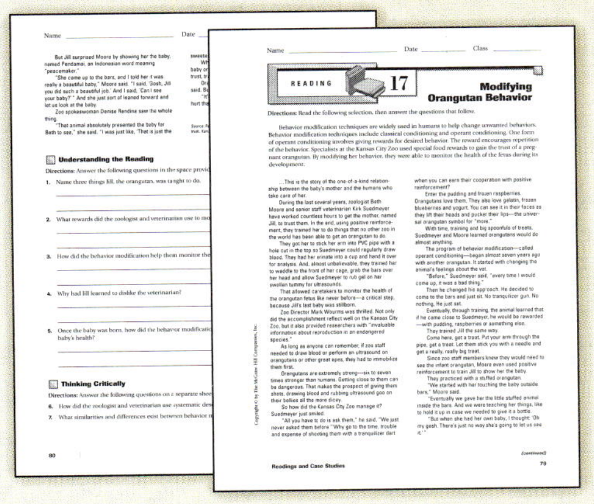
Reading 17 Modifying Orangutan Behavior

Psychology Case Study 17

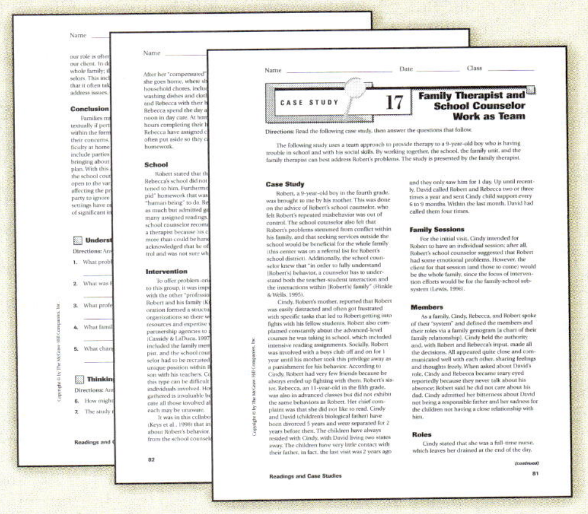
Case Study 17 Family Therapist and School Counselor Work as Team

PSYCHOLOGY Online

Visit glencoe.com for a Chapter Overview for **Chapter 17—Therapy and Change.**

GLENCOE TECHNOLOGY

PRESENTATION Plus!

For a preview of Chapter 17 content, see MindJogger Checkpoint on **Presentation Plus!**

PSYCHOLOGY JOURNAL

Recommend that students review Chapter 16 for symptoms of the various disorders mentioned in the text.

This journal activity provides the basis for the Psychology Journal activity exercise in the Chapter Assessment. ■

CHAPTER 17 Therapy and Change

PSYCHOLOGY Online

Chapter Overview
Visit the *Understanding Psychology* Web site at glencoe.com and click on **Chapter 17—Chapter Overviews** to preview the chapter.

PSYCHOLOGY JOURNAL

Recommend a treatment for the following problems: compulsive overeating, inability to finish work, severe depression. Write your recommendations in your journal. ■

TWO-MINUTE LESSON LAUNCHER

Tell students that as they study Chapter 17 they will learn that therapists must be able to interpret both verbal and nonverbal communications conveyed by their clients. Tell them that nonverbal communication is often referred to as *body language.* Provide students with a variety of photos or pictures of people in various types of situations showing different types of facial expressions or other obvious body language, such as folded arms. Display the photos or pictures so that the entire class can view them. Direct students to work in pairs to write captions interpreting the nonverbal clues.

SECTION 1

What Is Psychotherapy?

Reader's Guide

Main Idea

Psychotherapy is a general term for the several approaches used by mental health professionals to treat psychological disorders.

Vocabulary

- psychotherapy
- eclectic approach
- placebo effect
- empathy
- group therapy

Objectives

- Explain the nature of psychotherapy.
- Describe the role of a therapist.

EXPLORING PSYCHOLOGY

When Should You Seek Help?

Her husband had brought her to the hospital because she had refused to eat for about three days, slept fitfully, and spent long hours staring off into space. She would speak to those around her, but only after more or less continuous coaxing. In very slow monotonous speech, she commented that she was talking to her dead sister who was wearing a white gown, but with a face eaten up by worms and with part of her eyesocket missing. This hallucination was intermixed with some discussion between the patient and God that seemed to center around a mixture of pleading with Him to do something about her sister and reprimanding Him for letting her get into that condition.

—from *Abnormal Behavior, Psychology's View* by F.B. McMahon, 1976

At certain times of transition and crisis in life, we may feel an urgent need to find someone trustworthy with whom to share our doubts and problems. A parent, relative, or close friend is often helpful in such times of need. Many psychological problems, however, are too bewildering and complex to be solved in this way. When people become dissatisfied or distraught with life and suspect that the reason lies within themselves, they are likely to seek help from someone with training and experience in such matters. These people seek *therapy,* which refers to treatment of behavioral, bodily, or psychological disorders. Mental health professionals who have been trained to deal with the psychological problems of others include psychologists, psychiatrists, and

SECTION RESOURCES

Reproducible Masters

- Guided Reading Activity 17–1
- Vocabulary Activity 17–1
- Section Quiz 17–1

Transparencies

- Daily Focus Transparency 17–1

Multimedia

- *ExamView® Assessment Suite* CD-ROM
- Presentation Plus! Software

1 FOCUS

Section Objectives

1. Explain the nature of psychotherapy.
2. Describe the role of a therapist.

BELLRINGER
Motivational Activity

Project Daily Focus Transparency 17–1 and have students answer the questions.

Available as blackline master

Daily Focus Transparency 17–1

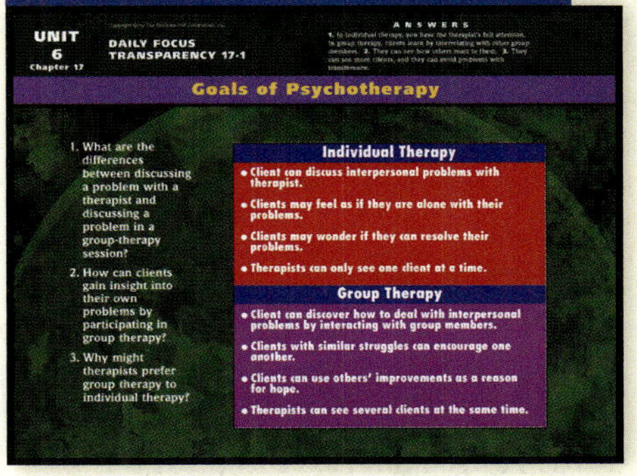

Reader's Guide

Use the Reader's Guide to introduce concepts and vocabulary.

Exploring Psychology

Ask students to read the **Exploring Psychology** feature and then discuss the following question: **Where would a therapist begin as he or she treats this client?**

Vocabulary Precheck

Have students write a definition of *psychotherapy* and *placebo effect* based on what they learned in earlier chapters. Ask them to compare these definitions to the Glossary definitions. Then have them write the Glossary definitions of the remaining terms.

2 TEACH

L1 Defining Psychotherapy
Read aloud the following definition of psychotherapy offered by Lewis Wolberg (1977):

Psychotherapy is the treatment, by psychological means, of problems of an emotional nature in which a trained person deliberately establishes a professional relationship with the patient with the object of (1) removing, modifying, or retarding existing symptoms; (2) mediating disturbed patterns of behavior; and (3) promoting positive personality growth and development.

Ask: What does Wolberg see as the main function of a psychotherapist? Point out that although all psychotherapists share this goal, they differ in the techniques used to achieve it. **BLOCK SCHEDULING**

Figure 17.1

Caption Answer Answers will vary. Students should consider how social and cultural changes have influenced the way we view people with psychological disorders.

psychotherapy: any treatment used by therapists to help troubled individuals overcome their problems

social workers. The special kind of help they provide is called psychotherapy. **Psychotherapy** involves three things: verbal interaction between a therapist and client; the development of a supportive and trusting relationship; and an analysis by the therapist of the client's problems, including suggestions for overcoming those problems.

THE NATURE OF PSYCHOTHERAPY

Psychotherapy literally means "healing of the soul," and in early times people often thought that psychological disturbances represented some sort of moral or religious problem. People with personal problems were sometimes viewed as being inhabited by demons, and treatment consisted of exorcism—the driving out of these demons by religious ceremonies or by physical punishment. Within the past 200 years, however, views of psychological disorders have changed. Psychological disorders slowly came to be thought of as diseases, and the term *mental illness* was applied to many psychological problems.

With the unchaining of mental patients at Bicetre hospital in France, Philippe Pinel (1745–1826) in 1793 marked the beginning of society's view that people with psychological disturbances are not possessed but ill, needing care and treatment. Nevertheless, many psychotherapists feel that the term *mental illness* has outlived its usefulness and that, in fact, it may now be doing more harm than good.

The trouble with letting a person think of himself as mentally ill is that he sees himself in a passive, helpless position. He sees his troubles as being caused by forces over which he has no control. By thinking of himself in this way, the person can avoid taking responsibility for his own situation and for helping himself change.

Figure 17.1 Is This Treatment?

In earlier times, people with serious psychological disorders were labeled *mad* or *lunatics*. These people were often tortured, hanged, burned at the stake, or sent to sea in "ships of fools" to be saved by fate. ***How do you think society regards people with psychological disorders today?***

Functions of Psychotherapy

One of the functions of psychotherapy is to help people realize that they are responsible for their own problems and that, even more importantly, they are the only ones who can really solve these problems. This approach does not imply that people become disturbed on purpose or that no one should need outside help. People often adopt certain techniques for getting along in life that seem appropriate at the time but that lead to trouble in the long run. Such patterns can be difficult for the individual to see or change. The major task of the therapist, therefore, is to help people examine their way of living, to understand

COOPERATIVE LEARNING ACTIVITY

Creating a Reference Book Organize students into small groups. Ask them to create a class reference book on the various types of therapists that work in your community. Each entry should be prepared on a separate page so that it can be alphabetically inserted into a binder. Encourage students to illustrate items and expand their information as necessary. The therapists listed in Figure 17.3 can serve as a starting point. Encourage students to identify other categories of therapists. Make the finished reference book available for the class to consult as they study Chapter 17. **BLOCK SCHEDULING**

how their present way of living causes problems, and to start living in new, more beneficial ways. The therapist can be thought of as a professional hired by the individual to help him find the source of his problems and some possible solutions.

Main Kinds of Therapy

There are many different kinds of therapy. However, only a few of them will be described in this chapter, including psychoanalysis, humanistic, cognitive, behavioral, and biological approaches to treatment (see Figure 17.2). Each one is based on different theories about how human personality works, and each one is carried out in a different style. Some psychotherapists stick rigorously to one style and consider the other styles less useful. Other psychotherapists use an **eclectic approach** to therapy, choosing methods from many different kinds of therapy and using the one that works best. Whatever the style or philosophy, all types of psychotherapy have certain characteristics in common.

Profiles In Psychology

Dorothea Dix

1802–1887

"I proceed, Gentlemen, briefly to call your attention to the *present* state of Insane Persons confined within this Commonwealth, in *cages, closets, stalls, pens! Chained, naked, beaten with rods,* and *lashed* into obedience!"

Although at the early age of 14 Dorothea Dix established her own school for young children, she is best remembered as an activist for the rights of the mentally ill. In 1841 a member of the clergy asked Dix to teach a Sunday school class at a local prison in Massachusetts. When she arrived at the prison, Dix became horrified to see mentally ill patients locked up with prisoners in dark, unheated, and filthy rooms.

Dix set out on a crusade that would last a lifetime. She toured similar jails throughout several states, reporting to the public the appalling things she witnessed. She saw people chained up and sitting in filth. She found people whose worst crimes were having psychological disorders confined and beaten in prisons. She observed men, women, and children thrown together in jail cells.

At a time when women were thought incapable of speaking in public, Dix reported her findings to state legislatures. Her struggles resulted in the reform of prisons and the treatment of people with psychological disorders.

eclectic approach: method that combines various kinds of therapy or combinations of therapies

Goals of Therapy

The primary goal of psychotherapy is to strengthen the patient's control over his or her life. People seeking psychotherapy need to change their thoughts, feelings, and behaviors. Over the years, they have developed not only certain feelings about themselves but also behaviors that reinforce those feelings. Their behaviors and feelings make it difficult or impossible for them to reach their goals.

Profiles In Psychology

Ask students to read the **Profiles In Psychology** feature and then discuss the following questions:

1. For what is Dorothea Dix best remembered? *(as an activist for the rights of the mentally ill)*
2. How did she raise awareness of the plight of the mentally ill? *(After seeing the inhumane condition in which the mentally ill were forced to live, she reported what she saw to the public and to state legislatures.)*
3. What were the results of her efforts? *(reforms in the prison systems and in the treatment of those with psychological disorders)*

Guided Reading Activity 17–1

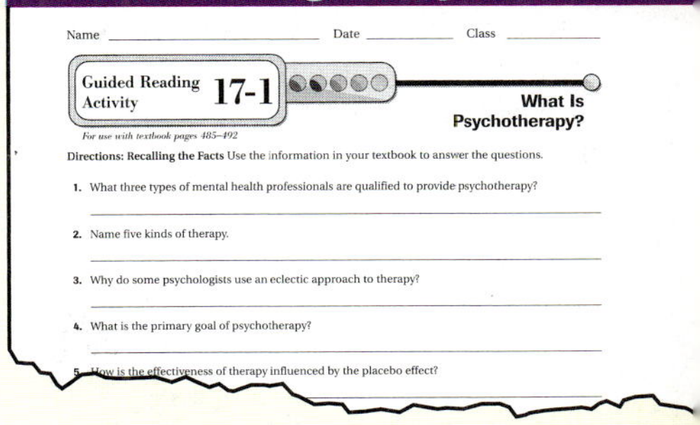
Name ______ Date ______ Class ______

Guided Reading Activity 17-1 — What Is Psychotherapy?

For use with textbook pages 485–492

Directions: Recalling the Facts Use the information in your textbook to answer the questions.

1. What three types of mental health professionals are qualified to provide psychotherapy?
2. Name five kinds of therapy.
3. Why do some psychologists use an eclectic approach to therapy?
4. What is the primary goal of psychotherapy?
5. How is the effectiveness of therapy influenced by the placebo effect?

MEETING SPECIAL NEEDS

Learning Style: Interpersonal Have students review the material in this section about self-help groups and then imagine they are part of a smoking cessation self-help group. Challenge students to write a dialogue of the first five minutes of a group session assuming the following: (1) one student has assumed the role of group facilitator; (2) there is a new group member who wants to stop smoking but has not quit yet; and (3) there are four others in attendance who have had various experiences with their battle to quit smoking. **L2**

Refer to ***Inclusion for the High School Social Studies Classroom Strategies and Activities*** in the TCR for strategies for students with different learning styles.

CHAPTER 17

Section 1, pages 485–492

Figure 17.2

Visual Instruction As a class, compare and contrast the main goals of each type of therapy.

Caption Answer Students' answers may vary. Most students will identify cognitive or behavior therapy as the most effective treatment for someone with an eating disorder.

FYI

Psychiatric nurses dispense medication or act as "contacts" in the long hours between counseling sessions. The nurses' words and gestures help clients deal with the day-to-day problems of emotional recovery. They are in a very real sense "the therapy in between the therapy."

CULTURAL CONNECTIONS

The Jack Brown Center treats Native American clients with substance abuse problems. One type of therapy it employs is art therapy. It describes the concept of art therapy as follows: ". . . all the marks we make on paper, all the colors and graphic gestures we choose and use, are extensions of ourselves and of what we think and feel. Art therapy is especially valuable for those to whom words come too easily or too hard." *Source:* Cherokee Nation Behavioral Health Service at www.cherokee.org/home.aspx?section=health&service=HealthServices.

Figure 17.2 Types of Psychotherapies

There are several types of therapies. The ones listed in this chart are commonly used methods. ***Which method would probably be most effective for treating someone with an eating disorder?***

Therapy Method	Main Technique(s)	Main Goal	Means of Achieving Goal
Psychoanalysis	free association, dream analysis, transference	reduce anxiety and guilt from unconscious urges	verbal processes
Humanistic Therapy	active listening, acceptance, support	fulfill one's potential and improve self-concept	verbal processes
Cognitive Therapy	talking, listening, role-playing, and completion of assignments	unite behaviors and thought	revising thoughts
Behavior Therapy	counterconditioning, operant conditioning, systematic desensitization	change one's unwanted or abnormal behaviors and acquire desirable behaviors	behavioral training

placebo effect: the influence that a patient's hopes and expectations have on his or her improvement during therapy

One of the most important factors in effective treatment is the patient's belief or hope that he can change. The influence that a patient's hopes and expectations have on his improvement is often called the **placebo effect.** This name comes from giving medical patients placebos, inert sugar pills, when they complain of ailments that do not seem to have any physiological basis. The patients take the tablets, and their symptoms disappear.

The placebo effect does not imply that problems can be solved simply by fooling the patient. It does demonstrate, however, the tremendous importance of the patient's attitude in finding a way to change. A patient who does not believe he can be helped probably cannot be. A patient who believes he can change and believes he has the power to change will find a way. Therapy goes beyond the placebo effect. It combines the patient's belief that he can change with hard work and professional guidance.

WHO ARE THERAPISTS?

In American society, there are many people who practice psychotherapy. Some, like clinical psychologists, are trained in psychological testing, assessment, and diagnosis. Counseling psychologists have been trained to deal with problems of adjustment. The various kinds of therapists and the training that each goes through before practicing psychotherapy are shown in Figure 17.3.

What Makes a Good Therapist?

Before going to a professional therapist, most people first turn to a friend or other nonprofessional for help and advice. Sometimes, this is exactly what's needed. Professional therapists, however, are likely to be more skillful in encouraging the person to examine uncomfortable feelings and problems.

CRITICAL THINKING ACTIVITY

Demonstrating Reasoned Judgment Tell students that several Web sites offer online psychotherapy through e-mail or live chat. Online clients cite convenience (time and place), lower cost, and reduced inhibition as reasons of use. Some say that they feel freer to express their innermost thoughts and feelings when they cannot see the therapist. Online critics charge that therapists cannot see a client's body language nor hear the client's tone of voice. They say that online psychotherapy is at best unethical and may be illegal. They charge that since most therapists are licensed in only one state, they are violating their license if they treat out-of-state patients online. Have students debate the ethical, legal, and human aspects of online psychotherapy. **L2**

There are three characteristics found in effective therapists. First, a therapist needs to be psychologically healthy. A therapist who is anxious, defensive, and withdrawn will not be able to see the patient's problems clearly. A second important characteristic is **empathy,** a capacity for warmth and understanding. Troubled people are usually fearful and confused about explaining their problems. The therapist needs to be able to give the patient confidence that he is capable of caring and understanding. Finally, a good therapist must be experienced in dealing with people and understanding their complexities. Only by having worked with many people can a therapist learn when to give support, when to insist that the patient stand on his own feet, and how to make sense of the things people say.

empathy: capacity for warmth and understanding

GROUP THERAPIES

In some forms of therapy, the patient is alone with the therapist. In **group therapy,** however, she is in the company of other patients. There are several advantages to this situation. A person in group therapy has a

group therapy: patients work together with the aid of a leader to resolve interpersonal problems

Figure 17.3 Kinds of Therapists

Clinical psychologists are therapists with a Ph.D. or a Psy.D., a Doctor of Psychology. They treat people with psychological disorders in hospitals, clinics, and community health centers.

Counseling psychologists generally have a master's or Ph.D. degree in counseling psychology. They usually work in educational institutions, where they are available for consultation about personal problems. They customarily refer clients with serious problems to clinical psychologists or psychiatrists.

Clinical Neuropsychologists have Ph.D. degrees. They have extensive education in neurophysiology regarding the mechanisms and operation of the brain. They typically work with patients who have a brain injury that is interfering with normal behavior. Such damage may result from drug use, accidents, or normal aging. Their primary role has been in assessing neurological damage; some are now involved in therapy, and some prescribe medicine.

Psychiatrists are medical doctors. They take postgraduate training in the causes and treatment of abnormal behavior. Because of their medical background, psychiatrists are licensed to prescribe medicines and are the only group that can perform operations.

Psychoanalysts are usually medical doctors who have taken special training in the theory of personality and techniques of psychotherapy of Sigmund Freud, typically at a psychoanalytic institute. They must themselves be psychoanalyzed before they can practice. Declining numbers of psychoanalysts still practice.

Psychiatric social workers are people with a master's degree in social work. They counsel people with everyday problems.

Psychiatric nurses have a standard nursing license and advanced training in psychology. They dispense medicine and act as a contact person between counseling sessions.

Counselors have a master's degree from a counseling program. They dispense advice and may or may not have any training in psychology. Nevertheless, more troubled people turn to counselors than to other kinds of therapists.

Several groups of people practice psychotherapy. Not all of them have professional training in psychology. ***What is the difference between a counselor and a psychoanalyst?***

PSYCHOLOGY Update

Bioenergetic Psychotherapy The connection between the mind and the body has long been studied and debated. Today, bioenergetic psychotherapy seeks to treat both the mind and the body to relieve psychological problems. In addition to traditional therapy, a bioenergetic psychotherapist may prescribe specific exercises to help the client change patterns of repressed emotions or feelings.

Figure 17.3

Visual Instruction List the various types of therapists on the board. For each type, have students list the education and special training required and the places in which they typically work.

Caption Answer Counselors have a master's degree and dispense advice. They may or may not have a degree in psychology. Psychoanalysts are medical doctors specially trained in psychoanalysis.

PSYCHOLOGY JOURNAL

Remind students that one goal of psychotherapy is to help people realize that they can resolve their own problems. Have students make a list of the ways a therapist can help someone find solutions to his or her problems. ■

PSYCHOLOGY LAB EXPERIMENT

Client and Therapist Interchange Divide the class into pairs to illustrate the listening-talking interchange that takes place during psychotherapy. Direct one student to play the part of the listener and the other the talker. For three minutes, the listener should silently pay attention to everything the other student says. Direct the listener to keep eye contact and to make no judgments or facial expressions. Direct the talker to speak about himself or herself. When the three minutes are up, have students change roles. In a follow-up discussion, ask students to share how they felt in each role. **L2** **ELL** **BLOCK SCHEDULING**

Reading Check Answer People in group therapy can relate to others struggling with the same problems and can correct mistaken views of themselves and others. People in group therapy also see others with similar problems recovering, giving them hope. Also, one therapist can help a large number of people.

Vocabulary Activity 17–1

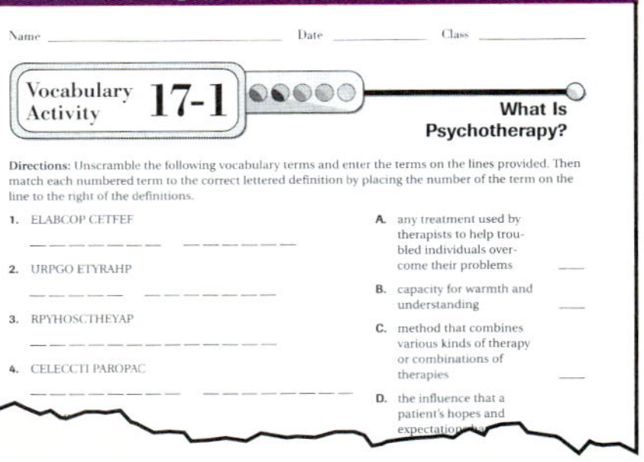
Name ______ Date ______ Class ______

Vocabulary Activity 17-1

What Is Psychotherapy?

Directions: Unscramble the following vocabulary terms and enter the terms on the lines provided. Then match each numbered term to the correct lettered definition by placing the number of the term on the line to the right of the definitions.

1. ELABCOP CETFEF
2. URPGO ETYRAHP
3. RPYHOSCTHEYAP
4. CELECCTI PAROPAC

A. any treatment used by therapists to help troubled individuals overcome their problems ___
B. capacity for warmth and understanding ___
C. method that combines various kinds of therapy or combinations of therapies ___
D. the influence that a patient's hopes and expectation...

TEACHER Tip

Tell students that group therapy works best when all members agree to keep everything discussed in the group confidential. Discuss why confidentiality is so important to group success.

Figure 17.4

Caption Answer The therapist can objectively make suggestions, clarify points, and keep activities from getting out of hand.

chance to see how other people are struggling with problems similar to her own, and she discovers what other people think of her. She, in turn, can express what she thinks of them, and in this exchange she discovers where she is mistaken in her views of herself and of other people and where she is correct (Drum, 1990). In group therapy she can also see other people with similar problems recovering, giving her the hope of recovery.

Reading Check What are the advantages of group therapy?

Another advantage to group therapy is that one therapist can help a large number of people at a reduced cost. Most group-therapy sessions are led by a trained therapist who makes suggestions, clarifies points, and keeps activities from getting out of hand. In this way, her training and experience are used to help as many as 20 people at once, although 8–10 is a more comfortable number. It is possible to use psychoanalytical, cognitive, and behavioral techniques in a group setting.

Family Therapy

Therapists often suggest, after talking to a patient, that the entire family unit should work at group therapy. In *family therapy*, the focus is on the interactions among the family members. This method is particularly useful because it untangles the twisted web of relationships that has led one or more members of the family to experience emotional suffering.

Often family members are unhappy because they are mistreating or are being mistreated by other family members in ways no one understands or wants to talk about. The family therapist can point out what is happening from an objective viewpoint and can suggest ways of improving communication and fairness in the family. Not all group therapies are run by professionals, however. Some of the most successful examples are provided in nonprofessional organizations, such as self-help groups.

Figure 17.4 Group Therapy

Many people who need help in dealing with their problems benefit from group therapy, which provides a supportive atmosphere in which other people are dealing with similar issues. ***What does a skilled therapist provide in a group-therapy session?***

Self-Help Groups

An increasing number of *self-help groups* have emerged in recent years. These voluntary groups, composed of people who share a particular problem, are often conducted without the active involvement of a professional therapist.

INTERDISCIPLINARY CONNECTIONS ACTIVITY

Government Request students to research the case of Joyce-Ann Brown (1987)—the first homeless person forced by New York City health officials to be hospitalized under a program for mentally ill street people. With the help of lawyers from the American Civil Liberties Union, Brown successfully fought for her right to live on her own. Have students present their findings in an oral report. Advise them to take into account the rights of the individual versus the rights of the public at large. In a general debate, explore student opinion on the Brown case. **L2**

During regularly scheduled meetings, members of the group come together to discuss their difficulties and to provide one another with support and possible solutions.

Self-help groups have been formed to deal with problems ranging from alcoholism, overeating, and drug addiction to child abuse, widowhood, single parenting, adjusting to cancer, and gambling. The best-known self-help group is Alcoholics Anonymous (AA), which was founded in 1935. Far more people find treatment for their drinking problems through AA than in psychotherapy or treatment centers. Many self-help groups have based their organizations on the AA model in which individual members can call on other members for help and emotional support.

AA logo

The purpose of Alcoholics Anonymous is "to carry the AA message to the sick alcoholic who wants it." According to AA, the only way for alcoholics to change is to admit that they are powerless over alcohol and that their lives have become unmanageable. Alcoholics must come to believe that some power greater than themselves can help them. Those who think they can battle the problem alone will not be successful. There are also AA-based groups, such as Al-Anon and Alateen, for family members for mutual support.

Members of AA usually meet at least once a week to discuss the meaning of this message, to talk about their experiences with alcohol, and to describe the new hope they have found with AA. Mutual encouragement, friendship, and an emphasis on personal responsibility are used to keep an individual sober.

DOES PSYCHOTHERAPY WORK?

In 1952 Hans Eysenck published a review of five studies of the effectiveness of psychoanalytic treatment and 19 studies of the effectiveness of eclectic psychotherapy, treatment in which several different therapeutic approaches are combined. Eysenck concluded that psychotherapy was no more effective than no treatment at all. According to his interpretation of these 24 studies, only 44 percent of the psychoanalytic patients improved with treatment, while 64 percent of those given eclectic psychotherapy had improved.

Most startling, Eysenck argued that even this 64 percent improvement rate did not demonstrate the effectiveness of psychotherapy, since it has been reported that 72 percent of a group of hospitalized neurotics improved without treatment. If no treatment at all leads to as much improvement as psychotherapy, the obvious conclusion is that psychotherapy is not effective. Eysenck (1966) vigorously defended his controversial position, which generated a large number of additional reviews and a great many studies of the effectiveness of psychotherapy.

Did You Know?

Conducting Therapy There are four areas of concern that a therapist might discuss with the patient.

1) Identify the problem behavior based on the classification scheme for psychological disorders.
2) Propose some ideas about the history and cause of the problem.
3) Explain the details of what is included in the treatment program.
4) Make a time line for the course of treatment.

EXTENDING THE CONTENT

Sensitivity Training Tell students that in 1993 the state of Connecticut enacted a law requiring all employers with 50 or more employees to send their managers to sensitivity training sessions to improve human interactions among employees in the workplace. The sessions were aimed primarily at eliminating sexual harassment in the workplace. In 1999, Pizza Hut agreed to provide racial-sensitivity training to thousands of employees as part of a settlement of a racial discrimination case. Most sensitivity training sessions are held in groups of 10 to 20 people and encourage participants to use empathy, understanding, and tolerance when interacting with others.

Looking @ the Issues

Group Therapy In the world of managed care and limited coverage of psychological services by most health insurers, group therapies have increased in popularity. Group therapies allow one therapist to treat more clients and make better use of time. Many group therapy sessions last for relatively brief periods, with 6 to 12 sessions common. Some insurers cover group therapy; others do not. Use the following question to direct a class discussion: **Should psychological services be covered as a standard part of all health insurance plans?**

3 ASSESS

Assign Section 1 Assessment as homework or as an in-class activity.

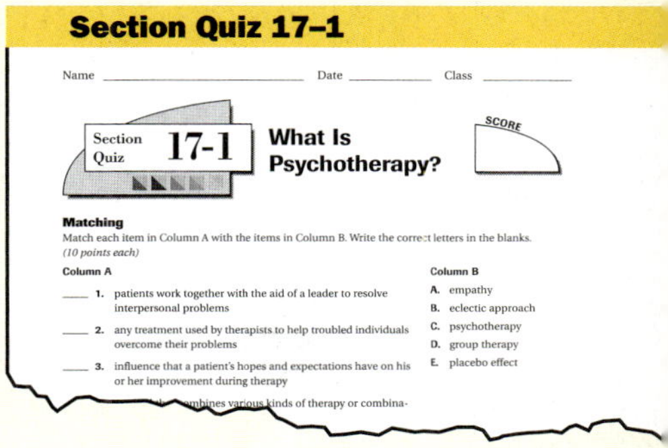
Section Quiz 17–1

Name ______ Date ______ Class ______

Section Quiz 17-1 What Is Psychotherapy?

SCORE

Matching

Match each item in Column A with the items in Column B. Write the correct letters in the blanks. *(10 points each)*

Column A

____ 1. patients work together with the aid of a leader to resolve interpersonal problems

____ 2. any treatment used by therapists to help troubled individuals overcome their problems

____ 3. influence that a patient's hopes and expectations have on his or her improvement during therapy

... combines various kinds of therapy or combina-

Column B

A. empathy
B. eclectic approach
C. psychotherapy
D. group therapy
E. placebo effect

Reteach
Have a class discussion in which half of the class supports Hans Eysenck's view that psychotherapy is not effective. The other half should support the position of Allen Bergin.

Enrich
Have students prepare a wall-size time line showing major events in the historical development of psychotherapy. Recommend *The Story of Psychology* by Morton Hunt or *Psychology in America: A Historical Survey* by Ernest R. Hilgard as possible sources.

4 CLOSE

Using several of the psychological disorders discussed in Chapter 16, ask students to identify the type(s) of therapy that could effectively treat the disorder.

More About...

Therapy and HMOs

Recent economic trends have affected the length of time a person spends in psychotherapy. People who receive their health care through health maintenance organizations (HMOs) pay a fixed amount of money per month for health care. The HMO will then pay for only a certain amount of therapy per month. The HMO in effect minimizes the amount of services a person can obtain, so a person who requires extensive therapy may not be able to get it unless he pays for it on his own.

Allen Bergin (1971) wrote one of the most thoughtful and carefully reasoned reviews. Bergin's review leads one to question the validity of Eysenck's sweeping generalization that psychotherapy is no more effective than no treatment at all. Much of Bergin's argument is based on differences of opinion about how patients should be classified. Precise criteria for improvement are difficult to define and apply. Some people may experience spontaneous remission, or the sudden, unaccountable disappearance of symptoms without any therapy at all. However, such people may have received help from unacknowledged sources—family, friends, relatives, religious advisers, or family physicians. If, as some researchers believe, the prime ingredient in therapy is the establishment of a close relationship, then spontaneous remission in people who have received continuing help from such sources is not spontaneous at all.

An analysis of nearly 400 studies on the effectiveness of psychotherapy, conducted by Mary Lee Smith and Gene V. Glass (1977), used elaborate statistical procedures to estimate the effects of psychotherapy. They found that therapy is generally more effective than no treatment and that on the average most forms of therapy have similar effects; that is, therapy may improve the quality of life for the patients. Will any therapy do for any client? Probably not. Smith and Glass were able to show that for some specific clients and situations, some forms of therapy would be expected to have a greater effect than others. Together, the psychologist and client may discuss the appropriate form of psychotherapy to achieve a cure.

SECTION 1 Assessment

1. **Review the Vocabulary** Cite and describe two examples of group therapy and how these types of therapy help patients.
2. **Visualize the Main Idea** In a diagram similar to the one below, list and describe the characteristics that make a good, effective therapist.

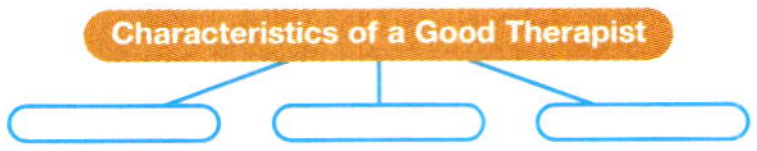

3. **Recall Information** What are the goals of therapy? What is the eclectic approach to therapy?
4. **Think Critically** When should a person seek psychotherapy? Explain your answer.
5. **Application Activity** You are unsure of yourself. You do not know what to do with your future. As a result, you decide that you need the help of a professional to get your personal life on track. Identify the kind of psychotherapist and the kind of therapy that might help you. Explain your answers.

SECTION 1 Assessment Answers

1. Family therapy helps families who are dealing with communication or family structure issues. Self-help groups such as AA allow people to help one another work through commonly shared problems.
2. Therapists should be psychologically healthy. They should have empathy. They should be experienced in dealing with people and understanding their complexities.
3. The primary goal of psychotherapy is to strengthen the patient's control over his or her life. The eclectic approach uses a variety of methods to help each patient achieve that goal.
4. Students' answers will vary. Many may suggest that psychotherapy is needed when a person is facing a crisis or transition in life or cannot function in everyday life.
5. Suggestions will vary. A counselor or a counseling psychologist will likely be the most common choices. Humanistic or cognitive therapies should be the chosen methods.

SECTION 2 Psychoanalysis and Humanistic Therapy

Reader's Guide

Main Idea

Psychoanalysis is an analysis of the conscious and unconscious mind based on the theories of psychoanalyst Sigmund Freud. Humanistic therapy helps people reach their full potential.

Vocabulary

- psychoanalysis
- insight
- free association
- resistance
- dream analysis
- transference
- humanistic therapy
- client-centered therapy
- nondirective therapy
- active listening
- unconditional positive regard

Objectives

- Describe psychoanalysis and its aims.
- Explain humanistic therapy and its goals.

EXPLORING PSYCHOLOGY

What Does This Dream Mean?

I was a child again, and riding my bicycle along the village street, but its wheels began to sink into sticky, muddy earth, so that I could barely move. Finally, however, the earth began to dry, and I found that I was able to cycle along quite easily once more.

—from *Parker's Complete Book of Dreams* by Julia and Derek Parker, 1995

The dream above was experienced by an elderly woman fighting a serious illness. Psychoanalysts might interpret the dream in the following manner: the earth symbolized the illness as well as the woman's concern that she might die. As a child, she had never been allowed to own a bicycle, so having one represented freedom. The bike symbolized something she badly wanted—good health. Psychoanalysts would then use this information—the dream interpretation—to help the woman understand the psychological dilemmas she faces.

SECTION RESOURCES

Reproducible Masters

- Guided Reading Activity 17–2
- Vocabulary Activity 17–2
- Section Quiz 17–2

Transparencies

- Daily Focus Transparency 17–2

Multimedia

- *ExamView® Assessment Suite* CD-ROM
- Presentation Plus! Software

1 FOCUS

Section Objectives

1. Describe psychoanalysis and its aims.
2. Explain humanistic therapy and its goals.

BELLRINGER
Motivational Activity

Project Daily Focus Transparency 17–2 and have students answer the questions.

Available as blackline master

Daily Focus Transparency 17–2

Reader's Guide

Use the Reader's Guide to introduce concepts and vocabulary.

Exploring Psychology

Ask students to read the **Exploring Psychology** feature and then discuss the following question: **How can dreams explain or help us understand our lives?**

Vocabulary Precheck

Have students read the Glossary definitions of the terms. Then have them create a word search puzzle using the definitions as clues. Ask students to trade puzzles with a classmate and complete the word search.

2 TEACH

L1 Demonstration To demonstrate free association, instruct students to write down every thought that comes into their heads for three minutes. Caution students to suspend all judgment and analysis. When the three minutes are up, allow students to do some self-analysis of their writing. **Ask: What, if any, patterns or surprising thoughts turned up?** Request volunteers to share their lists or to talk about feelings of resistance that they might have had during the exercise. **ELL**

Guided Reading Activity 17-2

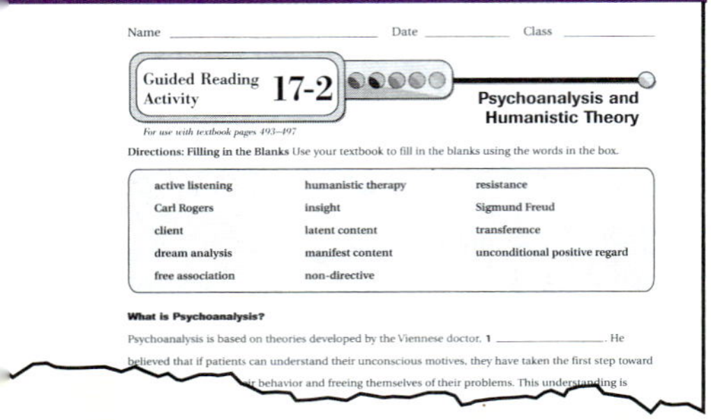
Name ______ Date ______ Class ______

Guided Reading Activity 17-2

Psychoanalysis and Humanistic Theory

For use with textbook pages 493–497

Directions: Filling in the Blanks Use your textbook to fill in the blanks using the words in the box.

active listening	humanistic therapy	resistance
Carl Rogers	insight	Sigmund Freud
client	latent content	transference
dream analysis	manifest content	unconditional positive regard
free association	non-directive	

What is Psychoanalysis?

Psychoanalysis is based on theories developed by the Viennese doctor. **1** ______. He believed that if patients can understand their unconscious motives, they have taken the first step toward ...ir behavior and freeing themselves of their problems. This understanding is

CURRICULUM CONNECTION

The Arts Drama used as therapy seeks to change behavior through the dramatic process. Drama therapists use many dramatic exercises such as pantomime and improvisation. Group members are given a specific situation and act out various scenarios based on that situation. Through these situations, group members learn ways to deal with their own problems. Drama therapists work with adolescents, adults, and senior citizens.

WHAT IS PSYCHOANALYSIS?

psychoanalysis: therapy aimed at making patients aware of their unconscious motives so that they can gain control over their behavior

For a long time **psychoanalysis** was the only formalized psychotherapy practiced in Western society. It was this type of therapy that gave rise to the classic picture of a bearded Viennese doctor seated behind a patient who is lying on a couch.

Psychoanalysis is based on the theories of Sigmund Freud. According to Freud, psychological disturbances are due to anxiety caused by hidden conflicts among the unconscious components of one's personality. (Freud's theory of personality is described in Chapter 14.) One job of the psychoanalyst, therefore, is to help make the patients aware of the unconscious impulses, desires, and fears that are causing the anxiety. Psychoanalysts believe that if patients can understand their unconscious motives, they have taken the first step toward gaining control over their behavior and freeing themselves of their problems. Such understanding is called **insight.**

insight: the apparent sudden realization of the solution to a problem

Free Association

Psychoanalysis is a slow procedure. It may take years of 50-minute sessions several times a week before the patient is able to make fundamental changes. Throughout this time, the analyst assists the patient in a thorough examination of the unconscious motives behind his or her behavior. This task begins with the analyst telling the patient to relax and talk about everything that comes to mind. This method is called **free association.** The patient may consider some passing thoughts too unimportant or too embarrassing to mention. The analyst suggests that everything should be expressed; the thought that seems most inconsequential may, in fact, offer insight into the unconscious.

free association: a method used to examine the unconscious; the patient is instructed to say whatever comes into his or her mind

As the patient lies on the couch, he or she may describe dreams, discuss private thoughts, or recall long-forgotten experiences. The psychoanalyst often says nothing for long periods of time. The psychoanalyst also occasionally makes remarks or asks questions that guide the patient. The analyst also may suggest an unconscious motive or factor that explains something the patient has been talking about, but most of the work is done by the patient.

The patient is understandably reluctant to reveal painful feelings and to examine lifelong patterns that need to be changed and, as the analysis proceeds, is likely to try unconsciously to hold back the flow of information. This phenomenon—in fact, any behavior that impedes the course of therapy—is called **resistance.** The patient may have agreed to cooperate fully, yet at times his or her mind is blank, and he or she feels powerless and can no longer think of anything to say. At such times the analyst will simply point out what is happening and wait for the patient to continue. The analyst may also suggest another line of approach to the area of resistance. By analyzing the patient's resistances, both the therapist and the patient can understand the source of the anxieties and how the patient deals with anxiety-provoking material.

resistance: the reluctance of a patient either to reveal painful feelings or to examine long-standing behavior patterns

COOPERATIVE LEARNING ACTIVITY

Designing a Flowchart Organize the class into small groups. Direct the groups to design a flowchart illustrating the main steps or stages in the psychoanalytical process. Students should illustrate the flowchart, showing the client-therapist relationship at the various stages. Encourage the groups to share their flowcharts with the class. Display the flowcharts around the classroom. **BLOCK SCHEDULING**

Dream Analysis

Freud believed that dreams express unconscious thoughts and feelings. In a technique known as **dream analysis,** the psychoanalyst interprets the client's dream to find the unconscious thoughts and feelings in it.

Freud believed that dreams contain manifest and latent content. *Manifest content* refers to what you remember about your dream. For instance, you recall seeing your house fall apart, brick by brick, in last night's dream. *Latent content* refers to the hidden meanings represented symbolically in the dream that the therapist interprets from the manifest content. Although a therapist might link your dream to your current health concerns, there is little research evidence linking dream content to a person's existing life-problems.

Figure 17.5 What Do Our Dreams Mean?

While we sleep, our dreams probably do not follow logical thought patterns. Because of this, Freud considered dreams the purest form of free association. ***What do therapists hope to learn from analyzing dreams?***

Transference

Sooner or later, the analyst begins to appear in the patient's associations and dreams. The patient may begin feeling toward the analyst the way she feels toward some other important figure in her life. This process is called **transference.**

If the patient can recognize what is happening, transference may allow her to experience her true feelings toward the important person. Often, instead of experiencing and understanding her feelings, the patient simply begins acting toward the therapist in the same way she used to act toward the important person, usually one of her parents.

The therapist does not allow the patient to resort to these tactics. Remaining impersonal and anonymous, the therapist always directs the patient back to herself. The therapist may ask, for example, "What do you see when you imagine my face?" The patient may see the therapist as an angry, frowning, unpleasant figure. The therapist never takes this personally, instead asking, "What does this make you think of?" Gradually, it will become clear to both patient and therapist that the patient is reacting to the neutral therapist as though he or she were a threatening parent, for example.

By understanding transference, the patient becomes aware of hidden feelings and motivations. She may begin to understand, for example, the roots of trouble with her boss at work. The boss, the therapist, or any person in a position of authority may be viewed in the same way that, as a child, she saw her parents.

The purpose of psychoanalysis is to show the role of the unconscious and to provide insight for the client. This type of classical psyche (mind) analysis, however, is not for everyone. It requires an average of 600 sessions and years of meeting with a psychoanalyst. Psychoanalysis has

dream analysis: a technique used by psychoanalysts to interpret the content of patients' dreams

transference: the process, experienced by the patient, of feeling toward an analyst or therapist the way he or she feels or felt toward some other important figure in his or her life

Figure 17.5

Caption Answer Therapists hope to discover an individual's unconscious thoughts and feelings.

TEACHER Tip

Make sure students understand the difference between *manifest content* and *latent content* of dreams. Tell students that trained therapists are best at interpreting the latent content of dreams.

Vocabulary Activity 17–2

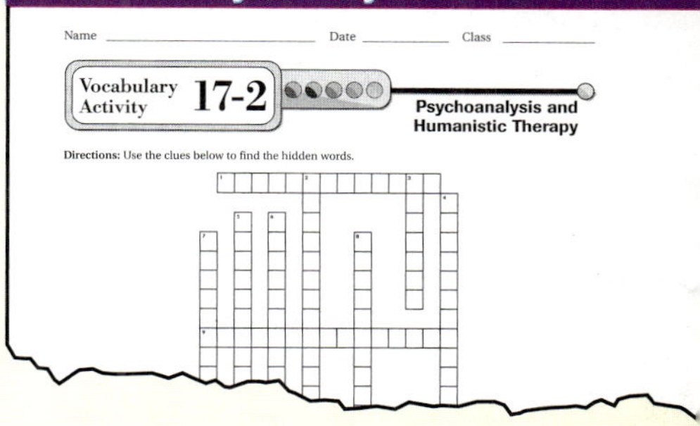

PSYCHOLOGY JOURNAL

Tell students that in client-centered therapy, the client is ultimately responsible for making positive changes. Have students explain how this approach is similar to or differs from traditional psychoanalysis. ■

MEETING SPECIAL NEEDS

Learning Style: Intrapersonal Challenge students to keep a dream diary for a week during which they will record the content of their dreams immediately upon waking. Have students write only the manifest content for each dream. At the end of the week, have students review the dreams and write an interpretation of the latent content. Encourage students to use library or Internet resources to find common meanings for the people and objects in their dreams. Have students write a summary of their beliefs concerning dream analysis and its usefulness in understanding oneself. **L2** **BLOCK SCHEDULING**

Figure 17.6

Caption Answer It focuses on the value of the person and encourages him to strengthen some of his skills to realize his full potential.

Reading Check Answer
The term *patient* places the person in a position of inferiority. The term *client* gives the person an equal relationship with the therapist. According to Rogers, therapy represents an equal relationship between therapist and client.

3 ASSESS

Assign Section 2 Assessment as homework or as an in-class activity.

Section Quiz 17–2

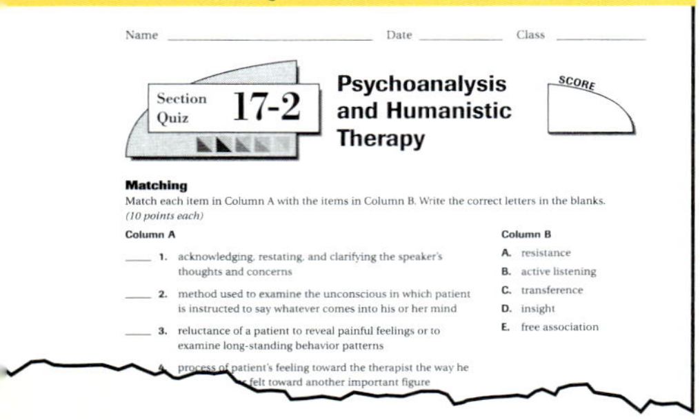
Name ____________ Date ________ Class ________

Section Quiz 17-2

Psychoanalysis and Humanistic Therapy

SCORE

Matching
Match each item in Column A with the items in Column B. Write the correct letters in the blanks.
(10 points each)

Column A

____ **1.** acknowledging, restating, and clarifying the speaker's thoughts and concerns

____ **2.** method used to examine the unconscious in which patient is instructed to say whatever comes into his or her mind

____ **3.** reluctance of a patient to reveal painful feelings or to examine long-standing behavior patterns

process of patient's feeling toward the therapist the way he ... felt toward another important figure

Column B

A. resistance
B. active listening
C. transference
D. insight
E. free association

Reteach

Have students create a chart to list and describe the basic techniques used in client-centered therapy.

changed with patients, disorders, and the prevailing cultures. There are many versions available today of this classical psychoanalysis. For example, *short-term dynamic psychotherapy* is a shortened version of psychoanalysis. This type of therapy focuses on a client's problems. The therapist uses a direct and more active approach in identifying and resolving the problems. This approach to therapy, along with psychoanalysis, works well for clients who are able to gain insight into their behavior. People who lose touch with reality—for instance, a person suffering from schizophrenia—will probably not benefit from psychoanalysis, though.

"Of course you have strengths, dear. It's just that you don't communicate them."

Figure 17.6 Humanistic Approaches to Therapy

Humanistic therapies attempt to help clients make better use of their own abilities. ***How does this cartoon reflect a humanistic approach?***

HUMANISTIC THERAPY

The goal of **humanistic therapy** is to help people fulfill their human potential. Humanistic psychology has given rise to several approaches to psychotherapy, known collectively as **client-centered therapy.** Humanistic psychologists stress the actualization of one's unique potentials through personal responsibility, freedom of choice, and authentic relationships.

humanistic therapy: focuses on the value, dignity, and worth of each person; holds that healthy living is the result of realizing one's full potential

client-centered therapy: reflects the belief that the client and therapist are partners in therapy

Client-Centered Therapy

Client-centered therapy, or person-centered therapy, is based on the theories of Carl Rogers (1951, 1977). This therapy depends on the person's own motivation toward growth and self-actualization. The use of the term *person* or *client* instead of *patient* gives one an insight into the reasoning behind Rogers's method. *Patient* may suggest inferiority or passivity, whereas *person* or *client* implies an equal relationship between the therapist and the individual seeking help. According to Rogers, this equal relationship reflects three therapeutic components—positive regard, empathy, and genuineness. Positive regard refers to the therapist's ability to demonstrate caring and respect for the client. Empathy is the ability to understand what the client is feeling. Genuineness refers to the therapist's ability to act toward the client in a real and nondefensive manner.

Client-centered therapists assume that people are basically good and that they are capable of handling their own lives. Psychological problems arise when the true self becomes lost and the individual comes to view the self according to the standards of others. One of the goals of therapy is to help the person recognize his or her own strength and confidence, thereby learning to be true to his or her own standards and ideas about how to live effectively.

Reading Check
Why did Rogers choose to refer to a patient as a "client"?

Techniques of Client-Centered Therapy In the course of an interview, the client is encouraged to speak freely about any troubling matters. The topics discussed are entirely up to the client. This method is called **nondirective therapy** because the therapist does not direct it. The therapist listens and encourages conversation but tries to avoid giving opinions.

nondirective therapy: the free flow of images and ideas, with no particular direction

CRITICAL THINKING ACTIVITY

Identifying Central Issues Challenge students to work in pairs to write a mock transcript from a client-centered therapy session. (If possible, have students locate an actual transcript from a collection of case studies to use as a model.) Instruct students to role-play the session and explore the feelings experienced by the client. Next, assign the pairs to rewrite the transcripts using another therapy approach. Conduct another role-play exercise having the same students play the client role. Challenge students to compare the different emotions, thoughts, and/or resistance evoked by the different therapies. Ask clients which they preferred and why. **L3**

BLOCK SCHEDULING

The therapist tries to echo back, as clearly as possible, the feelings the client has expressed. This communication technique is called **active listening.** The therapist may try to extract the main points from the client's hesitant or rambling explanations. Between them, the client and therapist form a clearer picture of how the client really feels about self, life, and important others.

Client-centered therapy is conducted in an atmosphere of emotional support that Rogers calls **unconditional positive regard.** The therapist never says what he or she thinks of the client or whether what the client has said is good or bad. Instead the therapist shows the client that anything said is accepted without embarrassment, reservation, or anger. The therapist's main responsibility is creating and maintaining a warm and accepting relationship with the client. This acceptance makes it easier for clients to explore thoughts about themselves and their experiences. They are able to abandon old values without fear of disapproval, and can begin to see themselves, their situations, and their relationships with others in a new light and with new confidence.

As they reduce tensions and release emotions, the clients feel that they are becoming more complete people. They gain the courage to accept parts of their personalities that they had formerly considered weak or bad. By recognizing their self-worth, they can set up realistic goals and consider the steps necessary to reach them. The clients' movements toward independence signal the end of the need for therapy; they can assume the final steps to independence on their own.

Although client-centered therapy has proved more effective than no treatment, it seems to be no more or less effective than other types of therapy. Client-centered therapy has helped, though, make therapists aware of the importance of developing supportive relations with their clients.

active listening: empathetic listening; a listener acknowledges, restates, and clarifies the speaker's thoughts and concerns

unconditional positive regard: a therapist's consistent expression of acceptance of the patient, no matter what the patient says and does

PSYCHOLOGY Online

Student Web Activity
Visit the *Understanding Psychology* Web site at glencoe.com and click on **Chapter 17—Student Web Activities** for an activity about psychotherapy.

SECTION 2 Assessment

1. **Review the Vocabulary** Cite and describe the techniques involved in client-centered therapy.
2. **Visualize the Main Idea** In a chart similar to the one below, list and describe the main processes involved in psychoanalysis.

Processes of Psychoanalysis
1
2
3
4

3. **Recall Information** What is the purpose of dream analysis? How do therapists use it?
4. **Think Critically** What are the main differences between psychoanalysis and humanistic therapy?
5. **Application Activity** Some therapists may view therapy as a process of teaching a client a philosophy of life. Do you think this therapy goal is appropriate? Does this goal assume the therapist has the *better* philosophy of life? Argue your point in an editorial-type essay.

SECTION 2 Assessment Answers

1. Client-centered therapy uses nondirective therapy and active listening in an atmosphere of unconditional positive regard.
2. Psychoanalysis uses free association and dream analysis techniques to understand unconscious thoughts and motives. Psychoanalysts will look for ways to overcome resistance to the free flow of information. Transference occurs when the client feels the same way toward the therapist that he or she feels toward some important figure in his or her life.
3. Dream analysis helps identify unconscious thoughts, feelings, and motives. Therapists use the latent content to help identify these unconscious thoughts.
4. Psychoanalysis places the therapist in the role of interpreter of a client's unconscious and gives the power to the therapist. Humanistic therapy seeks to make the client responsible for his or her own change. The therapist serves primarily as a facilitator.
5. Answers will vary but should reflect an understanding of the various therapies.

PSYCHOLOGY Online

Links and instructional guidelines can be found in the **Web Activity Lesson Plan** at glencoe.com.

Enrich

Have students create a list of tips that they and fellow classmates can use to help them become more assertive.

4 CLOSE

Tell students that Carl Rogers originally called his therapy *client-centered.* He later changed it to *person-centered* to indicate his belief that the same principles employed in counseling applied to all human interactions. Challenge students to use unconditional positive regard, empathy, and genuineness for 24 hours and report on the results.

Going Further

Freud's Development of Psychoanalysis

One of the cases that Sigmund Freud studied extensively to develop psychoanalysis was the case of Anna O. Anna experienced what would now be called conversion disorder, including hysterical blindness and partial paralysis. She was treated by Josef Breuer, a contemporary of Freud. During the treatment, Anna was encouraged to talk about herself. As she discovered repressed memories, her physical condition improved. Although Breuer did not call his process *free association*, the term describes the basic technique he used with Anna.

Anna also experienced transference. Breuer did not know how to deal with these intense feelings and eventually terminated treatment. When the sessions were terminated, not all of her symptoms had been relieved. She did, however, eventually recover.

Discussing the Case Study

Ask: What was Rat Man's fantasy? What was Freud's original hypothesis? Did Freud's hypothesis change during the course of the treatment? How do you see Rat Man overcoming resistance to his deepest feelings?

Case Studies

The Case of Rat Man

Period of Study: Early 1900s

Introduction: Sigmund Freud used psychoanalysis with a patient Freud referred to as *Rat Man.* A 29-year-old man came to Freud complaining of various fears, obsessions, and compulsions, or cravings, which had been occurring for approximately six years. These symptoms had prevented the man from completing his university studies and attaining success at work. Freud focused on Rat Man's uncontrollable fantasy in which the man would see his father and girlfriend tied down and being tortured by hungry rats strapped to their flesh.

Hypothesis: Freud's earliest hypothesis was that Rat Man maintained a conflict over whether he should marry his girlfriend or not. Since Rat Man was unable to decide consciously, he resolved this issue through his unconscious mind. These unconscious thoughts produced disturbing pictures in his mind, thus making him unable to carry out daily activities such as school and work. Freud also theorized that past love and hate issues between Rat Man and his father caused the father to be in Rat Man's dreams and fantasies.

Method: Freud began therapy with Rat Man by using a psychoanalytic technique called *free association*. Freud asked Rat Man to free-associate with the word *rats.* Rat Man came up with the word *rates,* referring to installments or money. In an earlier session, Rat Man indicated his girlfriend had little money and his father had always wanted him to marry a wealthy woman. Freud deduced the rat fantasies were related to the father's opposition to Rat Man's girlfriend.

In another instance during therapy, Rat Man described an event relayed to him by his mother, which had taken place when he was around four years of age. Rat Man claimed his mother had told him that as a little boy he had once bitten the nurse who was taking care of his father. Rat Man's father began to beat him immediately after the incident occurred. Rat Man responded to the beatings with a multitude of angry and harsh words directed toward his father. After hearing those words, Rat Man's father never beat him again. Freud suggested that the act of Rat Man biting the nurse was a sexual action. Since his father beat him for indulging in his sexual needs (biting), Rat Man's fear of fulfilling his needs for a relationship stemmed from fear he would be punished.

A major breakthrough occurred when Rat Man revealed another fantasy he had been having. In this fantasy, Rat Man was persuaded to marry Freud's daughter. These wishes came directly from Freud himself (according to Rat Man's fantasy). Freud immediately interrupted and stated that Rat Man was replacing the role of his father with Freud. Moments later Rat Man became emotionally enraged at his therapist, and this rage ended with an intense fear that Freud would beat him. This signified a chief discovery. Freud convinced Rat Man he was reliving the event with his father by placing the therapist in the father's role.

Results: Before therapy, Rat Man had never consciously experienced anger toward his father. This anger came out in therapy sessions. To Freud, the rats biting into and destroying Rat Man's father and girlfriend symbolized significant past events—Rat Man biting his first love, or the nurse, and in another essence *biting* his father with angry words. According to Freud, Rat Man's conscious acceptance of the feelings of fear and anger toward his father would lead to a recovery. However, Rat Man was never able to fully enjoy the newly found insights. Shortly after his sessions with Freud, Rat Man was killed in World War I.

Analyzing the Case Study

1. Why did Rat Man seek therapy?
2. What was Freud's strategy in treating Rat Man?
3. **Critical Thinking** How did Rat Man demonstrate transference? How did this transference help in therapy?

Answers for Analyzing the Case Study

1. He sought therapy in an attempt to overcome his paralyzing fears, obsessions, and compulsions. These symptoms had prevented him from completing his university studies and attaining success at work.
2. Freud used traditional psychoanalysis including free association. Freud hypothesized that Rat Man had unconscious thoughts that were disturbing him. He helped Rat Man overcome resistance. Eventually Rat Man's unconscious thoughts surfaced and Freud helped him gain insight from them.
3. Rat Man transferred his anger toward his father onto Freud. Freud used this to help Rat Man recognize and understand his feelings of fear and anger toward his father.

SECTION 3

Cognitive and Behavior Therapies

Reader's Guide

■ Main Idea

Cognitive and behavior therapies help clients develop new ways of thinking and behaving.

■ Vocabulary

- behavior modification
- cognitive therapy
- rational-emotive therapy (RET)
- behavior therapy
- systematic desensitization
- aversive conditioning
- contingency management
- token economy
- cognitive-behavior therapy

■ Objectives

- Describe cognitive therapies and their aims.
- Explain the processes and goals of behavior therapy.

EXPLORING PSYCHOLOGY

Imagine That!

Five times a day for several days, Brooks Workman stopped what she was doing and vividly imagined herself opening a soft drink can. She made a special point of picturing herself bringing the can to her mouth and placing her lips on it. Just as she was about to drink, hordes of roaches poured out of the can and scurried into her mouth, writhing, twitching, and wiggling their feelers.

—from *Toward a Self-Managed Life Style* by R.L. Williams and J.D. Long, 1979

Why would someone purposefully imagine the scene in the story above? Brooks's behavior was not as strange as it sounds. She was trying to cut down on the number of soft drinks she had each day. To achieve her goal, Brooks Workman used a method known as **behavior modification**—one of several forms of behavior therapy often used to eliminate or alter an undesirable voluntary behavior. In this section we will examine behavior and cognitive therapies.

behavior modification: a systematic method of changing the way a person acts and feels

COGNITIVE THERAPY

The goal of **cognitive therapies** focuses on changing the way people think (Beck, 1991). Basic assumptions that cognitive therapies share are that faulty cognitions—our irrational or uninformed beliefs, expectations, and

cognitive therapy: using thoughts to control emotions and behaviors

SECTION RESOURCES

Reproducible Masters

- Guided Reading Activity 17–3
- Vocabulary Activity 17–3
- Section Quiz 17–3

Transparencies

- Daily Focus Transparency 17–3

Multimedia

- *ExamView® Assessment Suite* CD-ROM
- Presentation Plus! Software

1 FOCUS

Section Objectives

1. Describe cognitive therapies and their aims.
2. Explain the processes and goals of behavior therapy.

BELLRINGER
Motivational Activity

Project Daily Focus Transparency 17–3 and have students answer the questions.

Available as blackline master

Daily Focus Transparency 17–3

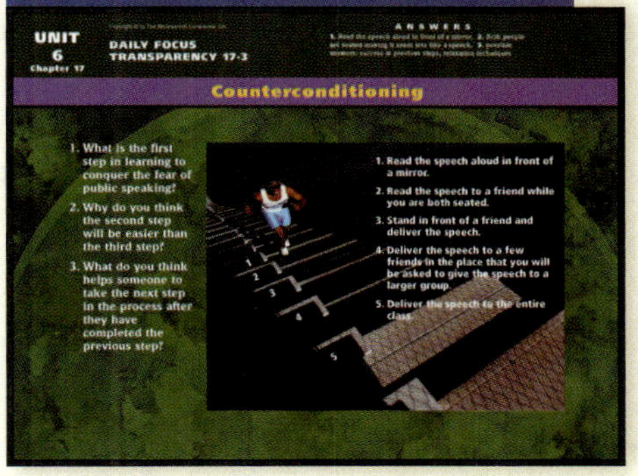

Reader's Guide

Use the Reader's Guide to introduce concepts and vocabulary.

■ Exploring Psychology

Ask students to read the **Exploring Psychology** feature and then discuss the following: **What other habits can be effectively changed using behavior modification?**

■ Vocabulary Precheck

Have students read the Glossary definitions of the vocabulary terms. Then challenge them to write a paragraph about cognitive and behavior therapies using as many of the terms as possible.

2 TEACH

L1 Identifying Distorted Thinking Tell students that there are many types of maladaptive thought patterns that lead to irrational thinking. Describe to students the following four common types of maladaptive thought patterns:

1. Catastrophizing (expecting a disaster to occur)
2. Mind reading (assuming that you know what someone else is thinking or feeling without the person expressing his or her thoughts)
3. Being right (needing to prove that your opinions and decisions are always right even in the face of evidence to the contrary)
4. Emotional reasoning (believing that what you feel must be true)

Have students develop irrational statements to match each of these types of distorted thinking. **BLOCK SCHEDULING**

Figure 17.7

Visual Instruction Ask: How is each of the statements irrational? Which parts of the statement are likely true and which are false?

Caption Answer The therapist would use techniques such as role-playing, modeling, humor, and specific practice exercises to teach the individual to think in realistic terms.

Guided Reading Activity 17–3

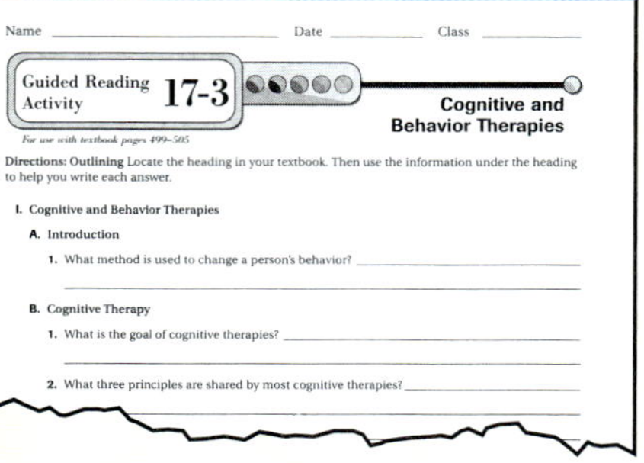
Name ____ Date ____ Class ____

Guided Reading Activity 17-3

Cognitive and Behavior Therapies

For use with textbook pages 499–505

Directions: Outlining Locate the heading in your textbook. Then use the information under the heading to help you write each answer.

I. Cognitive and Behavior Therapies

A. Introduction

1. What method is used to change a person's behavior? ____

B. Cognitive Therapy

1. What is the goal of cognitive therapies? ____

2. What three principles are shared by most cognitive therapies? ____

Figure 17.7 Examples of Irrational Thinking

Albert Ellis (1961) asserted that the irrational ideas we believe stand in the way of achieving lives that are free of anxiety. ***How might a RET therapist counter these irrational beliefs?***

Everything I do must be approved and loved by virtually everybody.
I have to be completely competent, totally in control, and successful in everything I do.
It is catastrophic when things are not going the way I want them to go.
My unhappiness is not my fault. People and events over which I have no control are responsible.
Anytime I encounter something that I fear, I need to be consumed with worries and upset about it.
It is easier to avoid life's difficulties and responsibilities than to develop a better system for meeting them.
My life and the people with whom I work should be changed from the way they are.
The best I can do for myself is to relax and enjoy life. Inaction and passivity are the best bet to maximize my own enjoyment.

ways of thinking—distort our behaviors, attitudes, and emotions. So to improve our lives, we must work to change our patterns of thinking.

In what other ways are cognitive therapies similar? According to some psychologists (Ross, 1977), all of these theories follow one or more of three principles—disconfirmation, reconceptualization, and insight. *Disconfirmation* means clients may be confronted with evidence that directly contradicts their existing beliefs. In *reconceptualization,* clients work toward an alternative belief system to explain their experiences or current observations. In *insight,* clients work toward understanding and deriving new or revised beliefs.

Rational-Emotive Therapy

rational-emotive therapy (RET): a form of psychological help aimed at changing unrealistic assumptions about oneself and other people

Albert Ellis developed a form of therapy called **rational-emotive therapy (RET)** (1973). Ellis believed that people behave in deliberate and rational ways, given their assumptions about life. Emotional problems arise when an individual's assumptions are unrealistic (see Figure 17.7).

Suppose a man seeks therapy when a woman leaves him. He cannot stand the fact that she has rejected him. Without her, his life is empty and miserable. She has made him feel utterly worthless. He must get her back. Like a spoiled child, the man is demanding that the woman love him. He expects, even insists, that things will always go his way. Given this assumption, the only possible explanation for her behavior is that something is dreadfully wrong, either with him or with her.

What is wrong, in the therapist's view, is the man's thinking. By defining his feelings for the woman as need rather than desire, he—not she—is causing his depression. When you convince yourself that you need someone, you will in fact be unable to carry on without that person in your life. When you believe that you cannot stand rejection, you will in fact fall apart when you encounter rejection. This kind of faulty thinking is based on unreasonable attitudes, false premises, and rigid roles for behaviors.

The goal of rational-emotive therapy is to correct these false and self-defeating beliefs. Rejection is unpleasant but not unbearable. A relationship may be desirable, but it is not irreplaceable. To teach the individual to think in realistic terms, RET therapists may use a

COOPERATIVE LEARNING ACTIVITY

Directing a Panel Discussion Request a volunteer to compile a list of all the different therapists mentioned in this chapter. Organize the class into small groups so that each group represents a different therapist. Assign the groups to find out as much as they can about the therapist and his or her theories and practices. Then conduct a mock panel discussion in which you pose questions about the therapists' various approaches to treatment, attitudes toward patients, and expected time frame for change. Each group should use its research to answer the questions about the therapist it represents. **BLOCK SCHEDULING**

number of techniques. One is *role playing* so that the person can see how his beliefs affect his relationships. Another technique is *modeling* to demonstrate other ways of thinking and acting. A third is *humor* to underline the absurdity of his beliefs. Still another technique is simple *persuasion*. The therapist may also assign homework to give the man practice in acting more reasonably. For example, the therapist may instruct him to ask women who are likely to reject him out on dates. Why? He will learn that he can cope with things not going his way.

Ellis liked to teach that behaviors are the result of the ABCs. *A* refers to the *Activating* event. *B* is the person's *Belief* system about the event. *C* refers to the *Consequences* that follow. Ellis claimed it is not the event that causes trouble but rather the way a person thinks about the event. In other words, A does not cause C, but instead B causes C (see Figure 17.8).

Figure 17.8 Ellis's ABCs

Many cognitive therapists believe that our emotional reactions to situations are the result not of the situations but of our beliefs about the situations or our interpretations of the situations. ***On what aspect—A, B, or C—do cognitive therapists focus? Why?***

A
Activating event
(e.g., a criticism)

B
Belief
(e.g., "I must be loved by everyone to be happy")

C
Consequent emotion
(e.g., unhappiness)

In therapy, the therapist and client work to change B, the belief. Ellis believes that the individual must take three steps to cure or correct himself. First, he must realize that some of his assumptions are false. Second, he must see that he is making himself disturbed by acting on false beliefs. Finally, he must work to break old habits of thought and behavior. He has to practice self-discipline and learn to take risks.

Beck's Cognitive Therapy

Aaron T. Beck (1967, 1970) introduced another form of cognitive therapy that is similar to Ellis's rational-emotive therapy. The primary difference in Beck's therapy is the focus on illogical thought processes (see Figure 17.9). Beck has therapists—through using persuasion and logic to change existing beliefs—also encourage clients to engage in actual tests of their own beliefs. For example, if a client believes that "I never have a good time," the therapist might point out that this is a hypothesis, not a fact. The therapist might then ask the client to

Figure 17.9 Beck's Maladaptive Thought Patterns

Beck believed that maladaptive thought patterns cause a distorted view of oneself and one's world, leading to various psychological problems. ***What is polarized thinking?***

Maladaptive Thought Patterns	Definition	Example
Overgeneralization	Making blanket judgments about oneself	I'm a failure.
Polarized Thinking	Categorizing information into two categories	Most people don't like me.
Selective Attention	Focusing on only one detail of many	People always criticize me.

Figure 17.8

Visual Instruction Tell students that the activating event (A) can be internal or external. Ask students to name examples of each.

Caption Answer Cognitive therapists focus on unreasonable beliefs (B) because they may lead to false assumptions (C).

PSYCHOLOGY JOURNAL

Ask students to write down examples of times when they engaged in maladaptive thought patterns. Have students analyze the incidents and identify whether the thought patterns were examples of overgeneralization, polarized thinking, or selective attention. ■

Figure 17.9

Visual Instruction Tell students that other examples of maladaptive thought patterns include filtering, personalization, perceiving total control by others, and blaming. Encourage students to find definitions or descriptions of these patterns.

Caption Answer categorizing information into two categories (seeing everything in terms of "black or white")

MEETING SPECIAL NEEDS

Learning Style: Intrapersonal Tell students to use Ellis's ABCs to analyze three recent events they have experienced in which an unreasonable belief resulted in emotional distress. Encourage students to be honest by telling them that the examples they write down will not be seen by anyone else. Challenge them to rewrite the beliefs eliminating all unrealistic beliefs. Have them reexamine their emotions after rewriting the beliefs. Ask students to write a brief analysis of this process evaluating whether reorienting their beliefs changed the consequent emotions. **L2** **BLOCK SCHEDULING**

CHAPTER 17

Section 3, pages 499–505

Quick Lab

Purpose Students will explore ways to overcome irrational fears.

Process Skills Understanding cause and effect, identifying central issues

Teaching Strategies

- Review the procedures to be used.
- Encourage students to list at least seven to ten aspects of the situation that could be frightening, including some items that would cause minimal fear.

Analysis

1. Answers will vary. Treatments should begin with the least frightening aspect and progressively move through the others.
2. Answers will vary. It helps to overcome all aspects of the fear and allows for progressive levels of success.

Readings and Case Studies in Psychology

Have students read the Chapter 17 Case Study selection in *Readings and Case Studies in Psychology* and answer the questions that follow the case study.

TEACHER Tip

Have students review the material on classical and operant conditioning from Chapter 9. **Ask: How are these techniques both a form of learning and a form of therapy?**

Quick Lab

How can someone overcome an irrational fear?

Systematic desensitization is most often used to help individuals overcome fears and anxieties. How is this technique applied?

Procedure

1. Identify a situation that makes someone you know fearful, or you can make up a fear for an imaginary person.
2. Imagine that you are that person. List all the aspects of the situation that you find frightening and rank them in order from the most frightening to least frightening.
3. Suggest a step-by-step plan. Apply the systematic desensitization technique to help overcome the fear.

Analysis

1. Prepare a flowchart showing the steps you would use to help the individual change his or her behavior.
2. Why do you think this technique is often effective in overcoming irrational fears?

See the Skills Handbook, page 622, for an explanation of designing an experiment.

test the hypothesis by looking at the evidence differently and note the times in her life when she actually did have a good time. The therapist's goal is to demonstrate to the client that her automatic thinking may be incorrect and that things are not as bad as they seem.

Beck's work has been very successful with people who are depressed. He believed that depressed people blame themselves instead of their circumstances. He also believed that depressed people focus on only negative events and ignore the positive events. They make pessimistic projections about the future. Finally, he believed they make negative conclusions about self-worth based on events that are not significant.

The goal of Beck's cognitive therapy is to change the way people think. The therapist's job is to determine the pace and direction of the therapy and to help the client detect negative thinking patterns. Therapists also help the client use more reasonable standards for self-evaluation.

Beck may also have clients do homework assignments to assess the true value of his or her beliefs. They may be asked to engage in behaviors that test these beliefs outside of the office. For example, a person who is not very assertive may be asked to cut into a line at the grocery store, to interrupt people who are talking, or to ask someone for a favor.

BEHAVIOR THERAPIES

behavior therapy: changing undesirable behavior through conditioning techniques

In **behavior therapy** there is emphasis on one's behavior rather than one's thoughts, as in cognitive therapy. Rather than spending large amounts of time going into the patient's past or the details of his or her dreams, the behavior therapist concentrates on determining what is specifically troubling in the patient's life and takes steps to change it. The goal of behavior therapy is to modify one's behavior.

The idea behind behavior therapy is that a disturbed person is one who has learned to behave in an undesirable way and that any behavior that is learned can be unlearned. The therapist's job, therefore, is to help the patient learn new behaviors. The reasons for the patient's undesirable behavior are not important; what is important is to change the behavior. By changing one's behavior, one's thoughts change as well. The person is asked to list concrete examples of desired behaviors and behavioral goals. Once these behaviors have been targeted, a program to achieve these goals is developed. To bring about such changes, the therapist uses conditioning techniques first discovered in animal laboratories.

CRITICAL THINKING ACTIVITY

Analyzing Information Read aloud the following quote from an interview with Albert Ellis printed in *Psychology Today.*

Patients temporarily felt better from all the talk and attention but they didn't seem to get better. . . . I began to wonder why I had to wait passively for weeks or months until a client showed that they were ready to accept my interpretation. Why . . . couldn't I help them with some pointed questions or remarks? So . . . I began to become more eclectic. . . .

Have students analyze why Ellis questioned psychoanalysis. Then have them create a chart that contrasts psychoanalysis and rational-emotive therapy (RET). **L2**

Counterconditioning

One technique used by behavior therapists is counterconditioning. This technique pairs the stimulus that triggers an unwanted behavior (such as the fear of snakes) with a new, more desirable behavior. The therapist helps the client reduce anxiety by pairing relaxation with anxiety-producing situations. Counterconditioning is a three-step process: (1) the person builds an anxiety hierarchy with the least feared situation on the bottom and the most feared situation on top; (2) the person learns deep muscle relaxation; (3) the person imagines or experiences each step in the hierarchy, starting with the least anxiety-provoking situation, while learning to be relaxed. Since it is impossible to maintain both relaxation and anxiety, the idea is to teach the person that the situation does not have to be anxiety producing. Using the anxiety hierarchy, the person progresses through each step after successfully completing the previous one.

systematic desensitization: a technique to help a patient overcome irrational fears and anxieties

Systematic desensitization is a counterconditioning technique used to overcome irrational fears and anxieties the patient has learned (Wolpe, 1961). The goal of systematic desensitization therapy is to encourage people to imagine the feared situation while relaxing, thus extinguishing the fear response (see Figure 17.10). For example, suppose a student is terrified of speaking in front of large groups—that, in fact, his stage fright is so tremendous that he is unable to speak when called upon in class. How would systematic desensitization therapy effectively change this person's behavior?

The therapist might have the student make a list of the frightening aspects of talking to others. Perhaps the most frightening aspect is actually standing before an audience, whereas the least frightening is speaking to a single other person. The client ranks these fears, from the most frightening on down. Then the therapist begins teaching the client muscle relaxation. Once he knows how to relax completely, the client is ready for the next step. The client tries to imagine as vividly as possible the least disturbing scene on his list of fears. Thinking about speaking to a single stranger may cause mild anxiety. Because the therapist has taught him how to relax, he learns to think about the experience without feeling anxious. The basic logic is that a person cannot feel anxious and relaxed at the same time. The therapist attempts to replace anxiety with its opposite, relaxation, through counterconditioning.

Figure 17.10 Losing Fears

Counterconditioning techniques, such as systematic desensitization, are used to help people overcome their irrational fears and anxieties. ***What steps might be used to desensitize a child's fear of the dark?***

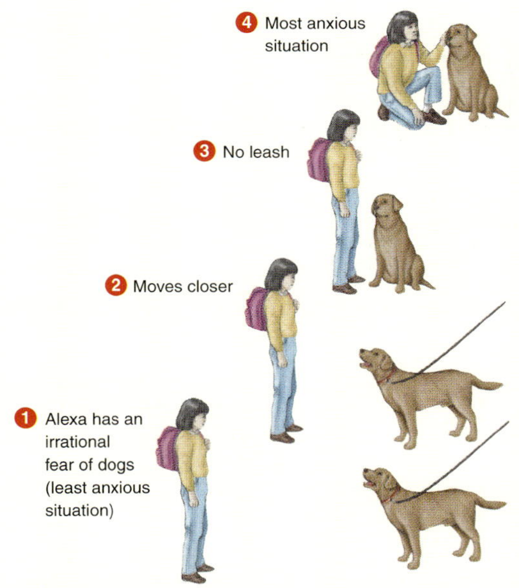

FYI

Crisis intervention programs, such as telephone hot lines, take an active approach to mental health. Counselors in such programs listen, provide encouragement, help people assess their situations realistically, and help people work out adaptive ways of coping with present and future crises.

Applying Psychology

Tell students to imagine that a friend has come to them upset about the way her boss at a part-time job treats her. She is thinking about quitting her job, but other than the boss' criticisms, she really likes her job and her coworkers. Have students suggest specific techniques of either rational-emotive therapy (RET) or cognitive therapy that may help the friend deal with the situation. Students should describe their suggestions in a two-page report.

Figure 17.10

Visual Instruction Explain to students that if undesirable behaviors are conditioned, or learned through reinforcement, counterconditioning can be used to learn adaptive behaviors.

Caption Answer Answers will vary but should show a gradual process from looking into a dark room to being able to sleep in a dark room all night.

PSYCHOLOGY LAB EXPERIMENT

Behavior Modification Review the behavioral approach to therapy with an emphasis upon contingency management. Have the class make a list of common bad habits most people would like to change. Then divide the class into small groups and assign one bad habit to each group. Challenge the group to develop a reward/reinforcement schedule that will help break this habit. If any volunteers choose to try the program, have them regularly report their progress to the class. (At some point, you might explore how these reports serve as a positive or negative stressor.) **L2** **BLOCK SCHEDULING**

CHAPTER 17

Section 3, pages 499–505

Vocabulary Activity 17-3

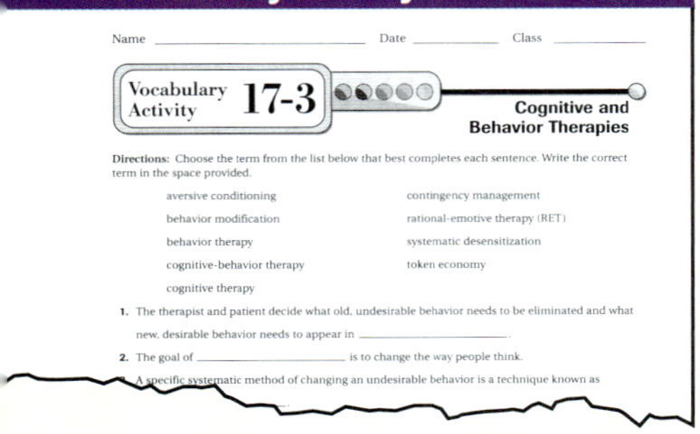
Name ______ Date ______ Class ______

Vocabulary Activity 17-3 — Cognitive and Behavior Therapies

Directions: Choose the term from the list below that best completes each sentence. Write the correct term in the space provided.

aversive conditioning	contingency management
behavior modification	rational-emotive therapy (RET)
behavior therapy	systematic desensitization
cognitive-behavior therapy	token economy
cognitive therapy	

1. The therapist and patient decide what old, undesirable behavior needs to be eliminated and what new, desirable behavior needs to appear in ______.
2. The goal of ______ is to change the way people think.
3. A specific systematic method of changing an undesirable behavior is a technique known as

Reading Check Answer Aversive conditioning pairs a negative result with an undesired behavior. Counterconditioning pairs a stimulus that causes an unwanted behavior with something desirable to create a new, desired behavior.

3 ASSESS

Assign Section 3 Assessment as homework or as an in-class activity.

Section Quiz 17-3

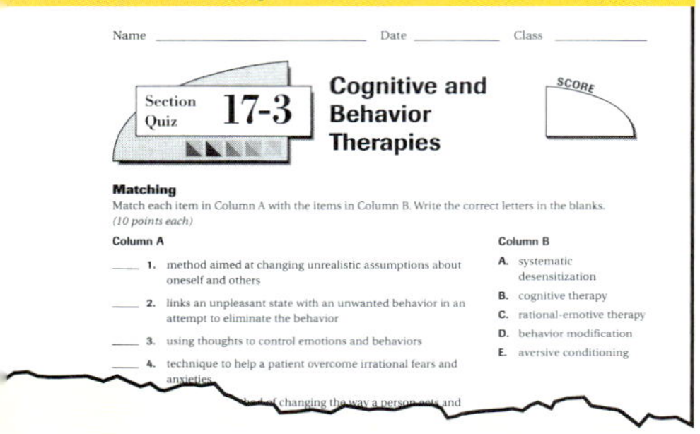
Name ______ Date ______ Class ______

Section Quiz 17-3 — Cognitive and Behavior Therapies — SCORE

Matching
Match each item in Column A with the items in Column B. Write the correct letters in the blanks. (10 points each)

Column A	Column B
___ 1. method aimed at changing unrealistic assumptions about oneself and others	A. systematic desensitization
___ 2. links an unpleasant state with an unwanted behavior in an attempt to eliminate the behavior	B. cognitive therapy
___ 3. using thoughts to control emotions and behaviors	C. rational-emotive therapy
___ 4. technique to help a patient overcome irrational fears and anxieties	D. behavior modification
___ 5. ... changing the way a person acts and	E. aversive conditioning

Did You Know?

Virtual-Reality Therapy Some therapists use virtual reality in therapy. They equip their clients with helmets that display a virtual-reality scene. For instance, if you are afraid of heights, your therapist might expose you to a virtual-reality scene in which you are riding a glass elevator to the 74th floor of a building. The therapist can closely monitor your situation and turn off the display or remove your helmet if you become too agitated.

The patient and therapist then progress step-by-step through the list of anxiety-arousing events. The patient reaches a point where he is able to imagine the most threatening situations without feeling anxiety. Now the therapist starts to expose the person to real-life situations that have previously frightened him. Therapy finally reaches the point where the student is able to deliver an unrehearsed speech to a full auditorium.

Flooding refers to another treatment in which a therapist exposes the client to a feared object or situation. For example, let's say that you are deathly afraid of snakes. Your therapist might have you imagine yourself in a room full of snakes or have you hold a snake. This makes your heart rate soar, but it cannot stay that way forever. Eventually your heart rate returns to normal, and you realize that you have survived this test—you have faced your fear. You have begun to overcome your fear.

Behavior therapists also use *modeling* to teach a client to do something by watching someone else do it. For example, when teaching clients how to be assertive, a therapist might demonstrate ways to be assertive. The client watches and then tries to imitate the behavior.

aversive conditioning: links an unpleasant state with an unwanted behavior in an attempt to eliminate the behavior

Aversive Conditioning In **aversive conditioning,** the goal is to make certain acts unpleasant so that they will be avoided. For example, alcoholics can be given medication that will make them sick when they take alcohol. The relearning process involved is to try to associate the aversive (negative) feeling with taking the alcohol and hence reduce its appeal and use. The rate of improvement for this method is about 50 percent, with the effect lasting about six months. Thus it is not a solution as much as a good beginning for a number of alcoholics (Ullmann & Krasner, 1969, 1975).

Reading Check How does aversive conditioning differ from counterconditioning?

Operant Conditioning

Operant conditioning is based on the assumption that behavior that is reinforced tends to be repeated, whereas behavior that is not reinforced tends to be extinguished. In **contingency management** the therapist and patient decide what old, undesirable behavior needs to be eliminated and what new, desirable behavior needs to appear.

contingency management: undesirable behavior is not reinforced, while desirable behavior is reinforced

Arrangements are then made for the old behavior to go unrewarded and for the desired behavior to be positively reinforced. In its simplest form, contingency management consists of the therapist agreeing with the patient: "If you do X, I will give you Y." This form of agreement is similar to systems of reward that people often use on themselves or parents use on children. For instance, a student may think, "If I get a good grade on the exam, I'll treat myself to a new CD." The reward is contingent (dependent) upon getting a good grade.

Contingency management is used in prisons, mental hospitals, schools, army bases, and with individual patients. In these situations it is

INTERDISCIPLINARY CONNECTIONS ACTIVITY

Music Tell students that the American Music Therapy Association defines music therapy as "the prescribed use of music by a qualified person to effect positive changes in the psychological, physical, cognitive, or social functioning of individuals with health or educational problems." Have students research the effect of music therapy on behavior and prepare a classroom demonstration of how music therapy can have a positive change on behavior. **L2** **BLOCK SCHEDULING**

possible to set up whole miniature systems of rewards, called **token economies.** For example, psychologists in some mental hospitals select behavior they judge desirable. Patients are then rewarded for these behaviors with tokens. Thus if a patient cleans his room or works in the hospital garden, he is rewarded with token money. The patients are able to cash in their token money for things they want, such as candy or cigarettes, or for certain privileges, such as time away from the ward. These methods are successful in inducing patients to begin leading active lives. They learn to take care of themselves and to take on responsibility instead of having to be cared for constantly.

token economy: desirable behavior is reinforced with valueless objects or points, which can be accumulated and exchanged for various rewards

COGNITIVE-BEHAVIOR THERAPY

Many therapists combine aspects of cognitive and behavior therapies. **Cognitive-behavior therapy** focuses on setting goals for changing a client's behavior and then, unlike other behavior therapies, placing more emphasis on changing the client's interpretation of his or her situation. This type of therapy seeks to help clients differentiate between serious, real problems and imagined or distorted problems. A cognitive-behavior therapist might work with a client to change certain behaviors by monitoring current behaviors and thought patterns, setting progressively difficult goals, reinforcing positive changes, substituting positive thoughts for negative thoughts, and practicing new behaviors in a safe setting. Many self-help programs use this approach. For example, you might begin a program of developing positive self-esteem by using these techniques. Cognitive-behavior therapies are becoming increasingly widespread and have proven effective for treating a wide range of problems.

cognitive-behavior therapy: based on a combination of substituting healthy thoughts for negative thoughts and beliefs and changing disruptive behaviors in favor of healthy behaviors

SECTION 3 Assessment

1. **Review the Vocabulary** How does cognitive therapy differ from behavior therapy?
2. **Visualize the Main Idea** In a diagram similar to the one below, list and describe rational-emotive therapy techniques.

3. **Recall Information** How does aversive conditioning work?
4. **Think Critically** Sheila was not picked to be a basketball captain in gym class. She thought the gym teacher didn't pick her because Sheila is short. Sheila became angry with the teacher and acted rudely in gym class. Explain this scenario using what psychologist Albert Ellis calls the *ABCs*.
5. **Application Activity** Pick something of which you are afraid. Construct a plan for using systematic desensitization to help you overcome this fear.

SECTION 3 Assessment Answers

1. Cognitivists seek to change beliefs that will change the way people feel about events. Behaviorists seek to change behaviors to resolve problems.
2. Role-playing allows the person to see how beliefs affect relationships. Modeling demonstrates ways of thinking and acting. Humor can point out the absurdity of beliefs. Specific homework assignments and simple persuasion can challenge the person to act more reasonably.
3. Aversive conditioning associates a negative feeling or result with an undesired behavior, allowing a person to change a behavior.
4. A: Sheila was not chosen. B: She was not chosen because she is short. The teacher doesn't want short basketball players in class. C: Sheila felt slighted and unwanted, therefore she acted up.
5. Students' answers will vary. The plan should show step-by-step counterconditioning.

Reteach

Divide the class in half for a discussion comparing behavioral and cognitive therapies. One half of the class will be behaviorists and take the position that people can best be helped by finding ways to change their behaviors. The other half of the class will be cognitivists and take the position that people can best be helped by changing their beliefs.

Enrich

Describe to students the hypothetical case of a teen who hasn't learned to drive because he has an intense fear of learning to drive an automobile. Tell students that the teen was recently in a car with his older brother when they had a minor accident. Have students design a course of therapy for this teen using one of the methods discussed in this section.

4 CLOSE

Have students draw a diagram showing how each of the counterconditioning methods works.

1 FOCUS

Section Objectives

1. Explain biological approaches to treatment.
2. Give examples of treatment medicines and their effects on patients.

BELLRINGER
Motivational Activity

Project Daily Focus Transparency 17–4 and have students answer the questions.

Also available as blackline master

Daily Focus Transparency 17–4

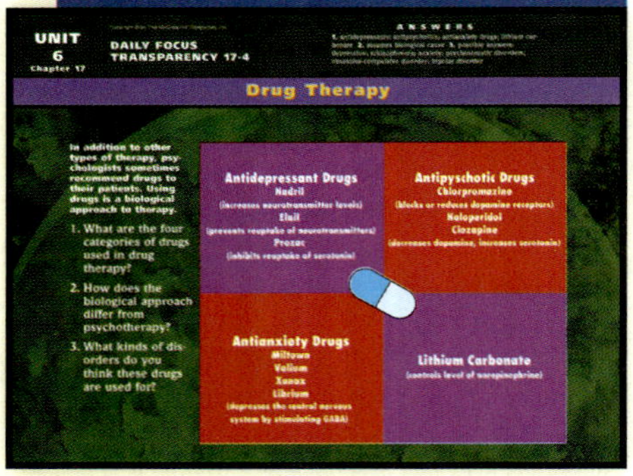

Reader's Guide

Use the Reader's Guide to introduce concepts and vocabulary.

Exploring Psychology
Ask students to read the **Exploring Psychology** feature and then discuss the following: **What reasons can you suggest for why medication works in some cases while psychotherapy does not?**

Vocabulary Precheck
Have students read the Glossary definitions of the terms. Then have them create flash cards with the terms on one side and definitions on the other. Students should use the flash cards to study the terms.

Use the **Vocabulary PuzzleMaker CD-ROM** to create crossword and word search puzzles.

SECTION 4 Biological Approaches to Treatment

Reader's Guide

Main Idea
Biological approaches to treatment rely on methods such as medications, electric shock, and surgery to help clients.

Vocabulary
- drug therapy
- antipsychotic drugs
- antidepressants
- lithium carbonate
- antianxiety drugs
- electroconvulsive therapy (ECT)
- psychosurgery
- prefrontal lobotomy

Objectives
- Explain biological approaches to treatment.
- Give examples of treatment medicines and their effects on patients.

EXPLORING PSYCHOLOGY

Medical Miracles?

Susan A. has spent most of her adult life fighting with people—her parents, her neighbors, her co-workers, and her husband. The 39-year-old Seattle woman has suffered bouts of depression and bulimia, abused drugs and alcohol, and twice tried to kill herself. She once sought relief in an antidepressant called doxepin, but she didn't like the way it made her feel.

Two years ago her therapist, Dr. Michael Norden, suggested she try a new drug called Prozac. She did. Within a month, Susan had given up psychotherapy in favor of school and a full-time job. She had also given up tranquilizers and street drugs. "I feel 1,000%," she said in a written note. "I actually like Mom and Dad now, I'm well liked at work, I don't ruminate on the negatives, I don't have murderous rages, my marriage is five times better."

—from "The Promise of Prozac" by G. Cowley, in *Newsweek*, March 26, 1990

People with ear infections are given antibiotics, and within about 10 days, most infections are gone. Could the same approach be used for people with psychological problems? According to Susan A.'s testimonial, the drug Prozac seemed to alleviate her psychological problems. Some experts believe that biological therapies, such as medications, should be reserved for people who fail to respond to psychotherapy. Other experts believe that a combination of psychotherapy and biological therapy is the answer for many patients.

SECTION RESOURCES

Reproducible Masters
- Guided Reading Activity 17–4
- Vocabulary Activity 17–4
- Section Quiz 17–4

Transparencies
- Daily Focus Transparency 17–4

Multimedia
- Vocabulary PuzzleMaker CD-ROM
- *ExamView*® *Assessment Suite* CD-ROM
- Presentation Plus! Software

BIOLOGICAL THERAPY

It is not possible for therapists to help all people with the therapies described so far in the chapter. The various talking and learning therapies have been aimed primarily at patients who are still generally capable of functioning within society.

Biological approaches to treatment assume there is an underlying physiological reason for the disturbed behavior, the faulty thinking, and the inappropriate emotions the person displays. Biological therapy uses methods such as medication, electric shock, and surgery to help people with psychological disorders.

Since these treatments are medical in nature, physicians or psychiatrists typically administer them. In recent years, some qualified psychologists also have begun prescribing drugs, but all may help decide whether a biological approach to treatment is appropriate for their patients.

Figure 17.11 Starting Biological Therapy

The patient is meeting with her doctor to discuss treatment and evaluate how she is doing and what should happen next. ***When would a psychiatrist suggest that a patient try medications?***

Drug Therapy

The most widely used biological therapy for psychological disorders is **drug therapy.** Drug therapy involves four main types of psychoactive medications: antipsychotic drugs, antidepressant drugs, lithium, and antianxiety drugs. Prescribed drug therapy medications relieve psychiatric symptoms and increase the usefulness of other forms of psychotherapy. They are a temporary cure, however. When patients undergoing drug therapy stop taking the medication, symptoms typically reappear. Often, drugs treat only the symptoms; drug therapy does not remove the causes of the disorder.

drug therapy: biological therapy that uses medications

Antipsychotic Drugs For a long time the most common method of helping dangerous or overactive schizophrenic patients was physical restraint—the straitjacket, wet-sheet wrapping, and isolation. Doctors calmed the patient by means of psychosurgery or electroconvulsive shock (discussed later).

Patients with schizophrenia are usually prescribed **antipsychotic drugs.** These drugs have helped schizophrenics stay out of mental institutions. Many patients with schizophrenia who take these drugs improve in a number of ways: they become more vigilant and attentive, with improved problem-solving and organization skills. However, it may reduce their fine motor skills (Dixon et al., 1995). One theory of schizophrenia proposes that when a person's dopamine neurotransmitter system somehow becomes overactive, that person develops schizophrenia. These medicines inhibit dopamine receptor sites. Drugs like chlorpromazine (such as Thorazine)

antipsychotic drugs: medication to reduce agitation, delusions, and hallucinations by blocking the activity of dopamine in the brain; tranquilizers

CHAPTER 17

Section 4, pages 506–510

2 TEACH

L1 Weighing Advantages and Disadvantages After students have reviewed the information on the biological treatment of psychological disorders with drugs, organize a panel discussion in which students debate the use of drug therapy for schizophrenia, depression, bipolar disorder, and anxiety. Assign panelists to represent the following points of view: a psychiatrist, a behavioral psychologist, a health care worker, an insurance company spokesperson, and several patients.

Figure 17.11

Caption Answer Medication is used for people who fail to respond to psychotherapy. The psychiatrist may suspect that there is an underlying physiological reason for the disturbed behavior.

Guided Reading Activity 17–4

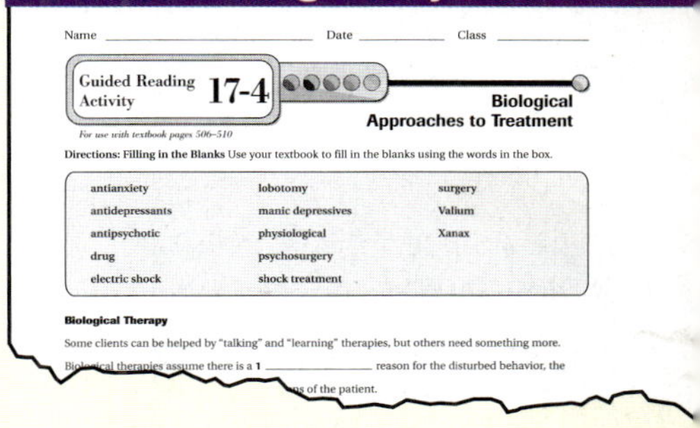

Name ______ Date ______ Class ______

Guided Reading Activity 17-4

Biological Approaches to Treatment

For use with textbook pages 506–510

Directions: Filling in the Blanks Use your textbook to fill in the blanks using the words in the box.

antianxiety	lobotomy	surgery
antidepressants	manic depressives	Valium
antipsychotic	physiological	Xanax
drug	psychosurgery	
electric shock	shock treatment	

Biological Therapy

Some clients can be helped by "talking" and "learning" therapies, but others need something more. Biological therapies assume there is a 1 ______ reason for the disturbed behavior, the ... of the patient.

COOPERATIVE LEARNING ACTIVITY

Creating a Fact Sheet Organize students into small groups to create a drug fact sheet that pharmacists can distribute with prescriptions. Assign each group one of the drugs discussed in the text or newer drugs that have received FDA approval, such as Risperdel, Luvox, or Zoloft. Have the groups use *The Physician's Desk Reference* (Medical Economics Company) or similar source for their research. You may want to check with a local pharmacist for samples of drug fact sheets that students could use as models. **BLOCK SCHEDULING**

Psychology and You

Use the following question to direct a class discussion after students have read the **Psychology and You** feature.

Ask: **What services besides food and shelter should society provide to the homeless?**

Vocabulary Activity 17–4

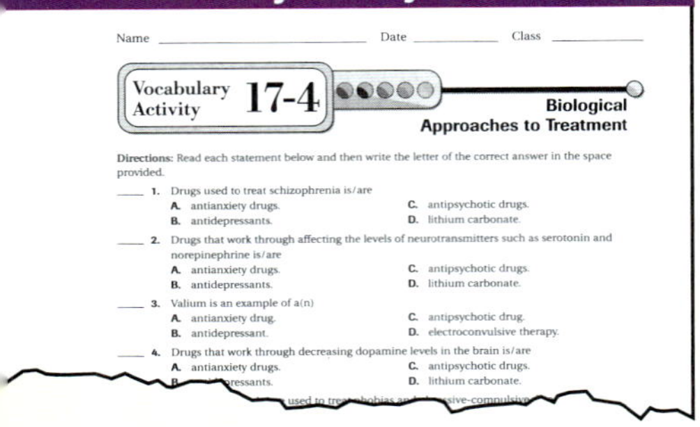
Name ______ Date ______ Class ______

Vocabulary Activity 17-4

Biological Approaches to Treatment

Directions: Read each statement below and then write the letter of the correct answer in the space provided.

____ **1.** Drugs used to treat schizophrenia is/are
A. antianxiety drugs. **C.** antipsychotic drugs.
B. antidepressants. **D.** lithium carbonate.

____ **2.** Drugs that work through affecting the levels of neurotransmitters such as serotonin and norepinephrine is/are
A. antianxiety drugs. **C.** antipsychotic drugs.
B. antidepressants. **D.** lithium carbonate.

____ **3.** Valium is an example of a(n)
A. antianxiety drug. **C.** antipsychotic drug.
B. antidepressant. **D.** electroconvulsive therapy.

____ **4.** Drugs that work through decreasing dopamine levels in the brain is/are
A. antianxiety drugs. **C.** antipsychotic drugs.
B. ...pressants. **D.** lithium carbonate.

Readings and Case Studies in Psychology

Have students read the Chapter 17 Case Study selection in *Readings and Case Studies in Psychology* and answer the questions that follow the case study.

PSYCHOLOGY JOURNAL

Tell students that a doctor has recommended to a family member that he or she receive ECT to treat severe depression. Have students write a series of questions that the family member should ask before agreeing to the treatment. ■

Psychology and You: Homelessness: A Legacy of Deinstitutionalization

Homelessness is a major problem in the United States, and it is likely that you come into contact with the homeless at least occasionally. When you do, you may be observing a person with a psychological disorder.

Estimates suggest that 20 to 25 percent of the homeless are mentally ill. This is not a direct result of deinstitutionalization, which released many people in the 1950s and 1960s. Rather, it apparently results from declining housing options and income. Denial of services and reduced care options forced by managed-care providers also may be involved (National Coalition for the Homeless, 2005).

Since the introduction of antipsychotic drugs in the 1950s, the number of patients confined to mental institutions has steadily dropped. Unfortunately, most antipsychotic drugs do not cure disorders. Rather, they merely control the more obvious symptoms of psychological disorders so that patients are no longer dangerous. Thus, there is no longer any reason to keep these people institutionalized.

Many patients who have been released from institutions often find it impossible to hold steady jobs or to live on their own. In this way, the noble goal of deinstitutionalization has contributed to the problem of homelessness.

and haloperidol (such as Haldol) block or reduce the sensitivity of dopamine receptors. Clozapine (such as Closaril) decreases dopamine activity and increases the serotonin level, which inhibits the dopamine system. While these drugs reduce symptoms, there can be unpleasant side effects, such as muscular rigidity, impaired coordination, and tremors.

Antidepressant drugs Another class of drugs, called **antidepressants,** relieves depression. Depression is accompanied by imbalances in the nuerotransmitters serotonin and norepinephrine. Monoamine oxidase (MAO) inhibitors, such as Nadril, elevate the levels of certain neurotransmitters by inhibiting their breakdown. Tricyclicantide-pressants, such as Elail, increase levels of these neurotransmitters by preventing the reuptake of these transmitters into the axon terminals. Antidepressants may have unpleasant side effects, such as dizziness, fatigue, forgetfulness, and weight gain. Selective serotonin reuptake inhibitors (SSRI), such as those in Prozac, work the same way but target the neurotransmitter serotonin.

antidepressants: medication to treat major depression by increasing the amount of one or both of the neurotransmitters noradrenaline and serotonin

lithium carbonate: a chemical used to counteract mood swings of bipolar disorder

antianxiety drugs: medication that relieves anxiety and panic disorders by depressing the activity of the central nervous system

Lithium Carbonate **Lithium carbonate** is widely used by people with a bipolar disorder to counteract extreme mood swings. While all of the other medications described here are synthetic, lithium is a natural chemical element that controls levels of norepinephrine. Lithium can cause side effects if not administered under proper supervision. Lithium salts reduce the symptoms of people with a bipolar disorder more so than for those with a unipolar depression. Many psychological and biological mechanisms provoke depression, but only a single brain network generates mania. It is likely that these are two different illnesses (Bower, 2000).

Antianxiety Drugs Commonly known as sedatives or mild tranquilizers, **antianxiety drugs** are used to reduce excitability and cause drowsiness. First the barbiturates, then Miltown (meprobamate), and eventually the benzodiazepines have been very popular prescriptions in recent decades. At one time Valium was the most popular prescription drug in the country. Now several benzodiazepines, which are prescribed for panic attacks and agoraphobia and include Xanax (alprazolam), have joined it among the 75 most prescribed drugs.

MEETING SPECIAL NEEDS

Learning Style: Naturalist Have students research some of the "natural" alternatives to traditional drug therapy, such as nutritional supplements, vitamins, and minerals. Challenge students to discover what psychological disorders these natural remedies claim to treat. Also, encourage them to discover the history of some of these remedies. Have students list the recognized benefits and dangers of using these natural alternatives. **L2** **BLOCK SCHEDULING**

Refer to ***Inclusion for the High School Social Studies Classroom Strategies and Activities*** in the TCR for strategies for students with different learning styles.

Figure 17.12 Deinstitutionalization

Over the past three decades the national policy has been one of deinstitutionalization. Deinstitutionalization refers to the release of patients from mental hospitals. These patients rejoin the community to attempt to lead independent lives. ***How has the number of days patients spend in mental hospitals changed since 1980?***

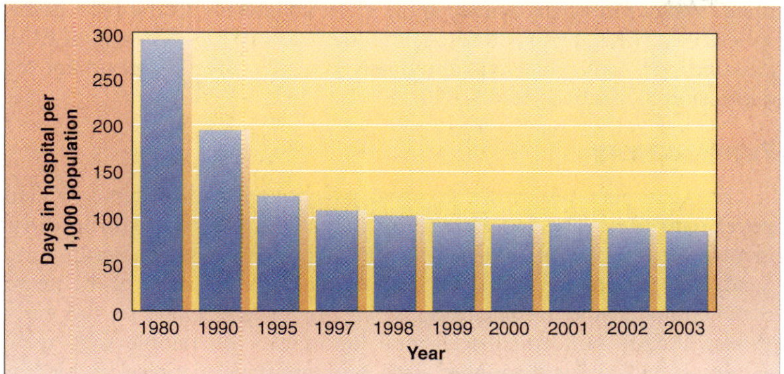

Source: U.S. Bureau of the Census, *Statistical Abstract of the United States*, 2003, 2006.

While these drugs are effective for helping normal people cope with difficult periods in their lives, they are also prescribed for the alleviation of various anxiety-based symptoms, psychosomatic problems, and symptoms of alcohol withdrawal. The major effect of Valium, Librium, and Miltown is to depress the activity of the central nervous system by stimulating the action of the neurotransmitter GABA (gamma-aminobutyric acid).

Reading Check What is the major effect of antianxiety drugs?

If antianxiety drugs are taken properly, the side effects are few and consist mainly of drowsiness. However, prolonged use may lead to dependence, and heavy doses taken along with alcohol can result in death. These drugs do reduce anxiety, but the best use seems to be for dealing with acute (temporary) rather than chronic (long-term) anxiety. (Mellinger, Balter, & Uhlenhuth, 1985).

Electroconvulsive Therapy

Electroconvulsive therapy (ECT), commonly called shock treatment, has proved extremely effective in the treatment of severe depression, acute mania, and some types of schizophrenia (Koop, 2001). No one understands exactly how it works, but it involves administering, over several weeks, a series of brief electrical shocks of approximately 70–150 volts for 0.1–1.0 seconds. The shock induces a convulsion in the brain similar to an epileptic seizure that may last up to a minute.

electroconvulsive therapy (ECT): an electrical shock is sent through the brain to try to reduce symptoms of mental disturbance

Many people consider ECT a controversial treatment. In the past, it was not always used judiciously. As a result, some people experienced extensive amnesia, as well as problems with language and verbal abilities. Today, electroconvulsive therapy entails very little discomfort for the patient. Prior to treatment, the

Figure 17.12

Visual Instruction Discuss as a class the reasons for the steep decline in the number of days spent in the hospital.

Caption Answer By 2003, the number was less than one-third what it was in 1980.

Reading Check Answer Antianxiety drugs reduce excitability and cause drowsiness. They help normal people cope with difficult periods in their lives and relieve anxiety-based symptoms, psychosomatic problems, and symptoms of alcohol withdrawal.

CULTURAL CONNECTIONS

In the United States, the American Psychiatric Association supports the use of ECT for severe mood disorders and other specific cases. It is not generally regarded as a useful treatment for schizophrenia. In India, ECT is frequently used to treat schizophrenia. *Source:* Shukla, G.D. (1989). Electroconvulsive therapy: A review. *Indian Journal of Psychiatry, 31,* 97–115.

3 ASSESS

Assign Section 4 Assessment as homework or as an in-class activity.

CRITICAL THINKING ACTIVITY

Identifying Central Issues Tell students that in Berkeley, California, voters passed a law to ban the use of ECT in their area. The courts later overturned the law. Have students review information on ECT. **Ask:** **What are the pros and cons of its use?** Working individually or in small groups, challenge students to write a position paper on the use of ECT in their community. The paper should address what, if any, legal restrictions should be applied to this form of treatment. Remind students to use standard grammar, spelling, sentence structure, and punctuation. **L2**

CHAPTER 17

Section 4, pages 506–510

Section Quiz 17–4

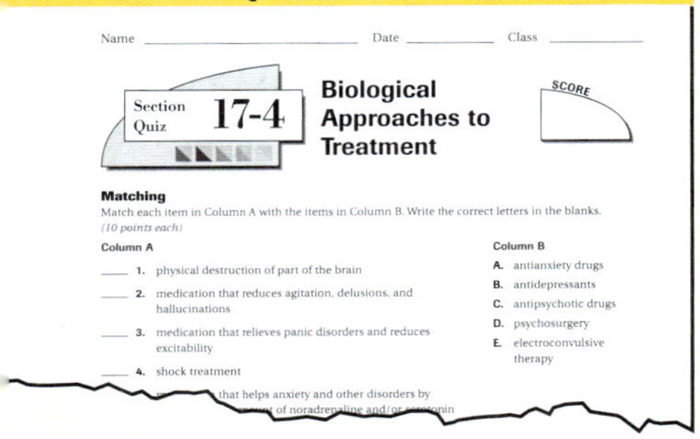
Name ____ Date ____ Class ____

Section Quiz 17-4 **Biological Approaches to Treatment**

SCORE

Matching

Match each item in Column A with the items in Column B. Write the correct letters in the blanks. *(10 points each)*

Column A

____ **1.** physical destruction of part of the brain

____ **2.** medication that reduces agitation, delusions, and hallucinations

____ **3.** medication that relieves panic disorders and reduces excitability

____ **4.** shock treatment

that helps anxiety and other disorders by ... of noradrenaline and/or serotonin

Column B

A. antianxiety drugs

B. antidepressants

C. antipsychotic drugs

D. psychosurgery

E. electroconvulsive therapy

Reteach

List the various categories of psychological disorders discussed in Chapter 16. For each, have students list the type of biological treatments that could be used, including the specific types of drugs that may be prescribed.

Enrich

Challenge students to find out how the cingulatomy and stereotaxic subcaudate tractotomy (SST) differ from prefrontal lobotomies.

4 CLOSE

Have students compare the effectiveness of biological therapies to other forms of treatment discussed in the chapter.

patient is given a sedative and injected with a muscle relaxant to alleviate involuntary muscular contractions. Even with these improvements, however, electroconvulsive therapy is a drastic treatment and must be used with great caution. Many people experience some memory problems after receiving this treatment. When ECT is applied bilaterally—with the electric current running across both of the brain's hemispheres—the patient may lose memory for events occurring one to two days before the treatment. Today physicians usually apply ECT unilaterally to the right hemisphere only. This technique results in little memory loss. The use of ECT has declined somewhat, but it remains a highly effective treatment for depression (Thienhaus et al., 1990).

Psychosurgery

psychosurgery: a medical operation that destroys part of the brain to make the patient calmer and freer of symptoms

prefrontal lobotomy: a radical form of psychosurgery in which a section of the frontal lobe of the brain is destroyed

Brain surgery performed to treat psychological disorders is called **psychosurgery.** The most common operation, **prefrontal lobotomy,** involves destruction of the front portion of the brain, just behind the forehead. This part of the brain, the frontal lobe, contains most of the nerve connections that control emotions. From the late 1930s to the early 1950s, doctors performed prefrontal lobotomies on people who were extremely violent or diagnosed with schizophrenia, depression, bipolar disorder, and obsessive-compulsive disorder. The use of prefrontal lobotomies decreased significantly in the mid-1950s, when newly developed drugs offered alternative treatments. At the same time, mounting evidence indicated that lobotomized patients showed an inability to plan. Furthermore, destroyed brain tissue never regenerates, so the effects are permanent. Patients may become apathetic and less creative after surgery. Although specific nerve tracts and areas of the brain can now be located very precisely, less than 200 prefrontal lobotomies are performed annually in the United States (Sabbatini, 1997).

SECTION 4 Assessment

1. **Review the Vocabulary** Describe how antipsychotic drugs, antidepressants, and antianxiety drugs work as therapy.
2. **Visualize the Main Idea** In a graphic organizer similar to the one below, list and explain the biological approaches to treatment.

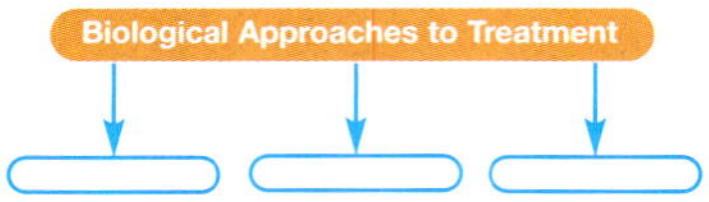

3. **Recall Information** Why is psychosurgery controversial? Why is it used?
4. **Think Critically** Describe a situation in which you believe a therapist would suggest biological therapy involving psychosurgery for a patient.
5. **Application Activity** Imagine that you have been asked to give a talk about the biological approaches to psychological problems. Create an outline for your speech.

SECTION 4 Assessment Answers

1. These approaches to treatment assume that there is an underlying physiological reason for the disturbed behavior. They treat only the symptoms of the disorders; they do not remove the causes.
2. Drug therapy treats symptoms of various disorders. ECT causes a convulsion and can help those with severe depression. Psychosurgery reduces aggressiveness and violent behavior in people with certain severe psychological disorders.
3. It cannot be reversed and may have unintended results. It may be used in extreme cases that have not responded to other forms of treatment.
4. A person who has lost contact with reality and cannot obtain insight from psychotherapy, or is suicidal, has a severe psychological disorder and has not responded to psychotherapy or drug therapy may be a candidate for psychosurgery.
5. Outlines should be well-ordered and address benefits and concerns of the various biological approaches.

CHAPTER 17

Summary and Vocabulary

People who suffer from emotional problems often seek therapy from mental health professionals. The help these professionals provide is called psychotherapy.

Section 1 What Is Psychotherapy?

Main Idea: Psychotherapy is a general term for the several approaches used by mental health professionals to treat psychological disorders.

- Mental health professionals who have been trained to deal with the psychological problems of others include counseling and clinical psychologists, psychiatrists, and social workers.
- An important function of psychotherapy is to help people realize that they are responsible for their own problems and that they are the only ones who can really solve these problems.

Section 2 Psychoanalysis and Humanistic Therapy

Main Idea: Psychoanalysis is an analysis of the conscious and unconscious mind based on the theories of psychoanalyst Sigmund Freud. Humanistic therapy helps people reach their full potential.

- A main goal of a psychoanalyst is to help make patients aware of the unconscious impulses, desires, and fears that are causing their anxieties.
- Humanistic psychology has given rise to several approaches to psychotherapy known as client-centered therapy.
- Client-centered therapists believe that psychological problems arise when the true sense of self becomes lost and the individual comes to view himself or herself according to the standards of others.

Section 3 Cognitive and Behavior Therapies

Main Idea: Cognitive and behavior therapies help clients develop new ways of thinking and behaving.

- Cognitive therapists focus on changing the way people think about their own problems.
- Behavior therapists concentrate on determining what is specifically troubling with a patient's life and taking steps to change it.

Section 4 Biological Approaches to Treatment

Main Idea: Biological approaches to treatment rely on methods such as medications, electric shock, and surgery to help clients.

- Biological approaches to treatment assume there is an underlying physiological reason for the disturbed behavior, faulty thinking, and inappropriate emotions an individual displays.
- Drug therapy involves four main types of medications—antipsychotic drugs, antidepressant drugs, lithium, and antianxiety drugs.
- Electroconvulsive therapy is a rare, drastic treatment that is used with great caution.
- Psychosurgery involves destroying part of the brain to free the patient of symptoms.

Chapter Vocabulary

psychotherapy (p. 486)
eclectic approach (p. 487)
placebo effect (p. 488)
empathy (p. 489)
group therapy (p. 489)
psychoanalysis (p. 494)
insight (p. 494)
free association (p. 494)
resistance (p. 494)
dream analysis (p. 495)
transference (p. 495)
humanistic therapy (p. 496)
client-centered therapy (p. 496)
nondirective therapy (p. 496)
active listening (p. 497)
unconditional positive regard (p. 497)
behavior modification (p. 499)
cognitive therapy (p. 499)
rational-emotive therapy (RET) (p. 500)
behavior therapy (p. 502)
systematic desensitization (p. 503)
aversive conditioning (p. 504)
contingency management (p. 504)
token economy (p. 505)
cognitive-behavior therapy (p. 505)
drug therapy (p. 507)
antipsychotic drugs (p. 507)
antidepressants (p. 508)
lithium carbonate (p. 508)
antianxiety drugs (p. 508)
electroconvulsive therapy (ECT) (p. 509)
psychosurgery (p. 510)
prefrontal lobotomy (p. 510)

17 Summary and Vocabulary

Using the Chapter 17 Summary and Vocabulary

Use the Chapter 17 Summary and Vocabulary to preview, review, condense, or reteach the chapter.

Preview/Review

Use the Chapter Vocabulary list to help students review and study.

Activity Ask students to list the terms on separate index cards or slips of paper. Have them match the terms to the following headings: *Psychoanalysis, Humanistic Therapy, Cognitive and Behavior Therapies, Biological Therapies,* and *Other.*

Vocabulary PuzzleMaker CD-ROM reinforces the vocabulary terms used in Chapter 17.

Condense

Have students read the Chapter 17 Summary.

Chapter 17 Guided Reading Activities

Reteach

Reteaching Activity 17

PERFORMANCE ASSESSMENT ACTIVITY

Statement of Criteria Explain that one of the problems of determining the effectiveness of psychotherapy is the lack of agreed-upon criteria for success. Tell students they are members of a task force formed by the the American Psychiatric Association to establish criteria for the effectiveness of psychotherapy. Remind them that their criteria should be in measurable form so that data can be collected and analyzed. As a guiding question, **ask:** **How would a therapist or client know that it is time to end therapy sessions?**

Refer to the ***Authentic Assessment*** booklet for additional activities and information about evaluating student performance.

17 Assessment

PSYCHOLOGY Online

Have students visit the Web site at glencoe.com to review Chapter 17 and take the **Self-Check Quiz**.

GLENCOE TECHNOLOGY

For a review of Chapter 17 content, see MindJogger Checkpoint on **Presentation Plus!**

CHAPTER 17 Assessment

PSYCHOLOGY Online

Self-Check Quiz
Visit the *Understanding Psychology* Web site at glencoe.com and click on **Chapter 17—Self-Check Quizzes** to prepare for the Chapter Test.

Reviewing Vocabulary

Choose the letter of the correct term or concept below to complete the sentence.

a. eclectic approach
b. empathy
c. insight
d. free association
e. active listening
f. unconditional positive regard
g. systematic desensitization
h. aversive conditioning
i. antipsychotic drugs
j. lithium carbonate

1. Some psychotherapists use a(n) __________ to therapy, using many different methods.
2. Patients with schizophrenia are often treated with __________.
3. A technique in which people are urged to imagine a feared situation in order to extinguish the fear is called __________.
4. In a communication technique called __________, the client-centered therapist tries to echo back the feelings the client has expressed.
5. __________, or people's understanding of their unconscious motives, is the first step toward gaining control over their behavior.
6. An effective psychotherapist has __________, or a capacity for warmth and understanding.
7. In a technique called __________, individuals learn to associate negative feelings with the behavior they want to avoid.
8. Talking about everything that comes to mind is called __________.
9. Client-centered therapy is conducted in an atmosphere of emotional support called __________.
10. __________ is often used to bring manic-depressive people to a state of equilibrium.

Recalling Facts

1. How do self-help groups help people deal with problems?
2. What is the goal of psychoanalysis? What does the therapist do to achieve this goal?
3. Using a diagram similar to the one below, describe the main techniques of client-centered therapy.

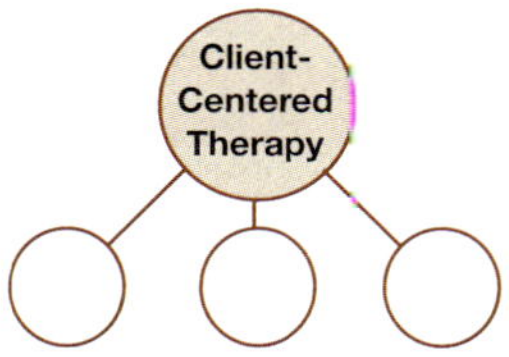

4. What steps does a rational-emotive therapist expect the client to take to solve his or her problems?
5. Identify the effects of antipsychotic drugs, antidepressants, and antianxiety drugs.

Critical Thinking

1. **Making Inferences** One technique that client-centered therapists use is active listening. What does this technique involve? Do you think active listening might be effective in improving day-to-day communication between people? Explain.
2. **Demonstrating Reasoned Judgment** Do you agree with Albert Ellis that it is not the event in a person's life that causes trouble but rather the way a person thinks about the event? Explain.
3. **Evaluating Information** Make a list of a few fears that you have. Rank them from least fearful to most fearful. Do you think any of your fears are based on conditioning? Describe a method of counterconditioning that you think would remove the fear or make it less intense.
4. **Making Comparisons** What do you think are the major differences between psychoanalysis and behavior therapy?
5. **Analyzing Information** Do you think psychosurgery should ever be used to treat psychological problems? Why?

Reviewing Vocabulary

1. a	**6.** b
2. i	**7.** h
3. g	**8.** d
4. e	**9.** f
5. c	**10.** j

Recalling Facts

1. They allow people to participate voluntarily and help one another work through problems shared in common.
2. The goal of psychoanalysis is to make the patient aware of unconscious motives, desires, and fears that are causing anxiety. The psychoanalyst uses free association, dream analysis, and verbal interaction over a long period of time.
3. nondirective therapy, in which the therapist listens and encourages conversation but does not give opinions; active listening, in which the therapist echoes back the feelings expressed by the client; unconditional positive regard, which is emotional support and acceptance provided by the therapist
4. Steps would include recognizing false assumptions, developing an awareness of how these assumptions affect behavior, and working to break old habits of thought and behavior.
5. Antipsychotic drugs reduce agitation, delusions, and hallucinations by decreasing dopamine activity. Antidepressants are used to treat major depression by regulating levels of serotonin and norepinephrine. Antianxiety drugs relieve anxiety and panic disorders by depressing activity of the central nervous system by stimulating the neurotransmitter GABA.

Critical Thinking

1. Active listening involves the therapist echoing back the feelings expressed by the client without making judgments or reaching conclusions. Active listening can avoid misunderstandings and allow people to focus on what others are really saying.
2. Answers will vary. Encourage students to provide specific examples supporting their points of view.
3. To encourage a true assessment of students' fears, tell them that they will not be required to share any private information if it makes them uncomfortable. Students should propose a logical counterconditioning technique to overcome their fears.
4. Psychoanalysis is a slow process in which the analyst helps the client examine the unconscious motives behind his or her behavior. Behavior therapy is more action-oriented and tends to take less time than psychoanalysis.
5. Psychosurgery may be warranted under extreme circumstances, after all other forms of therapy have failed.

Psychology Projects

1. Students should make arrangements to attend prior to the meeting. Advise students that some meetings are "closed" to observers to protect the privacy of the participants.

Psychology Projects

1. **What Is Psychotherapy?** Attend an open meeting of one of the following self-help support groups: Alcoholics Anonymous, Al-Anon, Alateen, Smokenders, Narcotics Anonymous, Weight Watchers, or Overeaters Anonymous. Go with a classmate so that you can share your observations and experiences. Notice and report to the class on the ways in which the group provides support for people.
2. **Humanistic Therapies** Research existential therapies and transactional analysis, which are two other types of client-centered therapies. What are the basic beliefs? Summarize your research and report your findings in an essay or brief presentation to the class.
3. **Behavior Therapies** Operant conditioning is based on the assumption that reinforced behavior tends to be repeated. Behavior therapy often involves a system of rewards called token economies. Propose a token economy that could be used in your school. Describe what rewards would be used and what behaviors they would reinforce.
4. **Biological Approaches to Treatment** Go to your local library or video store to find a movie that portrays mental illness. You might view *One Flew Over the Cuckoo's Nest* or *Awakenings*. Describe and classify some of the patients' symptoms and the kinds of treatments that were administered. Describe the effectiveness of the treatments in a written report.

Technology Activity

Search the Internet for sites that provide online psychotherapy services. Find out what types of problems are generally addressed in these sites. Report your findings in a written report.

Psychology Journal

Reread the recommendations for treatment that you wrote in your journal. How do the techniques you suggest resemble the therapies described in this chapter? Answer this question in your journal.

Building Skills

Interpreting a Graph Review the graph below, then answer the questions that follow.

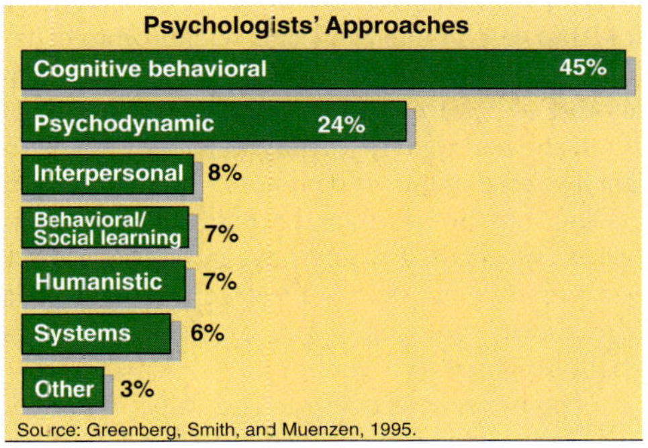

1. What percentage of psychologists uses behavior therapies? Interpersonal therapies?
2. Which type of psychotherapy is used by the greatest percentage of psychologists? Why do you think this is so?
3. Psychodynamic therapy (or short-term dynamic psychotherapy) is an approach that is similar to psychoanalysis. Why do you think more therapists practice psychodynamic therapy rather than classical psychoanalysis?
4. How popular do you think biological approaches are? Why do you think so? Investigate this question and report your findings to the class.

Practice and **assess** key social studies skills with **Glencoe Skillbuilder Interactive Workbook CD-ROM, Level 2.**

See the Skills Handbook, page 628, for an explanation of interpreting graphs.

Building Skills

1. 7%; 8%
2. cognitive behavioral; student answers will vary but may mention that the method combines cognitive and behavioral approaches, offering a wide range of treatments
3. Under managed care where the cost drives the decision, psychodynamic therapy is preferred because it takes less time than traditional psychoanalysis.
4. Answers will vary. Drug therapy will likely grow in importance because it is relatively inexpensive and reasonably effective at treating the major symptoms of some disorders.

GLENCOE TECHNOLOGY

CD-ROM
Glencoe Skillbuilder Interactive Workbook, Level 2

This interactive CD-ROM is designed to reinforce student mastery of essential social studies skills.

Chapter Bonus Test Question

This question may be used for extra credit on the Chapter Assessment.
Answer the following question:
I am the psychologist who questioned Hans Eysenck's view that psychotherapy is no more effective than no treatment at all. Who am I?
Answer: Allen Bergin

2. Challenge students to discover why these therapies are no longer popular.
3. Remind students that the goal of behavior therapy is behavior modification. Students may wish to review token economies by looking at Chapter 9.
4. Challenge students to present their ideas in the form of a case study.

Technology Activity

Ask students to speculate on the future of psychotherapy services on the Internet.

Psychology Journal

Answers will vary. Encourage students to revise their recommended treatments for these disorders based upon what they have learned in this chapter.

Readings in Psychology

Block Schedule

This activity works well for a block-scheduling framework.

Reinforcing Vocabulary

Review the **Reader's Dictionary** terms with students to be sure they understand any unfamiliar items.

Background Information

The Bell Jar is one vehicle that Sylvia Plath used to describe her own battle with depression, attempted suicide, and electroshock therapy. Her poems were her other vehicle. In them she expresses her deepest emotions—fear, loneliness, and depression.

Sylvia's own story does not have a happy ending. Although she was a successful poet and novelist, she did not win her battle with depression. She committed suicide on her third attempt. She was only 30 years old.

Her husband, British poet laureate Ted Hughes, did not speak publicly about his wife's suicide for 35 years. In 1998, he published *Birthday Letters,* which is a collection of poems about his relationship with Sylvia. In them he describes the ups and downs of their relationship and her battles with depression.

Readings In Psychology

In the novel *The Bell Jar,* nineteen-year-old Esther Greenwood wins a dream assignment on a New York fashion magazine, but she quickly finds herself sinking into despair. In this excerpt, Esther receives electroshock therapy at Belsize hospital after attempting to commit suicide. This novel is largely autobiographical—poet-author Sylvia Plath ended her own life a month after the book's publication in 1963.

Reader's Dictionary

alcove: a small recessed section of a room

electrotherapy: treatment or therapy that uses electricity; electroconvulsive therapy (ECT)

pallid: lacking sparkle or liveliness

THE BELL JAR

BY SYLVIA PLATH

The nurse rapped on my door and, without waiting for an answer, breezed in.

It was a new nurse—they were always changing—with a lean, sand-colored face and sandy hair, and large freckles polka-dotting her bony nose. For some reason the sight of this nurse made me sick at heart, and it was only as she strode across the room to snap up the green blind that I realized part of her strangeness came from being empty-handed.

I opened my mouth to ask for my breakfast tray, but silenced myself immediately. The nurse would be mistaking me for somebody else. New nurses often did that. Somebody in Belsize must be having shock treatments, unknown to me, and the nurse had, quite understandably, confused me with her.

I waited until the nurse had made her little circuit of my room, patting, straightening, arranging, and taken the next tray in to Loubelle one door farther down the hall.

Then I shoved my feet into my slippers, dragging my blanket with me, for the morning was bright, but very cold, and crossed quickly to the kitchen. The pink-uniformed maid was filling a row of blue china coffee pitchers from a great, battered kettle on the stove. . . .

"There's been a mistake," I told the maid, leaning over the counter and speaking in a low, confidential tone. "The new nurse forgot to bring me in my breakfast tray today."

I managed a bright smile, to show there were no hard feelings.

"What's the name?"

"Greenwood. Esther Greenwood."

"Greenwood, Greenwood, Greenwood." The maid's warty index finger slid down the list of names of the patients in Belsize tacked upon the kitchen wall. "Greenwood, no breakfast today."

I caught the rim of the counter with both hands. . . .

I strode blindly out into the hall, not to my room, because that was where they would come to get me, but to the alcove. . . .

I curled up in the far corner of the alcove with the blanket over my head. It wasn't the shock treatment that struck me, so much as the bare-faced treachery of Doctor Nolan. I liked Doctor Nolan, I loved her, I had given her my trust on a platter and told her everything, and she had promised, faithfully, to warn me ahead of time if ever I had to have another shock treatment.

If she had told me the night before I would have lain awake all night, of course, full of dread and foreboding, but by morning I would have been composed and ready. I would have gone down the hall between two nurses, past DeeDee and Loubelle and Mrs. Savage and Joan, with dignity, like a person coolly resigned to execution.

The nurse bent over me and called my name.

I pulled away and crouched farther into the corner. The nurse disappeared. I knew she would return, in a minute, with two burly men attendants,

ADDITIONAL READINGS ABOUT THE TOPIC

Cronkite, K. (1994). *On the Edge of Darkness: Conversations About Conquering Depression.* New York: Dell.

Plath, S. (1991). *The Journals of Sylvia Plath.* McCollough, F.M., & Hughes, T., eds. New York: Ballantine.

O'Connor, R. (1999). *Undoing Depression: What Therapy Doesn't Teach You and Medication Can't Give You.* New York: Little Brown & Company.

Stevenson, A. (1998). *Bitter Fame: The Life of Sylvia Plath.* Boston: Houghton Mifflin Co.

Yapko. M. (1998). *Breaking the Patterns of Depression.* New York: Bantam Doubleday Books for Young Readers.

and they would bear me, howling and hitting, past the smiling audience now gathered in the lounge.

Doctor Nolan put her arm around me and hugged me like a mother.

"You said you'd *tell* me!" I shouted at her through the dishevelled blanket.

"But I *am* telling you," Doctor Nolan said. "I've come specially early to tell you, and I'm taking you over myself."

I peered at her through swollen lids. "Why didn't you tell me last night?"

"I only thought it would keep you awake. If I'd known . . ."

"You *said* you'd tell me."

"Listen, Esther," Doctor Nolan said. "I'm going over with you. I'll be there the whole time, so everything will happen right, the way I promised. I'll be there when you wake up, and I'll bring you back again."

I looked at her. She seemed very upset.

I waited a minute. Then I said, "Promise you'll be there."

"I promise."

Doctor Nolan . . . led me down a flight of stairs into the mysterious basement corridors that linked, in an elaborate network of tunnels and burrows, all the various buildings of the hospital.

The walls were bright, white lavatory tile with bald bulbs set at intervals in the black ceiling. Stretchers and wheelchairs were beached here and there against the hissing, knocking pipes that ran and branched in an intricate nervous system along the glittering walls. I hung on to Doctor Nolan's arm like death, and every so often she gave me an encouraging squeeze.

Finally, we stopped at a green door with Electrotherapy printed on it in black letters. I held back, and Doctor Nolan waited. Then I said, "Let's get it over with," and we went in.

The only people in the waiting room besides Doctor Nolan and me were a pallid man in a shabby maroon bathrobe and his accompanying nurse. . . .

"Do you want to sit down?" Doctor Nolan pointed at a wooden bench, but my legs felt full of heaviness, and I thought how hard it would be to hoist myself from a sitting position when the shock treatment people came in.

"I'd rather stand."

At last a tall, cadaverous woman in a white smock entered the room from an inner door. I thought that she would go up and take the man in the maroon bathrobe, as he was first, so I was surprised when she came toward me. . . .

Through the slits of my eyes, which I didn't dare open too far, lest the full view strike me dead, I saw the high bed with its white, drumtight sheet, and the machine behind the bed, and the masked person—I couldn't tell whether it was a man or a woman—behind the machine, and other masked people flanking the bed on both sides.

Miss Huey helped me climb up and lie down on my back.

"Talk to me," I said.

Miss Huey began to talk in a low, soothing voice, smoothing the salve on my temples and fitting the small electric buttons on either side of my head. "You'll be perfectly all right, you won't feel a thing, just bite down. . . ." And she set something on my tongue and in panic I bit down, and darkness wiped me out like chalk on a blackboard.

Analyzing the Reading

1. What is the setting of this excerpt?
2. How does Esther realize that she is scheduled for a shock treatment that morning?
3. **Critical Thinking** Despite its risks, ECT is still used to treat severe depression. Do you think this is ethical? Under what circumstances would such treatment be administered?

Active Reading Strategy

Explain to students that as they read, they should evaluate whether the details support the author's thesis. After completing the selection, readers should compare their opinions and interpretations with those expressed by the author.

Psychology Journal

Have students write a poem about how they overcame a battle with loneliness, depression, or fear. ■

Teacher Tip

Discuss with students the difference between being in a down mood or feeling depressed and being clinically depressed.

Answers to Analyzing the Reading

1. It is set in a psychiatric ward of a hospital—Belsize Hospital.
2. The nurse enters her room in the morning without a breakfast tray. During her stay at the hospital, Esther has realized that this is what occurs when someone is scheduled for shock treatment.
3. Students' answers will vary. It does fit the APA guidelines for treatment. It is used for suicidal patients who have not responded to antidepressant drugs.

Unit 7 Planning Guide

National High School Psychology Standards

The national high school psychology standards identify what students in an introductory high school psychology course should learn. **The material covered in Unit 7 reflects content from one of the five content domains: *Sociocultural.*** To see a chapter-by-chapter correlation to the national standards, refer to pages xiv–xvii.

Content Domains for National High School Psychology Standards

Use this diagram to review the standards areas that are covered in Unit 7. Standards areas covered in this unit are highlighted in red in the diagram.

- **Methods**
  - Introduction and Research Methods
- **Sociocultural**
  - Individual Differences
  - Personality and Assessment
  - Psychological Disorders
  - Treatment of Psychological Disorders
  - **Social and Cultural Dimensions of Behavior**
- **Developmental**
  - Lifespan Development
- **Cognitive**
  - Learning
  - Memory
  - Thinking and Language
  - States of Consciousness
- **Biopsychological**
  - Biological Bases of Behavior
  - Sensation and Perception
  - Motivation and Emotion
  - Stress, Coping, and Health

BIBLIOGRAPHY

Readings for the Student

Aronson, E. (2003). *The Social Animal.* New York: W.H. Freeman & Co.

Cialdini, R.B. (1998). *Influence: The Psychology of Persuasion.* New York: Morrow.

Hall, E.T. (1990). *The Hidden Dimension.* New York: Anchor Books/Doubleday.

Readings for the Teacher

Brislin, R. (1999). *Understanding Culture's Influence on Behavior.* San Diego, CA: Harcourt Brace Jovanovich.

Donohue, W.A., & Kolt, R. (1992). *Managing Interpersonal Conflict.* Newbury Park, CA: Sage.

Huffman, K. (2005). *Psychology in Action.* New York: Wiley.

Multimedia Resources

Videocassette. *Understanding Prejudice* (two 30-minute programs). Thinking Allowed Video Collection. The natural tendency toward stereotyping and prejudice is discussed.

Film. *12 Angry Men* (95 minutes). MGM Home Entertainment. A drama about jury deliberations filmed in 1957 demonstrates leadership and small-group decision making.

Unit 7 Resource Manager

Note: The following materials may be used when teaching Unit 7. Chapter level support materials can be found on the chapter resource pages.

GLENCOE'S ASSESSMENT ADVANTAGE

Use the following tools to easily assess student learning in a variety of ways:

- Authentic Assessment with Rubrics
- Section Quizzes, Chapter Tests, and Unit Tests
- glencoe.com
- SAT/SAT II Test Practice
- *ExamView® Assessment Suite* CD-ROM

APPLICATIONS AND HANDS-ON

Psychology Lab Activities 7–1 and 7–2

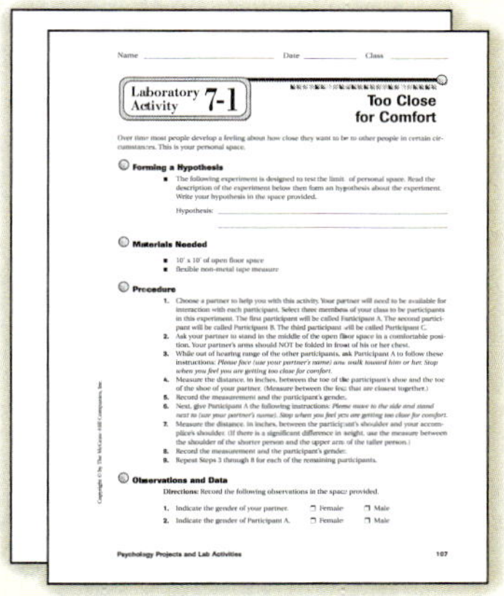
Laboratory Activity 7-1
Too Close for Comfort

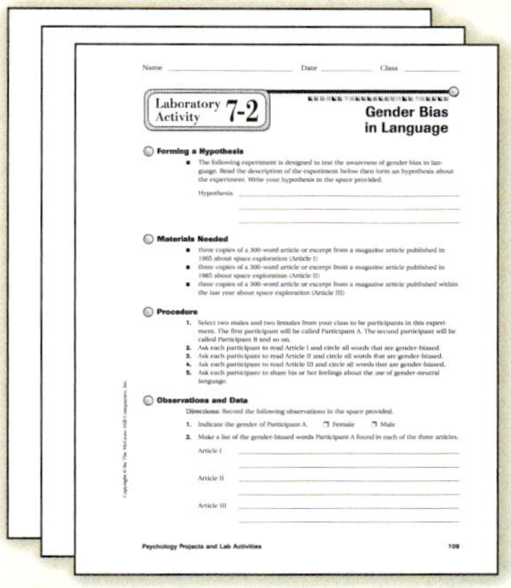
Laboratory Activity 7-2
Gender Bias in Language

ASSESSMENT

GLENCOE'S ASSESSMENT ADVANTAGE

Unit 7 Test, Form A

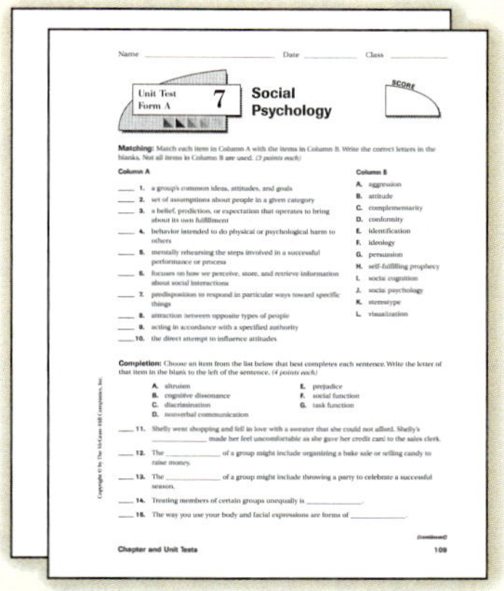
Unit Test Form A 7
Social Psychology

Unit 7 Test, Form B

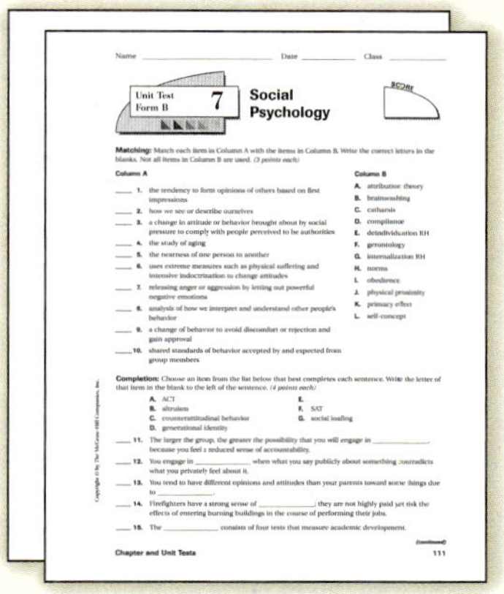
Unit Test Form B 7
Social Psychology

PRESENTATION Plus!

Use Glencoe's ***Presentation Plus!*** multimedia teacher tool to easily present dynamic lessons that visually excite your students. Using Microsoft PowerPoint® you can customize the presentations to create your own personalized lessons.

Introducing
UNIT 7

Unit Overview
This unit explores social psychology—an area of psychology in which we seek to explain our own and others' thoughts, feelings, perceptions, and behaviors. We also try to understand how we are influenced by the presence of and interactions with others. **Chapter 18** explores interpersonal attraction, social perceptions, and personal relationships. **Chapter 19** describes group behavior, conformity, obedience, conflict, and cooperation. **Chapter 20** investigates attitude formation and change, prejudice, and persuasion. **Chapter 21** explores careers in psychology and psychology's contributions to society.

Unit Objectives
After studying this unit, students will be able to:
1. Describe several factors that influence how we interpret others' behavior.
2. Define and explain different types of groups.
3. Describe the factors involved in attitude formation and change.
4. List several careers available in psychology.

UNIT 7

Social Psychology

Contents

A group experiencing the Okinawa, Japan aquarium

EXTRA CREDIT PROJECT
Influence Diary Ask students to keep a diary for one week. In the diary, students should describe the people or forces that influence their attitudes or beliefs each day. Tell students to look for examples of peer pressure, advertisements, parental pressure, and so on. At the end of the week, have students create a master list of the people and forces that have influenced them and the number of times during the week the influences were felt. **Ask:** **What patterns do you see in the forces that influence you? What forces influence you most often? How has this activity helped you understand persuasion processes?** **BLOCK SCHEDULING**

Why It's Important

How and why do we interact with others the way we do? *Social psychology* is an area of psychology in which we first study and seek to explain our own and others' thoughts, feelings, perceptions, and behaviors. Then we study how we are influenced by the presence of and interactions with one another. How do we form impressions? Why do prejudices exist? Why do we perceive social situations the way we do? Social psychologists examine these issues.

Psychology Fair Suggestion Box

Encourage students to get involved with a psychology fair. Here are some project suggestions for **Unit 7—Social Psychology:**

- Explore cultural differences in nonverbal communication or physical attractiveness.
- Examine how political correctness has influenced American society.
- Describe the influence of peer pressure across the human lifespan.
- Investigate a recent finding of psychological research that may have a significant impact on human society.

Refer to ***Psychology Projects and Lab Activities*** in the TCR for help with organizing a psychology fair.

PSYCHOLOGY *Online*

Visit glencoe.com, the *Understanding Psychology* Web site, for Chapter Overviews, Student Web Activities, Interactive Puzzles, and Self-Check Quizzes for every chapter of the text.

PORTFOLIO PROJECT

Conducting Interviews Direct students to create a set of interview questions about the groups to which people belong during high school. Students should include questions addressing the group's purpose or goals, its methods of ensuring conformity, member selection process, manner and frequency of exerting peer pressure, how being a member of the group was advantageous, and how important the group was once high school ended. Have students tape-record interviews with at least one person from each of the following age groups: 19–25, 26–34, 35–44, 45–54, 55 and older. Encourage students to explore interesting topics as they arise, rather than sticking rigidly to the script. Ask students to write a 2-page summary of their conclusions.

Chapter 18 Resource Guide

SECTION RESOURCES

Daily Objectives	Reproducible Resources	Multimedia Resources
Section 1 **Interpersonal Attraction** Explain how we depend on others to survive and the factors that influence our attraction to others.	Guided Reading Activity 18–1 Vocabulary Activity 18–1 Section Quiz 18–1	Daily Focus Transparency 18–1 *ExamView® Assessment Suite* CD-ROM Presentation Plus! Software
Section 2 **Social Perception** Describe the ways in which we explain the behavior of others by making judgments about them based on our perceptions of them.	Guided Reading Activity 18–2 Vocabulary Activity 18–2 Section Quiz 18–2	Daily Focus Transparency 18–2 *ExamView® Assessment Suite* CD-ROM Presentation Plus! Software
Section 3 **Personal Relationships** Explore the different types of love and relationships people experience throughout their lives.	Guided Reading Activity 18–3 Vocabulary Activity 18–3 Section Quiz 18–3	Daily Focus Transparency 18–3 *ExamView® Assessment Suite* CD-ROM Presentation Plus! Software

Blackline Master   CD-ROM   Transparency

Block Schedule

Activities that are particularly suited for use within the block-scheduling framework are identified throughout this chapter by the following designation: **BLOCK SCHEDULING**

KEY TO ABILITY LEVELS

Teaching strategies have been coded for varying learning styles and abilities.

- **L1** **BASIC** activities for all students
- **L2** **AVERAGE** activities for average to above-average students
- **L3** **CHALLENGING** activities for above-average students
- **ELL** **ENGLISH LANGUAGE LEARNER** activities

Chapter 18 Resource Guide

Timesaving Tools

TeacherWorks™ All-In-One Planner and Resource Center

- **Interactive Teacher Edition** Access your Teacher Wraparound Edition and your classroom resources with a few easy clicks.
- **Interactive Lesson Planner** Planning has never been easier! Organize your week, month, semester, or year with all the lesson helps you need to make teaching creative, timely, and relevant.

Use Glencoe's **Presentation Plus!** multimedia teacher tool to easily present dynamic lessons that visually excite your students. Using Microsoft PowerPoint® you can customize the presentations to create your own personalized lessons.

Activity

From the Classroom of...

Cathy Draeger
Garden Grove High School
Garden Grove, CA

Nonverbal Communication

Purpose: To examine how the nonverbal aspects of communication convey meaning

Organize the class into two groups. Ask one group to brainstorm and record several sentences that could have multiple meanings, depending on the emotion used to convey them.

Example: But I didn't sign the check, Mr. X, you did.

Have the other group write down different emotions on separate slips of paper. Encourage them to think beyond happy, sad, and mad. Perhaps citing some examples like trepidation, elation, and reluctance will help. More emotions than sentences will be needed.

Collect the sentences from each group. Ask for three volunteers, give them the same sentence, and have each draw a different emotion to express. Have the volunteers, one by one, say the sentence to express the emotion they have drawn. Make certain that the class focuses not on the speaker's words, but on the facial expression and body language. Have the class guess what emotion is being expressed, and then repeat the process with three new volunteers.

End the hour with a short discussion of the importance of nonverbal cues in communication.

Psychology Online

Use our Web site for additional resources. All essential content is covered in the Student Edition.

You and your students can visit glencoe.com, the Web site companion to *Understanding Psychology*. This innovative integration of electronic and print media offers your students a wealth of opportunities. The student text directs students to the Web site for the following options:

- Chapter Overviews
- Student Web Activities
- Self-Check Quizzes

Answers are provided for you in the **Web Activity Lesson Plan**. Additional Web resources and Interactive Puzzles are also available.

Chapter 18 Resource Guide

Note: The following materials may be used when teaching Chapter 18. Section level support materials are shown at point of use in the margins of the Teacher Wraparound Edition.

TEACHING TRANSPARENCIES

Chapter 18
Concept Transparencies

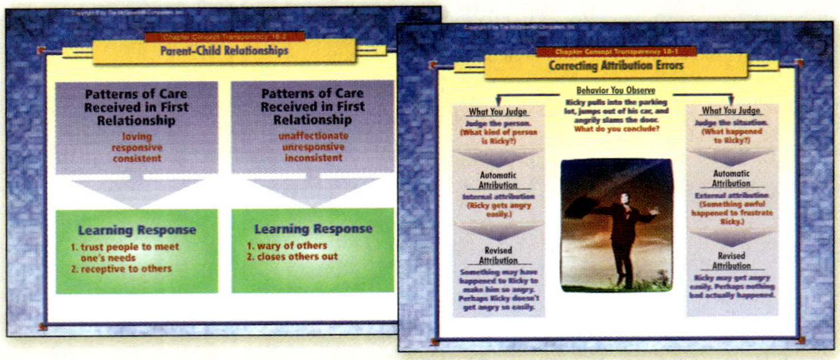

MULTIMEDIA

- **Vocabulary PuzzleMaker CD-ROM**
- ***ExamView® Assessment Suite* CD-ROM**
- **TeacherWorks™ CD-ROM**
- **Glencoe Skillbuilder Interactive Workbook, Level 2**
- **Presentation Plus! Software**

REVIEW AND REINFORCEMENT

Reteaching Activity 18

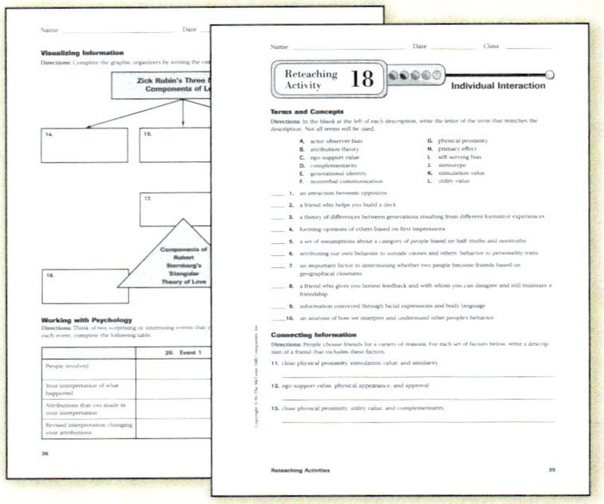

Graphic Organizer Activity 18

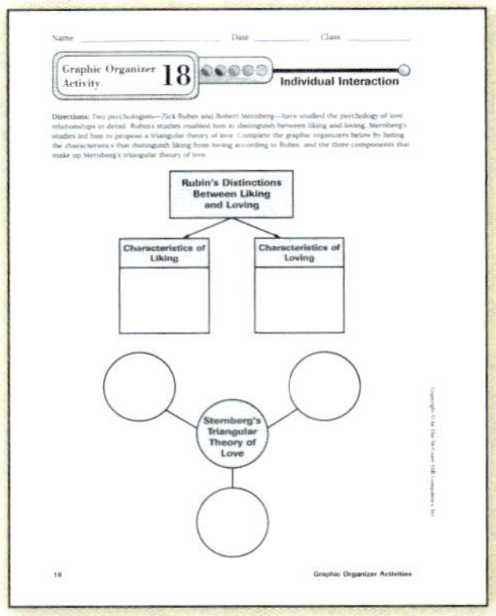

APPLICATION AND HANDS-ON

Psychology Projects 18–1 and 18–2

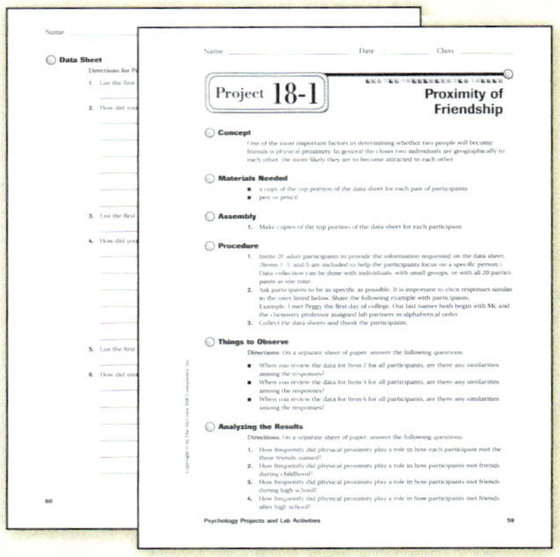

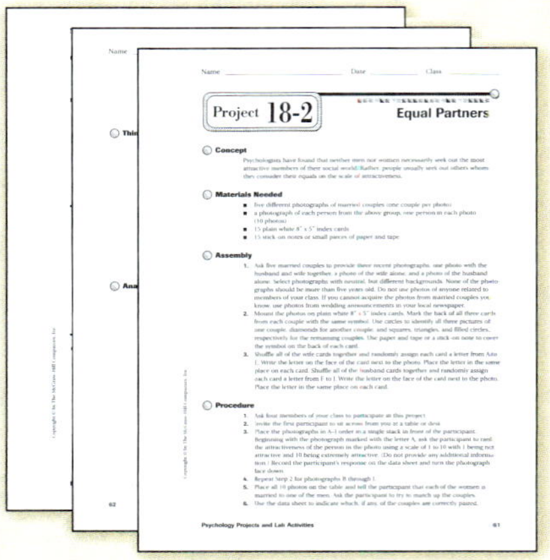

Application Activity 18

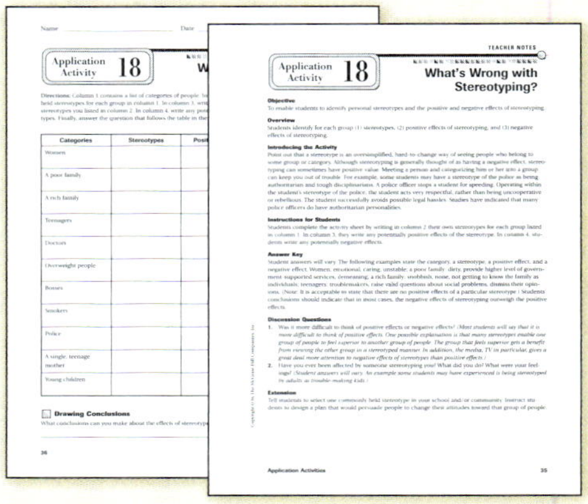

Chapter 18 Resource Guide

ASSESSMENT

GLENCOE'S ASSESSMENT ADVANTAGE

Chapter 18 Test, Form A

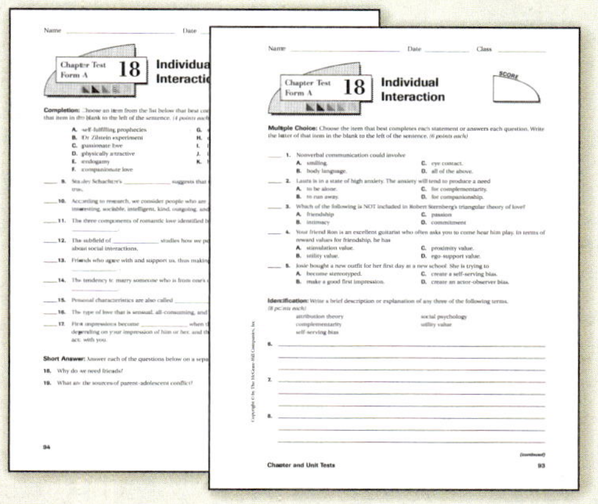

Chapter 18 Test, Form B

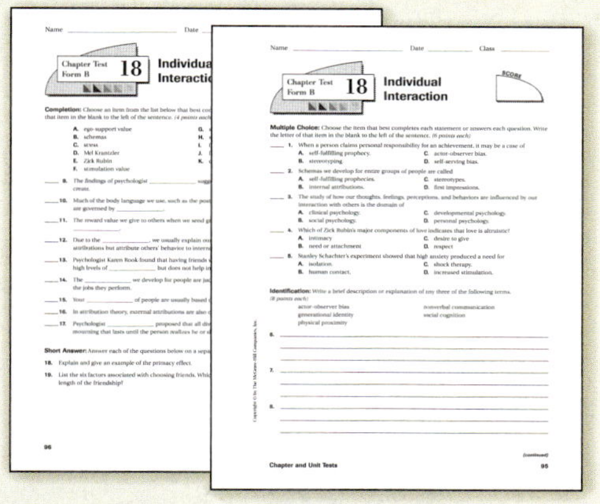

Authentic Assessment Activity 18

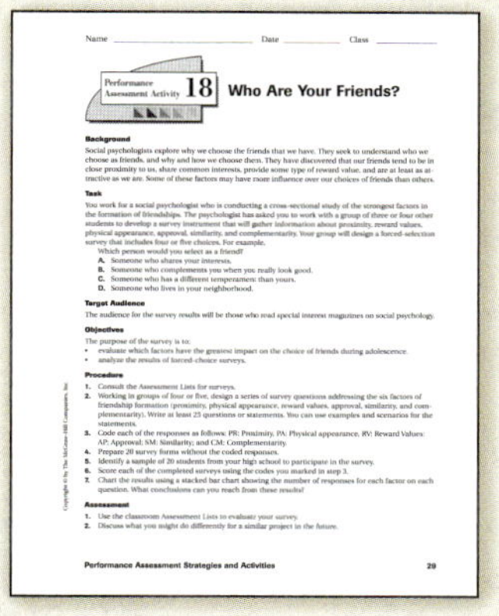

EXTENSION AND ENRICHMENT

Enrichment Activity 18

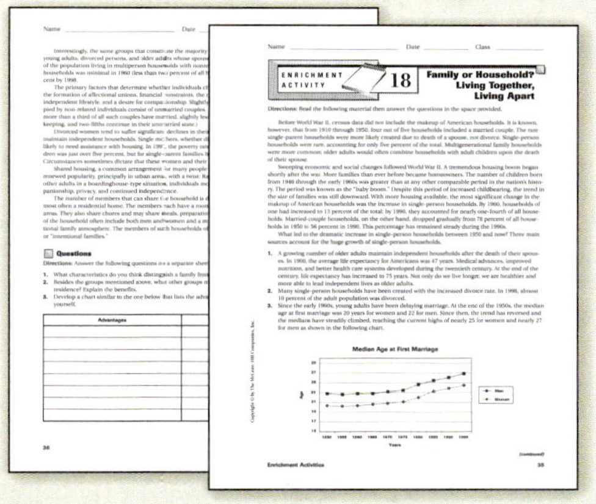

Critical Thinking Skills Activity 18

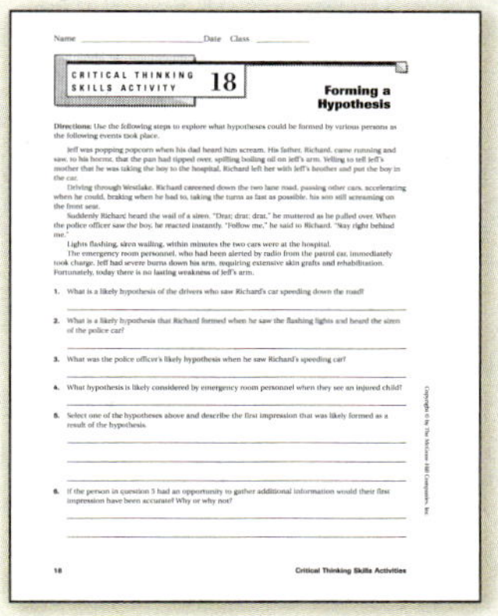

Psychology Reading 18

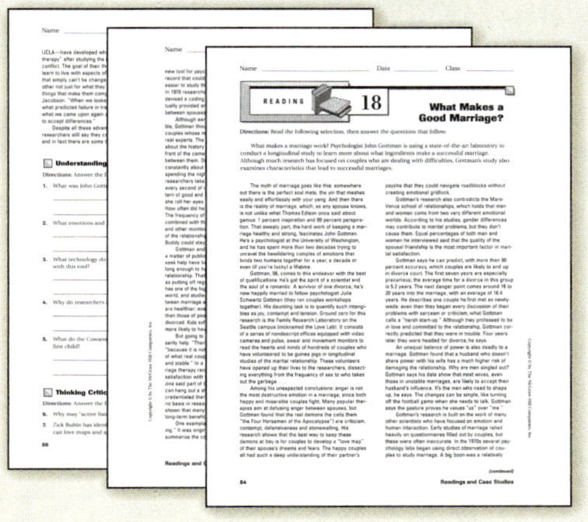

Psychology Case Study 18

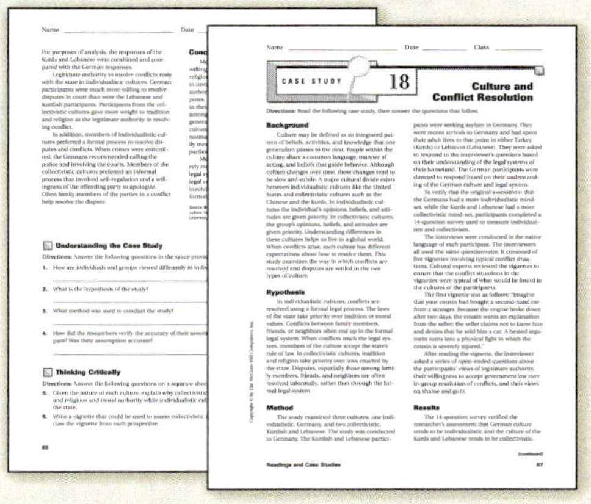

PSYCHOLOGY Online

Visit glencoe.com for a Chapter Overview for **Chapter 18—Individual Interaction.**

GLENCOE TECHNOLOGY

PRESENTATION Plus!

For a preview of Chapter 18 content, see MindJogger Checkpoint on **Presentation Plus!**

PSYCHOLOGY JOURNAL

Help students recognize the differences between the way they communicate with friends and the way they communicate with strangers.

This journal activity provides the basis for the Psychology Journal activity exercise in the Chapter Assessment. ■

CHAPTER 18 Individual Interaction

PSYCHOLOGY JOURNAL

Why do people choose to interact with certain people and not with others? How do you communicate with others? In your journal, keep a log for several days of the people you communicate with and how you communicate with them. For example, do you use only verbal communication, or do your friends and family realize what you are feeling by the look on your face or other signs? ■

PSYCHOLOGY Online

Chapter Overview

Visit the *Understanding Psychology* Web site at glencoe.com and click on **Chapter 18—Chapter Overviews** to preview the chapter.

TWO-MINUTE LESSON LAUNCHER

Tell students that some police departments have been accused of racial profiling for suspecting people of criminal behavior simply because of their race or ethnicity. Explain to students that while we all form first impressions of people, some of these impressions may be based on stereotypes. Give students rating sheets that have scales with opposite characteristics on each end. One scale could range from "Good to Bad," another from "Attractive to Unattractive." Provide scales for at least five pairs of characteristics. Then briefly show students pictures of people and have students rank them using the scales. **Ask: Are any of your ratings based on stereotypes? If so, what are they?**

SECTION 1 Interpersonal Attraction

Reader's Guide

Main Idea

We depend on others to survive. We are attracted to certain people because of factors such as proximity, reward values, physical appearance, approval, similarity, and complementarity.

Vocabulary

- social psychology
- social cognition
- physical proximity
- stimulation value
- utility value
- ego-support value
- complementarity

Objectives

- Discuss why we need friends.
- List and explain the factors involved in choosing friends.

EXPLORING PSYCHOLOGY

Alone and Safe?

The . . . story concerns a relative of a friend, who is an extremely wealthy industrialist. He, too, wanted to retire someplace safe from the congestion and crime of Europe. He bought a small island in the Bahamas, built a splendid estate, and surrounded himself with armed guards and attack dogs. At first he felt safe and comfortable, but soon worries began to appear. Were there enough guards to protect him in case his wealth attracted criminals to loot the island? Yet if he strengthened the guards, wouldn't he become increasingly weaker, more dependent on his protectors? In addition, the gilded cage soon became boring; so he fled back to the anonymity of a big city.

—from *The Evolving Self: A Psychology for the Third Millennium* by Mihaly Csikszentmihalyi, 1993

Is it possible to isolate ourselves to remain safe and also remain happy? As the man in the excerpt above found out, isolation has a price. Being with other people may not be safe, but it is often preferable. That is why we choose friends. This topic is the concern of **social psychology**—the study of how our thoughts, feelings, perceptions, and behaviors are influenced by our interactions with others. **Social cognition,** a subfield of social psychology, is the study of how we perceive, store, and retrieve information about these social interactions. Social psychologists might ask: Why did we choose the friends we have? What attracted us to

social psychology: the study of how our thoughts, feelings, perceptions, and behaviors are influenced by interactions with others

social cognition: focuses on how we perceive, store, and retrieve information about social interactions

SECTION RESOURCES

Reproducible Masters

- Guided Reading Activity 18–1
- Vocabulary Activity 18–1
- Section Quiz 18–1

Transparencies

- Daily Focus Transparency 18–1

Multimedia

- *ExamView® Assessment Suite* CD-ROM
- Presentation Plus! Software

1 FOCUS

Section Objectives

1. Discuss why we need friends.
2. List and explain the factors involved in choosing friends.

BELLRINGER
Motivational Activity

Project Daily Focus Transparency 18–1 and have students answer the questions.

Available as blackline master

Daily Focus Transparency 18–1

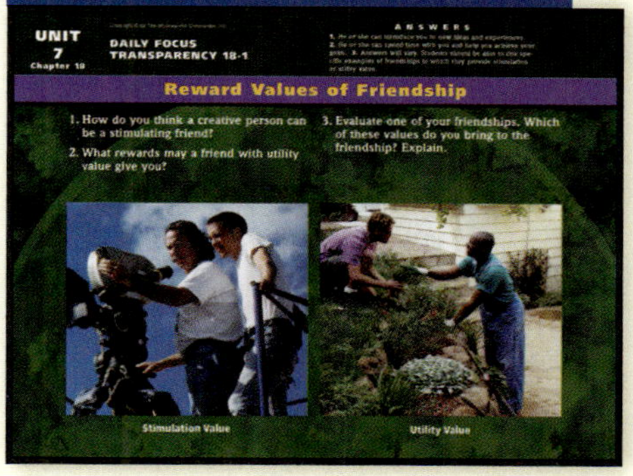

Reader's Guide

Use the Reader's Guide to introduce concepts and vocabulary.

Exploring Psychology

Ask students to read the **Exploring Psychology** feature and then discuss: **How do the people in your life influence the way you think, feel, and behave?**

Vocabulary Precheck

Have students read the Glossary definitions of the terms aloud. Then have them write a sentence using each vocabulary word.

them in the first place? Every day we are making judgments about others based on our perceptions of who they are. Then, when we interact with these people, we must adjust our judgments to explain their behavior and ours.

WHY YOU NEED FRIENDS

During infancy we depend on others to satisfy our basic needs. In this relationship we learn to associate close personal contact with the satisfaction of basic needs. Later in life we seek personal contact for the same reason, even though we can now care for ourselves.

Being around other human beings—interacting with others—has become a habit that would be difficult to break. Moreover, we have developed needs for praise, respect, love and affection, the sense of achievement, and other rewarding experiences. These needs, acquired through social learning, can only be satisfied by other human beings (Bandura & Walters, 1963).

Anxiety and Companionship

Social psychologists are interested in discovering what circumstances intensify our desire for human contact. It seems that we need company most when we are afraid or anxious, and we also need company when we are unsure of ourselves and want to compare our feelings with other people's.

Psychologist Stanley Schachter (1959) decided to test the old saying "Misery loves company." His experiment showed that people suffering from a high level of anxiety are more likely to seek out company than are those who feel less anxious. He arranged for a number of college women to come to his laboratory. One group of women was greeted by a frightening-looking man in a white coat who identified himself as Dr. Gregor Zilstein of the medical school. Dr. Zilstein told each woman that she would be given electric shocks to study the effect of electricity on the body. He told the women, in an ominous tone, that the shocks would be extremely painful. With a devilish smile, he added that the

Figure 18.1 Solitary and Social Animals

All newborn animals depend on others to fulfill basic biological needs. While snakes are solitary animals, some animals such as elephants and humans remain highly social even after they become self-sufficient. ***Why do we need friends?***

PSYCHOLOGY Online

Student Web Activity
Visit the *Understanding Psychology* Web site at glencoe.com and click on **Chapter 18—Student Web Activities** for an activity on individual interaction.

CHAPTER 18
Section 1, pages 519–525

2 TEACH

L1 Analyzing Information Tell students that Stanley Schachter set out to test the old saying "Misery loves company." He found that misery not only loves company, it loves *miserable* company. Ask students to explain how the old saying, "There's strength in numbers," might also apply to Schachter's findings. *(Companionship can offer people a feeling of security when they are feeling vulnerable.)* Ask students to cite examples of scenes or plots from movies or television shows that seem to support Schachter's findings. **BLOCK SCHEDULING**

PSYCHOLOGY Online

Links and instructional guidelines can be found in the **Web Activity Lesson Plan** at glencoe.com.

Figure 18.1

Caption Answer We need friends to meet basic needs for companionship, praise, respect, love, and other rewarding experiences.

Guided Reading Activity 18–1

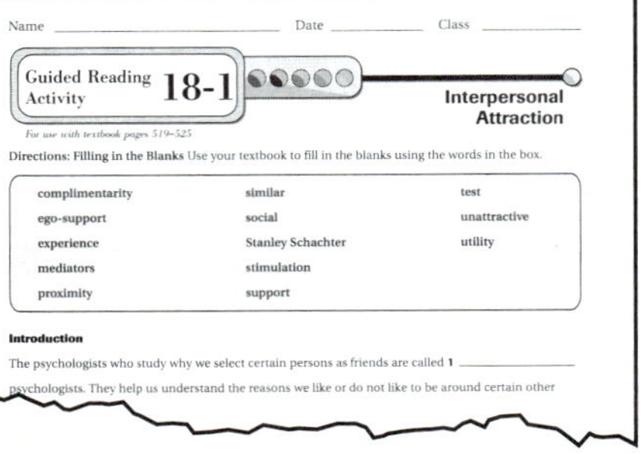
Name ______ Date ______ Class ______

Guided Reading Activity 18-1 — Interpersonal Attraction

For use with textbook pages 519–525

Directions: Filling in the Blanks Use your textbook to fill in the blanks using the words in the box.

complimentarity	similar	test
ego-support	social	unattractive
experience	Stanley Schachter	utility
mediators	stimulation	
proximity	support	

Introduction

The psychologists who study why we select certain persons as friends are called **1** ______ psychologists. They help us understand the reasons we like or do not like to be around certain other

COOPERATIVE LEARNING ACTIVITY

Quotation Search Organize students into small groups. Have each group find quotations that attempt to define what a friend or friendship is. They might explore books of quotations (such as *Bartlett's*), the Internet, or check the indexes of biographies and autobiographies of famous people (especially those who were known to have strong or stormy friendships). Tell students that another source might be the greeting card racks in stores. After they have gathered at least a dozen quotations, direct the teams to categorize them according to the three kinds of reward values: stimulation, utility, and ego support. The groups should present their findings in a chart. **BLOCK SCHEDULING**

shocks would cause no permanent skin damage. For obvious reasons, this group of women was referred to as the high-anxiety group. The doctor was friendly to the other group and told them that the shocks would produce only ticklish, tingling sensations, which they might even find pleasant. These women formed the low-anxiety group.

Zilstein told each participant that she would have to leave the laboratory while he set up the equipment. He then asked each woman to indicate on a questionnaire whether she wished to wait alone in a private room or with other participants in a larger room. Most women in the low-anxiety group chose to wait alone. The majority of high-anxiety women, however, preferred to wait with others. Thus, the experiment demonstrated that high anxiety tends to produce a need for companionship (see Figure 18.2).

Comparing Experiences and Reducing Uncertainty

People also like to get together with one another to reduce their uncertainties about themselves. For example, when you get tests back, you probably ask your friends how they did. You try to understand your own situation by comparing it to other people's. You learn your strengths and weaknesses by asking: Can other people do it, too? Do they do it better or worse? Many individuals use the performance of others as a basis for self-evaluation. According to this theory, one of the reasons why the women in the shock experiment sought company was to find out how they should respond to Dr. Zilstein. Should they feel fear or anger, or should they take the whole thing in stride? One way to get this information was to talk to others.

Schachter conducted another experiment to test this idea. It was essentially the same as the Dr. Zilstein experiment, but this time all the women were made anxious. Half of them were then given the choice between waiting alone and waiting with other women about to take part in the same experiment. The other half were given the choice between waiting alone and passing the time in a room where students were waiting to see their academic advisers.

As you might expect, the women who had a chance to be with other women in the same predicament seized the opportunity. These women wanted to compare their dilemma with others. Yet most of the women in the second group chose to spend the time alone rather than with the unconcerned students. As the experimenter put it, "Misery doesn't love just any kind of company; it loves only miserable company."

Other researchers have shown that the more uncertain a person is, the more likely he or she is to seek out other people. Like Schachter, Harold Gerard and J.M. Rabbie (1961) recruited volunteers for an experiment. When the volunteers arrived, some of them were escorted to a booth and attached to a machine that was supposed to measure emotionality. The machine was turned on, and the participants were able to see not only their own ratings but also the ratings of three other participants. In each case the dial for the participant registered 82 on a scale of 100; the dials for the other participants registered 79, 80, and 81. (As you have undoubtedly guessed, the machine was rigged.) A second group of participants was

Figure 18.2 Schachter's Results

These graphs show the results of Schachter's experiment about the effects of anxiety on affiliation. ***Which group was more likely to seek company? Why?***

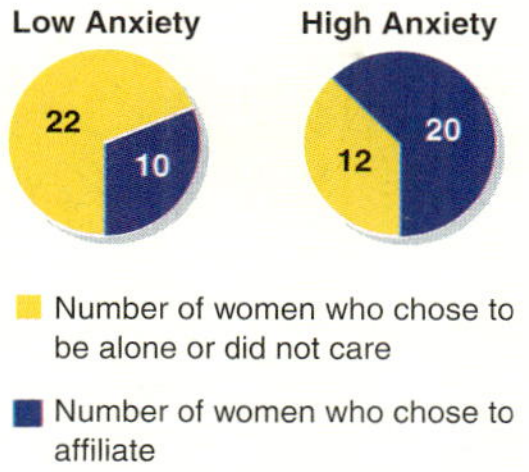

CHAPTER 18
Section 1, pages 519–525

Figure 18.2

Visual Instruction Ask students to use the information provided in the circle graphs to create bar graphs showing the results of Schachter's experiment.

Caption Answer those experiencing high anxiety because they were more likely to need companionship

TEACHER Tip

Help students understand that ego support has its limits as a reward value. Read aloud the following philosophical observation from Cicero's treatise *On Friendship:* "There is no greater bane to friendship than adulation, fawning, and flattery."

PSYCHOLOGY JOURNAL

Ask students to think of a person who was a good friend during elementary school but with whom they are no longer close. Ask students to write a paragraph describing what changed. Then have them analyze these changes in terms of how they choose friends. ■

MEETING SPECIAL NEEDS

Learning Style: Interpersonal Have students role-play based on the following recommendations for winning and keeping friends: (1) When you are talking to someone, spend at least 50 percent of the time listening to them; (2) Be an active rather than a passive listener; (3) Instead of focusing on yourself, ask questions about the person you are with; (4) Insincere approval is a turnoff. Be sure to praise only things the other person considers important. **L2**

BLOCK SCHEDULING

Refer to ***Inclusion for the High School Social Studies Classroom Strategies and Activities*** in the TCR for strategies for students with different learning styles.

Reading Check Answer They allow you to share information and ideas, mediate problems, and offer support.

CURRICULUM CONNECTION

History Benjamin Franklin described how he won the friendship of someone who had been his political opponent. The opponent had a very rare book in his collection. Franklin wrote him a note requesting to borrow the book. The opponent sent it to him immediately. Franklin returned the book after a week with a note expressing his gratitude. Franklin described what happened next:

When next we met in the House he spoke to me (which he had never done before), and with great civility; and he ever after manifested a readiness to serve me on all occasions, so that we became great friends and our friendship continued to his death. This is another instance of the truth of an old maxim I had learned, which says, "He that has once done you a kindness will be more ready to do you another than he whom you yourself have obliged." Source: Bigelow, J. (ed.). (1931). *The Autobiography of Benjamin Franklin.* San Francisco: Printed for members of the Limited Editions Club.

attached to a similar machine and shown their own ratings but not those of other participants. A third group was not given any information about themselves or other participants in the experiment. When asked whether they wanted to wait alone or with other participants, most of the people in the first group chose to wait alone. They had seen how they compared to others and felt they were reacting appropriately. Most of the participants in the other two groups, who had no basis for evaluating themselves, however, chose to wait with other people.

Friendship also offers support in trying times. Friends may serve as mediators if you have problems with another person. Friends are there to react to your ideas. In your social network, friends are your connections to a broad array of available support.

Reading Check How do friends reduce uncertainty?

Yet, as we will see, predicting the effects of friendship can be quite complex. Karen Rook (1987) found that having friends who offer support helped reduce very high stress. On the other hand, friends were no significant help in dealing with average amounts of stress. Perhaps, most surprisingly, the support of friends actually hindered people's ability to deal with low levels of stress. Rook theorizes that reviewing smaller problems again and again with your friends may actually increase your sensitivity to those problems.

HOW YOU CHOOSE FRIENDS

Most people feel they have a great deal of latitude in the friends they choose. Easy transportation, telephones, and the spare time available to most Americans would all seem to ease communication among them and, therefore, to permit them a wide range of individuals from whom to choose companions, friends, and lovers. In fact, we rarely venture beyond the most convenient methods in making contact with others.

Proximity

physical proximity: the distance of one person to another person

Would it surprise you to learn that one of the most important factors in determining whether two people will become friends is **physical proximity**—the distance from one another that people live or work? In general, the closer two individuals are geographically to one another, the more likely they are to become attracted to each other. Yet it is more than just the opportunity for interaction that makes the difference.

Psychologists have found that even in a small two-story apartment building where each resident was in easy reach of everyone else, people were more likely to become close friends with the person next door than with anyone else (see Figure 18.3). Psychologists believe that this is a result of the fears and embarrassments most people have about making contact with strangers. When two people live next door to one another, go to the same class, or work in the same place, they are able to get used to one another and to find reasons to talk to one another without ever seriously having to risk rejection. To make friends with someone you do not see routinely is much more difficult. You have to make it clear that you are interested and thus run the risk of making a fool of yourself—either because

Vocabulary Activity 18–1

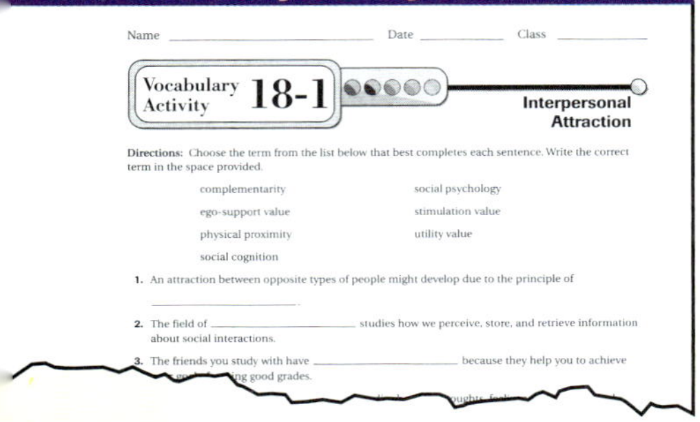
Name ____ Date ____ Class ____

Vocabulary Activity 18-1

Interpersonal Attraction

Directions: Choose the term from the list below that best completes each sentence. Write the correct term in the space provided.

complementarity	social psychology
ego-support value	stimulation value
physical proximity	utility value
social cognition	

1. An attraction between opposite types of people might develop due to the principle of ____.
2. The field of ____ studies how we perceive, store, and retrieve information about social interactions.
3. The friends you study with have ____ because they help you to achieve ... ing good grades.

CRITICAL THINKING ACTIVITY

Distinguishing Fact From Opinion Assign students to research whether or not people are instinctively biased against unattractive people. The research should seek to define what people mean by unattractive. Ask them to write an essay, drawing on their research and their general knowledge of psychology. Tell students that the essay should suggest ways people might learn to recognize this bias in themselves and to overcome it. Remind students to use standard grammar, spelling, sentence structure, and punctuation. You may extend this activity by having students participate in a debate on this topic, presenting their findings and recommendations.

L1 BLOCK SCHEDULING

the other person turns out to be less interesting than he or she seemed at a distance or because that person expresses no interest in you. Of course, it may turn out that both of you are very glad someone spoke up.

Reward Values

Proximity helps people make friends, but it does not ensure lasting friendship. Sometimes people who are forced together in a situation take a dislike to one another that develops into hatred. Furthermore, once people have made friends, physical separation does not necessarily bring an end to their relationship. What are the factors that determine whether people will like each other once they come into contact?

One reward of friendship is stimulation. A friend has **stimulation value** if he or she is interesting or imaginative or can introduce you to new ideas or experiences. A friend who is cooperative and helpful has **utility value;** he or she is willing to give time and resources to help you achieve your goals. A third type of value in friendship is **ego-support value**—sympathy and encouragement when things go badly, appreciation and approval when things go well. These three kinds of rewards—stimulation, utility, and ego support—are evaluated consciously or unconsciously in every friendship. One person may like another because the second is a witty conversationalist (stimulation value) and knows a lot about gardening (utility value). You may like a some people because they value your opinions (ego-support value) and because you have an exciting time with them (stimulation value). By considering the three kinds of rewards that a person may look for in friendship, it is possible to understand other factors that affect liking and loving.

stimulation value: the ability of a person to interest you in or to expose you to new ideas and experiences

utility value: the ability of a person to help another achieve his or her goals

ego-support value: the ability of a person to provide another person with sympathy, encouragement, and approval

Physical Appearance

A person's physical appearance greatly influences others' impressions of him or her. People feel better about themselves when they associate with people whom others consider desirable. In addition, we often consider those with physical beauty to be more responsive, interesting, sociable, intelligent, kind, outgoing, and poised (Longo & Ashmore, 1995). This is true of same-sex as well as opposite-sex relationships. Physical attractiveness influences our choice of friends as well as lovers.

In one study (Dion, Berscheid, & Walster, 1972), participants were shown pictures of men and women of varying degrees of physical attractiveness and were asked to rate their personality traits. The physically attractive people were consistently viewed more positively than the less attractive ones. They were seen as more sensitive, kind, interesting, strong, poised, modest, and sociable, as well as more sexually responsive. It

Figure 18.3 Proximity and Friendship

A set of apartments such as this was used in a study of friendship choice. It was found that the fewer doors there were between people, the more likely they were to become friends. ***How does physical proximity affect your choice of friends?***

CHAPTER 18
Section 1, pages 519–525

CULTURAL CONNECTIONS

A study examining cultural differences in the identification of beauty characteristics was conducted in 1991. During the study, participants from America and Canada (representing individualistic cultures) as well as South Korea (a collectivist culture) evaluated photographs of people. Using these ratings, researchers determined that both culture types agreed on the following characteristics of beauty:

sociable	extraverted
likeable	happy
popular	well-adjusted
friendly	mature
poised	sexually warm and responsive

Source: Eagly, A.H., Ashmore, R.D., Makhijani, M.G., & Longo, L.C. (1991). What is beautiful is good, but. . . : A meta-analytic review or research on the physical attractiveness stereotype. *Psychological Bulletin, 110.*

Figure 18.3

Caption Answer The smaller the physical distance between people, the more likely the people will become friends.

PSYCHOLOGY LAB EXPERIMENT

The Need for Friends Have students keep a contact log for at least one week. Instruct students to record each time a friend initiates contact, whether by telephone, letter, or in person. Tell students to identify the motivating factor underlying each contact: Was it to alleviate anxiety, compare experiences, or reduce uncertainty? Have students analyze their findings by preparing a bar graph showing the percentage of each type of contact. Students should prepare a brief oral report based on their findings to present in class. **L2** **BLOCK SCHEDULING**

CHAPTER 18

Section 1, pages 519–525

Figure 18.4

Caption Answer Answers will vary. Students will likely say that standards of beauty do vary, at least to some extent, based on one's culture.

3 ASSESS

Assign Section 1 Assessment as homework or as an in-class activity.

Section Quiz 18–1

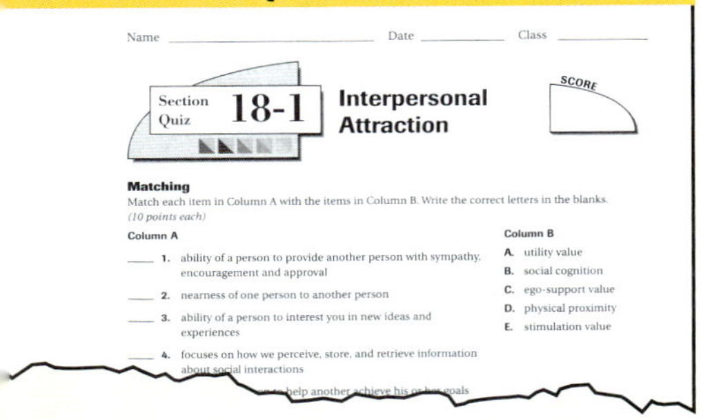
Name ______ Date ______ Class ______

Section Quiz 18-1 **Interpersonal Attraction**

SCORE

Matching

Match each item in Column A with the items in Column B. Write the correct letters in the blanks. *(10 points each)*

Column A

____ 1. ability of a person to provide another person with sympathy, encouragement and approval

____ 2. nearness of one person to another person

____ 3. ability of a person to interest you in new ideas and experiences

____ 4. focuses on how we perceive, store, and retrieve information about social interactions

Column B

A. utility value

B. social cognition

C. ego-support value

D. physical proximity

E. stimulation value

Reteach

Ask students to consider friendships they have formed during high school. Call on volunteers to describe the circumstances under which the friendships were formed. **Ask: Was physical proximity a key factor? What other factors were important?**

Figure 18.4 Standards of Beauty

Standards of physical attractiveness vary widely internationally. These photos are of people considered beautiful from Kenya, Japan, and Bali. ***Do you believe that your ideal of physical beauty is dependent on your culture? Explain.***

seems, therefore, that although we have heard that "beauty is only skin deep," we act as if it permeates one's entire personality.

People who do not meet society's standards for attractiveness are often viewed in an unfavorable light. Research has shown that obese adults are often discriminated against when they apply for jobs. Even children are targets of prejudice (see Figure 18.5). An unattractive child is far more likely to be judged to be bad or cruel for an act of misbehavior than is a more attractive peer (Dion, Berscheid, & Walster, 1972).

Interestingly, psychologists have found that both men and women pay much less attention to physical appearance when choosing a marriage partner or a close friend than when inviting someone to go to a movie or a party. Yet neither men nor women necessarily seek out the most attractive member of their social world. Rather, people usually seek out others whom they consider their equals on the scale of attractiveness (Folkes, 1982).

Approval

Another factor that affects a person's choice of friends is approval. All of us tend to like people who agree with and support us because they make us feel better about ourselves—they provide ego-support value.

Some studies suggest that other people's evaluations of oneself are more meaningful when they are a mixture of praise and criticism than when they are extreme in either direction. No one believes that he or she is all good or all bad. As a result, one can take more seriously a person who sees some good points and some bad points. When the good points come first, hearing the bad can make one disappointed and angry at the person who made them. When the bad points come first, the effect is opposite.

Similarity

People tend to choose friends whose backgrounds, attitudes, and interests are similar to their own. Often, husbands and wives have similar economic, religious, and educational backgrounds.

There are several explanations for the power of shared attitudes. First, agreement about what is stimulating, worthwhile, or fun provides the basis

INTERDISCIPLINARY CONNECTIONS ACTIVITY

The Media Have students find examples in popular magazines of personal beauty. In addition to physical beauty, have them look for articles on inner beauty or inner strength. From these examples, ask students to create a display of what they think American culture values as beautiful. Remind students that this may include inner and outer beauty. The displays should answer the question: Is beauty only skin deep in America? The displays should include visual elements and written descriptions. Encourage students to make a portion of the display interactive by including quick quizzes about the topic. **L1** **ELL**

for sharing activities. People who have similar interests are likely to do more things together and get to know one another.

Second, most of us feel uneasy around people who are constantly challenging our views, and we translate our uneasiness into hostility or avoidance. We are more comfortable around people who support us. A friend's agreement bolsters our confidence and contributes to our self-esteem. In addition, most of us are self-centered enough to assume that people who share our values are basically decent and intelligent.

Finally, people who agree about things usually find it easier to communicate with each other. They have fewer arguments and misunderstandings, and they are better able to predict one another's behavior and thus feel at ease with each other (Carli, Ganley, & Pierce-Otay, 1991).

Figure 18.5 Subject to Prejudice

In one experiment, women were shown photographs of children participating in a variety of antisocial behaviors. The adults tended not only to see the behaviors committed by the unattractive children as more antisocial but also to attribute a more negative moral character to these children than to the attractive ones (Dion et al., 1972). ***Why are we attracted to good-looking people?***

Complementarity

Despite the power of similarity, an attraction between opposite types of people—**complementarity**—is not unusual. For example, a dominant person might be happy with a submissive mate. Still, most psychologists agree that similarity is a much more important factor. Although the old idea that opposites attract seems reasonable, researchers continue to be unable to verify it (Swann et al., 1994).

complementarity: the attraction that often develops between opposite types of people because of the ability of one to supply what the other lacks

SECTION 1 Assessment

1. **Review the Vocabulary** Explain the differences among stimulation value, utility value, and ego-support value.
2. **Visualize the Main Idea** Using a diagram similar to the one below, list and describe the factors involved in choosing friends.

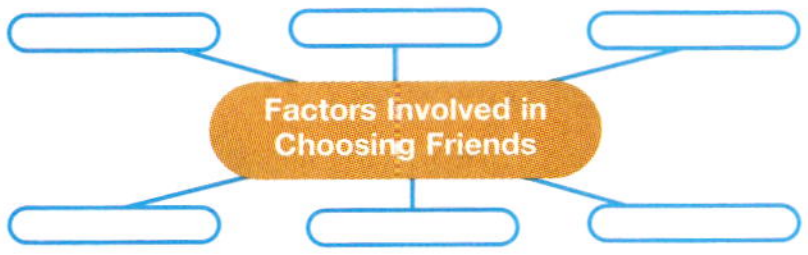

3. **Recall Information** Is the saying "misery loves company" accurate? Explain.
4. **Think Critically** There is a saying stating that "beauty is only skin deep." Do you think it is true? Do people act as if it is true? Explain.
5. **Application Activity** Go to a greeting card store and examine several types of cards to send to important people in your life. In a brief essay analyze the following question: What factors of interpersonal attraction do the cards emphasize?

Figure 18.5

Caption Answer We feel better about ourselves when we associate with people we consider desirable. We also tend to consider good-looking people to be more responsive, interesting, and intelligent.

Enrich

Instruct students to identify five traits they admire in their best friends and then identify five traits they think their best friends admire in them. Next, tell students to ask their best friends to draw up the same kind of list. Have them compare lists. Ask students to list the traits that they had in common with their friends. Compile the various traits to determine the ten qualities that seem to be the most important to teenagers.

4 CLOSE

Discuss the concept of complementarity using the characters of the television program *Will and Grace*. Ask students to identify some other examples of odd couples.

SECTION 1 Assessment Answers

1. Friends with stimulation value are interesting and imaginative and provide new experiences. Friends who are willing to give you time and resources provide utility value. Friends who offer sympathy, encouragement, approval, and appreciation provide ego-support value.
2. Diagrams should include the following: proximity, reward values, physical appearance, approval, similarity, and complementarity.
3. Students' answers will vary. Some will explain that those suffering high anxiety seek out the company of others. Students should note that according to Schachter's experiment, misery loves only miserable company; that is, people with high anxiety want to be with others who feel the same way.
4. Students' answers will vary. For some people this is true; however, many people seek friends whose beauty is an inner quality rather than an outer one.
5. Students' answers will vary. Encourage students to bring examples of cards showing the various factors.

Going Further

Social Conformity

Society tends to expect conformity to the norms it establishes. Physical appearance can be seen as just another example of this expectation. Unlike conforming to other social norms, physical conformity is more difficult because differences are so apparent and because our genetic makeup is a key ingredient to our physical appearance.

Studies during adolescence have shown that boys who mature late and girls who mature early face some daunting social challenges. Although some of the changes that occur during adolescence are not related to physical appearance, many of them are. Consider the boy who does not hit his growth spurt until he is 16 or 17 years old. He is likely to face ridicule and feelings of inferiority to his more physically mature classmates. His lack of conformity to the perceived standard cannot be altered in the short-term; he has to wait for his body to mature on its own time line. The effects of late maturity in boys has been demonstrated to affect them socially and emotionally well into their thirties.

Discussing the Case Study

Ask: **What has influenced your beliefs about the importance of physical appearance? Why is attractiveness difficult to define? Why do you think there is a connection between looks and social skills?**

Case Studies

What You See Is What You Get?

Period of Study: 1992

Introduction: Even though people are taught that "looks aren't everything" and "beauty is in the eye of the beholder," these beliefs do not always seem to be upheld within American society. For many years psychologists have disputed whether the importance of physical appearance is a learned concept, from such influences as television or magazines, or has a biological explanation. One consistency found is that physical attractiveness becomes less important as individuals mature.

There have been many studies focusing on the link between physical attractiveness and the behavior of individuals. In 1972 researchers (Dion, Berscheid, & Walster) administered a test to college students by showing them photographs of people with varying physical appearances. The college students would then describe a type of personality for each photograph. Other researchers (Stephan & Langlois, 1984; Karraker & Stern, 1990) researched feelings and perceptions of adults about the "cuteness" of an assorted group of newborn infants. In 1977 research was performed comparing the annual salaries of men and women of like qualifications but contrasting physical appearance (Dipboye, Arvey, & Terpstra). The results from all of these studies were similar—physical attractiveness was a key factor.

Hypothesis: Alan Feingold set out to study and compare personality traits of those individuals who were considered to be physically attractive with those who were not considered physically attractive. Feingold wanted to disprove the myth that attractive or good-looking individuals could possess superior personality traits.

Method: Defining the attractiveness of individuals for this type of research is not simple. There are far too many ways in which people can be classified in terms of beauty and personality. Much of this revolves around personal preferences of others. Feingold combined the results of numerous studies dealing with this issue.

Results: Feingold's research indicated no significant relationships between physical attractiveness and such traits as intelligence, leadership ability, self-esteem, and mental health. For unknown reasons, results seem to be reported and discussed more from the studies in which physical attractiveness dominates. Yet in actuality, Feingold's research indicated those type of results occurred far less. Perhaps relaying the cases in which physical attractiveness prevails shows humans that we still can be superficial when judging other people as a whole. Although Feingold found no relationship between physical attractiveness and distinguished personality traits, he did discover tendencies within the two defined groups. He discovered that those individuals who are considered attractive generally are more comfortable in social settings and are less likely to be lonely and anxious. They seem to be more socially skilled than their counterparts. Therefore, what seems to be important is how we define physical attractiveness and our perceptions of the personalities of those attractive people.

Analyzing the Case Study

1. What connection between personality and physical attractiveness did Feingold set out to study?
2. What connections between physical attractiveness and personality did Feingold discover?
3. **Critical Thinking** Do you think physical beauty influences a person's personality? Explain.

Answers for Analyzing the Case Study

1. Feingold wanted to disprove the myth that good-looking people have superior personality traits. He set out to study and compare the personality characteristics of individuals considered physically attractive with those not considered physically attractive.
2. Feingold found that physical attractiveness is not related to intelligence, leadership ability, self-esteem, or mental health. He did, however, find a correlation between looks and social skills. Feingold found that those individuals considered to be physically attractive are generally more comfortable in social situations.
3. Answers will vary. Encourage students to consider how our culture may influence their answers.

SECTION 2 Social Perception

Reader's Guide

Main Idea

We explain the behavior of others by making judgments about them. Our judgments are influenced by our perceptions of others.

Vocabulary

- primacy effect
- stereotype
- attribution theory
- fundamental attribution error
- actor-observer bias
- self-serving bias
- nonverbal communication

Objectives

- Explain how we use first impressions and schemas.
- Describe several factors that influence how we interpret others' behavior.

EXPLORING PSYCHOLOGY

First Meeting

We told a waitress that we had come to see Mr. Malcolm X. . . . In a moment Malcolm appeared at the rear door. His aura was too bright and his masculine force affected me physically. A hot desert storm eddied around him and rushed to me, making my skin contract, and my pores slam shut. He approached, and all my brain would do for me was record his coming. I had never been so affected by a human presence. . . .

"Ladies, *Salaam aleikum.*" His voice was black baritone and musical. Rosa shook hands, and I was able to nod dumbly. Up close he was a great red arch through which one could pass to eternity. His hair was the color of burning embers and his eyes pierced. . . .

—from *The Heart of a Woman* by Maya Angelou, 1981

Maya Angelou, a writer, remembers her first impression of 1960s Black Muslim leader Malcolm X. What influenced her first impression of Malcolm X? Based on what she knew and her own thoughts and feelings, Angelou instantly appraised him.

We often cannot explain our own behaviors. How then do we explain the behavior of others? It takes people very little time to make judgments about one another. From one brief conversation or even by watching a person across a room, you may form an impression of what someone is like, and first impressions influence the future of a relationship. If a person

SECTION RESOURCES

Reproducible Masters

- Guided Reading Activity 18–2
- Vocabulary Activity 18–2
- Section Quiz 18–2

Transparencies

- Daily Focus Transparency 18–2

Multimedia

- *ExamView® Assessment Suite* CD-ROM
- Presentation Plus! Software

1 FOCUS

Section Objectives

1. Explain how we use first impressions and schemas.
2. Describe several factors that influence how we interpret others' behavior.

BELLRINGER
Motivational Activity

Project Daily Focus Transparency 18–2 and have students answer the questions.

Available as blackline master

Daily Focus Transparency 18–2

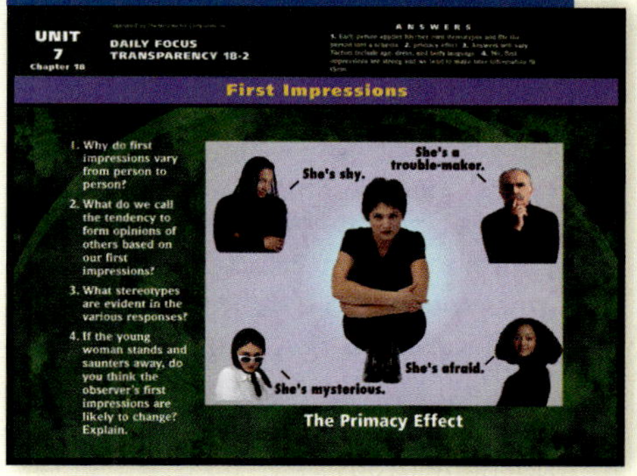

Reader's Guide

Use the Reader's Guide to introduce concepts and vocabulary.

Exploring Psychology

Ask students to read the **Exploring Psychology** feature and then discuss: **Who has made the strongest first impression on you? Describe that impression.**

Vocabulary Precheck

Have students read the Glossary definitions of the terms. Have them write a paragraph about social perception using four of the terms.

2 TEACH

L1 First Impressions Arrange to have a "stranger" interrupt your class, supposedly to deliver a message to you. Interact with the stranger for a few moments where all of the students can see. After the stranger is gone, ask students to write down what impressions they formed about the person. Call on students to read their impressions aloud and to compare them among themselves. Discuss why different students formed different impressions.

FYI

The tendency to attribute other people's behavior to personality rather than to situational forces is so pervasive that it often overrides common sense. It is not uncommon, for example, for people to initially misjudge strangers, assuming their actions are personality based and not the result of situational factors.

Guided Reading Activity 18–2

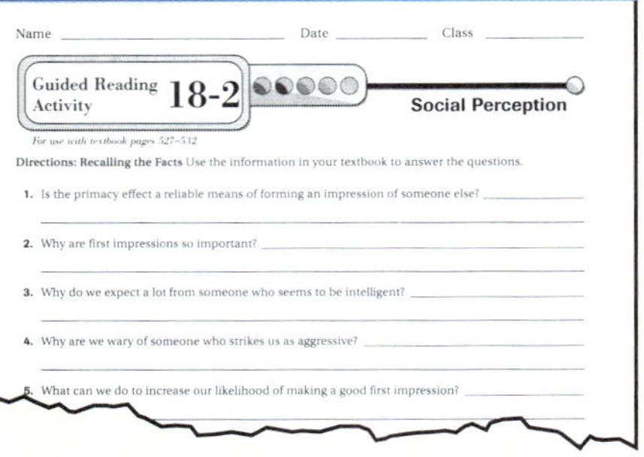
Name ____ Date ____ Class ____

Guided Reading Activity 18-2

Social Perception

For use with textbook pages 527–532

Directions: Recalling the Facts Use the information in your textbook to answer the questions.

1. Is the primacy effect a reliable means of forming an impression of someone else? ____
2. Why are first impressions so important? ____
3. Why do we expect a lot from someone who seems to be intelligent? ____
4. Why are we wary of someone who strikes us as aggressive? ____
5. What can we do to increase our likelihood of making a good first impression? ____

seems interesting, he or she becomes a candidate for future interaction. A person who seems to have nothing interesting to say—or too much to say—does not. We tend to be sympathetic toward someone who seems shy, to expect a lot from someone who impresses us as intelligent, and to be wary of a person who strikes us as aggressive.

Forming an impression of a person is not a passive process in which certain characteristics of the individual are the input and a certain impression is the automatic outcome. If impressions varied only when input varied, then everyone meeting a particular stranger would form the same impression of him or her. This, of course, is not what happens. One individual may judge a newcomer to be quiet, another may judge the same person to be dull, and still another person may think the person mysterious. These various impressions lead to different expectations of the newcomer and to different interactions with him or her.

FIRST IMPRESSIONS

Imagine that it is the first time you are meeting someone. How do you treat that person? Why? Your first impression of someone is usually based on that person's physical appearance (see Figure 18.6). You instantly make certain judgments based on how he or she looks. For example, if you meet a well-dressed woman in an office building, you might assume that she is a well-paid corporate executive. Should you meet a waiter in a local restaurant, you might assume that he does not make as much money as the corporate executive. You might interact with these people differently, just as you might interact differently with people of different genders, races, or socioeconomic classes.

These initial judgments may influence us more than later information does (Belmore, 1987). For example, one researcher invited a guest lecturer to a psychology class. Beforehand, all the students were given a brief description of the visitor. The descriptions were identical in all traits but one. Half the students were told that the speaker was a rather cold person, as well as being industrious, critical, practical, and determined; the others were told he was a very warm person, along with the other four attributes. After the lecture, the researcher asked all the students to evaluate the lecturer. Reading their impressions, you would hardly know that the two groups of students were describing the same person. The students who had been told he was cold saw a humorless, ruthless, self-centered person. The other students saw a relaxed, friendly, concerned person. The students used *cold* or *warm* to influence the meaning they assigned to the other four words, so *cold* and *warm* – the first words heard – exhibited a **primacy effect** on the other, previously neutral, words. The students interpreted the common words *practical* and *determined* in terms of the different words *warm* and *cold,* giving them greater, or primary, impact. Thus, to be warm and determined was perceived as dedicated; to be cold and determined was perceived as rigid. It also affected their behavior. Students in the "warm group" were warm themselves, initiating more conversations with the speaker than did the students in the other group (Kelley, 1950).

primacy effect: the tendency to form opinions about others based on first impressions

COOPERATIVE LEARNING ACTIVITY

Creating a Skit Organize the class into small groups. Ask each group to create a skit that demonstrates a fundamental attribution error. Challenge the groups to make the skits as realistic as possible, using situations that would be familiar to most teens. Have the groups perform their skits. After each skit, have the class identify the fundamental attribution error, discuss reasons the error exists, and name ways to avoid making this type of error. **BLOCK SCHEDULING**

What was your first impression of your teacher? Did that first impression ever change? These impressions sometimes become a self-fulfilling prophecy; that is, the way you act toward someone changes depending on your impression of him or her, and this in turn affects how that person interacts with you. For instance, suppose you showed up on the first day of class in a terrible mood. During the class period, you did not really pay attention to the lecture and even made a few jokes in class. Your teacher immediately labeled you as the class troublemaker and, therefore, did not treat you as an attentive and good student. You may have responded to that treatment by not studying nor caring about your grade in class. In reality, you may be a great student; you just had a bad day on the first day of class and now cannot seem to please your teacher. On many occasions we take first impressions into account. For example, when you first start dating someone, you try to look nice. When going for a job interview, you dress well.

Figure 18.6 Are You Attracted to These People?

Are you drawn to the people in these photos, or is your impression less favorable? Your answer depends in large part on the schemas you have developed. ***How do we use our schemas of people?***

Schemas

Forming impressions about others helps us place these people into categories. The knowledge or set of assumptions that we develop about any person or event is known as a *schema*. We develop a schema for every person we know. When you meet someone who seems unusually intelligent, you may assume she is also active, highly motivated, and conscientious. Another person in the group may have an altogether different schema for highly intelligent people—that they are boring, boastful, unfriendly, and the like. Whatever the person does can be interpreted as support for either theory. You are impressed by how animated your intelligent friend becomes when talking about work; another person does not care for how little attention your friend pays to other people. Both of you are filling in gaps in what you know about the person, fitting her into a type you have constructed in your mind.

Reading Check How do first impressions help us form schemas?

Sometimes we develop schemas for people we do not know but have heard about. Schemas can influence and distort our thoughts, perceptions, and behaviors. Think of a person you like. If that person smiles as you pass in the hallway, that smile looks friendly to you. Now think of a person whom you mistrust or do not really like. If that person smiles at you in the hallway, you may not interpret the smile as friendly but instead think of it as a guilty or fake smile.

We develop schemas for people and events. The schemas associated with people are judgments about the traits people possess or the jobs they

Figure 18.6

Caption Answer We use them to explain a person's past behavior and predict future behavior.

Reading Check Answer
They give us the initial information to begin forming our schema of that person.

Readings and Case Studies in Psychology
Have students read the Chapter 18 Case Study selection in *Readings and Case Studies in Psychology* and answer the questions that follow the case study.

PSYCHOLOGY JOURNAL
Have students make a list of stereotypes they hold. Then have them categorize the stereotypes as useful or potentially harmful. Challenge students to begin to consider how such stereotypes were formed and how they can be avoided in the future. Ask students to write about the connection between stereotypes and bias. ■

MEETING SPECIAL NEEDS

Learning Style: Auditory/Musical Ask students to work in groups to write a rhyme set to music or a rap about one of the following: how we can make inaccurate first impressions, a schema you have developed for a person, the dangers of stereotypes, an explanation of actor-observer bias, or an explanation of self-serving bias. Encourage students to perform the rhyme or rap either live for the class or on tape to be played in class. **L2**

Refer to ***Inclusion for the High School Social Studies Classroom Strategies and Activities*** in the TCR for strategies for students with different learning styles.

L1 Identifying Faulty Assumptions Have students discuss the advantages and disadvantages of stereotypes. Ask students to explain, for example, how they imagine some common, inoffensive stereotypes came about *(for example, Germans are hard-working and efficient; the Japanese are polite)*. Point out that many stereotypes are indeed true to some extent and arise from cultural rules of behavior *(for example, the Japanese do value politeness)*. The fallacy lies in thinking that the stereotype is always true. Have students brainstorm examples of how negative stereotyping has been used as a weapon of discrimination and hatred.

Vocabulary Activity 18–2

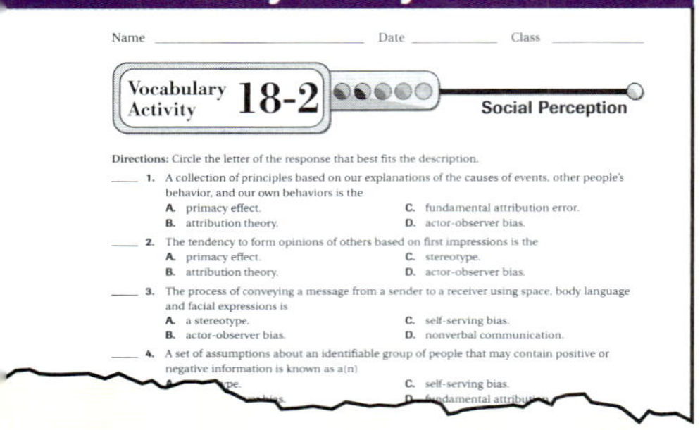
Name ______ Date ______ Class ______

Vocabulary Activity 18-2 — Social Perception

Directions: Circle the letter of the response that best fits the description.

____ **1.** A collection of principles based on our explanations of the causes of events, other people's behavior, and our own behaviors is the
A. primacy effect. **C.** fundamental attribution error.
B. attribution theory. **D.** actor-observer bias.

____ **2.** The tendency to form opinions of others based on first impressions is the
A. primacy effect. **C.** stereotype.
B. attribution theory. **D.** actor-observer bias.

____ **3.** The process of conveying a message from a sender to a receiver using space, body language and facial expressions is
A. a stereotype. **C.** self-serving bias.
B. actor-observer bias. **D.** nonverbal communication.

____ **4.** A set of assumptions about an identifiable group of people that may contain positive or negative information is known as a(n)
C. self-serving bias.

TEACHER Tip

To make sure students understand the difference between *dispositional* and *situational attributions*, provide specific situations and have students explain the action using each type of attribution.

3 ASSESS

Assign Section 2 Assessment as homework or as an in-class activity.

---

perform. Schemas about events consist of behaviors that we associate with certain events. For example, we know that we can yell and cheer at the basketball game but that we should be quiet and subdued at funerals.

What is the purpose of developing these schemas? With your schemas you are able to explain a person's past behavior and to predict his future behavior. Schemas allow us to organize information so that we can respond appropriately in social situations.

stereotype: a set of assumptions about people in a given category summarizing our experience and beliefs about groups of people

attribution theory: a collection of principles based on our explanations of the causes of events, other people's behav-

Stereotypes Sometimes we develop schemas for entire groups of people. You may have schemas for men, women, Asian Americans, African Americans, or certain religious groups. Such schemas are called stereotypes. A **stereotype** is a set of assumptions about an identifiable group of people. The belief that males are dominant and independent or that females are nurturing and emotional are examples. Stereotypes may contain positive or negative information, but primacy effects may cause stereotypes to bias us. If stereotypes influence our information about people and are not modified by experience, they may become self-fulfilling prophecies.

Schemas are useful because they help us predict with some degree of accuracy how people will behave. Without them, we would spend considerable energy observing and testing people to find out what they are like, whether we want to pursue a relationship with them, and so on. Like stereotypes, if the assumptions we make about people from our first impressions do not change as we get to know them better, then we are guilty of harboring prejudice.

More About...

Shyness

Studies show that about 40 percent of adults are shy (Henderson & Zimbardo, 1996). Shyness is a feeling of distress that results from feeling awkward in social situations and from fearing rejection. People may feel shy in front of authoritative figures, in one-on-one dating scenarios, with strangers, or with groups of people. Shyness is really a form of excessive self-focus. The shy person is preoccupied with his or her own thoughts, feelings, or physical reactions.

Shy people differ from others in how they attribute their own successes and failures. Whereas most people demonstrate the self-serving bias—taking credit for success and blaming failures on external causes—shy people reverse this bias and blame themselves for failure and externalize the causes of success. For example, whereas Roger may credit his strength and skill for winning a tennis match, shy Jackie may attribute her win to luck or to her opponent's poor performance.

Psychologists may treat shyness by exposing the patient to feared situations and teaching the patient how to control anxiety. In addition, psychologists may lead a patient to restructure his or her negative thoughts into positive affirmations.

ATTRIBUTION THEORY

You are waiting at a traffic light. Somebody behind you honks and gestures frantically for you to get out of the way. Not sure what is happening, you move your car—slowly, so they will not think you are a push-over—to allow the driver to pull even with you. As he does, the driver looks across at you and says, "Thanks. My wife's in labor. We're in a hurry!"

If you are like most of us, you feel foolish, but everyone has moments like that. You were facing a situation that many social psychologists study—trying to interpret and explain people's behavior by identifying what caused the behavior (Jones, 1990). The focus of study in this circumstance is called **attribution theory** (Heider, 1958), an analysis of how we interpret and understand other people's behavior. When you first heard the horn, you undoubtedly attributed the man's pushiness to personal characteristics—often called *internal attributions*. Once he thanked you and gave a

---

CRITICAL THINKING ACTIVITY

Analyzing Information Have students gather a series of sports articles in which players are quoted. Tell students to include examples of quotes from athletes who were victorious and athletes who were defeated. Ask students to analyze the examples to test the hypothesis that sports figures make internal attributions when they are victorious and external attributions when they suffer defeat. **Ask:** **Do your examples support the hypothesis? Is the method you used to test the hypothesis scientific? Why or why not? What other conclusions can you draw from these examples? L2**

valid reason for his urgency, your analysis immediately changed to credit his behavior to the needs of his wife—often called *external attributions.* Internal attributions are also known as *dispositional,* while external attributions are sometimes referred to as *situational.*

We can make errors when we decide whether behavior is caused by internal or external factors. A prominent example, the **fundamental attribution error,** is the tendency to attribute others' behavior to dispositional causes (Ross, 1977). In the traffic light example, you probably attributed the man's honking to pushiness, an internal cause, without considering possible external causes.

While we tend to focus on internal factors when explaining the behavior of others, we focus more on external factors when explaining our own behavior. This is called the **actor-observer bias** (Jones & Nisbett, 1972). We are an actor when we explain our own behavior, but an observer when we explain the behavior of others (see Figure 18.7). For example, the actor attributes an action to the situation: "I am smiling because it is a beautiful day." However, an observer likely attributes the same behavior to internal causes: "She is smiling because she is a cheerful person."

What causes actor-observer bias? Some psychologists propose that we realize that our own behavior changes from situation to situation, but we may not believe the same is true of others. The point is that we all actively perceive other people's actions. What we conclude about other people depends not only on what they do but also on our interpretations. This is true not just when we deal with individuals but also when we react to groups.

When there is glory to be claimed, we often demonstrate another form of error called a **self-serving bias.** In victory, we are quick to claim personal responsibility (internal attribution); in defeat, we pin the blame on circumstances beyond our control (external attribution). For example, if we receive an A on the test, we attribute our good grade to our hard work and intelligence. When we get a D on the test, however, we blame a biased test for our poor performance. In this way we try to keep ourselves in the best possible light.

NONVERBAL COMMUNICATION

Central to the development and maintenance of a relationship is the willingness to communicate aspects of yourself to others. Communication involves at least two people: a person who sends a message and a person who receives it. The message sent consists of an idea and some emotional component. Messages are sent verbally and nonverbally. "I like to watch you dance" is a verbal message, while a warm smile is an example of **nonverbal communication.**

Although most people are aware of what they are saying verbally, they are often unaware of their nonverbal messages. They are more aware of the nonverbal messages when they are on the receiving end of them. You have probably heard someone say, "It doesn't matter," speaking in a low voice and looking away; the unspoken message is "My feelings are hurt." You do not need to be told in so many words that a friend is elated or depressed,

fundamental attribution error: an inclination to over attribute others' behavior to internal causes (dispositional factors) and discount the situational factors contributing to their behavior

actor-observer bias: tendency to attribute one's own behavior to outside causes but attribute the behavior of others to internal causes

self-serving bias: a tendency to claim success is due to our efforts, while failure is due to circumstances beyond our control

nonverbal communication: the process through which messages are conveyed using space, body language, and facial expression

CHAPTER 18

Section 2, pages 527–532

L1 Developing a Glossary

Have students work in teams of writers and artists/photographers to develop a glossary of body language. Instruct the teams to decide on a consistent style and format for their glossary. For example, it could be organized in alphabetical order or grouped by visual elements such as facial and posture clues. Assign a team member to compile the glossary and oversee its publication. Distribute copies to all class members. ELL

BLOCK SCHEDULING

Section Quiz 18–2

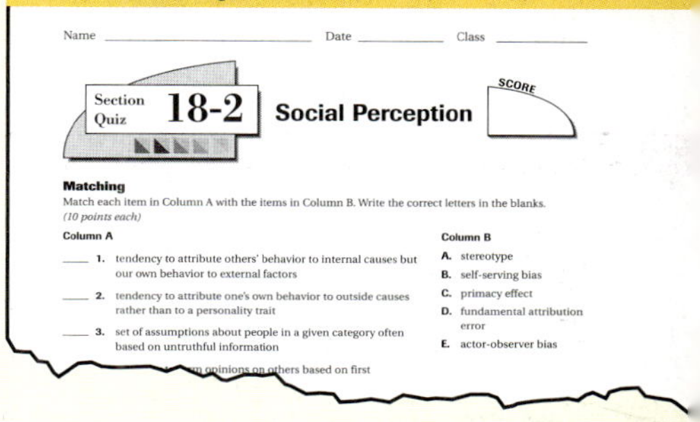
Name ____ Date ____ Class ____

Section Quiz 18-2 **Social Perception** SCORE

Matching

Match each item in Column A with the items in Column B. Write the correct letters in the blanks. *(10 points each)*

Column A

____ **1.** tendency to attribute others' behavior to internal causes but our own behavior to external factors

____ **2.** tendency to attribute one's own behavior to outside causes rather than to a personality trait

____ **3.** set of assumptions about people in a given category often based on untruthful information

...m opinions on others based on first

Column B

A. stereotype

B. self-serving bias

C. primacy effect

D. fundamental attribution error

E. actor-observer bias

Reteach

Ask students to list examples of cultural differences in body language. Such examples might include physical proximity, hand gestures, ways of sitting, touching, etc. Discuss these examples in terms of attribution errors. Ask students to explain how these cultural differences are often misinterpreted. Challenge students to identify ways to avoid misinterpreting cultural differences.

PSYCHOLOGY LAB EXPERIMENT

Conducting a Survey Have students ask ten people to describe their greatest success and their most disappointing failure. Students should record the responses, assuring each individual that he or she will remain anonymous. After they have collected the responses, have students review the answers to identify the attributions used by the participants in describing their successes and failures. Ask students to compile their results in chart form and write a brief summary of their findings. Remind students not to use individuals' names in their charts or summaries. L2 **BLOCK SCHEDULING**

Figure 18.7

Caption Answer We tend to assign internal attributions to others as a shortcut to understanding behavior. Some psychologists suggest that while we realize our own behavior is influenced by external circumstances, we may not believe that this is true of others.

Enrich

Ask students to monitor news reports for a week to find instances of self-serving bias in the behavior of politicians. Have students report and discuss their findings in class.

4 CLOSE

As a class, list various facial expressions, postures, and gestures used by teens. Then ask students to describe what nonverbal communication each gesture expresses. Finally, discuss the social rules that govern these communications. Ask students to explain why these social rules change over time.

angry or pleased, nervous or content. You sense these things. People communicate nonverbally, not only through facial expressions but also through their use of space and body language (posture and gestures).

The way you carry your body also communicates information about you. This is your *body language.* If you stand tall and erect, you convey the impression of self-assurance. If you sit and talk with your arms folded and legs crossed—a closed body position—you communicate that you are protecting yourself. When you unfold your arms and stretch out, your open body position may be saying that you are open to people.

Although the use of body language is often unconscious, many of the postures we adopt and gestures we make are governed by *social rules.* These rules are very subtle. Touching, for example, has rules—not just where, but who (Duncan, 1969). Your teacher or boss is much more likely to touch you than you are to touch him or her. Touching is considered a privilege of higher status, although the rules are changing.

Figure 18.7 Actor-Observer Bias

Our eyes point outward, away from ourselves, so that when we watch someone else perform an action we focus on the actor. When we perform an action, we see the surrounding environment, so we attribute behavioral causes to the situation. ***Why then do we attribute internal, or dispositional, causes to others' actions?***

SECTION 2 Assessment

1. **Review the Vocabulary** Explain the errors people sometimes make when using shortcuts to attribute behavior.
2. **Visualize the Main Idea** Using a diagram similar to the one below, list and describe the two components of attribution theory.

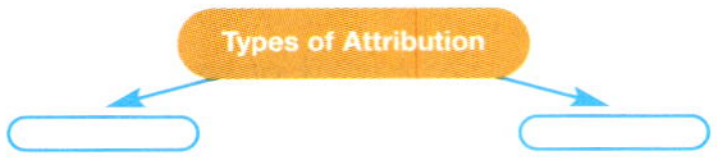

3. **Recall Information** What are *social rules?* Give an example of such a rule.
4. **Think Critically** Rate the following situations as external or internal attributions: (a) Your friend helped you wash your car because she is nice. (b)Your friend helped you wash your car because she wanted to impress your parents, who were watching. (c) Your friend helped you wash your car because she owed you a favor.
5. **Application Activity** Use information found in the library, on the Internet, or through personal interviews to find examples of nonverbal communication in other cultures. Be prepared to show at least two such examples to the class.

SECTION 2 Assessment Answers

1. People tend to put themselves in the best possible light by assigning external causes for failures and internal causes for successes. This is the self-serving bias. On the other hand, people tend to attribute others' behavior to internal attributions—representing a fundamental attribution error. Actor-observer bias attributes one's own behavior to outside forces rather than to personality traits.
2. The attributions we make are either internal (dispositional) or external (situational).
3. Social rules govern postures and gestures. For example, in America, it is unlikely for two men to be seen walking arm in arm.
4. (a) internal, (b) external, (c) external
5. Students' answers will vary. Challenge pairs of students to work together to demonstrate one or more of the examples they have found.

SECTION 3 Personal Relationships

Reader's Guide

■ Main Idea
People experience different types of love and relationships throughout their lives.

■ Vocabulary
- generational identity

■ Objectives
- Describe sources of parent-adolescent conflict.
- Describe different types of love.

EXPLORING PSYCHOLOGY

Raising Your Family

They had been so sweet when they were little. Granny wished the old days were back again with the children young and everything to be done over. It had been a hard pull, but not too much for her. When she thought of all the food she had cooked, and all the clothes she had cut and sewed, and all the gardens she had made—well, the children showed it. There they were, made out of her, and they couldn't get away from that. Sometimes she wanted to see John again and point to them and say, "Well, I didn't do so badly, did I?"

—from *The Jilting of Granny Weatherall* by Katherine Anne Porter, 1930

In the story above, Granny Weatherall looks back on her life—a life of raising and loving children. The relationships you have with your grandparents, parents, guardians, and others will influence and enrich your life. Your personal relationships with others bring meaning and substance to your everyday experiences.

PARENT-CHILD RELATIONSHIPS

Noted psychologists, including Erik Erikson, believed that early and persistent patterns of parent-child interaction could influence people's later adult expectations about their relationships with the significant people in their lives. If a young infant's first relationship with a caregiver is

SECTION RESOURCES

Reproducible Masters
- Guided Reading Activity 18–3
- Vocabulary Activity 18–3
- Section Quiz 18–3

Transparencies
- Daily Focus Transparency 18–3

Multimedia
- *ExamView® Assessment Suite* CD-ROM
- Presentation Plus! Software

CHAPTER 18
Section 3, pages 533–540

1 FOCUS

Section Objectives
1. Describe sources of parent-adolescent conflict.
2. Describe different types of love.

BELLRINGER
Motivational Activity

Project Daily Focus Transparency 18–3 and have students answer the questions.

Available as blackline master

Daily Focus Transparency 18–3

Reader's Guide

Use the Reader's Guide to introduce concepts and vocabulary.

■ Exploring Psychology
Ask students to read the **Exploring Psychology** feature and then discuss: **In what ways did Granny show her love for children?**

■ Vocabulary Precheck
Have students read the Glossary definition of the term. Then encourage them to have a discussion with an adult to identify examples of generational identity.

2 TEACH

L1 Identifying Alternatives Tell students evidence suggests that family violence is perpetuated in the behavior of the next generation, when the children themselves become parents. Ask students to draw on their knowledge of psychology to explain why this is likely to be true.

Next, organize students into groups. Tell the members of each group to imagine they are family psychologists drawing up a behavioral plan to help break the cycle of family abuse. Have them design alternative action plans for children of abusive parents to follow in their own family situations. Have students share their plans with the class. **BLOCK SCHEDULING**

Figure 18.8

Caption Answer Answers will vary. Parent-adolescent conflict will vary, culture by culture, depending on cultural beliefs, values, and differences in generational identities.

Guided Reading Activity 18–3

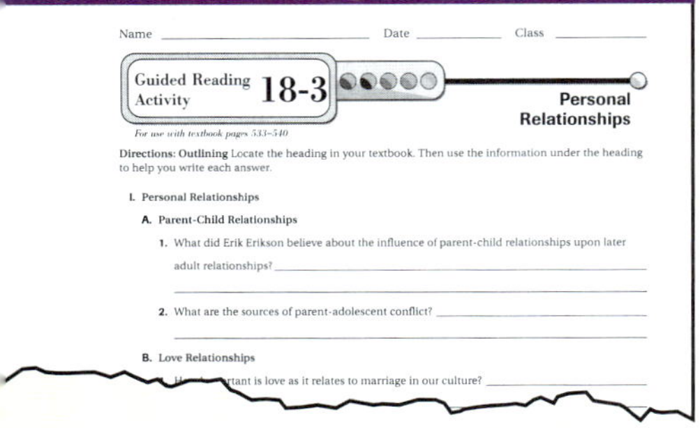
Name ______ Date ______ Class ______

Guided Reading Activity 18-3 — Personal Relationships

For use with textbook pages 533–540

Directions: Outlining Locate the heading in your textbook. Then use the information under the heading to help you write each answer.

I. Personal Relationships

A. Parent-Child Relationships

1. What did Erik Erikson believe about the influence of parent-child relationships upon later adult relationships? ______

2. What are the sources of parent-adolescent conflict? ______

B. Love Relationships

How important is love as it relates to marriage in our culture? ______

Figure 18.8 Parent-Child Relationships

Parenting styles vary among different families and different ethnic groups. ***Do you think adolescents all over the world experience the same types of conflicts with their parents? Explain.***

loving, responsive, and consistent, the child will develop a trust in the ability of other people to meet his or her needs. In turn, this trusting will encourage the person to be receptive to others. However, a child who has experienced unresponsive, inconsistent, or unaffectionate care in infancy will most likely be more wary or mistrustful of other people. Within the parent-child relationship, we learn how to manipulate others to have our needs met. A parent is likely to satisfy the wishes of a child who is well-behaved, that is, who does what the parent asks. The child may also learn to get attention by pouting or having temper tantrums.

As children develop and form relationships with people outside their families, they apply what they have learned about relationships. As a result of childhood experiences, an individual might, for example, believe that the only way to establish and maintain good relationships with friends is always to say what pleases them rather than speak the truth.

Your parents influence the quality of your adult relationships in other ways. They provide you with your first model of a marital relationship. As you watched your mother and father interacting with each other as husband and wife, you were most likely forming some tentative conclusions about the nature of relationships. Later on, you might use their example as a guide in selecting a future mate or in evaluating your relationships. If your parents have a happy marriage, you will most likely seek to duplicate it by imitating their patterns. Sadly, the reverse may also be true. Evidence suggests that being part of a violent family in childhood increases the likelihood that someone will use violence against his or her children and spouse (DeGenova & Rice, 2005).

Sources of Parent-Adolescent Conflict

In our society, parent-child conflict may develop during adolescence. Adolescence may be a period of inner struggles—goals versus fear of inability to accomplish them, desire for independence versus the realization that we are only human and have limitations. The adolescent thus needs parents who are sure of themselves, their identities, and their values. Such parents serve not only as models but also as sources of stability in a world that has become complicated and full of choices.

generational identity: the theory that people of different ages tend to think differently about certain issues because of different formative experiences

Each generation has a **generational identity.** This refers to the simple fact that adolescents and their parents tend to think differently about some things. Why does this happen? You are part of a generation that is distinct from others. Your generation has shared formative experiences that are different from those of other generations. For example, whereas conflicts such as the Vietnam War and political upheavals such as the civil rights movement shaped other generations' ideas, situations such as economic uncertainty, the prevalence of divorce, technological innovations, or a decreased sense of security may shape your generation's views. Your parents' or guardians' prominent flashbulb memories will not be the same as those for your generation, though all of us share the memory of September 11, 2001. Yet, such differences do not automatically lead to conflict. The conflicts that adolescents experience with their parents may result from a changing parent-child relationship, as well as from different ideologies and concerns.

COOPERATIVE LEARNING ACTIVITY

Conducting a Debate Organize the class into two teams and give them a few days to prepare strategies for a debate on the following question: **On what is the ideal relationship based—passionate love or companionate love?** Tell the members of each team that they will not be informed of the position they will argue until the day of the debate. Therefore, they should prepare arguments both for and against each kind of love relationship. On the day of the debate, have the teams select debate leaders, who should flip a coin to determine which position each team will take. **BLOCK SCHEDULING**

LOVE RELATIONSHIPS

While most people say that they love their parents, their friends, and maybe even their brothers and sisters, they attach a different meaning to love when referring to a boyfriend, girlfriend, or spouse. Love means different things to different people and within different relationships.

Love and Marriage

The idea of love without marriage is no longer shocking. The fact that a couple is developing a close and intimate relationship or even living together does not necessarily mean that they are contemplating marriage. The idea of marriage without love, however, remains unpopular to most Americans. Marrying for convenience, companionship, financial security, or any reason that does not include love strikes most of us as impossible or at least unfortunate.

This, according to psychologist Zick Rubin (1973), is one of the main reasons it is difficult for many people to adjust to love and marriage. Exaggerated ideas about love may also help explain the growing frequency of divorce. Fewer couples who no longer love one another are staying together for the sake of the children or to avoid gossip than did in the past. Let us begin at the beginning, though, with love.

Love Reflecting on almost two decades of studies, one psychologist (Hatfield, 1988) identified two common types of love. *Passionate love* is very intense, sensual, and all-consuming. It has a feeling of great excitement and of intense sexuality, yet there is almost an element of danger—that it may go away at any moment. In fact, it does usually fade in any

Profiles In Psychology

Sigmund Freud

1856–1939

"Martha is mine, the sweet girl of whom everyone speaks with admiration, who despite all my resistance captivated my heart at our first meeting, the girl I feared to court and who came toward me with high-minded confidence, who strengthened the faith in my own value and gave me new hope and energy to work when I needed it most."

It has been said that a person in love does not see his or her lover as others do. Freud obviously viewed his wife Martha Bernays in a unique manner. Freud believed that we see the lover as our ideal, and the more dissatisfied with ourselves we are, the more we need a lover to make up for our weaknesses, and the more inclined we are to idealize our lover.

Why do we do this? Freud believed that whenever we make a choice—such as choosing a lover—we are governed by hidden mental processes of which we are unaware and over which we have no control.

Freud's contributions to psychology are controversial. Although his ideas greatly influenced the development of the field of psychology, critics claim that Freud saw people as foolish, weak, and self-deluded. But it may be better to view people as basically good, though injured.

Profiles In Psychology

Ask students to read the **Profiles In Psychology** feature and then discuss the following questions:

1. How did Freud view a lover? *(as an ideal)*
2. When did Freud believe we needed a lover the most? *(when we are most dissatisfied with ourselves; the lover makes up for our weaknesses)*
3. What processes did Freud think are at work when we choose a lover? *(hidden mental processes over which we have no control)*
4. What fault do critics find with Freud's approach to psychology? *(He viewed people as foolish and weak, whereas the critics believe people should be viewed as basically good but injured.)*

Readings and Case Studies in Psychology

Have students read the Chapter 18 Reading selection in *Readings and Case Studies in Psychology* and answer the questions that follow the reading.

MEETING SPECIAL NEEDS

Learning Style: Naturalist Tell students to use naturalistic observation in a park or a mall to identify and observe at least five couples who appear to be in love. Have students keep a log of what the couples did or said that identified them as possibly being in love, as well as an estimate of the ages of the couples. Ask students to write a brief summary of their findings, using Rubin's three major components of romatic love as a reference. **L2**

Refer to ***Inclusion for the High School Social Studies Classroom Strategies and Activities*** in the TCR for strategies for students with different learning styles.

Vocabulary Activity 18–3

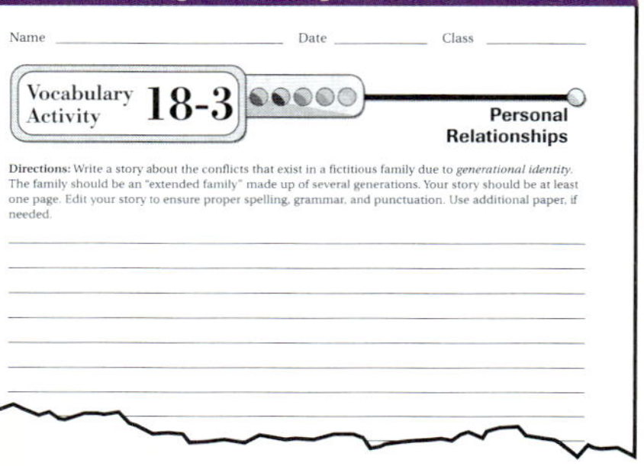
Name ____ Date ____ Class ____

Vocabulary Activity 18-3

Personal Relationships

Directions: Write a story about the conflicts that exist in a fictitious family due to *generational identity*. The family should be an "extended family" made up of several generations. Your story should be at least one page. Edit your story to ensure proper spelling, grammar, and punctuation. Use additional paper, if needed.

Figure 18.9

Caption Answer Caring allows us to give emotionally and express concern for the needs of loved ones. They, in turn, do the same for us. The result is a shared intimacy.

TEACHER Tip

Explain that mature, companionate love is characterized by empathy for the loved one (experiences are shared); concern for the welfare and happiness of the other person; finding pleasure in working for the loved one's welfare; and allowing the loved one freedom to do whatever he or she wishes.

PSYCHOLOGY JOURNAL

Have students write a poem about or to someone they love. Tell students that the poem can express passionate or companionate love. ■

romantic relationship. When passionate love subsides it may grow into *companionate love,* which includes friendship, liking someone, mutual trusting, and wanting to be with them. Companionate love is a more stable love that includes the commitment and intimacy identified by Robert Sternberg (1988). There are other views of love, however.

Some years ago Zick Rubin surveyed University of Michigan student volunteers. Couples who had been going together for anywhere from a few weeks to six or seven years filled out questionnaires about their feelings toward their partners and their same-sex friends. The answers enabled Rubin to distinguish between liking and loving.

Liking is based primarily on respect for another person and the feeling that he or she is similar to you. Loving is rather different. As Rubin wrote, "There are probably as many reasons for loving as there are people who love. In each case there is a different constellation of needs to be gratified, a different set of characteristics that are found to be rewarding, a different ideal to be fulfilled" (Rubin, 1973). Looking beyond these differences, however, Rubin identified three major components of romantic love: *need* or attachment, *caring* or the desire to give, and *intimacy*.

Figure 18.9 Different Types of Love

It is easy to think of love in a narrow context and consider only the sexual relationship that exists between a man and a woman. This view, however, omits the kinds of love that exist between children and grandparents, between people and their pets, between siblings and friends, and so on. ***Why are caring and need important in love?***

People in love feel strong desires to be with the other person, to touch, to be praised and cared for, to fulfill and be fulfilled. That love is so often described as a longing, a hunger, a desire to possess, a sickness that only one person can heal, suggests the role need plays in romantic love.

Equally central is the desire to give. Love goes beyond the cost-reward level of human interaction. It has been defined as "the active concern for the life and growth of that which we love" (Fromm, 1956) and as "that state in which the happiness of another person is essential to our own" (Heinlein, in Levinger & Snoek, 1972). This kind of love is very altruistic, very giving. Without caring, need becomes a series of self-centered, desperate demands; without need, caring is charity or kindness. In love, the two are intertwined.

Need and caring take various forms, depending on individual situations. What all people in love share is intimacy—a special knowledge of each other derived from uncensored self-disclosure. Exposing your true self to another person is always risky. It does not hurt so much if a person rejects a role you are trying to play, but it can be devastating if a person rejects the secret

CRITICAL THINKING ACTIVITY

Understanding Cause and Effect Have students search magazines, periodicals, and the Internet for articles that give advice to couples who are married or who are planning to be married. Have students identify the sources of difficulty in marriage relationships cited by the authors and how the authors suggest that couples resolve these problems. Have a class discussion about the recommendations made by the various authors. **Ask: How do the approaches to conflict resolution vary among the authors? L2**

longings and fears you ordinarily disguise or keep hidden. It hurts deeply if he or she uses that private information to manipulate you. This is one of the reasons why love so often brings out violent emotions—the highs and lows of our lives.

Rubin conducted a number of experiments to test common assumptions about the way people in love feel and act. He found that couples who rated high on his "love scale" did, indeed, spend more time gazing into each other's eyes (while waiting for the experimenter) than other couples did. He was unable, however, to prove that lovers sacrifice their own comfort for that of their partners.

Perhaps the most interesting discoveries in love research concern the differences between men and women. Rubin found that most couples were equal on the love scale; the woman expressed the same degree of love for her partner as he did for her. Women, however, tended to *like* their boyfriends—to respect and identify with them—more than their boyfriends liked them. Women also tended to love and share intimacies with their same-sex friends more often than men did with theirs.

As Rubin suggested, women in our society tend to specialize in the social and emotional dimensions of life. One revelation—that men carry out more romantic gestures than women—may seem surprising, but perhaps it should not. At a time when women usually worked at home, marriage basically determined their style of living. Now earning power is no longer such a powerful concern. More than half of all married women work outside the home, so both men and women contribute to family finance and have the ability to perform more romantic gestures. In fact, two psychologists (Fehr & Russell, 1991) reported that women are no longer different from men as to how "romantic" they are. Women participate equally in varying forms of passionate and companionate love.

A follow-up questionnaire, sent a year after Rubin's original study, indicated that when both a man and a woman express their interest in each other, the relationship is likely to progress; that is, they become more intimate and committed to each other. What is the implication of this finding? Love is not something that happens *to* you; it is something you seek and create. You must work at it and nurture it.

Reading Check What is the difference between passionate and companionate love?

Triangular Theory of Love A more comprehensive theory of the many forms of love has been proposed by Robert Sternberg (1986). Sternberg's triangular theory of love contends that love is made up of three parts: intimacy, passion, and commitment. The various combinations of these parts account for the many different ways love is experienced (see Figure 18.10).

Using Sternberg's model, we can see how different kinds of love are made of different degrees of intimacy, passion, and commitment. The love at first sight felt on a first date has a lot of passion but little commitment, whereas the love felt by a couple celebrating their fiftieth wedding anniversary has much commitment, and may have intimacy, but probably less passion. Yet, each combination yields a satisfying love for those experiencing it.

Reading Check Answer
Passionate love is intense, sensual, and all-consuming and usually fades over time. Companionate love includes friendship, trust, and desire to be together and is more stable over time.

Psychology Update

Endogamy In a 1999 study researchers Carl Bankston and Jacques Henry used census data to identify and attempt to explain the high rate of endogamy among the Cajun population of southwest Louisiana. The researchers noted that there had been a tendency among most ethnic minorities in the United States to marry outside their ethnic group. However, this was not true of the Cajun population living in southwest Louisiana. The occurrence of endogamy was even more surprising since Cajuns do not bear physical traits that distinguish them from the majority. Researchers concluded that socioeconomic homogamy may have been a more significant factor, in this case, than endogamy. They noted that those who did marry outside the ethnic group tended to be excluded by the group, and lost their ethnic identity.
Source: Bankston, C.L., & Henry, J. (1999). Endogamy among Louisiana Cajuns: A social class explanation. *Social Forces, 77.*

PSYCHOLOGY LAB EXPERIMENT

Designing a Survey Have students work in groups to create a survey based on the following questions: **What is the most important character trait in a friend? What is your favorite spare-time activity? What is the most important thing in life? What is the most important factor when choosing an occupation? What do you worry about most?** Ask the members of each group to administer the survey to 20 teens and 20 adults in their parents' age group. Have students compile and analyze results to determine if the survey revealed aspects of generational identity. Each group should create a visual and oral presentation of its findings. Combine all the groups' findings and discuss the results. **L2** **BLOCK SCHEDULING**

Quick Lab

Purpose Students will explore the traits males and females look for in their mates.

Process Skills Analyzing information, demonstrating reasoned judgment

Teaching Strategies
- Identify reasons for differences in preferences expressed by males and females.
- Discuss how the traits someone looks for in a mate may change as the person gets older.

Analysis
1. Answers will depend on the input from the participants. There will likely be some differences between the responses of males and females.
2. Answers will vary. Challenge students to consider how important traits may change as they mature.

Applying Psychology

Tell students that in 1994, the New Jersey Supreme Court awarded damages for emotional suffering to the girlfriend of a man who had seen him killed in a horrible traffic accident. Before this time, such awards had been limited to spouses. The court's ruling was based on the couple's attachment, caring relationship, and intimacy. **Ask: Do you agree with the court's ruling? What legal rights do you think couples in a committed dating relationship should have?**

3 ASSESS

Assign Section 3 Assessment as homework or as an in-class activity.

Quick Lab

What traits are important in a potential marriage partner?

About 90 percent of adults in the United States eventually marry. How do they decide which person is right for them?

Procedure
1. Ask at least 30 of your classmates and friends to identify one quality they consider essential in a potential mate.
2. Separate the results into responses from females and those from males. Tally the results in a chart.

Analysis
1. What traits did females consider most important in a potential partner? Males?
2. Based on the information in the chapter regarding love and marriage, do you think the traits listed by the people you surveyed are ones that are likely to result in a successful marriage? Explain.

See the Skills Handbook, page 622, for an explanation of designing an experiment.

Marriage A couple decides to make a formal and public commitment to each other. They marry. Will they "live happily ever after"? Their chances are good if they come from similar cultural and economic backgrounds, have about the same level of education, and practice (or reject) the same religion. Their chances are better still if their parents were happily married, they had happy childhoods, and they maintain good relations with their families. All of these are good predictors of marital success. Two principles tend to govern behavior leading to successful marriages: endogamy and homogamy.

Endogamy identifies the tendency to marry someone who is from one's own social group. Marriages are more likely to be successful when we marry someone similar to us (Buss, 1985). In addition, *homogamy* identifies our tendency to marry someone who has similar attributes, including physical attractiveness, age, and physique, to our own. A common observation is that people who marry tend to look similar to one another. It is now suspected that social processes operate that tend to cause this matching to happen. At a dance held at the University of Minnesota a number of years ago, a computer randomly matched students. Physical attractiveness was the only predictor of the likelihood that two randomly matched people would continue dating (Walster et al., 1966).

Marital Problems and Divorce In general, healthy adjustment to marriage seems to depend on three factors: whether the couple's needs are compatible, whether the husband's and wife's images of themselves coincide with their images of each other, and whether they agree on what the husband's and wife's roles in the marriage are.

External factors may make it impossible for one or both to live up to their own role expectations. A man who is unemployed cannot be the good provider he wants to be and may take out his frustrations on his family members, who constantly remind him of this. A woman trying to hold a job and raise a family in a slum tenement may have trouble keeping the kitchen clean with a broken sink, providing good meals for her family, or keeping her children safe.

Often couples just grow apart; the husband or wife may become totally engrossed in work, a hobby, raising children, or community affairs. Let us suppose they are unable or unwilling to fill each other's needs and role expectations through accommodation or compromise. Perhaps they cannot face their problems. For whatever reasons, they decide on divorce. What then?

In many ways, adjusting to divorce is like adjusting to death—the death of a relationship. Almost inevitably, divorce releases a torrent of

INTERDISCIPLINARY CONNECTIONS ACTIVITY

Literature Assign students to find two love poems—one that celebrates or bemoans passionate love and one that praises or laments companionate love. Ask students to look for poems from a variety of time periods and cultures. Tell the students to bring copies of their poems to class. Select a group of volunteers to read samples aloud. Ask students to determine where on Sternberg's triangular theory of love the poem falls. **L2** **BLOCK SCHEDULING**

emotions: anger (even if the person wanted a divorce), resentment, fear, loneliness, anxiety, and above all the feeling of failure. Both individuals are suddenly thrust into a variety of unfamiliar situations. A man may find himself cooking for the first time in years; a woman, fixing her first leaky faucet. Dating for the first time in 5 or 10 years can make a formerly married person feel like an adolescent. Friends may feel they have to choose sides. Some divorcing people may find it unsettling to think of giving up on a marriage or being unattached and free to do whatever they like. One of the biggest problems may be time—the free time a person desperately wanted but now has no idea how to fill.

All of this adds up to what Mel Krantzler (1973) calls "separation shock." Whatever the circumstances, most divorced people go through a period of mourning that lasts until the person suddenly realizes that he or she has survived. This is the first step toward adjusting to divorce. Resentment of his or her former spouse subsides. The pain left over from the past no longer dominates the present. The divorced person begins calling old friends, making new ones, and enjoying the fact that he or she can base decisions on his or her own personal interests. In effect, the divorcee has begun to construct a new identity as a single person.

Figure 18.10 Triangular Theory of Love

Intimacy refers to the feeling part of love—as when we feel close to another. Passion is love's motivating aspect—feeling physically aroused and attracted to someone. Commitment is the thinking component—when we realize that a relationship is love and we desire to maintain that relationship over time. ***What is consummate love?***

CHAPTER 18
Section 3, pages 533–540

Looking @ the Issues

Child Abuse Child abuse is a national epidemic—nearly 1 million children are abused each year. Every day at least three children die as a result of abuse. Violence in the home has been listed as a major factor contributing to these reports of child abuse and neglect. **Ask: What should society do to stop this epidemic of abuse? What action should you take if you suspect that a child is being abused or neglected?**

Figure 18.10

Visual Instruction Ask students to identify the seven forms of love identified in the illustration. Then have them identify the varying degrees of intimacy, commitment, and passion for each type of love.

Caption Answer a complete form of love characterized by intimacy, passion, and commitment

Section Quiz 18–3

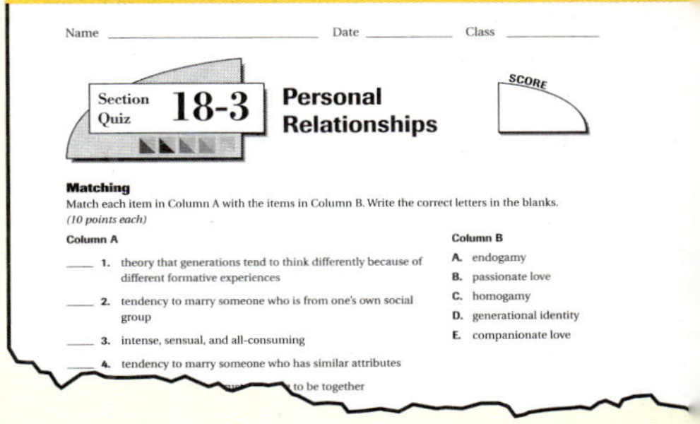
Name ______ Date ______ Class ______

Section Quiz 18-3 **Personal Relationships** SCORE

Matching
Match each item in Column A with the items in Column B. Write the correct letters in the blanks.
(10 points each)

Column A
____ 1. theory that generations tend to think differently because of different formative experiences
____ 2. tendency to marry someone who is from one's own social group
____ 3. intense, sensual, and all-consuming
____ 4. tendency to marry someone who has similar attributes

Column B
A. endogamy
B. passionate love
C. homogamy
D. generational identity
E. companionate love

EXTENDING THE CONTENT

Love Styles Tell students that Clyde and Susan Hendrick have identified six love styles, based on the six Greek words for love. They are as follows—*eros:* passionate, physical love; *ludus:* love played as a game and not taken seriously; *storge:* slow-growing love based on affection and friendship; *pragma:* pragmatic, or practical, love; *mania:* highly emotional love that is similar to a roller-coaster ride; *agape:* altruistic, giving love. The researchers developed a love attitudes scale based on these six styles. A copy of the scale instrument can be found in many social psychology texts.
Source: Hendrick, S.S., & Hendrick, C. (1986). A theory and method of love. *Journal of Personality and Social Psychology, 50.* **L2**

Reteach

Have students brainstorm a list of events or formative experiences for their generation and for their parents' generation. Ask students to identify how these events and experiences may contribute to parent-adolescent conflict.

Enrich

Have students gather love quizzes found in popular magazines. Ask them to analyze the quizzes in terms of Zick Rubin's three components of romantic love. **Ask: Are all components represented in these quizzes? Which components seem to be missing?**

4 CLOSE

Have students discuss with their parents the major events of the parents' childhood. These may include personal and family events, as well as world events. Then have students ask their parents how these experiences influenced who they are today. Have volunteers share their findings with the class. Then discuss as a class major events in their lives that are influencing their attitudes and will affect how they think and act as adults.

Children and Divorce Adjusting to divorce is usually far more difficult for children than for their parents. First, rarely do children want a divorce to occur; the conflict is not theirs but their parents'. Second, while the parents may have good reasons for the separation, children (especially very young children) are unlikely to understand those reasons. Third, children themselves rarely have any control over the outcome of a divorce. Such decisions as with whom they will live and how frequently they will be able to see the separated parent are out of their hands. Finally, children, especially young ones, cannot muster as much emotional maturity as their parents to help them through such an overwhelming experience.

A child of parents who divorce may exhibit behaviors ranging from emotional outbursts to depression or rebellion. The longevity of these behaviors may be determined by "the harmony of the parents' ongoing relationship, the stability of the child's life, and the adequacy of the caregiving arrangement"(Berger, 2005).

Adolescents experience special problems as a result of their parents' divorce because their developmental stage already involves the process of breaking family ties. When that separation takes place before the adolescent is ready to actively take part in it, the experience can be terribly unsettling. As one young person said, "[It was] like having the rug pulled out from under me" (Wallerstein & Kelly, 1974).

Like their parents, most children do eventually come to terms with divorce. They learn to put some distance between themselves and their parents' conflict, and they learn to be realistic about the situation and make the best of it. Adjustment is made easier when parents take special care to explain the divorce and allow children to express their feelings. Divorce is becoming a problem with which more and more children will have to cope.

SECTION 3 Assessment

1. **Review the Vocabulary** What is generational identity?
2. **Visualize the Main Idea** Using an outline similar to the one below, explain why children may have difficulty adjusting to their parents' divorce.

   I. Adjusting to Divorce
   A. ______
   B. ______
   C. ______
   D. ______

3. **Recall Information** What is the difference between endogamy and homogamy? Explain.
4. **Think Critically** In what ways are liking and loving different? Explain.
5. **Application Activity** Have you heard of "love at first sight"? Write a paragraph explaining what you think this phrase means. Interview an adult about their experience of love in terms of intimacy and commitment.

SECTION 3 Assessment Answers

1. It is the theory that generations tend to think differently about certain issues because of different formative experiences.
2. Children rarely want the divorce to occur. Children are unlikely to understand the reasons for the separation and divorce. Children rarely have any control over the outcome of the divorce. Children do not have the emotional maturity to overcome the hurt and pain.
3. Endogamy refers to the tendency to marry someone from one's own social group. Homogamy refers to the tendency to marry someone with similar attributes.
4. Liking is based on similarities and respect. Love is deeper in that it involves need, intimacy and caring.
5. Students' answers will vary. Encourage students to consider a time when they may have experienced "love at first sight." Ask them to consider how that relationship developed and how parent interviews will vary.

CHAPTER 18

Summary and Vocabulary

Psychologists have provided insights into why people choose to interact with some people and not with others. They also have provided insights into why people want to be around other people.

Section 1 Interpersonal Attraction

Main Idea: We depend on others to survive. We are attracted to certain people because of factors such as proximity, reward values, physical appearance, approval, similarity, and complementarity.

- Social psychologists have discovered that people need company most when they are afraid or anxious or when they are unsure of themselves and want to compare their feelings with other people's.
- The closer two individuals are geographically to one another, the more likely they are to become attracted to each other.
- Friendships provide three rewards—stimulation, utility, and ego support.

Section 2 Social Perception

Main Idea: We explain the behavior of others by making judgments about them. Our judgments are influenced by our perceptions of others.

- Forming impressions about others helps us place these people in categories.
- We form first impressions of people based on schemas.
- When people develop schemas for entire groups of people, they are developing stereotypes.
- People often try to interpret and explain others' behavior by identifying what caused the behavior.
- Communication in a relationship consists of both verbal and nonverbal messages.

Section 3 Personal Relationships

Main Idea: People experience different types of love and relationships throughout their lives.

- Children apply knowledge gained from parent-child relationships to relationships with others.
- There are two common types of love: passionate love and companionate love.
- Zick Rubin found that love in long-term relationships is based on attachment, caring, and intimacy.
- Robert Sternberg contends that love is made of intimacy, passion, and commitment.
- People tend to marry someone who is from their own social group and who has similar attributes.
- The success of a marriage seems to depend on whether the couple's needs are compatible, whether their images of themselves coincide with their images of each other, and whether they agree on what their roles in the marriage are.
- Parents and their children may have difficulty adjusting to divorce.

Chapter Vocabulary

social psychology (p. 519)
social cognition (p. 519)
physical proximity (p. 522)
stimulation value (p. 523)
utility value (p. 523)
ego-support value (p. 523)
complementarity (p. 525)
primacy effect (p. 528)
stereotype (p. 530)
attribution theory (p. 530)
fundamental attribution error (p. 531)
actor-observer bias (p. 531)
self-serving bias (p. 531)
nonverbal communication (p. 531)
generational identity (p. 534)

Using the Chapter 18 Summary and Vocabulary

Use the Chapter 18 Summary and Vocabulary to preview, review, condense, or reteach the chapter.

Preview/Review

Use the Chapter Vocabulary list to help students review and study.

Activity Ask students to make a set of flash cards with the vocabulary terms on one side and their definitions on the other. Encourage students to use the flash cards to review the vocabulary.

Vocabulary PuzzleMaker CD-ROM reinforces the vocabulary terms used in Chapter 18.

Condense

Have students read the Chapter 18 Summary.

Chapter 18 Guided Reading Activities

Reteach

Reteaching Activity 18

PERFORMANCE ASSESSMENT ACTIVITY

Creating an Exhibit Tell students they are curators of a museum planning an exhibit entitled "Human Interaction." Organize the class into three groups, and ask each group to find works of art related to one of the three chapter sections. Students should find photographs or reproductions of paintings and sculptures that depict people interacting in various ways. Students may use photocopies. Groups should prepare captions to accompany the works.

Refer to the ***Authentic Assessment*** booklet for additional activities and information about evaluating student performance.

PSYCHOLOGY Online

Have students visit the Web site at glencoe.com to review Chapter 18 and take the **Self-Check Quiz**.

GLENCOE TECHNOLOGY

Presentation Plus! For a review of Chapter 18 content, see MindJogger Checkpoint on **Presentation Plus!**

Reviewing Vocabulary

1. d
2. i
3. f
4. b
5. a
6. h
7. j
8. g
9. c
10. e

Recalling Facts

1. The most important factor is physical proximity. It increases the likelihood that two people will interact and become attracted to each other.
2. People are more likely to choose friends whose backgrounds, attitudes, and interests are similar to their own.
3. You should try to do well on the first test. The primacy effect is at work in this situation. This is the tendency for people to form opinions about others based on first impressions.
4. Rubin's three major components of romantic love are need or attachment, caring or the desire to give, and intimacy.
5. The three factors upon which marital happiness depends are (1) whether the couple's needs are compatible, (2) whether the husband's and wife's images of themselves coincide with their images of each other, and (3) whether they agree to what the husband's and wife's roles are in the marriage.

Critical Thinking

1. Answers will vary. Students should be able to identify all three forms of friendship rewards–stimulation value, utility value, and ego-support value.
2. Answers will vary. Students' answers should recognize the advantages and disadvantages of stereotypes.

CHAPTER 18 Assessment

PSYCHOLOGY Online

Self-Check Quiz

Visit the *Understanding Psychology* Web site at glencoe.com and click on **Chapter 18—Self-Check Quizzes** to prepare for the Chapter Test.

Reviewing Vocabulary

Choose the letter of the correct term or concept below to complete the sentence.

a. social cognition
b. physical proximity
c. stimulation value
d. utility value
e. complementarity
f. stereotype
g. attribution theory
h. self-serving bias
i. nonverbal communication
j. generational identity

1. A friend who is able to give you his or her time and resources to help you achieve your goal has __________.
2. Waving at someone to get his or her attention is an example of __________.
3. A(n) __________ is an exaggerated set of assumptions about an identifiable group of people.
4. __________ refers to the distance from one another that people live or work.
5. The study of how people perceive, store, and retrieve information about social interactions is called __________.
6. Claiming personal responsibility for positive occurrences and blaming circumstances beyond our control for negative occurrences is called a(n) __________.
7. The tendency for members of different generations to think differently about things refers to the __________.
8. An analysis of how we interpret and understand other people's behavior is called __________.
9. A friend who wants to try new experiences has __________.
10. An attraction between opposite types of people is called __________.

Recalling Facts

1. What is the most important factor in determining the start of a friendship? Why is this factor important?
2. In general, are you likely to choose as a friend a person who is similar to you or a person who complements your strengths and weaknesses?
3. If you want people to think that you are smart, should you try to do your best on the first, second, or last test in a class? Why?
4. Using a diagram similar to the one below, identify Rubin's three major components of romantic love.

5. Identify three factors upon which marital happiness depends.

Critical Thinking

1. **Evaluating Information** Think of people with whom you are friends. Which rewards do you get from these friendships?
2. **Analyzing Concepts** We may think that stereotyping does not influence us. Watch a television program about (a) a detective, (b) an African American family, (c) a white family, and (d) an independent woman. What traits does each character have? Are these stereotypes?
3. **Making Inferences** People sometimes are accused of saying one thing but meaning another. Do you think people's nonverbal communication sometimes conflicts with their verbal communication? Explain.
4. **Synthesizing Information** Pretend someone has just asked you, "How do I know if I'm in love?" How would you respond?
5. **Applying Information** How could understanding fundamental attribution error help you better explain the behavior of others?

3. Answers will vary. People's body language often conveys their real feelings, even those they may verbally deny.
4. Answers will vary. Students should consider Rubin's three major components of romantic love in their answers.
5. Answers will vary. You would understand that the behaviors you observe have situational, not just internal, causes. For example, a student sleeping in class may be sleep deprived due to home or work factors (and not disinterested, as one might first assume.)

Psychology Projects

1. Have students identify which types of rewards they are expecting from and adding to the friendship they have described in the ad.
2. Students' essays should reflect an understanding of the concepts discussed in this chapter. Challenge students to identify the source of one or more of these quotes.

Assessment

Psychology Projects

1. **Interpersonal Attraction** Prepare a want ad in which you advertise for a friend. Include the main characteristics you look for in a friend in the advertisement.
2. **Social Perception** In an essay, support or refute the following common-sense sayings with information you learned from the chapter:
   "Birds of a feather flock together."
   "Opposites attract."
   "Familiarity breeds contempt."
   "Beauty is only skin deep."
   "Absence makes the heart grow fonder."

Technology Activity

Several sites on the Internet are designed to help parents and teenagers deal with conflicts. Find these Web sites and evaluate the suggestions they offer.

Psychology Journal

Some claim that nonverbal communication shows true feelings better than verbal communication. Write an essay that argues both sides of the issue. Use standard grammar, spelling, sentence structure, and punctuation.

Building Skills

Interpreting a Chart Ten thousand people from different countries in the world were surveyed about the characteristics they look for in a mate. Review the results in the chart below (1 is most important; 18 is least important), then answer the questions that follow.

Practice and **assess** key social studies skills with **Glencoe Skillbuilder Interactive Workbook CD-ROM, Level 2.**

See the Skills Handbook, page 628, for an explanation of interpreting charts.

Rank Ordering of Desired Characteristics in a Mate

	China		South Africa Zulu		United States	
	Males	Females	Males	Females	Males	Females
Ambition and industriousness	10	5	8	7	11	6
Chastity (no prior sexual intercourse)	3	6	13	18	17	18
Dependable character	6	7	3	1	3	3
Desire for home and children	2	2	9	9	9	7
Education and intelligence	8	4	6	6	5	5
Emotional stability and maturity	5	1	1	2	2	2
Favorable social status or rating	14	13	17	14	14	14
Good cook and housekeeper	9	11	2	15	13	16
Good financial prospect	16	14	18	13	16	11
Good health	1	3	5	4	6	9
Good looks	11	15	14	16	7	13
Mutual attraction—love	4	8	10	5	1	1
Pleasing disposition	13	16	4	3	4	4
Refinement, neatness	7	10	7	10	10	12
Similar education	15	12	12	12	12	10
Similar political background	17	17	15	17	18	17
Similar religious background	18	18	16	11	15	15
Sociability	12	9	11	8	8	8

Source: Feldman, Robert. *Understanding Psychology.* Boston: McGraw-Hill College, 2005.

1. In which country were males and females most in agreement about the kinds of characteristics they looked for in a mate?
2. Which characteristic ranked the lowest among both males and females in each of the three countries included on the chart? How do you explain this?

Assessment

Building Skills

1. United States
2. In China, males and females rated similar religious backgrounds lowest. Among the Zulus, males rated good financial prospect lowest, while females rated chastity lowest. In the United States, males rated similar political background lowest, while women rated chastity lowest. Students' explanations should recognize the impact of the culture on these rankings.

GLENCOE TECHNOLOGY

CD-ROM
Glencoe Skillbuilder Interactive Workbook, Level 2

This interactive CD-ROM is designed to reinforce student mastery of essential social studies skills.

Chapter Bonus Test Question

This question may be used for extra credit on the Chapter Assessment.
Answer the following question:
Joseph Addison was quoted as saying: "________________ improves happiness, and abates misery, by doubling our joy, and dividing our grief." What word completes the quote?
Answer: friendship

Technology Activity

Have students ask for their parents' thoughts about these sites. Encourage them to share the addresses of the Web sites they found with the class.

Psychology Journal

Students' answers should express their ability to examine both sides of an issue and argue each point without identifying their own point of view.

Chapter 19 Resource Guide

SECTION RESOURCES		
Daily Objectives	**Reproducible Resources**	**Multimedia Resources**
Section 1 **Group Behavior** Explain that a group is a collection of people who interact, share common goals, and influence how members think and act. Explore how groups are unified by the attitudes and standards members share and their commitment to them.	Guided Reading Activity 19–1 Vocabulary Activity 19–1 Section Quiz 19–1	Daily Focus Transparency 19–1 *ExamView® Assessment Suite* CD-ROM Presentation Plus! Software
Section 2 **Conformity and Obedience** Describe how you may engage in behavior because of direct or indirect group pressure or in response to orders given by authorities.	Guided Reading Activity 19–2 Vocabulary Activity 19–2 Section Quiz 19–2	Daily Focus Transparency 19–2 *ExamView® Assessment Suite* CD-ROM Presentation Plus! Software
Section 3 **Conflict and Cooperation** Explore conflicts between groups that result because groups influence how individuals perceive and respond to situations.	Guided Reading Activity 19–3 Vocabulary Activity 19–3 Section Quiz 19–3	Daily Focus Transparency 19–3 Vocabulary PuzzleMaker CD-ROM *ExamView® Assessment Suite* CD-ROM Presentation Plus! Software

Blackline Master   CD-ROM   Transparency

Block Schedule

Activities that are particularly suited for use within the block-scheduling framework are identified throughout this chapter by the following designation: **BLOCK SCHEDULING**

KEY TO ABILITY LEVELS

Teaching strategies have been coded for varying learning styles and abilities.

L1 **BASIC** activities for all students

L2 **AVERAGE** activities for average to above-average students

L3 **CHALLENGING** activities for above-average students

ELL **ENGLISH LANGUAGE LEARNER** activities

Chapter 19 Resource Guide

Timesaving Tools

TeacherWorks™ **All-In-One Planner and Resource Center**

- **Interactive Teacher Edition** Access your Teacher Wraparound Edition and your classroom resources with a few easy clicks.
- **Interactive Lesson Planner** Planning has never been easier! Organize your week, month, semester, or year with all the lesson helps you need to make teaching creative, timely, and relevant.

Use Glencoe's **Presentation Plus!** multimedia teacher tool to easily present dynamic lessons that visually excite your students. Using Microsoft PowerPoint® you can customize the presentations to create your own personalized lessons.

ACTIVITY

From the Classroom of...

James Murray
St. Francis Indian School
St. Francis, SD

Stereotypes

Purpose: To examine how stereotypes are formed and how they affect students' lives.

Collect pictures of people from different ethnic and social groups. Show the pictures to the class and have students write down their basic assumptions about the people in the pictures. Conduct a class discussion about the results. Ask why certain assumptions were made, what items, clothing, and so on affected students' assumptions. Then discuss the concept of stereotyping and its effects. Ask students to identify examples of stereotypes they encounter in everyday life. Conclude by assigning a reflective essay on how stereotyping affects students' lives. Students should consider what stereotypes they have of others, and what stereotypes others have of them.

PSYCHOLOGY Online

Use our Web site for additional resources. All essential content is covered in the Student Edition.

You and your students can visit glencoe.com, the Web site companion to *Understanding Psychology*. This innovative integration of electronic and print media offers your students a wealth of opportunities. The student text directs students to the Web site for the following options:

- Chapter Overviews
- Student Web Activities
- Self-Check Quizzes

Answers are provided for you in the **Web Activity Lesson Plan**. Additional Web resources and Interactive Puzzles are also available.

Chapter 19 Resource Guide

Note: The following materials may be used when teaching Chapter 19. Section level support materials are shown at point of use in the margins of the Teacher Wraparound Edition.

TEACHING TRANSPARENCIES

Chapter 19
Concept Transparencies

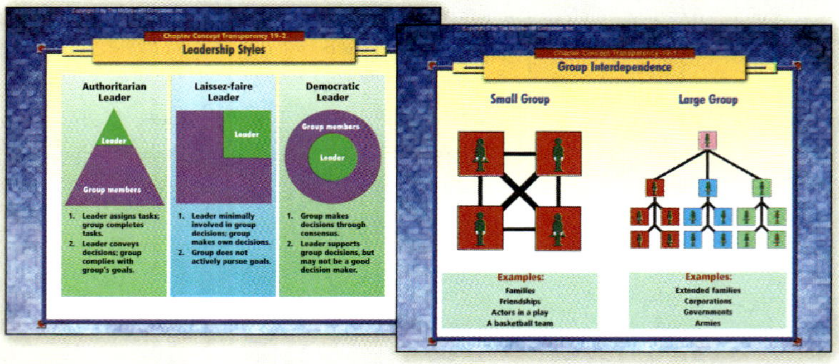

MULTIMEDIA

- **Vocabulary PuzzleMaker CD-ROM**
- ***ExamView® Assessment Suite* CD-ROM**
- **TeacherWorks™ CD-ROM**
- **Glencoe Skillbuilder Interactive Workbook, Level 2**
- **Presentation Plus! Software**

REVIEW AND REINFORCEMENT

Reteaching Activity 19

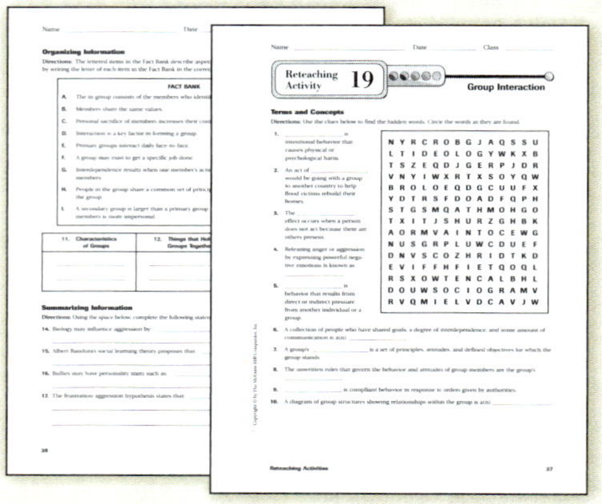

Graphic Organizer Activity 19

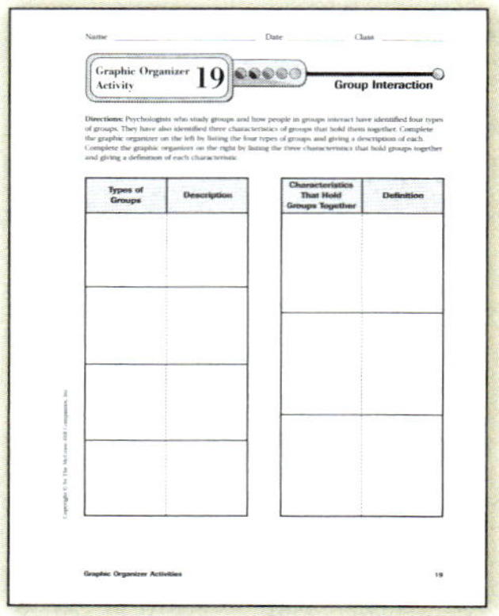

APPLICATION AND HANDS-ON

Psychology Project 19

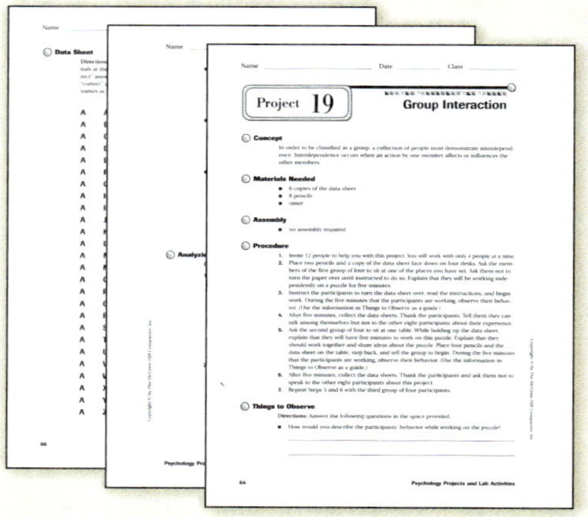

Application Activity 19

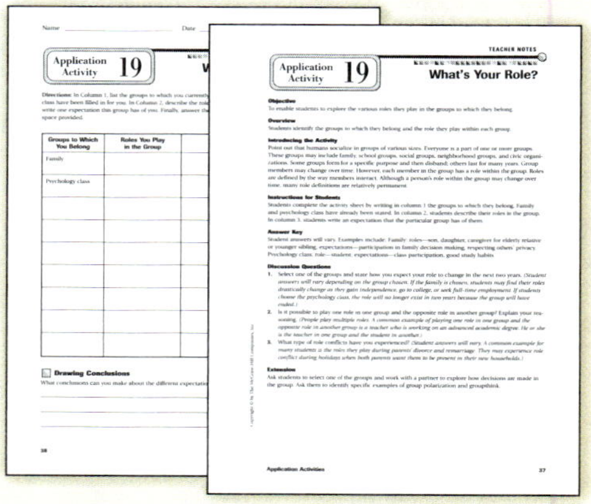

Chapter 19 Resource Guide

ASSESSMENT

Chapter 19 Test, Form A

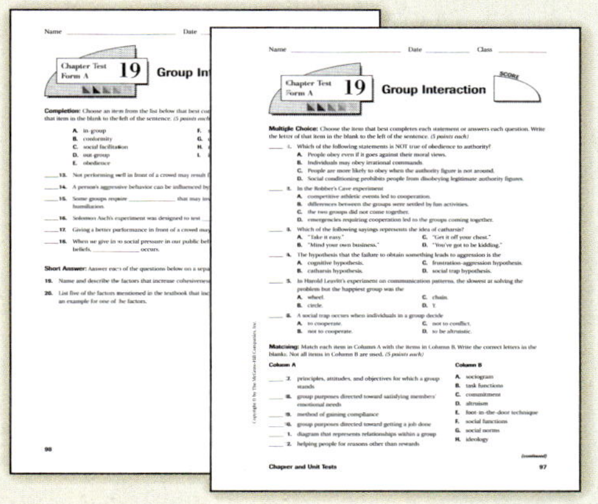

Chapter 19 Test, Form B

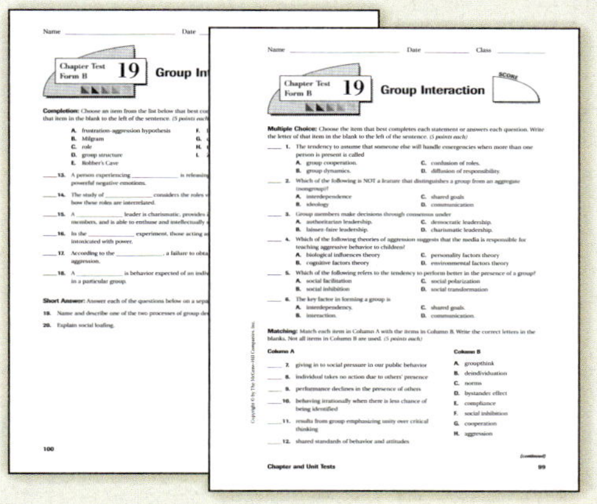

Authentic Assessment Activity 19

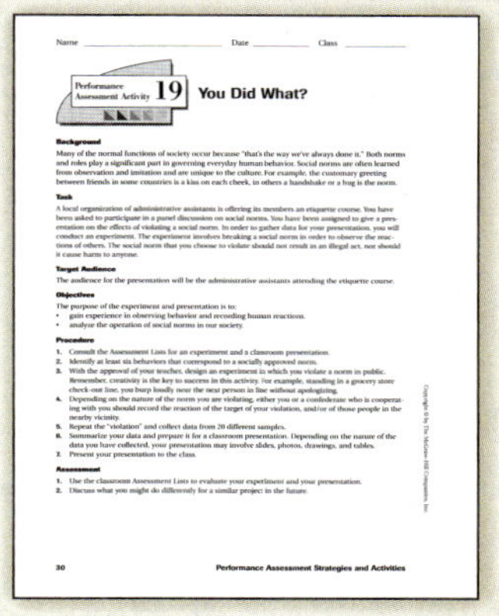

EXTENSION AND ENRICHMENT

Enrichment Activity 19

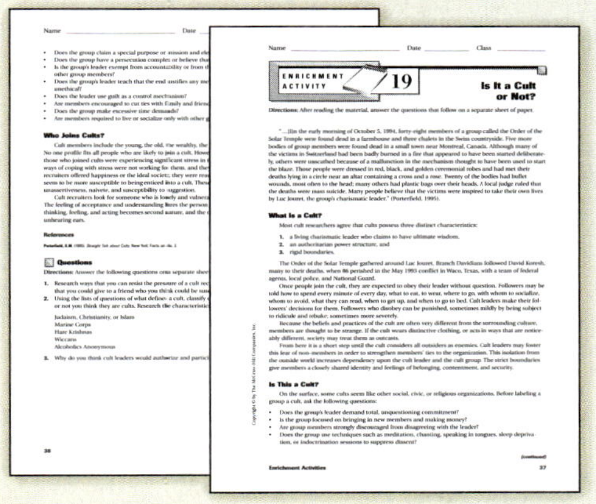

Critical Thinking Skills Activity 19

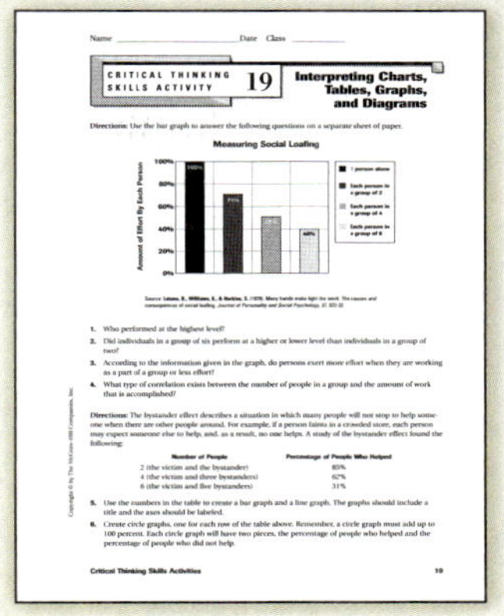

Psychology Reading 19

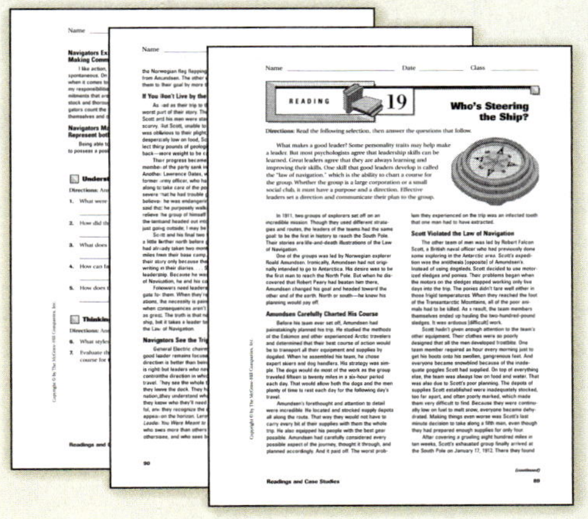

Psychology Case Study 19

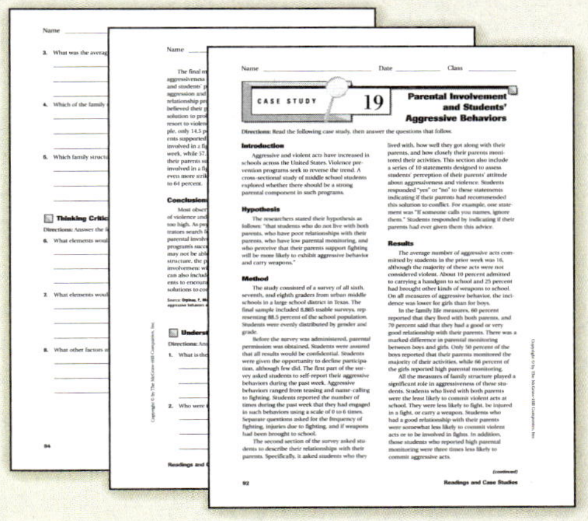

PSYCHOLOGY Online

Visit glencoe.com for a Chapter Overview for **Chapter 19—Group Interaction.**

GLENCOE TECHNOLOGY

For a preview of Chapter 19 content, see MindJogger Checkpoint on **Presentation Plus!**

Psychology Journal

Ask students to consider both positive and negative influences of the various groups to which they belong.

This journal activity provides the basis for the Psychology Journal activity exercise in the Chapter Assessment. ■

CHAPTER 19 Group Interaction

Psychology Journal

Think of the groups to which you belong—your family, your friends, the band, a sports team. What effect do these groups have on how you think, act, and feel? In your journal, describe any influences one of these has over you. ■

PSYCHOLOGY Online

Chapter Overview

Visit the *Understanding Psychology* Web site at glencoe.com and click on **Chapter 19—Chapter Overviews** to preview the chapter.

544

TWO-MINUTE LESSON LAUNCHER

Tell students that when people are in groups, deindividuation occurs. That is, the person's behavior becomes less inhibited. Explain that this lowered inhibition leads to an increase in impulsive acts, both positive and negative. Display pictures of groups performing uninhibited activities. First show pictures of people in groups enjoying activities such as dancing and celebrating a team's victory. Then show pictures of people in groups displaying aggression or antisocial behavior such as a college football crowd tearing down the goalpost or a riot. Ask students for their ideas on why people are less inhibited in large groups. Then ask for their ideas on how deindividuation can lead to violence and aggression.

SECTION 1 Group Behavior

Reader's Guide

Main Idea

A group—a collection of people who interact, share common goals, and influence how members think and act—is unified by the attitudes and standards members share and by their commitment to those beliefs.

Vocabulary

- group
- task functions
- social functions
- norms
- ideology
- social facilitation
- social inhibition
- group polarization
- groupthink
- sociogram

Objectives

- Define and explain different types of groups.
- Describe the interactive patterns within groups.

EXPLORING PSYCHOLOGY

Greasers Versus Socs

Anyway, I went on walking home, thinking about the movie, and then suddenly wishing I had some company. Greasers can't walk alone too much or they'll get jumped, or someone will come by and scream "Greaser!" at them, which doesn't make you feel too hot, if you know what I mean. We get jumped by the Socs. I'm not sure how you spell it, but it's the abbreviation for the Socials, the jet set, the West-side rich kids. It's like the term "greaser," which is used to class all us boys on the East Side.

—from *The Outsiders* by S.E. Hinton, 1967

In the passage above, S.E. Hinton's character Ponyboy tells his story, a story marked by the rivalry between two groups—the Socs and the Greasers. The differentiation between these groups influences Ponyboy's life to a great degree. What groups influence your life? Why?

WHAT ARE GROUPS?

What do the St. Stanislaus Parish Bowling Team, the AARP (American Association of Retired Persons), and country music's Dixie Chicks have in common? Each can be classified as a group. A **group** is a

group: a collection of people who have shared goals, a degree of interdependence, and some amount of communication

1 FOCUS

Section Objectives

1. Define and explain different types of groups.
2. Describe the interactive patterns within groups.

BELLRINGER
Motivational Activity

Project Daily Focus Transparency 19–1 and have students answer the questions.

Available as blackline master

Daily Focus Transparency 19–1

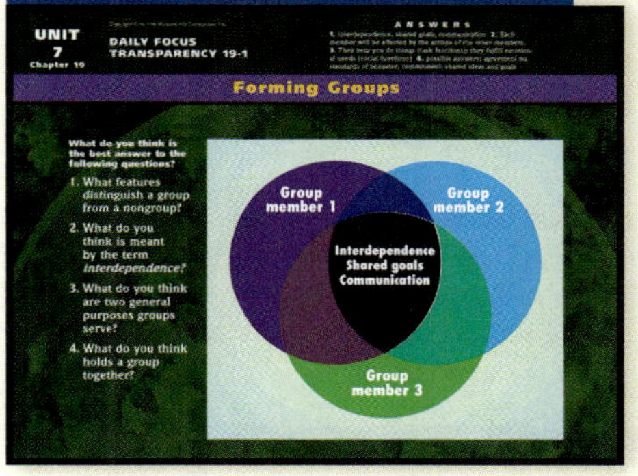

Reader's Guide

Use the Reader's Guide to introduce concepts and vocabulary.

Exploring Psychology
Ask students to read the **Exploring Psychology** feature. Ask: **What advantage does being a member of a group offer to individuals?**

Vocabulary Precheck
Have students create a word search puzzle using the Glossary definitions as clues for the terms.

SECTION RESOURCES

Reproducible Masters
- Guided Reading Activity 19–1
- Vocabulary Activity 19–1
- Section Quiz 19–1

Transparencies
- Daily Focus Transparency 19–1

Multimedia
- *ExamView® Assessment Suite* CD-ROM
- Presentation Plus! Software

CHAPTER 19

Section 1, pages 545–554

2 TEACH

L1 Writing a Case Study

Have students identify various groups within your school. List responses on the board. **Ask: Do certain norms apply to all the groups listed? What particular norms distinguish each group from all the others?** Divide the class into small groups. Ask each group to prepare a case study analyzing one of the school groups. The case study should identify the norms that pertain to each group. It should also identify each group's distinguishing ideology and the commitment of its members to the group. Share the case studies with the class and conduct a class discussion about the findings. **BLOCK SCHEDULING**

Figure 19.1

Caption Answer interdependence, shared goals, and communication

Guided Reading Activity 19–1

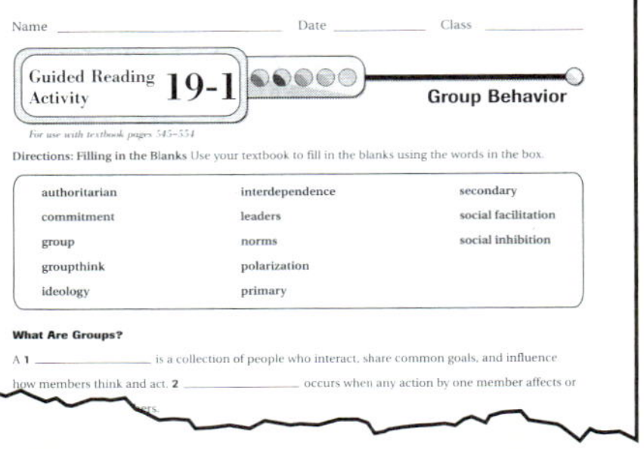
Name ______ Date ______ Class ______

Guided Reading Activity 19-1 — Group Behavior

For use with textbook pages 545–554

Directions: Filling in the Blanks Use your textbook to fill in the blanks using the words in the box.

authoritarian	interdependence	secondary
commitment	leaders	social facilitation
group	norms	social inhibition
groupthink	polarization	
ideology	primary	

What Are Groups?

A **1** ______ is a collection of people who interact, share common goals, and influence how members think and act. **2** ______ occurs when any action by one member affects or

PSYCHOLOGY JOURNAL

Ask students to write their thoughts on the following question: **Can a group formed for a task function become a group with a social function and vice versa?** ■

Figure 19.1 Teamwork

Whether or not the members of this surgical team get along outside the operating room does not matter. Their main purpose is to do a certain job. ***What are the features that groups share?***

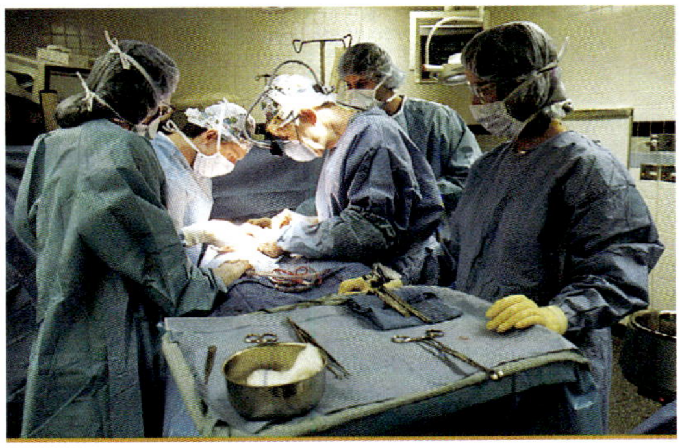

collection of people who interact, share common goals, and influence how members think and act. In general, members of a *group* are interdependent, have shared goals, and communicate with one another. People who congregate but do not interact are not considered a group but rather an *aggregate.* For example, a collection of people waiting to cross 4th Avenue at 33rd Street is not a group but just an aggregate. If the light refuses to change and enough people join, there is a common goal and there is interaction. When someone eventually starts across the street, the group will follow, exhibiting interdependence. *Interaction* is the key factor in forming a group.

Interdependence

To be classified as a group, a collection of people must be interdependent. Interdependence occurs when any action by one member will affect or influence the other members. For instance, in groups of athletes or roommates, each member has a certain responsibility to the rest of the group, and if he or she does not fulfill it, the other members will be affected. For the athletes, the consequence may be losing the game; for the roommates, a messy apartment. A person may be the group leader, the decision maker, the one who is the listener, or so on. If any person does not fulfill his or her role, the rest of the group is affected.

In small groups, members usually have a direct influence on one another: one member communicates directly with another. In larger groups, the influence may be indirect. The interdependence between you and the president of the United States is not a result of personal contact. Nevertheless, one of the things that makes the people of the United States a group is that the president's actions affect you and your actions, together with those of many other Americans, affect the president.

Communication

Whether it is boys or girls engaged in a neighborhood tug-of-war contest, a football team preparing for the big game, or a NASA launch team spread around the world, communication is crucial to the functions of a group. In some cases, the communication is directed outward as a declaration of group membership, such as when a member of the band wears a T-shirt or jacket with the school's logo or name.

In other instances, the communication is internal, intended for group members to discuss group activities and share common experiences. Direct communication aids members' feelings of belonging. It increases the likelihood that group members will respond differently to one another than to those who do not belong to the group. Communication encourages debate among members regarding individual goals and increases members' feelings of commitment to group goals.

COOPERATIVE LEARNING ACTIVITY

Building the Tallest Structure Organize groups into teams of three or four. Give each group 100 straws, ten paper clips, four thumb tacks, two feet of string, a pair of scissors, and a roll of masking tape. Ask each group to design and build the tallest structure possible (using only the supplied materials) that is also capable of supporting a golf ball. Tell them they have 20 minutes to complete the project. When each group is finished, test each structure by placing a golf ball within it. Also measure the height of each structure. Declare a winner. Afterwards, ask each group to analyze how interdependence, shared goals, norms, ideology, and commitment played a part in the group's successful completion of the assigned task (or its inability to do so). Have groups evaluate their areas of strength and weakness.

Shared Goals

Group members become interdependent because they share common goals. Groups are usually created to perform tasks or to organize activities that no individual could handle alone. Members of a consumer group, for example, share the common goal of working for consumer protection. Members of ethnic and religious groups desire to perpetuate a common heritage or set of beliefs.

The purposes groups serve are of two general kinds: **task functions,** those directed toward getting some job done; and **social functions,** those directed toward filling the emotional needs of members. In most groups, task and social functions are combined naturally and cannot be separated easily, although one dominates in any given group.

task functions: activities directed toward getting a job done

social functions: responses directed toward satisfying the emotional needs of members

Political parties, teams of surgeons, and crews of construction workers are all task-oriented groups. Although social interactions occur within each of these groups, their main purpose is to complete a project or achieve some change in the environment. Social functions are emphasized in more informal, temporary groups. When people take walks together, attend parties, or participate in conversations, they have formed a group to gain social rewards such as companionship and emotional support. Yet again, every group involves both task and social functions.

HOW GROUPS ARE HELD TOGETHER

The factors that work to hold a group together—that increase the group's *cohesiveness*—include shared attitudes and standards and the group's commitment to them.

norms: shared standards of behavior accepted by and expected from group members

Norms

Norms are unwritten rules that govern the behavior and attitudes of group members. They include rules—shared beliefs about the correct way to behave and what to believe. For example, there are rules about how to behave at home, at school, and at an amusement park. There are rules about what to say and how to communicate with brothers, sisters, parents, and friends. Would you use the same words and expressions with both your friends and your parents? Most people would not. These rules are not necessarily like rigid laws. They may be more like tendencies or habits, but group members are expected to act in accordance with group norms and are punished in some way if they do not. If a student consistently sneaks to the front of the lunch line, her friends would not hesitate to say something about it. Strangers might point and grow angry—simply because she violated a norm that you wait in line

Figure 19.2 Why Do We Join Groups?

Psychologists have proposed various reasons why we join groups. ***For what reason would you join a task-oriented group?***

They satisfy our need to belong.
We must compare ourselves to others who are similar to us.
We must compare our experiences with those of others who are similar to us.
We use group members as standards against which to evaluate ourselves.
Groups reduce our uncertainty.
Group members may offer us support in trying times.
Groups provide us with companionship.
Groups provide comfort and lessen our anxiety.
Groups help us accomplish things that we could not do alone.

CULTURAL CONNECTIONS

The United States is a country made up of a wide variety of ethnic groups, most of whom arrived as immigrants. Using 1990 census data, Gregory Rodriguez of Pepperdine University studied efforts that recent immigrants made to fit into the norms of American life. He examined several areas of commitment to norms including acquiring citizenship, learning English, and buying a home. He found that 75 percent of the immigrants who had been in America for at least 40 years had become citizens. The same percentage had learned English within 10 years of coming to the United States. In addition, within 20 years of coming to this country, more than 60 percent owned their own home. His conclusion is that the majority of immigrants accept the cultural norms of American life.

Figure 19.2

Visual Instruction Have students list two groups to which they belong. For each group, have them rank the items listed in the figure in order of importance.

Caption Answer to accomplish some goal or complete a job

MEETING SPECIAL NEEDS

Learning Style: Visual/Spatial Tell students to assume that they are part of an environmental awareness group that is planning a cleanup day. Have students develop a poster to attract people to a task-oriented group for the purpose of cleaning up a local park. Challenge them to use the poster to express the ideology of the group and to ask for a specific commitment. **L2** **BLOCK SCHEDULING**

Refer to ***Inclusion for the High School Social Studies Classroom Strategies and Activities*** in the TCR for strategies for students with different learning styles.

Figure 19.3

Caption Answer Answers will vary. Examples include sharing feelings and keeping group conversations confidential.

Looking @ the Issues

Online Communities Online communities are a relatively new type of group that allows members who share a common goal or interest to meet on the Internet. Like many groups, online communities face the challenge of membership commitment. These communities often have a core of supporters as well as peripheral members who are rarely, if ever, involved in the group. Online communities never meet face-to-face, and they can request membership participation but can do little if members choose not to comply. In addition, technical problems can discourage even interested members. However, as technology advances, more people will find themselves participating in online communities. **Ask: How might online membership in a group foster personal growth and development?**

PSYCHOLOGY Online

Links and instructional guidelines can be found in the **Web Activity Lesson Plan** at glencoe.com.

Figure 19.3 Group Norms

Social norms can be formal or informal. Formal norms are rules such as traffic laws. Informal norms are unwritten rules such as greeting friends and shaking your opponents' hands at the end of a game. ***What norms might be important to a group organized to serve social functions?***

after the people who arrived before you. Thus, the punishment may take the form of coldness or criticism from other group members. If the norm is very important to the group, a member who violates it may endure a more severe social reaction or may be excluded from the group.

Ideology

For a group to be cohesive, members must share the same values. In some cases, people are drawn together because they discover they have common ideas, attitudes, and goals—that is, a common **ideology.** In other instances, people are attracted to a group because its ideology provides them with a new way of looking at themselves and interpreting events, and a new set of goals and means for achieving them. The National Organization for Women (NOW), for example, has provided a focal point for resistance to discrimination on the basis of gender. The AARP (American Association of Retired Persons) lobbies for the rights of older people and retirees. Leaders, heroes and heroines, rallies, books and pamphlets, slogans, and symbols all help popularize an ideology, win converts, and create feelings of solidarity among group members.

ideology: the set of principles, attitudes, and defined objectives for which a group stands

Commitment

One factor that increases individual commitment is the requirement of personal sacrifice. If a person is willing to pay money, endure hardship, or undergo humiliation to join a group, he or she is likely to continue with it. For example, some groups in high school require initiation rites in order to join the group. College students who undergo embarrassing initiation rites to join sororities or fraternities tend to develop a loyalty to the group that lasts well beyond their college years. During your first year of high school, you also go through initiation rites. Seniors may tell new students about elevators that do not exist, stairwells that are blocked, or directions that lead to the wrong place. These common ordeals bind people to others in the group.

Another factor that strengthens group commitment is participation. When people actively participate in group decisions and share the rewards of the group's accomplishments, their feeling of membership increases—they feel that they have helped make the group what it is. For example, social psychologists have compared groups of workers who participate in decisions that affect their jobs with other workers who elect representatives to decision-making committees or workers who are simply told what to do. Those who participate have higher morale and accept change more readily than do the other workers (Coch & French, 1948). Other studies have highlighted the importance of supportive managers in maintaining

PSYCHOLOGY Online

Student Web Activity
Visit the *Understanding Psychology* Web site at glencoe.com and click on **Chapter 19—Student Web Activities** for an activity on group behavior.

CRITICAL THINKING ACTIVITY

Making Comparisons Ask students to attend a meeting of at least three different groups. Suggest that they consider community organizations and school organizations that have meetings open to the public. Have students analyze the leadership style of the person directing the meeting and the ways in which the group responds to the leader's style. After attending the different group meetings, students should prepare a report that compares the leadership styles of the groups' leaders and reaches a conclusion about the effectiveness of the various styles. Remind students to use standard grammar, spelling, sentence structure, and punctuation. **L2**

such worker involvement (Locke, Latham, & Erez, 1988).

The processes that hold a group together must work both ways. The individual must be responsive to the norms of the group, subscribe to its ideology, and be prepared to make sacrifices to be part of it. The group must also respond to the needs of its members. It cannot achieve cohesiveness if its norms are unenforceable, if its ideology is inconsistent with the beliefs of its members, or if the rewards it offers do not outweigh the sacrifices it requires.

Psychology and You

Social Norms

Visual behavior illustrates the effects of norms on our behavior. When you are passing someone in the hallway whom you do not know, you have two choices: to speak or not to speak. If you say hello, nod, or otherwise acknowledge the other person and he or she responds, then what? If you decide not to speak, then what?

In both instances, when you are between 10 and 18 feet in front of the person, accepted social rules are that you divert your eyes to the right. You might develop an interest in the bulletin board or simply look at the ceiling or floor. If you look at the person until your head is turned 90 degrees, it is considered pushy. If you turn and continue looking at the person as you walk down the hallway, it might be viewed as harassment or a challenge.

Similar norms operate in many different situations. For instance, it is customary for elevator riders to redistribute floor space more or less equally each time someone gets on or off. These norms are the unwritten rules that govern our social behavior.

TYPES OF GROUPS

Social psychologists are interested in what happens between groups of people. Groups can be differentiated by in-groups and out-groups and primary and secondary groups. When a group's members identify with their group, they are referred to as the *in-group.* The *out-group* includes everyone who is not a member of the in-group. Members of the out-group will be rejected by and could be hostile to the in-group.

A *primary* group is a group of people who interact daily face-to-face. Because of the frequency of these interactions, some situations may become emotionally charged. For example, you see your family members every day. You eat, sleep, and have fun with them, and you also fight with them. A *secondary* group is a larger group of people with whom you might have more impersonal relationships. For example, your psychology class is a secondary group.

Reading Check Name a primary and a secondary group with which you are involved.

SOCIAL FACILITATION VERSUS SOCIAL INHIBITION

Do you perform better or worse in front of a crowd? Have you heard of the "home team advantage"? This is another term for social facilitation. **Social facilitation** refers to the tendency to perform better in the presence of a group. At times, however, you may perform poorly in front of crowds. This is an example of **social inhibition.** Social facilitation and social inhibition may occur because the presence of a crowd increases one's drive or arousal.

Psychologist Robert Zajonc (1965) noticed that social facilitation seemed to occur when participants performed simple or well-learned tasks, whereas social inhibition occurred when participants performed more

social facilitation: an increase in performance in front of a crowd

social inhibition: a decrease in performance in front of a crowd

Psychology and You

Use the following questions to direct a class discussion after students have read the **Psychology and You** feature.

Ask: **Are the norms discussed in the feature universal or culturally based? How do social norms vary among cultures? Do social norms vary from generation to generation?**

Reading Check Answer Answers should indicate an understanding of the differences between the two types of groups.

Psychology Update

Control Groups When conducting experiments, researchers use an experimental group and a control group. Research on social facilitation usually uses people performing tasks alone as the control group. In a 1998 study, psychologists demonstrated that people who are assigned some task to perform alone will infer that they are being monitored. Since they assume they are being monitored, they should not be used as a control group to test the theory that people perform better in the presence of a group.

PSYCHOLOGY LAB EXPERIMENT

Examining Norms Use tape to outline an 8' x 8' square on the floor in front of the class. Tell students that the square represents an elevator. Designate a side of the square as the doorway. Call on students one at a time to enter the "elevator." Tell them to behave like strangers. Ask the rest of the class to observe the students' movements as the "elevator" fills to capacity. **Ask:** **Have all of the "passengers" arranged themselves facing the door? Have the males gravitated toward the sides and back?** After the "elevator" is full, call on two more students to enter. Have the class observe their behavior. After the demonstration, have a class discussion on the unwritten rules that govern elevator etiquette. L1 ELL

CHAPTER 19

Section 1, pages 545–554

Figure 19.4

Caption Answer Social inhibition might occur when performing a complex or unfamiliar task such as a difficult exam or a gymnastic feat in front of a crowd. Social inhibition may also occur when performing a complex task in front of an unfamiliar or expert crowd.

Vocabulary Activity 19–1

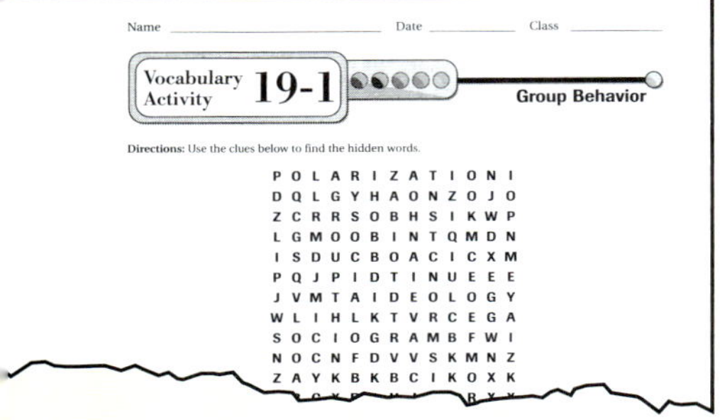
Name ______ Date ______ Class ______

Vocabulary Activity 19-1 Group Behavior

Directions: Use the clues below to find the hidden words.

P	O	L	A	R	I	Z	A	T	I	O	N	I
D	Q	L	G	Y	H	A	O	N	Z	O	J	O
Z	C	R	R	S	O	B	H	S	I	K	W	P
L	G	M	O	O	B	I	N	T	Q	M	D	N
I	S	D	U	C	B	O	A	C	I	C	X	M
P	Q	J	P	I	D	T	I	N	U	E	E	E
J	V	M	T	A	I	D	E	O	L	O	G	Y
W	L	I	H	L	K	T	V	R	C	E	G	A
S	O	C	I	O	G	R	A	M	B	F	W	I
N	O	C	N	F	D	V	V	S	K	M	N	Z
Z	A	Y	K	B	K	B	C	I	K	O	X	K

TEACHER Tip

Tell students that one way to increase cooperation between in-group and out-group members is to create opportunities for in-group members to interact with out-group members. One challenge of this strategy is that in-group members must be convinced that the out-group member they are interacting with is representative of other out-group members. If they do not believe that the person is representative, they will likely not change their attitude about the out-group.

Figure 19.4 Performance Factors

Some people perform better in front of crowds, and others do not. Whether you show social facilitation or social inhibition depends on your past experience, the task at hand, and the crowd itself. ***When might social inhibition occur?***

complex tasks or tasks that involved unfamiliar factors to the participants. So, in effect, how you perform in front of a crowd depends on what you are doing. For example, if you are an expert tennis player but a novice piano player, you may perform better in front of others while playing tennis but poorly in front of others when you are trying to play a rendition of "Heart and Soul."

The effect of a crowd on your behavior may also be a reflection of your concern about being evaluated. For example, you may play an excellent game of tennis in front of your friends and parents, but your performance may slip while playing in front of college recruiters.

INTERACTIONS WITHIN GROUPS

Providing an individual with values and a sense of identity is only one aspect of the group's meaning to him or her. The particular role he or she plays in the group's activities is also important. Each group member has certain unique abilities and interests, and the group has a number of different tasks that need to be performed. The study of the roles various members play in the group and how these roles are interrelated is the study of *group structure.*

There are many aspects to group structure: the personal relationships between individual members, such as liking relationships and trusting relationships; the rank of each member on a particular dimension, such as power, popularity, status, or amount of resources; and the roles various members play. A *role* is behavior expected of an individual because of his or her membership in a particular group. Thus, when your class meets, someone has the role of teacher, and others have the role of students. Is someone a student leader in your class? Does someone always remain silent? Is another person always making jokes? Each of us has *multiple roles* that shift as we merge with different groups. Occasionally, we may find ourselves in *role conflict,* such as if you switch schools and your old school plays your new school in football.

Decision Making

Most groups must make decisions. For example, you and your friends must decide what to do Saturday night. Jurors must decide whether a defendant is guilty or not guilty. A president's advisory committee must determine the proper solution to a company crisis. Group polarization and groupthink are two processes that affect group decision making.

group polarization: theory that group discussion reinforces the majority's point of view and shifts group members' opinions to a more extreme position

Group Polarization Have you ever expressed an opinion and discussed it with a group of friends? How did the discussion affect the strength of your opinion? According to **group polarization**, if you discuss an

INTERDISCIPLINARY CONNECTIONS ACTIVITY

Literature Fiction often provides keen insights into how norms govern social behavior. Assign students to research and find an example of a novel, short story, play, or fairy tale in which a character breaks a norm and suffers social consequences. (Nathaniel Hawthorne's *The Scarlet Letter* and Stephen Crane's *Red Badge of Courage* are classic examples.) Have students prepare a synopsis of their chosen work and present it orally to the class. **L2**

opinion with a group of people and a majority of the members argue for one side of the issue, the discussion typically pushes the majority to a more extreme view than they held before the discussion (see Figure 19.5). In this process, the majority's point of view is reinforced. The repetition of the same arguments results in stronger attitudes in support of the majority's view. If opinions of a group are equally split on an issue before a discussion, though, the group discussion usually results in compromise.

For example, say you think that bikers should wear helmets. One afternoon at lunch, the subject of bikers and helmets comes up. Most of your friends also believe that bikers should wear helmets. As your group discusses the issue, you and your friends use examples and your own reasoning to argue the point. You come away from the discussion feeling very strongly about the issue—much more strongly than before the discussion. You feel that it should be mandatory for bikers to wear helmets.

Groupthink Throughout history, government leaders have sometimes made poor decisions. When John F. Kennedy became president of the United States in 1961, he faced the problem of Fidel Castro, the Communist leader of Cuba. Castro formed a close alliance with the Soviet Union, and this alliance threatened the security of the United States. Kennedy ordered a secret invasion of Cuba to overthrow Castro. The invasion at the Bay of Pigs failed miserably, making Kennedy's administration look weak and bringing the world close to nuclear war. Why did Kennedy make this ill-fated decision? Kennedy and his administration were probably the victims of groupthink.

When groups stick together and fail to adequately appraise alternative courses of action, they are guilty of **groupthink.** When engaged in groupthink, the members of a group do not make the best decisions. Group members may refrain from criticizing one another, and they may not discuss opposing viewpoints or evaluate the situation critically.

While discussing the Bay of Pigs invasion, Kennedy's advisers failed to critically examine Kennedy's decision to invade. Instead, they

groupthink: poor group decision making that occurs as a result of a group emphasizing unity over critical thinking

Figure 19.5 Group Polarization

Each triangle represents the opinion of one individual. Before the group discussion, individuals are divided in the content and strength of their opinions. After the group discussion, individuals' opinions move toward a more extreme version from their initial opinions. ***Why do opinions become more extreme during group polarization?***

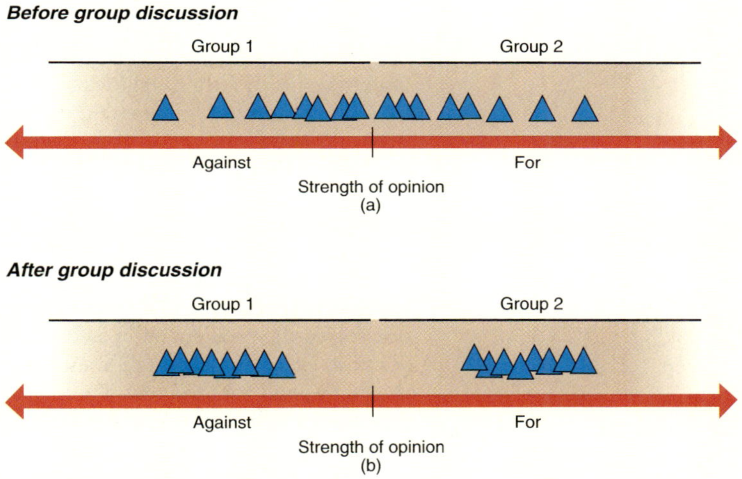

Source: Peter Gray, *Psychology*, 2006.

Looking @ the Issues

Group Polarization Studies of group polarization in the 1960s showed that groups will make riskier decisions than individuals within the group. However, more recent studies have shown that group decisions become stronger than individual opinions. For example, if the individuals in the group independently favor a conservative position, the group as a whole will likely take an even more conservative position than expressed by individual members. **Ask: Why do groups tend to take more extreme positions than the individual group members?**

Figure 19.5

Visual Instruction Have a class discussion listing the causes of group polarization. Ask students if one dissenting voice can make a difference in such a group. *(Studies show that one dissenting voice can reduce the strength of the group's decision but is not likely to change it.)*

Caption Answer The majority's point of view is being reinforced.

EXTENDING THE CONTENT

The Influence of Cultural Norms Cross-cultural studies using Choice Dilemma Questionnaires examine whether groups take riskier or less risky positions than the individuals in the group. The questionnaire presents a series of dilemmas. Participants identify the probability of success that they would require to select the riskiest alternative course of action. In the United States, where risky behavior is accepted and even applauded, groups tended to make riskier choices than the individuals in the group. In contrast, in Uganda where caution is valued over risk taking, groups tended to make more cautious decisions than the individuals in the group. Thus, group behavior is influenced by cultural norms.

Figure 19.6

Caption Answer Group members should make sure all viewpoints are expressed; group unity should not be the goal. Instead, groups should focus on keeping the lines of communication open and gathering enough information to make an unbiased decision.

Applying **Psychology**

Assign students to observe the interactions within a small group in the community or perhaps a group with which they are themselves affiliated. Instruct students to interview each member in the group to learn with which group member he or she would most likely interact. Then the students should analyze the group's hierarchical structure and represent it by constructing a sociogram like the ones pictured in Figure 19.7. Have students present their finished sociograms to the class and explain the interactions that they represent.

Readings and Case Studies in Psychology
Have students read the Chapter 19 Reading selection in *Readings and Case Studies in Psychology* and answer the questions that follow the reading.

3 ASSESS

Assign Section 1 Assessment as homework or as an in-class activity.

Figure 19.6 The *Challenger* Explosion

The decision to launch the *Challenger* U.S. space shuttle in below-freezing weather in January 1986 was the result of groupthink. Managers ignored the engineers' warnings about the dangers of launching. In full view of people on the ground and millions more on television, the space shuttle exploded just after its launch. ***How can groups prevent groupthink?***

sought to please the president and present a unified front. Several hundred members of the invading force at the Bay of Pigs lost their lives as a result of the decision.

How to Improve Group Decision Making Groups can avoid bad decision making and improve the quality of their decisions. Leaders should avoid strongly advocating their own views and, instead, encourage group discussion. During discussion, group members should hear all viewpoints and challenge one another's views. Minority viewpoints should be expressed and discussed. Also, group members should focus on the task—the issue to be discussed or the problem to be resolved. Group members should not focus on group unity when making decisions; however, they should focus on keeping the lines of communication open and gathering enough information to make an unbiased decision.

Communication Patterns

When studying groups, social psychologists use a technique called the **sociogram** to analyze group structure. All members of a group are asked to name those people with whom they would like to interact, those they like best, and those with whom they'd rather not work. For example, the members may be asked with whom they would like to go to a party, to discuss politics, to spend a vacation, or to complete a task. Their choices can then be diagrammed, as shown in Figure 19.7. Sociograms can help psychologists predict how that individual is likely to communicate with other group members. Another way to discover the structure of a group is to examine the communication patterns in the group—who says what to whom and how often.

sociogram: a diagram that represents relationships within a group, especially likes and dislikes of members for other members

An experiment on communication patterns in problem solving was conducted by Harold Leavitt in 1951. He gave a card with several symbols on it to each person in a group of five and put each person in a separate room or booth. By allowing group members to communicate only by written messages in a certain configuration, he was able to create the networks shown in Figure 19.8. Each circle represents a person, and the lines represent open channels. Participants placed in each position could exchange messages only with the person to whom they were connected by channels.

The people who were organized into a "circle" were the slowest at solving the problem presented on the cards but the happiest at doing it. In this group everyone sent and received a large number of messages until someone solved the problem and passed the information on. In the "wheel," by contrast, everyone sent a few messages to one central person, who solved the puzzle and told the rest. These groups found the answer quickly, but the people on the outside of the wheel did not enjoy the job.

Following the experiment, the members in each group were asked to identify the leader of their group. In the centralized groups (wheel, Y, and chain), the person in the center was usually chosen as the group leader.

PSYCHOLOGY LAB EXPERIMENT

Case Study Ask students to identify a school or community group that has failed or dissolved. If possible, have students interview members of the group to explore the reasons the group failed. If interviews are not possible, have students conduct research on the group's demise. From the interviews or the gathered facts, students should write a case study analyzing the reasons for failure based on the three cohesiveness factors—norms, ideology, and commitment. Encourage students to share their case studies with the class. **L2** **BLOCK SCHEDULING**

In the circle network, however, half the group members said they thought there was no real leader, and those who did say there was a leader disagreed on who that leader was. Thus a centralized organization seems more useful for task-oriented groups, whereas a decentralized network is more useful in socially oriented groups.

Leadership

All groups, whether made up of students, workers, Girl Scouts, or politicians, have leaders. A leader embodies the norms and ideals of the group and represents the group to outsiders. Within the group, a leader initiates action, gives orders, makes decisions, and settles disputes. An effective leader has a great deal of influence on the other members.

Leadership may be defined in several ways. Most of us think of leadership as a *personality trait.* To an extent, this is true. One psychologist (Stogdill, 1974) identified leadership as being an aspect of personality—the ability to get people to comply. It can be thought of as skills in social influence or persuasion or simply as social power. It has been found that leaders tend to be better adjusted, more self-confident, more energetic and outgoing, and slightly more intelligent than other members of their group (Gibb, 1969). Other researchers (Blake & Mouton, 1985) proposed a different model. They argue that leaders are concerned to some degree with both output (that is, the task) and the welfare of the people. Each dimension is separate, and any leader can be at any level on either dimension. A leader deeply concerned with both output and welfare would likely develop a team management program so that workers contribute to the group's goals. A leader concerned solely with output would stress obedience, and a leader whose primary concern was the worker might create a stress-free atmosphere with a friendly organization. A leader who cared little for output or welfare might encourage workers to do the minimum to keep things functioning (Blake & McCanse, 1991).

Another way to think of leadership is as the *end product of the reinforcements of the group* being led (Berry & Houston, 1993). In this way, leadership is simply the center or focus of group action, an instrument for achieving the group's goal or a result of group interaction (Stogdill, 1974). In this sense, the nature of the group in part determines who will lead. Different circumstances call for different kinds of leaders. A group that is threatened by internal conflict requires a leader who is good at handling people, settling disputes, and soothing tempers. A group that has a complex task to perform needs a leader with special experience in setting goals and planning strategies to achieve them (Fiedler, 1969).

Another kind of leadership is called a *transformational leadership.* This leadership produces large-scale organizational change by changing the goals of group members and deepening their commitment. Transformational leaders are charismatic, they provide individualized attention to group members, and they are able to enthuse and intellectually stimulate group members. Charisma refers to a leader's persuasive powers. This, in turn, is based on the followers' perceptions of the leader's talents and expertise. When a leader is charismatic, followers trust the correctness

Figure 19.7 Sociograms

In these sociograms, the blue arrows indicate admiration that is not returned, and the black arrows indicate a two-way friendship. The more a person is liked, the higher in the pattern he or she appears. The pattern of the bottom group shows a hierarchical structure. ***Who are the leaders in the bottom group?***

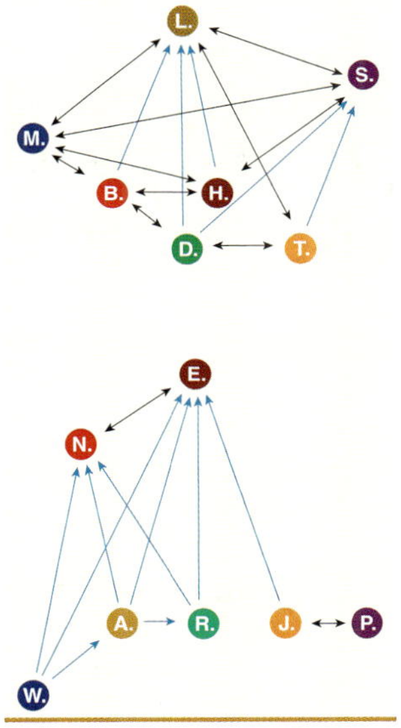

CHAPTER 19
Section 1, pages 545–554

Figure 19.7

Visual Instruction Ask students to define *sociogram* and to explain how researchers go about constructing them.

Caption Answer E and N

Section Quiz 19–1

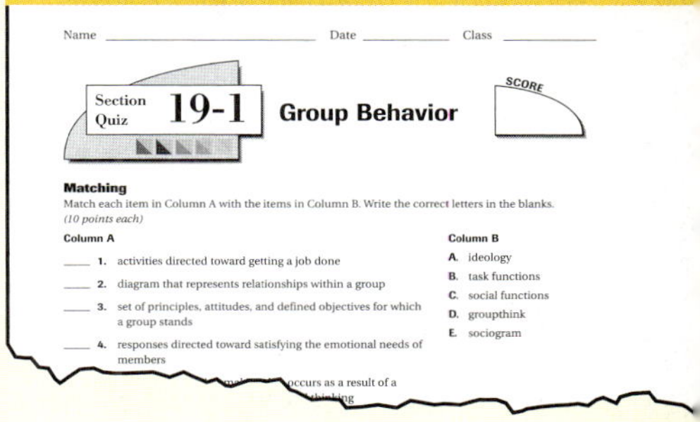

Name ______ Date ______ Class ______

Section Quiz 19-1 Group Behavior

SCORE

Matching

Match each item in Column A with the items in Column B. Write the correct letters in the blanks.
(10 points each)

Column A

___ 1. activities directed toward getting a job done

___ 2. diagram that represents relationships within a group

___ 3. set of principles, attitudes, and defined objectives for which a group stands

___ 4. responses directed toward satisfying the emotional needs of members

Column B

A. ideology
B. task functions
C. social functions
D. groupthink
E. sociogram

Reteach

Have students explain what is meant by "norms of behavior." Ask them to work in pairs to role-play the violation of a social norm. Encourage the class to identify the norm that is being violated.

EXTENDING THE CONTENT

What Makes a Leader? The ongoing debate among social scientists about how leaders are made may never be resolved. Many believe that leadership qualities are innate. Bruce Avolio and his colleagues have conducted research on leadership for more than 10 years. He believes that, with training, anyone can master the skills needed for leadership. He recommends the following: "Visualize obstacles; set goals and find someone who will hold you accountable to them; seek and incorporate feedback from colleagues; reflect on your best and worst moments; train gradually; broaden your model of leadership to include a full range of styles; and honor high ethical standards." *Source:* Avolio, B. (1999, September/October). Are leaders born or made? *Psychology Today, 32 (5),* 18. **L1**

CHAPTER 19
Section 1, pages 545–554

Figure 19.8

Visual Instruction Have students identify the dot in each figure that represents the group leader. *(The center dots in the "Chain," "Y," and "Wheel" models represent the group leaders. The "Circle" model has no primary leader.)*

Caption Answer Leavitt's findings show that centralized organizations are more useful for task-oriented groups, whereas a decentralized network is more useful in socially oriented groups.

Enrich

Ask pairs of students to arrange to interview human resource personnel to identify how teams are used in their companies. Have the pairs report their findings in oral reports.

4 CLOSE

Reproduce the Wheel and Circle models of communication networks (shown in Figure 19.8) on the board. Ask students to explain the kind of interaction that occurs in each model. Then ask them to explain why the Circle network is slower but more satisfying than the Wheel network for solving tasks.

Figure 19.8 Leavitt's Communication Network System

Each dot represents a person. The lines represent open channels. Participants could exchange messages only with the person to whom they were connected by channels. ***What were Leavitt's findings regarding centralized organizations?***

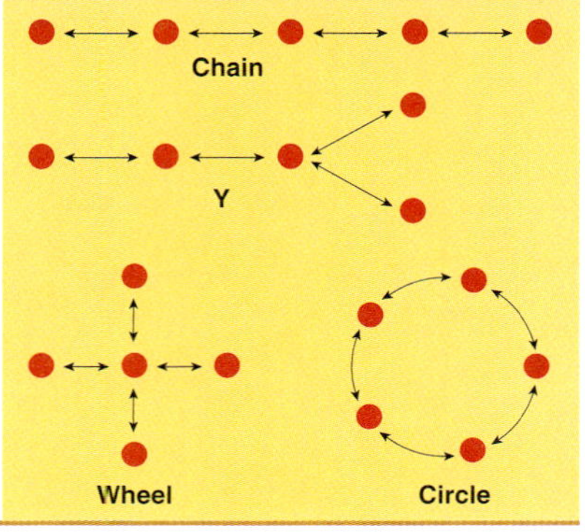

of the leader's views, obey the leader willingly, feel affection for the leader, and are motivated to perform at peak levels. Presidents Franklin D. Roosevelt and John F. Kennedy have been called charismatic leaders.

Leadership Styles The three leadership styles are authoritarian, laissez-faire, and democratic. An *authoritarian* leader makes all the decisions and assigns tasks to group members. These leaders are focused on completing tasks and compliance to group goals. Authoritarian leaders, such as Libyan leader Muammar al-Qaddhafi, tell other group members what to do and demand obedience. A *laissez-faire* leader is only minimally involved in a group's decision making. This leader encourages the group to make its own decisions. Under this type of leadership, it is the group's goals, not the leader's, that are pursued; group members make all the decisions. When leading a discussion, your teacher may be a good example of a laissez-faire leader—one who encourages group members to explore their own ideas. A *democratic* leader encourages group members to come to decisions through consensus. These leaders are often viewed as supportive but not good decision makers. Democratic leaders, such as those in the U.S. Congress, try to build a consensus among group members.

SECTION 1 Assessment

1. **Review the Vocabulary** Explain how groups organized for task functions differ from those organized for social functions. Give an example of a task and social group to which you belong.
2. **Visualize the Main Idea** Using a graphic organizer similar to the one below, identify and describe the three styles of leadership.

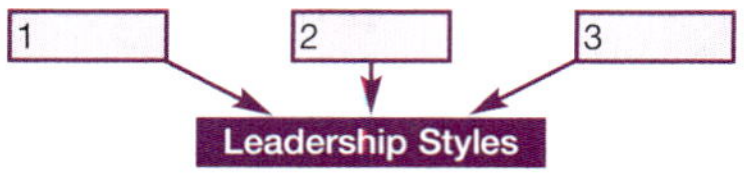

3. **Recall Information** What is the difference between an in-group and an out-group? Give an example of each.
4. **Think Critically** When might a group benefit from a laissez-faire style of leadership? When might a group benefit from authoritarian leadership?
5. **Application Activity** Describe an activity that you did in the past month in front of a crowd. How did you perform? Analyze in a brief report why you performed this way.

SECTION 1 Assessment Answers

1. Task function groups exist to complete a job. Social function groups exist to fulfill the emotional needs of members. Students' examples may vary but should reflect an understanding of the difference between task function groups and social function groups.
2. Authoritarian leaders make the decisions and assign tasks. Laissez-faire leaders are minimally involved and let the group make its own decisions. Democratic leaders encourage groups to make decisions through consensus.
3. In-group members identify with their group. All nonmembers of the group are in the out-group. An example is an athletic team that considers all people who are not members of the team as the out-group.
4. Answers will vary. Explanations should demonstrate an understanding of each leadership style
5. Students' answers will vary. Ask students to analyze their performance based on the difficulty of the task. Answers should also address the aspects of social facilitation and social inhibition.

SECTION 2

Conformity and Obedience

Reader's Guide

Main Idea

You may engage in behavior because of direct or indirect group pressure or in response to orders given by authorities.

Vocabulary

- conformity
- obedience

Objectives

- Identify ways that groups can influence an individual's behavior.
- Explain why most people tend to obey authority figures.

EXPLORING PSYCHOLOGY

Why Are They Running?

Suddenly someone began to run. It may be that he had simply remembered, all of a moment, an engagement to meet his wife, for which he was now frightfully late. Whatever it was, he ran east on Broad Street (probably toward the Maramor Restaurant, a favorite place for a man to meet his wife). Somebody else began to run, perhaps a newsboy in high spirits. Another man, a portly gentleman of affairs, broke into a trot. Inside of ten minutes, everybody on High Street, from the Union Depot to the Courthouse was running. A loud mumble gradually crystallized into the dread word "dam." "The dam has broke!" The fear was put into words by a little old lady in an electric car, or by a traffic cop, or by a small boy: nobody knows who, nor does it now really matter.

—from "The Day the Dam Broke" in *My Life and Hard Times* by James Thurber, 1933

The above passage is a good example of people conforming to group pressures. Why did they run? They ran because everyone else was running. Most of these individuals did not make a decision based on their own reasoning; rather, they conformed to a group decision—to run.

SECTION RESOURCES

Reproducible Masters

- Guided Reading Activity 19–2
- Vocabulary Activity 19–2
- Section Quiz 19–2

Transparencies

- Daily Focus Transparency 19–2

Multimedia

- *ExamView® Assessment Suite* CD-ROM
- Presentation Plus! Software

1 FOCUS

Section Objectives

1. Identify ways that groups can influence an individual's behavior.
2. Explain why most people tend to obey authority figures.

BELLRINGER
Motivational Activity

Project Daily Focus Transparency 19–2 and have students answer the questions.

Available as blackline master

Daily Focus Transparency 19–2

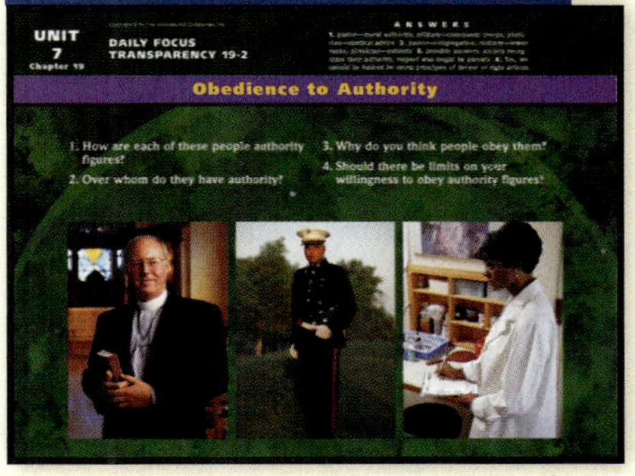

Reader's Guide

Use the Reader's Guide to introduce concepts and vocabulary.

Exploring Psychology

Ask students to read the **Exploring Psychology** feature. Ask: **How have you conformed to group pressure without seriously considering the alternatives?**

Vocabulary Precheck

Have students write a definition of the terms based on their own experiences. Then have them read the Glossary definitions and revise their own definitions.

2 TEACH

L1 Creative Writing To illustrate the influence of social norms on individual behavior, tell students to imagine that they have found a way to be invisible for 24 hours. Ask them to outline how they would spend the day. To encourage honesty, tell students that the outlines will not be collected.

Conduct an anonymous paper ballot poll, asking the students whether their activities while invisible would be classified as social or antisocial (watching people in a park, or sneaking into someone's house). Compile the ballots.

Tell students that a similar activity was conducted by social psychologist David K. Dodd. The study revealed that 36 percent of the stories involved antisocial activities such as "rob a bank." **Ask:** **What does this activity reveal about the effect of peer pressure on curbing antisocial behavior?**

Figure 19.9

Visual Instruction To set the stage for the series of photos in Figure 19.10, ask students to identify which comparison line in the bottom box matches the line in the top box.

Caption Answer Asch wanted to test the degree of conformity to pressure from one's peers.

Guided Reading Activity 19–2

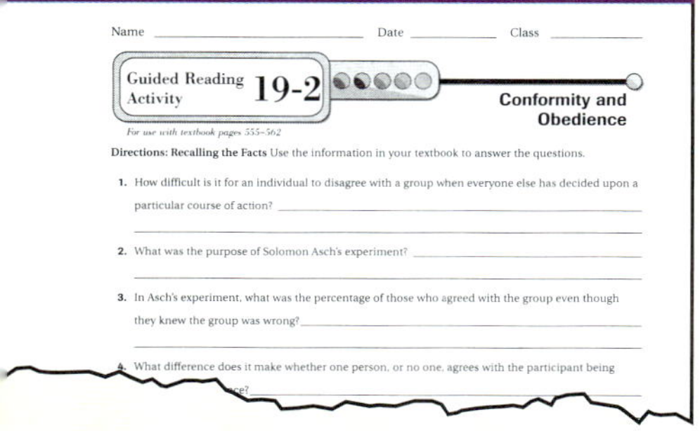
Name ______ Date ______ Class ______

Guided Reading Activity 19-2 — Conformity and Obedience

For use with textbook pages 555–562

Directions: Recalling the Facts Use the information in your textbook to answer the questions.

1. How difficult is it for an individual to disagree with a group when everyone else has decided upon a particular course of action? ______
2. What was the purpose of Solomon Asch's experiment? ______
3. In Asch's experiment, what was the percentage of those who agreed with the group even though they knew the group was wrong? ______
4. What difference does it make whether one person, or no one, agrees with the participant being ...ce? ______

GROUP PRESSURE TO CONFORM

Have you ever come home and surprised your parents by wearing the latest fad in clothing? Possibly the conversation that followed went something like this:

"How can you go around looking like that?"

"But everyone dresses like this."

Psychologist Solomon Asch (1952) designed what has become a classic experiment to test conformity to pressure from one's peers. **Conformity** involves any behavior that you engage in because of direct or indirect group pressure. He found that people may conform to other people's ideas of the truth, even when they disagree. The following is what you would have experienced if you had been a participant in this experiment.

conformity: acting in accord with group norms or customs

You and six other students meet in a classroom for an experiment on visual judgment. A line is projected on a screen in front of all seven participants. You are then shown another view of three lines and are asked to pick the one that is the same length as the first line. One of the three is exactly the same length. The other two lines are obviously different (see Figure 19.9). The experiment begins uneventfully. The participants announce their answers in the order in which they are seated in the room. You happen to be sixth, and one person follows you. On the first comparison, every person chooses the same matching line. The second set of lines is displayed, and once again the group is unanimous. The discriminations seem simple and easy, and you prepare for what you expect will be a rather boring experiment.

Figure 19.9 Asch's Experiment

These two choices were shown to participants in one trial of Asch's experiment on conformity. The participants' task was to determine whether the length of the standard line matches the length of the comparison lines. The actual discrimination is easy. ***What was the purpose of Asch's experiment?***

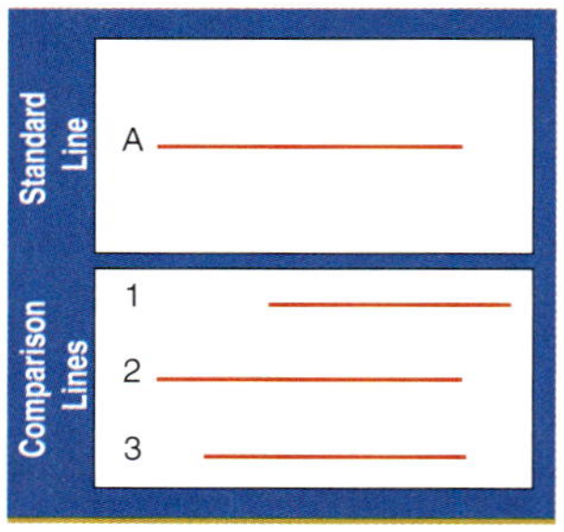

On the third trial, there is an unexpected disturbance. You are quite certain that line 2 is the one that matches the standard. Yet the first person in the group announces confidently that line 1 is the correct match. Then the second person follows suit, and he, too, declares that the answer is line 1; so do the third, fourth, and fifth participants. Now it is your turn. You are suddenly faced with two contradictory pieces of information; the evidence of your own senses tells you that one answer is clearly correct, but the unanimous and confident judgments of the five preceding participants tell you that you are wrong.

The dilemma persists through 18 trials. On 12 of the trials, the other group members unanimously give an answer that differs from what you clearly perceive to be correct. It is only at the end of the experimental session that you learn the explanation for the confusion. The six other participants were all actors, and they had been instructed to give incorrect answers on those 12 trials (see Figure 19.10).

How do most participants react to this situation? Asch found that about 75 percent of his participants conformed some of the time. These conformers he called the "yielders." Most yielders explained to Asch afterward that they knew which line was correct but that they yielded to group pressure to not appear different from the others. Asch called those who did not conform "independents." About 25 percent of the participants were independents. They gave the correct answer despite group pressure. Why so much conformity? According to one

COOPERATIVE LEARNING ACTIVITY

Researching Cults Organize the class into small groups. Ask each group to select a well-known cult catastrophe, such as Marshall Applewhite's Heaven's Gate, David Koresh and the Branch Davidians, or Jim Jones and the People's Temple. Have the group research the ways in which the cult demanded conformity and the ways in which it enforced its rules. Tell the groups to prepare a list titled "Lessons To Be Learned" in which they cite the warning signs of cult activity and how to avoid being influenced by such groups. **BLOCK SCHEDULING**

Figure 19.10 **Should He Conform?**

These photographs were taken during Asch's experiment on conformity. Participant 6 is the only real participant, and the others are collaborators with the experimenter. The participant listens to the others express identical judgments that differ from his own. He is in a dilemma: Does he express the judgment he knows to be correct and risk being different from the group, or does he conform to the group's judgment? ***Why does Participant 6 find himself in a dilemma? What were Asch's findings?***

theory, most children are taught the overriding importance of being liked and of being accepted. Conformity is the standard means of gaining this approval.

Reading Check Why did the yielders conform?

Why Do People Conform?

One of the most important findings of Asch's experiment was that if even one person among the first five failed to conform to the group's judgment, the participant was able to stick to his own perceptions. It seems that it is hardest to stand alone. Later researchers have shown that under some conditions, a minority view can come to win over the larger group (Moscovici, 1985). By disagreeing with the majority view, a person can actually reduce the pressure that others feel to conform. A minority dissenter may also serve an informational purpose by making others question whether the majority view is actually right. When people hear a dissenting opinion, they are more likely to examine the issue more closely, which can lead to a better solution.

In Asch's experiment, participants conformed; they responded to match the other group members' responses, yet they might not have actually changed their beliefs. This contrast between public behavior and private belief often characterizes *compliance.* Compliance occurs when we respond to the request of another person without necessarily changing our beliefs.

A method of gaining compliance is the *foot-in-the-door technique.* This occurs when you get a person to agree to a relatively minor request. This minor request, which the participant is likely to agree with, is really a set-up for a major request. For example, a car salesperson might get you into the showroom by saying, "Just come in, and we'll run a few numbers—no obligation." Once you are in the showroom, though, you

Figure 19.10

Caption Answer He must decide if he should stand alone against the rest of the group. Students should note that almost one-third of Asch's participants conformed at least half the time; that if the participant stood alone in his answer, he was more likely to accept the majority opinion.

Reading Check Answer They did not want to appear different from the rest of the group.

CURRICULUM CONNECTION

Social Studies President Franklin D. Roosevelt was concerned that Americans would lose the will to fight the war in the Pacific after achieving victory in Europe during World War II. Social psychologist Carl Hovland was assigned to study the effects of a series of documentary films created to increase soldier morale. His experiments with 200,000 soldiers revealed that the films had little effect on their attitudes about Japan. He did discover, however, that one-sided arguments (such as focusing on the dedication of the Japanese people) were more persuasive with people who already agreed that continuing the war was important. He also discovered that two-sided arguments (centered on America's advantages in war, while raising the possibility of a prolonged struggle) were more effective in convincing people who disagreed with the government's position.

MEETING SPECIAL NEEDS

Learning Style: Kinesthetic Ask students to put together a clothes combination that clearly does not conform to the current popular styles. Encourage students to wear the outfit to school and record student and teacher reactions to the outfit. Have students report to the class what they learned about conformity. **L2**

Refer to ***Inclusion for the High School Social Studies Classroom Strategies and Activities*** in the TCR for strategies for students with different learning styles.

Quick Lab

Purpose Students will explore the results of not conforming to group norms.

Process Skills Predicting outcomes, analyzing information

Teaching Strategies

- Review the procedures to be used.
- Caution students that the violation should not endanger or frighten either the student or the observer of the behavior.
- Review the students' ideas before they implement the experiments.

Analysis

1. Encourage students to keep a log of reactions. They may want to work in pairs with one person violating the norm and the other recording observations.
2. Answers will vary. Encourage students to be candid about their feelings. Tell them that this helps them learn how much social norms are a part of life.
3. Answers will vary. Encourage students to address these questions from the individual's viewpoint and from the viewpoint of society as a whole.

Psychology Journal

Tell students to write about times that they have seen the *foot-in-the-door* technique used to gain compliance. If possible, encourage them to include examples of solicitation letters that they or their parents or other family members have received that demonstrate this technique. ■

Quick Lab

How do we conform to group norms?

Norms are formalized rules for how members of groups should behave. They can exert strong influences on other members' behaviors. How do people react when group norms are not adhered to?

Procedure

1. Think of a norm that regulates what an individual should or should not do in a given situation. (Examples include standing a certain distance from a person when talking, not talking during a movie, or wearing certain types of clothing for given situations.)
2. Design and act out an experiment in which you do not adhere to the norm.

Analysis

1. What were the general reactions of other group members to you not adhering to the particular norm?
2. How did other people's reactions make you feel?
3. Do you think norms are always useful? Can they be harmful? Why do you think so?

See the Skills Handbook, page 622, for an explanation of designing an experiment.

are more likely to develop the attitude that you need a new car. Whereas initially, your commitment was minor, later you commit more intensely.

There are several factors that increase conforming behavior in people. The factors include:

- belonging to a group that emphasizes the role of groups rather than individuals
- the desire to be liked by other members of the group
- low self-esteem
- social shyness
- lack of familiarity with a task
- group size (Conformity increases as the size of the group grows to five or six people. After that, conformity levels off.)
- cultural influences

OBEDIENCE TO AUTHORITY

The influence other people have on your attitudes and actions is considerable. Sometimes this influence is indirect and subtle, and at other times it is quite direct. People may simply tell you what to believe and what to do. Under what conditions do you obey them?

Everyone in this society has had experiences with various authorities, such as parents, teachers, police officers, managers, judges, clergy, and military officers. **Obedience,** or behavior in response to orders given by these authorities, can be either useful or destructive. For instance, obeying the orders of a doctor or firefighter in an emergency would be constructive. Psychologists are more interested, however, in the negative aspects of obedience. They know from cases in history such as German Nazism and American atrocities in Vietnam that individuals frequently obey irrational commands. In fact, people often obey authority even when obedience goes against their conscience and their whole system of morality.

obedience: a change in attitude or behavior brought about by social pressure to comply with people perceived to be authorities

The Milgram Experiment

Psychologist Stanley Milgram conducted the most famous investigation of obedience in 1963 (see Figure 19.12). Milgram set up the experiment as follows. Two participants appeared for each session. They were told that they would be participating in an experiment to test the effects of punishment on memory. One of the participants was to be the "teacher" and the other, the "learner." In reality, the learner was not a volunteer participant; he was Milgram's accomplice. The teacher was to read into a microphone a list of words to be memorized by the learner, who would be

CRITICAL THINKING ACTIVITY

Identifying Central Issues Arrange for an authority figure in your school, such as the principal, to come into your class at the beginning of the class period (you should remain outside the classroom). Have the person give the following series of orders: "Everyone be seated." "Place everything on your desk on the floor and place your hands flat on the desk." "If you are wearing a necklace, please stand up." The authority figure should give additional, similar commands until you enter the class. **Ask:** **Did you do as the authority figure directed? Why? Did you question his or her authority? Did you continue to obey even if you questioned his or her authority? What have you learned about obedience to authority? L2**

in a nearby room. If the learner failed to recite the list back correctly, the teacher was to administer an electric shock. The alleged purpose of the experiment was to test whether the shock would have any effect on learning. In actuality, however, Milgram wanted to discover how far the teacher would follow his instructions and how much shock the teacher would be willing to give another human being. Milgram surveyed a group of psychology students before the experiment. All respondents predicted that very few participants would be willing to shock the learner.

As the experiment began, the learner continually gave wrong answers, and the teacher began to administer the prescribed shocks from an impressive-looking shock generator. The generator had a dial that ranged from 15 volts, which was labeled "Slight Shock," to 450 volts, which was labeled "Danger: Severe Shock." After each of the learner's mistakes, the teacher was told to increase the voltage by one level. The teacher believed that the learner was receiving these shocks because he had experienced a mild sample shock, had seen the learner being strapped into a chair, and had watched electrodes being attached to the learner's hands. However, the learner received no shocks at all during the experiment.

As the experiment progressed, the learner made many mistakes, and the teacher was instructed to give increasingly severe shocks. At 300 volts the learner pounded on the wall and refused to provide any further answers. At this point the experimenter (who wore a white lab coat) instructed the participant to treat the absence of an answer as a wrong answer and to continue the procedure. The experiment ended either when the maximum 450 volts was administered or when the teacher refused to administer any more shocks. If at any point the teacher indicated a desire to stop, the experimenter calmly said, "Whether the learner likes it or not, you must go on until he has learned all the word pairs correctly."

Sixty-five percent of the participants delivered the full range of shocks. These participants were not sadists. Many of them showed signs of extreme tension and discomfort during the session, and they often told the experimenter that they would like to stop. Despite these feelings, most continued to obey the experimenter's commands. They were ordinary people—salespeople, engineers, and postal workers—placed in an unusual situation.

What accounts for this surprisingly high level of obedience? Part of the answer is that the experimenter represents a legitimate authority. People assume that such authorities know what they are doing, even when their instructions seem to run counter to standards of moral behavior.

THE FAR SIDE By GARY LARSON

Laboratory peer pressure

Figure 19.11 Going With the Group

Conforming to a group has practical explanations. If you see people running out of a building, you may assume that they know something you do not—that the building is on fire, for example. ***What are other reasons for conforming with a group?***

CHAPTER 19
Section 2, pages 555–562

Figure 19.11

Caption Answer sense of belonging, low self-esteem, social shyness, lack of familiarity with a task, group size, and cultural influences

Vocabulary Activity 19–2

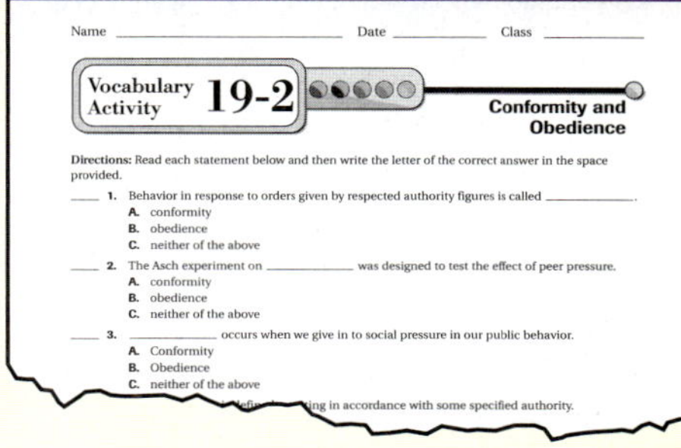
Name ______ Date ______ Class ______

Vocabulary Activity 19-2

Conformity and Obedience

Directions: Read each statement below and then write the letter of the correct answer in the space provided.

____ 1. Behavior in response to orders given by respected authority figures is called ______.
A. conformity
B. obedience
C. neither of the above

____ 2. The Asch experiment on ______ was designed to test the effect of peer pressure.
A. conformity
B. obedience
C. neither of the above

____ 3. ______ occurs when we give in to social pressure in our public behavior.
A. Conformity
B. Obedience
C. neither of the above

TEACHER Tip

Discuss with students one or more of the atrocities that occurred during the twentieth century, including the Holocaust, My Lai massacre, Turkish mass murder of Armenians during World War I, Joseph Stalin's reign of terror in Ukraine, the killing fields of Rwanda and Cambodia, and ethnic cleansing in Bosnia and Kosovo. **Ask: Where does obedience end and personal responsibility begin?**

PSYCHOLOGY LAB EXPERIMENT

Re-creating Asch's Experiment Have students re-create the experiment Asch conducted. Students should arrange for an informed group of six to eight collaborators. Have students explain the experiment and the collaborators' role in the experiment. Students should conduct 10 trials by having a series of student participants join the group as the uninformed lead student. Prior to the experiment, have students prepare the sets of cards as described in the text. After the experiment, **ask: How closely did the results match the Asch data? What might account for any differences?** Students should summarize their findings and observations in a 1- to 2-page report. **L2** **BLOCK SCHEDULING**

Figure 19.12

Caption Answer Answers will vary but might include the following: the experimenter represented legitimate authority, and social conditioning.

FYI

Tell students that when the Milgram experiment was altered so that the participants saw two other supposed participants refuse to continue, only 10 percent gave the highest level of shock.

CURRICULUM CONNECTION

History Until the sixteenth century, the Catholic Church in Rome was the absolute moral and cultural authority over the lives of Europeans. The Church wielded enormous political and social power because it claimed that obedience to the pope was the only route to eternal life. In 1517, Martin Luther posted his "Ninety-Five Theses" on the Wittenberg church door, questioning this absolute authority. He claimed that God gave eternal life and that blind obedience to papal authority was not the way to heaven. This heresy was condemned by the Church, and Luther was excommunicated and sentenced to death. However, the questions raised by Luther and others changed the power structure in Europe. As the Church's power diminished, the power of the individual countries increased.

Figure 19.12 Milgram's Experiment

(a) In Milgram's experiment on obedience, the "learner" is connected to the shock apparatus. (b) Milgram explains the procedure to the "teacher." (c) This participant refuses to administer shocks any further and angrily rises in protest. (d) Milgram explains the truth about the experiment. (© 1965 by Stanley Milgram. From the film *Obedience.* Distributed by New York University Film Library.) ***Why did many participants continue to administer shocks to the learner?***

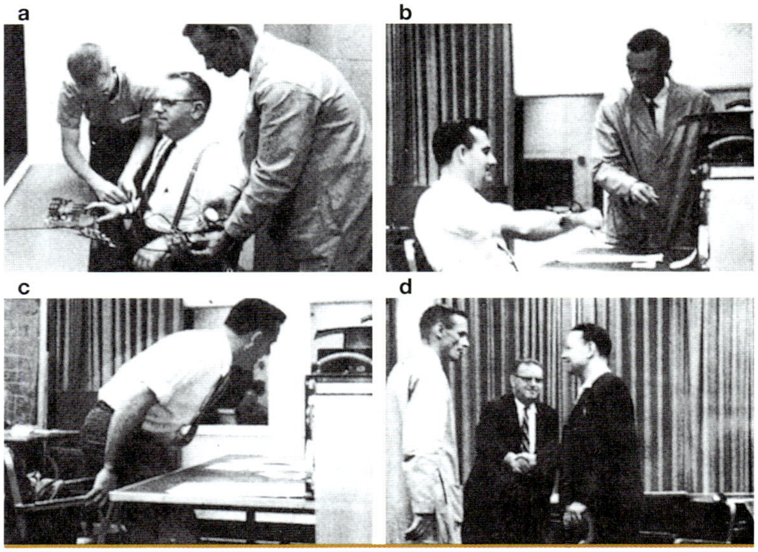

Milgram's participants could have walked out at any time; they had nothing to lose by leaving. Nevertheless, social conditioning for obeying legitimate authorities is so strongly ingrained that people often lack the words or the ways to do otherwise. Getting up and leaving would have violated powerful unwritten rules of acceptable social behavior.

Milgram's experiment is important because it questions so many different aspects of human behavior. The experiment also raised questions about the ethics of some psychological experiments. How would you feel if you had been one of Milgram's participants? How would you feel if you had been deceived into engaging in hurtful behavior? Since the experiment, the APA (2002) has changed its ethical standards for experiments. Today all experiments, especially those that have potential to cause psychological harm, are carefully screened by research committees. Informed consent prior to the experiment and complete disclosure of all design details after an experiment are absolute rights of participants in modern-day psychological studies.

INTERDISCIPLINARY CONNECTIONS ACTIVITY

History Tell students that at the Nuremberg Trials in 1945–46, former Gestapo officer Adolf Eichmann offered the following defense of his activities during the Holocaust: *I am not the monster I am made out to be. This mass slaughter* [the Holocaust] *is solely the responsibility of political leaders. My guilt lies in my obedience, my respect for discipline, my allegiance to the colors and the service* [of Germany]. **Ask: How does Eichmann's quote illustrate the negative aspect of obedience? When do humans have an obligation to disobey authority? L2**

The Stanford Prison Experiment

One Sunday summer morning, a siren shattered the silence, awakening Tommy Whitlow. As Tommy opened his eyes, a police cruiser pulled up, screeching its tires to a halt. The police arrested Tommy, charging him with a felony. They informed him of his rights, frisked and handcuffed him, and placed him in the police vehicle. At the station, police fingerprinted and booked Tommy. They then blindfolded him and led him to the Stanford County Prison. Once he was there, guards stripped him naked and sprayed him down with a disinfectant. He was ordered to wear a beige smock uniform with his identification number patched on the front. Police arrested eight other students that morning as well.

Tommy and the other students were actually participants in another experiment that caused ordinary people to act in extraordinary ways. So as not to unduly surprise the participants, only volunteers were used. Tommy and the other volunteers had answered a newspaper ad; they had no idea that the experiment involved a staged arrest.

The researchers randomly divided the male volunteers into two groups—prisoners and prison guards. Both groups were sent to live in a simulated prison set up in the basement of a Stanford University building. The guards were instructed to maintain order. Within two days, most of the guards had become intoxicated with power. They acted cruelly toward the prisoners, often without reason. The guards expected the prisoners to follow the rules without question. If the prisoners did not follow the rules, they lost the privilege to read or write letters. As the prisoners disobeyed more rules, the punishments increased. Sometimes the guards subjected the prisoners to embarrassment, humiliation, and mindless tasks such as push-ups and washing toilets with their bare hands.

At the same time, the prisoners began showing signs of extreme stress, often acting subdued and depressed. Sometimes the prisoners refused to follow the rules. They yelled back at the guards, made negative comments about the jail, and later became passive from defeat. Some of the prisoners became angry and disillusioned, while others developed psychological

More About...

Collectivism

Many Americans value individualism—a focus on defining oneself in individual terms and giving priority to personal goals. Other societies, though, focus on collectivism—defining oneself in terms of the groups to which one belongs and giving priority to the groups' goals. Individuals in collective societies, such as those in Africa, Asia, and Central and South America, work to control their behaviors and maintain harmonious relationships with others. These individuals are encouraged to be dependent on and submissive to the values of the group. People from collectivist cultures have different priorities and thus have different strategies in how they resolve conflicts and deal with others.

Figure 19.13 Other Cultures

Some cultures, such as the Mexican culture, place greater emphasis on the group than on the individual. Individuals are viewed as part of the family and society and must work hard to maintain harmonious relationships with others. ***How do you think the American culture views individuals' roles in groups?***

Figure 19.13

Caption Answer Answers will vary. Some students will point out that Americans have always valued individuality. However, with the increasing emphasis on teamwork in schools and companies, the trend may be changing.

3 ASSESS

Assign Section 2 Assessment as homework or as an in-class activity.

Section Quiz 19–2

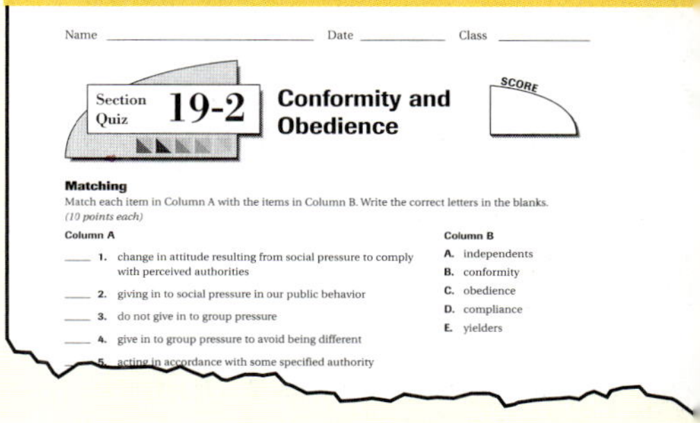
Name ______ Date ______ Class ______

Section Quiz 19-2 **Conformity and Obedience**

SCORE

Matching

Match each item in Column A with the items in Column B. Write the correct letters in the blanks. *(10 points each)*

Column A

____ 1. change in attitude resulting from social pressure to comply with perceived authorities

____ 2. giving in to social pressure in our public behavior

____ 3. do not give in to group pressure

____ 4. give in to group pressure to avoid being different

____ 5. acting in accordance with some specified authority

Column B

A. independents
B. conformity
C. obedience
D. compliance
E. yielders

EXTENDING THE CONTENT

Broken Window Theory Political scientist James Q. Wilson and criminologist George Kelling theorized that human behavior is strongly influenced by symbols of order and disorder. Neighborhoods that maintain their properties and a sense of order make people feel safe. Such neighborhoods are less likely to be plagued by criminals who prefer neighborhoods in which apathy and neglect reign. One unrepaired broken window in an otherwise orderly neighborhood, said Wilson and Kelling, can encourage troublemakers to break more windows, eventually creating a spiral into disorder. The theory's basic idea equates the appearance of care and tending with safety and order. *Source:* McKay, T. (1998). Security centered around self-respect. *Security Management, 42 (6),* 62–5.

CHAPTER 19
Section 2, pages 555–562

Figure 19.14

Caption Answer because the pilots can simply follow orders and avoid the emotional reactions of seeing the damage caused by their actions

Reteach

Have students work in pairs or small groups to create skits showing how groups encourage conformity.

Enrich

Have students research the *door-in-the-face* technique, which is another means of gaining compliance.

4 CLOSE

Tell students that recently three people died in a fire in a college dorm. Although the alarm sounded, there had been 18 false alarms in the same dorm in the four months preceding the fire. As a class, discuss how something like repeated false alarms can dull the senses to the point that antisocial or harmful behavior seems acceptable. Encourage students to bring examples of conformity from recent newspaper and magazine articles.

Figure 19.14 Obeying Orders

Military pilots do not witness the consequences of their actions. They identify and kill their enemies simply by targeting a blip on a radar screen. ***Why might military pilots find it less upsetting than soldiers on the ground to inflict damage?***

illnesses and rashes. The emotional reactions were so extreme that experimenters ended the planned two-week experiment after only six days. It seems that the prison environment was much stronger than individual personalities. Although the participants in this experiment were emotionally mature and stable (according to tests administered before the experiment), the roles these individuals adopted changed the way they acted. There may be other situations in everyday life that cause us and those around us to act in ways we do not expect.

In follow-up interviews, none of the participants reported any lasting effects. Some of the participants had difficulty understanding how powerful the experiment had become. The experiment not only changed the ethical standards of experimentation in psychology but it also demonstrated the power that situations can have in changing how we feel, think, and behave. The social situation of being in the prison changed the rules, roles, and expectations of the students (Zimbardo, 1975).

Why Do People Obey? Why did the Germans obey Adolf Hitler's commands to commit genocide during World War II? Why do cult members sometimes consent to their leaders' orders to commit suicide? After all, these leaders' commands are clearly unreasonable, right? Psychologists have proposed that people learn to obey authority figures. Throughout our lives, we obey parents, doctors, teachers, and religious leaders. Throughout our lives, we also have learned to follow orders. We follow traffic rules, school rules, and parental rules. However, we are more likely to follow these rules when the authority figure is actually present.

SECTION 2 Assessment

1. **Review the Vocabulary** Give an example of a way you show conformity.
2. **Visualize the Main Idea** Duplicate and complete the chart below, describing the Asch experiment.

The Asch Experiment

Hypothesis:	
Method:	
Results:	

3. **Recall Information** How is compliance related to conformity? Explain.
4. **Think Critically** Do you think that conforming to a group is always a negative thing to do? Explain.
5. **Application Activity** Try this experiment with your family or group of friends. Stare at the ceiling continuously for a time. Do other people start to look up at the ceiling also? Why or why not? Explain the principles behind this experiment.

SECTION 2 Assessment Answers

1. Answers will vary. Answers should reflect the knowledge that conformity is a result of direct or indirect group pressure.
2. Hypothesis: People will conform to a group decision even if they know it is wrong. Method: Students should describe the various trials and the results of each trial. Results: Students should describe the different results of yielders and independents.
3. Compliance is a change in behavior without an accompanying change in thinking. Outwardly, the person appears to be conforming.
4. No. Students should provide several examples of ways in which conformity is beneficial. Examples include being quiet during movies, following rituals in a visit to a new church, or waiting your turn in a line.
5. Answers will vary. Students should suggest that those individuals who looked up at the ceiling may have done so because of group pressure to conform.

Your Stripes or Your Morality

Period of Study: 1994

Introduction: Lawrence Rockwood, a captain in the United States Army, had served in the army for close to 20 years when he was ordered to lead a force of troops into Haiti. (A military government had come to power in Haiti. U.S. troops provided stability while the democratically elected government regained power.) Through the mission, President William J. Clinton intended to stop brutal crimes imposed on the Haitian people. Confident and eager about his mission, Rockwood strongly advocated human rights for people all over the world. Rockwood did not know, however, that his mission would clash intensely with his morals.

Hypothesis: Similar to the studies conducted by Asch and Milgram, the hypothesis was that when faced with pressure to conform, an individual would conform to the group or an authority.

Method: Immediately upon arrival in Haiti, U.S. leaders changed the mission from "stopping brutal crimes" to "forced protection," or keeping American troops safe from harm. Commanders ordered Captain Rockwood to survey local Haitian prisons and report on the conditions there. Rockwood found and reported horrible conditions in these prisons. Guards mistreated and tortured prisoners. Rockwood discovered that one of the prisons had about 30 inmates housed in one small cell and that one man had been confined in a position so long that portions of his skin had rotted off.

Outraged at these conditions, Captain Rockwood petitioned for special operations units to enter the prisons and enforce the rules and regulations involving prisoners of war. A senior officer listened to Rockwood's pleas. The officer recommended that special operations investigate the prisons. Special operations turned down the request.

This refusal prompted Rockwood to take matters into his own hands. Knowing his military career would be put on the line by way of court-martial, Rockwood disobeyed direct orders, climbed the outer fence of his base, and proceeded to a Haitian prison where he demanded to evaluate each prisoner. Four hours later, a United States major arrived at the prison and ordered Rockwood to leave. When Rockwood resisted, troops forced him out of the prison. Army psychiatrists evaluated Rockwood twice and found him sane. The army then charged him with disobeying direct orders. In Rockwood's own defense, he stated, "I am more sensitive to human rights concerns than the average officer."

Results: In 1995 the Army court-martialed Rockwood for his actions. The Army sentenced Rockwood to dismissal—equal to a dishonorable discharge—despite his perfect military record and stripped him of some pay and allowances. All of this occurred because Rockwood chose not to conform to the extreme pressures placed upon him by the military. He made the moral decision to come to the aid of his fellow human beings. Many people question the power the United States military possesses in making each and every soldier conform to and obey the ideology of each armed forces branch, no matter what the cost. The case of Captain Lawrence Rockwood and his squashed crusade for human rights demonstrates the power of an individual to resist conformity.

Analyzing the Case Study

1. Why did Rockwood refuse to conform to group pressure?
2. Does this case study support the findings of Milgram and Asch? Explain.
3. **Critical Thinking** Under what circumstances might Rockwood have obeyed his orders? Do you think that conformity depends upon the situation or the person? Or both? Explain your answer.

Answers for Analyzing the Case Study

1. His moral principles took precedence over his orders. He could not obey his orders to not help Haitian prisoners who were being mistreated and tortured. Rockwood felt it was morally wrong to deny his fellow human beings the help they needed.
2. The Asch and Milgram studies provide examples of people conforming and obeying an authority figure, though some resisted. The case of Lawrence Rockwood is an example of someone unwilling to conform and obey because of strong moral beliefs. So no, this case study does not support most of Milgram and Asch's findings.
3. Answers will vary. Students may suggest that Rockwood would have obeyed orders that he felt were moral or if he believed the prison situation would be addressed. If possible, have students discuss the study with someone who has served in the military to determine how his or her perspective differs from those of the students.

Going Further

Rockwood's Ongoing Battle

The Court of Appeals for the Armed Forces unanimously upheld Rockwood's conviction. They did not find any significant procedural or international law violations. In their opinion, Walter T. Cox, the chief judge for the Court of Appeals, wrote: "The difference between a military organization and a mob is the role of command and control in channeling, directing and restraining human behavior."

Discussing the Case Study

Ask: **How was Rockwood's situation similar to the participants' situation in the Asch experiment? How was it different? What dilemma did Rockwood face? What was his decision? What was the military's response? Do you think Rockwood made a wise decision? Explain.**

CHAPTER 19

Section 3, pages 564–570

1 FOCUS

Section Objectives

1. Explain causes of group conflict and cooperation.
2. Summarize how group dynamics promote or restrain altruism and aggression.

BELLRINGER
Motivational Activity

Project Daily Focus Transparency 19–3 and have students answer the questions.

Available as blackline master

Daily Focus Transparency 19–3

Reader's Guide

Use the Reader's Guide to introduce concepts and vocabulary.

■ **Exploring Psychology**

Ask students to read the **Exploring Psychology** feature and then discuss: **How do individuals in large groups act differently than they would alone?**

■ **Vocabulary Precheck**

Have students read the Glossary definitions of the terms. Then have them write a sentence using each of the terms.

Use the **Vocabulary PuzzleMaker CD-ROM** to create crossword and word search puzzles.

SECTION 3 Conflict and Cooperation

Reader's Guide

■ **Main Idea**

Conflicts between groups are a fact of everyday life. Individuals perceive and respond to situations differently in a group, sometimes giving up responsibility for their actions.

■ **Vocabulary**

- aggression
- catharsis
- altruism
- diffusion of responsibility
- bystander effect
- social loafing
- deindividuation

■ **Objectives**

- Explain causes of group conflict and cooperation.
- Summarize how group dynamics promote or restrain altruism and aggression.

EXPLORING PSYCHOLOGY

Watching From Above

This was the evening of April 29, 1992. The Los Angeles Riots were erupting below us. . . .

I peered though my side-window as the copter continued to circle in a steep bank. I could see the traffic was moving through the intersection below us. I watched as various cars whipped in a U-turn around to avoid the ominous chaos ahead. There were clusters of people milling around. They were throwing rocks and bottles at passing cars. There were no police officers around, just an unruly mob venting hate on innocent motorists who happened to find themselves in the wrong place at the wrong time.

—from *News at Ten: Fifty Years With Stan Chambers* by Stan Chambers, 1994

In April 1992, the media released footage of four white police officers beating an African American motorist. When jurors found the officers not guilty of charges including assault and excessive use of force, mob violence erupted in South Central Los Angeles. That violence continued for several days and fed on itself, resulting in 55 deaths and $1 billion in damage.

What causes group violence? Why did some people in Los Angeles harm others? Would they have committed those same lawless acts in a different and calmer atmosphere?

SECTION RESOURCES

Reproducible Masters

- Guided Reading Activity 19–3
- Vocabulary Activity 19–3
- Section Quiz 19–3

Transparencies

- Daily Focus Transparency 19–3

Multimedia

- Vocabulary PuzzleMaker CD-ROM
- *ExamView® Assessment Suite* CD-ROM
- Presentation Plus! Software

AGGRESSION

Any behavior that is intended to cause physical or psychological harm is called **aggression.** It seems that our society is being challenged by increasing violence and aggression. What causes humans to act in ways that harm others? Psychologists have proposed several theories to explain aggression.

Biological Influences

Some animals are naturally aggressive. For instance, you might know that when injured, some otherwise friendly dogs become vicious. This violent response is an innate biological reaction. Psychologists have proposed that humans also have innate biological factors that cause aggression. Neurotransmitters, such as serotonin, influence a person's aggressive behavior. When a person has diminished serotonin levels in the brain, he or she may experience violent outbursts.

Studies on mice indicate that mice whose genes have been altered so that their brains lack serotonin receptors attack other mice quicker and with more intensity than other mice (Shih, 1996). Psychologists, though, warn against labeling aggression as caused by only biological factors.

Figure 19.15 A Model of Aggression

This is just one model of aggression. Psychologists have proposed various biological, cognitive, and environmental factors that influence a person's response to the fight-or-flight dilemma. ***What leads to aggression in this model?***

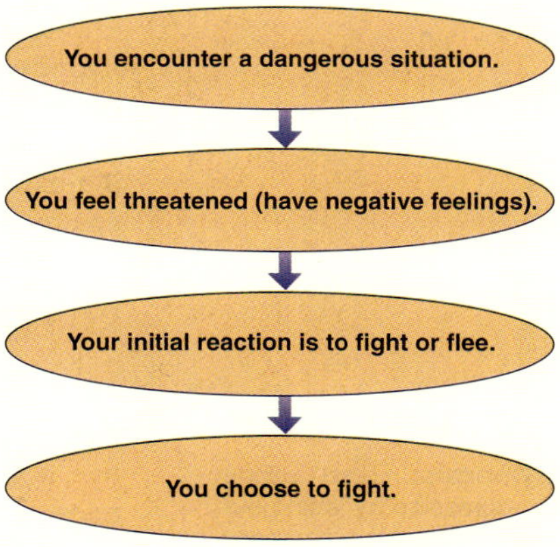

Cognitive Factors

Psychologist Albert Bandura proposes that children learn aggressive behavior by observing and imitating their parents. Bandura suggested that we watch models perform and then imitate the models' behavior. His social learning theory also proposes that aggressive behavior may be reinforced in several ways. Parents who use aggression to discipline their children may be teaching their children to use aggression.

aggression: behavior intended to do physical or psychological harm to others

The media—television, movies, video games, and music—may also be teaching aggressive behavior to children. By 18 years of age, the average American has witnessed an estimated 200,000 acts of violence on television (American Academy of Pediatrics, 1995). As children witness media violence, they grow immune to the horror of violence, gradually accept violence as a way to solve problems, imitate the violence they observe, and identify with certain characters whether they are victims or victimizers.

Personality Factors

Certain personality traits, such as impulsiveness and having little empathy, combined with favoring domination, can turn a person into a bully. Aggressive people also may be arrogant and egotistical. People often strike out at others to affirm their sense of superiority (Baumeister, Smart, & Boden, 1996). Can psychologists predict violent behavior based on personality factors? Usually, past experience is the best predictor. An aggressive child tends to become an aggressive adult.

2 TEACH

L1 Identifying Causes for Aggression Ask each student to find a newspaper or magazine article about someone or some group whose actions are violent or aggressive. Have each student summarize his or her article for the class. As a class, discuss possible reasons for these actions. **Ask:** **How would you feel in the aggressor's position? In the victim's position?** **BLOCK SCHEDULING**

Figure 19.15

Visual Instruction Provide students with several realistic scenarios and ask students to write "fight" or "flight" as their likely response to each. Collect the responses and chart the results for each scenario. Then discuss the results.

Caption Answer In this case, aggression is the response to a perceived threat in a dangerous situation.

COOPERATIVE LEARNING ACTIVITY

Controlling Aggression Organize students into small groups. Have each group develop a skit that would show a 7- to 9-year-old how to deal with feelings of aggression. Tell students that the skits should use a situation that a typical child might encounter. In the skits, aggressive feelings may be relieved using catharsis, accepting frustration and moving on, or reacting to a situation in nonaggressive ways. Have groups perform the skits in class and ask the class to identify the method used to control aggression. **BLOCK SCHEDULING**

Readings and Case Studies in Psychology

Have students read the Chapter 19 Case Study selection in *Readings and Case Studies in Psychology* and answer the questions that follow the case study.

Guided Reading Activity 19–3

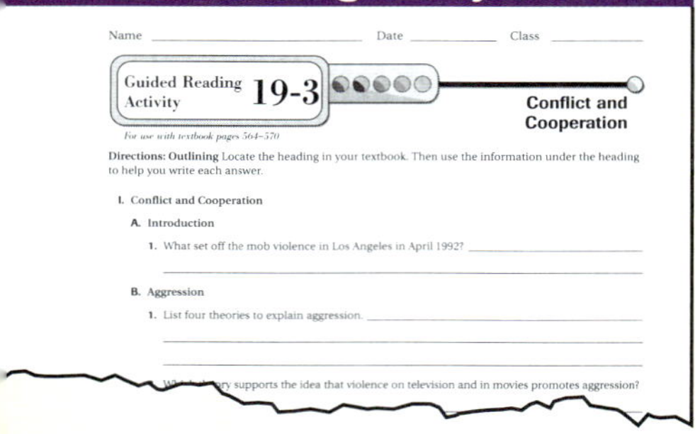
Name ______ Date ______ Class ______

Guided Reading Activity 19-3

Conflict and Cooperation

For use with textbook pages 564–570

Directions: Outlining Locate the heading in your textbook. Then use the information under the heading to help you write each answer.

I. Conflict and Cooperation

A. Introduction

1. What set off the mob violence in Los Angeles in April 1992? ______

B. Aggression

1. List four theories to explain aggression. ______

... supports the idea that violence on television and in movies promotes aggression?

PSYCHOLOGY JOURNAL

Have students write about an incident in which they used aggression to resolve a conflict. Then have them write about an incident in which they controlled their aggression. Ask students to compare the results and their feelings about the two incidents. ■

FYI

A 2004 report by the U.S. Department of Justice estimated that about 44 percent of rape victims are under 18 years old. A 2004 National Crime Victimization Survey found that 67 percent of rape victims were sexually assaulted by a friend, an acquaintance, or a family member. Only about 42 percent of rapes are reported to the police.

Environmental Factors

Sometimes something provokes you and you become violent. Maybe your friend borrowed something without telling you. Maybe another driver refused to let you merge into traffic. Psychologists explain acts of violence that arise from such situations with the *frustration-aggression hypothesis.* This is the idea that frustration or a failure to obtain something expected leads to aggression. The hypothesis, though, fails to note that frustration does not always lead to aggressive behavior. For instance, if your friend trips and falls into you, knocking a soda out of your hands, you may not feel angry once you realize that it was an accident.

Leonard Berkowitz (1989) proposed a modified frustration-aggression hypothesis. Berkowitz proposes that frustration leads to aggression only in certain instances. For example, when a stranger bumps into you, you may strike that person if you have done so before or if the person does not intimidate you. Other reactions to frustration may include withdrawal, apathy, anxiety, stress, or simple tolerance.

CONTROLLING AGGRESSION

Aggression, then, is a combination of biological, cognitive, personality, and environmental factors. Knowing this, how do we limit and control aggression? One method is through catharsis. **Catharsis** involves releasing anger or aggression by expressing powerful negative emotions. For instance, when you are angry, you should "get it off your chest." This might mean talking to a friend, playing a tough game of soccer, or hitting a punching bag for a while. Unfortunately, critics of catharsis believe that any expression of aggression is negative. They point out that expressing your aggression may lead to more aggression.

catharsis: releasing anger or aggression by letting out powerful negative emotions

Other strategies of controlling aggression include punishing children for violent behavior and cutting down on the violence they observe. Excessive punishment, though, may trigger aggressive behavior. People can also be taught to control their aggression. Aggressive behavior can be controlled by teaching people to accept frustrations and move on and to react to disappointments in ways other than violence. If people do not view violence as an option, then they will not resort to violence.

Did You Know?

American Violence Social psychologists blame our culture for the increasing amount of violence. They say that social changes have left people feeling isolated and disconnected. The American culture encourages self-centeredness and violence. Arnold Goldstein of the Center for Research on Aggression at Syracuse University commented, "We are a nation whose role models, presidents, and leaders on Wall Street have set the tone for the country—I'm going to get mine" (Benson & Roehlkepartain, 1993).

GROUP CONFLICT VERSUS COOPERATION

Conflicts between groups are a fact of everyday life: some level of hostility does exist between women and men, young and old, workers and bosses, African Americans and whites, Catholics and Protestants, and students and teachers. Why do these conflicts exist, and why do they persist? Let us consider the findings of a group of psychologists (Sherif & Hovland, 1961) who

MEETING SPECIAL NEEDS

Learning Style: Kinesthetic Explain that increased aggression may result because of crowding. In urban areas, architects plan ways to make people feel less crowded, even as more people move into the same limited amount of space. Ask students to create a plan to rearrange the classroom in a way in which students will feel crowded and a plan to arrange the classroom in a way to reduce these feelings. If possible, implement the plans and observe how students react. Have students discuss how the room arrangement made them feel. **L2**

Refer to ***Inclusion for the High School Social Studies Classroom Strategies and Activities*** in the TCR for strategies for students with different learning styles.

created a boys' camp to study intergroup relations. The camp at Robber's Cave offered all the usual activities, and the boys had no idea that they were part of an experiment.

From the beginning of the experiment, the boys were divided into two groups. The boys hiked, swam, and played baseball only with members of their own group, and friendships and group spirit soon developed. After a while the experimenters (working as counselors) brought the groups together for a tournament. The psychologists had hypothesized that when these two groups of boys were placed in competitive situations, where one group could achieve its goals only at the expense of the other, hostility would develop. They were right.

Although the games began in a spirit of good sportsmanship, tension mounted as the tournament continued. Friendly competition gave way to name calling, fistfights, and raids on enemy cabins. The psychologists had demonstrated the ease with which they could produce unity within the two boys' groups and hatred between them. The experimenters then tried to see what might end the conflict and create harmony between the two groups. They tried to bring the groups together for enjoyable activities, such as a movie and a good meal. This approach failed. The campers shoved and pushed each other, threw food and insults, and generally used the opportunity to continue their attacks.

Next, the psychologists deliberately staged a series of emergencies in which the boys either would have to help one another or lose the chance to do or get something they all wanted. For instance, one morning someone reported that the water line to the camp had broken. The boys were told that unless they worked together to find the break and fix it, they would all have to leave camp. By afternoon, they had jointly found and fixed the damage. Gradually, through such cooperative activities, intergroup hostility and tensions lessened. Friendships began to develop between individuals of the opposing groups, and eventually the groups began to seek out occasions to mingle. At the end of the camp period, members of both groups requested that they ride home together on the same bus.

The results of this experiment were striking. Two groups of boys from identical backgrounds had developed considerable hostility toward each other simply because they were placed in competition. The crucial factor in eliminating group hostility was cooperation.

The question of conflict is not confined just to small groups. It applies to large communities, too, but then the possibility of a *social trap* is greater. A social trap occurs when individuals in a group decide not to cooperate. Instead, they act selfishly and create a bad situation for all. An

More About...

Gangs

The Federal Bureau of Investigation (FBI, 2006) estimates that there are about 800,000 active gang members in the United States. In hundreds of cities throughout the nation, these gangs are harming the communities in which they operate. Police departments have identified three types of gangs.

Social gangs are relatively permanent groups that hang out in a specific location. Members often engage in organized group activities. Members may hold the norms and values of society in general. *Delinquent gangs* are organized around the principle of monetary gain. Members depend on one another to carry out planned activities. The leader is usually the member most skilled at stealing. *Violent gangs* are organized to obtain emotional gratification from violent activities. Members spend their time carrying out violent acts. Leaders are usually emotionally unstable—they have a need to control others. Group members overestimate the importance and power of their group, and there may be violence within the group (Austin Police Department Gang Suppression Unit, 1999).

Anyone may become a victim of gang violence. Gang members are constantly recruiting members, focusing on younger and younger recruits. Many delinquent and violent gang members become career criminals. How do we stop the spread of gangs? Children can learn self-control; they can be taught how to deal with problems. Communities can develop greater opportunities to involve all citizens.

TEACHER Tip

After students read the **More About** feature, make sure they understand the difference between the terms *social gangs* and *delinquent* and *violent gangs*. Ask students to find out how their community addresses gang violence.

Looking @ the Issues

Conflict Resolution Many companies have restructured their workplace environments into self-directed work teams. People on these teams work closely together to accomplish specific team goals. When people work closely together, conflicts are likely to arise. One critical ingredient to successful teamwork is the team's ability to resolve conflict among team members. Training in conflict resolution helps all team members learn that conflicts can be resolved constructively. They also learn that the resolution of conflicts can lead to stronger, more dynamic teams. **Ask: Why do conflicts arise in the workplace? How can teams help resolve conflicts constructively?**

CRITICAL THINKING ACTIVITY

Competition Versus Cooperation Create 30 sets of cards, each of which will contain the following four choices: Card 1/You win $5, Your friend wins $5; Card 2/You win $10, Your friend loses $10; Card 3/You lose $10, Your friend wins $10; Card 4/You lose $3, Your friend loses $3. (This is a version of "The Prisoner's Dilemma"). Group the students into pairs and pass a card set to each student. Explain that the purpose is to win as much imaginary money as possible. During a game turn, each student will secretly pick one of the cards. When ready, the students will show their opponents their cards and then compile the totals of both cards. Each student should keep a running total of overall gains and losses. The game lasts for 10 turns. Then ask the students to reveal their final totals and strategies. **Ask: Did you choose the competitive strategy or the cooperative one? Did a pattern of trust or distrust develop? L2**

CHAPTER 19
Section 3, pages 564–570

Reading Check Answer They placed the two groups in competitive situations in which one group could achieve its goals only at the expense of the other.

FYI

Professional athletes are paid high salaries and their actions frequently earn them the public's perception as self-centered and spoiled. However, some professional athletes like basketball star David Robinson and football greats Steve Young and Darrell Green demonstrate altruism by giving their time, money, guidance, and encouragement to various charitable causes.

Figure 19.16

Caption Answer Intergroup hostility develops when groups are placed in competition or have conflicting goals.

Applying Psychology

The National Center for Education Statistics reported the following statistics from a 2000 survey of 2,270 public schools around the country.

- Twenty percent of the schools had experienced one or more serious violent crimes in the past year. Serious violent crimes ranged from robbery to murder.
- The number of schools reporting at least one less serious violent episode ranged from 61 percent for elementary schools to 92 percent for high schools.
- More than 75 percent of schools have a formal violence prevention or reduction program.

Ask: **What factors trigger violence in schools? What can be done to prevent violence in schools? What security measures would you recommend?**

Reading Check How did experimenters create intergroup hostility at the Robber's Cave camp?

illustration of the social trap can be seen in the way Americans have responded to the problems of pollution. We know that automobile exhaust pollutes the air. We know that one way to reduce air pollution is to carpool or use public transportation. Yet the driver who commutes 30 miles a day alone and who knows that he or she is polluting the air thinks: "Yes, I know my car exhaust is bad, but I am only one person. If I stop driving, it won't make any difference." As long as we fall into that social trap, we continue to destroy our environment.

Rather than simply requiring cleaner exhaust (which encourages continued driving), cities are offering priority lanes for buses and access to High Occupancy Vehicle lanes for cars with two or more occupants. Other ways to change people's behavior include educating them concerning the issues and communicating the idea that "Yes, you do make a difference." By publicizing the problems and solutions and organizing groups to act, individuals begin to believe that what they do does have an impact, and their actions are reinforced by the group. In this way, people find it more beneficial to cooperate than to act in a purely selfish manner.

ALTRUISM

altruism: helping others, often at a cost or risk, for reasons other than rewards

Altruism means helping another, often with a cost to oneself, for reasons other than the expectation of a reward. Consider the following scene: You are walking on a crowded street and suddenly hear a scuffle off to the side. You turn to see a man trying to rip a woman's purse from her grasp. Everyone else just keeps on walking past the scuffle. What do you do? Whether you help or not may depend on the diffusion of responsibility.

Figure 19.16 **Us Versus Them**

Intergroup conflict results when a group no longer sees the enemy as individual humans and thus can treat them indecently. This occurred in Bosnia-Herzegovina in the late 1990s. ***How does intergroup hostility develop?***

Diffusion of Responsibility

Sometimes when several people are faced with a common problem and there is no opponent, they may not even see themselves as a group. There have been many famous examples of muggings, rapes, and murders that were committed in public while a large group of people watched without intervening or calling for help.

By studying artificial crises, psychologists have tried to find out why these people did not act. In one experiment, college students were asked to participate in a discussion of personal problems. They were asked to sit in separate rooms. Some were told that they would be communicating with only one other person, and others were given the impression that they would be talking with as many as five other people. All communication, the psychologist told each student, was to take place over microphones so that everyone would remain anonymous and thus would be able

PSYCHOLOGY LAB EXPERIMENT

Cooperation Organize the class into groups of three. Tell the groups that they will use the jigsaw classroom strategy to study for a test on this chapter. Explain this strategy as follows: Within the group, each person is assigned one section of the chapter. Each student is to become an expert in that section of the chapter. After students have had time to study their assigned section, the groups will meet. Each person will teach the material from his or her section. The other students should ask questions. Give the class a test on the chapter and encourage members to share their results with the group. As a class, discuss the effectiveness of this study method, both in terms of grades earned and in terms of learning to cooperate. **L2**
BLOCK SCHEDULING

to speak more freely. Each person was to talk in turn.

In reality, there were no other people—all the voices presenting each problem were on tape. As discussion of solutions started, the participant heard one of the other participants go into what sounded like an epileptic seizure. The victim began to make choking sounds and call for help. The experimenters found that 85 percent of the people who thought they were alone with the victim came out of their room to help him. Of those who believed there were five other people nearby, however, only 31 percent did anything to help.

Figure 19.17 Would You Help Someone in Need?

Whether we offer assistance to someone in need depends on several factors, including what other witnesses are doing. ***How does diffusion of responsibility affect our behavior in such situations?***

The experimenters suggested that this behavior was the result of **diffusion of responsibility.** In other words, because several people were present, each participant assumed someone else would help. The researchers found that in experiments where people could see the other participants, the same pattern emerged. In addition, bystanders reassured one another that it would not be a good idea to interfere. The **bystander effect** occurs when a person refrains from taking action because of the presence of others. These findings on diffusion of responsibility suggest that the larger the crowd or group of bystanders, the more likely any given individual is to feel that he or she is not responsible for trying to alter whatever is going on (Darley & Latané, 1968).

diffusion of responsibility: the presence of others lessens an individual's feelings of responsibility for his or her actions or failure to act

bystander effect: an individual does not take action because of the presence of others

Another influence that inhibits action is the tendency to minimize the need for any response. To act, you must admit that an emergency exists. You may not know exactly what is going on when you hear screams or loud thumps upstairs. You are likely to wait before risking the embarrassment of rushing to help where help is not needed or wanted. It is easier to persuade yourself that nothing needs to be done if you look around and see other people behaving calmly. Not only can you see that they think nothing is wrong but you also can see that not doing anything is "the norm." You are able to minimize the need to act and shift any responsibility to those around you. Both the presence of a leader and being familiar with the person needing help, however, increase the likelihood and speed of help being offered. The same is true of knowing what kind of help is required, seeing the correct form of assistance being modeled, or expecting future interactions with the person needing help. These situations increase the chances that assistance will be offered when it is most needed (Baron & Byrne, 2006).

Social Loafing

Your evaluations of a situation also may lead to social loafing. **Social loafing** occurs when you allow your contributions to the group to slack off because you realize that individual contributions

social loafing: the tendency to work less hard when sharing the workload with others

CHAPTER 19

Section 3, pages 564–570

Figure 19.17

Caption Answer When someone needs assistance, we are less likely to act when others are around because we each assume that someone else will help.

Vocabulary Activity 19–3

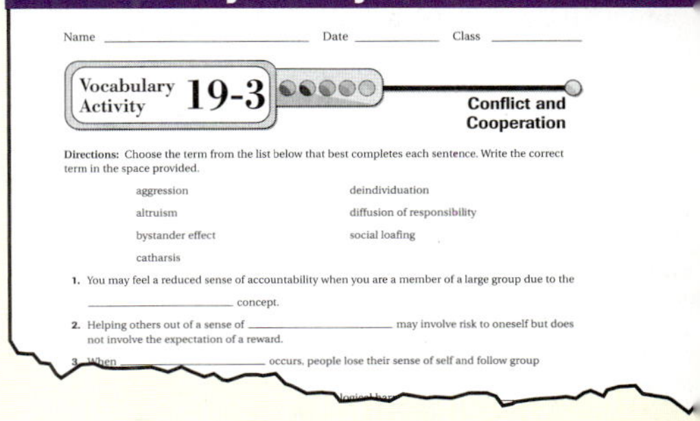
Name ______ Date ______ Class ______

Vocabulary Activity 19-3 — Conflict and Cooperation

Directions: Choose the term from the list below that best completes each sentence. Write the correct term in the space provided.

aggression; deindividuation; altruism; diffusion of responsibility; bystander effect; social loafing; catharsis

1. You may feel a reduced sense of accountability when you are a member of a large group due to the ______ concept.
2. Helping others out of a sense of ______ may involve risk to oneself but does not involve the expectation of a reward.
3. When ______ occurs, people lose their sense of self and follow group

3 ASSESS

Assign Section 3 Assessment as homework or as an in-class activity.

Section Quiz 19–3

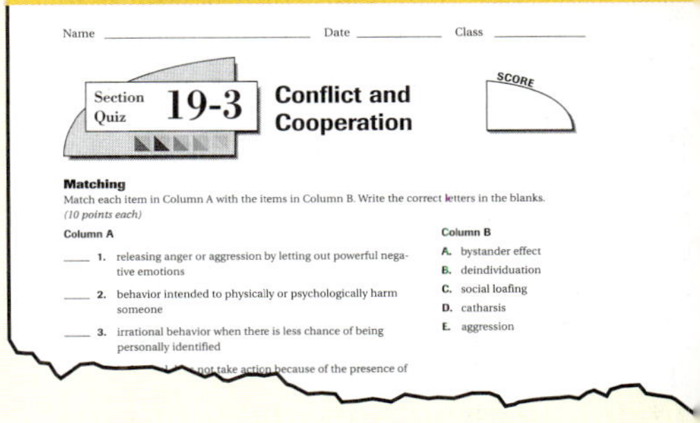
Name ______ Date ______ Class ______

Section Quiz 19-3 — Conflict and Cooperation

SCORE

Matching

Match each item in Column A with the items in Column B. Write the correct letters in the blanks. *(10 points each)*

Column A

____ 1. releasing anger or aggression by letting out powerful negative emotions

____ 2. behavior intended to physically or psychologically harm someone

____ 3. irrational behavior when there is less chance of being personally identified

Column B

A. bystander effect
B. deindividuation
C. social loafing
D. catharsis
E. aggression

INTERDISCIPLINARY CONNECTIONS ACTIVITY

The Media Organize the class into small groups. Ask each group to review newspaper accounts of the days following the September 11, 2001, terrorist attacks on the World Trade Center, looking for examples of altruism by professionals and ordinary citizens. Have each group prepare a display of the examples they have found. Place the displays around the classroom and allow groups time to share the stories they uncovered. **L2**

Reteach

Have students create a model of aggression for each of the theories of aggression, using Figure 19.15 as an example.

Enrich

Tell students to select an altruistic cause that they support. Challenge them to develop a multimedia presentation that could be used to encourage others to support the cause financially or by volunteering their time.

4 CLOSE

To demonstrate diffusion of responsibility and the bystander effect, arrange with a student beforehand to come late to class loaded down with an armful of books and supplies. Have the student accidentally trip and spill the items being carried. If possible, you should be as far away from the scene as possible. Have the student take the time to pick up the belongings and take a seat. The discussion that follows the incident will depend on the other students' responses to the student who spilled the belongings.

---

are not as apparent and easily measured in a group setting. When you are a member of a large group, for example, you may feel a reduced sense of accountability.

deindividuation: individuals behave irrationally when there is less chance of being personally identified

Deindividuation When people act as individuals, obey their consciences, and are concerned with self-evaluation, we think of them as *individualistic*. When **deindividuation** occurs, people lose their sense of self and follow group behaviors. The deindividuated person acts without thinking about self and goes along with the group. Why did normally pleasant people violently throw bottles and rocks at innocent people during the Los Angeles riots? Researchers believe that being in a crowd may reduce feelings of guilt or self-awareness that one ordinarily feels. People in crowds are anonymous—there is little chance of pinpointing who threw the rock and of being identified.

Social pressure can affect us in positive ways, too. Most people care deeply about what others think of them. This can be a powerful source of pressure for individuals to do what others believe they should do. Have you ever refrained from saying or doing something mean because you wanted others to think highly of you? Maybe you went out of your way to act compassionately while others witnessed your actions. Microsoft Corporation chairman Bill Gates and his wife, Melinda, have donated nearly $26 billion to their charitable foundation, which was established in 1994. Money from the Gates Foundation is used to fund health and education projects around the world. In 2006, financial expert Warren Buffet, the world's second-richest person, pledged to donate the bulk of his $44 billion fortune to the Gates Foundation. It is difficult to say whether these charitable acts resulted from social pressure, but social influence may have played a role.

SECTION 3 Assessment

1. **Review the Vocabulary** How does diffusion of responsibility affect individuals in a group?
2. **Visualize the Main Idea** Using a graphic organizer similar to the one below, compare and contrast aggression and altruism.

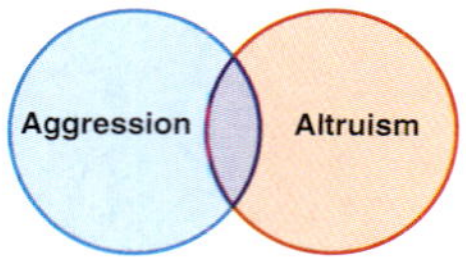

3. **Recall Information** What is deindividuation, and how does it occur?
4. **Think Critically** Do you think that most students work harder on projects they must complete alone for a grade or on team projects in which no individual grades are given? Explain your reasoning.
5. **Application Activity** Keep an anger diary for a week. In it include descriptions of several fight-or-flight situations that you experience or observe. Did any of the episodes lead to violence? Why or why not?

SECTION 3 Assessment Answers

1. Individuals are less likely to act and take responsibility when others are around because they expect someone else to act.
2. Aggression is intended to do physical or psychological harm to another person. Altruism is the act of helping others without expecting a reward, and even when it involves risk. The overlap exists in that both acts are voluntary and involve a choice by the individual.
3. Deindividuation is irrational behavior performed by an individual when there is little or no chance of being identified. It occurs when people lose their sense of self and let the group direct their behavior.
4. Students' answers will vary and will likely depend on the individual and the amount of pressure exerted by the group.
5. Students' answers will vary. Encourage students to be honest and to learn from the situations.

CHAPTER 19

Summary and Vocabulary

People belong to many groups for a variety of reasons. Groups can affect the way individuals behave in different situations.

Section 1 Group Behavior

Main Idea: A group—a collection of people who interact, share common goals, and influence how members think and act—is unified by the attitudes and standards members share and by their commitment to those beliefs.

- To be classified as a group, a collection of people must demonstrate interdependence, communication, and common goals.
- Groups serve two general purposes—task functions and social functions.
- To be part of a group, an individual must be responsive to the norms of the group, subscribe to its ideology, and be prepared to make sacrifices in order to be part of it.
- Groups can be differentiated by in-groups and out-groups and primary and secondary groups.
- Research has shown that social facilitation seems to occur when participants perform simple tasks, whereas social inhibition seems to occur when participants perform more complex tasks.
- Group polarization and groupthink are two processes of group decision making.

Section 2 Conformity and Obedience

Main Idea: You may engage in behavior because of direct or indirect group pressure or in response to orders given by authorities.

- Psychologists believe that people conform to gain approval.
- Compliance occurs when an individual gives in to social pressure in his or her public behavior but does not actually change private beliefs.
- Psychologists believe that people learn to obey authority figures and to follow orders and rules.

Section 3 Conflict and Cooperation

Main Idea: Conflicts between groups are a fact of everyday life. Individuals often give up responsibility for their actions by perceiving and responding to situations as a group.

- Aggression is a combination of biological, cognitive, personality, and environmental factors.
- Psychologists have found that the larger the crowd or group of bystanders, the more likely any given individual is to feel that he or she is not responsible for whatever is going on.
- Social loafing occurs when people allow their contributions to the group to slack off because they realize that individual contributions are not as apparent and easily measured in a group setting.
- When deindividuation occurs, people lose their sense of self and follow group behaviors.

Chapter Vocabulary

group (p. 545)
task functions (p. 547)
social functions (p. 547)
norms (p. 547)
ideology (p. 548)
social facilitation (p. 549)
social inhibition (p. 549)
group polarization (p. 550)
groupthink (p. 551)
sociogram (p. 552)
conformity (p. 556)
obedience (p. 558)
aggression (p. 565)
catharsis (p. 566)
altruism (p. 568)
diffusion of responsibility (p. 569)
bystander effect (p. 569)
social loafing (p. 569)
deindividuation (p. 570)

19 Summary and Vocabulary

Using the Chapter 19 Summary and Vocabulary

Use the Chapter 19 Summary and Vocabulary to preview, review, condense, or reteach the chapter.

Preview/Review

Use the Chapter Vocabulary list to help students review and study.

Activity Have students create a word search using examples or definitions as the clues for the terms. Have pairs of students trade and complete word search puzzles.

Vocabulary PuzzleMaker CD-ROM reinforces the vocabulary terms used in Chapter 19.

Condense

Have students read the Chapter 19 Summary.

Chapter 19 Guided Reading Activities

Reteach

Reteaching Activity 19

PERFORMANCE ASSESSMENT ACTIVITY

Bylaws of a Group Ask students to imagine they are in the process of founding a task function group to perform community service. Instruct students to draw up bylaws to help ensure group cohesiveness and address such issues as norms, ideology, and commitment. They should also outline the communication pattern that will operate within the group and set guidelines for the selection and responsibilities of leaders. **BLOCK SCHEDULING**

Refer to the ***Authentic Assessment*** booklet for additional activities and information about evaluating student performance.

19 Assessment

PSYCHOLOGY Online

Have students visit the Web site at glencoe.com to review Chapter 19 and take the **Self-Check Quiz**.

GLENCOE TECHNOLOGY

PRESENTATION Plus!

For a review of Chapter 19 content, see MindJogger Checkpoint on **Presentation Plus!**

Reviewing Vocabulary

1. d
2. g
3. a
4. e
5. c
6. j
7. h
8. b
9. f
10. i

Recalling Facts

1. Diagrams should include the following: interdependence, shared goals, and communication.
2. Shared norms, a common ideology, and high commitment and participation of group members work to hold a group together. Commitment increases when the individuals can share in group decisions and share the rewards and when there is a requirement of personal sacrifice.
3. People conform to increase their sense of belonging to a group and to avoid standing out.
4. The cognitive theory assumes aggression is learned in childhood by observing and imitating the behavior of models.
5. Diffusion of responsibility and the bystander effect inhibit individual action within a group setting. Diffusion of responsibility occurs when the presence of others lessens an individual's feeling of responsibility. When a person refrains from taking action because of the presence of others, it is known as the bystander effect.

Critical Thinking

1. Encourage students to talk to persons whom they admire as leaders. Have them ask about their backgrounds, how they became leaders, and what they think makes an effective leader. Students should note such things as personality traits when discussing the characteristics of leadership.

CHAPTER 19 Assessment

PSYCHOLOGY Online

Self-Check Quiz
Visit the *Understanding Psychology* Web site at glencoe.com and click on **Chapter 19—Self-Check Quizzes** to prepare for the Chapter Test.

Reviewing Vocabulary

Choose the letter of the correct term or concept below to complete the sentence.

a. ideology
b. social facilitation
c. social inhibition
d. group polarization
e. conformity
f. obedience
g. aggression
h. catharsis
i. bystander effect
j. deindividuation

1. __________ occurs when the majority's point of view is reinforced and an extreme view dominates.
2. A behavior that is intended to cause physical or psychological harm is called __________.
3. A group with a common __________ shares a set of principles, attitudes, and defined objectives for which the group stands.
4. __________ involves any behavior that an individual engages in because of direct or indirect group pressure.
5. The tendency to perform poorly in front of a group is known as __________.
6. __________ occurs when people lose their sense of self and follow group behaviors.
7. Punching a pillow to release anger is a form of __________.
8. The tendency to perform better in the presence of a group is known as __________.
9. __________ is behaving according to the authority of group norms or customs.
10. The __________ occurs when a person refrains from taking action because of the presence of others.

Recalling Facts

1. Using a diagram similar to the one below, identify the characteristics of a group.

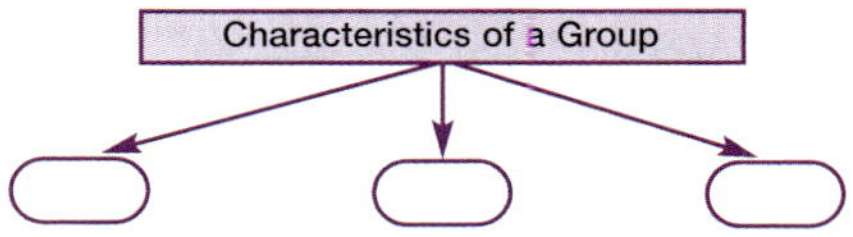

2. What factors work to hold a group together? What factors increase the commitment of a person to the group?
3. Why do people conform?
4. How does the cognitive theory explain aggression?
5. What are two factors that inhibit individual action within a group setting?

Critical Thinking

1. **Evaluating Information** Choose a person in your community whom you consider to be a leader. What qualities does this person have that make him or her a leader? How does the person demonstrate the characteristics of leadership?
2. **Analyzing Concepts** Do you think it is possible for an individual to never have to conform to a group? Explain your answer.
3. **Demonstrating Reasoned Judgment** Which psychological theory discussed in the chapter do you think best explains the reasons for aggression? Provide reasons for your opinion.
4. **Applying Concepts** Do you think knowing the causes of aggression is important in finding ways to help reduce violence in society? Explain your answer.
5. **Synthesizing Information** Think about what you have learned from your reading and classroom discussions about altruistic or helping behavior. How might it be possible to increase altruistic behavior in people? What factors might prevent this from occurring?

2. Answers will vary. Unless totally isolated, every person conforms to some degree. Remind students that conforming can be positive. Encourage students to think of everyday types of conformity like eating with utensils rather than with hands.
3. Students' explanations should clearly support the theory or combination of theories they have chosen.
4. Students' answers will vary. Remind them that anytime a cause is known, the likelihood of altering the effects increases.
5. Students' answers will vary. Ask students when altruism ends and conformity begins.

Psychology Projects

1. The oral reports should describe the incident and suggest ways in which groupthink could have been avoided.
2. Students should describe the personality characteristics of both the leader and the participants of such groups. Ask how the interaction of these personality characteristics contributed to the conformity.
3. Encourage students to use strong visuals and clear messages to make their points.

CHAPTER 19

Assessment

Psychology Projects

1. **Group Behavior** Groupthink occurs when group discussions stress agreement rather than critical thinking. The Bay of Pigs invasion was one result of groupthink. Research other historical events that were the result of groupthink, such as Watergate or the *Challenger* disaster. Find out the background of these events and how groupthink contributed to the outcomes. Present your findings in an oral report.
2. **Conformity and Obedience** Research examples of extreme group conformity and obedience. You might find out about David Koresh and the Branch Davidians or Jimmy Jones and the Jonestown cult. Research the general characteristics of the people who joined the groups and the reasons given for the leaders' ability to command such obedience. Share your findings in a documentary report or presentation.
3. **Conflict and Cooperation** Create an illustrated, captioned poster that provides strategies for teenagers to use to control aggression. Display your poster in the classroom.

Technology Activity

Think of a cause or an issue about which you feel strongly. Use the library and the Internet to find task-oriented groups that address this cause or issue. Find the e-mail address of the organization and send an e-mail to find out more about the group's goals and the ways that you might become involved. Share the information you collected, your sources, and any e-mail responses with the class.

Psychology Journal

Reread the journal entry you wrote at the beginning of the chapter. Using what you have learned, select one group to which you belong and describe it. Answer the following questions: What is the purpose of the group? What kind of group is it? Why do you belong to it? Do you conform to any ideals of the group? Why? What might happen if you did not conform to the group's ideals or norms?

Building Skills

Interpreting a Graph Milgram was upset about the willingness of his participants to obey an authority. In later experiments, he tried to find ways to reduce obedience. He found that distance between the teacher and the learner had an effect. The graph at right shows the percentage of "teachers" who obeyed orders at three different physical distances. Review the graph, then answer the questions below.

1. What percentage of teachers obeyed orders when they could only hear the learner?
2. What happened to the percentage of teachers who obeyed orders when they were in the same room and could see the learner? When they were asked to touch the learner?
3. What reasons can you give for the differences in the percentage of participants obeying authority in the three physical distances illustrated in the graph?

Practice and **assess** key social studies skills with **Glencoe Skillbuilder Interactive Workbook CD-ROM, Level 2.**

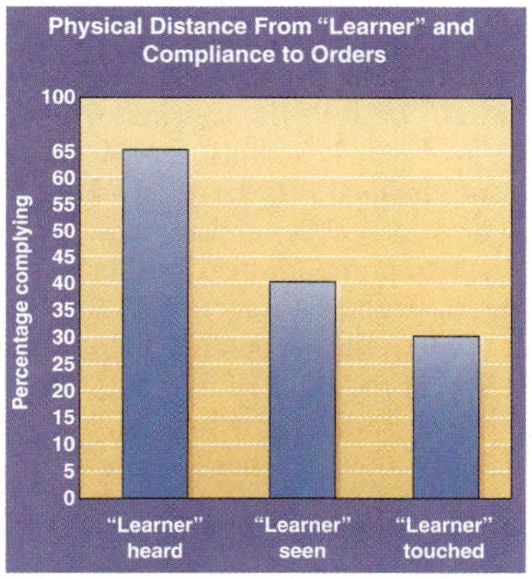

See the Skills Handbook, page 628, for an explanation of interpreting graphs.

Building Skills

1. 65 percent
2. The percentages declined to 40 percent and 30 percent, respectively.
3. Answers will vary but should explain that the better one knows a person or the closer one physically is to a person, the less likely one will be to harm that person. Students may suggest that it is easier to harm another when you do not witness the consequences of your own harmful behavior.

GLENCOE TECHNOLOGY

CD-ROM

Glencoe Skillbuilder Interactive Workbook, Level 2

This interactive CD-ROM is designed to reinforce student mastery of essential social studies skills.

Chapter Bonus Test Question

This question may be used for extra credit on the Chapter Assessment.

Answer the following question:

I have just been hired by a large company that was once a leader in the marketplace but has not kept up with the changes in technology. I have been told that I have three years to make the company profitable. What kind of leader do I need to be?

Answer: transformational leader

Technology Activity

Caution students not to make a commitment to a group until they have thoroughly researched the organization. Tell students that some groups use seemingly good causes and the anonymity provided by the Internet to defraud people.

Psychology Journal

Encourage students to use these basic questions as they consider joining new groups.

Readings in Psychology

Block Schedule

This activity works well for a block-scheduling framework.

Reinforcing Vocabulary

Review the **Reader's Dictionary** terms with students to be sure they understand any unfamiliar terms.

Background Information

This fascinating story is based on a real classroom experiment in which a teacher, Ron Jones, attempted to show this students the dangers of conformity. By allowing the students to experience the lesson, he hoped to show them the ease with which individuals sublimate their personal values in order to become accepted members of a group. Never envisioning the students' enthusiastic response, Mr. Jones found his lesson on Nazi Germany taking on a frightening life of its own. Within a week of its inception, the "Third Wave," as it was originally called, had permeated the entire school, its membership growing from less than 30 to over 200. Mr. Jones brought the lesson to a conclusion by calling for a members' only rally. During the rally he explained the real purpose behind his lesson, concluding his talk with a film of Hitler appearing before the enthralled masses at Nuremberg. He asked that the class rally and its revelations be kept secret. The students, many shocked and weeping, complied. They were all willing to remember the lesson, while forgetting how easily they became involved. In the four years that followed, Mr. Jones did not remember one person ever admitting attendance at the Third Wave rally.

Ask: **Why was it so easy for the students to become Wave enthusiasts? What did the Wave offer that made it so attractive to so many people? Do you think it was ethical for Mr. Jones to conduct this experiment on his class?**

Readings In Psychology

Todd Strasser's *The Wave* is based on a true incident that occurred in 1969 in a California classroom. Read this excerpt from the book to find out what happened when teacher Ben Ross took an unusual approach to teaching his class about the control of the Nazi party.

Reader's Dictionary

punctual: prompt; arriving on time

precise: exact; definite; strictly following rules

THE WAVE

BY TODD STRASSER

For the next twenty minutes the class practiced getting out of their seats, wandering around in apparent disorganization and then, at their teacher's command, quickly returning to their seats and the correct seated posture. Ben shouted orders more like a drill sergeant than a teacher. Once they seemed to have mastered quick and correct seating, he threw in a new twist. They would still leave their seats and return. But now they would return from the hallway and Ross would time them with a stopwatch.

On the first try, it took forty-eight seconds. The second time they were able to do it in half a minute. Before the last attempt, David had an idea.

"Listen," he told his classmates as they stood outside in the hall waiting for Mr. Ross's signal. "Let's line up in the order of who has to go the farthest to reach their desks inside. That way we won't have to bump into each other."

The rest of the class agreed. As they got into the correct order, they couldn't help noticing that Robert was at the head of the line. "The new head of the class," someone whispered as they waited nervously for their teacher to give them the sign. Ben snapped his fingers and the column of students moved quickly and quietly into the room. As the last student reached his seat, Ben clicked the stopwatch off. He was smiling. "Sixteen seconds."

The class cheered.

"All right, all right, quiet down," their teacher said, returning to the front of the room. To his surprise, the students calmed down quickly. The silence that suddenly filled the room was almost eerie. Normally the only time the room was that still, Ross thought, was when it was empty.

"Now, there are three more rules that you must obey," he told them. "One. Everybody must have pencils and note paper for note-taking. Two. When asking or answering a question, you must stand at the side of your seats. And three. The first words you say when answering or asking a question are, 'Mr. Ross.' All right?"

Around the room, heads nodded.

"All right," Mr. Ross said. "Brad, who was the British Prime Minister before Churchill?"

Still sitting at his seat, Brad chewed nervously on a fingernail. "Uh, wasn't it—"

But before he could say more, Mr. Ross quickly cut him off. "Wrong, Brad, you already forgot the rules I just told you." He looked across the room at Robert. "Robert, show Brad the proper procedure for answering a question."

Instantly Robert stood up next to his desk at attention. "Mr. Ross."

"Correct," Mr. Ross said. "Thank you, Robert."

"Aw, this is dumb," Brad mumbled.

"Just because you couldn't do it right," someone said.

"Brad," Mr. Ross said, "who was the Prime Minister before Churchill?"

This time Brad rose and stood beside his desk. "Mr. Ross, it was, uh, Prime Minister, uh."

"You're still too slow, Brad," Mr. Ross said. "From now on, everyone make your answers as short as possible, and spit them out when asked. Now, Brad, try again."

This time Brad snapped up beside his seat. "Mr. Ross, Chamberlain."

ADDITIONAL READINGS ABOUT THE TOPIC

Aronson, E. (2003). *The Social Animal* (9th ed.). New York: Freeman.

Cialdini, R. (1998). *Influence: The Psychology of Persuasion.* New York: Harper.

Pratkanis, A.R., & Aronson, E. (2001). *The Age of Propaganda: The Everyday Use and Abuse of Persuasion.* New York: Freeman.

Zimbardo, P.G., & Leippe, M.R. (1991). *The Psychology of Attitude Change and Social Influence.* New York: McGraw-Hill.

Ben nodded approvingly. "Now that's the way to answer a question. Punctual, precise, with punch. Andrea, what country did Hitler invade in September of 1939?"

Andrea, the ballet dancer, stood stiffly by her desk. "Mr. Ross, I don't know."

Mr. Ross smiled. "Still, a good response because you used proper form. Amy, do you know the answer?"

Amy hopped up beside her desk. "Mr. Ross, Poland."

"Excellent," Mr. Ross said. "Brian, what was the name of Hitler's political party?"

Brian quickly got out of his chair. "Mr. Ross, the Nazis."

Mr. Ross nodded. "That's good, Brian. Very quick. Now, does anyone know the official name of the party? Laurie?"

Laurie Sanders stood up beside her desk. "The National Socialist—"

"No!" There was a sharp bang as Mr. Ross struck his desktop with a ruler. "Now do it again correctly."

Laurie sat down, a confused look on her face. What had she done wrong? David leaned over and whispered in her ear. Oh, right. She stood up again. "Mr. Ross, the National Socialist German Workers Party."

"Correct," Mr. Ross replied.

Mr. Ross kept asking questions, and around the room students jumped to attention, eager to show that they knew both the answer and the correct form with which to give it. It was a far cry from the normally casual atmosphere of the classroom, but neither Ben nor his students reflected on that fact. They were too caught up in this new game. The speed and precision of each question and answer were exhilarating. Soon

Ben was perspiring as he shouted each question out and another student rose sharply beside his or her desk to shout back a terse reply.

"Peter, who proposed the Lend-Lease Act?"

"Mr. Ross, Roosevelt."

"Right. Eric, who died in the death camps?"

"Mr. Ross, the Jews."

"Anyone else, Brad?"

"Mr. Ross, gypsies, homosexuals, and the feeble-minded."

"Good. Amy, why were they murdered?"

"Mr. Ross, because they weren't part of the superior race."

"Correct. David, who ran the death camps?"

"Mr. Ross, the S.S."

"Excellent."

Out in the hall, the bells were ringing, but no one in the classroom moved from their seats. Still carried by the momentum of the class's progress that period, Ben stood at the front of the room and issued the final order of the day. "Tonight, finish reading chapter seven and read the first half of chapter eight. That's all, class dismissed." Before him the class rose in what seemed like a single movement and rushed out into the hall.

"Wow, that was weird, man, it was like a rush," Brian gasped in uncharacteristic enthusiasm. He and some of the students from Mr. Ross's class were standing in a tight pack in the corridor, still riding on the energy they'd felt in the classroom.

Analyzing the Reading

1. How is student participation different during this class?
2. What are the students' attitudes toward the new rules?
3. **Critical Thinking** Why do you think the students participated in the new system? Did pressure from the rest of the class have any influence on participation? Explain.

Answers to Analyzing the Reading

1. It is structured and has to conform to rules. Students are eager to show that they know the correct answers in the proper form.
2. Students are hesitant at first, but this soon gives way to overwhelming enthusiasm.
3. Answers will vary. Positive reinforcement from Mr. Ross and classmates encouraged participation, as did group pressure.

Active Reading Strategy

Remind students that rereading a confusing part and relating information to previous knowledge might clarify their understanding. Explain that good readers often pause to reread, question, or think about what they read.

Psychology Journal

Tell students to write a short story about a time when they conformed to group pressure. ■

Teacher Tip

Tell students to write about a time when they felt pressured to participate in something with which they disagreed. Have them describe the ways in which they were pressured and how they made their decision to participate or to refuse to participate.

Chapter 20 Resource Guide

SECTION RESOURCES

Daily Objectives	Reproducible Resources	Multimedia Resources
Section 1 **Attitude Formation** Describe how our attitudes are the result of conditioning, observational learning, and cognitive evaluation. Explain how attitudes help us define ourselves and our place in society, evaluate people and events, and guide our behavior.	Guided Reading Activity 20–1 Vocabulary Activity 20–1 Section Quiz 20–1	Daily Focus Transparency 20–1 *ExamView® Assessment Suite* CD-ROM Presentation Plus! Software
Section 2 **Attitude Change and Prejudice** Explore how attitudes are formed through compliance, identification, and internalization. Explore how attitudes may be changed as a result of cognitive dissonance.	Guided Reading Activity 20–2 Vocabulary Activity 20–2 Section Quiz 20–2	Daily Focus Transparency 20–2 Vocabulary PuzzleMaker CD-ROM *ExamView® Assessment Suite* CD-ROM Presentation Plus! Software
Section 3 **Persuasion** Explain how persuasion is a direct attempt to influence attitudes and how we determine the credibility of a message by evaluating when, where, and how a message is presented, as well as the message itself.	Guided Reading Activity 20–3 Vocabulary Activity 20–3 Section Quiz 20–3	Daily Focus Transparency 20–3 Vocabulary PuzzleMaker CD-ROM *ExamView® Assessment Suite* CD-ROM Presentation Plus! Software

Blackline Master CD-ROM Transparency

Block Schedule

Activities that are particularly suited for use within the block-scheduling framework are identified throughout this chapter by the following designation: **BLOCK SCHEDULING**

KEY TO ABILITY LEVELS

Teaching strategies have been coded for varying learning styles and abilities.

L1 **BASIC** activities for all students
L2 **AVERAGE** activities for average to above-average students
L3 **CHALLENGING** activities for above-average students
ELL **ENGLISH LANGUAGE LEARNER** activities

Chapter 20 Resource Guide

Timesaving Tools

TeacherWorks™ All-In-One Planner and Resource Center

- **Interactive Teacher Edition** Access your Teacher Wraparound Edition and your classroom resources with a few easy clicks.
- **Interactive Lesson Planner** Planning has never been easier! Organize your week, month, semester, or year with all the lesson helps you need to make teaching creative, timely, and relevant.

Use Glencoe's **Presentation Plus!** multimedia teacher tool to easily present dynamic lessons that visually excite your students. Using Microsoft PowerPoint® you can customize the presentations to create your own personalized lessons.

Activity

From the Classroom of...

Robert Windemuth
Chambersburg Area Senior High School
Chambersburg, PA

Attitude Formation

Time: 1 class period (45 minutes)

Materials Needed: A newspaper for each student; blank sheets of paper for each student; adhesive tape and scissors; and headlines the teacher has prepared in advance to be used in debriefing

Tell students they are going to read through the newspaper to form a general impression about whether, in their opinion, the news is negative, positive, or neutral. After they are finished, ask students to write a paragraph describing their position and how they arrived at it. Then ask them to cut out five headlines that support the position they have taken and tape them to the paper on which they have written their paragraphs. Students can then join small groups and compare their papers. Afterward, ask for volunteers who saw the news in different ways to share their opinions with the group. Debrief by showing the headlines you had prepared in advance and discussing them.

A variation of this activity would be to pre-select a variety of headlines and ask students to rate them as positive, negative, or neutral and then discuss student opinions.

Psychology Online

Use our Web site for additional resources. All essential content is covered in the Student Edition.

You and your students can visit glencoe.com, the Web site companion to *Understanding Psychology*. This innovative integration of electronic and print media offers your students a wealth of opportunities. The student text directs students to the Web site for the following options:

- Chapter Overviews
- Student Web Activities
- Self-Check Quizzes

Answers are provided for you in the **Web Activity Lesson Plan**. Additional Web resources and Interactive Puzzles are also available.

Chapter 20 Resource Guide

Note: The following materials may be used when teaching Chapter 20. Section level support materials are shown at point of use in the margins of the Teacher Wraparound Edition.

TEACHING TRANSPARENCIES

Chapter 20 Concept Transparencies

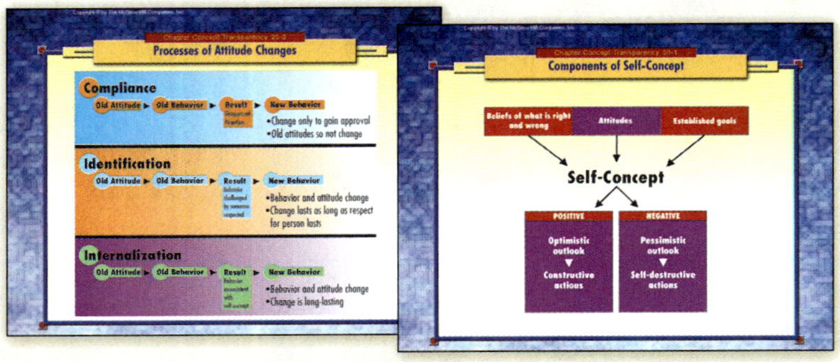

MULTIMEDIA

- Vocabulary PuzzleMaker CD-ROM
- *ExamView® Assessment Suite* CD-ROM
- TeacherWorks™ CD-ROM
- Glencoe Skillbuilder Interactive Workbook, Level 2
- Presentation Plus! Software

REVIEW AND REINFORCEMENT

Reteaching Activity 20

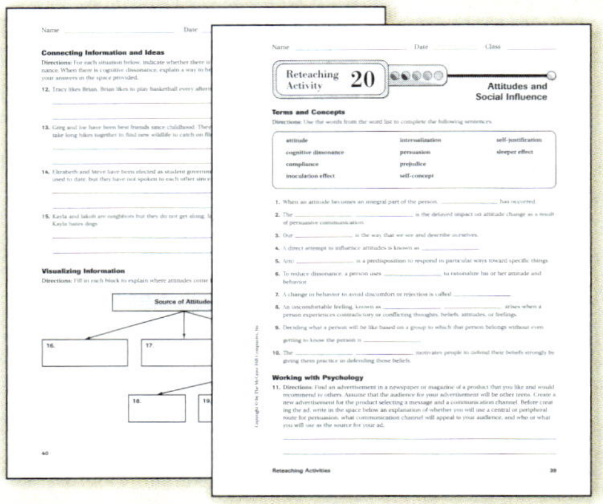

Graphic Organizer Activity 20

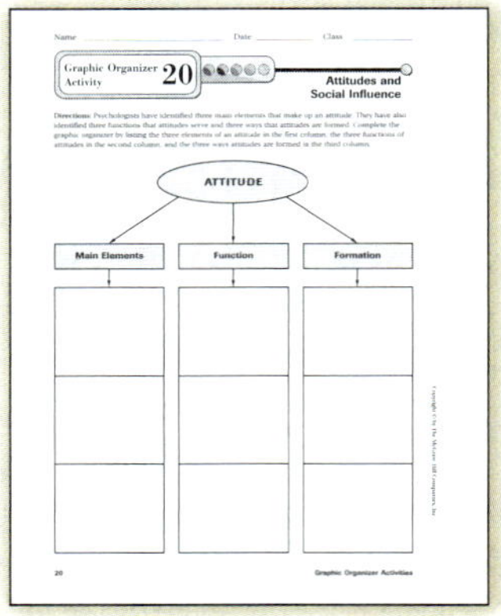

APPLICATION AND HANDS-ON

Psychology Project 20

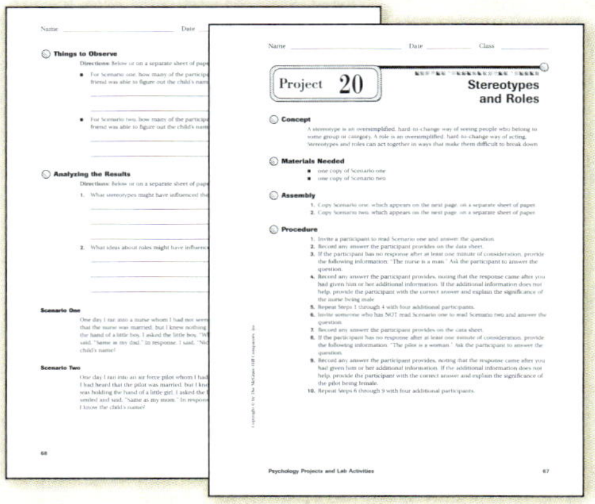

Application Activity 20

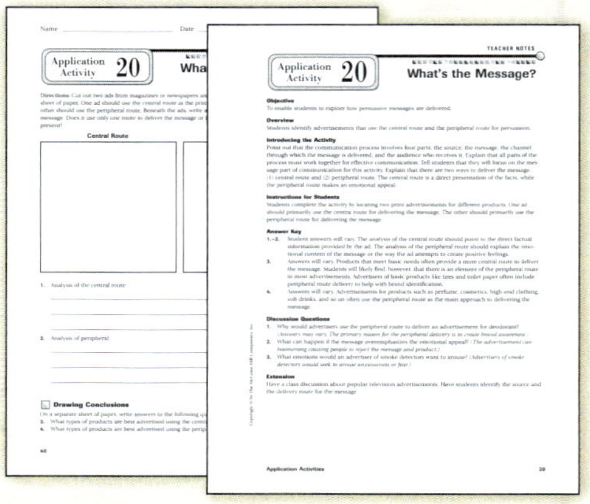

Chapter 20 Resource Guide

ASSESSMENT

Chapter 20 Test, Form A

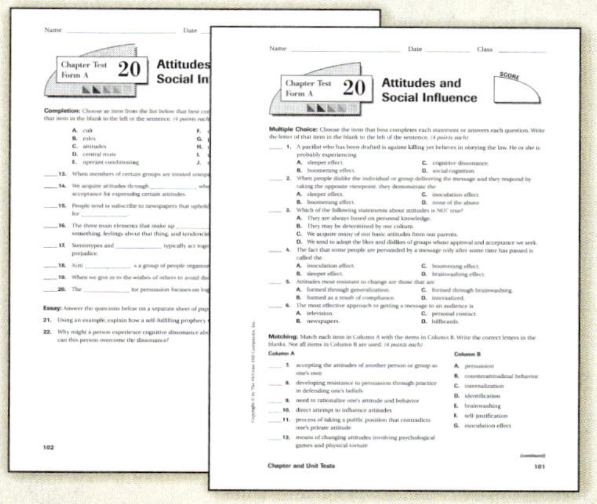
Chapter Test Form A 20 Attitudes and Social Influence

Chapter 20 Test, Form B

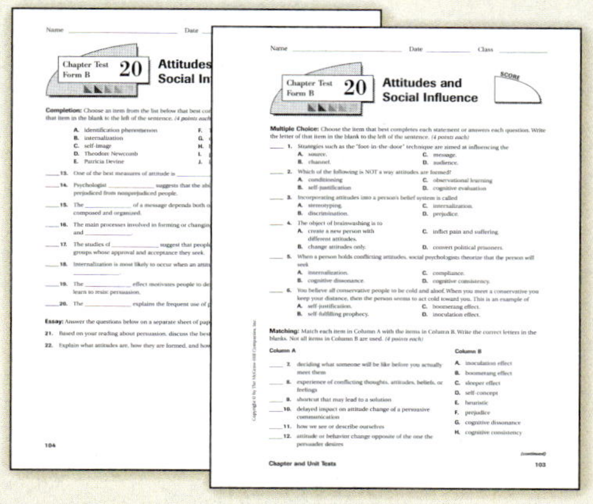
Chapter Test Form B 20 Attitudes and Social Influence

Authentic Assessment Activity 20

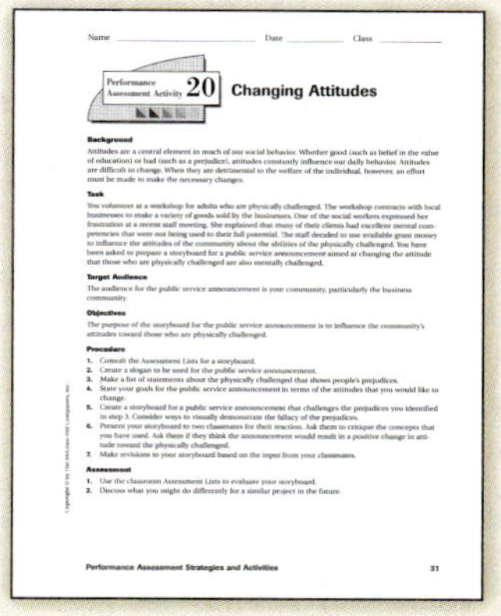
Performance Assessment Activity 20 Changing Attitudes

EXTENSION AND ENRICHMENT

Enrichment Activity 20

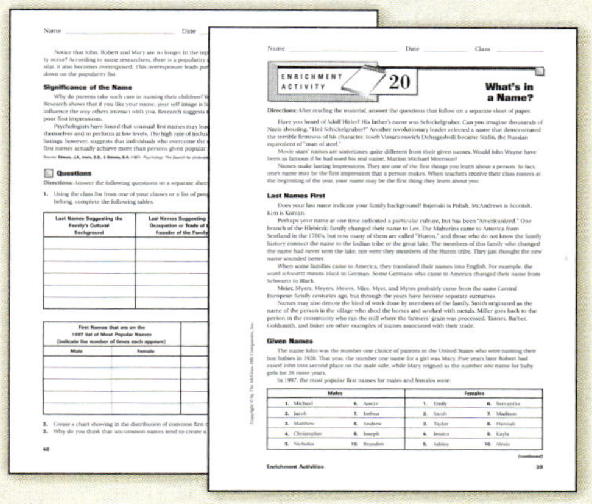
Enrichment Activity 20 What's in a Name?

Critical Thinking Skills Activity 20

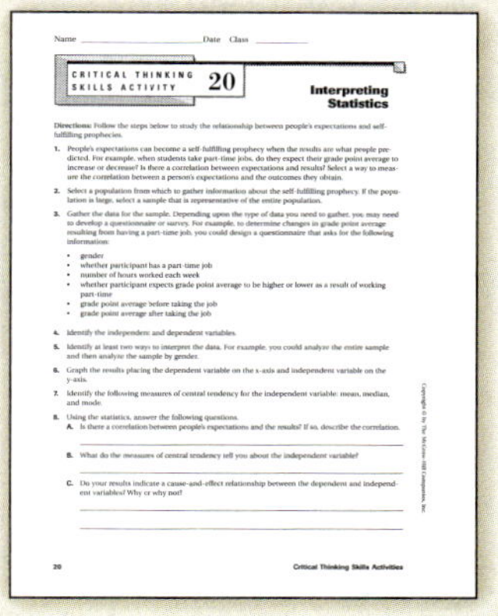
Critical Thinking Skills Activity 20 Interpreting Statistics

Psychology Reading 20

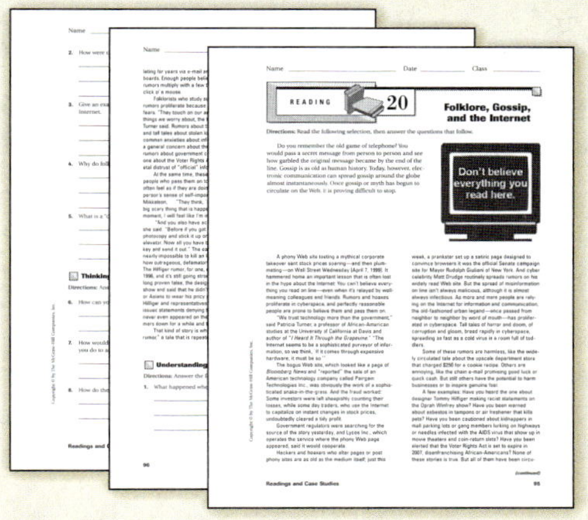
Reading 20 Folklore, Gossip, and the Internet

Psychology Case Study 20

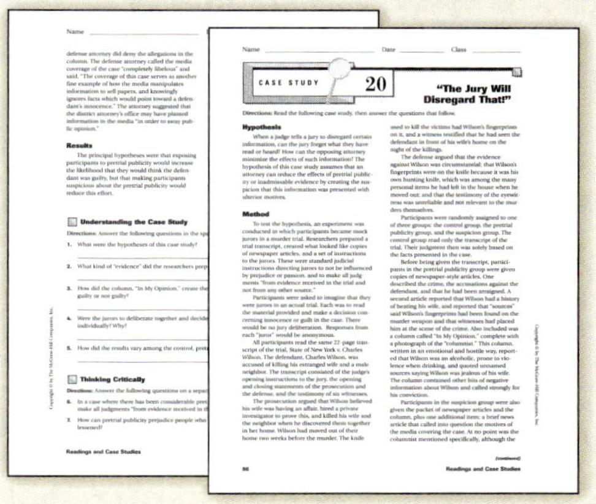
Case Study 20 "The Jury Will Disregard That!"

PSYCHOLOGY Online

Visit glencoe.com for a Chapter Overview for **Chapter 20—Attitudes and Social Influence.**

GLENCOE TECHNOLOGY

For a preview of Chapter 20 content, see MindJogger Checkpoint on **Presentation Plus!**

PSYCHOLOGY JOURNAL

Encourage students to consider the ramifications of prejudiced thinking. ■

This journal activity provides the basis for the Psychology Journal activity exercise in the Chapter Assessment.

CHAPTER 20

Attitudes and Social Influence

PSYCHOLOGY JOURNAL

Write a definition of prejudice in your journal, and list four examples of prejudiced thinking. ■

PSYCHOLOGY Online

Chapter Overview
Visit the *Understanding Psychology* Web site at glencoe.com and click on **Chapter 20—Chapter Overviews** to preview the chapter.

TWO-MINUTE LESSON LAUNCHER

Psychology professors Anthony Greenwald and Mahzarin Banaji have developed implicit association tests that can be taken online. The tests allow a person to test his or her own level of age, race, and gender prejudice. To date, the tests indicate that between 90 and 95 percent of participants have shown some form of unconscious prejudice. If possible, have students visit implicit.harvard.edu/implicit/ and take one or more of the tests. If it is not possible for students to visit the site, conduct a brief test of ageism in class by showing students pictures of young and old faces and having students list adjectives to describe the faces. Explore as a class how some of these adjectives could be considered prejudiced.

SECTION 1 Attitude Formation

Reader's Guide

■ Main Idea

Our attitudes are the result of conditioning, observational learning, and cognitive evaluation. Our attitudes help us define ourselves and our place in society, evaluate people and events, and guide our behavior.

■ Vocabulary

- attitude
- self-concept

■ Objectives

- Trace the origin of attitudes.
- Describe the functions of attitudes.

EXPLORING PSYCHOLOGY

An Attitude of Disbelief

On July 20, 1969, Astronaut Neil Armstrong emerged from a space capsule some 250,000 miles from Earth and, while millions of television viewers watched, became the first man to set foot upon the moon. Since that time other astronauts have experienced that same monumental unique experience in space, yet there are in existence today numerous relatively intelligent, otherwise normal humans who insist it never happened—that the masses have been completely deluded by some weird government hoax—a conspiracy of monumental proportions! There is even a well-publicized organization in England named "The Flat Earth Society," which seriously challenges with interesting logic all such claims of space travel and evidence that the earth is round.

—from *Story of Attitudes and Emotions* by Edgar Cayce, 1972

What do you accept as fact? What do you call products of fantasy? Your attitudes can lead you to believe that something is fact when it is really imaginary or that something is not real when it really is fact. An **attitude** is a predisposition to respond in particular ways toward specific things. It has three main elements: (1) a belief or opinion about something, (2) feelings about that thing, and (3) a tendency to act toward that thing in certain ways. For example, what is your attitude toward the senators from your state? Do you *believe* they are doing a good job? Do you *feel* you trust or distrust them? Would you *act* to vote for them?

attitude: predisposition to act, think, and feel in particular ways toward a class of people, objects, or an idea

1 FOCUS

Section Objectives

1. Trace the origin of attitudes.
2. Describe the functions of attitudes.

BELLRINGER
Motivational Activity

Project Daily Focus Transparency 20–1 and have students answer the questions.

Available as blackline master

Daily Focus Transparency 20–1

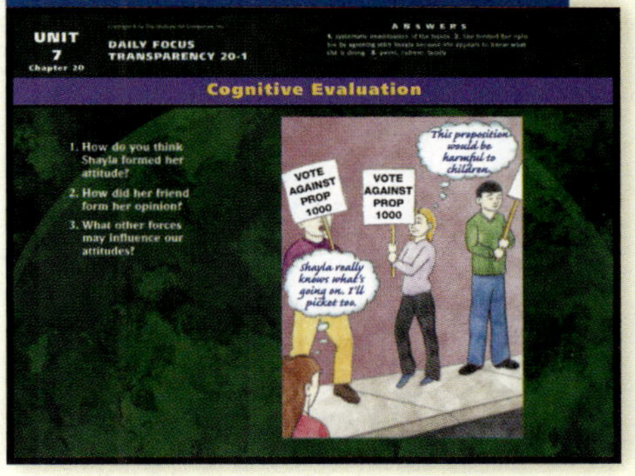

Reader's Guide

Use the Reader's Guide to introduce concepts and vocabulary.

■ Exploring Psychology
Ask students to read the **Exploring Psychology** feature. Then ask: **What would cause someone to act contrary to logic?**

■ Vocabulary Precheck
Have students write a definition of each term. Then have them read the Glossary definitions of the terms. Ask them to revise their definitions as needed.

SECTION RESOURCES

Reproducible Masters
- Guided Reading Activity 20–1
- Vocabulary Activity 20–1
- Section Quiz 20–1

Transparencies
- Daily Focus Transparency 20–1

Multimedia
- *ExamView® Assessment Suite* CD-ROM
- Presentation Plus! Software

CHAPTER 20
Section 1, pages 577–581

2 TEACH

L1 Analyzing Viewpoints

Read aloud the following statements, and ask students to write down whether they agree or disagree with each one.

1. Rap music should be censored for use of profanity and violence.
2. Employers should have the right to test employees at random for drug use.
3. Parents should have the right to approve all their children's decisions until children reach age 18.
4. The federal government should have the right to ban violent television programs from prime-time television.

Tell students that their responses to each of these statements involved an attitude or belief. **Ask:** **On which, if any, of these issues might you and your parents disagree? Why?**

Guided Reading Activity 20–1

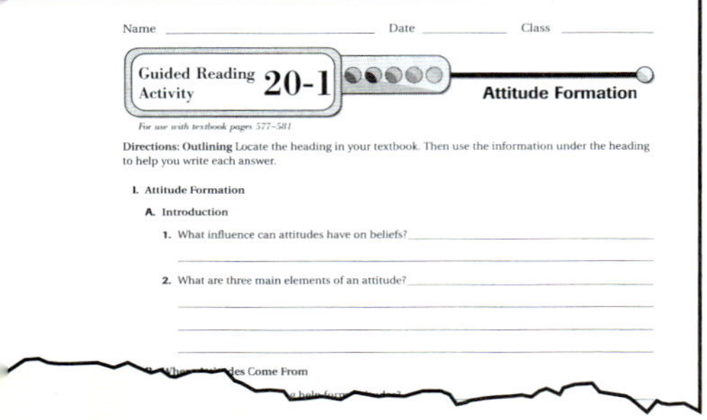
Name ____ Date ____ Class ____

Guided Reading Activity 20-1 — Attitude Formation

For use with textbook pages 577–581

Directions: Outlining Locate the heading in your textbook. Then use the information under the heading to help you write each answer.

I. Attitude Formation

A. Introduction

1. What influence can attitudes have on beliefs? ____

2. What are three main elements of an attitude? ____

Figure 20.1

Visual Instruction Have students use the diagram to work through other examples of attitudes formed through classical conditioning.

Caption Answer Jane and embarrassing remarks

WHERE ATTITUDES COME FROM

We have very definite beliefs, feelings, and responses to things about which we have no firsthand knowledge. Where do these attitudes come from? Attitudes are formed through conditioning, observational learning, and cognitive evaluation.

Conditioning

Classical conditioning (discussed in Chapter 9) can help you learn attitudes in different situations (see Figure 20.1). When a new stimulus (the conditioned stimulus) is paired with a stimulus that already causes a certain reaction (the unconditioned stimulus), the new stimulus begins to cause a reaction similar to the one caused by the original stimulus. For instance, scientist Ivan Pavlov's dog had a positive innate response to meat (he liked to eat it). When Pavlov paired the meat with the ringing of the tuning fork, the dog formed a positive conditioned response to the sound of the tuning fork. So when Pavlov's dog heard the sound of the tuning fork, he wagged his tail and salivated. We also acquire attitudes through operant conditioning; we receive praise, approval, or acceptance for expressing certain attitudes or we may be punished for expressing other attitudes.

Cognitive Evaluation

Sometimes we develop attitudes toward something without stopping to think about it. For example, if our friend feels strongly about politics and uses many statistics or big words when speaking about a specific political issue, we may agree with her simply because she sounds like she knows what she is talking about. If we do this, we have used a *heuristic,* a mental shortcut, to form an attitude.

However, we may sit down and systematically think about an issue that affects us directly. For example, if your friend speaks strongly about State College and its credentials, you may not simply accept her

Figure 20.1 Attitude Formation Through Classical Conditioning

Suppose you meet Jane. Jane seems to enjoy making comments that embarrass you. After a few encounters with Jane, even the sound of her voice upsets you. So you learn to avoid her. ***What factors were paired to produce your avoidance response?***

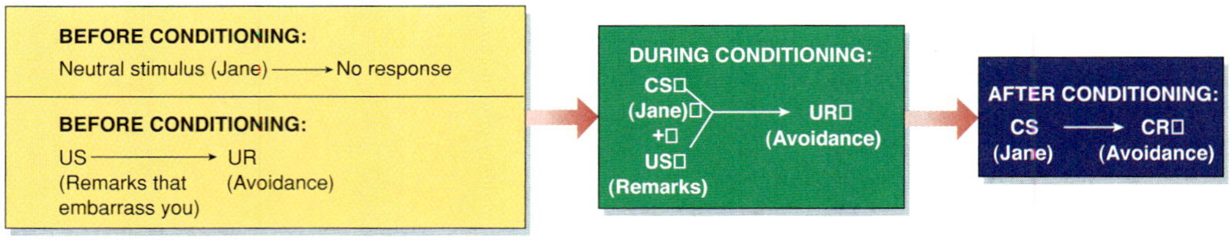

COOPERATIVE LEARNING ACTIVITY

Creating a Chart Organize students into small groups. Write the following categories on the board: politics, education, clothing styles, dating choices, and personal values. Ask the groups to develop a chart that lists the following influencers: parents, other respected adults, peers, the media, and society. For each category, the groups should use a 10-point scale to rate each influencing factor, with 1 representing no influence and 10 as having great influence. Discuss the similarities and differences among the charts prepared by each group.

BLOCK SCHEDULING

argument. You may list and evaluate the pros and cons of State College versus State University when you are selecting the college to attend. This matter is important, and you do not want to rely on shortcuts.

Other Sources

Your attitudes are also shaped by other forces. You may develop your attitudes by watching and imitating others—through observational learning. These forces are at work when you interact with others. For example, you may adopt your parents' political views or dress very much like your friends do. The culture in which you grew up, the people who raised you, and those with whom you associate all shape your attitudes. You also learn many of your attitudes through direct experience. For instance, once you drive the new BMW, you may develop a favorable attitude toward it.

Culture Culture influences everything from our taste in food to our attitudes toward human relationships and our political opinions. For example, most (if not all) Americans would consider eating grubs, curdled milk spiced with cattle blood, or monkey meat disgusting. Yet in some parts of the world these are considered delicacies.

The list of culturally derived attitudes is endless. Indeed, it is only by traveling and reading about other ways of life that we discover how many of the things we take for granted are *attitudes,* not facts.

Parents There is abundant evidence that all of us acquire many basic attitudes from our parents (see Figure 20.2). How else would you account for the finding that a high percentage of elementary schoolchildren favor the same political party as their parents? As adults, more than two-thirds of all voters continue to favor the political party their parents supported. Parental influence wanes as children get older, of course.

Peers It is not surprising that parental influence declines as children get older and are exposed to many other sources of influence. In a now classic study, Theodore Newcomb (1943) questioned and requestioned students at Bennington College in Vermont about their political attitudes over a period of four years. Most of the young women came from wealthy, staunchly conservative families. In contrast, most Bennington faculty members were outspoken liberals. Newcomb found that many of the students adopted the liberal point of view of the faculty. In 1936, 54 percent of the juniors and seniors supported Franklin D. Roosevelt and the New Deal over the conservative Republican candidate Alf Landon. Newcomb contacted the participants of his study 25 years after they had graduated and found that most had maintained the attitudes

Did You Know?

The Exposure Effect One determinant of attitudes is the mere exposure effect—the more frequently people encounter an object or idea, the more favorably they evaluate it. You may have experienced this by listening to a song over and over again and growing to like that song. Candidates for political office use this effect by constantly advertising during political campaigns.

Figure 20.2 Learning Attitudes

Children are skilled at detecting their parents' attitudes. Often children learn to react in the same way as their parents to various events or things. ***How do we develop attitudes through observational learning?***

CHAPTER 20

Section 1, pages 577–581

Psychology Journal

Ask students to write about an experience they have had when they have encountered the influence of another culture. ■

Readings and Case Studies in Psychology

Have students read the Chapter 20 Case Study selection in *Readings and Case Studies in Psychology* and answer the questions that follow the case study.

Vocabulary Activity 20–1

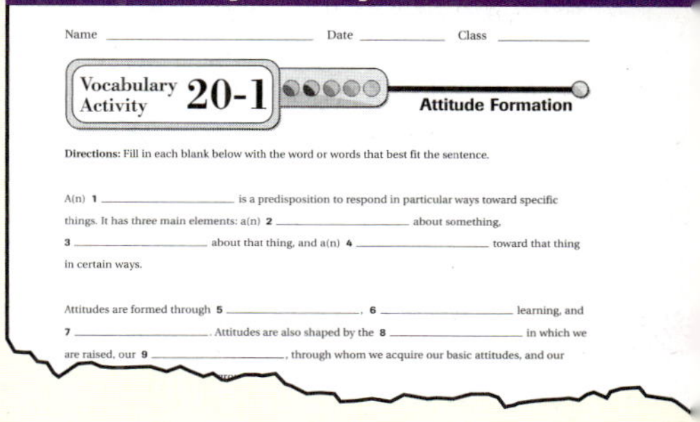
Name ______ Date ______ Class ______

Vocabulary Activity 20-1

Attitude Formation

Directions: Fill in each blank below with the word or words that best fit the sentence.

A(n) **1** ______ is a predisposition to respond in particular ways toward specific things. It has three main elements: a(n) **2** ______ about something, **3** ______ about that thing, and a(n) **4** ______ toward that thing in certain ways.

Attitudes are formed through **5** ______, **6** ______ learning, and **7** ______. Attitudes are also shaped by the **8** ______ in which we are raised, our **9** ______, through whom we acquire our basic attitudes, and our

Figure 20.2

Caption Answer We adopt attitudes by watching and imitating others, like parents and friends.

MEETING SPECIAL NEEDS

Learning Style: Logical/Mathematical Ask students to obtain a copy of the Constitutional Bill of Rights. Have them select 2 of the 10 amendments and create two posters that show either in words or in pictures the values, ideals, and beliefs explicitly stated or implied by the amendments. Display the posters around the classroom. Discuss how the Bill of Rights has influenced the attitudes of the American people. **L2**

Refer to ***Inclusion for the High School Social Studies Classroom Strategies and Activities*** in the TCR for strategies for students with different learning styles.

CHAPTER 20
Section 1, pages 577–581

Quick Lab

Purpose Students will explore the similarities between their views and their parents' views.

Process Skills Making comparisons, analyzing information

Teaching Strategies
- Tell students that they must complete the questionnaire before administering it to their parents.
- Encourage students to word the questions so that their viewpoints are not obvious.

Analysis
1. Answers will vary. Ask students if they were surprised by any of the results.
2. Answers will vary. Ask students if they think their attitudes will change over time. Ask them if they believe their parents' attitudes have changed over time.

3 ASSESS

Assign Section 1 Assessment as homework or as an in-class activity.

Section Quiz 20–1

Name ________ Date ________ Class ________

Section Quiz 20-1 **Attitude Formation**

SCORE

Matching
Match each item in Column A with the items in Column B. Write the correct letters in the blanks.
(10 points each)

Column A
____ 1. results from watching and imitating others
____ 2. systematically thinking about an issue
____ 3. how we see or describe ourselves
____ 4. predisposition to act, think, and feel in particular ways toward people, objects, or ideas
____ 5. mental shortcut

Column B
A. self-concept
B. heuristic
C. attitude
D. observational learning
E. cognitive evaluation

Reteach

Write the following words on the board: *conditioning, observational learning, cognitive evaluation, culture, parents,* and *peers*. Have students discuss attitudes that originate from these sources.

Quick Lab

How similar are your views to your parentsÕviews?

Studies have shown that parents are an important source of many of our basic attitudes and beliefs. What is the degree of similarity between your parents' views and your views on selected issues?

Procedure
1. Generate a list of 10 statements about social issues, such as political affiliation, nuclear energy, mandatory retirement, equal pay, and paternity leave.
2. Develop a questionnaire based on these issues in which a person can respond by agreeing or disagreeing with the statements. Use a five-point scale ranging from 1 (strongly agree) to 5 (strongly disagree) to rate your opinions.
3. Complete the questionnaire and ask your parents to do the same.

Analysis
1. Analyze your parents' responses. On what issues did you agree and disagree?
2. Why do you think your parents have been influential in shaping some of your attitudes and not others?

See the Skills Handbook, page 622, for an explanation of designing an experiment.

self-concept: how we see or describe ourselves; our total perception of ourselves

they had acquired in college. One reason was that they had chosen friends, spouses, and careers that supported liberal values (Newcomb et al., 1967). People tend to adopt the likes and dislikes of groups whose approval and acceptance they seek.

FUNCTIONS OF ATTITUDES

Why do we have attitudes? How do they help us in everyday functions and interactions with others? Attitudes reflect our beliefs and values as we define ourselves, interpret the objects and events we encounter, and determine how we may act in given situations.

Attitudes as a Self-Defining Mechanism

Ask a friend to describe herself. How does she do it? Along with a physical description, she may include her attitudes, or values, about certain things. For example, she may claim that she likes helping others, tries to be a good student, or is a strong supporter of equal rights. These attitudes help her define who she is. They refer to what she considers right or wrong and establish her goals. These attitudes make up her self-concept. Our **self-concept** refers to how we see or describe ourselves. If you have a positive self-concept, you will tend to act and feel optimistically and constructively; whereas if you have a negative self-concept, you will tend to act and feel pessimistically or self-destructively.

Social groups as well as individuals hold attitudes. People living in the same conditions and who frequently communicate with one another have attitudes in common because they are exposed to the same information and may have formed as a group partly because of their similar attitudes.

Attitudes as Cognitive Guidelines and Guides to Action

Our attitudes serve as guidelines for interpreting and categorizing people, objects, and events. Attitudes also guide us to behave in certain ways (see Figure 20.3). In effect, attitudes guide us toward or away from particular people, objects, and events. For instance, we may link negative feelings with walking in unlit and dirty alleyways or we may link positive feelings with friendly and happy people. These attitudes tell us to avoid the former and approach the latter.

Sometimes, though, our attitudes are not consistent with our behaviors. For example, although we may disagree with littering, we may throw a candy wrapper on the ground. Your behavior may reflect your attitudes

CRITICAL THINKING ACTIVITY

Classifying Information Direct students to write down four of their strongest beliefs. Next to each item, have them list some of the ways this belief influences their behavior. For example, after Bennington students adopted liberalism, how did this belief influence their voting patterns? Based on this exercise, ask students to write a one-page essay evaluating the validity of the following text statement: "Our attitudes serve as guidelines for interpreting and categorizing other people, objects, and events. Attitudes also guide us to behave in certain ways." **L2**

Figure 20.3 A Theory of Planned Behavior

Psychologists have proposed a theory that three factors determine a person's behavior. The strength or weakness of each of these three factors explains why certain people behave differently despite shared attitudes (Ajzen, 1991; Sheppard, Hartwick, & Warshaw, 1988). ***What factors other than attitude determine a person's behavior?***

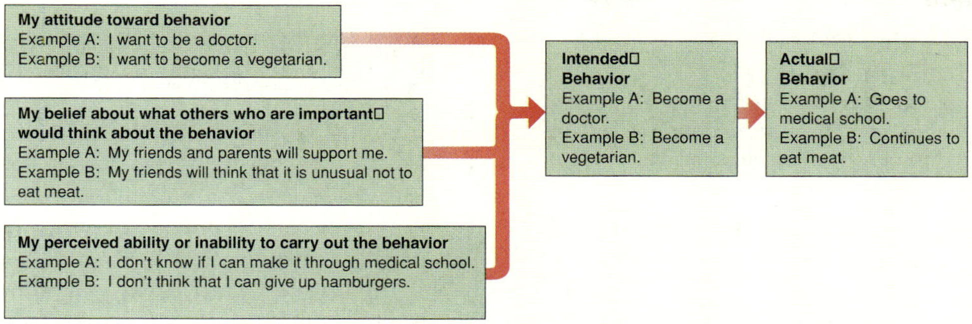

more strongly, though, depending on why you have formed a certain attitude. Many psychologists argue that the attitudes that most strongly predict behavior are those that are acquired through direct experience. For example, if you do not eat meat because in the past you have become sick after eating it, the smell and sight of meat may automatically remind you of being sick. In this case, you are unlikely to eat meat. If you disagree with eating meat because of strictly moral reasons, however, you may not automatically remember your attitude when you smell and see meat. So, attitudes do play a role in determining behavior, but this role varies in different circumstances.

Reading Check How do our attitudes help us organize our reality?

SECTION 1 Assessment

1. **Review the Vocabulary** What are the three elements of an attitude?
2. **Visualize the Main Idea** Using a diagram similar to the one below, list and describe the functions of attitudes.

3. **Recall Information** How do family and peers affect our attitudes?
4. **Think Critically** How can attitudes help keep us out of dangerous situations?
5. **Application Activity** Investigate how advertisers use classical conditioning to influence our attitudes. Bring an example of such an advertisement to class and, in a brief report, analyze the advertiser's technique.

Figure 20.3

Caption Answer beliefs, others' beliefs, and perceived ability or inability to carry out the behavior

Reading Check Answer Attitudes help us interpret and categorize people, objects, and events.

Enrich

Ask students to draw a circle on a sheet of paper and label it "Self." Around the circle have students write all the positive words they can think of to describe themselves. Tell them to read that list three or four times during the day. Tomorrow, have students share the effects these descriptions had on their attitudes and mood the previous day.

4 CLOSE

Have pairs of students role-play typical behaviors of teens in school. Ask the class to identify the underlying attitude of each character.

SECTION 1 Assessment Answers

1. The three elements of an attitude are (1) belief or opinion, (2) feelings, and (3) a tendency to act in certain ways.
2. Attitudes help us (1) evaluate our own beliefs and values to define ourselves, (2) interpret the objects and events we encounter, and (3) determine how to act in given situations.
3. Student answers will vary. People tend to adopt the attitudes of those groups whose approval they seek.
4. Attitudes guide us toward or away from certain situations. For example, we develop negative attitudes toward dangerous situations and so avoid those situations. Students may use specific examples to make their points.
5. Have students present their examples in class and see if the class agrees with each student's analysis of the advertiser's technique.

CHAPTER 20
Section 2, pages 582–588

1 FOCUS

Section Objectives

1. Cite the sources of attitude change.
2. Describe prejudice and its relationship to stereotypes and roles.

BELLRINGER
Motivational Activity

Project Daily Focus Transparency 20–2 and have students answer the questions.

Also available as blackline master.

Daily Focus Transparency 20–2

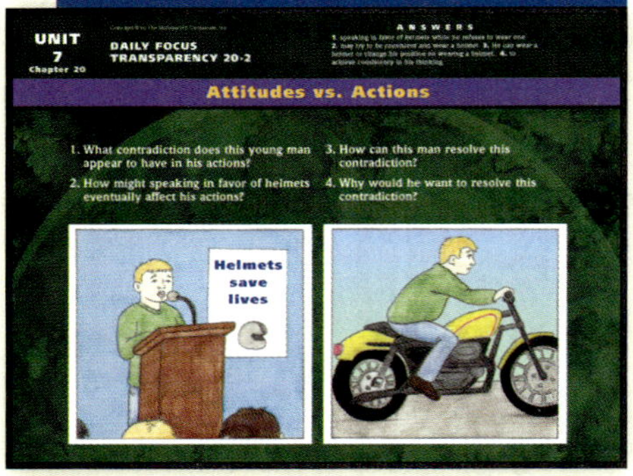

Reader's Guide

Use the Reader's Guide to introduce concepts and vocabulary.

Exploring Psychology

Ask students to read the **Exploring Psychology** feature and then discuss: **How can assumptions lead to prejudice?**

Vocabulary Precheck

Have students create a crossword puzzle using the definitions of the terms for the clues. Ask pairs of students to trade and complete each other's puzzles.

Use the **Vocabulary PuzzleMaker CD-ROM** to create crossword and word search puzzles.

SECTION 2

Attitude Change and Prejudice

Reader's Guide

Main Idea

Attitudes are formed through compliance, identification, and internalization. Attitudes may be changed as a result of cognitive dissonance.

Vocabulary

- compliance
- identification
- internalization
- cognitive dissonance
- counterattitudinal behavior
- self-justification
- self-fulfilling prophecy
- prejudice
- discrimination

Objectives

- Cite the sources of attitude change.
- Describe prejudice and its relationship to stereotypes and roles.

EXPLORING PSYCHOLOGY

Can You Figure It Out?

I met my friend the test pilot, who had just completed an around-the-world flight by balloon. With the pilot was a little girl of about two.

"What's her name?" I asked my friend, whom I hadn't seen in five years and who had married in that time.

"Same as her mother," the pilot replied.

"Hello, Susan," I said to the little girl.

How did I know her name if I never saw the wedding announcement?

—from "Steve's Primer of Practical Persuasion and Influence" [Web site], 1996

Did you figure out the answer to the thought problem above? You see, the author knew the name of the little girl because the test pilot was a woman—the little girl's mother. Thus the mother and daughter share the same first name. You may have had trouble coming up with the answer because you assumed that the test pilot was male. Also, we usually do not expect women to name their daughters after themselves. If you had trouble with this thought problem, you were the victim of cognitive consistency—that is, you tried to fit this new situation into your existing assumptions. You made a prejudgment about the situation that prevented you from considering all the possibilities.

ATTITUDE CHANGE

Having suggested where attitudes come from, we can now look at how they develop. The three main processes involved in forming or changing attitudes are compliance, identification, and internalization (Kelman, 1961).

SECTION RESOURCES

Reproducible Masters
- Guided Reading Activity 20–2
- Vocabulary Activity 20–2
- Section Quiz 20–2

Transparencies
- Daily Focus Transparency 20–2

Multimedia
- Vocabulary PuzzleMaker CD-ROM
- *ExamView® Assessment Suite* CD-ROM
- Presentation Plus! Software

If you praise a certain film director because everyone else does, you are complying. If you find yourself agreeing with everything a friend you particularly admire says about the director, you are identifying with your friend's attitudes. If you genuinely like the director's work and, regardless of what other people think, consider it brilliant, you are expressing an internalized attitude.

Compliance

One of the best measures of attitude is behavior. If a man settles back into his chair after dinner, launches into a discussion of his support of the women's rights movement, then shouts to his wife—who is in the kitchen washing the dishes—to bring more coffee, you probably would not believe what he had been saying. His actions speak louder than his words. Yet the same man might hire women for jobs he has always considered "men's work" because the law requires him to do so. He also might finally accept his wife's going to work because he knows that she, their children, and many of their friends would consider him old-fashioned if he did not. People often adapt their actions to the wishes of others to avoid discomfort or rejection and to gain support. This is called **compliance.** Under such circumstances, social pressure often results in only temporary compliance, and attitudes do not really change. Later in this chapter, however, we shall see that compliance can sometimes affect one's beliefs.

compliance: a change or maintenance of behavior to avoid discomfort or rejection and to gain approval

Identification

One way in which attitudes may be formed or changed is through the process of **identification.** Suppose you have a favorite uncle who is everything you hope to be. He is a successful musician, has many famous friends, and seems to know a great deal about everything. In many ways you identify with him and copy his behavior. One night, during an intense conversation, your uncle asks you why you do not vote. At first, you feel defensive and argumentative. You contend that it does not matter, that your vote would not make a difference. As you listen to your uncle, however, you find yourself starting to agree with him. If a person as knowledgeable and respectable as your uncle believes it is important to vote, then perhaps you should, too. Later you find yourself eager to take part in the political process. You have adopted a new attitude because of your identification with your uncle.

identification: seeing oneself as similar to another person or group and accepting the attitudes of another person or group as one's own

Identification occurs when a person wants to define himself or herself in terms of a person or group and therefore adopts the person's or group's attitudes and ways of behaving. Identification is different from compliance because the individual actually believes the newly adopted views. Yet because these attitudes are based on emotional attachment to another person or group rather than the person's own assessment of the issues, they are fragile. If the person's attachment to that person or group fades, the attitudes may also weaken.

Previously, you read that adolescents move away from peer groups and toward independence as they grow older. If this is true, do attitudes stabilize with age? Two psychologists (Krosnick & Alwin, 1989) studied

2 TEACH

L1 Debating an Issue Request volunteers to cite examples of legal compliance. *(The text mentions a man who hires a woman for "men's work" because the law requires it. Another example might be obeying a 30-mile-per-hour speed limit on a little-traveled road rather than risking a ticket.)* List these items on the board. Then explore the difference between *compliance* and *identification*. Based on this discussion, have students resolve the following conflict through debate: *Resolved—Behavior at school is determined more by identification than by compliance.* **BLOCK SCHEDULING**

Psychology Journal

Have students write a paragraph describing their feelings when their behavior was predicated on compliance. ■

COOPERATIVE LEARNING ACTIVITY

Relocation Handout Organize students into groups of four. Tell students to imagine that they are cross-cultural trainers hired by a major United States multinational corporation. Their job is to relocate American employees to one of the following countries: Japan, India, Kenya, Egypt, China, Turkey, or Colombia. Have each group choose a country and research culturally derived attitudes of which the relocated employees must be made aware. Groups should present their findings in the form of a relocation handout. At least one part of the handout should list "Dos" and "Don'ts." (For example: "Do not wear your shoes in a traditional Turkish household.") Compile the handouts from the various groups into a booklet and distribute them to the class.

Reading Check Answer

Attitudes formed by internalization are the most stable and long-lasting.

Looking @ the Issues

Politics and Cognitive Dissonance In the presidential campaign of 2000, Republican candidate John McCain of Arizona presented a consistent message about the need for campaign finance reform. He, and others, specifically wanted to eliminate or severely restrict the amounts of money that come from special-interest groups. The message created cognitive dissonance with many voters because his campaign continued to accept funds from special-interest groups. Voters felt that his message did not match his actions. **Ask:** **Does cognitive dissonance cause people to be apathetic about politics? Explain. What other examples of cognitive dissonance in politics can you cite?**

Guided Reading Activity 20–2

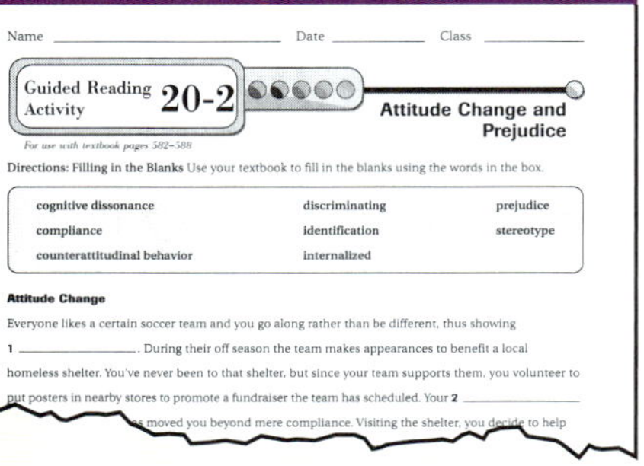
Name ____________ Date ________ Class ________

Guided Reading Activity 20-2 — Attitude Change and Prejudice

For use with textbook pages 582–588

Directions: Filling in the Blanks Use your textbook to fill in the blanks using the words in the box.

cognitive dissonance	discriminating	prejudice
compliance	identification	stereotype
counterattitudinal behavior	internalized	

Attitude Change

Everyone likes a certain soccer team and you go along rather than be different, thus showing **1** ____________. During their off season the team makes appearances to benefit a local homeless shelter. You've never been to that shelter, but since your team supports them, you volunteer to put posters in nearby stores to promote a fundraiser the team has scheduled. Your **2** ____________ ...s moved you beyond mere compliance. Visiting the shelter, you decide to help

the political and social attitudes of groups of people of various ages over an extended period. Those in the 18 to 25 age group were the most likely to change their attitudes; those age 34 and older held attitudes that were essentially stable. As self-critiquing and self-analysis decline through late adolescence and into adulthood, attitudes become more stable.

Internalization

internalization: incorporating the values, ideas, and standards of others as a part of oneself

The wholehearted acceptance of an attitude is **internalization.** The attitude becomes an integral part of the person. Internalization is most likely to occur when an attitude is consistent with a person's basic beliefs and values and supports his or her self-image. The person adopts a new attitude because he or she believes it is right to do so, not because he or she wants to be like someone else.

Internalization is the most lasting of the three sources of attitude formation or change. Your internalized attitudes will be more resistant to pressure from other people because your reasons for holding these views have nothing to do with other people. They are based on your own evaluation of the merits of the issue. A Bennington student put it this way: "I became liberal at first because of its prestige value; I remain so because the problems around which my liberalism centers are important. What I want now is to be effective in solving problems" (Newcomb, 1943).

Reading Check Which attitudes are the most stable and long-lasting—those formed by compliance, identification, or internalization?

As this example suggests, compliance or identification may lead to the internalization of an attitude. Often the three overlap. You may support a political candidate in part because you know your friends will approve, in part because someone you admire speaks highly of the candidate, and in part because you believe his or her ideals are consistent with your own.

COGNITIVE CONSISTENCY

Many social psychologists have theorized that people's attitudes change because they are always trying to get things to fit together logically inside their heads. This is called *cognitive consistency* (see Figure 20.4). Holding two opposing attitudes can create great conflict in an individual, throwing him or her off balance. A doctor who smokes and a parent who is uncomfortable with children have one thing in common: they are in conflict.

cognitive dissonance: the uncomfortable feeling when a person experiences contradictory or conflicting thoughts, attitudes, beliefs, or feelings

According to Leon Festinger (1957), people in such situations experience cognitive dissonance. **Cognitive dissonance** is the uncomfortable feeling that arises when a person's behavior conflicts with thoughts, beliefs, attitudes, feelings, or behaviors. To reduce dissonance, it is necessary to change either the behavior or the conflicting attitudes.

People reduce dissonance in several ways. First, some people just deny the dissonance. They pretend it did not happen. When faced with information on the health hazards of smoking, a smoker simply treats the information as nonsense or propaganda by antismoking groups. Some people attempt to evade dissonance by avoiding situations or exposure to information that would create conflict. For example, they may make a point of subscribing to newspapers and magazines that uphold their political

MEETING SPECIAL NEEDS

Learning Style: Intrapersonal Provide students with the following excerpt from a profile on social psychologist Thomas Pettigrew: *Pettigrew was influenced early in life by his Scottish-born grandmother. . . . When young Tom returned from a school trip to Richmond's St. John Church and exuberantly recounted how Patrick Henry had uttered his immortal line, "Give me liberty or give me death!" his grandmother admonished him . . . "Ah yes, 'tis a fine story, lad. . . . Did they happen to mention that he owned 22 slaves?". . . The question . . .* [stayed with Pettigrew] *into adulthood.* Ask students to prepare an essay describing someone who has strongly influenced their attitudes or beliefs. **L2** **BLOCK SCHEDULING**

attitudes, of surrounding themselves with people who share the same ideas, and of attending only those speeches and lectures that support their views. It is not surprising that such people get quite upset when a piece of conflicting information finally does get through. Some people change their attitude and/or reevaluate the event. Because the new information they received does not agree with their old attitude, they revise their attitude. The smoker might consider the research on the dangers of smoking and make an attempt to quit smoking. The process of dissonance reduction does not always take place consciously, but it is a frequent and powerful occurrence.

Figure 20.4 Balance Theory

According to Fritz Heider's Balance Theory—another means of analyzing cognitions related to attitudes—people are inclined to achieve consistency in their attitudes by balancing their beliefs and feelings about an object, person, or event against their attitudes about other people. When someone we care about strongly disagrees with us, an uncomfortable state of imbalance occurs. ***What do you think we do when we become involved in a state of imbalance?***

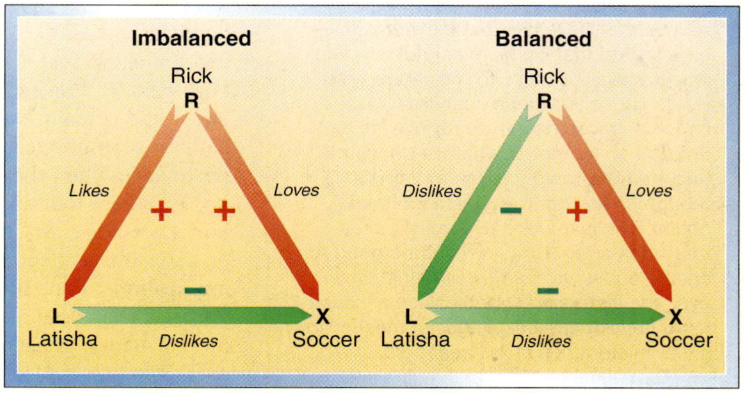

ATTITUDES AND ACTIONS

Social psychologists have discovered several interesting relationships between attitudes and actions. Obviously, your attitudes affect your actions: if you like Fords, you will buy a Ford. Some of the other relationships are not so obvious.

Doing Is Believing

It turns out, for example, that if you like Fords but buy a Chevrolet for some reason (perhaps you can get a better deal on a Chevy), you will end up liking Fords less. In other words, actions affect attitudes.

In many instances, if you act and speak as though you have certain beliefs and feelings, you may begin to *really* feel and believe this way. This phenomenon is called **counterattitudinal behavior**, and it is a method of reducing cognitive dissonance. For example, people accused of a crime have confessed to crimes they did not commit. They confessed to relieve the pressure; but having said that they did the deed, they begin to believe that they really *are* guilty.

counterattitudinal behavior: the process of taking a public position that contradicts one's private attitude

One explanation for this phenomenon comes from the theory of cognitive dissonance. If a person acts one way but thinks another, he or she will experience dissonance. To reduce the dissonance, the person will

Figure 20.4

Visual Instruction Ask each student to draw upon a personal experience to create an imbalanced situation. Then ask each student to draw the balanced situation showing how the issue was resolved. Ask for volunteers to share their situations. Set the ground rules that participation is optional and that the examples should not reveal information that is too private or might hurt someone else's feelings.

Caption Answer We change one or both of the conflicting attitudes to achieve balance.

TEACHER Tip

To make sure that students understand cognitive dissonance, ask them to think of examples from their own lives.

Applying Psychology

Tell students to think of a time when they went to a great deal of effort to accomplish a goal. For example, they may have spent extra hours studying in order to raise their grades, or they may have worked for years to buy a car. Have students list their goals and the efforts necessary to achieve them. **Ask: Was the goal worth the effort? Did you use self-justification to explain your actions? Did you exaggerate any of your efforts?**

CRITICAL THINKING ACTIVITY

Making Generalizations Ask students to collect advertisements that use children to sell products. Tell them to study the way in which the child actors depict the role(s) of children. Have students consider how these advertisements use stereotypes in their depiction of children. Use the following questions to conduct a discussion that distinguishes how advertisements use stereotypes to convey positive and negative characteristics. **Ask: What kind of clothes do the children wear? In what situations do the children appear? What attitudes or behaviors do the ads assign to children? How might these ads affect the way children see themselves? L2**

CHAPTER 20
Section 2, pages 582–588

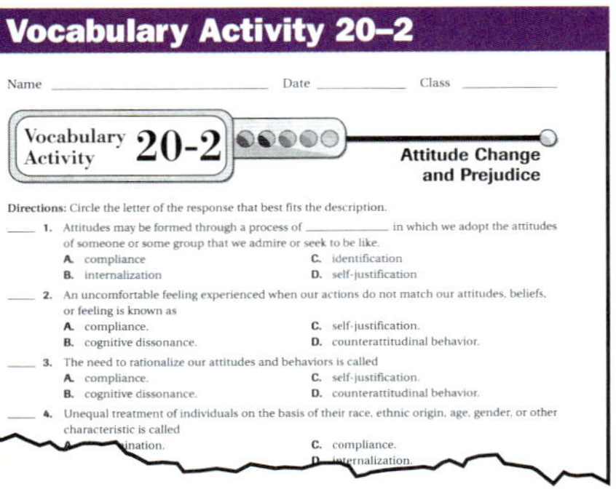
Vocabulary Activity 20–2

Name ______ Date ______ Class ______

Vocabulary Activity 20-2

Attitude Change and Prejudice

Directions: Circle the letter of the response that best fits the description.

____ 1. Attitudes may be formed through a process of ______ in which we adopt the attitudes of someone or some group that we admire or seek to be like.
A. compliance C. identification
B. internalization D. self-justification

____ 2. An uncomfortable feeling experienced when our actions do not match our attitudes, beliefs, or feeling is known as
A. compliance. C. self-justification.
B. cognitive dissonance. D. counterattitudinal behavior.

____ 3. The need to rationalize our attitudes and behaviors is called
A. compliance. C. self-justification.
B. cognitive dissonance. D. counterattitudinal behavior.

____ 4. Unequal treatment of individuals on the basis of their race, ethnic origin, age, gender, or other characteristic is called
A. ...ination. C. compliance.
D. internalization.

PSYCHOLOGY Update

First Impressions and Self-Fulfilling Prophecies In a recent study, researchers found that people tend to form first impressions based on the stranger's most distinctive trait. If that trait is associated with positive characteristics, the person views the stranger positively. If the trait is associated with negative characteristics, the stranger is viewed negatively. Once the positive or negative first impression is made, the study showed that it became a self-fulfilling prophecy when the two people interacted. *Source:* Nelson, L.J., & Klutas, K. (2000). The distinctiveness effect in social interaction: Creation of a self-fulfilling prophecy. *Personality and Social Psychology Bulletin, 26 (1):* 126–135.

FYI

Supreme Court Justice Oliver Wendell Holmes wrote the following in 1901: "The mind of a bigot is like the pupil of the eye, the more light you pour upon it the more it will contract."

More About...

The Just-World Bias

When watching some movies, we expect the evil character to get punished. Sometimes we may even hear ourselves saying, "He'll get what he deserves." Psychologists label this tendency the *just-world bias* (Lerner, 1980). We need to believe that life is fair, that the world is orderly, and that we have control over our environment, because to think otherwise would cause too much cognitive dissonance. For instance, if we believe life is unfair, then no matter what we do, something terrible could happen to us. That thought is an extremely uncomfortable notion. The just-world hypothesis, then, motivates us to work hard and be good to ensure our survival and well-being. However, the just-world hypothesis may cause us to develop prejudice against those who suffer misfortunes or mistreatment.

To maintain our belief that life is fair, we reason that those who are worse off than we are somehow deserve their lot. We blame the victim. For example, we may say that the woman who was robbed last night should not have been walking alone at night.

have to change either the behavior or the attitude. A similar explanation is that people have a need for **self-justification**—a need to justify their behavior.

In an experiment that demonstrated these principles, participants were paid either $1 or $20 (roughly $5 and $100 in today's currency) to tell another person that a boring experiment in which they both had to participate was really a lot of fun. Afterward, the experimenters asked the participants how they felt about the experiment. They found that the participants who had been paid $20 to lie about the experiment continued to believe that it had been boring. Those who had been paid $1, however, came to believe that the experiment had actually been fairly enjoyable. These people had less reason to tell the lie, so they experienced more dissonance when they did so. To justify their lie, they had to believe that they had actually enjoyed the experiment (Festinger & Carlsmith, 1959).

The phenomenon of self-justification has serious implications. For example, how would you justify to yourself that you had intentionally injured another human being? In another psychological experiment, participants were led to believe that they had injured or hurt other participants in some way (Glass, 1964). The aggressors were then asked how they felt about the victims they had just harmed. It was found that the aggressors had convinced themselves that they did not like the victims of their cruelty. In other words, the aggressors talked themselves into believing that their defenseless victims had deserved their injury. The aggressors also considered their victims to be less attractive after the experiment than before—their self-justification for hurting another person was something like "Oh, well, this person doesn't amount to much, anyway."

self-justification: the need to rationalize one's attitude and behavior

Self-Fulfilling Prophecy

Another relationship between attitudes and actions is rather subtle but extremely widespread. It is possible, it seems, for a person to act in such a way as to make his or her beliefs come true. This phenomenon is called a **self-fulfilling prophecy.** Self-fulfilling prophecies can influence all kinds of human activity. Suppose you believe that people are basically friendly and generous. Whenever you approach other people, you are friendly and open. Because of your smile and positive attitude toward yourself and the world, people like you. Thus your belief that people are friendly produces your friendly behavior, which in turn causes people to respond favorably toward you. Suppose you turn this example around. Imagine that you believe people are selfish and cold. Because of your negative attitude, you tend to avert your eyes from other people, to act gloomy, and to appear

self-fulfilling prophecy: a belief, prediction, or expectation that operates to bring about its own fulfillment

PSYCHOLOGY LAB EXPERIMENT

Identifying Stereotypes Organize students into small groups and have them create a list of commonly held stereotypes about age and gender. From the list, have the groups create a short questionnaire that asks people the degree to which they agree or disagree with the statements. The rating scale should have five choices ranging from Completely Agree to Completely Disagree. Caution students not to use the word *stereotype* in describing the activity to the participants. Have each group find 25 people of various ages to complete the questionnaire. The groups should chart their results and present their findings to the class. As a class, brainstorm ideas for reducing stereotyping. **L2** **BLOCK SCHEDULING**

rather unfriendly. People think your actions are strange, and consequently, they act coldly toward you. Your belief produced the behavior that made the belief come true.

PREJUDICE

Prejudice means, literally, prejudgment. Prejudice means deciding beforehand what a person will be like instead of withholding judgment until it can be based on his or her individual qualities or behavior. To hold a stereotype about a group of people is not to be prejudiced unless the stereotype is not revised in light of experience in interacting with people from that group. Prejudice is not necessarily negative—men who are prejudiced against women are often equally prejudiced in favor of men, for example.

prejudice: preconceived attitudes toward a person or group that have been formed without sufficient evidence and are not easily changed

Stereotypes and Roles

Prejudice is strengthened and maintained by inflexible stereotypes and roles. A *stereotype* is a generalization about all members of a group. Racial groups, scientists, women, and the rich, for example, often have been viewed and treated only as stereotypes rather than as individuals. A *role* is a response pattern structured by group membership. Stereotypes and roles can act together in a way that makes them difficult to alter. For example, many whites once had a stereotype of minority racial groups, believing them to be irresponsible, superstitious, or unintelligent. Whites who believed this expected members of the racial group to act out a role that was consistent with a stereotype. Members of the targeted racial group were expected to be submissive, deferential, and respectful toward whites, who acted out the role of the superior, condescending parent. In the past, many people accepted these roles and looked at themselves and each other according to these stereotypes. In the past several decades, however, many people have worked to step out of these roles and drop these stereotypes, and many have been successful.

Patricia Devine (1989) proposed a model to explain the relationships between stereotypes and prejudice. She theorizes that if a specific stimulus is encountered, it automatically activates your stereotype mechanism. For example, if you see an old man or woman, it activates your stereotype of old people. Devine suggests that what separates prejudiced from nonprejudiced people is their ability to inhibit negative attitudes. If you can do so, your response will be nonprejudiced; if you cannot restrain your negative beliefs, you will behave in a prejudiced manner.

Psychology and You

Illusory Correlation

An illusory correlation occurs when we see a relationship between variables that aren't really related. Philip Zimbardo, recent president of the American Psychological Association, gives an excellent example of illusory correlation. Many years ago a failure in a mid-Atlantic power station caused a blackout to sweep the East Coast one evening. A Little Leaguer in Boston was on his way home from a game, swinging his bat at everything as he walked. He swung at a lamppost, and just as his bat hit the post, the lights of all Boston blinked out before his disbelieving eyes. It was an illusory correlation.

Psychology and You

Use the following question to direct a class discussion after students have read the **Psychology and You** feature.
Ask: **What might change an illusory correlation?**

3 ASSESS

Assign Section 2 Assessment as homework or as an in-class activity.

Section Quiz 20–2

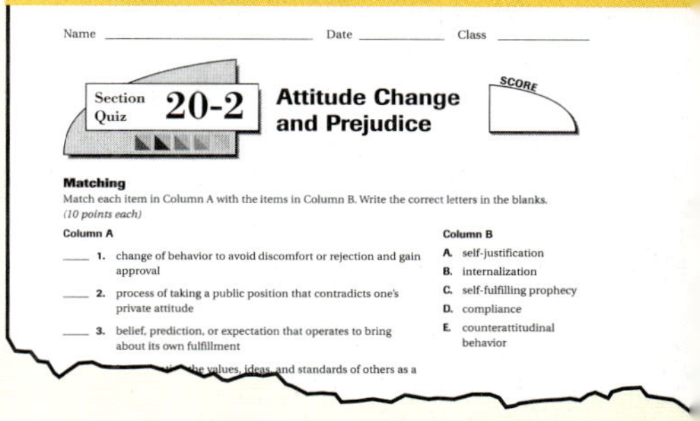
Name ______ Date ______ Class ______

Section Quiz 20-2 **Attitude Change and Prejudice**

SCORE

Matching
Match each item in Column A with the items in Column B. Write the correct letters in the blanks.
(10 points each)

Column A
____ **1.** change of behavior to avoid discomfort or rejection and gain approval
____ **2.** process of taking a public position that contradicts one's private attitude
____ **3.** belief, prediction, or expectation that operates to bring about its own fulfillment

Column B
A. self-justification
B. internalization
C. self-fulfilling prophecy
D. compliance
E. counterattitudinal behavior

INTERDISCIPLINARY CONNECTIONS ACTIVITY

History Explain that during wars, each side generally views the other in stereotypical ways, leading to extreme prejudice. During World War II, the anger and fear generated by Pearl Harbor fell heaviest upon Japanese Americans living in California and other parts of the western United States. Have students research the forced relocation of thousands of Japanese Americans to internment camps. Advise them to include the 1988 Senate apology and tax-free payment of $20,000 to each of the 60,000 surviving *Nisei* (U.S. citizens born of Japanese parents) in their research. (One highly readable source is *Desert Exile* by Yoshiko Uchida.) Ask students to prepare oral reports on the causes and effects of misdirected prejudice. **L2**

Reteach

Ask students to explain how stereotyping can lead to people assuming dominant and submissive roles in accordance with the applied stereotype. Ask students to describe how such situations arise in the workplace, school, and society in general.

Enrich

Have students list their attitudes on each of the following topics: human rights, animal rights, the environment, politics, and religion. Then have students identify how they formed their attitudes. **Ask:** **What conclusions can you draw about the way in which you form important attitudes?**

4 CLOSE

Write on the board a list of 10 different professions or jobs, such as construction worker, teacher, and hairdresser. Have students brainstorm stereotypes associated with each of these jobs. **Ask:** **Does every stereotype hold a grain of truth? Why or why not?**

Another psychologist, Thomas Pettigrew, suggests that in situations where a dominant group and a deferential group can be identified, members of each group may play roles that foster and maintain their respective positions. A member of a dominating group, for example, will speak first, interrupt more often, and talk louder and longer. A member of the deferential group will show courtesy and concern for the dominant member and do more listening and less interrupting.

Prejudice and Discrimination

There are many possible causes for prejudice. Prejudice can be based on social, economic, or physical factors. Psychologists have found that people may be prejudiced against those less well-off than themselves—these people seem to justify being on top by assuming that anyone of lower status or income must be inferior. People who have suffered economic setbacks also tend to be prejudiced; they blame others for their misfortune. Prejudice also arises from "guilt by association." People who dislike cities and urban living, for example, tend to distrust people associated with cities. Also, people may be prejudiced in favor of those they see as similar to themselves and against those who seem different. Whatever the original cause, prejudice seems to persist. One reason is that children who grow up in an atmosphere of prejudice conform to the prejudicial norm. That is, they are encouraged to conform to the thoughts and practices of their parents and other teachers.

discrimination: the unequal treatment of individuals on the basis of their race, ethnic group, age, gender, or membership in another category rather than on the basis of individual characteristics

Prejudice, which is an attitude, should be distinguished from **discrimination,** the unequal treatment of members of certain groups. It is possible for a prejudiced person not to discriminate. He or she may recognize his or her prejudice and try not to act on it. Similarly, a person may discriminate, not out of prejudice, but in compliance with social or economic pressures.

SECTION 2 Assessment

1. **Review the Vocabulary** Describe the relationship between attitudes and behavior in counterattitudinal behavior, self-justification, and self-fulfilling prophecy.
2. **Visualize the Main Idea** Using a diagram similar to the one below, list and describe the three main processes involved in forming or changing attitudes.

Processes of Forming/Changing Attitudes

3. **Recall Information** How do stereotypes and roles strengthen prejudice?
4. **Think Critically** How do theories of cognitive dissonance explain why certain people may be attracted to some information while they avoid other information? Explain.
5. **Application Activity** List 10 makes and models of cars (such as Saturn Sky, Honda Civic) and ask 15 people to choose from a wide range of adjectives (such as serious, reliable, dishonest) that best describes someone who drives that type of car. Analyze the results of your survey to see if people are stereotyped by the cars they drive.

SECTION 2 Assessment Answers

1. Counterattitudinal behavior—public behavior contradicts private attitudes; self-justification—to reduce dissonance, either behavior or attitudes must be justified; self-fulfilling prophecy—person behaves in such a way as to make the attitude true
2. Answers should describe compliance, identification, and internalization.
3. Stereotypes are oversimplified and difficult-to-change beliefs. Roles are oversimplified and difficult-to-change ways of acting. They work together to create prejudice and interact in such a way that makes the cycle hard to break.
4. Answers will vary but should explain how people are attracted to information that reinforces their opinions and they ignore information that runs counter to their ideals (all to avoid cognitive dissonance).
5. Recommend that students survey people in various age groups and compare the results.

Feelings vs. Actions

Period of Study: 1934

Introduction: In the early days of psychology, researchers assumed that people's behavior could be predicted by measuring their attitudes and opinions. In 1934, researcher Richard LaPiere conducted a study designed to evaluate a person's attitudes and actions with situations regarding race. He studied the social attitudes of individuals and examined the connection between an individual's real behavior and an individual's symbolic behavior. *Symbolic behavior* refers to a person's statements regarding his or her actions in a hypothetical situation. With this idea in mind, LaPiere set out to test individuals' symbolic racial responses compared with their actual racial responses.

Hypothesis: LaPiere came up with the idea of studying racial behavior when he traveled across the United States with a young Chinese couple to conduct research on a different topic. During the 1930s, much racial prejudice targeted Asian Americans. LaPiere wondered if his companions would encounter racism in the form of compromised or denied service.

Method: LaPiere and the couple visited various restaurants, attempted to check in to hotels, and frequented other public service businesses. LaPiere recorded significant data, such as how the couple was treated, if they were served, if they were asked to leave, and other important information. He noted that only one of the 251 establishments they visited refused service to his friends.

Given the climate of prejudice against people from Asia, LaPiere was curious about this observation. He decided to investigate the issue by sending questionnaires to the establishments that the Chinese couple had visited. The questionnaires simply asked if that establishment would provide services to a Chinese husband and wife. He received 128 completed questionnaires, or 51 percent of the total mailed.

Results: Only one of the 128 responding businesses said that it would serve a Chinese couple. The vast majority (90 percent) said that they would not serve the couple. Yet during the trip, only one establishment actually denied LaPiere's companions service. Thus, the attitudes reported by the business owners (symbolic behavior) did not seem to match their actual behaviors.

Even though mailing questionnaires is not an ideal way to measure the relationship between symbolic and actual behavior, this study suggested that the attitudes people report do not necessarily predict behavior. Conversely, people's behavior may reflect attitudes that are different than what they report. Later studies confirmed and refined this general conclusion. The relationship between attitudes and behavior has proven to be a rich topic of study for social psychologists.

Analyzing the Case Study

1. What is the difference between symbolic behavior and actual behavior? Explain.
2. What was LaPiere's hypothesis?
3. **Critical Thinking** If LaPiere performed this experiment today, do you think that his results would be the same? Why or why not?

Going Further

Sexual Harassment

Sexual harassment in the workplace is a violation of the Civil Rights Act of 1964. Today most large businesses and many small businesses have written official sexual harassment policies. However, having a written policy about harassment and having an aggressive program to prevent sexual harassment are two different things. One represents the company's symbolic behavior toward sexual harassment. The other demonstrates the company's real commitment to preventing harassment in the workplace.

Supreme Court decisions support the idea that a company must do more than include a written policy about harassment in employee handbooks. Companies that are serious about preventing harassment in the workplace should provide training to employees and supervisors, should discuss sexual harassment policies with all new employees, and should have sound procedures in place to resolve reported cases of sexual harassment.

Discussing the Case Study

Ask: **Why is LaPiere's study still included in textbooks? What factors may have affected the actual behavior of the business owners, causing it to contradict their symbolic behavior? In general, why are attitudes not necessarily a predictor of actual behavior?**

Answers for Analyzing the Case Study

1. Symbolic behavior refers to how people say they will behave as opposed to the way they actually behave in the same situation.
2. LaPiere wondered whether his Asian friends would be denied service due to racism. LaPiere was curious to see if people's symbolic behavior would match their actual behavior.
3. Answers will vary. Students should support their position with clear reasoning about the attitudes they think would be common today. Ask students to consider current racial attitudes and how they might affect the results of an experiment like LaPiere's.

1 FOCUS

Section Objectives

1. Describe the factors involved in the communication process.
2. Explain the different types of persuasion processes.

BELLRINGER
Motivational Activity

Project Daily Focus Transparency 20–3 and have students answer the questions.

Also available as blackline master

Daily Focus Transparency 20–3

Reader's Guide

Use the Reader's Guide to introduce concepts and vocabulary.

Exploring Psychology
Ask students to read the **Exploring Psychology** feature and then discuss: **How does the frequency of advertisements influence behavior, especially in children?**

Vocabulary Precheck
Have students create a set of flash cards with the terms on one side and the definitions on the other. Encourage students to use the flash cards as a study tool.

Use the **Vocabulary PuzzleMaker CD-ROM** to create crossword and word search puzzles.

SECTION 3 Persuasion

Reader's Guide

Main Idea
Persuasion is a direct attempt to influence attitudes. We evaluate when, where, and how a message is presented, as well as the message itself, when determining the credibility of the message.

Vocabulary
- persuasion
- boomerang effect
- sleeper effect
- inoculation effect
- brainwashing

Objectives
- Describe the factors involved in the communication process.
- Explain the different types of persuasion processes.

EXPLORING PSYCHOLOGY

Why Do Kids Love McDonald's?

By switching the channel on a Saturday morning, a child can watch "Ronald McDonald" in up to a dozen, colorful, fast-paced commercials *each hour;* perhaps this is one reason why the chain sells so many billions of hamburgers.

—from *The Social Animal* by Elliot Aronson, 2006

Advertisers use persuasion to encourage consumers to buy their products. McDonald's uses at least one method of persuasion—familiarity. Most American kids know what McDonald's is; most American kids have seen a McDonald's commercial or advertisement. What methods of persuasion lure you?

PERSUASION

persuasion: the direct attempt to influence attitudes

Persuasion is a direct attempt to influence attitudes. At one time or another everyone engages in persuasion. When a smiling student who is working her way through college by selling magazine subscriptions comes to the door, she attempts to persuade you that reading *TIME* magazine or *Sports Illustrated* will make you better informed and give you lots to talk about at parties. Parents often attempt to persuade a son or daughter to conform to their values about life. Similarly, some young people try to persuade their parents that all their friends' parents are buying them iPods. In each case, the persuader's main hope is that by changing the other person's attitudes, he or she can change that person's behavior as well.

SECTION RESOURCES

Reproducible Masters
- Guided Reading Activity 20–3
- Vocabulary Activity 20–3
- Section Quiz 20–3

Transparencies
- Daily Focus Transparency 20–3

Multimedia
- Vocabulary PuzzleMaker CD-ROM
- *ExamView® Assessment Suite* CD-ROM
- Presentation Plus! Software

The Communication Process

Enormous amounts of time, money, and effort go into campaigns to persuade people to change their attitudes and behavior. Some succeed on a grand scale, while others seem to have no effect. Discovering the elements of an effective persuasive communication is one of the most difficult problems confronted by social psychologists.

The communication process can be broken down into four parts. The *message* itself is only one part. It is also important to consider the *source* of the message, the *channel* through which it is delivered, and the *audience* that receives it.

The Source How a person sees the source of a message may be a critical factor in his or her acceptance of it. The person receiving the message asks himself or herself three basic questions: Is the person giving the message trustworthy and sincere? Does he or she know anything about the subject? Is he or she likable (Pratkanis & Aronson, 2001)? If the answers are yes, the message is more likely to be accepted (see Figure 20.5).

Suppose, for example, that you wrote a paper criticizing a short story for your English class. A friend who reads the paper tells you about an article that praises the story and asks you to reconsider your view. The article was written by Agnes Stearn, a college student. You might change your opinion, or you might not. Suppose your friend tells you the same critique was written by Stephen King. Chances are that you would begin to doubt your own judgment. Three psychologists tried this experiment. Not surprisingly, many more students changed their minds about a piece of writing when they thought the criticism was written by a famous writer (Aronson, Turner, & Carlsmith, 1963).

A person receiving the message also asks, "Do I like the source?" If the communicator is respected and admired, people will tend to go along with the message, either because they believe in his or her judgment or because they want to be like him or her. This identification phenomenon explains the frequent use of athletes in advertisements. Football players and Olympic champions are not (in most cases) experts on deodorants, electric razors, or milk. Indeed, when an athlete endorses a particular brand of deodorant on television, we all know he or she is doing it for the money. Nevertheless, the process of identification makes these sales pitches highly effective (Wu & Shaffer, 1987).

However, attempts to be friendly and personal can backfire. When people dislike the individual or group delivering a message, they are likely to respond by taking the opposite point of view. This

Figure 20.5 The Source

National newscasters, such as Katie Couric, appear attractive, honest, and credible. We are likely to believe sources that seem trustworthy and are attractive. ***What is the identification phenomenon?***

2 TEACH

L1 Persuasion at Work Write the following list of products on the board: *soft drinks, cars, shampoo, soap, blue jeans,* and *cereal.* Ask students for brand name examples. List as many brand names below the product as possible.

Call on volunteers to explain why they chose those specific brands. Explore how students learn about and/or choose a brand. **Ask: Which of the following most influences you to buy a product for the first time: advertising appeal, the opinions of friends, product quality, or some other reason?** ELL

Figure 20.5

Caption Answer If the communicator, or source of the message, is liked and admired, people tend to accept the message because they believe in the communicator's judgment or because they want to be like him or her.

COOPERATIVE LEARNING ACTIVITY

Flowcharts As a class, brainstorm some of the features of an effective message *(clarity, pertinence to the subject, appropriate language, and so on).* Then explore factors that ensure delivery, or communication, of the message. Based on this discussion, assign small groups to design illustrated flowcharts showing the four main parts in the communication process. Direct students to create descriptive captions to explain the flow of information. Encourage groups to share their finished flowcharts with the class. **BLOCK SCHEDULING**

CHAPTER 20

Section 3, pages 590–596

Guided Reading Activity 20-3

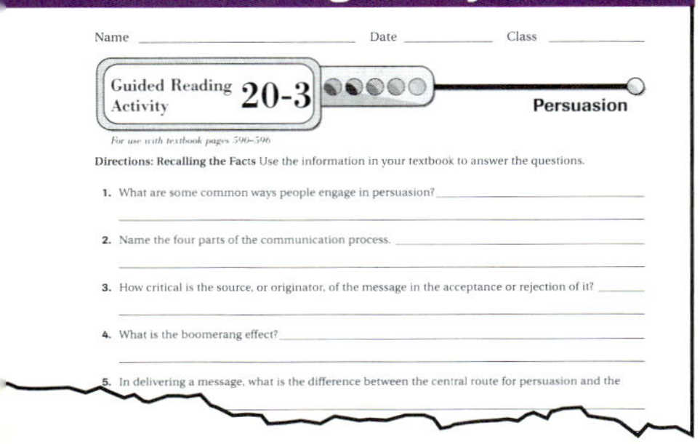
Name ______ Date ______ Class ______

Guided Reading Activity 20-3 Persuasion

For use with textbook pages 590–596

Directions: Recalling the Facts Use the information in your textbook to answer the questions.

1. What are some common ways people engage in persuasion? ______
2. Name the four parts of the communication process. ______
3. How critical is the source, or originator, of the message in the acceptance or rejection of it? ______
4. What is the boomerang effect? ______
5. In delivering a message, what is the difference between the central route for persuasion and the

Figure 20.6

Caption Answer This is an example of a peripheral route for persuasion because it appeals to the emotions.

Psychology Journal

Have students find an example of an advertisement in a magazine or other print source that they think is effective. Tell them to attach the sample to their journal and describe what makes the advertisement effective. ■

FYI

Doubling the size of an advertisement does not necessarily double the readership. A color advertisement also will not automatically guarantee readers. A black-and-white ad surrounded by color ads may get more notice. Research indicates that the most effective place to run a magazine advertisement is on the inside covers.

boomerang effect: a change in attitude or behavior opposite of the one desired by the persuader

is known as the **boomerang effect.** For example, the sales of a product may go down after the well-known spokesperson for the product is arrested for breaking the law, or the well-intentioned comments of a politician may offend certain groups and, thereby, damage his popular appeal.

The Message Suppose two people with opposing viewpoints are trying to persuade you to agree with them. Suppose further that you like and trust both of them. In this situation, the message becomes more important than the source. The persuasiveness of a message depends on the way in which it is composed and organized as well as on the actual content.

There are two ways to deliver a message. The *central route for persuasion* focuses on presenting information consisting of strong arguments and facts—it is a focus on logic. The *peripheral route for persuasion* relies on emotional appeals, emphasizing personal traits or positive feelings.

Should the message arouse emotion? Are people more likely to change their attitudes if they are afraid or angry or pleased? The answer is yes, but the most effective messages combine emotional appeal with factual information and argument. A moderately arousing message typically causes the largest shift of opinion. Similarly, a message that deviates moderately from the attitudes of the target audience will tend to move that audience furthest. A communication that overemphasizes the emotional side of an issue may boomerang. The peripheral route sometimes arouses fear (see Figure 20.6). If the message is too upsetting, people may reject it. For example, showing pictures of accident victims to people who have been arrested for drunken driving may convince them not to drive when they have been drinking. Yet if the film is so bloody that people are frightened or disgusted, they may also stop listening to the message. On the other hand, a communication that includes only logic and information may miss its mark because the audience does not relate the facts to their personal lives.

In addition to considering the route of the appeal, communicators must also decide whether or not to present both sides of an issue. For the most part, a two-sided communication is more effective because the audience tends to believe that the speaker is objective and fair-minded. A slight hazard of presenting opposing arguments is that they might undercut the message or suggest that the whole issue is too controversial to warrant a decision.

People usually respond positively to a message that is structured and delivered in a dynamic way. A communication that is forceful to the point of being pushy, however, may produce negative results. People generally resent being pressured. If listeners infer from a message that they are being left with no choice but to agree with the speaker's viewpoint, they may reject an opinion for this reason alone.

Figure 20.6 Appealing to Your Fears

Advertisements, such as this, are effective only if you believe the danger is real and if you believe that you can do something to reduce the danger. ***Is this an example of a central or peripheral route for persuasion?***

MEETING SPECIAL NEEDS

Learning Style: Visual/Spatial Ask students to select a product marketed for teens. Then ask them to create two advertisements for the product. Tell them that one should appeal to the central route for persuasion and the other should appeal to the peripheral route for persuasion. The students may create either an advertisement for a print medium or a storyboard for a television advertisement. Encourage students to share their advertisements with the class. **L2**

BLOCK SCHEDULING

Refer to ***Inclusion for the High School Social Studies Classroom Strategies and Activities*** in the TCR for strategies for students with different learning styles.

The Channel Where, when, and how a message is presented also influences the audience's response. In general, personal contact is the most effective approach to an audience. For example, in one study in Ann Arbor, Michigan, 75 percent of voters who had been contacted personally voted in favor of a change in the city charter. Only 45 percent of those who had received the message in the mail and 19 percent of those who had seen only ads in the media voted for the change (Eldersveld & Dodge, 1954).

As we saw earlier, however, personal contact may boomerang: people may dislike the communicator or feel that they are being pressured. Besides, you can reach a great many more people through mailings and radio and television broadcasts than you can in person.

There is some evidence that television and films are more effective media of persuasion than printed matter. People tend to believe what they see and hear with their own senses (even if they know the information has been edited before it is broadcast). In one experiment, 51 percent of people who had watched a film could answer factual questions about the issue in question—compared to 29 percent of those who had seen only printed material. In addition, more of the people who had viewed the film altered their viewpoints than did people who had read about the issue (Hovland, Lumsdaine, & Sheffield, 1949).

The Audience Finally, the most effective channel also depends in part on the audience. The audience includes all those people whose attitudes the communicator is trying to change. Persuading people to alter their views depends on knowing who the audience is and why they hold the attitudes they do. Despite the power of persuasion, most people accept information about things they find interesting, and they avoid information that does not support their beliefs (Pratkanis & Aronson, 2001). Suppose, for example, you are involved in a program to reduce the birthrate in a heavily populated area. The first step would be to inform people of various methods of birth control as well as how and where to obtain them—but will they do so? To persuade them to use available contraceptives, you need to know why they value large families. In some areas of the world, people have as many children as they can because they do not expect most to survive. In this case, you might want to tie the family-planning campaign to programs of infant care. In some areas, children work to bring in needed income. In this case, you might want to promote an incentive system for families who limit themselves to two or three children.

If the people are not taking advantage of available means of birth control, you will want to know who is resisting. Perhaps men believe fathering a child is a sign of virility. Perhaps women consider motherhood an essential element of femininity. Perhaps both sexes see parenthood as a symbol of maturity and adulthood (Coale, 1973). Knowing who your audience is and what motivates its members are crucial.

Several strategies effectively involve the audience. One strategy that has been studied extensively is the *foot-in-the-door technique,* which involves first making a very small request that someone is almost sure to agree to and then making a much more demanding request (Dillard, 1991). In one

Readings and Case Studies in Psychology

Have students read the Chapter 20 Reading selection in *Readings and Case Studies in Psychology* and answer the questions that follow the reading.

CURRICULUM CONNECTION

History When Franklin D. Roosevelt became president in March 1933, the nation was trapped in a deep economic depression. His Inaugural Address provided a clear message of courage and hope as he spoke the following words: *This is preeminently the time to speak the truth, the whole truth, frankly and boldly. Nor need we shrink from honestly facing conditions in our country today. This great Nation will endure as it has endured, will revive and will prosper. So, first of all, let me assert my firm belief that the only thing we have to fear is fear itself—nameless, unreasoning, unjustified terror which paralyzes needed efforts to convert retreat into advance. In every dark hour of our national life a leadership of frankness and vigor has met with that understanding and support of the people themselves which is essential to victory. I am convinced that you will again give that support to leadership in these critical days.*

CRITICAL THINKING ACTIVITY

Classifying Information Assign students to take notes on commercial advertisements shown during prime-time television. Suggest that they organize data collection by setting up a chart with the following heads: *Product Being Sold, Visual Messages, Auditory Messages, Persuasion Techniques,* and *Appeal to Prejudices.* Have students report their findings to the class. **Ask:** **How does knowledge of the advertising process help you better resist persuasion techniques? L2**

CHAPTER 20
Section 3, pages 590–596

PSYCHOLOGY Online

Links and instructional guidelines can be found in the **Web Activity Lesson Plan** at glencoe.com.

Reading Check Answer
The foot-in-the-door technique involves making a small request and then making a more demanding request. The door-in-the-face technique involves making a very large request and then following it with a more reasonable request.

TEACHER Tip

To illustrate people's unconscious awareness of the *sleeper effect,* point out the use of such expressions as "Let me think about it" or "Let me sleep on it."
Ask: What other similar phrases can you suggest? Do you feel most people need time for the message to sink in? Why or why not?

CULTURAL CONNECTIONS

Paraguay has an authoritarian government, which means that the government controls all media channels and effectively censors all dissenting views. As a result, dissenters have found it difficult to express their opposition. The leading opposition groups in Paraguay have found graffiti the most effective means available to them to express their dissent. Political graffiti messages have become an inexpensive and accessible channel that reaches a wide audience.

PSYCHOLOGY Online

Student Web Activity
Visit the *Understanding Psychology* Web site at glencoe.com and click on **Chapter 20—Student Web Activities** for an activity on attitudes and influence.

Reading Check
How does the foot-in-the-door technique differ from the door-in-the-face technique?

experiment, two researchers (Freedman & Fraser, 1966) asked residents of Palo Alto, California, for permission to place a small sign reading "Be a Safe Driver" in a window of their homes. Two weeks later, another person asked residents for permission to stake a large "Drive Carefully" sign in the front yard. Nearly 56 percent of those who had agreed to the first request also agreed to the second request. However, only 17 percent of the residents who heard only the second request but not the first agreed to put the sign in their yard.

Another strategy is sometimes called the *door-in-the-face technique.* It works like this: To encourage people to agree to a moderate request that might otherwise be rejected, you make a major request—likely to be rejected. When it is, you follow up immediately with a more minor request. For example, you might ask a friend, "I'm helping my parents move this weekend. Would you come over and help us Saturday and Sunday until we're done?" "No? Well, then, could you come over Saturday morning and just help me move our grand piano?" You have a much higher likelihood of success on the second request following the first than if you had made only the second request.

Models of Persuasion

As discussed earlier, a message leads to thinking, but how much and at what depth are determined both by the message and the needs of the person receiving it. Two different levels of activity are possible—central route processing (when the recipient thoughtfully considers the issues and arguments) and peripheral route processing (characterized by considering other cues rather than the message itself). Another model of persuasion is the heuristic model (Chaiken, 1987). A *heuristic* is a rule of thumb or a shortcut that may lead to but does not guarantee a solution (see Figure 20.7).

The heuristic model proposes two ways in which attitudes may be changed. If an individual is not interested in an issue under discussion, he or she is likely to rely on heuristic processing, a very casual, low-attention form of analyzing evidence. In this kind of processing, the recipient tunes in to the peripheral aspects of the message—the likability of the source, the number of arguments, and the tone of voice.

On the other hand, if the recipient is deeply interested or curious about the topic of a message, the likely result is sometimes called systematic processing, or central route processing. Advertisers use heuristics to get you to buy their products. For instance, they may sprinkle their ads with numbers and nice-sounding words such as *integrity,* employ celebrities to endorse their products, or state that their product is the most popular one.

The Sleeper Effect Changes in attitudes are not always permanent. In fact, efforts at persuasion usually have their greatest impact immediately and then fade away. However, sometimes people seem to reach different conclusions about a message after a period of time has elapsed. This curious **sleeper effect** has been explained in several ways.

sleeper effect: the delayed impact on attitude change of a persuasive communication

One explanation of the delayed-action impact depends on the tendency to retain the message but forget the source. As time goes by, a positive source no longer holds power to persuade nor does a negative

PSYCHOLOGY LAB EXPERIMENT

Discovering How We Respond to Messages Invite a guest speaker to participate in an experiment with the class. If possible, contact a person who is knowledgeable in advertising or marketing. Arrange for students to come to class in two shifts. For the first shift, ask the speaker to deliver a warm, friendly, and/or humorous message on the art of advertising. For the second shift, have the speaker deliver the same message in a cold, matter-of-fact manner. In the next class session, have students write a review of the talk, including the main impact points. After comparing results, discuss the importance of the source in audience acceptance of a message. **L2** **BLOCK SCHEDULING**

source undercut the message. When the memory of the source fades, the message then stands on its own merit, and more people may accept it (Kelman & Hovland, 1953).

The problem is that this requires forgetting one thing and retaining another, with no obvious reason why that should occur. Researchers (Pratkanis et al., 1988) conducted experiments to verify their differential decay hypothesis. They argued that if the message is heard first, followed by a discounting cue (such as a low-credibility source), the two balance each other out—no effect is observed. Over time, however, the negative aspects of the cue dissipate more rapidly than the impact of the highly elaborated message. It is easier to remember your own position than the details of an argument. If the cue decays rapidly and the argument more slowly, what remains is the effect on an attitude. It may also be that it simply takes time for people to change their minds. As the message sinks in, attitudes change more.

The Inoculation Effect

What can you do to resist persuasion? Research has shown that people can be educated to resist attitude change. This technique can be compared to an inoculation (McGuire, 1970). Inoculation against persuasion works in much the same way as inoculation against certain diseases. When a person is vaccinated, he is given a weakened or dead form of the disease-causing agent, which stimulates his body to manufacture defenses. If an inoculated person is attacked by a more potent form of the agent, he is immune to infection. Similarly, a person who has resisted a mild attack on his beliefs is ready to defend them against an onslaught that might otherwise have been overwhelming.

The **inoculation effect** can be explained in two ways: it motivates individuals to defend their beliefs more strongly, and it gives them some practice in defending those beliefs. The most vulnerable attitudes you have, therefore, are the ones that you have never had to defend. For example, you might find yourself hard put to defend your faith in democracy or in the healthfulness of vegetables if you have never had these beliefs questioned.

Brainwashing

The most extreme means of changing attitudes involves a combination of psychological gamesmanship and physical torture, called **brainwashing.** The most extensive studies of brainwashing have been done on Westerners

Figure 20.7 Using Heuristics

We use heuristics, or shortcuts, to evaluate many messages. This saves us time and energy. ***Which heuristic is this advertiser using?***

1. If the message contains many numbers and large words, it must be based on facts.
2. If the message focuses on values I have, it is probably right.
3. Famous or successful people conveying the message are probably right.
4. If most people support this product or believe this, it is probably true.

inoculation effect: developing resistance to persuasion by exposing a person to arguments that challenge his or her beliefs so that he or she can practice defending them

brainwashing: extreme form of attitude change; uses peer pressure, physical suffering, threats, rewards, guilt, and intensive indoctrination

CHAPTER 20

Section 3, pages 590–596

Figure 20.7

Caption Answer This advertiser is using numbers with the thought that people will believe the ad if it contains statistics. A second heuristic at work here is the belief that if most people support the product, the ad is probably true. (Pampers are a well-known and established product.)

Vocabulary Activity 20-3

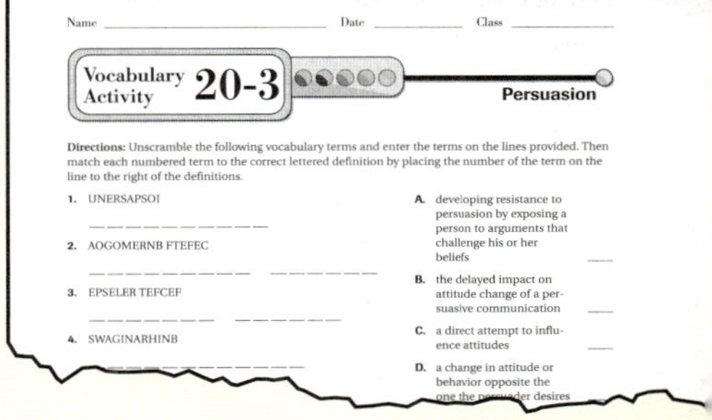
Name ______ Date ______ Class ______

Vocabulary Activity 20-3 Persuasion

Directions: Unscramble the following vocabulary terms and enter the terms on the lines provided. Then match each numbered term to the correct lettered definition by placing the number of the term on the line to the right of the definitions.

1. UNERSAPSOI
2. AOGOMERNB FTEFEC
3. EPSELER TEFCEF
4. SWAGINARHINB

A. developing resistance to persuasion by exposing a person to arguments that challenge his or her beliefs ___
B. the delayed impact on attitude change of a persuasive communication ___
C. a direct attempt to influence attitudes ___
D. a change in attitude or behavior opposite the one the persuader desires

3 ASSESS

Assign Section 3 Assessment as homework or as an in-class activity.

Section Quiz 20-3

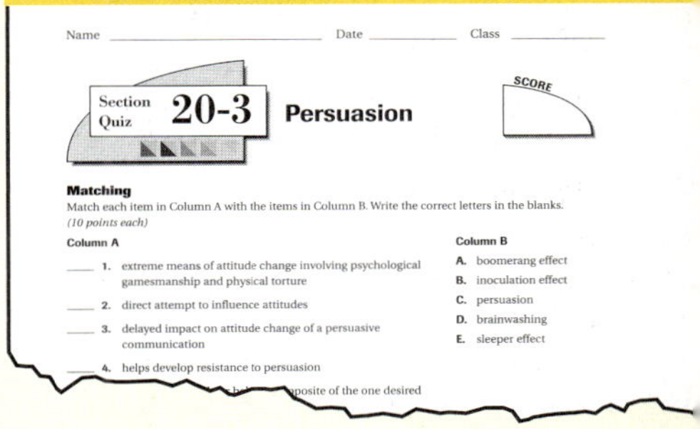
Name ______ Date ______ Class ______

Section Quiz 20-3 Persuasion

SCORE

Matching

Match each item in Column A with the items in Column B. Write the correct letters in the blanks. *(10 points each)*

Column A

___ 1. extreme means of attitude change involving psychological gamesmanship and physical torture
___ 2. direct attempt to influence attitudes
___ 3. delayed impact on attitude change of a persuasive communication
___ 4. helps develop resistance to persuasion

Column B

A. boomerang effect
B. inoculation effect
C. persuasion
D. brainwashing
E. sleeper effect

INTERDISCIPLINARY CONNECTIONS ACTIVITY

The Media Introduce the nonprofit groups Population Communications International (PCI) and the Population Council. These groups are using psychology to change attitudes about family size in countries like Mexico, India, and Kenya. The cultures of all three countries value large families. Tell students that researchers have found that the most effective method of changing attitudes about family size has been the use of soap opera-type programs, such as Kenya's *Tushuriane* ("Let's Talk About It"). Assign students to work in groups to write a script for a soap opera episode that one of these organizations might run in an attempt to change attitudes on family size in Mexico, India, or Kenya. Remind students that the most effective episodes will take into account cultural factors that shape attitudes. **L2**

Reteach

Organize the class into small groups. Give each group a common household product like laundry detergent, pet food, and so on. Ask each group to create an advertising campaign around the product. Students will develop slogans and methods of persuasion, identify the likely audience, and determine the channels (when, where, and how the message is presented). Have the groups use this information to prepare a storyboard showing how they would advertise the product.

Enrich

Have groups of students imagine that they are psychologists interested in deprogramming former cult members. Challenge them to devise the most effective strategies for helping the individuals readjust. As they are planning their strategies, they may want to explore the methods used by psychologists such as Margaret Thaler Singer.

4 CLOSE

Bring to class a variety of advertisements for everyday products. Include advertisements for competing brands. As a class, discuss the possible heuristics that the advertisers were using.

who had been captured by the Chinese during the Korean War and subjected to "thought reform." Psychiatrist Robert Jay Lifton (1963) interviewed several dozen prisoners released by the Chinese, and from their accounts, he outlined the methods used to break down people's convictions and introduce new patterns of belief, feeling, and behavior.

The aim in brainwashing is as much to create a new person as to change attitudes. So the first step is to strip away all identity and then subject the person to intense social pressure and physical stress. Prison is a perfect setting for this process. The person is isolated from social support, is a number not a name, is clothed like everyone else, and can be surrounded by people who have had their thoughts "reformed" and are contemptuous of "reactionaries." So long as the prisoner holds out, he is treated with contempt or exhorted to confess by his fellow prisoners. He is interrogated past the point of exhaustion and is humiliated and discomfited by being bound at all times, even during meals or elimination. The prisoner is rewarded for cooperating. Cooperation involves confessing to crimes against the people in his former way of life. With every act of compliance, prison life is made a little more pleasant. Finally, by a combination of threat, peer pressure, systematic rewards, and other psychological means, the prisoner comes to believe his confession.

It is difficult to say where persuasion ends and brainwashing begins. Some researchers believe that brainwashing is just a very intense form of persuasion. Drawing this line has become particularly important to the courts—especially in cases such as lawsuits regarding the deprogramming of members of religious cults. A cult is a group of people who organize around a strong authority figure. Cults use influence techniques and deception to attain psychological control over members and new recruits.

SECTION 3 Assessment

1. **Review the Vocabulary** Explain how the boomerang, sleeper, and inoculation effects influence your attitudes.
2. **Visualize the Main Idea** Use a diagram similar to the one below to outline the parts of the communication process.

3. **Recall Information** How does brainwashing work? Why is it used?
4. **Think Critically** When evaluating a message that is very important to you, do you rely on systematic processing or heuristics? Explain.
5. **Application Activity** Pretend that you are a car dealer and you are persuading a young couple to purchase an automobile from your dealership. Write a brief script between the dealer and the couple that incorporates aspects of persuasion techniques both might use.

SECTION 3 Assessment Answers

1. Boomerang—effect on attitude that is opposite of the one intended; sleeper—delayed change in attitude; inoculation—resistance to changing attitudes that results from having to defend one's beliefs
2. Diagrams should include the following: the source, the message, the channel, and the audience.
3. Brainwashing is an extreme form of attitude change that involves a combination of psychological gamesmanship (such as peer pressure, threats, rewards, and guilt), and physical torture. It is used to break down people's convictions and introduce new beliefs, behaviors, and feelings.
4. You rely on systematic processing. Because you are interested in the topic, you want logical arguments to support your position.
5. Answers will vary but should include knowledge of the four components of the communication process: source, message, channel, and audience.

CHAPTER 20 Summary and Vocabulary

Everyone has a variety of opinions, attitudes, and beliefs. Psychologists study where they come from and how they change.

Section 1 Attitude Formation

Main Idea: Our attitudes are the result of conditioning, observational learning, and cognitive evaluation. Our attitudes help us define ourselves and our place in society, evaluate people and events, and guide our behavior.

- Attitudes may be formed through classical conditioning.
- The culture in which you grew up, the people who raised you, and those with whom you associate all shape your attitudes.
- People living in the same conditions and who frequently communicate with one another tend to have attitudes in common because they are exposed to the same information.
- Our attitudes serve as guidelines for interpreting and categorizing people, objects, and events.

Section 2 Attitude Change and Prejudice

Main Idea: Attitudes are formed through compliance, identification, and internalization. Attitudes may be changed as a result of cognitive dissonance.

- People often adapt their actions to the wishes of others to avoid discomfort or rejection and to gain support.
- Identification occurs when a person wants to define himself or herself in terms of a person or group and therefore adopts the person's or group's attitudes and ways of behaving.
- Internalization is the most lasting of the three sources of attitude formation or change.
- People's attitudes change because they are always trying to get things to fit together logically.
- A person's actions can affect his or her attitudes.
- Prejudice means deciding beforehand what a person will be like instead of withholding judgment until it can be based on a person's individual qualities.

Section 3 Persuasion

Main Idea: Persuasion is a direct attempt to influence attitudes. We evaluate when, where, and how a message is presented, as well as the message itself, when determining the credibility of the message.

- The process of communication involves four elements: the message itself, the source of the message, the channel through which it is delivered, and the audience that receives it.
- The audience may process a message by systematically thinking about it or by using heuristics.
- The most effective messages combine moderate emotional appeal with factual information and argument.

Chapter Vocabulary

attitude (p. 577)
self-concept (p. 580)
compliance (p. 583)
identification (p. 583)
internalization (p. 584)
cognitive dissonance (p. 584)
counterattitudinal behavior (p. 585)
self-justification (p. 586)
self-fulfilling prophecy (p. 586)
prejudice (p. 587)
discrimination (p. 588)
persuasion (p. 590)
boomerang effect (p. 592)
sleeper effect (p. 594)
inoculation effect (p. 595)
brainwashing (p. 595)

20 Summary and Vocabulary

Using the Chapter 20 Summary and Vocabulary

Use the Chapter 20 Summary and Vocabulary to preview, review, condense, or reteach the chapter.

Preview/Review

Use the Chapter Vocabulary list to help students review and study.

Activity Ask students to create a word search using examples or definitions as the clues for the terms. Have pairs of students trade and complete word search puzzles.

Vocabulary PuzzleMaker CD-ROM reinforces the vocabulary terms used in Chapter 20.

Condense

Have students read the Chapter 20 Summary.

Chapter 20 Guided Reading Activities

Reteach

Reteaching Activity 20

PERFORMANCE ASSESSMENT ACTIVITY

Analyzing Letters to the Editor Letters to the Editor are direct attempts by the writer to sway the reader to the writer's point of view. Assign students to collect three Letters to the Editor from newspapers. Ask students to identify the issues presented, the writers' attitudes, and determine whether the writers used the central route or the peripheral route for persuasion. **Ask:** **How persuasive was each of the letters? Did the letters present one side of an issue or did they present a two-sided argument? Of the two methods, which was more effective?** **BLOCK SCHEDULING**

Refer to the ***Authentic Assessment*** booklet for additional activities and information about evaluating student performance.

PSYCHOLOGY Online

Have students visit the Web site at glencoe.com to review Chapter 20 and take the **Self-Check Quiz**.

GLENCOE TECHNOLOGY

Presentation Plus! For a review of Chapter 20 content, see MindJogger Checkpoint on **Presentation Plus!**

Reviewing Vocabulary

1. a	**6.** j
2. i	**7.** b
3. e	**8.** h
4. c	**9.** f
5. g	**10.** d

Recalling Facts

1. Attitudes are formed by compliance, identification, and internalization. Compliance occurs when people adapt to the wishes of others to avoid rejection and gain support. Identification occurs when a person wants to define himself or herself in terms of a person or group and, therefore, adopts the person's or group's attitudes and behavior. Internalization is the incorporation of values, ideas, and standards of others as part of oneself.
2. Diagrams should include the following—central processing route and peripheral processing route. The central route focuses on presenting information consisting of strong facts and arguments. The peripheral route focuses on emotional appeals, emphasizing personal traits or positive feelings.
3. self-justification; They are rationalizing their attitudes and behavior.
4. Some listeners may take the opposite point of view (boomerang effect) or stop listening completely.
5. The purpose is to break down people's convictions and introduce new beliefs and behaviors. Methods include the following: subject person to intense personal pressure and stress; inflict punishment for unreformed behavior; give rewards for cooperation and inoculation of new attitudes.

Critical Thinking

1. Answers will vary. Encourage students to consider when these attitudes were formed and who or what was the primary influence.
2. Answers should include examples of compliance, identification, and internalization. Internalization is the most lasting process because a person's reasons for holding certain views have nothing to do with other people. They are based on that person's own evaluation of the issue.
3. Answers will vary but might mention avoiding prejudgement and treating people as individuals, not members of a group.
4. In assessing the effect of advertising on purchasing decisions, students should use specific examples and mention components of the communication process.
5. Encourage students to bring to class print advertisements demonstrating each processing route. If students are aware of any video or audio advertisements, encourage them to record the advertisements and share them with the class.

Psychology Projects

1. Projects should include visuals that represent the culture being explored.
2. Display the cartoons around the class and give students time to review one another's work. Then review as a class the suggestions for eliminating stereotypes.
3. Challenge students to create storyboards showing how they would get the message across.
4. If no campaigns are ongoing, suggest that students

CHAPTER 20 Assessment

PSYCHOLOGY Online

Self-Check Quiz
Visit the *Understanding Psychology* Web site at glencoe.com and click on **Chapter 20—Self-Check Quizzes** to prepare for the Chapter Test.

Reviewing Vocabulary

Choose the letter of the correct term or concept below to complete the sentence.

a. attitude	**f.** discrimination
b. compliance	**g.** self-concept
c. identification	**h.** boomerang effect
d. internalization	**i.** sleeper effect
e. self-justification	**j.** brainwashing

1. A(n) __________ is a predisposition to respond in particular ways toward specific things.
2. A(n) __________ occurs when people seem to reach different conclusions about a message after a period of time has elapsed.
3. Trying to explain one's behavior to reduce cognitive dissonance is called __________.
4. __________ occurs when a person wants to define himself or herself in terms of a person or group and therefore adopts the person's or group's attitudes.
5. Your __________ is how you see or describe yourself.
6. The most extreme means of changing attitudes is called __________.
7. __________ occurs when a person yields to the desires or demands of others to avoid discomfort or to gain approval.
8. A(n) __________ occurs when people dislike the individual delivering a message and respond by taking the opposite point of view.
9. The unequal treatment of members of certain groups is called __________.
10. __________ occurs when a person wholeheartedly accepts an attitude, and the attitude becomes an integral part of the person.

Recalling Facts

1. In what three ways are attitudes formed?
2. Using a diagram similar to the one below, identify and describe two methods of delivering a persuasive message.

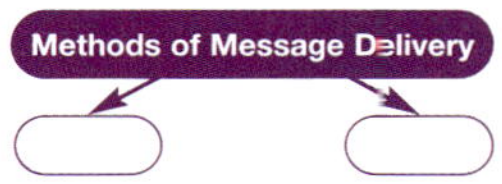

3. Which cognitive act are people engaging in when they convince themselves that they did not like the victim of their aggressive act?
4. What will be the effect on listeners if you use a very emotional appeal or if you pressure them to adopt your point of view?
5. What is the goal of brainwashing? How does brainwashing work?

Critical Thinking

1. **Evaluating Information** Attitudes come from a variety of sources. Using the information in the chapter, what source do you think was most influential in establishing your attitudes? Why do you think so?
2. **Analyzing Information** There are three processes involved in changing attitudes. Provide examples of an attitude being changed in each of the three ways. Explain which process is the most lasting process for changing attitudes and why.
3. **Applying Concepts** What are two ways that you can help reduce prejudice in your school or community?
4. **Making Inferences** One of the primary objectives of advertising is to get the viewers or listeners to remember the product. To what extent do you think familiarity with brand names influences your choices in the market?
5. **Synthesizing Information** Think of a recent local or national political campaign. Focus on the kinds of persuasion techniques used by the candidates. How did they use central route processing? Peripheral route processing?

CHAPTER 20 Assessment

Psychology Projects

1. **Attitude Formation** Use a variety of sources to find examples of the ways in which culture influences attitudes. Find out about attitudes in other places of the world and compare those attitudes to ones in this country. Present your findings in an illustrated, captioned poster.
2. **Prejudice** Use magazine and newspaper articles to find out about common stereotypes toward groups such as teenagers and the elderly. Create a cartoon illustrating these stereotypes and provide suggestions for eliminating them.
3. **Persuasion** Choose some issue on which you have a strong opinion. If you were given an unlimited budget, how would you go about persuading people to agree with you? In a written report, describe the sources you would employ, the channels you would use, the content of your message, and the audience you would try to reach.
4. **Attitude Change** Study a recent or ongoing political campaign. What attitudinal change and persuasive strategies are being used? Collect examples of the strategies and report your findings in a brief presentation.

Technology Activity

Locate examples of persuasion techniques used by advertisers on the Internet. Print out pages of the advertisements and explain the techniques used to influence consumers. How effective do you think these advertisements are in changing people's attitudes?

Psychology Journal

After reading the chapter and class discussions, would you revise the definition of prejudice that you wrote at the beginning of this chapter's study? In your journal, write a one-page paper explaining whether or not prejudice is unavoidable.

Building Skills

Identifying Cause-and-Effect Relationships Review the advertisement below, then answer the questions that follow.

1. Which function of attitudes does this advertisement illustrate?
2. Do you think this advertisement is an effective persuasive communication tool? Explain your answer.

Practice and assess key social studies skills with **Glencoe Skillbuilder Interactive Workbook CD-ROM, Level 2.**

See the Skills Handbook, page 624, for an explanation of identifying cause-and-effect relationships.

Building Skills

1. The advertisement was created to alter the reader's attitude and act as a guideline to action.
2. Answers will vary, but might include references to models of persuasion or elements of the communication process.

GLENCOE TECHNOLOGY

CD-ROM

Glencoe Skillbuilder Interactive Workbook, Level 2

This interactive CD-ROM is designed to reinforce student mastery of essential social studies skills.

Chapter Bonus Test Question

This question may be used for extra credit on the Chapter Assessment.
Answer the following question:
When people's attitudes and behavior match, they have achieved what?
Answer: cognitive consistency

explore a local or national issue and identify the persuasive strategies being employed by each side of the issue.

Technology Activity

As a class, discuss whether Internet advertising should be regulated. If so, describe the regulations and who should do the regulating. If not, discuss the potential impact of violent or sexually explicit advertising on children.

Psychology Journal

Encourage students to consider how prejudice is harmful and helpful. Students' revised definitions should reflect insights obtained after reading the chapter.

TIME REPORTS

Reader's Dictionary

Review the following terms with students to help them read and understand the article.

contrition: remorse for one's actions; penitence
affirmative-action policies: regulations designed to provide equal opportunities to groups harmed by discrimination
regents: members of the board of governors of an institution
laudable: praiseworthy
reparations: money or other action to compensate for past damages
proxies: alternates empowered to act in the place of another
PSY: 14A

CLICK HERE

TIME REPORTS

Visit **www.time.com/teach** for the complete text of this article, as well as related articles on the subject.

Block Schedule

This activity works well for a block-scheduling framework.

TIME REPORTS

Coloring the Campus

It's like the 1960s in reverse: the schools are trying to integrate, and the courts won't let them

By ADAM COHEN

YOU MIGHT THINK THAT THE president of a major university would show some contrition after being slapped down by a panel of federal judges. But when an appeals court ruled last month that the University of Georgia had discriminated against white applicants in favor of blacks—and had systematically violated the 14th Amendment—UGA president Michael Adams calmly turned the other cheek. "Sometimes," he said, "you are defined by the battles in which you engage rather than by those you win."

"Our policy is fully constitutional," echoed Lee Bollinger, president of the University of Michigan, whose law school is fighting a similar lawsuit charging it with discriminating against whites. "This is not the moment to back away."

In other words, buzz off.

That's right: courts and universities are at each other's throats, and once again the issue is race. If you are old enough to remember black-and-white TV, you saw the footage the last go-round: federal judges ordering all-white universities in the South to open their doors to blacks. But in the new millennium, the sides have flipped. Now the schools are the ones trying to usher in minority students with broad affirmative-action policies. And the courts—and, in California, voters and the regents—have been striking down those policies.

Each side in this legal tug-of-war is fighting for a deeply held principle. Backers of the recent rulings say the courts are ushering in a laudable "post-affirmative action" era—when people will be judged as individuals, not as members of groups. But opponents argue—as did many reparations advocates at the recently concluded U.N. racism conference in South Africa—that the slave trade's effects have not yet been erased, and it is far too soon to dismantle programs designed to increase minorities' access to higher education.

What has academic administrators around the country so worried is that they know rulings like the UGA decision could dramatically change the racial makeup of their campuses. The Berkeley campus of the University of California saw this firsthand when it was forced by California's Proposition 209 to switch to race-blind admissions. Underrepresented minorities in the student body dropped sharply, from 25% to 11%. At the University of Texas School of Law, the number of black first-years fell to just four the year after the school was ordered to adopt race-blind admissions—from 38 the year before.

Universities are not openly defying the courts. In states where they have been ordered—as UGA was—to stop using formulas that give extra points to minority applicants, they have complied. But what they can do—and have done—is fight back with a range of new programs and policies designed to maintain minority enrollment while walking the new legal lines set by the courts. No school has worked harder to do this than U.T.'s law school, which in 1996 was hit by a suit, *Hopwood v. Texas*; the ruling in that case removed race as a consideration in admissions.

The law school has since enlisted high-profile alumni such as Dallas mayor Ron Kirk and Texas secretary of state Henry Cuellar to write to minority applicants to encourage them to come. A Texas state senator talked airlines into donating tickets so out-of-state blacks can visit the campus. And although the school itself is prohibited from offering race-based scholarships, U.T. alumni have stepped in to help. Last year U.T.'s alumni association, the Texas Exes, gave nearly $400,000 in aid to 31 Hispanics,

COOPERATIVE LEARNING ACTIVITY

Surveying Attitudes Toward Affirmative Action Organize students into groups of four. Ask each group to prepare and conduct a survey to investigate attitudes toward affirmative action. For example, the surveys might ask if a respondent thinks affirmative-action policies should be expanded, kept at the same level, or reduced. Have each group collect 25 responses from teens and 25 responses from adults. Be sure the surveys are totally anonymous; age (teen or adult) should be the only biographical information on the questionnaires. Each group should graph and present its data to the class. **BLOCK SCHEDULING**

RON SHERMAN—STONE

28 blacks and one Native American. The payoff: black enrollment is up—to 16 this fall from the low of four the year after *Hopwood*.

The state of Texas responded to *Hopwood* with the now-famous "top 10%" law that guarantees a place in the state university system to any student who graduates in the top 10% of his or her class. Because many Texas high schools are not well integrated, the top 10% in some schools is almost all minorities. U.T. officials have boosted the program by offering scholarships to top percenters at 70 high schools in Dallas, Houston, San Antonio and other underrepresented—and heavily black and Latino—areas. Minority enrollment in the U.T. undergraduate program is actually higher today than before *Hopwood* rewrote the rules.

These programs and policies are generating a new debate. To supporters of affirmative action, they work to keep higher education inclusive while staying within the letter of the law. But opponents of affirmative action are crying foul. Ward Connerly, the regent who wrote California's Proposition 209, argues that many of the ideas being proposed in California, like reducing the academic track, are "designed to be proxies for points"—ways of tipping the scales without engaging in the kind of blatant favoritism struck down in Georgia.

Both sides of this debate claim to be working for diversity. The Georgia appeals court said UGA's inflexible formula, which assigned extra points to blacks, made the mistake of assuming that groups, rather than individuals, add diversity to a campus. "A white applicant from a disadvantaged rural area in Appalachia may well have more to offer a Georgia public university such as UGA—from the standpoint of diversity—than a nonwhite applicant from an affluent family and a suburban Atlanta high school," the court wrote.

But supporters of more traditional approaches to affirmative action say race remains key. "You can be diverse and not have affirmative action," says Richard Black, U.C. Berkeley's associate vice chancellor for admissions and enrollment. "But the kind of diversity that you get from bringing oboe players and stamp collectors together is different."

The Georgia, Michigan and Texas suits all focused on admissions formulas and the extra points given to minority applicants. But if those decisions hold up, expect to see affirmative-action critics turn their attention to the newer, subtler affirmative-action policies. The same week the court issued the UGA ruling, the University of Florida announced, in response to an Office of Civil Rights directive, that it was changing its scholarship criteria to reduce the role of race. The move was a reminder that in the ongoing assault on affirmative action, these secondary forms of assistance—including outreach programs, new admissions criteria and targeted scholarships—may be the next battleground. ■

—For the complete text of this article and related articles from TIME, please visit www.time.com/teach

Analyzing the Article

1. Describe the two sides of today's affirmative-action debate.
2. CRITICAL THINKING Do you think U.S. society is ready to move into a "post-affirmative action" era? Why or why not?

Answers to Analyzing the Article

1. One side feels that affirmative action is no longer necessary. This side maintains we are ready to treat individuals strictly on merit. The other side feels affirmative action is still needed. In this view, the harsh effects of racism and discrimination are still felt; therefore, society needs affirmative-action policies to create equal opportunities for all people.
2. Answers will vary. Some students may suggest that much progress has been made and that affirmative action is no longer necessary. Others may believe that society does not yet offer people of different races equal opportunities.

TIME REPORTS

Active Reading Strategy

Explain to students that *connecting* means relating what they already know about a subject to what they are now reading about the subject.

Questions for Discussion

Use the following questions for a class discussion after students have read the article.

1. How might the phenomenon of self-fulfilling prophecy affect attempts to integrate society? *(People who hold negative stereotypes of other groups will be inclined to treat individuals from that group in a cold, unfriendly fashion. This sort of treatment will likely get a negative response, which a prejudiced person then interprets as evidence the prejudice is justified.)*
2. What motives or factors might affect an individual's attitude toward affirmative-action policies? *(Encourage students to discuss both social justice and any hidden motives that might exist. For example, a person in a privileged position may be afraid of losing power, money, or prestige if affirmative-action policies are instituted.)*
3. Do you think schools will be able to recruit minority students if the courts continue to strike down affirmative-action policies? *(Answers will vary. Encourage students to discuss alternative measures being taken in states where affirmative-action policies are no longer in place.)*

Chapter 21 Resource Guide

SECTION RESOURCES

Daily Objectives	Reproducible Resources	Multimedia Resources
Section 1 **Careers in Psychology** Explain how human behavior plays a key role in many areas of study. Understand that the study of psychology can prepare you for many career opportunities.	Guided Reading Activity 21–1 Vocabulary Activity 21–1 Section Quiz 21–1	Daily Focus Transparency 21–1 *ExamView® Assessment Suite* CD-ROM Presentation Plus! Software
Section 2 **Psychology's Contributions** Describe the many contributions that psychology has made to society by promoting human welfare, clarifying assessment methods, explaining human behavior, and helping humans better understand their world.	Guided Reading Activity 21–2 Vocabulary Activity 21–2 Section Quiz 21–2	Daily Focus Transparency 21–2 Vocabulary PuzzleMaker CD-ROM *ExamView® Assessment Suite* CD-ROM Presentation Plus! Software

Blackline Master   CD-ROM   Transparency

Block Schedule

Activities that are particularly suited for use within the block-scheduling framework are identified throughout this chapter by the following designation: **BLOCK SCHEDULING**

KEY TO ABILITY LEVELS

Teaching strategies have been coded for varying learning styles and abilities.

- **L1** **BASIC** activities for all students
- **L2** **AVERAGE** activities for average to above-average students
- **L3** **CHALLENGING** activities for above-average students
- **ELL** **ENGLISH LANGUAGE LEARNER** activities

Chapter 21 Resource Guide

Timesaving Tools

TeacherWorks™ All-In-One Planner and Resource Center

- **Interactive Teacher Edition** Access your Teacher Wraparound Edition and your classroom resources with a few easy clicks.
- **Interactive Lesson Planner** Planning has never been easier! Organize your week, month, semester, or year with all the lesson helps you need to make teaching creative, timely, and relevant.

Use Glencoe's **Presentation Plus!** multimedia teacher tool to easily present dynamic lessons that visually excite your students. Using Microsoft PowerPoint® you can customize the presentations to create your own personalized lessons.

Activity

From the Classroom of...

Art Friedman
formerly of
James Logan High School
Union City, CA

Interest Assessment

Purpose: To help students consider career options that are available in the field of psychology

Tell students that they will be taking a nonscientific interest assessment test. Tell them that there are no right or wrong answers. They will use the answers to the questions to help them identify the areas of psychology that interest them the most. Ask students to write answers to the following questions or statements:

1. What do you have fun doing?
2. What do you do well?
3. List things you feel strongly about.
4. What are your dreams for the future?
5. What is the most exciting thing you have done this school year?

Provide students with a list of various specialties in psychology. Tell students to imagine that they have decided on a career in psychology. Tell them to examine their answers to the five questions and identify the areas of psychology that would be of the most interest to them. For example, an avid athlete may decide that his or her area of interest is sports psychology.

Psychology Online

Use our Web site for additional resources. All essential content is covered in the Student Edition.

You and your students can visit glencoe.com, the Web site companion to *Understanding Psychology*. This innovative integration of electronic and print media offers your students a wealth of opportunities. The student text directs students to the Web site for the following options:

- Chapter Overviews
- Student Web Activities
- Self-Check Quizzes

Answers are provided for you in the **Web Activity Lesson Plan**. Additional Web resources and Interactive Puzzles are also available.

Chapter 21 Resource Guide

Note: The following materials may be used when teaching Chapter 21. Section level support materials are shown at point of use in the margins of the Teacher Wraparound Edition.

TEACHING TRANSPARENCIES

Chapter 21 Concept Transparencies

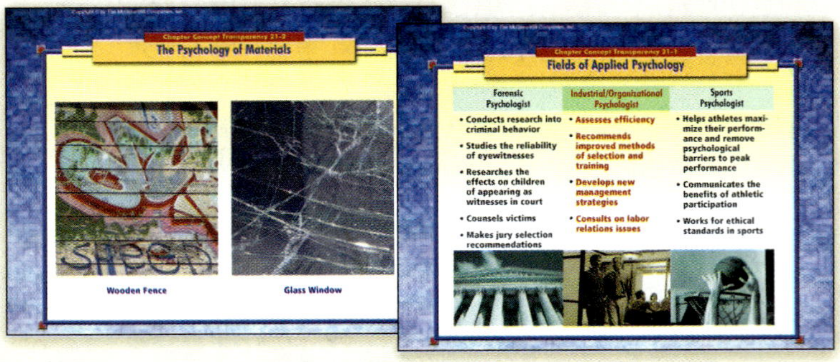

MULTIMEDIA

- Vocabulary PuzzleMaker CD-ROM
- *ExamView® Assessment Suite* CD-ROM
- TeacherWorks™ CD-ROM
- Glencoe Skillbuilder Interactive Workbook, Level 2
- Presentation Plus! Software

REVIEW AND REINFORCEMENT

Reteaching Activity 21

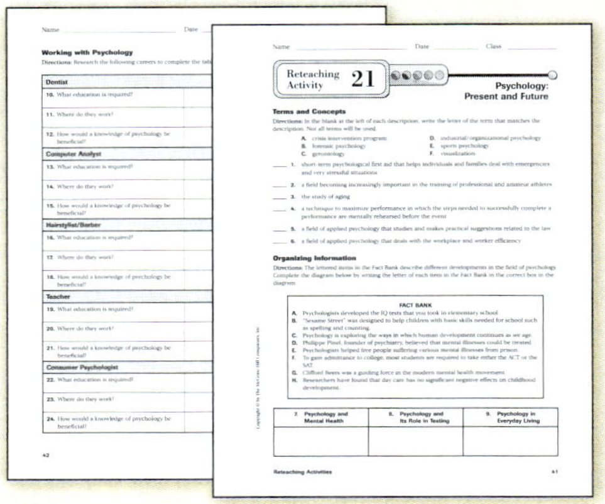

Graphic Organizer Activity 21

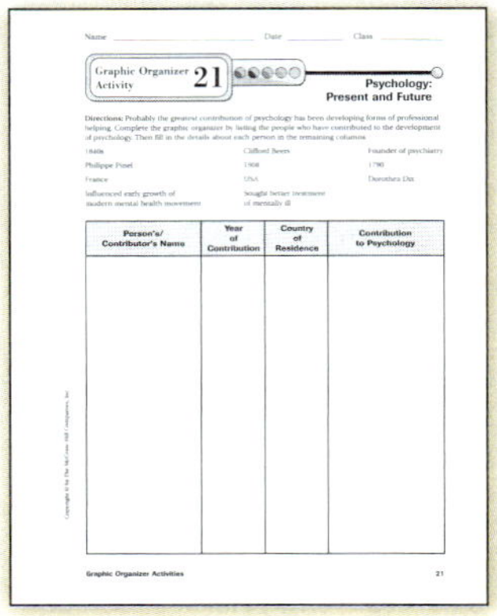

APPLICATION AND HANDS-ON

Psychology Project 21

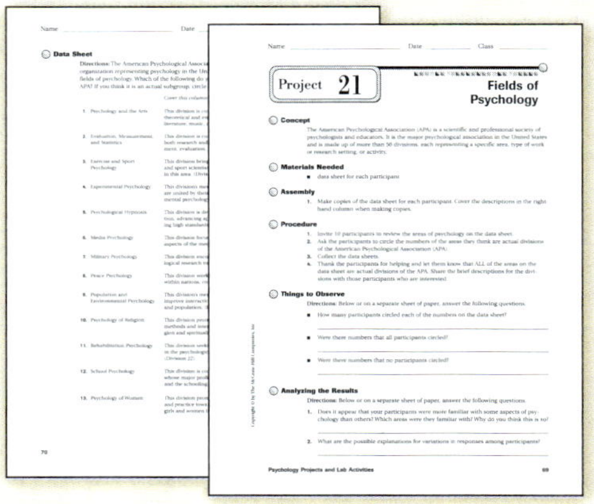

Application Activity 21

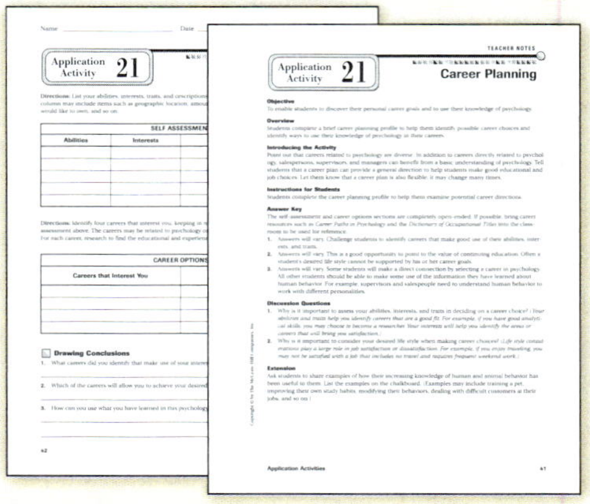

Chapter 21 Resource Guide

ASSESSMENT

Chapter 21 Test, Form A

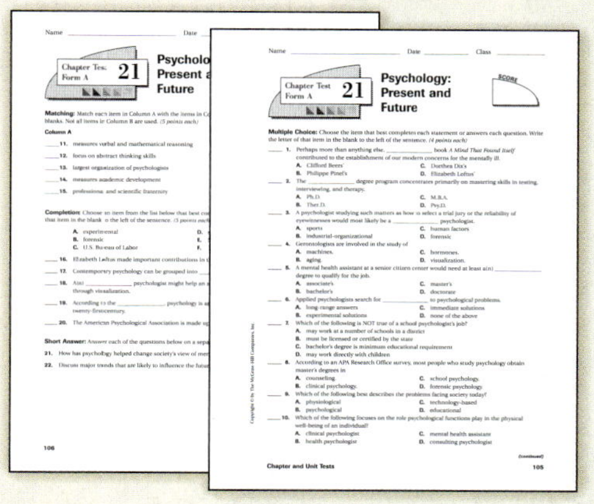

Chapter 21 Test, Form B

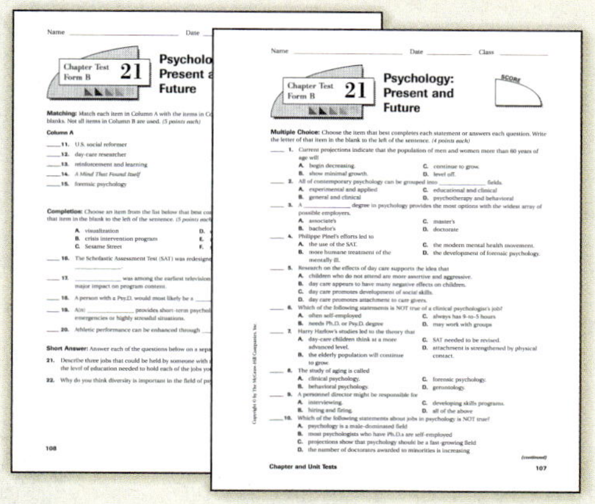

Authentic Assessment Activity 21

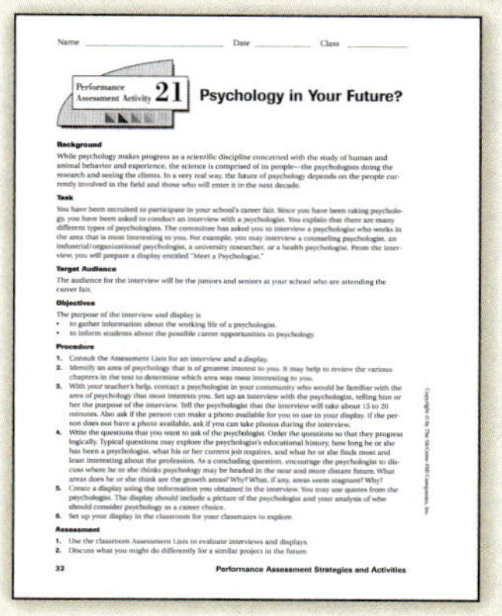

EXTENSION AND ENRICHMENT

Enrichment Activity 21

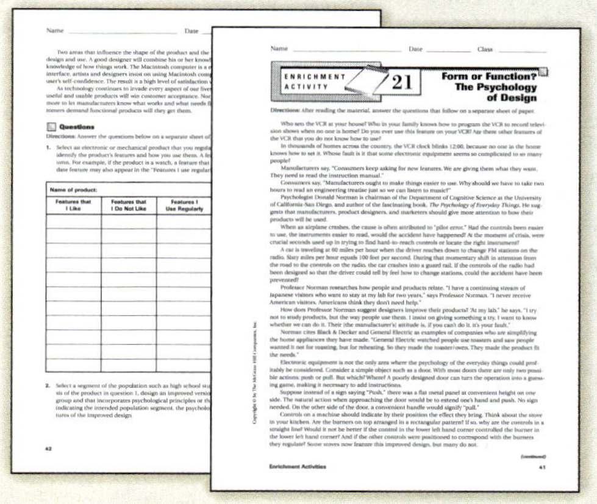

Critical Thinking Skills Activity 21

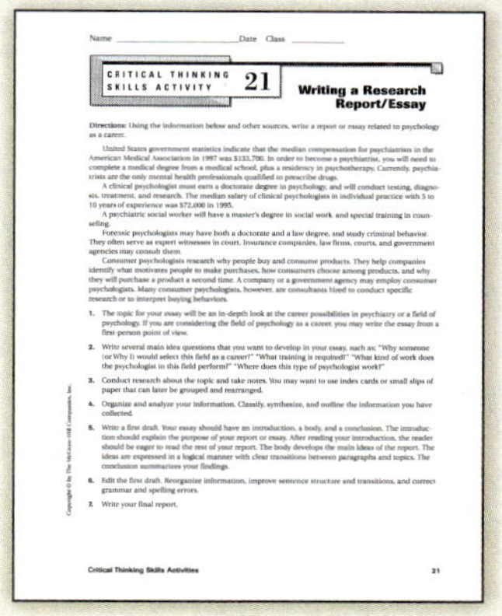

Psychology Reading 21

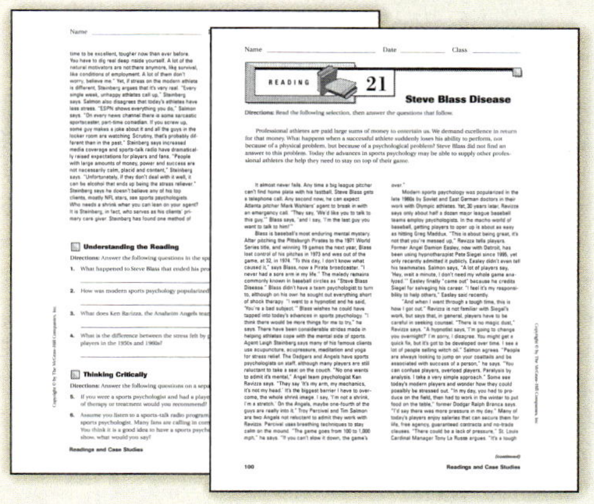

Psychology Case Study 21

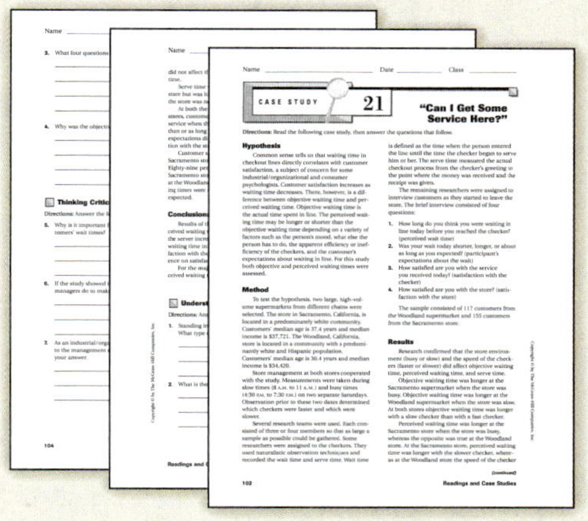

CHAPTER 21 *Introduction*

PSYCHOLOGY Online

Visit glencoe.com for a Chapter Overview for **Chapter 21—Psychology: Present and Future.**

GLENCOE TECHNOLOGY

PRESENTATION Plus! For a preview of Chapter 21 content, see MindJogger Checkpoint on **Presentation Plus!**

PSYCHOLOGY JOURNAL

Help students get started by suggesting categories of problems such as the environment, crime, education, racial and ethnic conflict, and so on.

This journal activity provides the basis for the Psychology Journal activity exercise in the Chapter Assessment. ■

CHAPTER 21

Psychology: Present and Future

PSYCHOLOGY JOURNAL

What do you think will be the most serious problem in this century? Write your answer in your journal. ■

PSYCHOLOGY Online

Chapter Overview
Visit the *Understanding Psychology* Web site at glencoe.com and click on **Chapter 21—Chapter Overviews** to preview the chapter.

602

TWO-MINUTE LESSON LAUNCHER

Explain that the *Annual Review of Psychology* contains predictions for future developments in psychology. For example, a recent review discusses the effect of health-enhancing and health-impairing behaviors on life-threatening diseases. These discoveries may revolutionize the way we think about the workings of the mind. There also may be advances made by new, testable theories and new technologies. Ask students to brainstorm examples of mysteries about the human mind and human behavior that we do not yet fully understand. Then ask them to rank these examples to identify what they think are the three most important mysteries that psychology can still unlock.

SECTION 1 Careers in Psychology

Reader's Guide

■ Main Idea

Human behavior plays a key role in many areas of study. Studying psychology can prepare you for many career opportunities.

■ Vocabulary

- crisis intervention program

■ Objectives

- Outline the requirements needed to become a psychologist.
- List several careers available in psychology.

EXPLORING PSYCHOLOGY

Choosing My Destiny

Many of the students at the school had been given intelligence tests and scored at the lowest and most handicapped level. Yet it was evident that these young people had skills that were relevant to their culture. I recall a Down's syndrome child who could beat out complex rhythms on the drum, young women who learned to card and weave rugs from foster grandparents, and Yazzie, our survival artist, who could go for days in very severe weather conditions with little clothing or food and would turn up in a distant town days later seemingly no worse for wear. Obviously, the intelligence tests were missing something that was very important.

—from "Pathways to Change and Development: The Life of a School Psychologist" by Stephen F. Poland, in *Career Paths in Psychology,* edited by Robert J. Sternberg

In the passage above, author Stephen Poland describes his experiences with teaching a group of mentally challenged Navajo children. This adventure led him to seek his destiny and his career—becoming a school psychologist.

CAREERS IN PSYCHOLOGY

"What are you going to do when you get out of school?"

"Beats me. My grandparents want me to learn the shoe business and take over when they retire. Mom and Dad want me to think about law as

SECTION RESOURCES

Reproducible Masters

- Guided Reading Activity 21–1
- Vocabulary Activity 21–1
- Section Quiz 21–1

Transparencies

- Daily Focus Transparency 21–1

Multimedia

- *ExamView® Assessment Suite* CD-ROM
- Presentation Plus! Software

1 FOCUS

Section Objectives

1. Outline the requirements needed to become a psychologist.
2. List several careers available in psychology.

BELLRINGER
Motivational Activity

Project Daily Focus Transparency 21–1 and have students answer the questions.

Available as blackline master

Daily Focus Transparency 21–1

Reader's Guide

Use the Reader's Guide to introduce concepts and vocabulary.

■ Exploring Psychology

Ask students to read the **Exploring Psychology** feature and then discuss the following question: **What types of intelligence are now recognized by psychologists?**

■ Vocabulary Precheck

Have students read the Glossary definition of the term. Then have them make a list of the crises for which your community may offer intervention programs.

CHAPTER 21

Section 1, pages 603–608

2 TEACH

L1 Role-Play Explain to students that working as a crisis hot line adviser is just one of the many practical applications of psychology. Bring a telephone directory to class, and point out the listings for the various kinds of hot lines that serve your community. Call on various pairs of volunteers to improvise the crises that different kinds of hot line advisers might be expected to handle. After each skit, ask the participants to discuss how they felt. **Ask:** **What, if any, stress did the adviser experience? How did the caller feel about the effect of the conversation?** Encourage the class to share their observations about how the two actors responded to the situation.

Figure 21.1

Visual Instruction Assign students to research each field of psychology listed and give a brief report to the class about what is involved in the specialty.

Caption Answer Clinical/Counseling/School psychology has experienced the greatest amount of growth over the past 30 years.

Reading Check Answer Psychology is an area of study focused on how people perceive, think, feel, and act. It is also a career that applies psychological principles to help people.

Figure 21.1 Areas of Expertise of Ph.D. Psychologists

Over the past 30 years, the number of people receiving doctorate degrees in the field of psychology has grown by nearly 170 percent. ***Which area of expertise has enjoyed the greatest growth?***

	1975	1995	2004
Clinical/Counseling/School	35%	50%	53%
Experimental/Comparative/Physiological	17%	16%	2%
Developmental/Child/Social/Personality	14%	13%	2%
Educational	5%	3%	7%
Industrial/Organizational	3%	3%	2%
Other psychology subfields	26%	15%	34%

Sources: NSF/SRS Surveys of Doctorate Recipients; *Digest of Education Statistics*, 2005.

a career. I was leaning toward business administration, but my sister just graduated with an M.B.A. I don't want to be just like her. I've got more choices than I can handle."

This conversation is imaginary but typical for juniors and seniors in high school. You do have many options. Because you have spent a period of time studying psychology, it may be beneficial to respond to questions about psychology: What will I do with what I have learned? Was it worth it if this is the only psychology course I ever take? What careers in psychology are open to me? To help you find answers to these questions, this section offers several descriptions of opportunities in psychology careers. The careers described here, though, are only a few in the vast field of psychology and related fields.

What Are Employers Looking For?

Employers are most likely to hire someone who offers special skills. In psychology, as in many other fields, job choices are limited if you have only a high school diploma. Surprisingly, when you have a Ph.D., you also have relatively few choices, but by that time you have chosen to fine-tune your education and experience for a specific kind of job; you are a specialist.

Those with a bachelor's degree in psychology may have the most options with the widest array of possible employers. Moreover, psychology is a logical undergraduate major for those planning graduate work in such fields as sociology, social work, law, medicine, or education. Human behavior plays a key role in all of these areas.

Some Career Options

Reading Check How is psychology both a science and a profession?

Psychology is both a science and a profession. As a science, psychologists study how people perceive, think, feel, and act. In the professional arena, careers that are based on psychological principles seek to predict how people will act; help people modify their behavior; and help organizations, businesses, and communities to change.

Crisis Hot Line Adviser

crisis intervention program: short-term psychological first aid that helps individuals and families deal with emergencies or highly stressful situations

Employer: a large hospital

Can you do it? A person holding this job might be a senior in high school. For **crisis intervention programs,** applicants must complete a comprehensive training program. A county hospital, for instance, might offer

COOPERATIVE LEARNING ACTIVITY

Writing a Monologue Organize students into seven groups, and assign each team one of the job categories discussed in this section. Instruct students to write a short monologue in which a person describes what he or she does for a living. Tell students to avoid using the job title or any words that directly refer to it. When the groups have prepared the activity, request a member of each group to deliver the monologue. Challenge other students to guess the job being described. **BLOCK SCHEDULING**

such training over three weekends. Following training, a typical assignment would involve two 4-hour shifts a week.

What's involved? Crisis hot line personnel respond primarily to two kinds of problems. One involves the immediate, possibly life-threatening situation that can arise as a result of a personal or family crisis—perhaps an argument or the unexpected death of a loved one. Drug use, whether from withdrawal or overdose, can also bring about an immediate need for help. The other type of problem is the crisis evolving from long-term stress, such as that experienced in the family, on the job, or in a failure to develop one's career. Crises like these are not as threatening, but still need to be resolved.

A person handling a hot line will have a list of psychologists and counselors as well as information about a wide array of treatment facilities and programs operating in the vicinity. This job requires being able to calm the caller, identify his or her problem, and help that caller to see the wisdom—once the immediate crisis has been dealt with—of contacting the most appropriate agency or professional for long-term follow-up.

Word Processor Salesperson

Employer: a local computer dealer

Can you do it? People with an interest in psychology are likely to have a higher-than-average interest in behavior—both theirs and others. That interest, even if backed only by a high school diploma, is a vital element of the successful salesperson. One report suggests that the best salespeople are motivated by the need for status, control, respect, routine, accomplishment, stimulation, and honesty. With those needs met, a salesperson will feel happy regardless of level of education. A basic understanding of people's driving forces—their needs for achievement, affiliation, and safety—is but one aspect of psychology that would aid someone seeking a career in sales.

What's involved? The key requirement may be experience. One psychologist has suggested that you cannot educate someone to be good in sales, but sensitivity to others can be improved by training. You must also be persistent, skillful at language, able to query prospective customers, and able to relate their needs to those answered by the product you are offering.

Mental Health Assistant

Employer: a senior citizen service center

Can you do it? This is a new career field, usually requiring at least an associate degree. An associate degree is

Psychology and You

Try Out a Career in Psychology

As you search the want ads in your local newspaper, you may not see very many entry-level job openings for psychologists. There are jobs, though, that can expose you to psychology-related work. Look for jobs that utilize people skills, such as communicating or relating to people; analytical skills, such as figuring out and resolving problems; writing skills, such as writing logical reports; and research skills, such as using statistics or tables to analyze issues. These skills are called for in a variety of jobs, such as working for case workers, business managers, probation or corrections officers, city managers, and human services.

Psychology Journal

Tell students to imagine that they are a salesperson in a technology store. Instruct them to write a sales pitch to sell a DVD player to another teen. Challenge them to identify how their knowledge of psychology has helped them formulate the sales pitch. ■

Guided Reading Activity 21-1

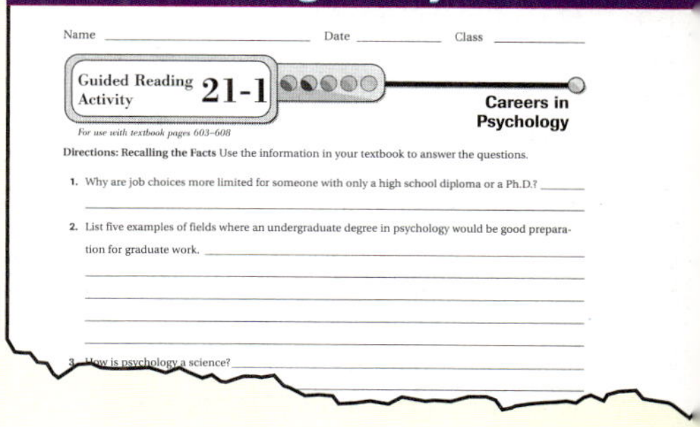
Name ______ Date ______ Class ______

Guided Reading Activity 21-1 — Careers in Psychology

For use with textbook pages 603–608

Directions: Recalling the Facts Use the information in your textbook to answer the questions.

1. Why are job choices more limited for someone with only a high school diploma or a Ph.D.? ______
2. List five examples of fields where an undergraduate degree in psychology would be good preparation for graduate work. ______
3. How is psychology a science? ______

Readings and Case Studies in Psychology

Have students read the Chapter 21 Case Study selection in *Readings and Case Studies in Psychology* and answer the questions that follow the case study.

Psychology and You

Use the following question to direct a class discussion after students have read the **Psychology and You** feature.

Ask: Why do so many jobs use the skills you have learned about in this psychology course?

MEETING SPECIAL NEEDS

Learning Style: Intrapersonal Ask students to write their educational, career, and personal goals for the next five years. Tell students that goals should state their dreams in measurable terms. Then ask students to examine their goals and write a paper that describes how they will use the knowledge gained in the psychology class to set and reach intermediate and terminal goals. Have students include a paragraph on each goal and the related insights from psychology class that will help them attain it. **L2** **BLOCK SCHEDULING**

Refer to ***Inclusion for the High School Social Studies Classroom Strategies and Activities*** in the TCR for strategies for students with different learning styles.

Profiles In Psychology

Ask students to read the **Profiles In Psychology** feature and then discuss the following questions:

1. How does Linda McCarley help people? *(She helps people create drawings, paintings, sculptures, and other art forms that provide glimpses into their inner worlds.)*
2. How can artmaking help people? *(It provides avenues of self-expression, helps release tension, and is life-enhancing.)*
3. How do art therapists help their clients? *(They set the stage for self-discovery and healing by facilitating their clients' creative expressions.)*

Vocabulary Activity 21–1

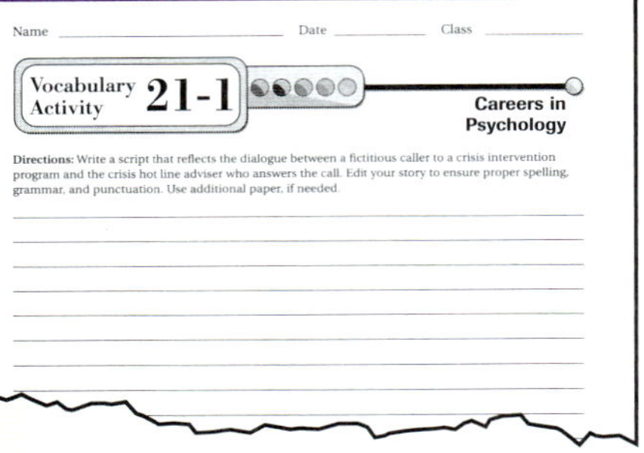
Name ______ Date ______ Class ______

Vocabulary Activity 21-1 — Careers in Psychology

Directions: Write a script that reflects the dialogue between a fictitious caller to a crisis intervention program and the crisis hot line adviser who answers the call. Edit your story to ensure proper spelling, grammar, and punctuation. Use additional paper, if needed.

TEACHER Tip

Make sure students understand the difference between a Doctor of Philosophy (Ph.D.), a Doctor of Psychology (Psy.D.), and a Doctor of Medicine (M.D.).

Profiles In Psychology

Linda L. McCarley

1946–

"Artmaking opens windows to the inner world."

Linda L. McCarley, an art therapist, is founder and director of the Art Therapy Institute in Dallas, Texas. She helps people create drawings, paintings, sculptures, and other art forms that provide a glimpse into their inner world.

How does art therapy work? Have you ever felt better after expressing yourself with music, dance, drama, or art? That is because words may not adequately express some of your deepest feelings or life experiences. Artmaking provides another avenue of self-expression, helps release tension, and is known to be life enhancing. As we can see by studying the images etched on the walls of caves dating back to ancient times, people have always relied upon imagery to express their most significant life experiences. The art made by people throughout history enriches our understanding of those people.

Similarly, art therapists gain an understanding of their clients through the process of making art in therapy. Art therapists set the stage for self-discovery and healing by facilitating their clients' creative expressions.

awarded after a two-year course preparing for paraprofessional occupations in nursing homes, community mental health centers, centers dealing with mental retardation, or even special-education centers for the variously disabled in public schools.

What's involved? Typically supervised by a staff psychologist, an assistant helps with or conducts admission interviews. He or she may be responsible—under supervision—for administering various psychological tests, either to new patients or to assess the progress of those already admitted.

Personnel Director

Employer: a large department store, for example

Can you do it? The successful applicant is likely to have a bachelor's degree in psychology, having concentrated on courses involving interviewing, test construction and interpretation, statistics, and law. Such a person might also have taken a minor in management courses in a university's College of Business Administration. He or she would stress organizational and quantitative skills. This is not an entry-level job, however. Some prior experience with the employer's policies is a definite requirement.

What's involved? A personnel director may participate in a wide array of activities, depending on the nature and interest of his or her employer. This person's responsibility would include some involvement in the decisions to hire and fire, especially for the support staff in an organization. Such a person might also develop programs to improve or maintain staff skills in sales, interpersonal sensitivity, or any other area involved in conducting the company's business.

CRITICAL THINKING ACTIVITY

Demonstrating Reasoned Judgment Provide the following statistics about various fields in which psychologists work (taken from the 2003 Survey of Doctorate Recipients, National Research Council and National Science Foundation): *Independent Practice, 6.0%; University/College, 28.2%; Other Educational Settings, 11.5%; Government, 21.9%, Private for Profit, 27.8%, and Private, Nonprofit, 4.2%.* Ask students to present this data in the form of a circle or bar graph. Based on these graphs, **ask:** **In what fields do most psychologists work? In which field do you think each of these might work: (a) experimental psychologist, (b) psychoanalyst, (c) mental health assistant, and (d) industrial/organizational psychologist?** Students should be able to explain each choice. **L2**

School Psychologist

Employer: a city school system

Can you do it? A master's degree is a must for this position; an undergraduate major in psychology is desirable. In addition, most school psychologists must be licensed or certified in their state of employment, which involves taking a test.

What's involved? In bigger districts, you might stay in one school, but many school psychologists divide their time among a number of schools. They usually work with children experiencing the normal array of problems in school. A school psychologist might give reading, aptitude, interest, or intelligence tests and must be skillful in interpreting them. At other times he or she might work directly with the children or young adults in school or with the families of those students.

Clinical Psychologist

Employer: self-employed, government, business, hospital, prison, or nonprofit organization

Can you do it? To use this title in most states requires a Ph.D. (a Doctor of Philosophy) or a Psy.D. (a Doctor of Psychology). The Psy.D. is a degree developed in the 1970s. In a Psy.D. program, a student gains skill in psychotherapy, undergoing intensive training in testing, interviewing, and giving supervised therapy.

What's involved? A practicing clinical psychologist is often self-employed. Thus, required skills include those needed to run any small business, in addition to knowledge of testing and practical experience with the limits and strengths of various forms of therapy. He or she must develop working relations with other clinicians in the area—psychiatrists, medical doctors, and other contacts in local hospitals and mental health facilities. From such sources come the patient/client referrals that are vital to one's success as a psychotherapist.

A typical day might involve 8 to 10 hours in various stages of psychotherapy with different individuals. The hours have to be offered at times when clients are free to visit, so this may not be a traditional 9-to-5 job. Other types of therapy a clinical psychologist might offer are group therapy or consultation with other therapeutic organizations, such as Alcoholics Anonymous. It is also possible, of course, to utilize the same skills as a clinical psychologist in a state-supported mental hospital, a Veterans Administration hospital, or a community mental health center.

Figure 21.2 Consumer Psychology

Consumer psychologists study the processes people go through as they purchase goods and services. Organizations hire them to research and answer questions such as "What do consumers think of us?" and "How can we better serve our customers?" ***Why might consumer psychologists be involved in employee training?***

More About...

Human Factors Engineering

Human factors engineers, or engineering psychologists, help design machines and equipment, such as computer systems, automobiles, office equipment, and household appliances, to match human abilities and limitations. Their goal is to create equipment that can be operated efficiently and safely. Human factors engineers draw on physics, anatomy, psychology, sociology, and contributions from teachers and communications experts to analyze and solve problems. Consider this example: Why is the gas pedal on the right side of your car's floor rather than on the left? The reason is for more efficient use. Most people are right-side dominant and use the gas pedal more than the brake.

Figure 21.2

Caption Answer They may train salespeople and customer service representatives to anticipate, understand, or respond better to customers' wants and needs.

PSYCHOLOGY Update

Student-Counselor Ratios Experts agree that the student-counselor ratio in middle and high schools should be 300 to 1. In the 1999–2000 school year, the ratio in Los Angeles County averaged 890 to 1. Counselors often have contact with 100 to 200 adolescents per day, most for just a minute or two. Often, minor problems have to become serious before the counselors have time to help. The challenge faced by society is to acknowledge the importance of school counselors and find a way to increase the funding to hire more of them.

3 ASSESS

Assign Section 1 Assessment as homework or as an in-class activity.

PSYCHOLOGY LAB EXPERIMENT

Conducting a Product Survey Tell students they are consumer psychologists working for a large food manufacturer. The company is developing a new health bar that contains all the nutrients needed for a meal with only 25 percent of the calories. Assign students to work in pairs to develop a survey that will find out what flavors, colors, and sizes are preferred by the following categories: men and women, 15- to 20-year-olds, 21- to 25-year-olds, and 26- to 30-year-olds. The survey should provide a description of the product and then ask 3 to 5 questions to determine the preferences. Students should chart the results and use them to make a written recommendation to the product development team. **L2**

CHAPTER 21

Section 1, pages 603–608

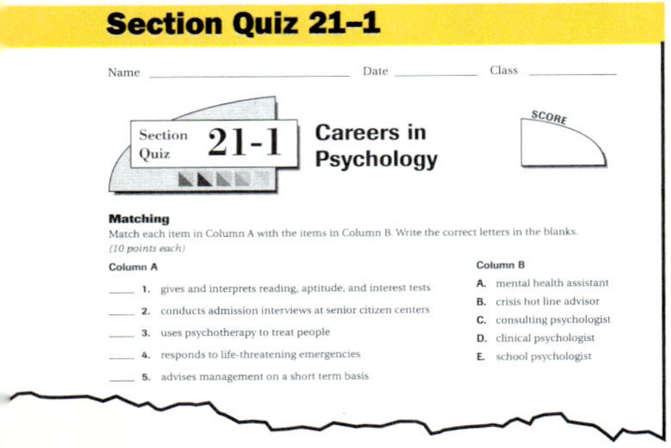

Section Quiz 21-1

Name ________ Date ________ Class ________

Section Quiz 21-1 **Careers in Psychology**

SCORE

Matching

Match each item in Column A with the items in Column B. Write the correct letters in the blanks. *(10 points each)*

Column A	Column B
____ 1. gives and interprets reading, aptitude, and interest tests	A. mental health assistant
____ 2. conducts admission interviews at senior citizen centers	B. crisis hot line advisor
____ 3. uses psychotherapy to treat people	C. consulting psychologist
____ 4. responds to life-threatening emergencies	D. clinical psychologist
____ 5. advises management on a short term basis	E. school psychologist

Reteach

Ask students to brainstorm a list of jobs that seem interesting to them. For each job on the list, students should identify the special skills that may be required for success. Then have students explain how their knowledge of psychology could help them in that job.

Enrich

Have students select one of the careers mentioned in this section. For that career, have students write a personality profile for someone who would be good at that career.

4 CLOSE

Ask students to reread the job descriptions in this section. Then have them discuss the advantages and disadvantages of each of them.

Did You Know?

Postwar Psychology The demand for the services of counseling and clinical psychologists always increases dramatically toward the end of a war. This occurred at the end of World War II, the Korean War, the Vietnam War, and the Persian Gulf War. Counseling psychologists are needed to help servicemen and women adjust to civilian life, shift war-industry workers, and rehabilitate the wounded and emotionally disturbed war veterans.

Consulting Psychologist

Employer: a management consulting firm

Can you do it? A Ph.D. is required for this job. Such a person might spend graduate school in an industrial/organizational psychology program learning management practices, testing strategies, interpersonal behavioral strategies, and intervention techniques in complex organizations.

What's involved? By the very nature of his or her job, a consultant must offer an array of skills not normally represented among the full-time employees of companies that hire consultants. Thus, a consultant's job tends to be short term. A consultant might, for instance, advise a company's top management on how to take human performance limits into account in the design of a control board for a nuclear power plant. He or she might be involved in all aspects of the design of an interstate highway—signs, bridges and crossover devices, and lane-flow control.

Future Psychology Career Options

As psychologists in every specialty area meet new challenges, new areas of psychology begin to develop. Often a new area of psychology develops as a result of a merging of other areas. For example, the relatively new area of health psychology combines aspects of physiological, social, counseling, and clinical psychology. Health psychologists focus on the role the psychological functions of an individual play on the health of that individual. A health psychologist might research the origins of obesity and try to find and apply effective treatments. A health psychologist might also deal with how stress is related to illness.

SECTION 1 Assessment

1. **Review the Vocabulary** What types of situations does a crisis intervention program handle?
2. **Visualize the Main Idea** Use a graphic organizer similar to the one below to list a possible psychology career under each discipline.

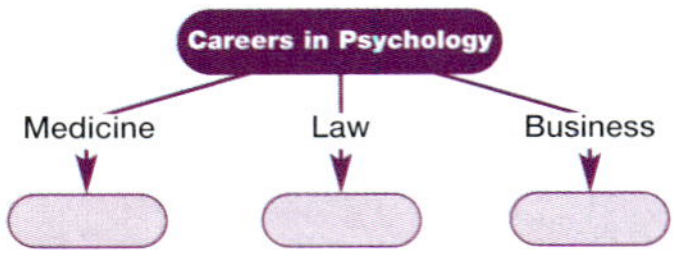

3. **Recall Information** What qualities are most employers seeking in employees?
4. **Think Critically** How might a degree in psychology help you design a popular Web page or market yourself as an up-and-coming actor?
5. **Application Activity** Explore your long-term goals by outlining a possible educational and career path that you might follow. In your outline be sure to indicate your career goal and how you plan to achieve that goal. Explain why you have selected that goal.

SECTION 1 Assessment Answers

1. They handle immediate, life-threatening family or personal situations, or problems involving long-term stress.
2. Medicine—mental health adviser; law—law enforcement; business—consulting psychologist
3. Employers want people with specialized skills. Students may also suggest that employers would want employees who are mature, responsible, cooperative, and so on.
4. Students' answers will vary. Students' answers should reflect an understanding of the basic psychological concepts discussed in this book. Examples include persuasion techniques used to attract people to your Web page.
5. Tell students that it is often helpful to break long-term goals into measurable short-term objectives. Also, remind them that goals can change over time.

Case Studies

Parapsychology

Period of Study: 1882 and 1975

Introduction: Scientists sometimes investigate behavior or events that seem to have fantastic origins. In psychology, this area of study is known as *parapsychology*, which means "alongside psychology." Parapsychology is not considered to be in the mainstream of psychology, but its controversial issues have attracted many people. Parapsychologists suggest that humans possess senses other than the known seven—vision, hearing, taste, smell, touch, balance, and body senses. People skeptical of this suggestion point to the fact that the evidence supporting parapsychology's claims never stands up to rigorous testing.

Hypothesis: Parapsychology's advocates often state their claims in such a way that they are not subject to disproof; in other words, the claims are not testable, scientific hypotheses. As a result, many investigators approach these claims by trying to eliminate all other reasonable explanations for the observed behaviors.

Method: In 1882, scientists established the first organization to study parapsychology, the Society of Psychical Research, in London. The American version of this society was formed in Boston three years later. These organizations focused on mediumship, or communication with those who have died. As time passed, other phenomena began to be studied, such as telepathy (the ability of people to communicate without using ordinary senses), clairvoyance (the ability to experience an event without physically being there), and psychokinesis (controlling objects with the mind).

Perhaps the most famous attempts to demonstrate psychokinesis were made by Uri Geller. Geller claimed he could bend and break metal objects by using his mind. On nonscientifically controlled occasions, Geller did appear to bend or break objects without touching them. In 1974, psychologists filmed several encounters with Geller. In one instance, Geller unbalanced a precision scale, and in another, he appeared to bend a steel band. Many people believed Geller really did all this with psychokinetic power; however, skeptics debunked Geller's claims.

Results: The events surrounding Geller were highly controversial; for him, they were highly profitable. He began making appearances in various locations, bending spoons or similar objects. He eventually received an invitation to appear on national television, but when it was time to perform, Geller failed to deliver. It was discovered that he had access before all of his performances to the objects he was hoping to bend. On television, however, his personal set of objects had been switched with a new set, and Geller was left to claim that something was blocking his amazing "abilities."

Geller's claim that his abilities were blocked illustrates one difference between science and belief. Scientists accept the results of well-designed tests, whether their hypotheses are supported or not. Geller rejected the disconfirming observations, adding a vague explanation after the fact to explain unsatisfying results. The effects allegedly produced by parapsychological phenomena have much simpler explanations—sleight of hand or prior manipulation to bend spoons, hidden magnets to deflect compasses, and the like. Perhaps breakthroughs will occur in the study of parapsychology. However, for now, healthy skepticism prevails.

Analyzing the Case Study

1. What is parapsychology?
2. What abilities did Geller claim to have?
3. **Critical Thinking** Do you believe that some people have parapsychological abilities? Why or why not?

Going Further

Testing the Paranormal

One argument against the existence of paranormal phenomena is that the alleged occurrences cannot be replicated under scientific conditions. Testing often reveals simpler explanations for the observed behavior.

A humorous, yet revealing, example of science explaining a supposedly paranormal event took place in 1994. In England, a man claimed that a dog had psychic powers and was able to sense when its absent owner had begun her homeward journey. Allegedly, the dog would run to the porch at that precise moment, and there await its owner's imminent arrival.

When a television crew arrived at the house to film the occurrence, the animal appeared to perform as advertised. Two psychologists were then called in to set up an experiment in order to test the animal. Making sure the dog received no sensory clues from any of the observers or participants, and randomly selecting the owner's departure and return times, the scientists carefully monitored the dog through four trials. In each, the animal failed to detect when its owner began her journey home. They did discover, though, that the dog frequently ran to the porch at the approach of children, animals, people, cars, and sometimes at random. Thus, the dog was often sitting on the porch when its owner arrived. The source of the animal's behavior was not the paranormal, it was just chance related.

Discussing the Case Study

Ask: **How might someone's claim to have these perceptions be proved or disproved? What is the most likely explanation for Gellar's failure to perform his abilities on national television?**

Answers for Analyzing the Case Study

1. Parapsychology is the study of behavior and events that cannot be explained by mainstream psychology. Parapsychology suggests that humans possess senses other than the known seven.
2. He claimed to be able to bend and break metal objects by using mind control only.
3. Answers will vary. Ask students to back up their points of view with specific examples.

1 FOCUS

Section Objectives

1. Describe psychologists' contributions in everyday life.
2. Summarize psychology's challenges for the future.

BELLRINGER
Motivational Activity

Project Daily Focus Transparency 21–2 and have students answer the questions.

Also available as blackline master

Daily Focus Transparency 21–2

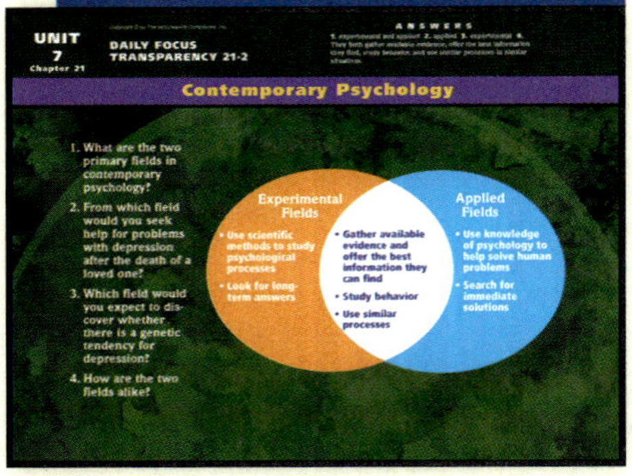

Reader's Guide

Use the Reader's Guide to introduce concepts and vocabulary.

Exploring Psychology
Ask students to read the **Exploring Psychology** feature and then discuss the following question: **What was the taxi driver's view of what psychologists do?**

Vocabulary Precheck
Have students create a crossword puzzle using the definitions of the terms for the clues. Then have pairs of students trade and complete each other's puzzles.

Use the **Vocabulary PuzzleMaker CD-ROM** to create crossword and word search puzzles.

SECTION 2 Psychology's Contributions

Reader's Guide

Main Idea

Psychology has made many contributions to society by promoting human welfare, clarifying assessment methods, explaining human behavior, and helping humans better understand their world.

Vocabulary

- ACT
- SAT
- forensic psychology
- industrial/organizational psychology
- sports psychology
- visualization
- gerontology

Objectives

- Describe psychologists' contributions in everyday life.
- Summarize psychology's challenges for the future.

EXPLORING PSYCHOLOGY

Misinformed

A few years ago, a psychology professor, famous in his field for developing new experimental and statistical methods, got into a taxi. He started a friendly conversation with the driver and when asked what he did for a living, the professor replied that he was a psychologist. "Oh yeah? My sister went to see a psychologist," replied the driver. "She's really a nut-case. Hey wait, can you read my mind? I'd better be careful what I say!" The professor reports that he now replies to such questions by saying that he is a "research scientist."

—from *Opportunities in Psychology Careers* by Donald E. Super and Charles M. Super, 2001

Although most people seem to have an accurate idea of what doctors or lawyers do, many people do not realize what psychologists do. These people probably do not realize, then, the many contributions to life that the science of human behavior has produced.

PSYCHOLOGY'S ROLE IN MENTAL HEALTH

Of all of psychology's contributions, perhaps its most significant is the development of forms of professional helping, including psychotherapy. An early step forward came in the 1790s through the pioneering efforts of Philippe Pinel, a French physician and a founder of psychiatry. Pinel unchained patients who were held in mental wards, some of whom had

SECTION RESOURCES

Reproducible Masters

- Guided Reading Activity 21–2
- Vocabulary Activity 21–2
- Section Quiz 21–2

Transparencies

- Daily Focus Transparency 21–2

Multimedia

- Vocabulary PuzzleMaker CD-ROM
- *ExamView®* *Assessment Suite* CD-ROM
- Presentation Plus! Software

been restrained for more than 20 years. Pinel argued against the prevailing belief that the mentally ill were possessed by demons. Moreover, he thought mental illness could be treated. Mainly due to his efforts, France became a leader in improving conditions for the mentally ill.

Despite the progress in France, more than half a century passed before similar efforts were exerted in the United States. After discovering that the mentally ill were being jailed along with criminals, teacher and social reformer Dorothea Dix (1802–1887) became the chief spokesperson for reform. Her personal crusade in the 1840s aroused interest in the problems of mental illness and led to more enlightened treatment of the mentally ill in Canada and Great Britain, as well as in the United States.

A former mental patient, Clifford Beers (1876–1943) became the guiding force in the early growth of the modern mental health movement. Beers's own account of his illness and recovery, *A Mind That Found Itself* (1908), first published nearly 100 years ago, has motivated many concerned individuals to promote better psychological care in communities, in schools, and in hospitals. The book set into motion Beers's plan to improve conditions in mental hospitals. In 1908 Beers founded the Connecticut Society for Mental Hygiene, the first organization of its type. In its charter, the Connecticut Society pledged to eliminate restraints on patients, improve standards of care for the mentally retarded, prevent mental disorders, preserve mental health, and provide information on mental illness to the public.

Figure 21.3 **Before Psychological Illnesses Were Understood**

Often described as the father of scientific psychiatry, Philippe Pinel argued that the mentally ill required humane treatment, sympathy, and guidance, not the beatings, imprisonment, and ridicule they so often suffered. ***Why was Pinel's behavior considered revolutionary?***

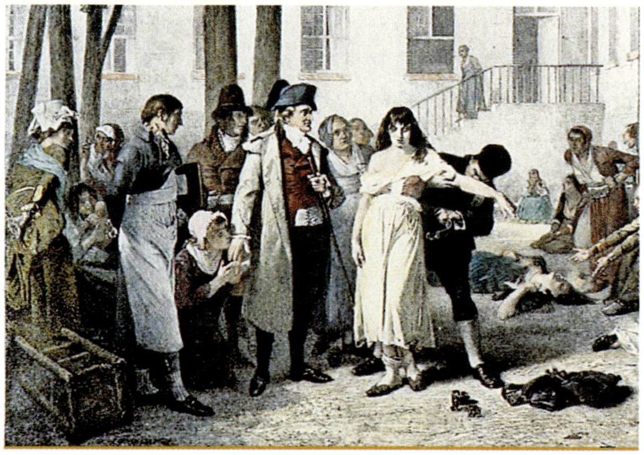

PSYCHOLOGY'S ROLE IN TESTING

Most students are given IQ tests or other tests at an early age. Psychologists have played a leading role in devising and updating these tests, as well as other tests in higher education that assess personal skills. Many of you have taken or will take one or both of the two major standardized college entrance exams: the Scholastic Assessment Test (SAT) and the American College Testing Proficiency Examination Program (ACT). Developed in 1959, the current **ACT** places greater emphasis on scientific concepts and abstract reading skills and less emphasis on factual material than the earlier version. Nearly 1.2 million high school seniors take the ACT each year. The **SAT**, taken by about 1.5 million high school seniors annually, was redesigned in 2005 and now assesses critical reading, math concepts and reasoning, and development and expression of ideas in writing.

ACT: a standardized test that consists of four assessment tests that measure academic development

SAT: a standardized test that is an admission requirement at some colleges; the test measures verbal and mathematical reasoning and writing abilities

2 TEACH

L1 Illustrating an Idea Organize students into nine groups, and assign them the task of creating posters that illustrate the title of this section: "Psychology's Contributions." Assign three groups to focus on contributions to the work environment. Three other groups should focus on contributions to the development of mental health care. The final three groups should explore new areas of research. When the groups have finished their task, have them present their posters to the class. ELL
BLOCK SCHEDULING

Figure 21.3

Caption Answer Pinel argued against the prevailing practices of beating, imprisioning, and ridiculing the mentally ill. He believed mental illness could be treated, and his actions helped change the treatment of the mentally ill.

Guided Reading Activity 21–2

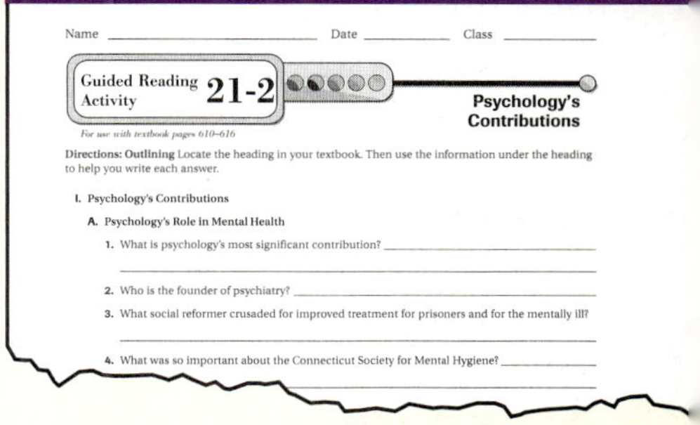
Name ______ Date ______ Class ______

Guided Reading Activity 21-2

Psychology's Contributions

For use with textbook pages 610–616

Directions: Outlining Locate the heading in your textbook. Then use the information under the heading to help you write each answer.

I. Psychology's Contributions

A. Psychology's Role in Mental Health

1. What is psychology's most significant contribution? ______
2. Who is the founder of psychiatry? ______
3. What social reformer crusaded for improved treatment for prisoners and for the mentally ill? ______
4. What was so important about the Connecticut Society for Mental Hygiene? ______

COOPERATIVE LEARNING ACTIVITY

Creating a Time Line Organize students into groups. Assign each group a time period, and have the groups research those periods to find significant events in the history of psychology to include in a master time line. Tell the groups that they may use Figure 21.5 as a guideline. Also, have each group find at least one quote about human behavior that belongs to its assigned time period. When the groups have finished, create a master time line by connecting each group's contributions. Ask the members of each group to share the quote they selected and the reasons for their choice. **BLOCK SCHEDULING**

PSYCHOLOGY Online

Links and instructional guidelines can be found in the **Web Activity Lesson Plan** at glencoe.com.

Psychology Journal

Ask students to reflect on what they have learned in this course. Have them write about the things that surprised them most about psychology, and also the things that disappointed them the most. ■

Cultural Connections

Since World War II, the world has become increasingly interdependent. Today, the countries of the world are linked by trade, travel, the Internet, and so on. At one time, the work of promoting cooperation belonged to diplomats. But today they are joined by cross-cultural psychologists who investigate the similarities and differences in the psychological functioning of different cultures and ethnic groups. These professionals study everything from child-rearing practices to perceptions of beauty. Cross-cultural psychology is predicted to become one of the fastest-growing psychological fields in the twenty-first century.

Figure 21.4

Caption Answer Psychologists answer questions about human behavior, help design learning tools, and provide explanations for the challenges faced as we age.

PSYCHOLOGY Online

Student Web Activity Visit the *Understanding Psychology* Web site at glencoe.com and click on **Chapter 21—Student Web Activities** for an activity about psychology's contributions.

PSYCHOLOGY'S ROLE IN EVERYDAY LIVING

With more than half of all mothers and an even higher percentage of fathers working outside the home, day-care and out-of-home nurturing and learning are significant developmental issues. Researchers note that day care appears to have few negative effects on children and actually promotes development of social skills (Bukatko & Daehler, 2004). Children with experience in day care tend to be more assertive and aggressive. Alison Clarke-Stewart (1993) has suggested that this may result from the fact that day-care children tend to think at a more advanced level but have not yet developed the social skills to smoothly implement their plans for action. Much remains to be learned about how children grow and learn.

Harry Harlow's work led to the idea that the attachment of children to their caregivers is made stronger by physical contact. That, in turn, led to the demonstration that breast-feeding versus bottle-feeding makes little difference in the parent-child attachment. It is the holding, not the feeding, that is most important.

Psychologists play a role in designing and assessing tools for learning in a variety of media; for example, their understanding of the principles of learning contributed to the development of the PBS series *Sesame Street*. Studies show that almost 60 percent of the preschool children who watch that program at least five times a week can recite the entire alphabet correctly. Originally designed to provide creative ways to educate children with skills required in school—such as spelling, counting, and new words—this program, as the data indicate, has met its goal.

Some of B.F. Skinner's ideas on learning have been implemented into computer software designs. The ideas of feedback, prior knowledge and knowledge of results, and reinforcement play important roles in games as well as educational programs.

The work of many psychologists led to a clearer understanding about challenges facing men and women as they age. As the American population ages, increased understanding of the abilities of the aged is an area in which psychology must make continued contributions.

Figure 21.4 Then and Now

Although it is considered a new science, psychology has come a long way. Some of the questions of early psychologists, such as how perception works or why we reason, have been mostly answered. Other questions, such as nature versus nurture, remain the focus of research. ***What have psychologists contributed to everyday living?***

PSYCHOLOGY TODAY

Contemporary psychology can be grouped into experimental fields and applied fields. Experimental

MEETING SPECIAL NEEDS

Learning Style: Verbal/Linguistic Assign students to research countries in which patients with psychological disorders still receive inadequate care. Challenge them to write a speech to be delivered before the United Nations on behalf of these patients. In addition to citing the specific inadequacies in the country's mental health care, the speech should recommend specific suggestions for reform. **L2** **BLOCK SCHEDULING**

Refer to ***Inclusion for the High School Social Studies Classroom Strategies and Activities*** in the TCR for strategies for students with different learning styles.

Figure 21.5 **Some Significant Dates in the History of Psychology**

The history of psychology reflects the origins of many contemporary psychological issues and questions. ***In 1649 René Descartes suggested that the body and soul are separate. How might contemporary psychologists label the "body" and "soul" today?***

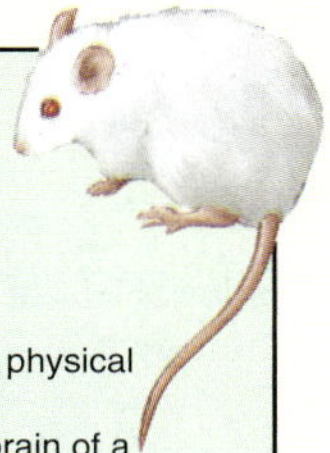

- **170 B.C.** • Claudius Galeno describes the anatomy of the human brain.
- **1649** • René Descartes proposes that the body and soul are totally separate.
- **1651** • Thomas Hobbes argues in *Leviathan* that all human behavior is the result of physical processes.
- **1848** • Jean-Baptiste Bouillard offers 500 francs to anyone who can show him the brain of a human who suffered from speech disturbance and did not have damage to the left frontal lobe.
- **1859** • Karl Marx proposes the idea that social being determines consciousness in *A Contribution to the Critique of Political Economy*.
- **1860** • Paul Broca claims that a specific area (left frontal lobe) of the human brain is responsible for speech.
- **1879** • Wilhelm Wundt establishes the first psychological laboratory at Leipzig University.
- **1884** • William James argues that human behavior can be understood in terms of its purposes or functions.
- **1890** • James McKeen Cattell develops the first psychological tests for individual differences.
- **1891** • American Psychological Association formed at Clark University
- **1901** • Ivan Pavlov discovers the conditioned reflex.
- **1905** • Binet-Simon scale, the first intelligence scale, formulated
- **1912** • William Stern develops the intelligence quotient (IQ).
- **1913** • John B. Watson advocates behaviorism.
- **1920** • Hermann Rorschach develops the inkblot test.
- **1930** • Karl Lashley concludes that complex behavior is the result of neural programs in the brain.
- **1933** • Lev Vygotsky argues that the human mind is a product of history and culture.
- **1951** • Simone de Beauvoir publishes a landmark book on the rights of women *(The Second Sex)*.
- **1954** • The U.S. Supreme Court rules that racially segregated education is inherently illegal in *Brown* v. *Board of Education*, resulting in many psychological studies of social issues.
- **1955** • A federal commission reports that more than 50 percent of the 1,500,000 hospital beds in the U.S. are devoted to patients with mental illness, making mental illness the greatest single U.S. health problem.
- **1966** • The first federal act to protect animal research subjects is enacted in the United States.
- **1971** • B.F. Skinner argues that human behavior is a product of environmental stimuli.
- **1980** • It is estimated that 1 of 10 doctorates granted in the United States is in psychology.
- **1990s** • Various psychologists argue that behavior is determined by social and cultural influences.
- **1995** • First issue of *Psychology, Public Policy, and Law* appears.

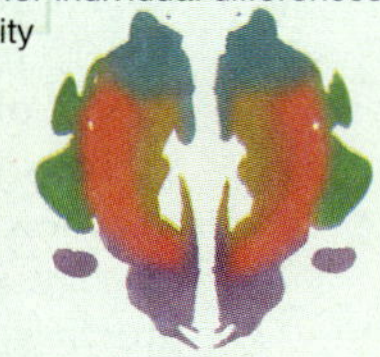

psychologists use a variety of scientific methods to study human and animal behavior. Applied psychologists put knowledge of psychology to work solving human problems. Yet this distinction is not always sharp. Both experimental and the applied psychologists gather the available evidence and offer the best explanation they find. Both study behavior, and both use similar processes in similar situations. A major difference is that applied psychlogists search for immediate solutions, experimental psychologists for long-range answers.

Figure 21.5

Visual Instruction Make sure students know how to read the time line. Then have them select one of the events and explain what they learned about the event or person during this course.

Caption Answer Most psychologists recognize the connection between the mind and the body. Psychologists might label the body as our physiological state and the mind as our cognitive state.

Readings and Case Studies in Psychology

Have students read the Chapter 21 Reading selection in *Readings and Case Studies in Psychology* and answer the questions that follow the reading.

Applying **Psychology**

Explain that psychology makes important contributions to understanding human behavior on a regular basis. Assign students to find five contributions that psychology has made to humanity during their lifetimes. Students should prepare a 2- to 3-page report discussing their findings.

CRITICAL THINKING ACTIVITY

Identifying Central Issues Assign students to research the current and projected demographics of aging in the United States. **Ask:** **What changes in America's politics, social programs, health care systems, and businesses do futurists foresee as the elderly become a larger segment of the overall population?** Ask students to present their statistical findings and their opinions on these questions in the form of a written report or a multimedia presentation. **L2**

Reading Check Answer

Experimental psychologists use the scientific method to study psychological processes. Applied psychologists use the accumulated knowledge gained by psychological studies and experiments to help people solve everyday problems.

Vocabulary Activity 21–2

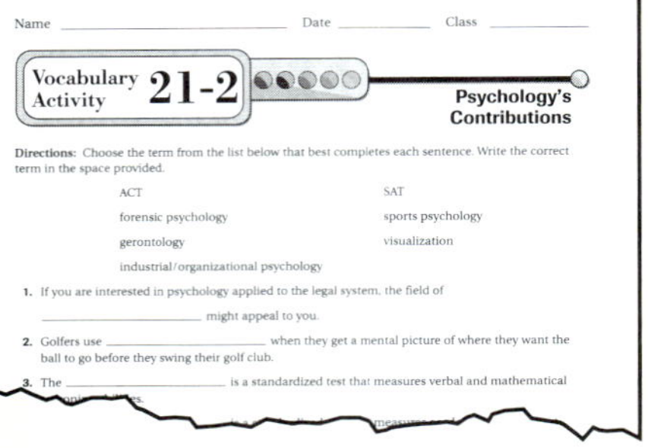
Name ____ Date ____ Class ____

Vocabulary Activity 21-2 Psychology's Contributions

Directions: Choose the term from the list below that best completes each sentence. Write the correct term in the space provided.

ACT	SAT
forensic psychology	sports psychology
gerontology	visualization
industrial/organizational psychology	

1. If you are interested in psychology applied to the legal system, the field of ____ might appeal to you.
2. Golfers use ____ when they get a mental picture of where they want the ball to go before they swing their golf club.
3. The ____ is a standardized test that measures verbal and mathematical

TEACHER Tip

If students have ever wondered how reports of new psychological discoveries manage to find their way into the news media, chances are the reports originated in the APA's Public Affairs Office. Each year this office generates thousands of news releases about psychological advances that could benefit individuals and society.

Figure 21.6

Visual Instruction Explain to students the difference between nonprofit and for-profit private businesses. This may lead to a discussion of the role of profit in making decisions about health care.

Caption Answer Most people who earn a Ph.D. in psychology work in universities and colleges.

Psi Chi is the national honor society of psychology.

Reading Check

How does the work of experimental and applied psychologists differ?

Current Trends

The American Psychological Association (APA) is a scientific and professional society of psychologists and educators. Founded in 1892, it is the major psychological association in the United States and is made up of more than 50 divisions, each representing a specific area, type of work or research setting, or activity. Some divisions are research-oriented, while others are advocacy groups. Together they are a cross section of the diverse nature of psychology.

Beginning in the 1970s, some members expressed dissatisfaction with the direction of the APA. These critics feared that the APA was becoming a professional instead of an academic organization. As a result, a new organization for academic and science-oriented psychologists, the Association for Psychological Science (APS), was founded in 1988; in five years it grew to a membership of 15,000, with slightly more now. With 150,000 members and affiliates, the APA is the world's largest organization of psychologists.

Another organization, Psi Chi, a professional and scientific honor society, has chapters on many college and university campuses. Members of Psi Chi hold meetings and help orient psychology students to the field.

According to the most recent survey completed by the APA Research Office (1996, 1999), about 43 percent of those who study psychology obtain master's degrees in counseling, 32 percent in clinical psychology, and 15 percent in school psychology. The remaining respondents to the survey obtained their degrees in traditional research and other subfields, such as industrial/organizational psychology, general and educational psychology, and experimental psychology (see Figure 21.6).

The United States Bureau of Labor places psychology among the fastest-growing fields into the twenty-first century. In addition, the number of women in psychology has been increasing rapidly. In the early 1990s, women held 60 percent of the civilian jobs in psychology, and women received more than two-thirds of the bachelor's and master's degrees conferred during that time. Although psychology is still a male-dominated field, the proportion of women in psychology is greater than in most other scientific disciplines (APA, 2005).

Ethnic minorities have indeed been a minority in the field of psychology. This trend, however, also seems to be changing. In the past decade, a relatively

Figure 21.6 Employment of Ph.D. Psychologists

Psychology is one of the most diverse fields to enter. Almost all psychologists are trained at colleges and universities, and therefore all psychologists are familiar with the academic setting. ***Where do most people who obtain Ph.D.s in psychology work?***

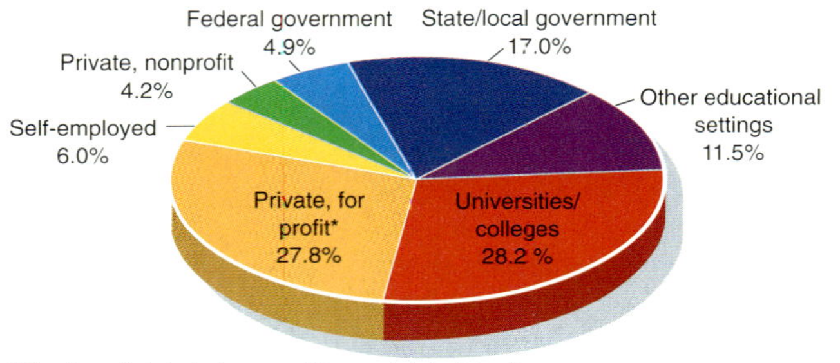

*This category includes businesses and incorporated private practices.

Source: 2003 Survey of Doctorate Recipients, National Research Council and National Science Foundation. Compiled by APA Research Office, August 2005.

PSYCHOLOGY LAB EXPERIMENT

Designing a Visualization Exercise Explain that visualization involves a mental rehearsal of the steps involved in a successful performance or process. Ask students to select an activity that they do well. (Tell students that they are not limited to sporting activities. Examples may include performing in a play, providing first aid, or any other activity with which they are familiar.) Have students write out a visualization plan that could be memorized and quickly rehearsed before performing the activity. If possible, have students try their visualization process and orally report their findings to the class. **L2** **BLOCK SCHEDULING**

larger number of doctorates have been awarded to members of minority groups. The increasing diversity of the field of psychology is important. As diverse people enter the field, they offer new perspectives on issues of psychology and behavior. Although new perspectives can be controversial, they pave the way for scientific advancement (Super & Super, 2001).

Did You Know?

Funding The United States federal government invests about one twenty-fifth of 1 percent of the national budget in psychological research. The APA and APS send representatives to Capitol Hill to appeal for more support. The government spends painfully little to study the nature of human behavior.

Fields of Psychology

Forensic psychology is a branch of applied psychology that studies and makes practical suggestions about the workings of the law. The work of psychologist Elizabeth Loftus has played a pivotal role (see Chapter 10). Many forensic psychologists study criminal behavior. Still others do work on the reliability of eyewitnesses, the effects on children who appear in court, counseling victims, and the jury selection process. A lawyer-psychologist often has both a Ph.D. and a law degree (Hofer, 1991).

Work and the working environment are the provinces of **industrial/organizational psychology,** or, as the field is often called, organizational psychology (Schneider et al., 2005). Psychologists in this field apply their findings to help businesses and industries operate more efficiently and humanely through improving methods of selection and training, and developing new organizational and management strategies. Other industrial/organizational psychologists concentrate on such issues as labor-union relations, rules defining harassment, job satisfaction, and worker motivations and incentives.

Sports psychology, a field that developed during the 1980s, is an important part of training for many amateur and professional athletes. Sports psychologists apply the principles of psychology to sports activities. Some focus on maximizing athletic performance through **visualization**—mentally rehearsing the steps of a complete, successful performance—improving concentration or relaxation or reducing negative thoughts that may interfere with performance. Other areas of study include the psychological and physiological benefits of sports participation, violence, ethics in sports, and the design of safe equipment (Durkin, 1991).

The Challenges for Psychology

Social change, urban problems, early learning, the neural bases of behavior, psychology and minorities, and the reduction of violence are psychology's challenges today. One way to determine future directions of psychology is by analyzing the trends of age in the population. The average age of the citizens in North America is going steadily upward; there are more people over age 65 in the United States and Canada now than at any time in the history of either country. That creates new problems for psychologists to study and new careers in both research and service. It also suggests a growing specialty in the field of developmental psychology—**gerontology,** the study of aging.

forensic psychology: the study of the diagnosis, evaluation, treatment, and testimony regarding the law and criminal behavior

industrial/organizational psychology: the study of behavioral elements of the workplace

sports psychology: the study of athletics and athletic performance

visualization: mentally rehearsing the steps involved in a successful performance or process

gerontology: the study of aging

CURRICULUM CONNECTION

Health With the steady decline of deaths due to infectious and communicable diseases (smallpox, tuberculosis, and cholera), America faces a changing pattern of disease. Approximately half of all deaths in the United States can now be attributed to behavioral factors, such as smoking, alcohol use, and diet/activity. Psychologists are being challenged to conduct research, design, develop, and implement health care strategies that will assist people in changing their behaviors and implementing positive lifestyle changes.

3 ASSESS

Assign Section 2 Assessment as homework or as an in-class activity.

Section Quiz 21–2

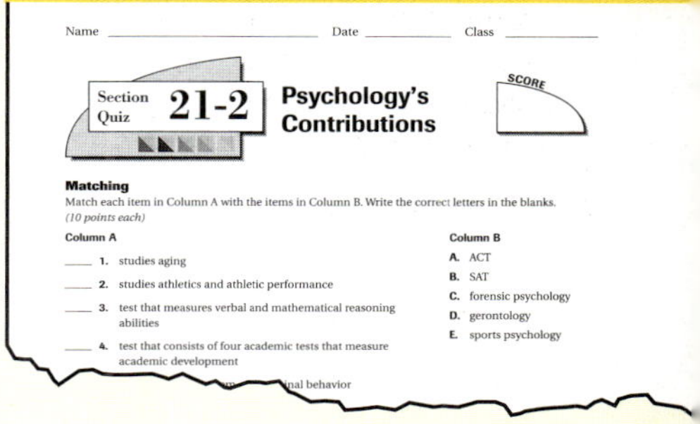
Name ________ Date ________ Class ________

Section Quiz 21-2 **Psychology's Contributions** SCORE

Matching
Match each item in Column A with the items in Column B. Write the correct letters in the blanks. *(10 points each)*

Column A	Column B
____ 1. studies aging	A. ACT
____ 2. studies athletics and athletic performance	B. SAT
____ 3. test that measures verbal and mathematical reasoning abilities	C. forensic psychology
____ 4. test that consists of four academic tests that measure academic development	D. gerontology
	E. sports psychology

INTERDISCIPLINARY CONNECTIONS ACTIVITY

Daily Life Tell students that many families today must make decisions about the care of an elderly relative, usually a grandparent. Gerontologists have found in their research that most older people prefer their independence. When that is no longer possible, the older person and his or her family may decide to create an intergenerational household with at least three generations living in the same house. This transition is often difficult for all members of the family. Ask students to research how families can avoid conflict when creating an intergenerational household. Then have them create a checklist that will assist families to make a smooth transition from a traditional to an intergenerational home. **L2**

Reteach

Organize students into small groups. Have each group prepare an explanation of how psychology affects our everyday life. Ask each group to present its explanations. Then, in a class discussion, have the class create one concise explanation of the role of psychology in everyday life.

Enrich

Have students find a recent newspaper or popular magazine article about psychology. Ask students to analyze the author's evidence and conclusions. **Ask: Does the author's evidence support his or her conclusions?**

4 CLOSE

Have volunteers write or search online for information about the APA and APS. Ask the volunteers to report on the organizations' goals, memberships, and future directions.

At the other end of the age spectrum are a different set of factors that may impact future jobs for psychologists. Consider the traditional killers of children—measles, chicken pox, scarlet fever, rheumatic fever, mumps, tuberculosis, and polio. Assuming a child has had his or her proper vaccinations, all of these problems are gone. The top three killers of children and adolescents in our society now are accidents, violence, and drugs. These are not *physiological* or medical problems like our old enemies, they are *psychological* or behavioral problems. Many of the dangers that face society today are rooted in social problems; that is, they can be solved only through changing behavior and attitudes of individuals and communities.

Where Do You Go From Here?

As you come to the end of this textbook, it is important to consider not only the future of psychology but also how psychology plays a role in your future. Whether you choose further education and a career in psychology or not, you should not stop thinking critically about and seeking to explain your behavior and the behavior of others.

The information presented in this textbook does not represent the absolute truth. Psychology is a science—it is a *process* of trying to understand the world around us. As you encounter articles in newspapers and magazines concerning psychology, try to read them critically. Read the material, think about it, and question it. Analyze the evidence and the author's conclusions. Remember, though, that all conclusions are tentative. Ask yourself: Are there better ways to approach this issue or question? Use what you have learned in this course to determine your own hypotheses and theories and to critically analyze what you read, hear, and experience every day.

SECTION 2 Assessment

1. **Review the Vocabulary** What do sports psychologists do?
2. **Visualize the Main Idea** Using a graphic organizer similar to the one below, outline the challenges psychologists face.

3. **Recall Information** Why must psychologists study aging?
4. **Think Critically** Consider what you have learned in this psychology course. What information will be most useful to you during your lifetime? Why? In what types of situations during your life do you think you will use this information? Explain.
5. **Application Activity** Visit a large bookstore and browse through the titles of books dealing with psychology. What topics seem to be the most popular? Which books seem to be the most helpful? Which books seem most interesting to you? Why? Based on your observations, forecast several topics that could result in a popular psychology book.

SECTION 2 Assessment Answers

1. Sports psychologists help athletes prepare to perform their best. They also research the benefits of sports participation and explore violence in competition.
2. Social change, urban problems, psychology and minorities, the neural bases of behavior, and the reduction of violence are psychology's challenges today.
3. The population of senior citizens continues to increase. This creates new issues for psychologists to study and new careers in both research and service.
4. Students' answers will vary. Challenge students to consider concrete ways to apply what they have learned.
5. Have students visit different bookstores and compare their findings. Ask them to determine whether the majority of the books are generalized (popular, mass market) or science-based.

CHAPTER 21 Summary and Vocabulary

Psychology has made many contributions to society in the past. Its place in the future is secure because it helps people resolve issues and problems. The field of psychology is among the fastest-growing in the twenty-first century.

Section 1 Careers in Psychology

Main Idea: Human behavior plays a key role in many areas of study. Studying psychology can prepare you for many career opportunities.

- A bachelor's degree in psychology affords many options with a wide array of possible employers.
- As a profession, careers that are based on psychological principles seek to predict how people will act; help people modify their behavior; and help organizations, businesses, and communities change.

Section 2 Psychology's Contributions

Main Idea: Psychology has made many contributions to society by promoting human welfare, clarifying assessment methods, explaining human behavior, and helping humans better understand their world.

- The most significant contribution of psychology is the development of forms of professional helping, including psychotherapy.
- Psychologists have played a leading role in devising and updating educational testing programs.
- The study of psychology has implications for everyday living, especially in the areas of raising children, improving learning, and understanding the process of aging.
- The common link in careers in psychology is the desire to understand behavior.
- Psychology can be grouped into experimental fields and applied fields.
- Experimental psychologists use a variety of scientific methods to study human and animal behavior.
- Applied psychologists put knowledge of psychology to work solving human problems.
- According to the United States Bureau of Labor, psychology is among the fastest-growing fields in the twenty-first century.
- The American Psychological Association (APA) is a scientific and professional society of psychologists and educators.
- The American Psychological Society (APS) is an organization for academic and science-oriented psychologists.
- Fields of psychology that have potential for future growth include forensic psychology, industrial/organizational psychology, and sports psychology.
- Many problems that face society today, such as violence, drugs, and AIDS, require behavioral solutions.

Chapter Vocabulary

- crisis intervention program (p. 604)
- ACT (p. 611)
- SAT (p. 611)
- forensic psychology (p. 615)
- industrial/organizational psychology (p. 615)
- sports psychology (p. 615)
- visualization (p. 615)
- gerontology (p. 615)

21 Summary and Vocabulary

Using the Chapter 21 Summary and Vocabulary

Use the Chapter 21 Summary and Vocabulary to preview, review, condense, or reteach the chapter.

Preview/Review

Use the Chapter Vocabulary list to help students review and study.

Activity Have students create a word search puzzle using definitions or examples as the clues for the puzzle. Then have pairs of students exchange and complete each other's puzzles.

Vocabulary PuzzleMaker CD-ROM reinforces the vocabulary terms used in Chapter 21.

Condense

Have students read the Chapter 21 Summary.

Chapter 21 Guided Reading Activities

Reteach

Reteaching Activity 21

PERFORMANCE ASSESSMENT ACTIVITY

Create a Recruiting Brochure Assign students to work in pairs or small groups. Tell them that psychology is not taken by many students because it is an elective course. Explain that you would like to get more students to enroll in the course because you believe it can help them in many areas of life. Ask students to create a brochure that would entice more students to sign up for the course. **BLOCK SCHEDULING**

Refer to the ***Authentic Assessment*** booklet for additional activities and information about evaluating student performance.

21 Assessment

PSYCHOLOGY Online

Have students visit the Web site at glencoe.com to review Chapter 21 and take the **Self-Check Quiz**.

GLENCOE TECHNOLOGY

PRESENTATION Plus! For a review of Chapter 21 content, see MindJogger Checkpoint on **Presentation Plus!**

CHAPTER 21 Assessment

PSYCHOLOGY Online

Self-Check Quiz

Visit the *Understanding Psychology* Web site at glencoe.com and click on **Chapter 21—Self-Check Quizzes** to prepare for the Chapter Test.

Reviewing Vocabulary

Choose the letter of the correct term or concept below to complete the sentence.

- **a.** ACT
- **b.** SAT
- **c.** forensic psychologist
- **d.** industrial/organizational psychologist
- **e.** sports psychology
- **f.** visualization
- **g.** gerontology
- **h.** crisis intervention program
- **i.** clinical psychologist
- **j.** school psychologist

1. A(n) __________ is often involved in helping businesses operate more efficiently.
2. A(n) __________ may give reading, aptitude, interest, or intelligence tests to middle or high school students.
3. __________ is the study of aging.
4. A(n) __________ is often self-employed, practicing some form of psychotherapy.
5. Athletes sometimes use the process of __________—mentally rehearsing the steps of a successful performance—to reduce negative thoughts that may interfere with performance.
6. Nearly 1.2 million high school seniors take the __________, which emphasizes scientific concepts and abstract reading skills.
7. About 1.5 million seniors take the __________, which was redesigned in 2005 to give more weight to abstract thinking skills and writing.
8. A(n) __________ can respond to an individual's life-threatening situation or long-term stress.
9. A(n) __________ is involved in working on the reliability of witnesses in a court proceeding.
10. An important part of training for many professional athletes is the field of __________.

Recalling Facts

1. Explain the findings of research about the effects of day care on children.
2. Explain the projections for the elderly population in the twenty-first century. How does this impact psychology?
3. Using a diagram similar to the one below, list the similarities and differences in the work of applied psychologists and experimental psychologists.

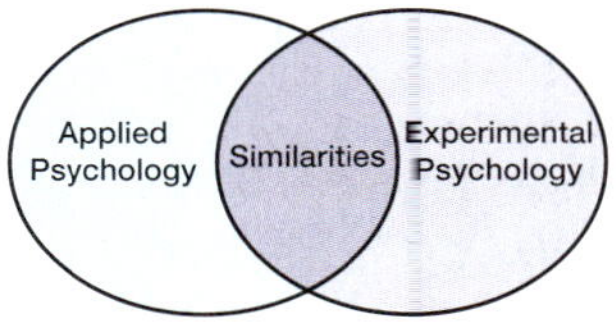

4. List three organizations for psychologists and/or students of psychology.
5. Identify two careers that require a background in psychology and briefly describe the careers.

Critical Thinking

1. **Analyzing Concepts** Define job satisfaction in your own words. Do you think it is possible to measure job satisfaction? Explain.
2. **Evaluating Information** Do college admission tests really predict success in college? Why or why not?
3. **Synthesizing Information** There are many types of mental health professionals. What common characteristics do they all share?
4. **Making Inferences** Name three jobs in psychology that you think will offer good opportunities for employment and explain why. Name three jobs that you think will offer few opportunities and explain why.
5. **Comparing and Contrasting** Compare and contrast the educational requirements and the responsibilities of a crisis hot line adviser, a mental health assistant, and a consulting psychologist.

Reviewing Vocabulary

1. d
2. j
3. g
4. i
5. f
6. a
7. b
8. h
9. c
10. e

Recalling Facts

1. Day care appears to have few negative effects and promotes social skills. Children with experience in day care do tend to be more assertive and aggressive. This, however, may be a result of day care children thinking at an advanced level but not yet possessing the social skills to implement their plans smoothly.
2. The average age of citizens in North America is going steadily upward; there are more people over 65 in the United States and Canada now than at any time in history. This creates new problems for psychologists to study. It has led to the creation and growth of gerontology.
3. Similarities–They both study human behavior, gather the available evidence, and offer the best solution possible. Differences–Applied psychologists search for immediate solutions by putting the knowledge of psychology to work, while experimental psychologists search for long-term answers by using the scientific method to study psychological processes.
4. The American Psychological Association (APA) is a scientific and professional society of psychologists and educators. The American Psychological Society (APS) is an organization geared toward academic and science-oriented psychologists. Psi Chi is a professional and scientific honor society with chapters on many college and university campuses.
5. Answers will vary. Some careers, such as mental health adviser, do not require an advanced degree. However, most careers as a full-time psychologist do involve advanced degrees. The careers vary depending on whether the person is involved in an experimental or applied field. The place of employment also makes a difference.

Critical Thinking

1. Answers will vary. Students should consider such factors as stimulation and rewards.
2. Answers will vary. Encourage students to make reasoned arguments for their positions.
3. Help students realize that all mental health professions share an interest in human behavior and a concern for people's welfare.
4. Answers will vary. Most fields of psychology are considered as growth areas. However, fields like behavioral psychology are not currently as popular as they once were.
5. Have students review the educational requirements listed in Section 1 of this chapter.

CHAPTER 21 Assessment

Psychology Projects

1. **Psychology's Contributions** Find out about the historical treatment of psychological problems. You might focus on the treatments used in the Middle Ages and in the early nineteenth century. Share your findings in an oral report.
2. **Psychology Today and in the Future** In recent years, astronauts in the U.S. space program have spent extended time in space in cramped and crowded quarters. A recent field of psychology is space psychology. Psychologists in this field study the behavioral challenges of spaceflight. Find out about this field and the kinds of issues it addresses. Present your findings in an informational pamphlet.

Technology Activity

One of the major contributions of psychology is in the designing and assessing of tools for learning. Find examples of educational computer software. Find out what approach to learning is incorporated in the software—feedback, reinforcement, and so on. Evaluate the effectiveness of the software.

Psychology Journal

Review your journal entry. Do you feel optimistic or pessimistic that those problems can be solved? Why or why not? In what specific ways might psychology help solve these problems? Write answers in your journal.

Building Skills

Interpreting a Graph Job satisfaction—studied by industrial/organizational psychologists—is an issue for many people. Various factors contribute to job satisfaction. Review the graph, then answer the questions that follow.

1. According to this graph, what three job characteristics do most people find important for job satisfaction?
2. With which job characteristic were people most satisfied? Least satisfied?
3. Select an area on the graph. How might an industrial/organizational psychologist help managers and/or employees in this area?

Practice and **assess** key social studies skills with **Glencoe Skillbuilder Interactive Workbook CD-ROM, Level 2.**

See the Skills Handbook, page 628, for an explanation of interpreting graphs.

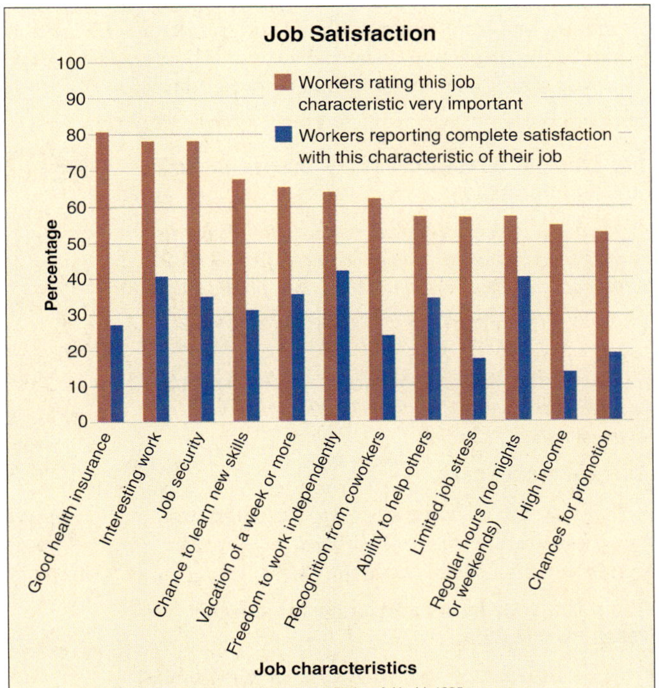

Source: Hugick & Leonard, 1991; based on Rathus & Nevid, 1995.

Building Skills

1. Most people list good health insurance, interesting work, and job security as the most important issues for job satisfaction.
2. most satisfied: interesting work, freedom to work independently, and regular hours; least satisfied: limited job stress and high income
3. Answers will vary. Encourage students to identify items that a manager is likely to be able to control.

GLENCOE TECHNOLOGY

CD-ROM

Glencoe Skillbuilder Interactive Workbook, Level 2

This interactive CD-ROM is designed to reinforce student mastery of essential social studies skills.

Chapter Bonus Test Question

This question may be used for extra credit on the Chapter Assessment.
Answer the following question:
I am a former mental patient whose book *A Mind That Found Itself* motivated better care from the mental health community. Who am I?
Answer: Clifford Beers

Psychology Projects

1. After presenting their reports, have students discuss how treatments have changed as the body of psychological knowledge has increased.
2. If possible, have students go to the NASA Web site, which provides a wealth of information about the current and future space program.

Technology Activity

Suggest that students recommend the types of software that would be effective for various age groups, starting with preschoolers and extending through adulthood.

Psychology Journal

If students have a difficult time answering this question, suggest that they review the problems at the beginning of the twentieth century and see how many of them were successfully resolved. Have students reflect on what this tells them about human ability to find solutions to problems.

Skills Handbook

TEACH

Forming a Hypothesis Place a list of questions on the board about the behavior of teens. Review the importance of asking questions to find research topics. Select one of the questions and have students develop a hypothesis. For example, "Why do so many students fall asleep in their first class of the day?" A possible hypothesis based on this question is "Students who get six hours of sleep or less are more likely to fall asleep in their first class of the morning." Explain that it is important to state the hypothesis in a way that it can be proved or not proved.

Tell students that researchers make educated guesses in forming hypotheses. Disproving a hypothesis does not mean that the researcher has failed; it means that the explanation can be eliminated and new research can be explored. Explain that this is the basic method of social scientific reasoning. Have students read the skill and complete the practice application.

Answers to Apply the Skill

Although students' answers may vary, possible hypotheses are:

- A water temperature at or slightly above one's body temperature causes muscles to relax.
- Mothers can calm their babies before putting them to sleep by bathing them in warm water.

Additional Practice

Critical Thinking Skills Activities 3 and 18

Psychology Skills

Forming a Hypothesis

A researcher in the study of psychology analyzes information and asks a research question. The researcher then forms a **hypothesis,** or an educated guess that answers the research question. A hypothesis allows a person to make sense of unorganized, separate observations and bits of information by placing them within a structured and coherent framework. The researcher has some evidence for suspecting a specific answer. The hypothesis expresses the researcher's reasoning in such a way that it can be confirmed or not confirmed.

For example, a researcher may analyze the following information:

There are several different methods for trying to quit smoking. Most people, however, fail at their attempts to quit. Studies show that people who attend "quit smoking" clinics have a better chance of kicking the smoking habit.

Fear tactics, such as describing health hazards, have been used successfully to motivate people to modify their behavior.

The researcher asks:

Can fear tactics, such as describing the health hazards of smoking, increase the number of smokers who sign up for "quit smoking" clinics?

The researcher forms a hypothesis from this research question:

Using fear tactics, such as describing the health hazards of smoking, increases the number of smokers who sign up for "quit smoking" clinics.

Learn the Skill

1. Analyze information to identify a specific problem or question.
2. Use the specific problem or question to form a hypothesis.
3. Test the hypothesis by gathering additional information.
4. Use the additional information to reanalyze the original hypothesis. If necessary, restate the hypothesis.

Apply the Skill

Read the information below. Form a hypothesis using the four steps discussed in *Learn the Skill.*

People who bathe in warm water relax more quickly than people who bathe in cold water.

Some mothers complain that they are unable to calm their babies in order to get them to sleep.

EXTENSION ACTIVITY

Forming a Hypothesis Supply several copies of your local newspaper to the class. Have students work in pairs to develop at least 10 research questions based on articles in the newspaper. Then have each pair of students formulate two hypotheses based on one of the research questions. Have them gather additional information to test the hypotheses and report their findings. L2 BLOCK SCHEDULING

Interpreting Statistics

Statistics are mathematical processes used to organize, summarize, and analyze data collected by researchers. Interpreting statistics helps us use data to support a generalization or conclusion.

Learn the Skill

There are three things to consider when interpreting statistics: nonrepresentative sample, correlation, and statistical significance.

1. Suppose that a psychologist wants to test the following hypothesis: *Teenagers who eat large breakfasts have high grades.* Since it is impossible to study all teenagers, the researcher must pick a **sample,** or a relatively small population, of students that represents the population of students as a whole. A **nonrepresentative sample** is a sample that does not represent the entire population and, therefore, may affect the results of the study. For example, a sample that includes only females would be a nonrepresentative sample. What information can you learn about the sample by looking at Skills Figure 1?

2. A **correlation** is the association or relationship between two or more variables. For example, if data show that students who eat large breakfasts have high grades, this would be a positive correlation. If the data show that students who eat large breakfasts have low grades, this would be a negative correlation. What type of correlation do the statistics in the Skills Figure 1 show?

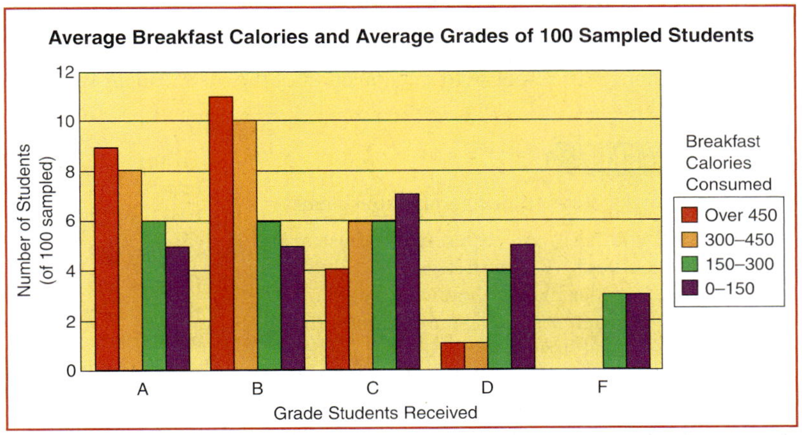

Skills Figure 1

3. When interpreting statistics, researchers must decide whether the data support a generalization or whether the data are due to chance. The results are called **statistically significant** if the probability that the data support a generalization is 95 percent or higher. Do you think the data in Skills Figure 1 support a generalization or are due to chance? Explain.

Apply the Skill

Develop a survey for which you believe the data might show a correlation. For example, "Do you have a regular exercise routine that you follow?" and "Do you have enough energy to make it through the day?" Pick a representative sample of people and conduct the survey. Organize and interpret your statistics.

TEACH

Interpreting Statistics Tell students that psychological research often entails gathering a data sample from the population. For example, when pollsters report the likely winners in political campaigns, they make their predictions based on a sample of likely voters. To help ensure the accuracy of the results, the sample must be random and unbiased. In a national political poll, a random sample would include voters from all parts of the country.

Tell students that when two things are correlated, you cannot assume that one thing causes the other. For example, if students who scored the highest on a recent test were found to have eaten a particular breakfast cereal on the morning of the test, it would not mean that the cereal was the reason for the good performance. Other reasons such as the time spent studying or the amount of sleep the night before might be the real reason. Have students read the skill and complete the practice application.

Answers to Apply the Skill
Students' answers will vary. Possible survey topics might include the number of speeding tickets that a person has and the frequency with which he or she exceeds the speed limit. In selecting a representative sample for this topic, the sample should include both genders and people driving different makes, models, and colors of vehicles.

Additional Practice
Critical Thinking Skills Activities 2 and 20

EXTENSION ACTIVITY

Interpreting Statistics Ask students to select two items that they believe may be correlated, such as the number of extracurricular activities a student participates in and his or her grade point average. Have them conduct a survey or use an appropriate research method to gather the information. Then have students analyze and chart their results showing measures of central tendency, a frequency distribution, and a scatterplot. **L2** **BLOCK SCHEDULING**

TEACH

Designing an Experiment As researchers design their experiments, they must identify the factors, or variables, that will be altered and measured. Explain the importance of conducting experiments in which variables can be controlled. When researchers can control the variables, they can formulate theories based on the results.

Review the importance of experimental and control groups. The experimental group is the one for which the independent variable is changed. The control group does not experience this change. By comparing the results between the two groups, the researcher can be reasonably certain that any change in the dependent variable is the result of the change in the independent variable. Have students read the skill and complete the practice application.

Answers to Apply the Skill
The specific design of students' experiments will vary. Students should have a complete list of materials and procedures before they conduct the experiment. The analysis of the results of their experiment should compare the experimental and control groups. Further breakdowns, such as by gender and age, may also be possible depending on the sample size and number of trials.

Additional Practice
Critical Thinking Skills Activities 4 and 8

Skills Handbook

Psychology Skills

Designing an Experiment

An **experiment** is a series of carefully planned steps that test a hypothesis. Psychologists establish cause-and-effect relationships by performing experiments. Experiments allow the researcher to control the situation and narrow the possibilities as to what can influence the results. In designing experiments, researchers think in terms of **variables,** or factors and conditions that can change or vary. Researchers test the relationship between two factors by deliberately producing a change in one factor and observing the effect the change has on the other factor. An **independent variable** is the factor that researchers change or alter so they can observe its effects. The **dependent variable** is the one that changes in response to manipulation of the independent variable.

Learn the Skill

Use the following steps to design an experiment:

1. Make a hypothesis. All experiments must start with a hypothesis. A **hypothesis** is an educated guess a researcher makes about some phenomenon. The researcher should state the hypothesis in clear, concrete language to rule out any confusion or error in its meaning. To be valid, a hypothesis must be testable by experimentation.
2. Brainstorm a list of ways to test the hypothesis. You might include surveys or questionnaires, but in order to be an experiment, one variable must be manipulated.
3. Identify the independent and dependent variables that will be measured.
4. From the list created in Step 2, design an experiment to test one variable identified in Step 3.
5. List materials needed for the experiment. This step includes determining the number of participants to be tested. Researchers should use at least two groups of participants in every experiment. The **experimental group** is the group of participants who are exposed to the independent variable. For example, if your hypothesis was that hot temperatures cause aggression in humans, then you would expose the members of the experimental group to hot temperatures and observe their reactions. Members of the **control group** are treated the same as the members of the experimental group in every way except they are not exposed to the independent variable (in this case hot temperatures).
6. Gather the data.
7. Decide how you can display the results. From the data collected, you will draw a conclusion and make a statement about your results. If your conclusion supports your hypothesis, then you may say that your hypothesis is confirmed. (Researchers use statistical procedures to determine if their results are statistically significant—that is, not due to chance.) If your conclusions did not support your hypothesis, then you would have to make additional observations, state a new hypothesis, and test it against the available data.

Researchers often repeat experiments many times before they are confident that the answers they found are correct. That is why the results of new studies and experiments are often questioned until other researchers have a chance to repeat the experiments and come up with the same conclusions.

Apply the Skill

Read the hypothesis below. Design an experiment using the steps discussed in *Learn the Skill.*

People exposed to the smell of certain foods prior to eating a meal have a smaller appetite than people who are not exposed to the smell of those foods.

EXTENSION ACTIVITY

Designing an Experiment Tell students that when we feel in control of a situation, we experience less stress. Have students work in small groups to design an experiment based on the following hypothesis: *During the road experience portion of driver's education, the person in the car experiencing the least amount of stress is the driver.* Tell groups that their experiment design should include a list of materials, a set of procedures, a description of the sample to be used, and an explanation of how they will analyze and present the data. **L2** **BLOCK SCHEDULING**

Psychology Skills

Using the Scientific Method

The **scientific method** is a series of planned steps used to solve problems. It is an objective, logical, and systematic way of collecting data and drawing conclusions. Psychology researchers use the scientific method to analyze data, to draw conclusions, and to prevent their own biases from interfering with the research process.

Researchers **analyze the data** collected in an experiment by looking for patterns and relationships in the facts obtained. Analyzing the data leads to **drawing conclusions.** After careful analysis of the data, the researcher asks: Was the hypothesis supported by the facts? Was it not supported? Are more data needed? **Inferences** are logical conclusions based on observations and are made after careful analysis of all the available data. Inferences are a means to explain or interpret observations.

Researchers also use reasoning to draw conclusions. **Inductive reasoning** involves first considering a number of specific statements or observations and then drawing a conclusion—reasoning from particular facts to a broad generalization. An example of inductive reasoning might be:

Observations: *That woman is a jogger. She is wearing sneakers.* Conclusion: *People who wear sneakers are joggers.*

However, just because someone is wearing sneakers does not necessarily mean that the person is a jogger. This generalization might be too broad.

Deductive reasoning involves using past knowledge or general rules to decide or predict how probable or accurate a certain conclusion is—reasoning from general to particular. An example of deductive reasoning might be:

General rule: *People who jog wear sneakers.* Past Knowledge: *That woman is a jogger.* Conclusion: *She probably wears sneakers when she jogs.*

Researchers must use both deductive and inductive reasoning in forming and testing hypotheses.

Learn the Skill

The following steps are used in the scientific method:

1. **Question** Ask a question about an observation you have made.
2. **Hypothesis** Make a hypothesis about the observation you have made.
3. **Experiment** Design an experiment to test the hypothesis.
4. **Data** Collect data through observation and organize it into graphic form.
5. **Draw Conclusions** Analyze your data and determine if your hypothesis is true or false.

Apply the Skill

Read the problem below. Use the steps in the scientific method to design a plan to solve this problem.

Robert is having difficulty learning to play the tuba. He is not sure if he learns better practicing by himself, with another tuba player, or with his tuba instructor.

TEACH

Using the Scientific Method

As students enter the classroom, write "Quiz Today" on the board. After a few minutes, ask students to discuss the conclusions they drew from the message and how it made them feel. Tell them that humans constantly analyze the world around them and draw conclusions about what they experience. Psychologists do much the same thing, but they use a specific technique known as the scientific method to gather, objectively analyze, and interpret information. By using this formal process, psychologists avoid reaching conclusions based on just their own experiences or feelings. Have students read the skill and complete the practice application.

Answers to Apply the Skill

Students' specific design of the steps in the scientific method will vary but should demonstrate an understanding of the steps of the scientific method.

Additional Practice

Critical Thinking Skills Activity 12

EXTENSION ACTIVITY

Using the Scientific Method As a class, brainstorm a list of behaviors that students have observed while traveling to and from school. Working in pairs, have students select one of the behaviors listed and investigate using the scientific method. Have each pair create a folder with one sheet of paper for each step in the scientific method. On the first sheet they will write questions about the observation. On the second sheet they will write their hypotheses about the observation, indicating which hypothesis they will test. The third will explain their experiment, while the fourth will describe the data collected. The last sheet will explain the accuracy of the hypothesis. Have them share the results of their investigations. **L2** **BLOCK SCHEDULING**

Reading and Critical Thinking Skills

TEACH

Identifying Cause-and-Effect Relationships To show students a few clear-cut cases of cause and effect, have them explain how or why the following diseases occur in human beings: malaria *(bite of infected mosquito)* and rickets *(lack of vitamin D)*. Ask how the causes of these diseases were discovered. *(observation, experimentation, logic)* Have students read the skill and complete the practice application.

Answers to Apply the Skill
Possible answers include:
Cause: children give gift to teacher; Effect: children feel happy about gift
Cause: teacher finds something wrong with gift; Effect: some children decide their gift was bad

Additional Practice
Critical Thinking Skills Activity 5

TEACH

Comparing and Contrasting Many television ads are based on comparisons. Ask two volunteers, with different preferences in breakfast cereals, to bring an empty box of the cereal to class, along with the price they paid for it. Have volunteers put the nutrition information, net weight, and price on the board. Ask a student to calculate the price per ounce of each cereal. Based on this information, have the class list the similarities and differences between the two products. Have students read the skill and complete the practice application.

Identifying Cause-and-Effect Relationships

When reading information, it is important to determine cause-and-effect relationships in order to understand why an event occurred. A **cause** is the action or situation that produces an event. An **effect** is the result or consequence of an action or situation. The connection between what happens and what makes it happen is known as a **cause-and-effect relationship.**

Learn the Skill

1. Begin by asking questions about why events occur. Look for related problems and actions, since these are potential causes of the event.
2. Look for clue words that may help you identify whether one event caused the other. Words or phrases such as *because, led to, brought about, produced, as a result of, so that, for this reason, as a consequence, as an outgrowth, if, since,* and *therefore* indicate cause-and-effect relationships.
3. Identify the outcome or impact of the event or situation. Look for relationships between events. Be sure to check for other, more complex, connections beyond the immediate cause and effect. For example, in a chain of events, an event often becomes the cause of multiple events.

CAUSE➜EFFECT (CAUSE)➜EFFECT

Takes drugs to reduce stress➜Becomes dependent on drugs➜Steals to support drug habit

Apply the Skill

Read the passage below and then identify the causes and effects by creating a cause-and-effect diagram. In a paragraph, discuss the immediate effects and possible later effects.

In a recent study of 107 kindergarten students in New York City, [Dr. Carol] Dweck confirmed the notion that negative reactions to failure and criticism start early. Dweck asked the children to role-play a scene in which they pretended to give their teacher a gift they had made. Almost all of them were happy with the gift they gave. But, after the teacher found something wrong with it, nearly half of them decided that the gift they had made was "bad," while the rest of them still considered the gift "good" (Azar, 1996).

Comparing and Contrasting

Often it is necessary to use comparing and contrasting to understand concepts, to make decisions, or to solve problems. Making comparisons is a good way to organize information, extend understanding, and learn more about the behavior of people. As long as two things share one common quality, they can be compared. To make a comparison, students must examine two or more groups, situations, events, or documents. Then students must identify **similarities,** or ways they are alike, and **differences,** or ways they are not alike. **Comparing** means identifying similarities. **Contrasting** means identifying differences.

EXTENSION ACTIVITY

Identifying Cause-and-Effect Relationships Instruct students to find an article relating to psychology in a magazine, journal, or newspaper. Students should isolate one cause-and-effect relationship in the article and consider how the remaining details are related to it. Encourage students to chart the relationship and summarize their findings in a short paper. **L1**

BLOCK SCHEDULING

Learn the Skill

1. Identify what is being compared and contrasted.
2. Determine the purpose for comparing and contrasting. Ask: What do these events or items have in common? What would you compare using these two events or items? What is the purpose of this comparison? What question do you want to answer by comparing the events or items? By answering these questions, you are deciding what items are to be compared.
3. Now you must decide what characteristics will be used to compare the items. Note and list similarities in the characteristics of the items being compared. When comparing items, look for clue words that indicate two things are alike. Such clue words include *all, both, like, as, likewise,* and *similarly.*
4. List differences in the characteristics of the items. When contrasting, look for clue words that show how things differ, such as *different, differ, unlike, however,* and *on the other hand.*
5. At this point you should review the similarities and differences that you have found. Ask: Why are there similarities and differences in these items? What might have caused the differences? Point out information related to the similarities and differences found.
6. Finally, recall the research question or the purpose of comparing the events or items (from Step 2). Ask yourself: Does this comparison answer this research question? How?

Apply the Skill

Research to compare and contrast the beliefs of any two of the following psychologists.

John B. Watson	Wilhelm Wundt	William James
Wolfgang Köhler	Sigmund Freud	Carl Rogers

Distinguishing Fact From Opinion

It is necessary to distinguish between fact and opinion in order to think critically and to make decisions. A **fact** is a statement that can be proved to be false or true and is supported by evidence. For example, the statement *Tobacco is the most widely used and abused drug today; it contributed to 435,000 deaths in 2000* (Mokdad et al., 2004) is a fact because it can be proved. An **opinion** expresses a personal belief, viewpoint, or emotion. For example, the statement *The best method to use to cope with stress is meditation* is an opinion since it cannot be proved and it is not supported with any evidence.

Learn the Skill

The following guidelines will help you distinguish between fact and opinion.

1. When listening to or reading a statement, keep in mind the meanings of *fact* and *opinion.* It is a fact if the statement is supported with evidence. It is an opinion if the statement is not or cannot be supported with evidence.
2. Identify facts by looking for words and phrases that indicate specific information about people, places, events, dates, times, and statistics.
3. Identify opinions by looking for words and phrases such as *I believe, I think, most likely, in my judgment, in my view, may, might, could,* and *seems to me.*

Apply the Skill

Find a newspaper or magazine article about a psychological study. Use the guidelines in *Learn the Skill* to help you identify five statements in the article as being either facts or opinions. Give a reason why each statement is either a fact or an opinion.

Reading and Critical Thinking Skills

Answers to Apply the Skill
Students' answers will vary. The primary area of research or point of view of each psychologist is as follows: **John B. Watson:** only observable behavior should be studied; **Wilhelm Wundt:** developed introspection as a way of collecting information about the mind; **William James:** focused on the functions of the conscious mind; **Wolfgang Köhler:** a Gestalt psychologist who helped explain perception; **Sigmund Freud:** personality develops in early childhood as a result of sexual tension; and **Carl Rogers:** people should relate to one another with unconditional positive regard.

Additional Practice
Critical Thinking Skills Activities 9 and 16

TEACH

Distinguishing Fact From Opinion Explain that we are confronted with facts and opinions every day in the media. **Ask:** **Where would you look in the newspaper for opinions? Where would you find solid facts in a newspaper?** Have students find examples of headlines that state facts and those that express opinions. Make a display of the two types of headlines. Have students read the skill and complete the practice application.

Answers to Apply the Skill
Students may find articles about psychology in the newspaper, in health magazines, or on the Internet. Statements of fact usually convey specific information. Statements of opinion make broad, general statements.

Additional Practice
Critical Thinking Skills Activities 6 and 17

EXTENSION ACTIVITIES

Comparing and Contrasting Have students survey classmates or friends about an issue, such as their attitudes toward political candidates in an upcoming election. Students should compare and contrast results in a graphic organizer. Remind students to begin this activity by asking a research question. **L2** **BLOCK SCHEDULING**

Distinguishing Fact From Opinion Have students research an issue about which they have strong feelings. Have students use their research findings to prepare a persuasive speech to encourage fellow students to support their point of view. As the class is listening to the speeches, have them identify the facts and the opinions expressed. **L1**

TEACH

Using Critical Methods of Inquiry Write the following headline on the board: *Worst Fire in City's History Kills 25.* **Ask: What is the headline claiming? What kind of information do you need to prove the claim made in the headline?** Have students discuss where they might find the information needed to verify the claim. **Ask: Which of these sources would be most reliable? Least reliable?** Explain that identifying primary and secondary sources of information and determining their reliability are essential steps when trying to prove a claim. Have students read the skill and complete the practice application.

Answers to Apply the Skill
Possible sources of articles include science and health magazines, and newspaper sections that report on health, medicine, and science.

Additional Practice
Critical Thinking Skills Activities 13 and 15

TEACH

Organizing and Analyzing Information Ask students to write detailed directions on how to get from the classroom to the cafeteria. Have students exchange directions with a classmate. Then pass out copies of the school map. Have students compare the written directions with the map. **Ask: How do the sources compare? Will they both lead you to the same point?** Tell students that when they conduct research, they must be able to classify and synthesize information. Have students read the skill and complete the practice application.

Using Critical Methods of Inquiry

It is important to use critical methods of inquiry when conducting research. Once you have decided on a topic for your research report, use the library's card catalog, the Internet, or a computerized referral service to find suitable reference sources. Resource materials can be accessed through the World Wide Web. Information on the Web is organized according to category and is stored at an address, or *URL*—Universal Resource Locator. Web browsers and search engines help you locate material on the Internet.

Learn the Skill

There is a vast amount of information in libraries and on the Internet. Use the following steps in analyzing sources:

1. Determine if the material is a *primary source,* which is a firsthand account, or a *secondary source,* which is a description or interpretation of events. Primary sources are helpful because they provide a close-up view of research results. Secondary sources are helpful tools because the writer has the advantage of knowing what theories and research results were proved or disproved, thus providing a broad perspective.
2. Read the material to identify main ideas and supporting details. Consider the nature of the material. Is it scientific or is it telling a story?
3. Distinguish fact from opinion. Psychologists often express their beliefs, but make sure these beliefs are based on facts.
4. Check for bias or faulty reasoning. Search for evidence presented by the writer that supports the conclusion.
5. If possible, find more than one source to check for accuracy.
6. Consider the origin of the source. Does the writer have credibility in the field of psychology? Does the writer have a degree and experience in the subject area?
7. Search for information on the Internet written by a well-known source. Do not use information on the Internet that does not list a source.

Apply the Skill

Select an article from a psychology magazine, journal, or book. Analyze the source by using the steps in *Learn the Skill.*

Organizing and Analyzing Information

Information for research reports must be organized and analyzed. To do this, it is important to know how to classify information you gather as you conduct your research, synthesize information from different sources and mediums, and create an outline of the information as it should appear in the research report.

Learn the Skill

1. **Classifying Information** As you read about your topic, identify information that has similar characteristics. List this information on separate note cards. Label the note cards with categories. Then add facts to the categories as you continue your research.

EXTENSION ACTIVITIES

Using Critical Methods of Inquiry Ask students to list three fields of psychology that are of most interest to them. Have students research the trends in that field by exploring primary and secondary sources. Then have them prepare a question-and-answer sheet that describes the field and the trends in research with source material references. **L2** **BLOCK SCHEDULING**

Organizing and Analyzing Information Find several relatively short newspaper articles about events with which the students are familiar. Cut the articles into sections by paragraph, placing the sections on separate sheets of paper. Have students work in small groups to put the articles back into the correct order. Have a volunteer from each group read the article to you.

Remember that when classifying, you are grouping objects or events for a purpose. The purpose could be general, such as for ease of finding an item. Once you have classified the material, look for patterns and relationships among the facts. It is at this point that you may make comparisons, draw conclusions, and develop questions or hypotheses for further study.

2. **Synthesizing Information** When using more than one source for a research report, you need to synthesize, or combine, the information. Look for connections and relationships among different sources. You may want to include both primary and secondary sources in your report. Combine the information so that each source adds to the understanding of your topic.

3. **Outlining Information** Outlines are also very useful when researching and writing essays or reports. Use outlines to help clarify and organize your thoughts, to decide what main ideas to include, and to flesh out each main idea with subtopics and supporting details. A good outline summarizes information and shows how ideas and facts are connected. In an outline, information is arranged in three categories—main ideas; subtopics, or parts of each main idea; and supporting details. Outlines begin with broad ideas, followed by more specific ideas. Put your information in order. Determine what information will be part of the introduction, the body, and the conclusion of your report. Use main ideas as headings in your outline. Use supporting details as subheadings under the appropriate headings in your outline.

Apply the Skill

Select a topic for research. Organize and analyze the information you collect using the steps in *Learn the Skill.*

Writing a Research Report/Essay

You will be asked to write research reports and essays in most of the subjects you take in school. There are basic steps to follow when writing research reports or essays.

Learn the Skill

1. Choose a topic and identify your purpose for the research report or essay.
2. Write several main idea questions you want to answer about your topic. Organize these questions into an outline.
3. Conduct research about the topic and take notes.
4. Organize and analyze your information. Classify, synthesize, and outline the information collected.
5. Write a first draft. A research report or essay has an introduction, a body, and a conclusion. The *introduction* explains the purpose of the report or essay. The *body* develops the main ideas of the report or essay. Be sure to use proper transitions between paragraphs in the body. The *conclusion* summarizes your findings.
6. Edit the first draft. Reorganize information, and use standard grammar, spelling, sentence structure, and punctuation.
7. Write your final report or essay.

Apply the Skill

Write a psychology research report using the steps in *Learn the Skill.*

Research and Writing Skills

Answers to Apply the Skill

Recommend that students select a specific topic for research. Require students to complete and submit for review an outline of their report before they begin writing.

Additional Practice

Critical Thinking Skills Activities 1 and 14

TEACH

Writing a Research Report/Essay Have students review the process of choosing a topic. Practice this process with them by suggesting a number of general topics about psychology that students must narrow down. General topics might include perception, memory, or childhood development. These could be narrowed down to the perception of touch, long-term memory, and emotional development of children from birth to three years old. Have students read the skill and complete the practice application.

Answers to Apply the Skill

Students should select a specific topic in an area of psychology that is of interest to them. Recommend that students look through the topics in chapters that have not yet been studied for additional ideas.

Additional Practice

Critical Thinking Skills Activities 11 and 21

EXTENSION ACTIVITIES

Acknowledge whether the order is correct, close, or incorrect. ELL L1 BLOCK SCHEDULING

Writing a Research Report/Essay Have each student create a folder in which he or she will collect newspaper and magazine articles about psychology. The sources can be varied but should be noted with the item. Ask students to collect at least 10 articles during a one-week period and sort the articles by general topic. Tell students that these types of articles serve as great resource material to generate ideas for research reports. Have them identify at least three possible research topics from the material they have collected. L1

TEACH

Interpreting Charts, Tables, Graphs, and Diagrams Remind students that graphs, charts, and tables are used to show quantitative information, but there are differences in the best ways to show such information. Write *line graph, bar graph,* and *circle graph* on the board. **Ask: Which of these would best show: changes in the stock market** *(line graph)*; **the number of people in class having green, blue, or brown eyes** *(bar graph)*; **comparison of gas versus electricity use in your community for a year** *(circle or bar graph).*

Answers to Apply the Skill

Possible figures from the text that students could analyze would be Figure 4.10 and Figure 5.1. Figure 4.10 focuses on juvenile arrests in the United States. This is a table that shows the number of juvenile arrests for various crimes and the percentage decrease in juvenile arrests for these crimes over specific time periods. Figure 5.1 presents a time line showing physical changes that occur as we age.

Additional Practice

Critical Thinking Skills Activities 7 and 19

Visual Literacy Skills

Interpreting Charts, Tables, Graphs, and Diagrams

Data gathered in psychology research are often presented in charts, tables, graphs, and diagrams. These visual representations of data organize the information to make it quicker and easier to read, compare, and contrast.

Charts and tables are divided into columns and rows. The column title usually lists items to be compared. The row headings usually list the specific characteristics being compared among those items. There are three main types of graphs. A **line graph** shows the relationship between two variables. The independent variable usually goes on the x-axis, or the horizontal axis. The dependent variable usually goes on the y-axis, or the vertical axis. Refer back to page 472, Figure 16.4, for an example. A **bar graph** is similar to a line graph, except bars are used to show comparisons between data or to display data that do not continuously change. Thick bars are used instead of dots and lines (see Skills Figure 3 below). A **circle graph** shows the parts of a whole (see Skills Figure 2 below). Each section represents one part of the whole. A **diagram** is a drawing that shows what something is or how something is done. Diagrams may have several parts that show steps in a process. The parts of a diagram are usually labeled.

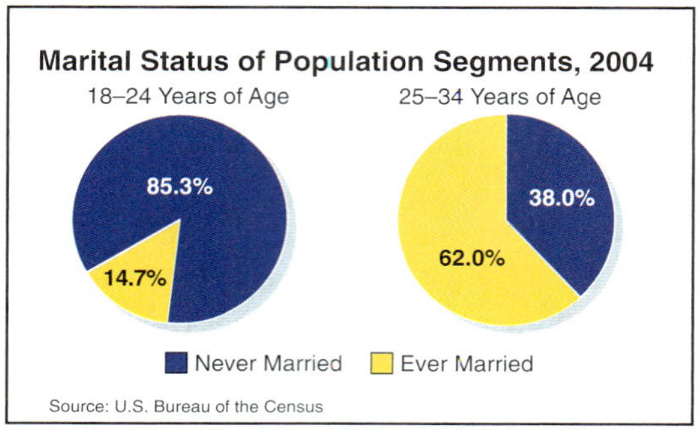

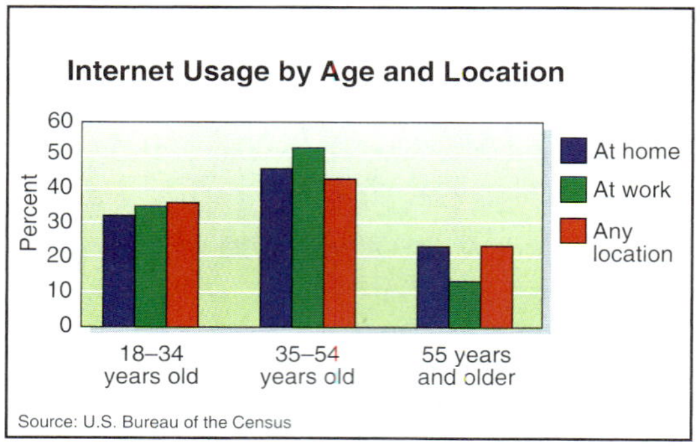

Learn the Skill

1. **Read the title.** The title tells you the purpose of the visual information.
2. **Look for clues.** Study the parts of the visual information. For a chart or table, read the columns and rows to identify what data are being presented. For a line graph or bar graph, read the x-axis and y-axis. For a circle graph, read the sections to find out what parts of a whole are being presented. For a diagram, read the parts that are labeled.
3. **Analyze the information.** Ask yourself questions such as: How do the data change over time? What is the relationship of the parts to the whole?
4. **Put the data to use.** Draw conclusions based on the data.

Apply the Skill

Find examples of visual information in your psychology text. Use the steps in *Learn the Skill* to interpret the visuals.

EXTENSION ACTIVITY

Interpreting Charts, Tables, Graphs, and Diagrams Collect several examples of newspaper articles that include charts or graphs from sources like *USA Today.* Organize the class into groups of three and give each group one of the charts without the supporting article. Have students prepare a brief written explanation of the chart or table. Then supply the group with the article. **Ask: What changes would you make to your explanation based on reading the article?** Have the groups share their results with the class. **L2** **BLOCK SCHEDULING**

Reading and Making Graphic Organizers

A **graphic organizer** is a type of diagram that shows the relationship among ideas and helps you organize information in a visual context. A graphic organizer can make abstract ideas more concrete and help you better understand the ideas and terms you are studying. A graphic organizer can show the interaction of a series of events, present a hierarchy of procedures, or describe the steps in a process.

Graphic organizers come in many forms. There are network trees, concept webs, events chain maps, cycle concept maps, and others. There may be more than one way to construct a graphic organizer. As you make a graphic organizer, you may realize that there is a better way to show the information on a map. In that case, change the format or how the information is displayed. Graphic organizers can be used to help you review and study information.

The graphic organizer below is a network tree. To read it, begin by reading the term at the top of the network tree that shows the main concept—the nervous system. Next, find the two divisions of the nervous system—central nervous system and peripheral nervous system—that branch out from the main concept. Now look at how the parts of these divisions branch out. Finally, see how the divisions of the autonomic system branch out.

Divisions of the Nervous System

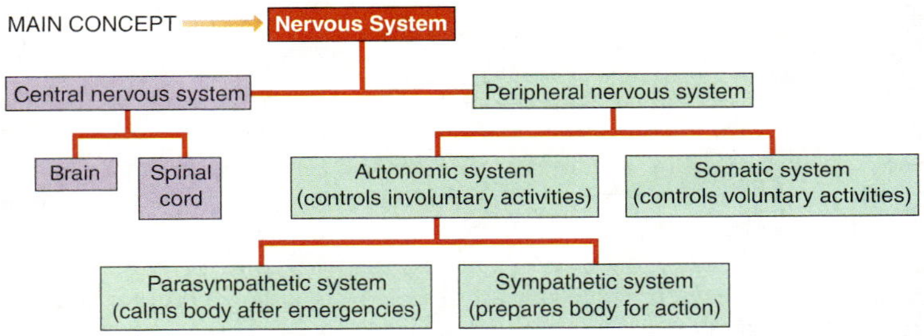

Learn the Skill

Follow the steps below when creating a graphic organizer.

1. State the main concept.
2. Branch the related concepts from the main concept. Use lines to connect the branches.
3. Continue to branch out more specific details from the related concepts.
4. You may write words on the lines to help explain the relationship of related concepts.

Apply the Skill

Construct a graphic organizer. Choose one of the following main concepts, or choose your own. Use information from your text and the steps in *Learn the Skill* to help you make your graphic organizer.

- Endocrine System
- Classical Conditioning
- Processes of Memory
- Development of Language
- Changes in Old Age
- Personality Theory

EXTENSION ACTIVITY

Reading and Making Graphic Organizers Have the class brainstorm a list of topics in psychology that can be compared and contrasted. Examples are the similarities and differences between clinical and counseling psychologists or the similarities and differences in parenting styles. Have pairs of students select one of the topics and develop a list of similarities and differences. Then have them prepare a Venn diagram using overlapping circles. Remind them to insert the similarities in the overlapping area and write the differences in the distinct areas. Encourage students to share their completed diagrams with the class. **L2** **BLOCK SCHEDULING**

TEACH

Reading and Making Graphic Organizers Provide the class with an example of the school's organizational chart. Tell students that the chart is a form of a graphic organizer. It represents the relationships among employees in a graphic way. Have students explore what the different levels and lines mean. Explain the connecting networks of information using the chart to guide you. Then have students read the skill and complete the practice application.

Answers to Apply the Skill

Possible organizers include:
Endocrine System—glands and the hormones they release;
Classical Conditioning—process of a neutral stimulus becoming a conditioned stimulus when paired with an unconditioned stimulus;
Process of Memory—flow diagram of encoding, processing, and storage;
Development of Language—a time line showing the development from birth through five years old,
Changes in Old Age—a concept web showing physical, emotional, and mental changes that occur in old age;
Personality Theory—a Venn diagram comparing and contrasting theories

Additional Practice

Critical Thinking Skills Activity 10

Glossary-Glosario

A

absolute threshold the weakest amount of a stimulus that a person can detect half the time (p. 209)

umbral absoluto magnitud más débil de un estímulo que puede detectar un individuo la mitad de las veces (pág. 209)

abstinence a choice to avoid harmful behaviors including premarital sex and use of drugs and alcohol (p. 99)

abstinencia elección de evitar conductas perjudiciales, incluido el coito premarital y el uso de drogas y alcohol (pág. 99)

accommodation the process by which a person changes his or her old methods or schemas to adjust or deal with new situations (p. 71)

ajuste proceso mediante el cual un individuo cambia sus métodos o esquemas previos para ajustarse o lidiar con nuevas situaciones (pág. 71)

achievement test an instrument used to measure the amount of knowledge a person has learned in a given subject or area (p. 360)

prueba de progreso instrumento empleado para medir la cantidad de conocimiento que un individuo aprendió sobre un tema o área dados (pág. 360)

acoustic codes when people try to remember something by saying it out loud or to themselves repeatedly (p. 274)

códigos acústicos cuando se intenta recordar algo mediante repetición en voz alta o repitiéndolo a uno mismo (pág. 274)

acquisition the process by which a conditioned response is established or strengthened (p. 244)

adquisición proceso por el cual se establece o refuerza una respuesta condicionada (pág. 244)

ACT American College Testing Proficiency Examination Program; a standardized test (p. 611)

ACT Programa de Exámenes de Pruebas de Destreza de los Colegios Americanos; una prueba estandarizada (pág. 611)

active listening empathetic listening in which the listener acknowledges, understands, restates, and clarifies the speaker's thoughts and concerns (p. 497)

escucha activa escucha empática en la cual el receptor reconoce, entiende, enuncia de nuevo y aclara los pensamientos y preocupaciones del hablante (pág. 497)

actor-observer bias tendency to attribute one's own behavior to outside causes but attribute the behavior of others to internal causes (p. 531)

prejuicio del actor-observador tendencia de atribuir a causas externas el comportamiento propio, pero atribuir el comportamiento ajeno a causas internas (pág. 531)

addiction a self-destructive pattern of drug abuse characterized by an overwhelming and compulsive desire to obtain and use the drug (p. 476)

adicción un patrón autodestructivo de abuso de drogas caracterizado por un deseo irrefrenable y compulsivo de obtener y usar la droga (pág. 476)

ageism prejudice or discrimination based on age, especially against the elderly (p. 138)

discriminación etaria prejuicio o discriminación en base a la edad, especialmente contra los ancianos (pág. 138)

aggression the initiation of hostile or destructive behavior intended to do physical or psychological harm to others (pp. 119, 565)

agresión inicio de una conducta hostil o destructiva con la intención de causar daño físico o psicológico a otros (págs. 119, 565)

agoraphobia extreme fear of being in a public place (p. 457)

agorafobia miedo extremo de estar en un lugar público (pág. 457)

algorithm a step-by-step procedure for solving a problem that leads to a solution (p. 299)

algoritmo procedimiento por pasos para resolver un problema que conduce a una solución (pág. 299)

altruism unselfishly helping others, often at a cost or risk, for reasons other than rewards (p. 568)

altruismo ayudar a otros sin egoísmo, con frecuencia a un costo o riesgo, por razones diferentes a obtener recompensas (pág. 568)

Alzheimer's disease currently an irreversible, incurable condition that destroys a person's ability to think, remember, relate to others, and care for herself or himself (p. 143)

enfermedad de Alzheimer condición actualmente incurable e irreversible que destruye la capacidad de una persona para pensar, recordar, relacionarse con otros y cuidar de sí mismo(a) (pág. 143)

amnesia severe loss or deterioration of memory that occurs after damage to the brain (temporary or permanent) following drug abuse or severe psychological stress (p. 286)

amnesia pérdida o deterioro severo de la memoria que ocurre tras un daño cerebral (temporal o permanente) después de abusar de las drogas o por un estrés psicológico severo (pág. 286)

anal stage the stage at which children associate erotic pleasure with the elimination process (p. 82)

etapa anal etapa en la cual los niños asocian el placer erótico con el proceso de evacuación (pág. 82)

androgynous combining or blending traditionally male and female characteristics (p. 117)

andrógino combinación o mezcla de características femeninas y masculinas tradicionales (pág. 117)

Glossary-Glosario

anger a strong feeling of displeasure, resentment, or hostility, with an irate reaction likely to result from frustration (pp. 145, 422)

anorexia nervosa a serious eating disorder where the fear of gaining weight results in prolonged self-starvation and dramatic weight loss (p. 114)

antianxiety drugs a type of medication that relieves anxiety disorders and panic disorders by depressing the activity of the central nervous system (p. 508)

antidepressants a type of medication used to treat major depression by increasing the amount of neurotransmitters believed to be involved in the regulation of emotions and moods (p. 508)

antipsychotic drugs a type of medication used to reduce agitation, delusions, and hallucinations; also called tranquilizers (p. 507)

antisocial personality a personality disorder characterized by a pattern of irresponsibility, shallow emotions, lack of conscience, and violating the rights of others without feeling guilt or remorse (p. 475)

anxiety an unpleasant psychological state characterized by a vague, generalized apprehension or feeling that one is in danger (pp. 422, 456)

applied science discovering ways to use scientific findings to accomplish practical goals (p. 11)

approach-approach conflict a type of conflict situation in which the individual must choose between two positive but mutually exclusive alternatives (p. 414)

approach-avoidance conflict a type of conflict situation in which the individual wants to do something but fears or dislikes it at the same time (p. 415)

aptitude test an instrument used to predict or estimate the probability that a person will be successful in learning a specific new skill or skills in the future (p. 360)

archetype an inherited idea, image, or concept based on the experiences of one's ancestors that shapes one's perception of the world (p. 384)

assimilation the process of fitting objects and experiences into one's schemas to deal with new situations and to understand the environment (p. 71)

asynchrony the condition during adolescence in which the growth or maturation of bodily parts is uneven (p. 96)

attitude a predisposition to act, think, and feel in a particular way toward a class of people, objects, or an idea (p. 577)

attribution theory a collection of principles based on our explanations of the causes of events, other people's behaviors, and our own behaviors (p. 530)

ira fuerte sensación de incomodidad, resentimiento u hostilidad, con una reacción iracunda que probablemente proviene de la frustración (págs. 145, 422)

anorexia nerviosa trastorno alimenticio severo en donde el miedo a ganar peso resulta en un período prolongado de pasar hambre y una dramática pérdida de peso (pág. 114)

medicamentos antiansiolíticos tipo de medicina que disminuye los trastornos de ansiedad y los trastornos de pánico al disminuir la actividad del sistema nervioso central (pág. 508)

antidepresivos tipo de medicamento empleado para tratar depresiones fuertes al aumentar la cantidad de neurotransmisores que se consideran presentes en la regulación de las emociones y los estados de ánimo (pág. 508)

medicamentos antisicóticos tipo de medicamento usado para reducir la agitación, delirios y alucinaciones; llamados también tranquilizantes (pág. 507)

personalidad antisocial trastorno de personalidad caracterizado por un patrón de irresponsabilidad, emociones superficiales, pérdida de conciencia y la violación de los derechos ajenos sin sentir culpa o remordimiento (pág. 475)

ansiedad estado psicológico desagradable caracterizado por una aprensión vaga generalizada o por el sentimiento de que uno está en peligro (págs. 422, 456)

ciencia aplicada descubrir maneras de usar hallazgos científicos para lograr objetivos prácticos (pág. 11)

conflicto de acercamiento-acercamiento tipo de situación conflictiva en la cual el individuo debe elegir entre dos alternativas positivas, pero mutuamente excluyentes (pág. 414)

conflicto de acercamiento-evasión tipo de situación conflictiva en la cual el individuo quiere hacer algo, pero le teme o desagrada al mismo tiempo (pág. 415)

prueba de aptitud instrumento empleado para predecir o estimar la probabilidad de tener éxito al aprender una nueva habilidad o habilidades específicas en el futuro (pág. 360)

arquetipo idea, imagen o concepto heredado, basado en la experiencia de los antepasados de un individuo que moldea su percepción del mundo (pág. 384)

asimilación proceso de adecuación de objetos y experiencias en los esquemas de un individuo para lidiar con nuevas situaciones y para entender el ambiente (pág. 71)

asincronía condición durante la adolescencia en la cual el crecimiento o maduración de las partes corporales es desigual (pág. 96)

actitud predisposición a actuar, pensar y sentir de una manera en particular hacia una clase de personas, objetos o una idea (pág. 577)

teoría de atribución colección de principios basada en nuestras propias explicaciones de las causas de los eventos, de las conductas de otras personas y de nuestro propio comportamiento (pág. 530)

Glossary-Glosario

auditory nerve the nerve that carries impulses from the inner ear to the brain, resulting in the perception of sound (p. 218)

authoritarian family family in which parents attempt to control, shape, and evaluate the behavior and attitudes of children in accordance with a set code of conduct (p. 79)

authoritarian leader a person who makes all the decisions and assigns tasks to group members (p. 554)

autonomic nervous system (ANS) the portion of the peripheral nervous system that controls internal biological functions such as heart rate, breathing, and blood pressure (p. 158)

autonomy the ability to take care of oneself and make one's own decisions independently (p. 437)

aversive conditioning a type of counterconditioning that links an unpleasant state with an unwanted behavior in an attempt to eliminate the behavior (p. 504)

aversive control the process of influencing behavior by means of unpleasant stimuli (p. 256)

avoidance-avoidance conflict a type of conflict situation in which the individual must choose between two negative or undesirable alternatives (p. 415)

avoidance conditioning the training of an organism to respond so as to prevent the occurrence of an unpleasant stimulus (p. 257)

axon a single, threadlike structure within the neuron that extends from and carries signals away from the cell body to neighboring neurons, organs, or muscles (p. 157)

axon terminals small fibers branching out from the end of an axon (p. 157)

nervio auditivo nervio que conduce los impulsos del oído interno al encéfalo, lo cual resulta en la percepción del sonido (pág. 218)

familia autoritaria familia en la cual los padres intentan controlar, moldear o evaluar el comportamiento y las actitudes de los hijos de acuerdo con un código de conducta establecido (pág. 79)

líder autoritario individuo que toma todas las decisiones y asigna tareas a los miembros del grupo (pág. 554)

sistema nervioso autónomo (SNA) la porción del sistema nervioso periférico que controla las funciones biológicas internas, como el ritmo cardiaco, la respiración y la presión sanguínea (pág. 158)

autonomía capacidad para responsabilizarse de sí mismo y de tomar decisiones propias de manera independiente (pág. 437)

condicionamiento aversivo tipo de contra condicionamiento que relaciona un estado desagradable con una conducta indeseada en un intento de eliminar la conducta (pág. 504)

control aversivo el proceso de influir sobre la conducta por medio de estímulos desagradables (pág. 256)

conflicto evasión-evasión tipo de situación conflictiva en que el individuo debe elegir entre dos alternativas negativas o desagradables (pág. 415)

condicionamiento de evasión entrenamiento de un organismo de modo de prevenir la ocurrencia de un estímulo desagradable (pág. 257)

axón estructura neuronal, individual y semejante a una hebra, que se extiende desde el cuerpo celular y transmite señales a partir de éste y hacia las neuronas, órganos o músculos vecinos (pág. 157)

terminales axónicos pequeñas fibras que se ramifican a partir del extremo de un axón (pág. 157)

B

basic science the pursuit of knowledge about natural phenomena for its own sake (p. 11)

behaviorism the belief that the proper subject matter of psychology is objectively observable behavior and nothing else (p. 387)

behaviorist a psychologist who analyzes how organisms learn or modify their behavior based on their response to events in the environment (p. 20)

behavior modification a systematic application of learning principles to change people's actions and feelings (pp. 263, 499)

behavior therapy a form of therapy that begins with clear, well-defined behavioral goals aimed at changing undesirable behavior through conditioning techniques (p. 502)

binocular depth cues depth cues that depend upon the movement of both eyes (p. 228)

ciencia básica la búsqueda del conocimiento sobre los fenómenos naturales por el conocimiento mismo (pág. 11)

conductualismo la creencia de que la apropiada materia del estudio de la psicología es el comportamiento objetivamente observable y nada más (pág. 387)

conductualista psicólogo que analiza cómo los organismos aprenden o modifican su comportamiento en base a su respuesta a eventos del ambiente (pág. 20)

modificación de conducta aplicación sistemática de principios de aprendizaje para cambiar las acciones o sentimientos de los individuos (págs. 263, 499)

terapia conductual forma de terapia que comienza con metas conductuales claras y bien definidas, encaminadas a cambiar comportamientos indeseados a través de técnicas de condicionamiento (pág. 502)

señas binoculares de profundidad claves de profundidad que dependen del movimiento de ambos ojos (pág. 228)

binocular fusion the process of combining the images received from the two eyes into a single, fused image (p. 216)

biofeedback the process of learning to control bodily states by monitoring the states to be controlled (pp. 194, 434)

bipolar disorder a disorder in which a person's mood inappropriately alternates between feelings of mania (euphoria) and depression (p. 471)

body language an often unconscious but sometimes conscious way of communicating by the way a person carries his or her body to convey an impression (p. 532)

boomerang effect a change in attitude or behavior opposite to the one desired by the persuader (p. 592)

brainwashing the most extreme form of attitude change, accomplished through peer pressure, physical suffering, threats, rewards for compliance, manipulation of guilt, intensive indoctrination, and other psychological means (p. 595)

bulimia nervosa a serious eating disorder characterized by compulsive overeating usually followed by self-induced vomiting or abuse of laxatives (p. 115)

bystander effect the tendency of a person to be less likely to give aid if other bystanders are present (p. 569)

fusión binocular proceso de combinar imágenes recibidas de los dos ojos en una sola imagen fusionada (pág. 216)

retroalimentación biológica proceso de aprendizaje para controlar estados corporales mediante monitoreo de los estados a controlarse (págs. 194, 434)

trastorno bipolar afección en que el estado anímico de un individuo se alterna inadecuadamente entre sentimientos de manía (euforia) y depresión (pág. 471)

lenguaje corporal forma de comunicación a menudo inconsciente, aunque en ocasiones consciente, por la que un individuo utiliza su cuerpo para transmitir una impresión (pág. 532)

efecto boomerang un cambio de actitud o conducta opuesto al deseado por el persuasor (pág. 592)

lavado cerebral la manera más extrema de cambio de actitud, lograda por presión de pares, sufrimiento físico, amenazas, recompensas por cumplimiento, manipulación de culpa, adoctrinamiento intensivo y otros medios psicológicos (pág. 595)

bulimia nerviosa trastorno alimenticio grave caracterizado por comer excesiva y compulsivamente, seguido por vómito autoinflingido o abuso de laxantes (pág. 115)

efecto transeúnte tendencia en que un individuo es menos probable que brinde ayuda al estar presentes otros transeúntes (pág. 569)

C

cardinal trait a characteristic or feature that is so pervasive the person is almost identified with it (p. 400)

career a chosen pursuit, profession, or occupation in which a person works at least a few years (p. 440)

case study an in-depth research method that involves an intensive investigation of one or more subjects (p. 37)

catharsis a psychological process through which anger or aggressive energy is released by expressing or letting out powerful negative emotions (p. 566)

central nervous system (CNS) the part of the nervous system that consists of the brain and spinal cord (p. 156)

central route for persuasion a way to deliver a message by focusing on presenting information consisting of strong arguments and facts (p. 592)

central tendency a number that describes something about the "average" score of a distribution (p. 51)

central trait the trait that best describes a person, such as shy, loyal, friendly, or generous (p. 400)

cerebral cortex the gray mass surrounding the subcortex, which is the information-processing center that controls the higher brain functions, such as reading and problem solving (p. 161)

rasgo fundamental característica o rasgo tan dominante que la persona prácticamente se identifica con ella (pág. 400)

profesión ocupación, profesión o meta elegida en que un individuo trabaja al menos por unos cuantos años (pág. 440)

estudio de casos método de investigación a fondo que significa una investigación intensiva de uno o más temas (pág. 37)

catarsis proceso psicológico a través del cual se libera la ira o energía agresiva al expresar o liberar poderosas emociones negativas (pág. 566)

sistema nervioso central (SNC) parte del sistema nervioso que consiste en el encéfalo y la médula espinal (pág. 156)

ruta central de persuasión manera de transmitir un mensaje enfocada en presentar información que consiste en argumentos o hechos sólidos (pág. 592)

tendencia central número que describe algo acerca del valor "promedio" de una distribución (pág. 51)

rasgo central característica que mejor describe a un individuo, como tímido, leal, amigable o generoso (pág. 400)

corteza cerebral materia gris que rodea la subcorteza, que es el centro de procesamiento de información que controla las funciones cerebrales superiores, como la lectura y la solución de problemas (pág. 161)

Glossary-Glosario

child abuse inadequate care or acts by a caregiver (physical or emotional abuse) that puts a child in danger, causes physical harm or injury, or involves molestation (p. 80)

chunking combining separate items of information into a larger unit, or chunk, and then remembering chunks of information rather than an individual item (p. 277)

circadian rhythm a regular sequence of biological processes such as temperature and sleep that occurs every 24 hours (p. 186)

classical conditioning a learning procedure in which associations are made between a neutral stimulus and an unconditioned stimulus (p. 241)

client-centered therapy an approach developed by Carl Rogers that reflects the belief that the client and therapist are partners in therapy (p. 496)

climacteric all the psychological and biological changes that occur in a woman between the ages of 45 and 50 (p. 131)

clinical psychologist a psychologist who diagnoses and treats people with emotional disturbances (p. 25)

clique a small, exclusive group of people within a larger group (p. 110)

cognitive having to do with an organism's thinking and understanding (p. 7)

cognitive appraisal the interpretation of an event that helps determine its stress impact (p. 431)

cognitive-behavior therapy a treatment based on a combination of substituting healthy thoughts for negative thoughts and beliefs and changing disruptive behaviors in favor of healthy behaviors (p. 505)

cognitive consistency the theory that people's attitudes change because they are always trying to get things to fit together logically inside their heads (p. 584)

cognitive dissonance a state of unpleasant psychological tension that arises when a person experiences contradictory or conflicting thoughts, attitudes, beliefs, or feelings (p. 584)

cognitive learning a form of learning that involves mental processes and may result from observation or imitation (p. 260)

cognitive map a mental picture of spatial relationships or relationships between events (p. 260)

cognitive therapy an approach in which thoughts are used to control emotions and behaviors (p. 499)

cognitivist a psychologist who studies how we process, store, retrieve, and use information and how thought processes influence our behavior (p. 20)

cohesiveness the factors that work to hold groups together (p. 547)

collective unconscious the part of the mind that contains inherited instincts, urges, and memories common to all people (p. 384)

abuso infantil atención o acciones inadecuadas de un cuidador (abuso físico o emocional) que pone a un infante en peligro, le causa daños o heridas físicas o implica abusos inmorales (pág. 80)

fragmentación combinación de diferentes elementos de información en una unidad más grande o segmento, para luego recordar porciones de información en lugar de elementos individuales (pág. 277)

ritmo circadiano secuencia regular de procesos biológicos, tales como temperatura y sueño, que ocurre cada 24 horas (pág. 186)

condicionamiento clásico procedimiento de aprendizaje donde se hacen asociaciones entre un estímulo neutro y un estímulo incondicionado (pág. 241)

terapia centrada en el cliente enfoque desarrollado por Carl Rogers que refleja la creencia de que el cliente y el terapista son compañeros de terapia (pág. 496)

climatérico todos los cambios psicológicos y biológicos que le ocurren a la mujer entre los 45 y 50 años de edad (pág. 131)

psicólogo clínico psicólogo que diagnostica y trata a individuos con trastornos emocionales (pág. 25)

camarilla grupo pequeño y exclusivo de individuos dentro de un grupo mayor (pág. 110)

cognitivo lo relativo al razonamiento y entendimiento de un organismo (pág. 7)

evaluación cognitiva interpretación de un evento que ayuda a determinar sus efectos sobre el estrés (pág. 431)

terapia cognitiva de conducta tratamiento basado en la combinación de un reemplazo de pensamientos y creencias negativos por pensamientos saludables y un cambio de conductas perturbadoras a favor de conductas saludables (pág. 505)

consistencia cognitiva teoría de que las actitudes personales cambian debido a que los individuos siempre tratan de ajustar las cosas en forma lógica en la mente (pág. 584)

disonancia cognitiva estado de tensión psicológica desagradable que surge cuando un individuo experimenta pensamientos, actitudes, creencias o sentimientos contradictorios o conflictivos (pág. 584)

aprendizaje cognitivo forma de aprendizaje en que participan procesos mentales y puede provenir de la observación o la imitación (pág. 260)

mapa cognitivo imagen mental de relaciones espaciales o relaciones entre eventos (pág. 260)

terapia cognitiva enfoque que usa los pensamientos para controlar las emociones y las conductas (pág. 499)

cognitivista psicólogo que estudia cómo procesamos, almacenamos, recuperamos y usamos la información y cómo influyen los procesos del pensamiento en nuestro comportamiento (pág. 20)

cohesividad factores que operan para mantener la unión en los grupos (pág. 547)

inconsciente colectivo parte de la mente que contiene instintos heredados, impulsos y memorias comunes a todas las personas (pág. 384)

community psychologist a psychologist who may work in a mental health or social welfare agency operated by the government or a private organization (p. 26)

companionate love a condition associated with trusting and tender feelings for someone whose life is closely bound up with one's own (p. 536)

comparable worth the concept that women and men should receive equal pay for jobs calling for comparable skill and responsibility (p. 441)

complementarity the attraction that often develops between opposite types of people because of the ability of one to supply what the other lacks (p. 525)

compliance a change or maintenance of behavior to avoid discomfort or rejection and to gain approval (p. 583)

compulsion an apparently irresistible urge to repeat an act or engage in ritualistic behavior such as hand washing (p. 458)

computerized axial tomography (CT) an imaging technique in which low levels of X rays are passed through the brain, and a computer measures the amount of radiation absorbed by the brain cells and produces a relatively good image of the brain (p. 167)

concept a way to group objects, events, or characteristics on the basis of some common property they share (p. 296)

conditioned response (CR) a response elicited by the conditioned stimulus; it is similar to the unconditioned response, but not identical in magnitude or amount (p. 242)

conditioned stimulus (CS) a once-neutral event that elicits a given response after a period of training in which it has been paired with an unconditioned stimulus (p. 242)

conditioning a type of learning that involves stimulus-response connections in which the response is conditional on the stimulus (p. 241)

conditions of worth the conditions a person must meet in order to regard himself or herself positively (p. 395)

cones visual receptors that are adapted for color vision, daytime vision, and detailed vision (p. 215)

confabulation the act of filling in memory with statements that make sense but that may be untrue (p. 284)

conflict situation a situation in which a person must choose between two or more options that tend to result from opposing motives (p. 414)

conformity acting in accord with group norms or customs (pp. 111, 556)

consciousness an individual's state of awareness, including a person's feelings, sensations, ideas, and perceptions (p. 183)

conservation according to Piaget, the principle that a given quantity does not change when its appearance is changed (p. 73)

psicólogo comunitario psicólogo que puede trabajar en un organismo de salud mental o de beneficencia social administrada por el gobierno o una organización privada (pág. 26)

amor compañero condición asociada con sentimientos tiernos y de confianza hacia alguien cuya vida está estrechamente ligada con la propia (pág. 536)

valor comparable concepto de que las mujeres y los hombres deben recibir salarios iguales por trabajos que requieren de destreza y responsabilidad comparables (pág. 441)

complementariedad la atracción que frecuentemente se desarrolla entre tipos opuestos de individuos debido a la capacidad de algunos de ellos de proporcionar lo que el otro carece (pág. 525)

adecuación cambio de conducta para evitar incomodidad o rechazo y para ganar aprobación (pág. 583)

compulsión necesidad aparentemente irresistible para repetir un acto o participar en un comportamiento ritualista como lavarse las manos (pág. 458)

tomografía axial computarizada (CT) técnica de generación de imágenes en la cual se hacen pasar niveles bajos de rayos X a través del encéfalo y una computadora mide la cantidad de radiación que absorben las células encefálicas y produce una imagen relativamente óptima del encéfalo (pág. 167)

concepto manera de agrupar objetos, eventos o características en base a algunas propiedades compartidas (pág. 296)

respuesta condicionada (RC) respuesta provocada por el estímulo condicionado; es semejante a la respuesta incondicionada, pero no idéntica en magnitud o cantidad (pág. 242)

estímulo condicionado (EC) evento anteriormente neutral, que provoca cierta respuesta tras un período de entrenamiento en el cual se pareó con un estímulo incondicionado (pág. 242)

condicionamiento tipo de aprendizaje que concierne conexiones estímulo–respuesta en las cuales la respuesta se condiciona al estímulo (pág. 241)

condiciones de valor condiciones que un individuo debe cumplir para estimarse positivamente(a)(pág. 395)

conos receptores visuales adaptados para la visión a color, visión diurna y visión detallada (pág. 215)

confabulación el acto de ocupar la memoria con enunciados que tienen sentido, pero que pueden ser falsos (pág. 284)

situación conflictiva situación en la cual se debe elegir entre dos o más opciones que tienden a resultar de motivos opuestos (pág. 414)

conformidad actuar de acuerdo con normas o costumbres del grupo (págs. 111, 556)

conciencia el estado mental de un individuo, incluido sus sentimientos, sensaciones, ideas y percepciones (pág. 183)

conservación de acuerdo con Piaget, el principio de que una cantidad dada no cambia al modificarse su apariencia (pág. 73)

constancy the tendency to perceive certain objects in the same way regardless of changing angle, distance, or lighting (p. 229)

content validity similarity between the items in a test and the information the test is meant to measure (p. 360)

contingencies of reinforcement the occurrence of rewards or punishments following particular behaviors (p. 388)

contingency management a form of behavior therapy in which undesirable behavior is not reinforced, while desirable behavior is reinforced (p. 504)

control group in an experiment, a group of participants that is treated in the same way as the experimental group except that the experimental treatment (the independent variable) is not applied (p. 40)

convergence the process by which your eyes turn inward to look at nearby objects (p. 228)

convergent thinking a way of thinking that depends heavily on symbols, concepts, and rules (p. 297)

conversion disorder a somatoform disorder characterized by changing emotional difficulties into a loss of a specific voluntary body function (p. 461)

correlation the measure of a relationship between two variables or sets of data (p. 39)

correlation coefficient a statistic that describes the direction and strength of the relationship between two sets of variables (p. 52)

counseling psychologist an individual who has a Ph.D. in psychology or education who helps people deal with problems of living (p. 25)

counterattitudinal behavior the process of taking a public position that contradicts one's private attitude (p. 585)

creativity the ability to use information, invent new solutions to problems, or create original and ingenious materials (p. 300)

crisis intervention program a short-term psychological first aid that helps individuals and families deal with emergencies or highly stressful situations (p. 604)

critical period a stage or point in development when certain skills or abilities are most easily learned (p. 75)

cross-sectional studies a research method in which data are collected from groups of participants of different ages and compared so that conclusions can be drawn about differences due to age differences (p. 38)

cultural bias an aspect of an intelligence test in which the wording used in questions and the experiences on which they are based may be more familiar to people of one social group than to another group (p. 356)

constancia la tendencia a percibir ciertos objetos de la misma forma, a pesar de cambios de ángulo, distancia o iluminación (pág. 229)

validez de contenido semejanza entre los elementos de una prueba y la información que la prueba pretende medir (pág. 360)

contingencias de reforzamiento incidencia de recompensas o castigos como consecuencia de ciertos comportamientos (pág. 388)

manejo de contingencias forma de terapia conductual en la cual no se refuerza el comportamiento indeseado y se refuerza el deseable (pág. 504)

grupo de control en un experimento, grupo de participantes que se trata de la misma manera que el grupo experimental, excepto que no se le aplica el tratamiento experimental (la variable independiente) (pág. 40)

convergencia el proceso por el cual tus ojos giran hacia adentro para observar objetos cercanos (pág. 228)

pensamiento convergente una forma de razonamiento que depende fuertemente de símbolos conceptos y reglas (pág. 297)

trastorno de conversión un trastorno somatoforme caracterizado por transformar problemas emocionales en la pérdida de una función corporal voluntaria específica (pág. 461)

correlación la medida de una relación entre dos variables o conjuntos de datos (pág. 39)

coeficiente de correlación una estadística que describe la dirección y fortaleza de la relación entre dos conjuntos de variables (pág. 52)

psicólogo consejero individuo con un doctorado en psicología o educación que ayuda a lidiar con sus problemas cotidianos (pág. 25)

comportamiento contraactitudinal el proceso de tomar una postura pública que contradice la actitud privada propia (pág. 585)

creatividad la capacidad para usar información, inventar nuevas soluciones a los problemas o crear materiales originales e ingeniosos (pág. 300)

programa de intervención de crisis una ayuda psicológica preliminar a corto plazo que ayuda a los individuos y familias a lidiar con emergencias o situaciones altamente estresantes (pág. 604)

período crítico una etapa o punto del desarrollo donde se aprenden más fácilmente ciertas destrezas o habilidades (pág. 75)

estudios transversales método de investigación en que se recopilan y comparan datos de grupos de participantes de distintas edades para poder obtener conclusiones sobre discrepancias atribuibles a diferencias etarias (pág. 38)

sesgo cultural aspecto de una prueba de inteligencia donde la redacción de las preguntas y las experiencias en que se basan puede resultar más familiares a individuos de cierto grupo social que a las de otro (pág. 356)

D

decay fading away of memory over time (p. 285)

declarative memory stored knowledge of facts or events such as scenes, stories, words, faces, or daily events that can be called forth consciously as needed (p. 279)

decremental model of aging a theory that holds that progressive physical and mental decline is inevitable with age (p. 138)

defense mechanisms certain specific means by which the ego unconsciously protects itself against unpleasant impulses or circumstances (p. 380)

deindividuation individuals behave irrationally when there is less chance of being personally identified (p. 570)

delusions false beliefs, as of persecution or grandeur, that a person maintains in the face of contradictory evidence (p. 466)

democratic/authoritative family family in which adolescents participate in decisions affecting their lives (p. 79)

democratic leader a person who encourages group members to come to decisions through consensus (p. 554)

dendrites the branchlike extensions of a neuron that receive impulses from other neurons, muscles, or sense organs and conduct them toward the cell body (p. 157)

denial a defense coping mechanism in which a person refuses to admit that a problem exists (pp. 145, 381, 431)

dependent variable in an experiment, the factor that is being measured that may or may not change when the independent variable is changed (p. 40)

depression a psychological disorder characterized by extreme sadness, an inability to concentrate, and feelings of helplessness and dejection (p. 145)

descriptive statistics the listing and summarizing of data in a practical, efficient way such as through graphs and averages (p. 48)

developmental friendship the type of friendship in which the partners force each other to reexamine their basic assumptions and perhaps adopt new ideas and beliefs (p. 438)

developmental psychologist a psychologist who studies the emotional, physical, cognitive, biological, personal, and social changes that occur as an individual matures (p. 26)

developmental psychology the branch of psychology that studies the emotional, physical, cognitive, biological, personal, and social changes that occur throughout an individual's life cycle (p. 61)

deterioro desvanecimiento de la memoria con el tiempo (pág. 285)

memoria declarativa conocimiento almacenado de hechos o eventos como escenas, historias, palabras, caras o eventos cotidianos que pueden recordarse conscientemente al requerirse (pág. 279)

modelo decremental de envejecimiento teoría que sostiene que el deterioro físico y mental progresivo resulta inevitable con la edad (pág. 138)

mecanismos de defensa ciertos medios específicos por los cuales el ego se protege inconscientemente de impulsos o circunstancias incómodas (pág. 380)

desindividualización los individuos se comportan irracionalmente cuando hay menor probabilidad de que se les identifique personalmente (pág. 570)

delirios falsas creencias, como de persecución o grandeza, que mantiene un individuo a pesar de existir evidencia contradictoria (pág. 466)

familia democrática/autoritaria familia en la cual los adolescentes participan en las decisiones que afectan sus vidas (pág. 79)

líder democrático persona que anima a los miembros del grupo a tomar decisiones a través de consensos (pág. 554)

dendritas extensiones ramificadas de una neurona que reciben impulsos de otras neuronas, músculos u órganos sensoriales y los conducen hacia el cuerpo celular (pág. 157)

negación mecanismo de defensa en el cual un individuo se niega a admitir que existe un problema (págs. 145, 381, 431)

variable dependiente en un experimento, el factor a medir, que podría cambiar o no al hacerlo la variable independiente (pág. 40)

depresión un trastorno psicológico caracterizado por extrema tristeza, inhabilidad para concentrarse y sentimientos de impotencia y abatimiento (pág. 145)

estadística descriptiva enumerar y resumir datos de manera práctica y eficiente, como gráficas y promedios (pág. 48)

amistad del desarrollo tipo de amistad en la cual los compañeros se esfuerzan mutuamente para reexaminar sus suposiciones básicas y quizá adoptar nuevas ideas y creencias (pág. 438)

psicólogo del desarrollo psicólogo que estudia los cambios emocionales, físicos, cognitivos, biológicos, personales y sociales que ocurren al madurar un individuo (pág. 26)

psicología del desarrollo rama de la psicología que estudia los cambios emocionales físicos, cognitivos, biológicos, personales y sociales que ocurren a lo largo del ciclo vital de un individuo (pág. 61)

difference threshold the smallest change in a physical stimulus that can be detected half the time (p. 210)

umbral de diferencia el menor cambio en un estímulo físico que puede detectarse la mitad del tiempo (pág. 210)

diffusion of responsibility when the presence of others lessens an individual's feelings of responsibility for his or her actions or failure to act (p. 569)

difusión de responsabilidad cuando la presencia de otros disminuye los sentimientos de responsabilidad de un individuo por sus acciones u omisiones (pág. 569)

directed thinking a systematic and logical attempt to reach a specific goal, such as a solution to a problem (p. 297)

razonamiento dirigido un intento sistemático y lógico por alcanzar una meta específica, como la solución de un problema (pág. 297)

disconfirmation one of three principles in cognitive therapy where clients may be confronted with evidence that directly contradicts their existing beliefs (p. 500)

desconfirmación uno de los tres principios de la terapia cognitiva donde los clientes pueden confrontarse con evidencia que contradice directamente sus creencias existentes (pág. 500)

discrimination the ability to respond differently to similar but distinct stimuli (p. 244); the unequal treatment of individuals on the basis of their race, ethnic group, age, gender, or membership in another category rather than on the basis of individual characteristics (p. 588)

discriminación la capacidad para responder de manera diferente a estímulos similares pero distintivos (pág. 244); tratamiento desigual de individuos en base a su raza, grupo étnico, edad, género o afiliación en otra categoría, en vez de basarse en las características individuales (pág. 588)

displacement a defense mechanism that shifts the desires, feelings, or impulses from their proper object to a substitute (p. 383)

desplazamiento mecanismo de defensa que traslada los deseos, sentimientos o impulsos de su objeto apropiado a un sustituto (pág. 383)

dissociative amnesia a dissociative disorder characterized by the inability to recall important personal events or information and usually associated with stressful events (p. 462)

amnesia disociativa trastorno disociativo caracterizado por la incapacidad de recordar información o eventos personales importantes y generalmente asociado con eventos estresantes (pág. 462)

dissociative disorder a disorder characterized by a disruption, split, or breakdown in a person's normally integrated and functioning memory, identity, or consciousness (p. 462)

trastorno disociativo trastorno caracterizado por la perturbación, resquebrajamiento o colapso de la memoria, identidad o conciencia normalmente integrada y funcional de un individuo (pág. 462)

dissociative fugue a dissociative disorder in which a person suddenly and unexpectedly travels away from home or work and is unable to recall the past (p. 462)

fuga disociativa trastorno disociativo en el cual un individuo repentina e inesperadamente viaja lejos de su hogar o trabajo y es incapaz de recordar el pasado (pág. 462)

dissociative identity disorder a dissociative disorder in which a person exhibits two or more personality states, each with its own patterns of thinking, perceiving, behaving, and relating in the world (p. 462)

trastorno de identidad disociativa trastorno disociativo en que un individuo presenta dos o más estados de personalidad, cada uno con sus propias pautas de pensamiento, percepción, comportamiento y forma de relacionarse con el mundo (pág. 462)

distress the type of stress that stems from acute anxiety or pressure and is damaging or negative (p. 414)

aflicción tipo de estrés que proviene de la ansiedad o presión aguda y que es dañino o negativo (pág. 414)

divergent thinking a way of thinking that consists of a free flow of thoughts with no particular plan and depends more on images (p. 297)

razonamiento divergente forma de razonamiento que consiste en el flujo libre de pensamientos sin ningún plan en particular y que depende más de las imágenes (pág. 297)

door-in-the-face technique a method of gaining compliance by first making an outrageous request and then replying to the refusal with a more reasonable request (p. 594)

técnica de portazo en la cara método para obtener conformidad al hacer primero una solicitud desmesurada y luego responder a la negativa con una solicitud mucho más razonable (pág. 594)

double approach-avoidance conflict a situation in which the individual must choose between two or more alternatives, each of which has attractive and unattractive aspects (p. 415)

conflicto doble de evasión-acercamiento situación en que el individuo debe elegir entre dos o más alternativas, cada una de las cuales tiene aspectos atractivos y desagradables (pág. 415)

double-blind experiment an experiment in which neither the experimenter nor the participants know which participants receive which treatment (p. 43)

experimento doblemente anónimo experimento en el cual ni el investigador ni los participantes saben qué participantes reciben qué tratamientos (pág. 43)

dream analysis a technique used by psychoanalysts to interpret the content of patients' dreams (p. 495)

análisis de sueños técnica que usan los psicoanalistas para interpretar el contenido de los sueños de los pacientes (pág. 495)

drive a condition of arousal or tension produced by a need that motivates an organism toward a goal (p. 315)

motivación condición de excitación o tensión producida por una necesidad que motiva a un organismo hacia una meta (pág. 315)

drug therapy a form of biological therapy that uses medications (p. 507)

terapia medicinal forma de terapia biológica que emplea medicamentos (pág. 507)

DSM-IV the fifth version of the American Psychiatric Association's Diagnostic and Statistical Manual of Mental Disorders (p. 451)

DSM-IV la quinta versión del Manual Diagnóstico y Estadístico de Trastornos Mentales de la Asociación Psiquiátrica Estadounidense (pág. 451)

E

echoic memory the sensory register in which traces of sounds are held and may be retrieved within several seconds (p. 275)

eclectic approach an approach to therapy in which the psychotherapist combines techniques and ideas from many different schools of thought (p. 487)

educational psychologist a psychologist who is concerned with helping students learn (p. 26)

ego the part of the personality that is in touch with reality and strives to meet the demands of the id and the superego in socially acceptable ways (p. 380)

egocentric a young child's inability to understand another person's perspective (p. 73)

ego-support value the ability of a person to provide another person with sympathy, encouragement, and approval (p. 523)

eidetic memory the ability to remember with great accuracy visual information on the basis of short-term exposure (p. 284)

elaborative rehearsal a memory device that creates a meaningful link between new information and material that is already known (p. 287)

electroconvulsive therapy (ECT) a radical treatment for psychological disorders in which an electrical shock is sent through the brain (p. 509)

electroencephalograph (EEG) a machine used to record the electrical activity of large portions of the brain (p. 165)

emotion a state of feeling that involves a set of complex reactions to a stimulus involving subjective feelings, physiological arousal, and observable behavior (p. 329)

emotional intelligence the ability to perceive, imagine, and understand emotions and to use that information in decision making (pp. 329, 351)

empathy the capacity for warmth and understanding (p. 489)

encoding placing or storing information such as images, events, or sounds in memory by making mental representations so the nervous system can process it (p. 274)

endocrine system a chemical communication system located throughout the body that uses hormones to send messages through the bloodstream to particular organs of the body (p. 171)

memoria ecoica el registro sensorial donde se conservan los rastros de sonidos y éstos pueden recuperarse en cuestión de segundos (pág. 275)

enfoque ecléctico aproximación a la terapia en donde el psicoterapeuta combina técnicas e ideas de muchas escuelas de pensamiento diferentes (pág. 487)

psicólogo educacional psicólogo cuya preocupación es ayudar a los estudiantes a aprender (pág. 26)

ego la parte de la personalidad que está en contacto con la realidad y que se esfuerza por cumplir con las demandas del id y del súper ego en formas socialmente aceptables (pág. 380)

egocéntrico la incapacidad de un niño pequeño para entender la perspectiva de otra persona (pág. 73)

valor de apoyo al ego la capacidad de un individuo para proporcionarle simpatía, ánimo y aprobación a otro individuo (pág. 523)

memoria eidética la habilidad de recordar con gran precisión información visual en base a una exposición a corto plazo (pág. 284)

ensayo elaborado instrumento de memoria que crea un enlace significativo entre la información nueva y el material ya conocido (pág. 287)

terapia electroconvulsiva (ECT) tratamiento radical para trastornos psicológicos en que se envía una descarga eléctrica a través del encéfalo (pág. 509)

electroencefalógrafo (EEG) máquina que se usa para grabar la actividad eléctrica de grandes porciones del encéfalo (pág. 165)

emoción estado anímico que incluye un conjunto de reacciones complejas a un estímulo que presenta sentimientos subjetivos, excitación fisiológica y comportamiento observable (pág. 329)

inteligencia emocional la capacidad de percibir, imaginar y entender emociones y usar esta información en la toma de decisiones (págs. 329, 351)

empatía capacidad de afecto y entendimiento (pág. 489)

codificar colocar o almacenar información tales como imágenes, eventos o sonidos en la memoria mediante representaciones mentales a fin de que el sistema nervioso pueda procesarlo (pág. 274)

sistema endocrino sistema de comunicación química localizado en todo el organismo, que emplea hormonas para enviar mensajes a través del torrente sanguíneo a ciertos órganos corporales (pág. 171)

Glossary-Glosario

endogamy the tendency to marry someone who is from one's own social group (p. 538)

environmental psychologist a psychologist who studies the effects of the environment on people (p. 27)

episodic memory chronological retention of the events of one's life (p. 279)

escape conditioning the training of an organism to remove or terminate an unpleasant stimulus (p. 257)

estrogen one of the major female sex hormones (p. 172)

ethics methods of conduct or standards for proper and responsible behavior (p. 40)

eustress positive stress, which results from motivating strivings and challenges (p. 414)

experimental group the group of participants to which an independent variable is applied (p. 40)

experimental psychologist a psychologist who studies sensation, perception, learning, motivation, and/or emotion in carefully controlled laboratory conditions (p. 28)

extinction in classical conditioning, the gradual disappearance of a conditioned response because the reinforcement is withheld or because the conditioned stimulus is repeatedly presented without the unconditioned stimulus (p. 245)

extrasensory perception (ESP) a group of psychic experiences that involves perceiving or sending information (images) outside normal sensory processes or channels; includes four general abilities: telepathy, precognition, clairvoyance, and psychokinesis (p. 230)

extravert an outgoing, active person who directs his or her energies and interests toward other people and things (p. 401)

extrinsic motivation engaging in certain activities or behaviors that either reduce biological needs or help a person obtain external incentives (p. 316)

endogamia la tendencia a casarse con alguien que pertenece al propio grupo social (pág. 538)

psicólogo ambiental psicólogo que estudia los efectos del ambiente sobre los individuos (pág. 27)

memoria episódica retención cronológica de los eventos experimentados durante la vida de un individuo (pág. 279)

condicionamiento de escape entrenamiento de un organismo para eliminar o terminar un estímulo desagradable (pág. 257)

estrógeno una de las principales hormonas sexuales femeninas (pág. 172)

ética métodos de conducta o estándares para un comportamiento apropiado y responsable (pág. 40)

eustrés estrés positivo, que resulta de esfuerzos y retos motivadores (pág. 414)

grupo experimental grupo de participantes al cual se le aplica la variable independiente (pág. 40)

psicólogo experimental psicólogo que estudia sensación, percepción, aprendizaje, motivación y/o emoción en condiciones de laboratorio cuidadosamente controladas (pág. 28)

extinción en condicionamiento clásico, la desaparición gradual de una respuesta condicionada debido a que se retiene el reforzamiento o debido a que el estímulo condicionado se presenta repetidamente sin el estímulo instintivo (pág. 245)

percepción extrasensorial (ESP) grupo de experiencias psíquicas que implica percibir o enviar información (imágenes) fuera de los procesos o canales sensoriales normales; incluye cuatro capacidades generales: telepatía, precognición, clarividencia y psicoquinesis (pág. 230)

extrovertido individuo activo y desenvuelto que enfoca sus energías e intereses hacia otros individuos y cosas (pág. 401)

motivación extrínseca participar en ciertas actividades o comportamientos, que reducen necesidades biológicas o ayudan a un individuo a obtener incentivos externos (pág. 316)

F

factor analysis a complicated statistical technique used to identify the underlying reasons variables are correlated (p. 401)

family therapy a form of therapy aimed at understanding and improving relationships that have led one or more members in a close social unit to experience emotional suffering (p. 490)

fear the usual reaction when a stressor involves real or imagined danger (p. 422)

fight-or-flight response a state of increased physiological arousal that helps us cope with and survive threatening situations (p. 421)

fixed-interval schedule a pattern of reinforcement in which a specific amount of time must elapse before a response will elicit reinforcement (p. 254)

análisis de factores técnica estadística complicada que se emplea para identificar las razones subyacentes por las que se correlacionan las variables (pág. 401)

terapia familiar forma de terapia enfocada a entender y mejorar las relaciones que conllevan a uno o más miembros de una unidad social cercana a experimentar sufrimiento emocional (pág. 490)

miedo la reacción usual cuando un estresor presenta peligro real o imaginario (pág. 422)

respuesta de pelea o huída estado de excitación fisiológica aumentada que nos ayuda a enfrentar y sobrevivir situaciones amenazantes (pág. 421)

programa de intervalo fijo patrón de reforzamiento en que debe pasar una cantidad específica de tiempo antes de que una respuesta provoque reforzamiento (pág. 254)

fixed-ratio schedule a pattern of reinforcement in which a specific number of correct responses is required before reinforcement can be obtained (p. 253)

flexibility the ability to overcome rigidity (p. 301)

flooding therapy for a phobia in which the person is suddenly exposed to the object of the phobia (p. 504)

foot-in-the-door technique a method of gaining compliance by getting a person to agree to a relatively minor request first (pp. 557, 593)

forebrain the largest part of the brain that covers the brain's central core, responsible for sensory and motor control and the processing of thinking and language (p. 161)

forensic psychology a branch of psychology that deals with diagnosis, evaluation, treatment, and testimony regarding the law and criminal behavior (p. 615)

fraternal twins twins who come from two different eggs fertilized by two different sperm (p. 176)

free association a Freudian technique used to examine the unconscious; the patient is instructed to say whatever comes into his or her mind (p. 494)

frequency distribution an arrangement of data that indicates how often a particular score or observation occurs (p. 49)

fully functioning an individual whose person and self coincide (p. 396)

functional fixedness a mental set characterized by the inability to imagine new uses for familiar objects (p. 300)

functionalist a psychologist who studied the function (rather than the structure) of consciousness (p. 16)

fundamental attribution error an inclination to over attribute others' behavior to internal causes (dispositional factors) and discount the situational factors contributing to their behavior (p. 531)

fundamental needs biological drives or needs that must be satisfied in order to maintain life (p. 326)

programa de razón fija patrón de reforzamiento en el cual se requiere un número específico de respuestas correctas antes de que pueda obtenerse el reforzamiento (pág. 253)

flexibilidad capacidad para superar la rigidez (pág. 301)

inundación terapia para una fobia en que un individuo se expone súbitamente al objeto de la fobia (pág. 504)

técnica del pie en la puerta método que logra conformidad al hacer que un individuo acceda primero a un solicitud relativamente pequeña (págs. 557, 593)

prosencéfalo la sección más grande del encéfalo que cubre su parte central; es la responsable del control sensorial y motor y el procesamiento del pensamiento y el lenguaje (pág. 161)

psicología forense rama de la psicología que se ocupa del diagnóstico, evaluación, tratamiento y testimonio relacionado con la ley y la conducta criminal (pág. 615)

gemelos fraternos gemelos que provienen de dos óvulos diferentes fecundados por dos espermatozoides diferentes (pág. 176)

asociación libre técnica freudiana empleada para examinar el subconsciente; se le instruye al paciente a que diga cualquier cosa que le venga a su mente (pág. 494)

distribución de frecuencia arreglo de datos que indica la frecuencia con que se presenta un valor u observación particular (pág. 49)

funcionalmente completo individuo cuya persona y su yo coinciden (pág. 396)

fijación funcional esquema mental caracterizado por la incapacidad de imaginar nuevos usos para objetos familiares (pág. 300)

funcionalista psicólogo que estudia la función (más que la estructura) de la conciencia (pág. 16)

error de atribución fundamental inclinación para atribuir en demasía el comportamiento ajeno a causas internas (factores de disposición) y descontar los factores situacionales que contribuyen a su comportamiento (pág. 531)

necesidades fundamentales impulsos o necesidades biológicas que deben satisfacerse para mantener la vida (pág. 326)

G

gate control theory of pain the theory that we can lessen some pains by shifting our attention away from the pain impulses or by sending other signals to compete with the pain signals (p. 221)

gender identity the sex group (masculine or feminine) to which an individual biologically belongs; an individual's subjective sense of being male or female (p. 117)

gender role the sex group (masculine or feminine) with which an individual feels identification; the set of behaviors that society considers appropriate for each sex (p. 117)

teoría del control de la compuerta del dolor la teoría de que podemos atenuar algunos dolores al desviar nuestra atención de los impulsos dolorosos o al enviar otras señales que compitan con las señales dolorosas (pág. 221)

identidad de género grupo sexual (masculino o femenino) al cual pertenece biológicamente un individuo; el sentido subjetivo de un individuo de ser masculino o femenino (pág. 117)

papel de género el grupo sexual (masculino o femenino) con el que se identifica un individuo; el conjunto de conductas que una sociedad considera apropiadas para cada sexo (pág. 117)

gender schema a set of behaviors organized around how either a male or female should think and behave (p. 122)

esquema de género conjunto de conductas organizadas alrededor de cómo debe pensar y comportarse un hombre o mujer (pág. 122)

gender stereotype an oversimplified or distorted generalization about the characteristics of men and women (p. 117)

estereotipo de género generalización sobresimplificada o distorsionada sobre las características de los hombres y mujeres (pág. 117)

general adaptation syndrome according to Selye, a series of three stages—alarm, resistance, and exhaustion—that correspond to the three different reactions of the body to stressful situations (p. 421)

síndrome de adaptación general según Selye, una serie de tres etapas: alarma, resistencia y agotamiento, que corresponden a las tres reacciones corporales diferentes a situaciones estresantes (pág. 421)

generalization in classical conditioning, the tendency for a stimulus that is similar to the original conditioned stimulus to elicit a response that is similar to the conditioned response (p. 244)

generalización en el condicionamiento clásico, la tendencia de un estímulo semejante al estímulo condicionado original de provocar una respuesta semejante a la respuesta condicionada (pág. 244)

generational identity the theory that people of different ages tend to think differently about certain issues because of different formative experiences (p. 534)

identidad generacional la teoría de que las personas de diferentes edades tienden a pensar de manera diferente sobre ciertos asuntos debido a experiencias formativas distintas (pág. 534)

generativity the desire in middle age to use one's accumulated wisdom to guide future generations (p. 135)

generatividad en la mediana edad, el deseo de usar la sabiduría acumulada propia para guiar a las generaciones futuras (pág. 135)

genes the basic building blocks of heredity (p. 175)

genes los bloques básicos de la herencia (pág. 175)

genital stage Freud's fifth and final psychosexual stage during which an individual's sexual satisfaction depends as much on giving pleasure as on receiving it (p. 82)

etapa genital quinta y última etapa psicosexual de Freud durante la cual la satisfacción sexual de un individuo depende tanto del placer que proporciona como del que recibe (pág. 82)

gerontology the study of aging (p. 615)

gerontología el estudio del envejecimiento (pág. 615)

Gestalt the experience that comes from organizing bits and pieces of information into meaningful wholes (p. 224)

Gestalt experiencia que proviene de la organización de fragmentos y elementos de información en unidades integrales significativas (pág. 224)

grammar a set of rules for combining words into phrases and sentences to express an infinite number of thoughts that can be understood by others (p. 66)

gramática conjunto de reglas para combinar palabras en frases y enunciados con el fin de expresar un número infinito de pensamientos que puedan entender los demás (pág. 66)

grasping reflex an infant's clinging response to a touch on the palm of his or her hand (p. 62)

reflejo de aprehensión respuesta de aferramiento de un lactante a que se le toque la palma de la mano (pág. 62)

group a collection of people who have shared goals, a degree of interdependence, and some amount of communication (p. 545)

grupo colectivo de individuos que compartieron metas, un grado de interdependencia y cierta cantidad de comunicación (pág. 545)

group polarization the theory that group discussion reinforces the majority's point of view and shifts group members' opinions to a more extreme position (p. 550)

polarización grupal teoría que establece que las discusiones grupales refuerzan el punto de vista de la mayoría y cambian las opiniones de los miembros del grupo hacia posiciones más extremas (pág. 550)

group therapy a form of therapy in which patients work together with the aid of a leader to resolve interpersonal problems (p. 489)

terapia grupal forma de terapia donde los pacientes trabajan juntos con la ayuda de un líder para resolver problemas interpersonales (pág. 489)

groupthink poor group decision making that occurs as a result of a group emphasizing unity over critical thinking (p. 551)

razonamiento grupal toma deficiente de decisiones grupales que ocurre como resultado de un grupo que favorece la unidad sobre el razonamiento crítico (pág. 551)

H

hallucinations false sensory perceptions that have no direct external cause (pp. 199, 466)

alucinaciones percepciones sensoriales falsas que carecen de causa externa directa (págs. 199, 466)

hallucinogens drugs that often produce hallucinations (p. 200)

alucinógenos drogas que frecuentemente producen alucinaciones (pág. 200)

hardiness the personality traits of control, commitment, and challenge that help us reduce the stress we feel (p. 432)

hassles common, relatively minor day-to-day stressors (p. 418)

health psychologist a psychologist who studies the interaction between physical and psychological health factors (p. 27)

heredity the genetic transmission of characteristics from parents to their offspring (p. 174)

heritability a measure of the degree to which a characteristic is related to inherited genetic factors (p. 355)

heuristic a rule-of-thumb, problem-solving strategy that reduces the number of operations or allows us to take shortcuts in solving problems (pp. 299, 594)

hindbrain a part of the brain located at the rear base of the skull that is involved in the basic processes of life such as sleeping, waking, coordinating body movements, and regulating vital reflexes (p. 160)

histogram a graph similar to a bar graph except that histograms show frequency distribution by means of rectangles whose widths represent class intervals and whose areas are proportionate to the corresponding frequencies (p. 50)

homeostasis the tendency of all organisms to correct imbalances and deviations from their normal state (p. 315)

homogamy the tendency to marry someone who has similar attributes, including physical attractiveness, age, and physique, to our own (p. 538)

hormones chemical substances produced by the endocrine glands that carry messages through the body in blood and regulate specific body functions (p. 171)

hospice a type of care for terminally ill patients; an organization that provides such care (p. 147)

humanist a psychologist who believes that each person has freedom in directing his or her future and achieving personal growth (p. 20)

humanistic psychology a school of psychology that emphasizes personal growth and the achievement of maximum potential for each unique individual (p. 392)

humanistic therapy an approach to psychology that focuses on the value, dignity, and worth of each person and holds that healthy living is the result of realizing one's full potential (p. 496)

hypnosis a state of consciousness resulting from a narrowed focus of attention and characterized by heightened suggestibility (p. 191)

hypnotic analgesia a reduction of pain reported by patients after undergoing hypnosis (p. 194)

hypochondriasis a somatoform disorder characterized by being preoccupied with imaginary ailments (p. 461)

hypothesis an assumption or prediction about behavior or an educated guess about the relationship between two variables that is tested through scientific research (pp. 11, 40)

firmeza características personales de control, compromiso y desafío que ayudan a reducir el estrés que sentimos (pág. 432)

dificultades estresores cotidianos comunes, relativamente menores (pág. 418)

psicólogo de salud psicólogo que estudia la interacción entre factores de salud físicos y psicológicos (pág. 27)

herencia traspaso genético de características de padres a progenie (pág. 174)

heredabilidad medida del grado con que un rasgo se relaciona con factores genéticos heredados (pág. 355)

heurístico estrategia empírica de solución de problemas que reduce el número de operaciones o que nos permite tomar atajos para resolver problemas (págs. 299, 594)

mielencéfalo parte del encéfalo localizada en la base trasera del cráneo que se encarga de los procesos vitales básicos, como dormir, despertarse, coordinar movimientos corporales y regular los reflejos vitales (pág. 160)

histograma gráfica parecida a una gráfica de barras excepto que los histogramas muestran la distribución de frecuencia mediante rectángulos cuyas áreas representan intervalos de clase y cuyas áreas son proporcionales a las frecuencias correspondientes (pág. 50)

homeostasis tendencia de todos los organismos de corregir los desequilibrios y desviaciones de su estado normal (pág. 315)

homogamia tendencia a casarse con alguien que posee atributos semejantes a los propios, incluidos el atractivo físico, la edad y el físico (pág. 538)

hormonas sustancias químicas que producen las glándulas endocrinas, que transportan mensajes a través del cuerpo por la sangre y regulan funciones corporales específicas (pág. 171)

hospicio tipo de cuidado para pacientes desahuciados; organización que proporciona tal cuidado (pág. 147)

humanista psicólogo que cree que cada persona tiene libertad de dirigir su futuro y de lograr su crecimiento personal (pág. 20)

psicología humanista escuela de psicología que enfatiza el crecimiento personal y la consecución del potencial máximo para cada individuo único (pág. 392)

terapia humanista aproximación a la psicología que se enfoca en la estima, dignidad y valía de cada persona y sostiene que la vida saludable es el resultado de la realización del potencial completo del individuo (pág. 496)

hipnosis estado consciente que resulta de enfocar la atención en un espacio restringido y se caracteriza por una sugestibilidad aumentada (pág. 191)

analgesia hipnótica reducción del dolor informado por pacientes tras someterse a hipnosis (pág. 194)

hipocondriasis trastorno somatoforme caracterizado por la preocupación con dolencias imaginarias (pág. 461)

hipótesis suposición o predicción acerca del comportamiento o una conjetura razonable sobre la relación entre dos variables y que se prueba a través de una investigación científica (págs. 11, 40)

hysteria more commonly used in Sigmund Freud's time to refer to unexplainable fainting, paralysis, or deafness (p. 461)

histeria término usado más comúnmente en la época de Sigmund Freud para referirse a desmayo, parálisis o sordera inexplicables (pág. 461)

I

iconic memory the sensory register that briefly holds mental images of visual stimuli (p. 275)

memoria icónica registro sensorial que mantiene brevemente imágenes mentales de estímulos visuales (pág. 275)

id in psychoanalytic theory, that part of the unconscious personality that contains our needs, drives, and instincts, as well as repressed material (p. 379)

id en teoría psicoanalítica, la parte de la personalidad inconsciente que contiene nuestras necesidades, impulsos e instintos, así como material reprimido (pág. 379)

identical twins twins who develop from one fertilized egg; twins having the same heredity and genes (p. 175)

gemelos idénticos gemelos desarrollados de un óvulo fecundado; gemelos que poseen la misma herencia y genes (pág. 175)

identification in psychoanalytic theory, the process by which a child adopts the values and principles of the same-sex parent (p. 82); the process of seeing oneself as similar to another person or group and accepting the attitudes of another person or group as one's own (p. 583)

identificación en teoría psicoanalítica, el proceso por el cual un niño adopta los valores y principios del padre del mismo sexo (pág. 82); el proceso de verse a sí mismo como semejante a otra persona o grupo y aceptar las actitudes de otra persona o grupo como propias (pág. 583)

identity crisis a period of inner conflict during which adolescents worry intensely about who they are (p. 105)

crisis de identidad período de conflicto interno durante el cual los adolescentes se preocupan intensamente sobre quiénes son (pág. 105)

ideology the set of principles, attitudes, and defined objectives for which a group stands (p. 548)

ideología conjunto de principios, actitudes y objetivos definidos de los cuales es partidario un grupo (pág. 548)

illusions perceptions that misrepresent physical stimuli (pp. 229, 436)

ilusiones percepciones que representan erróneamente estímulos físicos (págs. 229, 436)

image a visual, mental representation of a specific event or object (p. 296)

imagen representación mental visual de un evento u objeto específico (pág. 296)

immune system the body's natural defense system that fights off bacteria, viruses, and other foreign or toxic substances (p. 426)

sistema inmunológico sistema de defensa natural del cuerpo que combate bacterias, virus y otras sustancias tóxicas o extrañas (pág. 426)

imprinting inherited tendency of some newborn animals to follow the first moving object they see (p. 75)

impronta tendencia heredada que despliegan algunos animales recién nacidos de seguir el primer objeto móvil que ven (pág. 75)

incentive environmental factor such as an external stimulus, reinforcer, or reward that motivates our behavior (p. 316)

incentivo factor ambiental, tal como un estímulo externo, refuerzo o recompensa que motiva nuestro comportamiento (pág. 316)

independent variable in an experiment, the factor that the researcher deliberately controls or manipulates to test its effect on another factor (p. 40)

variable independiente en un experimento, el factor que el investigador controla o manipula deliberadamente para probar su efecto sobre otro factor (pág. 40)

individualistic when people act as individuals, obey their consciences, and are concerned with self-evaluation (p. 570)

individualista cuando las personas actúan como individuos, obedecen a sus conciencias y se interesan en la autoevaluación (pág. 570)

industrial/organizational psychologist a psychologist who uses psychological concepts to make the workplace a more satisfying environment for employees and managers (p. 26)

psicólogo industrial/organizacional psicólogo que usa conceptos psicológicos para hacer del lugar del trabajo un ambiente más satisfactorio para empleados y administrativos (pág. 26)

industrial/organizational psychology a branch of psychology that deals with the psychology of the workplace (p. 615)

psicología industrial/organizacional rama de la psicología que trata con la psicología del lugar de trabajo (pág. 615)

inferential statistics numerical methods used to determine whether research data support a hypothesis or whether results were due to chance (p. 53)

estadística inferencial métodos numéricos que se usan para determinar si los datos de la investigación apoyan una hipótesis o si los resultados se deben a la casualidad (pág. 53)

inferiority complex a pattern of avoiding feelings of inadequacy and insignificance rather than trying to overcome their source (p. 385)

in-group group members who identify with their group (p. 549)

initiation rites a ceremony or ritual in which an individual is admitted to a new status or accepted into a new position (p. 94)

innate part of a person's biological inheritance (p. 330)

inoculation effect a method of developing resistance to persuasion by exposing a person to arguments that challenge his or her beliefs so that he or she can practice defending them (p. 595)

insight the apparent sudden realization or understanding of the solution to a problem (pp. 301, 494)

insomnia a sleep disorder characterized by recurring problems in falling asleep or staying asleep (p. 187)

instincts innate tendencies that determine behavior (p. 314)

intellectualization a coping mechanism in which the person analyzes a situation from an emotionally detached viewpoint (p. 431)

intelligence the ability to acquire new ideas and new behavior, learn from experience, and adapt to new situations (p. 348)

intelligence quotient (IQ) standardized measure of intelligence based on a scale in which 100 is defined as average (p. 352)

interest inventory measures a person's preferences and attitudes in a wide variety of activities (p. 361)

interference the process that occurs when new information appears in short-term memory and replaces what was already there (p. 286)

internalization the process of incorporating the values, ideas, and standards of others as a part of oneself (p. 584)

intimacy the component of love associated with feeling close and connected to someone (p. 536)

intrinsic motivation engaging in certain activities because they are personally rewarding or because they fulfill our beliefs and expectations (p. 316)

introspection a method of self-observation in which participants report on their thoughts and feelings (p. 16)

introvert a reserved, withdrawn person who is more preoccupied with his or her inner thoughts and feelings than in what is going on around him or her (p. 401)

complejo de inferioridad patrón de evitar sentimientos de inconveniencia e insignificancia, en vez de intentar la superación de la causa de estos sentimientos (pág. 385)

grupo de pertenencia miembros que se identifican con su grupo (pág. 549)

ritos de iniciación ceremonia o ritual mediante el cual se admite un individuo a un estatus nuevo o se le acepta en una posición diferente (pág. 94)

innato parte de la herencia biológica de un individuo (pág. 330)

efecto de inoculación método de desarrollo de resistencia a la persuasión que expone al individuo a argumentos que desafían sus creencias y de modo que pueda practicar a defenderlas (pág. 595)

discernimiento darse cuenta o entender de manera aparentemente repentina la solución de un problema (págs. 301, 494)

insomnio trastorno del sueño caracterizado por problemas recurrentes para dormirse o permanecer dormido (pág. 187)

instintos tendencias innatas que determinan la conducta (pág. 314)

intelectualización mecanismo para sobrellevar el estrés, en el cual un individuo analiza una situación desde un punto de vista emocionalmente distante (pág. 431)

inteligencia capacidad para adquirir nuevas ideas o conductas, aprender de la experiencia y adaptarse a nuevas situaciones (pág. 348)

coeficiente de inteligencia (IQ) medida estandarizada de la inteligencia que se basa en una escala en la cual 100 se define como el promedio (pág. 352)

medidas de inventario de intereses preferencias y actitudes de un individuo dentro una amplia gama de actividades (pág. 361)

interferencia proceso que ocurre cuando aparece información nueva en la memoria a corto plazo y reemplaza a la que estaba allí (pág. 286)

internalización proceso de incorporación de valores, ideas y estándares ajenos como parte de uno mismo (pág. 584)

intimidad componente del amor asociado con sentirse cercano y conectado a alguien (pág. 536)

motivación intrínseca comprometerse con ciertas actividades porque nos gratifican personalmente o satisfacen nuestras creencias y expectativas (pág. 316)

introspección método de autoobservación en el cual los participantes informan sobre sus pensamientos y sentimientos (pág. 16)

introvertido individuo reservado y abstraído que se preocupa más por sus propios pensamientos y sentimientos que por lo que sucede a su alrededor (pág. 401)

Glossary-Glosario

J

just noticeable difference (JND) the smallest increase or decrease in the intensity of a stimulus that a person is able to detect (p. 210)

diferencia apenas notable (DAN) el menor aumento o disminución en la intensidad de un estímulo que es capaz de detectar un individuo (pág. 210)

K

kinesthesis the sense that provides information about the position and movement of individual body parts (p. 222)

cinestesia el sentido que proporciona información sobre la posición y movimiento de partes corporales individuales (pág. 222)

L

laissez-faire leader a person who is only minimally involved in a group's decision making (p. 554)

language a system of communication that involves using rules to make and combine symbols in ways that produce meaningful words and sentences (p. 304)

language-acquisition device (LAD) innate brain structures that include inborn mechanisms that guide a person's learning of the unique rules of his or her native language (p. 306)

latency stage the fourth stage of Freud's psychosexual development at which sexual desires are pushed into the background and the child becomes involved in exploring the world and learning new skills (p. 82)

latent content refers to the hidden meanings represented symbolically in a dream (p. 495)

latent learning learning that is not demonstrated by an immediate, observable change in behavior (p. 260)

lateral hypothalamus (LH) the part of the hypothalamus that produces hunger signals (p. 320)

learned helplessness a condition in which repeated attempts to control or influence a situation fail, resulting in the belief that the situation is uncontrollable and that any effort to cope will fail (p. 261)

learning a relatively permanent change in behavior that results from experience (p. 241)

lens a flexible, elastic, transparent oval structure in the eye that changes its shape to focus light on the retina; the lens is attached to muscles that adjust the curve of the lens, which in turn adjusts the focus (p. 215)

linguistic relativity the idea that a person's language influences his or her thoughts (p. 308)

lithium carbonate a chemical used to counteract mood swings of bipolar disorder (p. 508)

lobes the different regions into which the cerebral cortex is divided (p. 162)

líder liberal individuo que sólo participa de una manera mínima en la toma de decisiones de un grupo (pág. 554)

lenguaje sistema de comunicación que concierne el uso de reglas para formar y combinar símbolos en formas que producen palabras y enunciados significativos (pág. 304)

mecanismo de adquisición de lenguaje (LAD) estructuras encefálicas innatas que incluyen mecanismos connaturales que guían el aprendizaje individual de las reglas particulares de su lengua nativa (pág. 306)

etapa de latencia la cuarta etapa del desarrollo psicosexual de Freud en la cual los deseos sexuales pasan a segundo término y el niño se interesa en la exploración del mundo y en el aprendizaje de nuevas destrezas (pág. 82)

contenido latente se refiere a los significados ocultos que se representan simbólicamente en un sueño (pág. 495)

aprendizaje latente aprendizaje que no se demuestra por un cambio observable e inmediato en el comportamiento (pág. 260)

hipotálamo lateral (HL) parte del hipotálamo que produce las señales de hambre (pág. 320)

impotencia adquirida condición producida al fracasar repetidamente los intentos de controlar o influir en una situación, lo cual resulta en la creencia de que la situación es incontrolable y que fallará cualquier esfuerzo para superarla (pág. 261)

aprendizaje cambio conductual relativamente permanente que resulta de la experiencia (pág. 241)

lente estructura ocular oval, transparente, elástica y flexible, que cambia de forma para enfocar luz sobre la retina; la lente se une a unos músculos que ajustan su curvatura, que a su vez ajustan el enfoque (pág. 215)

relatividad lingüística idea que el lenguaje de un individuo influye en sus pensamientos (pág. 308)

carbonato de litio sustancia química empleada para contrarrestar los cambios de ánimo del trastorno bipolar (pág. 508)

lóbulos las diferentes regiones en que se divide la corteza cerebral (pág. 162)

longitudinal study research method in which data are collected about a group of participants over a number of years to assess how certain characteristics change and remain the same during development (p. 38)

LSD (lysergic acid diethylamide) an extremely potent psychedelic drug that produces hallucinations (p. 200)

estudio longitudinal método de investigación en que se recopilan datos sobre un grupo de participantes durante varios años para averiguar cómo cambian y se mantienen ciertas características durante el desarrollo (pág. 38)

dietilamida del ácido lisérgico (LSD) droga psicodélica extremadamente potente que produce alucinaciones (pág. 200)

M

magnetic resonance imaging (MRI) an imaging technique that passes nonharmful frequencies through the brain; a computer measures the interaction with brain cells and transforms this interaction into an incredibly detailed image of the brain (or body) (p. 167)

maintenance rehearsal a system for remembering that involves repeating information to oneself without attempting to find meaning in it (p. 276)

major depressive disorder a severe form of depression marked by at least two weeks of continually being in a bad mood, having no interest in anything, and getting no pleasure from activities (p. 470)

manifest content what a person remembers about a dream (p. 495)

marijuana the dried leaves and flowers of Indian hemp (*Cannabis sativa*) that produce an altered state of consciousness when smoked or ingested (p. 198)

maturation the internally programmed growth of a child that occurs as a result of automatic, genetically determined signals (p. 64)

mean the arithmetic average of all the individual measurements in a distribution (p. 51)

median the score that divides a distribution of rank-ordered observations in half; the middle score (p. 51)

meditation a systematic narrowing of attention on an image, thought, bodily process, or external object with the goal of clearing one's mind and producing relaxation (pp. 195, 434)

memory the input, storage, and retrieval of what has been learned or experienced (p. 274)

menarche a female's first menstrual period (p. 96)

menopause the biological event in which a woman's production of sex hormones is sharply reduced (p. 131)

mental set the tendency to approach a new problem in a way that has been successful in the past (p. 299)

metacognition the awareness of or thinking about one's own cognitive processes (p. 297)

midbrain the small part of the brain above the pons that arouses the brain, integrates sensory information, and relays it upward (p. 161)

generación de imágenes por resonancia magnética (MRI) técnica de generación de imágenes que pasa frecuencias no perjudiciales a través del encéfalo; una computadora mide la interacción con las células encefálicas y la transforma en una imagen encefálica (o corporal) increíblemente detallada (pág. 167)

ensayo de mantenimiento sistema para recordar que implica repetir información para sí mismo sin intentar hallarle un significado (pág. 276)

trastorno depresivo grave aguda forma de depresión caracterizada por al menos dos semanas continuas de mal humor, sin mostrar interés en nada y sin obtener ningún placer de las actividades realizadas (pág. 470)

contenido manifiesto lo que un individuo recuerda sobre un sueño (pág. 495)

marihuana hojas y flores deshidratadas del cáñamo de la India (*Cannabis sativa*), que producen un estado alterado de conciencia al fumar o ingerirse (pág. 198)

maduración crecimiento internamente programado de un niño que ocurre como resultado de señales automáticas genéticamente determinadas (pág. 64)

media promedio aritmético de todas las mediciones individuales en una distribución (pág. 51)

mediana la magnitud que divide por la mitad una distribución de observaciones ordenadas por rango; el valor intermedio (pág. 51)

meditación enfoque sistemático de atención a una imagen, pensamiento, proceso corporal u objeto externo con el fin de aclarar la mente y producir relajación (págs. 195, 434)

memoria adquisición, almacenamiento y recuperación de lo que se aprendió o se experimentó (pág. 274)

menarquía el primer período menstrual de una mujer (pág. 96)

menopausia evento biológico en el cual se reduce agudamente la producción de hormonas sexuales de una mujer (pág. 131)

esquema mental tendencia de enfrentar un nuevo problema de una manera que resultó exitosa en el pasado (pág. 299)

metacognición conciencia de o pensamiento de un individuo acerca de sus propios procesos cognitivos (pág. 297)

mesencéfalo la parte más pequeña del encéfalo sobre el puente de Varolio, que integra la información sensorial y la transmite hacia la parte superior (pág. 161)

mnemonic devices techniques of memorizing information by forming vivid associations or images, which facilitate recall and decrease forgetting (p. 288)

instrumentos nemotécnicos técnicas para memorizar información que forman asociaciones o imágenes vivas que facilitan el recuerdo y disminuyen el olvido (pág. 288)

mode the most frequent score in a distribution of observations (p. 51)

moda el dato más frecuente en una distribución de observaciones (pág. 51)

modeling the process of learning behavior through observation and imitation of others; copying behavior (pp. 262, 504)

modelado proceso de aprendizaje de conductas a través de la observación e imitación de otros; comportamiento copiado (págs. 262, 504)

monocular depth cues depth cues produced by signals from a single eye (p. 227)

señas de profundidad monocular claves de profundidad producidas por señales que parten de un solo ojo (pág. 227)

morpheme the smallest unit of meaning in a given language, such as a prefix or suffix (p. 305)

morfema la unidad más pequeña con significado en un idioma dado, como un prefijo o sufijo (pág. 305)

motion parallax the apparent movement of stationary objects relative to one another that occurs when the observer changes position (p. 228)

movimiento paralaje movimiento aparente entre cuerpos estacionarios relacionados que ocurre al cambiar de posición el observador (pág. 228)

motivation various physiological and psychological factors that activate behavior and energize and direct that behavior toward a goal (p. 314)

motivación varios factores fisiológicos y psicológicos que activan el comportamiento y lo potencian y dirigen hacia una meta (pág. 314)

motive to avoid success a theory that suggests that some people are (or were) raised with the idea that being successful in all but a few careers is odd and unlikely (p. 325)

motivo para evitar el éxito teoría que sugiere que algunos individuos se crían (o se criaron) con la idea que ser exitosos es raro y poco probable, excepto en unas cuantas profesiones (pág. 325)

Munchausen's syndrome a disorder in which an individual develops great sensitivity to emotional pain and will use any method possible to avoid feeling it (p. 464)

síndrome de Munchausen trastorno en que un individuo desarrolla una gran sensibilidad al dolor emocional y usa cualquier método posible para evitar sentirlo (pág. 464)

myelin sheath a tubelike white fatty substance that insulates the axons and enables rapid transmission of neural impulses (p. 157)

envoltorio mielínico sustancia blanca grasosa con forma de tubo que aísla los axones y permite la rápida transmisión de impulsos neuronales (pág. 157)

N

narcolepsy a condition characterized by suddenly falling asleep or feeling very sleepy during the day (p. 188)

narcolepsia condición caracterizada por quedarse dormido repentinamente o sentirse muy adormilado durante el día (pág. 188)

naturalistic observation a research method in which the psychologist observes the subject in a natural setting and without manipulation or control on the part of the observer (p. 37)

observación naturalista método de investigación en el cual el psicólogo observa al sujeto en un escenario natural y sin manipulación o control por parte del observador (pág. 37)

need a biological or psychological requirement for the well-being of an organism (pp. 314, 536)

necesidad requerimiento biológico o psicológico para el bienestar de un organismo (págs. 314, 536)

negative correlation a relationship between two variables in which one variable increases as the other variable decreases (p. 39)

correlación negativa relación entre dos variables donde una de ellas aumenta mientras que la otra disminuye (pág. 39)

negative reinforcement increasing the strength of a given response by removing or preventing a painful stimulus when the response occurs (p. 256)

reforzamiento negativo incrementar la intensidad de una respuesta dada al eliminar o prevenir un estímulo doloroso cuando se presenta la respuesta (pág. 256)

neurons the long, thin cells that constitute the structural and functional unit of nerve tissue along which messages travel to and from the brain (p. 157)

neuronas células largas y delgadas que constituyen la unidad estructural y funcional del tejido nervioso, a través de las cuales se transportan los mensajes hacia y desde el encéfalo (pág. 157)

neurotransmitters the chemicals released by neurons, which determine the rate at which other neurons fire (p. 158)

neurotransmisores sustancias químicas liberadas por neuronas que determinan la velocidad a la cual responden otras neuronas (pág. 158)

neutral stimulus a stimulus that does not initially elicit any part of an unconditioned response (p. 242)

nightmares unpleasant dreams that contain frightening and anxiety-producing images (p. 188)

night terrors sleep disruptions that occur during Stage IV of sleep, involving screaming, panic, or confusion that is seldom remembered (p. 188)

nondirective therapy the free flow of images and ideas, occurring with no particular goal (p. 496)

nonverbal communication conveying messages using space, body language, and facial expression (p. 531)

normal curve a graph of frequency distribution shaped like a symmetrical, bell-shaped curve; a graph of normally distributed data (p. 51)

norms standards of comparison for test results developed by giving the test to large, well-defined groups of people (p. 346); shared standards of behavior accepted by and expected from group members (p. 547)

estímulo neutral estímulo que inicialmente no provoca ninguna parte de una respuesta incondicional (pág. 242)

pesadillas sueños desagradables que contienen imágenes que generan temor y ansiedad (pág. 188)

terrores nocturnos perturbaciones que ocurren durante la etapa IV del sueño, donde se presentan gritos, pánico o confusión escasamente recordados (pág. 188)

terapia no direccional libre flujo de imágenes e ideas que ocurre sin ningún objetivo en particular (pág. 496)

comunicación no verbal transmisión de mensajes que usa el espacio, el lenguaje corporal y las expresiones faciales (pág. 531)

curva normal gráfica de distribución de frecuencias con forma de curva acampanada simétrica; gráfica de datos distribuidos normalmente (pág. 51)

normas estándares comparativos de resultados de pruebas que se desarrollan al aplicarlas a grupos grandes y bien definidos de individuos (pág. 346); estándares de conducta compartidos que aceptan y esperan los miembros de un grupo (pág. 547)

O

obedience a change in attitude or behavior brought about by social pressure to comply with people perceived to be authorities (p. 558)

objective test a limited- or forced-choice test (in which a person must select one of several answers) designed to study personality characteristics (p. 364)

object permanence a child's realization that an object exists even when he or she cannot see, hear, or touch it (p. 72)

observational learning learning by observing and imitating the behavior of others (pp. 262, 389)

obsession a recurring thought or image that seems to be beyond control (p. 458)

obsessive-compulsive disorder an anxiety disorder consisting of obsessions and compulsions (p. 458)

olfactory nerve the nerve that transmits information about odors from the nose to the brain (p. 220)

operant conditioning a form of learning in which a certain action is reinforced or punished, resulting in corresponding increases or decreases in the likelihood that similar actions will occur again (p. 250)

optic nerve the nerve that carries impulses from the retina to the brain (p. 215)

optimist a person whose thoughts lead him or her to believe and expect that good things will happen (p. 433)

oral stage Freud's first stage of psychosexual development, in which infants associate erotic pleasure with the mouth (p. 82)

out-group everyone who is not a member of the in-group (p. 549)

obediencia un cambio de actitud o conducta generado por presión social para cumplir con individuos que se perciben como autoridades (pág. 558)

prueba de objetivos una prueba de selección múltiple (en la cual un individuo debe seleccionar una de entre varias respuestas) diseñada para estudiar características de personalidad (pág. 364)

permanencia de objeto cuando un niño se da cuenta que un objeto existe aún sin poder ver, oír o tocarlo (pág. 72)

aprendizaje por observación aprendizaje adquirido al observar e imitar el comportamiento ajeno (págs. 262, 389)

obsesión pensamiento o imagen recurrente que aparenta estar fuera de control (pág. 458)

trastorno obsesivo compulsivo trastorno de ansiedad que consiste en obsesiones y compulsiones (pág. 458)

nervio olfativo nervio que transmite información sobre los olores de la nariz al encéfalo (pág. 220)

condicionamiento operante una forma de aprendizaje que refuerza o penaliza una cierta reacción y resulta aumentos o disminuciones respectivos en la probabilidad de que ocurran nuevamente semejantes acciones (pág. 250)

nervio óptico nervio que transporta impulsos nerviosos de la retina al encéfalo (pág. 215)

optimista persona cuyos pensamientos lo llevan a creer y a esperar que sucederán cosas buenas (pág. 433)

etapa oral primera etapa del desarrollo psicosexual de Freud, en la cual los lactantes asocian el placer erótico con la boca (pág. 82)

grupo de no-pertenencia todos los que no son miembros del grupo de pertenencia (pág. 549)

Glossary-Glosario

ovaries the female sex glands (p. 172)

overgeneralization a common error during language acquisition in which children apply a grammatical rule to cases where it should not be used (p. 68)

overjustification effect when people are given more extrinsic motivation than necessary to perform a task, their intrinsic motivation declines (p. 317)

ovarios glándulas sexuales femeninas (pág. 172)

sobregeneralización error común durante la adquisición del lenguaje en que los niños aplican reglas gramaticales en casos donde no debieran emplearse (pág. 68)

efecto de sobrejustificación efecto que ocurre cuando se les da a las personas más motivación extrínseca de la necesaria para llevar a cabo una tarea y su motivación intrínseca disminuye (pág. 317)

P

panic a feeling of sudden, helpless terror (p. 457)

panic disorder an extreme anxiety that manifests itself in the form of panic attacks (p. 457)

parapsychology the study of behavior types that seem to deviate from normal behavior and are sometimes left unexplained; literally means "alongside psychology" (p. 609)

passionate love a condition that is associated with continuously thinking about a loved one and accompanied by warm sexual feelings and powerful emotional reactions (p. 535)

percentile system a system for ranking test scores that indicates the ratio of scores lower and higher than a given score (p. 346)

perception the organization and interpretation of sensory information into meaningful experiences (p. 208)

peripheral nervous system (PNS) a network of nerves branching beyond the spinal cord that conduct information from the bodily organs to the central nervous system and take information back to the organs (p. 156)

peripheral route for persuasion a way to deliver a message by relying on emotional appeals, emphasizing personal traits or positive feelings (p. 592)

permissive/laissez-faire family family in which children have the final say; parents are less controlling and have a nonpunishing, accepting attitude toward children (p. 79)

personal construct theory George Kelly's theory that our processes are psychologically channelized by the ways in which each of us anticipates events (p. 396)

personality all the consistent, stable, enduring, and unique ways in which the behavior of one person differs from that of others (p. 375)

personality disorders maladaptive or inflexible ways of dealing with others and one's environment (p. 475)

personality test an instrument used to measure a person's traits, behaviors, and unobservable characteristics and to identify problems (p. 363)

pánico sentimiento de terror repentino e inevitable (pág. 457)

trastorno de pánico ansiedad extrema que se manifiesta en forma de ataques de pánico (pág. 457)

parapsicología estudio de tipos de comportamiento que parecen desviarse de su comportamiento normal y algunas veces se quedan sin explicación; literalmente significa "al lado de la psicología" (pág. 609)

amor apasionado condición asociada con el pensar continuamente en el ser amado, acompañado de sentimientos sexuales cálidos y reacciones emotivas poderosas (pág. 535)

sistema percentil sistema de ordenamiento de resultados de pruebas que indica la razón de resultados por encima y por debajo de un valor dado (pág. 346)

percepción organización e interpretación de información sensorial en experiencias significativas (pág. 208)

sistema nervioso periférico (SNP) red de nervios que se ramifican más allá de la médula espinal que conducen información de los órganos corporales al sistema nervioso central y que lleva de vuelta información a los órganos (pág. 156)

ruta periférica para persuasión manera de entregar un mensaje al confiar en apelaciones emocionales que enfatizan características personales o sentimientos positivos (pág. 592)

familia permisiva/liberal familia en la cual los hijos tienen la última palabra; los padres son menos controladores y tienen una actitud de aceptación, no punitiva hacia ellos (pág. 79)

teoría de construcción personal teoría de George Kelly que establece que nuestros procesos se canalizan psicológicamente por la forma en que cada uno anticipa los eventos (pág. 396)

personalidad todas las maneras consistentes, estables, duraderas y únicas en que el comportamiento de un individuo difiere del de otros (pág. 375)

trastornos de personalidad maneras desadaptadas o inflexibles de tratar con otros y el propio ambiente (pág. 475)

prueba de personalidad instrumento que se emplea para medir los rasgos, los comportamientos y las características no observables de un individuo y para identificar problemas (pág. 363)

persuasion the direct attempt to influence attitudes (p. 590)

pessimist a person whose thoughts lead him or her to believe and expect that bad things will happen (p. 433)

phallic stage in this stage, Freud's third psychosexual stage, children associate sexual pleasure with their genitals (p. 82)

phobia an intense and irrational fear of a particular object or situation (p. 456)

phoneme an individual sound that is the basic structural element of language (p. 305)

physical proximity the distance of one person to another person (p. 522)

physiological having to do with an organism's physical needs (pp. 7, 616)

pituitary gland the center of control of the endocrine system that hangs directly below the hypothalamus and secretes a large number of hormones (p. 171)

placebo effect a change in a participant's illness or behavior that results from a belief that the treatment will have an effect rather than from the actual treatment (pp. 45, 488)

positive correlation a relationship between variables in which one variable increases as the other variable also increases (p. 39)

positive regard viewing oneself in a favorable light due to supportive feedback received from interaction with others (p. 395)

positive reinforcer a stimulus that increases the likelihood that a response will occur again (p. 251)

positron emission tomography (PET) an imaging technique used to see which areas of the brain are being activated while performing tasks (p. 167)

posthypnotic suggestion a suggestion made during hypnosis about performing a particular behavior in response to a predetermined cue that influences the participant's behavior afterward (p. 193)

post-traumatic stress disorder disorder in which victims of catastrophes or other traumatic events experience the original event in the form of dreams or flashbacks (pp. 423, 459)

preattentive process a method for extracting information automatically and simultaneously when presented with stimuli (p. 213)

precocious puberty premature puberty (p. 100)

predictive validity ability of a test's scores to predict real-world performance (p. 345)

prefrontal lobotomy a radical form of psychosurgery in which a section of the frontal lobe of the brain is destroyed (p. 510)

prejudice preconceived, unjustifiable, and usually negative attitude toward a person or group that has been formed without sufficient evidence (p. 587)

persuasión intento directo de influir sobre actitudes (pág. 590)

pesimista individuo cuyos pensamientos lo llevan a creer y a esperar que ocurran cosas malas (pág. 433)

etapa fálica en ésta, la tercera etapa psicosexual de Freud, los niños asocian el placer sexual con sus genitales (pág. 82)

fobia miedo intenso e irracional hacia un objeto o situación particular (pág. 456)

fonema sonido individual que constituye el elemento estructural básico del lenguaje (pág. 305)

proximidad física distancia entre un individuo y otro (pág. 522)

fisiológico lo relativo a las necesidades físicas de un organismo (págs. 7, 616)

glándula pituitaria centro de control del sistema endocrino que cuelga directamente debajo del hipotálamo y secreta una gran cantidad de hormonas (pág. 171)

efecto placebo cambio en la enfermedad o comportamiento de un participante que resulta de creer que el tratamiento tendrá un efecto, en lugar del tratamiento en sí (págs. 45, 488)

correlación positiva relación entre variables en que aumenta una variable mientras que aumenta también la otra (pág. 39)

consideración positiva verse a sí mismo de forma positiva debido a la retroalimentación de apoyo recibida de la interacción con otros (pág. 395)

reforzador positivo estímulo que aumenta la probabilidad de que ocurrirá de nuevo una respuesta (pág. 251)

tomografía de emisión de positrones (PET) una técnica de generación de imágenes empleada para observar qué áreas del encéfalo se activan al desempeñar ciertas tareas (pág. 167)

sugestión posthipnótica sugestión hecha durante la hipnosis sobre el desempeño de cierta conducta como respuesta a un impulso predeterminado que influye sobre la conducta posterior del participante (pág. 193)

trastorno de estrés postraumático trastorno donde las víctimas de catástrofes u otros eventos traumáticos experimentan el evento original en forma de sueños u escenas retrospectivas (págs. 423, 459)

proceso preatencional método de extraer información automática y simultáneamente al presentarse un estímulo (pág. 213)

pubertad precoz pubertad prematura (pág. 100)

validez predictiva capacidad de los resultados de una prueba para predecir el desempeño en el mundo real (pág. 345)

lobotomía prefrontal forma radical de psicocirugía en la cual se destruye una sección del lóbulo frontal del encéfalo (pág. 510)

prejuicio actitud preconcebida, injustificada y generalmente negativa hacia un individuo o grupo generada sin suficiente evidencia (pág. 587)

Glossary-Glosario

primacy effect the tendency to form opinions about others based on first impressions (p. 528)

primary appraisal one's immediate evaluation of a situation (p. 416)

primary group a group of people who interact daily face-to-face (p. 549)

primary-recency effect the fact that most people are better able to recall information presented at the beginning and end of a list (p. 277)

primary reinforcer a stimulus, such as food or water, that is naturally rewarding and satisfying and requires no learning on the part of the subject to become pleasurable (p. 252)

proactive interference a forgetting process in which information that we learned earlier blocks or disrupts the retrieval of related new information (p. 286)

procedural memory permanent storage of learned skills that does not require conscious recollection (p. 279)

progesterone a female sex hormone (p. 172)

progressive relaxation an exercise performed by lying down comfortably and tensing and releasing the tension in each major muscle group in turn (p. 434)

projection unconsciously transferring one's own undesirable attitudes, feelings, or thoughts to others (p. 382)

projective test an unstructured test of personality in which a person is asked to respond freely, giving his or her own interpretation of various ambiguous stimuli (p. 366)

prototype a representative example of a concept (p. 296)

psychiatry a branch of medicine that deals with mental, emotional, or behavioral disorders (p. 25)

psychoactive drugs chemicals that affect the nervous system and result in altered consciousness or awareness, influence sensations and perceptions, and modify moods and cognitive processes (p. 197)

psychoanalysis a form of therapy aimed at making patients aware of their unconscious motives so that they can gain control over their behavior and free themselves of self-defeating patterns (p. 494)

psychoanalyst a psychologist who studies how unconscious motives and conflicts determine human behavior, feelings, and thoughts (p. 19)

psychobiologist a psychologist who studies how physical and chemical changes in our bodies influence our behaviors (p. 21)

psychological the emotional and behavioral characteristics of an individual or group (p. 616)

psychological dependence a strong, repetitive desire for use of a drug to such an extent that a person feels nervous and anxious without it (p. 476)

efecto de primacía tendencia a formarse opiniones sobre los demás en base a primeras impresiones (pág. 528)

valoración primaria evaluación individual inmediata de una situación (pág. 416)

grupo primario grupo de individuos que interactúan diariamente cara a cara (pág. 549)

efecto de primacía-reciente el hecho de que la mayoría de los seres humanos son más capaces de recordar información presentada al inicio y al final de una lista (pág. 277)

reforzador primario estímulo, como alimento o agua, naturalmente gratificante y satisfactorio que no requiere aprendizaje por parte del sujeto para tornarse placentero (pág. 252)

interferencia proactiva proceso de olvido en que la información que aprendimos anteriormente bloquea o afecta la recuperación de nueva información relacionada (pág. 286)

memoria procesal almacenaje permanente de destrezas aprendidas que no requieren de un recuerdo consciente (pág. 279)

progesterona hormona sexual femenina (pág. 172)

relajación progresiva ejercicio que se realiza al tenderse cómodamente y a la vez tensar y liberar la tensión en cada grupo muscular principal (pág. 434)

proyección transferir inconscientemente a otros las actitudes, sentimientos o pensamientos indeseados propios (pág. 382)

prueba de proyección prueba de personalidad no estructurada en la cual se le solicita a un individuo que responda libremente al dar su propia interpretación de varios estímulos ambiguos (pág. 366)

prototipo ejemplo representativo de un concepto (pág. 296)

psiquiatría rama de la medicina que trata con trastornos mentales, emocionales o conductuales (pág. 25)

drogas psicoactivas sustancias químicas que afectan el sistema nervioso y producen estados alterados de consciencia o conocimiento, influyen en las sensaciones y percepciones y modifican los estados de ánimo y procesos cognitivos (pág. 197)

psicoanálisis forma de terapia dirigida a concientizar a los pacientes de sus motivos inconscientes para que puedan tomar control de su comportamiento y liberarse de patrones autoderrotistas (pág. 494)

psicoanalista psicólogo que estudia cómo los motivos y conflictos inconscientes determinan la conducta, los sentimientos y los pensamientos humanos (pág. 19)

psicobiólogo psicólogo que estudia cómo los cambios físicos y químicos de nuestros cuerpos influyen en nuestro comportamiento (pág. 21)

psicológico(a) características emocionales o conductuales de un individuo o grupo (pág. 616)

dependencia psicológica deseo intenso y repetitivo por usar una droga hasta tal punto que un individuo se siente nervioso y ansioso sin ella (pág. 476)

psychological needs urges to belong and to give and receive love and urges to acquire esteem through competence and achievement (p. 326)

necesidades psicológicas impulsos por pertenecer y por dar y recibir amor; impulsos por adquirir estima a través de competencia y logros (pág. 326)

psychologist a scientist who studies the mind and behavior of humans and animals (p. 25)

psicólogo científico que estudia la mente y el comportamiento de humanos y animales (pág. 25)

psychology the scientific, systematic study of behaviors and mental processes (p. 9)

psicología estudio científico y sistemático de las conductas y los procesos mentales (pág. 9)

psychophysics the study of the relationships between sensory experiences and the physical stimuli that cause them (p. 208)

psicofísica estudio de las relaciones entre las experiencias sensoriales y los estímulos físicos que los causan (pág. 208)

psychosocial development life periods in which an individual's goal is to satisfy desires associated with social needs (p. 83)

desarrollo psicosocial períodos de vida en que el objetivo de un individuo es satisfacer deseos asociados con necesidades sociales (pág. 83)

psychosocial hunger factors external cues that affect eating (p. 321)

factores psicosociales del hambre impulsos externos que afectan la forma de comer (pág. 321)

psychosurgery a medical operation that destroys part of the brain to make the patient calmer and freer of symptoms (p. 510)

psicocirugía operación médica que destruye parte del encéfalo para calmar más al paciente y liberarlo un poco más de sus síntomas (pág. 510)

psychotherapy a general term for the application of psychological principles and techniques for any treatment used by therapists to help troubled individuals overcome their problems and disorders (p. 486)

psicoterapia término general para la aplicación de principios y técnicas psicológicas para cualquier tratamiento que usan los terapistas para ayudar a individuos conflictivos a sobreponerse a sus problemas y trastornos (pág. 486)

puberty the period of sexual maturation; the end of childhood and the point when reproduction is first possible (p. 95)

pubertad período de maduración sexual; fin de la infancia y el punto cuando es posible la reproducción por primera vez (pág. 95)

pupil the opening in the iris that regulates the amount of light entering the eye (p. 215)

pupila abertura en el iris que regula la cantidad de luz que entra al ojo (pág. 215)

R

random sample a sample group of a larger population selected in such a way that each subject within the population has an equal chance of being selected (p. 37)

muestra aleatoria grupo muestral de una población más grande, seleccionada de manera que exista igual oportunidad de selección entre los sujetos que integran la población (pág. 37)

range the lowest score in a distribution subtracted from the highest score (p. 52)

rango la calificación más baja en una distribución que se le resta a la calificación más alta (pág. 52)

rational-emotive therapy (RET) a confrontational cognitive form of therapy aimed at changing unrealistic assumptions about oneself and other people (p. 500)

terapia racional-emotiva (RET) forma de terapia cognitiva confrontativa dirigida a cambiar suposiciones no realistas sobre sí mismo y sobre otros (pág. 500)

rationalization a process whereby an individual seeks to explain an often unpleasant emotion or behavior in a way that will preserve his or her self-esteem (pp. 102, 381)

racionalización proceso por el cual un individuo busca explicarse una emoción o conducta no placentera de una manera que conserve su autoestima (págs. 102, 381)

reaction formation a defense mechanism by which the ego unconsciously replaces an unacceptable feeling or urge with its opposite (p. 382)

reacción formativa mecanismo de defensa mediante el cual el ego reemplaza inconscientemente con su opuesto, un sentimiento o impulso no aceptable (pág. 382)

recall the type of memory retrieval in which a person reconstructs previously learned material without the aid of or with very few external cues (p. 283)

recuerdo tipo de recuperación de memoria por el cual un individuo reconstruye material previamente aprendido sin la ayuda de o con muy pocas indicaciones externas (pág. 283)

recognition the type of memory retrieval in which a person is required to identify an object, idea, or situation as one he or she has or has not experienced before (p. 283)

reconocimiento tipo de recuperación de memoria mediante la cual se le solicita a un individuo que identifique un objeto, idea o situación como algo experimentado o no previamente (pág. 283)

recombination rearranging the elements of a problem in order to arrive at an original solution (p. 301)

recombinación reorganizar los elementos de un problema para llegar a una solución original (pág. 301)

reconceptualization one of three principles in cognitive therapy where clients work toward an alternative belief system to explain their experiences or current observations (p. 500)

reconstructive processes the alteration of a recalled memory that may be simplified, enriched, or distorted, depending on an individual's experiences, attitudes, or inferences (p. 284)

regression a defense mechanism in which an individual retreats to an earlier stage of development or pattern of behavior in order to deal with a threatening or stressful situation (p. 383)

reinforcement a stimulus or event that follows a response and increases the likelihood that the response will be repeated (p. 251)

reliability the ability of a test to give the same results under similar conditions (p. 344)

REM sleep a stage of sleep characterized by rapid eye movements, a high level of brain activity, a deep relaxation of the muscles, and dreaming behind closed eyelids (p. 186)

replicate to repeat a research study to confirm the results of the original study (p. 40)

representational thought the intellectual ability of a child to picture something in his or her mind (p. 72)

repression the exclusion from conscious awareness of a painful, unpleasant, or undesirable memory (pp. 286, 381)

resistance in psychoanalysis, the reluctance of a patient either to reveal painful feelings or to examine longstanding behavior patterns (p. 494)

response chain the learned reactions that follow one another in sequence, each reaction producing the signal for the next (p. 256)

resynthesis the process of combining old ideas with new ones and reorganizing feelings in order to renew one's identity (p. 439)

retina the light-sensitive innermost coating of the back of the eye that contains the rods, cones, and neurons that process visual stimuli (p. 215)

retinal disparity a binocular cue for perceiving depth based on the differences between the images stimulating each eye (p. 216)

retrieval the process of obtaining information that has been stored in memory (p. 274)

retroactive interference the hampering of recall of learned material by the recall of other material learned more recently (p. 286)

rods visual receptor cells in the retina that are sensitive to light but not color, allowing us to see in dim light but to see only black, white, and shades of gray (p. 215)

role behavior expected of an individual because of his or her membership in a particular group (pp. 550, 587)

role taking an important aspect of children's play that involves assuming adult roles, thus enabling the child to experience different points of view firsthand (p. 84)

reconceptualización uno de los tres principios de la teoría cognitiva en donde los clientes intentan hallar un sistema de creencias alternativo para explicar sus experiencias u observaciones actuales (pág. 500)

procesos reconstructivos alteración de una memoria recordada que puede simplificarse, enriquecerse o distorsionarse según las experiencias, actitudes o inferencias individuales (pág. 284)

regresión mecanismo de defensa en el cual un individuo regresa a una etapa de desarrollo o patrón conductual anterior para tratar con una situación amenazadora o estresante (pág. 383)

reforzamiento estímulo o evento que sigue a una respuesta e incrementa la probabilidad de repetición de la misma (pág. 251)

confiabilidad propiedad de una prueba para dar los mismos resultados bajo condiciones semejantes (pág. 344)

sueño MOR etapa del sueño caracterizada por movimientos oculares rápidos, un elevado nivel de actividad encefálica, una relajación muscular profunda y sueños de párpados cerrados (pág. 186)

réplica repetir el estudio de una investigación para confirmar los resultados del estudio original (pág. 40)

pensamiento representativo capacidad intelectual de un niño para visualizar algo en su mente (pág. 72)

represión exclusión de la conciencia de una memoria dolorosa, desagradable o indeseada (págs. 286, 381)

resistencia en psicoanálisis, renuencia de un paciente a revelar sentimientos dolorosos o a examinar patrones de conducta duraderos (pág. 494)

cadena de respuestas reacciones aprendidas que siguen una secuencia, donde cada reacción produce una señal para la siguiente (pág. 256)

resíntesis proceso de combinación de ideas antiguas con ideas nuevas y reorganización de sentimientos para renovar nuestra identidad (pág. 439)

retina el recubrimiento más interno sensible a la luz en la parte posterior del ojo, que contiene los bastones, conos y neuronas que procesan los estímulos visuales (pág. 215)

disparidad retinal impulso binocular para percibir la profundidad en base a las diferencias entre las imágenes que estimulan cada ojo (pág. 216)

recuperación proceso de obtención de información almacenada en la memoria (pág. 274)

interferencia retroactiva entorpecer el recuerdo de algún material aprendido al recordar otro aprendido recientemente (pág. 286)

bastones células receptoras visuales en la retina sensibles a la luz pero no al color, que sólo nos permiten ver en luz tenue el negro, el blanco y los tonos grises (pág. 215)

papel conducta que se espera de un individuo debido a su afiliación en un cierto grupo (págs. 550, 587)

adopción de papeles aspecto importante de los juegos infantiles que implica asumir papeles de adulto, lo cual le permite a los niños experimentar diferentes puntos de vista de primera mano (pág. 84)

rooting reflex an infant's response in turning toward the source of touching that occurs anywhere around his or her mouth (p. 62)

reflejo de búsqueda respuesta de un infante de voltearse hacia la fuente de contacto que ocurre en cualquier parte alrededor de su boca (pág. 62)

rule a statement of relation between concepts (p. 297)

regla enunciado de relación entre conceptos (pág. 297)

S

sample the small group of subjects, out of the total number available of a target population, that a researcher studies (p. 36)

muestra grupo pequeño de sujetos, de entre el número total disponible de una población objetivo, que estudia un investigador (pág. 36)

SAT Scholastic Assessment Test; a standardized test (p. 611)

SAT Prueba de Rendimiento Académico; una prueba estandarizada (pág. 611)

scatterplot a graph of scores that demonstrates the direction of the relationship between two variables (p. 53)

diagrama de dispersión gráfica de resultados que demuestra la dirección de la relación entre dos variables (pág. 53)

schema an idea or mental framework a person uses to organize and interpret information and make sense of the world (pp. 71, 284, 529)

esquema idea o estructura mental que usa un individuo para organizar e interpretar información y darle sentido al mundo (págs. 71, 284, 529)

schizophrenia a group of severe psychotic disorders characterized by confused and disconnected thoughts, emotions, behavior, and perceptions (p. 466)

esquizofrenia conjunto de trastornos sicóticos agudos caracterizados por emociones, conductas, percepciones y pensamientos confusos e inconexos (pág. 466)

scientific method a general approach to gathering information and answering questions so that errors and biases are minimized (p. 12)

método científico enfoque general para reunir información y responder a preguntas de modo que se minimicen errores y prejuicios (pág. 12)

seasonal affective disorder (SAD) a pattern of depressive symptoms that cycle with the seasons, typically beginning in fall or winter (p. 472)

trastorno afectivo de temporada (SAD) patrón de síntomas depresivos que se repite con las estaciones y comienza típicamente en el otoño o invierno (pág. 472)

secondary group a larger group of people with whom you might have impersonal relationships (p. 549)

grupo secundario grupo más grande de individuos con los cuales podrías mantener relaciones impersonales (pág. 549)

secondary reinforcer a stimulus such as money that becomes rewarding through its link with a primary reinforcer (p. 252)

reforzamiento secundario estímulo como el dinero que se vuelve gratificante a través de su vínculo con un reforzador primario (pág. 252)

secondary traits transient or less consistent traits found in individuals, such as food and music preferences (p. 400)

rasgos secundarios características temporales o menos consistentes que existen en los individuos, como preferencias gastronómicas y musicales (pág. 400)

self one's experience or image of oneself, developed through interaction with others (p. 395)

el yo experiencia propia o imagen de sí mismo desarrollada a través de la interacción interpersonal (pág. 395)

self-actualization the humanist term for realizing one's unique potential (pp. 392, 449)

auto-actualización término humanista para el desarrollo del propio potencial (págs. 392, 449)

self-actualization needs the pursuit of knowledge and beauty or whatever else is required for the realization of one's unique potential (p. 326)

necesidades de realización personal búsqueda del conocimiento y la belleza o cualquier otra cosa que se requiera para el desarrollo del propio potencial (pág. 326)

self-concept how we see or describe ourselves; our total perception of ourselves (p. 580)

concepto de sí mismo la manera cómo nos vemos o nos describimos; percepción total de nosotros mismos (pág. 580)

self-efficacy a person's view of his or her ability to succeed (p. 390)

autoeficacia apreciación personal de la propia capacidad para triunfar (pág. 390)

self-fulfilling prophecy a belief, prediction, or expectation that operates to bring about its own fulfillment (pp. 42, 586)

profecía de autocumplimiento creencia, predicción o expectativa que opera para provocar su propio cumplimiento (págs. 42, 586)

self-help group a type of therapy in which a group of individuals share a common problem and meet to discuss it without the active involvement of professional therapists (p. 490)

grupo de autoayuda tipo de terapia en la cual un grupo de individuos comparten un problema común y se reúnen para discutirlo sin la participación activa de terapistas profesionales (pág. 490)

self-justification the need to rationalize one's attitude and behavior (p. 586)

autojustificación necesidad de racionalizar la actitud y conducta propias (pág. 586)

Glossary-Glosario

self-serving bias the tendency to view one's successes as stemming from internal factors and one's failures as stemming from external factors (p. 531)

semantic codes ways in which a person tries to remember something by making sense of it, such as associating a letter with a word (p. 274)

semantic memory a type of declarative memory consisting of factual knowledge of language, including its rules, words, and meanings (p. 279)

semantics the study of meaning in language (p. 305)

senile dementia a collective term to describe decreases in mental abilities experienced by some people after the age of 65 (p. 142)

sensation the stimulation of sensory receptors and the transmission of sensory information to the brain (p. 208)

sensory memory very brief memory storage immediately following initial stimulation of a receptor (p. 274)

separation anxiety distress that is sometimes experienced by infants when they are separated from their primary caregivers (p. 76)

set-point the weight around which your day-to-day weight tends to fluctuate (p. 321)

shaping technique of operant conditioning in which the desired behavior is "molded" by first rewarding any act similar to that behavior and then requiring ever-closer approximations to the desired behavior before giving the reward (p. 255)

short-term dynamic psychotherapy a shortened version of psychoanalysis in which the therapist uses a direct and more active approach in identifying and resolving problems (p. 496)

short-term memory memory that is limited in capacity to about seven items for a short period of time (p. 276)

signal-detection theory the study of people's tendencies to make correct judgments, misses, and false alarms in detecting the presence of stimuli (p. 212)

single-blind experiment an experiment in which the participants are unaware of which participants received the treatment (p. 43)

sleep apnea a sleep disorder in which a person stops breathing for intervals of 10 seconds or longer, wakes up briefly, resumes breathing, and returns to sleep (p. 187)

sleeper effect the delayed impact on attitude change of a persuasive communication (p. 594)

sleepwalking walking or carrying out behaviors while still asleep (p. 188)

social cognition a subfield of social psychology that focuses on cognitive processes and how we perceive, store, and retrieve information about social interactions (p. 519)

prejuicio de autoservicio tendencia que considera que el éxito propio proviene de factores internos y que los fracasos propios provienen de factores externos (pág. 531)

códigos semánticos modos en los cuales un individuo intenta recordar algo al tratar de entenderlo, como asociar una letra con una palabra (pág. 274)

memoria semántica un tipo de memoria declarativa que se compone de conocimientos objetivos del lenguaje, incluido sus reglas, palabras y significados (pág. 279)

semántica el estudio del significado en el lenguaje (pág. 305)

demencia senil término colectivo para describir disminuciones en las capacidades mentales que experimentan algunas personas después de los 65 años de edad (pág. 142)

sensación estimulación de los receptores sensoriales y la transmisión de información sensorial al encéfalo (pág. 208)

memoria sensorial almacenamiento muy breve de memoria que sigue a la estimulación inicial de un receptor (pág. 274)

ansiedad de separación aflicción que experimentan en ocasiones los niños al separarse de sus cuidadores primarios (pág. 76)

punto fijo biológico peso alrededor del cual tiende a fluctuar tu peso de un día a otro (pág. 321)

formado técnica de condicionamiento operante que "moldea" la conducta deseada al recompensar primero cualquier acto semejante a esa conducta y luego requiere aproximaciones cada vez más parecidas a la conducta deseada antes de proporcionar la recompensa (pág. 255)

psicoterapia dinámica a corto plazo versión abreviada del psicoanálisis en la cual el terapista usa un enfoque más directo y activo para identificar y resolver problemas (pág. 496)

memoria de corto plazo memoria limitada en capacidad a aproximadamente siete artículos durante un período corto de tiempo (pág. 276)

teoría de detección de señales estudio de las tendencias de las personas a hacer juicios correctos, fallas y falsas alarmas al detectar la presencia de estímulos (pág. 212)

experimento anónimo sencillo un experimento en el cual los participantes desconocen cuáles de ellos recibieron el tratamiento (pág. 43)

apnea del sueño trastorno del sueño en el cual un individuo deja de respirar a intervalos de 10 o más segundos, despierta brevemente, respira nuevamente y vuelve a dormirse (pág. 187)

efecto durmiente impacto postergado en el cambio de actitud de una comunicación persuasiva (pág. 594))

sonambulismo caminar o realizar conductas mientras aún se está dormido (pág.188)

conocimiento social una subdivisión de la psicología social que se enfoca en los procesos cognitivos y en cómo percibimos, almacenamos y recuperamos información sobre interacciones sociales (pág. 519)

social facilitation an increase in performance in front of a crowd (p. 549)

social functions responses directed toward satisfying the emotional needs of members (p. 547)

social inhibition a decrease in performance in the presence of a crowd (p. 549)

socialization the process of learning the rules of behavior of the culture within which an individual is born and will live (p. 81)

social learning form of learning in which the organism observes, explores, and imitates the behavior of others (p. 259)

social learning theory theory that individuals develop by interacting with others (p. 107)

social loafing the tendency for people to work less hard when sharing the workload with others than when they are working alone (p. 569)

social psychology a broad field of psychology that involves the study of how our thoughts, feelings, perceptions, and behaviors are influenced by interactions with others (p. 519)

social support information that leads someone to believe that he or she is cared for, loved, respected, and part of a network of communication and mutual obligation (p. 428)

social trap a situation that occurs when individuals in a group decide not to cooperate (p. 567)

sociogram a diagram that represents relationships within a group, especially likes and dislikes of members for other members (p. 552)

somatic nervous system (SNS) the division of the peripheral nervous system that controls voluntary movement of skeletal muscles (p. 158)

somatoform disorder a psychological disorder marked by a pattern of recurring physical symptoms for which there is no apparent physical cause (p. 461)

source trait a stable characteristic that can be considered to be at the core of personality (p. 401)

spermarche a period during which males achieve first ejaculation (p. 96)

spinal cord the bundle of nerves within the spine that runs down the length of the back and transmits most messages back and forth between the body and brain (p. 156)

spontaneous recovery the reappearance of an extinguished conditioned response after some time has passed (p. 245)

sports psychology a branch of psychology that studies athletics and athletic performance (p. 615)

stagnation a discontinuation of development and a desire to recapture the past, characteristic of some middle-aged people (p. 135)

standard deviation a measure of variability that describes an average distance of every score from the mean of the scores (p. 52)

facilitación social aumento del desempeño frente a una multitud (pág. 549)

funciones sociales respuestas dirigidas a satisfacer las necesidades emocionales de los miembros (pág. 547)

inhibición social disminución del desempeño en presencia de una multitud (pág. 549)

socialización proceso de aprendizaje de las reglas de conducta de la cultura dentro de la que nace y vivirá un individuo (pág. 81)

aprendizaje social forma de aprendizaje en que los organismos observan, exploran e imitan la conducta ajena (pág. 259)

teoría de aprendizaje social teoría de que los individuos se desarrollan al interactuar con otros (pág. 107)

holgazanería social tendencia de los individuos a trabajar con menos esfuerzo al compartir la carga de trabajo con otros que al trabajar solos (pág. 569)

psicología social un campo amplio de la psicología que busca explicar cómo se influencian nuestros pensamientos, sentimientos, percepciones y conductas al interactuar con otros (pág. 519)

apoyo social información que lleva a alguien a creer que es amado y respetado, que se preocupan por él y que es parte de una red de comunicación y obligación mutua (pág. 428)

trampa social situación que se presenta cuando los individuos de un grupo deciden no cooperar (pág. 567)

sociograma diagrama que representa las relaciones dentro de un grupo, especialmente las filiaciones y aversiones de miembros por otros miembros (pág. 552)

sistema nervioso somático (SNS) la división del sistema nervioso periférico que controla el movimiento voluntario de los músculos esqueléticos (pág. 158)

trastorno somatoforme trastorno psicológico caracterizado por un patrón de síntomas físicos recurrentes para los que no hay una causa física aparente (pág. 461)

rasgo fuente característica estable que se considera está en el núcleo de la personalidad (pág. 401)

espermarca período durante el cual el varón logra su primera eyaculación (pág. 96)

medula espinal haz de nervios dentro de la espina dorsal que recorre toda la espalda y transmite la mayor parte de los mensajes entre el cuerpo y el encéfalo en ambas direcciones (pág. 156)

recuperación espontánea reaparición de una respuesta condicionada extinta después de pasar algún tiempo (pág. 245)

psicología deportiva rama de la psicología que estudia los deportes y el desempeño deportivo (pág. 615)

estancamiento interrupción del desarrollo y un deseo de recapturar el pasado, característico en algunas personas de edad madura (pág. 135)

desviación estándar medida de variabilidad que describe la distancia promedio de cada puntaje de la media de los puntajes (pág. 52)

state-dependent learning the idea that we recall information more easily when we are in the same physiological or emotional state or setting as when we originally encoded the information (p. 284)

statistically significant effect that has a low probability of having arisen by chance (p. 54)

statistics the branch of mathematics concerned with summarizing and making meaningful inferences from collections of data (p. 48)

stereotype a set of assumptions about people in a given category, either positive or negative, often based on half-truths and. nontruths (pp. 530, 587)

stimulation value the ability of a person or participant to interest or expose another to new ideas and experiences (p. 523)

stimulus any aspect of or change in the environment to which an organism responds (p. 208)

storage the process of placing encoded information into relatively permanent mental storage for later recall (p. 274)

stranger anxiety the fear of strangers that infants commonly display (p. 76)

stratified sample a sample group of a larger population in which subgroups within the larger population are represented proportionally (p. 37)

stress a person's physical and mental reaction to his or her inability to cope with a certain tense event or situation (p. 413)

stressor an event or situation that produces stress (p. 414)

stress reaction the body's response to a stressor (p. 414)

structuralist a psychologist who studied the basic elements that make up conscious mental experiences (p. 16)

sublimation the process of redirecting sexual impulses into learning tasks (p. 82); redirecting a forbidden desire into a socially acceptable desire (p. 383)

subliminal messages brief auditory or visual messages that are presented below the absolute threshold so that their chance of perception is less than 50 percent (p. 226)

subliminal perception the ability to notice stimuli that affect only the unconscious mind (p. 227)

superego the part of the personality that is the source of conscience and counteracts the socially undesirable impulses of the id (p. 380)

surface trait a stable characteristic that can be observed in certain situations (p. 401)

survey a research method in which information is obtained by asking many individuals a fixed set of questions about their attitudes or behavior (p. 38)

aprendizaje dependiente del estado idea de que recordamos información más fácilmente cuando estamos en el mismo estado o situación psicológica o emocional que cuando registramos originalmente la información (pág. 284)

estadísticamente significativo efecto con baja probabilidad de haberse presentado por casualidad (pág. 54)

estadística rama de las matemáticas que se encarga de resumir y de hacer inferencias significativas de conjuntos de datos (pág. 48)

estereotipo conjunto de suposiciones positivas o negativas sobre los individuos en una categoría dada, frecuentemente basado en verdades a medias y falsedades (págs. 530, 587)

valor de estimulación capacidad de un individuo o participante de interesar o exponer a otros a nuevas ideas y experiencias (pág. 523)

estímulo cualquier aspecto de o cambio en el ambiente al cual responde un organismo (pág. 208)

almacenamiento proceso de colocar información cifrada en una reserva mental relativamente permanente para recordarlo posteriormente (pág. 274)

ansiedad de extraños el temor a los extraños que comúnmente exhiben los niños (pág. 76)

muestra estratificada un grupo muestral de una población más grande en la cual se representan proporcionalmente los subgrupos dentro de dicha población (pág. 37)

estrés reacción física o mental de un individuo a su incapacidad para manejar una situación o evento tenso (pág. 413)

agente estresor evento o situación que produce estrés (pág. 414)

reacción de estrés respuesta del cuerpo al agente estresor (pág. 414)

estructuralista psicólogo que estudia los elementos básicos que conforman las experiencias mentales concientes (pág. 16)

sublimación proceso de desviar impulsos sexuales hacia el aprendizaje de tareas (pág. 82); desviar un deseo prohibido hacia un deseo socialmente aceptable (pág. 383)

mensajes subliminales breves mensajes auditivos o visuales que se presentan por debajo del umbral absoluto, de modo que su posibilidad de percepción es menos del 50 por ciento (pág. 226)

percepción subliminal capacidad de notar estímulos que sólo afectan la mente inconsciente (pág. 227)

súper ego parte de la personalidad que es la fuente de la conciencia y contrarresta los impulsos socialmente indeseados del id (pág. 380)

rasgo superficial característica estable que puede observarse en ciertas situaciones (pág. 401)

encuesta método de investigación mediante el cual se obtiene información al preguntar a muchos individuos un conjunto fijo de preguntas sobre sus actitudes o conductas (pág. 38)

symbol an abstract unit of thought that represents an object or quality; anything that stands for or represents something else (p. 296)

synapse the gap that exists between the axon terminals of the sending neuron and the dendrites of the receiving neuron (p. 157)

syntax the set of language rules that govern how words can be combined to form meaningful phrases and sentences (p. 305)

systematic desensitization a counterconditioning technique used by behavior therapists to help a patient overcome irrational fears and anxieties (p. 503)

símbolo unidad abstracta de pensamiento que representa un objeto o cualidad; cualquier cosa que representa algo más (pág. 296)

sinapsis espacio entre los terminales del axón de la neurona emisora y las dendritas de la neurona receptora (pág. 157)

sintaxis conjunto de reglas del lenguaje que establecen cómo pueden combinarse las palabras para formar frases y enunciados significativos (pág. 305)

insensibilización sistemática técnica de contra-condicionamiento que emplean los terapistas conductuales para ayudar a los pacientes a sobreponerse al miedo o ansiedades irracionales (pág. 503)

T

task functions activities directed toward getting a job done (p. 547)

telegraphic speech the kind of verbal utterances offered by young children in which articles, prepositions, and parts of verbs are left out, but the meaning is usually clear (p. 67)

testes the male sex gland (p. 172)

testosterone the male sex hormone that stimulates the growth of genital organs and the development of secondary sexual characteristics (p. 172)

thalamus a structure of the brain that relays messages from the sense organs to the cerebral cortex (p. 161)

thanatology the study of dying and death (p. 144)

theory a set of assumptions used to explain why something is the way it is and happens the way it does (p. 11)

therapy treatment of behavioral, bodily, or psychological disorders (p. 485)

thinking mental activity that involves changing and reorganizing of the information stored in memory in order to create new information (p. 296)

thyroid gland the gland in the endocrine system that produces several hormones, including thyroxine (p. 171)

token economy form of conditioning in which desirable behavior is reinforced with valueless objects or points that can be accumulated and exchanged for privileges or other rewards (pp. 264, 505)

tolerance the reaction of the body and brain to regular drug use, whereby a person needs an increased amount in order to produce the original effect (p. 476)

trait an aspect of personality with a tendency to react to a situation in a way that remains stable over time (p. 398)

transference process of feeling toward an analyst or therapist the way a patient feels or felt toward some other important figure in his or her life (p. 495)

triarchic theory Robert Sternberg's theory of intelligence that proposes that a person's intelligence involves analytical, creative, and practical thinking (p. 350)

funciones de tarea actividades dirigidas hacia la culminación de un trabajo (pág. 547)

discurso telegráfico tipo de expresión verbal emitida por niños pequeños en que los artículos, las preposiciones y parte de los verbos se omiten, pero cuyo significado es generalmente claro (pág. 67)

testículos glándula sexual masculina (pág. 172)

testosterona hormona sexual masculina que estimula el crecimiento de los órganos genitales y el desarrollo de características sexuales secundarias (pág. 172)

tálamo estructura cerebral que transmite mensajes de los órganos de los sentidos a la corteza cerebral (pág. 161)

tanatología el estudio del proceso de morir y la muerte (pág. 144)

teoría conjunto de suposiciones usadas para explicar por qué algo es como es y sucede de la manera en que lo hace (pág. 11)

terapia tratamiento de trastornos conductuales, corporales o psicológicos (pág. 485)

razonamiento actividad mental que implica el cambio y reorganización de la información almacenada en la memoria para crear información nueva (pág. 296)

glándula tiroides glándula del sistema endocrino que produce diversas hormonas, incluido la tiroxina (pág. 171)

economía simbólica forma de condicionamiento en la cual la conducta deseable se refuerza con objetos o puntos sin valor que pueden acumularse e intercambiarse por privilegios u otras recompensas (págs. 264, 505)

tolerancia reacción del cuerpo y el encéfalo al uso frecuente de drogas, en que un individuo requiere una mayor cantidad para producir el efecto original (pág. 476)

rasgo aspecto de la personalidad con tendencia a reaccionar a una situación de una manera que permanece estable con el tiempo (pág. 398)

transferencia proceso de sentir hacia un analista o terapista de la misma manera que un paciente se siente o sentía hacia alguna otra figura importante en su vida (pág. 495)

teoría triárquica teoría de la inteligencia de Robert Sternberg que propone que la inteligencia de un individuo incluye razonamiento analítico, creativo y práctico (pág. 350)

two-factor theory Charles Spearman's theory of intelligence that proposes that a person's intelligence is composed of a general ability level and specific mental abilities (p. 349)

teoría de los dos factores teoría de la inteligencia de Charles Spearman que propone que la inteligencia de un individuo se compone de un nivel de capacidad general y capacidades mentales específicas (pág. 349)

U

unconditional positive regard the perception that individuals' significant others value them for what they are, in their entirety, which leads the individuals to grant themselves the same unconditional positive regard (pp. 396, 497)

concepto positivo incondicional la percepción de que los seres queridos de los individuos los valoran por lo que son en su totalidad, lo cual lleva a los individuos a concederse a ellos mismos el mismo concepto positivo incondicional (págs. 396, 497)

unconditioned response (UR) an organism's automatic (or natural) reaction to a stimulus (p. 242)

respuesta incondicional (RI) la reacción automática (o natural) de un organismo a un estímulo (pág. 242)

unconditioned stimulus (US) an event that elicits a certain predictable response without previous training (p. 242)

estímulo incondicional (EI) un evento que provoca una cierta respuesta predecible sin previo entrenamiento (pág. 242)

unconscious according to Freud, the part of the mind that holds mostly unacceptable thoughts, wishes, feelings, and memories of which we are unaware but that strongly influences conscious behaviors (p. 379)

inconsciente según Freud, la parte de la mente que contiene pensamientos inaceptables, deseos, sentimientos y memorias de los cuales no estamos conscientes, pero que influyen fuertemente sobre las conductas conscientes (pág. 379)

uninvolved parents parents who are typically very self-centered in their child rearing, seemingly uncommitted to their role, and quite distant from their children (p. 79)

padres distantes padres que típicamente están muy centrados en sí mismos durante la crianza de sus hijos, aparentemente no comprometidos con su papel y bastante distantes de ellos (pág. 79)

uplifts small, positive events that make a person feel good (p. 419)

animadores pequeños eventos positivos que hacen sentir bien a un individuo (pág. 419)

utility value the ability of a person or participant to help another achieve his or her goals (p. 523)

valor de utilidad capacidad de un individuo o participante para ayudar a que otros logren sus metas (pág. 523)

V

validity the ability of a test to measure what it is intended to measure (p. 345)

validez capacidad de una prueba para medir lo que se intenta medir (pág. 345)

variability a measure of difference, or spread of data (p. 52)

variabilidad medida de la diferencia o la distribución de los datos (pág. 52)

variable in an experiment, any factor that is measured or controlled and is capable of change (p. 40)

variable en un experimento, cualquier factor que se mide o controla y es capaz de cambiar (pág. 40)

variable-interval schedule a pattern of reinforcement in which changing amounts of time must elapse before a response will obtain reinforcement (p. 255)

programa de intervalo de variables patrón de reforzamiento donde deben transcurrir cantidades variables de tiempo antes de que una respuesta obtenga refuerzo (pág. 255)

variable-ratio schedule a pattern of reinforcement in which an unpredictable number of responses is required before reinforcement can be obtained each time (p. 254)

programa de razón de variables patrón de reforzamiento en el cual se requiere un número impredecible de respuestas antes de que pueda obtenerse el reforzamiento en cada ocasión (pág. 254)

ventromedial hypothalamus (VMH) the part of the hypothalamus that causes one to slow down or stop eating altogether if stimulated (p. 321)

hipotálamo ventromedial (HVM) parte del hipotálamo que ocasiona que un individuo coma menos o deje de comer al estimularse (pág. 321)

vestibular system three semicircular canals located in the inner ear that provide the sense of balance (p. 220)

sistema vestibular tres canales semicirculares localizados en el oído interno que proporcionan el sentido del equilibrio (pág. 220)

visual codes a way a person tries to remember something by keeping a mental picture in his or her mind (p. 274)

códigos visuales forma en que un individuo intenta recordar algo mediante una imagen mental (pág. 274)

visualization mentally rehearsing the steps involved in a successful performance or process (p. 615)

visualización ensayar mentalmente los pasos envueltos en un desempeño o proceso exitoso (pág. 615)

W

Weber's law a psychophysics law stating that for any change (Δs) in a stimulus to be detected, a constant proportion of that stimulus (s) must be added or subtracted (p. 211)

withdrawal the symptoms that occur after a person discontinues the use of a drug to which he or she has become addicted (p. 477)

working memory a system that processes and works with current information; also called short-term memory (p. 278)

ley de Weber una ley psicofísica que establece que para detectar cualquier cambio (Δ) en un estímulo, debe sumarse o restarse una proporción constante de ese estímulo o estímulos (pág. 211)

síndrome de abstinencia síntomas que ocurren después de que un individuo descontinúa el uso de una droga a la cual se ha vuelto adicto (pág. 477)

memoria operativa sistema que procesa y trabaja con información actual; también llamada memoria de corto plazo (pág. 278)

Index

Italicized page numbers refer to illustrations. Preceding the page number, abbreviations refer to a chart (c), photograph or other picture (p), graph (g), cartoon (crt), painting (ptg). Quoted material is referenced with the abbreviation (q) before the page number.

SUBJECT INDEX

A

Index

Index

Index

Index

G

H

Index

Index

Index

R

S

Index

Index

T

U

NAME INDEX

Index

References

A

AAA Foundation for Traffic Safety. (1997). *Road Rage: How to Avoid Aggressive Driving.* New York: AAA Foundation for Traffic Safety.

Abramson, L.Y., Seligman M., & Teasdale, J.D. (1987). Learned helplessness in humans: Critique and reformulation. *Journal of Abnormal Psychology, 87,* 49–74.

Adler, A. (1959). *What Life Should Mean to You.* New York: Putnam. (paper).

Ahrens, R. (1954). Beitrag zur Entwicklung des Physiognomie-und Mimiker-kennens. Z. exp. angew. Psychol., 2, 412–454.

Ainsworth, M.D.S. (1989). Attachments beyond infancy. *American Psychologist,* 44, 709–716.

Ainsworth, M.D.S., & Bowlby, J. (1991). An ethnological approach to personality development. *American Psychologist,* 46, 333–341.

Alexander, B.K. (1990). The empirical and theoretical bases for an adaptive model of addiction. *Journal of Drug Issues,* 20, 37–65.

Allgeier, A.R. (1983). Sexuality and gender roles in the second half of life. In A.R. Allgeier & N. McCormick (Eds.), *Changing Boundaries.* Palo Alto, CA: Mayfield.

Allport, G. (1937). *Personality: A Psychological Interpretation.* New York: Henry Holt.

______. (1954). *The Nature of Prejudice.* Garden City, NY: Doubleday. (paper).

______. (1961). *Pattern and Growth in Personality.* New York: Holt, Rinehart and Winston.

______. (Ed.). (1965). *letters from Jenny.* New York: Harcourt, Brace & World.

American Academy of Pediatrics. (1995). Media violence policy statement. Retrieved September 2, 1999 from the World Wide Web: **http://www.aap.org/**

American Demographics. (1997). Longer lives mean longer marriages. Retrieved August 16, 1999 from the World Wide Web: **http://www.demographics.com/**

American Foundation for Suicide Prevention. (2006). Suicide facts. Retrieved June 10, 2006 from the World Wide Web: **http://www.afsp.org**

American Psychiatric Association. (1993). APA online public information: The insanity defense. Retrieved July 9, 1999 from the World Wide Web: **http://www.psych.org/public_info/insani~1.htm**

______. (1994). *Diagnostic and Statistical Manual of Mental Disorders* (4th ed.). Washington, DC.

American Psychological Association. (2002). *Ethical Principles of Psychologists and Code of Conduct.* Washington, D.C.: American Psychological Association.

______. (1993). 1993 Profile of APA Membership. Washington, DC.

______. (1996). *Master's, Specialist's, and Related Degrees Employment Survey.* Washington, DC: Author.

______. (1999). APA research office–Survey reports. Washington, DC: Author. Retrieved September 15, 1999 from the World Wide Web: **http://research.apa.org/reports.html**

______. (2001). *Inside APA.* Washington, DC: American Psychological Association. Retrieved October 5, 2001 from the World Wide Web: **http://www.apa.org/about/homepage.html**

______. (2005). *2003 Doctorate Employment Survey.* Washington, DC: American Psychological Association. Retrieved July 3, 2006 from the World Wide Web: **http://research.apa.org/des03.html**

American Psychological Association, Commission on Violence and Youth. (1993). Violence & youth: Psychology's response (Vol. 1) [Summary Report]. Washington, DC: Author.

American Psychological Society. (2001). *About APS.* Washington, DC: American Psychological Society. Retrieved October 5, 2001 from the World Wide Web: **http://www.psychologicalscience.org/aboutaps.html**

Anand, V. (1997). *More questions than answers.* Retrieved July 24, 2001 from the World Wide Web: **http://www.research.ibm.com/deepblue/home/may11/story_3.html**

Archer, J. (1997). On the origins of sex differences in social behavior: Darwinian and non-Darwinian accounts. *American Psychology, 52,* 1383–1384.

Arkoff, A. (1968). *Adjustment and Mental Health.* New York: McGraw-Hill.

Arnett, J.J. (1999). Adolescent storm and stress, reconsidered. *American Psychologist, 54 (5),* 317–326.

Aronson, E. (2006). The Social Animal. New York, NY: W.H. Freeman & Co.

Aronson, E., Turner, J., & Carlsmith, M. (1963). Communicator credibility and communicator discrepancy as determinants of opinion change. *Journal of Abnormal and Social Psychology, 67,* 31–36.

Asch, S. (1940). Studies in the principles of judgments and attitudes: Determination of judgments by group and ego standards. *Journal of Social Psychology, 12,* 433–465.

______. (1952). *Social Psychology.* New York: Prentice-Hall.

______. (1956). Studies of independence and conformity: A minority of one against a unanimous majority. *Psychological Monographs, 70,* Whole No. 416.

______. (1965). Effects of group pressure upon the modification and distortion of judgments. In J. Proshansky & B. Seidenberg. (Eds.), *Basic Studies in Social Psychology,* (pp. 393–401). New York: Holt, Rinehart and Winston.

Atkinson, J.W. (Ed.). (1958). *Motives in Fantasy, Action, and Society.* New York: Van Nostrand Reinhold.

Austin Police Department Gang Suppression Unit. (1999). Basic gang facts. Retrieved September 2, 1999 from the World Wide Web: **http://www.austingangbusters.org/**

Averill, J. (1983). Studies on anger and aggression: Implications for theories of emotion. *American Psychologist, 38,* 1145–1160.

Axsom, D., Yates, S., & Chaiken, S. (1987). Audience response as a heuristic cue in persuasion. *Journal of Personality and Social Psychology, 53,* 30–40.

Ayer, E.H. (1998). *Everything You Need to Know About Stress.* New York: The Rosen Publishing Group, Inc.

Azar, B. (1996, June). Schools the source of rough transitions. *APA Monitor,* 14.

B

Bahrick, H.P., Bahrick, P.O., & Wittinger, R.P. (1974, December). Those unforgettable high school days. *Psychology Today.*

Bailey, A.J. (1995). The biology of autism. *Psychological Medicine, 23,* 7–11.

Baillergeon, R., Graber, M., Decops, J., & Black, J. (1990). Why do young infants fail to search for hidden objects? *Cognition,* 36, 255–284.

Ball, S.A., Carroll, K. M., Babor, T.F., and Rounsaville, B.J. (1995). Subtype of cocaine abusers: Support for a Type A-Type B distinction. *Journal of Consulting and Clinical Psychology, 63(1),* 115–124.

Ballieux, R. E. (Ed.) (1984). *Breakdown in Human Adaptation to 'Stress:' Towards a Multidisciplinary Approach.* Vol. 2, Part 3. Boston, MA: Martinus Nijhoff Publishers.

Baltes, P.P., & Schaie, K.W. (1977). Aging and IQ: The myth of the twilight years. In S.H. Zarit (Ed.), *Readings in Aging and Death: Contemporary Perspectives.* New York: Harper & Row.

Baltrusch, H.J., Stangel, W., & Titze, I. (1991). Stress, cancer, and immunity: New developments in biopsychosocial and psychoneuroimmunologic research. *Acta Neurologica, 13,* 315–327.

Bandura, A. (1964). The stormy decade: Fact or fiction? *Psychology in the Schools, 1,* 224–231.

______. (1965). Influence of models' reinforcement contingencies on the acquisition of imitative responses. *Journal of Personality and Social Psychology, 1,* 589–595.

References

______. (1971). Analysis of modeling processes. In A. Bandura (Ed.), *Psychological Modeling: Conflicting Theories,* (pp. 1–62). Chicago: Aldine-Atherton.

______. (1977). *Social Learning Theory.* Englewood Cliffs, NJ: Prentice-Hall.

______. (1986). *Social Foundations of Thought and Action: A Social Cognitive Theory.* Englewood Cliffs, NJ: Prentice-Hall.

_____. (1997). *Self-Efficacy: The Exercise of Control.* New York: W.H. Freeman.

Bandura, A., & Walters, R.H. (1963). *Social Learning and Personality Development.* New York: Holt, Rinehart and Winston.

Barber, T.X. (1965). Measuring 'hypnotic-like' suggestibility with and without 'hypnotic induction': psychometric properties, norms, and variables influencing response to the Barber suggestibility scale (BSS). *Psychological Reports, 16,* 809–844.

Baron, R.A., & Byrne, D. (2006). *Social Psychology: Understanding Human Interaction* (10th ed.). Boston: Allyn and Bacon.

Bartoshuk, L. (1989). Taste: Robust across the life span? *Annals of the New York Academy of Sciences, 561,* 65–75.

Baumeister, R.F., Smart, L., & Boden, J.M. (1996). Relation of threatened egotism to violence and aggression: The dark side of high self-esteem. *Psychological Review, 103,* 5–33.

Baumrind, D. (1971). Current patterns of parental authority. *Developmental Psychology Monographs, 4* (1), Pt. 2.

______. (1973, February). Will a day care center be a child development center? *Young Children, 28,* 154–169.

Beck, A.T. (1967). *Depression: Causes and Treatment.* Philadelphia: University of Pennsylvania Press.

______. (1970). Cognitive therapy: Nature and relation to behavior therapy. *Behavior Therapy, 1,* 184–200.

Beck, A.T., & Rush, A.J. (1989). Cognitive therapy. In H.I. Kaplan & B. Sadock (Eds.), *Comprehensive Textbook of Psychiatry* (Vol 5). Baltimore, MD: Williams & Wilkins.

Beck, J.T. (1995). *Cognitive Therapy: Basic and Beyond.* New York: Guilford Publications.

Beebe-Center, J.G. (1949). Standards for the use of Gust scale. *Journal of Psychology, 28,* 411–419.

Belmore, S.B. (1987). Determinants of attention during impression formation. *Journal of Experimental Psychology: Learning, Memory, and Cognition, 13,* 480–489.

Belsky, J. (1984). The determinants of parenting: A process model. *Child Development, 55,* 83–96.

Bem, D.J. (1970). *Beliefs, Attitudes and Human Affairs.* Belmont, CA: Brooks/Cole.

Bem, S.L. (1975, September). Androgyny vs. the little lives of fluffy women and chesty men. *Psychology Today, 8,* 59–62.

______. (1981). Gender schema theory: A cognitive account of sex typing. *Psychological Review, 88,* 354–364.

______. (1983). Gender schema theory and its implications for child development: Raising gender-aschematic children in a gender-schematic society. *Signs, 8,* 598–616.

______. (1985). Androgyny and gender schema theory: A conceptual and empirical integration. In T.B. Sonderegger (Ed.), *Nebraska Symposium on Motivation: Psychology and Gender.* Lincoln, NE: University of Nebraska Press: 179–266.

______. (1993). *The Lenses of Gender: Transforming the Debate on Sexual Inequality.* New Haven, CT: Yale University Press.

Benson, P.L., & Roehlkepartain, E. Youth violence in Middle America. Retrieved September 7, 1999 from the World Wide Web: **http://www.ncrel.org/**

Berger, K.S. (2005). *The Developing Person Through the Life Span* (6th ed.). New York: Worth Publishers.

Bergin, A.E. (1971). The evaluation of therapeutic outcomes. In A.E. Bergin & S.L. Garfield (Eds.), *Handbook of Psychotherapy and Behavior Change: An Empirical Analysis.* New York: Wiley.

Berkowitz, L. (1962). *Aggression: A Social Psychological Analysis.* New York: McGraw-Hill Book Company.

______. (1989). Frustration-aggression hypothesis: Examination and reformulation. *Psychological Bulletin, 106,* 59–73.

Berman, M.E., Tracy, J.I., & Coccaro, E.R. (1997). The serotonin hypothesis of aggression revisited. *Clinical Psychology Review, 17,* 651–665.

Berndt, T.J. (1992). Friendship and friends' influence in adolescence. *Current Directions in Psychological Science, 1,* 156–159.

Berry, L.M., & Houston, J.P. (1993). *Psychology at Work: An Introduction to Industrial and Organizational Psychology.* Madison, WI: WCBrown and Benchmark Publishers.

Biernat, M., & Wortman, C.B. (1991). Sharing of home responsibilities between professionally employed women and their husbands. *Journal of Personality and Social Psychology, 60,* 844–860.

Bischof, L. (1969). *Adult Psychology.* New York: Harper & Row.

Bjorkqvist, K., Lagerspetz, K., & Kaukiainen, A. (1992). Do girls manipulate and boys fight? Developmental trends in regard to direct and indirect aggression. *Aggressive Behavior, 18,* 117–127.

Blake, R.R., & McCanse, A.A. (1991). *Leadership Dilemmas: Grid Solutions.* Houston, TX: Gulf Publishing Company.

Blake, R.R., & Mouton, J.S. (1985). *The Managerial Grid III: The Key to Leadership Excellence* (3rd ed.). Houston, TX: Gulf Publishing Company.

Block, R., & Ghoneim, M. (1993). Effects of chronic marijuana use on human cognition. *Psychopharmacology, 110* (1–2), 219–228.

Blum, R.W., Beuhring, T., Shew, M. L., Bearinger, L. H., Sieving, R. E., and Resnick, M. D. (2000). The effects of race/ethnicity, income, and family structure on adolescent risk behaviors. *American Journal of Public Health, 90(12),* 1879–1884.

Bootzin, R.R. (1975). *Behavior Modification and Therapy: An Introduction.* Cambridge, MA: Winthrop.

Bornstein, R.F. (1989). Subliminal techniques as propaganda tools: Review and critique. *Journal of Mind and Behavior, 10,* 231–262.

Bouchard, T.J., Jr., & McGue, M. (1981). Familial studies of intelligence: A review. *Science, 212,* 1055–1059.

Bower, B. (2000). Pushing the mood swings: Social and psychological forces sway the course of manic depression. *Science News, 157 (15),* 232.

Bowlby, J. (1960–1961). Separation anxiety: A critical review of the literature. *Journal of Child Psychology and Psychiatry, 1,* 251–269.

______. (1965). *Child Care and Growth of Love* (2nd ed.). Baltimore: Penguin.

______. (1973). *Attachment and Loss: Vol. 2 Separation: Anxiety and Anger.* New York: Basic Books.

Brady, J.V. (1958, October). Ulcers in 'executive' monkeys. *Scientific American, 199,* 95–100.

Brett, J.F., Brief, A.P., Burke, M.J., George, J.M., & Webster, J. (1990). Negative affectivity and the reporting of stressful life events. *Health Psychology, 9,* 57–68.

Briton, N., & Hall, J. (1995). Beliefs about female and male nonverbal communication. *Sex Roles, 32,* 79–90.

Brooks-Gunn, J., & Peterson, A.C. (1983). *Girls at Puberty: Biological and Psychosocial Perspectives.* New York: Plenum Press.

Brown, R. (1973). A First Language: *The Early Stages.* Cambridge, MA: Harvard University Press.

Buck, L., & Axel, R. (1991). A novel multigene family may encode odorant receptors: A molecular basis for odor recognition. *Cell, 65,* 175–187.

Budzynski, T.H., et al. (1973). EMG biofeedback and tension headache: A controlled outcome study. *Psychosomatic Medicine, 35,* 484–496.

Bukatko, D., & Daehler, M.W. (2004). *Child Development: A Thematic Approach.* Boston: Houghton-Mifflin Company.

Buss, D.M. (1985). Human mate selection. *American Scientist, 73,* 47–51.

Buss, D. M. (2000). *The Dangerous Passion: Why Jealousy Is as Necessary as Love and Sex.* New York, NY: The Free Press.

Buss, D. M. & Malamuth, N. M. (1996). *Sex, Power, Conflict: Evolutionary and Feminist Perspectives.* New York, NY: Oxford University Press.

C

Campbell, D. (1992). *CISS* (Campbell Interest and Skill Survey). NCS.

Cann, A., Sherman, S.J., & Elkes, R. (1975). Effects of initial request size and timing of a second request on compliance: The foot-in-the-door and the door-in-the-face. *Journal of Personality and Social Psychology, 32,* 774–782.

Cannon, T. D., Rosso, I. M., Hollister, J. M., Bearden, C. E., Sanchez, L. E., & Hadley, T. (2000). A prospective cohort study of genetic and perinatal influences in the etiology of schizophrenia. *Schizophrenia Bulletin, 26(2),* 351–366.

Cannon, W.B. (1929). *Bodily Changes in Pain, Hunger, Fear and Rage.* Appleton, NY.

Carey, S. (1978). The child as word learner. In M. Halle, J. Bresnan, & G.A. Miller (Eds.), *Linguistic Theory and Psychological Reality.* Cambridge, MA: MIT Press.

Carli, L.L., Ganley, R., & Pierce-Otay, A. (1991). Similarity and satisfaction in roommate relationships. *Personality and Social Psychology Bulletin, 17,* 419–426.

Carlsson, A. (1988). The current status of the dopamine hypothesis of schizophrenia. *Neuropsychopharmacology, 1,* 179–186.

Carson, R.C., & Butcher, J.N. (1992). *Abnormal Psychology and Modern Life* (9th ed.). New York: HarperCollins Publishers.

Carson, R.C., & Sanislow, C.A., III. (1992). The schizophrenias. In H.E. Adams & P.B. Surkur (Eds.), *Comprehensive Handbook of Psychopathology* (2nd ed.). New York: Plenum.

Carsten, J.M., & Spector, P.E. (1987). Unemployment, job satisfaction, and employee turnover: A meta-analytic test of the Muchinsky model. *Journal of Applied Psychology, 72,* 374–381.

Carter, E.A., & McGoldrick, M. (1988). Overview: The changing family life cycle; A framework for family therapy. In E.A. Carter & M. McGoldrick (Eds.), *The Changing Family Cycle: A Framework for Family Therapy* (2nd ed.). New York: Gardner Press.

Cartwright, R. (1993). Who needs their dreams? The usefulness of dreams in psychotherapy. *Journal of the American Academy of Psychoanalysis, 8 (4),* 539–547.

Ceci, S.J. (1991). How much does schooling influence general intelligence and its cognitive components? A reassessment of the evidence. *Developmental Psychology, 27,* 703–722.

Centers for Disease Control and Prevention. (2004). Youth risk behavior trends from CDC's 1991–2003 Youth Risk Behavior Surveys. Retrieved May 12, 2006 from the World Wide Web: **http://www.cdc.gov/HealthyYouth/yrbs/index.htm**

_____. (2005). *Health, United States, 2005.* Retrieved May 27, 2006 from the World Wide Web: **http://cdc.gov/nchs/data/hus/hus05.pdf**

Chaiken, S. (1987). The heuristic model of persuasion. In M.P. Zanna, J.M. Olson, & C.P. Herman (Eds.), *Social Influence: The Ontario Symposium* (Vol 5), (pp. 3–39). Hillsdale, NJ: Lawrence A. Eribaum.

Chamberlain, K., & Zika, S. (1990). The minor events approach to stress: Support for the use of daily hassles. *British Journal of Psychology, 81,* 469–481.

Chand, I.P., Crider, D.M., & Willets, F.K. (1975). Parent-youth disagreement as perceived by youth: A longitudinal study. *Youth and Society, 6,* 365–375.

Chang, E.C. (1996). Cultural differences in optimism, pessimism, and coping: Predictors of subsequent adjustment in Asian American and Caucasian American college students. *Journal of Counseling Psychology, 43,* 113–123.

Cherry, F., & Deaux, K. (1978). Fear of success versus fear of gender-inappropriate behavior. *Sex Roles, 4,* 97–102.

Child Maltreatment 2003. (2005). U. S. Department of Health and Human Services. Retrieved May 9, 2006 from the World Wide Web: **http://www.acf.dhhs.gov/programs/cb/pubs/cm03/index.htm**

Chomsky, N. (1957). *Syntactic Structures.* The Hague: Mouton.

Chukovsky, K. (1963). *From Two To Five.* Berkeley: University of California Press.

Ciaranello, R. D. (2001). The neurobiology of infantile autism. *NARSAD Research Newsletter.* Retrieved August 14, 2001 from the World Wide Web: **http://www.mhsource.com/narsad/autism.html**

Clarke-Stewart, A. (1993). *Daycare,* (rev. ed.). Cambridge, MA: Harvard University Press.

Clay, R.A. (2003). An empty nest can promote freedom, improved relations. *APA Monitor, 34 (4),* 40–41.

Coale, A.J. (1973). The demographic transition reconsidered. *In International Population Conference,* Liège.

Cobb, S. (1976, September-October). Social support as a moderator of life stress. *Psychosomatic Medicine, 38,* 300–314.

Cobb, S., & Rose, R. (1973). Hypertension, peptic ulcers, and diabetes in air traffic controllers. *Journal of the American Medical Association, 224,* 489–492.

Coch, L., & French, J.R.P., Jr. (1948). Overcoming resistance to change. *Human Relations, 1,* 512–532.

Cohen, A., Glass, D., & Phillips, S. (1977). Environment and Health. In H.E. Freeman, S. Levine, & L.G. Reeder (Eds.), *Handbook of Medical Sociology.* Englewood Cliffs, NJ: Prentice-Hall.

Cohen, A.R. (1964). *Attitude Change and Social Influence.* New York: Basic Books.

Cohen, S. (1988). Psychosocial models of the role of social support in the etiology of physical disease. *Health Psychology, 7,* 269–297.

Cohen, S., Glass, D., & Singer, J. (1973). Apartment noises, auditory discrimination and reading ability in children. *Journal of Experimental Social Psychology, 9,* 407–422.

Cohen, S., & Lezak, A. (1977). Noise and inattentiveness to social cues. *Environment and Behavior, 9,* 559–572.

Cohen, S., Tyrrell, D.A., & Smith, A.P. (1991). Psychological stress and susceptibility to the common cold. *New England Journal of Medicine, 325,* 606–612.

Colby, A., Kohlberg, L., Gibbs, J., & Lieberman, M. (1983). A longitudinal study of moral judgment. *Monographs of the Society for Research in Child Development, 48,* 1–124.

Coles, R. (1971). Life in Appalachia: The case of Hugh McCaslin. In G. Armstrong (Ed.), *Life at the Bottom,* (pp. 26–42). New York: Bantam.

Collins, J. (1998, October 19). Seven kinds of smart. *Time.*

Compas, B.E., Hinden, B.R., & Gerhardt, C.A. (1995). Adolescent development: Pathways and processes of risk and resilience. *Annual Review of Psychology, 46,* 265–293.

Costa, P.T., Jr., McCrae, R.R., & Dye, D.A. (1991). Facet scales for agreeableness and conscientiousness: A revision of the NEO personality inventory. *Personality and Individual Differences, 12,* 887–898.

Crooks, R. L., & Stein, J. (1988). *Psychology: Science, Behavior, and Life.* New York, NY: Holt, Rinehart and Winston, Inc.

References

Csikszeutmihalyi, M. (1993). The evolving self: A psychology for the third millennium. New York, NY: HarperCollins.

Czeisler, C.A., Duffy, J.F., Shanahan, T.L., Brown, E.N., Mitchell, J.F., Rimmer, D.W., Ronda, J.M., Silva, E.J., Allan, J.S., Emens, J.S., Dijk, D., & Kronauer, R.E. (1999). Stability, precision, and the near-24-hour period of the human circadian pacemaker. *Science, 284,* 2177–2181.

D

Damasio, A.R. (1994). *Descartes' Error: Emotion, Reason, and the Human Brain.* New York: G.P. Putnam's Sons.

Darley, J.M., & Latané, B. (1968). Bystander intervention in emergencies: Diffusion of responsibility. *Journal of Personality and Social Psychology, 8,* 377–383.

Darwin, C. (1967). *The Expression of Emotions in Man and Animals.* Chicago: University of Chicago Press. (Original work published 1872).

Dasen, P.R., & Heron, A. (1981). Cross-cultural tests of Piaget's theory. In H. Triandis (Ed.), *Handbook of Cross-Cultural Psychology. Vol. 4: Developmental Psychology.* Boston: Allyn and Bacon.

Davis, K. (1985, February). Near and dear: Friendship and love compared. *Psychology Today, 19,* 22–30.

Davison, G. C., & Neale, J. M. (2001). *Abnormal Psychology* (8th ed.). New York, NY: John Wiley & Sons.

Deci, E.L. (1971). Effects of externally mediated rewards on intrinsic motivation. *Journal of Personality and Social Psychology, 18,* 105–115.

Deci, E.L., & Ryan, R.M. (1987). The support of autonomy and the control of behavior. *Journal of Personality and Social Psychology, 53,* 1024–1037.

DeGenova, M.K., & Rice, F.P. (2005). *Intimate Relationships, Marriages, and Families.* (6th ed.). New York: McGraw-Hill.

Delgado, J.M.R. (1969). *Physical Control of the Mind.* New York: Harper & Row.

Delongis, A., Folkman, S., & Lazarus, R.S. (1988). The impact of daily stress on health and mood: Psychological and social resources as mediators. *Journal of Personality and Social Psychology, 54,* 486–495.

Dement, W. (1976). *Some Must Watch While Some Must Sleep.* New York: Norton.

Dement, W., & Wolpert, E. (1958). Relation of eye movements, bodily mobility, and external stimuli to dream content. *Journal of Experimental Psychology, 55,* 543–553.

Dennis, W. (1960). Causes of retardation among institutional children: Iran. *Journal of Genetic Psychology, 96,* 47–59.

______. (1966). Creative productivity between the ages of twenty and eighty years. *Journal of Gerontology, 21,* 1–8.

Deutsch, M., & Collins, M. (1951). *Interracial Housing: A Psychological Evaluation of a Social Experiment.* Minneapolis: University of Minnesota Press.

Devine, P.G. (1989). Stereotypes and prejudice: Their automatic and controlled components. *Journal of Personality and Social Psychology, 56,* 5–18.

Diamond, A. (1985). Development of the ability to use recall to guide action, as indicated by infants' performance on AB. *Child Development, 56,* 868–883.

Dillbeck, M.C., & Ome-Johnson, D.W. (1987). Physiological differences between transcendental meditation and rest. *American Psychologist, 42,* 879–881.

Dion, K.L., Berscheid, E., & Walster, E. (1972). What is beautiful is good. *Journal of Personality and Social Psychology, 24,* 285–290.

Dipboye, R.L., Arvey, R.D., & Terpstra, D.E. (1977). Sex and physical attractiveness of raters and applicants as determinants of resume evaluations. *Journal of Applied Psychology, 62,* 288–294.

Dixon, L.B., Lehman, A.F., & Levine, J. (1995). Conventional antipsychotic medications for schizophrenia. *Schizophrenia Bulletin, 21 (4),* 567–577.

Doob, L.W. (1990). Forward. In M.H. Segall, et al. (Eds.), *Human Behavior in Global Perspective: An Introduction to Cross-cultural Psychology.* New York: Pergamon Press.

Drum, D. J. (1990). Group therapy review. *Counseling Psychologist. 18(1),* 131–138.

Dubas, J.S., Graber, J.A., & Peterson, A.C. (1991). A longitudinal investigation of adolescents' changing perceptions of pubertal timing. *Developmental Psychology, 27,* 580–589.

Duncan, S. (1969). Nonverbal communication. *Psychological Bulletin, 72,* 118–137.

Duncker, K. (1945). On problem solving. (L.S. Lees, trans.). *Psychological Monographs, 58,* (270).

Durkin, J. (1991). The sports psychologist. In R. Gifford (Ed.), *Applied Psychology: Variety and Opportunity.* Boston: Allyn and Bacon.

E

Eccles, J.S., Wigfield, A., & Byrnes, J. (2003). Cognitive development in adolescence. In R.M. Lerner, M.A. Easterbrooks, & J. Mistry (Eds.), *Handbook of Psychology* (Vol 6). New York: Wiley.

Edwards, J.N., & Brauburger, M.B. (1973). Exchange and parent-youth conflict. *Journal of Marriage and the Family, 35,* 101–107.

Ekman, P. (1984). Expression and the nature of emotion. In K.R. Scherer & P. Ekman (Eds.), *Approaches to Emotion.* Hillsdale, NJ: Erlbaum.

______. (1985). *Telling Lies: Clues to Deceit in the Marketplace, Politics, and Marriage.* New York: W.W. Norton & Company.

Ekman, P., Friesen, W.V., & Ellsworth, P. (1972). *Emotion in the Human Face: Guidelines for Research and an Integration of Findings.* Elmsford, NY: Pergamon.

Ekman, P., Levenson, R., & Friesen, W. (1983). Autonomic nervous system activity distinguishes among emotions. *Science, 221,* 1208–1210.

Eldersveld, S., & Dodge, R. (1954). Personal contact or mail propaganda? An experiment in voting turnout and attitude change. In D. Katz, et al. (Eds.), *Public Opinion and Propaganda,* (pp. 532–542). New York: Dryden Press.

Eliot, L. (2000). *What Going on in There? How the Brain and Mind Develop in the First Five Years of Life.* New York, NY: Bantam Books.

Elkin, I., et al. (1989). National institute of mental health treatment of depression collaborative research program: General effectiveness of treatments. *Archives of General Psychiatry, 46,* 971–982.

Elkind, D. (1984). *All Grown Up and No Place to Go.* Reading, MA: Addison-Wesley.

______. (1985). Egocentrism redux. *Developmental Review, 5,* 218–226.

Ellis, A. (1973). Rational-emotive therapy. In R. Corsini (Ed.), *Current Psychotherapies,* (pp. 167–206). Itasca, IL: Peacock.

Eppley, K.R., Abrams, A.I., & Shear, J. (1989). Differential effects of relaxation techniques on trait anxiety: A meta-analysis. *Journal of Clinical Psychology, 45,* 957–974.

Erickson, M.F., Egeland, B., & Pianta, R. (1989). The effects of maltreatment on the development of young children. In D. Cicchetti, et al. (Eds.), *Child Maltreatment: Theory and Research on the Causes and Consequences of Child Abuse and Neglect,* (pp. 647–684). New York: Cambridge University Press.

Erikson, E. (1950). *Childhood and Society.* New York: Norton.

______. (1968). *Identity: Youth and Crisis.* New York: Norton.

Ettinger, R. H., Crooks, R. L., & Stein, J. (1994). *Psychology: Science, Behavior and Life,* (3rd ed.). New York, NY: Harcourt Brace College Publishers.

Evans, G. W., Bullinger, M., & Hygge, S. (1998). Chronic noise exposure and physiological response: A prospective study of children living under environmental stress. *Psychological Science, 9(1),* 75–77.

Ewen, R.B. (2003). *An Introduction to Theories of Personality,* (6th ed.). Mahwah, NJ: Lawrence Erlbaum Associates.

Eysenck, H.J. (1952). The effects of psychotherapy: An evaluation. *Journal of Consulting Psychology, 16,* 319–324.

______. (1966). *The Effects of Psychotherapy.* New York: International Science Press.

______. (1970). *The Structure of Human Personality.* London: Metheun.

______. (1990). Biological dimensions of personality. In L.A. Pervin (Ed.), *Handbook of Personality Theory and Research,* (pp. 244–276). New York: Guilford Press.

F

Fall, G.S. (1904). *Adolescence.* New York: Appleton.

Fantz, R.L. (1961). The origins of form perception. *Scientific American, 204,* 66–72.

Federal Bureau of Investigation (2006). Violent gangs. Retrieved June 26, 2006 from the World Wide Web: **http://ww2.fbi.gov/hq/cid/ngic/violent_gangs.htm**

Fehr, B. (1996). *Friendship Processes.* Thousand Oaks, CA: Sage Publications.

Fehr, B., & Russell, J.A. (1991). The concept of love viewed from a prototype perspective. *Journal of Personality and Social Psychology, 60,* 425–438.

Feingold, A. (1992). Good-looking people are not what we think. *Psychological Bulletin, 111,* 304–341.

Feist, J. (1985). *Theories of Personality.* New York: Holt, Rinehart and Winston.

Feldman, R. S. (2005). *Understanding Psychology* (7th ed.). New York, NY: McGraw-Hill Book Company.

Festinger, L., (1957). *A Theory of Cognitive Dissonance.* Stanford, CA: Stanford University Press.

Festinger, L,. & Carlsmith, J.M. (1959). Cognitive consequences of forced compliance. *Journal of Abnormal and Social Psychology, 58,* 203–210.

Fiedler, F.E. (1969). Style or circumstance: The leadership enigma. *Psychology Today, 2,* 38–43.

Fischer, K.W. (1973). *Piaget's Theory of Learning and Cognitive Development.* Chicago: Markham.

Fisher, S., & Greenberg, R.P. (1977). *The Scientific Credibility of Freud's Theories and Therapy.* New York: Basic Books.

Flavell, J.H. (1963). *The Developmental Theory of Jean Piaget.* New York: Van Nostrand.

Flavell, J.H., Green, F., & Flavell, E. (1995). Young children's knowledge about thinking. *Monographs of the Society for Research in Child Development, 60* (1, Serial No. 243).

Folkes, V.S. (1982). Forming relationships and the matching hypothesis. *Personality and Social Psychology Bulletin, 8,* 631–636.

Forsen, A. (1991). Psychosocial stress as a risk for breast cancer. *Psychotherapy and Psychosomatics, 55,* 176–185.

Foulkes, D. (1966). *The Psychology of Sleep.* New York: Scribner's.

Frankl, V. (1970). *Man's Search for Meaning: An Introduction to Logotherapy.* New York: Clarion.

Franklin, B. (1818; reprinted in 1949). *The Autobiography of Benjamin Franklin.* As cited in Gray, 1999. Berkeley: University of California Press.

Freedman, J.L. (1975). *Crowding and Behavior.* San Francisco: Freeman.

Freedman, J.L., & Fraser, S.C. (1966). Compliance without pressure: The foot-in-the-door technique. *Journal of Personality and Social Psychology, 4,* 195–202.

French, S., & Gendreau, F. (2003). Safe and humane corrections through effective treatment. Retrieved June 6, 2006 from the World Wide Web: **http://www.csc-scc.gc.ca/text/rsrch/reports/r139/r139_e.pdf**

Freud, E.L. (Ed.) (1960). *Letters of Sigmund Freud.* New York: Dover Publications, Inc.

Freud, S. (1943). *A General Introduction to Psychoanalysis.* (J. Riviere, trans.). Garden City, NY: Garden City Publishing.

______. (1949). *An Outline of Psychoanalysis.* (J. Strachey, ed. and trans.). New York: Norton. (Original work published 1940).

______. (1965). *The Interpretation of Dreams,* (3rd English ed.). (P.A. Fried & J. Strachey, eds. and trans.). New York: Avon Books.

Friedman, M., & Rosenman, R.H. (1974). *Type A behavior and your heart.* New York: Knopf.

Friedman, M., & Ulmer, D. (1984). *Treating Type A Behavior–and Your Heart.* New York: Alfred A. Knopf.

Friman, P.C., Allen, K.D., Kerwin, M.L.E., & Larzelere, R. (1993). Changes in modern psychology: A citation analysis of the Kuhnian displacement thesis. *American Psychologist, 48,* 658–664.

Fromm, E. (1947). *Man for Himself: An Inquiry Into the Psychology of Ethics.* New York: Holt, Rinehart and Winston.

______. (1956). *The Art of Loving.* New York: Harper & Row.

Furstenberg, F.F., & Cherlin, A.J. (1991). *Divided Families: What Happens to Children When Parents Part.* Cambridge, MA: Harvard University Press.

Furth, H. (1969). *Piaget and Knowledge.* Englewood Cliffs, NJ: Prentice-Hall.

G

Galanter, M. (1990). Cults and zealous self-help movements: A psychiatric perspective. *American Journal of Psychiatry, 147,* 543–551.

Galton, F. (1869). *Hereditary Genius: An Inquiry into Its Laws and Consequences.* London: Macmillan.

Garcia, J., & Koelling, R.A. (1966). The relation of cue to consequence in avoidance. *Learning. Psychonomic Science, 4,* 123–124.

Gardner, H. (1983). *Frames of Mind: The Theory of Multiple Intelligences.* New York: Basic Books.

______. (1999). *Intelligence Reframed.* New York, NY: Basic Books.

Gardner, R.A., & Gardner, B.T. (1969). Teaching sign language to a chimpanzee. *Science, 1965,* 644–672.

Gerard, H.B., & Rabbie, J.M. (1961). Fear and social comparison. *Journal of Abnormal and Social Psychology, 62,* 586–592.

Gerrig, R.J., & Zimbardo, P.G. (2005). *Psychology and Life,* (17th ed.). Boston, MA: Allyn & Bacon.

Gerst, M.S. (1971). Symbolic coding processes in observational learning. *Journal of Personality and Social Psychology, 19,* 9–17.

Gesell, A., & Thompson, H. (1929). Learning and growth in identical twin infants. *Genetic Psychological Monograph, 6,* 1–124.

Gibb, C. (1969). Leadership. In G. Lindsey & E. Aronson (Eds.), *The Handbook of Social Psychology, Vol. 4,* (2nd ed.). Reading, MA: Addison-Wesley.

Gibson, E.J., & Walk, R.D. (1960). The "visual cliff." *Scientific American, 202,* 64–71.

Gilligan, C. (1977). In a different voice: Women's conceptions of self and morality. *Harvard Educational Review, 47,* 481–517.

______. (1982). *In a Different Voice: Psychological Theory and Women's Development.* Cambridge, MA: Harvard University Press.

Gilligan, C., & Attanucci, J. (1988). Two moral orientations: Gender differences and similarities. *Merrill-Palmer Quarterly, 34,* 223–237.

Ginsburg, H., & Opper, S. (1969). *Piaget's Theory of Intellectual Development: An Introduction.* Englewood Cliffs, NJ: Prentice-Hall.

Gladwin, T. (1964). Culture and logical process. In N. Goodenough (Ed.), *Explorations in Cultural Anthropology: Essays in Honor of George Peter Murdoch.* New York: McGraw-Hill.

Glass, D.C. (1964). Changes in linking as a means of reducing cognitive discrepancies between self-esteem and aggression. *Journal of Personality, 32,* 531–549.

Gollaher, D. (1995). *Voice for the Mad: The Life of Dorothea Dix.* New York: The Free Press.

Goodenough, F.L. (1932). Expression of the emotions in a blind-deaf child. *Journal of Abnormal and Social Psychology, 27,* 328–333.

References

Goodman, B. (1994). *When the Body Speaks Its Mind: A Psychiatrist Probes the Mysteries of Hypochondria and Munchausen's Syndrome.* New York: G.P. Putnam's Sons.

Gottesman, I.I. (1991). *Schizophrenia Genesis: The Origins of Madness.* New York: W.H. Freeman.

Gottesman, I.I., & Shields, J. (1982). *Schizophrenia: The Epigenetic Puzzle.* Cambridge, England: Cambridge University Press.

Gough, H. (1987). *California Psychological Inventory: Administrator's Guide.* Palo Alta: Consulting Psychologists Press.

Graber, J.A., Seeley, J.R., Brooks-Gunn, J., & Lewinsohn, P.M. (2004). Is pubertal timing associated with psychopathology in young adulthood? *Journal of the American Academy of Child & Adolescent Psychiatry, 43 (6),* 718–726.

Grambs, J.D. (1990). *MMPI-2: Assessing Personality and Psychopathology.* New York: Oxford University Press.

Gray, Paul. (1999, January 11). Cursed by eugenics. *Time.*

Gray, Peter. (2006). *Psychology.* New York, New York: Worth Publishers.

Green, D.M., & Swets, J.A. (1996). *Signal Detection Theory and Psychophysics.* New York: Wiley.

Green, J. P., Lynn, S. J., & Malinoski, P. (1998). Hypnotic pseudomemories, prehypnotic warnings, and the malleability of suggested memories. *Applied Cognitive Psychology, 12,* 431–444.

Greenberg, S. (2001). *Elder Action: Action Ideas for Older Persons and Their Families–Looking Out For Depression.* Washington, DC: Administration of Aging. . . . Retrieved July 17, 2001 from the World Wide Web: **http://www.aoa.dhhs.gov/aoa/eldractn/deprssn.html**

Greenberg, S., Smith, I. L., & Muenzen, P. M. (1995). *Study of the Practice of Psychology in the United States and Canada.* New York, NY: Professional Examination Service.

Greenblatt, M., et al. (Eds.). (1965). *Drugs and Social Therapy in Chronic Schizophrenia.* Springfield, IL: Charles C. Thomas.

Gregory, R.L. (1970). *The Intelligent Eye.* New York: McGraw-Hill, (paper).

Guilford, J.P. (1959). *Personality.* New York: McGraw-Hill.

Gura, T. (1997). Obesity sheds its secrets. *Science, 275,* 751–753.

Gustavson, C.R., et al. (1974). Coyote predation control by aversive conditioning. *Science, 184,* 581–583.

H

Haber, R.N. (1970). How we remember what we see. *Scientific American, 222,* 104–112.

Hall, C.S. (1954). *A Primer of Freudian Psychology.* Cleveland: World, (paper).

Hall, C.S., & van de Castle, R.L. (1966). *The Content Analysis of Dreams.* New York: Appleton-Century-Crofts.

Hall, E.T. (1959). *The Silent Language.* Garden City, NY: Doubleday.

______. (1966). *The Hidden Dimension.* Garden City, NY: Doubleday.

Hall, E.T., & Hall, M. (1990). *Understanding Cultural Differences.* Yarmouth, ME: Intercultural Press, Inc.

Hammen, C., & Brennan, P.A. (2001). Depressed adolescents of depressed and nondepressed mothers: Tests of an interpersonal impairment hypothesis. *Journal of Consulting and Clinical Psychology, 69(2),* 284–294.

Hanson, D.R., & Gottesman, I.I. (2005). Theories of schizophrenia. *BMC Medical Genetics 6,* 7. Retrieved June 23, 2006 from the World Wide Web: **http://www.biomedcentral.com**

Harkins, E.B. (1978). Effect of empty nest transition on self-report of psychological and physical well-being. *Journal of Marriage and the Family, 40,* 549–556.

Harlow, H.F. (1949). The formation of learning sets. *Psychological Review, 56,* 51–65.

______. (1961). The development of affectional patterns in infant monkeys. In B.M. Foss (Ed.), *Determinants of Infant Behavior,* (pp. 75–100). New York: Wiley.

Harlow, H.F., & Zimmerman, R.R. (1959). Affectional responses in the infant monkey. *Science, 140,* 421–432.

Harris, B. (1979). Whatever happened to little Albert? *American Psychologist, 34,* 151–160.

Harris, C.S. (1978). *Fact Book on Aging: A Profile of America's Older Population.* Washington, DC: National Council on the Aging.

Harris, J.R. (1999). *The Nurture Assumption: Why Children Turn Out the Way They Do.* New York: The Free Press.

Harris, M.J., Milich, R., Corbitt, E.M., Hoover, D.W., & Brady, M. (1992). Self-fulfilling effects of stigmatizing information on children's social interactions. *Journal of Personality and Social Psychology, 63,* 41–50.

Hartup, W.W. (1970). Peer interaction and Social organization. In P.H. Mussen (Ed.), *Carmichael's Manual of Child Psychology, Vol. 3.* New York: Wiley.

Hassett, J. (1978). *A Primer of Psychophysiology.* San Francisco: Freeman.

Hatfield, E., & Walster, G. (1981). *A New Look at Love.* Reading, MA: Addison-Wesley.

Hathaway, S.R., & McKinley, J.C. (1940). A multiphasic personality schedule (Minnesota): I. construction of the schedule. *Journal of Psychology, 10,* 249–254.

Havighurst, R.J. (1972). *Developmental Tasks and Education* (3rd ed.). New York: McKay.

Hays, W.L. (1963). *Statistics for Psychologists.* New York: Holt, Rinehart and Winston.

Hebb, D.O. (1974). What psychology is about. *American Psychologist, 29,* 71–79.

Heider, F. (1958). *The Psychology of Interpersonal Relationships.* New York: John Wiley.

Herrnstein, R. (1971). I.Q. *Atlantic, 228,* 43–64.

Herron, J. (1976, March). Southpaws: How different are they? *Psychology Today,* 50–56.

Hess, E.H. (1958). 'Imprinting' in animals. *Scientific American, 198,* 81–90.

______. (1972). 'Imprinting' in a natural laboratory. *Scientific American, 227,* 24–31.

Hess, R., & Torney, J. (1967). *The Development of Political Attitudes in Children.* Chicago: Aldine.

Higgins-Trenk, A., & Gaite, A.J.H. (1971). Elusiveness of formal operational thought in adolescents. *Proceedings of the Seventy-ninth Annual Convention of the American Psychological Association.*

Hilgard, E.R. (1965). *Hypnotic Susceptibility.* New York: Harcourt Brace Jovanovich.

______. (1986). *Divided Consciousness: Multiple Controls in Human Thought and Action* (expanded ed.). New York: Wiley-Interscience.

______. (1987). *Psychology in America: A Historical Survey.* New York: Harcourt Brace Jovanovich.

Hiroto, D.S. (1972). Locus of control and learned helplessness. *Journal of Experimental Psychology, 102,* 187–193.

Hofer, P. (1991). The lawyer-psychologist. In R. Gifford (Ed.), *Applied Psychology: Variety and Opportunity.* Boston: Allyn and Bacon.

Hoffman, B. (1962). *The Tyranny of Testing.* New York: Collier, (paper).

Holden, C. (1980). Identical twins reared apart. *Science, 207,* 1323–1328.

Holland, G.A. (1973). Transactional analysis. In R. Corsini (Ed.), *Current Psychotherapies,* (pp. 353–400). Itasca, IL: Peacock.

Hollon, S.D., & Beck, A.T. (1986). Cognitive and cognitive-behavioral therapies. In S.L. Garfield & A.E. Bergin (Eds.), *Psychotherapy and Behavior Change* (3rd ed.). New York: Wiley.

Holmes, D.L., & Morrison, F.J. (1979). *The Child: An Introduction to Developmental Psychology.* Monterey, CA: Brooks/Cole.

Holmes, D.S., & Roth, D.L. (1988). Effects of aerobic exercise on cardiomuscular activity during psychological stress. *Journal of Psychosomatic Research, 32,* 469–474.

Holmes, T.H., & Rahe, R.H. (1967). The social readjustment scale. *Journal of Psychosomatic Research, 11,* 213.

Honig, W.H. (Ed.). (1966). *Operant Behavior: Areas of Research and Application.* New York: Appleton-Century-Crofts.

Horn, J.L. (1982). The aging of human abilities. In *Handbook of Developmental Psychology,* (pp. 847–870). Englewood Cliffs, NJ: Prentice Hall.

Horner, M.S. (1970). Femininity and successful achievement: A basic inconsistency. In J. Bardwick, et al. (Eds.), *Feminine Personality and Conflict.* Belmont, CA: Brooks/Cole.

______. (1972). Towards an understanding of achievement-related conflicts in women. *Journal of Social Issues, 28,* 157–175.

Horney, K. (1937). *The Neurotic Personality in Our Time.* New York: Norton.

Horrocks, J.E., & Benimoff, M. (1967). Isolation from the peer group during adolescence. *Adolescence, 2,* 41–52.

______. (1981). *Work Stress and Social Support.* Reading, MA: Addison-Wesley.

Horrocks, J.E., Landis, K.R., & Umberson, D. (1988). Social relationships and health. *Science, 241,* 540–545.

Hovland C., Lumsdaine, A., & Sheffield, F. (1949). *Experiments on Mass Communication.* Princeton, NJ: Princeton University Press.

Hovland, C., & Sears, R. (1940). Minor studies of aggression: Correlation of lynching with economic indices. *Journal of Psychology, 9,* 301–310.

Hrushesky, W. (1994 July/August). Timing is everything. *The Sciences,* 32–37.

Hubel, D.H., & Wiesel, T.N. (1962). Receptive fields, binocular interaction, and functional architecture in the cat's visual cortex. *Journal of Physiology, 160,* 106–154.

Hull, C. (1943). *Principles of Behavior: An Introduction to Behavior Theory.* New York: Appleton-Century-Crofts.

Hunt, M. (1993). *The Story of Psychology.* New York: Doubleday.

Hunt, S. (1997). Taste is not only relative, it's genetic. Retrieved July 20, 2001 from the World Wide Web: **http://exn.ca/stories/1997/02/10/07.asp**

Huston, A., Watkins, B.A., & Kunkel, D. (1989). Public policy and children's television. *American Psychologist, 44,* 424–433.

Hyde, J., & Linn, M. (1988). Gender differences in verbal ability: A meta-analysis. *Psychological Bulletin, 104,* 53–69.

I

Inhelder, B. (1969). Memory and intelligence in the child. In D. Elkind & J.F. Flavell (Eds.), *Studies in Cognitive Development,* (pp. 337–364). New York: Oxford University Press.

Inhelder, B., & Piaget, J. (1964). *The Early Growth of Logic in the Child.* New York: Harper & Row.

Itard, J.M.G. (1894). *The Wild Boy of Aveyron.* New York: Appleton-Century-Crofts.

Izard, C.E. (1971). *The Face of Emotion.* New York: Appleton-Century-Crofts.

______. (1972). Patterns of Emotions: *A New Analysis of Anxiety and Depression.* New York: Academic Press.

J

Jackson, R., Creemers, J., Ohagi, S., Raffin-Sanson, M., Sanders, L., Montague, C., Hutton, J., & O'Rahilly, S. (1997). Obesity and impaired prohormone processing associated with mutations in the human prohormone convertase 1 gene. *Nature Genetics, 16,* 303–306.

James, W. (1890). *Principles of Psychology.* New York: Holt, Rinehart and Winston.

John, O.P. (1990). The big five factor taxonomy: Dimensions of personality in the natural language and in questionnaires. In L.A. Pervin (Ed.), *Handbook of Personality Theory and Research,* (pp. 67–100). New York: Guilford Press.

Jones, E.E. (1990). *Interpersonal Perception.* New York: W.H. Freeman.

Jones, E.E., & Davis, K.E. (1965). From acts to dispositions: The attribution process in person perception. In Leonard Berkowitz (Ed.), *Advances in Experimental Social Psychology,* Vol. 2, (pp. 219–266). New York: Academic Press.

Jones, E.E., & Nisbett, R.E. (1972). The actor and the observer: Different perceptions of the cause of behavior. In E.E. Jones, et al. (Eds.), *Attribution: Perceiving the Causes of Behavior.* Morristown, NJ: General Learning Press.

Jones, M.C. (1924). The elimination of children's fears. *Journal of Experimental Psychology, 29,* 383–390.

______. (1965). Psychological correlates of somatic development. *Child Development, 36,* 899–911.

Jones, M.C., Albert, P., & Watson, J.B. (1974). *American Psychologist,* (August), 581–583.

Jouvet, M. (1967). The stages of sleep. *Scientific American, 216,* 62–72.

Jung, C.G. (1963). *Memories, Dreams, Reflections.* (A. Jaffe, Ed., R. & C. Winston, Trans.). New York: Pantheon.

K

Kalat, J. W. (2006). *Biological Psychology,* (9th ed.). Belmont, CA: Wadsworth Publishing.

______. (2005). *Introduction to Psychology.* Belmont, CA: Wadsworth Publishing Company.

Kaplan, B. (Ed.). (1964). *The Inner World of Mental Illness.* New York: Harper & Row, (paper).

Karasek, R., & Theorell, T. (1990). *Healthy Work: Stress, Productivity, and the Reconstruction of Working Life.* New York: Basic Books.

Karraker, K.H., & Stern, M. (1990). Infant physical attractiveness and facial expression: Effects on adult perception. *Basic and Applied Psychology, 11,* 371–385.

Kasschau, R. A. (2000). *Psychology: Exploring Behavior.* Orlando, FL: (AI)^2.

Kelley, H.H. (1950). The warm-cold variable in first impressions of persons. *Journal of Personality, 18,* 431–439.

______. (1967). Attribution theory in social psychology. In D. Levine (Ed.), *Nebraska Symposium on Motivation, Vol. 15,* (pp. 192–238). Lincoln, NE: University of Nebraska Press.

Kelley, G.A. (1958). The theory and technique of assessment. *Annual Review of Psychology, 9,* 323–352.

______. (1991). *The Psychology of Personal Constructs, Volume One: A Theory of Personality.* London: Routledge.

Kelman, H.C. (1961). Processes of opinion change. *Public Opinion Quarterly, 21,* 57–78.

Kelman, H.C., & Hovland, C.I. (1953). 'Reinstatement' of the communicator in delayed measurement of opinion change. *Journal of Abnormal and Social Psychology, 48,* 327–335.

Kendrick, D. (1987). Gender, genes, and the social environment. In F.L. Denmark & M.A. Pauldi (Eds.), *Psychology of Women: A Handbook of Issues and Theories.* Westport, CT: Greenwood Press.

Kessler, R.C., & McRae, J.A. (1981). Trends in the relationship between sex and psychological distress. *American Sociological Review, 46,* 443–452.

Kimmel, D.C. (1980). *Adulthood and Aging* (2nd ed.). New York: Wiley.

Kissin, B. (1986). *Conscious and Unconscious Programs in the Brain.* New York: Plenum Press.

Klapper, J.T. (1960). *The Effects of Mass Communications.* New York: Free Press.

Kleitman, N. (1960, November). Patterns of dreaming. *Scientific American, 203,* 82–88.

______. (1963). *Sleep and Wakefulness* (rev. ed.). Chicago: University of Chicago Press.

Klüver, H., & Bucy, P.C. (1937). Psychic blindness and other symptoms following bilateral temporal lobectomy in rhesus monkeys. *American Journal of Physiology, 119,* 532–535.

Koffka, K. (1963). *Principles of Gestalt Psychology.* New York: Harcourt Brace Jovanovich.

Kohlberg, L. (1968, September). The child as moral philosopher. *Psychology Today, 2,* 25–30.

______. (1969a). The development of children's orientations toward a moral order: I. sequence in the development of moral thought. *Vita Humana, 6,* 11–33.

______. (1969b). Stage and sequence: The cognitive-developmental approach to socialization. In D.A. Goslin (Ed.), *Handbook of Socialization Theory and Research.* Chicago: Rand-McNally.

References

Kohlberg, L., & Kramer, R. (1969). Continuities and discontinuities in child and adult moral development. *Human Development, 12,* 93–120.

Kohlberg, L., & Tunel, E. (1971). *Research in Moral Development: The Cognitive-Developmental Approach.* New York: Holt, Rinehart and Winston.

Köhler, W. (1976). *The Mentality of Apes.* New York: Liveright.

Kolata, G. (1993, February). Does brain exercise work? *Reader's Digest, 142,* 108–110.

Koop, C. E. (2001). Electroconvulsive Therapy. College Park, MD: University of Maryland. Retrieved October 24, 2001 World Wide Web: **http://umm.drkoop.com/conditions/ency/article/003324.htm**

Krantzler, M. (1973). *Creative Divorce.* New York: Evans.

Krosnick, J.A., & Alwin, D.F. (1989). Aging and susceptibility to attitude change. *Journal of Personality and Social Psychology, 57,* 416–425.

Ksir, C.J., Hart, C.L., & Ray, O.S. (2006). *Drugs, Society, and Human Behavior* (11th ed.). New York: McGraw-Hill.

Kübler-Ross, E. (1969). *On Death and Dying.* New York: Macmillan.

L

Lachman, S. (1996). Processes in perception: Psychological transformations of highly structured stimulus material. *Perceptual and Motor Skills, 83,* 411–418.

Lakoff, R. (1973). Language and women's place. *Language and Society, 2,* 45–79.

Lange, C.G., & James, W. (1922). *The Emotions.* (K. Dunlap, Ed., I.A. Haupt, Trans.). Baltimore: Williams & Wilkins.

Lashley, K.S. (1929). *Brain Mechanisms and Intelligence.* Chicago: University of Chicago Press.

Lauer, J., & Lauer, R. (1985). Marriages made to last. *Psychology Today, 16, (6),* 22–26.

Lazarus, R.H. (1993). From psychological stress to the emotions: A history of changing outlooks. *Annual Review of Psychology, 44,* 1–21.

Lazarus, R.S., DeLongis, A., Folkman, S., & Gruen, R. (1985). Stress and adaptational outcomes: The problem of confounded measures. *American Psychologist, 40,* 770–779.

Lazarus, R.S., et al. (1965). The principle of short-circuiting of threat: Further evidence. *Journal of Personality, 3,* 622–635.

Learman, L.A., Avorn, J., Everitt, D.E., & Rosenthal, R. (1990). Pygmalion in the nursing home: The effects of caregiver expectations on the patient outcomes. *Journal of the American Geriatrics Society, 38,* 797–803.

Leavitt, H.J. (1951). Some effects of certain communication patterns on group performance. *Journal of Abnormal Social Psychology, 46,* 38–50.

Lerner, M.J. (1980). *The Belief in a Just World: A Fundamental Delusion.* New York: Plenum Press.

Levinger, G. K., & Shoek, J. D. (1972). Attraction in relationships: A new look at interpersonal attraction. Morristown NJ: General Learning Press.

Levinson, D.J. (1978, May 1). Living with dying. *Newsweek,* 52–61.

______. (1986). A conception of adult development. *American Psychologist, 41,* 31.

Levinson, D.J., Darrow, C.M., Klein, E.G., Levinson, M.H., & McKee, B. (1978). *The Seasons of a Man's Life.* New York: Alfred A. Knopf.

Levy, J. (1985, May). Right brain, left brain: Fact and fiction. *Psychology Today.*

Levy, S. (1997, May 5). Man vs. machine. *Newsweek.*

Lichtman, A., Dimen, K., & Martin, B. (1995). Systematice or intrahippocampal cannabinoid administration impairs spatial memory in rats. *Psychopharmacology, 119,* 282–290.

Liebert, R.M., & Spiegler, M.D. (1994). *Personality: Strategies and Issues* (7th ed.). Pacific Grove: Brooks/Cole.

Lifton, R.J. (1963). *Thought Reform and the Psychology of Totalism: A Study of Brainwashing in China.* New York: Norton. (paper).

Locke, E.A., Latham, G.P., & Erez, M. (1988). The determinants of goal commitment. *Academy of Management Review, 13,* 23–29.

Loftus, E. (1974). Reconstructing memory: The incredible eyewitness. *Psychology Today, 8, 7,* 116–119.

______. (1979). *Eyewitness Testimony.* Cambridge, MA: Harvard University Press.

______. (1980a). Trial by data: Psychological research as legal evidence. *American Psychologist, 35,* 270–283.

______. (1980b). *Memory: Surprising New Insights Into How We Remember and Why We Forget.* Reading, MA: Addison-Wesley.

Loftus, E., & Loftus, G.R. (1980). On the performance of stored information in the human brain. *American Psychologist, 35,* 409–420.

Loftus, E., & Palmer, J.C. (1974). Reconstruction of automobile destruction: The influence of the wording of a question. *Journal of Verbal Learning and Verbal Behavior, 13,* 585–589.

Longo, L.C., & Ashmore, R.D. (1995). The looks-personality relationship: Global self-orientations as shared precursors of subjective physical attractiveness and self-ascribed traits. *Journal of Applied Social Psychology, 25,* 371–398.

Loranger, A.W., Prout, C.T., & White, M.A. (1961). The placebo effect in psychiatric drug research. *Journal of the American Medical Association, 176 (11),* 920–925.

Lorayne, H., & Lucas, J. (1974). *The Memory Book.* New York: Ballantine. (paper).

Lorenz, K.Z. (1972). *Studies in Animal and Human Behavior,* trans. by Robert Martin, 2 vols. Cambridge, MA: Harvard University Press.

Lovaas, O.I., et al. (1967, August). Establishment of imitation and its use for the development of complex behavior in schizophrenic children. *Behavior Research and Therapy, 5,* 171–181.

Lubin, B., Larsen, R.M., & Matarazzo, J.D. (1984). Patterns of psychological test usage in the United States: 1935–1982. *American Psychologist, 39,* 451–454.

Luce, G.G., & Segal, J. (1966). *Sleep.* New York: Coward, McCann & Geoghegan.

Luria, A.R. (1968). *The Mind of a Mnemonist.* New York: Basic Books.

Lykken, D.T. (1974). Psychology and the lie detector industry. *American Psychologist, 29,* 725–739.

______. (1988). Detection of guilty knowledge: A commitment on Forman and McCauley. *Journal of Applied Psychology, 73,* 303–304.

M

Maccoby, E.E. (1992). The role of parents in the socialization of children: An historical overview. *Developmental Psychology, 28,* 1006–1017.

Maccoby, E.E., & Martin, J. (1983). Socialization in the context of the family. In P. Mussen & E.M. Hetherington (Eds.), *Handbook of Child Psychology: Socialization, Personality, and Social Development, Vol. 4* (4th ed.). New York: Wiley.

Maccoby, E.E., & Masters, J.C. (1970). Attachment and dependency. In P.H. Mussen (Ed.), *Manual of Child Psychology, Vol. 2,* (pp. 159–260). New York: Wiley.

MacKay, C. (1932). *Extraordinary Popular Delusions and the Madness of Crowds.* New York: Farrar, Straus & Giroux.

Madison, P. (1969). *Personality Development in College.* Reading, MA: Addison-Wesley.

Marcia, J.E. (1966). Development and validation of ego identity status. *Journal of Personality and Social Psychology, 3,* 551–558.

Marlatt, G., & Rohsenow, D. (1981, December). The think-drink effect. *Psychology Today, 15,* 60–70.

Martin, C. L., & Fabes, R. A. (2001). The stability and consequences of young children's same-sex peer interactions. *Developmental Psychology, 37(3),* 431–446.

Maslow, A.H. (1970). *Motivation and Personality* (rev. ed.). New York: Harper and Row.

Masters, W.H., & Johnson, V.E. (1970). *Human Sexual Inadequacy.* Boston: Little, Brown.

References

Matlin, M.W. (1993). *The Psychology of Women* (2nd ed.). Fort Worth, TX: Harcourt Brace Jovanovich.

Matthews, K., Scheier, M., Brunson, B., & Carducci, B. (1989). Why do unpredictable events lead to reports of physical symptoms? In T.W. Miller (Ed.), *Stressful Life Events.* Madison, CT: International Studies Press.

May, R. (1969). *Existential Psychology* (2nd ed.). New York: Random House.

______. (1977). *The Meaning of Anxiety.* Rev. ed. New York: Norton.

Mayer, J.D., & Salovey, P. (1997). What is emotional intelligence? In P. Salovey & D. Sluyter (Eds.), *Emotional Development and Emotional Intelligence: Implications for Educators.* New York: Basic Books.

McCarley, R.W. (1978, December). Where dreams come from: A new theory. *Psychology Today, 12,* 54–65.

McClelland, D.C. (1958). Risk taking in children with high and low need for achievement. In J.W. Atkinson (Ed.), *Motives in Fantasy, Action, and Society,* (pp. 306–321). Princeton, NJ: Van Nostrand.

______. (1965). Need achievement and entrepreneurship: A longitudinal study. *Journal of Personality and Social Psychology, 1,* 389–392.

McClelland, D.C., et al. (1953). *The Achievement Motive.* New York: Appleton-Century-Crofts.

McClelland, D.C., & Harris, T.G. (1971, January). To know why men do what they do: A conversation with David C. McClelland. *Psychology Today, 4,* 35–39.

McCoy, K. (1982). *Coping With Teenage Depression.* New York: Mosby.

McDougall, W. (1908). *Social Psychology.* New York: Putnam.

McGuire, W.J. (1970, February). A vaccine for brainwash. *Psychology Today, 3,* 36–39, 62–64.

McIntosh, D.N. (1996). Facial feedback hypothesis: Evidence, implications, and directions. *Motivation and Emotion, 20,* 121–147.

McMillan, J., Clifton, A., McGrath, D., & Gale, W. (1977). Woman's language: Uncertainty or interpersonal sensitivity and emotionality? *Sex Roles, 3,* 545–560.

Mead, M. (1935). *Sex and temperament in three primitive societies.* New York: William Morrow & Co.

______. (1973). *Coming of Age in Samoa : A Psychological Study of Primitive Youth for Western Civilization.* New York: William Morrow & Co.

Mednick, M., & Thomas, V. (1993). Women and the psychology of achievement: A view from the eighties. In F.L. Denmark & M.A. Paludi (Eds.), *Psychology of Women: A Handbook of Issues and Theories.* Westport, CT: Greenwood Press.

Mellinger, G.D., Balter, M.B., & Uhlenhuth, E.H. (1985). Insomnia and its treatment: Prevalence and correlates. *Archives of General Psychiatry, 42,* 225–232.

Melzack, R., & Wall, P.D. (1965). Pain mechanisms: A new theory. *Science, 150,* 971–979.

Miedzian, M. (1991). *Boys Will Be Boys: Breaking the Link Between Masculinity and Violence.* New York: Doubleday.

Milgram, S. (1964). *Obedience to Authority.* New York: Harper & Row.

______. (1965). Some conditions of obedience and disobedience to authority. *Human Relations, 18,* 56–76.

______. (1970). The experience of living in cities. *Science, 167,* 1461–1468.

______. (1974). *Obedience to Authority.* New York: Harper and Row.

Miller, G.A. (1956). The magical number seven, plus or minus two: Some limits on our capacity for processing information. *Psychological Review, 63,* 81–97.

Miller, G.R., & Schneider, R. (1970). The use of a token system in Project Headstart. *Journal of Applied Behavior Analysis, 3,* 213–220.

Miller, N.E. (1944). Experimental studies of conflict. In J. Hunt (Ed.), *Personality and the Behavior Disorders.* New York: Ronald Press.

Miller, S., & Seligman, M. (1982). The reformulated model of helplessness and depression: Evidence and theory. In N. W. Newfield (Ed.), *Psychological Stress and Psychopathology.* New York: McGraw-Hill.

Mintz, R.S. (1968). Psychotherapy of the suicidal patient. In H.L.P. Resnik (Ed.). *Suicidal Behaviors.* Boston, MA: Little, Brown.

Miskhin, M., Saunders, R., & Murray, E. (1984). Further evidence that amygdala and hippocampus contribute equally to recognition memory. *Neuropsychologia, 22,* 785–796.

Mitchell, T. R., Thompson, L., Peterson, E., & Cronk, R. (1997). Temporal adjustments in the evaluation of events. The "rosy view." *Journal of Experimental Social Psychology 33,* 421–448.

Mokdad, A.H., Marks, J.S., Stroup, D.F., & Gerberding, J.L. (2004). Actual causes of death in the United States, 2000. *Journal of the American Medical Association 291,* 1238–1245.

Montague, C., Farooqi, I., Whitehead, J., Soos, M., Rau, H., Wareham, C., Sewter, C., Digby, J., Mohammed, S., Hurst, J., Cheetham, C., Earley, A., Barnett, A., Prins, J., & O'Rahilly, S. (1997). Congenital leptin deficiency is associated with severe early-onset obesity in humans. *Nature, 387,* 903–908.

Morris, C.G. (1990). *Contemporary Psychology and Effective Behavior* (7th ed.). New York: HarperCollins Publishers.

______. (2005). *Psychology: An Introduction.* (12th ed.) Upper Saddle River, New Jersey: Prentice Hall.

Morris, C.G., & Maisto, A.A. (2005). *Psychology: An Introduction* (12th ed.). Upper Saddle River, NJ: Prentice-Hall.

Mortensen, P. B., Pedersen, C. B., Westergaard, T., Wohlfahrt, J., Ewald, H., Mors, O., Andersen, P. K., & Melbye, M. (1999). Effects of family history and place and season of birth on the risk of schizophrenia. *New England Journal of Medicine, 340(8),* 603–608.

Moscovici, S. (1985). Social influence and conformity. In G. Lindsay & E. Aronson (Eds.), *Handbook of Social Psychology* (3rd ed.). New York: Random House.

Motley, M.T. (1985). Slips of the tongue. *Scientific American, 253,* 116–127.

Mowrer, O.H., & Mowrer, M. (1938). Enuresis: A method for its study and treatment. *American Journal of Orthopsychiatry, 8,* 436–459.

Mulligan, T., & Moss, C.R. (1991, February). Sexuality and aging in male veterans: A cross-sectional study of interest, ability, and activity. *Archives of Sexual Behavior, 20,* 17–25.

Murray, H.A. (1943). *Thematic Apperception Test manual.* Cambridge, MA: Harvard University Press.

Murray, H.A., et al. (1934). *Exploration in Personality.* New York: Oxford University Press.

Myers, D.G. (1983). *Social Psychology.* New York: McGraw-Hill.

N

Nathan, P.E., & Harris, S.L. (1975). *Psychopathology and Society.* New York: McGraw-Hill.

National Center for Education Statistics. (1997). Statistical analysis report: Fathers' involvement in their children's schools, October. Retrieved September 15, 1999 from the World Wide Web: **http://nces.ed.gov/pubs98/fathers/**

National Coalition for the Homeless. (2005). NCH Fact Sheet #5. Retrieved June 15, 2006, from the World Wide Web: **http://www.nationalhomeless.org**

National Institute of Mental Health (NIMH). (2006). *Facts about Anxiety Disorders.* Washington, DC: National Institute of Mental Health.

National Institute of Mental Health (NIMH). (2005). *Schizophrenia.* Retrieved June 8, 2006 from the World Wide Web: **http://www.nimh.nih.gov/publicat/schizoph.cfm**

National Task Force on the Prevention and Treatment of Obesity. (1994). Weight cycling. *Journal of the American Medical Association, 272,* 1196–1202.

References

National Television Violence Study (NTVS). (1998). Thousand Oaks, CA: Sage Publications.

Neher, A. (1991). Maslow's theory of motivation: A critique. *Journal of Humanistic Psychology, 31,* 89–112.

Neugarten, B., et al. (1963). Women's attitudes toward the menopause. *Vita Humana, 6,* 140–151.

New York Times. (1958, May 19). Huxley fears new persuasion methods could subvert democratic procedures, 45.

______. (1983, April 17). Parents on the brink of child abuse get crisis aid. 1, 29.

Newcomb, T. (1943). *Personality and Social Change.* New York: Dryden Press.

Newcomb, T., et al. (1967). *Persistence and Change: Bennington College and Its Students After 25 Years.* New York: Wiley.

Nolen-Hoeksema, S. (1987). Sex differences in unipolar depression: Evidence and theory. *Psychological Bulletin, 101,* 259–282.

O

Oakes, P.J., & Turner, J.C. (1990). Is limited information processing capacity the cause of social stereotyping? *European Review of Social Psychology, 9,* 147–152.

O'Donnell, S.A. (1999). Breathe your way out of an asthma attack. *Prevention, 51,* 36.

O'Farrell, T.J., Allen, J.P., & Litten, R.Z. (1995). Disulfram (Antabuse) contracts in treatment of alcoholism. In L.S. Onken, J.D. Blaine, & J.J. Boren (Eds.), *Integrating Behavioral Therapies with Medications in the Treatment of Drug Dependence.* Washington, DC: National Institute of Drug Abuse.

Offer, D., & Offer, J. (1975). *From Teenage to Young Manhood.* New York: Basic Books.

Offer, D., & Schonert-Reichl, K.A. (1992). Debunking the myths of adolescence: Findings from recent research. *Journal of the American Academy of Child and Adolescent Psychiatry, 31,* 1003–1013.

Olds, J., & Olds, M.E. (1965). Drives, rewards and the brain. In F. Barron, et al. (Eds.), *New Directions in Psychology II.* New York: Holt, Rinehart and Winston.

O'Leary, A. (1990). Stress, emotion, and human immune function. *Psychological Bulletin, 108,* 363–382.

Orne, M.T. (1959). The nature of hypnosis: Artifact and essence. *Journal of Abnormal and Social Psychology, 58,* 277–299.

P

Palmore, E. (1977). What can the USA learn from Japan about aging? In S.H. Zarit (Ed.), *Readings in Aging and Death: Contemporary Perspectives.* New York: Harper & Row.

Paludi, M.A. (1984). Psychometric properties and underlying assumptions of four objective measures of fear of success. *Sex Roles, 10,* 765–781.

Parke, R., & Lewis, N. (1980).The family in context: A multilevel interactional analysis of child abuse. In R.W. Henderson (Ed.), *Parent-Child Interaction: Theory, Research and Prospect.* New York: Academic Press.

Parke, R., & Slaby, R. (1983). Aggression: A multilevel analysis. In P.H. Mussen & M.E. Hetherington (Eds.), *Handbook of Child Psychology. Vol. 14. Socialization, Personality and Social Development* (4th ed.). New York: Wiley.

Pavlov, I.P. (1927). *Conditioned Reflexes.* (G.V. Anrep, Trans.). London: Oxford University Press.

Payne, W.A., Hahn, D.B., & Pinger, R.R. (1991). *Drugs: Issues for Today.* St. Louis, MO: Mosby-Year Book, Inc.

Pear, R. (2006). Medicare deadline spurs a debate over penalties. *New York Times,* May 15.

Pearlson, G.D., Kim, W.S., Kubos, K., Moberg, P., Jarayam, G., Bascom, M., Chase, G., Goldfinger, A., & Tune, L. (1989). Ventricle-brain ratio, computed tomographic density, and brain area in 50 schizophrenics. *Archives of General Psychiatry, 46.*

Pellegrini, A.D. (1987). Rough and tumble play: Developmental and educational significance. *Educational Psychologist, 22,* 23–43.

Penfield, W. (1969). Consciousness, memory, and man's conditioned reflexes. In K.H. Pribram (Ed.), *On the Biology of Learning.* New York: Harcourt Brace Jovanovich.

Perls, F., Hefferline, R.F., & Goodman, P. (1965). *Gestalt Therapy.* New York: Dell.

Perris, C. (1982). The distinction between bipolar and unipolar affective disorders. In E.S. Paykel (Ed.), *Handbook of Affective Disorders.* New York: Guilford Press.

Peterson, A.C. (1988). Adolescent development. *Annual Review of Psychology, 39,* 583–607.

Pfungst, O. (1911). *Clever Hans.* New York: Holt.

Phillips, D. (1998). Is a culture a factor in air crashes? *The Washington Post,* March 18, A17.

Piaget, J. (1926). *The Language and Thought of the Child.* London: Routledge & Kegan Paul.

Piaget, J., & Inhelder, B. (1969). *The Development of Physical Number Concepts in Children: Maintenance and Atomism.* Stuttgart, Germany: Ernst Klett.

Pines, M. (1970, November 29). Infants are smarter than anybody thinks. *The New York Times Magazine.*

______. (1981, September). The civilizing of Genie. *Psychology Today,* 28–34.

Plomin, R. (1990). The role of inheritance in behavior. *Science, 248,* 183–188.

Plomin, R. (1997). Scientist finds first gene for intelligence. Cited in *The Boston Globe, Offbeat News.* Retrieved August 5, 2001 from the World Wide Web: **http://www.boston.com/globe/offbeat/daily/03/gene.htm**

Plomin, R., Owen, M.J., & McGuffin, P. (1994). The genetic bias of complex human behaviors. *Science 264,* 1733–1739.

Plotnik, R. (2005). *Introduction to Psychology,* (7th ed.). Belmont, CA: Wadsworth Publishing Company.

Polsdorfer, J. R. (1999). Jet lag. Gale *Encyclopedia of Medicine.* Detroit: Gale Research.

Pope, H., & Yurgelun-Todd, D. (1996). The residual cognitive effects of heavy marijuana use in college students. *Journal of the American Medical Association, 275,* 521–527

Pratkanis, A. R., & Aronson, E. (2001). *Age of Propaganda: The Everyday Use and Abuse of Persuasion.* New York, NY: W. H. Freeman and Company.

Pratkanis, A. R., Greenwald, A. G., Leippe, M. R., & Baumgardner, M. R. (1988). The sleeper effect is dead: Long live the sleeper effect. *Journal of Personality and Social Psychology, 54(2),* 203–218.

Pressey, S.L. (1926). Experiments looking toward fundamental changes in instructional methods in professional courses for teachers. *Studies in Education, 15,* 45–49.

Prutkin, J., Duffy, V. B., Etter, L., Fast, K., Gardner, E., Lucchina, L. A., Snyder, D. J., Tie, K., Weiffenbach, J., & Bartoshuk, L. M. (2000). Genetic variation and inferences about perceived taste intensity in mice and men. *Physiology and Behavior, 69,* 161–173.

Q

Quinn, R., Seashore, S., Kahn, R., Mangione, T., Campbell, D., Staines, G., & McCullough, M. (1971). *Survey of Working Conditions.* Washington, DC: U.S. Government Printing Office.

R

Rahe, R.H. (1975). Life changes and near-future illness reports. In L. Levi (Ed.), *Emotions: Their Parameters and Measurement.* New York: Raven Press.

Raichle, M.E. (1994). Visualizing the mind. *Scientific American, 270,* 58–64.

Rathbone, D. B., & Huckabee, J. C. (1999). *Controlling Road Rage: Literature Review and Pilot Study.* AAA Foundation for Traffic Safety.

Ray, R.D. (2004). Adaptive computerized educational systems. In D. Moran & R. Mallott (Eds.), *Evidence-Based Educational Methods.* San Diego, CA: Elsvier.

Reinisch, J., & Beasley, R. (1990). *The Kinsey Institute New Report on Sex.* New York: St. Martin's Press.

Reisman, D., Glazer, N., & Denney, R. (1953). *The Lonely Crowd.* New Haven, Conn.: Yale University Press, (paper).

Reisman, J., & Shorr, S. (1978). Friendship claims and expectations among children and adults. *Child Development, 49,* 913–916.

Repetti, R.L. (1993). Short-term effects of occupational stressors on daily mood and health complaints. *Health Psychology, 12 (2),* 125–131.

Reppucci, N.D., & Saunders, J.T. (1974). Social psychology of behavior modification. *American Psychologist, 29,* 649–660.

Reynolds, G.S. (1968). *A Primer of Operant Conditioning.* Glenview, IL: Scott, Foresman.

Rhine, J.B. (1964). *Extra-Sensory Perception.* Boston: Branden.

Rhine, L.E. (1961). *Hidden Channels of the Mind.* New York: Apollo, (paper).

Rhoads, K. (1997). Cults: Questions & answers. Retrieved August 16, 1999 from the World Wide Web: **http://www.influenceatwork.com/**

Rice, F.P. (1990). *The Adolescent: Development, Relationships, and Culture* (6th ed.). Boston: Allyn & Bacon, pp. 434–441.

______. (1992a). *The Adolescent: Development, Relationships, and Culture* (7th ed.). Boston: Allyn & Bacon, pp. 410–419.

______. (1992b). *Human Development: A Life-Span Approach.* Englewood Cliffs, NJ: Prentice Hall.

______. (2001). *Human Development: A Life-Span Approach* (4th ed.). Englewood Cliffs, NJ: Prentice Hall.

Rice, K.G., Cunningham, T.J., & Young, M.B. (1997). Attachment to parents, social competence, and emotional well-being: A comparison of black and white late adolescents. *Journal of Counseling Psychology, 44 (1),* 89–101.

Ridge, R. D., & Reber, J. S. (1998). *Women's responses to men's flirtations in a professional setting: Implications for sexual harassment.* Paper presented at the annual meeting of the American Psychological Society, Washington, DC.

Rierden, J., Koff, E., & Stubbs, M. (1988). Gender, depression, and body image in early adolescents. *Journal of Early Adolescence, 8,* 109–117.

Roediger, H.L., III. (1990). Implicit memory: Retention without remembering. *American Psychologist, 45,* 1043–1056.

Roethlisberger, F.J., & Dickson, W.J. (1939). *Management and the Worker.* Cambridge, MA: Harvard University Press.

Rogers, C.R. (1951). *Client-centered Therapy.* Boston: Houghton Mifflin.

______. (1961). *On Becoming a Person.* Boston: Houghton Mifflin.

______. (1977). *On Personal Power: Inner Strength and Its Revolutionary Impact.* New York: Delacorte.

______. (1980). *A Way of Being.* Boston: Houghton Mifflin.

Rogers, D. (1977). *The Psychology of Adolescence* (3rd ed.). Englewood Cliffs, NJ: Prentice-Hall.

______. (1986). *The Adult Years: An Introduction to Aging* (3rd ed.). Englewood Cliffs, NJ: Prentice-Hall.

Roid, G.H. (2003). *Stanford-Binet Intelligence Scale.* (5th ed.). Technical Manual. Itasca, IL: Riverside.

Rokeach, M. (1971). Long-range experimental modification of values, attitudes, and behavior. *American Psychologist, 26,* 453–459.

Rook, K.S. (1987). Social support versus companionship: Effects on life stress, loneliness, and evaluations by others. *Journal of Personality and Social Psychology, 52,* 1132–1147.

______. (1990). Parallels in the study of social support and social strain. *Journal of Social and Clinical Psychology, 9,* 118–132.

Rosenfeld, M. (1998, March 26). Reexamining the plight of young males. *Washington Post.*

Rosenhan, D., & Seligman, M. (1984). *Abnormal Psychology.* New York: W.W. Norton and Company.

Rosenthal, R., & Rosnow, R.L. (Eds.). (1969). *Artifact in Behavioral Research.* New York: Academic Press.

Ross, L. (1977). The intuitive psychologist and his shortcomings. In L. Berkowitz (Ed.), *Advances in Experimental Social Psychology, Vol. 10.* New York: Academic Press.

Rossi, P.H. (1990). The old homeless and the new homelessness in historical perspective. *American Psychologist, 45,* 954–959.

Roth, D.L., & Holmes, D.S. (1987). Influence of aerobic exercise training and relaxation training on physical and psychologic health following stressful life events. *Psychosomatic Medicine, 49,* 355–365.

Rubin, Z. (1970). Measurement of romantic love. *Journal of Personality and Social Psychology, 16,* 265–273.

______. (1973). *Liking and Loving.* New York: Holt, Rinehart and Winston.

Rubin, Z., & Mitchell, C. (1976). Couples research as couples counseling: Some unintended effects of studying close relationships. *American Psychologist, 31(1),* 17–25.

Russell, J. (1994). Is there universal recognition of emotion from facial expression? A review of the cross-cultural studies. *Psychological Bulletin, 115,* 102–141.

S

Sabbatini, R. M. E. (1997). The History of Psychosurgery, *Brain & Mind, Vol. I* (Mar-May) Retrieved October 24, 2001 from the World Wide Web: **http://www.epub.org.br/cm/home_i.htm**

Samuelson, R. (1997, January 22). The two-earner myth. *Washington Post.*

Sapolsky, R.M. (2004). *Why Zebras Don't Get Ulcers.* (3rd ed.). New York: Henry Holt.

Sarbin, I., (1979). Hypnosis and psychopathology: Replacing old myths with fresh metaphors. *Journal of Abnormal Psychology, 88,* 506–526.

Sarbin, I., & Coe, W. (1972). *Hypnosis: A Social Psychological Analysis of Influence Communication.* New York: Holt, Rinehart and Winston.

Savage-Rumbaugh, E.S. (1990). Language acquisition in a nonhuman species: Implications for the innateness debate. *Developmental Psychology, 26,* 599–620.

______. (1998, January 19). Cited in S. Begley, Aping language. *Newsweek.*

Savage-Rumbaugh, E.S., Murphy, J., Sevcik, R., Brakke, K., Williams, S., & Rumbaugh, D. (1993). Language comprehension in ape and child. *Monographs of the Society for Research in Child Development, 58*(3–4).

Savage-Rumbaugh, E.S., Sevcik, R., Brakke, K., & Rumbaugh, D. (1992). Symbols: Their communicative use, communication, and combination by bonobos (Pan paniscus). In L.P. Lipsitt & C. Rovee-Collier (Eds.), *Advances in Infancy Research, Vol. 7,* (pp. 221–278). Norwood, NJ: Ablex.

Schachter, S. (1959). *The Psychology of Affiliation.* Stanford, CA: University Press.

______. (1971). *Emotion, Obesity, and Crime.* New York: Academic Press.

______. (1978). Second thoughts on biological and psychological explanations of behavior. In L. Berkowitz (Ed.), *Cognitive Theories in Social Psychology.* New York: Academic Press.

Schachter, S., & Singer, J. (1962). Cognitive, social, and physiological determinants of emotional state. *Psychological Review, 69,* 379–399.

References

Schaie, W.K., & Strother, C. (1968). A cross-sectional study of age changes in cognitive behavior. *Psychological Bulletin, 70,* 671–680.

Schneider, F.W., Gruman, J., & Coutts, L.M. (2005). *Applied Social Psychology.* Thousand Oaks, CA: Sage Publications.

Schneider, K. (1984). The cognitive basis of task choice in preschool children. *Advances in Motivation and Achievement, 3,* 57–72.

Schreiber, F.R. (1973). *Sybil.* New York: Warner.

Schulman, J., et al. (1973, May). Recipe for a jury. *Psychology Today, 6,* 37–44.

Schultes, R.E. (1976). *Hallucinogenic Plants.* New York: Golden Press.

Schwartz, A.N., & Peterson, J.A. (1979). *Introduction to Gerontology.* San Francisco: Holt, Rinehart and Winston.

Sears, D.O., Peplau, L.A., & Taylor, S.E. (1991). *Social Psychology* (7th ed.). Englewood Cliffs, NJ: Prentice-Hall.

Seeland, I.B., Klagsbrun, S.C., DeBellis, R., Kutscher, A.H., Avellanet, C., & Dennis, J. (Eds.). (1991). *The Final 48 Hours: Observations on the Last Days of Life.* Philadelphia: The Charles Press.

Seigel, R.K. (1977, October). Hallucinations. *Scientific American, 237,* 132–140.

Seligman, M.E.P. (1975). *Helplessness.* San Francisco: Freeman.

______. (1991). *Learned Optimism.* New York: Alfred A. Knopf.

Seligman, M. E. P., Walker, E. F., & Rosenhan, D. L. (2000). *Abnormal Psychology* (4th ed.). New York, NY: W. W. Norton & Company.

Selye, H. (1956). *The Stress of Life.* New York: McGraw-Hill.

______. (1974). *Stress Without Distress.* Philadelphia: Lippincott.

______. (1976). *Stress in Health and Disease.* Woburn, MA: Butterworth.

______. (1982). History and present status of the stress concept. In L. Goldberger & S. Breznitz (Eds.), *Handbook of Stress: Theoretical and Clinical Aspects.* New York: Free Press.

Selye, H., & Cherry, L. (1978, March). On the real benefits of eustress. *Psychology Today, 11,* 60–70.

Sexton, V., & Hogan, J.D. (Eds.). (1992). *International Psychology: Views From Around the World.* Omaha: University of Nebraska Press.

Shapiro, D. (1973). Preface. In D. Shapiro, et al. (Eds.), *Biofeedback and Self-Control 1972.* Chicago: Aldine-Atherton.

Shaver, P. (1976). Questions concerning fear of success and its conceptual relatives. *Sex Roles, 2,* 305–320.

Sheehy, G. (1976). *Passages.* New York: Dutton.

Shepard, R.N., & Metzler, J.N. (1971). Mental rotation of three-dimensional objects. *Science, 171,* 701–703.

Sheppard, B.H., Hartwick, J., & Warshaw, P.R. (1988). The theory of reasoned action: A meta-analysis of past research with recommendations for modifications and future research. *Journal of Consumer Research, 15,* 325–343.

Shermer, M. (1998). The truth is out there & Ray Hyman wants to find it: An interview with a co-founder of Modern Skepticism. *Skeptic, 6(2),* 90–96.

Shih, J.C. (1996, June 6). Of mice and mayhem. Cited in T. Monmaney, *Los Angeles Times,* B-2.

Simons, R.L., Whitbeck, L.B., Conger, R.D., & Wu, C.I. (1991). Intergenerational transmission of harsh parenting. *Developmental Psychology, 27,* 159–171.

Singer, J., & Singer, D. (1983). Psychologists look at television: Cognitive, developmental, personality and social policy implications. *American Psychologist, 38,* 826–834.

Sizemore, C.C., & Pittillo, E.S. (1977). *I'm Eve.* Garden City, NY: Doubleday Books.

Skinner, B.F. (1961). *The Behavior of Organisms.* New York: Appleton-Century-Crofts.

______. (1962). *Walden Two.* New York: Macmillan. (Original work published 1948.)

______. (1971). *Beyond Freedom and Dignity.* New York: Knopf.

______. (1974). *About Behaviorism.* New York: Knopf.

______. (1983). Intellectual self-management in old age. *American Psychologist, 38,* 239–244.

Smith, D. (1982). Trends in counseling and psychotherapy. *American Psychologist, 37,* 802–809.

Smith, M.L., & Glass, G.V. (1977). Meta-analysis of psychotherapy outcome studies. *American Psychologist, 32,* 752–760.

Snellgrove, L. (1967). *Psychological Experiments and Demonstrations.* New York: McGraw-Hill.

Snyder, H. (2005). *Juvenile Arrests 2003.* Washington, DC: Office of Juvenile Justice and Delinquency Prevention. *OJJDP Statistical Briefing Book.* Retrieved May 20, 2006 from the World Wide Web: **http://ojjdp.ncjrs.org**

Social Security Administration. (2001). Social Security Amendments of 1983, signed on April 20, 1983. History page of social security online. Retrieved July 17, 2001 from the World Wide Web: **http://www.ssa.gov/history/1983amend.html**

Solomon, R.L., & Corbit, J.D. (1974). An opponent-process theory of motivation. *Psychological Review, 81,* 119–145.

Spearman, C. (1904). "General intelligence" objectively determined and measured. *American Journal of Psychology, 15,* 201–293.

Sperling, G. (1960). The information available in brief visual presentations. *Psychological Monographs, 74,* no. 11.

Spirduso, W.W., & MacRae, P.G. (1990). Motor performance and aging. In J.E. Birren & K.W. Schaie (Eds.), *Handbook of the Psychology of Aging* (3rd ed.). San Diego, CA: Academic Press.

Squire, L.R. (1987). *Memory and Brain.* New York: Oxford University Press.

Stephan, C.W., & Langlois, J.H. (1984). Baby beautiful: Adult attributions of infant competence as a function of infant attractiveness. *Child Development, 55,* 576–585.

Stephens, R., Roffman, R., & Simpson, E. (1994). Treating adult marijuana dependence: A test of the relapse prevention model. *Journal of Consulting and Clinical Psychology, 62 (1),* 92–99.

Sternberg, R. (1985). *Beyond IQ: A Triarchic Theory of Human Intelligence.* New York: Cambridge University Press.

______. (1986). A Triangular Theory of Love. *Psychological Review, 93,* 119–135.

______. (1988). *The Triangle of Love: Intimacy, Passion, Commitment.* New York: Basic Books.

Stogdill, R.M. (1974). *Handbook of Leadership: A Survey of Theory and Research.* New York: Free Press.

Strasser, T. (1981). *The Wave.* New York: Dell Publishing.

Stroebe, M., et al. (1992). Broken hearts or broken bonds: Love and death in historical perspective. *American Psychologist, 47,* 1205–1212.

Sulloway, F.J. (1996). *Born to Rebel: Birth Order, Family Dynamics and Creative Lives.* New York: Pantheon Books.

Super, D.E. & Super, C.M., (2001). *Opportunities in Psychology Careers.* Chicago, IL: VGM Career Horizons, a division of the NTC Publishing Group.

Swann, W.B., Stein-Seroussi, A., & Gleiser, R.B. (1992). Why people self-verify. *Journal of Personality and Social Psychology, 62,* 392–401.

Szasz, T. S. (1984). *The Myth of Mental Illness: Foundations of a Theory of Personal Conduct* (Revised ed.). New York, NY: HarperCollins.

T

Tanner, J.M., Whitehouse, R.H., & Takaishi, M. (1966). Standards from birth to maturity for height, weight, height velocity, and weight velocity for British children, 1965, Parts I and II. *Archives of Disease in Childhood, 41.*

Taylor, S. E., & Brown, J. D. (1988). Illusion and well-being: A social psychological perspective on mental health. *Psychological Bulletin, 103,* 193–210.

Taylor, S. E. & Brown, J. D. (1994). Positive illusions and well-being revisited: Separating fact from fiction. *Psychological Bulletin, 116,* 21–27.

Teigen, K. (1994). Yerkes-Dodson: A law for all seasons. *Theory and Psychology, 4*(4), 525–547.

Thelin, A.G. (1998). Working environment conditions in rural areas according to psychosocial indices. *Annals of Agricultural and Environmental Medicine, 5(2),* 139–145.

Thienhaus, O. J., Margletta, S., & Bennett, J. A. (1990). A study of clinical efficacy of maintenance ECT. *Journal of Clinical Psychiatry, 51(4),* 141–144.

Thomas, A., Chess, S., & Birch, H.G. (1968). *Temperament and Behavior Disorders in Children.* New York: New York University Press.

Thornton, B., & Maurice, J. K. (1999). Physical attractiveness contrast effect and the moderating influence of self-consciousness. *Sex Roles: A Journal of Research, 40(5/6),* 379–392.

Thurstone, L.L. (1938). *Primary Mental Abilities.* Chicago: University of Chicago Press.

Treisman, A.M. (1964). Verbal cues, language, and meaning in selective listening. *American Journal of Psychology, 77,* 206–219.

Trotter, R. (1983, August). Baby face. *Psychology Today, 17,* 15–20.

Tulving, E. (1972). Episodic and semantic memory. In E. Tulving & W. Donaldson (Eds.), *Organization of Meaning.* New York: Academic Press.

Turner, P., & Gervai, J. (1995). A multidimensional study of gender typing in preschool children and their parents: Personality, attitudes, preferences, behavior, and cultural differences. *Developmental Psychology, 31,* 759–772.

U

United States Bureau of Labor Statistics (2005). Women in the labor force: A databook. Retrieved June 22, 2006 from the World Wide Web: **http://www.bls.gov/cps/wlf-databook-2005.pdf**

United States Census Bureau (2005). 65+ in the United States. Retrieved May 20, 2006 from the World Wide Web: **http://www.census.gov/prod/2006pubs/p23-209.pdf**

______. (2006). *Statistical Abstract of the United States, 2006.* Washington, DC: Government Printing Office.

University of Michigan, Survey Research Center. (2005). Monitoring the future. Retrieved May 30, 2006 from the World Wide Web: **http://www.monitoringthefuture.org**

V

Valvo, A. (1971). *Sight Restoration After Long-Term Blindness: The Problems and Behavior Patterns of Visual Rehabilitation.* New York: American Foundation for the Blind.

Van der Linden, W.J., & Glas, C.A.W. (Eds.). (2000). Computerized Adaptive Testing. St. Paul, MN: Assessment Systems Corporation.

Vernon, P.E. (1987). The demise of the Stanford Binet scale. *Canadian Psychology, 28,* 251–258.

Vokey, J.R., & Read, J.D. (1985). Subliminal messages, between the devil and the media. *American Psychologist, 40,* 1231–1239.

W

Wadden, T.A., & Stunkard, A.J. (1987). Psychopathology and obesity. *Annals of the New York Academy of Science, 499,* 55–65.

Wade, C., & Cirese, S. (1991). *Human Sexuality* (2nd ed.). San Diego, CA: Harcourt Brace Jovanovich.

Wald, G. (1964). The receptors of color vision. *Science, 145,* 1007–1016.

Wallerstein, J., & Kelly, J. (1974). The effects of parental divorce: The adolescent experience. In J. Anthony & C. Koupernik (Eds.), *The Child in His Family: Children at Psychiatric Risk,* (pp. 479–505). New York: Wiley.

Walster, E., Aronson, V., Abrahams, D., & Rottman, L. (1966). Importance of physical attractiveness in dating behavior. *Journal of Personality and Social Psychology, 4,* 508–516.

Warden, C.H. (1997). Gene heats up obesity research. Cited in R. Plotnik, *Science News, 151,* 142.

Waterson, E. J., & Murray-Lyon, I.M. (1990). Preventing alcohol related birth damage: *A Review. Social Science and Medicine, 30,* 349–364.

Watkinson, B. (1990). 36- and 48-month neurobehavioral follow-up of children prenatally exposed to marijuana, cigarettes, and alcohol. *Development and Behavioral Pediatrics, 11,* 49–58.

Watson, J.B. (1970). *Behaviorism.* New York: Norton. (Original work published 1924.)

Watson, J.B., & Rayner, R. (1920). Conditioned emotional reactions. *Journal of Experimental Psychology, 3,* 1–14.

Wechsler, D. (1997). WAIS III Administration and Scoring Manual. San Antonio, TX: Psychological Corporation.

______. (2003). *The WISC-IV Technical and Interpretive Manual.* San Antonio, TX: Psychological Corporation.

Weiss, J.M. (1971). Effects of coping behavior in different warning-signal conditions on stress pathology in rats. *Journal of Comparative and Physiological Psychology, 77,* 1–13.

______. (1972). *Influence of Psychological Variables on Stress-Induced Pathology. In Physiology, Emotion and Psychosomatic Illness (Ciba Foundation Symposium 8).* New York: American Elsevier.

White, B.L. (1969). Child development research: An edifice without a foundation. *Merrill-Palmer Quarterly of Behavior and Development, 15,* 49–79.

White, R. (1959). Motivation reconsidered: The concept of competence. *Psychological Review, 66,* 297–333.

______. (1964). *The Abnormal Personality.* New York: Ronald.

______. (1966). *Lives in Progress: A Study of the Natural Growth of Personality* (2nd ed.). New York: Holt, Rinehart and Winston.

Whorf, B. (1956). *Language, Thought, and Reality.* New York: Wiley.

Wilson, E.O. (1975). *Sociobiology: A New Synthesis.* Cambridge, MA: Harvard University Press.

Wilson, T.D., Kraft, D., & Dunn, D.S. (1989). The disruptive effects of explaining attitudes: The moderating effects of knowledge about the attitude object. *Journal of Experimental Social Psychology, 25,* 379–400.

Windle, M., & Windle, R. C. (2001). Depressive symptoms and cigarette smoking among middle adolescents: Prospective associations and intrapersonal and interpersonal influences. *Journal of Consulting and Clinical Psychology, 69(2),* 215–226.

Wispe, L., & Drambarean, N. (1953). Physiological need, word frequency, and visual duration thresholds. *Journal of Experimental Psychology, 46,* 25–31.

Wolfe, J.B. (1936). Effectiveness of token-rewards for chimpanzees. *Comparative Psychological Monographs, 12,* 5.

Wolman, B.B. (Ed.). (1965). *Handbook of Clinical Psychology.* New York: McGraw-Hill.

______. (Ed.). (1973). *Handbook of General Psychology.* Englewood Cliffs: NJ: Prentice-Hall.

Wolpe, J. (1961). The systematic desensitization treatment of neuroses. *Journal of Nervous and Mental Disease,* 132: 189–203.

Woods, N.F., & Mitchell, E.S. (1999). Anticipating menopause. *Menopause, 6 (2),* 167–173.

Woods, S.C., & Clegg, D.J. (2003). In U. Eiholzer, D. L'Allemand, & W.B. Zipf (Eds.). Prader-Willi syndrome as a model for obesity. International Symposium, Zurich, 2002. Basel, Karger, 15–30.

Woolfolk, R.L. (1975). Psychophysiological correlates of meditation. *Archives of General Psychiatry, 32,* 1326–1333.

World Almanac Books (2006). *World Almanac and Book of Facts.* New York: World Almanac Books.

References

Wu, C., & Shaffer, D.R. (1987). Susceptibility to persuasive appeals as a function of source credibility and prior experience with the attitude object. *Journal of Personality and Social Psychology, 4,* 195–202.

Wyatt, R. J., & Susser, E. S. (2000). Editor's introduction: U. S. birth cohort studies of schizophrenia: A sea of change. *Schizophrenia Bulletin 26(2),* 255–256.

Y

Yarrow, L.J., & Goodwin, M.S. (1973). The immediate impact of separation reactions of infants to a change in mother figures. In L.J. Stone, T.J. Smith, & L.B. Murphy (Eds.), *The Competent Infant.* New York: Basic Books.

Z

Zajonc, R.B. (1965). Social facilitation. *Science, 149,* 269–274.

Zajonc, R.B., & Markus, G.B. (1976). Birth order and intellectual development. *Psychological Review, 82,* 74–88.

Zigler, E., & Muenchow, S. (1992). *Head Start: The Inside Story of America's Most Successful Educational Experiment.* New York: Basic Books.

Zigler, E., Styfco, S.J., & Gilman, E. (1993). The national Head Start Program for disadvantaged preschoolers. In E. Zigler & S.J. Styfco (Eds.), *Head Start and Beyond: A National Plan for Extended Childhood Intervention.* New Haven, CT: Yale University Press.

Zimbardo, P.G. (1975). On transforming experimental research into advocacy for social change. In *Psychology and Life* (10th ed.). Glenview, IL: Scott, Foresman.

______. (1997, May). What messages are behind today's cults? *APA Monitor.*

Acknowledgments and Credits

Acknowledgments
From AN ANTHROPOLOGIST ON MARS by Oliver Sacks Copyright © 1995 by Oliver Sacks. Reprinted by permission of Alfred A. Knopf, Inc., a Division of Random House, Inc.

Photo Credits

COVER Mick Wiggins

xii file photo; **xiv** Roger Ressmeyer/CORBIS; **1** file photo; **2–3** David Muir/Masterfile; **4** S. Purdy Matthews/Tony Stone Images/Getty Images; **6** age fotostock/SuperStock; **8** Comstock/SuperStock; **11** Archivo Iconografico, S.A./CORBIS; **13** Bettmann/CORBIS; **15** North Wind Picture Archive; **17** (t)Archives of the History of American Psychology/The University of Akron; (b)www.ScienceCartoonsPlus.com; **18** (l)Musee du Louvre, Paris/SuperStock; (r)First Image; **19** Archives of History of American Psychology/The University of Akron; **25** (l)Gabe Palmer/CORBIS; (r)Spencer Grant/PhotoEdit; **31** CALVIN AND HOBBES ©1999 Bill Watterson. Reprinted with permission of UNIVERSAL PRESS SYNDICATE. All rights reserved; **34** Shehzad Noorani/Peter Arnold, Inc. **36** Bios (M. Gunther)/Peter Arnold, Inc.; **45** Arthur Beck/CORBIS; **46** Archives of the History of American Psychology/The University of Akron; **58 59 60** Javier Pierini/Getty Images; **63** Aaron Haupt; **66 67** Enrico Ferorelli; **69 72** First Image; **73** Archives of the History of American Psychology/The University of Akron; **76** (t)Nina Leen/Time Life Syndication; (b)Martin Rogers/Tony Stone Images/Getty Images; **79** Yoichi Nagata/Getty Images; **81** Michael Ventura/Photo Edit; **84** (l)Tony Stone Images/Getty Images; (r)Robert Essel/CORBIS; **89** Ross Products Division/Abbott Laboratories; **92** SuperStock; **94** Dugald Bremner/Tony Stone Images/Getty Images; **97** Jeff Zaruba/CORBIS; **98** For Better or For Worse reprinted by permission of United Feature Syndicate, Inc.; **102** Terry Vine/Tony Stone Images/Getty Images; **106** Ted Streshinsky/CORBIS; **108** CORBIS; **111** For Better or For Worse reprinted by permission of United Feature Syndicate, Inc.; **112** Kwame Zikomo/SuperStock; **114** SuperStock; **118** Stockbyte/Getty Images; **119** K.M. Westermann/CORBIS; **120** Cathy Guisewite/Universal Press Syndicate; **128** Lori Adamski Peek/Getty Images; **132** (l)Getty Images; (r)First Image; **134** First Image; **138** For Better or For Worse reprinted by permission of United Feature Syndicate, Inc.; **139** Ariel Skelley/CORBIS; **143** Biophoto Associates/Photo Researchers; **145** Reuters/Ken Ross/Archive Photos; **146** David Hiser/Tony Stone Images/Getty Images; **147** Pete Saloutos/CORBIS; **148** Pugliano/Getty Images; **153** Anatomyworks/the Stock Shop/Medichrome; **154** CJ Gunther/CORBIS; **157** Biophoto Associates/Photo Researchers; **159** (l)J. Silver/SuperStock; (tr)Adam Hart-Davis/Science Photo Library/Photo Researchers; **164** Svenskt Pressefoto/Archive Photos; **166** AJPhoto/Photo Researchers; **168** The Stock Shop/ Medichrome; **173** Arnulf Husmo/Tony Stone Images/Getty Images; **176** Rick Gomez/CORBIS; **182** David Pu'u/CORBIS; **189** Smithsonian American Art Museum, Washington, DC/Art Resource, NY; **192** North Wind Picture Archive; **195** The Newark Museum/Art Resource, NY; **196** Charles Gupton/CORBIS; **200** Icon Images; **201** David R. Frazier Photography; **206** Bettmann/CORBIS; **209** Archives of the History of American Psychology/The University of Akron; **218** Lester V. Bergman/ CORBIS; **228** (l)Craid Aurness/CORBIS; (r)Paul Jonason/SuperStock; **230** Kenneth Rogers/CORBIS; **231** Baron Wolman/Woodfin Camp & Associates; **232** Lightstone/CORBIS; **237** Lien/Nebauer Photography/ Liaison Agency; **238–239** David Stoecklein/CORBIS; **240** Christine Kennedy/Getty Images; **244** The Far Side ©1993 FARWORKS, INC. Used by permission. All rights reserved; **245** Culver Pictures; **249** courtesy Professor Benjamin Harris/University of Wisconsin-Parkside; **252** Nina Leen/Life Magazine/Getty Images; **255** J. Sekowski; **256** (t) Lew Long/CORBIS; (b)Mark A. Johnson/CORBIS; **258** CALVIN AND HOBBES ©1999 Bill Watterson. Reprinted with permission of UNIVERSAL PRESS SYNDICATE. All rights reserved; **260** Reprinted by permission of Sidney Harris; **263** First Image; **265** Andersen Ross/Getty Images; **272** Owen Edelsten/Masterfile; **278** Getty Images; **281** Mitch York/Tony Stone Images/Getty Images; **285** courtesy Elizabeth Loftus, Ph.D./University of Washington; **286** Reprinted by permission of Sidney Harris; **293** Pete Salutos/CORBIS; **294** Uripos/eStock Photo; **300** First Image; **303 306** AP/Wide World Photos; **312–313** Bryan Reinhart/Masterfile; **315** courtesy the Harlow Primate Laboratory; **317** Jonathan Ernst/REUTERS; **318** Bernd Kappelmeyer/Getty Images; **321** courtesy Dr. Neil E. Miller, Yale Dept. of Psychology; **326** Gail Meese/Meese Photo Research; **330** (l)VCG/Getty Images; (r)file photo; **331** courtesy Dr. Paul Ekman; **340–341** Raoul Minsart/Masterfile; **342** Gail Meese/Meese Photo Research; **344** Geoff Butler; **348** David Hiser/Network Aspen; **350** courtesy Dr. Howard Gardner; **353** Jose L. Pelaez/CORBIS; **358** Don Mason/CORBIS; **360** Rick Gomez/Masterfile; **366 367** Spencer Grant/PhotoEdit; **371** THE FAR SIDE, FARWORKS, INC. Used by permission. All rights reserved; **374** Andrew Olney/Masterfile; **376** George Doyle/Getty Images; **377** Cathy Guisewite/Universal Press Syndicate; **381** Mike Baldwin/CartoonStock; **384** CORBIS; **385** Warner Bros./ZUMA/CORBIS; **386** (l)Hugh Sitton/Tony Stone Images/Getty Images; (r)AFP/CORBIS; **388** Reprinted by permission of Sidney Harris; **392** Ralph Morse/Life Magazine/Getty Images; **393** CORBIS; **394** PEANUTS reprinted by permission of United Feature Syndicate, Inc.; **395** Time Life Syndication; **397** Jose Luiz Pelaez/Getty Images; **399** The New Yorker Collection, 1977 Henry Martin from cartoonbank.com. All Rights Reserved; **404** Michael Shay/Getty Images; **407** The New Yorker Collection, 1991 Mick Stevens from cartoonbank.com All Rights Reserved; **409** Tristen Paviot/Tony Stone Images/Getty Images; **410–411** Reza Estakhrian/Tony Stone Images/Getty Images; **412** SuperStock; **414** Lawrence Manning/CORBIS; **421** Nicholas Devore/Network Aspen; **422** (bl)First Image; (br)Gail Meese/Meese Photo Research; Robert Llewellyn/SuperStock; **423** Evan Agostini/Getty Images; **424** Vincent Laforet/Pool/Reuters/CORBIS; **426** Prof. S.H.E. Kaufman & Dr. J.R. Golecki/Photo Researchers; **428** Mike Powell/Getty Images; **436** file photo; **439** Simon Wikinson/Getty Images; **440** Dilbert reprintd by permission of United Feature Syndicate, Inc.; **446** Shadow/Getty Images; **448 449** Ian O'Leary/Tony Stone Images/Getty Images; **451** CORBIS; **453** SuperStock; **456** Charles Gupton/CORBIS; **459** Joe Raedle/Getty Images; **461** PEANUTS reprinted by permission of United Feature Syndicate, Inc.; 463 furnished for publication by Chris Costner Sizemore/The Jerry Naylor Company; **464** ChiselVision/CORBIS; **467** Paul Brown/Photo Researchers; **468** First Image; **469** courtesy Ms. Edna Morlok; **471** Robert Essel/CORBIS; **477** Oscar Burriel/Photo Researchers; **484** Nobuo Kuwahara/Photonica/Getty Images; **486** North Wind Picture Archive; **490** Michael Newman/PhotoEdit; **491** file photo; **495** H. Sakuramoto/Photonica/Getty Images; **496** The New Yorker Collection, 1977 Lee Lorenz from cartoonbank.com. All Rights Reserved; **498** Tom McHugh/Photo Researchers; **507** Cliff Moore Photography; **515** Studiohio; **516–517** Koichi Kamoshida/Getty Images; **518** Matt Meadows; **520** (l)Lynn M. Stone; (c)Stan Osolinski/Getty Images; (r)Don Smetzer/Tony Stone Images/Getty Images; **523** First Image; **524** (l, r)Art

Acknowledgments and Credits

Wolfe/Getty Images; (c)Nicholas DeVore/Getty Images; **525** Jose L. Pelaez/CORBIS; **526** Mitchell Gerber/CORBIS; **529** (l)Ken Chernus/Getty Images; (c)Ralf Gerard/Getty Images; (r)Gail Meese/Meese Photo Research; **532** (l)Richard Price/Getty Images; (r)Carl Schneider/Getty Images; **534** Nicholas DeVore/Tony Stone Images/Getty Images; **535** Archive/Photo Researchers; **536** (t)Telegraph Colour Library/Getty Images; (bl)Ronnie Kaufman/CORBIS; (br)Gail Meese/Meese Photo Research; **544** Lori Adamski Peek/Getty Images; **546** Phil Schermeister/Network Aspen; **548** Bruce Ayres/Getty Images; **550** Dana White/PhotoEdit; **552** Liaison Agency; **557** William Vandivert; **559** The Far Side ©1984 FARWORKS, INC. Used by permission. All rights reserved.; **560 561** file photo **562** Aero Graphics, Inc./CORBIS; **563** First Image; **568** AP/Wide World Photos; **569** First Image; **575** Eyewire/Getty Images; **576** Jose Luis Pelaez/Getty Images; **579** age fotostock/SuperStock; **589** Joe Sohm/CORBIS; **591** Mario Anzuoni/REUTERS; **592** Liaison Agency; **595** Gaslight Ad Archives; **602** Erich Lessing/Art Resource, NY; **606** courtesy Linda Lea McCarley; **607** Ed Lallo/Liaison Agency; **609** First Image; **611** North Wind Picture Archive; **612** (l)North Wind Picture Archive; (r)Jeff Isaac Greenberg/Photo Researchers; **614** First Image